Seabrook's Bible Dictionary

of Traditional and Mystical Christian Doctrines

☙ THE LOCHLAINN SEABROOK COLLECTION ❧

Everything You Were Taught About the Civil War is Wrong, Ask a Southerner!
Everything You Were Taught About American Slavery is Wrong, Ask a Southerner!
Everything You Were Taught About African-Americans and the Civil War is Wrong, Ask a Southerner!
Confederate Flag Facts: What Every American Should Know About Dixie's Southern Cross
Give This Book to a Yankee! A Southern Guide to the Civil War For Northerners
Honest Jeff and Dishonest Abe: A Southern Children's Guide to the Civil War
Confederacy 101: Amazing Facts You Never Knew About America's Oldest Political Tradition
Slavery 101: Amazing Facts You Never Knew About America's "Peculiar Institution"
The Great Yankee Coverup: What the North Doesn't Want You to Know About Lincoln's War!
Confederate Blood and Treasure: An Interview With Lochlainn Seabrook
A Rebel Born: A Defense of Nathan Bedford Forrest - Confederate General, American Legend (winner of the 2011 Jefferson Davis Historical Gold Medal)
A Rebel Born: The Screenplay
Nathan Bedford Forrest: Southern Hero, American Patriot - Honoring a Confederate Icon and the Old South
The Quotable Nathan Bedford Forrest: Selections From the Writings and Speeches of the Confederacy's Most Brilliant Cavalryman
Give 'Em Hell Boys! The Complete Military Correspondence of Nathan Bedford Forrest
Forrest! 99 Reasons to Love Nathan Bedford Forrest
Saddle, Sword, and Gun: A Biography of Nathan Bedford Forrest For Teens
Nathan Bedford Forrest and the Battle of Fort Pillow: Yankee Myth, Confederate Fact
Nathan Bedford Forrest and the Ku Klux Klan: Yankee Myth, Confederate Fact
Nathan Bedford Forrest and African-Americans: Yankee Myth, Confederate Fact
The Quotable Jefferson Davis: Selections From the Writings and Speeches of the Confederacy's First President
The Quotable Alexander H. Stephens: Selections From the Writings and Speeches of the Confederacy's First Vice President
The Alexander H. Stephens Reader: Excerpts From the Works of a Confederate Founding Father
The Quotable Robert E. Lee: Selections From the Writings and Speeches of the South's Most Beloved Civil War General
The Old Rebel: Robert E. Lee As He Was Seen By His Contemporaries
The Articles of Confederation Explained: A Clause-by-Clause Study of America's First Constitution
The Constitution of the Confederate States of America Explained: A Clause-by-Clause Study of the South's Magna Carta
The Quotable Stonewall Jackson: Selections From the Writings and Speeches of the South's Most Famous General
Abraham Lincoln: The Southern View - Demythologizing America's Sixteenth President
The Unquotable Abraham Lincoln: The President's Quotes They Don't Want You To Know!
Lincolnology: The Real Abraham Lincoln Revealed in His Own Words - A Study of Lincoln's Suppressed, Misinterpreted, and Forgotten Writings and Speeches
The Great Impersonator! 99 Reasons to Dislike Abraham Lincoln
The Quotable Edward A. Pollard: Selections From the Writings of the Confederacy's Greatest Defender
Encyclopedia of the Battle of Franklin - A Comprehensive Guide to the Conflict that Changed the Civil War
Carnton Plantation Ghost Stories: True Tales of the Unexplained from Tennessee's Most Haunted Civil War House!
The McGavocks of Carnton Plantation: A Southern History - Celebrating One of Dixie's Most Noble Confederate Families and Their Tennessee Home
Jesus and the Law of Attraction: The Bible-Based Guide to Creating Perfect Health, Wealth, and Happiness Following Christ's Simple Formula
The Bible and the Law of Attraction: 99 Teachings of Jesus, the Apostles, and the Prophets
Christ Is All and In All: Rediscovering Your Divine Nature and the Kingdom Within
Jesus and the Gospel of Q: Christ's Pre-Christian Teachings As Recorded in the New Testament
Seabrook's Bible Dictionary of Traditional and Mystical Christian Doctrines
The Way of Holiness: The Story of Religion and Myth From the Cave Bear Cult to Christianity
Christmas Before Christianity: How the Birthday of the "Sun" Became the Birthday of the "Son"
Autobiography of a Non-Yogi: A Scientist's Journey From Hinduism to Christianity (with Amitava Dasgupta)
Britannia Rules: Goddess-Worship in Ancient Anglo-Celtic Society - An Academic Look at the United Kingdom's Matricentric Spiritual Past
The Book of Kelle: An Introduction to Goddess-Worship and the Great Celtic Mother-Goddess Kelle, Original Blessed Lady of Ireland
The Goddess Dictionary of Words and Phrases: Introducing a New Core Vocabulary for the Women's Spirituality Movement
Princess Diana: Modern Day Moon-Goddess - A Psychoanalytical and Mythological Look at Diana Spencer's Life, Marriage, and Death (with Dr. Jane Goldberg)
Aphrodite's Trade: The Hidden History of Prostitution Unveiled
UFOs and Aliens: The Complete Guidebook
The Caudills: An Etymological, Ethnological, and Genealogical Study - Exploring the Name and National Origins of a European-American Family
The Blakeneys: An Etymological, Ethnological, and Genealogical Study - Uncovering the Mysterious Origins of the Blakeney Family and Name

Five-Star Books & Gifts From the Heart of the American South

☙ SeaRavenPress.com ❧

Seabrook's Bible Dictionary

Of Traditional & Mystical Christian Doctrines

An Introduction to the Hidden Mysteries of the Church

Illustrated by the Author, Colonel

Lochlainn Seabrook

JEFFERSON DAVIS HISTORICAL GOLD MEDAL WINNER

DILIGENTLY RESEARCHED FOR THE ELUCIDATION OF THE READER

Sea Raven Press, Nashville, Tennessee, USA
2016

SEABROOK'S BIBLE DICTIONARY

Published by
Sea Raven Press, Cassidy Ravensdale, President
PO Box 1484, Spring Hill, Tennessee 37174-1484 USA
SeaRavenPress.com • searavenpress@gmail.com

Copyright © 2016 Lochlainn Seabrook
in accordance with U.S. and international copyright laws and regulations, as stated and protected under the Berne Union for the Protection of Literary and Artistic Property (Berne Convention), and the Universal Copyright Convention (the UCC). All rights reserved under the Pan-American and International Copyright Conventions.

1st Sea Raven Press paperback edition (978-1-943737-33-8): August 2016
1st Sea Raven Press hardcover edition (978-1-943737-34-5): August 2016

ISBN: 978-1-943737-33-8 (paperback)
Library of Congress Control Number: 2016932898

This work is the copyrighted intellectual property of Lochlainn Seabrook and has been registered with the Copyright Office at the Library of Congress in Washington, D.C., USA. No part of this work (including text, covers, drawings, photos, illustrations, maps, images, diagrams, etc.), in whole or in part, may be used, reproduced, stored in a retrieval system, or transmitted, in any form or by any means now known or hereafter invented, without written permission from the publisher. The sale, duplication, hire, lending, copying, digitalization, or reproduction of this material, in any manner or form whatsoever, is also prohibited, and is a violation of federal, civil, and digital copyright law, which provides severe civil and criminal penalties for any violations.

Seabrook's Bible Dictionary of Traditional and Mystical Christian Doctrines, by Lochlainn Seabrook. Includes endnotes and bibliographical references.

Front & back cover design & art, book design, layout, & interior art by Lochlainn Seabrook
All images, graphic design, graphic art, & illustrations copyright © Lochlainn Seabrook
Cover design copyright © Lochlainn Seabrook
Portions of this book have been adapted from the author's other works

The religious and spiritual views documented in this book are those of the publisher.

☙ All are thrice spirit-blessed who read this little book ❧

The paper used in this book is acid-free and lignin-free. It has been certified by the Sustainable Forestry Initiative and the Forest Stewardship Council and meets all ANSI standards for archival quality paper.

PRINTED & MANUFACTURED IN OCCUPIED TENNESSEE, FORMER CONFEDERATE STATES OF AMERICA

DEDICATION

To the Followers of the Way,

Epigraph

"But we speak the wisdom of God in a mystery, even the hidden wisdom, which God ordained before the world unto our glory."

Paul, 1 Corinthians 2:7

Contents

Notes to the Reader 14
Preface 19
Introduction 53

ENTRIES

A

Abraham 81
Adam 84
Adversary 85
Alpha and Omega 86
amen 87
Ancient of Days 87
angels 87
anointing 88
antichrist 88
Apostles 88
ark 89
Ascension 90
astrology 90
atonement 94

B

Babylon 96
baptism 96
Beast 98
Bethlehem 98
Bible 99
birth of Jesus 99
Blood of the Lamb 100
born again 101
bread 102
Brethren 102
Buddha 102

C

calf 109
Cana wedding 109
Christ 109
Christ Consciousness 115
Christianity 116
Christmas 143
Church 147

closet 149
Comforter 149
Conscious Mind 151
cross 152
crown 155
Crucifixion 156

D

death of Jesus 159
Devil 162
Divine Mind 163
divinity of Jesus 164
door 167
dove 168

E

ears 171
east 172
Ecclesia 172
Eden 173
Ego 174
Egypt 174
Elias 175
Elisha 179
enlightenment 179
Enoch 180
Essenes 183
Eucharist 191
Eve 191
evil 191
Exodus 192
eyes 194

F

Fall of Man 196
Father 197
First-Born Son of God 198
fish 198
Flood of Noah 199
Forbidden Fruit 202
forgiveness 203
Four Horsemen 203

G

Galilee 206
Garden of Eden 206
Gnosis 207
Gnosticism 209

	God	239
	Goddess	246
	gods and goddesses	249
	gold, frankincense, and myrrh	251
	Golgotha	252
	Good News	252
	Good Shepherd	254
	Gospel	255
	Gospel of Jesus Christ	264
	Gospel of Q	265
	Gospel of the Kingdom of God	267
	Gospel of Thomas	271
H		
	Heaven	273
	Hell	275
	Herod Antipas	275
	Hidden Man of the Heart	275
	Higher Self	275
	Holy Ghost	276
	Holy Spirit	276
	Holy Trinity	277
I		
	I AM	281
	Indwelling Christ	284
	Inner Man	284
	inward man	284
	Israel	284
J		
	Jehovah	286
	Jerusalem	286
	Jesus	288
	John the Baptist	306
	Jordan River	308
K		
	karma	311
	Keys of the Kingdom of Heaven	316
	king	317
	Kingdom of God	318
	Kingdom of Heaven	320
	Krishna	320
	Kyrios	322
L		
	Lamb of God	325
	Lazarus	326

light 326
Logos 328
Lower Self 330
Lucifer 330

M

manna 334
mansions 335
Mary 335
Massacre of the Innocents 336
mass mind 337
Melchizedek 337
Messiah 337
Mithra 340
monotheism 353
Moses 355
Mother 357
mountain 358
mouth of God 358
Myth of Christ 359

N

Nativity 363
Nazarenes 378
neighbor 379
Noah 379
number of the Beast 380
numbers 383

O

oil 389
Only Begotten Son 393
original sin 395
Osiris 397
outward man 402

P

parable 404
Paraclete 404
Passion of Jesus 404
Paul 404
peace and sword 416
Pearl of Great Price 418
Peter 418
Pharisees 421
Pilate 421
Pool of Bethesda 421
prayer 421

R

precious stones 422
purple 423
Pythagoras 423

rainbow 428
raising the dead 430
rebirth 430
Redeemer 430
redemption 433
reincarnation 433
Resurrection of Jesus 444
revelation 449
righteousness 452
river 453
rock 455

S

Sacrament 459
salvation 464
Satan 468
Savior 469
Scheme of Salvation 473
Second Coming of Christ 473
serpent 474
seven stars 477
Silent Years 479
sin 492
Solomon 492
Son of God 492
Son of Man 495
Soul 500
Spirit 502
Star of Bethlehem 503
Subconscious Mind 504
Sun 505
Sun of Righteousness 512
Superconscious Mind 513

T

Teacher of Righteousness 515
Temple of God 516
tetramorph 517
thealogy 524
theology 524
Theosis 525
Third Ear 531

U

Third Eye	531
three days	532
Transfiguration of Jesus	534
Tree of Life	536
Tribes of Israel	539
Trinity	541
Twelve	541
Underworld	545
union with God	545
unrighteousness	547
Upper Room	547

V

valley	549
virgin birth	549
Virgo	555
voice of God	555

W

walking on water	558
washed in the blood of the Lamb	558
washing the feet	561
water	562
Way of the Lord	566
wine	567
Wise Men	567
Word	570
Word of God	570

Y

Yahweh	573
yoke of Jesus	576

Z

Zion	579
Zodiac	579
Appendix A: A List of Christian Mystics	584
Appendix B: The Mystic's Creed	585
Notes	586
Bibliography	684
Meet the Author	720

444

Notes to the Reader

GENERALITIES
✠ As different cultures view spiritual doctrines and symbols differently in different time periods, no two traditional Christian or mystical Christian schools of thought agree on every one of the definitions contained in this reference work. As such, there is great fluidity of meaning across the various entries, the truth therein which must be spiritually discerned by the reader.

THE MYSTICAL CHURCH
✠ While throughout this book I use the phrase "mystical Christian Church," I do not intend this to mean that Christian mystics possess a physical or even an official Church. Rather I am referring to the body of mystical believers, who read their Bible *intuitively* (as interpreted by the Holy Spirit), as opposed to the body of traditional believers, who read their Bible *literally* (as interpreted by the clergy).

CHURCH DIVISIONS
✠ Christianity is normally placed into three divisions: 1) Orthodox, 2) Catholic, and 3) Protestant, with the mystical branch, or what has been devilishly misnamed the "heterodox" or "heretical" branch, being completely disregarded. For this book, however, I have done away with this archaic and inaccurate arrangement. In its place I have divided the Church into two basic segments: 1) traditional, 2) mystical.

In my system the *traditional Christian* branch includes Catholicism, Protestantism, Greek Orthodoxy, and all other related Christian denominations, sects, cults, and associations. My *mystical Christian* branch includes all non-traditional Christian groups and spiritual belief systems that have been labeled "unorthodox" by mainline Christianity, and which proudly fall under the heading of Christian mysticism.

Thus in this volume I refer to, for example, Catholicism and Evangelical Christianity as "traditional," "conventional," "mainstream," "mainline," "organized," "institutional," or "orthodox"—though the latter word normally applies to the Greek Orthodox Church.

QUOTATIONS
✠ When quoting early writers, in nearly every case I have reproduced the exact wording, including spellings peculiar to pre-21st-Century writing. However, in some cases I have broken up long-running paragraphs for ease of reading.

NEW TESTAMENT AUTHORS
✠ Though most of the Bible's books are pseudepigraphical (that is, their authors are unknown or, more often, are falsely attributed), for simplicity's sake I use the authors ascribed by Christian tradition; for example, "Mark" for the Gospel of Mark, "Paul" for the letter to the Ephesians, "Isaiah" for the book of Isaiah, etc.

BIBLE VERSION: KING JAMES
✠ All canonical Bible passages are from the King James Version (KJV), unless otherwise noted. As a result, my readings and interpretations may differ from those found in other versions. Because of this, I highly recommend the use of the KJV in combination with *Seabrook's Bible Dictionary*.

THIS BOOK'S UNIVERSAL MESSAGE
✠ Though this work is geared toward Christians, because Jesus' message is truly universal, anyone of any faith, or even nonbelievers (for much of Christian spirituality agrees with modern sciences like psychology and quantum physics), can benefit from studying these pages. As the Quakers teach, every man and woman is born with the "seed of God" (that "Divine Spark" known to Christian mystics as "the Christ") within them, no matter what their nationality or personal beliefs.[1]

MY VIEW OF THE BIBLE
✠ I do not agree with traditional Christians that the Bible is "inerrant" and "infallible," or that "everything in the Bible is literally true." In fact, as this very book amply illustrates, there are grave dangers to accepting an infallible literalist view of the Old and New Testaments—or of any ancient sacred texts, for that matter. At the same time I do not hold the view, as so many of my fellow Christian mystics do, that the miracles, myths, and supernatural events presented in the Bible are all literary inventions or folkloric in origin. In fact, as a genuine mystic, I believe that "with God all things are possible,"[2] which means that anything and everything in the Bible *could* be true. I can attest to this, for I am one who has seen and personally experienced countless "miracles," as well as a host of paranormal and supernatural phenomena, firsthand, and continue to do so on a daily basis.

This being said, it must be admitted by every honest individual who has given the Bible even the most cursory reading, that it contains a mass of both unintentional and intentional errors, syncretistic discrepancies, weird discontinuities, ludicrous impossibilities, bizarre additions, surprising doublets, odd omissions, doltish misinterpretations, out-of-place accretions, violent interpolations, jarring recensions, obtrusive apologetics, intrusive emendations, conspicuous contrivances, outlandish distortions, extraordinary conflations, explicit contradictions, unaccountable repetitions, "premeditated perversions,"[3] appalling obscenities,[4] and scores of obvious late and often abrupt revisions and redactions by thousands of uneducated, politically-oriented, anti-mystical ecclesiastical hands.[5] How can we honestly continue to claim then that, word for word, the Bible is "revealed"?

Freud likened the tampering of biblical texts with murder,[6] and for good reason: millions of lives have been damaged or even destroyed by a misunderstanding of the Bible's 31,102 verses. One historian, Arthur Findlay, found that the English revisers working on the King James Version of the New

Testament alone made 36,191 "changes" during their translation from the original Greek text, a staggering average of 4.5 redactions in each of its 7,960 verses.[7] Objective Bible scholars have long accepted the fact that *every* New Testament book has undergone extensive ancient editing, resulting in thousands of variants in the earliest Greek copies. The 4th-Century Pope Damasus I noted that 2nd-Century Latin translations in particular had undergone so much copying and recopying that now, "full of errors and dubious passages," each copy had literally become a different version in its own right.[8]

What all of this means is that in its present form the New Testament does not and cannot contain the original wording of its original authors, whoever they were. Rather it is a patchwork quilt that for centuries has been almost continually "improved" by a myriad of anonymous "contributors"; the end result of a long and complex series of editorial processes which can never be unraveled due to the paucity of evidence.[9]

Strauss rightly noted that since "all things contained in religions which contradict each other cannot have been revealed, we are compelled to exercise a critical discrimination."[10] Baigent and Leigh refer to the four canonical Gospels as historical black holes, infamously untrustworthy and lacking any reliable historical context,[11] a view backed by centuries of industrious and typically earnest and objective form, source, textual, canonical, narrative, redaction, psychological, rhetorical, and socioscientific criticism (often performed by Bible-believing Christian scholars).

Thus, I maintain, along with the great Victorian Bible critics, that all ancient histories, including the Good Book, should be approached with the same objective eye, whether they be Hindu, Buddhist, Mesopotamian, Celtic, Scandinavian, Native-American, Egyptian, Jewish, or Christian. To the mystic everything is grist for the esoteric mill, where, to test their truthfulness, spiritual ideas must be put through an allegorical interpretive process. As this book shows, there is almost nothing in the Bible that is itself either not mystical in nature, or is not connected to mysticism in one way or another. For me, as a Christian mystic, this makes the Bible the world's greatest book of mysticism—as the following pages will show.

LEARN MORE

✠ Not even 100 large volumes could contain everything that is known about the very important and complex topic of traditional and mystical Christian doctrines. As such, this small work is meant only as an introduction, and the reader is encouraged to explore the vast array of literature that is available, from ancient to modern. In particular I direct those interested to my other works on Jesus, spirituality, and the Word of God, listed on page 2.

Keep Your Body, Mind, & Spirit Vibrating at Their Highest Level

YOU CAN DO SO BY READING THE BOOKS OF

SEA RAVEN PRESS

There is nothing that will so perfectly keep your body, mind, and spirit in a healthy condition as to think wisely and positively. Hence you should not only read this book, but also the other books that we offer. They will quicken your physical, mental, and spiritual vibrations, enabling you to maintain a position in society as a healthy erudite person.

KEEP YOURSELF WELL-INFORMED!

The well-informed person is always at the head of the procession, while the ignorant, the lazy, and the unthoughtful hang onto the rear. If you are a Spiritual man or woman, do yourself a great favor: read Sea Raven Press books and stay well posted on the Truth. It is almost criminal for one to remain in ignorance while the opportunity to gain knowledge is open to all at a nominal price.

We invite you to visit our Webstore for a wide selection of wholesome, family-friendly, well-researched, educational books for all ages. You will be glad you did!

Five-Star Books & Gifts From the Heart of the American South

SeaRavenPress.com

"Three things shine before the world and cannot be hidden.
The Moon, the Sun, and the Truth."

buddha

Preface

"I AM NOT YOUR MASTER, FOR YOU HAVE SIPPED FROM
THE SACRED WATERS THAT I HAVE LADLED OUT."[12]

JESUS TO THE APOSTLES

THERE are thousands of Bible dictionaries. Why write another? For one thing it is rare to read about the esoteric side of Christianity. Nearly all Bible dictionaries are penned by the orthodox, and few if any of these authors provide the mystical, inner, symbolic, or spiritual meaning of the Good Book's many passages. More to the point, in modern times none have been written comparing traditional and mystical Christian doctrines. My book intends to fill these empty spaces left by both the passage of time and mainstream Church theologians and writers.

There are, however, a number of other reasons a book like this is vitally important today. To begin with, it was not the human mind which first responded to Jesus. It was the human heart, and by this I mean that our Lord was first experienced by others non-intellectually, outside the analytical mind, via an indescribable state of consciousness that is commonly referred to as "mystical."[13]

This is precisely what one would expect considering that *all* "personal religious experience has its roots and center in mystical states of consciousness,"[14] *all* religions have their beginnings in mysticism, and *all* religious ideas are expressed mystically, that is, through symbolism.[15] Indian mystics go as far as to hold mysticism to be the very foundation of human civilization and culture.[16] And yet, nearly *all* of the controversies, divisiveness, and dissension that exist between the various Christian denominations and sects have arisen due to a misunderstanding of mysticism and its arcane symbols.[17] To the Christian mystic this is a momentous calamity, for "everything is symbolic of something more."[18]

Why mystical symbols? the traditional Christian asks. Why are they, as well as mysticism itself, so important to the Faith? And why are these things not taught more often and openly in the mainstream Church?

Let us answer these questions.

Symbolism is not only the original and innate language of religion, mysticism, and philosophy, it is the language of all of Nature, for every material form is but a symbol of the Divine Energy which created it.[19] Thus to view biblical figures like "Jonah," "Ruth," and "Job" as literal historical people rather than as what they really are, symbolic literary inventions, is to completely miss the intended mystical meaning behind them.[20] Of these facts Pike writes:

> Symbols were the almost universal language of ancient theology. They were the most obvious method of instruction; for, like nature herself, they addressed the understanding through the eye; and the most ancient expressions denoting communication of religious knowledge, signify ocular exhibition. The first teachers of mankind borrowed this method of instruction; and it comprised an endless store of pregnant hieroglyphics. These lessons of the olden time were the riddles of the Sphynx, tempting the curious by their quaintness, but involving the personal risk of the adventurous interpreter. "The Gods themselves," it was said, "disclose their intentions to the wise, but to fools their teaching is unintelligible;" and the King of the Delphic Oracle was said not to declare, nor on the other hand to conceal; but emphatically to "intimate or signify."
>
> The Ancient Sages, both barbarian and Greek, involved their meaning in similar indirections and enigmas; their lessons were conveyed either in visible symbols, or in those "parables and dark sayings of old," which the Israelites considered it a sacred duty to hand down unchanged to successive generations. The explanatory tokens employed by man, whether emblematical objects or actions, symbols or mystic ceremonies, were like the mystic signs and portents either in dreams or by the wayside, supposed to be significant of the intentions of the Gods; both required the aid of anxious thought and skillful interpretation. It was only by a correct appreciation of analogous problems of nature, that the will of Heaven could be understood by the Diviner, or the lessons of Wisdom become manifest to the Sage.[21]

This is how we know that Christianity began as a mystical religion (in Egypt it was born out of Gnosticism, in Palestine out of Essenism),[22] and that its first leaders and teachers, men such as Jesus,[23] Paul, John, and James, were superlative mystics and hierophants[24] who spoke and taught in mystical terms, using allegory, symbols, simile, metaphor, numerology, ciphers, astrology, parables, key words, sacred alphabets, cryptic hand signals, passwords, geometric shapes, and mythology to relay profound spiritual verities, hidden knowledge, and concealed wisdom to their followers. For, after all, "myth is the garment of mystery,"[25] and the fable is the truth clothed in allegory.[26]

Indeed, early Christianity possessed far more sacred mysteries, esoteric secrets, and occult principles than Paganism did. This is proven in part by biblical words such as "mystery," which, when used by Jesus and other highly evolved spiritual masters, does not refer to a complex principle that it is difficult to understand (the modern definition), but rather to a *secret revelation*; in other words, "that which is known only to the initiated."[27]

This makes the Bible itself, like the Bhagavad Gita[28] and nearly every other ancient holy book, one great mythic allegory—in this case, concerning personal redemption—from beginning to end.[29] The hidden knowledge contained within the Bible then can only be ascertained by reading it allegorically.[30] But since ancient allegory is unfamiliar to the modern Bible student, one hoping to gain even an infinitesimal understanding of its mystical teachings will need a key to unlock them. This book is that key.

This is doubly important since orthodox Christians have not only Paganized and apotheosized Jesus, *and* carefully imitated and copied Pagan art,[31] they have also literalized, distorted, and perverted authentic Christian doctrine beyond recognition, making "the word of God of none effect through their tradition . . . teaching for doctrines the commandments of men" instead of the Father's.[32]

What was the purpose of this, a nefarious process that has been rightly called the "Scheme of Salvation"?[33] And what were the conditions that prompted and allowed it to be concocted?

In answer to the second question, there was, following Jesus' death, a bitter disappointment due to the delay of the Parousia (which both Jesus[34] and later Paul[35] are shown incorrectly predicting to occur within the lifetimes of their 1st-Century followers), as well as the failed appearance of the long awaited *political* messiah, who, it was hoped, would liberate Israel from the crushing domination of Roman rule. These two components created ideal conditions for belief in a second "anointed one," a *spiritual* messiah,[36] one that had long been prophesied and hoped for—based on a vague passage in Zechariah[37]—by Jewish sects like the Essenes.[38]

In answer to the first question, after the Jerusalem Conference about A.D. 50, in which a major schism split Jewish Christians from Gentile (Pagan) Christians,[39] many of the former began to return to Judaism.[40] This left Pagans as the main source of converts for the growing orthodox Church.[41] As personal spiritual beliefs are never simply dropped when one changes their religion,[42] in order to attract these myth-loving polytheistic "heathens" into the fold,[43] Church officials deemphasized Jesus's humanity, then deified Him,[44] a non-biblical,[45] "self-contradictory deception"[46] that not only turned Him into a spiritual (as opposed to a political) messiah, but also a standard pre-Christian Pagan Sun/Son-god who is born at the Spring Equinox (Easter), reaches His peak strength at the Summer Solstice (Midsummer), ages at the Autumnal Equinox (Halloween), and dies and is reborn at the Winter Solstice (Christmas). Along the way the historical Jesus was forgotten, replaced by the religious Christ.[47] Thus, as Frazer writes,

> the Church has skillfully contrived to plant the seeds of the new faith on the old stock of paganism.[48]

The astrological passion play upon which this story was built is indeed "old stock," for it is thousands of years older than Christianity.[49] Some 5,000 years ago, for instance, the ancient Egyptian festival known as the "Mysteries of Osiris" featured an eight-day theatrical pageant in which the entire life cycle of this African Sun/Son-god was depicted, from his birth, life, and death to his burial, ascension, and resurrection.[50] In truth, all of the early Mystery Religions were built upon this same mythological scaffolding: the Spring birth and Winter death of the dying and rising solar-god,[51] perhaps the commonest type of deity, one known from at least 4000 B.C.[52]

The 1st Century A.D. was the Age of Syncretism (or Theocrasia) after all, so the process of developing "The Christ Myth" was just as natural in Jerusalem as it was in Rome, Athens, or Alexandria,[53] and Church Fathers like Irenaeus, Tertullian, and Augustine only helped further establish it by knowingly endorsing and expanding its many accompanying Pagan motifs.[54] More help came from ordinary Pagans and Christians during these early centuries, who were used to worshiping the emperor, the state god, and Jesus as deities, and who thus found it easy to switch back and forth between Pagan Sun-worship and Christian Son-worship; or even embrace both simultaneously, as Constantine the Great did.[55]

Along with these momentous changes, any and all writings and sects which revealed that many of Jesus' teachings derived from pre-Christian Christian sources, such as the Essenes and the Gnostics, were suppressed and even obliterated. Jesus' beautiful and mystical "Gospel of the Kingdom of God,"[56] a clear "danger to the sacred interest of the Church,"[57] was replaced with the plain and literal "Gospel of Jesus Christ,"[58] and His original, flexible, subjective, mystical, meaningful doctrines were literalized, historicized, and trivialized, transforming them into unchangeable, concretized, objective, often meaningless, Christian dogma.

How unfortunate. For, as was their custom, in the interest of apologetics, propaganda, and good story-telling,[59] the mystical Oriental authors of the Bible had freely and intentionally used figurative language, gross exaggeration, and striking ancient mythic elements to lend interest and color to their often dull narratives, never once expecting them to be taken literally.[60]

One example of this can be found in Mark 14:30, where the second Evangelist has Jesus say to Peter: "Before the cock crow twice, thou shalt deny me thrice." Not understanding that this was merely a common Hebrew idiom, an everyday Jewish form of emphasis, the other three subsequent Gospelers literalized the passage, making Peter actually deny Jesus three times.[61] Jewish scholar Hugh J. Schonfield notes that the real meaning of this Marcan scripture is simply that Peter will deny Jesus like everyone else, not that he will do so *three times* specifically.[62] Mainstream Church authorities, of course, have long withheld such historical knowledge from the laity, which is why it comes as such a surprise to those Christians who are first exposed to it.

Christianity itself was turned into a complex system of codes, creeds, beliefs, concepts, rituals, doctrines, and regulations that had never existed during Jesus' lifetime, and which "required" a priesthood to explain them to the masses[63]—this despite the fact that Jesus, whose Gospel was simple and childlike, never once refers to a priesthood![64] By the 4th Century A.D. Churchianity was born: a soulless demystified religion comprised of empty fabricated rules and peculiar and often nonsensical biblical stories and figures, all perverted beyond recognition by orthodox Christian priests and their equally unenlightened scribes.

This sharp and artificial division between the first Christians, the mystics, and the second Christians, the so-called "traditionalists," was exacerbated by an important psychological element: in order to feel a complete sense of solidarity, the early Catholic masses needed to vent their animosity on an "outside minority," as Freud labeled it. In this case that outside minority was the Gnostic-Essenic Church, the mystical branch of Christianity—and its original root—which, due to its numerical weakness, literally invited suppression by its stronger rival.[65]

In an 1856 article Bishop C. J. Ellicott writes of both the distortion of sacred scripture and the outright deception that was involved in the creation of the mainstream Church:

> But credulity is not the only charge which these early ages have to sustain. They certainly cannot be pronounced free from the influence of pious frauds. . . . *It was an age of literary frauds. Deceit, if it had a good intention, frequently passed unchallenged.* . . . . However unwilling we may be to admit it,

history forces upon us the recognition of pious fraud as a principle which was by no means inoperative in the earliest ages of Christianity.[66]

Jeremiah Jones writes:

> To *make testimonies out of forgeries and spurious books to prove the very foundation of the Christian revelation*, was a method much practised by some of the Fathers, especially Justin Martyr, Clemens Alexandrinus, and Lactantius.[67]

B. H. Cowper, a well-known defender of traditional Christianity, confessed that Christianity's earliest officials, priests, and scribes had little regard for truth, fact, or authentic history:

> *Ancient invention and industry went even further*, and produced sundry scraps about Herod, Veronica, Lentulus, and Abgar, wrote epistles for Christ and his mother, and I know not how much besides. *No difficulty stood in the way; ancient documents could easily be appealed to without necessarily existing*; spirits could be summoned from the other world by a stroke of the pen, and be made to say anything; sacred names could be written and made *a passport to fictions*, and so on *ad libitum*.[68]

Mosheim makes mention of

> a variety of [early Christian] commentaries filled with impostures or fables on our Savior's life and sentiments, composed soon after his ascent into heaven, by men who, without being bad, perhaps, were superstitious, simple, and piously deceitful. To these were afterwards added other writings falsely accredited to the most holy apostles by fraudulent individuals. . . . A pernicious maxim which was current in the schools, not only of the Egyptians, the Platonists, and the Pythagoreans, but also of the Jews, was very early recognised by the Christians, and soon found among them numerous patrons—namely, that *those who made it their business to deceive with a view of promoting the cause of truth were deserving rather of commendation than censure*.[69]

Professor of Theology at Gottingen, Dr. Gieseler, writes:

In reference to the advancement of various Christian interests, and in like manner also to the confirmation of those developments of doctrine already mentioned, the spurious literature which had arisen and continually increased among the Jews and Christians, was of great importance. *The Christians made use of such expressions and writings as had already been falsely attributed by Jews, from partiality to their religion, to honored persons of antiquity, and altered them in parts to suit their own wants, such as the book of Enoch and the fourth book of Ezra. But writings of this kind were also fabricated anew by Christians, who quieted their conscience respecting the forgery with the idea of their good intention, for the purpose of giving greater impressiveness to their doctrines and admonitions by the reputation of respectable names, of animating their suffering brethren to steadfastness, and of gaining over their opponents to Christianity.*[70]

"What a distortion did his doctrine and memory suffer in the same, in the next, and the following ages!" complained Emerson bitterly about what the Church has done to Jesus and His teachings.[71] Of the early Christian Church, Plutarch might have said that in

> *mistaking the sign for the thing signified*, [they] fell into a ridiculous superstition; while others, in avoiding one extreme, plunged into the no less *hideous gulf of irreligion and impiety*.[72]

Of this tragic religious scheming, Christian mystic and New England Transcendentalist William Ellery Channing writes:

> There is much reason to believe that *Christianity is at this moment dishonoured by gross and cherished corruptions*. If you remember the darkness which hung over the Gospel for ages; if you consider the impure union which still subsists in almost every Christian country between the church and state, and which enlists men's selfishness and ambition on the side of *established error*; if you recollect in what degree *the spirit of intolerance has checked free inquiry*, not only before but since the Reformation; you wilt see that *Christianity cannot have freed itself from all the human inventions which disfigured it under the Papal tyranny*.
>
> No. Much stubble is yet to be burned; much rubbish

to be removed; *many gaudy decorations which a false taste has hung around Christianity must be swept away*; and the earth-born fogs which have long shrouded it must be scattered, before this divine fabric will rise before us in its native and awful majesty, in its harmonious proportions, in its mild and celestial splendours.[73]

Albert Pike, here in the American South an honored Confederate officer during Lincoln's War on the Constitution,[74] a leader in the Scottish Rite of Freemasonry, and a great defender of the Ancient Mysteries, gives the following explanation of how pure religion (that is, mysticism) and its sacred spiritual symbols "degenerated" into "popular religion," with its many Pagan motifs, figures, myths, and doctrines:

> *In the Ancient Orient, all religion was more or less a mystery and there was no divorce from it of philosophy. The popular theology, taking the multitude of allegories and symbols for realities, degenerated into a worship of the celestial luminaries, of imaginary Deities with human feelings, passions, appetites, and lusts, of idols, stones, animals, reptiles.* The Onion was sacred to the Egyptians, because its different layers were a symbol of the concentric heavenly spheres. Of course the popular religion could not satisfy the deeper longings and thoughts, the loftier aspirations of the Spirit, or the logic of reason. *The first, therefore, was taught to the Initiated in the mysteries. There, also, it was taught by symbols. The vagueness of symbolism, capable of many interpretations, reached what the palpable and conventional creed could not. Its indefiniteness acknowledged the abstruseness of the subject: it treated that mysterious subject mystically:* it endeavored to illustrate what it could not explain; to excite an appropriate feeling, if it could not develop an adequate idea; and to *make the image a mere subordinate conveyance for the conception, which itself never became obvious or familiar.*
>
> Thus the knowledge now imparted by books and letters, was of old conveyed by symbols; and the priests invented or perpetuated a display of rites and exhibitions, which were not only more attractive to the eye than words, but often more suggestive and more pregnant with meaning to the mind.
>
> Masonry, successor of the [early] mysteries, still follows the ancient manner of teaching. Her ceremonies are like the ancient mystic shows,—not the reading of an essay,

but the opening of a problem, requiring research, and constituting philosophy the arch-expounder. Her symbols are the instruction she gives. The lectures are endeavors, often partial and one-sided, to interpret these symbols. He who would become an accomplished Mason must not be content merely to hear, or even to understand, the lectures; he must, aided by them, and they having, as it were, marked out the way for him, *study, interpret, and develop these symbols for himself.*

. . . But Masonry teaches, and has preserved in their purity, the cardinal tenets of the old primitive faith, which underlie and are the foundation of all religions. *All that ever existed have had a basis of truth; and all have overlaid that truth with errors. The primitive truths taught by the Redeemer [Jesus] were sooner corrupted, and intermingled and alloyed with fictions than when taught to the first of our race.* Masonry is the universal morality which is suitable to the inhabitants of every clime, to the man of every creed. It has taught no doctrines, except those truths that tend directly to the well-being of man; and those who have attempted to direct it toward useless vengeance, political ends, and Jesuitism, have merely perverted it to purposes foreign to its pure spirit and real nature. . . . *So it has always been that allegories, intended as vehicles of truth, to be understood by the sages, have become or bred errors, by being literally accepted.*

. . . *The dunces who led primitive Christianity astray, by substituting faith for science, reverie for experience, the fantastic for the reality; and the inquisitors who for so many ages waged against Magism [that is, Christian mysticism] a war of extermination, have succeeded in shrouding in darkness the ancient discoveries of the human mind; so that we now grope in the dark to find again the key of the phenomena of nature.*

. . . *To all this the absurd reading of the established Church, taking literally the figurative, allegorical, and mythical language of a collection of Oriental books of different ages, directly and inevitably led.*[75]

Pike understood the importance of allegory, whether it concerned Freemasonry or Christianity:

[Freemasonry has been] from the earliest times the custodian and depository of the great philosophical and religious truths, unknown to the world at large, and handed down from age to age by an unbroken current of tradition, embodied in symbols, emblems, and allegories. . . . It is of little importance whether [its background] . . . is in anywise historical. For [Freemasonry's] value consists in the lessons which it inculcates, and the duties which it prescribes to those who receive it. The parables and allegories of the Scriptures are not less valuable than history. Nay, they are more so, because ancient history is little instructive, and *truths are concealed in and symbolized by the legend and the myth.*[76]

Similarly Parker writes:

> *On the authority of the written word man was taught to believe impossible legends, conflicting assertions; to take fiction for fact, a dream for a miraculous revelation of God, an oriental poem for a grave history of miraculous events, a collection of amatory idyls for a serious discourse "touching the mutual love of Christ and the church;" they have been taught to accept a picture sketched by some glowing eastern imagination, never intended to be taken for a reality, as a proof that the Infinite God spoke in human words, appeared in the shape of a cloud, a flaming bush, or a man who ate, and drank, and vanished into smoke; that he gave counsels to-day, and the opposite to-morrow; that he violated his own laws, was angry, and was only dissuaded by a mortal man from destroying at once a whole nation—millions of men who rebelled against their leader in a moment of anguish.*
>
> Questions in philosophy, questions in the Christian religion, have been settled by an appeal to that book. The inspiration of its authors has been assumed as infallible. Every fact in the early Jewish history has been taken as a type of some analogous fact in Christian history. The most distant events, even such as are still in the arms of time, were supposed to be clearly foreseen and foretold by pious Hebrews several centuries before Christ. It is assumed at the outset, with no shadow of evidence, that those writers held a miraculous communication with God, such as he has granted to no other man. What was originally a presumption of bigoted Jews became an article of faith, which Christians were burned for not believing. This has been for centuries the general opinion of the Christian church, both Catholic and

Protestant, though the former never accepted the Bible as the only source of religious truth. It has been so.

Still worse, it is now the general opinion of religious sects of this day. Hence the attempt, which always fails, to reconcile the philosophy of our times with the poems in Genesis writ a thousand years before Christ. Hence the attempt to conceal the contradictions in the record itself. Matters have come to such a pass that even now he is deemed an infidel, if not by implication an atheist, whose reverence for the Most High forbids him to believe that God commanded Abraham to sacrifice his son, a thought at which the flesh creeps with horror; to believe it solely on the authority of an oriental story, written down nobody knows when or by whom, or for what purpose; which may be a poem, but cannot be the record of a fact, unless God is the author of confusion and a lie.

Now, this idolatry of the Old Testament has not always existed. Jesus says that none born of a woman is greater than John the Baptist, yet the least in the kingdom of heaven was greater than John. Paul tells us the law—the very crown of the old Hebrew revelation—is a shadow of good things, which have now come; only a schoolmaster to bring us to Christ; and when faith has come, that we are no longer under the schoolmaster; that it was a law of sin and death, from which we are made free by the law of the spirit of life. Christian teachers themselves have differed so widely in their notion of the doctrines and meaning of those books, that *it makes one weep to think of the follies deduced therefrom.*

But modern criticism is fast breaking to pieces this idol which men have made out of the scriptures. It has shown that here are the most different works thrown together; that their authors, wise as they sometimes were, pious as we feel often their spirit to have been, had only that inspiration which is common to other men equally pious and wise; that they were by no means infallible, but were mistaken in facts or in reasoning—uttered predictions which time has not fulfilled; men who in some measure partook of the darkness and limited notions of their age, and were not always above its mistakes or its corruptions.

The history of opinions on the New Testament is quite similar. *It has been assumed at the outset, it would seem with no sufficient reason, without the smallest pretence on its writers' part, that all of its authors were infallibly and miraculously inspired, so that they could commit no error of doctrine or fact. Men have been* bid to close their eyes at the obvious difference between Luke and John—the serious disagreement between Paul and Peter; to believe, on the smallest evidence, accounts which shock the moral sense and revolt the reason, and tend to place Jesus in the same series with Hercules, and Apollonius of Tyana; accounts which Paul in the Epistles never mentions, though he also had a vein of the miraculous running quite through him. Men have been told that all these things must be taken as part of Christianity, and if they accepted the religion, they must take all these accessories along with it; that the living spirit could not be had without the killing letter.

All the books which caprice or accident had brought together between the lids of the Bible were declared to be the infallible word of God, the only certain rule of religious faith and practice. Thus the Bible was made not a single channel, but the only certain rule of religious faith and practice. To disbelieve any of its statements, or even the common interpretation put upon those statements by the particular age or church in which the man belonged, was held to be infidelity, if not atheism. In the name of him who forbid us to judge our brother, good men and pious men have applied these terms to others, good and pious as themselves. That state of things has by no means passed away. *Men, who cry down the absurdities of paganism in the worst spirit of the French "free-thinkers," call others infidels and atheists, who point out, though reverently, other absurdities which men have piled upon Christianity. So the world goes.*

An idolatrous regard for the imperfect scripture of God's word is the apple of Atalanta, which defeats theologians running for the hand of divine truth. *But the current notions respecting the infallible inspiration of the Bible have no foundation in the Bible itself. Which evangelist, which apostle of the New Testament, what prophet or psalmist of the Old Testament, ever claims infallible authority for himself or for others? Which of them does not in his own writings show that he was finite, and, with all his zeal and piety, possessed but a limited inspiration, the bound whereof we can sometimes discover? Did Christ ever demand that men should assent to the doctrines of the Old Testament, credit its stories, and take its poems for histories, and believe equally two accounts that contradict one another?*

Has he ever told you that all the truths of his religion, all the beauty of a Christian life, should be contained in the writings of those men who, even after his resurrection, expected him to be a Jewish king; of men who were sometimes at variance with one another, and misunderstood his divine teachings? Would not those modest writers themselves be confounded at the idolatry we pay them? Opinions may change on these points, as they have often changed—changed greatly and for the worse since the days of Paul. They are changing now, and we may hope for the better; for God makes man's folly as well as his wrath to praise him, and continually brings good out of evil.[77]

As "Christianity borrowed lavishly from its competitors,"[78] and fabricated much of its own self-supporting scripture and literature, it is all too "evident that this professedly historical Jesus is not a purely historical figure, but one which has been artificially transplanted into history" by a syncretistic, dogma-loving, but mysticism-hating organized Church.[79] In this way the human Jesus became an awkward, confusing, contradictory, composite, Pagan, godlike personage, one who our Lord Himself, a Jew, would have regarded as entirely blasphemous.[80]

It is for this reason that I refer to modern traditional, mainstream, conservative, evangelical, conventional, fundamentalist, formalized, institutional Christianity as "Pagan Christianity."[81] For it was only by adopting and assimilating Pagan ideas, rules, and rituals that the real human Jesus (the "Son of Man") and His mystical anti-formalistic teachings could be suppressed, replaced by a fabricated Pagan deity (the "Son of God") who preached doctrines that accorded with the orthodox branch of the Church. This sinister Paganization and literalization of Spiritual Truth orthodox Church officials have long disingenuously called "ecclesiastical necessity"!

But the truth is that there is very little of the authentic teachings of Jesus in popular Christianity today. Just a manmade *religious* belief system combining ancient Jewish-Pagan and modern politically correct doctrines intended to promote Churchianity rather than true Christianity.[82] Why is this a problem that confronts all Christians? Because Jesus taught a *spiritual* belief system, one without today's "uniformity of creeds" and "doctrinal divisions"; one that was meant to be a way of life rather than a religion.[83] This is what He meant when

He made the mystical comment that "my kingdom is not of this world."[84] Yet Christian literalists have made our Lord's kingdom a worldly one, with a Paganized deity named "Jesus Christ" as its royal monarch. Of these facts Pike writes:

> The God of nineteen-twentieths of the Christian world is only Bel, Moloch, Zeus, or at best Osiris, Mithras, or Adonai, under another name, worshipped with the old Pagan ceremonies and ritualistic formulas. It is the Statue of Olympian Jove, worshipped as the Father, in the Christian Church that was a Pagan Temple; it is the Statue of Venus, become the Virgin Mary.[85]

The ramifications and dire consequences of replacing the authority of Jesus with the authority of the Church,[86] the Church's adoption of Pagan imperial dress, pomp, holidays, and ceremony,[87] and the traditional Church's perversion of the Bible and the falsification of Jesus' life story and teachings, indeed, have lasted into the present day, and with devastating effects. Fundamentalist Christians, for example, are not preserving the "fundamentals" of Christianity, as their name implies, for what they consider "fundamental Christianity" is actually invented Christianity, a fabricated form of the faith that was unknown to Jesus, and which was begun only after He died—when He was no longer able to oppose it.

How do we know this is true?

Because we can read the history of these manmade decrees and doctrines as they were created and adopted, not only in the New Testament (for example, in Ephesians and the three Pastoral letters,[88] we begin to see the emphasis changing from the freeform mystical spirituality of Jesus to an institutionalized hierarchical Church, along with a degeneration of faith into formalism and dogmatism),[89] but also in the records of the Church's many ecclesiastical councils over the past 1700 years.[90]

What was invented at these meetings were *not* the fundamentals of our Lord, but the fundamentals of the Church,[91] which has proven over and over again that it wants nothing to do with the earthly human Jesus[92]—the great prophet, teacher, and healer who never mentioned either a church or a priesthood, and who taught that we are all gods,[93] that we could and would do greater works than He did,[94] and that the kingdom of Heaven is within us![95]

No doubt the most serious consequence of this drastic changeover—the disastrous attempt to merge incompatible Pagan and Jewish doctrines, concepts, beliefs, and myths[96]—is that not only was Jesus turned from a brilliant human educator, a superlative oracle, and an altruistic physician, into a strange, unrelatable composite figure that some have called a "pathological egoist,"[97] but that much of sacred scripture no longer makes sense, a phenomenon that causes skeptics, non-believers, agnostics, atheists and other religion-haters to regard the Bible with contempt; as nothing more than a monstrous book of fairy tales meant to anaesthetize, delude, and control the unthinking masses. Christian mystics, who have long strongly lamented orthodoxy's sweeping literalist revision of the Bible, have sympathy with this reaction. Pike writes:

> *To understand literally the symbols and allegories of Oriental books [like the Bible] as to ante-historical matters, is willfully to close our eyes against the Light. To translate the symbols into the trivial and commonplace, is the blundering of mediocrity.*

All religious expression is symbolism; since we can describe only what we see, and the true objects of religion are The Seen. *The earliest instruments of education were symbols*; and they and all other religious forms differed and still differ according to external circumstances and imagery, and *according to differences of knowledge and mental cultivation. All language is symbolic,* so far as it is applied to mental and spiritual phenomena and action. All words have, primarily, a material sense, howsoever they may afterward get, for the ignorant, a spiritual nonsense. "To refract,'" for example, is to draw back, and when applied to a statement, is symbolic, as much so as a picture of an arm drawn back, to express the same thing, would be. The very word "spirit" means "breath," from the Latin verb *spiro*, breathe.

To present a visible symbol to the eye of another, is not necessarily to inform him of the meaning which that symbol has to you. Hence the philosopher soon superadded to the symbols explanations addressed to the ear, susceptible of more precision, but less effective and impressive than the painted or sculptured forms which he endeavored to explain. *Out of these explanations grew by degrees a variety of narrations, whose true object and meaning were gradually forgotten, or lost in contradictions and incongruities. And when these were abandoned, and Philosophy resorted to definitions and formulas, its language was but a more complicated symbolism, attempting in the dark to grapple with and picture ideas impossible to be expressed. For as with the visible symbol, so with the word: to utter it to you does not inform you of the exact meaning which it has to me; and thus religion and philosophy became to a great extent disputes as to the meaning of words.* The most abstract expression for Deity, which language can supply, is but a sign or symbol for an object beyond our comprehension, and not more truthful and adequate than the images of Osiris and Vishnu, or their names, except as being less sensuous and explicit. We avoid sensuousness, only by resorting to simple negation. We come at last to define spirit by saying that it is not matter. Spirit is—spirit.[98]

Let us look at just one example of the confusion caused by biblical tampering.

The traditional Christian view of Jesus, as a Paganesque "*Only* Begotten Son of God" (rather than what He really was, a universal *human* example of what each person can become) renders His teachings incomprehensible and His life and death meaningless. For if, Parker writes,

> as some early Christians began to do, you take a heathen view, and make him a god, the Son of God in a peculiar and exclusive sense, much of the significance of his character is gone. His virtue has no merit, his love no feeling, his cross no burden, his agony no pain. His death is an illusion, his resurrection but a show. For if he were not a man, but a god, what are all these things? what his words, his life, his excellence of achievement?
>
> It is all nothing, weighed against the illimitable greatness of him who created the worlds and fills up all time and space! Then *his resignation is no lesson, his life no model, his death no triumph to you or me, who are not gods, but mortal men*, that know not what a day shall bring forth, and walk by faith "dim sounding on our perilous way." *Alas! we have despaired of man, and so cut off his brightest hope.*[99]

There is also the important matter of the doctrine of Original Sin: since it is not found in the Bible, it is obviously manmade.[100] But if it is manmade then the Virgin Birth as well as the death and resurrection of Jesus were unnecessary, and institutional Christianity serves no purpose. How to explain this overt contradiction to the Christian laity? Hence the need for a priesthood,[101] to interpret what Emerson called the Church's "gross superstitions,"[102] which Channing referred to as the "fictions of theologians,"[103] which Bauer referred to as the "web of deceit" spun by the four Evangelists,[104] and which Burkitt called the "regrettable accretions foisted on by superstition to the pure morality of the original Gospel."[105]

As many have discovered and as mystics have always known, the countless difficulties in the Bible vanish when one stops reading it literally and begins to view it allegorically.[106] Thus, for instance, because it is interior, spiritual, mental, and psychological, Christian mysticism can easily explain the death and resurrection of Jesus. Hence no need for a priesthood—as noted, an organizational body which Jesus never referred to in any *authentic* passage.[107] This is why Christian mystics have been persecuted and their writings have been suppressed by institutional Christianity for over 1,500 years: mystical Christianity is personal, spiritual, unorganized, passive, tolerant, and apolitical, while traditional Christianity is corporate, religious, organized, aggressive, intolerant, and political. It is the age old fight between liberalism and conservatism, dressed in religious garb.

The early orthodox branch of the Church desired far more than merely theological power over the masses, however. The "scheme" of Paganizing Jesus, historicizing unrelated Old Testament prophecies, and concretizing Christian doctrine handily fulfilled another ambition of Christian literalists, formalists, and dogmatists: the social, economic, and political takeover of the Empire by the Mother Church at Rome,[108] which finally occurred in the early 4th Century after the proclamation of Constantine the Great as emperor in A.D. 306.[109] The religiously intolerant Christian Emperor Theodosius the Great finished the job at the Council of Nicaea in 325 and the Council of Constantinople in 381, after which his many severe prohibitions against Paganism opened the door for the catholicization of the Empire. In this way Christian truth became Christian falsehood, Christian falsehood became Christian truth, and the traditional Church came to be regarded by mystics as the enemy of both Christ and free thought. So it has remained to this day among the orthodox, for having invented the Paganized version of Christianity after the death of Jesus, it must continue to subscribe to it in order to sustain the ruse.[110]

Now we can better understand the infamous statement of Pope Leo X, who in the 16th Century admitted that "it has served us well, this myth of Christ,"[111] as well as those early Church Fathers who maintained that "these officious lies [about Jesus] were devised for a good end."[112]

But the Truth that the orthodox has suppressed, buried, ignored, ridiculed, besmirched, slandered, and tried to obliterate for nearly two millennia still survives in the doctrines of the mystical Christian Church, and I have made many of them available in this very book.

The Truth that is revealed within these pages goes far beyond the Church's manufactured, carefully engineered teachings, not to mention the self-righteous morality and self-serving platitudes that one so often hears spouted from mainstream pulpits, and which never passed over the lips of our Lord. As it turns out, the root message of *true* and *original* Christianity, that is, mystical Christianity,[113] is the same one that is found in every other religion, from ancient

Rome, Greece, China, and Mesopotamia, to the Americas, Africa, Australia, and India: the archetypal threefold process of "generation, degeneration, and regeneration"[114]—which every human soul must successfully pass through on his or her path to their glory (that is, spiritual perfection). What follows is my personal interpretation of this mystical doctrine, of spiritual involution and evolution, which is presented in the New Testament as "the Life of Jesus."

SEABROOK'S MYSTICAL DOCTRINE OF THE CHRIST

1) In the Spirit Plane a Soul, the Universal Indwelling Christ, decides to come to earth to advance its spiritual growth, and selects a father and mother to come through (the "Annunciation").[115] The incoming incarnating Christ-Soul (the "Baby Jesus")[116] drops downward from the Spirit Plane (the "Immaculate Conception")[117] and onto the Material Plane, planting itself (as spirit) inside the mother's womb (the "Incarnation").[118]

2) Now on earth the Soul encases itself ("Baptism")[119] in a fetus or physical body (the "Cross"),[120] is born (the "Virgin Birth")[121] on a predetermined day ("Christmas"), and carefully tended into adolescence (the "Adoration"). During young adulthood the Soul progresses in knowledge and wisdom[122] (Jesus' "Silent Years," from 12 to 30 years old),[123] learning chiefly through experiencing the suffering caused by the tension between materiality and spirituality—which leads, in adulthood, to the final triumph over the physical plane (the "Temptation").[124] This stage ends in enlightenment (the "Transfiguration"),[125] accompanied by the realization and acceptance of the painful reality (the "Passion")[126] that it must sacrifice its physical body in order to return to God (the "Crucifixion").[127]

3) The Soul is rewarded by then being released (the "Resurrection")[128] to return upward, back to the world of Spirit (the "Ascension").[129] Once the Soul has been completely perfected through this repetitive process (either via physical reincarnation[130] or psychologically being "born again"),[131] it is allowed to stay in the highest Heaven (the seventh)[132] for all eternity ("Exaltation").[133]

From the Christian mystic's viewpoint, the entire Gospel story of Jesus is thus but an allegory of this divine process (which, viewed psychologically, was called "individuation" by Jung),[134] one which we all must experience.

Here we have the true "Redemption" of humanity: the final salvation of every person is assured,[135] for each Soul (not God or Satan) is in control of his or her own destiny—here on Earth and in the Afterlife. And what controls our conditions, circumstances, and experiences here, as well as our very fate in the World To Come? It is our *thoughts*,[136] the power of thought being "the true savior of humanity,"[137] which is exactly what the mystical writer of Proverbs proclaimed:

> For as a man thinketh in his heart, so is he.[138]

This is pure psychology, both Western and Eastern, one of whose primary principles is that whatever we focus on most consistently eventually becomes a part of us.[139] Thus the Hindu Maitri Upanishad states:

> What ever one doth thinketh, that doth one will become. This is the mystery of the ages.[140]

From this we glean the mystical meaning of the word psychology: *psyche*, the "Soul," and *logia*, "science." Or in German, *Seelenkunde*: *Seele*, meaning "Soul," and *kunde*, "the science of." Literally, Soul-Science,[141] or more generally, the "scientific study of the Soul," the Soul being another word for the human Mind.

Mastery of the Lower Self (Ego-Satan-Devil) is salvation, freeing the Higher Self to spend eternity in Spirit without having to go through the involutionary-evolutionary process again and again (reincarnation). In other words, we must "win" and enter a "difficult-to-obtain" human body[142] (according to Buddha, not an easy task),[143] and *while still in it* complete our "initiation," or soul growth, by realizing our infinite Divinity.[144] Only by coming to Earth School and taking on a human body (becoming "bound" on the material plane) can we fulfill this,[145] which is the very purpose of creation (that is, to become "unbound" by realizing our divine nature).[146] Some have likened this concept to a wild animal, which cannot appreciate freedom (that is, life in a spiritual body on the Heavenly Plane) until it has experienced captivity (that is, life in a physical body on the Earth Plane). Thus Hartmann writes:

> A soul cannot develop and progress without an appropriate body, because it is the physical body that furnishes the material for its development.[147]

The ancients held the selfsame view, as Pike notes:

> . . . the ancient Philosophers regarded the soul of man as having had its origin in Heaven. That was, Macrobius says, a settled opinion among them all; and they *held it to be the only true wisdom, for the soul, while united with the body, to look ever toward its source, and strive to return to the place whence it came.*

Among the fixed stars it dwelt, until, *seduced by the desire of animating a body, it descended to be imprisoned in matter.* Thenceforward it has no other resource than recollection, and is ever attracted toward its birth place and home. The means of return are to be sought for in itself. *To re-ascend to its source, it must do and suffer in the body.*[148]

Of this reality Heckethorn writes:

All light is born out of darkness, and must pass through the fire to arrive at the light; there is no other way but through darkness, or death, or hell—an idea which we find enunciated and represented in all the mysteries.[149]

Accordingly, God has given us the power to accomplish this very task. The Eastern masters say that those who do not come to understand this simple principle are "no better than a stone."[150]

To the mystic this is the true "Good News" of Christianity, and those who read this work from cover to cover will discover this truth for themselves. But it will not come by way of my words, nor can you ask your pastor, rabbi, priest, or priestess about it. It must come through your heart (*kardia*), the ancient codeword for the "Core of Your Being,"[151] or "Seat of Intelligence,"[152] that is, the Subconscious Mind (intuition),[153] the only instrument, as Emerson declared, that can finally determine religious truth once and for all.[154] Hence, Gnostic-Christians taught that the historical life of Jesus (including His crucifixion and resurrection) was not only an unfathomable mystery, but that viewing it literally would only lead the truth-seeker further astray.[155]

Like the celebrated "Boston Brahmin," I myself fall firmly on the mystical side of the Christian spectrum. For as a Christian mystic and Southern Transcendentalist I have, since earliest childhood, always perceived a second hidden and deeper meaning in every biblical passage. But unlike many of the conservative authors of traditional Bible dictionaries—most who like to interpret scripture to mean what they already believe it to mean;[156] who write polemically not in order to enlighten, but to persuade, influence, and propagandize; who engage in what has been aptly called "evangelical mind-control";[157] and who often contemptuously refer to my kind as the "lunatic fringe," "schismatics," "fanatics," "extremists," "heretics,"[158] and even "psychopaths"[159]—as a Christian mystic I do not seek to convert anyone to Christian mysticism, or even to the mystical method of interpreting the Bible.

My spiritual sister, the great Christian mystic Saint Teresa, once said: "For what reason would you want everyone to believe as you do?"[160] How true.

Which is why I follow the mystic's custom, espoused by the Unitarians, that each and every Christian should be free to view life, religion, even God himself, in any way he or she sees fit.[161]

The truth is that religious "heterodoxy" (mysticism) and religious "orthodoxy" (literalism) both derive from the same source, and are thus but two different variations on a single theme:[162] Man's effort to find God. And, as is patently clear from a thorough study of the New Testament, it contains no "strict doctrinal unity"[163] (for there was no single "pure" form of Christianity in the early Church,[164] and to this day there never has been),[165] I respect all views concerning the Faith, the Word of God, and our Lord. We are all in different "grades" here in Earth School, so it is only right that each one of us "work out our own salvation," in our own time and in our own way, just as both Paul[166] and Buddha commanded.[167]

Nonetheless, it is hoped that the once traditional, now "nontraditional," Christian doctrines found in this little volume will achieve the following:

☞ Bring the reader closer to both the human Jesus (Jesuology) and the mystical Christ (Christology).
☞ Engender discussion and questions concerning the Good Book.
☞ Aid those who are interested in a deeper form of biblical exegesis than their Church allows or teaches.
☞ Show that there are many alternative meanings, explanations, and interpretations of Christian scripture, and that, through mutual respect, tolerance, and understanding, these can exist harmoniously alongside orthodox ones.
☞ Reveal that our Father in Heaven purposefully influenced the writers of the Old and New Testaments to write mystically, in a "beautiful, humanitarian, and transcendent code,"[168] in order that we, depending on our level of intelligence, spiritual maturity, and receptivity, can absorb exactly what it is that we are ready and need to hear at each stage in our life.
☞ Assist the reader in realizing his or her inner divinity, known as "the Christ," which forwards our spiritual growth, our main purpose for coming to earth (known to mainline Christians as "glorifying God").
☞ Learn, as all the great Christian mystics have taught, that as god-men and god-women we humans can and are meant to have a direct relationship with the Divine.
☞ Provoke a rethinking of traditional Christian principles.

The last item listed here is especially important. For mysticism seeks, as Aldous Huxley remarked, to free Christianity from its "idolatrous preoccupation" with literal events—along with its "unfortunate servitude to historic fact"—and replace these with a more "spiritualized and universalized Christianity."[169]

Why is this important?

This is the exact type of "Christianity" that Jesus taught, an Essenic-Gnostic mysticism that can only be accessed by spiritually seeking God with "the Mind of Christ,"[170] that is, the open-minded receptivity and Christlike behavior of a "little child"[171]—identical to the "beginner's mind" of Zen Buddhism.[172] Only then can we gain entrance to our Lord's "Kingdom of Heaven Within."[173] Why is this? It is because the human Soul itself is divine,[174] and thus, like God, it sees, thinks, dreams, and communicates symbolically. Hence, mystical symbols, when correctly comprehended, feed and nourish that which is our true essence: Spirit.[175]

It is the Christian mystic's belief that the true path to God is not found in a literal interpretation of biblical precepts, but through self-interpretation, which is why the Protestant Reformers taught that "scripture is its own interpreter,"[176] and that each Christian, under the direction of the Holy Spirit, must construe the Bible for himself or herself.[177] This is because, as a highly evolved man once said, "the spiritual [that is, the inner] meaning of anything is its real meaning."[178]

This is part of the beauty and grandeur of Christian mysticism: its secrets, mysteries, symbols, metaphors, and allegories "are truer than history, for they take us to the inside of things," whereas the literalism of conventional Christianity "only shows us the outside."[179] This is why Anaxagoras invented the allegorical mode of interpretation to begin with,[180] and it is why Jung held that the one-sided, extraverted, literalization of the Bible trivializes spirituality, for in doing so it denigrates and suppresses the two-sided, introverted, mystical aspect of religion that is so vital to a living and vibrant Christianity.[181]

Literalizing the Bible is not just injurious to Christian spirituality and to our relationship with God, on a more practical level its dangers spill out into our everyday lives. For one thing, as Keck has pointed out, if we were to live literally according to the Bible's dictates, men would not be allowed to shave, women would not be able to wear jewelry, foods containing pork, crab, and rabbit would be banned, children found guilty of crimes would be executed, and children born out of wedlock would be shunned.[182] And as Bishop Spong has noted, a literal view of the Bible would mean that women could not sing in the choir, participate in the liturgy, teach Sunday School, or be ordained to the clergy.[183]

A quick glance at the Old Testament reveals a host of ancient commandments that, if taken at face value and strictly enforced by the mainstream Church, would overturn modern Western society as we know it.

According to the Bible, all of the following, for example, are punishable by death:

- Family members who are not of the same faith.[184]
- Breaking the Sabbath[185] (crimes which include "gathering sticks" or "kindling a fire" on the Sabbath).[186]
- Eating leavened bread during Passover.[187]
- Eating the fat of ox, sheep, or goats.[188]
- Being a sex-worker.[189]
- Committing adultery.[190]
- Being involved in Wicca,[191] or any other Pagan religion.[192]

Such facts underscore the absurdity of literalizing every word in the Bible.

More importantly, to see only the literal meaning of sacred scripture, as Christian traditionalists do, is to look only superficially, at the veneer. Christian mystics seek to study the wood beneath, where the true beauty lies, unveiling the real significance of mysticism: because *mystics experience God directly*, their "religion" is permanent and indestructible, for it is built upon spiritual interiority; an inner personal orientation that, being contained within one's own mind, lies beyond the corrosive influences of outside human logic and manmade doctrines. On the other hand, *traditionalists believe in God indirectly*, making their religion frail and perishable, for it is built upon spiritual exteriority; an outer corporate orientation that can only exist by reason and intellect, and which is thus subject to the predominate popular beliefs of mass society.[193] Such individuals, as William James pointed out, are likely to possess a faith that is merely "faith in somebody else's faith,"[194] rather than having their own unique and personal relationship with God.

The Christian mystic therefore seeks to practice the same Christianity that the first Christians, the Essenes and Gnostics, did; desiring to recapture the pure Faith that existed before the Church was organized and imbued with a corruptible priestly hierarchy and erroneous manmade doctrines; a period when a pre-ecclesiastical, open-ended *spiritual* Christianity (that joyfully and easily encompassed scores of different types of Christianity) was the only one available; one in which the only qualification for membership was the guidance of one's own heart. In this sense the modern Christian mystic is perfectly inline with George Fox and the Quakers: spiritual truth can only be transmitted directly from God to the human soul (that is, without a human intermediary), and one's faith can only be real if it derives from immediate personal experience.[195] The 17th-Century German Christian mystic Jakob Böhme wrote:

> Spiritual knowledge cannot be communicated from one

intellect to another, but must be sought for in the spirit of God.[196]

Likewise Whitman correctly noted:

> Wisdom is of the soul; [and it] cannot be passed from one having it to another not having it.[197]

After he attained enlightenment (by moving from a literal faith to a mystical one), the biblical Job came to understand this sentiment perfectly, writing:

> I have heard of thee [God] by the hearing of the [physical] ear: but now mine [spiritual] eye seeth thee.[198]

Tennyson too captured the essence of the personal "state of transcendent wonder" that is experienced by Christian mystics:

> Moreover, something is or seems,
> That touches me with mystic gleams,
> Like glimpses of forgotten dreams—
>
> Of something felt, like something here;
> Of something done, I know not where;
> Such as no language may declare.[199]

It certainly is no accident that hermeneutics,[200] the science of interpreting biblical texts,[201] was named after Hermes,[202] the god of communication, and the most mysterious and most mystically oriented deity in the ancient Pagan Pantheon.[203] Swedenborg writes:

> *The spiritual sense is not the sense that shines forth from the sense of the letter of the Word when one is studying it and so construing it as to confirm some dogma of the church. That may be called the literal and ecclesiastical sense of the Word. The spiritual sense is not apparent in the sense of the letter; it is interiorly within it as the soul is in the body*, as the thought of the understanding is in the eyes, or the love's affection in the face.
>
> *It is that sense chiefly that makes the Word spiritual*, not only for men but for angels also; and therefore by means of that sense the Word has communication with the heavens. *As*

the Word is inwardly spiritual it was written purely by correspondences [symbols and allegories]; and because it was written by correspondences in its outmost sense it was written in a style like that of the Prophets, the Gospels, and the Apocalypse, which, although commonplace in appearance, still conceals within it Divine wisdom and all angelic wisdom.[204]

Pike writes:

> The human mind still speculates upon the great mysteries of nature, and still finds its ideas anticipated by the ancients, whose profoundest thoughts are to be looked for, *not in their philosophies, but in their symbols*, by which they endeavored to express the great ideas that vainly struggled for utterance in words, as they viewed the great circle of phenomena,—Birth, Life, Death, or Decomposition, and New Life out of Death and Rottenness,—to them the greatest of mysteries. Remember, while you study their symbols, that they had a profounder sense of these wonders than we have. To them the transformations of the worm were a greater wonder than the stars; and hence the poor dumb scarabaeus or beetle was sacred to them. Thus their faiths are condensed into symbols or expanded into allegories, which they understood, but were not always able to explain in language; for *there are thoughts and ideas which no language ever spoken by man has words to express.*[205]

For millennia this truth has been known among the mystics of all the great religions, a group who share the same central doctrines, one known as the "*Perennial Philosophy*"[206]—which is almost entirely missing from traditional mainstream Christianity. And yet, as Kingsford and Maitland point out:

> Maimonides, the most learned of the Rabbis, speaking of the Book of Genesis, says, *"We ought not to take literally that which is written in the story of the Creation, nor entertain the same ideas of it as are common with the vulgar [the masses]. If it were otherwise, our ancient sages would not have taken so much pains to conceal the sense, and to keep before the eyes of the uninstructed the veil of allegory which conceals the truth it contains."* In the same spirit it was observed by [the Church Father] Jerome, that *"the most difficult and obscure of the holy books contain as many secrets as they*

do words, concealing many things even under each word."

"All the Fathers of the second century," says Mosheim, "attributed a hidden and mysterious sense to the words of Scripture." Papias, Justin Martyr, Irenaeus, Clemens Alexandrinus, Gregory of Nazianzen, Gregory of Nyssa, and Ambrose, held that the Mosaic account of Creation and of the Fall was a series of allegories. The opinion of Origen on the same subject was plainly expressed. "What man," he asks, "is so simple as to believe that God personifying a gardener, planted a garden in the East? that the tree of Life was a real tree which could be touched, and of which the fruit had the power of conferring immortality?"[207]

The original Christian Church was indeed mystical, not what we now think of as traditional or orthodox. Indeed, up until A.D. 692, various aspects of Sunday worship were celebrated in secret, to protect what Paul called the "hidden wisdom"[208] (*apokrupto sophia*) from the unenlightened masses. That year, for the first time, Church authorities voted to allow all believers to view and hear the entire service. Yet vestiges of the original Christian Mysteries survive, such as in the Greek Orthodox Church, where the priest still performs certain rites behind a curtain.[209]

Augustine acknowledged the idea of the Christian Mysteries, which Jesus referred to as "the mysteries of the kingdom of heaven,"[210] for, as the great saint held, the uninitiated laity would not be able to understand them and thus might mock them.[211] Saint Basil noted how the Church Fathers

> were well instructed to preserve the veneration of the [Christian] mysteries by silence. For how could it be proper, publicly to proclaim in writing the doctrine of those things, which no unbaptized person may so much as look upon?[212]

Clement of Alexandria also wrote of the early Church's method of concealing secret knowledge, or Gnosis, from the general public, saying:

> And the Gnosis itself is that which has descended by transmission to a few, having been imparted unwritten by the Apostles [Jesus' inner circle of 12 initiates].[213]

Stirling writes:

> St. Clement declared that the barbarian [Pagan] Scriptures were all symbolical, and to be understood required "an

interpreter and guide. For they considered that, receiving truth from those who knew it well, we should be more earnest and less liable to deception;" and speaking of his own [Christian] tenets, he says, "Rightly, therefore, the divine Apostle [Paul] says, *'By revelation the mystery was made known to me,'*[214] for without a guide or interpreter to reveal the meaning of the Scriptures, the mysteries are hidden and dark." Such a revelation was given by St. John, only his "Revelation" is as obscure as the Parable which it is supposed to lay bare. A plain explanation of the Gospel was handed down by oral tradition only, as St. Clement intimates, for "fear of the *swinish and untrained hearers.*" "Even now I fear, as it is said, 'to cast pearls before swine, lest they tread them under foot, and turn and rend us!' . . . . *For scarcely could anything which they would hear be more ludicrous than those to the multitude.*" Thus without disguise he gives the reason why *"the mysteries of faith are not to be divulged to all."* All old philosophers and priests, Christian or otherwise, had the same dread of the vulgar and profane, and had the same motive for concealing their mystical doctrine from the people, namely, lest it should be turned into ribaldry.[215]

Thus, Pike observes that the writings of the first Christians, the Essenes,

were full of mysticism, parables, enigmas, and allegories. They believed in the esoteric and exoteric meanings of the Scriptures; and . . . they had a warrant for that in the Scriptures themselves. *They found it in the Old Testament, as the Gnostics found it in the New. The Christian writers, and even Christ himself, recognized it as a truth, that all Scripture had an inner and outer meaning.* Thus we find it said as follows, in one of the Gospels:

> "Unto you it is given to know the mystery of the Kingdom of God; but unto men that are without, all these things are done in parables; that seeing, they may see and not perceive, and hearing, they may hear and not understand." . . . And the disciples came and said unto him, "Why speakest Thou the truth in parables?"—He

> answered and said unto them, "Because it is given unto you to know the mysteries of the Kingdom of Heaven, but to them it is not given."

Paul, in the 4th chapter of his Epistle to the Galatians, speaking of the simplest facts of the Old Testament, asserts that they are an allegory. In the 3rd chapter of the second letter to the Corinthians, he declares himself a minister of the New Testament, appointed by God; "Not of the letter, but of the spirit; for the letter killeth." *Origen and St. Gregory held that the Gospels were not to be taken in their literal sense; and Athanasius admonishes us that "should we understand sacred writ according to the letter, we should fall into the most enormous blasphemies."* Eusebius said, "Those who preside over the Holy Sepulchres, philosophize over them, and expound their literal sense *by allegory*."[216]

As mentioned above, Pike notes that Paul himself, Christianity's greatest mystic after Jesus, admitted that the Old Testament stories were allegories hiding profound spiritual truths. There was no New Testament at the time, but we can be sure that Paul would have said the same thing about its 27 books—which included some of his own highly mystical letters. Of the Genesaic story of Abraham, for example, the Thirteenth Apostle says:

> For it is written, that Abraham had two sons, the one by a bondmaid, the other by a freewoman. But he who was of the bondwoman was born after the flesh; but he of the freewoman was by promise. *Which things are an allegory*: for these are the two covenants; the one from the mount Sinai, which gendereth to bondage, which is Agar. For this Agar is mount Sinai in Arabia, and answereth to Jerusalem which now is, and is in bondage with her children. But Jerusalem which is above is free, which is the mother of us all.[217]

Like all of the earliest Christians, mystic Paul held that one of the primary goals for becoming a follower of Jesus was to become united with the Lord's very nature; a deep mystical union in which the Indwelling Christ fuses with the individual.[218] Thus, Paul could say:

> I am crucified with Christ: nevertheless I live; yet not I, but

Christ liveth in me: and the life which I now live in the flesh I live by the faith of the Son of God, who loved me, and gave himself for me.[219]

Channing writes:

> The highest truths are not those which we learn from abroad. No outward teaching can bestow them. *They are unfolded from within, by our very progress in the religious life*. New ideas of perfection, new convictions of immortality, a new consciousness of God, a new perception of our spiritual nature, *come to us as revelations*, and open upon us with a splendour which belongs not to this world.[220]

Yes, the Divine must be discovered not through tuition (meaning "to be taught from without") but through intuition (meaning "to be taught from within").[221] For as the main channel of revelation and the wellspring of religion itself, intuition is the primary method by which God speaks to us.[222] Hence, Paramahansa Yogananda once said that "all authentic religions are based on intuitive knowledge," making this the only guaranteed method of comprehending spiritual truth.[223] And so must the Word of God as relayed in the Bible, a book that is theology not history; and mystical theology at that.

Now theology is by nature abstract,[224] and abstract concepts allow us to more easily understand archetypes, along with general correlations and relationships between religious ideas, myths, figures, and doctrines. Pike comments:

> The Jewish-Greek School of Alexandria is known only by two of its Chiefs, Aristobulus and Philo, both Jews of Alexandria in Egypt. Belonging to Asia by its origin, to Egypt by its residence, to Greece by its language and studies, it strove to show that all truths embedded in the philosophies of other countries were transplanted thither from Palestine. *Aristobulus declared that all the facts and details of the Jewish Scriptures were so many allegories, concealing the most profound meanings*, and that Plato had borrowed from them all his finest ideas.
>
> Philo, who lived a century after him, following the same theory, endeavored to show that *the Hebrew writings, by their system of allegories, were the true source of all religious and philosophical doctrines. According to him, the literal meaning is for the vulgar alone.* Whoever has meditated on philosophy,

purified himself by virtue, and raised himself by contemplation, to God and the intellectual world, and received their inspiration, *pierces the gross envelope of the letter, discovers a wholly different order of things, and is initiated into mysteries, of which the elementary or literal instruction offers but an imperfect image. A historical fact, a figure, a word, a letter, a number, a rite, a custom, the parable or vision of a prophet, veils the most profound truths; and he who has the key of science will interpret all according to the light he possesses.*[225]

Of Christianity's Holy Scripture Clymer writes:

The Bible is the greatest book of the Mystic and Occult we have. It contains the secrets of all true Alchemy and Mysticism; it contains the secret of Transmutation of the baser metals into pure and shining gold, and shows the way to find the hidden meaning of the Rose and the Cross. The Bible [therefore] must not be taken in its literal sense.[226]

This is why the Prophets, Jesus, Paul, and the Apostles, all wrote or spoke in mystical terms, terms that cannot be understood by the intellect.[227] It would be difficult, if not almost impossible, for example, to cite a single statement made by our Lord that is not mystical, symbolic, allegorical, cryptic, arcane, or occultic in one form or another. Indeed, not only did Jesus Himself come to earth as a mystery, to His followers He was the "Mystery of

Mysteries."[228] His words are actually known as "mystical sayings" to theologians, one of whom correctly refers to Jesus as "the last representative of a mysticism that draws its nutriment from other Oriental religions."[229]

Furthermore, it is well-known, even among many mainstream Bible scholars, that when it came to teaching divine principles, Jesus' intent was not to explain, but to challenge;[230] to mystify and conceal, not to clarify and reveal—and this is precisely how mysticism operates. For as I have repeatedly emphasized here, "absolute truth cannot be embodied in human thought. It must always be clothed in symbols."[231] And it was to protect these holy symbols, these precious spiritual gemstones, from abuse by the uninitiated that the Master Jesus gave the following aforementioned commandment:

Give not that which is holy unto the dogs, neither cast ye your
pearls before swine, lest they trample them under their feet,
and turn again and rend you.[232]

This explains our Lord's constant use of the parabolic method of teaching,[233] which as He Himself states in Mark, is purposefully esoteric and cryptic; meant to separate the spiritually mature (receptive) from the spiritually immature (unreceptive).[234] Again, though the following was cited earlier, it is so important to an understanding of the focus of this dictionary that we will repeat it once more:

And when he [Jesus] was alone, they that were about him
with the twelve asked of him the parable. And he said unto
them, "Unto you it is given to know the mystery of the
kingdom of God: but unto them that are without, all these
things are done in parables: That seeing they may see, and not
perceive; and hearing they may hear, and not understand; lest
at any time they should be converted, and their sins should be
forgiven them." . . . And with many such parables spake he
the word unto them, as they were able to hear it. But
without a parable spake he not unto them: and when they
were alone, he expounded all things to his disciples.[235]

Certainly *all* of Jesus' statements which include "he who has ears to hear, let him hear,"[236] indicate a concealed mystical meaning,[237] the Master's code-phrase to the initiated that He was speaking occultly.[238] In addition, not only did He allegorize his own parables,[239] He also made declarations such as the "Father is Spirit,"[240] an idea that goes wholly against traditional Christianity, which typically images God as an anthropomorphic being, a stern old man with white hair and a beard sitting on a throne in Heaven.

But our Lord's meaning is clear: God does not make his abode in the letter of the law, but rather in the spirit of the law. This is why one must "worship Him in Spirit";[241] that is, using the intuitive (spiritual) faculty, rather than the tuitive (intellectual) one.[242]

At Caesarea Philippi, where Peter proclaimed Jesus the Christ, Jesus did not praise the Apostle because he learned this from a book or teacher ("flesh and blood"). Instead he says to Peter:

Blessed art thou, Simon Barjona: for flesh and blood hath not
revealed it unto thee, but my Father which is in heaven.[243]

In this particular case, the "Father which is in heaven" here is a mystical metaphor for intuition, which is spiritual as opposed to intellectual. Since the Prince of Peace spoke mystically, is it not absolutely vital that we learn how to read and interpret the Bible mystically? Christian mystics say yes.

This, the mystical approach to exegesis, has been promoted, endorsed, and even taught by some of Christianity's greatest thinkers. John Calvin once said that because the Word of God is spiritual it cannot be perceived by the mind, only by the spirit[244]—and the spirit is subjective (mystical), *not* objective (literal). Erasmus defended the personal interpretation of scripture, saying:

> To be learned falls to the lot of but few, but there is no one who cannot be a Christian, no one who cannot be pious; I may add this boldly: *no one who cannot be a theologian.*[245]

Likewise John Knox notes:

> The Word of God is plain in itself; and, if there appear any obscurity in one place, the Holy Ghost, who is never contrary to Himself, explains the same more clearly in other places: so that there can remain no doubt, but to such as obstinately remain ignorant.[246]

Zwingli writes:

> When some seven or eight years ago I began to devote myself entirely to the study of Holy Scripture, theological and philosophical questions would persist in intruding themselves on my attention. At last I was driven to say to myself, "Thou must leave everything on one side and just find out the pure mind of God from his own simple word." Then I began to ask God for light, and the Scriptures became much clearer, although I merely read them.
>
> *The Holy Spirit must give to man immediate certainty of the truth. If we rely on the external word without the witness of the Spirit in us, we shall be relying on a creature, which can neither help us nor prove a substitute for the fellowship of God.* Nor may we ascribe saving power either to the outward word or to the Sacraments. *What the living word has alone to do is to impel us to seek Christ, in order that he may speak and work in us by his Spirit and give us the experience of his consolations and fellowship.*
>
> This is the *inner word* which has its seat in the souls of

believers; the *inner teacher* who has power to renovate the *inner man*. When this inner teacher has worked, we shall profitably call the letter, the outward words and signs, to mind. *Their purpose is to stir us up to seek the truth inwardly. Words are signs, a spur, which drives, does not run. It is the inner word that first makes the outer sure and certain.*[247]

This personal approach to reading the Bible and attaining atonement, that is, at-one-ment with the Divine, is far older than Christianity, and was, as discussed, later acknowledged by many early Church authorities. Again, one of these was esotericist Paul, whose statement, "the letter killeth, but the spirit giveth life,"[248] is the very foundation of both mystical Christianity and this book, whose primary crusade is against Christian "ignorance, intolerance, fanaticism, superstition, uncharitableness, and error."[249]

To the spiritually immature the mystical doctrines laid out in this work will be nothing but silly mythology and perverse occultism. To the spiritually mature, however, they will be received as sublime philosophy and inspired religion,[250] which rightly Jesus called the "Bread of Life."[251] This is the essential difference between traditional and mystical Christianity. Those who have "ears to hear" will understand.[252] Those who do not, but wish to, need only harken to the Christ Within,[253] and, as the Psalmist declares, God "wilt light your candle and enlighten your darkness."[254]

In the end the Bible must not be exempt from the rules of scholarship which are applied to every other work of literature.[255] The Christian mystic accepts, even welcomes, this approach. When we have authentic belief and understanding, we are never afraid to examine the inner workings of our religion. Jesus taught us to live fearlessly,[256] for living in dauntless faith always brings us closer to the Truth. *Deus est lux.*

LOCHLAINN SEABROOK
God-written
Nashville, Tennessee, USA
August 2016
1 Thessalonians 5:16-18

"If the doors of perception were cleansed, everything would appear to man as it is, infinite. For man has closed himself up, till he sees all things through the narrow chinks of his cavern."
— William Blake, 1790

INTRODUCTION

BY LOCHLAINN SEABROOK

"THE SYMBOLS OF THE WISE ARE THE IDOLS OF THE VULGAR."[257]
ALBERT PIKE

THE Bible is the most revered, most popular, bestselling book in the English-speaking world. And yet it is the least read book. This is because, even with dozens of English translations available, it is the least understood.[258] And it is the least understood because, in an effort to maintain control over its lay members, the mainstream Church refuses to teach them the inner message—that is, the mystical meaning—of its many often strange and bewildering words and phrases (mystery engenders allegiance).[259] Instead, authorities continue the ancient orthodox tradition of teaching the Bible literally, which only leads to more confusion since the original writers were mystics who wrote in a mystical language. Hence, the need for a modern dictionary comparing traditional Christian doctrines with mystical ones.

As I mentioned in the Preface, not only is such a modern work currently nonexistent, and therefore of utmost importance, but Jesus and the Apostles taught using both a traditional approach and a mystical approach,[260] the former meant to be absorbed through the intellect (tuition via an *outer* "schoolmaster"), the latter (which our Lord was especially known for)[261] to be absorbed through the spirit (intuition via the *inner* "schoolmaster").[262] Certainly if this method was used by our Lord, it is our responsibility as Christians to learn as much as we can about it.

Those who are familiar with the Christian doctrine called "progressive revelation" well know that we are all at different levels in our spiritual evolution, and that because of this God approaches us at our current stage of growth, and works with us based on our personal beliefs and conceptions as they exist in this moment.[263] Spiritually, intellectually, psychologically, we are not all of one cast. Thus God, in his perfection and love, appears to us as we image Him, in a shape that is determined by our expectations.[264]

How does this work? It works through *Gnosis*: "cognizance by intuition."[265] Protestant Reformer Martin Luther held that we should allow the

Holy Spirit (the female or intuitive aspect of the brain) to interpret the Bible for us; in Latin, *Scriptura sacra sui ipsius interpres*: "Scripture is its own interpreter."[266] To the Christian mystic it is not possible to learn biblical truths in Church, from a pastor, or even from a book (including this one). *Self-interpretation* of Christian doctrine is the only true path to understanding it, for no two individuals are on the exact same rung on the ladder of spiritual growth.

We do not attempt to teach a six year old what we teach a 16 year old, for the younger one could not begin to comprehend what the older one can, and we would not expect it to be otherwise. Why do the orthodox think that God would approach his own human children any differently? We place our youngsters in different grades to expedite their academic learning. And God is not dissimilar when it comes to religion and his earthly children, making the age-old conflict between "heretical" Christian esotericists and "orthodox" Christian exotericists a fool's errand.[267]

Thus, as this work will make readily apparent, Jesus and Paul, actually, all of the great early spiritual leaders, used three different teaching methods for the three basic and differing grades of people:

1) An *Exoteric*, outer, or objective method for the spiritually unevolved.
2) A *Mesoteric*, middle, or intermediate method for those partially spiritually evolved.
3) An *Esoteric*, inner, or subjective method for the spiritually evolved.

Buddhists, likewise, teach by a similar though slightly different discipline using what they refer to as "The Three Secret Doctrines":

1) The External or Exoteric, for beginners.
2) The Internal or Esoteric, for intermediates.
3) The Transcendental or non-Exoteric and non-Esoteric (that is, non-Dualistic), for the advanced.[268]

If, as Buddhists aptly maintain, someone were to be taught the Sacred Truths without this initiatory process, it would be like pouring water into an earthen pot that has not yet been fired in a kiln.[269]

I am often asked if there is biblical evidence for my assertion that Jesus and the Apostles, and later the early Christian Church, taught using the Three-Grade System, and the answer is yes.

The following introductory material, some of it excerpted from my book *Jesus and the Law of Attraction*, will illustrate my claim while providing irrefutable proof.

INNER & OUTER CIRCLES

Contrary to what we have been taught, the early Church was not a "catholic" faith; that is, a universal religion whose simplistic teachings could be understood by all people. In fact, according to the Bible, first and second generation Christian preachers were very careful about who they shared the Good News with, that great "mystery which was kept secret since the world began."[270] As we will see, this is why Jesus taught the masses in parables, saving His "inner teachings" for His close circle of handpicked neophytes. "The wise can understand; the foolish have no need to know," He asserts in *The Aquarian Gospel of Jesus the Christ*,[271] a statement supported by the recently discovered Secret Gospel of Mark.[272]

In a 17th-Century copy of a letter penned by Clement of Alexandria, the 2nd-Century Church Father mentions that Mark composed a "more spiritual" covert version of his public (canonical) Gospel,[273] one that contains the "hierophantic [esoteric] teachings of the Lord," which are to be read "only to those who are being initiated into the great mysteries."[274] From this it is clear that Jesus was a hierophant who taught the "higher truths" to special initiates in a graded school system or sacred order, using an exoteric Gospel which He made available to the unenlightened masses and an esoteric Gospel which He presented to His most advanced students and followers.[275]

Some believe that this centuries-old letter may not be genuine. But even if it is not, we still have evidence that Jesus headed a secret initiatic school in which He imparted hierophantic knowledge to his closest associates.[276] How do we know this? Because He Himself says so in the New Testament. Here are the Master's own words from the Gospel of Luke:

> And he said [to the Apostles], "Unto you it is given to know the mysteries of the kingdom of God: but to others [the masses] in parables; that seeing they might not see, and hearing they might not understand."[277]

No amount of word-twisting by mainstream Christians can change our Lord's words: the Apostles, His inner circle of initiates, were permitted to learn about the Mysteries, but the general public was not.

HOW JESUS PROTECTED THE LAW FROM BEING MISUSED

Some of the more important "mysteries" Jesus is referring to concern Theosis (God in Man), the Divine Mind, the Law of Thought, the Law of the Word, the Law of Healing, the Law of Faith, and the Law of Attraction, all which can be used to create one's own "kingdom of God," that is, our ideal life in the here and now.

Like all of the world's great spiritual teachers, Jesus considered the knowledge of these teachings so incredibly powerful that they could be hazardous in the wrong hands. He had come to learn that the safest method of preserving Divine Truth, and of communicating it to the worthy while concealing it from the unworthy, was to speak it using *allegory* and *parables* and write it using *esoteric symbols* (such as squares, triangles, crosses, circles, etc.), *esoteric emblems* (such as the numbers seven, 12, 40, 120, etc.), and *esoteric words* (such as "the Father," "wine," "mustard seed," "ears," "the temple," "the word," "fishers of men," "rock," "keys," "bread," "fruits," "vineyard," "kingdom of God," "eagles," etc.).[278]

Clement—who was well aware of the Master's occult practices and doctrines—understood, saying that Jesus would not share His secret teachings with strangers, the "Profane," as he called them, because it would be like giving a sword to a child: dangerous and unwise.[279] Synesius, the 5th-Century Greek Christian Bishop of Ptolemaïs, and also a Kabbalist, writes:

> *The people will always mock at things easy to be understood; it must needs have impostures.* A Spirit that loves wisdom and contemplates the Truth close at hand, is forced to disguise it, to induce the multitudes to accept it. . . . *Fictions are necessary to the people, and the Truth becomes deadly to those who are not strong enough to contemplate it in all its brilliance.* If the sacerdotal laws allowed the reservation of judgments and the allegory of words, I would accept the proposed dignity on condition that I might be a philosopher at home, and abroad a narrator of apologues and parables. . . . *In fact, what can there be in common between the vile multitude and sublime wisdom? The truth must be kept secret, and the masses need a teaching proportioned to their imperfect reason.*[280]

Pike describes why Freemasons, like every other secret society, encrypt their sacred doctrines:

> Masonry, like all the Religions, all the Mysteries, Hermeticism and Alchemy, *conceals its secrets from all except the Adepts and Sages, or the Elect, and uses false explanations and misinterpretations of its symbols to mislead those who deserve only to be misled; to conceal the Truth, which it calls Light, from them, and to draw them away from it. Truth is not for those who are unworthy*

or unable to receive it, or would pervert it. So God Himself incapacitates many men, by color-blindness, to distinguish colors, and leads the masses away from the highest Truth, *giving them the power to attain only so much of it as it is profitable to them to know. Every age has had a religion suited to its capacity.*

The Teachers, even of Christianity, are, in general, the most ignorant of the true meaning of that which they teach. There is no book of which so little is known as the Bible. To most who read it, it is as incomprehensible as the Sohar.

So Masonry jealously conceals its secrets, and intentionally leads conceited interpreters astray.[281]

The same held true for the Knights Templar, the Medieval monastic military order that sought to preserve the original mystical teachings of Jesus.[282] Though written in the negative by an "enemy" of the Templars, the following description helps illuminate our topic:

> The secret thought of Hugues de Payens, in founding his Order, was not exactly to serve the ambition of the Patriarchs of Constantinople. There existed at that period in the East *a Sect of Johannite Christians, who claimed to be the only true initiates into the real mysteries of the religion of the Saviour. They pretended to know the real history of Yesus [Jesus] the Anointed*, and, adopting in part the Jewish traditions and the tales of the Talmud, *they held that the facts recounted in the Evangels [four Gospels] are but allegories*, the key of which Saint John gives, in saying that the world might be filled with the books that could be written upon the words and deeds of Jesus Christ; words which, they thought, would be only a ridiculous exaggeration, if he were not speaking of an allegory and a legend, that might be varied and prolonged to infinity.
>
> *The Johannites ascribed to Saint John the foundation of their Secret Church*, and the Grand Pontiffs of the Sect assumed the title of *Christos, Anointed*, or *Consecrated*, and claimed to have succeeded one another from Saint John by an uninterrupted succession of pontifical powers. He who, at the period of the foundation of the Order of the Temple, claimed these imaginary prerogatives, was named Theoclet; he knew Hugues De Payens, he initiated him into the

mysteries and hopes of his pretended church, he seduced him by the notions of Sovereign Priesthood and Supreme royalty, and finally designated him as his successor.

Thus the Order of Knights of the Temple was at its very origin devoted to the cause of opposition to the tiara of Rome and the crowns of Kings, and *the Apostolate of Kabalistic Gnosticism was vested in its chiefs. For Saint John himself was the Father of the Gnostics*, and the current translation of his polemic against the heretical of his Sect and the pagans who denied that Christ was the Word, is throughout a misrepresentation, or misunderstanding at least, of the whole Spirit of that Evangel.

The tendencies and tenets of the Order were enveloped in profound mystery, and it externally professed the most perfect orthodoxy. The Chiefs alone knew the aim of the Order: the Subalterns followed them without distrust.

To acquire influence and wealth, then to intrigue, and at need to fight, to establish the Johannite or Gnostic and Kabalistic dogma, were the object and means proposed to the initiated Brethren. The Papacy and the rival monarchies, they said to them, are sold and bought in these days, become corrupt, and to-morrow, perhaps, will destroy each other. All that will become the heritage of the Temple: the World will soon come to us for its Sovereigns and Pontiffs. We shall constitute the equilibrium of the universe, and be rulers over the Masters of the World.

The Templars, like all other Secret Orders and Associations, had two doctrines, one concealed and reserved for the Masters, which was Johannism; the other public, which was the Roman Catholic. Thus they deceived the adversaries whom they sought to supplant. Hence Free-Masonry, vulgarly imagined to have begun with the Dionysian Architects or the German Stone-workers, adopted Saint John the Evangelist as one of its patrons, associating with him, in order not to arouse the suspicions of Rome, Saint John the Baptist, and thus covertly proclaiming itself the child of the Kabalah and Essenism together. *[Thus] the Johannism of the [Templar] Adepts was the Kabalah of the earlier Gnostics.*[283]

We can see from such comments why Jesus often did things "in secret,"[284] why He formed a secret school at Capernaum comprised of 120 hand-selected initiates,[285] and why He divided into 12 classes each class of ten pupils headed by one of the 12 Apostles.[286] This is also why, as in the Great Mystery Schools,[287] He taught important spiritual truths only to those he considered spiritually mature, such as the 12 Apostles (His inner circle), directly and openly, but he taught it to the multitudes (His outer circle) in an arcane manner, in this case in parables: imaginative allegorical stories that relay deep spiritual and moral concepts through symbols, figures, words, images, ideas, myths, numbers, and emblems. Thus canonical Mark says:

> And with many such parables spake he [Jesus] the word unto them [the spiritually immature masses], as they were able to hear it [that is, according to their level of spiritual evolvement]. But without a parable spake he not unto them: and when they were alone, he expounded all things [openly] to his [spiritually mature] disciples.[288]

In *The Aquarian Gospel of Jesus the Christ*, our Lord explains that some are too spiritually undeveloped to understand the deeper meanings of many of His teachings, and so He must educate them using allegorical tales or parables:

> Now, his disciples were beside him in the boat, and Thomas asked, "Why do you speak in parables?" And Jesus said, "My words, like every master's words, are dual in their sense. To you [advanced spiritual initiates] who know the language of the soul, my words have meanings far too deep for other men to comprehend. The other sense of what I say is all the multitude [spiritual beginners] can understand; these [outer] words are food for them; the inner thoughts are food for you. Let every one reach forth and take the food that he is ready to receive."[289]

But, as Jesus well knew, not even the Apostles, His inner secret circle of 12 initiates, were spiritually mature enough to be able to understand everything about the "mysteries." This is why, in the Gospel of John, He tells them: "I have yet many things to say unto you, but ye cannot bear them now."[290]

Parabolic teaching was a common practice among the ancient Mystery Schools of the Roman Empire, and Jesus was only one of many early religious teachers who used it. In fact, parabolization has been employed by spiritually evolved men and women around the world for millennia. Here, for instance, is a passage from the Hindus' Mundaka Upanishad:

> Let a man tell this science of Brahman *to those only who have performed all necessary acts*, who are versed in the Vedas, and firmly established in the lower Brahman, who themselves offer as oblation the one Rishi, full of faith, and by whom the rite of carrying fire on the head has been performed, according to the rule of the Atharvanas.[291]

Buddha understood this principle, which is why he taught his followers using a three-stage system that he compared to a farmer sowing seeds in three types of soil: poor, mediocre, and excellent—a theme, incidently, borrowed 500 years later by Jesus.[292] Buddha's "poor" soil represents those who were new to his teachings; the "mediocre" soil those who were casual practitioners; the "excellent" soil those who were advanced Buddhists.[293] As we will now see, spiritual instructors have good reason for protecting sacred doctrines by tactfully teaching according to a student's capacity and their level of spiritual maturity.

THE THREE SPIRITUAL LANGUAGES OF THE BIBLE
Jesus' "Gospel of the Kingdom"[294] (which is completely different than the traditional Church's "Gospel of Jesus Christ")[295] is like a powerful double-edged sword that can benefit one or hurt one. Thus He was careful who He revealed its secrets to. And, in fact, we have further evidence of this in the Good Book. Not just in the arcane methods by which Jesus and other biblical figures taught the Gospel, but also as revealed in the cryptic manner in which the Bible itself was written. First a little background.

As part of the ancient program to protect the "mysteries of the Kingdom of God" from being used for evil purposes, the Bible was written in three languages. I am not speaking of the linguistic languages Hebrew, Aramaic, and Greek, but of the three spiritual languages.

1) THE EXOTERIC LANGUAGE & SPIRITUAL ELEMENTARY SCHOOL
The Exoteric Language forms the outer, obvious, verbatim, and literal meanings of the Bible's many words and phrases. It is meant for the general public; the masses of the spiritually unevolved; the uninitiated or the unenlightened, who correlate with what we call Elementary School; that is, those in the beginning levels, kindergarten through fifth grades, of Spiritual School. They have no real awareness, and thus no true understanding, of what Jesus called "the mysteries of the Kingdom of God."[296] They are psychomics (from the word *psychoma*,

"soul sleep").²⁹⁷ Being spiritually asleep, they are not aware of the true profound nature of life. This class makes up the vast majority of the orthodox or traditional branches, denominations, and cults of Christianity, and are the ones most likely to abuse the sacred "mysteries."

Members of this group are usually regular church goers and place great emphasis on accepted mainstream doctrine. Thus, they maintain, we are born in sin, only Jesus' death can save us, and God is a corporeal, transcendent, anthropomorphic deity who lives outside of us, and whose "Kingdom" exists only in the Afterlife. Jesus Himself is the one and only Son of God, the personal savior of Christian believers, who came to earth to die on the cross for our sins. These individuals know Him as "Jesus Christ."²⁹⁸ Spirituality is largely a foreign concept. Religion, religious duties, religious rules, religious rituals are the main concerns in life. There is an "us versus them" bunker mentality. There is only one true religion, one pathway to Heaven: Christianity (and often it is found only through their particular denomination).

Likewise, this group accepts the scriptural hermeneutics (interpretations) of their clergy and catechists, usually without question. As biblicists, when they do read the Bible, it is literally, never probing beneath the surface. The spiritual life is lived solely from the outside in, and spiritual knowledge is absorbed from exterior sources. Typically neophobic, they often stubbornly resist new ideas and concepts that promise to expand their consciousness by throwing additional light on conventional Christianity.

Those in this group are commonly known as "Conservative Christians." Of this, the conventional Christian, noted American physician, philosopher and psychologist William James describes him this way:

> His religion has been made for him by others, communicated to him by tradition, determined to fixed forms by imitation, and retained by habit.²⁹⁹

2) THE MESOTERIC LANGUAGE & SPIRITUAL MIDDLE SCHOOL

The Mesoteric Language forms the middle, partially veiled meanings of the Bible's many words and phrases. It is meant for those who have begun to grasp the mysteries of the Kingdom of God, but are not yet able to put them into practice. These are the incompletely evolved, who correlate with what we call Middle School, the sixth through ninth grades of Spiritual School. They have some understanding and some knowledge of the mysteries of the Kingdom of God, but are not yet ready to graduate, as more "inner work" is needed.

This class, which makes up only a small percentage of the laity, attends church sporadically and is considered to be "falling away" from the faith by the more orthodox, literal-minded Exoteric Language group. At the same time, these individuals are starting to realize that other religions may also have merit, and begin to take an interest in non-Christian belief systems. With the realization that Jesus was a man (as Matthew, Luke, John, and the author of Hebrews clearly tell us),[300] and that "Christ" is not a surname but a title (though one with deep metaphysical meaning), they know the Lord as "Jesus *the* Christ"—the same appellation by which the Lord knew Himself.[301]

Members of this group may enjoy reading and studying the inner meanings of the Bible, but are not advanced enough to begin actually living these principles yet. They have begun to seriously question if not completely reject the literalistic, formalistic, scriptural interpretations of their clergy and religious teachers. The spiritual life is lived both from the outside in and the inside out, and spiritual knowledge is absorbed from both external sources (books, teachers, etc.) and internal sources (self-reflection, prayer, meditation, etc.). Those in this group are typically known as "middle of the road Christians," or "lukewarm Christians."

3) THE ESOTERIC LANGUAGE & SPIRITUAL HIGH SCHOOL

The Esoteric Language forms the inner, cryptic, allegorical, and symbolic meanings of the Bible's many words and phrases, that is, their *true* meaning. It is meant for those who have advanced to the highest levels of spirituality and who have full understanding and use of the mysteries of the Kingdom of God. These are the "initiated," the "enlightened," who correlate with what we call High School; that is, those in the upper final levels, tenth through twelfth grades, of Spiritual School. This class makes up a tiny minority of the Christian faith, probably less than 1 percent.

Essentially mystical, these individuals easily recognize the Indwelling Christ[302] and perceive themselves and God as one and the same.[303] Indeed, they see God in everyone and everything. The Kingdom of God is here and now, in this lifetime, as Jesus affirmed,[304] and as gods and goddesses ourselves, we possess the same powers as the Father.[305]

The idea of original sin is rejected and our innate perfection,[306] as creatures made "complete"[307] in the pure image of the perfect God,[308] is acknowledged and accepted.[309] Jesus is seen as the world's premier example of the fully enlightened "prototypical Ideal Man";[310] the "ideal virtuous man" of Luke,[311] a "model for mankind,"[312] the "Perfect Man,"[313] the "Archetypal Man,"[314] a "pattern for the sons of men,"[315] sent to earth to remind us of our divine nature,[316] our oneness with the Father,[317] and to show us that what He achieved we can also achieve.[318] For due to the Indwelling Christ,[319] we are all sons of Gods, just as Paul and John taught.[320]

This high consciousness group fully understands the spiritual import and gnomic connotations behind the names "Jesus Christ" and "Jesus the Christ," and so does not take them literally, as the previous two groups do. They perceive the word Christ to be a mystical title ("anointed"), representing the Higher Self that exists within each one of us—meaning that we are each a Christ in our own right, as the Bible reveals.[321]

Known in mystical Christianity as the "Indwelling Christ," or "Christ Within," the Christ has always existed and always will, for it is eternal and universal;[322] it is the real you, the immortal you, the divine you; for you, as Paul declared, "are the temple of the living God."[323] As such, the preexistent Christ lived before Jesus,[324] a fact that He Himself openly teaches in the Gospel of Matthew:

> While the Pharisees were gathered together, Jesus asked them, saying, "what think ye of Christ? whose son is he?" They say unto him, "the Son of David." He saith unto them, "how then doth David in spirit call him 'Lord,' saying, 'the Lord said unto my Lord, sit thou on my right hand, till I make thine enemies thy footstool?'[325] If David then call him Lord, how is he his son?" And no man was able to answer him a word, neither durst any man from that day forth ask him any more questions.[326]

Transdenominational and ecumenically oriented, this group recognizes the unity of all religions, seeing the all-embracing nature of spirituality wherever and however it manifests in the world. Thus, respecting all faiths, non-Christian religions are acknowledged as other pathways to the Almighty—for spiritually speaking, this group maintains, "all roads lead to Rome."[327] They do not, in other words, confuse the messenger with the message, as the orthodox do, glorifying Jesus, who glorified not Himself, but God.

These individuals have usually lost the need to attend church, and have rejected nearly all of the so-called "traditional" interpretations of the Bible as well as the authority of the clergy. Avid readers of the Bible, they grasp the full meaning of the biblical teachings that Jesus, Paul, and others purposefully concealed from the formalistic.

Members of this group are seen by institutional Christians as "apostates," "the faithless," "mystics," "New Agers," and even "atheists." However, though they are now essentially nonreligious, they are the most *spiritual* of the three groups. For them, the external trappings of religion, so important to the orthodox, have lost all meaning and importance. The spiritual life is lived purely from the inside out, and spiritual knowledge is absorbed only from one internal source: the Higher Self (self-knowledge, self-realization, self-illumination). Those in this group are typically known as "Liberal Christians," though many would call themselves mystical Christians.[328]

THE THREE SPIRITUAL EDUCATIONAL LEVELS OF THE CHURCH

Observing these three naturally occurring gradations of spiritual awareness among the masses,[329] the ancient, pre-Christian, Pagan Mystery Schools divided their educational system into three levels, degrees, or stages—material, mental, and spiritual[330]—a concept that was adopted by the new Christian Church in the 1st Century[331] from the three-tiered teaching method of Jesus.[332] These were, starting from the lowest or least spiritually mature and moving upward:

1) The Beginners (initiates), or the *Somatics* (that is, the "Bodies").
2) The Progressing (intermediates), or the *Psychics* (that is, the "Souls").
3) The Perfect (advanced), or the *Pneumatics* (that is, the "Spirituals").[333]

These three degrees, which correspond exactly with the three spiritual languages of the Bible as described above (Exoteric, Mesoteric, and Esoteric), were known in the early Christian Church by other names as well, including:

1) The Auditors, the Material, or the Purification (Beginners).
2) The Catechumens, the Initiation, the Awakening, or the Intellectual (Progressing).
3) The Faithful, the Accomplishment, the Illumination, or the Spiritual (Perfect).[334]

Pike writes of these three classes of spiritual and intellectual capacity:

> *In the early days of Christianity, there was an initiation like those of the Pagans. Persons were admitted on special conditions only. To arrive at a complete knowledge of the doctrine, they had to pass three degrees of instruction.* The initiates were consequently divided into three classes; the first, *Auditors*, the second, *Catechumens*, and the third, the *Faithful*. The Auditors were a sort of novices, who were prepared by certain ceremonies and certain instruction to receive the dogmas of Christianity. A portion of these dogmas was made known to the Catechumens; who, after particular purifications, received

baptism, or the initiation of the *theogenesis* (divine generation); but in the grand mysteries of that religion, the incarnation, nativity, passion, and resurrection of Christ, none were initiated but the Faithful. These doctrines, and the celebration of the Holy Sacraments, particularly the Eucharist, were kept with profound secrecy. These mysteries were divided into two parts; the first styled the Mass of the Catechumens; the second, the Mass of the Faithful.[335]

As evidence of these facts we have the written testimony of the early Church Fathers, many who, as in Mark's aforementioned "Secret Gospel," openly discussed the existence of a Hidden Knowledge, Jesus' initiatic teaching, and a three-degree Christian school. In Clement's work, *Hypotyposes*, for example, a book accepted even by the Catholic Church, we read:

> The Lord after his resurrection imparted [a higher] knowledge to [His brother] James the Just and to John and Peter, and they imparted it to the rest of the apostles, and the rest of the apostles to the seventy, of whom Barnabas was one.[336]

Along with Bishop Clement, the following Fathers also recognized the Christian Mysteries: Saint Chrysostom, Tertullian, Origen, Bishop Archelaus of Cascara, Bishop Cyril of Jerusalem, Saint Basil, Saint Gregory of Nazianzus, Saint Ambrose, Saint Augustine, Saint Cyril of Alexandria, and Bishop Theodoret of Cyropolis, among many others.[337] Ancient Pagans too, like Roman attorney Minucius Felix, noted the early Christian practice of a three-tiered initiation process in what Paul referred to, in the Pagan tradition, as the "Mysteries of God."[338] As the exoteric and esoteric teaching method was also employed in pre-Christian rabbinical circles, we should not be surprised that Jesus and His Apostles used it, or that it was later adopted by the early orthodox Church.[339]

PAUL & THE "HIDDEN WISDOM"
This three-level educational system was undertaken by early Christian teachers, such as Paul, because they understood that we are all in different spiritual grades in "Earth School." We do not, for example, teach differential calculus to first-graders and we do not teach basic math to college graduates. As such, Jesus' doctrines were dispersed in a different manner to each of the three grades, just

as we do with children of different ages. As Paul states mystically to his followers at Corinth, Greece:

> There is one glory of the sun [the Perfect], and another glory of the moon [the Progressing], and another glory of the stars [the Beginners]: for one star differeth from another star in glory.[340]

Paul uses the word "glory" here to mean spiritual awareness. Thus, he taught what he called the "hidden wisdom,"[341] or the "deep things of God,"[342] to these three groups using the Exoteric, Mesoteric, and Esoteric methods; or as he put it: "in the spirit [we] speaketh mysteries."[343]

The Thirteenth Apostle, who revealingly refers to himself as one of the "stewards of the mysteries of God,"[344] refers openly to all three groups in this same letter, as we will now see. The key to understanding it is that Paul calls his most advanced followers the "Perfect" or the "Spiritual," his intermediate followers the "Natural," and his beginner followers the "Carnal" or the "Babes." This part of his letter to the Corinthians is addressed to the latter, the spiritually immature, who had earlier asked Paul why he used a different language when instructing the various groups of his followers:

> "Howbeit we speak wisdom among them that are *perfect* [the Advanced]: yet not the wisdom of this world, nor of the princes of this world, that come to nought: but *we speak the wisdom of God in a mystery*, even *the hidden wisdom*, which God ordained before the world unto our glory: which none of the princes of this world knew: for had they known it, they would not have crucified the Lord of glory.
> "But as it is written, 'eye hath not seen, nor ear heard, neither have entered into the heart of man, the things which God hath prepared for them that love him.' But *God hath revealed them unto us by his Spirit*: for the Spirit searcheth all things, yea, *the deep things of God*. For what man knoweth the things of a man, save the spirit of man which is in him? even so the things of God knoweth no man, but the Spirit of

God.

"Now we have received, not the spirit of the world, but the spirit which is of God; that we might know the things that are freely given to us of God. Which things also we speak, not in the words which man's wisdom teacheth, but which the Holy Ghost teacheth; comparing spiritual things with spiritual. But the *natural* man [the Intermediates] receiveth not the things of the Spirit of God: for they are foolishness unto him: neither can he know them, because they are [that is, can only be] spiritually discerned.

"But he that is *spiritual* [the Advanced] judgeth all things, yet he himself is judged of no man. For who hath known the mind of the Lord, that he may instruct him? But *we have the mind of Christ* [Christ Consciousness]. And I, brethren, could not speak unto you as unto *spiritual* [the Advanced], but as unto *carnal* [the Beginners], even as unto *babes* in Christ.

"I have fed you with milk [elementary exoteric doctrines], and not with meat [advanced esoteric doctrines]: for hitherto ye were not able to bear it, neither yet now are ye able. For ye are yet *carnal* [unenlightened]: for whereas there is among you envying, and strife, and divisions, are ye not *carnal* [spiritually immature] and walk as men?"[345]

It is especially telling that Paul's use of the word mystery here (in Greek *musterion*) refers not to an unknown riddle, the common modern definition, but to "a secret teaching confided only to the initiated," the ancient mystic's definition.

It is also interesting to note that some of the Christian Perfect (Pneumatics) at Corinth[346] arrogantly began to see themselves as spiritual royalty, spiritual "kings," as they called themselves, far above and beyond the uninitiated, that is, the Beginners (Somatics). Because of this haughty attitude, in his letter Paul had to remind them to be careful of succumbing to pride.[347]

JESUS & HIS ADVANCED INITIATES
Of this particular group, the Perfect, Jesus made numerous comments as well. Among them:

> Be ye therefore *perfect*, even as your Father which is in heaven is *perfect*.[348]

> If thou wilt be *perfect*, go and sell that thou hast, and give to the poor, and thou shalt have treasure in heaven: and come and follow me.[349]
>
> I in them, and thou in me, that they may be made *perfect* in one; and that the world may know that thou hast sent me, and hast loved them, as thou hast loved me.[350]
>
> The disciple is not above his master: but every one that is *perfect* shall be as his master.[351]

The inner meaning of this last passage:

> My Beginner (initiate) and my Progressing (intermediate) students have not yet attained my degree of spiritual maturity; however, my Perfect (advanced) students have. They are now just like me.[352]

In the understandably famous Gospel of Thomas we find this interesting exchange between Peter and our Lord:

> Simon Peter said to Him, "Let Mary leave us, for women [used here as a symbol of the Somatics or unenlightened class] are not worthy of Life." Jesus said, "I myself shall lead her in order to make her male [a symbol of the Pneumatics or enlightened class], so that she too may become a living spirit resembling you males [the Perfect]. For every woman [spiritual beginner] who will make herself male [spiritual expert] will enter the Kingdom of Heaven."[353]

In The Gospel of Thomas the Contender, when Thomas asks Jesus a question about a specific teaching, the Lord gives the following answer regarding the spiritually mature, that is, the Perfect:

> Thomas, you are referring to the doctrine of *the perfect*. And if you want to become *perfect*, you will follow it.[354]

PAUL ENCOURAGES HIS INITIATES TO ATTAIN THE PERFECT
Paul too encouraged his lower ranked followers to reach for the highest degree of his esoteric brotherhood, the Perfect. Here are a few examples:

> For we are glad, when we are weak, and ye are strong: and this also we wish, even your *perfection*. . . . Finally, brethren, farewell. Be *perfect*, be of good comfort, be of one mind, live in peace; and the God of love and peace shall be with you.[355]
>
> Till we all come in the unity of the faith, and of the knowledge of the Son of God, unto a *perfect* man, unto the measure of the stature of the fulness of Christ.[356]
>
> Not as though I had already attained, either were already *perfect*: but I follow after, if that I may apprehend that for which also I am apprehended of Christ Jesus.[357]
>
> Let us therefore, as many as be *perfect*, be thus minded: and if in any thing ye be otherwise minded, God shall reveal even this unto you.[358]
>
> Whom we preach, warning every man, and teaching every man in all wisdom; that we may present every man *perfect* in Christ Jesus.[359]
>
> Epaphras, who is one of you, a servant of Christ, saluteth you, always labouring fervently for you in prayers, that ye may stand *perfect* and complete in all the will of God.[360]
>
> That the man of God may be *perfect*, throughly furnished unto all good works.[361]
>
> God having provided some better thing for us, that they without us should not be made *perfect*.[362]

JAMES & PETER COMMENT ON THE PERFECT
Here is what Jesus' brother, James the Just, said about the most advanced spiritual class, the Perfect:

> But let patience have her *perfect* work, that ye may be *perfect* and entire, wanting nothing.[363]
>
> For in many things we offend all. If any man offend not in word, the same is a *perfect* man, and able also to bridle the

whole body.[364]

The Apostle Peter recognized the Perfect group as well:

> But the God of all grace, who hath called us unto his eternal glory by Christ Jesus, after that ye have suffered a while, make you *perfect*, stablish, strengthen, settle you.[365]

In the Essenic Letter to the Hebrews[366] we find these passages concerning the spiritual progress of Jesus' followers, encouraging them not to fall back down to the lower levels of spiritual school:

> . . . let us go on unto *perfection*; not laying again the foundation of repentance from dead works, and of faith toward God, of the doctrine of baptisms, and of laying on of hands, and of resurrection of the dead, and of eternal judgment. And this will we do, if God permit. For it is impossible for those who were *once enlightened*, and have tasted of the heavenly gift [the Law of Attraction], and were made partakers of the Holy Ghost, and have tasted the good word of God, and the powers of the world to come, if they shall fall away, to renew them again unto repentance; seeing they crucify to themselves the Son of God afresh, and put him to an open shame.[367]

THE ANCIENT WISDOM: THE GOSPEL OF THE INNER CHRIST

"The hidden wisdom of God in a mystery" that Paul speaks of above refers to Jesus' secret teachings on the Universal Divine Mind and Man's oneness with God (Theosis).[368] It is, Paul declares,

> the mystery of God, and of the Father, and of Christ; in whom are hid all the treasures of wisdom and knowledge.[369]

The Bible itself bears witness to Paul's statement, for the vast majority of Jesus' parables were about the mysterious treasure-filled "Kingdom of God." The "Kingdom," for example, is mentioned 119 times in the four canonical Gospels, but the word "atonement" does not appear even once. Based on this fact alone, it is clear which doctrine Jesus considered most important!

Paul would have agreed, which is why he preached about the salvific benefit of living according to the Gospel of the Indwelling Christ:

For I am not ashamed of *the gospel of [the Indwelling] Christ*: for it is the power of God unto salvation to every one that believeth; to the Jew first, and also to the Greek [non-Jews]. For therein is the righteousness of God revealed from faith to faith: as it is written, "The just shall live by faith."[370]

PAUL CALLS THE OT STORIES "ALLEGORIES" & "JEWISH FABLES"
These same sacred truths—known collectively as the "Ancient Wisdom," or biblically, as the "mystery which hath been hid from ages and from generations"[371]—were also concealed in the Old Testament under layers of arcane language, symbolism, parables, folklore, myth, and allegories.

Thus Paul, like every early Christian teacher of Theosis, taught that many of the Old Testament stories are not literal, true-life historical events.[372] Rather, they are he said, "Jewish fables,"[373] spiritual "allegories" meant to hide ancient occult knowledge and wisdom concerning powerful sacred doctrines from the uninitiated.[374] (Peter preached the same doctrine, noting, for example, that the waters of Noah's flood symbolized baptism.)[375]

For Paul, the "uninitiated" were those who were not part of his secret brotherhood,[376] and those who did not adhere to his own personal gospel.[377] As such, those Christian biblicists who take such tales literally, according to Paul, are committing a grave sin. Why? Because the literal (outer) meaning is merely a literary device to hide the true (inner) meaning from the spiritually immature, and it is this inner meaning that we are meant to try and discover and understand. As the saint himself asserted: "The letter killeth, but the spirit giveth life."[378] The true believer lives, he continued, according to the heart, not according to a strict literal interpretation of religious law:[379]

> But now we are delivered from the law [of Moses], that being dead wherein we were held; that we should serve in *newness of spirit*, and not in the *oldness of the letter*.[380]

THE CODED LANGUAGE OF JESUS & PAUL
We should not be surprised to learn that Jesus too taught the "mysteries of the Kingdom of God" using the three-tier system of the ancient mystery schools, designed to personally cater to the capabilities and temperaments of His students and followers.[381] Many times throughout the Gospels He speaks of employing the *Exoteric Method* (primarily through parables) to teach the multitudes (the uninitiated), the *Mesoteric Method* to teach His inner school of 120 Disciples (the intermediates),[382] and the *Esoteric Method* to educate His Apostles (the advanced).[383] According to Matthew it was to His Disciples or

intermediates, for example, that He addressed His celebrated Sermon on the Mount, not to the general public.[384]

The question is why did Jesus, Paul, and the teachers of countless other early Christian secret brotherhoods, Jewish rabbinical schools, and Pagan Mystery Cults use the three spiritual languages to teach inner and outer doctrines, such as Theosis, the Law of Thought, the Law of Karma, and the Golden Rule, to their three-tiered followers, the Beginners, the Progressing, and the Perfect?

First, concerning Jesus specifically. He had many enemies (mainly religiously strict Jews, such as the Pharisees)—whom He referred to as "the children of the wicked one"[385]—who wanted to trick Him into saying something blasphemous, illegal, or treasonous. Though the Master often spoke openly and boldly, even in the midst of His critics, there were times when He felt it was best to protect Himself, His followers, and especially His inner teachings from those who would do them harm. After all, when the unenlightened try to teach arcane spiritual principles, the teacher and his students, not to mention the sacred doctrines themselves, all fall further and further away from the Truth.

It was to protect both the Word and Himself from these types of dangers that Jesus relied on parabolic language. Other ancient spiritual teachers, such as Paul, had similar reasons for speaking selectively, esoterically, and even secretly to those "as they were able to hear it."[386]

Second, ancient religious teachers believed that if their spiritually immature and uninitiated aspirants (the Beginners), along with the unilluminated masses, were to get hold of the "hidden wisdom"—such as the all-powerful Law of Attraction principles that enable one to alter physical reality—they might abuse or misuse this very special and formidable power of God, perhaps even for evil purposes.

Because of this, sacred information was taught to them in a coded language, the Esoteric Language, so that they could only grasp the outer meaning of the secret "principles of the oracles of God."[387] Those who were more spiritually evolved, such as the Progressing class, would glean what they could, while the upper class, the Perfect, would have full access[388] to these oracles, the "hidden wisdom" (inner meaning), due to their enlightened state.[389] Speaking to the "babes" (the Beginners) among his followers, Paul phrased the situation like this:

> Of whom we have many things to say, and hard to be uttered, seeing ye are dull of hearing [spiritually immature]. For when for the time ye ought to be teachers [advanced initiates], ye have need that one teach you again which be the first principles of the oracles of God [divine secrets of the Father]; and are become such as have need of milk [basic spiritual teachings], and not of strong meat [advanced spiritual teachings].
>
> For every one that useth milk is unskilful in the word of righteousness: for he is a babe [a Beginner]. But strong meat belongeth to them that are of full age [the Perfect], even those who by reason of use have their senses exercised to discern both good and evil [the Progressing or Intermediates]. Therefore leaving the principles of the doctrine of [the Indwelling] Christ, let us go on unto *perfection* [that is, work toward the highest spiritual level, the Perfect]; not laying again the foundation of repentance from dead works, and of faith toward God . . .[390]

Again, note that the author speaks of the simple doctrines he teaches to his Beginners as "milk" for "a babe," and the more complex ones he teaches to his advanced students, the Perfect, those who are of "full age," as "strong meat."

JESUS ADDRESSES HIS SECRET INNER CIRCLE
Jesus goes into great detail replying to the following question put to Him by His Disciples: why do you withhold the mysteries from the outer circle (the masses), but teach them to your inner circle (the Disciples)?[391] Here is the story as told by Mark:

> And when he was alone, they that were about him with the twelve [Apostles, or advanced initiates] asked of him the parable. And he said unto them, "Unto you it is given to know the mystery of the kingdom of God: but unto them that are without, all these things are done in parables: that seeing they may see, and not perceive; and hearing they may hear, and not understand; lest at any time they should be converted, and their sins should be forgiven them."[392]

Matthew goes into more detail in his account:

And the disciples came, and said unto him, "Why speakest thou unto them [the multitudes] in parables?" He answered and said unto them, "Because it is given unto you to know the mysteries of the kingdom of heaven, but to them it is not given. For whosoever hath, to him shall be given, and he shall have more abundance: but whosoever hath not, from him shall be taken away even that he hath. Therefore speak I to them in parables: because they seeing see not; and hearing they hear not, neither do they understand. And in them is fulfilled the prophecy of Esaias [Isaiah], which saith,

> "By hearing ye shall hear, and shall not understand; and seeing ye shall see, and shall not perceive: for this people's heart is waxed gross, and their ears are dull of hearing, and their eyes they have closed; lest at any time they should see with their eyes, and hear with their ears, and should understand with their heart, and should be converted, and I should heal them."[393]

But blessed are your [inner] eyes, for they see [deep spiritual things]: and your [inner] ears, for they hear [deep spiritual things]. For verily I say unto you, that many prophets and righteous men have desired to see those things which ye see, and have not seen them; and to hear those things which ye hear, and have not heard them.[394]

Jesus then uses a parable to describe the three groups He teaches using the standard Mystery School allegory, which was practiced centuries earlier by spiritual masters like Buddha:[395]

> Hear ye therefore the parable of the sower. When any one heareth the word of the kingdom, and understandeth it not, then cometh the wicked one, and catcheth away that which was sown in his heart. This is he which received seed by the way side. But he that received the seed into stony places, the same is he that heareth the word, and anon with joy receiveth it; Yet hath he not root in himself, but dureth for a while: for when tribulation or persecution ariseth because of the

word, by and by he is offended. He also that received seed among the thorns is he that heareth the word; and the care of this world, and the deceitfulness of riches, choke the word, and he becometh unfruitful. But he that received seed into the good ground is he that heareth the word, and understandeth it; which also beareth fruit, and bringeth forth, some an hundredfold, some sixty, some thirty.[396]

Now let us reread these passages stripped of Jesus' coded language, so that everything will be made plain:

> The Disciples came to Jesus and asked him: "Why do you teach the masses using allegories?" Jesus replied: "Because I have chosen you, my closest and spiritually mature followers, to understand the secret teachings of the Gospel of the Kingdom, while the masses have not been chosen because, being spiritually immature, they are not ready, posing a danger to themselves and society. For those who already comprehend and practice the principles of the Gospel of the Kingdom are always receiving from the Father, while those who know nothing about them, and so do not practice them, from them more and more is taken away, even what little they have to begin with.
>
> "This is why I teach to the masses using allegories; because even though they can see with their physical eyes, they cannot see with their spiritual eyes; and even though they can hear with their physical ears, they cannot hear with their spiritual ears. And so they are incapable of truly understanding anything about the inner workings of the Gospel of the Kingdom. It is these very people, the uninitiated masses, that have fulfilled the prophecy of Isaiah:
>
>> 'Though listening through physical ears you hear, you will not understand; and though looking through physical eyes you see, you will not perceive: For the masses' subconscious minds have been struck dumb, and their ears are blocked off, and their eyes are closed; otherwise they might have to see with their spiritual

eyes and hear with their spiritual ears; then comprehending through the Divine Mind, they would be transformed into spiritually mature individuals, and I would then be able to heal them.'

"But Disciples, my spiritually mature followers, you should be very happy because you are able to see with your spiritual eyes and hear with your spiritual ears. I tell you truly that many of the most important, powerful, and admirable men in history have longed to be able to see spiritually like you, but were unable to, and to hear spiritually like you, but could not.

"Let me explain further by telling you the allegory of the farmer and the three levels or degrees of spiritual awareness.

"The third or lowest level is comprised of the Beginner or *Somatic* (the 'Body'), a completely unenlightened person. He is so spiritually immature that he is not even open to hearing about the Gospel. If you try to teach it to him, he will not be able to understand it. For Satan—that is, his Ego—will negate the positive thoughts that you have tried to plant in his Subconscious Mind, making him feel unworthy of happiness, health, and abundance. This is like the farmer who sows his crop seeds on a hard dry road instead of on moist black soil: there will be no growth.

"The second or middle level is made up of the Progressing or the *Psychic* (the 'Soul'), a semi-enlightened person. He is open to hearing about the Gospel, and will even be happy to learn about it. But being a spiritually intermediate, he is not deeply grounded in spiritual truth. So when the first stressful event comes along in his life, he loses his faith and forgets the teaching. This is like the farmer who sows his crop seeds on rocky soil: the seeds try to grow but cannot take root. Similarly we have the man who at first seems to understand the teachings of the Gospel, but is soon seduced away by the false promises of materialism. This is like the farmer who sows his crop seeds amid thorns: they suffocate the seedlings before they can sprout, making them unfertile.

"The first or highest degree is formed around the Perfect or the *Pneumatic* individual (the 'Spiritual'). This man is fully spiritually mature and thus fully spiritually receptive. As such, when he hears about the Gospel of the Kingdom of God for the first time, he understands it immediately, for it is not learned from a book, but from the Higher Self (intuition; that is, self-knowledge or Gnosis). He accepts it and begins to practice it. He soon starts to create his ideal life on the visible plane (the Good News). This is like the farmer who sows his crop seeds on healthy, fertile, freshly tilled soil: his harvest will be thirty, sixty, even 100 times what he originally planted."[397]

Thus spoke the Master of Galilee to his band of privately initiated followers, a group that included an even deeper inner circle of "secret Disciples" comprised of individuals such as Joseph of Arimathea,[398] who like Jesus, his parents Joseph and Mary, John the Baptist, the 12 Apostles, and Nicodemus, was also probably a member (or student) of the Essenes.[399]

JAMES, JOHN, & PETER: JESUS' MOST SECRET INNER CIRCLE

The first Christians, the Gnostic-Christians—one group who wrote an entire text in honor of the Pneumatics or Perfect called: "The Thunder: Perfect Mind"[400]—held that the Apostles James (mystically representing judgment and the Conscious Mind), John (love and the Superconscious Mind), and Peter (faith and the Subconscious Mind) were the only ones Jesus considered spiritually mature enough to be able to comprehend the most deeply occult secrets of what he revealingly called, not "the Gospel of Jesus Christ," but "the Gospel of the Kingdom"[401]—a timeless arcane philosophy so fascinating that even "angels desire to look into it."[402]

This view is not "heterodox" as some would have you believe. Rather it is orthodox, for it is confirmed by the canonical Gospels themselves.[403] Additionally, Clement of Alexandria, according to Eusebius, corroborates it in a 2nd-Century document in which he discusses the secret "Hidden Wisdom":[404]

> Christ, after his resurrection, communicated it [the Sacred Gnosis] to James the Just, John, and Peter; these delivered it to the rest of the Apostles; from them it passed to the Seventy, [one] of whom was Barnabas, the writer of the Epistle; and from these it was by God's grace *transmitted without writing* through a few deserving persons from father

to son down to ourselves.[405]

In short, parables were necessary in Jesus' day, and are still necessary in our day, because, as *The Aquarian Gospel of Jesus the Christ* states:

> Man is not far enough advanced to live by faith; he cannot comprehend the things his eyes see not, he yet is [a] child, and during all the coming age he must be taught by pictures, symbols, rites, and forms. His God must be a human God; he cannot see a God by faith. And then he cannot rule himself; the king must rule; the man must serve.[406]

Those who want to understand and literally *live* the Gospel of the Kingdom, however, must become the opposite and strive to be Perfect.[407] That is, they must learn to live both by Spiritual Law (which God "put into our hearts and minds ")[408] and by faith,[409] learn to spiritually comprehend things that their physical eyes cannot see,[410] and learn to trust in the "eternal, immortal, invisible" God of Jesus[411] rather than the visible "human" God of modern Pagan Christianity.[412] Only then can we come to realize what Jesus taught us we truly are: kings of our own personal Inner Realm,[413] that magical but real place that the Lord called the "Kingdom Within,"[414] and which He preached as "the Gospel of the Kingdom,"[415] with its emphasis on the doctrine of immortal God in Man[416]—in mystical Christianity the one and only true Good News.

In this way, he who comes to understand the mystical inner meaning of the Bible is "born again," and is then, as the Gospel of Philip teaches, "no longer a Christian but a Christ."[417] This Truth, as well as the thousands of others contained within the pages of this book, will not be revealed to you by flesh and blood, but by the Father in Heaven.[418]

ENTRIES

"EVERY ONE THAT HEARKENS TO THESE
WORDS SHALL NEVER TASTE DEATH."

JESUS

GOSPEL OF THOMAS

"You poor ignorant idiots" said the Gnostic Christians to the orthodox Church Fathers, "you have mistaken the mysteries of old for modern history, and accepted literally all that was only meant mystically." — GERALD MASSEY, 1883

ABRAHAM: In traditional Christianity Abraham is the founder of the Hebrew people,[419] the first patriarch,[420] the first to profess monotheism,[421] a wealthy owner of concubines and slaves,[422] the father of the three great monotheistic religions (Judaism, Christianity, and Islam),[423] and the Hebrew with whom God made a lasting covenant.[424] He worshiped God not as Yahweh or Jehovah, but as El Shaddai,[425] the name of a Mesopotamian mountain-god.[426] Under Abraham the Pagan rite of circumcision was adopted as a "covenantal sign."[427] Clement of Rome held that Abraham was redeemed "by faith and hospitality."[428]

Famed for having been asked by God to sacrifice his only son Isaac,[429] and as a military hero, blessed by Melchizedek the priest-king of Salem,[430] Abraham was later recognized as a "spiritual ancestor" of the Christian Church.[431] Judeo-Christian tradition holds that he was the first man whose hair turned white.[432] As Jesus descended from Abraham, non-Jews who believe in Jesus are considered the spiritual "seed of Abraham."[433]

In mystical Christianity, as with countless other important ancient founders and leaders (including Jesus),[434] Abraham is said to have been born in a cave,[435] a symbol of the womb of the great Mother-Goddess,[436] known in early Judaism as Asherah.[437] Abraham seems to have been the result of two mythical figures combined.[438] At first a Pagan, he worshiped at the shrine of the Oak-god at Mamre in Hebron,[439] whose sacred day is Thor's Day (Thursday),[440] and was buried in the oracular cave of Machpelah.[441] His journey from Mesopotamia into Canaan[442] is a crossing-the-threshold myth, symbolic of the passing of the soul from an ego state to a non-ego state; that is, from the earth plane to Heaven.[443]

Not only is he considered a symbol of unconditional sacrifice[444] and obedient faith,[445] whose sacred animal is the ram (the astrological Sun-sign Aries),[446] and whose life span, 175 years,[447] is the numerological equivalent of 13 (a symbol of the Sun and the 12 Sun-signs), his very name esoterically represents the divine nature of the human soul;[448] that is, Theosis: God in Man.

Abraham's biography itself suggests that he is an ancient legendary version of Jesus, the archetypal Christ: Abraham and his barren wife Sarah ("Queen"), who bears their son Isaac miraculously, are prefigures of Jesus and the Virgin Mary; his willingness to sacrifice his son as commanded by God prefigures the crucifixion of the "Only Begotten Son"; his 12 grandsons prefigure the 12 Apostles, who in turn represent the 12 astrological Sun-signs. Even the "Abrahamic" ritual of circumcision is not original to Abraham; it was assimilated from the Persians[449] and the ancient Egyptians,[450] just as Herodotus testified.[451] Abraham then is an early type of father-god or Christ,[452] a personification of the Creative Principle,[453] and a representation of the awakening of faith[454] who symbolizes the eternal Indwelling Spirit of God in Man.

"Ye are gods," Jesus declares to the orthodox Jews in the canonical Gospel of John,[455] the same mysterious "three words" he utters to the Apostles in the non-canonical Gospel of Thomas.[456] What makes us each a god or goddess in our own right, as the Lord taught? It is the Christ or I AM, which according to Paul indwells not just Jesus, but each and every human being.[457] Being unlimited, boundless, and ubiquitous, the Indwelling Christ existed prior to the birth of Jesus, as He Himself acknowledged.[458] The Lord, in His usual mystical way, explained it like this: "Before Abraham was, I AM."[459]

The magnificent import of this statement can be seen in the occult fact that Abraham's birth name was Abram,[460] which means "exalted Father." The "Father" is the Divine Mind, the Great Cosmic Spirit, the Cosmic Intellect, or what the ancient Egyptians knew as "Father Mind" or "Supreme Mind."[461] The Sanskrit word for this, the immanent and infinite "One Absolute Reality," is Brahman. Thus Abram was the ancient Hebrew version of the Hindu Brahman: "a Brahman," in fact, who was later renamed A-Brahman,[462] that is, Abraham[463]—whose name means "Father of a multitude," the "multitude" being everything in the Universe.[464]

Further proof that the two are one comes from the occult meaning behind the name *Abrm* or rather Abraham: *Ab* means "father"; *Br* means "son"; *Am* is Aum, Om, or Amen ("divine power"); and *Rm* means "he is lifted up."[465]

The following scripture ties in perfectly with several others in the Near Eastern Gnostic, canonical Gospel of John, which some believe was written by the Gnostic teacher Cerinthus.[466] Again, speaking as the Indwelling Christ, His Higher Self, Jesus says to the Pharisees, who represent the human Ego, or on a broader scale, the Lower Self of humanity:

> "Ye are from beneath; I am from above: ye are of this world; I am not of this world. I said therefore unto you, that ye shall die in your sins: for if ye believe not that I am he, ye shall die in your sins. . . . I have many things to say and to judge of you: but he that sent me is true; and I speak to the world those things which I have heard of him." They understood not that *he spake to them of the Father.* Then said Jesus unto them, "When ye have lifted up the Son of man, then shall ye know that I am he, and that *I do nothing of myself;* but as my Father hath taught me, I speak these things.[467]

The inner meaning:

"You act out of your Lower Selves; I act out of my Higher Self; you are religious; I am spiritual; therefore I say that if you do not believe in the Universal I AM that I AM, you will suffer due to your disbelief." . . . The Pharisees did not understand that Jesus was talking about the Divine Mind, so He said to them: "When you honor the Son of Man, the human Jesus, you will realize that I AM that I AM; and that I do nothing for my own honor; but only those things that the Divine Mind has directed me to say and do."[468]

Here, as He so often did, Jesus is telling us that the Universal Indwelling Christ[469] is one with the Father ("I AM"),[470] that is, with Divine Mind;[471] for, as Paul taught, Christ possesses the full nature of God.[472]

Now if, as the Master asserted, "I and my Father are one,"[473] and we are one with Christ[474]—in fact, He is *in* us[475] and we are *in* Him[476]—then we humans are also one with the Father,[477] and can therefore be nothing less than gods and goddesses ourselves.[478] For Christ and the Father are one and the same, and we are one with both.[479]

By definition there is only a single "One": one Source, one Substance, one Fire, one Mind, one Brahman, one God over all people, be they Christian, Jew, or Pagan[480]—and we are all one with it.[481] Why is there only one ultimate Source, one God? For the same reason we have only one heart: it would be impossible to synchronize two hearts. The second would always be slightly out of alignment with the first, disrupting the entire system.

And so it is with the God of our Universe, a word that derives from the Latin *uni*, meaning "one" or "single." The Father himself said:

> I am the Lord: that is my name: and my glory will I not give to another, neither my praise to graven images.[482]

There can be only one, and that "one" is the "living God,"[483] who has expressed Himself in us as the I AM or Indwelling Christ.[484] It is this, the Christ Within, who Paul described as

> *the image of the invisible God, the firstborn of every creature*: for by him were all things created, that are in heaven, and that are in earth, visible and invisible, whether they be thrones, or dominions, or principalities, or powers: *all things were created by him, and for him: and he is before all things, and by him all things consist.*[485]

Because we are one with the One, just as Zen Buddhism holds that we are each a Buddha,[486] Jesus taught that each one of us is *a Brahman*; that is, we are each an "Abraham," whose real self is the immortal Christ that has always existed and will always exist.[487] See ADAM, CHRIST, MOSES, NOAH, THEOSIS.

ADAM: In traditional Christianity Adam is the first human being, said to be buried on Golgotha, the site of Jesus' crucifixion.[488] Adam was not born but uniquely made by the hand of God on the sixth day of Creation.[489] He died at the age of 930 years.[490] He was the "old Adam" or "First Adam" who prefigured the "new Adam" or "Second Adam," Jesus,[491] as well as the "father of humanity," which gives all people one common ancestor.[492] Thus, as Genesis stresses, because of Adam (and Eve) we are all one race: the human race.[493] Jesus is said to have freed Adam from Hell during his visit to the Underworld.[494]

Created in God's image, Adam and his wife Eve ("life"), the first woman, were placed in the Garden of Eden, where they disobeyed God. In the organized Church this disobedience, "original sin," has been passed down from the First Couple to all mankind, necessitating Jesus' death on the cross for the remission of human sin.[495] Surprisingly, the man who most ardently campaigned to make this idea a mainstream Christian doctrine was a former Gnostic-Christian,[496] Saint Augustine, whose unbiblical views are with us still.[497]

One old Christian legend states that three seeds from the Tree of Life were planted in Adam's mouth after his death. Over the millennia the wood from the resulting trees was used in the magic wand of Noah, plantings from it grew into the burning bush of Noah, and pieces of it were used in the Ark of the Covenant and the pillars of the Jewish Temple at Jerusalem. Finally its wood was said to have been used by the Romans to construct the cross upon which Jesus was crucified.[498]

In mystical Christianity Adam was not a historic figure (his name does not even appear in the first of the two creation accounts in Genesis),[499] for he was merely the Hebrew version of the "first man" in an archetypal myth that is found in every known civilization (in Greece, for example, he was called Hephaestus). Since Adam was figurative there can be no, and there is no, such thing as "original sin."

Not even Judaism treats Adam as a real person. Instead modern Jews see him symbolically as the "primal source," and as the father of the human race representing the unity and equality of humanity,[500] while Christian mystics view him as a symbol of the human race.[501] Thus, an individual named "Adam" is noticeably absent from many Jewish histories of Israel and the Jewish people.[502]

The word-name "Adam" gives away his true nature: he is a symbol of Theosis, the Divine Spark of God incarnate on the material plane. He is thus another type of Christ, as the New Testament itself proclaims.[503]

Adam is connected to the Hebrew word *adom*, meaning "red," the color of dirt, clay, or dust,[504] while his name derives from the Hebrew word *adama*, "earth." Adam is, in fact, the common noun in Hebrew for "humankind,"[505] as his initials illustrate in the Greek names for the four compass points:

*A*natole: east
*D*ysis: west
*A*rctos: north
*M*esembria: south[506]

The man-created-from-clay myth was common around the world in ancient times.[507] All of this explains the inner meaning of the following passage from the book of Genesis:

> And the Lord God formed man of *the dust of the ground*, and breathed into his nostrils the breath of life; and man became a living soul.[508]

The occult Christian schools also view Adam as a symbol of the generic man (that is, the entire human race embodied in one individual),[509] the "creative genetic principle in matter,"[510] and the archetypal Wise Old Man. In Jungian psychology he is the "Cosmic Human," while in alchemy Adam is the *prima materia*, the primeval matter or fundamental substance of the Universe[511] out of which the Big Bang was born. His name and image have appeared on amulets throughout history, used for protection and magic.[512] The pre-Christian Gnostic text, The Revelation of Adam, describes how Adam disclosed to his son Seth the manner in which Noah was saved from drowning during the Great Deluge.[513] According to one Jewish mystical story, the Garden of Eden contained a magical light which enabled Adam to see "from one end of the world to the other."[514]

Adam's age at death, 930, reveals his genuine symbolic nature: in numerology 930 is both a 12 and a three number, the former being the number of the 12 Sun-signs of the Zodiac, and three being the number of the Holy Trinity: Man, Woman, and Child; Mind, Spirit, and Body; Conscious Mind, Subconscious Mind, and Superconscious Mind; Brahma, Vishnu, and Shiva; Jupiter, Juno, and Minerva; Zeus, Apollo, and Athena; Odin, Frigg, and Balder; Mitra, Indra, and Varuna; God, Christ, and the Holy Spirit; etc. See EDEN, EVE, GARDEN OF EDEN, HOLY TRINITY, SERPENT, TETRAMORPH, TREE OF LIFE, TRINITY.

ADVERSARY (THE): In traditional Christianity the Adversary is the same as the "tempter" Satan, God's opposition.[515] In mystical Christianity the Adversary is also Satan, but here Satan is not real, unless we think him into existence through consistent belief and fear. For thoughts are things,[516] and so what we think becomes real for us, just as the Bible teaches.[517] Thus Christian mystics view the Adversary as the personification of the human Ego, Matter, or the reasoning analytical mind, which cannot truly know or understand that which is spiritual—as Man himself surely is. In the Christian Mystery Schools the title Adversary has arcane significance because physicality and materialism hinder us from seeing the Truth;[518]

namely, that Man is Divine.[519] All religions were founded and continue to exist primarily to assist humanity in this most noble of all endeavors.[520] See BEAST, DEVIL, EGO, EGYPT, EVIL, GODS AND GODDESSES, HELL, LOWER SELF, LUCIFER, MASS MIND, NUMBER OF THE BEAST, SATAN, SERPENT, SIN.

ALPHA AND OMEGA: In traditional Christianity Alpha and Omega are the first and last letters of the Greek alphabet, thus representing the eternal aspect of Jesus, who is "the first and the last"; that is, the beginning and the end of all things.[521] The phrase comes from the occultic book of Revelation (patterned on the Essenes' "War Scroll"), written by the Gnostic-Christian mystic "John,"[522] the most highly spiritually evolved of the four Gospelers:[523]

> I was in the Spirit on the Lord's day, and heard behind me a great voice, as of a trumpet, saying "I AM Alpha and Omega, the first and the last: and, what thou seest, write in a book, and send it unto the seven churches which are in Asia; unto Ephesus, and unto Smyrna, and unto Pergamos, and unto Thyatira, and unto Sardis, and unto Philadelphia, and unto Laodicea." And I turned to see the voice that spake with me. And being turned, I saw seven golden candlesticks; And in the midst of the seven candlesticks one like unto the Son of man, clothed with a garment down to the foot, and girt about the paps with a golden girdle.[524]

Since the passage in question begins with the sacred "I AM," and since Om-ega is the Greek version of the Hindu Om (Aum), mystical Christians view the Alpha and Omega as a symbol of the Higher Self or universal Indwelling Christ,[525] and thus as an esoteric emblem of Man's immortal Soul.[526]

It is clear that the Alpha and Omega figure described in the above passage as "girt about the paps with a golden girdle"[527] cannot be Jesus, as the mainstream Church believes, for men's breasts are not called "paps," nor do men wear girdles.[528] So a deeper meaning was obviously intended by the Revelator, and that deeper meaning is that Alpha and Omega represents the "the true Light, which lighteth every man that cometh into the world," as the same author put it.[529] That is, it is a sibylline emblem of the divine spark within each one of us,[530] made in the exact image of God.[531]

The idea back of the Alpha and Omega is purely Pagan and is found as far distant as ancient Egypt.[532] As noted, in India, for example, the Alpha and Omega is known as AUM (the I AM or the Amen of the Bible),[533] with "A" representing the beginning, "U" representing transition, and "M" representing the end.[534] Thus in the Bhagavad Gita, Krishna (the Hindu Christ) declares: "I AM the beginning and the middle and also the end of existing things," while the Egyptian Sun/Son-god

Horus said: "I AM yesterday, today, and tomorrow."[535] See AMEN, ASTROLOGY, CHRIST, I AM, KRISHNA, OSIRIS, WAY OF THE LORD.

AMEN: In traditional Christianity amen derives from a Hebrew word meaning "so be it," thus it is often used to end prayers and liturgies.[536] But Jesus, being a universal mystic, used the word amen in an occult manner, opening many of His declarations with it (though this fact has been concealed under the mistranslated word "verily").[537] Christian mystics have long understood amen to be a christianized Graceo-Roman version of the arcane term I AM, identical to the Hindu Aum or Om,[538] the Persian Hom,[539] the Jewish Amam, the Tibetan Hum,[540] the ancient Egyptian Amon, and the Gnostic-Christian Logos.[541] All refer to the Divinity Within, that is, the Christ, which, according to Paul, indwells all living things,[542] and which John the Revelator mystically refers to as "the Amen."[543] See CHRIST, I AM, JESUS, MOUTH OF GOD, ONLY BEGOTTEN SON, YAHWEH.

ANCIENT OF DAYS: In traditional Christianity the Ancient of Days is a term for God, one found only in Daniel, where he appeared to the prophet in this guise.[544] In mystical Christianity it is a term for the unborn, unformed, uncreated, indestructible, eternal Higher Self: the Indwelling Christ.[545] Since the Higher Self or Christ is made in God's image[546] and is therefore a manifestation of the universal Spirit that is "given to every man,"[547] both the traditional and the mystical meanings are identical. See CHRIST, CHRIST CONSCIOUSNESS, I AM.

ANGELS: An Oriental Pagan concept found in numerous pre-Christian religions,[548] most notably Zoroastrianism, from which the idea of angels was borrowed by the Hebrews, and from them the Christians.[549] Unsurprisingly, the earliest known artistic representation of an angel is found in the ancient ruins of Babylon.[550] Our English word angel comes from the Greek *aggelos* (*angelos*), meaning "messenger." Christian fundamentalists (as well as many Christian mystics) consider angels to be real beings,[551] "superhuman agents of God," arranged in various orders and hierarchies, each assigned his or her own specific task.[552] Some deliver messages from God, some guard over individuals, some act in similar fashion to the Pagan nature spirit, presiding over various material substances.[553]

In some cases the Christian angel is clearly patterned on the Pagans' "Four Compass Gods,"[554] overseeing the four directions (east, west, north, south), the four winds, the four corners of the earth, the four seasons, the four elements (fire, water, earth, air),[555] the four cardinal virtues (temperance, fortitude, prudence, justice),[556] the four occult worlds (Aziluth: emanation; Briarth: creation; Jezirath: forms; Aziath: materiality),[557] etc. In ancient astrology these evolved into the four well-known quaternary Sun-signs: Aquarius the Waterman,[558] Leo the Lion, Taurus the Bull, and Aquila the Eagle (later to become Scorpio the Scorpion).[559]

In the mystical Christian Church angels are "spiritual influences" that minister to the human soul, aiding our Higher Self in its spiritual growth and evolution. As an essence of God, here angels are "voices of the Lord"; that is, mental or psychological messengers working through our conscience, urging us in the direction of righteousness, peace, love, truth, and the Light.[560] See COMFORTER, GOD, TETRAMORPH.

ANOINTING: In traditional Christianity anointing is the act of placing oil on people, animals, or objects out of a sign of respect, for burial and sacralizing, or for use in medicine. Pagan and Jewish prophets, priests, and kings were routinely anointed or christed with oil, usually olive oil,[561] sometimes in religiosexual ceremonies related to Goddess-worship and fertility-vegetation cults.[562] In mystical Christianity anointing is a symbol of Divine Love being poured into the human soul.[563] Thus the Psalmist's occult prayer:

> Thou preparest a table before me in the presence of mine enemies: Thou hast anointed my head with oil; my cup runneth over.[564]

See CHRIST, OIL, PETER, ROCK.

ANTICHRIST: In traditional Christianity the antichrist is a "man of sin" who will attack the people of God in the last days.[565] The word, *antichristos*, appears only in 1 John[566] and 2 John.[567] In mystical Christianity the antichrist is the Lower Self (or Satan), which is in constant combat with the Higher Self (or Christ).[568] It is, in other words, anything or anyone who opposes the goodness of Spirit.[569] See ADVERSARY, BEAST, DEVIL, EGO, EGYPT, EVIL, GODS AND GODDESSES, HELL, LOWER SELF, LUCIFER, MASS MIND, NUMBER OF THE BEAST, SATAN, SERPENT, SIN.

APOSTLES (THE 12): In traditional Christianity the Apostles are the 12 men chosen by Jesus to aid Him in His earthly ministry.[570] As Matthew, Mark, Luke, and Acts do not agree on either their names or their order,[571] and as most of the ancient religious teachers, founders, and gods had 12 apostles (for example, Buddha, Mithra, Roland, Ra, Odin, etc.), and as Jesus Himself is referred to as an "Apostle" in the New Testament,[572] it is clear that the mainstream view of the 12 Apostles does not go below the veneer of superficial literalism.

In mystical Christianity the 12 Apostles of Jesus are seen as symbols of the 12 highest virtues of the Indwelling Christ. These virtues are in turn esoterically represented in the Bible as the 12 astrological Sun-signs (which "orbit" around the Sun, or Christ), the 12 Tribes of Israel, the 12 running springs in Helim, the 12 stones in Aaron's breastplate, the 12 loaves of shew-bread, the 12 spies sent by

Moses, the 12 stars of the bride's crown, the 12 foundations of the New Jerusalem and her 12 gates and 12 precious stones, and so on.[573] Mystic Apostle Paul derogatorily described James, Peter, and John as "pillar" Apostles; that is, as unenlightened literalists belonging to the orthodox branch of the early Church.[574] See ASTROLOGY, JESUS, PAUL, PETER, TRIBES OF ISRAEL, TWELVE, ZODIAC.

ARK (NOAH'S): In traditional Christianity the ark was a ship designed by God and made by Noah[575] at the former's command, which enabled the patriarch and his family to save themselves from the Great Flood.[576] But as Noah is merely an ancient Hebrew version of countless archetypal flood-men, such as the Greek Deucalion,[577] the Hindu Manu,[578] the Hawaiian Nu'u,[579] the Sumerian Ziusudra,[580] and the Mesopotamian Utnapishtim,[581] and as the Hebrew word *tebah* (translated "ark"), is from the ancient Egyptian word *tba*, "chest,"[582] we must turn to the Christian arcana to discover the ark's true inner meaning. For like all ancient symbols this sealed "chest" contains sacred mysteries, one whose lock can only be opened with the key of mystical knowledge.

In mystical Christianity Noah's Ark is a symbol of what is known as the causal body;[583] that is, the Spirit, or the spiritual aspect of human consciousness;[584] also known as the mental body, seed body, or *Karan Sharir*. The causal body is the real Self, the Higher Self, the Mind or Indwelling Christ, made in the image of God.[585] It is sheathed in the astral body, commonly known as the Soul, and also as the subtle body, light body, rainbow body, or *Sukhsham Sharir*, and the astral body is sheathed in the physical body; that is, the material body, desire body, gross body, or *Isthul Sharir*.[586]

These three bodies (mental, astral, and physical) are symbolized by the three stories of the ark; the seven people who accompany Noah symbolize the Seven Heavens, or additionally the "completion" of the Higher Self[587] (the number three representing the Masculine Principle, which added to four, representing the Feminine Principal, equals seven: perfection); the rainbow is a symbolic bridge between the material plane and the spiritual plane (and thus an emblem of enlightenment); and the animals on the ark represent Man's base impulses, that is, his Lower Nature or Lower Self (Ego/Satan), all which are "baptized" (spiritualized) by the flood waters of "divine truth."

The waters of the deluge can also be a dark emblem of godlessness or evil. Here the "ark" symbolizes the refuge to which our Spirit flees when overly influenced by worldly matters,[588] or it can be a "chest" containing the salvific Gnosis, which we access through intuition. Jung sees Noah's ark as a symbol of the "maternal womb,"[589] while Graves views it as the archetypal "chest of re-birth" (found in ancient myths from Ireland to Egypt), which derives from an Asian tale in which the Spirit of the Sun annually rides aboard a Moon-ship around the 12 astrological signs.[590] See CHRIST, DOVE, FLOOD OF NOAH, GNOSIS, NOAH,

RAINBOW, RIVER, WATER.

ASCENSION: In traditional Christianity the Ascension is the act of Jesus leaving earth to return to the Father.[591] In mystical Christianity the Ascension of Jesus is spiritual not physical,[592] for countless other Sun-gods, son-gods, saviors, christs, and messiahs, such as Hercules,[593] also ascended to Heaven after physical death. Thus, the true meaning of ascension is the upward movement of the human soul from the earth plane to the spirit plane, as it progresses toward oneness with God. The mystical view is proven by the fact that in the four *original* canonical Gospel texts, there is not a single reference to the Ascension of our Lord.[594] See BIRTH OF JESUS, CHRIST, CRUCIFIXION, DEATH OF JESUS, JESUS, RESURRECTION OF JESUS, TRANSFIGURATION OF JESUS.

ASTROLOGY: Astrology would appear to have no connection to traditional Christianity, and indeed according to modern mainstream Christians, it does not. But contrary to today's teachings of the Ecclesia (the organized institutionalized Christian Church),[595] astrology was clearly an integral part of early Judaism and Christianity, a fact so obvious to those with "eyes to see"[596] that some actually view the Bible as a veritable "astrological textbook."[597] Speaking with the voice of an astrologer,[598] Jesus, the very man after whom Christianity was named, once said:

> And there shall be signs in the sun, and in the moon, and in the stars[599] . . . and great signs shall there be from heaven.[600]

More overt evidence comes from ancient Christian artwork and Medieval iconography, which often featured the 12 Sun-signs, as well as a variety of other obvious astrological elements. One example is "The Zodiac Window," located in Chartres Cathedral at Paris, France. Its South Ambulatory Window contains the 12 Pagan Zodiacal Sun-signs in panes of beautifully colored glass. Starting at the bottom and going upward, they are:

1) January, Aquarius
2) February, Pisces
3) March, Aries
4) April, Taurus
5) May, Gemini
6) June, Cancer
7) July, Leo
8) August, Virgo,
9) September, Libra
10) October, Scorpio
11) November, Sagittarius
12) December, Capricorn

At the pinnacle of this "Christian" Zodiac sits Jesus, with the Greek letters Alpha and Omega on either side.[601]

If this is not enough evidence showing the early Church's mystical association with astrology, we have the Bible, which brims with passages related to the ancient art, much of it stemming not just from Pagan sources, but from the "long tradition" of astrological knowledge found in the Talmud, Midrash, and Judaic mystical writings.[602] The following scriptures represent just a small sampling. Note that some of these passages must be read with the Spiritual or Third Eye (that is, figuratively, using intuition) rather than the physical eyes (that is, literally, using tuition or the intellect).

EXAMPLES OF BIBLICAL ASTROLOGY (partial list)
Genesis 1:14-15; 37:9-11
Deuteronomy 4:19, 24
Judges 5:20
Job 3:1-10; 9:7; 38:4-7, 32
Psalms 19:1-4; 84:11
Ecclesiastes 3:1-8
Isaiah 14:12-14
Jeremiah 8:1-2
Ezekiel 1:10
Malachi 4:2
Matthew 2:1-10; 12:32; 13:39-40; 17:2; 24:3; 28:20
Luke 1:78; 18:29-30; 21:25
John 1:4-9; 8:12; 12:46
1 Corinthians 3:6-8; 10:11
Ephesians 1:21; 5:14
Hebrews 6:5; 9:26
2 Peter 1:19
Revelation 1:7, 16; 2:27-29; 4:6-7; 8:16; 12:1; 15:3; 22:16

As is clear from the last entry, the book of Revelation alone makes numerous esoteric references to astrology, such as the 12 gates made of pearls[603] and the 12 "precious stones" which "garnished the wall" of the holy city, the New Jerusalem,[604] both which are emblems of the 12 Sun-signs of the Zodiac. Such knowledge is not recent. Some believe that Man has had an interest in and an understanding of the Zodiac for some 5 million years.[605]

The sacred gemology of the Pagan-Jewish-Christian astrological tradition is with us to this day. The ancient and modern birth stones of the 12 Sun-signs are a near perfect match with the 12 "precious stones" mentioned in Revelation 2,000 years ago:

1) Aries: amethyst
2) Taurus: emerald
3) Gemini: sapphire
4) Cancer: ruby

5) Leo: onyx
6) Virgo: peridot
7) Libra: sapphire
8) Scorpio: ruby

9) Sagittarius: topaz
10) Capricorn: agate

11) Aquarius: garnet
12) Pisces: jasper[606]

Though there is no *modern* traditional Christian connection to astrology, in the mystical branch of the Church the Zodiac is viewed as a symbol of the cycle of life, divided into the 12 stages of soul evolution one must ascend through in order to attain at-one-ment with God (enlightenment, nirvana, samadhi, etc.). In other words, the human soul or Self (Indwelling Christ) is the "Sun" and archetypal Man is the "year," separated into 12 parts representing the soul's cyclic progression from the lowest spiritual level (Aries) to the highest (Pisces).[607] This cycle is often depicted as a circle, just as a natal horoscope is drawn as a ring containing the 12 Sun-signs. The author of the book of Proverbs made reference to this band of astrological symbols:

> When he prepared the heavens I was there: when he set a circle upon the face of the depth.[608]

Jesus Himself has deep connections to astrology: born in the Age of Aries the Ram (which began around 2220 B.C.),[609] a constellation known to pre-Christian Pagans as "the Lamb of God" and the "Savior,"[610] the Lord took on these titles as well.[611] Later, because His ministry started during the Age of Pisces (the Two Fishes), His sacred symbol became the fish, *ichthys* (Greek for "fish") being an acronym for "Jesus, Christ, of God, Son, Savior."

Even the 12 Apostles—patterned on such pre-Christian Pagan deities as the 12 Titans of Greek mythology, the 12 Aesirs of Scandinavian mythology, the 12 Aditya of Hindu mythology, and the 12 Helpers of Egyptian mythology—became associated with the 12 star-signs of astrology, who annually "orbited" their Divine Father Jesus, known to 4th-Century Christians as the great Pagan Sun-god *Sol Invictus*.[612]

In chronological order we have what I call the 12 Apostolic Powers of Man as emblemized in the 12 Sun-signs:

1) James, Aries the Ram: judgement.
2) Andrew, Taurus the Bull: strength.
3) Thomas, Gemini the Twins: understanding.
4) Nathaniel, Cancer the Crab: imagination.
5) Judas, Leo the Lion: acquisitiveness.
6) James the Just, Virgo the Virgin: self-denial.
7) Jude, Libra the Scales: orderliness.
8) John, Scorpio the Scorpion: love.
9) Philip, Sagittarius the Archer: power.
10) Simon, Capricorn the Goat: emotion.

11) Matthew, Aquarius the Water Bearer: the will.
12) Peter, Pisces the Two Fishes: faith.⁶¹³

The "Twelve Days of Christmas" were also modeled on these ancient Pagan-Christian connections, beginning with James (Aries) on December 26, ending with Peter (Pisces) on January 6.

Additionally, in mystical Christianity the 12 Apostles are connected to the 12 Mental Faculties (closely related to the 12 Apostolic Powers above). There are many interpretations, including:

1) Peter, the deductive mind.
2) Andrew, faith.
3) James, hope.
4) John, love.
5) Philip, courage.
6) Bartholomew, perseverance.
7) Thomas, truth-seeking.
8) James Alpheus, modesty.
9) Simon, gentleness.
10) Judas (brother of James), compassion.
11) Matthew, critical thinking.
12) Judas Iscariot, prudence.⁶¹⁴

In Hinduism the Sacred 12 are symbolic of Cosmic Man, and are thus associated with the Sahasrara (seventh) Chakra (that is, the Christ, the Sun, the Son, or Crown Chakra) and the six lower spinal "flowers" or "wheels," which owing to their dual positive and negative energies, are doubled, thus equaling 12:

Sixth: Ajna Chakra
Fifth: Vishudda Chakra
Fourth: Anahata Chakra
Third: Manipura Chakra
Second: Svadhishthana Chakra
First: Muladhara Chakra

Here, the human body—along with its millions of "subjects" (cells)—is considered a "kingdom," ruled over by a "king"; namely, the Indwelling Christ, who exists as the Crown Chakra in the skull (behind the Third Eye), which is known to Christian mystics as the "Temple of Wisdom"⁶¹⁵ or "Holy of Holies."⁶¹⁶ The skull is symbolized in Christian legend as Golgotha (the "place of the skull"), the skullcap-shaped hill at Jerusalem where Jesus is believed by some to have been crucified.⁶¹⁷

Luke calls Golgotha *kranion* in Greek, which is cranium in English. King

James' scribes translated *kranion* as "Calvary."[618] The English word Calvary derives from *calvariae locus*, the Latin translation of the Greek *kraniou topos* (the "location of the cranium"). According to Eusebius, the Romans later built a temple honoring the goddess Aphrodite over Golgotha.[619] This was long ago torn down, however, and replaced with a Christian church, the first construction which was begun by the Crusaders in the 12th Century.[620]

Aphrodite was also known as the "Virgin-Mother," "Stella Maris,"[621] and Mari, the "Sea" (the Egyptians knew her as Ay-Mari), the same names Christian mythologists later appended to the mother of Jesus. The Easter month of April (*Aphrilis*) was named after Aphrodite,[622] the month in which Jesus is said to have risen from the dead. Aphrodite, like Jesus, known as the "Morning Star" (Venus),[623] is the Greek version of the ancient Hebrew mother-goddess Ashtoreth or Asherah,[624] as well as the Phoenician love-goddess Astarte, the "Queen of Heaven" and virgin-mother who gave birth to the Solar-God (the Christ) every 12 months on December 25 (Christmas).[625]

Many of the popes relied on astrology for planning the dates of important events. As late as the 16th Century, Pope Leo X established a "Chair of Astrology" at a noted university,[626] while in the early 17th Century German professor, Catholic preacher, and Jesuit priest Jeremias Drexel published a popular astrological book, *Zodiacus Christianus* (the "Christian Zodiac"), which likened the 12 Virtues of Christianity to the 12 signs of the Zodiac.[627] See GOLGOTHA, TRIBES OF ISRAEL, TWELVE, UPPER ROOM, ZODIAC.

ATONEMENT: As with many other biblical doctrines, the idea of atonement too has been mistranslated (in many cases, intentionally), and thus its truly salvific power has long been denied the masses. Mainstream Christianity teaches that atonement is the reconciliation of God and humankind through the sacrificial blood and death of Jesus.[628] This is merely the outer (exoteric) meaning, however.

The inner (esoteric) meaning is that atonement is a reminder or spiritual restoration of our *at-one-ment*, our union, our complete and perfect oneness, with the "Father" (Superconscious Mind), "the Christ" (Conscious Mind), and the "Holy Ghost" (Subconscious Mind). Contrary to orthodox Christian teaching, Jesus never used the word atonement, and in fact, it only appears once in the entire New Testament (in Paul's letter to the Romans).[629] Everything else taught about it is manmade, not Jesus-made.

Despite this, Jesus insured that His teachings on the topic of at-one-ment were clear and available to all who have ears to hear (that is, those at the proper spiritual level to understand them): we are one with God, Christ, and the Holy Spirit,[630] all part of the "great mystery of godliness" Paul referred to.[631] See CHRIST, CHRIST CONSCIOUSNESS, GOD, PRAYER, REDEEMER, REDEMPTION, SALVATION, UNION WITH GOD.

"Believe not because some old manuscripts are produced, believe not because it is your national belief, because you have been made to believe from your childhood, but reason truth out, and after you have analyzed it, then, if you find it will do good to one and all, believe it, live up to it, and help others to live up to it." — BUDDHA

B

BABYLON: In traditional Christianity Babylon, the Greek form of Babel (meaning "gate of Bel"),[632] is both the capital of the Babylonian Empire (Chaldea) and a symbol of opposition to God.[633] Its temple, a ziggurat or stepped tower, was dedicated to the Pagan deity Bel (Marduk),[634] and is the "Tower of Babel" of Genesis.[635] The Hanging Gardens of Babylon were once considered one of the Seven Wonders of the World.[636]

In the book of Revelation Babylon is the "City of Satan,"[637] where it represents the anti-Christian city of Rome,[638] "the mother of harlots and abominations of the earth,"[639] a godless place of corruption and perversion, the opposite of the Heavenly Jerusalem.[640]

In mystical Christianity Babylon is a symbol of the earth plane or world of materiality,[641] as well as spiritual chaos and confusion, which inevitably give rise to the "Beast": the base impulses of humanity.[642] Babylon is thus a metaphor for both materialism and Man's Lower Self, the nature of desire and sensation, which imprisons the soul in the physical.[643]

Despite the negative reputation given to Babylon by biblical authors, it was a magnificent and sophisticated society and is still considered by many to be the "cradle of civilization." Its religion possessed an early Holy Trinity (made up of the deities Shamash, Ishtar, and Sin), and its poetry and literature influenced the Bible itself. The Epic of Gilgamesh, for example, was used by ancient Hebrew writers as a pattern for the myth of Noah and the Great Flood.[644] See BEAST, DEVIL, EGYPT, EVIL, NUMBER OF THE BEAST, PHARISEES, PILATE, SATAN.

BAPTISM: In traditional Christianity there are two forms of baptism: baptism by water (a symbol of Truth), implemented by John the Baptist, which cleanses the Soul of sin, and baptism by fire (a symbol of Spirit), implemented by Jesus, which signals a new life of righteousness in Christ. Baptism is a means of admitting the individual into the mainstream Church.[645] Christian baptism derives from Judaism and Judaism borrowed it from Paganism. It is first known in India (Hinduism),[646] and was later practiced by such people as the Roman Pagans (who were baptized in the *Taurobolium*,[647] where they were drenched in the blood of bulls)[648] and the mystical Jewish Essenes (of whom John the Baptist, Jesus, and the 12 Apostles may have been members),[649] who practiced ritual baptism before and during the 1st Century A.D.[650]

In mystical Christianity baptism by water and baptism by fire are essentially the same. The first is a form of spiritual purification which prepares the Soul for the descent of the Holy Spirit. The latter represents psychological and physical rebirth. Both are symbolic of spiritual regeneration.

Jesus never taught the ritual of *water* baptism specifically,[651] for there is no clear biblical passage in which He formally institutes baptism by immersion, nor is He shown baptizing anyone with water,[652] or even commanding that any of His converts be baptized.[653] Then there is the thief who was crucified alongside Jesus, who was saved without baptism or receiving communion.[654] Furthermore, many, such as the first Christians, the Gnostics, have rightly pointed out that John's form of baptism was one of repentance of sin.[655] This being true, why then did Jesus, who was sinless, need to be baptized by John?[656]

For these reasons and many others, the rite of baptism by immersion was not considered essential in the Church until after Jesus' death,[657] and Swiss Reformer Ulrich Zwingli correctly denied its necessity.[658] Our Lord Himself did not discuss or command it until *after* His resurrection in a suspicious passage attributed to the risen Christ, by now the second member of the Holy Trinity.[659] But as the doctrine of the Trinity was not part of the earliest Church (it is nowhere mentioned in any authentic Bible passage, and was not officially adopted until the 4th or 5th Century),[660] this scripture is an obvious late interpolation.[661]

Even then, the primitive Christian form of baptism was derived not from Jesus, but from John the Baptist. Thus the spiritual importance the traditional Church puts on baptism by immersion is wholly misplaced.[662]

This is because the form of baptism our Lord insisted on was not physical but mystical; one in which, as the Gnostic-Christians taught, the Indwelling Christ "descends upon" an individual.[663] John the Baptist hinted at this in his declaration:

> I indeed baptize you with water unto repentance: but he that cometh after me is mightier than I, whose shoes I am not worthy to bear: he shall baptize you with the Holy Ghost, and with fire.[664]

As noted above, Jesus' injunction to "go ye therefore, and teach all nations, baptizing them in the name of the Father, and of the Son, and of the Holy Ghost,"[665] is a late 4th-Century interpolation, one that is not mentioned by earlier Church Fathers. In his writings Eusebius, for example, who lived from about A.D. 260 to about 340, cites this same passage from Matthew numerous times without any reference to the "Father, the Son, and the Holy Ghost," and instead records the original verse as simply:

> Go, and make disciples of all nations in my Name.[666]

This statement perfectly matches an earlier one in Matthew made by our Lord:

> This gospel of the Kingdom shall be preached in all the world for a witness unto all nations.[667]

This is why, after Jesus' Resurrection, Peter ordered fellow Christians to be baptized, not "in the name of the Father, and of the Son, and of the Holy Ghost," but simply "in the name of Jesus Christ."[668] See FLOOD OF NOAH, HOLY SPIRIT, HOLY TRINITY, RIVER, TRINITY, WASHING THE FEET, WATER.

BEAST (THE): In modern traditional Christianity "the Beast" of Revelation is an apocalyptic symbol of any nonhuman force that opposes God.[669] Though often vaguely described as a "devilish creature,"[670] most Christians view it very specifically as the Devil or Satan.[671] To the Christians who lived at the time Revelation was written, however, the Beast was the Roman Emperor Nero, whose name in Aramaic is spelled *Nron Ksr* (without vowels) and in Greek, *Neron Kaisar* (that is, "Nero Caesar").[672] In mystical Christianity the Beast is the human Ego (known in the orthodox Church as "Satan"), the godless rebellious aspect of human nature. See ADVERSARY, ANTICHRIST, DEVIL, EGO, EGYPT, EVIL, GODS AND GODDESSES, HELL, LOWER SELF, LUCIFER, MASS MIND, NUMBER OF THE BEAST, PHARISEES, PILATE, SATAN, SERPENT, SIN.

BETHLEHEM: In traditional Christianity Bethlehem is the city of Jesus' birth.[673] Bethlehem means the "House (*beyt* or *beth*) of Bread (*lechem* or *lehem*)";[674] that is, the Abode of Christ, for occultly bread is a symbol of spiritual food or spiritual truth.[675] Thus in mystical Christianity Bethlehem, the House of Bread or the House of Sustenance, is a symbol of both the spiritual substance that makes up the Indwelling Christ[676] and the purified mind in which the Christ is born.[677]

As far back as the 4th Century Christians were aware that the word "Bethlehem" contained esoteric connotations that hid beneath a literal interpretation. One of these was the Church Father St. Ambrose, who wrote:

> Wherefore every soul which receives that bread which comes down from heaven is the house of bread, that is, the Bread of Christ, being nourished and supported and having its heart strengthened by that heavenly bread which dwells within it. Hence Paul also says, "For we being many are one bread."[678] Every faithful soul is Bethlehem, as Jerusalem also is said to be, which has the peace and tranquillity of that Jerusalem which is above, in heaven. That is the true Bread which, when broken into pieces, fed all men.[679]

As Bethlehem contained a shrine to the Syrian dying and rising savior-god Adonis (or Tammuz), one of the many prototypes of the Paganized Jesus, it was only natural that early Christian writers and mythographers would want to connect our Lord with the town known as the House of Bread. Even Adonis' words were put into Jesus' mouth:[680] "I am the good shepherd; the good shepherd giveth his life for the sheep."[681] See BREAD, CHRIST, CHRISTMAS, EGYPT, GALILEE, ISRAEL, JERUSALEM, SACRAMENT, WASHING THE FEET, WATER, WINE.

BIBLE: In the traditional Church the Bible is an infallible God-inspired work whose theme is that human faith and action are consummated in the New Testament.[682] To Jews the Bible begins and ends with the Old Testament. To atheists the Bible is merely a diverse assortment of ancient and often childish myths.

In the mystical Christian Church the Bible is the ultimate handbook on the mysteries of birth, life, and death; a highly occult work filled—if one knows how to read it—from the first chapter of Genesis to the last chapter of Revelation with vital sacred truths, doctrines, wisdom (Sophia), and knowledge (Gnosis), all which is meant to aid one in the spiritual growth of his or her Soul.[683]

And herein lies one of the greatest differences between the traditional Church and the mystical Church. In the former the Bible is master rather than servant. In the latter the Bible is servant rather than master.[684] See CHRISTIANITY, GNOSTICISM, GOSPEL, MYTH OF CHRIST.

BIRTH OF JESUS: In the traditional Christian Church the miraculous virgin birth of Jesus is taken literally, word for word—despite the fact that it is described very differently by different authors and is not even mentioned by writers like Mark and Paul. In the mystical Christian Church the birth of Jesus is a universal allegory representing the descent of Spirit into matter, an act known to esotericists as "involution." Kingsford and Maitland write:

> Christ cannot be conceived save of a soul immaculate and virgin as to matter, and meet to become the spouse of the Divine Spirit. Therefore, as the soul as Eve gives consent to the annunciation of the Serpent, so, as Mary, become virgin, she gives consent to the annunciation of the Angel, and understands the mystery of the Motherhood of the man regenerate. She has no acts of her own, all the acts of her Son are hers also. She participates in his nativity, in his manifestation, in his passion, in his resurrection, in his ascension, in his pentacostal gift. He himself is her gift to the world. But it is always he who operates; she who asks, acquiesces, consents, responds. Through her he outflows into the mind and external man, and, so, into life and conduct. As Augustine says, "All graces pass to

us through the hands of Mary." For the purified soul is the mediatrix, as she is the genetrix, of the Divine presence.

The Church speaks of the Ascension of Christ, and of the Assumption of Mary. Christ being deific in nature and of heavenly origin, ascends by his own power and will. But the soul is "assumed," or drawn up by the power and will of her Son. Of herself she is nothing; he is her all in all. Where he abides, thither must she be uplifted, by force of the divine union which makes her one with him. Henceforth she abides in the real, and has the illusions of sense for evermore under foot. It is not of herself that Mary becomes Mother of *God in man*. The narrative of the Incarnation implies a conjunction of human—though not physical—and Divine potencies. Mary receives her infant by an act of celestial energy overshadowing and vitalising her with the Divine life. This is because the pure soul is as a lens to the Divine rays, polarising them and kindling fire therefrom. Having this attitude towards God, she has kindled in her that holy flame which becomes the light that enlightens the world.[685]

In other words, because the Christ (our Higher Self, our true self, our spirit body) is a piece of God,[686] it is invisible and eternal, uncreated and indestructible. Thus it is not, and cannot be, born carnally via physical reproduction, as the human body is. Instead it is implanted in the earthly body (sometime between conception and birth) by a mysterious divine process that mystics, struggling with the limitations of language, refer to as a "virgin birth." In occult Christian terms, this means that every person experiences the "birth of Jesus," for we are each a "Christ child" born of a "Virgin-Mother"—which is exactly what the New Testament Nativities reveal to those who have "eyes to see."[687] See CHRIST, CHRISTIANITY, GOSPEL, JESUS, NATIVITY.

BLOOD OF THE LAMB: In the traditional Christian Church the Blood of the Lamb is the literal physical blood of Jesus, which washed away the sins of humanity at the crucifixion.[688] In mystical Christianity blood itself signifies the Soul, the Life Force, and solar energy,[689] while the Blood of the Lamb is a symbol of spiritual rebirth,[690] the Divine Energy of God, and Divine Truth. Thus Swedenborg says:

> Blood is mentioned in many parts of the Word, and everywhere signifies, in a spiritual sense, the divine truth of the Lord, which also is the divine truth of the Word; and, in an opposite sense, the divine truth of the Word falsified or profaned . . .[691]

Kingsford and Maitland write:

> To live the Divine Life is to be partaker in the blood of Christ and to drink of Christ's cup. It is to know the love of Christ which "passeth understanding," the love which is Life, or God, and whose characteristic symbol is the blood-red ray of the solar prism. By this mystical blood we are saved,—this blood, which is no other than the secret of the Christs, whereby man is transmuted from the material to the spiritual plane, the secret of inward purification by means of Love. For this "blood," which, throughout the sacred writings is spoken of as the essential principle of the "Life," is the spiritual Blood of the spiritual Life,—Life in its highest, intensest, and most excellent sense,—not the mere physical life understood by materialists,—but the very substantial Being, *the inward Deity in man*. And it is by means of this Blood of Christ only—that is by means of Divine Love only—that we can "come to the Father," and inherit the kingdom of heaven. For, when it is said that "the blood of Christ cleanseth from all sin," it is signified that sin is impossible to him who is perfect in Love.[692]

As the pre-Christian Pagan symbol of the Universal Savior, the lamb became the natural symbol of Christ in both the mystical and traditional Churches, its four feet representing the four Gospels, and its blood an emblem of the solar life that pours forth onto and over the earth via the Sun-sign Aries,[693] which ruled the astrological Age in which Jesus was born.[694] Among the Quakers, as with many other mystical Christian groups, the Blood of Christ is seen as a metaphor for the "Light Within," that is the all-inclusive Indwelling Christ,[695] which Gnostic John the Evangelist described as "the true Light, which lighteth every man that cometh into the world."[696] See GOOD SHEPHERD, LAMB OF GOD.

BORN AGAIN: In the mainstream Church being "born again" means that one is baptized and accepts Jesus as his or her personal savior, known to traditionalists theologically as "regeneration through the Holy Spirit."[697] In the mystical Church being "born again" refers to an inner rebirth of one's entire being, allowing entrance into the Kingdom of Heaven, that blissful state of consciousness that is only open to those who have taken on a new and pure spiritual consciousness: "the mind of Christ."[698]

For those who embrace the doctrine of the transmigration of souls literally, being "born again" means reincarnation, which, this school maintains, is a necessary refining process that perfects the human Soul over numerous earthly lifetimes.[699] Among some Christian occultists being "born again" has yet another meaning, one mystically referred to as being "twice-born." We are born first into the material world and we are "born" secondly into the spirit world at the time of so-called "death."[700] Thus Jesus said: "Except a man be born again, he cannot see the kingdom of God."[701] See GOSPEL, NATIVITY, REINCARNATION.

BREAD: In the traditional Christian Church bread is literally bread,[702] though sometimes it can be a generic symbol for food or a word indicating the presence of God.[703] In the mystical Christian Church bread is a symbol of spiritual food or spiritual truth.[704] Hence, Jesus, speaking as the universal Indwelling Christ, says:

> I am the bread of life: he that cometh to me shall never hunger;
> and he that believeth on me shall never thirst.[705]

See BETHLEHEM, SACRAMENT, WATER, WINE.

BRETHREN (THE): In the traditional Church the ancient appellation "the Brethren" was simply a name given to fellow Christians after Jesus' death and the Jerusalem conference, which took place around A.D. 33.[706] In the mystical Church "the Brethren" was the name given to that early Jewish brotherhood popularly known today as the Essenes (the New Testament "Nazarenes")[707]—whose most famous community was located at Qumran (in modern Israel's West Bank), and whose best known religious works are the misnamed "Dead Sea Scrolls," or the "Great Essene Library," as they should more properly be called.[708] The Free Masons, who claim descent from the Essenes, still refer to themselves as "the Brethren." In fine, "the Essenes were the early Christians in disguise," which is why historians such as Josephus never mention Christians or Christianity,[709] but do mention the Essenes,[710] of which John the Baptist, Jesus, his parents Joseph and Mary, the 12 Apostles, Joseph of Arimathea, and many others linked to our Lord, were almost certainly members.[711]

Jesus was not a Christian, and knew nothing of the term or the religion.[712] The word "Christian," in fact, was invented *after* His death by Pagans, particularly those at Antioch, as a derogatory term for His followers. This is one reason Jesus never referred to Himself, the Apostles, or His followers as "Christians," and it is why the Apostles never called each other "Christians." The word appears just three times in the entire Bible,[713] and was only accepted as a legitimate designation for Jesus' followers long after His Crucifixion. Hence, the first Christians in Palestine, the Jewish Essenic "Brotherhood" of Christ, called themselves "the Brethren."[714] See CHRISTIANITY, ENOCH, ESSENES, GNOSTICISM, NAZARENES.

BUDDHA: Buddha, who lived some 500 years before Jesus, does not appear by name in the Christian Bible, of course. But he is included here because he, like Attis, Osiris, Mithra, Apollo, Tammuz, Helios, Bacchus, Dionysus, and a thousand other deities, is recognized by Christian mystics as one of the principal pre-Christian saviors[715] upon whom the figure of the Paganized pseudo-Jesus was built and developed over the centuries during the Catholic Church's monstrous process known as the "Scheme of Salvation."[716]

There is another important reason why Buddha appears in this work, however. Buddhism, like the other major Eastern faiths, can be seen to have had a strong influence on the doctrines of Gnosticism and Essenism, original Christianity[717]—which is why we find Buddhist elements in the introductory narratives of the Gospel of Luke, the teachings of Jesus,[718] and the letters of Paul,[719] as just three examples. The similarities between the two Faiths are so great that numerous volumes have been written on the subject, including Arthur Lillie's *The Influence of Buddhism on Primitive Christianity* and *Buddhism in Christendom*; William Hübbe-Schleiden's *Jesus a Buddhist?*; Ernest De Bunsen's *The Angel-Messiah of Buddhists, Essenes, and Christians*; and Thomas S. Berry's *Christianity and Buddhism: A Comparison and Contrast*.[720]

A brief excerpt from Kersey Graves' *The World's Sixteen Crucified Saviors* will suffice to illustrate these bold facts of history, providing deeper insight into both Jesus and Buddha:

> Buddha believed and taught his followers that all sin is inevitably punished, either in this or the future life; and so great were his sympathy and tenderness, that he condescended to suffer that punishment himself, by an ignominious death upon the cross, after which he descended into Hades (Hell), to suffer for a time (three days) for the inmates of that dreadful and horrible prison, that he might show he sympathized with them. After his resurrection, and before his ascension to heaven, as well as during his earthly sojourn, he imparted to the world some beautiful, lofty, and soul-elevating precepts.
>
> "The object of [Buddha's] mission," says a writer, "was to instruct those who were straying from the right path, and expiate the sins of mortals by his own suffering, and procure for them a happy entrance into Paradise by obedience to his precepts and prayers to his name. His followers always speak of him as one with God from all eternity." His most common title was "the Savior of the World." He was also called "the Benevolent One," "the Dispenser of Grace," "the Source of Life," "the Light of the World," "the True Light," etc.
>
> [Buddha's] mother [Maya or Maira] was a very pure, refined, pious and devout woman; never indulged in any impure thoughts, words or actions. She was so much esteemed for her virtues and for being the mother of a God, that an escort

of ladies attended her wherever she went. The trees bowed before her as she passed through the forest, and flowers sprang up wherever her foot pressed the ground. She was saluted as "the Holy Virgin, Queen of Heaven."

It is said that when her divine child was born, he stood upright and proclaimed, "I will put an end to the sufferings and sorrows of the world." And immediately a light shone around about the young Messiah. He spent much time in retirement, and like Christ in another respect, was once tempted by a demon who offered him all the honors and wealth of the world. But he rebuked the devil, saying, "Begone; hinder me not."

Buddha began, like Christ, to preach his gospel and heal the sick when about twenty-eight years of age. And it is declared, "the blind saw, the deaf heard, the dumb spoke, the lame danced and the crooked became straight." Hence, the people declared, "He is no mortal child, but an incarnation of the Deity." His religion was of a very superior character. He proclaimed, "My law is a law of grace for all." His religion knew no race, no sex, no caste, and no aristocratic priesthood.

"It taught," says Max Müller, "the equality of all men, and the brotherhood of the human race." "All men, without regard to rank, birth or nation," says Dunckar, "form, according to Buddha's view, one great suffering association in this earthly vale of tears; therefore, the commandments of love, forbearance, patience, compassion, pity, brotherliness of all men." Klaproth (a German professor of oriental languages) says this religion is calculated to ennoble the human race. "It is difficult to comprehend," says a French writer (M. Leboulay), "how men, not assisted by revelation, could have soared so high, and approached so near the truth."

Dunckar says this oriental God "taught self-denial, chastity, temperance, the control of the passions, to bear injustice from others, to suffer death quietly, and without hate of your persecutor, to grieve not for one's own misfortunes, but for those of others." An investigation of their history will show that they lived up to these moral injunctions. "Besides the five great commandments," says a Wesleyan missionary (Spense Hardy) in his Dahmma Padam, "every shade of vice, hypocrisy, anger, pride, suspicion, greediness, gossiping, and cruelty to animals is guarded against by special precepts. Among the virtues recommended, we find not only reverence for parents, care for children, submission to authority, gratitude, moderation in all things, submission in time of trial, equanimity at all times, but virtues, unknown in some systems of morality, such as the duty of forgiving injuries, and not rewarding evil for evil." And we will add, both charity and love are specially recommended.

We have it also upon the authority of Dunckar that "Buddha proclaimed that salvation and redemption have come for all, even the lowest and most abject classes." For he broke down the iron caste of the Brahminical code which had so long ruled India, and aimed to place all mankind upon a level. His followers have been stigmatized by Christian professors as "idolaters." But Sir John Bowling, in his "Kingdom and People of Siam," denies that they are idolaters—"because," says he, "no Buddhist believes his image to be God, or anything more than an outward representation of Deity." Their deific images are looked upon with the same views and feelings as a Christian venerates the photograph of his deceased friend. Hence, if one is an idolater, the other is also. With respect to the charge of polytheism, Missionary Hue says, "that although their religion embraces many inferior deities, who fill the same offices that angels do under the Christian system, yet,"—adds M. Huc—"monotheism is the real character of Budhism;" and confirms the statement by the testimony of a Tibetan.

It should be noted here that although Buddhism succeeded in converting about three hundred millions, or one-third of the inhabitants of the globe, it was never propagated by the sword, and never persecuted the disciples of other religions. Its conquests were made by a rational appeal to the human mind. Mr. Hodgson says, "It recognizes the infinite capacity of the human intellect." And St. Hilaire declares, "Love for all beings is its nucleus; and to love our enemies, and not prosecute, are the virtues of this people." Max Müller says, "Its moral code, taken by itself, is one of the most perfect the world has ever known." Its five commandments are:

1. Thou shalt not kill.
2. Thou shalt not steal.
3. Thou shalt not commit adultery or any impurity.
4. Thou shall not lie.
5. Thou shalt not intoxicate thyself.

To establish the above cited doctrines and precepts,

Buddha sent forth his disciples into the world to preach his gospel to every creature. And if any convert had committed a sin in word, thought or deed, he was to confess and repent. One of the tracts which they distributed declares, "There is undoubtedly a life after this, in which the virtuous may expect the reward of their good deeds. . . . . Judgment takes place immediately after death."

Buddha and his followers set an example to the world of enduring opposition and persecution with great patience and non-resistance. And some of them suffered martyrdom rather than abandon their principles, and gloried in thus sealing their doctrines with their lives.

A story is told of a rich merchant by the name of Purna, forsaking all to follow his lord and master [Buddha]; and also of his encountering and talking with a woman of low caste at a well, which reminds us of similar incidents in the history of Christ. But his enemies, becoming jealous and fearful of his growing power, finally crucified him near the foot of the Nepaul mountains, about 600 B.C. But after his death, burial and resurrection, we are told he ascended back to heaven, where millions of his followers believed he had existed with Brahma from all eternity.[721]

Likewise Müller notes:

That there are striking coincidences between Buddhism and Christianity cannot be denied; and it must likewise be admitted that Buddhism existed at least four hundred years before Christianity.[722]

The similarities continue: Buddha started in the religion of his parents (Hinduism) and ended up inadvertently launching another (Buddhism); while Jesus began life in the religion of His parents (Judaism) and ended up inadvertently launching another (Christianity). Both taught the extinction of the Ego,[723] which Buddhists call the "individual personality"[724] and which Jesus called "Satan."[725] Both taught the parable of the Prodigal Son,[726] used the image of the mustard seed,[727] and urged their followers to "let your light shine before the world."[728] Buddha called his gospel "The Way of Truth,"[729] and was known by the titles "the Way," "the Truth," and "the Life,"[730] while Jesus, speaking as the Universal Indwelling Christ, said "I am the Way, the Truth, and the Life."[731]

Buddha viewed his neighbor as his own self,[732] as did Jesus.[733] Buddha taught his gospel using the example of three types of soil,[734] Jesus taught His gospel using precisely the same theme.[735] Buddha taught the Eight-Fold Path,[736] Jesus taught the Eight-Fold Beatitudes.[737] Additionally, as Graves mentions above, Buddha became enlightened around age 30,[738] while Jesus was imbued with the Holy Spirit at the same age,[739] and the virgin births of both were attended by natural and supernatural phenomena, such as miracles, angels, and heavenly music. Lillie correctly states that "Buddha and Christ taught much the same doctrine,"[740] a fact patently clear to all but the most entrenched literalists and exotericists.[741] See GOSPEL, JESUS, KRISHNA, MESSIAH, MITHRA, NATIVITY, OSIRIS, PYTHAGORAS, SAVIOR, TEACHER OF RIGHTEOUSNESS.

Buddha choosing his 12 Apostles.

Birth of Jesus.

Entering Noah's Ark.

Ascension of Jesus.

CALF (MOLTEN): In the traditional Church the molten calf was an object of Pagan worship that was adopted by some early Jewish groups.[742] In mystical Christianity the molten calf or golden calf is a symbol of superstition[743] and gross materiality.[744] See DEVIL, EGYPT, GODS AND GODDESSES, PILATE, SATAN.

CANA WEDDING: In the mainstream Church the Cana wedding was a ceremony that Jesus attended, and where he famously turned water into wine.[745] In some Christian sects and cults the Cana wedding was Jesus' own marriage, to Mary Magdalene.[746] But as "marriage" is often used as an occult term in sacred writings,[747] and since many pre-Christian saviors (such as Bacchus and Dionysus) also transformed water into wine,[748] Christian mystics turn to mysticism for a true understanding of this biblical "event."

In the mystical Church the Cana wedding is a symbol of the Hieros Gamos[749] or "Sacred Marriage" between the Subconscious Mind and the Superconscious Mind,[750] or rather the Feminine Principle (earth) and the Masculine Principle (heaven)—which is itself an emblem of spiritual enlightenment. Plutarch called the Hiero Gamos or Holy Union "the basis of all the Mysteries."[751] See CROSS, JESUS, OIL, SACRAMENT, SEVEN STARS, WASHING THE FEET, YAHWEH.

CHRIST: In the institutional Church Christ is the literal surname of Jesus, and hence another name for the Christian Messiah.[752] As Jesus bore no known last name (though some believe it may have been Pandira),[753] and as He referred to Himself not as "Christ" but as "*the* Christ"[754] (as did the original 12 Apostles),[755] throughout the ages critical thinkers have rightly questioned this notion. The first Christians, the Gnostic-Christians,[756] too distinguished between "Jesus" and "the Christ,"[757] seeing them as entirely separate entities. Thus it is not surprising that the mystical Evangelist John (or more likely the Pagan philosopher Cerinthus),[758] the Gnostic author of the mystical book of Revelation,[759] did as well, writing:

> The kingdoms of this world are become the kingdoms of *our Lord, and of his Christ*; and he shall reign for ever and ever.[760]

Orthodox Church Father Irenaeus angrily pointed out how the Gnostic-

Christians differentiated between Jesus and the Indwelling Christ in the matter of baptism:

> They maintain that those who have attained to perfect knowledge must of necessity be regenerated into that power which is above all. For it is otherwise impossible to find admittance within the Pleroma [divine power], since this [regeneration] it is which leads them down into the depths of Bythus [the unknowable true God]. For the baptism instituted by *the visible Jesus* was for the remission of sins, but the redemption brought in by *that [invisible] Christ who descended upon Him*, was for perfection; and they allege that *the former is animal, but the latter spiritual*. And the baptism of John was proclaimed with a view to repentance, but the redemption by Jesus was brought in for the sake of perfection. And to this He refers when He says, "And I have another baptism to be baptized with, and I hasten eagerly towards it" (Luke 12:50).[761]

Frothingham writes:

> *Jesus is the name of a man; Christ, or rather The Christ, is the name of an idea. The history of Jesus is the history of an individual; the history of the Christ is the history of a doctrine.* An essay on the Christ-idea touches the person of Jesus, only as he is associated with the Christ-idea or is made a representative of it. Had he not been associated with that idea, either through his own design or in the belief of his countrymen, the omission of all mention of his name would provoke no criticism.
>
> *The common opinion that he was in some sense the Christ; that but for him the Christ-idea would not have been made conspicuous in the way and at the time it was; that the existence of the Christian Church, the conversion of Paul, the composition of the New Testament, the course of religious thought in the eastern and western world was directed by his mind . . . [is thus incongruous].*[762]

The reason for this, as I make clear in my entry on "Christianity," is that our religion existed long prior to the birth of our Lord. Thus portraying the word Christ as Jesus' surname must be counted as one of the greatest errors perpetuated amongst the "wooden creeds" and "petrified doctrines" of organized Christianity,[763] for the word Christ is not a proper name at all, nor is it even Christian. It is a pre-Christian Pagan title that once signified a heathen ruler who had been "anointed" (that is, "christed") with a type of sanctified olive oil known as *chrism*.[764]

This shining oil was associated with the shining Sun and the deity who ruled it, the great Sun-god, known by thousands of names throughout the ancient world. In other words, the original "Christ" was the god of the Sun, the universal symbol of the Higher Self, the "Word made flesh."[765] As proof of this we need only look at the origin of the word *chrism*, which derives from the ancient Babylonian word for the Chaldean Sun-god *Chris*, whose name in Hebrew was spelled *Hrs*, or with vowels, *Heres*.[766]

Anointing or christing with chrism was an act performed chiefly on important religious and political leaders, and was thus an emblem of nobility and royalty, and sometimes more specifically of kingship;[767] for a king is always a christ and a christ is always a king—either literally or symbolically.[768] Such associations, between the Christ, chrism, royalty, and immortality, began long ago in ancient Egypt, where we find the crucified and resurrected mummy-god *Karast* (*Krst*),[769] meaning (risen) "mummy,"[770] whose name became *Chrestus* in Rome, *Christos* in Greece, and *Christ* in England.

The apotheosization and christing of human rulers was a pre-Christian tradition that continued well into the ancient Roman world, where emperors were regarded as both gods and christs. This same idea passed into early Judaism, and can still be seen in the Old Testament. Here, Hebrew kings,[771] as well as lower ranked religious authorities, were viewed as christs.[772] Our own Santa Claus is nothing but a modern European version of the ancient universal Sun-god, annually reborn in late December at the Winter Solstice, and christened king of the New Year by pouring sacred oil on his head. Hence his alternate name: Kris Kringle, meaning the "Christ child," reborn ever year—as was the tradition of pre-Christian gods, such as Mithra—on December 25.[773]

In the mystical Church the word Christ denotes spiritual law or Divine Law,[774] which includes the Laws of Love, Karma, the Word, Forgiveness, and Attraction. Here, the Christ, *Chrestus*, or *Christos*, is identical to the human Soul, the Divine Self or Higher Self of each individual,[775] idealized in Jesus as the archetypal "virtuous man,"[776] but which also exists in each one of us as a potential state of heavenly consciousness, for as Plotinus declared, "God is the root of the Soul,"[777] and the Soul is Christ.

The word Christ is paralleled in the name of the Indian god Krishna or Chrishna: *krs* means "universal," while *na* loosely means "self." Thus Krishna gives us the meaning of the "Universal Self." This is attested to in colloquial Bengali, in which Krishna is sometimes spelled Krista, meaning "Christ."[778] This is why, along with Buddha, both Jesus and Krishna are known as "The Lords of Enlightened Love."[779]

Mystically speaking, though there was only one Jesus and only one Gautama (both Sun/Son symbols of fully enlightened Man), there are billions of Christs and billions of Buddhas,[780] for God has personally christed or buddhaed ("anointed")[781] each and every one of us himself,[782] lovingly forming the "Son *in* you and me."[783] Hence, the Lord warned: "If any man shall say unto you, 'Lo, here is Christ,' or 'there'; believe it not."[784] Christ and His "kingdom" are not external to us. They are within us.[785] Böhme writes:

> For *Jesus Christ*, the son of God, the Eternal Word in the Father (who is the glance, or brightness, and the power of the light eternity), *must become man, and be born in you,* if you will know God; otherwise you are in the dark stable, and go about groping and feeling, and look always for Christ at the right hand of God, *supposing that he is a great way off*; you cast your mind aloft above the stars and seek God, as *the sophisters teach you, who represent God as one afar off, in heaven.*[786]

Known in mystical Christianity as the doctrine of Theosis, that is, the deification of Man,[787] Paul plainly and openly called our Indwelling Christ the "Christ in you,"[788] for "ye are the temple of the living God."[789] This is why he asserted that "Christ is all, and in all."[790] Solomon described it more mystically: "The spirit of man is the candle of the Lord."[791] In other words, God's fire (Spirit) lights (enlightens) us through that part of us which was made in the spiritual image of God: the Christ.[792] Of the Christ Kingsford and Maitland write:

> The first Adam is of the earth, earthy, and liable to death. The second is "from heaven," and triumphant over death. For "sin has no more dominion over him." He, therefore, is the product of *a soul purified from defilement by Matter, and released from subjection to the body. Such a soul is called virgin. And she has for spouse, not Matter—for that she has renounced—but the Divine Spirit, which is God. And the man born of this union is in the image of God, and is God made man; that is, he is Christ, and it is the Christ thus born in every man who redeems him and endows him with eternal life. For in him the man becomes transmuted from Matter into Spirit.* He is the man himself, by regeneration become a son at once of man and of God. Generation, degeneration, regeneration,—in these three terms is comprised the whole process of the soul's history.[793]
>
> . . . For, as cannot be too clearly and forcibly stated, between the man who becomes a Christ, and other men, there is no difference whatever of kind. The difference is alone of condition and degree, and consists in difference of unfoldment of the spiritual nature possessed by all in virtue of their common derivation. "All things," as has repeatedly been said, "are made of the divine Substance." And Humanity represents a stream

which, taking its rise in the outermost and lowest mode of differentiation of that Substance, flows inwards and upwards to the highest, which is God. And the point at which it reaches the celestial, and empties itself into Deity, is "Christ." *Any doctrine other than this—any doctrine which makes the Christ of a different and non-human nature—is anti-Christian and sub-human.* And, of such doctrine the direct effect is to cut off man altogether from access to God, and God from access to man.[794]

The Universal Indwelling Christ, also known as the World-Christ, has always existed and always will.[795] For it is "without father, without mother, without descent, having neither beginning of days, nor end of life; but made like unto the Son of God."[796] Being unborn, unmade, unformed, imperishable, immortal, eternal, undying, changeless, incorporeal, immanent, indestructible, and timeless, the Christ Within existed, of course, before Jesus (as He Himself acknowledged),[797] and lives on in each one of us as what Hindus call the Supreme Self or Brahman,[798] what Buddhists call the father-less and mother-less "self-born Buddha,"[799] and what Emerson called the Oversoul.[800]

The truth of the Christ and the human Soul has long been described using symbols derived from Nature and from farming, in particular those connected to the planting, growing, and harvesting of crops. Irving writes:

> You may depend upon it. . . that the laws of all life, vegetable, animal, mental (soulal), and spiritual, are one and the same, though different in degree; and all derived from one and the same sacrifice of our blessed Lord and Saviour, offered from all eternity; without which there would have been no life, but an universal death. And you may rest assured also, that the lower is always typical of the higher; and that the knowledge of the higher is best ascended into through the progression of the lower. We ought not to wonder, therefore, that the Holy Spirit continually useth the emblems or symbols derived from vegetable and human life—the sowing of the seed and the harvest, the birth of the child and the full-grown man—to set forth spiritual things withal. And you ought not to say, they are finely chosen similitudes, but, they are rightly appropriated types. And, however much our men of taste and sentiment do laugh at the spiritualisings of our fathers, I dare to believe and to say, that to spiritualise nature is rightly to interpret nature; and that the greater part of our Lord's discourses are nothing but divine exercises of this kind; and so of His parables also.[801]

Holy Scripture asserts that the Indwelling Christ is indeed "everlasting,"[802] for He "abideth for ever."[803] Hence, speaking as the Indwelling Christ, Jesus said: "Before Abraham was I AM,"[804] and "Lo, I AM with you alway, even unto the end of the world."[805] When we realize our oneness, that is, our at-one-ment, with God, we attain what mystical Christians refer to as Christ Consciousness[806] or Cosmic Consciousness, or what Paul named "the mind of Christ."[807] We become the Christ: the Archetypal Man.[808] "Let this mind be in you, which was also in Christ Jesus," said the Thirteenth Apostle.[809]

According to Jesus, those who follow His teachings are those who love the Indwelling Christ, and it is to these individuals that the Indwelling Christ reveals itself.[810] Our Lord describes the Indwelling Christ as humble, gentle, and modest,[811] like a shy young child who must be coaxed to come out and play.[812] We come into a relationship with the Indwelling Christ through wisdom, faith, and love, which are the results of right thinking, right feeling, right speaking, and right action (true Christianity). Conversely, we prevent oneness with the Christ via the enemies of Spirit, ignorance (caused by mob rule), superstition (caused by Church rule), and fear (caused by state rule), which are formed through wrong thinking, wrong feeling, wrong speaking, and wrong action (false Christianity).[813]

And here is the mystical meaning of the Atonement: *we achieve at-one-ment with Christ by being Christlike*, that is, by conquering what Buddhists called The Five Poisons: 1) lust; 2) anger; 3) sloth; 4) jealousy; and 5) selfishness.[814] The Indwelling Christ, speaking through Jesus, tells us what will happen as a result:

> If a man love me, he will keep my words: and my Father will love him, and we will come unto him, and make our abode with him.[815]

The inner (mystical) meaning of the words of James now becomes understandable:

> Draw nigh to God, and he will draw nigh to you.[816]

We are truly the apple of God's eye,[817] which is why he gives us the following promise:

> Have not I commanded thee? Be strong and of a good courage; be not afraid, neither be thou dismayed: for the Lord thy God is with thee whithersoever thou goest.[818]

"Sing and rejoice, for I will dwell in the midst of thee!" says God in Zechariah.[819] "I help those who walk in my path," declares the Hindu Indwelling Christ, Krishna, in the Bhagavad Gita.[820] Why and how does this particular principle work? When Man obeys

Divine Law ("Christ"), Divine Law obeys Man.[821] In other words, by following spiritual law we gain the power to use spiritual law to create anything we like.[822] Truly, the *"Christ in you* is the hope of glory" saith Paul.[823] Understanding this ancient mystical doctrine is the first step toward acknowledging our divine perfection, the fire of Christos that burns in us all.[824]

Though He was the perfect embodiment of the Christ Within, Jesus did not want attention focused on His physical being (that is, on Jesus the man, the human son of Joseph and Mary);[825] but on the "Father" (*Divine Mind*) and on the "Christ" (*Divine Law*), both which reside within all individuals. Thus He said:

> But be not ye called Rabbi ["teacher"]: for one is your Master, even Christ; and all ye are brethren. And call no man your father upon the earth: for one is your Father, which is in heaven. Neither be ye called masters: for one is your Master, even Christ.[826]

One of the many Eastern names for Christ is Buddha, which means "The Awakened"[827] or "The Enlightened One"; that is, the Light One, the Sun/Son-god. As the title Christ was appended to the man known as Jesus, the so-called "founder of Christianity," so the title Buddha was appended to the man known as Siddhartha Gautama, the so-called "founder of Buddhism."[828] And as the individual named Gautama was deified,[829] so was the individual named Jesus,[830] and this is the same man who said: "I AM in my Father, and ye [are] in me, and I [AM] in you."[831]

Thus we are all Christs; or as John and Paul mystically called us, "Sons of God,"[832] for it is the Christ which, as the ancient Egyptians, and later John the Gnostic-Christian Evangelist, noted,[833] is "the true Light, which lighteth every man that cometh into the world."[834] This makes Jesus, who strongly rejected the idea that He was a political Messiah,[835] not the *focus* of Christianity, as in the traditional Church, but the *locus* of Christianity, as in the mystical Church.[836] See BUDDHA, CHRISTIANITY, DIVINITY OF JESUS, GOD, JESUS, KRISHNA, MITHRA, OSIRIS, PYTHAGORAS, SON OF GOD, TEACHER OF RIGHTEOUSNESS.

CHRIST CONSCIOUSNESS: In traditional Christianity there is no such thing as "Christ Consciousness," for it is not mentioned by that name in the Bible. In mystical Christianity it is seen as being referenced hundreds of times in the Bible, most notably by Paul, who calls it "the mind of Christ,"[837] which is identical to the Eastern ideas of satori, bodhi, kensho, wu wei, Buddhahood, samadhi, or moksha ("liberation"); that is, self-realization, spiritual enlightenment, or what Zen Buddhists call *atma-bodha*, "self-awakening," or *atma-jnana*, "self-knowledge."[838]

It is this same divine mental state that Dante called "Beatrice," Balzac called "Seraphita," Whitman called "My Soul," and Paul called "the Christ."[839] Nirvana, in particular, perfectly describes this elevated state of mind: a Buddhist word, it means to "breathe out." Thus we get the meaning of "letting go," of having enough faith in the Father to release ourselves to his care. In other words, when we give up our material attachments and turn ourselves over to Spirit, we find God.[840] This is the experience of Christ Consciousness.

Jesus Himself referred to Christ Consciousness as "the Kingdom of God,"[841] for the "king" of the Inner Kingdom is the Indwelling Christ,[842] our Higher Self, our true self, which is made in the "image of the invisible God."[843] This image, as Jukes explains,

> is the mind of God; for Christ is that Mind or Word to rule in us. The Man is Christ, the perfect mind of God.[844]

Christ Consciousness or Christhood is not strictly Christian. Thus Hindus have their own name for it: the "Brahmic Splendor,"[845] or *Kutastha Chaitanya*,[846] known to Buddhists as "Buddhahood," which springs from one's "Buddha Nature," an inner spiritual "treasure" that is available to everyone.[847] For since we all possess what Christian mystics know as the Indwelling Christ[848] (the Spark of Divinity),[849] we have the potential of recognizing that we are already spiritually illuminated.[850] This gives Christ Consciousness its more usual and widely known appellation: *Cosmic Consciousness*, which is often instantly bestowed on one by grace; but in other cases, only after years of diligent Christlike behavior, prayer, and meditation.[851]

The characteristics of one who has attained this celestial state of mind—normally occurring between the ages of 30 and 40—are nearly identical to Paul's description of divine love,[852] and include: gentleness, modesty, longsuffering, simplicity of lifestyle, happiness, peacefulness, altruism, an increased sense of morality, tolerance, a sure knowledge of immortality, a complete loss of the sense of sin as well as the fear of death, and a disinterest in both traditional education (college) and traditional religion (church)[853]—for all outer education is deemed "learned ignorance" by the metaphysically minded.[854]

None are left out of God's great salvific plan for Divine Man and Woman,[855] for we are all "partakers of the divine nature."[856] To further illustrate this truth, I have coined the following additional names for Christ Consciousness: Buddha Consciousness, Moses Consciousness, Jupiter Consciousness, Juno Consciousness, Krishna Consciousness, Zeus Consciousness, Hera Consciousness, Dagda Consciousness, Morrigan Consciousness, Abraham Consciousness, Sarah Consciousness, Yahweh Consciousness, Asherah Consciousness, Jesus Consciousness, Mary (Magdalene) Consciousness, Rama Consciousness, Sita Consciousness, Odin Consciousness, and Freya Consciousness. See CHRIST, CROWN, ENLIGHTENMENT, KINGDOM OF GOD, UNION WITH GOD.

CHRISTIANITY: In the traditional Church Christianity is a religion founded by Jesus around the year A.D. 30, at which time it became the "one and only true

Faith." However, the doctrine that one can only be "saved" from damnation by being baptized in the Christian Church was not adopted until the 4th Century. Thus this marks the actual beginning of orthodox Christianity.[857] We will note here that there was no single "pure" form of Christianity before then, or even afterward,[858] and there is still not one today.[859] And the New Testament, which contains no "strict doctrinal unity," reflects this fact.[860]

Thus, the traditional belief regarding the start of Christianity during our Lord's lifetime cannot be literally true. And in fact many mainstream Christians correctly today acknowledge that because the Paganistic doctrines of the Incarnation and the Resurrection were alien to Jewish tradition, they could not have and did not become established beliefs until *after* Jesus' death, at which time a religion began to be built around them by non-Jews, that is, Pagans ("Gentiles").[861]

Additionally, though Judaism had long been both recognized and authorized by Rome, as late as the beginning of the 1st Century the Empire had not yet acknowledged the followers of Jesus as either a "religion" or even as a religious "association." Indeed, it was still a capital crime to profess the faith of the small Nazarene movement that traditional Pagans knew pejoratively as "Christian."[862] Thus Jesus could not have founded Christianity, for it did not exist as an official or even a distinguishable religion until the 4th Century, when it was authorized by Rome for the first time under Constantine the Great.[863]

The mystical Church handily resolves this entire "difficulty" by understanding that Christianity is an ancient pre-Christian *universal* religion that was already in existence at the time of Jesus' birth, and which He only resuscitated and reintroduced to a forgetful and increasingly unspiritual humanity. For great spiritual teachers, prophets, and avatars never come to earth to preserve religious dogma. They come to reinstate eternal spiritual principles,[864] universal mystical doctrines that have always existed, and which are not bound by religious ideologies, boundaries, or prejudices.

For those who doubt the mystical view, please ask yourself this question: if God's Truth, which the Bible says has existed "from the beginning,"[865] and which being "the same yesterday, and to day, and for ever,"[866] is immortal and unchanging, how then could Jesus have been the originator of it? Being enlightened, He well understood that you cannot "found" a religion that has always existed and that will never perish. This is why Voltaire said that Plato—who was born four centuries *before* Jesus—was "one of the greatest teachers of Christianity."[867]

Jesus Himself, a Jewish mystic, asserted that He had no desire to found a new religion.[868] Saith the Master:

> Think not that I am come to destroy the law [of Moses], or the prophets: I am not come to destroy, but to fulfil.[869]

Here is how the venerable Church Father Saint Augustine viewed this topic:

> That, in our times, is the Christian religion, which to know and to follow is the most sure and certain health, called according to that name, but not according to that thing itself, of which it is the name; for *the thing itself which is now called the Christian religion really was known to the ancients, nor was wanting at any time from the beginning of the human race until the time when Christ came in the flesh, from whence the true religion, which had previously existed, began to be called Christian; and this in our days is the Christian religion.*[870]

Eusebius, the well-known ancient Roman Christian historian and the bishop of Caesarea in the early 4th Century, made a similar statement:

> The names of Jesus and Christ were both known and honored by the ancients [that is, pre-Christian peoples]. . . . *That which is called the Christian religion is neither new nor strange*, but—if it be lawful to testify the truth—*was known to the ancients.*[871]

Early Gnostic-Christians preached the identical doctrine. In their work entitled The Tripartite Tractate, we read:

> Not only did the Christ exist from the very beginning [of time], but *so did the Church.*[872]

In his famous Gnostic-tinged "second letter,"[873] Clement claims that the Christian Church is a "pre-existent, spiritual reality," which only later took on physical form in the flesh of Jesus.[874]

We have canonical evidence for these views as well. Paul, for example, acknowledged that the Indwelling Christ, and therefore Christianity, were both known to his own henotheistic ancestors, the Israelites, who, according to Jewish tradition, crossed the Red Sea some 1,500 years before the birth of Jesus:

> Moreover, brethren, I would not that ye should be ignorant, how that *all our fathers* were under the cloud, and all passed through the sea; and were all baptized unto Moses in the cloud and in the sea; and *did all eat the same spiritual meat; and did all drink the same spiritual drink: for they drank of that spiritual Rock that followed them: and that Rock was Christ.*[875]

In his letter to the Ephesians, Paul asserts that Jesus (the Indwelling Christ) chose us to be His "adopted children" even prior to the earth being formed:

According as he hath chosen us in him *before the foundation of the world*, that we should be holy and without blame before him in love: *having predestinated us unto the adoption of children by Jesus Christ to himself*, according to the good pleasure of his will . . .[876]

In his letter to the Colossians, Paul makes this cosmic statement about the Indwelling Christ,

> . . . who is the image of the invisible God, the firstborn of every creature: for by him were all things created, that are in heaven, and that are in earth, visible and invisible, whether they be thrones, or dominions, or principalities, or powers: all things were created by him, and for him: and *he is before all things*, and by him all things consist.[877]

In the same letter Paul confirms what has been known to every great mind: the Gospel was taught long before the time of either Paul or Jesus. Writing only a few decades after our Lord's death, he declares an impossibility—unless Christianity has always existed:

> . . . the gospel . . . *was* preached to every creature which is under heaven.[878]

The Apostle Peter wrote that the Christ has always been recognized, but for the benefit of humanity, was made known physically in the form of Jesus 2,000 years ago:

> Who verily was foreordained *before the foundation of the world*, but was manifest in these last times for you . . .[879]

The prophet Daniel, who lived some 600 years before the birth of the Lord, was well aware of the World-Christ and His "everlasting" church:

> I saw in the night visions, and, behold, one like *the Son of man* came with the clouds of heaven, and came to the Ancient of days, and they brought him near before him. And there was given him dominion, and glory, and a kingdom, that all people, nations, and languages, should serve him: *his dominion is an everlasting dominion, which shall not pass away, and his kingdom that which shall not be destroyed*.[880]

The Essenic Hebraist noted that because the Christ "continueth forever, he hath an unchangeable priesthood,"[881] while Jesus Himself had this to say on the subject of the eternalness of the Christ Within:

> "I am Alpha and Omega, the beginning and the ending," saith the Lord, "which is, and *which was*, and which is to come, the Almighty."[882]

Again, speaking as the Indwelling Christ, Jesus once commented on "the glory which I had with God *before the world was*,"[883] openly declaring: *"Before Abraham was, I AM."*[884] The universal unfading omnipresence of the Christ Within is also mentioned by Jesus in this pantheistic passage from The Gospel of Thomas:

> If you are alone, fear not, I am with you. Lift up any rock and there I AM. Cut open any piece of wood, and you will find me.[885]

Buddhism, of course, teaches the same principle, for "the Buddha" (not the man, but the Spirit) is the Asian Christ, therefore, like the Christ, there is no place in the Universe where he is not present. For the Buddha-Christ is unborn, unmade, unformed, and imperishable.[886]

During one of his verbal conflicts with the Pharisees, Jesus makes it perfectly clear that the Christ, and hence the religion is His name, has existed since the beginning of time. The following exchange, for instance, was recorded by Matthew:

> While the Pharisees were gathered together, Jesus asked them, saying, "what think ye of Christ? whose son is he?" They say unto him, "the Son of David." He saith unto them, "how then doth David in spirit call him 'Lord,' saying, 'the Lord said unto my Lord, sit thou on my right hand, till I make thine enemies thy footstool?'[887] If David then call him Lord, how is he his son?" And no man was able to answer him a word, neither durst any man from that day forth ask him any more questions.[888]

According to Titcomb,

> Justin Martyr, in his dialogue with Trypho, says that there exist not a people, civilized or semi-civilized, who have not offered up prayers in the name of a crucified Saviour to the Father and Creator of all things.[889]

Reverend Robert Taylor made these comments on this subject:

> What short of an absolute surrender of all pretence to an existence distinctive and separate from Paganism is that never-to-be-forgotten, never-to-be overlooked, and I am sure never-to-be-answered capitulation of their [the Christians'] Melito, Bishop of Sardis, in which in an apology delivered to the emperor, Marcus Antoninus, in the year 170, he complains of certain annoyances and vexations which Christians were at that time subjected to, and for which he claims redress from the justice and piety of that emperor: first, on the score that none of his ancestors had ever persecuted the professors of the Christian faith; Nero and Domitian only, who had been equally hostile to their subjects of all persuasions, having been disposed to bring the Christian doctrine into hatred, and even their decrees had been reversed, and their rash enterprises rebuked, by the godly ancestors of Antoninus himself. . . . And secondly, the good bishop claims the patronage of the emperor for *the Christian religion, which he calls our philosophy, on account of its high antiquity, as having been imported from countries lying beyond the limits of the Roman empire, in the reign of his ancestor Augustus*, who found its importation ominous of good fortune to his government.[890]

The ancient philosopher Celsus noted that

> the Christian religion contains nothing but what Christians hold in common with heathen; nothing new.[891]

Caecilius declared:

> All these fragments of crack-brained opiniatry and silly solaces played off in the sweetness of song by deceitful [Pagan] poets, by you too credulous creatures [that is, the Christians] have been shamefully reformed and made over to your own god.[892]

In writing to Augustine, Faustus made these statements:

> You have substituted your agape for the sacrifices of the Pagans; for their idols your martyrs, whom you serve with the very same honors. You appease the shades of the dead with wine and feasts; you celebrate the solemn festivals of the Gentiles, their

calends, and their solstices; and as to their manners, those you have retained without any alteration. *Nothing distinguishes you from the Pagans, except that you hold your assemblies apart from them.*⁸⁹³

Christian writer M. Turretin spoke of Christianity in the 4ᵗʰ Century, saying that

> it was not so much the [Pagan Roman] empire that was brought over to the [Christian] faith, as the faith that was brought over to the empire; *not the Pagans who were converted to Christianity, but Christianity that was converted to Paganism.*⁸⁹⁴

The great English historian Edward Gibbon writes:

> It must be confessed that the ministers of the Catholic Church imitated the profane model which they were impatient to destroy. The most respectable bishops had persuaded themselves that the ignorant rustics would more cheerfully renounce the superstitions of Paganism if they found some resemblance, some compensation, in the bosom of Christianity. The religion of Constantine achieved in less than a century the final conquest of the Roman empire; but *the victors themselves were insensibly subdued by the arts of their vanquished rivals.*⁸⁹⁵

The 2ⁿᵈ-Century Church Father Tertullian was originally a Pagan, inspiring these assertions on the heathen origins of Christianity:

> I find no other means to prove myself to be impudent with success, and happily a fool, than by my contempt of shame,—as, for instance, I maintain that the Son of God was born. Why am I not ashamed of maintaining such a thing? Why, but because it is itself a shameful thing. I maintain that the Son of God died. Well, that is wholly credible, because it is monstrously absurd. I maintain that after having been buried he rose again; and that I take to be manifestly true, because it was manifestly impossible.⁸⁹⁶

Being essentially Essenic in nature,⁸⁹⁷ early Christians were accused of worshiping the Sun, and many Pagans, such as Emperor Hadrian, believed that Christians were identical to followers of the ancient Egyptian Sun-god Serapis. Thus when the Emperor penned a letter to the Consul Servianus, he said:

There are there [that is, in Egypt] Christians who worship Serapis and devoted to Serapis are those who call themselves "Bishops of Christ."[898]

In the 1860s British scholar Charles W. King wrote:

There is very good reason to believe that as in the East the worship of Serapis was at first combined with Christianity, and gradually merged into it with an entire change of name, not substance, carrying with it many of its ancient notions and rites; so in the West a similar influence was exerted by the Mithraic religion. Seel is of opinion that "as long as the Roman dominion lasted in Germany we find also traces of the Mosaic Law; as there were single Jewish, so were there also single Christian families existing amongst the Gentiles. The latter, however, for the most part ostensibly paid worship to the Roman gods in order to escape persecution, holding secretly in their hearts the religion of Christ. It is by no means improbable that under the permitted symbols of [the Pagan Sun-god] Mithras they worshipped the Son of God and the mysteries of Christianity. In this point of view the Mithraic monuments so frequent in Germany are evidences of the secret faith of the early Christian Romans."

That such a connexion was actually declared by the partisans of Mithraicism when in its decline, is proved by the express statement of Augustine: "I know that the priests of him [Mithras] in the [Phrygian] cap used at one time to say, 'our capped one is himself a Christian.'" In this asserted affinity we find also an explanation of the motive which induced Constantine to adopt for the most general reverse upon his copper coinage, retained long after his conversion, the figure of the Sun, with the legend, "To the Invincible Sun, my companion (or guardian);" as being a personification either of the ancient [Sun-god] Phoebus or the new Sun of Righteousness, equally acceptable to both Christian and Gentile, from the double interpretation of which that type was susceptible.

Similarly the ancient festival held on the 25th day of December in honour of the "Birthday of the Invincible One," and celebrated by the "Great Games" of the Circus, was afterwards transferred to the commemoration of the Birth of Christ, the precise day of which many of the Fathers confess was then unknown. Thus Chrysostom quotes the above direction of the Kalendar, and rightly understands it as referring to the Birthday of the Invincible Mithras, adding, "On this day also the Birthday of Christ was lately fixed at Rome in order that whilst the heathen were busied with their profane ceremonies, the Christians might perform their holy rites undisturbed." Again he exclaims, "But they call this day the Birthday of the Invincible One: who so invincible as the Lord that overthrew and vanquished Death? Or because they style it the Birthday of the Sun? He is the Sun of Righteousness of whom Malachi saith, "Upon you, fearful ones, the Sun of Righteousness shall arise with healing in his wings." And Leo the Great blames those Christians who gave offence to the weaker souls through the shameful persuasion of some by whom this festival of ours is reverenced not so much on account of Christ's Birth as on that of the "Rising of the New Sun," to use their own words. . . . [Furthermore in] the second century the syncretistic sects that had sprung up in Alexandria, the very hotbed of Gnosticism, found out in Serapis a prophetic type of Christ, or the Lord and Creator of all.[899]

Egyptian scholar James Bonwick notes:

There were many circumstances that gave color to the accusation, since in the second century they had left the simple teaching of Jesus for a host of assimilations with surrounding Pagan myths and symbols. Still, the defence made by Tertullian, one of the Fathers of the Church, was, to say the least of it, rather obscure. "Others," wrote he, "believe the sun to be our god. If this be so, we must not be ranked with the Persians; though we worship not the sun painted on a piece of linen, because in truth we have him in our own hemisphere. Lastly, this suspicion arises from hence because it is well known that we pray toward the quarter of the east."[900]

Titcomb writes:

The Essenes always turned to the east to pray. They met once a week, and spent the night in singing hymns, etc., until the rising of the sun. They then retired to their cells, after saluting one another. Pliny says the Christians of Bithynia met before it was light, and sang hymns to Christ, as to a God. After their service they saluted one another. It is just what the Persian

Magi, who were sun-worshippers, were in the habit of doing.

There are not many circumstances more striking than that of Christ being originally worshipped under the form of a lamb. The worship of the constellation Aries was the worship of the sun in his passage through that sign. This constellation was called by the ancients the Lamb, or the Ram. It was also called "the Saviour," and was said to save mankind from their sins. It was always honored with the appellation of Dominus, or "Lord." It was called by the ancients "the Lamb of God which taketh away the sins of the world." The devotees addressed it in their litany, constantly repeating the words, "O Lamb of God, that taketh away the sins of the world, have mercy upon us; grant us thy peace."

On an ancient medal of the Phoenicians, brought by Dr. Clark from Citium this "Lamb of God" is described with the cross and rosary.

. . . The oldest representation of Jesus Christ is a figure of a lamb, to which sometimes a vase was added, into which the blood of the lamb flowed. A simple cross, which was the symbol of eternal life among the ancients, was sometimes placed alongside of the lamb. In the course of time the lamb was put on the cross, as the ancient Israelites had put the Paschal lamb centuries before. Jesus was also represented in early art as the "Good Shepherd,"—that is, as a young man with a lamb on his shoulders, just as the Pagan [gods] Apollo, Mercury, and others were represented centuries before.[901]

Justin Martyr, the celebrated 2nd-Century Christian philosopher and apologist, was born a Pagan and was educated in Pagan philosophy (Stoicism, Platonism, etc.). Thus, when he defended Christianity against Paganism in his *Apologies* he readily admitted the countless similarities between the two faiths. To his Pagan neighbors he writes:

> And when we [Christians] say also that the Word, who is the first-birth of God, was produced without sexual union, and that He, Jesus Christ, our Teacher, was crucified and died, and rose again, and ascended into heaven, we propound nothing different from what you believe regarding those whom you esteem sons of Jupiter. For you know how many sons your esteemed writers ascribed to Jupiter: Mercury, the interpreting word and teacher of all; Aesculapius, who, though he was a great physician, was struck by a thunderbolt, and so ascended to heaven; and Bacchus too, after he had been torn

limb from limb; and Hercules, when he had committed himself to the flames to escape his toils; and the sons of Leda, and Dioscuri; and Perseus, son of Danae; and Bellerophon, who, though sprung from mortals, rose to heaven on the horse Pegasus. For what shall I say of Ariadne, and those who, like her, have been declared to be set among the stars? And what of the emperors who die among yourselves, whom you deem worthy of deification, and in whose behalf you produce some one who swears he has seen the burning Caesar rise to heaven from the funeral pyre? And what kind of deeds are recorded of each of these reputed sons of Jupiter, it is needless to tell to those who already know.

. . . Moreover, the Son of God called Jesus, even if only a man by ordinary generation, yet, on account of His wisdom, is worthy to be called the Son of God; for all writers call God the Father of men and gods. And if we assert that the Word of God was born of God in a peculiar manner, different from ordinary generation, *let this, as said above, be no extraordinary thing to you, who say that Mercury is the angelic word of God [that is, the Word or Logos]. But if any one objects that He was crucified, in this also He is on a par with those reputed sons of Jupiter of yours, who suffered as we have now enumerated. . . . And if we even affirm that He was born of a virgin, accept this in common with what you accept of Perseus. And in that we say that He made whole the lame, the paralytic, and those born blind, we seem to say what is very similar to the deeds said to have been done by Aesculapius.*[902]

Massey understood the true origins of Christianity; how it derived out of a preexisting astrological or "equinoctial" Christolatry that was taught by the pre-Christian Gnostics (*gnosis* is the Greek word for *inner* or *revealed* "knowledge"); that this made Christianity a direct descendant of Gnosticism—which had already been in existence from at least the time of ancient Egypt, and no doubt long before:

The ancient wisdom of Egypt and Chaldea lived on with the men who knew [and taught the secrets and mysteries of the Christ], called the Gnostics. They had directly inherited the gnosis that remained oral, the sayings uttered from mouth to ear that were to be unwritten, the mysteries performed in secret, the science kept concealed. *The continuity of the astronomical mythos of Equinoctial Christolatry and of the total typology is proved by the persistence of the type*—the ancient genitrix, the two sisters, the hebdomad of inferior and superior powers, the trinity in unity represented by *Iao*, the tetrads male and female, the double Horus, or Horus and Stauros, the system of Aeons, the Kamite divinities, Harpocrates and Sut-Anubis, Isis and Hathor. *Theirs was the Christ not made flesh, but the manifester of the seven powers and perfect star of the pleroma.* The figure of eight, which is a sign of the Nnu or associate gods in Egypt, who were the primary Ogdoad, is reproduced as a gnostic symbol, a figure of the pleroma and fellow-type of the eight-rayed star. *The "Lamb of God" was a gnostic sign.* "Lord, thou art the Lamb" (and "our Light") *was a gnostic formula.* The *"Immaculate Virgin" was a gnostic type.* On one of the sard stones Isis stands before Serapis holding the sistrum in one hand, in the other a wheatsheaf, the legend being "Immaculate is our Lady Isis," which proves the continuity from Kam.

It was gnostic art that reproduced the Hathor-Meri and Horus of Egypt as the Virgin and child-Christ of Rome, and the icons of characters entirely ideal which served as the sole portraits of the historical Madonna and Jesus the Christ. The report of Irenaeus sufficed to show the survival of the true tradition. He complains of the oral wisdom of the Gnostics, and says rightly they read from things unwritten—i.e., from sources unknown to him and the Fathers in general. Chief of these sources was the science of astronomy. *He testifies that Marcus [the Evangelist Mark] was skilled in this form of the gnosis, and enables us to follow the line of unbroken continuity, and to confute his own assertion that Gnosticism had no existence prior to Marcion and Valentinus; which shows he did not know, or else he denied the fact, that the Suttites, the Mandaites, the Essenes, and Nazarenes were all Gnostics; all of which sects preceded the cult of the carnalized Christ.* Hippolytus informs us that Elkesai said the Christ born of a Virgin was *aeonian*. The Elkesites maintained that Jesus the Christ had continually transformed and manifested in various bodies at many different times. This shows they also were in possession of the gnosis, and that the Christ and his repeated incarnations were Kronian. Hence we are told that they occupied themselves "with a bustling activity in regard to astronomical science." Epiphanius also bears witness that the head and front of the gnostic boast was astronomy, and that Manes wrote a work on astronomy, *astronomy being the root of the whole matter concerning Equinoctial Christolatry.*

Nothing is more astounding, on their own showing, than the ignorance of the [Church] Fathers about the nature, the significance, the descent of Gnosticism, and its rootage in the remotest past. They knew nothing of evolution or the survival of types, and for them the new beginning with Christ carnalized obliterated all that preceded. Such a thing as priority, natural genesis, or the doctrine of development did not trouble those who considered that the more the myth the greater was the miracle which proved the divinity.

  Also, it has been asserted from the time of Irenaeus down to that of Mansel that the Gnostic heretics of the second century invented a number of spurious Gospels in imitation of or in opposition to the true gospel of Christ, which has descended to us as canonical, authentic, and historic. *This is a popular delusion, false enough to damn all belief in it from the beginning until now. The ignorance of the past manifested by men like Irenaeus is the measure of the value of their testimony to the origins of Equinoctial Christolatry. They who pretend to know all concerning the founding and the founder know nothing of the foundations.*

  . . . Gnosticism, according to those who are ignorant of its origin and relationships, was supposed and assumed to have originated in the second century [A.D.]; the first [Century A.D.] being carefully avoided, only proves that the A-Gnostics [that is, Agnostics, anti-Gnostics, or anti-knowledge: the orthodox Church Fathers], who had literally adopted the pre-Christian types, and believed they had been historically fulfilled, *were then for the first time becoming conscious of the cult that preceded theirs and face to face with those who held them to be the heretics. Gnosticism was no birth or new thing in the second century [A.D.], it was no perverter or corrupter of Christian doctrines divinely revealed, but the voice of an older cult growing more audible in its protest against a superstition as degrading and debasing now as when it was denounced by men like Tacitus, Pliny, Julian, Marcus Aurelius, and Porphyry.* For what could be more shocking to any sense really religious than the belief that the very God himself had descended on earth as an embryo in a virgin's womb, to run the risk of abortion and universal miscarriage during nine months *in utero*, and then dying on a cross to save his own created world or a portion of its people from eternal perdition? *The [Gnostic-Christian] opponents of the latest [orthodox Christian] superstition were too intelligent to accept a dying deity.*

  Never were men more perplexed and bewildered than the A-Gnostic Christians [again, the orthodox Church Fathers] of the third and fourth centuries—who had started from a new beginning altogether, which they had been taught to consider solely historic—when they turned to look back for the first time to find that an apparition of their faith was following them one way and confronting them in another; a shadow that threatened to steal away their substance, mocking them with its aerial unreality; the ghost of the body of truth which they had embraced as a solid and eternal reality claiming to be the rightful owner of their possessions; a phantom Christ without flesh or bone; a crucifixion that only occurred in cloudland; a parody of the drama of salvation performed in the air, with never a cross to cling to, not a nail-wound to thrust the fingers into and hold on by, not one drop of blood to wash away their sins. It was horrible [they cried]. It was devilish. It was the devil, they said, and thus they sought to account for Gnosticism and fight down their fears. "You poor ignorant idiotai!" said the Gnostics, *"you have mistaken the mysteries of old for modern history, and accepted literally all that was only meant mystically."*—"You spawn of Satan!" responded the Christians, "you are making the mystery by converting our accomplished facts into your miserable fables; you are dissipating and dispersing into thin air our only bit of solid foothold in the world, stained with the red drops of Calvary. You are giving a Satanic interpretation to the word of revelation and falsifying the oracles of God. You are converting the solid facts of our history into your new-fangled allegories."—"Nay," replied the Gnostics, "it is you who have *taken the allegories of mythology for historic facts."* And they were right. It was in consequence of their taking the allegorical tradition of the fall for reality that the Christian Fathers considered woman to be accursed, and called her a serpent, a scorpion, the devil in feminine form.[903]

Westbrook writes:

> The Gnostics are said by Gibbon to have been "the most polite, the most learned, and the most wealthy of the Christian name." They were finally forbidden by Theodosias I to assemble at their places of meeting or to teach their doctrines. Their books, too, were burned, so that we have now no full account of them. Only those who lied about them have been permitted a hearing.
> *The very fact that all the apparently historic events in the life of Jesus have an astrological and metaphoric character lifts him out of the category of physical humanity into that of the ideal.* We may relegate him thither, and yet leave no vacant place in the arena

of common life. This would be in perfect keeping with ancient usage. Among the reputed founders of philosophic systems we have no evidence of the existence of such great teachers as Manu, Kapila, Vyasa, Kanada, or Gotama [Buddha], and the founding of the principal commonwealths was ascribed to demigods and fictitious eponymous heroes. Rome, Athens, Sparta, Thebes, and indeed every ancient city of note, was said to be established after that manner. *Even leaders and teachers actually existing have been disguised by myth or the characteristics of the doctrine which they taught. Confucius and Zoroaster are hidden from view by the character assigned to them by later writers. Even Socrates as he appears and speaks in the Platonic Dialogues is little else than a personification of the Academic philosophy. When we consider that he [Jesus] is closely assimilated to the sages and hero-gods of the other worships, and that every significant point in his history conforms to astrological periods and to similar characteristics in the pagan religions, we cannot well avoid the conclusion that he too is an ideal.*

Mr. William Oxley of England, in his great work on Egypt, takes the ground that *the account we have of Jesus in the Gospels is substantially drawn from Egyptian sources.*

Amenoph III was one of the greatest of the old Egyptian kings. Amongst other gigantic works, he built the temple at Luxor, much of which is buried in sand and covered over by native houses. It is on the walls of this temple that very remarkable sculptures are portrayed relating to the birth, etc. of Amenoph III; they are on the inner wall of the sacred shrine, the holy of holies, and the sculptured scenes represent the annunciation, the conception, the incarnation, birth, and adoration of the divine man-child (Amenoph III) born from Mut-em-Sa. The two latter syllables mean "the Alone," or Only One, and the whole title means "the mother who gave birth to the Only One."

One fact is established beyond all cavil, and that is that the New Testament is the product of an order of men well versed in astronomy, and who by the aid of that science produced, on lines laid down by the ancient Egyptian hierophants, a new version of the old myths and allegories. We have as a fact the actual names and dates plagiarized from an Egypto-Arabic source, which undoubtedly betrays its origin, and the interpretation of this, and numberless instances besides, in strict accordance with the astrological formula and system, with its Graeco-Egyptian zodiacal pictorial representations.

Oxley says: "Apropos to this doctrine, I have in my possession two statuettes—one dating from the twenty-second dynasty, 900 B.C.—of Isis, crowned and nursing the babe

Horus. On my return from Egypt through Italy, I obtained a statuette of Mary, crowned and nursing the babe Jesus, which is an exact copy of the Virgin and Child in the church of St. Augustine in Rome. *The figures are identical.*"

Face to face with such a fact, who dare assert that the Egyptian Isis and Horus are a myth, and that the Christian Mary and Jesus are really historical? Some simple-minded ones beguile themselves with the delusion that these Egyptian and other heathen beliefs are prophecies of the real Jesus who in the fulness of time came down from heaven and was born of a virgin. But against this we have not only the actual claim of several Egyptian kings to be the "son of God according to promise or prophecy" (sixteen hundred years before Christ was born), but we have the fact of a whole nation *for thousands of years* resting their hopes of eternal salvation upon a belief that *"the son of God, Osiris, came down from heaven, took upon himself the mortal form, was slain by wicked hands, rose again from the dead, and ascended into heaven, where he became the great judge of all mankind."*

What adds to the difficulty is that *no dates* are given in the writings of the early Christian authors, and, what is more, many of their names are evidently *noms de plume*; for instance, the arch-heretic Arius and the great Nicene Council seem to resolve themselves simply into a controversy relating to the sun-god under the form of Aries (the Ram or Lamb); and as to dates in connection therewith, they are simply Masonic points with an astronomical reference and symbolical meaning. *In plain terms, nearly the whole of both the Old and New Testaments is an allegorical record of astral, solar, and planetary phenomena, with personages substituted for zodiacal signs; and with this key in hand the Hermetic student can unravel the allegories which are presented in such a form as to read like literal history.*[904]

Such astute observations could be multiplied indefinitely.

What does all of this mean in plain English?

Christianity was not "founded" in the 1st Century A.D. by Jesus or anyone else. It has always existed as the one true faith, which is why it is the foundation of every other religion. Why is this not better known? Because it went by a variety of other names prior to the 1st Century. As Gandhi asserted: "The soul of religion is one, but it is encased in a multitude of forms." Thus, Christianity was called "Hermeticism" in ancient Egypt, "Orphism" in Greece, "Zoroastrianism" in Persia, "Shintoism" in Japan, "Hinduism" in India, "Taoism" in China,[905] and "Judaism" in Israel.[906] Evidence that Orphism, for example, was but a pre-Christian form of

Christianity comes from the many descriptions of this ancient Greek faith. Pike writes:

> The doctrine of the Unity of God . . . was taught by Orpheus. Of this his hymn or palinode is a proof; fragments of which are quoted by many of the Fathers, as Justin, Tatian, Clemens of Alexandria, Cyril, and Theodoret, and the whole by Eusebius, quoting from Aristobulus. The doctrine of the Logos (word) or the Nous (intellect), his incarnation, death, resurrection or transfiguration; of his union with matter, his division in the visible world, which he pervades, his return to the original Unity, and the whole theory relative to the origin of the soul and its destiny, were taught in the [Orphic] mysteries, of which they were the great object.[907]

Emerson makes this analogy:

> For all things proceed out of the same spirit, which is differently named love, justice, temperance, in its different applications, just as the ocean receives different names on the several shores which it washes.[908]

It is plain then that Christianity was a universal spiritual belief system that was already in existence, in a thousand different forms, long before the birth of our Lord, just as the more spiritually evolved of the early Church Fathers, and Jesus Himself, maintained. This being so, the Prince of Peace did not come to found a *new* truth, an impossibility to begin with. For the great spiritual masters never incarnate on earth to start up exclusive religions; but rather to restore the one cosmic religion that has existed from before the beginning of time: God-realization.[909]

As we have seen, truth is eternal, imperishable, birthless, deathless, and perpetual. Thus Jesus could have only come to the material plane to reestablish the *original* truth, saying: "Ye shall know the truth, and the truth shall make you free."[910] Why was this necessary? Because the Theosistic Truth about *God in Man* had been forgotten by most people in His day—just as it has by the majority of people in our day.

According to mystical Christian hermeneutics, Jesus' "religion" was indeed not a religion at all, but rather a simple informal belief system,[911] a unitive spirituality that stressed a personal relationship with the Divine,[912] and which was therefore based on the individual (rather than the group),[913] unconditional love for ourselves and others,[914] unqualified forgiveness,[915] knowledge of our oneness with God,[916] a universal spirituality or "church within"[917]—that is, the "true tabernacle,"[918] headed by our Higher Self, the everlasting "high priest" (Christ Within),[919] love of the Universal Brotherhood of Man (for all souls are equal),[920] the unconditional love, mercy, and kindness of God for us (whether merited or not),[921] and complete faith in the Father (Divine Mind).[922]

At the time, all that was required to join the Lord's group was belief;[923] not in a particular religion, but belief in the Great I AM within;[924] that is, the Inner God,[925] the Indwelling Christ,[926] and the Holy Ghost Within[927]—all three which existed before Jesus and which exist in each one of us now, for they are immortal, timeless, ineffable, ageless, changeless, exhaustless, incorruptible, and universal.[928] This is the same Inner Triune God that Hindus refer to as the "unborn, undying, indestructible Lord of all things living." Here we have, Pike correctly asserts,

> the universal, eternal, immutable religion, such as God planted it in the heart of universal humanity. No creed has ever been long-lived that was not built on this foundation. It is the base, and they are the superstructure.[929]

And it is this same universalist religion, Pike continues, that was taught by the ancient Druids, who preached

> devotion to friends, indulgence for reciprocal wrongs, love of deserved praise, prudence, humanity, hospitality, respect for old age, disregard of the future, temperance, contempt of death, and a chivalrous deference to woman.
>
> Listen to these maxims from the [Scandinavian] *Hava Maal*, or "Sublime Book of Odin":
>
>> "If thou hast a friend, visit him often; the path will grow over with grass, and the trees soon cover it, if thou dost not constantly walk upon it. He is a faithful friend, who, having but two loaves, gives his friend one. Be never first to break with thy friend; sorrow wrings the heart of him who has no one save himself with whom to take counsel. There is no virtuous man who has not some vice, no bad man who has not some virtue. Happy [is] he who obtains the praise and good-will of men; for all that depends on the will of another is hazardous and uncertain. Riches flit away in the twinkling of an eye; they are the most

inconstant of friends; flocks and herds perish, parents die, friends are not immortal, thou thyself diest; I know but one thing that doth not die, the judgment that is passed upon the dead. Be humane toward those whom thou meetest on the road. If the guest that cometh to thy house is a-cold, give him fire; the man who has journeyed over the mountains needs food and dry garments. Mock not at the aged; for words full of sense come often from the wrinkles of age. Be moderately wise, and not over-prudent. Let no one seek to know his destiny, if he would sleep tranquilly. There is no malady more cruel than to be discontented with our lot. The glutton eats his own death; and the wise man laughs at the fool's greediness. Nothing is more injurious to the young than excessive drinking; the more one drinks the more he loses his reason; the bird of forgetfulness sings before those who intoxicate themselves, and wiles away their souls. Man devoid of sense believes he will live always if he avoids war; but, if the lances spare him, old age will give him no quarter. Better live well than live long. When a man lights a fire in his house, death comes before it goes out."

And thus said the Indian books:

"Honor thy father and mother. Never forget the benefits thou hast received. Learn while thou art young. Be submissive to the laws of thy country. Seek the company of virtuous men. Speak not of God but with respect. Live on good terms with thy fellow-citizens. Remain in thy proper place. Speak ill of no one. Mock at the bodily infirmities of none. Pursue not unrelentingly a conquered enemy. Strive to acquire a good reputation. The best bread is that for which one is indebted to his own labor. Take counsel with wise men. The more one learns, the more he acquires the faculty of learning. Knowledge is the most permanent wealth. As well be dumb as ignorant. The true use of knowledge is to distinguish good from evil. Be not a subject of shame to thy parents. What one learns in youth endures like the engraving upon a rock. He is wise who knows himself. Let thy books be thy best friends. When thou attainest an hundred years, cease to learn. Wisdom is solidly planted, even on the shifting ocean. Deceive no one, not even thine enemy. Wisdom is a treasure that everywhere commands its value. Speak mildly, even to the poor. It is sweeter to forgive than to take vengeance. Gaming and quarrels lead to misery. There is no true merit without the practice of virtue. To honor our mother is the most fitting homage we can pay the Divinity. There is no tranquil sleep without a clear conscience. He badly understands his interest who breaks his word."

Twenty-four centuries ago, these were the Chinese Ethics:

"The Philosopher [Confucius] said, 'San! my doctrine is simple, and easy to be understood.' Thseng-tseu replied, 'that is certain.' The Philosopher having gone out, the disciples asked what their master had meant to say. Thseng-Tseu responded, 'The doctrine of our Master consists solely in being upright of heart, and loving our neighbor as we love ourself.'"

About a century later, the Hebrew law said, "If any man hate his neighbor . . . then shall ye do unto him, as he had thought to do unto his brother . . . Better is a neighbor that is near, than a brother afar off . . . Thou shalt love thy neighbor as thyself."

In the same fifth century before Christ, Socrates the Grecian said, "Thou shalt love thy neighbor as thyself."

Three generations earlier, Zoroaster had said to the Persians: "Offer up thy grateful prayers to the Lord, the most just and pure Ormuzd, the supreme and adorable God, who thus declared to his Prophet Zerdusht: 'Hold it not meet to do unto others what thou wouldst not desire done unto thyself; do that unto the people, which, when done to thyself, is not disagreeable unto thee.'"

The same doctrine had been long taught in the schools of Babylon, Alexandria, and Jerusalem. A Pagan declared to the Pharisee Hillel that he was ready to embrace the Jewish religion, if he could make known to him in a few words a summary of the whole law of Moses. "That which thou likest not done to thyself," said Hillel, "do it not unto thy neighbor. Therein is all the law: the rest is nothing but the commentary upon it."

"Nothing is more natural," said Confucius, "nothing more simple, than the principles of that morality which I endeavor, by salutary maxims, to inculcate in you . . . It is humanity; which is to say, that universal charity among all of our species, without distinction. It is uprightness; that is, that rectitude of spirit and of heart, which makes one seek for truth in everything, and desire it, without deceiving one's self or others. It is, finally, sincerity or good faith; which is to say, that frankness, that openness of heart, tempered by self-reliance, which excludes all feints and all disguising, as much in speech as in action."[930]

Such was the universal spiritual belief system of our Lord!

Jesus' spirituality, His "religion," as some incorrectly call it, was actually all-inclusive and incorporated even those who did not follow Him: "He that is not against us is for us," said the all-wise Teacher and Healer.[931] This story from *The Aquarian Gospel of Jesus the Christ* aptly illustrates my point:

> And John said, "Master, who may seek and save the lost? and who may heal the sick, and cast the demons out of those obsessed? When we were on the way we saw a man who was not one of us, cast demons out and heal the sick. He did it by the sacred Word and in the name of Christ; but we forbade

him, for he did not walk with us."

And Jesus said, "You sons of men, do you imagine that you own the powers of God? And do you think that all the world must wait for you to do the works of God? God is not man that he should have a special care for any man, and give him special gifts. Forbid not any man to do the works of God.

"There is no man who can pronounce the sacred Word, and in the name of Christ restore the sick, and cast the unclean spirits out, who is not [a] child of God. The man of whom you speak is one with us. Whoever gathers in the grain of heaven is one with us. Whoever gives a cup of water in the name of Christ is one with us; so God shall judge."[932]

Thus, the severe religiocentrism that burgeoned among a number of early Jewish groups,[933] and later among some of Jesus' followers after His Ascension[934] (and which is still very much alive today in many Christian communities),[935] completely opposes the Lord's true and original teachings on religious tolerance.[936]

Furthermore, Jesus' goal for every person was the attainment of the "Kingdom of God,"[937] entrance into which requires the innocence, humility, faith, and mental flexibility of "little children"[938]—a receptive state of consciousness that Zen Buddhists call "beginner's mind."[939] Being manmade, religious rituals, creeds, philosophies, rules, ceremonies, tenets, theologies, and doctrinal beliefs do not fill the heart of those who truly hunger after God. It is how you live that is important, how you treat others; it is the motivation behind your thoughts, words, and actions that count to God.[940] Thus saith Zoroaster.[941] And thus saith the Christ.[942] And his half-brother James the Just agreed:

> *Pure religion* and undefiled before God and the Father *is this*, to visit the fatherless and widows in their affliction, and *to keep himself unspotted from the world.*[943]

Not even history's greatest Christians focused on the Church. Saint Francis of Assisi, for instance, taught that one should simply "obey the teachings of Jesus and imitate him in every way possible."[944] Paul, as another example, also never addressed the topic of religion specifically. Instead, he urged us to live a life of gentleness, humility, and patience, with charity toward all, enmity toward none.[945]

In short, the "religion" of Jesus is not a religion at all, and 1st-Century mainstream Jews made the same mistake that modern mainstream Christians do in believing Him to be the founder of a new *earthly* institutional Faith (for which the former had Him executed).[946] The so-called "religion" of our Lord was and is simply love, mercy, and forgiveness; that is right-thinking, right-speaking, and right-acting, or what the ancients called righteousness;[947] a spiritual belief system that both Christian mystics and liberal Christians, such as Theodore Parker, refer to as the "perfect" Faith.[948] It is a universal, non-denominational philosophy, Parker writes, that is

> absolute, pure morality; absolute, pure religion; the love of man; the love of God acting without let or hindrance. *The only creed it lays down is the great truth which springs up spontaneously in the holy heart—there is a God. Its watchword is, "Be perfect as your Father in heaven." The only form it demands is a divine life; doing the best thing in the best way, from the highest motives; perfect obedience to the great law of God. Its sanction is the voice of God in your heart; the perpetual presence of him who made us and the stars over our head; Christ and the Father abiding within us. All this is very simple—a little child can understand it; very beautiful—the loftiest mind can find nothing so lovely.* Try it by reason, conscience, and faith—things highest in man's nature—we see no redundance, we feel no deficiency. Examine the particular duties it enjoins—*humility, reverence, sobriety, gentleness, charity, forgiveness, fortitude, resignation, faith,* and *active love*; try the whole extent of Christianity, so well summed up in the command, "Thou shalt love the Lord thy God with all thy heart, and with all thy soul, and with all thy mind"—"thou shalt love thy neighbor as thyself;" and is there anything therein that can perish? No, *the very opponents of Christianity have rarely found fault with the teachings of Jesus.*[949]

Similarly Pike writes:

> None can deny that Christ taught a lofty morality. "Love one another: forgive those that despitefully use you and persecute you: be pure of heart, meek, humble, contented: lay not up riches on earth, but in heaven: submit to the powers lawfully over you: become like these little children, or ye cannot be saved, for of such is the Kingdom of Heaven: forgive the repentant; and cast no stone at the sinner, if you too have sinned: do unto others as ye would have others do unto you:" such, and not abstruse questions of theology, were his simple and sublime teachings.
>
> *The early Christians followed in his footsteps. The first preachers of the faith had no thought of domination.* Entirely animated by his saying, that he among them should be first, who

should serve with the greatest devotion, they were humble, modest, and charitable, and they knew how to communicate this spirit of the inner man to the churches under their direction. These churches were at first but spontaneous meetings of all Christians inhabiting the same locality. A pure and severe morality, mingled with religious enthusiasm, was the characteristic of each, and excited the admiration even of their persecutors. Everything was in common among them; their property, their joys, and their sorrows. In the silence of night they met for instruction and to pray together. Their love-feasts, or fraternal repasts, ended these reunions, in which all differences in social position and rank were effaced in the presence of a paternal Divinity. *Their sole object was to make men better, by bringing them back to a simple worship, of which universal morality was the basis*; and to end those numerous and cruel sacrifices which everywhere inundated with blood the altars of the Gods. Thus did Christianity reform the world, and obey the teachings of its founder. It gave to woman her proper rank and influence; it regulated domestic life; and by admitting the slaves to the love-feasts, it by degrees raised them above that oppression under which half of mankind had groaned for ages.

This, in its purity, as taught by Christ himself, was the true primitive religion, as communicated by God to the Patriarchs. *It was no new religion, but the reproduction of the oldest of all; and its true and perfect morality is the morality of Masonry, as is the morality of every creed of antiquity.*[950]

All of this makes the Lord's "faith" identical to the ancient Wisdom Religion, or what Hindus call *Sanatana Dharma*, the "Eternal Way." This is the One Universal Religion that is known by hundreds of thousands of different names around the globe, and which John refers to when he says, "God so loved *the world* that he gave his only begotten Son . . ."[951] For at the core of Sanatana Dharma lies those three immortal and timeless spiritual truths upon which all religions are ultimately founded: *love, compassion,* and *wisdom*. These concepts are found in all religions, from Baha'i[952] and Buddhism[953] to Wicca[954] and Zoroastrianism.[955] Thus, if we were to give a name to Jesus' "religion," it would be "The Way"[956]—which is exactly what He[957] and His followers called it.[958]

But just as Christianity was not original to Jesus, neither was this name. He was simply borrowing one that was commonplace among the great spiritual teachers throughout pre-Christian history, from the Old Testament authors, such as Moses,[959] Jeremiah,[960] Job,[961] and the Psalmist,[962] to the ancient philosopher-priest Hermes Trismegistus[963] and the famed Chinese teacher Lao Tzu, the founder of the religion literally known as "The Way": Tao (Taoism).⁹⁶⁴

Some 750 years before Jesus' birth, Micah articulated the Lord's spiritual belief system, The Way, perfectly:

> What doth the Lord require of thee, but to do justly, and to love mercy, and to walk humbly with thy God?⁹⁶⁵

That the Wisdom Religion, The Way of Jesus, is universal and eternal, can be seen in the fact that its cardinal principles, "Deity, the Immortality of the Soul, and the Brotherhood of Man," were taught by Pythagoras (born 586 B.C.), and are still being taught right into the modern day by such secret societies as Free Masonry.⁹⁶⁶ Our Lord's Gospel has also been articulated as "liberty of thought, equality of all men in the eye of God, and universal fraternity."⁹⁶⁷ This is the same "religion" that Deist and American Founding Father Thomas Paine wrote about in his famous pamphlet, *The Age of Reason*:

> I believe in one God, and no more; and I hope for happiness beyond this life. I believe in the equality of man, and I believe that religious duties consist in doing justice, loving mercy, and endeavoring to make our fellow-creatures happy.⁹⁶⁸

Thomas Jefferson practiced the same Faith:

> Say nothing of my religion. It is known to my God and myself alone. Its evidence before the world is to be sought in my life; if that has been honest and dutiful to society, the religion which has regulated it cannot be a bad one.⁹⁶⁹

Likewise Confucius taught:

> Love thy neighbor as thyself: Do not to others what thou wouldst not wish should be done to thyself: Forgive injuries. Forgive your enemy, be reconciled to him, give him as, assistance, invoice God in his behalf!⁹⁷⁰

Zoroaster too preached the following principles:

> Be good, be kind, be humane, and charitable; love your fellows; console the afflicted; pardon those who have done you wrong.⁹⁷¹

The great Buddha said:

I do not care to know your various theories about God. What is the use of discussing all the subtle doctrines about the soul? Do good and be good. And this will take you to whatever truth there is.⁹⁷²

Of this universal faith Hartmann writes:

> This Wisdom Religion has been, and is to-day, the inheritance of the saints, prophets, and seers, and of the illuminated ones of all nations, no matter to what external system of religion they may have given their adherence. It was taught by the ancient Brahmins, Egyptians, and Jews in temples and caves, *Gautama Buddha and Jesus of Nazareth preached it*, it formed the basis of the Eleusinian and Bacchic mysteries of the Greeks, and *the true religion of the eternal Christ is resting upon it. It is the religion of Humanity, that has nothing to do with opinions and forms.*
>
> Now, as in times of old, its truths are misunderstood and misrepresented by men who profess to be teachers of men. The Pharisees and Sadducees of the New Testament were the prototypes of modern churchmen and scientists existing to-day. Now, as then, the truth is daily crucified between superstition and selfishness and laid in the tomb of ignorance. Now, as then, the spirit has fled from the form, being driven away by those that worship the letter and ignore the spirit.
>
> Wisdom will for ever remain a secret science to the idolators *adoring the form*, even if it were proclaimed from the housetops and preached at a marketplace. The dealer in pounds and pennies, absorbed by his material interests, may be surrounded by the greatest beauties of nature and not comprehend them, the speculative reasoner will ask for a sign and not see the signs by which he is continually surrounded.
>
> *The tomb from which the Saviour will arise is the heart of mankind; if the God in Humanity awakens to self-consciousness of his Divinity then will he appear as a sun, shedding its light upon a better and happier generation.*⁹⁷³

Sadly, many of those who had the privilege of hearing Jesus teach His "religion" in person "understood not the things which he spake unto them."⁹⁷⁴ To this very day many followers of Christianity still do not understand that the purpose of our faith is not to find the historical Jesus. It is to find the spiritual Christ: God.⁹⁷⁵ Parker put it this way:

> *The end [purpose] of Christianity seems to be to make all men one with*

God as Christ was one with him; to bring them to such a state of obedience and goodness that we shall think divine thoughts and feel divine sentiments, and so keep the law of God by living a life of truth and love. Its means are purity and prayer; getting strength from God, and using it for our fellow-men as well as ourselves. It allows perfect freedom. *It does not demand all men to think alike, but to think uprightly, and get as near as possible at truth; not all men to live alike, but to live holy, and get as near as possible to a life perfectly divine.* Christ set up no pillars of Hercules, beyond which men must not sail the sea in quest of truth. He says, "I have many things to say unto you, but ye cannot bear them now. . . Greater works than these shall ye do."

Christianity lays no rude hand on the sacred peculiarity of the individual genius and character. But *there is no Christian sect which does not fetter a man. It would make all men think alike, or smother their conviction in silence.* Were all men Quakers or Catholics, Unitarians or Baptists, there would be much less diversity of thought, character, and life, less of truth active in the world, than now. But Christianity gives us the largest liberty of the sons of God; and *were all men Christians after the fashion of Jesus, this variety would be a thousand times greater than now: for Christianity is not a system of doctrines, but rather a method of attaining oneness with God.* It demands, therefore, a good life of piety within, of purity without, and gives the promise that whoso does God's will shall know of God's doctrine.

In an age of corruption, as all ages are, Jesus stood and looked up to God. There was nothing between him and the Father of all; no old world, be it of Moses or Esaias, of a living rabbi, or sanhedrin of rabbis; no sin or perverseness of the finite will. As the result of this virgin purity of soul and perfect obedience, the light of God shone down into the very depths of his soul, bringing all of the Godhead which flesh can receive. *He would have us do the same; worship with nothing between us and God; act, think, feel, live, in perfect obedience to him; and we never are Christians as he was the Christ, until we worship, as Jesus did, with no mediator, with nothing between us and the Father of all. He felt that God's word was in him; that he was one with God.* He told what he saw, the truth; he lived what he felt, a life of love.

The truth he brought to light must have been always the same before the eyes of all-seeing God, nineteen centuries before Christ, or nineteen centuries after him. *A life supported by the principle and quickened by the sentiment of religion, if true to both, is always the same thing in Nazareth or New England. Now that divine man received these truths from God, was illumined more clearly by "the light that lighteth every man," combined or involved all the truths of religion and morality in his doctrine, and made them manifest in his life.* Then his words and example passed into the world, and can no more perish than the stars be wiped out of the sky.

The truths he taught; his doctrines respecting man and God; the relation between man and man, and man and God, with the duties that grow out of that relation—are always the same, and can never change till man ceases to be man, and creation vanishes into nothing. No; forms and opinions change and perish, but the word of God cannot fail. *The form religion takes, the doctrines wherewith she is girded, can never be the same in any two centuries or two men*; for since the sum of religious doctrines is both the result and the measure of a man's total growth in wisdom, virtue, and piety, and since men will always differ in these respects, so religious doctrines and forms will always differ, always be transient, as Christianity goes forth and scatters the seed she bears in her hand.

But the Christianity holy men feel in the heart, the Christ that is born within us, is always the same thing to each soul that feels it. This differs only in degree, and not in kind, from age to age, and man to man.[976]

This is *true* Christianity, the Christianity of Jesus, the mystic universalist. Not a strict social and religious system of dogmatic doctrines, but a personal method of attaining at-one-ment with God. Today's organized Christian Church would be completely unrecognizable to the man for whom it was named. See BUDDHA, CHRIST, FISH, GNOSTICISM, GOSPEL, JESUS, KRISHNA, MITHRA, OSIRIS, PYTHAGORAS, SON OF GOD, TEACHER OF RIGHTEOUSNESS, UNION WITH GOD, WAY OF THE LORD.

CHRISTMAS: Christmas, the birth of Jesus, the "Mass of Christ," was not celebrated by the first Christians, hence it is not mentioned in the Bible. It was not until many centuries later that the day began to be thought of as holy. Since no one knew the exact day, month, or even the year Jesus was born, in the 4th Century the traditional Pagan Sun-god's birthday was selected to stand in its stead: December 25,[977] to accord with the early Pagan belief that the Sun-god was born three days after the Winter Solstice on December 22.[978] Just as Jesus' death day was placed on March 25 to accord with the Pagan celebration of the death of the Phrygian savior-god Attis,[979] Christmas then is a Christian substitute for the Roman Winter

Solstice festival[980] devoted to the Sun-God Sol (Sol Invictus),[981] a popular ancient celebration then known as *Natalis Invicti*;[982] or more fully as *Dies Natalis Solis Invicti*: "Birthday of the Unconquered Sun."[983]

Of the many difficulties, developments, and opinions regarding the birth date of Jesus, Hampson writes:

> The birth of our Lord has been variously assigned to the years 748, 749, 750 and 751, from the foundation of Rome. The same uncertainty prevails respecting the day and month, on both which, Scriptures, our only authority, are profoundly silent. Many, from the time of Clement of Alexandria, maintain that he was born in the Spring; and Paul, bishop of Middleburgh, fixes the day on the 25th of March, exactly at the time of the vernal equinox, but the reason assigned is based on a vague hypothesis. Beroaldus, who has many followers, says that he was born in Autumn; and J. Harduin fixes on September, about the time of the Autumnal equinox. Another class maintain that he was born on the 6th of January, which is now the Epiphany; and *Cassian says that the Egyptians celebrated the Nativity on this day*. According to the vulgar opinion, which was generally received in the time of Theophilus, bishop of Caesaria in the reigns of Commodus and Severus, he was born on Dec. 25; and *Victorinus Pictavensis affirms that, in the third century, the Nativity was celebrated about the winter solstice. This custom was retained and confirmed by the councils of Basil and Florence, and, consequently, adopted by the compilers of martyrologies, breviaries, diaries, and kalendars*. Polydore Vergil, without any notice of the day of the Nativity, places the festival among those which originated with the apostles. Theophilus of Antioch, in 170, mentions it in his Paschal Epistle, as quoted by Nicephorus; and L'Estrange mentions the sermon on the Nativity by Gregory Nazianzen, in the fourth century. The progress of the English name, from the Saxon [*Christenmesse*] to the present appellation [*Christmas*], is nearly as above: *at first midwinter, the appellation of the 25th of December as the solstitial, though referring to the pagan rites of Yule, was used indifferently with* Cristes maesse daeg *(Christ's Mass-day)*. In the Chronicle, it constantly occurs up to the year 973, when it is mentioned in a poetical specification of the date, as the Nativity: "And then were passed ten hundred winters from the birth-time of the illustrious king, the guardian of light."[984]

Over time the traditional Pagan Winter Solstice celebratory accouterments were added to Jesus' Holy Day as well. For instance: the Christmas tree, Kris Kringle (Santa Claus), the Yule Log, mistletoe, holly, plum pudding, wreathes, mince pie, hot cider, nuts, boar's head, turkey, candles, lights, fires, carols, pantomime, candies, pastries, fruits, and gift-giving, to name only a few.

This major alteration to the biography of our Lord aided the Catholic Church in its quest to dehumanize and then deify Him, transforming Him from the Son of Man (a natural man) into the Son of God (a supernatural being). The apotheosization and Paganization of Jesus, an all too *human* Jewish mystic, is certainly one of the greatest coverups in religious history. Carpenter writes that:

> The Jesus-story . . . has a great number of correspondences with the stories of former Sungods and with the actual career of the Sun through the heavens—so many indeed that they cannot well be attributed to mere coincidence or even to the blasphemous wiles of the Devil! Let us enumerate some of these.
>
> There are (1) the birth from a Virgin mother; (2) the birth in a stable (cave or underground chamber); and (3) on the 25th December (just after the winter solstice). There is (4) the Star in the East (Sirius) and (5) the arrival of the Magi (the "Three Kings"); there is (6) the threatened Massacre of the Innocents, and the consequent flight into a distant country (told also of Krishna and other Sun-gods).
>
> There are the Church festivals of (7) Candlemas (2nd February), with processions of candles to symbolize the growing light; of (8) Lent, or the arrival of Spring; of (9) Easter Day (normally on the 25th March) to celebrate the crossing of the Equator by the Sun; and (10) simultaneously the outburst of lights at the Holy Sepulchre at Jerusalem.
>
> There is (11) the Crucifixion and death of the Lamb-God, on Good Friday, three days before Easter; there are (12) the nailing to a tree, (13) the empty grave, (14) the glad Resurrection (as in the cases of Osiris, Attis and others); there are (15) the twelve disciples (the Zodiacal signs); and (16) the betrayal by one of the twelve.
>
> Then later there is (17) Midsummer Day, the 24th June, dedicated to the Nativity of John the Baptist, and corresponding to Christmas Day; there are the festivals of (18) the Assumption of the Virgin (15th August) and of (19) the Nativity of the Virgin (8th September), corresponding to the movement of the god through Virgo; there is the conflict of Christ and his disciples with the autumnal asterisms, (20) the

Serpent and the Scorpion; and finally there is the curious fact that the Church (21) dedicates the very day of the winter solstice (when any one may very naturally doubt the rebirth of the Sun) to St. Thomas, who doubted the truth of the Resurrection!

These are some of, and by no means all, the coincidences in question. But they are sufficient, I think, to prove—even allowing for possible margins of error—the truth of our general contention.[985]

Brewster likewise writes:

> One curious fact or coincidence yet confronts us, that this date [December 25] exactly corresponds both in its inception and the length of the festival with the great festival of pagan Rome, the Saturnalia.
>
> Though Christian nations have thus from an early period in the history of the church celebrated Christmas about the period of *the winter solstice or the shortest day*, it is well known that many and indeed the greater number of the popular festive observances by which it is characterized, are referable to a much more ancient origin. *Amid all the pagan nations of antiquity there seems to have been a universal tendency to worship the sun as the giver of life and light and the one visible manifestation of the Deity. Various as were the names bestowed by different peoples on this object of their worship, the sun was still the same divinity. Thus at Rome he appears to have been worshipped under one of the characters attributed to Saturn, the father of the gods; among the Scandinavian nations he was known under the name of Odin or Woden, the father of Thor, who seems afterwards to have shared with his parent the adoration bestowed on the latter as the divinity of which the sun was the visible manifestation; whilst with the ancient Persians the appellation for the god of light was Mithras, apparently the same as the Irish Mithr, and with the Phoenicians or Carthaginians it was Baal or Bel, an epithet familiar to all students of the Bible.*
>
> In the early ages of Christianity its ministers frequently experienced the utmost difficulty in inducing the converts to refrain from indulging in the popular amusements which were so largely participated in by their pagan countrymen. Among others the revelry and license which characterized the Saturnalia called for special animadversion. *But at last, convinced partly of the inefficacy of such denunciations, and partly influenced by the idea that the spread of Christianity might thereby be advanced, the Church*

> endeavoured to amalgamate as it were the old and new religions, and sought by transferring some of the heathen ceremonies to the solemnities of the Christian festivals to make them subservient to the cause of religion and piety.
>
> Thus it has been suggested, and not without some reason, that in the selection of this day for Christmas, instead of the time-honoured Epiphany, the Holy Father may have been influenced.
>
> The name given by the ancient Goths and Saxons to the festival of the winter solstice was *Jul* or *Yule*, the latter term forming to the present day the designation in the Scottish dialect of Christmas, and preserved also in the name of the yule log. Perhaps the etymology of no term has excited any greater discussion among antiquaries. The most probable derivation of the word is from the Gothic *gigul* or *hiul*, the origin of the modern word wheel, and bearing the same signification. According to this very probable explanation the yule festival received its name from its being the turning point of the year or the period at which the fiery orb of day made a revolution in its annual circuit and entered his northern journey. A confirmation of this view is afforded by the circumstance that in the old Clog almanacs a wheel is the device employed for marking the season of yule-tide.[986]

Historicizing dozens of ancient Pagan myths and appending them to the figure of Jesus (elements that even many evangelical Christian leaders regard as "foreign materials"),[987] however, has not been able to conceal the truth from Christian mystics. As we see it, due to the fact that traditional "Christianity borrowed lavishly from its competitors,"[988] Jesus the Christian *Son* of God is now little different than the archetypal Pagan *Sun* of God on whom much of his biography was patterned. Though this nefarious transmutation, known as the "Scheme of Salvation,"[989] has been a great loss to Christians everywhere, much of the true and original Jesus can still be ascertained in ancient books like The Gospel of Q[990] and The Gospel of Thomas, both which have retained many elements of the authentic man.[991] See BUDDHA, CHRISTMAS, GOOD NEWS, GOSPEL OF Q, KRISHNA, MITHRA, MYTH OF CHRIST, NATIVITY, OSIRIS, PYTHAGORAS, TEACHER OF RIGHTEOUSNESS, THREE DAYS, STAR OF BETHLEHEM.

CHURCH (THE CHRISTIAN): In mainstream Christianity the Church is the total membership of that organization, and which is known as the "body of Christ."[992] In mystical Christianity the "Church" is not physical. It is internal, mental, or spiritual, for as the Bible itself declares: "The most High dwelleth not in temples made with hands."⁹⁹³ This can only mean that the temple the "most High" *does* dwell in was made by God Himself, and this "temple," of course, is the human form, just as Paul and other Christian mystics have long taught.⁹⁹⁴

In mystical Christianity there is an outward church (physical) and an inward church (spiritual), the latter being the relevant one. The Indwelling Christ (our Soul) is the eternal "high priest"⁹⁹⁵ of our personal "church within,"⁹⁹⁶ which the Hebraist called "the one and only true church, made by the hands of God, not man."⁹⁹⁷ Of this mystical doctrine Channing writes:

> There have been men of eminent piety who, from conscience, have separated themselves from all denominations of Christians and all *outward worship*. Milton, that great soul, in the latter years of his life, forsook all temples made with hands, and worshipped wholly in the *inward sanctuary*. So did William Law, the author of that remarkable book, *The Serious Call to a Devout and Holy Life*. His excess of devotion (for in him devotion ran into excess) led him to disparage all occasional acts of piety. He lived in solitude, that he might make life a perpetual prayer. . . . With such examples before us, we learn not to exclude men from God's favour because severed from the outward church.
>
> The doctrine of this discourse is plain. *Inward sanctity, pure love, disinterested attachment to God and man, obedience of heart and life, sincere excellence of character, this is the one thing needful, this the essential thing in religion; and all things else, ministers, churches, ordinances, places of worship, all are but means, helps, secondary influences, and utterly worthless when separated from this. To imagine that God regards anything but this, that He looks at anything but the heart, is to dishonour Him, to express a mournful insensibility to his pure character, Goodness, purity, virtue, this is the only distinction in God's sight.*
>
> This is intrinsically, essentially, everlastingly, and by its own nature, lovely, beautiful, glorious, divine. It owes nothing to time, to circumstance, to outward connections. It shines by its own light. It is the sun of the spiritual universe. *It is God Himself dwelling in the human soul*. Can any man think lightly of it because it has not grown up in a certain church, or exalt any church above it?
>
> My friends, *one of the grandest truths of religion is the supreme importance of character, of virtue, of that divine spirit which shone out in Christ. The grand heresy is to substitute anything for this, whether creed, or form, or church. One of the greatest wrongs to Christ is to despise his character, his virtue, in a disciple who happens to wear*

a different name from our own.[998]

See BIBLE, CHRIST, CHRISTIANITY, ECCLESIA, JESUS, WORD OF GOD.

CLOSET: The biblical Greek word for closet is *tameion*, whose traditional meaning is a small "storeroom." Jesus taught that when we pray, we should "enter into thy closet, and when thou hast shut thy door, pray to thy father which is in secret; and thy Father which seeth in secret shall reward thee openly."[999] In the mainstream Church this is seen as a literal injunction to pray privately.

The mystical meaning, however, goes much deeper. In the esoteric Christian school closet means the inner sanctum of consciousness, and Jesus' teaching is a call to pray to or mediate upon the God Within, which the Bible calls a "still small voice,"[1000] otherwise known as the Universal Mind, or the Divine Soul, which Jesus knew as the "Father."[1001] Hence, the inner meaning of the Master's words:

> Meditate on Divine Mind, and He who perceives you telepathically will manifest in the physical all that you pray for in the spiritual.[1002]

See GOD, PRAYER, UNION WITH GOD, WORD OF GOD.

COMFORTER: In traditional Christianity the Comforter is considered identical to the Holy Spirit or Holy Ghost,[1003] yet in the mystical Church it has a specific meaning of its own: spiritual understanding, the inner light, which gives us peace of mind and a sense of security; of being taken care of, comforted, and loved unconditionally by God. Jesus referred to this sensation, this elevated spiritual level of consciousness, as the Comforter; in Greek, *Parakletos*, "helper," "assistant."[1004]

The Lord promised that after His physical life ended, the Comforter, the Christ Within,[1005] would take care of us and guide us, just as He had while here fulfilling His earthly mission: to reestablish within humanity the doctrine of Theosis, the concept of the Indwelling Christ, God in Man[1006] that had been suppressed by conventional Judaism (biblically represented by the Pharisees)—and which is still being suppressed by today's Pharisaical Christianity.[1007] Thus Jesus said, before I go

> I will pray the Father, and he shall give you another Comforter, that he may abide with you for ever; Even the Spirit of truth; whom the world cannot receive, because it seeth him not, neither knoweth him: but ye know him; for he dwelleth with you, and shall be in you. . . . the Comforter, which is the Holy Ghost, whom the Father will send in my name, he shall teach

you all things, and bring all things to your remembrance, whatsoever I have said unto you.[1008]

Like the Father,[1009] the Christ,[1010] and the Holy Ghost,[1011] the Comforter (intuition) also dwells within us, not outside of us.[1012] Augustine writes:

> Jesus knew what was most expedient for the Disciples, because *that inward sight*, wherewith the Holy Spirit was yet to comfort them, was undoubtedly superior; not by bringing a human body into the bodies of those who saw, but by infusing Himself into the hearts of those who believed.[1013]

As early religions, being innately mystical, viewed the Comforter or Holy Spirit as female, Christian mystics have long done so as well. She is "that inward sight" or "inner teacher" whom the ancients personified as the goddesses Sophia (Greek), Sapientia (Roman), Epinoia (Gnostic-Christian), and Shekinah (Hebrew); that is, spiritual "wisdom."[1014] Concerning the 3rd-Century Syrian Christian writer Aphraates, Burkitt writes:

> I must not omit to point out one remarkable feature of Aphraates's doctrine of the Spirit. When we speak in the Creed of "the Lord, the Giver of Life," we are obliged to assign a sex to the Holy Spirit. We have to choose between Lord and Lady. The Greek *pneuma* is of course neuter. But in Semitic languages there is no neuter, and *Ruh* [ruach] the word for wind or spirit, is feminine; in the older Syriac literature, therefore, before the influence of Greek theology made itself felt, the Holy Spirit also is feminine. Thus in the old Syriac version of John 14:26 we actually read *The Spirit, the Paraclete, she shall teach you everything*. Thus it is only in accordance with the earliest usage that in a doxology Aphraates ascribes "glory and honour to the Father and to His Son and to His Spirit, the living and holy," where living and holy are feminine adjectives in the older MS. But he goes further: it is not a question only of grammatical nicety with Aphraates. In the treatise *On Virginity Against the Jews* he says:

>> "We have heard from the law that a man will leave his father and his mother and will cleave to his wife, and they will be one flesh; and truly a prophecy great and excellent is this. What father and mother doth he forsake that taketh a wife? This is

the meaning: that when a man not yet hath taken a wife, he loveth and honoureth God his Father, and *the Holy Spirit his Mother*, and he hath no other love. But when a man taketh a wife he forsaketh his Father and his Mother, those namely that are signified above, and his mind is united with this world; and his mind and his heart and his thought is dragged away from God into the midst of the world, and he loveth and cherisheth it, as a man loveth the wife of his youth, and the love of her is different from that of his Father and of his Mother."

We shall come across this view of the Holy Spirit again when we consider the *Acts of Thomas*. Here I must remind you that there is very early Christian authority for it.

In the ancient *Gospel according to the Hebrews*, as quoted by Origen and S. Jerome, our Lord Himself speaks of the Holy Spirit as His Mother. Origen, who is concerned to show that all things, including the Holy Spirit, came into existence through the Logos, does not reject this saying as "apocryphal," but explains it away. *He argues that the Holy Spirit does the will of the Father, and therefore may rightly be described as the Mother of Christ, in accordance with Matthew 12:50.* Perhaps *it was inevitable that the thought of the Holy Spirit as the Queen of Heaven should be eliminated from Christian theology*, but before we condemn the doctrine altogether let us remember that the theology of the age which followed its final disappearance, at the bidding of popular sentiment, by a false application of logic to Divine affairs, degraded the Christian vocabulary with the word *Theotokos* [that is, "Mother of God"].[1015]

See CHRIST, FATHER, GOD, GODDESS, HOLY SPIRIT, I AM, JESUS.

CONSCIOUS MIND: In the Bible the Conscious Mind is personified in the form of the human Jesus,[1016] the mortal son of Joseph and Mary (here, as always in Christian mysticism, distinguished from the Christ).[1017] In mystical Christianity then, our Conscious Mind is one aspect of the Holy Trinity, along with the Subconscious Mind (the Holy Spirit) and the Superconscious Mind (God).[1018]

In patriarchal religions the Conscious Mind is known as the "Son"; in matriarchal religions it is the "Sun." In mystical religions it is the "Christ" or

"Higher Self."

I call the Conscious Mind "The Thinker," for it is a symbol of wisdom, and is related to the physical plane and the material body. Thoughts and ideas are generated here, and, as the "Master," it conveys thoughts to the Subconscious Mind (the "Servant"), which stores our most dominant thoughts as beliefs. The Subconscious then passes these beliefs onto the Superconscious Mind (the "Creator"), which manifests them in the physical plane as our experiences and circumstances.

The Conscious Mind plays a vital role in working with the biblical Law of Attraction as laid out in the book of Proverbs: "For as a man thinketh in his heart, so is he."[1019] In other words, what we send out we get back, for as science itself has proven, a human being is like a living radio: it transmits and receives information and energy from the Universe.[1020] Thus, learning to control the thoughts coming out of the Conscious Mind is imperative if we wish to achieve health, wealth, and happiness.

The Conscious Mind correlates with the left side of the brain, which operates the right (male) side of the body. Its keywords are: logical, sequential, analytical, objective, masculine, daytime, knowledge, earthly, ideas, facts, science.[1021] See DIVINE MIND, GOD, JESUS, KEYS OF THE KINGDOM OF HEAVEN, SUBCONSCIOUS MIND, SUPERCONSCIOUS MIND.

CROSS: In modern mainstream Christianity the cross is a purely Christian symbol of the church,[1022] a call to totally surrender to God.[1023] Sometimes it can be a figurative emblem of the suffering[1024] a Christian undergoes.[1025] Most commonly, however, it is a traditional symbol of the redeeming crucifixion of Jesus, whose spilt blood delivered humanity from original sin.[1026] Even though Jesus only made one statement regarding the theological symbolism of the cross,[1027] its hold on the Church is profound enough that it is venerated as an idol by many Christians.[1028]

Despite all of this, the cross as a symbol of Jesus and his victory over death was unknown in the early Church, which used the sacrificial lamb or Good Shepherd carrying a lamb, as its sacred image—the latter patterned on such pre-Christian Pagan gods as Hermes and Osiris, both who were known by the title "Good Shepherd."[1029] Though the first (dated) cross used by Christians is from the year 134 (at Palmyra, Syria),[1030] it was not until the 7th Century that the cross began to be seen as a true Christian symbol,[1031] and it was not until the 9th Century, nearly a thousand years after Jesus' death, that it was officially accepted by the Church.[1032]

In the mystical Christian branch it is recognized that the cross is not specifically Christian. In fact, as an integral element of nature worship,[1033] it is both Pagan in origin and archetypal in nature, which is why it has been used by every known society, culture, religion, and civilization dating back to prehistoric times,[1034] when it was artistically utilized by the Cro-Magnon people.[1035]

The X-shaped "Cross of Saint Andrew," for example, has been found etched into prehistoric bones, while in more modern times crosses have been discovered among peoples as widely dispersed as the Minoans of ancient Crete, the ancient Egyptians (the ankh),[1036] the pre-Christian Norwegians, the early Chinese, and the pre-Columbian Incas[1037]—as well as a myriad of other pre-European Native American societies.[1038] The "Latin Cross" has been used in pre-Christian Japan, China, Buddhism, Tibet, Chaldea, Phoenicia, Assyria, Greece, and Druidism.[1039]

Educated Christian authorities are well aware of these facts. The celebrated Bishop of the Church of England, John William Colenso, writes:

> *From the dawn of organized Paganism in the Eastern world, to the final establishment of Christianity in the West, the cross was undoubtedly one of the commonest and most sacred of symbolical monuments. Apart from any distinctions of social or intellectual superiority, of caste, color, nationality, or location in either hemisphere, it appears to have been the aboriginal possession of every people in antiquity.*
>
> Diversified forms of the symbol are delineated more or less artistically, according to the progress achieved in civilization at the period, on the ruined walls of temples and palaces, on natural rocks and sepulchral galleries, on the hoariest monoliths and the rudest statuary; on coins, medals, and vases of every description; and in not a few instances, are preserved in the architectural proportions of subterranean as well as superterranean structures of tumuli, as well as fanes.
>
> Populations of essentially different culture, tastes, and pursuits—the highly civilized and the semi-civilized, the settled and the nomadic—vied with each other in their superstitious adoration of it, and in their efforts to extend the knowledge of its exceptional import and virtue amongst their latest posterities.
>
> Of the several varieties of the cross still in vogue, as national and ecclesiastical emblems, and distinguished by the familiar appellations of St. George, St. Andrew, the Maltese, the Greek, the Latin, etc., *there is not one amongst them the existence of which may not be traced to the remotest antiquity. They were the common property of the Eastern nations.*
>
> That each known variety has been derived from a common source, and is emblematical of one and the same truth may be inferred from the fact of forms identically the same, whether simple or complex, cropping out in contrary directions, in the Western as well as the Eastern hemisphere.[1040]

The cross is universal because it symbolizes the human form, Man and

Woman, with arms outstretched and feet together: a four-pointed emblem representing the sacred number four (the four seasons, the four winds, the four directions, the four corners of the earth, the four seasons, the four ages of the world, the four worlds, the four elements, the four cardinal virtues, etc.).[1041] A variation of the cross is the star or pentacle, with five points representing the head and two arms and two legs outstretched,[1042] often seen in the iconographic artwork of cathedrals.[1043]

However it is depicted, in the mystic Christian tradition the cross is the ultimate symbol of life, not death. Man and Woman themselves are "living crosses," with the horizontal beam (the outstretched arms) representing the Divine Feminine or Subconscious Mind, which is pierced from above by the vertical beam (the downward-pointing leg) representing the Divine Masculine[1044] or Superconscious Mind.[1045] Here the four-pointed cross is an emblem of the *Hieros Gamos*, or "Sacred Union" of the male (spiritual) and female (material) energies, uniting in a representation of spiritual oneness or wholeness between a positive polarity (the Divine Male) and a negative polarity (the Divine Female), equaling spiritual enlightenment. (This same theme is found in the hexagram or Star of David, whose downward-pointing triangle symbolizes the masculine energy, which overlays the upward-pointing triangle symbolizing the feminine energy.)[1046]

The cross is thus another symbol of the sacred Pagan and Christian Tetramorph, with the four fixed astrological Sun-signs (Taurus, Leo, Scorpio/Aquila, and Aquarius) at the end of each point, signifying the two solstices and the two equinoxes,[1047] which are themselves associated with the four Evangelists—a Christian version of the Four Regents of Hindu-Buddhist mythology.[1048]

In some mystical schools the upright beam is the *Axis Mundi* or Tree of Life (a symbol of spirit growing up from out of materiality),[1049] and the cross beam is the line separating the higher and lower natures, or the spirit plane and the earth plane.[1050] This proves the millennia old mystical symbolism of the cross: the human body is the "Tree of Life" of the Old Testament and the "cross" of the New Testament.[1051]

Early Pagan myths tell of savior-gods being sacrificed on trees at the Spring Equinox (a symbol of the victory of light over darkness),[1052] so that their "procreative" blood would run into the soil, thereby fructifying Mother-Earth in the hopes of producing a rich crop.[1053] Such tree-slain Pagan saviors include Dodonian Zeus, Marsyas, Odin, and Chrishna or Krishna.[1054] Additionally, long before the rise of Christianity countless Pagan "Sons of God" were already associated with both sacred trees and the cross, saviors such as Apollo, Wotan, Aton, Sarapis, Osiris, Attis, Buddha, Adonis, and Tammuz.[1055] The deep Pagan roots of the "Christian" cross are still evident in those biblical passages which speak of Jesus being hanged not on a cross, but on a tree, like his heathen forerunners.[1056] Its many Pagan associations are precisely why the early Christian fathers renounced the cross, and it is why it took so long to be officially embraced by the Church.[1057]

There are some 400 variations of the cross,[1058] from the Latin Cross, Celtic Cross, and Maltese Cross, to the Cross Saltire, Cross Fourchée, and Swastika. It is not known what shape Jesus' cross was,[1059] or even if it was a cross;[1060] nor it is known if he was nailed or tied to the structure, which some believe was a "T"-shaped cross known as the *Tau*.[1061]

What we do know is that the cross is the world's oldest[1062] and most universal of all cosmic symbols,[1063] with numenistic meanings and significance that transcend religion itself. See CHRIST, CHRISTIANITY, CROWN, CRUCIFIXION, GNOSTICISM, JESUS, KARMA, TETRAMORPH.

CROWN: In traditional Christianity the crown is a literal coronet worn on the head,[1064] and sometimes used throughout the Bible as a symbol indicating the "top of the head."[1065] As always, mystical Christianity picks up where the mainstream Church leaves off.

To the Christian esotericist the biblical "crown" is a symbol of the Crown Chakra, located at the top of the head, which is itself a symbol of spiritual enlightenment or Christ Consciousness, Cosmic Consciousness, Buddha Consciousness, Moses Consciousness, Asherah Consciousness, Osiris Consciousness, Isis Consciousness, Wotan Consciousness, Freya Consciousness, Mac Gréine Consciousness, Eriu Consciousness, etc.[1066]

Early Christian mystics had their own names for the Crown Chakra, including the "Crown of Rejoicing,"[1067] "Crown of Righteousness,"[1068] "Crown of Life,"[1069] "Crown of Glory,"[1070] and the "Golden Crown."[1071] Peter knew the Crown Chakra (symbolized by the royal crown) as the "crown of glory,"[1072] while Paul referred to it as the "incorruptible crown."[1073] The human skull, the site of the "Crown," is thus known to Christian mystics as the "Temple of Wisdom,"[1074] the "Holy of Holies,"[1075] or biblically as "Golgotha"[1076] or the "Upper Room."[1077]

The archetypal crown has played an important role in ancient myth, and in particular myths surrounding tree crucifixion—which was eventually replaced by cross crucifixion for the sake of convenience. Tree crucifixion was a popular element in pre-Christian myths concerning Pagan Sun-gods/Son-gods specifically. Such deities included the Phrygian savior Attis, the Greek savior Prometheus, the Nordic savior Odin, and the Hindu savior Krishna (or Chrishna). All were hanged on trees while wearing the foliage crown of each tree's respective deity. By way of the overly imaginative mythographer Mark, the first canonical Gospel writer to introduce legendary Pagan elements into the biography of our Lord,[1078] Jesus is also shown wearing the heathens' foliage crown during His crucifixion.[1079]

The Pagan crown is used in various other ways throughout the Bible. For instance, the "woman arrayed with the sun, and the moon under her feet, and upon her head a crown of 12 stars," as described in the book of Revelation,[1080] is wearing a Zodiacal crown representing the 12 Sun-signs of the astrological year, a christianization of the great Hindu Goddess Aditi,[1081] queen of the 12 astrological Sun-signs and the mother of the Sun/Son-god Surya.[1082] See CHRIST CONSCIOUSNESS, CROSS, CRUCIFIXION, UPPER ROOM.

CRUCIFIXION: In the traditional Church the Crucifixion is the literal execution of Jesus on the cross.[1083] In mystical Christianity the Crucifixion is a symbol of the death of the human ego,[1084] which combines with the human soul (the Christ;[1085] the "Sun"[1086] or "Son"[1087]) on the plane of matter (earth), but which must be sacrificed in order to re-ascend to the plan of spirit (heaven), home of God the Father—the same goal found in Buddhism.[1088] In 1847 Neander wrote of the mystical symbolism of the Crucifixion from the Gnostic-Christian viewpoint:

> *This seeming transaction symbolized the crucifixion of the soul, sunk in matter, which the Spirit of the Sun would raise up to itself.* As the crucifixion of that soul which was dispersed through all matter, served but to accomplish the destruction of the kingdom of darkness, so much more was this the effect of the seeming crucifixion of the Supreme Soul. Hence [the Gnostic Christian] Mani said, "The adversary, who was hoping to crucify the Saviour, the Father of the righteous, was crucified himself. What seemed to be done in this case is one thing; what was really done, another." *The Manichean theory, which represented the doctrine of Christ as a mere symbol*, is clearly set forth in an apocryphal account of the travels of the apostles. During the agony on the cross, Christ appears to the afflicted John, and tells him that all this is done but for the sake of the lower populace in Jerusalem. The human person of Christ now vanishes, and instead of it appears a cross of pure light, surrounded by a countless multitude of other forms, still representing, however, but one shape and one image, (*a symbol of the various forms under which the soul manifests itself, although it is in truth but one and the same.*) A divine voice, full of sweetness, issues from the cross, saying to him, "The cross of light is, for your sakes, called sometimes the Word, sometimes Christ; sometimes the Door, sometimes the Way; sometimes the Bread, sometimes the Sun; sometimes the Resurrection, sometimes Jesus; sometimes the Father, sometimes the Spirit; sometimes the Life, sometimes the Truth; sometimes Faith, and sometimes Grace."[1089]

The doctrine of the Crucifixion, being pre-Christian and universal, leads us back to its original mystical meaning and away from the modern literal one as formulated by the traditional Church. Indeed, thousands of Pagan saviors, christs, Sun/Son-gods, and god-men were said to have been crucified, among them: Adonis, Apollo, Attis, Bacchus, Buddha, Horus, Indra, Ixion, Jupiter, Krishna, Mithra, Osiris, Prometheus, Pythagoras, Quetzalcoatl, Gucumatz, Amaru, and Semiramis.[1090]

All have one thing in common: at the mystical level their crosses or trees are symbols of the human body and their crucifixions are symbolic of the death of the Ego,[1091] a spiritual act which allows for the attainment of the Kingdom of God, also known as nirvana, samadhi, satori, kensho, moksha, wu wei, self-realization, the Brahmic Splendor, Cosmic Consciousness, or Christ Consciousness. This is true at-one-ment with God, the realization of our divinity,[1092] the very basis of every religion, from Buddhism (which teaches that one must "die on the Cross of Sangsara")[1093] to Christianity (which teaches that one must "die daily"[1094] on the Cross of the Indwelling Christ).[1095] See ASCENSION, BAPTISM, BIRTH OF JESUS, CHRIST, CHRIST CONSCIOUSNESS, CROSS, DEATH OF JESUS, DIVINITY OF JESUS, JESUS, MYTH OF CHRIST, RESURRECTION OF JESUS, SON OF GOD, SON OF MAN, TRANSFIGURATION OF JESUS.

Christianity: The religion of the Indwelling Christ.

Crucifixion of Jesus.

The mystical Crown.

The Cross of Lorraine, one of hundreds of cross styles.

Miracle at Cana.

DEATH OF JESUS: In the traditional Church the death of Jesus is seen as a necessary aspect of His redemptive act upon the cross.[1096] His passing is said to have been accompanied by darkness ("until the ninth hour," or 3:00 PM), the rending of the Temple veil, an earthquake, and the opening up of the graves of the saints.[1097] Afterward His body was placed in a tomb to be attended by His female followers.[1098] Jesus was then resurrected into Heaven, but briefly returned to earth to leave His disciples one final commandment: to go out into the world and preach the Gospel.[1099]

While the orthodox Christian generally accepts this story without question, not so the mystical Christian. For one thing, he or she asks, why were these various momentous phenomena not recorded by contemporary historians living at the time? Gibbon takes up this inquiry into the earth-shaking events that were said to have occurred at the death of our Lord:

> . . . how shall we excuse the supine inattention of the Pagan and philosophic world, to those evidences which were presented by the hand of Omnipotence, not to their reason, but to their senses? During the age of Christ, of his apostles, and of their first disciples, the doctrine which they preached was confirmed by innumerable prodigies. The lame walked, the blind saw, the sick were healed, the dead were raised, daemons were expelled, and the laws of Nature were frequently suspended for the benefit of the church. But the sages of Greece and Rome turned aside from the awful spectacle, and pursuing the ordinary occupations of life and study, appeared unconscious of any alterations in the moral or physical government of the world.
>
> Under the reign of Tiberius, the whole earth, or at least a celebrated province of the Roman Empire, was involved in a praeternatural darkness of three hours. Even this miraculous event, which ought to have excited the wonder, the curiosity, and the devotion of mankind, passed without notice in an age of science and history. It happened during the lifetime of Seneca and the elder Pliny, who must have experienced the immediate effects, or received the earliest intelligence of the

prodigy. Each of these philosophers, in a laborious work, has recorded all the great phenomena of Nature, earthquakes, meteors, comets, and eclipses, which his indefatigable curiosity could collect. *Both the one and the other have omitted to mention the greatest phenomenon to which the mortal eye has been witness since the creation of the globe.*

A distinct chapter of Pliny is designed for eclipses of an extraordinary nature and unusual duration; but he contents himself with describing the singular defect of light which followed the murder of Caesar, when, during the greatest part of a year, the orb of the sun appeared pale and without splendour. This season of obscurity, which cannot surely be compared with the preternatural darkness of the Passion, had been already celebrated by most of the poets and historians of that memorable age.[1100]

What the Christian mystic perceives from such facts are numerous hints of legend, not history. Thus, in the mystical Christian Church the natural phenomena, numbers, names, literary devices, and supernatural occurrences attending the death of Jesus indicate an allegorical tale concealing profound spiritual truths, hidden knowledge, and secret wisdom.

Let us look at this topic from the viewpoint of comparative religion.

Among Jesus' nearly 1,000 titles, he was variously known as the "Lion of the Tribe of Judah,"[1101] the "Sun of Righteousness,"[1102] the "Great Physician,"[1103] the "Only Begotten Son,"[1104] the "Word,"[1105] "Wisdom,"[1106] the "Wise Master Builder,"[1107] the "Way,"[1108] the "Truth,"[1109] the "Life,"[1110] the "Prince of Peace,"[1111] the "Good Shepherd,"[1112] the "Light of the World,"[1113] "the Anointed,"[1114] "the Christ,"[1115] the "Messiah,"[1116] the "Savior of the World,"[1117] the "Way of Holiness,"[1118] and "Eternal Life."[1119]

These titles are of great interest to us, for all of them, along with the natural phenomena at our Lord's death, were prefigured in the life stories of a number of great religious teachers who came before Him; in particular Buddha—*who lived five centuries earlier.* Titcomb writes:

> At the death of Buddha, the earth trembled, the rocks were split and phantoms and spirits appeared. He descended to hell and preached to the spirits of the damned. When Buddha was buried, the coverings of the body unrolled themselves, the lid of his coffin was opened by supernatural powers, and he ascended bodily to the celestial regions. Marks on the rocks of a high mountain are shown, which are believed to be the last imprint of his footsteps in this world.

He was called the Lion of the Tribe of Sakya, the King of Righteousness, the Great Physician, the God among Gods, the Only Begotten, the Word, the All-wise, the Way, the Truth, the Life, the Intercessor, the Prince of Peace, the Good Shepherd, the Light of the World, the Anointed, the Christ, the Messiah, the Saviour of the World, the Way of Life and Immortality. Indeed in Ceylon the name of Buddha has twelve thousand synonyms.

When the time came for him to depart, he told his disciples to no longer remain together, but to go out in companies, and proclaim the doctrines he had taught them,—to found schools and monasteries, build temples, and perform acts of charity,—that they might obtain merit, and gain access to the blessed abode of Nigban, which he told them he was about to enter. The ever-faithful women were to be found at the last scene in the life of Buddha.[1120]

One must also confront the fact that many of the New Testament books, such as Luke's all-important Acts (which purports to chronicle the history of the early orthodox branch of the Church), completely lack a "theology of the cross," and never once mention anything about the atoning significance of Jesus' death.[1121] If the Master's crucifixion was a historical event, why the silence?

In the mystical Church then, the death of Jesus, like the deaths of Osiris (the ancient Egyptian savior), Attis (the ancient Phrygian savior), Lugh (the ancient Celtic savior), and Balder (the ancient Scandinavian savior), is a symbol of spiritual involution, otherwise known to the ancients as the *Aphanism* ("disappearance"); that is, the descent of spirit into matter—just as its opposite, the birth and also the resurrection of Jesus, represent spiritual evolution, or as it was known to the ancients, the *Euresis* ("finding"):[1122] the ascent of spirit back into spirit,[1123] or at-one-ment with God (Christ Consciousness), signified in the East as the Third Eye (pineal gland)—while the two thieves who died alongside Him (spiritual balance) are symbols of the anterior and posterior lobes of the pituitary gland.[1124]

Thus, to view the New Testament account of our Lord's death literally is to lead the Bible reader down a dark and confusing path from which few return. Many of the early churches were certainly aware of these occult facts, which is no doubt one reason they transferred the day of Jesus' death to March 25, the day on which the far older Pagan savior-god Attis was said to have died.[1125]

Here we have yet another of the numerous dissimilarities between the traditional Christian and the mystical Christian: the traditionalist bases his faith on the *death* of Jesus; the mystic bases his faith on the *life* of Jesus. See BUDDHA, CHRIST, CHRIST CONSCIOUSNESS, GOSPEL, JESUS, KRISHNA, MITHRA, NATIVITY, OSIRIS, PYTHAGORAS, REINCARNATION, RESURRECTION,

TEACHER OF RIGHTEOUSNESS, TRANSFIGURATION OF JESUS.

DEVIL (THE): In traditional Christianity the Devil is a title for Satan, the principle fallen angel and the arch enemy of God who destroys man through temptation.[1126] According to fundamentalist Christian mythology, he will be cast into Hell on Judgement Day.[1127] Through the syncretizing process of theocrasia the Church absorbed the concept of the Devil from early Judaism, which adopted it from the dualistic Zoroastrian religion thousands of years ago.[1128] Thus, while orthodox Christians resolutely condemn Paganism, they themselves continue to embrace and advance countless Pagan ideas and beliefs.

Identical to Satan and Lucifer, the Devil differs in Indo-European etymology only: the word derives from one of the names of the Hindu word for God, *deva* ("divine"), which is related to the English word deity, which comes from the Latin word *divus*, meaning a "god" or "goddess."[1129] The Devil's traditional horns, cloven hooves, and pointed tail were borrowed by inventive early Christian mythographers from the Greek nature-god Pan[1130] (a satyr identical to the ancient Roman nature-god Faunus, who gives us our modern word fauna).[1131]

Our Lord Jesus, the ultimate teacher of mystical spiritual doctrines, utterly rejected the idea of evil and the alleged existence of a real physical Devil-Lucifer-Satan, and asked us to do the same by practicing nonresistance to all that is negative.[1132] For thoughts are things.[1133] Thus, resisting what we perceive of as "evil" merely energizes it, using our defiant thoughts to strengthen itself into evermore realistic form.[1134]

In the mystical branch of Christianity the biblical Devil is an ancient personification of the human Ego,[1135] which, due to its self-centered atheistic nature, sees itself as separate and distinct from God. The Ego will stop at nothing to get us to take our focus off the Spiritual and put it on the Material. When the Bible speaks of multiple devils, such as the "seven devils" in Luke,[1136] mystics interpret this phrase to mean "negative habits" or "improper desires."[1137]

As Lucifer, the Devil is the "Bringer of Light" (that is, spiritual enlightenment), making him simultaneously both righteous and wicked, the *Demon est Deus Inversus* (the "Devil is God Inverted") of the ancient Mystery Schools.[1138] God himself admitted that it is he alone who creates light and darkness,[1139] and this is Pan, whose name means "all." Thus to Christian mystics the Devil is not a living being, as is taught in the traditional Church, but an invisible force, one that we know as "free will," which can be used for good or evil.[1140] Mystically this makes "Satan" and "Christ" two sides of the same coin: personal volition.

With this new understanding, the allegorical nature of Matthew's story of the "temptation of Christ" by the Devil (Ego) is now fully comprehensible *and* meaningful.[1141] See ADVERSARY, ANTICHRIST, BEAST, EGO, EGYPT, EVIL, HELL, HEROD ANTIPAS, KARMA, LOWER SELF, LUCIFER, MASS MIND, NUMBER OF THE BEAST, PHARISEES, PILATE, SATAN, SERPENT, SIN.

DIVINE MIND: Unknown in the traditional Church, Divine Mind is well-known in the mystical one, where it is held to be identical to God.[1142] As God is the Christ which indwells each one of us, our minds are all powerful, without limitations of any kind, for Mind is the essence of the Universe: it is our mind which survives death and which carries on for eternity as what we here on earth refer to as our "Spirit."

Everything begins in Spirit (cause), and then manifests on the material plane (effect). Because a piece of Divine Mind resides in us, we become what we think, just as the Old Testament writers declared.[1143] This is because, as the ancient Gnostic-Christians, stated: "God is all mind and mind is all God."[1144] Thus one of their Greek names for God was *Nous* ("Mind").[1145] And, in fact, the entire Gnostic-Christian system is based on the concept of Mind and its product: thoughts. The Gnostic Creation Myth, for instance, explains the evolution of Divine Mind like this. Spirit works through Thought (*Ennoia*) and Forethought (*Pronoia*), finally attaining enlightenment or spiritual Fullness (*Plemora*). Those who lack Wisdom (*Sophia*) find themselves in a state of Mindlessness (*Aponoia*) that can only be restored to wholeness by the divine Afterthought (*Epinoia*).[1146] Thus the earthly mind is actually a piece of the all-powerful Spirit, which operates from Heaven downward to the physical plane.

The ancient esoteric Christian teaching "as above, so below" now makes perfect sense. It is the ancient equivalent of the scientific maxim, "like attracts like," embodied in what early esotericists called the Law of Reciprocity or more commonly the Law of Attraction. This law works because everything in the visible (material) universe has a counterpart in the invisible (spiritual) universe.[1147] Thus, whatever thought is *consistently* formed in the mind ("above") eventually manifests on the physical ("below"). Or to put it another way, just as water always flows downhill, spiritual energy (thought or "heaven") always flows from the invisible down to the visible (matter or "earth").

As part of His teachings on the Law of Attraction, Jesus commented on this particular aspect in the "Lord's Prayer," instructing us to pray as follows:

> Our Father which art in heaven, hallowed be thy name. Thy kingdom come. Thy will be done, as in heaven, so in earth.[1148]

Here is the inner meaning of this scripture:

> The Divine Mind (the "Father") that is located in my spiritual center ("heaven") is sacred. Through this mind, my perfect life ("kingdom") will manifest on the physical plane. For the Law is that whatever is commanded on the spiritual level ("heaven") will be brought forth on the physical level ("earth").[1149]

In the Gospel of Matthew, Jesus spells out the Law in no uncertain terms:

> Verily I say unto you, whatsoever ye shall bind on earth shall be bound in heaven: and whatsoever ye shall loose on earth shall be loosed in heaven. Again I say unto you, that if two of you shall agree on earth as touching any thing that they shall ask, it shall be done for them of my Father which is in heaven.[1150]

According to our Lord this amazing spiritual power is one of the great "Keys to the Kingdom of Heaven," which He gave to Peter:

> And I will give unto thee the keys of the kingdom of heaven: and whatsoever thou shalt bind on earth shall be bound in heaven: and whatsoever thou shalt loose on earth shall be loosed in heaven.[1151]

In more recent times philosophers such as George Berkeley have held that "the Universe is permeated by and governed by Mind." This means, as quantum physics now shows, that material objects are nothing but "fabrications of the mind."[1152]

This being true, Divine Mind, God the Father, has provided us with the greatest gift: the "supernatural" power of thought (known to Christians as "faith"), enabling us to control and design our life, our circumstances, and our very fate.[1153] This is because, as every spiritual master knows, matter is energy and energy is created by Mind. Without Mind there can be neither.[1154] In short, the mind (spirit) controls biology (body), both the implications and the applications of which were superbly taught and demonstrated by our Lord.[1155] See CONSCIOUS MIND, CROWN, GOD, SUBCONSCIOUS MIND, SUPERCONSCIOUS MIND.

DIVINITY OF JESUS: In the traditional Church the divinity of Jesus is considered of paramount importance. Here, Jesus and only Jesus is divine; He is the only Christ, the "Only Begotten Son," the only Son of God—born of a virgin via the Holy Spirit, without an earthly father.[1156]

But this is not what the New Testament writers, including two of the 12 Apostles, say about our Lord. Preserving the original pre-Christian tradition concerning Jesus' real parents, and in particular His biological father, Matthew, for example, shows Jesus' neighbors asking:

> *Is not this the carpenter's son? Is not his mother called Mary? and his brethren, James, and Joses, and Simon, and Judas?*[1157]

Luke writes:

Now *his parents* went to Jerusalem every year at the feast of the passover.[1158]

Mary herself refers to Joseph as Jesus' father:

> And when they saw him [alone at the Temple], they were amazed: and his mother said unto him, "*Son*, why hast thou thus dealt with us? behold, *thy father and I* have sought thee sorrowing."[1159]

Luke again writes:

> And Jesus himself began to be about thirty years of age, being (*as was supposed*) *the son of Joseph*.[1160]

Luke:

> And all bare witness of him, and wondered at the gracious words which proceeded out of his mouth. And they said, "*Is not this Joseph's son?*"[1161]

Our Gnostic mystic John the Evangelist[1162] records an incident in which Philip introduces Nathanael to Jesus, not as "the son of Mary," but as "the son of Joseph":

> Philip findeth Nathanael, and saith unto him, "We have found him, of whom Moses in the law, and the prophets, did write, *Jesus of Nazareth, the son of Joseph*."[1163]

John also left us the words of Jesus' neighbors:

> And they said, "*Is not this Jesus, the son of Joseph, whose father and mother we know?*"[1164]

Revealingly, Mark refers to our Lord's siblings not as "half brothers" and "half sisters" (as the traditional Church does), but as *full* "brothers" and *full* "sisters":

> Is not this the carpenter, the son of Mary, the brother of James, and Joses, and of Juda, and Simon? and are not his sisters here with us?[1165]

The unknown author of Hebrews makes numerous references to Jesus as "this man":

> For *this man* was counted worthy of more glory than Moses, inasmuch as he who hath builded the house hath more honour than the house.[1166]

> But *this man*, because he continueth ever, hath an unchangeable priesthood.[1167]

> But *this man*, after he had offered one sacrifice for sins for ever, sat down on the right hand of God.[1168]

As for Jesus being "the one and only Christ," Paul says:

> Christ is all, and *in all*.[1169]

And Jesus could not be the "only begotten son of God" because John writes that:

> But *as many as received him, to them gave he power to become the sons of God.*[1170]

> Behold, what manner of love the Father hath bestowed upon us, that we should be called the sons of God. . . . Beloved, *now are we the sons of God.*[1171]

Paul makes it very clear that:

> *For as many as are led by the Spirit of God, they are the sons of God.*[1172]

Jesus Himself says that we are all gods and goddesses, with the divine potential to do greater works than He did:

> Is it not written in your law, "I said '*Ye are gods*'"? If he called them gods, unto whom the word of God came, and the scripture cannot be broken.[1173]

> Verily, verily, I say unto you, *He that believeth on me, the works that I do shall he do also; and greater works than these shall he do*; because I go unto my Father.[1174]

The Church Fathers were familiar with this view as well. Eusebius writes that both Jesus and His brother James were known as "the children of Joseph," and that Joseph was in turn known as "the father of Christ."[1175] He does not say stepfather or adoptive-father, but "the father." Many more biblical illustrations of this sort of thing could be provided.

If every believer is a son of God, possessed of the Christ, what then does the divinity of Jesus signify?

In the mystical Church Jesus is seen as a natural born, though fully spiritually enlightened, human being who serves as a living example of what all men and women can be. If He were an immortal Pagan-like deity, as the traditional Church depicts Him, this would not be possible: being a god or God, He would have an enormous spiritual advantage over mortal men and women; a hurtle that humanity could never overcome let alone approach. As we saw above, He repudiated this false dogmatic view in the most emphatic terms.[1176] Thus, He incarnated as a human being so that "the men of earth might see the possibilities of man."[1177] In *The Aquarian Gospel of Jesus the Christ* our Lord says:

> I come to manifest the Christ to men . . .[1178] *What I am, all men will be* . . .[1179] *What I have done all men can do . . . for every man is God made flesh.*[1180]

See BIRTH OF JESUS, CHRIST, CHRISTIANITY, GOSPEL, NATIVITY, ONLY BEGOTTEN SON, SON OF GOD, SON OF MAN, THEOSIS, WAY OF THE LORD, YOKE OF JESUS.

DOOR: In the traditional Church Jesus is the symbolic door that leads to redemption and salvation.[1181] This is based on the following passages from John:

> Then said Jesus unto them again, "Verily, verily, I say unto you, I AM the door of the sheep. All that ever came before me are thieves and robbers: but the sheep did not hear them. I AM the door: by me if any man enter in, he shall be saved, and shall go in and out, and find pasture."[1182]

In the mystical Christian Church, however, it is not Jesus the man who is the "door." It is Christ the spirit, for when He spoke of "Himself," he was not referring to the human being named "Jesus," as He repeatedly stated. He was speaking of the Indwelling Christ, the divine spark that resides in *every* individual;[1183] "the true Light, which lighteth every man that cometh into the world," as John put it.[1184]

The phrase that unveils this, the inner meaning, in the scripture above is "I AM," which is one of the Bible's many codewords for the Higher Self or Christ Within. Hindus know the I AM as "Aum" or "Om," the Persians as "Hom,"[1185] the Jews as "Amam," the Tibetans as "Hum,"[1186] the ancient Egyptians as "Amon," Gnostic-Christians as the "Logos," and the ancient Greeks, Romans, and Christians as "the Amen."[1187] Thus, in the mystical Church the "door" is not only a symbol of the mental-spiritual portal that leads to Christ Consciousness[1188] (Paul's "mind of Christ"),[1189] it is the divine human Soul, for this is Christ itself.[1190] See CHRIST, CHRIST CONSCIOUSNESS, DIVINITY OF JESUS, JESUS, SON OF GOD.

DOVE: In the mainstream Church the dove is a symbol of the Holy Spirit descending onto Jesus at the moment of His baptism.[1191] As the Evangelist John wrote of this event:

> And John [the Baptist] bare record, saying, "I saw the Spirit descending from heaven like a dove, and it abode upon him. And I knew him not: but he that sent me to baptize with water, the same said unto me, 'Upon whom thou shalt see the Spirit descending, and remaining on him, the same is he which baptizeth with the Holy Ghost.'"[1192]

The confusion surrounding the dogmatic orthodox view of Jesus' baptism hints at a deeper mystical meaning: aside from the problematic Adoptionist issue, as well as the facts that the Virgin Mary, the Apostles, and the redeemed thief who was crucified with our Lord, are never shown being baptized, John the Baptist is said to have practiced a "baptism of repentance for the remission of sins."[1193] Yet, Jesus was sinless.[1194] Why then did He require water baptism by John? In The Gospel of the Nazoreans, when His mother and brothers encourage Jesus to go with them to have their sins cleansed by John the Baptist, our Lord replies:

> In what way have I sinned? I have not. Why then should I be baptized by him?[1195]

A clue to this mystery comes from the ancient arcana regarding goddess-worship and the dove.

In the mystical Church the dove is a symbol of the Divine Spark of God, the Indwelling Christ, descending into Mankind.[1196] Ancient Pagans viewed the human spirit as female, which is why in pre-Christian times the "feminine" dove was associated with the Earth-Mother-Goddess, not the Heavenly-Father-God. In the Near East, for example, the dove was the sacred animal of the goddess Ishtar, in Phoenicia of Astarte, in Greece of Aphrodite,[1197] and in Rome of Venus Columba (later Christianized as the fictitious "Saint Columba").[1198] Living doves were raised and cared for by her followers in goddess temples, carved on her monuments, and generously portrayed on her coins and jewelry.[1199]

Another important dove-connected goddess was Sophia, the Greek female deity of wisdom (in Judaism known as Shekina, in Rome as Sapientia), whose cult imaged the dove as a symbol of the Hieros Gamos or "Sacred Union" between the

Divine Feminine (Spirit) and the Divine Masculine (Matter). Unlike Western Christians, Eastern Christians understood the spiritual "wisdom" of the goddess and her holy bird, which is why they erected one of the most beautiful shrines in the world to her: Hagia Sophia at Constantinople. Sophia's sacred dove motif was so popular that the Christian Church had little choice but to adopt it, which it did, transforming the gentle bird into a symbol of the Holy Spirit[1200]—itself an overt Christianization of the Mother-Goddess or Holy Female.[1201]

Christians also borrowed Jesus' statement, "Be ye therefore wise as serpents, and harmless as doves,"[1202] from Paganism. Originally this sentence was part of an invocation to the Syrian Mother-Goddess, whose followers saw the dove as an emblem of "life." This type of symbolism was derived directly from Pagan iconography, such as that found across the Roman Empire, which portrayed Spirit as a dove descending from the Great Mother in order to vivify the human body.[1203]

To this day mystics of all religions continue to view the New Testament dove as a symbol of the spiritual eye or Third Eye,[1204] located in the forehead between the two physical eyes. During deep meditation one will see this "eye of light," the activating principle of the Holy Ghost, as a gold halo encircling a blue sphere, at whose center shines a brilliant white five-pointed star (the points appearing to some as "wings"). This experience, in which the individual becomes enlightened to the fact that he and God are one,[1205] is what biblical writers describe as "the Holy Ghost descending in a bodily shape like a dove."[1206] This is the attainment of Christ Consciousness, the "Mind of Christ,"[1207] and like its symbol, the dove, it is itself spiritual peace and purity;[1208] one that bestows profound wisdom on the recipient.[1209]

The sacred dove of the old Pagan Mother-Goddess continues to be venerated in the Church under the Christianized title, *Columba Spiritus Sancti*: "Dove of the Holy Spirit."[1210] See BAPTISM, CHRIST, GODDESS, HOLY SPIRIT.

The Trinity, with the Sacred Dove of the Pagan Goddess at the center representing the Holy Spirit.

"The controversy which is so perseveringly carried on in our own day between supernaturalists and rationalists . . . rests on the failure to recognise the allegorical nature of all religion." — ARTHUR SCHOPENHAUER, 1876

EARS: According to literalistic orthodox Christianity, when Jesus uses the word ears, as in "he who has ears to hear, let him hear,"[1211] He is referring to our physical ears. In mystical Christianity, however, the Lord is referring here not to the physical ones, but to the Inner Ear or "Third Ear," meaning spiritual or inner perception (intuition) as opposed to intellectual or outer perception (tuition, using the two physical ears).[1212] Augustine wrote:

> *God speaks with a man not by means of some audible creature dinning in his ears*, so that atmospheric vibrations connect Him that makes with him that hears the sound, nor even by means of a spiritual being with the semblance of a body, such as we see in dreams or similar states; for even in this case He speaks as if to the ears of the body, because it is by means of the semblance of a body He speaks, and with the appearance of a real interval of space,—for visions are exact representations of bodily objects. Not by these, then, does God speak, but by the truth itself, if any one is prepared to *hear with the mind rather than with the body*. For He speaks to that part of man which is better than all else that is in him, and than which God Himself alone is better.
>
> For since man is most properly understood (or, if that cannot be, then, at least, believed) to be *made in God's image*, no doubt it is that part of him by which he rises above those lower parts he has in common with the beasts, which *brings him nearer to the Supreme*. But since the mind itself, though naturally capable of reason and intelligence, is disabled by besotting and inveterate vices not merely from delighting and abiding in, but even from tolerating His unchangeable light, until it has been gradually healed, and renewed, and made capable of such felicity, it had, in the first place, to be impregnated with faith, and so purified.
>
> And that in this faith it might advance the more confidently towards the truth, the truth itself, God, God's Son, assuming humanity without destroying His divinity, established and founded this faith, that there might be *a way for man to man's*

God through a God-man. For this is the Mediator between God and men, *the man Christ Jesus. For it is as man that He is the Mediator and the Way.* Since, if the way lieth between him who goes, and the place whither he goes, there is hope of his reaching it; but if there be no way, or if he know not where it is, what boots it to know whither he should go? Now the only way that is infallibly secured against all mistakes, is when *the very same person is at once God and man, God our end, man our way.*[1213]

See EYES, GNOSIS, GNOSTICISM, THEOSIS, THIRD EAR, THIRD EYE.

EAST (THE): In traditional Christianity east is merely the direction east, the place of the Sunrise.[1214] Mystical Christianity digs deep below this literal surface view. Here, the east is a symbol of the rising awareness that the Higher Self is an actual piece of God—that is, made in the image of God.[1215]

For countless millennia the Higher Self, also known as Christ or more accurately the Christ, has been symbolized by the Sun, which was personified in the figures of thousands of major Sun-gods, minor solar-deities, saviors, messiahs, lords, and sons of God, including Jesus, whom the Bible overtly refers to as "the Sun of Righteousness."[1216] In short, the rising Sun in the east represents the path of the human soul as it traverses upward across the "sky" of spiritual evolution (the 12 Sun-signs of the Zodiac) toward at-one-ment with God.[1217] See CHRIST, CHRIST CONSCIOUSNESS, CHRISTMAS, NATIVITY, STAR OF BETHLEHEM, SUN, SUN OF RIGHTEOUSNESS, VIRGIN BIRTH, VIRGO, WISE MEN.

ECCLESIA: A Greek word meaning "assembly," but mistranslated by King James' English scribes as "church."[1218] In my literary works I use the term Ecclesia to indicate the mainstream (institutionalized) Christian Church as opposed to the less conventional, unorthodox, independent, free-thinking, so-called "heterodox" Christian denominations, sects, and cults;[1219] that is, the mystical branches.

The Ecclesia, whether it be Catholic or Protestant, has ruled Christianity (politically, and often ruthlessly) since it began to take form shortly after Jesus' Ascension. The great irony is that Jesus Christ, after whom the ecclesiastical Christian Church was named, espoused a decidedly unconventional, unecclesiastical spirituality, one He encapsulated in what He called "the Gospel of the Kingdom,"[1220] an informal creed that was in stark contrast to what the Church would later teach in His name, and which—confusing the message with the messenger—they still wrongfully refer to as "the Gospel of Jesus Christ."[1221]

Indeed, not only were Jesus' esoteric teachings considered iconoclastic by contemporary orthodox Jewish authorities (and later by orthodox Christian authorities—who labeled them "heresy"),[1222] but His "heterodoxical" doctrines concerning the oneness of God and Man[1223] were actually what led to His execution on the cross,[1224] for in Mosaic Law, this concept, Theosis or "God in Man,"[1225] was considered blasphemy,[1226] and was punishable by death.[1227]

While in traditional Christianity Jesus was the literal founder of the religion and its corresponding orthodox Church (the Ecclesia), in mystical Christianity it is held that He had nothing to do with either this or the subsequent development of "the Gospel of Jesus Christ"—which was not only wholly unknown to Him, but would have been completely alien and even repugnant to Him.

According to Jesus' own words, even though He was extremely critical of the old religion (Judaism),[1228] He did not intend to overturn it, nor did He intend to create a new faith in His name—not Christianity or any other religion:[1229]

> Think not that I am come to destroy the law [of Moses], or the prophets [Judaism]: I am not come to destroy, but to fulfil.[1230]

Indeed, as His Essene-inspired Sermon on the Mount patently illustrates,[1231] the Lord's intention rather was to initiate a return to a more mystical form of spirituality, one based on love; free of the pseudorighteousness, dogmatic formalism, pathological creeds, petrified rites, empty ceremonialism, censorious diatribes, and imperious fundamentalism of the religious Pharisees,[1232] militaristic Herodians,[1233] and political Sadducees,[1234] whom Jesus is shown repeatedly cursing, damning, and vilifying.[1235] See APOSTLES, CHRIST, CHRISTIANITY, CHURCH, GNOSTICISM, JESUS, PHARISEES, WAY OF THE LORD.

EDEN: In traditional Christianity Eden is a literal place where God placed Adam and Eve prior to the Fall of Humanity and the onset of Original Sin.[1236] In mystical Christianity Eden is a symbol of spiritual wisdom and perfected godly love. Thus Swedenborg says:

> And Jehovah God planted a garden eastward in Eden, and there he put the man whom he had formed. By a garden is signified intelligence, by Eden, love, by the east, the Lord: consequently, by the garden of Eden eastward, is signified the intelligence of the celestial man, which flows in by love from the Lord.[1237]

Hebrew scholar Isaac Myer writes that

> Eden or Paradise was considered by the learned of the ancient Israelites as the place of understanding and Wisdom, the Intellect. . . . [Likewise, the Zohar says:] "The higher wisdom is also called, the Higher Eden."[1238]

According to Lewis H. Berens, the 17th-Century Christian mystic Gerrard Winstanley "came to regard the whole Biblical narrative as an allegory":

> The Creation is mankind. The Garden of Eden is the mind of man, which he describes as originally filled with herbs and pleasant plants, "as love, joy, peace, humility, delight, and purity of life." The serpent he holds to be self-love, the forbidden fruit to be "selfishness," following the promptings of which "the whole garden becomes a stinking dunghill of weeds, and brings forth nothing but pride, envy, discontent, disobedience, and the whole actings of the spirit and power of darkness."[1239]

In short, "Eden" is an interior, mental (spiritual) place, not a physical one; which is why its exact geographical location has never been found—and never will. See ADAM, EGYPT, EVE, GARDEN OF EDEN, SERPENT, TREE OF LIFE.

EGO: From the Latin word *ego*, meaning "I." In mystical Christianity (as opposed to the meaning used in modern psychology) the Ego is identical to the biblical Satan/the Devil/Lucifer. Thus in the East the Ego is called the *Chit-jada granthi*, the "knot" that connects the sentient Self (spirituality or God) with the insentient physical body (materiality or Satan).[1240]

Occultly, the "Crucifixion" is meant to be that of the Ego,[1241] which is attached to the physical body: the dissolving of our Lower Self, the godless, self-centered aspect of human nature, which either ignores or disdains God, and believes that we are separate from Him. Sadly, the latter idea, which goes completely contrary to Jesus' teachings on the at-one-ment of God and Man, is still very much alive in many Ego-centered Christian denominations.

By "crucifying" the atheistic Ego, or what Paul called "our old man," we are "born again" and realize our oneness with God.[1242] We are then free to live out of the Higher Self, the Indwelling Christ,[1243] the Great I AM,[1244] where happiness, health, and prosperity reign.[1245] Such doctrines reveal that both Jesus and Paul possessed a deep knowledge of Buddhism (and in particular Hathayoga),[1246] one of whose primary goals is the extinction of the Ego.[1247] See ADVERSARY, ANTICHRIST, BEAST, BUDDHA, DEVIL, EGYPT, ENLIGHTENMENT, HELL, HEROD ANTIPAS, HIGHER SELF, JESUS, LOWER SELF, LUCIFER, MASS MIND, NUMBER OF THE BEAST, PAUL, PHARISEES, PILATE, SATAN, SERPENT, SIN, SILENT YEARS, THEOSIS, WAY OF THE LORD.

EGYPT: In traditional Christianity Egypt is of interest primarily because of its connection with the Exodus of Moses[1248] and the infant Jesus.[1249] In mystical Christianity, however, Egypt is an important symbol of the Lower Self or Ego, also known occultly as Satan, the Devil, Lucifer, or the Adversary, the opposite of the Higher Self or Spirit, also known occultly as God, the Son/Sun, and the Christ.

Thus, esoterically Egypt is "the land of darkness," that is, of spiritual ignorance, and also of material consciousness, as opposed to "the land of light" (symbolically Israel), that is, of spiritual enlightenment and spiritual consciousness.[1250] The word implies "outer darkness" or "wilderness of thought."[1251] This is denoted by the ancient Egyptians' own name for their country: *Keme* or *Khem*, meaning "dark earth"[1252] or "the Black Land."[1253] As such, biblically and mystically speaking, the ancient Egyptians symbolize the lower traits of the physical plane (darkness), in opposition to the Israelites who symbolized the higher traits of the spiritual plane (light). Kingsford and Maitland write:

> In denoting the world and the body, Egypt denotes the lessons to be derived from both of these, the learning of which is indispensable to the soul's development. . . . The ladder of evolution must be climbed painfully and with labour from the lowest step again and again, for each fresh branch of experience that is necessary for the soul's full development.[1254]

Swedenborg noted that:

> By Egypt is signified the natural man who trusts in his own strength . . . [Egypt also has the symbolic meaning of] science and reasoning from self-derived intelligence, and thus the falsification of the truth of the Word . . .[1255]

Among Christian mystics the Exodus of Moses from Egypt is especially revealing, for here the African country is seen as an allegory of the ascending progression of the human soul from the depths of materialism and earthly desire upward toward salvation in Spirit.[1256] This image, of soul evolution, has often been mythologized as the archetypal "Son-coming-out-of-Egypt" legend. The New Testament has retained elements of this Pagan myth, for example, in the Gospel of Matthew: "Out of Egypt have I called my son."[1257] This passage takes on an entirely new meaning for those who read it with the Third Eye (intuition) rather than the two physical eyes (tuition). See ADVERSARY, ANTICHRIST, BEAST, BETHLEHEM, DEVIL, EGO, ENLIGHTENMENT, EXODUS, GODS AND GODDESSES, ISRAEL, HELL, JERUSALEM, LOWER SELF, LUCIFER, MASS MIND, MOSES, NUMBER OF THE BEAST, PILATE, SATAN, SERPENT, SIN.

ELIAS (ELIJAH): In traditional Christianity Elias (in Hebrew, Elijah) was a 9th-Century B.C., miracle-working prophet from Gilead[1258] who fought against Hebrew syncretism (the blending of Paganism with what is now known as

Judaism), and who, because of this, was later hailed as the "messenger of the Lord."[1259] In mystical Christianity he is a symbol of the awakening of our Higher Self. This gives the occult meaning of the phrase "the Lord's Messenger."[1260]

Many mystical Christian schools embrace, or at least accept the possibility of, reincarnation, and hold that as the "forerunner of Christ" John the Baptist was Elias reincarnated. The canonical words of Jesus indicate as much:

> And his disciples asked him, saying, "Why then say the scribes that 'Elias must first come'?" And Jesus answered and said unto them, "Elias truly shall first come, and restore all things. *But I say unto you, that Elias is come already, and they knew him not*, but have done unto him whatsoever they listed. Likewise shall also the Son of man suffer of them." *Then the disciples understood that he spake unto them of John the Baptist.*[1261]

Ancient Gnostic-Christians held the same view. In their book known as Pistis Sophia ("Faith Wisdom"), Jesus says:

> It came to pass, when I had passed through the midst of the rulers of the aeons, that I looked down on the world of men, by order of the first mystery; I found Elizabeth, mother of John the Baptist, before she had conceived him; I cast into her a power which I had received from the hand of the little Iao, the good, who is in the midst, that he might preach before me and prepare my way, and baptise in the water of the remission of sins. This power, then, is in the body of John.
>
> Moreover, in the region of the soul of the rulers, destined to receive it, I found the soul of the prophet Elias, in the aeons of the sphere, and I took him, and receiving his soul also, I brought it to the virgin of light, and she gave it to her receivers; they brought it to the sphere of the rulers, and cast it into the womb of Elizabeth. Wherefore the power of the little Iao, who is in the midst, and the soul of Elias the prophet, are united with the body of John the Baptist. For this cause have ye been in doubt aforetime, when I said unto you, "John said, 'I am not the Christ'"; and ye said unto me, "It is written in the Scripture, that when the Christ shall come, Elias will come before him, and prepare his way." And I, when ye had said this unto me, replied unto you, "Elias verily is come, and hath prepared all things, according as it is written; and they have done unto him whatsoever they would." And when I perceived that ye did not understand that I had spoken concerning the soul

of Elias united with John the Baptist, I answered you openly and face to face with the words, "If ye will receive it, John the Baptist is Elias who, I said, was for to come."[1262]

Additionally, mystics around the world, Christian, Pagan, and Jewish alike, believe that Jesus was Elisha reincarnated, and that Elisha was to Elias as Joshua was to Moses: a disciple and successor to his elder, one who performed many miracles[1263] and became the "spiritual guide of the people."[1264] If the mystical Christian Church is correct, then Jesus and John the Baptist developed a soul-bond in a previous lifetime together around 900 B.C., with Elias-John acting as guru and Elisha-Jesus as his student. Occult biblical evidence for this comes from numerous scriptures. For example, the following is from 1 Kings:

> And the Lord said unto him [Elias-Elijah-John the Baptist], "Go, return on thy way to the wilderness of Damascus: and when thou comest, anoint Hazael to be king over Syria: And Jehu the son of Nimshi shalt thou anoint to be king over Israel: and Elisha [Jesus] the son of Shaphat of Abelmeholah shalt thou anoint to be prophet in thy room." . . . So he departed thence, and found Elisha the son of Shaphat, who was plowing with twelve yoke of oxen before him, and he with the twelfth: and Elijah passed by him, and cast his mantle upon him.[1265]

From this it is clear to Christian mystics that God appointed Elias to be the guru (teacher) of Elisha. Elias selects Elisha as he works, just as Jesus would later select His Apostles as they worked. The "twelve yoke of oxen" symbolize the future 12 Apostles with whom Jesus would plow the human soul. And the phrase "cast his mantle upon him" is an esoteric reference to initiation or spiritual baptism, in which one is officially made a student of a teacher.[1266]

Just before Elias' death the following event occurred, as recorded in 2 Kings. It shows the depth of the soulmate relationship between Jesus (Elisha) and John the Baptist (Elias or Elijah), one which spanned lifetimes and thousands of years:

> And it came to pass, when the Lord would take up Elijah into heaven by a whirlwind, that Elijah went with Elisha from Gilgal. And Elijah said unto Elisha, "Tarry here, I pray thee; for the Lord hath sent me to Bethel." And Elisha said unto him, "As the Lord liveth, and as thy soul liveth, I will not leave thee" . . .
> And it came to pass, when they were gone over [the River] Jordan, that Elijah said unto Elisha, "Ask what I shall do for thee, before I be taken away from thee." And Elisha said, "I

pray thee, let a double portion of thy spirit be upon me." And he said, "Thou hast asked a hard thing: nevertheless, if thou see me when I am taken from thee, it shall be so unto thee; but if not, it shall not be so."

And it came to pass, as they still went on, and talked, that, behold, there appeared a chariot of fire, and horses of fire, and parted them both asunder; and Elijah went up by a whirlwind into heaven. And Elisha saw it, and he cried, "My father, my father, the chariot of Israel, and the horsemen thereof." And he saw him no more: and he took hold of his own clothes, and rent them in two pieces.

He took up also the mantle of Elijah that fell from him, and went back, and stood by the bank of Jordan; And he took the mantle of Elijah that fell from him, and smote the waters, and said, "Where is the Lord God of Elijah?" and when he also had smitten the waters, they parted hither and thither: and Elisha went over.

And when the sons of the prophets which were to view at Jericho saw him, they said, "The spirit of Elijah doth rest on Elisha." And they came to meet him, and bowed themselves to the ground before him.[1267]

The "double portion of thy spirit" is another occult reference to the guru-devotee relationship between Elias (Elijah) and Elisha.

Some 900 years later the two would again reincarnate together, this time near Jerusalem—and, it would seem, as Essenes[1268]—in order to begin their God-ordained mission of baptizing with water (Earth) and fire (Spirit); an attempt to rid religion of its rigid masculine formalism, literalism, and dogmatism, and reintroduce the Divine Feminine virtues of love, spirituality, peace, and forgiveness.

Because they reject reincarnation, modern traditional Christians often cannot understand how John the Baptist (Elias) could be superior to Jesus (Elisha); how he could be the teacher of our Lord. They are used to thinking of Jesus as God (superior) and John as merely human (inferior). But this is not how Jesus viewed their relationship. In the Gospel of Luke the Master says:

> For I say unto you, among those that are born of women there is not a greater prophet than John the Baptist.[1269]

Jesus was a prophet. Thus He is including Himself here as one who was below John in spiritual ranking.

Jesus not only publicly identified John the Baptist as Elias,[1270] but it was

Elias who appeared to Him during His Transfiguration,[1271] at which time the Lord's "face did shine as the sun," for he is the Sun. And mystically, what is the Sun? It is the universal symbol of the Indwelling Christ (the "Only Begotten Son" possessed by all). And the "high mountain" where the transfiguration took place is, like the "Upper Room,"[1272] another symbol of the top of the human head, site of the Crown Chakra or Christ Consciousness: spiritual enlightenment.[1273] See BAPTISM, BORN AGAIN, CHRIST CONSCIOUSNESS, ELISHA, JESUS, JOHN THE BAPTIST, REBIRTH, REINCARNATION, SON OF GOD, UPPER ROOM.

ELISHA: In the traditional Church Elisha was a wonderworking prophet of Israel, the son of Shaphat,[1274] whose biography has been overly embellished with marvelous legends and ancient mythic elements.[1275] In the mystical Church Elisha is a symbol of the Indwelling Christ, and was, in fact, a pre-Christian incarnation of Jesus and a devotee of (in Greek) Elias (in Hebrew, Elijah), His guru or teacher—a former incarnation of John the Baptist. As Elias and Elisha, the two worked as a team in combating the empty formalism of Paganism, then reincarnated together nearly a millennium later in Jerusalem to continue their work.[1276] Jesus mentions Elisha in the Gospel of Luke,[1277] while He discusses Elias in all three of the Synoptic Gospels.[1278] See BORN AGAIN, ELIAS, JESUS, JOHN THE BAPTIST, REBIRTH, REINCARNATION, SON OF GOD, SON OF MAN.

ENLIGHTENMENT: In the mainstream Church the word enlightenment, when it is even recognized, simply indicates the personal revelation that Jesus is the Messiah and Savior of all mankind. In the mystical Church this word has much richer and deeper meanings.

Here enlightenment (literally "the light within") is the realization that we are an individualization, an expression, a manifestation, a differentiation, an extension of God; that there is no such thing as "death" and that we are immortal; that we are one with all things, and in particular with God; and that our Higher Self, the Supreme Self, the Indwelling Christ,[1279] is in fact God, the Father, Divine Mind.[1280] In other words, when you realize in your soul that you are a god, as Jesus taught, you have attained enlightenment.[1281] John, the Church's Gnostic-Christian Evangelist,[1282] borrowing from the ancient Egyptians,[1283] said it best: the Christ is the "true light which lighteth every man that cometh into the world."[1284] Comprehending the meaning of this "light," and living it, is spiritual enlightenment.

Enlightenment is the opposite of spiritual darkness, ignorance, and immaturity, as well as scientific atheism. The only thing that can block us from enlightenment is the Ego (Satan), which being vain and dualistic, sees "you" as being separate from God.

Throughout the Bible enlightenment is variously symbolized as light, a flame, fire, candles, and more generally the ever constant, ever circling, ever present Sun. Thus in Psalms, God is called "my light and my salvation,"[1285] while in Malachi the Indwelling Christ is referred to as the "Sun of Righteousness."[1286] Psalms also gives us this beautiful passage:

> For thou wilt light my candle: the Lord my God will enlighten my darkness.[1287]

As enlightenment takes place in the mind, ancient artists portrayed enlightened individuals with nimbuses, halos, or bright auras around their heads, Christian symbols of what Hindus know as the "Crown Chakra,"[1288] what mystics call the "Temple of Wisdom,"[1289] and what Peter referred to as the "crown of glory."[1290] Paul called attaining enlightenment "having the mind of Christ,"[1291] and also "the helmet of salvation."[1292]

The mainstream Christian word for enlightenment is indeed "salvation," the mystical Christian term is "gnosis."[1293] Both are identical or similar in meaning to the related words: nirvana, satori, epiphany, bodhi, theophany, theaphany, mar'eh, wu wei, hierophany, tapas, kensho, Abraham Consciousness, Moses Consciousness, Krishna Consciousness, Krishnahood, Buddha Consciousness, Buddhahood, Christ Consciousness, Christhood, Cosmic Consciousness, self-realization, ananda, sat-chit-ananda, moksha, hazon, kaivalya, christophany, mukti, yogasema, apavarga, darshan, sukha, fana, illumination, turiya, and samadhi.

In very general terms all of these indicate the same thing: the realization that our Higher Self, the omnipresent indestructible Indwelling Christ, is one with God. Jesus not only said that we are one with God,[1294] but that we literally are gods.[1295] Again, understanding this, knowing this with full undeviating faith, is true enlightenment. See CHRIST, CHRIST CONSCIOUSNESS, CROWN, DIVINE MIND, GOD, SALVATION, SUN, THEOSIS, TRANSFIGURATION OF JESUS.

ENOCH (BOOK OF): In traditional Christianity the book of Enoch is part of the Apocrypha, which has been "understandably" banned from the Bible.[1296] In mystical Christianity the book of Enoch, though not mentioned by name in the Bible, is important for at least one very good reason: it was acknowledged, endorsed, and loved by Jesus, his brother Jude, by Paul, and by many of the early Church Fathers. Our Lord, for example, paraphrases it on numerous occasions, while his sibling Jude quotes it verbatim.[1297] It is said that Paul carried the book of Enoch with him wherever he went, using it as a sort of pocket reference, while the earliest Fathers—important Church leaders such as Barnabas, Athenagoras, Clement of Alexandria, Irenaeus, and Tertullian—accepted it as literal scripture.[1298]

Below are the secret passages in which Jesus cites this outlawed book, but which are hiding in plain sight in the Bible. The corresponding words and elements in Enoch are italicized:

- Jesus: The water that I shall give him shall be in him a well of

water springing up into everlasting life.[1299]
• Enoch: All *the thirsty drank, and were filled with wisdom*, having their habitation with the righteous, the elect, and the holy.[1300]

• Jesus: That ye may be called the children of light.[1301]
• Enoch: And now will I call the spirits of the good from *the generation of light*, and will change those who have been born in darkness; who have not in their bodies been recompensed with glory, as their faith may have merited.[1302]

• Jesus: Ye also shall sit upon twelve thrones, judging the twelve tribes of Israel.[1303]
• Enoch: I will bring them into the splendid light of those who love my holy name: and *I will place each of them on a throne of glory, of glory peculiarly his own.*[1304]

• Jesus: Woe unto that man through whom the Son of man is betrayed! It had been good for that man if he had not been born.[1305]
• Enoch: Where will the habitation of sinners be? and where the place of rest for those who have rejected the Lord of spirits? *It would have been better for them, had they never been born.*[1306]

• Jesus: The Father judgeth no man, but hath committed all judgment unto the son.[1307]
• Enoch: He sat upon the throne of his glory; and *the principal part of the judgment was assigned to him, the Son of man.*[1308]

• Jesus: Between us and you there is a great gulf fixed.[1309]
• Enoch: And in the same way likewise are *sinners separated when they die*, and are buried in the earth; judgment not overtaking them in their lifetime. Here *their souls are separated*. Moreover, abundant is their suffering until the time of the great judgment, the castigation, and the torment of those who eternally execrate, whose souls are punished and bound there for ever. And thus has it been from the beginning of the world. Thus has *there existed a separation between the souls* of those who utter complaints, and of those who watch for their destruction, to slaughter them in the day of sinners.[1310]

• Jesus: And every one that hath forsaken houses, or brethren, or sisters, or father, or mother, or wife, or children, or lands, for my name's sake, shall receive an hundredfold, and shall inherit everlasting life.[1311]

• Enoch: And the fourth [angel], who presides over repentance, and the hope of those who *will inherit eternal life*, is Phanuel.[1312]

• Jesus: In my Father's house are many mansions.[1313]
• Enoch: In that day shall the Elect One sit upon a throne of glory; and *shall choose their conditions and countless habitations* (while their spirits within them shall be strengthened, when they behold my Elect One), shall choose them for those who have fled for protection to my holy and glorious name.[1314]

• Jesus: Blessed are the meek, for they shall inherit the earth.[1315]
• Enoch The elect shall possess light, joy and peace, and *they shall inherit the earth*.[1316]

• Jesus: Wo unto you that are rich! for ye have received your consolation.[1317]
• Enoch: *Woe to you who are rich*, for in your riches have you trusted; but from your riches you shall be removed.[1318]

These scriptures beg the question: why was a book that was admired and quoted by our Lord and His family, and even accepted as authentic and divinely inspired by the earliest Fathers, eventually banished and censored? There are two primary reasons:

1) To hide the fact that many of the most famous and beloved doctrines taught by Jesus, and in turn later by the Church, were not original to Him, and thus were not uniquely Christian.[1319]
2) To conceal the fact that not only was there an overt connection between the Essenes and Christianity, Essenism *was* original Christianity[1320]—at least in Palestine. (We will note here that the Alexandrian Church, in contrast, derived directly from Gnosticism,[1321] and that both spiritual belief systems shared the same mystical doctrines and elements).[1322]

Thus, by the 4th Century, when these facts were finally realized, the Church barred the book of Enoch from the canon under such Fathers as Hilary, Jerome, and Augustine. It then went out of circulation and became one of the Bible's many "lost" books—that is, until its rediscovery in the Great Essene Library deceptively known as the "Dead Sea Scrolls"![1323]

There was another problem with Enoch and his book, however. Enoch was a type of Sun/Son-God whose life span, 365 years,[1324] was a symbol of the yearly procession of the Solar deity through the 12 Sun-signs. Jesus too was venerated by early Christians as a Sun/Son-God,[1325] whose 12 Apostles were closely identified with the 12 months of the year and their accompanying 12 astrological Sun-signs (in Judaism symbolized by the 12 Tribes of Israel).[1326] Thus, it is obvious that parts of Jesus' biography were patterned on the pre-Christian, Jewish-Pagan figure of Enoch, a fact that continues to be suppressed by the mainstream Church.

Lastly, if the book of Enoch was written by the Gnostic-Hindu-Persian-Buddhist-influenced Essenes,[1327] as is clear and as Christian mystics have long maintained, outlawing Enoch and excluding it from the Bible would help conceal the ancient belief that Jesus spent a portion of his 18 "Silent Years" (ages 12 through 30) studying with this mysterious Jewish sect, which taught many other pre-Christian ideas and doctrines now considered "traditional" and "orthodox" by the mainstream Church. Indeed, this is one of the very reasons any mention of the Essenes has been deleted from the Bible.[1328] The primary reason, however, is that they, along with their Qumran library (the intentionally misnamed "Dead Sea Scrolls"), undermine what the mainstream Church likes to consider the "uniqueness" of both Jesus and Christianity.[1329]

But none of this is an issue for Christian mystics, who acknowledge and accept the obvious syncretism of our Faith. See BIBLE, BRETHREN, CHRISTIANITY, ESSENES, GOSPEL, GNOSTICISM, SILENT YEARS.

ESSENES: The Essenes were a mystical pre-Christian Jewish sect,[1330] heavily influenced by Gnostic, Hindu, Persian, Buddhist, Roman, and Greek doctrines,[1331] out of which the Christian Church at Palestine was formed. Owing to the great number of Essenic elements in their teachings, Jesus and John the Baptist themselves were probably members, as were Jesus' parents Joseph and Mary, his siblings,[1332] the 12 Apostles, Joseph of Arimathea, and Nicodemus, among many others.[1333] At the very least these individuals must have studied under the Essenes,[1334] who were, in fact, Jewish Gnostics.[1335]

Enemies of the Judeo-Christian mystic Paul, a man whose writings show an intimate familiarity with Essene doctrine,[1336] refer to him as a "ringleader" of the Essenes under their New Testament codename, "Nazarenes,"[1337] while Jesus too is called a "Nazarene"[1338] (that is, an Essene).[1339] Purported ancient documents uncovered in the 25 miles of bookshelves at the Vatican Library[1340] show Jesus preaching vegetarianism (an Essene custom),[1341] while others, one from the 2nd-Century Church historian Hegesippus, state that Jesus' brother James, a post-resurrection Nazarene (Essene) leader,[1342] was a vegetarian as well.[1343] Our Lord's own carpentry occupation,[1344] as well as His father's,[1345] may have derived from the Essenes, who were known to have specialized in woodworking.[1346] Buttressing these views is a mysterious ancient book entitled, *The Crucifixion by an Eye-Witness*, written by an Essene who claims to have known Jesus personally, not only as the son of an Essene teacher, but as a member of the Essene community Himself.[1347]

That the Jewish splinter sect the Nazarenes, the Essenes, is the "proven Mother of Christianity," has long been known, both inside and outside the orthodox Church.[1348] Epiphanius, one of the early Church Fathers, observed that "the Nazarene sect was before Christ"[1349] and that "at that time all Christians alike were called Nazoraeans [Nazarenes]."[1350] Just as significant, the Nazarenes were long recognized as being the same as the Ebionites, a Jewish Gnostic (or perhaps Gnosticizing) sect from Palestine[1351] which held that Jesus was the human son of Joseph and Mary,[1352] and a virtuous man, but not divine.[1353] Both the Essenes (also known as the Esseans, Ossenes, the Osim, the Jessaeans, the Therapeutae, the Nozrei ha-Brit, the Nozrim, and the Nasrani) and the Christians maintained a "ruling body" at Jerusalem, and both referred to themselves as "followers of the Way."[1354] Based on these few facts alone, the Essene community at Qumran could have only been the equivalent of the early Christian Church.[1355]

The celebrated Church historian Eusebius too took it for granted that the Essenes and Christians were one and the same, admitting that

> the ancient Therapeute were Christians; and that their ancient writings were our Gospels and Epistles.[1356]

As mentioned, so did Bishop Epiphanius, who writes:

> They who believed on Christ were called *Jessaei* [that is, Jessaeans, Esseans, or Essenes] before they were called Christians. They derived their constitution from the signification of the name "Jesus," which in Hebrew signifies the same as Therapeutes, that is, a saviour or physician.[1357]

We will note here that, like Buddha,[1358] not only did Jesus' followers often call Him *Didaskalos* ("Doctor" or "Physician"),[1359] but His Greek name, *Iesous*, literally means "the Healer,"[1360] which was translated in ancient times as *Therapeutes*.[1361] I myself like to refer to Him as the "Eternal Physician," for healing was a major aspect of the ministry of both the Essenic Jesus[1362] and the Essenes themselves,[1363] whose name derives from an ancient Syrian word meaning "physician."[1364] Godfrey Higgins writes:

> The Essenes were called physicians of the soul, or Therapeutae; being resident in both Judea and Egypt, they probably spoke or had their sacred books in [the] Chaldee [language]. They were Pythagoreans, as is proved by all their forms, ceremonies, and doctrines, and they called themselves sons of Jesse.[1365]

Jesus, of course, was a descendant of Jesse (the father of David),[1366] and was thus called "a root of Jesse,"[1367] or Jessaean, one of the names of the Essenes. Higgins continues:

> If the Pythagoreans, or Conenobitae, as they were called by Jamblicus, were Buddhists, *the Essenes were Buddhists*. The Essenes called *Koinobii* lived in Egypt, on the lake of Parembole or Maria, in monasteries. These are the very places in which we formerly found the *Gymnosophists* or *Samaneans*, or Buddhist priests, to have lived, which Gymnosophists are placed also by Ptolemy in northeastern India.
>
> Their [the Essenes] parishes, churches, bishops, priests, deacons, festivals are all identically the same [as the Christians]. They had apostolic founders, the manners which distinguished the immediate apostles of Christ, scriptures divinely inspired, the same allegorical mode of interpreting them which has since obtained among Christians, and the same order of performing public worship. They had missionary stations or colonies of their community established in Rome, Corinth, Galatia, Ephesus, Philippi, Colossae, and Thessalonica, precisely such and in the same circumstances, as were those to whom Saint Paul addressed his letters in those places. All the fine moral doctrines which are attributed to the Samaritan Nazarite [Essene], and I doubt not justly attributed to him, are to be found among the doctrines of the ascetics.[1368]

Arthur Lillie has this to say on the topic:

> It is asserted by calm thinkers like Dean Mansel, that within two generations of the time of Alexander the Great, *the missionaries of Buddha made their appearance at Alexandria*. This theory is confirmed in the east by the Asoka monuments, in the west by Philo. He expressly maintains the identity in creed of the higher Judaism and that of the Gymnosophists of India who abstained from the "sacrifice of living animals,"—in a word, the Buddhists. It would follow from this that the priestly religions of Babylonia, Palestine, Egypt, and Greece were undermined by certain kindred mystical societies organized by Buddha's missionaries under the various names of Therapeutes, Essenes, Neo-Pythagoreans, Neo-Zoroastrians, etc. *Thus Buddhism prepared the way for Christianity*.[1369]

Titcomb has noted that:

We find Saint Paul, the first Apostle of the Gentiles, avowing that he was made a minister of the Gospel which had already been preached to every creature under heaven,[1370] and preaching a God manifest in the flesh, who had been believed on in the world,—therefore before the commencement of his ministry,—and who could not have been Jesus of Nazareth, who had certainly not been preached at that time, nor generally believed on in the world till ages after. Saint Paul owns himself a deacon, which is the lowest ecclesiastical grade of the Therapeutan church.[1371]

Bauer likewise holds that the spirit of the new religion

> *came from the west, the outward frame was furnished by Judaism. The new movement had two foci, Rome and Alexandria. Philo's "Therapeutae" were real people; they were the forerunners of Christianity. Under Trajan the new religion began to be known. Pliny's letter asking for instructions as to how to deal with the new movement is its certificate of birth—the original form of the letter, it must be understood, not the present form, which has undergone editing at the hands of Christians.*[1372]

Gfrörer writes:

> *The Christian Church grew out of the Essene Order by giving a further development to its ideas, and it is impossible to explain the organisation of the Church without taking account of the regulations of the Order.*[1373]

Bunsen writes:

> *The Gospel of which Paul's Epistles speak had been extensively preached and fully established before the time of Jesus by the Therapeutae or Essenes, who believed in the doctrine of the Angel-Messiah, the Aeon from heaven; the doctrine of the "Anointed Angel," of the man from heaven, the Creator of the world; the doctrine of the atoning sacrificial death of Jesus by the blood of his cross; the doctrine of the Messianic antetype of the Paschal lamb and of the Paschal omer, and thus of the resurrection of Jesus Christ the third day according to the Scriptures,—these doctrines of Paul can with more or less certainty be connected with the Essenes. . . . It becomes almost a certainty that Eusebius was right*

in surmising that Essenic writings have been used by Paul and the evangelists. Not Jesus, but Paul, is the cause of the separation of the Jews from the Christians.[1374]

Titcomb continues:

> The very ancient and Eastern doctrine of an Angel-Messiah had been applied to Gautama-Buddha, who predicted that another Avatar would come upon earth in six hundred years after his death. This time had nearly expired; so Jesus of Nazareth was proclaimed as the expected Messiah by these Buddhist Jews, and the sun-myths were interwoven with his real history. Jesus unquestionably possessed a nature as divine as it is possible for a human being to possess, or he would not otherwise have been received as the Angel-Messiah by a sect so pure and holy as were the Essenes.[1375]

Based on a 2,000 year old tradition, Venturini made the following observation:

> Jesus . . . was the son of a member of the Essene Order. The child was watched over by the Order and prepared for His future mission. He entered on His public ministry as a tool of the Essenes, who after the crucifixion took Him down from the cross and resuscitated Him.[1376]

Doane writes of this subject:

> The sacred books of Hindoos and Buddhists were among the Essenes, and in the library at Alexandria. *The Essenes, who were afterwards called Christians*, applied the legend of the Angel-Messiah—"the very ancient Eastern doctrine," to Christ Jesus. It was simply a transformation of names, a transformation which had previously occurred in many cases. After this came additions to the legend from other sources. Portions of the legends related of the Persian, Greek and Roman Saviours and Redeemers of mankind, were, from time to time, added to the already legendary history of the Christian Saviour. *Thus history was repeating itself. Thus the virgin-born God and Saviour, worshiped by all nations of the earth, though called by different names, was but one and the same.*[1377]

Scholarly research reveals that there are numerous commonalities between the Gospel and epistles of John and the Essenes, as well as the Gospel of

Matthew and some of Paul's writings. The Letter to the Hebrews (probably written by the Essenes)[1378] presents Jesus as both a priestly Messiah (descended from Aaron) and a royal Messiah (descended from David),[1379] a common dualistic belief in Essenic messianism.[1380] Furthermore, the organization of the primitive Christian Church and the Essene community at Qumran (in modern day Israel) were similar, and both referred to their council members as "the Many."[1381] The Christian community had three primary leaders (James, John, and Peter) and 12 Apostles, while the Essenic Community had three priestly leaders and 12 Councilmen.[1382] The Essenic "Inspector" bore a resemblance to the Christian bishop, and the liturgical "solemn meal" of the Essenes has affinities with the Lord's Supper.[1383]

Due to the discovery of the purposefully misnamed "Dead Sea Scrolls," numerous biblical passages, long believed to have been original to Jesus and the New Testament writers, have been shown to come directly from the Essenes. This is, of course, a great embarrassment to the institutional Church, whose very foundation partially rests on the idea that both Jesus and Christianity are thoroughly unique[1384]—a folly of extraordinary proportions considering that it is well-known that at least 90 percent of Jesus' ethical precepts alone were derived from Jewish teachers who came before Him.[1385]

Portions of the Sermon on the Mount are almost exact quotes from the Essenic scrolls,[1386] while the concept of the Good News or kerygma, John the Baptist's phrase "to fulfill all righteousness," and even the name of the New Testament itself, all derive from the Essenes, who referred to themselves as the "Community of the *New Covenant*" (that is "New Testament").[1387] In one Lukan passage Jesus Himself seems to attribute the concept of the Kingdom of God, the core of His Gospel,[1388] to His predecessor John the Baptist.[1389] The Golden Rule, preached by our Lord,[1390] is Pagan in origin, predating Christianity by millennia. Confucius, for example, taught this universal principle some 500 years before the 1st Century A.D.[1391] And as I show in numerous other entries, a great many of Jesus' teachings came from Buddhism, Hinduism, Zoroastrianism, and ancient Egypt.

Additionally, not only does the mystical Hellenized Gospel of John[1392] contain various elements of Hermetic thought,[1393] it is built around the dualistic doctrine of the conflict between light (the "Sons of Light") and darkness (those "walking in darkness"),[1394] a common theme in such Essenic texts as The Manual of Discipline.[1395] These themes and phrases are found almost exclusively in the Fourth Gospel,[1396] which reflects a Gnostic (that is, Essenic) tradition and background rather than a Synoptic one.[1397]

Owing to the great similarities between the Essenes (secretly called the Nazarenes)[1398] and early Christians, many believe that John the Baptist and Jesus were Essenes.[1399] As we have seen, Jesus was widely known as a "Nazarene,"[1400] and Paul was called a "ringleader" of the Nazarenes (Essenes).[1401] And though their beliefs were not identical in every way, as is clear from those cited above, the two Jewish sects shared much in common at the time.

As further examples: both the Nazarenes and the Essenes used the term "Son of God";[1402] both venerated the Sun of Righteousness (that is, the "Son")[1403] as well as the Teacher of Righteousness (the Indwelling Christ); both emphasized poverty as well as purity before God; both taught esoterically; both observed a eucharistic meal; both lived simply and communally; and both practiced baptism by water. Indeed, the Essenes sometimes referred to themselves as "The Bathers" or "The Daily Baptists."[1404]

To Christian mystics such evidence (and there is much more) is compelling, which is why we hold that the Essenes are "the (Christian) Brethren" of the New Testament.[1405] This certainly explains two theories for why the Essenes are not mentioned by that name in the Bible:

1) The Essenes were identical to the first Christians, which had not been given that name yet, but were then called "the Brethren."
2) Even the mere discussion of pre-Christian Jewish sects whose teachings were similar to or the same as those of Jesus was and still is discouraged, and early on the names of these groups were expunged by the institutional Church from texts under consideration for inclusion in the New Testament canon. One of these sects was the Sun-worshiping Essenes (the "Saints," from the Aramaic word *Chasya*, "saint"),[1406] whose mysterious "leader," the "Teacher of Righteousness," shares a host of commonalities with Jesus, the "Sun of Righteousness"[1407]—and may even be identical to Him, as many have argued.[1408]

As a result, Qumran, one of the 1st Century's most important, best known, and most prevalent Jewish communities (one that had a demonstrable influence on the Lord and His teachings), is not mentioned anywhere in the Talmud, the Old Testament, or the New Testament. Since the Essenes were proto-Christians,[1409] that is, "the intermediate step between Judaism and Christianity," and their Teacher of Righteousness was an obvious prototype of Jesus,[1410] Jews expunged their writings as "too Christian" while Christians expunged their writings as "too Jewish." The foremost example of this severe double censorship was the Essenic book of Enoch, which was suppressed by both religions[1411]—even though it was a favorite of our Lord and his brother Jude![1412]

In short, the Essenes were suppressed because they wrote much of the pseudepigraphical and so-called "apocryphal" Jewish literature (composed during the time between the end of the Old Testament and the beginning of the New Testament), which contains doctrines, statements, teachings, concepts, ideas, and beliefs that had once been considered original to Christianity.[1413]

Nonetheless, the Essenes were discussed by numerous early important

Church Fathers and historians, including Philo, Pliny the Elder, and, as we have seen, Epiphanius. Foremost among this group was the ancient historian Josephus, who named the Essenes as one of the four primary Jewish sects of his day (the other three were the Pharisees, the Sadducees, and the Galileans or Zealots).[1414] Josephus devotes some seven fascinating pages to the Essenes, from which the following brief selection has been taken:

> For there are three *philosophical* sects among the Jews. The followers of the first of which are the Pharisees, of the second the Sadducees, and the third sect, which pretends to a severer discipline, are called Essenes. These last are Jews by birth, and seem to have a greater affection for one another than the other sects have. These Essenes reject pleasures as an evil, but esteem continence, and the conquest over our passions to be virtue. They neglect wedlock, but choose out other persons' children while they are pliable, and fit for learning, and esteem them to be of their kindred, and form them according to their own manners. They did not absolutely deny the fitness of marriage, and the succession of mankind thereby continued; but they guard against the lascivious behaviour of women, and are persuaded that none of them preserve their fidelity to one man.
>
> These men are depisers of riches, and so very communicative as raises our admiration. Nor is there any one to be found among them who hath more than another; for it was a law among them, that those that come to them must let what they have be common to the whole order, insomuch that among them all, there is no appearance of poverty, or excess of riches, but every one's possessions are intermingled with every other's possessions, and so there is, as it were, one patrimony among all the brethren. They think that oil is a defilement; and if any of them be anointed without his own approbation, it is wiped off his body; for they think to be sweaty is a good thing, as they do also to be clothed in white garments. They also have stewards appointed, to take care of their common affairs, who everyone of them have no separate business for any, but what is for the use of them all.[1415]

Christian mystics maintain that Jesus studied under or actually joined the Essenes during His "silent years," the 18 years between ages 12 and 30. It is probable that during this period he picked up the mystical title the "Son of Man" (He never called Himself the "Son of God").[1416] Some evidence, such as the aforementioned book of Enoch, clearly confirms this: in the New Testament Jesus paraphrases this work on numerous occasions. Thus, it seems clear that He derived some of His teachings, and even patterned His own mission, around the cryptic Essenic figure, the "Teacher of Righteousness," who was venerated as the sect's messiah, came into conflict with orthodox Jewish authorities, and was eventually executed by them due to his "radical" teachings.[1417]

There are other tantalizing pieces of circumstantial evidence, such as the fact that the Last Supper took place in what was then considered the "Essene Quarter" of Jerusalem. Jesus could have called this gathering anywhere. Why did He choose to meet his Apostles for the last time in this specific location? The debate on the many connections between Judaism, Christianity, Jesus, the Essenes, the Nazarenes, and the Dead Sea Scrolls (the "Great Essene Library") continues.[1418] See BRETHREN, CHRISTIANITY, ENOCH, GNOSIS, GNOSTICISM, JESUS, SON OF GOD, SON OF MAN, TEACHER OF RIGHTEOUSNESS.

EUCHARIST: The Eucharist is the same as the SACRAMENT. See also BETHLEHEM, BREAD, GOSPEL, JESUS, WATER, WINE.

EVE: In the mainstream Church Eve is the "first woman," the wife of the "first man" Adam, and the "mother of all living." She gave into the "serpent" (Satan), who tempted her to eat the forbidden fruit. This caused the "Fall of Man," necessitating the redemptive death of Jesus on the Cross to expiate the "original sin" of mankind.[1419]

In the mystical Church, Eve is the first "Mary" and a symbol of the human soul, as opposed to Adam, who is the first "Jesus" and a symbol of the human body.[1420] Here, Eve was not a historic person; merely a symbol of the "First Woman," a motif which appears in the religious myths of nearly every known culture and society (in ancient Greece, for example, she was called Pandora).[1421]

Her true symbolical nature is revealed in her name: Eve is Hebrew for "life" or "living," an esoteric euphemism for the all-embracing, all-loving, life-giving conceptive spirit of the Divine Feminine. See ADAM, EDEN, GARDEN OF EDEN, GODDESS, ORIGINAL SIN, SERPENT, SIN, TREE OF LIFE, YAHWEH.

EVIL: From the Old English word *yfel*, meaning "the antithesis of good" (that is, the opposite of God), and thus, in traditional Christianity, connoting the "Evil One," that is, the "Devil." In the traditional Christian Church evil is an independent force under the rule of Satan, which every human being is subject to when he or she submits to temptation and falls from the path of God's righteousness. Since, according to conventional Christianity, God is all good, the very existence of evil presents what the orthodox Church admits is a "major theoretical and practical problem," one that can never be "completely solved."[1422]

In the mystical Christian Church, however, there are no such issues when it comes to evil. According to what is known as the "Ancient Wisdom," evil is simply the absence of God, or separation from God, Divine Mind, not an autonomous power or real entity. For there is nothing evil outside of us, the Devil (or Satan) himself merely being the biblical personification of our Lower Self. Naturally this negative energy can become personified into a living being by thought. But this thought, or belief, must be deeply ingrained and held onto consistently and intensely for this to occur. This is precisely why neither evil nor the Devil exist or have any impact in the lives of the spiritually enlightened: they simply refuse to think about either, and so, due to the psychospiritual Law of Thought and Attraction (that is, we create what we think of most often),[1423] the spiritually mature never experience evil. Thus as Whitman said, for those who reject the concept, "there is in fact no evil."[1424]

In the mystical Christian Church evil is believed to be created by wrong-thinking, and is therefore a product of the human mind (Ego).[1425] Thus, according to Jesus' Gospel of the Kingdom of God principles, if we believe in evil, we attract it. If we do not believe in evil, it cannot harm us. The only things that can come into our lives are those which we invite through prolonged and persistent thought—positive or negative.[1426]

Mystic Jesus wisely taught: "Resist not evil."[1427] This is because resistance to evil is recognizing it as a reality, which energizes it, and thus draws more of it to you. By not resisting evil, it disappears as the manmade illusion that it is.[1428]

Why does God allow evil to exist? It is part of his great gift to us: he has given us total freedom to do anything we like with our lives and to be anyone we wish—without any interference from him. For our freedom to be truly complete, however, we must not only be free to do good, we must also be free to do evil. For every light casts a shadow.[1429] Thus when we choose to incarnate on earth and take on the total freedom of humanhood, we also take on an enormous responsibility: that of learning to choose good over evil. We must remember then that the mirage-like "existence" of evil here on earth is not a curse, but a blessing; not a penalty, but a gift; a special inheritance from the One, the Divine, the Supreme Father/Mother,[1430] without which we would be choiceless spiritual slaves imprisoned in physical bodies.[1431]

There is solace in the fact that, as the ancient Mystery Religions taught, the evil and darkness of this world are temporary, while the light and goodness of Heaven are eternal.[1432] See ADVERSARY, ANTICHRIST, BEAST, DEVIL, EGO, EGYPT, GODS AND GODDESSES, HELL, KARMA, LOWER SELF, LUCIFER, MASS MIND, MOSES, NUMBER OF THE BEAST, PILATE, SATAN, SERPENT, SIN.

EXODUS (THE): In the traditional Church the Exodus comprises Israel's escape, under Moses, from slavery in Egypt and her journey through the wilderness to the Promised Land—considered to be the most theologically and historically important event in the Old Testament.[1433]

There is no mention in any ancient record that some 2 million Israelites (600,000 of whom were men, the rest were women and children) left Egypt around 1442 B.C. Not even the obsessive record-keeping Egyptians themselves mentioned it. All of this despite the fact that the Bible tells us that half of the country's population one day suddenly up and left (if this had been the case, Egypt would have certainly collapsed into financial ruin and social chaos). Nor is there any archaeological evidence that 2 million people traveled through and camped in the Sinai Desert for 40 years. This is one of the most geologically sensitive regions in the world, where the bone-dry conditions preserve such things as footprints and campfires for thousands of years. A caravan of 2 million people and their livestock would have left overt traces all over Sinai—if they had actually crossed over it.[1434]

Today no credible historian views the biblical account of the Exodus as anything other than an ancient religious fiction,[1435] containing, as it does, affinities with other early myths, such as the *Aeneid*.[1436] Most of the great civilizations of antiquity had their "Moses," including Arabia, Phoenicia, and Assyria, the Hebrew version himself who was based on earlier semi-mythic figures like Sargon I.[1437]

In the mystical Church the Exodus was indeed not a historical event, but rather an esoteric symbol of, as Dante put it, "the Soul's liberation from sin."[1438] Here Egypt is a symbol of Satan, of bondage to materiality and all of its delusions and pitfalls, while Israel is a symbol of God, of freedom in spirituality with all of its beauties and rewards. The "Exodus" then refers mystically to the emancipation of the Spirit from earthly imprisonment. Thus Bishop Christopher Wordsworth writes:

> The Exodus of Israel, their deliverance from their enemies, and their passage through the Red Sea, and the destruction of their enemies in its waters, were figures of the liberation of Mankind from the dominion and bondage of Satan, and of his overthrow by Christ in the Red Sea of His blood.[1439]

Augustine had this to say about the occult meaning of the Exodus:

> . . . we have been led out of Egypt, where we were slaves to the devil as to Pharaoh; where we applied ourselves to works of clay, engaged in earthly desires, and where we toiled exceedingly. And to us, while labouring, as it were, at the bricks, Christ cried aloud, "Come unto me, all ye that labour and are heavy laden." Thence we were led out by baptism as through the Red Sea,—red because consecrated by the blood of Christ. All our enemies that pursued us being dead, that is, all our sins being blotted out, we have been brought over to the other side. At the present time, then, before we come to the

land of promise, namely, the eternal kingdom, we are in the wilderness in tabernacles. They who acknowledge these things are in tabernacles; for it was to be that some would acknowledge this. For that man, who understands that he is a sojourner in this world, is in tabernacles. That man understands that he is travelling in a foreign country, when he sees himself sighing for his native land.

But whilst the body of Christ is in taberncles, Christ is in tabernacles; but at that time He was so, not evidently but secretly. For as yet the shadow obscured the light; when the light came, the shadow was removed. Christ was in secret: He was in the feast of tabernacles, but there hidden. At the present time, when these things are already made manifest, we acknowledge that we are journeying in the wilderness: for if we know it, we are in the wilderness. What is it to be in the wilderness? In the desert waste. Why in the desert waste? Because in this world, where we thirst in a way in which is no water. But yet, let us thirst that we may be filled.

For, "Blessed are they that hunger and thirst after righteousness, for they shall be filled." And our thirst is quenched from the rock in the wilderness: for "the Rock was Christ," and it was smitten with a rod that the water might flow. But that it might flow, the rock was smitten twice: because there are two beams of the cross." All these things, then, which were done in a figure, are made manifest to us. And it is not without meaning that it was said of the Lord, "He went up to the feast-day, but not openly, but as it were in secret." For Himself in secret was the thing prefigured, because Christ was hid in that same festal-day; for that very festal-day signified Christ's members that were to sojourn in a foreign land.[1440]

See CHRIST, EGYPT, ISRAEL, MOSES, SATAN.

EYES: In the traditional Church when Jesus uses the word "eyes," He is referring to our physical eyes. In mystical Christianity, however, when Jesus, Paul, and other enlightened biblical figures use the word "eyes," in many cases they are referring not to our two physical ones, but to our Inner Eye, or "Third Eye," meaning spiritual or inner perception (intuition)[1441] as opposed to intellectual or outer perception (tuition).[1442]
See DIVINE MIND, THIRD EAR, THIRD EYE.

Jesus the Essene Master.

Egyptian Sun worship.

The antediluvian patriarch Enoch.

Worshiping the molten calf.

FALL OF MAN: In the mainstream Church the Fall of Man is humanity's alienation from God through disobedience in the Garden of Eden, where Adam and Eve were tempted by the serpent and voluntarily sinned. This tainted the entire human race with "original sin," requiring the redemptive death of Jesus, the "Second Adam," on the cross.[1443] Since the Fall of Man motif is universal (found in hundreds of disparate cultures and religions around the world), and since biblical elements like the "First Man," "First Woman," and the "serpent" were all borrowed from far earlier tales, such as the Mesopotamian story known as the Epic of Gilgamesh,[1444] Christian mystics see past the literal narrative and into its occult nature.

Here, the Fall of Man is a symbol of involution, or the descent of the Soul into materiality, the Lower Nature, or the underworld.[1445] Alice Gardner writes of the esoteric meaning behind "the Fall of Man":

> To come to man the microcosm, the human trinity, made in the image of God, but fallen from its original glory, we have already seen that Scotus [John the Scot] attributes that fall to a self-willed turning away from man's proper nature and first principle of being. In following the story in Genesis, he gives an allegoric interpretation to its several parts, following in general the commentaries of the Fathers, especially Gregory of Nyssa and Maximus the Monk, though sometimes showing how the authorities differ and which view he personally prefers. It may seem superfluous to say that *the Fall is not regarded as an event in time, nor Paradise as a definite locality.* Again and again he recurs to the idea, on which Maximus also liked to dwell, that man before the Fall, or man according to his divine nature, was sexless. The division into male and female is a defect in humanity.
>
> The story of the forbidden fruit is interpreted as the leading away of the mind (= the man) by sensibility (= the woman), so as to seek pleasure in the things of sense and not in pure wisdom. The punishments inflicted have a hidden meaning:—"In sorrow shalt thou bring forth children," points to the efforts necessary for attaining knowledge; "thy desire

shall be to thy husband, and he shall rule over thee," promises the ultimate subjugation of sense by reason. The labours imposed on the man have a purgatorial end, and "thou shalt return" is spoken in hope. The return is not by way of new creation, but through a cleansing process, such as that which purifies from leprosy. When man can contemplate the Divine Goodness, he attains restoration, for the image remains in his nature even after the Fall.[1446]

Kingsford and Maitland write:

> [As to the] . . . the philosophical reading of our Parable [of the Fall], we find that on this plane the Man is the Mind or rational Intellect, out of which is evolved the Woman, the Affection or Heart; that the Tree of Knowledge represents Maya or Illusion; the Serpent, the Will of the Body; the Tree of Life, the Divine Gnosis—or interior knowledge; and the sin which has brought and which brings ruin on mankind, Idolatry.
>
> In this aspect of the Fall, we have presented to us the decline of Religion from the celestial to the astral. The affection of the unfallen mind is fixed on things above, spiritual and real, and not on things beneath, material and phantasmal. Idolatry is the adoration of the shadow instead of the substance, the setting up of the eidolon in the place of the God. It is thus no specific act, but the general tendency towards Matter and Sense, that constitutes the Fall. And of this tendency the world is full, for it is the "original sin" of every man born of the generation of "Adam", and only that man is free of it who is "born again of the Spirit" and made "one with the Father," the central and divine Spirit of man's system.[1447]

See ADAM, EVE, GARDEN OF EDEN, KARMA, ORIGINAL SIN, SERPENT.

FATHER: In traditional Christianity (which is patriarchal) the "Father" is one of the many names for God, who is anthropomorphized as a humanlike parent of humanity. In mystical Christianity "Father" is an esoteric codeword for the Divine Mind, which is precisely how Jesus used it.[1448] In matriarchal religions the Supreme Being was (and still is) known as "Mother" or "Goddess." As such, all three belief systems agree as to the meaning: God, though the definitions of God may differ.

Since earliest times it has been the practice of enlightened spiritual teachers, like Jesus, to depict the Divine Mind as a parent, in order to make the concept more accessible to the spiritually immature and the metaphysically undeveloped masses. Thus in male-based religions (theology) the Divine Mind has always been imaged as a masculine parent, in female-based religions (thealogy) as a feminine one.

In some faiths God has been portrayed as an androgynous being, or even as a multitude of deities, such as in early Judaism. Here the polytheistic Hebrew term *Elohim*, meaning a "plurality of gods or goddesses," is used. To hide this fact the word *Elohim* is mistranslated in the Old Testament as the singular word "God."[1449] The device is given away, however, in the book of Genesis, where it is written: "And God said, 'Let *us* make man in *our* image, after *our* likeness."[1450]

The first Christians, the Gnostics, however, made no pretense about God's androgynic nature, calling him/her *Metropator*, that is, "Mother-Father,"[1451] for we humans are each and all part material ("female") and part spiritual ("male"), having been born, as the Essenes would say, "of the Earthly Mother and the Heavenly Father."[1452] See GOD, GODDESS, JEHOVAH, MOTHER, YAHWEH.

FIRST-BORN SON OF GOD: The First-Born Son of God is identical to the ONLY BEGOTTEN SON. See also JESUS, SON OF GOD, SON OF MAN.

FISH: In the traditional Church Jesus is associated with the fish symbol due to the fact that the first five letters of the Greek word for "fish," *ichthys*, is an acrostic that forms the acronym for "Jesus, Christ, of God, Son, Savior."[1453] But in the mystical Church it is understood that the real origins, as with nearly everything else "Christian," derive from Paganism, and in this case more specifically with Pagan astrology and Goddess-worship.

Jesus was born in the Age of Aries the Ram (which began around 2220 B.C.),[1454] a constellation known to pre-Christian Pagans as "the Lamb of God" and the "Savior."[1455] Thus early on these titles were appended to him.[1456] Later, because His ministry started during the Age of Pisces (the Two Fishes),[1457] His sacred symbol became the fish, long a universal savior emblem due to the fact that it lives in the primordial ocean, the salvific "life-giving" sea, the archetypal amniotic fluid of the Great Virgin-Mother-Goddess.[1458]

The fish is thus linked to salvation, fertility, and to female deities in general. Hence, many goddesses have names comprised of the ancient elements *ma* ("mother") or *mar* ("sea"), such as: Ma Ma, Maerin, Maid Marian, Mar, Mara, Marah, Mari, Maria, Mariam, Marie, Marratu, Mary, Maya, Meri, etc.[1459] Other examples of associations between the Great Mother and water:

- The Greek goddess Aphrodite, whose name means "born of the (sea) foam."[1460]
- The Canaanite goddess Astarte, who was known as "Lady of the Sea."[1461]
- The ancient Egyptian Virgin-Goddess Isis, who gave her title *Stella Maris*, "Star of the Sea,"[1462] to the Virgin Mary.[1463]

It is worth remarking here that rivers all over Europe retain the names of the goddesses they were once associated with (such as Ireland's Rivers Boyne, Shannon, Lagan, and Bride),[1464] and that cities, regions, and even countries and continents, also take their names from goddesses. For example: Scotland, Ireland, Italy, Albania, Scandinavia, Crete, Britain, Venice, Athens, Rome, Greece, Holland, Africa, Romania, Denmark, etc.[1465]

Other ancient links between Jesus, fish, the sea, salvation, and goddesses:

- Early Christian converts were known as *pisciculi*, "little fish."[1466]
- Jesus Himself became an emblem of the Pagan fish-man, a symbol of the Life Principle Within (the Mother-Goddess' amniotic ocean), even comparing Himself to another celebrated fish-man, Jonah, who spent three nights in the "whale's belly."[1467]
- Jesus was a "fisher of men."[1468]
- Many of Jesus' Apostles were "fishermen."[1469]
- The Catholic rule to eat fish (in place of warm-blooded meat) on Fridays derives from the Roman love-goddess Venus (in Greece Aphrodite), also known as Fri, Frigg, Frigga, or Freya, whose sacred day was named after her: Fri's Day.[1470] Known to ancient Romans as *Dies Veneris* (Latin for the "Day of Venus"), Friday was thus held to be the proper day for lovemaking, said to be enhanced by eating fish—then as now considered an "aphrodisiac."[1471] To attract and appease converting Pagans, the goddess' Friday fish ritual was adopted by the Church and christianized.
- The Virgin Mary, the "Star of the Sea," is often portrayed with the *Vesica Piscis* ("fish bladder"), with its double crescent moons and sacred Yoni,[1472] a mystical Christian symbol of the procreative power of the Divine Feminine (the Hindu Mother-Goddess Aditi was often depicted standing on a crescent moon[1473] wearing a crown of 12 Zodiacal stars,[1474] imagery later appended to Mary).[1475]

See CHRISTIANITY, DOVE, FLOOD OF NOAH, RAINBOW, WATER.

FLOOD OF NOAH: In the traditional Church the Flood of Noah is a literal worldwide deluge that wiped out every living thing except Noah, his family, and the animals he was commanded to take aboard the ark. The cause of the flood was Mankind's sinful ways; the deluge was God's judgement.[1476]

Since there is not a single trace of a global flood in the sediment of any country on earth,[1477] and since—as even mainstream Protestants are now forced to admit[1478]— nearly every pre-biblical society and civilization possessed a flood myth of one kind or another,[1479] it is obvious that the "Flood of Noah" was not meant by its biblical authors to be taken literally. The story of the Great Deluge was intended as a metaphor or allegory of hidden knowledge and deep spiritual truths, and that is precisely how the mystical Church views it.

Here, the Great Flood is a symbol of the falsity and deception of the Ego (Satan),[1480] which bathes the human soul in an ocean of material illusion in an attempt to separate it from its divine origin: God. Thus Philo writes that

> in the inward meaning, the flood is symbolically representative of spiritual dissolution. When therefore by the grace of the Father we desire to throw away and to wash off all sensible and corporeal qualities by which the intellect was infected as by swelling sores, then the muddy slime is got rid of as by a deluge, sweet waters and wholesome fountains supervening. . . . [Hence] with respect to the inner sense of the passage, since the deluge of the mind arises from two things, for it arises partly from counsel, as if from heaven, and in another degree also from the body and from sense, as if from earth, the vices being reciprocally introduced by the passions and the passions by the vices, it was inevitably necessary that the word of the divine physician entering in as a salutary visitation for the purpose of healing the disease, should prevent both kinds of overflow for the future . . .[1481]

The writers of Genesis had access to a host of earlier local flood myths, and freely borrowed from them, two of the most notable being the ancient Mesopotamian tale known as the "Epic of Gilgamesh,"[1482] and the far older Babylonian legend called the "Epic of Atrahasis."[1483] They also adopted numerous elements from the Hurrian version of the Great Flood, even naming the biblical hero Noah after the Hurrian one: *Nahmizuli*, whose name bears the vowel-less Hebrew word for Noah, *Nhm*, in its first three letters.[1484] Doane writes:

> There is scarcely any considerable race of men among whom there does not exist, in some form, the tradition of a great deluge, which destroyed all the human race, except their own progenitors. The first of these which we shall notice, and the one with which the Hebrew agrees most closely, having been copied from it, is the Chaldean, as given by Berosus, the Chaldean historian. It is as follows:
>
>> "After the death of Ardates (the ninth king of the Chaldeans), his son Xisuthrus reigned eighteen sari. In his time happened a great deluge, the history of which is thus described: The deity Cronos appeared to

him (Xisuthrus) in a vision, and warned him that upon the fifteenth day of the month Desius there would be a flood, by which mankind would be destroyed. He therefore enjoined him to write a history of the beginning, procedure, and conclusion of all things, and to bury it in the City of the Sun at Sippara; and to build a vessel, and take with him into it his friends and relations, and to convey on board everything necessary to sustain life, together with all the different animals, both birds and quadrupeds, and trust himself fearlessly to the deep. Having asked the deity whither he was to sail, he was answered: 'To the Gods'; upon which he offered up a prayer for the good of mankind. He then obeyed the divine admonition, and built a vessel five stadia in length, and two in breadth. Into this he put everything which he had prepared, and last of all conveyed into it his wife, his children, and his friends. After the flood had been upon the earth, and was in time abated, Xisuthrus sent out birds from the vessel; which not finding any food, nor any place whereupon they might rest their feet, returned to him again. After an interval of some days, he sent them forth a second time; and they now returned with their feet tinged with mud. He made a trial a third time with these birds; but they returned to him no more: from whence he judged that the surface of the earth had appeared above the waters. He therefore made an opening in the vessel, and upon looking out found that it was stranded upon the side of some mountain; upon which he immediately quitted it with his wife, his daughter, and the pilot. Xisuthrus then paid his adoration to the earth, and, having constructed an altar, offered sacrifices to the gods."

This account, given by Berosus . . . agrees in almost every particular with that found in Genesis, and with that found by George Smith of the British Museum on terra cotta tablets in Assyria . . .[1485]

Now let us look at the pre-Jewish Hindu version of the Great Flood:

> Many ages after the creation of the world, Brahma resolved to destroy it with a deluge, on account of the wickedness of the people. There lived at that time a pious man named Satyavrata, and as the lord of the universe loved this pious man, and wished to preserve him from the sea of destruction which was to appear on account of the depravity of the age, he appeared before him in the form of Vishnu (the Preserver) and said:
>
>> "In seven days from the present time . . . the worlds will be plunged in an ocean of death, but in the midst of the destroying waves, a large vessel, sent by me for thy use, shall stand before thee. Then shalt thou take all medicinal herbs, all the variety of feeds, and, accompanied by seven saints, encircled by pairs of all brute animals, thou shalt enter the spacious ark, and continue in it, secure from the flood, on one immense ocean without light, except the radiance of thy holy companions. When the ship shall be agitated by an impetuous wind, thou shalt fasten it with a large sea-serpent on my horn; for I will be near thee (in the form of a fish), drawing the vessel, with thee and thy attendants."[1486]

Like much of the rest of the Bible, the Flood of Noah is nonsensical, nonscientific, confusing, and irrational if read literally, but perfectly understandable as a spiritual allegory—which is precisely how the biblical writers intended it to be read.[1487] See ARK, DOVE, NOAH, RAINBOW, RIVER, WATER.

FORBIDDEN FRUIT: In traditional Christianity the "Forbidden Fruit" is the fruit of the Tree of Knowledge of Good and Evil, of which God forbade Adam and Eve to partake.[1488] It is traditionally imaged as an apple, though the Bible does not specify what kind of fruit it was. In mystical Christianity the Forbidden Fruit is a symbol of the knowledge of Theosis (God in Man). More commonly, however, it represents the experience of the physical act of union between Man and Woman.[1489]

Known as horasis, the Hebrew word is *yada*: spiritual enlightenment through sex. In the Old Testament the biblical scholars working under King James translated *yada* as the words "knew," "know," or "knowing."[1490] In the New Testament the Greek word for horasis is *ginosko*, which was also translated as "knew,"[1491] to this day still a euphemism for the procreative act. See ADAM, ANOINTING, EVE, GARDEN OF EDEN, OIL, ORIGINAL SIN, THEOSIS.

FORGIVENESS: In traditional Christianity only God (or an ordained priest) can offer true forgiveness. This is based on repentance of sin, necessary because of the "Fall of Man" in the Garden of Eden ("Original Sin"). This, in turn, requires Man's atonement or reconciliation with God, which could only be achieved by Jesus' sanctifying death on the cross.[1492]

In mystical Christianity there is no such thing as "original sin" (which is manmade and therefore nonbiblical), and thus there is no need for God's forgiveness.[1493] This does not mean forgiveness is not necessary or important to mystical Christians. Only that it does not come from an external anthropomorphic deity. It derives from self-forgiveness via the God Within, the Indwelling Father,[1494] in whose image we are made[1495] and with whom we are one.[1496]

Because of its manmade rules and noncanonical doctrines, however, mainstream Christianity has created a conflict by teaching that self-forgiveness is not biblical and therefore anti-Christian. This is incorrect. In his letter to the Colossians we find Paul offering the following commandment on forgiveness:

Forbearing one another, and forgiving *one another* . . .[1497]

The Greek root word for the two italicized words, "one another," is *heautou*, which means "themselves." But it also means "*ourselves*" and "*yourselves*." Thus, this scripture actually reads:

Forbearing one another, and forgiving one another *as well as ourselves* (or *yourselves*).[1498]

See BORN AGAIN, JESUS, ORIGINAL SIN, REDEEMER, REDEMPTION.

FOUR HORSEMEN: In the traditional Church the Four Horsemen are merely bizarre emblems in the book of Revelation presaging the Parousia or Second Coming of Christ.[1499] But since even Jesus is shown wrongly predicting the time of "the Son of Man coming in his kingdom,"[1500] it is obvious that the Four Horsemen are symbols concealing esoteric doctrines. This is particularly true of the book of Revelation, which contains the same consecrated teachings that were preached by the ancient Egyptians, Gnostics, Chaldeans, Syrians, Tibetans, Greeks, Pythagoreans, and Druids.[1501] Thus, in the mystical Church the Four Horsemen are emblems related to astrology:

1) The first horse, which is white and whose rider is wearing a crown, represents the planet Venus and its ruling deity the Goddess of Women and Love: Venus (in Greece Aphrodite).[1502] (In some mystical Christian schools also a symbol of Jupiter and fire.)[1503]
2) The second horse, which is red and whose rider carries a sword, represents the planet Mars and its ruling deity the God of Men and War: Mars (in Greece Aries).[1504] (In some mystical Christian schools also a symbol of Juno and air.)[1505]
3) The third horse, which is black and whose rider holds a pair of balances, represents the planet Saturn and its ruling deity the God of Time: Saturn (in Greece Cronus).[1506] (In some mystical Christian schools also a symbol of Neptune and water.)[1507]
4) The fourth horse, which is pale and whose rider is named "Death," represents the planet Mercury and its ruling deity the God of Thought: Mercury (in Greece Hermes).[1508] (In some mystical Christian schools also a symbol of Vesta and earth.)[1509]

The Four Horsemen are, in other words, another Christian version of the Pagan Tetramorph, one that long predated Christianity in such religions as Mithraism, where we find the "Cosmic Quadriga," made up of four horses symbolizing the four natural elements of fire, air, water, and earth.[1510]

While a thorough study of astrology is helpful, the true metaphysical meaning of the Four Horsemen can only be perceived through intuition (as opposed to tuition)—the One True Way of the Christian mystic. See ASTROLOGY, KINGDOM OF GOD, SON OF MAN, TETRAMORPH, TWELVE, ZODIAC.

The Great Flood.

"Those who wish to seek out the cause of miracles and to understand the things of nature as philosophers, and not to stare at them in astonishment like fools, are soon considered heretical and impious, and proclaimed as such by those whom the mob adores as the interpreters of nature and the gods. For these men know that, once ignorance is put aside, that wonderment would be taken away, which is the only means by which their authority is preserved." — BARUCH SPINOZA, 1677

GALILEE: In traditional Christianity Galilee is the Palestinian province in which Jesus spent most of his ministry.[1511] In mystical Christianity Galilee is a symbol of Heaven, the abode we attain when we discover and accept our Christhood. Thus our Lord, the world's greatest mystic, spoke the following; not as the human Jesus, but as the Indwelling Christ:

> But after I AM raised up, I will go before you into Galilee.[1512]

Of the hidden meaning behind "Galilee" Dante wrote:

> Matthew said: "The Angel of the Lord descended from Heaven, and came and rolled back the stone from the door, and sat upon it. His countenance was like lightning, and his raiment white as snow."[1513] The Angel is this Nobility of ours which comes from God, as it has been said, of which our argument speaks, and says to each one of these sects, that is, to whoever seeks perfect Happiness in the Active Life, that it is not here; but go and tell the disciples and Peter, that is, tell those who seek for it and those who are gone astray like Peter, who had denied Him, that He will go before them into Galilee; meaning that the Beatitude or Happiness will go before us into Galilee, that is, into Contemplation; Galilee is as much as to say, Whiteness. Whiteness is a colour full of material light, more so than any other; and thus, Contemplation is more full of Spiritual light than any other thing which is below.[1514]

The meaning of the word Galilee reveals its mystical connotation: *galilaia* is Hebrew for "circuit," "ring," or "circle."[1515] When we complete the evolution of our spiritual journey and experience at-one-ment with the Father, our path then leads us to "Galilee," where we come full circle, emerging totally free in the Christ.[1516] See BETHLEHEM, CROWN, HEAVEN, I AM, JERUSALEM.

GARDEN OF EDEN: In the mainstream Church the Garden of Eden is the walled-in paradise where God placed Adam and Eve, after which they were banished for committing the first sin.[1517] Like the rest of the Bible's geographical settings, orthodoxy has literalized the Garden of Eden, locating it in Southern Mesopotamia near the Pishon and Gihon Rivers.[1518]

The myth that the first man and woman lived in an earthly Shangri-la is universal, and is known in pre-biblical cultures and societies all over the world.[1519] Most revealingly it is found in Sumeria, Akkadia, Persia, Babylonia, and India, where the idea of the Hebrew Garden of Eden legend had its beginnings. The Sumerians, for instance, possessed a "Land of Dilmun," while Babylonian mythology speaks of the "Garden of Siduri."[1520]

In mystical Christianity the literal interpretation of the Garden of Eden is exchanged for an esoteric one. Here it is a symbol of that blissful state we experience when we achieve Christhood: the realization of our own immortal divinity as beings made in the image of God.[1521] It is thus identical to Jesus' doctrine of the Kingdom of God, Paul's doctrine of the Christ, and Buddha's doctrine of Nirvana. See ADAM, EDEN, EVE, GARDEN OF EDEN, KINGDOM OF GOD, ORIGINAL SIN, SERPENT, SIN, THEOSIS, TREE OF LIFE.

GNOSIS: Gnosis is the Greek word for "knowledge." It was used by the first Christians, known today by the name the Gnostics (the *Gnostikoi*), to refer to inner self-knowledge (Higher Knowledge, the unchangeable Truth that Hindus refer to as *vidya*) as opposed to outer academic-knowledge (Lower Knowledge, the relative Truth that Hindus refer to as *avidya*). Gnosis means, in essence, "cognizance by intuition,"[1522] for it is rooted, not in reason, but in a direct personal experience of the divine,[1523] which Zen Buddhists call *atma-jnana*, "self-knowledge."[1524]

The entire catalog of universal knowledge (Gnosis) and wisdom (Sophia) is contained within us, but it cannot be accessed through the intellect (tuition). Only through the spirit (intuition). In Hinduism this great mass of inner Gnosis is known as the "Divine Library Within," thus Thomas Paine said: "My mind is my own church."

Self-revealed knowledge is necessary because we are all at different degrees of spiritual awareness, each one of us requiring a different level of teaching. Thus, as it should be, each individual interprets the Bible differently. This is why God made it impossible for us to use human knowledge to either understand sacred scripture[1525] or to know Him.[1526] This type of knowledge (Gnosis) can never come by reading a book; it can never be taught to us by a pastor, instructor, or school teacher. Only through self-revealed Gnosis, via the wisdom of the Indwelling Christ,[1527] can we attain the faith to discover the God Within.[1528] This is what Paul meant when he said:

> Before faith came, we were kept under the law, shut up unto the faith which should afterwards be revealed. Wherefore the law was our schoolmaster to bring us unto Christ, that we

might be justified by faith. But after that faith is come, *we are no longer under a schoolmaster.*[1529]

In other words, Christians who attain Cosmic or Christ Consciousness,[1530] which Paul calls "the mind of Christ,"[1531] are *self-taught* in the "Ways of the Lord"[1532] and "the mysteries of the Kingdom of Heaven"[1533] by the *Spirit Within*.[1534]

To reemphasize, this is because Gnosis is a type of knowledge that cannot be intellectually discerned. It must be, as Paul put it, "spiritually discerned."[1535] In the East this fact has long been understood: celestial knowledge simply cannot be conveyed using words.[1536] Lao Tzu taught that anything which is articulated is not and cannot be Divine Truth. As soon as it is defined, written, spoken, organized, or delineated in any way, it is no longer Divine Truth.[1537]

Thus those who attain or experience what is variously known as Christ Consciousness, Cosmic Consciousness, Moses Consciousness, Buddha Consciousness, etc., are the kind of men and women who are almost invariably "independent of education, and most of them . . . think it useless or worse."[1538] Thus Blake says:

> There is no use in education: I hold it to be wrong. It is a great sin.[1539]

Whitman writes:

> You shall no longer feed on the spectres in books.[1540]

Buddha declares:

> The noble truths were not among the doctrines handed down, but there arose within him [the enlightened individual] the eye to perceive them.[1541]

Jesus concurred with this view because He experienced it firsthand, having gained all of His spiritual wisdom directly through intuition, or what He called the "Father."[1542] Saith our Lord:

> As the Father hath said unto me so I speak.[1543]

These are all examples of how spiritually illuminated individuals view Gnosis.

As noted, an entire branch of early Christianity takes its name from the word Gnosis (divine inner knowledge): the pre-Christian Gnostics,[1544] who later became the first Christians.[1545] They held that a true understanding of God can only come from self-revelation, which includes meditation, prayer, intuition, epiphanies, theophanies, theaphanies, inspiration, visions, imagination, dreams, and the like. Many of these freethinking Christian sects also taught the true Gospel, "the Gospel of the Kingdom,"[1546] or rather "the Gospel of the Kingdom of God,"[1547] which included Jesus' doctrines on the Sacred Christ Within,[1548] our innate oneness with the Father,[1549] and such spiritual concepts as the laws of Healing, the Word, Karma, the Golden Rule, and Attraction.[1550] "For what thou see, thou shall become," taught the Gnostics.[1551]

Because of this very teaching, Gnostic Christianity was considered a threat to the Ecclesiastics (the hierarchy of the Catholic Church), and so Gnostic Christians were persecuted, tortured, and murdered, and their sacred books put to the torch.[1552] As a result, much of Jesus' authentic Gnostic teachings were lost.[1553] Yet, evidence of the Master's belief in self-revealed knowledge, and that of many of His followers, can still be found in the canonical Bible,[1554] and in numerous recently discovered Gnostic-Christian texts.[1555] See GNOSTICISM, WAY OF THE LORD.

GNOSTICISM: In traditional Christianity Gnosticism was an enemy of the early Church;[1556] a devilish imitation of Christianity which first arose in the 2nd Century A.D.[1557] In the mystical Church the opposite view is held; namely that Gnosticism was the original Christianity,[1558] a pre-Christian esoteric belief system[1559] upon which the orthodox Church in Alexandria was later built.[1560] To the Gnostics or *Gnostikoi* it was plain that this, the institutionalized branch, was created by Satan to oppose the Gnostic Church, mislead the masses, and conceal the Truth about Theosis (God in Man).[1561] Historically speaking, the Gnostics were right, as we shall now see.

Gnosis means "knowledge," and is similar to the Hebrew word "kabbalah,"[1562] which means "received," in this case mystically received knowledge.[1563] In other words, Gnosis is not book-learned knowledge (tuition), but rather self-revealed knowledge (intuition), a type which cannot be transmitted by reason, but only by insight. This is one of the primary reasons that the traditional Church has always been opposed to Gnosticism. For Gnostic Christianity does not require a priesthood, salvation, redemption, baptism, or even a church. It is founded on the idea of a direct, one-on-one experience of God, of the Divine, of the numenistic. Christian Gnostics, like Christian mystics, are led purely by the Holy Spirit, which makes its home *within* Man and Woman.[1564] Thus, the *outer religion* of the orthodox Christian is eschewed for an *inner spirituality* that seeks a personal relationship with the Almighty. For these views the early Gnostics were burned at the stake!

Contrary to conventional thought, many of the early orthodox Fathers thoroughly understood and openly embraced the Gnosis; that is, the Gnostic mysticism that was inherent to the primitive Church; a profound occultic doctrine that Paul referred to as the "mystery which was kept secret since the world began."[1565] One such individual was Clement of Alexandria, who declared:

> And the Gnosis itself is that which has descended by transmission to a few, having been imparted unwritten by the Apostles.[1566]

Stirling asserts that the widely held traditional notion that the Church Fathers unilaterally repudiated the Gnostics and their beliefs is nothing but a "priestly artifice" meant to veil the truth:

> From expressions of this kind [like Clement's above] it becomes apparent that the importance, attached to the unbroken continuity of the Apostolic succession, was due to the necessity for securing the transmission of the oral Tradition or Gnosis unimpaired, in order that the true interpretation of the Gospel might be insured to succeeding generations. *The works of Irenaeus, Hippolytus, and Epiphanius have numerous references to the Gnostic practices of the Christians, and particularly to the Cabalistic process of Gematria* [the mystical Jewish system of assigning numbers to letters, words, and phrases]. *The fact, that the numerical system of the Cabalists and Gnostics is generally condemned by the Fathers, appears to be no more than a priestly artifice, intended to deceive the vulgar, and prevent inquisitive people from prying too deeply into the mysteries, which were retained as the exclusive property of the few, referred to by St. Clement.* That the Greek philosophy rested upon the same secret [Gnostic] tradition, which was accepted and retained as the basis of the Christian theology, in common with other religious and philosophical systems, seems to be borne out by another passage from . . . [Clement's] *Miscellanies*: "Peter says in his 'Preaching,' Know that there is one God, . . . who made all things by the 'Word of His power,' that is, *according to the Gnostic Scripture, His Son.*" Then he adds: 'Worship this God, not as the Greeks'—signifying plainly, that *the excellent among the Greeks worshipped the same God as we, but that they had not learned by perfect knowledge that which was delivered by the Son.* 'Do not then worship,' he did not say the God whom the Greeks worship, but 'as the Greeks'—changing the manner of the worship of God, *not announcing another God.* . . . Neither worship as the Jews; for they, thinking that they only know God, do not know Him, adoring as they do angels and archangels, the month, and the moon. . . . For what belonged to the Greeks and the Jews is old. But we, who worship him in a new way, in the third form, are Christians."[1567]

We know that this view, that of the Christian mystic, is true, in great part, because of the orthodox Church Fathers themselves: as heresy-hunters they specifically identified the Gnostics as Christians—though naturally they portrayed them as heterodox in nature.[1568]

The truth is that it was the institutional Church that was and still is heterodox, as Parker states:

> The stream of Christianity has come to us in two channels—one within the church, the other without the church—and it is not hazarding too much to say, that *since the fourth century the true Christian life has been out of the established church, and not in it, but rather in the ranks of dissenters.*[1569]

Yes, the mystical Church was the original orthodox Church, and technically speaking, it still is. And we have the many sacred Gnostic texts from Nag Hammadi to prove it.[1570] Ghillany writes:

> The whole Eastern world was at that time impregnated with Gnostic ideas, which centered in the revelation of the Divine in the human [Theosis]. In this way there arose, for example, a Samaritan Gnosis, independent of the Christian. *Christianity itself is a species of Gnosis.*[1571]

Pike makes note of the great Syncretistic Age in which Jesus lived:

> At the time when John the Baptist made his appearance in the desert, near the shores of the Dead Sea, all the old philosophical and religious systems were approximating toward each other. A general lassitude inclined the minds of all toward the quietude of that amalgamation of doctrines for which the expeditions of Alexander and the more peaceful occurrences that followed, with the establishment in Asia and Africa of many Grecian dynasties and a great number of Grecian colonies, had prepared the way.
>
> After the intermingling of different nations, which resulted from the wars of Alexander in three-quarters of the globe, the doctrines of Greece, of Egypt, of Persia, and of India, met and intermingled everywhere. All the barriers that had formerly kept the nations apart, were thrown down; and while the People of the West readily connected their faith with those of the East, those of the Orient hastened to learn the traditions of Rome and the legends of Athens. While the Philosophers of

Greece, all (except the disciples of Epicurus) more or less Platonists, seized eagerly upon the beliefs and doctrines of the East,—the Jews and Egyptians, before then the most exclusive of all peoples, yielded to that eclecticism which prevailed among their masters, the Greeks and Romans. *Under the same influences of toleration, even those who embraced Christianity, mingled together the old and the new, Christianity and Philosophy, the Apostolic teachings and the traditions of Mythology. The man of intellect, devotee of one system, rarely displaces it with another in all its purity. The people take such a creed as is offered them.*

Accordingly, the distinction between the esoteric and the exoteric doctrine, immemorial in other creeds, easily gained a foothold among many of the Christians; and it was held by a vast number, even during the preaching of Paul, that the writings of the Apostles were incomplete; that they contained only the germs of another doctrine, which must receive from the hands of philosophy, not only the systematic arrangement which was wanting, but all the development which lay concealed therein. The writings of the Apostles, they said, in addressing themselves to mankind in general, enunciated only the articles of the vulgar faith; but transmitted the mysteries of knowledge to superior minds, to the Elect,—mysteries handed down from generation to generation in esoteric traditions; and to this science of the mysteries they gave the name of Gnosis.

The Gnostics derived their leading doctrines and ideas from Plato and Philo, the Zend-avesta and the Kabalah, and the Sacred books of India and Egypt; and thus introduced into the bosom of Christianity the cosmological and theosophical speculations, which had formed the larger portion of the ancient religions of the Orient, joined to those of the Egyptian, Greek, and Jewish doctrines, which the Neo-Platonists had equally adopted in the Occident.[1572]

Centuries ago Boulanger recorded the Gnostic-Christian perspective:

The Marcionists, (a [Gnostic] Christian sect) assured [us] that the evangelists were filled with falsities. The Manicheans, who formed a very numerous sect at the commencement of Christianity, rejected as false, all the New Testament; and shewed other writings quite different that they gave for authentic. The Cerinthians, like the Marcionists, admitted not the Acts of the Apostles. The Encratites, and the Sevenians, adopted neither the Acts nor the Epistles of Paul. Chrysostome, in a homily which he made upon the Acts of the Apostles, says, that in his time, about the year 400, many people knew nothing either of the author or of the book.

St. Irene, who lived before that time, reports that the Valentinians, like several other sects of the Christians, accused the scriptures of being filled with imperfections, errors, and contradictions. The Ebionites or Nazareens [that is, the Essenes], who were the first Christians, rejected all the Epistles of Paul, and regarded him as an impostor. They report, among other things, that he was originally a Pagan, that he came to Jerusalem, where he lived sometime; and that having a mind to marry the daughter of the high priest, he caused himself to be circumcised: but that not being able to obtain her, he quarrelled with the Jews, and wrote against circumcision, and against the observation of the sabbath, and against all the [Jewish] legal ordinances.[1573]

Yes, the Gnostics (and their Palestinian counterparts, the Essenes) were the first Christians. But this truth has been vigorously, and even violently at times, suppressed by the mainstream Church and utterly concealed from the laity. How? Chiefly through the destruction of Gnostic writings, the development of the pretense that the Gnostics came *after* Christianity, and the demonization of Gnosticism and its leaders, an uninformed polemical movement that continues within mainline Christianity to this day.

In ancient times, after condemning the Gnostics' literature and throwing their books into the fire,[1574] Irenaeus and numerous other traditional Church Fathers wrote scores of scathing books against Gnosticism during the savage anti-Gnostic crusade that swept Christianity during the 1st Millennium. The purpose was not only suppression, but, as mentioned, an effort to make it appear as if Gnosticism arose *subsequently* to Christianity, which, of course, turned it into the so-called imitator of the "original" Church. That the opposite was true did not disturb this group of deceitful and unscrupulous Churchmen.[1575]

Gnostic-Christians and their Pagan supporters did not take this repressive, totalitarian, brutal, and bloody religious cleansing lying down, however. In the 2nd Century A.D., for instance, the celebrated Pagan philosopher Celsus wrote a work called *The True Word*, exposing the many falsities of so-called "orthodox Christianity." But the Church ordered it burned in an effort to prevent the truth from being exposed. Today we know nothing about Celsus' work except the title, which is exactly what the Catholic Church intended. The great 3rd-Century philosopher Porphyry wrote a massive 15-volume work which described in detail the errors of "traditional" Christianity. But Christian magistrates had every copy torched and today almost nothing is known of it.[1576]

In 1444 William Caxton published the first book ever to be printed in England. Cardinal Wolsey, the Bishop of London, immediately recognized the immense threat the printing press posed to the Church, which is why in 1474 he announced to his fellow clergymen: "If we do not destroy this dangerous invention, it will one day destroy us." By "us" the crafty archpriest was surreptitiously referring to what his kind privately called "*The Myth of Christ*," the intentionally embellished biography of the historical Jesus,[1577] who the Church had willfully, and with malice aforethought, deified and apotheosized to attract Pagan converts[1578] during the first few centuries A.D.,[1579] posthumously putting words into His mouth He never spoke,[1580] turning a human Jewish prophet into not just the Son of God, but into God himself.[1581] As the 16th-Century Socinians declared, and as 21st-Century Unitarians and even many of today's most lauded theologians agree, "pronouncing the divinity of Christ as accepted by the [established mainstream] Church is unbiblical."[1582]

In light of such facts Archdeacon Paley was similarly moved to declare that when it came to Jesus and the true history of the Church, "he could ill afford to have a conscience," while Pope Leo X[1583] infamously avowed that "it is well known how profitable *this myth of Christ* has been to us."[1584]

Dr. Draper gives the following account of how The Myth of Christ was further developed by way of the traditional Church's "Scheme of Salvation":

> *Great is the difference between Christianity under Severus (born 146) and Christianity under Constantine (born 274). Many of the doctrines which at the latter period were pre-eminent, in the former were unknown. Two causes led to the amalgamation of Christianity with Paganism: 1) The political necessities of the new dynasty; 2) The policy adopted by the new religion to insure its spread.*
>
> Though the Christian party had proved itself sufficiently strong to give a master to the empire, *it was never sufficiently strong to destroy its antagonist, Paganism. The issue of the struggle between them was an amalgamation of the principles of both.* . . . Constantine continually showed by his acts, that he felt he must be the impartial sovereign of all his people, not merely the representative of a successful faction. Hence, if he built Christian churches, he also restored Pagan temples; if he listened to the clergy, he also consulted the haruspices [Pagan diviners]; if he summoned the Council of Nicea, he also honored the statue of Fortune; if he accepted the rite of Baptism, he also struck a medal bearing his title of "God." His statue, on top of the great porphyry pillar at Constantinople, consisted of an ancient image of [the Sun-God] Apollo, whose features were replaced by those of the emperor, and its head surrounded by the nails feigned to have been used at the crucifixion of Christ, arranged so as to form a crown of glory.
>
> *Feeling that there must be concessions to the defeated Pagan*

party, in accordance with its ideas, he looked with favor on the idolatrous movements of his court. In fact, the leaders of these movements were persons of his own family.

To the emperor,—a mere worldling—a man without any religious convictions, doubtless it appeared best for himself, best for the empire, and best for the contending parties, Christian and Pagan, *to promote their union or amalgamation as much as possible.* Even sincere Christians do not seem to have been averse to this; perhaps they believed that the new doctrines would diffuse most thoroughly by incorporating in themselves ideas borrowed from the old; that Truth would assert herself in the end, and the impurities be cast off. In accomplishing this amalgamation, Helen, the Empress-mother, aided by the court ladies, led the way.

As years passed on, the faith described by Tertullian (A.D. 150-195) was transformed into one more fashionable and more debased. It was incorporated with the old Greek mythology. Olympus was restored, but the divinities passed under new names.

. . . Heathen rites were adopted, a pompous and splendid ritual, gorgeous robes, mitres, tiaras, wax-tapers, processional services, lustrations, gold and silver vases, were introduced.

The festival of the Purification of the Virgin was invented to remove the uneasiness of heathen converts on account of the loss of their Lupercalia, or feasts of [the nature-god] Pan.

The apotheosis of the old Roman times was replaced by canonization; tutelary mints succeeded to local mythological divinities. Then came the mystery of transubstantiation, or the conversion of bread and wine by the priest into the flesh and blood of Christ. As centuries passed, the paganization became more and more complete.[1585]

Of this dark and shameful period in the history of traditional Christianity, Doane writes:

Beside forging, lying, and deceiving for the cause of Christ, the Christian Fathers destroyed all evidence against themselves and their religion, which they came across. Christian divines seem to have always been afraid of too much light. In the very infancy of printing, Cardinal Wolsey foresaw its effect on Christianity, and in a speech to the clergy, publicly forewarned them, that, if they did not destroy the Press, the Press would destroy them. There can be no doubt, that had the objections of Porphyry, Hierocles, Celsus, and other opponents of the Christian faith, been permitted to come down to us, the plagiarism in the Christian Scriptures from previously existing Pagan documents, is the specific charge they would have presented us. But these were ordered to be burned, by the prudent piety of the Christian emperors.

In Alexandria, in Egypt, there was an immense library, founded by the Ptolemies. This library was situated in the Alexandrian Museum; the apartments which were allotted for it were beautifully sculptured, and crowded with the choicest statues and pictures; the building was built of marble. This library eventually comprised *four hundred thousand volumes*. In the course of time, probably on account of inadequate accommodation for so many books, an additional library was established, and placed in the temple of Serapis. The number of volumes in this library, which was called the daughter of that in the museum, was eventually three hundred thousand. There were, therefore, *seven hundred thousand volumes in these royal collections.*

In the establishment of the museum, Ptolemy Soter, and his son Philadelphus, had three objects in view:

1. *For the perpetuation of knowledge.* Orders were given to the chief librarian to buy, at the king's expense, whatever books he could. A body of transcribers was maintained in the museum, whose duty it was to make correct copies of such works as their owners were not disposed to sell. Any books brought by foreigners into Egypt were taken at once to the museum, and when correct copies had been made, the transcript was given to the owner, and the original placed in the library. Often a very large pecuniary indemnity was paid.

2. *For the increase of knowledge.* One of the chief objects of the museum was that of serving as the home of a body of men who devoted themselves to study, and were lodged and maintained at the king's expense. In the original organization of the museum the residents were divided into four faculties,—Literature, Mathematics, Astronomy, and Medicine. An officer of very great distinction presided over the establishment, and had general charge of its interests. Demetius Phalareus, perhaps the most learned man of his age, who had been Governor of Athens for many years, was the first so appointed. Under him was the librarian, an office sometimes held by men whose names have descended to our times, as Eratosthenes and Apollonius Rhodius. In connection with the

museum was a botanical and a zoological garden. These gardens, as their names imply, were for the purpose of facilitating the study of plants and animals. There was also an astronomical observatory, containing armillary spheres, globes, solstitial and equatorial armils, astrolabes, parallactic rules, and other apparatus then in use, the graduation on the divided instruments being into degrees and sixths.

3. *For the diffusion of knowledge.* In the museum was given, by lectures, conversation, or other appropriate methods, instruction in all the various departments of human knowledge.

There flocked to this great intellectual centre, students from all countries. *It is said that at one time not fewer than fourteen thousand were in attendance. Subsequently even the Christian church received from it some of the most eminent of its Fathers, as Clemens Alexandrinus, Origen, Athanasius, etc.*

The library in the museum was burned during the siege of Alexandria by Julius Caesar. To make amends for this great loss, the library collected by Eumenes, King of Pergamus, was presented by Mark Antony to Queen Cleopatra. Originally it was founded as a rival to that of the Ptolemies. It was added to the collection in the Serapion, or the temple of Serapis.

It was not destined, however, to remain there many centuries, as *this very valuable library was willfully destroyed by the Christian Theophilus*, and on the spot where this beautiful temple of Serapis stood, in fact, on its very foundation, was erected a church in honor of the "noble army of martyrs," who had never existed.

This we learn from the historian Gibbon, who says that, *after this library was destroyed, "the appearance of the empty shelves excited the regret and indignation of every spectator, whose mind was not totally darkened by religious prejudice."*

The destruction of this library was almost the death-blow to free-thought—wherever Christianity ruled—for more than a thousand years.

The death-blow was soon to be struck, however, which was done by *Saint Cyril*, who succeeded Theophilus as Bishop of Alexandria.

Hypatia, the daughter of Theon, the mathematician, endeavored to continue the old-time [Gnostic] instructions. Each day before her academy stood a long train of chariots; her lecture-room was crowded with the wealth and fashion of

Alexandria. They came to listen to her discourses on those questions which man in all ages has asked, but which have never yet been answered: "What am I?" Where am I? What can I know?"

  Hypatia and Cyril; philosophy and bigotry; they cannot exist together. As Hypatia repaired to her academy, she was assaulted by (Saint) Cyril's mob—a mob of many [Christian] monks. Stripped naked in the street, she was dragged into a church, and there killed by the club of Peter the Reader. The corpse was cut to pieces, the flesh was scraped from the bones with shells, and the remnants cast into a fire. For this frightful crime Cyril was never called to account.

  It seemed to be admitted that the end sanctifies the means. So ended Greek philosophy in Alexandria, so came to an untimely close the learning that the Ptolemies had done so much to promote.

  The fate of Hypatia was a warning to all who would cultivate profane knowledge. Henceforth there was to be no freedom for human thought. Every one must think as ecclesiastical authority ordered him; A.D. 414. In Athens itself philosophy awaited its doom. Justinian at length prohibited its teaching and caused all its schools in that city to be closed.

  After this followed the long and dreary dark ages, but the sun of science, that bright and glorious luminary, was destined to rise again.

  The history of this great Alexandrian library is one of the keys which unlock the door, and exposes to our view the manner in which the Hindoo incarnate god Crishna, and the meek and benevolent Buddha, came to be worshiped under the name of Christ Jesus. For instance, we have just seen:

  1. That, "orders were given to the chief librarian to buy at the king's expense whatever books he could."

  2. That, "one of the chief objects of the museum was that of serving as the home of a body of men who devoted themselves to study."

  3. That, "any books brought by foreigners into Egypt were taken at once to the museum and correct copies made."

  4. That, "there flocked to this great intellectual centre students from all countries."

  5. That, "the Christian church received from it some of the most eminent of its Fathers."

  6. That, the chief doctrines of the Gnostic Christians

"had been held for centuries before their time in many of the cities in Asia Minor. There, it is probable, they first came into existence as 'Mystae,' *upon the establishment of a direct intercourse with India under the Seleucidse and the Ptolemies."*

7. That, *"the College of Essenes at Ephesus, the Orphics of Thrace, the Curetes of Crete, are all merely branches of one antique and common religion, and that originally Asiatic."*

8. That, *"the introduction, of Buddhism into Egypt and Palestine affords the only true solution of innumerable difficulties in the history of religion."*

9. That, "Buddhism had actually been planted in the dominions of the Seleucidae and Ptolemies (Palestine belonging to the former) before the beginning of the third century B.C., and is proved to demonstration by a passage in the edicts of Asoka."

10. That, *"it is very likely that the commentaries (Scriptures) which were among them (the Essenes) were the Gospels."*

11. That, *"the principal doctrines and rites of the Essenes can be connected with the East, with Parsism, and especially with Buddhism."*

12. That, *"among the doctrines which the Essenes and Buddhists had in common was that of the Angel-Messiah."*

13. That, *"they (the Essenes) had a flourishing university or corporate body, established at Alexandria, in Egypt, long before the period assigned for the birth of Christ."*

14. That, *"the very ancient and Eastern doctrine of the Angel-Messiah had been applied to Gautama Buddha, and so it was applied to Jesus Christ by the Essenes of Egypt and Palestine, who introduced this new Messianic doctrine into Essenic Judaism and Essenic Christianity."*

15. That, *"we hear very little of them (the Essenes) after A.D. 40; and there can hardly be any doubt that the Essenes as a body must have embraced Christianity."*

Here is the solution of the problem [of how Christianity got its start]. *The sacred books of Hindoos and Buddhists were among the Essenes, and in the library at Alexandria. The Essenes, who were afterwards called Christians, applied the legend of the Angel-Messiah—"the very ancient Eastern doctrine," which we have shown throughout this work—to Christ Jesus. It was simply a transformation of names, a transformation which had previously occurred in many cases. After this came additions to the legend from*

> *other sources. Portions of the legends related of the Persian, Greek and Roman Saviours and Redeemers of mankind, were, from time to time, added to the already legendary history of the Christian Saviour. Thus history was repeating itself. Thus the virgin-born God and Saviour, worshiped by all nations of the earth, though called by different names, was but one and the same.*[1586]

Of the original mystical Gnostic-Essenic Christian Church Pike writes:

> During the persecutions in the early ages of Christianity, the Christians took refuge in the vast catacombs which stretched for miles in every direction under the city of Rome, and are supposed to have been of Etruscan origin. There, amid labyrinthine windings, deep caverns, hidden chambers, chapels, and tombs, the persecuted fugitives found refuge, and there they performed the ceremonies of the Mysteries.
>
> The Basilideans, a sect of Christians that arose soon after the time of the Apostles, practised the Mysteries, with the old Egyptian legend. They symbolized Osiris by the Sun, Isis by the Moon, and Typhon by Scorpio; and wore crystals bearing these emblems, as amulets or talismans to protect them from danger; upon which were also a brilliant star and the serpent. They were copied from the talismans of Persia and Arabia, and given to every candidate at his initiation.
>
> Irenaeus tells us that the Simonians, one of the earliest sects of the Gnostics, had a Priesthood of the Mysteries.
>
> Tertullian tells us that the Valentinians, the most celebrated of all the Gnostic schools, imitated, or rather perverted, the Mysteries of Eleusis. Irenaeus informs us, in several curious chapters, of the mysteries practised by the Marcosians; and Origen gives much information as to the mysteries of the Ophites; and there is no doubt that all the Gnostic sects had mysteries and an initiation. *They all claimed to possess a secret doctrine, coming to them directly from Jesus Christ, different from that of the Gospels and Epistles, and superior to those communications, which, in their eyes, were merely exoteric [that is, superficial].* This secret doctrine they did not communicate to every one; and among the extensive sect of the Basilideans hardly one in a thousand knew it, as we learn from Irenaeus. We know the name of only the highest class of their initiates. They were styled Elect or *Elus*, and Strangers to the World. They had at least three degrees—the *Material*, the *Intellectual*,

and the *Spiritual*; and the lesser and greater mysteries: and the number of those who attained the highest degree was quite small.

Baptism was one of their most important ceremonies; and the Basilideans celebrated the 10th of January, as the anniversary of the day on which Christ was baptized in Jordan.

They had the ceremony of laying on of hands, by way of purification; and that of the mystic banquet, emblem of that to which they believed the Heavenly Wisdom would one day admit them, in the fullness of things.

Their ceremonies were much more like those of the Christians than those of Greece; but they mingled with them much that was borrowed from the Orient and Egypt: and taught the primitive truths, mixed with a multitude of fantastic errors and fictions.[1587]

The discipline of the secret was the concealment (*occultatio*) of certain tenets and ceremonies. So says Clemens of Alexandria.

To avoid persecution, the early Christians were compelled to use great precaution, and to hold meetings of the Faithful [of the Household of Faith] in private places, under concealment by darkness. They assembled in the night, and they guarded against the intrusion of false brethren and profane persons, spies who might cause their arrest. They conversed together figuratively, and by the use of symbols, lest cowans and eavesdroppers might overhear: and there existed among them a favored class, or Order, who were initiated into certain mysteries which they were bound by solemn promise not to disclose, or even converse about, except with such as had received them under the same sanction. They were called Brethren, the Faithful, Stewards of the Mysteries, Superintendents, Devotees of the Secret, and Architects.

In the *Hierarchies*, attributed to St. Dionysius the Areopagite, the first Bishop of Athens, *the tradition of the sacrament is said to have been divided into three degrees, or grades, purification, initiation, and accomplishment or perfection*; and it mentions also, as part of the ceremony, the bringing to sight.

The Apostolic Constitutions, attributed to Clemens, Bishop of Rome, describe the early church, and say: *"These regulations must on no account be communicated to all sorts of persons, because of the mysteries contained in them."* They speak of the Deacon's duty to keep the doors, that none uninitiated should enter at the oblation. *Ostiarii*, or doorkeepers, kept guard, and gave notice of the time of prayer and church-assemblies; and also by private signal, in times of persecution, gave notice to those within, to enable them to avoid danger. The mysteries were open to the *Fideles* or Faithful only; and no spectators were allowed at the communion.

Tertullian, who died about A.D. 216, says in his *Apology*:

> "None are admitted to the religious mysteries without an oath of secrecy. We appeal to your Thracian and Eleusinian mysteries; and we are specially bound to this caution, because if we prove faithless, we should not only provoke Heaven, but draw upon our heads the utmost rigor of human displeasure. And should strangers betray us? They know nothing but by report and hearsay. Far hence, ye Profane! is the prohibition from all holy mysteries."

Clemens, Bishop of Alexandria, born about A.D. 191, says, in his *Stromata*, that he cannot explain the mysteries, because he should thereby, according to the old proverb, put a sword into the hands of a child. He frequently compares the Discipline of the Secret with the heathen Mysteries, as to their internal and recondite wisdom.

Whenever the early Christians happened to be in company with strangers, more properly termed *the Profane*, they never spoke of their sacraments, but indicated to one another what they meant, by means of symbols and secret watchwords, disguisedly, and as by direct communication of mind with mind [telepathy], and by enigmas.

Origen, born A.D. 134 or 135, answering Celsus, who had *objected that the Christians had a concealed doctrine*, said:

> "Inasmuch as the essential and important doctrines and principles of Christianity are openly taught, it is foolish to object that there are other things that are recondite; for *this is common to Christian discipline with that of those philosophers in whose teaching some*

things were exoteric and some esoteric: and it is enough to say that it was so with some of the disciples of Pythagoras."

The formula which the primitive church pronounced at the moment of celebrating its mysteries, was this: *"Depart, ye Profane! Let the Catechumens, and those who have not been admitted or initiated, go forth."*

Archelaus, Bishop of Cascara in Mesopotamia, who, in the year 278, conducted a controversy with the Manichaeans, said:

"These mysteries the church now communicates to him who has passed through the introductory Degree. They are not explained to the Gentiles at all; nor are they taught openly in the hearing of Catechumens; but *much that is spoken is in disguised terms, that the Faithful, who possess the knowledge, may be still more informed, and those who are not acquainted with it, may suffer no disadvantage.*"

Cyril, Bishop of Jerusalem, was born in the year 315, and died in 386. In his *Catechesis* he says:

"The Lord spake in parables to his hearers in general; but to his disciples he explained in private the parables and allegories which he spoke in public. The splendor of glory is for those who are early enlightened: obscurity and darkness are the portion of the unbelievers and ignorant. Just so the church discovers its mysteries to those who have advanced beyond the class of Catechumens: we employ obscure terms with others."

St. Basil, the Great Bishop of Caesarea, born in the year 326, and dying in the year 376, says:

"We receive the dogmas transmitted to us by writing, and those which have descended to us from the Apostles, beneath the mystery of oral

> tradition: *for several things have been handed to us without writing, lest the vulgar, too familiar with our dogmas, should lose a due respect for them.* . . . *This is what the uninitiated are not permitted to contemplate; and how should it ever be proper to write and circulate among the people an account of them?"*

St. Gregory Nazianzen, Bishop of Constantinople, A.D. 379, says:

> *"You have heard as much of the mystery as we are allowed to speak openly in the ears of all; the rest will be communicated to you in private; and that you must retain within yourself.* . . . *Our mysteries are not to be made known to strangers."*

St. Ambrose, Archbishop of Milan, who was born in 340, and died in 393, says in his work *De Mysteriis*:

> *"All the mystery should be kept concealed, guarded by faithful silence, lest it should be inconsiderately divulged to the ears of the Profane.* . . . *It is not given to all to contemplate the depths of our mysteries that they may not be seen by those who ought not to behold them; nor received by those who cannot preserve them."*

And in another work:

> *"He sins against God, who divulges to the unworthy the mysteries confided to him. The danger is not merely in violating truth, but in telling truth, if he allow himself to give hints of them to those from whom they ought to be concealed. Beware of casting pearls before swine! Every mystery ought to be kept secret; and, as it were, to be covered over by silence, lest it should rashly be divulged to the ears of the Profane. Take heed that you do not incautiously reveal the mysteries!"*

St. Augustine, Bishop of Hippo, who was born in 347, and died in 430, says in one of his discourses:

> "Having dismissed the Catechumens, we have retained you only to be our hearers; because, besides those things which belong to all Christians in common, *we are now to discourse to you of sublime mysteries, which none are qualified to hear, but those who, by the Master's favor, are made partakers of them.* . . . *To have taught them openly, would have been to betray them.*"

And he refers to the Ark of the Covenant, and says that it signified a mystery, or secret of God, shadowed over by the cherubims of glory, and honored by being veiled.

St. Chrysostom and St. Augustine speak of initiation more than fifty times. St. Ambrose writes to those who are initiated; and initiation was not merely baptism, or admission into the church, but it referred to initiation into the mysteries. To the baptized and initiated the mysteries of religion were unveiled; they were kept secret from the Catechumens; who were permitted to hear the Scriptures read and the ordinary discourses delivered, in which *the mysteries, reserved for the Faithful*, were never treated of. When the services and prayers were ended, the Catechumens and spectators all withdrew.

Chrysostom, Bishop of Constantinople, was born in 354, and died in 417. He says:

> "*I wish to speak openly: but I dare not, on account of those who are not initiated. I shall therefore avail myself of disguised terms, discoursing in a shadowy manner.* . . . *Where the holy mysteries are celebrated, we drive away all uninitiated persons, and then close the doors.*"

He mentions the acclamations of the initiated; "which," he says, "I here pass over in silence; for it is forbidden to disclose such things to the Profane."

Palladius, in his life of Chrysostom, records, as a great outrage, that, a tumult having been excited against him by his enemies, they forced their way into the *penetralia*, where the uninitiated beheld what was not proper for them to see; and Chrysostom mentions the same circumstance in his epistle to Pope Innocent .

St . Cyril of Alexandria, who was made Bishop in 412, and died in 444, says in his 7th Book against Julian:

> "These mysteries are so profound and so exalted, that they can be comprehended by those only who are enlightened. I shall not, therefore, attempt to speak of what is so admirable in them, lest by discovering them to the uninitiated, I should offend against the injunction not to give what is holy to the impure, nor cast pearls before such as cannot estimate their worth. . . . I should say much more, if I were not afraid of being heard by those who are uninitiated: *because men are apt to deride what they do not understand. And the ignorant, not being aware of the weakness of their minds, condemn what they ought most to venerate.*"

Theodoret, Bishop of Cyropolis in Syria, was born in 393, and made Bishop in 420. In one of his three Dialogues, called the Immutable, he introduces *Orthodoxus*, speaking thus:

> "Answer me, if you please, in mystical or obscure terms: for perhaps there are some persons present who are not initiated into the mysteries."

And in his preface to Ezekiel, tracing up the secret discipline to the commencement of the Christian era, he says:

> "These mysteries are so august, that we ought to keep them with the greatest caution."

Minucius Felix, an eminent lawyer of Rome, who lived in 212, and wrote a defence of Christianity, says:

> "Many of them [the Christians] know each other by tokens and signs (*notis et insignibus*),

and they form a friendship for each other, almost before they become acquainted."

The Latin Word, *tessera*, originally meant a square piece of wood or stone, used in making tesselated pavements; afterward a tablet on which anything was written, and then a cube or die. Its most general use was to designate a piece of metal or wood, square in shape, on which the watchword of an army was inscribed; whence *tessera* came to mean the watchword itself. There was also a *tessera hospitalis*, which was a piece of wood cut into two parts, as a pledge of friendship. Each party kept one of the parts; and they swore mutual fidelity by Jupiter. To break the *tessera* was considered a dissolution of the friendship. The early Christians used it as a mark, the watchword of friendship. With them it was generally in the shape of a fish, and made of bone. On its face was inscribed the word "fish," the initials of which represented the Greek words [in English]: "Jesus Christ, the Son of God, the Saviour."

St. Augustine (*de Fide et Symbolis*) says:

> "This is the faith which in a few words is given to the Novices to be kept by a symbol; these few words are known to all the Faithful; that by believing they may be submissive to God; by being thus submissive, they may live rightly; by living rightly, they may purify their hearts and with a pure heart may understand what they believe."

Maximus Taurinus says:

> "The *tessera* is a symbol and sign by which to distinguish between the Faithful and the Profane."[1588]

Let us reemphasize: the mystical Gnostics (and Essenes) were the first Christians,[1589] which is why in so many regions of the Roman Empire most Christians were Gnostics.[1590] As noted above, Gnosticism was so integral to the first Church that Saint Ambrose held that it was a "sin against God" to divulge the "mysteries of the Kingdom of God"[1591] to uninitiated Christians.[1592]

As further evidence for these facts we have the words of the anti-Gnostic Church Father Epiphanius, Bishop of Salamis. In his work *Panarion* he makes three astounding admissions:

1) "The Nazarene sect was before Christ."[1593]
2) "At that time all Christians alike were called Nazoraeans [Nazarenes]."[1594]
3) The Nazarenes were identical to the Gnostic sect known as the Ebionites.[1595]

As is clear from these statements alone, reluctantly admitted by one of the Church's most orthodox and virulent anti-Gnostic crusaders, just as Palestinian Christianity began as an Essenic sect, Alexandrian Christianity started off as a Gnostic sect.[1596] Because these two branches of the Church share the same spiritual foundation,[1597] it is clear that both were completely Gnostic-Essenic, that is, mystical, in origin.

To bring this line of thought to its logical conclusion: *the historical reality is that the orthodox Christian Church was and is heterodox, while the mystical Church was and is orthodox.* And indeed, as we saw above, early Gnostic-Christians taught this exact doctrine, one that is held by Christian mystics to this day: *the organized Church was founded by the Devil after the mystical Church in order to pervert the true faith and to prevent Man and Woman from realizing their divine nature.*[1598] This is why we can still find "clear traces" of Gnosticism "in almost every part of the New Testament," particularly in the writings of the great Christian mystics Paul and John.[1599]

As Paul did,[1600] Jesus Himself taught various Gnostic doctrines,[1601] among them that His mortal being and the spiritual Christ were separate entities.[1602] He would often, for example, refer to Himself not as "Christ," but as "*the* Christ"[1603]—the former *word* being an expression of that which is earthly and personal (ancient kings, for example, were considered "anointed ones" or "Christs"),[1604] the latter *phrase* being an expression of that which is heavenly and universal (all people possess an Indwelling Christ,[1605] that piece of God in whose spiritual image we are formed).[1606]

Another Gnostic belief held and preached by Jesus was that of the "invisible Father," a loving Supreme Being with whom we can freely communicate and depend on to help direct our lives.[1607] According to Jesus' Gnostic view, God is *not* an angry, judgmental, anthropomorphic being dwelling far off in Heaven, as traditional Christianity images him. God is pure "Spirit," the Master declared,[1608] a mysterious nonmaterial presence that resides within us,[1609] and which responds to our every sincere faith-filled prayer.[1610] We will note here that mystic Paul preached the same doctrine, referring to the universal Indwelling Christ as "the image of the invisible God, the firstborn of every creature,"[1611] the "spirit of God which dwells in you."[1612]

Scholarly research into the time period supports Epiphanius' view that the first Christians, the Nazarenes, were Gnostics. Both Jewish and Hellenistic Gnosticism (which assimilated and mixed Oriental philosophy and mythology) existed long before the rise of the Catholic Church.[1613] For there is an overt and direct Gnostic current of doctrine and ritual beginning in ancient Egypt that stretches all the way up into the period in which our Lord Jesus lived,[1614] most notably among the Essenes[1615]—the mystical Jewish sect of which Jesus and John the Baptist were almost certainly members or students.[1616] Now a sub-sect of the Essenes were the Nazarenes,[1617] who, as we have just seen, were the same as the Gnostic Ebionites,[1618] later known as Christians in Antioch.[1619]

The New Testament itself was the result of the arguments, debates, and confusion created by the conflicts between the first Christians, the Gnostics, and the second Christians, the Catholics. Being the original Church, the Gnostics were, of course, the first to attempt to end the contention by establishing the first authoritative collection of sacred Christian writings, which were created by the so-called "heretic" Marcion around A.D. 150. Naturally this book, *the first real New Testament*, was rejected by the mainline branch, which followed up with its own canon in A.D. 367 under the auspices of the "Father of Orthodoxy," Athanasius, Bishop of Alexandria. His list was the first to contain the current 27 books of the New Testament and no others.[1620]

Though the Gnostics are not mentioned by this name in the New Testament, three Gnostic-Christian leaders are: Simon Magus, Hymenacus, and Philetus.[1621] Gnosticism itself is tacitly referenced hundreds of times, for Jesus,[1622] Paul,[1623] James,[1624] John,[1625] and others often show deep Gnostic tendencies, even espousing a number of overt Gnostic doctrines. Paul goes as far as to describe his type of Christianity as a "heresy."[1626] Why? Because his mystical beliefs were already coming under attack from orthodox Jewish and Christian elements. His enemies even portrayed him as a "ringleader" of the Nazarenes or Essenes,[1627] the mystical Jewish Gnostic sect out of which Christianity itself would spring. Paul is shown practicing Nazarite-Essenic rituals,[1628] while Jesus is literally called a "Nazarene," that is, an Essene,[1629] the sect which Church Father Epiphanius said existed "before Christ."[1630]

Gnosticism is also, of course, denigrated throughout the New Testament by the up and coming orthodox Christians, upon whose literalistic dogma the Catholic Church would one day be founded.[1631] Most of these passages are obvious late interpolations, introduced into the Bible by ecclesiastical priests and scribes seeking to consolidate Christian political, social, economic, and theological power at Rome.[1632]

Gnostic-Christians inflamed orthodox Christians with doctrines that ran counter to their own. For instance, while the institutional Church was based on scripture, law, and doctrine as laid down by the Fathers, the leaderless Gnostic Church was based on self-revealed knowledge or *gnosis*—the opposite of intellectually obtained knowledge. In other words, the tuitive literalistic (mainstream) Church was corporate and worshiped a transcendent anthropomorphic God; the intuitive mystical Church was personal and worshiped an immanent pneumamorphic God.[1633]

Thus, while the orthodox were experiencing God through their pastors,

Gnostic-Christians were experiencing God directly, through their own minds and hearts, for as mystics they refused to rely on what others told them about the Divine. They had to experience it firsthand,[1634] just as Jesus taught—the same man who never once referred to a Christian "priesthood," a Christian "Church," or even "Christianity."[1635] This rendered the orthodox priesthood both irrelevant and obsolete, further infuriating an already angry traditional clergy.

Another example: Gnostic-Christians embraced the concept of an inner resurrection, one that takes place within each believer as a "spiritual reality." They expounded upon this idea in such Gnostic-Christian works as The Treatise on the Resurrection, The Exegesis on the Soul, and The Gospel of Philip.[1636] Little wonder that the Gnostics viewed the orthodox (that is, those who took the Bible *literally*) as "spiritually immature," while they saw themselves (who viewed the Bible *intuitively*) as "spiritually mature."[1637]

It was for these very types of mystical beliefs that Irenaeus, Epiphanius, and other conventional Church Fathers eviscerated their esoterically oriented Christian brethren in writing. The Church itself went on to burn their sacred books, imprison and torture them, and even execute them by the thousands. But this did not destroy or even stop the growth of Gnostic Christianity. It merely went underground.[1638]

As noted, the early Gnostic-Christian Church did not simply accept the prejudice, persecution, and barbarities of the orthodox Church. They fought back in the only way open to them: in writing. In the Gnostic-Christian work The Apocalypse of Peter, for example, Jesus lambasts the spiritually ignorant (orthodox Christians) who persecute and mislead the spiritually enlightened (mystical Christians), saying to Peter:

> *I tell you that these people are spiritually deaf and blind. They are ignorant, and have no inner perception. They cling to a dead man, but this is an error, and it opens them up to evil, dogma, and heterodoxy. They pervert the truth, for they do not understand the mystery. As opposers of truth they are the couriers of falsehood. They do business in my name, and take on the titles "bishop" and "deacon," as if they were ordained by God Himself. But they are merely empty river beds. They are fake and will destroy themselves. Thus I say, leave them be, for they speak ignorance. Be strong and brave and have no fear of them. Peace be with you Peter!*[1639]

The New Testament too records Jesus' impatience and even disgust with the orthodox of His time, the dogmatic, literalistic, unspiritual but highly religious Pharisees, who always put the letter of the law before the spirit of the law. The entire twenty-third chapter of the Gospel of Matthew is devoted to one of the Master's many anti-orthodox speeches. Here is but a single sample, this one full of menacing "woes":

> Woe unto you, scribes and Pharisees, hypocrites! for ye devour widows' houses, and for a pretence make long prayer: therefore ye shall receive the greater damnation. Woe unto you, scribes and Pharisees, hypocrites! for ye compass sea and land to make one proselyte, and when he is made, ye make him twofold more the child of hell than yourselves.
>
> Woe unto you, ye blind guides, which say, "Whosoever shall swear by the temple, it is nothing; but whosoever shall swear by the gold of the temple, he is a debtor!" Ye fools and blind: for whether is greater, the gold, or the temple that sanctifieth the gold? And, whosoever shall swear by the altar, it is nothing; but whosoever sweareth by the gift that is upon it, he is guilty. Ye fools and blind: for whether is greater, the gift, or the altar that sanctifieth the gift?
>
> Woe unto you, scribes and Pharisees, hypocrites! for ye pay tithe of mint and anise and cummin, and have omitted the weightier matters of the law, judgment, mercy, and faith: these ought ye to have done, and not to leave the other undone. Ye blind guides, which strain at a gnat, and swallow a camel. Woe unto you, scribes and Pharisees, hypocrites! for ye make clean the outside of the cup and of the platter, but within they are full of extortion and excess.
>
> Thou blind Pharisee, cleanse first that which is within the cup and platter, that the outside of them may be clean also. Woe unto you, scribes and Pharisees, hypocrites! for ye are like unto whited sepulchres, which indeed appear beautiful outward, but are within full of dead men's bones, and of all uncleanness. Even so ye also outwardly appear righteous unto men, but within ye are full of hypocrisy and iniquity.
>
> O Jerusalem, Jerusalem, thou that killest the prophets, and stonest them which are sent unto thee, how often would I have gathered thy children together, even as a hen gathereth her chickens under her wings, and ye would not! Behold, your house is left unto you desolate.[1640]

For the facts concerning the *true* history of Gnosticism, Gnostic-Christianity, and orthodox Christianity, we turn to one of the greatest authorities on the subject, Kerr Cranston Anderson:

> *If there is one thing that has been proved by recent scholarship it is that*

the Gnostics were the first Christians. The various clauses of the Old Roman Symbol and of the Apostles' Creed were added as the idea of an historical interpretation of the Gospel arose. They were not added to guard against the heresies of the day, but to defend an innovation. The Apostles' Creed alleges seven historical facts about Jesus Christ the son of the Creator, his birth, crucifixion, burial, resurrection, ascension, session at the right of God, and second coming, and all the seven emphasize the reality of the life of Jesus as against the older view. *The truth is that the Old Roman Symbol and the Apostles' Creed are evidence that the church had lost the faculty of spiritual vision and had become a prey to the besetting sin of all ecclesiasticisms—the worship of the letter.*

What confirms us in all this is the fact that when we go back to the first century we find that there were other communities or churches besides those which were organized around the tradition of a historical Jesus. The Epistles of Paul are evidences of this fact. It is impossible to believe that the churches or communities to whom Paul preached his view of a spiritual Christ or Messiah revealed to him by his own ecstatic experiences or visions were derived from the church of Jerusalem of which Peter and James and John were the founders and which was organized around the story of a historic Jesus. Paul was at variance with Peter and James and John whom he called "pillar apostles" not in a very complimentary way. *In the letters of Paul we are introduced to communities or churches entirely different from those which took the synoptic Gospels as their inspiration and guides.*

Paul does not follow the synoptic tradition at all; he follows a Christ of his own and speaks of his own gospel. To Paul the views of the "pillar apostles" seemed decidedly materialistic. It is indeed difficult to believe that there was any such record of the life and teaching of Jesus in existence as the synoptic Gospels contain in the possession of the church at Jerusalem; for with an authority such a record would imply, how could Paul have had any chance of successfully withstanding the "pillar apostles," or of persuading the communities or churches formed by them to leave them and follow him? The immense probability is that *both "Jesus" and "Christ" were divine names before the Christian era, that both were equally unhistorical, and that they were brought together as denoting a single being by the movement that afterwards became historical Christianity.* Whether this be so or not, Paul's Epistles bear witness to the existence of churches or communities which had been long in existence when Paul visited them. Paul's words and phrases are the same as those in use in these communities or churches; they knew what he was speaking about, so that he did not need to define his terms. *Paul had no affinity with churches based upon the tradition of a historical Jesus such as we have in the synoptic Gospels; but he has a very close affinity with those other churches or communities whose members believed in a mystic Christ and whose technical terms were all borrowed from Gnosticism which recent research has proved to be pre-Christian.*

Paul was not converted to belief in a historical Jesus. He was changed from being an official persecutor of the Messianic sects to a preacher of a mystic Christ or spiritual Messiah, the conception of which, he declares, he did not derive from man; that is to say, the Christ he preached was born of his own immediate experience and revelation. He got a chance of a hearing for his spiritual gospel because it was on a level with the belief in Jesus. If one had been historical and the other not, he would have been as one beating the air. *What emerges clear as daylight is that the churches or communities he founded, as well as those he found already established when going on his missionary journeys, were not communities which believed in a historical Jesus; they were of a mystical nature resembling the Therapeutae of whom Philo tells us in his "On the Contemplative Life"—people devoted to the cultivation of the life of contemplation and of union with God.* It is not an unlikely supposition that it was with some one of those communities that Paul spent his three years after his conversion, and that it was the light and inspiration he received from that source which emboldened him to be the apostle he afterwards became. *It is here doubtless that we are to find the oldest form of the Christian faith. What we have in the synoptic Gospels is a teaching decidedly lower in spiritual insight and tone than that current in the mystical sects to which Paul ministered. They believed in a Saviour who was a heavenly being; belief in the Logos was a fundamental part of their creed; and if there was a historical Jesus at all, the great probability is that he was a member of one of the mystic sects of which the age was full. It is extremely unlikely that the historical Jesus shared the ignorant views of the people as the synoptic Gospels represent him as doing. The probability is that in these representations of the synoptic Gospels we have just that kind of misunderstanding which always takes place when a mystical teacher attempts to communicate truth to people on a lower level of life and experience. The supreme misunderstanding was the identification of the historical Jesus with the mystical Christ, the Logos.*

The real Saviour of men, as the real Jesus would doubtless have been the first to declare, is not a historical person, but a divine being who dwells in the soul as Paul teaches. This belief in a mystic Christ, in a heavenly being, in a divine Logos, long antedated the beginning of our era, both in Jewry and among the Greeks.

Now just as those mystic sects of the first century and before, represented by Paul, embodied a more spiritual conception of religion and of life than that embodied in the synoptic Gospels, so the communities or churches of the second century represented a phase of Christianity that was different from, and opposed to, that taught by the growing and triumphant Catholic church. *And it is to be noticed further that this form of Christianity was the original one and that the Christianity of the Catholic church was a development of that. This original form of Christianity is known as Gnosticism.*

All the apocryphal Gospels and Acts are saturated with Gnosticism. Here is where recent investigations into the genesis and development of Gnosticism help us greatly to discover the first form of the Christian faith. Instead of Gnosticism being an outgrowth of Christianity as has long been supposed—a heresy which was persecuted and finally expelled out of existence—the various forms of Gnosticism, Jewish and Christian, of the early centuries, were only particular cases within a movement that included much more. The apocryphal Gospels and Acts tell us what Gnosticism was much better than the school dogmas of Basilides and Valentinus which we know only through the reports of their ecclesiastical enemies, because they formed the main means of Gnostic public propaganda. *There was a very wide circulation of such Gospels and Acts in the second century. They are deeply spiritual in their meaning* though the outward form was often fantastic and grotesque enough. But we must remember that it is only to the modern mind that they seem fantastic and grotesque. They were not so to the men of the second century: to every shade of mind of that age they were equally and entirely credible. *And it was not the mythical and legendary element that offended the orthodox party of the day; it was the inner spiritual teaching, and that they assailed with misrepresentation, and tried to overwhelm with ridicule.* It is just to say that we of this age would be repelled by the marvelous nature of the stories they relate. The apocryphal Gospels and Acts which embody the inner spiritual teachings of those Gnostics read to us like wild romances, but to them they symbolized actual occurrences of the inner life, facts of direct spiritual consciousness. *The teaching is for those who knew the nature of the inner life by direct experience; for all others they were foolishness.* We have the principle stated by Paul in his letter to the Corinthians: "The natural man perceiveth not the things of the spirit of God, for they are foolishness unto him; neither can he know them, for they are spiritually discerned."[641]

It has always been a mystery how such wild imaginings and learned subtleties as the doctrines of the Gnostics seem to be (as represented by the orthodox Church Fathers) could make any deep impression on the minds of men of that age or indeed of any age. The mystery is explained when we turn our attention to the popular literature of the movement as embodied in the apocryphal Gospels and Acts of the second century; and when, especially, we are able to look below the surface and discern the inner spiritual meaning of the narratives. They were so popular in the second century that they could not be disposed of by ridicule simply, and the orthodox Church Fathers had to have recourse to other means to meet them. It is because of this fact that we have these apocryphal Gospels and Acts at all. *The orthodox Church Fathers boldly adopted the most popular narratives from the heretical books, and after carefully eliminating what they deemed the "poison of false doctrine," replaced them in this purified form in the hands of the people. Fortunately for us this purification has not been complete, and some of the "poison" has been preserved.* Many things of great beauty are found in these Gospels and Acts amid much that seems fantastic and grotesque. But, as I have said, they are so because we do not possess the key that will open up the meaning. This key is found in the man-mystery, the man-myth, or man-doctrine, which was central in all the mystery institutions of antiquity.

Briefly put, *it is the story of the descent of man from his heavenly home and his return to that state of glory after having mastered the powers of the world. There is nothing so ancient as this doctrine*; it is lost in the mists of antiquity, and in the centuries immediately preceding the beginning of our era it was a well-developed doctrine in the whole Graeco-Roman world. It was the jealously guarded secret of every mystery institution of antiquity. The whole ancient world was honeycombed with these mystery institutions. They were practically universal, being found in Chaldea, Phoenicia, Palestine, Egypt, Phrygia and Greece; *and in every one of them the central doctrine was this* myth or mystery of man. In Plato, whose writings were the Bible of the Greeks, we have allegory upon allegory describing the soul of man in his heavenly home. The state of man in this world these Gnostics called a state of death. We have a hint of this in Paul's letter to the Colossians where he describes man as "dead" and his "life as hid with Christ in God."[1642] *He means that the true life of man is buried in matter and awaits resurrection, which does not mean resuscitation of a dead body, but the awakening of the spirit of man into consciousness of its divine life.* In the Epistle to the Ephesians the apostle quotes a part of a Gnostic hymn: "Awake thou that sleepest, and arise from the dead, and the Christ shall shine upon thee,"[1643] and this does not mean a call upon dead bodies to come out of graves, which would be absurd, but a call upon the spirit to awaken out of its state of unconsciousness and realize its true life. *With the Gnostics of the apocryphal Gospels and Acts the death of Jesus was the symbol of a profound experience which the individual spirit must pass through on its upward journey as a condition of its further advancement. The resurrection of Jesus they similarly looked upon as a symbol of the new birth of illumination of the spirit, its coming to life from its previous death state.* The instruction given in the apocryphal Gospels and Acts, as well as in many Gnostic treatises, such as *Pistis Sophia*, is represented as having been given by Jesus to his disciples after his resurrection, which means that *the truth taught is what the soul sees in its state of illuminated consciousness.* The germ of the Christ life, the spark of divinity which the poet Browning says "*disturbs our clod,*" the image of God all men bear,[1644] the light which every man brings with him into the world,[1645] must descend into matter; the "dead" with the Gnostic writers and with Paul are those in whom the consciousness of the divine has not been awakened. Resurrection is the awakening of this germ to life. This is the real resurrection of which the historicized rising from the dead of the body of Jesus the canonical Gospels speak of is a symbol. *The story of the descent of the soul into matter, its gradual conquest of matter, its awakening to its true life, and its return to its former state having mastered the powers of the world is the myth of man found in all the ancient mysteries. It is the same story which the New Testament tells in the form of a symbolic life.*

Now from a human point of view *it was necessary that such a form of Christianity should not become the Christianity of the church.* For very soon came the fall of the Western Empire and the inrush of the barbarians from the north. Very soon *a wild sea of savage tribes surged and heaved where once the cultured fields of the Old World* had been. It was impossible that the strong virile minds of Goth, Hun, and Vandal could comprehend the religion that satisfied these philosophers of the East. A cruder faith was needed and a cruder faith became the faith of the Catholic church. The purer faith became a heresy and was bitterly opposed by the dominant church. As the Catholic church grew in power it grew too in priestly claim and in arrogance. Even as early as the latter part of the second century it had become a visible hierarchy. We find Irenaeus uttering the famous dictum that where the church is—and even as early as his day the church was a visible organization with its clergy and sacraments—there is the spirit of God, and where the spirit of God is there is the church.

A proud, arrogant, ambitious church in the course of its history has been guilty of many crimes, but perhaps *the blackest record its history can show is its persecution of these Gnostics*. These people had a long ancestry. "The method of history," says Prof. G. P. Fisher of Yale, "is never magical. In proportion to the magnitude of the event are the length of time and the variety of agencies which are employed in producing it." Professor Fisher applies this remark to the Reformation of the sixteenth century, showing that "never was a historical criticism more elaborately prepared for, and this through a train of causes which reach back into the remote past." But the words apply specially to the advent of Christianity; for as a matter of fact *Christianity was in the womb of the pagan world for centuries. As Gnosticism was the child of paganism, so Christianity was the child of Gnosticism.* The words of St. Augustine are strictly true.

> "The very thing which now is called the Christian religion existed among the ancients, nor was it absent in the beginning of the human race before Christ came in the flesh, since when the true religion which already existed began to be called Christian."

In the nicknames which the heresy hunters of the time hurled at the Gnostics we have a clue to the question whence they derived their teaching. The orthodox Church Fathers were neither sparing nor nice in the names they applied to the Gnostic heretics—devils, snakes, hounds, wolves, vipers, and firstborn of Satan. These names of course do not give us much light except upon those who used them; but when less thoroughly aroused with theological passion, and consequently in less bitter mood, *they said that the Gnostics derived their teaching from Pythagoras and Plato and Heraclitus and Cleanthes, and from the mystery institutions of Greece, Egypt and the East generally. This was the truth, but instead of being a reproach it was their glory. This meant that the teaching was the best in the religious teaching of the ancient world. Instead of coming into a world of universal darkness with its one divine light of truth, Christianity came from the same source as Gnosticism. In the Epistles of Paul we have echoes of what was taught in Egypt and Greece two or three hundred years before.*

There is nothing of which we are so sure as the existence of a well-developed and well-defined doctrine in the Hellenistic world of the first centuries before Christ, of the descent of man from the heavenly or archetypal man, and of his return to pristine glory with the experience he has gathered from his contact with, and conquest of, the world of matter and form. This Paul calls the "mystery" of Christ, the mystery hid from ages and generations, but now made manifest.[1646]

The story of a Christ who was the Saviour of the world, the divine man who was the representative of a great spiritual process, the mediator between God and men, the ideal man who was overcome in his struggles for human salvation but conquered in being overcome, is the story which the world has repeated to itself over and over again. It is not original with the New Testament, every feature of it was familiar to those who were initiated into the mysteries. This should be enough to show us that we are not in the presence of literal fact. There is no doubt that the crucifixion as Paul conceived it had cosmic significance—it is not merely the death of a martyr. The center and soul of the gnosis of the ancient world was the Cross. The technical phrase for it among the Gnostics is one used by Paul, the "cross the power of God."[1647] *Wherever the gnosis had established itself the kernel was the cross. It is obvious that in these places it could not mean the death of Jesus for that was a local happening. It meant the great world-passion, the sacrifice of God in the creation, Deity laying down his life in the universe of matter and form. And to Paul the cross was the symbol of this heart-moving conception.*[1648]

As such, concerning Gnosticism, Argentinian author Jorge Luis Borges rightly noted that if the Gnostic Christianity of Alexandria had triumphed rather than the Catholic Christianity of Rome, the "extravagant and muddled stories" of the Gnostics would today "be coherent, majestic, and perfectly ordinary."[1649]

Gnosticism is still very much alive in the 21st Century; not only as a strong stream of spiritual belief among mystical-minded Christians everywhere, but within small groups scattered throughout Western Europe (most who follow the doctrines espoused by the great Gnostic leader Valentinus).[1650] A sect of Gnostics also continues to flourish in Iraq and Iran: the Mandeans, whose name means "Knowers" (that is, Gnostics).[1651] Among the ancient practices of this enduring community are initiation, ecstasy, and various rituals that closely resemble those of the Freemasons—itself a descendant of Gnosticism.[1652]

The Mandean religion, or perhaps its roots, derives from the same period as primitive Christianity, and was, in fact, an offshoot of 1st-Century Gnostic Judaism.[1653] Not surprisingly then, it is among the Mandeans—who, like Gnostics in general, have been heavily influenced by Iranian, Mesopotamian, and Indian elements—that we find one of the sources, if not the principle or very first source, for the orthodox Christian concept of the 6,000 year old dying and rising Christ figure,[1654] which was later appended to the man Jesus. His name is *Enos Uthra*. According to Mandean sacred writings and beliefs, this pre-Christian Gnostic "heavenly redeemer," also known as *Manda da Hayye* (the "knowledge of life"), long ago incarnated on earth in order to subdue the powers of darkness, and guide human souls (which had been entrapped in physical bodies) back to the Realm of Light, their true home.[1655]

Revealingly, the Mandeans refer to themselves as the "Nazoreans," that is, the Nazarenes.[1656] And so we come full circle. As has been long well-known to Christian mystics, this makes Gnosticism, along with its Hebraic sibling Essenism, the original form of Christianity and the first Christian Church. See BRETHREN, CHRISTIANITY, ENOCH, ESSENES, GNOSIS, JESUS, NAZARENES, THEOSIS.

GOD: Though the Bible does not precisely define who or what God is,[1657] in traditional Christianity he is the Heavenly Father who created and rules over the entire Universe, often portrayed as a stern, bearded, manlike deity sitting on his throne in the clouds of Heaven, with a scepter in one hand and a lightning bolt in the other.

This is not the God of Jesus, however, and therefore it is not the true *Christian* God. In fact, the description above is of the archetypal *Pagan* Father-God, which some of the more overly imaginative Old Testament writers borrowed from, among others, ancient Mesopotamian, Egyptian, Phoenician, Akkadian, Hittite, Indian, Persian, Babylonian, Ugarite, Sumerian, Roman, and Greek mythology.

As was the custom at the time, nearly all of the primary male deities of early societies and religions were portrayed in the same way. Several of these ancient father-gods or sky-gods, in particular the Egyptian Ra, the Greek Zeus, the Indian Vishnu, the Tibetan Vajrapani, the Roman Jupiter, and the Canaanite Baal, were used as models upon which the Old Testament version of God was patterned—as ancient statues of these deities clearly show.[1658] Indeed, according to God himself, he was at one time literally known as "Baal" by his Hebrew followers:

> "And it shall be at that day," saith the Lord, "that thou shalt . . . call me no more Baal."[1659]

So deeply was the Pagan concept of the Father embedded among the ancient Hebrews that they also knew him as both the Pagan deity El Elyon (the name of a Canaanite city-god)[1660] and as the Pagan deity El Shaddai[1661] (the name of a pre-Mosaic Semitic mountain-god).[1662]

Jesus did away with this idolatry, this ancient Pagan, carnalized, anthropomorphic view of an angry, violent, transcendent, corporeal God sitting imperiously on his heavenly throne;[1663] the heartless "man of war" of the book of Exodus,[1664] who cruelly ordered the death penalty for such minor things as gathering sticks[1665] or kindling a fire on the Sabbath Day,[1666] for eating leavened bread during Passover,[1667] and for promiscuity,[1668] blasphemy,[1669] and heresy.[1670]

Jesus completely overturned the Old Testament notion of the tempestuous "Lord" who sanctioned or even commanded the wholesale slaughter of children and even entire nations;[1671] the ever-demanding "jealous God"[1672] who bellows, blusters, and threatens his way through the pages of such books as Micah, Nahum, Habakkuk, and Zephaniah.[1673]

In place of this human-fabricated Hebrew Zeus,[1674] Jesus declared once and for all that "God is Spirit." In other words, he is not a physical deity, he is the animating "spark" of the entire Universe and everything in it.[1675] Thus, Jesus said:

> . . . the Father himself, which hath sent me, hath borne witness of me. Ye have neither heard his voice at any time, nor seen his shape.[1676]

> No man hath seen God at any time; the only begotten Son [that is, the Indwelling Christ], which is in the bosom of the Father, he hath declared him.[1677]

The traditional Church's portrayal of a humanlike Supreme Being stems, in part, from the inability of Bible literalists and exoteric scholars and writers to understand this famous passage from Genesis:

> So God created man in his own image, in the image of God created he him; male and female created he them.[1678]

Since we have a physical *human* body, the literalist believes that God does as well. But as Jesus correctly taught, the Father is pure spiritual energy. Therefore the image God created us in is his *spirit*, for he *is* Spirit.[1679]

This is why only those who have entered the Kingdom of God (Cosmic or Christ Consciousness)[1680] have actually "seen" God. For since "God" is the Divine Mind, we can only "see" him through our spiritual (non-physical) eyes, just as Jesus declared:

> Not that any man hath seen the Father, save he which is of God, he hath seen the Father.[1681]

John echoed the views of our Lord, reaffirming that God lives inside of those who are loving:

> No man hath seen God at any time. If we love one another, God dwelleth in us, and his love is perfected in us.[1682]

In the Gnostic-Christian text known as The Apocryphon of John, Jesus rightly says that *what men call "God" is actually "the invisible Spirit, and it is not right to view him as a god."*[1683] And it is this "invisible spirit," the Christ Within, that indwells every one of us as our immortal Soul.[1684] Thus we are each gods and goddesses in our own right, just as our Lord taught. "Ye are gods," he asserted,[1685] the same mysterious "three words" that are tacitly referred to but not spelled out in The Gospel of Thomas.[1686] It was due to this very doctrine, known as Theosis, that Jesus was executed for blasphemy,[1687] and it is why many mainline Christians often mistakenly view Christian mystics as atheists. Pike writes:

> As the world grows in its development, it necessarily outgrows its ancient ideas of God, which were only temporary and provisional. *A man who has a higher conception of God than those about him, and who denies that their conception is God, is very likely to be called an Atheist by men who are really far less believers in a God than he.* Thus the Christians, who said the Heathen idols were no Gods, were accounted Atheists by the People, and accordingly put to death; and Jesus of Nazareth was crucified as an unbelieving blasphemer, by the Jews.[1688]

Let us note here that Jesus was not against Pagan gods because there is something inherently evil about them, as so many modern Christian authorities teach. After all, each ancient god and goddess was merely a symbol, a personification, of one of the many universal divine principles, the same principles that are taught to this day in both the mainstream and the mystical branches of the Christian Church, and in every other religion in fact.[1689]

Jesus was against praying to manmade deities because it is a waste of our time. Why? Because being mythological, there is no one to hear us. The divinities of Paganism, having been fabricated by the imagination of Man, are truly nothing but lifeless "graven images."[1690] Of them Jesus has this to say in *The Aquarian Gospel of Jesus the Christ*:

> These gods possess no ears to hear, no eyes to see, no heart to sympathize, no power to save. . . these gods are made of air, and clothed with shadows of a thought.[1691]

Hence the Lord always refers to the Pagans' God, the human Ego, as "the God of the dead," and the true God, Divine Mind, as "the God of the living."[1692] Jesus explains this doctrine in the following account from Mark:

> Then come unto him [Jesus] the Sadducees, which say there is no resurrection; and they asked him, saying, "Master, Moses wrote unto us, 'If a man's brother die, and leave his wife behind him, and leave no children, that his brother should take his wife, and raise up seed unto his brother.' Now there were seven brethren: and the first took a wife, and dying left no seed. And the second took her, and died, neither left he any seed: and the third likewise. And the seven had her, and left no seed: last of all the woman died also. In the resurrection therefore, when they shall rise, whose wife shall she be of them? for the seven had her to wife."
>
> And Jesus answering said unto them, "Do ye not therefore err, because ye know not the scriptures, neither the power of God? For when they shall rise from the dead, they neither marry, nor are given in marriage; but are as the angels which are in heaven. And as touching the dead, that they rise: have ye not read in the book of Moses, how in the bush God spake unto him, saying, 'I am the God of Abraham, and the God of Isaac, and the God of Jacob'? He is not the God of the dead, but the God of the living: ye therefore do greatly err."[1693]

Yes, just as Jesus teaches, God is pneumamorphic; that is, he has a "spirit body,"[1694] and a piece of this *spiritual* body lives within each one of us[1695] as what the Old Testament calls that "still small voice,"[1696] and which Job refers to as "a spirit in man."[1697] This is why individuals who have near-death experiences or NDEs never actually "see" God during their temporary journeys to Heaven.[1698] Instead, as they themselves testify, they "feel" him as an all-encompassing sensation of pure love that fills every atom of the Universe. He truly is, Paul said, "the invisible God[1699] . . . whom no man hath seen, nor can see,"[1700] and who "dwelleth not in temples made with hands."[1701] Where does he dwell then? He lives within your "inner church,"[1702] "the true tabernacle of faith, constructed by the Lord, not man."[1703] This is why the Indian spiritual masters teach God's own doctrine:

> To each one I appear to be what he thinks I am.[1704]

The following is straight from the Bhagavad Gita:

> However people choose to worship me, I manifest myself to them in that form. All men and women are seeking me, even if they think they are not.[1705]

Though He preached an omnipresent, immanent, circumambient, and unseeable God, Jesus knew that future teachers would fall back into idolatry and try to anthropomorphize both the invisible spiritual Father[1706] and the invisible Indwelling Christ[1707]—just as they did in His day. He admonished His followers to beware of these types of men and the "false Christs," or humanlike saviors, that they would extol to the masses. They will try to deceive even the most spiritually advanced souls with this erroneous doctrine, He warned.[1708]

But be not led astray, He continued, for even as God is Spirit, God's realm, the Kingdom of Heaven, is also invisible, for it is "within you,"[1709] that is, the "kingdom is within the soul."[1710] However, the day will come when all will recognize their oneness with the Divine Mind, and their own divine nature will shine forth.[1711] It will be at that time, Jesus said, that "the true worshippers shall worship the Father in spirit and in truth: for the Father seeketh such to worship him."[1712] Such are the doctrines that are embraced by Christian mystics concerning God.

The mystical Church believes that the word God has the highest vibratory rate of any word in any language, and that thus it should be used with complete faith as often as possible everyday. In fact, this word cannot be used too often.[1713] Its vibratory rate, 186,000 beats per second, can change physical matter, including biology, and thus has the power to heal, alter, and totally transform, beginning at the level of molecules and cells.[1714]

Like Hindu mystics Christian mystics define the word God as a religious word representing the ultimate and supreme reality; esoterically it is the sum total of all three minds: the Superconscious, the Conscious, and the Subconscious, which together form the Divine Mind. Ideas and thoughts are generated in the Conscious Mind (the "Son"); these are sent to the Subconscious Mind ("Holy Spirit"), where they become beliefs; these are then communicated to the Superconscious Mind (the "Father"), where they are generated into material reality. God is thus the Creator, the One, the Source of All.[1715]

In some metaphysical schools God is the Superconscious Mind alone, while scientists refer to him as the "Unified Field," "the laws of physics," or simply "Nature"—for God is everything and everything is God.[1716] In matriarchal religions God is a "she" who "is known in her palaces" as Goddess or Mother-Goddess.[1717]

Actually, as the Old Testament plural word Elohim (meaning "God/Goddess") reveals,[1718] "God" embodies both the Male Principle and the Female Principle,[1719] and is therefore called by some, such as the ancient Gnostic-Christians, *Metropator* ("Mother-Father"),[1720] the "Androgynous One,"[1721] or the "Androgynous Father."[1722] Thus in the mystical Christian tradition Jehovah means "the ever living male-and-female principle."[1723] This is literally true, for as human beings we are created from two substances: materiality (the "Earthly Mother," the conceptive force) and spirituality (the "Heavenly Father," the generative force).[1724]

There is nothing that is not God, so true pure atheism is impossible,[1725] making the word atheism itself an oxymoron.[1726] The atheist who denies God is himself or herself a piece of God! We dwell, breathe, swim in God, whatever label we choose to put on it. Paul said that in him/her/it "we live, and move, and have our being."[1727] The Hindus call God "Brahman," the name of the Creator-God of the Indian Holy Trinity, Trimurti. According to the ancient Christian doctrine of Theosis (embraced by the early Church Fathers), like Christ,[1728] the Holy Spirit[1729] and its mystical double, the Comforter or Paraclete,[1730] God also dwells within us,[1731] making up our Divine Inner Trinity.[1732] Our triform inner deity is comprised of a "Creator," a "Preserver," and a "Destroyer,"[1733] for due to the Divine Law of Thought, as gods and goddesses[1734] we possess the power to create, preserve, or destroy our lives![1735]

The Theosis doctrine of Jesus has been embraced by Christian mystics since the time of our Lord right into the present day. Gardner, for instance, writes:

> Man can name and can think of God because in his inmost substance *he is of God.* "All divine things," says Dionysius [the Areopagite], "in so far as they are manifested to us, are known only by participation therein." To the Unknown, Unnamed, he feels an affinity, in that he recognizes a "power by which we are joined, in a way that passes comprehension, to the Unspeakable and Unknowable, in that union which is stronger than any strength of mind or intellect." And similarly Scotus [John the Scot]: "In so far as (man) partakes of divine and heavenly existence, he is not animal, but through his reason and intellect and his thoughts of the Eternal, *he shares in celestial being.* . . . In *that part of him then, is he made in the image of God,* with which alone God holds converse in men that are worthy." And Maximus [the Confessor], who in many points is to be regarded as a mean term between Dionysius and Scotus, says: "As the air illuminated by the sun appears to be nothing but light: not that

it loses its own nature, but because light prevails in it: so *human nature, joined to God, is said in all things to be God: not that it ceases to be human nature, but that it receives a participation in Divinity so that in it God alone is found.*"[1736]

Swedenborg:

Concerning God they said, All who come into heaven have their place allotted them there, and thence everlasting joy, according to their idea of God, because this idea reigns universally in every particular of worship; the idea of an invisible God is not determined to any god, nor does it terminate in any, therefore it ceases and perishes; the idea of God as a spirit, when a spirit is thought of as ether or air, is an empty idea; but *the idea of God as a man is a just idea, for God is divine love and divine wisdom, with every quality belonging thereto, and the subject of these is man*, and not ether or wind.[1737]

William Ellery Channing:

My friends, how little do we know ourselves! How unjust are we to ourselves! We study everything else but *the Divine Principle within our own persons*. The truth may be on our lips. But in how few hearts does it live! We need a new revelation—not of Heaven or of Hell—but of *the Spirit within ourselves*.[1738]

For the Christian mystic, Jesus' statement that "the kingdom of God is within you"[1739] is quite literally true. It only follows then that if God's kingdom resides within us, that the God of that kingdom does as well, just as both our Lord and the Apostles taught:

- Jesus: "Ye are gods."[1740]
- John: The Christ is "the true light, which lighteth every man that cometh into the world."[1741]
- Paul: "Christ is all, and in all."[1742]
- Peter: We are all "partakers of the divine nature."[1743]
- The Hebraist: The spiritually mature will become "partakers of his holiness."[1744]

We can now understand why our Lord's focus was always on God rather than on Himself, the human being named Jesus.[1745] For Man's Higher Self is a veritable portion of God, the "true light" known variously as the Indwelling Christ or I AM—a Divine Spark that resides in everyone.[1746]

But we are not just "made in the image of God."[1747] The original Sanskrit word for image meant "exactness."[1748] We are exact replicas of the Infinite Divine Power, without any limitations except those we impose on ourselves.[1749] Now we can better understand Jesus' mystical statements, "I and my Father are one,"[1750] thus "he that hath seen me hath seen the Father."[1751] The I AM, the Christ in every individual, is actually *one and the same* as God, the unfathomable, unnameable, indescribable Source of All.[1752] Thus truly "we are gods," just as our Lord declared.[1753] For the Christian mystic, repeating "I AM God"[1754] is one of the most powerful and effective methods of achieving perfect health and happiness here on earth (at-one-ment),[1755] or what the Prince of Peace called the here-and-now "Kingdom Within."[1756] See ATONEMENT, CHRIST, CHRIST CONSCIOUSNESS, FATHER, GODDESS, GODS AND GODDESSES, JEHOVAH, JESUS, KINGDOM OF GOD, MOTHER, MOUTH OF GOD, SON OF GOD, TEMPLE OF GOD, THEALOGY, THEOLOGY, THEOSIS, UNION WITH GOD, VOICE OF GOD, WORD OF GOD, YAHWEH.

GODDESS: Traditional Christians hold that there is no Goddess, that is, a female Supreme Being, in the Faith. For one thing, they maintain, there is no Jewish or Christian goddess in the Old or New Testaments. For another, this idea does not appear in the teachings of Jesus, the Apostles, or the Church.

As Christian mystics from Julian of Norwich to William Blake, and even many Christian sects (from the Shakers[1757] to the Mormons),[1758] have noted over the centuries, however, this view is wholly incorrect.[1759]

To begin with, throughout the Bible the Supreme Being is portrayed in a variety of forms and genders. Though best known as a male,[1760] "God" is also depicted as an androgynous being, half-male, half-female[1761] (known to the first Christians as *Metropator*, "Mother-Father"),[1762] as a polytheistic group of seven (or 12) deities,[1763] the *Elohim*,[1764] and most interestingly pertaining to this entry, as a solely female divinity, *Goddess*.[1765]

As early as the second verse of the first chapter of Genesis, God is said to "*brood* upon the face of the waters." The Hebrew word here, *rachaph*, is commonly, and intentionally, mistranslated by patriarchal scholars as "moved," but its real outer meaning is "to hover" while its true inner meaning is "to brood." But "hovering," "brooding," and incubating—that is, sitting upon a nest of eggs—is a female attribute.[1766]

The idea of a female Supreme Being is far older than the idea of a male one. In prehistoric matriarchal religions (pre-6000 B.C.), during what has been called the Matriarchate (the nearly worldwide phenomenon of female-headed, though largely egalitarian, societies), Goddess was the name for the Supreme Being, who, at that time, was imaged as female.[1767] Later, after the rise of the idea of a male Supreme Being (post-6000 B.C.), the word Goddess was used to denote the feminine aspect of God, at which time she became God's "wife" or "consort."[1768]

As patriarchy spread across the West and Near East during the early historic period, mainstream Christianity and Judaism eventually suppressed her worship, which is repeatedly condemned[1769] throughout both the Old Testament[1770] and the New Testament.[1771] But she did not completely disappear. In the orthodox Christian Church she was metamorphisized into the figure of the Virgin Mary, the Holy Spirit or Holy Ghost, and various fictitious female saints, while in Judaism she continues to be venerated among Jewish mystics in her old Hebrew form as Asherah or Ashtoreth,[1772] known in Canaan as Astarte, in Mesopotamia as Ishtar.[1773] All three of these goddesses bore the title "Queen of Heaven."[1774]

The first known artistic portrayals of the Great Mother-Goddess date from the Acheulian Period of the Lower Paleolithic Age, some 500,000 years ago, at which time *Homo erectus* was carving crude female figures in her honor. Both the Neanderthal and Cro-Magnon peoples also produced a panoply of beautiful artistic representations of Goddess, the second group creating, most notably, the renowned but misnamed "Venus" figurines.[1775]

Unbeknownst to many traditional Christians but long well-known to mystical Christians, Jews and Christians have been venerating goddess as the Great Virgin-Mother in one form or another for millennia. In the book of Revelation we have, for example, the "woman arrayed with the sun, and the moon under her feet, and upon her head a crown of twelve stars."[1776] This is none other than a christianization of the old Hindu mother-goddess Aditi,[1777] queen of the 12 astrological Sun-signs and the mother of the Sun/Son-god Surya.[1778]

The mystical view of the Christian version of Goddess was noted by Kingsford and Maitland:

> This triumphant consummation of the soul's course is . . . celebrated in the Apocalypse. "I beheld," says the seer, "a great wonder in heaven: a woman clothed with the sun, having the moon under her feet, and on her head a crown of twelve stars." This is the soul invested with the light of supreme knowledge attained through the experiences undergone in the long series of her past existences; standing on the moon as victor over materiality and firm in the faith of a full intuition,—states denoted respectively by the dark and light portions of the moon; and superior evermore to the changes and chances of mortal destiny, the stars which represent this being the jewels of her crown, each of them denoting one of the "twelve labours" necessary to be endured by the soul on her path to her final perfectionment, and the spiritual gifts and graces acquired in the process.[1779]

While the great Jewish mother-goddess Ashtoreth or Asherah[1780]—the Hebrew Astarte or Ishtar,[1781] and the wife-consort of the father-god Yahweh or Jehovah—appears throughout the Old Testament in various guises and under a myriad of names[1782] (the Hebrews often worshiped her in sacred tree groves),[1783] the most outstanding example of Christian goddess-worship is that of the Virgin Mary, who, as discussed, is a Christian version of the universal Great Virgin-Mother, known around the world by thousands of names, including: Ma Ma, Maerin, Maid Marian, Mar, Mara, Marah, Mari, Maria, Mariam, Marie, Marratu, Mary, Maya, and Meri, to name but a few. To this day Jesus' mother Mary is still widely known by the ancient Pagan title that the Catholic Church borrowed from the Greek love-goddess Aphrodite:[1784] *Stella Maris* ("Star of the Sea").[1785] Aphrodite's name itself means "risen from sea-foam."[1786]

Why the water motif?

Many early female deities, and more specifically the Great Mother-Goddess, were mystically linked with the ocean, a symbol of the maternal "amniotic fluid" out of which the Universe was born. Thus, their names were given elements relating to the "Mother-Sea": *ma* ("mother") and *mar* ("sea").[1787]

Additionally, the female pudenda or yoni has long been likened to the scalloped marine seashell, which is why the shellfish came to be a goddess symbol of birth and regeneration and its pearl an emblem of love and marriage.[1788] Goddess' most common Pagan yoni symbol, the mandorla ("almond"), was absorbed by Christianity as the Vesica Piscis ("Vessel of the Fish"), a pointed oval that is still used artistically to enclose Mary and sometimes Jesus. This yonic emblem is truly ancient, and was connected to Aphrodite's Fish Rites at Paphos (under the Sun-sign Pisces, the "fish"), the Egyptian Virgin-Mother Isis, the Hindu goddess Kali, and the Scandinavian Freya. Pre-16th-Century Irish church buildings still bear the carvings of the Sheila-Na-Gig, the squatting, naked, life-and-death goddess whose predominant vesica piscis was meant to provide protection and bestow good luck.[1789]

Aphrodite, who was known in Syria as the "Lady of Pearls" and at Antioch as "Margarito," was said to have been created from a conch shell. As a Pagan symbol of regeneration, the goddess' scallop shell easily passed into Christianity as a symbol of resurrection,[1790] while numerous elements of Aphrodite herself, as well as those of hundreds of other goddesses, were assimilated into the biography and character of the Virgin Mary.[1791]

Why the worldwide popularity of Goddess-worship? The great Indian sage Sri Ramakrishna posed the question and answer this way:

> Why does the God-lover find such pleasure in addressing the Deity as Mother? Because the child is more free with its mother, and consequently she is dearer to the child than any one else.[1792]

See CANA WEDDING, CHRISTMAS, DOVE, FATHER, FISH, GOD, GODS AND GODDESSES, HOLY SPIRIT, HOLY TRINITY, I AM, MARY, MOTHER, THEALOGY, THEOLOGY, VIRGIN BIRTH, VIRGO.

GODS AND GODDESSES: In traditional Christianity the many minor gods and goddesses of Paganism are considered devilish shallow imitations of the one true God.[1793] In mystical Christianity these same divinities are seen more correctly as but individualized manifestations of the one true God,[1794] or more commonly, as personifications of the various aspects of Nature,[1795] which is merely one of science's many names for God. Modern mainstream Christians have thus been misled as to the truth of the subordinate deities of the Pagan Pantheon, who were and are nothing more than secret mystical emblems of important "immortal principles."[1796]

Furthermore, ancient Pagans did not "worship" these minor deities, as orthodox Christianity erroneously teaches, and neither do modern Pagans. They merely use them as embodiments to help illustrate and emphasize the various traits of the single Supreme Being.[1797] Hence, Swedenborg says:

> They are called gods who are in divine truths from the Lord, and abstractly, the truths themselves.[1798]

Picus Mirandulanus writes:

> The names of the gods, of whom Orpheus sings, are not the titles of deceiving demons but the designations of divine virtues.[1799]

Augustine states:

> We have the opinion of Plato affirming that all the gods are good, and that there is not one of the gods bad.[1800]

Plutarch made these comments on the subordinate Pagan deities:

> But those theorists engender horrible and impious notions, who apply the names of [the many Pagan] deities to natural productions and to things that be without sense, without life, and necessarily consumed by men in want of and making use of them. For these things themselves it is impossible to conceive as gods (for we cannot conceive God as an inanimate thing, subject to man), but from these productions we have drawn the inference that they who created them, and bestow, and dispense

them to us constantly and sufficiently, are gods—*not different gods amongst different people, nor Barbarian or Grecian, of the South or of the North*—*but like as the Sun, Moon, Sky, Earth, Sea, are the common property of all men, but yet are called by different names by different nations; in the same manner, as one reason regulates all things, and one Providence directs, and subordinate Powers are appointed over all things, yet different honours and titles are by custom assigned to them amongst different peoples: and these have established, and do employ, symbols, some obscure, some more intelligible, in order to lead the understanding into things divine.* And this not without danger: for some having entirely missed their meaning, have slid into superstition; whilst others shunning every superstition like a quagmire, have unknowingly fallen into Atheism as down a precipice.[1801]

Though he was monotheistic, Paul acknowledged and accepted the existence of the countless minor gods and goddesses of the Pagan Pantheon (a belief known as henotheism), saying:

For though there be that are called gods, whether in heaven or in earth, (as there be gods many, and lords many,) but to us there is but one God, the father, of whom are all things . . .[1802]

The Bhagavad Gita states unequivocally that the one true God appears to his followers in the form which they imagine him to be, even if that form is a multiplicity of deities. Said Krishna, the Hindu Christ, to Arjuna:

I serve men in the way in which they approach me. Men follow my path from every side. . . . To those who serve me alone, and who are thus constantly engaged in my service, I bring full assurance of happiness. Those also who serve other gods with a firm belief, in doing so, worship even me . . .[1803]

In a famous ancient myth, Isis the great Egyptian Mother-Goddess appears to Lucius in a vision "as a beautiful female, over whose divine neck her long thick hair hung in graceful ringlets." Addressing him, the deity says of herself in the third person:

The parent of Universal nature attends thy call. The mistress of the Elements, initiative germ of generations, Supreme of Deities, Queen of departed Spirits, first inhabitant of Heaven, and uniform type of all the Gods and Goddesses, propitiated by thy prayers, is with thee. She governs with her nod the luminous heights of the firmament, the salubrious breezes of the ocean; the silent deplorable depths of the shades below; *one Sole Divinity under many forms, worshipped by the different nations of the Earth under many titles, and with various religious rites.*[1804]

Of this topic, which he correctly terms "the pagan monotheism,"[1805] Cumont writes:

> The imperial policy [of ancient Rome] gave the first place in the official religion to the Sun, of which the sovereign was the emanation, just as in the Chaldaean speculations propagated by the Mithraists the royal planet held sway over the other stars. On both sides, *the growing tendency was to see in the brilliant star that illuminated the universe the only God, or at least the sensible image of the only God, and to establish in the heavens a monotheism in imitation of the monarchy that ruled on earth.* Macrobius (A.D. 400), in his *Saturnalia*, has learnedly set forth that *the gods were ultimately reducible to a single Being considered under different aspects, and that the multiple names by which they were worshipped were the equivalent of that of Helios (the Sun).*[1806]

Ironically, despite traditional Christianity's purported "monotheism," it is one of the world's most polytheistic faiths, openly practicing the very tradition which it has long criticized in other religions. Paul inadvertently admitted as much.[1807] Indeed, due to the Church's overt theoxenia (openness toward foreign deities), it eagerly adopted the ancient Pagan syncretizing philosophy of theocrasia, in which the traits of multiple non-Christian gods are combined into one; in this case, Jesus.

Those seeking Christian signs of the assimilation of the polytheism of the Old Religion need look no further than the Bible itself, which presents the reader with an overwhelming Judeo-Christian Pantheon of innumerable gods, goddesses, spirits, demons, beasts, monsters, dragons, devils, angels, powers, and principalities,[1808] an ever growing list to which can be added our modern saints[1809]—many, incidentally, which are now admitted to be early priestly fabrications.[1810] Freud correctly observed that modern Christians have remained essentially unchanged from their ancient ancestors: primitively polytheistic.[1811] See GOD, GODDESS, HOLY TRINITY, MONOTHEISM, MOTHER, TRINITY.

GOLD, FRANKINCENSE, & MYRRH: In the traditional Church gold, frankincense, and myrrh were the three gifts given to the infant Jesus by the (three) Wise Men or Magi:

And when they were come into the house, they saw the young child with Mary his mother, and fell down, and worshipped him: and when they had opened their treasures, they presented unto him gifts; gold, and frankincense, and myrrh.[1812]

In the mystical Church these three gifts are symbols of deeper truths: gold represents the abundance of Spirit and right aspiration; frankincense represents the charm of Spirit and right perception; and myrrh represents the immortality of Spirit and right judgement.[1813] In Swedenborg's opinion:

The reason why they [the Magi] offered these three, was, because gold signifies celestial good, frankincense spiritual good, and myrrh natural good, and from these three goods all worship is derived.[1814]

See BIRTH OF JESUS, CHRISTMAS, GOOD NEWS, GOSPEL, NATIVITY, STAR OF BETHLEHEM, VIRGIN BIRTH, VIRGO, WISE MEN.

GOLGOTHA: From the Aramaic *gulgulta*, "skull." In the traditional Church Golgotha is the skull-shaped hill upon which Jesus is said to have been crucified.[1815] Although there is a Christian structure (the Church of the Holy Sepulcher) located at the traditional site of Golgotha today, the authentic spot is not known,[1816] for no archaeological evidence has ever been found that would definitively identify it.[1817]

For Christian mystics, however, there is a simple reason for this: Golgotha was not a real physical hill. As its esoteric name reveals, the "skull" is a mystical symbol of the head, the location of the Crown Chakra (James' "Crown of Life"),[1818] or what mystics call the "Temple of Wisdom" or "Holy of Holies."[1819] The skull or head in turn represents the Indwelling Christ,[1820] the Universal Living Christ-Soul,[1821] made in the exact image of God,[1822] and which is the "true light which lighteth *every man* that cometh into the world."[1823] See CHRIST, CHRIST CONSCIOUSNESS, CROSS, CROWN, CRUCIFIXION, DEATH OF JESUS, SUN, UNION WITH GOD, UPPER ROOM, WORD OF GOD, ZODIAC.

GOOD NEWS (THE): In traditional Christianity the Good News is the Gospel of Jesus Christ, whose main message is that His redemptive death on the cross saves us from eternal damnation. The Greek word for gospel is *euangelion*, which means "good news."[1824]

In mystical Christianity, however, it is recognized that the Good News is not about the man Jesus, nor is it even Christian. The term *euangelion* was common in pre-Christian Rome, for example, where Pagans held that appearances by the emperor, as well as his inauguration, decrees, and birthdays, were "gospels" or "good news."[1825] Some 500 years before Jesus was born Buddha referred to his own gospel, "The Way of Truth,"[1826] as "good news."[1827] Additionally, Christian mystics understand, based on the New Testament, that Jesus never once preached or even knew about "the Gospel of Jesus Christ." Rather He taught "the Gospel of the Kingdom of God,"[1828] one whose focus was God the Father, not Himself.[1829]

As our Lord explicitly states in His Gospel of the Kingdom, every man is a god and every woman is a goddess in his or her own right,[1830] with the ability to perform feats, deeds, and miracles even greater than He Himself.[1831] According to Jesus, in fact, as divine beings we have the power to mold, sculpt, and guide, not just our everyday lives, but ultimately our fate and our destiny as well. In my opinion, and no doubt that of nearly every other Christian mystic, these doctrines, which center around the ancient concept of Theosis (God in Man) form what was the first and true "Good News" of Christianity.[1832]

Tragically, the organized Church later found our Lord's original Good News, the Jesus-less Gospel of the Kingdom of God, to be a major hindrance to its goal of political, theological, social, and economic domination of the Roman Empire—which it finally achieved with the rise of Constantine the Great in the 4th Century.[1833] And so the Catholic Church suppressed the genuine first Gospel and replaced it with a second manmade version: "the Gospel of Jesus Christ." Eventually Jesus' Gospel of the Kingdom of God disappeared from mainstream Christianity, and divine authority was transferred from Jesus to the Church, a tragic worldwide coverup, known as the "Scheme of Salvation," that continues to be accepted, concealed, and maintained by mainstream Christianity to this day.

Still, traces of our Lord's authentic Good News remain, not only in the four canonical Gospels, but in a host of recently discovered ancient books. Such texts have preserved both many of Jesus' suppressed secret teachings and those of His mystical posthumous followers. A partial list includes:

The Gospel of Thomas
The Secret Gospel of Mark
The Secret Book of James
The Dialogue of the Savior
The Gospel of the Egyptians
The Gospel of Truth
The Gospel of Mary
The Gospel of Peter
The Secret Book According to John
The Gospel of the Nazoreans
The Infancy Gospel of Thomas
The Book of Thomas the Contender
The Apocalypse of Paul
The Acts of Peter and the Twelve Apostles
The Thunder, Perfect Mind

The Gospel of the Ebionites
The Hymn of the Pearl
The Infancy Gospel of James
The Gospel of the Hebrews
The Gospel of Philip
The Hypostasis of the Archons
The Apocalypse of Adam[1834]

What then is the genuine Good News according to the mystical branch of Christianity? It is the dual message preached by Jesus:

1) We humans are god-men and god-women; specially created beings whose real Self is Divine; immortal "sparks of God" who are birthless, ageless, deathless, indestructible, and immortal.[1835]

2) Being one with God the Father,[1836] and with the Christ as our Higher Self,[1837] we possess the power to control *all* of our own experiences and conditions, including the limitless ability to heal, prosper, and flourish in any area of our lives.[1838] See GNOSTICISM, GOSPEL, GOSPEL OF JESUS CHRIST, GOSPEL OF THE KINGDOM OF GOD, GOSPEL OF Q, GOSPEL OF THOMAS, MYTH OF CHRIST, NATIVITY, SCHEME OF SALVATION, WAY OF THE LORD, WORD OF GOD.

GOOD SHEPHERD (THE): In the traditional Church the Good Shepherd is a title for Jesus, owing, in part, to his association with the Jewish sacrificial lamb (Passover) and the subsequent adoption of the Pagan symbol the *Agnus Dei*, "Lamb of God." In the mystical Church the "Good Shepherd" is another symbol of the Higher Self,[1839] or Indwelling Christ. John has Jesus declare:

> Verily, verily, I say unto you, I AM the door of the sheep. All that ever came before me are thieves and robbers: but the sheep did not hear them. I AM the door: by me if any man enter in, he shall be saved, and shall go in and out, and find pasture.
>
> The thief cometh not, but for to steal, and to kill, and to destroy: I AM come that they might have life, and that they might have it more abundantly. I AM the good shepherd: the good shepherd giveth his life for the sheep. But he that is an hireling, and not the shepherd, whose own the sheep are not, seeth the wolf coming, and leaveth the sheep, and fleeth: and the wolf catcheth them, and scattereth the sheep. The hireling fleeth, because he is an hireling, and careth not for the sheep.
>
> I AM the good shepherd, and know my sheep, and am known of mine. As the Father knoweth me, even so know I the Father: and I lay down my life for the sheep. And other sheep

I have, which are not of this fold: them also I must bring, and they shall hear my voice; and there shall be one fold, and one shepherd. Therefore doth my Father love me, because I lay down my life, that I might take it again.[1840]

Here the mystical inner meaning of the "Good Shepherd" is revealed by the words "I AM," one of the Bible's many codewords, not for the man Jesus, but for the spirit Christ, which indwells all human beings as the Higher Self or Soul,[1841] for as Paul said: "Ye are the temple of the living God."[1842]

Like nearly everything else considered "uniquely Christian," the title "Good Shepherd" too has its roots in Paganism, for the vast majority of pre-Christian saviors were attributed with the role of the Good Shepherd, who lovingly tends his "flock" of souls in the Afterlife. Among these were the Greek savior Adonis, the Babylonian savior Tammuz,[1843] the Sumerian savior Dumuzi, the Greek savior Hermes, the Roman god Mercury,[1844] and the Pelasgian Christ known as *Hermes Kriophoros*, "Hermes the sheep-bearer," who was portrayed carrying a lamb over his shoulders centuries before the rise of Christianity. Later, his function as protector of flocks and herds was given to the god Apollo Nomius,[1845] whose temple stood at Corcyra.[1846]

One of the oldest usages of the term Good Shepherd was in ancient Egypt, where the land's rulers were given the insignias of the shepherd (the crook and lash), a bucolic figure that began as a Pagan symbol of the archetypal caring protective father.[1847] The "Good Shepherd" was one of the titles of the Egyptian deity Osiris, who, like all savior-gods, was an occult symbol of the Divine Logos, Higher Self, or Indwelling Christ.[1848] In Egyptian funerary art we see Osiris depicted carrying the shepherd's crook or cross, this too later appended to the figure of Jesus and adopted by Christian bishops as their official scepter.[1849] From the Latin word for shepherd we derive the word *pastor*, as well as the term for clerical communications with church members: "pastoral letters."[1850]

Despite these Church "traditions," the roots of the Good Shepherd are pre-Christian, dating back, as noted, through ancient Greece and depictions of the "guardian of flocks," the god *Hermes Kriophorus*, to Mesopotamia where we find millennia-old images of the archetypal herdsman carrying a lamb on his shoulders. It is interesting to note that the Nature-god Pan, also a type of "Good Shepherd,"[1851] and popular with the shepherds of Arcadia,[1852] was later personified by traditional Christianity as the Devil,[1853] giving additional meaning to the term *Demon est Deus Inversus* (the "Devil is God Inverted").[1854] See BLOOD OF THE LAMB, KRISHNA, LAMB OF GOD, OSIRIS, WASHED IN THE BLOOD OF THE LAMB.

GOSPEL (THE): In traditional Christianity the Gospel is the life story of Jesus Christ and his salvific message to humanity, which includes the "infallible" details of His birth, life, ministry, death, and resurrection.[1855] Christian mystics, however, do not take the Gospel literally, which is owed, in part, to the many problems contained within the New Testament.[1856] For example there is:

- Mark's "Messianic Secret," in which Jesus is shown commanding His followers not to announce His messiahship but to keep silent about it.[1857]
- Mark's reference to Herod Antipas as a "king"[1858] (he was a tetrarch, as the more historically accurate Luke notes).[1859]
- John, one of the 12 Apostles, and the man who took care of the Virgin Mary after Jesus' death,[1860] neglects to mention the miraculous conception of our Lord.[1861]
- John's similar failure to mention the Sermon on the Mount,[1862] the institution of the Eucharist,[1863] the Transfiguration,[1864] the Great Commission,[1865] and the Ascension,[1866] *though he was present at all these events.*[1867]
- Jesus' failure to connect the coming Kingdom of God with the title Christ.[1868]
- Jesus' failed prediction that the Parousia would occur during the lifetimes of His followers;[1869] this despite the fact that He is portrayed as the Son of God,[1870] or even God himself,[1871] and is thus all-knowing (omniscient).[1872]
- Jesus' failure to ever mention His own miraculous birth.[1873]
- the fact that Matthew and Luke give Jesus two completely different genealogies,[1874] an issue so insurmountable that many Bible scholars consider it "impossible to reconcile."[1875] Note: Matthew traces Jesus' descent from David, which could only come through Joseph, who, according to the Nativity,[1876] was *not* Jesus' biological father; and as Strauss points out, Joseph's legal adoption of Jesus would not have been enough to meet the strict requirements of a "flesh and blood" descendant of David.[1877]
- Mary's silence in concealing her supernatural pregnancy from her husband Joseph.[1878]
- Mary's odd and unaccountable ignorance of her son's true identity, fully displayed when she confronts the 12 year old Jesus at the Temple.[1879]
- the four New Testament lists of the 12 Apostles[1880] differ in name and arrangement.[1881]
- the fact that the four canonical Gospels sharply contradict one another in form, features, chronology, and content.[1882]
- the late obvious ecclesiastic additions to Matthew,[1883] Mark,[1884] Luke,[1885] and John,[1886] all four Gospels which bear the overtly distinguishable marks of a multitude of different hands and unknown Christian storytellers, mythologists, and apologists.[1887]
- the fact that the Gospels describe in detail what occurred while Jesus was praying in *solitary* in the Garden of Gethsemane. Luke, for example, depicts the Lord's sweat appearing "like drops of blood."[1888] How does he know if neither he or anyone else was present? The only one there was Jesus, and

He never mentions this particular and dies shortly afterward. Matthew says that Jesus took Peter, James, and John with him to the garden, all who quickly fell asleep; despite this, the first Evangelist records everything Jesus says.[1889] (Gnostic-mystic John wisely forgoes any mention of the Agony at Gethsemane.)[1890] Plainly what we have here are invented narratives masquerading as eyewitness accounts, intended to fill in a blank page in the biography of our Lord (which had a beginning and end but no middle) and which the orthodox have literalized and historicized.[1891]

- the confused and misplaced sentence in the Lord's Prayer, "lead us not into temptation,"[1892] which attributes evildoing to the Heavenly Father,[1893] whom John defines as "love."[1894]
- the four Evangelists' frequent misunderstanding and hence misinterpretation of Old Testament passages, which they put forth as "prophecies" related to Jesus. Another possibility: they knew these scriptures were *not* Jesuine prophecies but presented them as such anyway. This would mean that Matthew, Mark, Luke, and John are guilty of either incompetence or fraud.[1895]
- the fact that we have no real idea what the original authors of the New Testament actually said,[1896] for we do not possess a single *original* and *complete* manuscript of any of its 27 books.[1897]
- the fact that even our earliest New Testament manuscripts are hand-copied copies of copies of the originals,[1898] which allowed for the possibility of the introduction of untold thousands of errors and artificial insertions and removals.
- the fact that the important figure of Nicodemus is only mentioned by John.[1899]
- the fact that after Jesus' death Joseph of Arimathea asks for the Lord's "body" (*soma*) rather than His "corpse" (*ptoma*),[1900] lending support to the popular ancient tradition that Jesus survived the Crucifixion[1901] and lived into old age.[1902]
- the fact that after His death Jesus' female followers planned to return to His tomb to pay their respects and anoint His body,[1903] revealing that they, like most if not of all of the Lord's other followers, did not expect there to be a resurrection.[1904]
- the fact that no two surviving ancient manuscripts of the New Testament completely agree in every detail.[1905]
- the fact that the New Testament was at first *not* considered "infallible," for early copyists, translators, and writers never hesitated to alter its words.[1906] Numerous details, for example, have been discovered that were obviously invented by the four Evangelists to accord with alleged prophetic requirements, but which Old Testament writers would never have intended to be linked to Jesus.[1907] Matthew and Luke specifically

certainly did not regard Mark as "inerrant," for they thought nothing of editorializing the second Gospel,[1908] adding to it, subtracting from it, and rewriting whatever it was that best suited their particular needs.[1909] (Matthew, for instance, purposely cut out Mark's important mention of Jesus' use of spittle.)[1910] Jesus Himself regarded various passages in the Old Testament as fallible, archaic, and disposable, and often reworded them to suit His own beliefs,[1911] and even quoted from scripture, like the book of Enoch, that was later banned from the Bible by the mainstream Church.[1912]

- the fact that the most impressive miracle story in the New Testament, the raising of Lazarus (Martha and Mary's brother) from the dead, is only mentioned by John.[1913] Furthermore, the Synoptic tradition is aware of Martha and Mary, but not Lazarus.[1914] Why? Even mainstream theologians admit that this is an "old and unsolvable problem."[1915]
- the fact that after Jesus' death on the cross Matthew states that the Roman soldiers guarding the Master's tomb "became as dead men,"[1916] yet a few sentences later he has them returning to the city to report to officials "all the things that were done."[1917]
- the fact that Luke's story of the two disciples on the road to Emmaus (suspiciously found only in Luke)[1918] derives some of its elements from the ancient Roman novel *The Golden Ass* by Lucius Apuleius.[1919]
- Luke's over reliance on the works of Josephus, numerous elements from which he freely "borrowed" for use in the third Gospel. One of the more noteworthy of these plagiarized items is the visit by the 12 year old Jesus to the Jerusalem Temple,[1920] which Luke took wholesale from Josephus' autobiography.[1921]
- the fact that Matthew first shows John the Baptist clearly identifying and baptizing Jesus as the Messiah.[1922] But later, after Jesus has selected the 12 Apostles, Matthew, confusingly, has John send messengers to Jesus asking for proof that He is indeed the awaited Messiah.[1923]
- the original primitive Christian view (found, for example, in the Gospel of Q and the Gospel of Thomas) concerning Jesus was that He was not God or even a god, but a very special human prophet, teacher, and healer, born naturally of two human parents.[1924] Writing within a few years after Jesus' death, Paul makes no mention of most of what would later become some of Christianity's greatest figures, stories, doctrines, rituals, and beliefs; among other things, he does not mention Jesus' miracles, the 12 Apostles, or the empty tomb—the latter being the very foundation of orthodox Christianity. Writing a generation later Mark now insists that Jesus was divine and that this divinity was revealed at the time of His baptism.[1925] Matthew and Luke, writing a generation later than Mark, however, assert that this "fact" was known at the time of His birth.[1926]

John, writing some three generations after Jesus' death, now claims that Jesus' divinity had existed all along, even prior to the creation of the world.[1927] As with many other New Testament elements, this developmental storyline clearly shows that the Gospel story evolved over time, through thousands of artificially appended additions.
- the fact that the four Evangelists have so muddled the sequence of events during the Passion Week that, despite the best efforts of the greatest minds over many centuries, they have never been resolved, and among honest academics the hope of ever doing so has completely evaporated.[1928]
- the fact that all four of the Gospels portray Jesus as the Messiah, a word He never used for Himself, a role He never openly claimed for Himself,[1929] and an idea which He once even publicly repudiated.[1930]
- the fact that the Synoptic writers base Jesus' *one-year* ministry in *Galilee*, while John places the Lord's *three-year* ministry in *Judea* (near Jerusalem). Both cannot be right, which means that either the Synoptics are false on this score, or John is, leaving open the possibility of numerous other erroneous statements, often of significant nature, throughout the New Testament.[1931]
- the fantastical reality that the Gospel was written by men who frequently disagreed with one another on the most basic of facts,[1932] seldom understood Jesus and His teachings[1933] (even when they were repeatedly and explicitly explained to them,)[1934] and even deserted Him in His final hour.[1935] Even after our Lord's resurrection appearances many of these same individuals continued to misunderstand and doubt.[1936]

Thousands more such examples could be provided, and many critical, objective, brilliant, and highly respected volumes have been penned on these problems, as well as scores of others.[1937]

Let us consider the following single fact: not only was the Gospel story written by individuals who did not fully comprehend Jesus, but at least two, if not all four, of the Evangelists never knew Jesus personally.[1938] The same could be, and has been, said of the rest of the New Testament writers.[1939] And yet it is from these two groups that the entire Gospel tradition derives,[1940] with all of its astonishing contradictions, errors, omissions, misconceptions, alterations, additions, subtractions, impossibilities, inconsistencies, revisions, mistranslations, rewrites, modifications, interpolations, gaps, emendations, redactions, bowdlerizations, incongruities, recensions, deletions, "corrections," misstatements, faults, expurgations, obscenities,[1941] and thousands of often incoherent and disconnected elements.[1942]

Bible scholars estimate that the Good Book has been so extensively revised and rewritten for doctrinal purposes that there is no longer a single sentence in, for instance, the New Testament in which the scriptural tradition is consistent and uniform. As a result, there are over 250,000 differences in our current inventory of New Testament manuscripts. One of our oldest complete copies of the New Testament, the Codex Sinaiticus (4th Century), reveals the avalanche of alterations that have been introduced: academics haves counted some 14,800 modifications and margin notes that have been made or added by at least nine unknown "correctors" over time.[1943]

Avoiding these thorny issues altogether, in the great mystic tradition the Christian Gospel is seen as an allegory of the human soul's descent into the material plane (involution or *aphanism*), its ascent into the spiritual plane (evolution or *euresis*),[1944] and its final merging (at-one-ment) with God,[1945] or what esotericists know as the three-phase journey toward attaining Godhood: "generation, degeneration, and regeneration."[1946] To make this, the Christian mystic's view of the Gospel, more understandable, I here offer my own interpretation of this arcane spiritual process. It reveals the inner meaning of those common terms given by Bible literalists and Christian traditionalists to the primary stages, events, and experiences in the life of our Lord, as they apply to the individual human Soul:

SEABROOK'S MYSTICAL DOCTRINE OF THE CHRIST

1) In the Spirit Plane a Soul, the Universal Indwelling Christ, decides to come to earth to advance its spiritual growth, and selects a father and mother to come through (the "Annunciation").[1947] The incoming incarnating Christ-Soul (the "Baby Jesus")[1948] drops downward from the Spirit Plane (the "Immaculate Conception")[1949] and onto the Material Plane, planting itself (as spirit) inside the mother's womb (the "Incarnation").[1950]

2) Now on earth the Soul encases itself ("Baptism")[1951] in a fetus or physical body (the "Cross"),[1952] is born (the "Virgin Birth")[1953] on a predetermined day ("Christmas"), and carefully tended into adolescence (the "Adoration"). During young adulthood the Soul progresses in knowledge and wisdom[1954] (Jesus' "Silent Years," from 12 to 30 years old),[1955] learning chiefly through experiencing the suffering caused by the tension between materiality and spirituality—which leads, in adulthood, to the final triumph over the physical plane (the "Temptation").[1956] This stage ends in enlightenment (the "Transfiguration"),[1957] accompanied by the realization and acceptance of the painful reality (the "Passion")[1958] that it must sacrifice its physical body in order to return to God (the "Crucifixion").[1959]

3) The Soul is rewarded by then being released (the "Resurrection")[1960] to return upward, back to the world of Spirit (the "Ascension").[1961] Once the Soul has been completely perfected through this repetitive process (either via physical reincarnation[1962] or psychologically being "born again"),[1963] it is allowed to stay in the highest Heaven (the seventh)[1964] for all eternity ("Exaltation").[1965]

The reason the Gospel is based around this single theme is because it is the most important spiritual truth of all: the Soul must take on a human body (known as an "initiation" into "soul growth"),[1966] and realize its divinity while in that body, before it will finally be freed to permanently return to Heaven (its true home) and rejoin God.[1967] Of this topic Kingsford and Maitland write:

> ... *the Gospel narrative*, while related—in Scripture fashion—as of an actual particular person, and in terms derived from the physical plane—*is a mystical history only of any person, and implies the spiritual possibilities of all persons. And hence, while using terms implying, or derived from, actual times, places, persons and events, it does not really refer to these or make pretence to historical precision, its function and purpose being, not to relate physical facts, which can have no relation to the soul, but to exhibit and illustrate processes and principles which are purely spiritual.* Thus regarded, the Gospels—even though having in view a special personality as their model [Jesus]—constitute *a parable rather than a history*.[1968]

Strauss writes:

> At an earlier period, Horst presented this symbolical view of the history of Jesus with singular clearness. Whether, he says, all that is narrated of Christ happened precisely so, historically, is a question indifferent to us, nor can it now be settled. Nay, if we would be candid with ourselves, *that which was once sacred history for the Christian believer, is, for the enlightened portion of our contemporaries, only fable*: the narratives of the supernatural birth of Christ, of his miracles, of his resurrection and ascension, must be rejected by us as at variance with the inductions of our intellect. Let them however only be no longer interpreted merely by the understanding as history, but by the feelings and imagination, as poetry; and it will be found that *in these narratives nothing is invented arbitrarily, but all springs from the depths and divine impulses of the human mind.*
>
> Considered from this point of view, we may annex to the history of Christ all that is important to religious trust, animating to the pure dispositions, attractive to the tender feelings. That history is *a beautiful, sacred poem of the human race*—a poem in which are embodied all the wants of our religious instinct; and this is the highest honour of Christianity, and the strongest proof of its universal applicability. *The history of the gospel is in fact, the history of human nature conceived ideally,*

and exhibits to us in the life of an individual, what man ought to be, and, united with him by following his doctrine and example, can actually become.[1969]

William Ralph Inge writes:

> What especially interested St. Paul about the death and resurrection was the light which they throw on the spiritual life of human beings. *The life and death and rising again of Christ [that is, the Gospel] are to him a kind of dramatisation of the normal psychological experience.* We, too, must die to sin and rise again to righteousness; nay, we must die daily, crucifying the old man and putting on the new man—the true likeness of Him who created us. And this is why the identification of Christ with the world-principle was so essential for him.
>
> The "whole process of Christ" (as some of our English divines called it) was thus proved to be the great spiritual law under which we all live. Whatever it behoved Christ to do and to suffer, that we, as members of His body, must be prepared to do and suffer also. If God was pleased highly to exalt Him who in human form did and suffered such things, then for us too death has lost its sting and the grave its victory. The law of the universe is proved to be not the law of sin and death, but the law of redemption through suffering, ending in triumph over sin and death.
>
> *This I believe is the leading thought in St. Paul's theology; and it is easy to see that it is in no way dependent on any historical details about the human Christ. Having once accepted the "revelation" made to him about the Person of Christ, he was, we may say boldly, independent of the history.* . . . The Gospel narrative [then] is to be studied *"in order that we may know"*: it does not convey knowledge immediately. "Getting to know" is a gradual process, a progressive inner experience. *God reveals Himself within us as we are able to receive Him*, and at each stage the figure of the historical Christ becomes clearer and more intelligible to us. *In this way the faith that began as an experiment ends as an experience; the body of teaching which we at first received from outside becomes part of our very selves.*[1970]

Likewise Basilides held that

> the life of Christ was the beginning of a progressive shaping and

forming of the individual souls of believers, as thoughts of God, out of the shapeless form of unconscious material or psychical experience. . . . This is the process, according to Basilides, not only of history, but of the whole creation itself. The history of mankind is the type of the evolution of creation.[1971]

This important Gospel message, part of the true Good News that our Lord preached, has been borne out on a personal level untold times throughout history. In the late 1800s, for example, Bucke recorded the following personal account from a woman who had experienced Christ Consciousness, or what he terms "Cosmic Consciousness": a mystical, overwhelming, sudden illumination of the heart, mind, and spirit, which fills one with indescribable wonder, peace, and joy, and enigmatically answers many of life's greatest questions. As she was going through this intense "psychological experience," she wrote:

> The great truth that life is a spiritual evolution, that this life is but a passing phase in the soul's progression, burst upon my astonished vision with overwhelming grandeur. Oh, I thought, if this is what it means, if this is the outcome, then pain is sublime! Welcome centuries, eons, of suffering if it brings us to this! . . . I had learned the grand lesson, that suffering is the price which must be paid for all that is worth having; that in some mysterious way we are refined and sensitized, doubtless largely by it, so that we are made susceptible to nature's higher and finer influences—this, if true of one, is true of all.[1972]

In the end, as Buddhism teaches, the Divine Truth that is embodied in sacred texts, such as the Christian Gospel, cannot be communicated from person to person. For as soon as we speak it or write it, "it" is no longer "it."[1973] Truth must come directly from God himself, via the Indwelling Christ (intuition). The printed word has no power or knowledge in and of itself, for as soon as we label Spirit or try to describe it, we falsify God—who is ultimately unknowable and therefore unnameable and indescribable.[1974] This is why those who worship and literalize the Bible's words will never find the Truth, for "the letter killeth."[1975] Thus Jesus, speaking as the Universal Christ Within, warned:

> Search the scriptures; for in them ye think ye have eternal life . . . And [yet] ye will not come to me, that ye might have life.[1976]

See BORN AGAIN, CHRIST, CROWN, ENOCH, GOOD NEWS, GOSPEL OF JESUS CHRIST, GOSPEL OF Q, GOSPEL OF THE KINGDOM OF GOD,

GOSPEL OF THOMAS, JESUS, NATIVITY, REBIRTH, REINCARNATION, WAY OF THE LORD.

GOSPEL OF JESUS CHRIST: In the traditional Church the Gospel of Jesus Christ is the one and only Gospel. No other is recognized or even discussed. Yet, this is not the Gospel our Lord Himself taught. He was not even aware of the Gospel of Jesus Christ,[1977] for this was formulated in His name long after His Death. He certainly would not have approved of it, for His Gospel, the true one, called by Him "the Gospel of the Kingdom of God,"[1978] focused not on Himself, but on the Father, hence the name He gave it.

In essence, *the early orthodox Church founded a religion on the messenger rather than on His message, contrived a gospel about Jesus rather than about His teachings, and glorified Him who commanded that we glorify only God.*[1979] In other words, it decided to *worship the symbol rather than the substance.* In this way, as Freud observed, the Father religion of the Hebrews became the Son religion of the Christians,[1980] an error of gargantuan proportions, for Jesus taught only the Father religion. Bultmann phrased it this way: "The proclaimer became the proclaimed."[1981] Pike put it this way: "They worshipped the Creature instead of the Creator . . . confounded the symbol with the thing itself . . . the type with the archetype . . . and worshipped the sign as if it were itself Deity."[1982] These facts are so obvious that they are acknowledged by many of the most respected Bible scholars today.[1983]

In the process, Jesus' "Gospel of the Kingdom of God" was ousted and replaced with the Church's own invention, "the Gospel of Jesus Christ." The Truth Jesus taught was discarded, and He Himself became the "Truth," and His authority was usurped and supplanted by the Church's authority.[1984] This was not what our Lord intended, however, as a close reading of the New Testament reveals to all those who take the time to study it.

The fact that the true Gospel of our Lord is no longer acknowledged let alone taught in our churches, the fact that the emphasis is now on Jesus rather than on God (as He preached), the fact that the orthodox have confused the messenger with the message, these must all be counted as a great and solemn tragedy for Christianity, and certainly one of the most significant coverups and conspiracies in the history of Western civilization. That many holding this book will be reading about this outrage for the first time is a testament to the magnitude of this unconscionable and offensive scandal.

Thankfully, despite the orthodox Church's 1,600 year vigorous and often violent campaign to wipe it out, the mystical Church continues to preserve the true Gospel of our Lord: the Gospel of the Kingdom of God, many of whose suppressed teachings are contained within this very book. See CHRISTIANITY, GNOSTICISM, GOOD NEWS, GOSPEL, GOSPEL OF Q, GOSPEL OF THE KINGDOM OF GOD, GOSPEL OF THOMAS, JESUS, MYTH OF CHRIST.

GOSPEL OF Q: In the traditional Church the Gospel of Q is largely unknown, and where it is known it is largely misunderstood and persistently ignored—and, as we will see, for good reason. However, it is included in this dictionary because it is actually part and parcel of the canonical Bible. In the mystical Church the Gospel of Q is all important, for it contains many of the original, authentic pre-Christian doctrines of Jesus as recorded in the New Testament, and which have been disregarded, misinterpreted, and even suppressed.

What is the Gospel of Q?

In essence, it was a document written in Aramaic (the language Jesus spoke) containing the earliest and thus original teachings of Jesus (in oral form)[1985] as they were remembered and recorded by His first followers, the Q community.[1986] It was discovered when scholars began studying the four Gospels in order to see which was written first. It immediately became clear that there were two correspondences:

1) The Gospels of Matthew and Luke only agree when they follow Mark; meaning that Mark was the earliest Gospel.[1987]
2) Matthew and Luke contain a large amount of Jesus' sayings material that is not in Mark, and most of which is identical; indicating that Matthew and Luke had used a second written document in addition to Mark.[1988]

It is this second source which has come to be known as the Gospel of Q.

After Jesus' death this document found its way into the hands of Matthew and Luke, who used it, along with the Gospel of Mark, as a foundation on which to construct an elaborate biography of our Lord; one which they intertwined with Pagan myths, beliefs, symbols, and doctrines, supernatural aspects that were not part of the life of the historical Jesus, and which He never taught and which He would never have condoned.[1989] The Q of the canonical Gospelers then is an orthodox revision, tidied up for a literalistic audience.[1990]

In short, the Gospel of Q is made up of the identical sayings material found in Matthew and Luke but which is not found in Mark—although I (and others) have shown that Mark did use Q to some extent.[1991] (We will note that John seems to have had no knowledge of Q; or if he did, he showed no interest in it.) Thus, the Synoptic Gospels, particularly Matthew and Luke, contain precious remnants of the Lord's actual thoughts and words, revealingly known to the first Christians, the Gnostics, as "The Secret Sayings of Jesus,"[1992] and which modern scholars call the "Wisdom Gospel."[1993] As such, Q may derive from the same oral tradition as the famed Gnostic Gospel of Thomas, or the Gospel of Thomas may in fact be the Gospel of Q (or a version of it).[1994]

The Gospel of Q derives its name from the German word *quelle*, "source," because it is the source of much of the secondary material in Matthew and Luke, but which is generally missing from Mark and completely absent from John.[1995]

The original Q document is, of course, now lost, though it was mentioned by both the 2nd-Century Bishop Papias of Hierapolis[1996] and by Paul[1997] before it finally disappeared.[1998] This occurred because in the minds of the Q people (Q's authors), once Q was absorbed into Matthew and Luke (and Mark)—not to mention numerous other noncanonical Gospels and works—there was little reason to preserve it. Thus, it gradually fell out of use and eventually vanished. After all, it was considered a theological document, not a historical one, and so, at the time, little or no importance was attached to it. Even what has been reconstructed from Matthew and Luke is missing at least 40 percent of the original Q document.[1999]

As paleographic evidence shows, the Gospel of Q—which, for example, lacks an incipit, and also the narrative framework of the four canonical Gospels—long predates the Synoptics, with the earliest "layer" (known as Q1) probably being recorded as early as the 30s (shortly after Jesus' death),[2000] Q2 being composed sometime in the 40s and 50s, and Q3 written as late as the year 75.[2001]

I refer to the Gospel of Q as *Christianity's most important document*, for it records the pre-Christian Jesus as He lived and taught before His doctrines were distorted and literalized, and before He Himself was Paganized into a Sun/Son-god by the orthodox Church. In other words, Q represents the authentic Jesus (the "Son of Man") of primitive Christianity (pure spirituality) rather than the subsequent supernatural Christ (the "Son of God") of orthodox Christianity (pure Paganism).

How do we know this? It is because the Gospel of Q, written long prior to the letters of Paul and to the four Gospels, does not mention or delve into the life of Jesus, His birth, baptism, messiahship, transfiguration, the Last Supper, the Passion, His trial, crucifixion, death resurrection, ascension, or even the kerygma.[2002] In fact, it completely lacks any kind of Christology.[2003] Its earliest layer, Q1, also contains no apocalyptic warnings, no martyrological dogma, no complex theodicies, no salvific creeds, no named apostles, and no rules or instructions on how to organize and maintain the community of Q—or any future type of "church" for that matter.[2004]

Rather, as one would expect from the earliest followers of the Master (who were not "Christians" and never thought of themselves as such), Q centers not on Jesus, but on Jesus' *teachings*, all of which were contained in what He called "the Gospel of the Kingdom (of God),"[2005] or what I term "the Good News about the Realm of Divine Mind."[2006] Other Jesuine teachings from the Gospel of Q that are found in the New Testament are the Lord's Prayer, the Golden Rule, and the Beatitudes. Of this mysterious and fascinating Gospel Harnack writes:

> Q is a compilation of discourses and sayings of our Lord, the arrangement of which has no reference to the Passion, with an horizon which is as good as absolutely bounded by Galilee, without any clearly discernible bias, whether apologetic,

didactic, ecclesiastical, national, or anti-national. So far as any purpose at all—beyond that of imparting catechetical instruction—can be discovered in the compilation, it consisted perhaps in an endeavour to give, with a certain degree of completeness, a representation of the main features of our Lord's relationship with His environment.[2007]

Q is, as Harnack noted, the true Gospel in its purest and most pristine form as it existed before it was contaminated by orthodox theological and political features.[2008] This is why I have devoted an entire book to it, *Jesus and the Gospel of Q*, which provides the complete Q canon as found in the New Testament (KJV).[2009] See CHRIST, CHRISTIANITY, GOSPEL, GOSPEL OF THE KINGDOM OF GOD, GOSPEL OF THOMAS, JESUS, MYTH OF CHRIST, NATIVITY.

GOSPEL OF THE KINGDOM OF GOD: In traditional Christianity the Gospel of the Kingdom of God, or Gospel of the Kingdom for short, is virtually unknown, for it has been displaced, and indeed completely replaced, by the Church's own posthumous fabrication, one known as "the Gospel of Jesus Christ," a gospel that Jesus did not teach, was not aware of, and which He would have soundly denounced had He been aware of it.

A little fact-based history.

The concept of "The Gospel" as we know it today did not exist during Jesus' life, which is why this term was not applied to His words and deeds until the middle of the 2nd Century.[2010] Indeed, the word "gospel" is not found anywhere in the so-called "Gospel" of John, a book that was given this title long after it was originally written. Even when the Synoptic writers mention the "Gospel," they are not referring to the four written Gospels as we know them. They are referring to Jesus' personal teachings.[2011] What were these teachings and what were they called?

As just noted, contrary to popular thought, there are two completely different Gospels presented in the New Testament: the first preached by Jesus during His ministry, which He called *"the Gospel of the Kingdom of God,"*[2012] and the second preached by His followers after His death, which they referred to as *"the Gospel of Jesus Christ."*[2013]

The former, Jesus' *Gospel of the Kingdom of God*, did not include anything relating to our Lord Himself.[2014] What it did include were His Gnostic-Essenic doctrines on love,[2015] justice,[2016] the divinity of Man (Theosis),[2017] faith and healing,[2018] reincarnation,[2019] vegetarianism,[2020] the Third Eye,[2021] the Way,[2022] occultic biology, bilocation, astral projection,[2023] the Golden Rule,[2024] the Law of Prosperity,[2025] purification of the body, the immortality of the Soul, spiritual alchemy, the Law of the Triangle, the attainment of spiritual beauty and divine power, the human aura,[2026] the path to eternal life, raising of the dead (using ancient works like the Egyptian *Book of the Dead*), moral law, civic duty, anti-formalism, spiritual psychology, the Law of Karma,[2027] the Law of Faith,[2028] the Law of Prayer,[2029] the Law of Word Power,[2030] the Law of Nonresistance,[2031] the Law of Forgiveness,[2032] the materialization and dematerialization of the body[2033] and of physical objects,[2034] the Law of Attraction,[2035] and our at-one-ment with the Father and the Indwelling Christ,[2036] all which made up the original "Good News" of Jesus.[2037] Small portions of this, the true Gospel, can still be discovered in both the Gospel of Q and the Gospel of Thomas, and in those sections of the Synoptics where Matthew, Mark, and Luke utilized these two older Gospels.[2038]

The latter or second Gospel, *the Gospel of Jesus Christ*, was created by His followers after His death, and was constructed around a Paganistic-Jewish-Catholic Christology centering on Jesus as the messianic Savior of Mankind,[2039] a title He never used for Himself, and a role He never intended to play.[2040] Thus, it was not the four "Evangelists" who authored the Gospel tradition. It was the Church.[2041]

Because Jesus' God-centered "Spiritual Gospel," *the Gospel of the Kingdom*,[2042] threatened both Catholic hegemony and the priesthood, over many centuries it was gradually suppressed and replaced by the Paganesque *Gospel of Jesus Christ*,[2043] the "Material Gospel," the one still followed by mainstream Christianity to this day.[2044] In this way "the profanity of men's lives has debauched and blinded their understanding as to Jesus."[2045] Of this tragic event Kingsford and Maitland write:

> In assigning to the Gospels their proper meaning, it is necessary to remember that, *as mystical Scriptures*, they deal, primarily, not with material things or persons, but with spiritual significations. Like the "books of Moses," therefore, and others, which, in *being mystical*, are, in the strictest sense, prophetical, *the Gospels are addressed, not to the outer sense and reason, but to the soul. And, being thus, their object is, not to give an historical account of the physical life of any man whatever, but to exhibit the spiritual possibilities of humanity at large, as illustrated in a particular and typical example.* The design is, thus, that which is dictated by the nature itself of Religion. *For Religion is not in its nature historical and dependent upon actual, sensible events, but consists in processes, such as Faith and Redemption, which, being interior to all men, subsist irrespectively of what any particular man has at any time suffered or done.* That alone which is of importance, is what God has revealed. And therefore it is that *the narratives concerning Jesus are rather parables founded on a collection of histories, than any one actual history, and have a spiritual import capable of universal application. And it is with this spiritual import, and not with physical facts, that the Gospels are concerned.*

Such were the principles which, long before the Christian era, and under divine control, had led the Mystics of Egypt, Persia, and India, to select Osiris, Mithras, and Buddha as names or persons representative of the Man Regenerate and constituting a full manifestation of the qualities of Spirit. And it was for the same purpose and under the same impulsion that the Mystics of the West, who had their head-quarters at Alexandria, *selected Jesus, using him as a type whereby to exhibit the history of all souls which attain to perfection*; *employing physical occurrences as symbols, and relating them as parables, to interpret which literally would be to falsify their intended import.* Their method was, thus, to *universalise that which was particular, and to spiritualise that which was material; and, writing, as they did, with full knowledge of previous mystical descriptions of the Man Regenerate, his interior history and his relations to the world,*—notable among which descriptions was the fifty-third chapter of the miscellaneous fragmentary prophetic utterances collected together under the typical name of Isaiah,—they would have had no difficulty in presenting a character consistent with the general anticipation of those who were cognisant of the meaning of the term "Christ," even without an actual example.

The failure to interpret the mystical Scriptures by the mystical rule, was due to the loss, by the Church, of the mystical faculty, or inner, spiritual vision, through which they were written. Passing under a domination exclusively sacerdotal and traditional, and losing thereby the intuition of things spiritual, the Church fell an easy prey to that which is *the besetting sin of priesthoods,—Idolatry; and in place of the simple, true, reasonable Gospel, to illustrate which the history of Jesus had been expressly designed, fabricated the stupendous and irrational superstition which has usurped his name.*

Converted by the exaltation of the Letter and the symbol in place of the Spirit and the signification, into an idolatry every whit as gross as any that preceded it, Christianity has failed to redeem the world. Christianity has failed, that is, not because it was false, but because it has been falsified. And the falsification, generally, has consisted in removing the character described under the name of Jesus, from its true function as the portrait of that of which every man has in him the potentiality, and referring it exclusively to an imaginary order of being between whom and man could be no possible relation, even were such a being himself possible. Instead of recognising the Gospels as a written hieroglyph, setting forth, under terms derived from natural objects and persons, processes which are purely spiritual and impersonal, the Churches have—one and all—fallen into that lowest mode of fetish-worship, which consists in the adoration of a mere symbol, entirely irrespective of its true import.

To the complaint that will inevitably be made against this exposition of the real nature of the Gospel history,—that it has "taken away the Lord,"—the reply is no less satisfactory than obvious. For he has been taken away only from the place wherein so long the Church has kept him, that is,—the sepulchre. There, indeed, it is, with the dead,—bound about with cerements, a figure altogether of the past,—that Christians have laid their Christ. But at length the "stone" of Superstition has been lifted and rolled away by the hand of the Angel of Knowledge, and the grave it concealed is discovered to be empty. No longer need the soul seek her living Master among the dead. Christ is risen,—risen into the heaven of a living Ideal, whence he can again descend into the hearts of all who desire him, none the less real and puissant, because a universal principle, and not merely an historical personage; none the less mighty to save because, instead of being a single Man Regenerate, he is every Man Regenerate, ten thousand times ten thousand,—the " Son of Man" himself.[2046]

Thankfully, the truth of Jesus and the authentic Spiritual Gospel, the universal Gospel of the Kingdom of God, has been kept alive by the mystical Christian Church. Origen wrote the following 1,800 years ago:

We must bear in mind, that as the law contains a shadow of good things to come, which are indicated by that law which is announced according to truth, so *the Gospel also teaches a shadow of the mysteries of Christ*, the Gospel which is thought to be capable of being understood by any one. What John calls the eternal Gospel, and *what may properly be called the spiritual Gospel*, presents clearly to those who have the will to understand, all matters concerning the very Son of God, both *the mysteries* presented by His discourses and those matters of which His acts were *the enigmas.*[2047]

While the institutional Church has ousted the first and authentic "Good News" for its own manmade one, interest in the true Gospel of Jesus continues among the mystically inclined and the spiritually mature. Peter said that the topic of the genuine Gospel, the Gospel of the Kingdom of God, is so enthralling that even "the angels desire to look into it."[2048] See CHRIST, GOOD NEWS, GOSPEL,

GOSPEL OF JESUS CHRIST, GOSPEL OF Q, GOSPEL OF THOMAS, JESUS.

GOSPEL OF THOMAS: In traditional Christianity the Gospel of Thomas is completely ignored by Church officials and is all but unknown to the mainstream laity. In mystical Christianity, however, it is considered the second most important document after the Gospel of Q.[2049] This is because, like Q, it is another important source for Jesus' original and authentic, and thus "secret,"[2050] pre-Christian teachings—a source that could itself be a version of the Gospel of Q, for at least 35 percent of the words in the Gospel of Thomas parallel or perfectly match those of Q.[2051] Revealingly, both focus on communicating the "hidden wisdom,"[2052] an esoteric Gnosis that is meant to unlock the mysteries of life and death.[2053]

Many of the sibylline doctrines of this "sayings gospel" are paralleled not only in the New Testament, but were once recognized by various early Christian mystics, some who cited them in their writings. More importantly, many of the sayings found in Thomas are much older than those found in the four canonical Gospels.[2054] Thomas, like the Gnostics' Apocryphon of James, The Book of Thomas, and The Apocryphon of John, contains material that almost certainly dates from the time of the historical Jesus, and thus reflects His actual words. The Parable of the Sower in Thomas, for example, reveals an earlier more primitive form than the one found in the New Testament.[2055]

The Gospel of Thomas, and its 114 sayings, or doctrines of Jesus, was discovered at Nag Hammadi, Egypt, in 1945, with the first English translation coming out in 1959. This particular (physical) document has been dated to around the year A.D. 340, although earlier corroborating finds at Oxyrhynchus, Egypt, date back to at least A.D. 130.[2056] Due to the style, wording, and tone of the Gospel of Thomas, however, the Nag Hammadi and Oxyrhynchus fragments must have been based on a scroll containing the core sayings of Jesus that was composed as early as the 30s or 40s A.D. I am speaking here of the Gospel of Q. Thus, the original Gospel of Thomas was probably written sometime between A.D. 50 and 75.[2057] This makes the Gospel of Thomas—which, as stated, may be a version of Q—of particular importance to those who are interested in learning about the pre-Paganized, pre-apotheosized, pre-politicized, pre-Catholicized figure of Jesus, His original teachings, and His original followers, the Jesus community of Q.[2058] See BIBLE, BRETHREN, CHRIST, CHRISTIANITY, ESSENES, GNOSIS, GNOSTICISM, GOOD NEWS, GOSPEL, GOSPEL OF Q, JESUS.

Krishna crushing the Serpent.

Adam and Eve in the Garden of Eden.

North end of the Dead Sea.

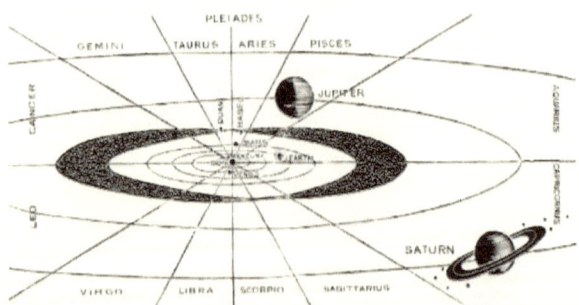
The Solar System, showing the position of the 12 astrological signs.

HEAVEN: In traditional Christianity Heaven is a literal place we go to after an earthly life of good Christian living.[2059] In this case the mystical Christian view does not differ much from the mainstream one; only it allows for other interpretations, the most common being that Heaven is a symbol of Spirituality (as Hell is a symbol of Materiality).

Christian mystics also understand Heaven as a state of consciousness here and in the Afterlife, rather than a specific location. This is due to the cosmic doctrine known as the Law of Reciprocity ("like attracts like"),[2060] which means that what we consistently believe, think, and feel eventually becomes real for us—just as the Bible teaches.[2061] Thus Jesus declared that the Kingdom of God (Heaven) is not outside of you. It is "within you."[2062]

Ancient Pagan, Jewish, and Christian tradition states that there are "Seven Heavens," or rather seven levels of one Heaven.[2063] Thousands of years ago these were patterned on the then seven known gods of the Zodiac: Sun, Moon, Mercury, Venus, Mars, Jupiter, Saturn (after which the seven days of our week are respectively named).[2064] The ancient Greeks held that each of the Seven Heavens and their accompanying deities were associated with one of the seven sacred vowels, which, when sung together, produce the "perfect harmony" of the Spheres:

First Heaven (the lowest): A or Alpha.
Second Heaven: E or Epsilon.
Third Heaven: H or Eta.
Fourth Heaven: I or Iota;
Fifth Heaven: O or Omicron.
Sixth Heaven: Υ or Upsilon.
Seventh Heaven (the highest): Ω or Omega.[2065]

Orthodox Christians reject the concept of Seven Heavens, even though it is referenced in the Bible many times. Paul, for example, states very plainly that he once had an out of body experience in which he visited the "third heaven." "I was," he said, "caught up into paradise, and heard unspeakable words, which it is not lawful for a man to utter."[2066] In the book of Revelation mystic John refers specifically to the First and Second Heavens,[2067] as well as to the Seven Heavens (*Ouranos*) themselves.[2068] Jesus alludes to various heavenly levels on several occasions:

> Whosoever therefore shall break one of these least commandments and shall teach men so, he shall be called *the least in the Kingdom of Heaven*; but whosoever shall do and teach them, the same shall be *called great in the Kingdom of Heaven*.[2069]

> *In my Father's house are many mansions*; if it were not so, I would have told you; for I go to prepare a place for you.[2070]

The doctrine of Heaven is universal, and is found in every religion around the globe. In ancient Greece, for instance, it was known as Elysium,[2071] in Scandinavia it is Valhalla,[2072] and in Tibet it is called Shambhala (the English Shangri-La).[2073] Hindu scriptures too hold that there are seven "astral planes" available to us after "death," the plane one arrives at depending on one's behavior while on earth.[2074] Indeed, according to the "dead" themselves (who speak through spiritualists and mediums) the level of Heaven you go to will be filled with people just like you—individuals with your exact temperament, attitudes, beliefs, perfections, imperfections, and overall state of spiritual consciousness.[2075]

Atheists, scientists, skeptics, and Christian fundamentalists take note: Christian mystics and Pure Land Buddhists, like esotericists from all religions, often portray Heaven using similar even identical language and images. The Buddhist Heaven, the "Western Paradise" known as *Sukhavati* (Sanskrit for "Land of Bliss"),[2076] for example, is described as a region of eternal happiness filled with "jewel trees" composed of various precious metals and stones (such as gold, silver, beryl, crystal, coral, pearl, and emeralds); breathtaking lotus flowers up to ten miles in circumference; countless agreeably scented rivers (filled with flowers and various gems) with bottom sand made of gold and which emit "heavenly music" as they flow over the landscape; endless miles of beautiful parks and palaces; a "Buddha-field" where there is no day or night, only constant beatific light; where life is guided and created by the mind alone; where one can eat, dress, and live according to one's wishes. Sukhavati, also delightfully known as "Happy Land," has much in common with the Christian Heaven described in the book of Revelation.[2077]

As spiritual masters have taught for millennia,[2078] and as the deceased have repeatedly told us through spirit communication (seances),[2079] we experience a bit of (at least one of the levels of) Heaven each night during the dream state, when our spirit temporarily departs the physical body (though it is still attached by the "silver cord" which connects the spirit and the body until the moment of death),[2080] and freely explores the infinite reaches of the Celestial Realms—where everything, as all spiritual masters have taught, is based on thought.[2081] See HELL.

HELL: In institutional Christianity Hell is a physical place of punishment and anguish located in the Christian Underworld, the destination of all sinners in the Afterlife.[2082] In Jesus' original language (Aramaic), however, Hell means "mental torment"; in other words, when you sin ("miss the mark"),[2083] that is, when you do something that is unspiritual, Spiritual Law brings suffering by drawing more disharmony to you.

In the New Testament the word "Hell" is written in three ways. The first is Hades, which is not Hell but rather the personal name of the Greek god of the Underworld (as such he is identical to the Roman underworld-god Orcus).[2084]

The second word, the Hebrew *Geenna* or *Gehenna*, also has nothing to do with the Hell of mainstream Christianity. *Geenna* refers to a real geographical site in ancient Israel: the Valley of Hinnom, just south of Jerusalem, which once served as a landfill for the town's refuse.[2085]

The third reference to Hell uses the Greek word *Tartaroo* (in English, Tartarus), which like Hades, is the name of both an ancient Grecian god and sometimes the Greek Underworld itself. In this case, Tartarus is the lowest, darkest level of Hell.[2086]

According to both early Christians[2087] and modern mainstream Christians,[2088] Jesus briefly visited Hell after His burial in the tomb, a belief intimated by Paul in his letter to the Ephesians.[2089] Christian mystics have long held that Hell, like evil and Satan, is a creation of the mind, which *always* turns our most consistent thoughts and beliefs into reality—whether they are negative or postive.[2090] See ADVERSARY, ANTICHRIST, BEAST, DEVIL, EGO, EGYPT, EVIL, HEAVEN, KARMA, LOWER SELF, LUCIFER, MASS MIND, NUMBER OF THE BEAST, ORIGINAL SIN, SATAN, SERPENT, SIN.

HEROD ANTIPAS: In traditional Christianity the semi-Pagan ruler Herod Antipas governed Galilee and Perea, and had John the Baptist executed.[2091] Jesus calls him a "fox,"[2092] while Mark incorrectly labels him a "king" (he was a tetrarch),[2093] just one of the many "infallibility" problems in the New Testament.[2094] In mystical Christianity his father, Herod the Great, is a symbol of Satan, sin, and human pride,[2095] which is why Mary Baker Eddy occultly refers to him as representing "the grossest element of mortal mind."[2096] Esoterically, these traits describe his son Herod Antipas as well. See DEVIL, EGYPT, HELL, JERUSALEM, LOWER SELF, MASSACRE OF THE INNOCENTS, MASS MIND, PHARISEES, PILATE, SATAN.

HIDDEN MAN OF THE HEART: The Hidden Man of the Heart is one of Peter's terms for the HIGHER SELF.[2097]

HIGHER SELF: The Higher Self is another name for the Christ. It is, in other words, the "true light which lighteth *every man* that cometh into the world."[2098] Paul called it the "inward man,"[2099] as opposed to the "outward man," or Lower Self.[2100] See CHRIST, INWARD MAN, LOWER SELF, OUTWARD MAN, ZION.

HOLY GHOST: The Holy Ghost is another, and less accurate, name for the HOLY SPIRIT.

HOLY SPIRIT: In traditional Christianity the Holy Spirit is considered the anthropomorphized third person of the Godhead, possessing actual humanlike qualities. These include the power to intercede,[2101] convict of sin,[2102] and inspire holy writ.[2103] Fundamentalists accord various personality traits to the Holy Spirit, such as will,[2104] mind,[2105] thought, knowledge,[2106] and love.[2107] All of this despite the fact that Jesus makes little reference to the Holy Spirit, and left us neither a christology or a pneumatology.[2108]

In the mystical branch of Christianity the Holy Spirit is the ancient biblical codename for the Subconscious Mind, which is feminine in nature.[2109] This is why some of the first Christians, the Ebionites, regarded the Holy Spirit as "the Mother of Jesus,"[2110] it is why many other early Christians knew it as Sophia-Sapientia, a personification of the great Pagan Mother-Goddess Mater Dei,[2111] and it is why the Clementine Gnostics held that the Virgin Mary was the vessel of the Holy Spirit.[2112]

The idea of the Holy Spirit began in ancient matriarchal religions as Goddess, the Great Cosmic Mother,[2113] one of whose sacred animals was the dove (a symbol of spiritual "peace"), which is why "the spirit of God" descended on Jesus "like a dove" at His baptism.[2114] Thus, in the noncanonical Gospel of the Hebrews, Jesus refers to the Holy Spirit as "my mother."[2115]

De-feminized, marginalized, masculinized, and Christianized in the 1st and 2nd Centuries, the great Mother-Goddess and her many manifestations (minor goddesses) were gradually absorbed by way of theacrasia,[2116] becoming the Holy Spirit or Holy Ghost, the third member of the Catholic Church's Holy Trinity.[2117] Her true origins, however, are still evident in the New Testament. Here both the words ghost and spirit are written *pneuma* in Greek, which means "breath," "wind," or "movement of air," making the true translation of Holy Ghost, the "Holy Breath." Hence, Jesus ordained His Disciples by breathing on them, a ritual known as insufflation, which implanted them with the Holy Spirit.[2118]

The Holy Breath (Subconscious Mind) is, of course, connected to the Word or Logos (Conscious Mind); that is, the divine power of thought,[2119] and was used by God in the creation of our species, *Homo sapiens*.[2120] The Holy Spirit is identical to the Comforter or Paraclete who "dwelleth with you, and shall be in you."[2121] But its female nature is given away by the Hebrew word for spirit, *ruach*, which is feminine.[2122]

Paul tells us that the Holy Spirit is a gift from God,[2123] one that He intentionally planted "in our hearts."[2124] Thus like the Father (Divine Mind),[2125] the Son (the Indwelling Christ),[2126] and the Comforter (Paraclete),[2127] the Holy Spirit also dwells within us.[2128] Mystically speaking then, the Holy Spirit is, in short, the *Whole Spirit* acting in every form in the Universe.[2129]

This doctrine of activity in association with the Holy Spirit is paralleled in Hinduism, where it is equated with the sacred I AM or the sacred three-letter name AUM. Here, the "A" derives from *Akara*, the creative vibration; "U" derives from *Ukara*, the preservative vibration; and "M" derives from *Makara*, the destructive vibration.[2130] This triune word, the Life-Giver, the Life-Preserver, and the Life-Destroyer,[2131] is yet another version of the universal Holy Trinity, one that in the East can have the meaning "Yes"—that is, the positive aspect of all and everything.[2132] See COMFORTER, DOVE, GODDESS, HOLY TRINITY, I AM, MARY, MOTHER, TRINITY, VIRGIN BIRTH, VIRGO.

HOLY TRINITY: The Holy Trinity is the threefold symbol of the great triune God, known to Christian mystics as the Divine Mind,[2133] comprised of the Conscious Mind, the Subconscious Mind, and the Superconscious Mind.[2134] Neither the doctrine of[2135] or the word "Trinity" appear in the Bible,[2136] and as the writings of Church Fathers, such as Eusebius, have shown, the infamous statement supposedly made by Jesus in Matthew 28:19[2137] is an obvious and late interpolation.[2138] In fact, mainstream Christianity did not adopt the idea of the Holy Trinity until the 12th Century, after which it proclaimed that while the Father is God,[2139] the Son is God,[2140] and the Holy Spirit is God,[2141] all are in fact one.[2142] Understandably, the concept of the Trinity, a blatant christianized form of Pagan polytheism,[2143] has been rejected by many Protestant sects for centuries.

To help canonize the idea of the Holy Trinity and firmly establish it among the Catholic masses, the Church forged 1 John 5:7 (the "three that bear record in heaven"), artificially adding it to John's letter sometime as late as the 9th Century.[2144] (As with so many other well-known Bible scriptures, this one too is absent from our earliest complete and original Bible manuscripts, such as the Codex Sinaiticus. This particular passage, in fact, got its start as a scribe's comment in the margin of an ancient Greek manuscript.)[2145]

In some mystical Christian schools the Father is "Mind" (Thought) the Son is "Idea" (Word) and the female Holy Spirit is "Expression" (Action), which correlates with the threefold nature of man: Spirit (Superconscious Mind, the "Father," the great "I AM"), Body (Conscious Mind, the "Son"), and Soul (Subconscious Mind, the "Holy Spirit"). Hence, ancient Gnostic-Christians referred to the Trinity as "the Father, the Mother, and the Son, the perfect power."[2146] "John's" interpolated passage on our Cosmic Inner Trinity reads in full:

> For there are three that bear record in heaven [enlightenment, harmony, nirvana, samadhi], the Father [Superconscious Mind], the Word [Conscious Mind], and the Holy Ghost [Subconscious Mind]: and these three are one.[2147]

The idea of the Holy Trinity did not originate with Christianity of course. Rather, it is a universal concept found worldwide in countless Pagan religions, dating back to the dawn of history, where it began as a simple familial triad based on the father, mother, and child family unit—the same one still being used by Gnostic-Christians in the 1st Century A.D.[2148] Over the millennia this idea became evermore sophisticated, and patriarchal. In India, for example, the Hindu Holy Trinity, known as Trimurti, is comprised of Brahma the Creator (male), Vishnu the Preserver (male), and Shiva the Destroyer (male).[2149] Hindu scriptures refer to what we Christians call the Father as "Sat," the Son as "Tat," and the Holy Ghost as "Aum" (identical to Om, I AM, and Amen). Brahma is sometimes depicted as a three-faced image,[2150] a trinitarian symbol of the one true God, one adopted by the Church and often seen in Christian art.[2151] Pike writes:

> Now the Egyptians arranged their deities in Triads,—the Father, or the Spirit or Active Principle or Generative Power; the Mother, or Matter, or the Passive Principle, or the Conceptive Power; and the Son, Issue or Product, the universe, proceeding from the two principles. These were Osiris, Isis, and Horus. In the same way, Plato gives us Thought, the Father; Primitive Matter the Mother; and Kosmos the World, the Son, the universe animated by a soul. Triads of the same kind are found in the Kabalah.[2152]

The archetypal religious triad, however, first sprang from out of early matriarchal societies, where it was imaged as an all-female trinity known as the Triple-Goddess.[2153] This is due to the fact that paternity, the male's role in reproduction, was unknown in prehistoric times. Thus, the female was worshiped as a magical parthenogenic goddess,[2154] with men playing a subservient (or sometimes an equal) role in society and religion (an example: the Minoans of ancient Crete).[2155]

Naturally then, as the archaeological record confirms, the first artistic depictions of a Supreme Being were female, for as Graves correctly asserts, "history began with female rule."[2156] This matriarchalism gave rise to the worship of the Great Mother-Goddess, or Universal Earth-Mother. And indeed, artistic portrayals of male deities, such as statues and cave etchings of male gods, do not appear until much later—*after* paternity was discovered through the domestication of wild animals (circa 10,000-6,000 B.C.).[2157] Thus the Divine Feminine and the all-female trinity were the forerunners of the Great Father-God, or Heavenly Father, and the gender-mixed trinity that we find in Christianity today: God the Father (male), the Son (male), and the Holy Spirit (female).[2158]

As an archetype found in one form or another in the majority of pre-Christian societies around the world, the Triple-Goddess is known far and wide, from, for instance, ancient Ireland,[2159] Norway,[2160] Rome,[2161] and Greece,[2162] to Palestine, India, and Africa.[2163] The Triple-Goddess symbolizes the three-fold nature of humanity (body, mind, and spirit); the three phases of the moon (waxing, full, waning); the three ages of Man and Woman: childhood (the "maiden" or "prince"), adulthood (the "mother" or "father"), and seniorhood (the "crone" or "grandfather"); the three periods of time: past, present, and future; and so on.

As ancient goddesses in general, and in particular the Great Mother-Goddess, were associated with the ocean (the maternal "amniotic fluid" from which all life sprang), their names are often comprised of the *ma* ("mother") and *mar* ("sea") elements, meaning "Mother-Sea." For example, we have the early goddess names: Ma Ma, Maerin, Maid Marian, Mar, Mara, Marah, Mari, Maria, Mariam, Marie, Marratu, Mary, Maya, and Meri, to name but a few. To this day Jesus' mother Mary is still widely known by the ancient Pagan title that the Catholic Church "borrowed" from the Greek love-goddess Aphrodite:[2164] *Stella Maris* ("Star of the Sea").[2165]

Like nearly all mythological Pagan figures, the Triple-Goddess too was eventually Christianized, absorbed through theocrasia into Christian myth[2166] as the "Three Marys" who "stood by the cross of Jesus" during His crucifixion.[2167]

As the first spiritual triad to appear in the archeological record (the earliest and most rudimentary depictions of the Triple-Goddess are roughly made triangular-shaped yonic stones, made by the Neanderthal people between 100,000 and 40,000 years ago),[2168] it is clear that the prehistoric Triple-Goddess served as prototype not only for the Christian Holy Trinity of the 12th Century, but for all historic religious trinities. See CHRISTMAS, DIVINITY OF JESUS, FATHER, GODDESS, I AM, MARY, MOTHER, SON OF MAN, TRINITY, YAHWEH, VIRGO.

Heaven and Hell, with the Gnostic Trinity of Father, Mother, and Son.

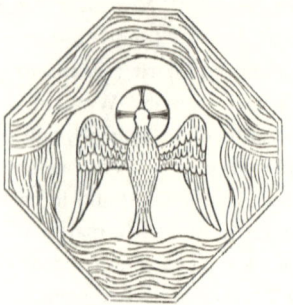

The Christian Holy Spirit.

Egyptian resurrection.

Gnostic symbols.

The Christian Holy Trinity.

I

I AM: In traditional Christianity "I AM" (in Hebrew, *Hayah*) is nothing more than a common Old Testament designation for God.[2169] In mystical Christianity I AM (or *Eimi*) is the secret and sacred name of the Universal **Immanent** God, revealed to Moses by his Third Eye (intuition)[2170] or EYE AM (I AM).[2171] Esoterically the term means self-generating "Being," and is personified in ancient religion and myth as the archetypal Virgin-Mother-Goddess, who reproduces parthenogenically; that is, who creates life alone without the aid of a male partner.

Since we are one with God[2172] we also contain the I AM, or what I refer to as the Great I AM Within.[2173] It is our real self, our Higher Self, our Divine Self, and is identical to the Indwelling Christ,[2174] or what Hindus call the "imperishable" Atman.[2175] Our realization of our oneness with God, our at-one-ment with Divine Mind, is one of the most important steps we can achieve in life,[2176] which is why the Hindu sage Ramana Maharshi called it "self-realization,"[2177] and it is why Jesus called it "salvation."[2178]

In Hinduism the I AM is written "Aum" or "Om," and being a positive word that can mean "the Yes,"[2179] is often used as a mantra or spiritual chant. In Hebrew it is "Amam," in Tibet it is "Hum," in ancient Egypt it was "Amon," and in traditional Christianity it is "Amen,"[2180] yet another symbolic manifestation of the ever creative Word, known as the "Logos"[2181] in Gnostic Christianity.[2182]

Pliny called the I AM, *Artifex Omnium Natura*, the "Creator of All Nature." Descartes said: "I think, therefore I AM." The Apostle John was well versed in the Gnosis of the Great I AM or Om: he used it occultly as the Greek word "Om-ega" (Omega),[2183] and also as "the Amen [I AM], the faithful and true witness, the beginning of the creation of God."[2184]

Having long ago rejected Jesus' secret teachings on the Great I AM, institutional Christianity does not recognize it, even though it is clearly revealed in the Bible, not only in God's statement, "I AM that I AM,"[2185] and Jesus' statement "before Abraham was, I AM,"[2186] but also as the book of Revelation's "voice of many waters."[2187] Since the I AM is God,[2188] since God is the "ground of being,"[2189] since "in him we live, and move, and have our being,"[2190] nothing is required to discover the I AM. As God himself proclaims in the Bible, merely "be still and know that I AM God."[2191]

In mystical Christianity the I AM is used in various ways by those on the path toward spiritual enlightenment. This is why, when practicing the Law of

Attraction, affirmations for specific desires should start off with "I AM" in order to form a magnetic union between the thought and God. This increases the vibrational intensity of the affirmation, speeding it on its way from the Conscious Mind (the "Son"), to the Subconscious Mind (the "Holy Spirit"), and from there onto the Superconscious Mind (the "Father," Divine Mind).[2192]

According to mystical Christian doctrine, whenever Jesus used the Great I AM in a sentence, it is always in reference to the Indwelling Christ that we all possess. This is not surprising, as Jesus had obliterated his personal Ego, becoming completely merged with the Universal Christ.[2193]

In the 1st Century A.D. the pronoun "I" did not necessarily refer to the speaker or writer.[2194] This practice helps us better understand the Bible's esoteric terminology. Thus mystically (psychologically) speaking, for example, Jesus' statement, "I AM the way, the truth, and the life: no man cometh unto the Father, but by me,"[2195] actually means "no one can connect to the Divine Mind except by way of the Christ Within."[2196] Jesus confirmed that the Great I AM is eternal, unborn, unformed, unmade, imperishable, timeless, and unchanging: "Lo, I AM with you alway[s], even unto the end of the world."[2197]

As noted, the I AM is not your Ego, your false self, your human self, your Lower Self—which will perish with your material body (for "all flesh is grass").[2198] It is your eternal God-Nature, your lucent Divine Self, your immortal God-Self; the "Christ that is formed in us,"[2199] that is "in all of us,"[2200] as Paul put it. It is that spiritual part of you which God "created in his own image":[2201] the *perfect* and *imperishable* you.

It is your Higher Self, your Divine Self, the incorporeal Supreme Self, the mystics' Cosmic Man, the Hindus' "Atman," Paul's "inner man"[2202] or "inward man,"[2203] Peter's "hidden man of the heart,"[2204] Luke's "Holy One,"[2205] Daniel's "Ancient of Days";[2206] it is that part of you that was never born and will never die, and which is "the same yesterday, and to day, and for ever."[2207] It is that aspect of you that is "without father, without mother, without descent, having neither beginning of days, nor end of life, but made like to the Son of God."[2208] For the Indwelling "Christ abideth for ever."[2209] No better definition of our Divine Spark, the Indwelling Christ, the "true light which lighteth *every man* that cometh into the world,"[2210] has ever been written.

Because the I AM is one more common term for the Immortal Indwelling Christ that lies at the core of us all,[2211] Jesus, like other ancient spiritual teachers, often used it to announce His divinity to others: "I AM he," he once told a group of startled Pharisees, who then "fell to the ground."[2212] Here is another revealing exchange He had with this rigidly religious Jewish sect:

> Again the high priest asked him, and said unto him, "Art thou *the Christ*, the Son of the Blessed?" And Jesus said, "*I AM* . . ."[2213]

Jesus used the mystical I AM title repeatedly. Here are some other examples:

"I AM from above."[2214]
"I AM the bread of life."[2215]
"I AM the door of the sheep."[2216]
"I AM the good shepherd."[2217]
"I AM the light of the world."[2218]
"I AM he that liveth."[2219]
"I AM Master and Lord."[2220]
"I AM meek and lowly in heart."[2221]
"I AM a king."[2222]
"I AM the way, the truth, and the life."[2223]
"I AM the true vine."[2224]
"I AM the Christ."[2225]

Similarly, in the Gospel of Thomas we find Jesus testifying not of Himself as the I AM, but to its cosmic universality:

> Wherever there are two, they are not without God, and wherever there is one alone, I say, I AM with him. Raise the stone, and there thou shalt find me; cleave the wood, and there AM I.[2226]

Being an expression of God, of the Divine Mind, the Indwelling Christ or great I AM is the power of thought incarnate in Man. It is "the Word [thought] made flesh."[2227]

Thousands of years before Christianity, and even long prior to the writing of the Bible, knowledge of the Great I AM as the human Soul is already in evidence far and wide. In the Egyptian *Book of the Dead*, for instance, the phrase is used thousands of times. A sampling:

> *I AM Yesterday, Today, and Tomorrow, and I have the power to be born a second time; I AM the divine hidden soul* who createth the gods. . . . I AM the rudder of the east, the possessor of two divine faces wherein his beams are seen. I AM the lord of the men who are raised up. . . I AM Bet, the first-born son of Osiris. . . . *I AM the divine Soul.* . . I AM the great god who gave birth to himself.[2228]

Likewise, thousands of years before Christianity the great Egyptian Mother-Goddess Isis was celebrated for her divine declaration:

I AM what was and is and is to come. No mortal hath yet unveiled me.²²²⁹

Sadly, the doctrine of the Universal I AM²²³⁰ as the Higher Self, the Christ Within,²²³¹ the Indwelling God,²²³² which is known in one form or another in every religion, is the same one that the Jews in Jesus' day called "blasphemy,"²²³³ and in Paul's day "heresy,"²²³⁴ and which many uninformed Christian authorities today still wrongly think of as an impious sacrilege. Yet it forms the very core of our Lord's "Gospel of the Kingdom of God."²²³⁵ See CHRIST, CROWN, FATHER, GOD, JESUS, KINGDOM OF GOD, THEOSIS, UNION WITH GOD.

INDWELLING CHRIST: The Indwelling Christ is the same as the CHRIST.²²³⁶

INNER MAN: The Inner Man is one of Paul's terms for the HIGHER SELF.²²³⁷

INWARD MAN: In traditional Christianity the "inward man" is Paul's term for the human soul.²²³⁸ In mystical Christianity it refers to the Higher Self (as opposed to the Lower Self). See CHRIST, CHRIST CONSCIOUSNESS, HEROD ANTIPAS, HIGHER SELF, LOWER SELF, KING, OUTWARD MAN.

ISRAEL: In traditional Christianity Israel is the general region of Jesus' homeland and ministry, as well as the name given to Abraham's grandson Jacob, and hence to the Israelites.²²³⁹ In mystical Christianity the biblical nation of Israel is a symbol of spiritual light or enlightenment, as opposed to biblical Egypt, a symbol of spiritual darkness or ignorance.²²⁴⁰

Mystically speaking, the word Israel derives from the names of three ancient Pagan deities: the Egyptian Mother-Goddess Isis ("to Save," that is, wisdom), the Egyptian Father-God Ra ("Sun," that is, truth), and the Canaanite Father-God El ("Deity," that is, power), giving Isis-Ra-El, or IsRaEl.²²⁴¹ In mainstream Christianity Israel is a Hebrew word meaning "God prevails," or more accurately, "he struggles with [the Pagan god] El."²²⁴²

It is from the mystical definition that we derive its occult (inner) meaning, which can be further elaborated thus: ancient Israel symbolizes the Spirit, perfection, monotheism, and enlightened Man, which was at odds with Egypt, a mystical symbol of materialism, imperfection, polytheism, and unenlightened Man.²²⁴³ In essence, Israel means: *"Spiritual Truth is the Salvific Power."* See BETHLEHEM, EGYPT, GALILEE, GOD, JERUSALEM, YAHWEH, ZION.

Triadic fish symbol.

A Pre-Christian Good Shepherd.

Heaven and Hell.

The Goddess Demeter.

JEHOVAH: Same as God. The word Jehovah, however, is a "false reading";[2244] that is, it is a creation of 16th-Century English priests, who combined the Tetragrammaton, JHVH—the Hebrew name of God (without vowels),[2245] and also spelled YHWH, that is, Yahweh—with the vowels of the word Adonai (a, o, a), resulting in the word J-a-H-o-V-a-H, or in Medieval English, Jehovah.[2246]

Adonai is the plural form of Adon, the name of a Canaanite fertility-god, known more familiarly as the Greek love-god Adonis.[2247] JHVH or Jehovah derives its mystic sacrality from its letters: "Y" is *Yod*, meaning the Father; "H" is *He*, meaning the Mother; and "V" is *Vau*, the Son."[2248] Thus, we have "Father-Mother-Son (child)," the original paleolithic Holy Trinity, and the one upon which all subsequent trinities were formed.

In ancient Greece, as well as in Kabbalah (Jewish Gnosticism) and Pagan Gnosticism, Jehovah was imaged as the god of the material world (earth) only, a subordinate being who is to be differentiated from the superior God of the spirit world (Heaven), "Lord of All," "the One," known to Christian Gnostics as Bythus, the one true God.[2249] Bythus' inferior was known to the Gnostics as the Demiurge, to the Tibetans as Vajrapani, to the Greeks as Zeus, to the Romans as Jupiter, to the Hindus as Indra, and to the Hebrews as JHVH or Yahweh; that is, Jehovah.[2250] See FATHER, GOD, TRINITY, WAY OF THE LORD, YAHWEH.

JERUSALEM: In the mainstream Church Jerusalem is the world's most important holy city due to its association with the life, death, and resurrection of Jesus. Jerusalem means "foundation of [the god] Shalim [that is, Salem: 'peace'],"[2251] a vestige of the polytheistic and henotheistic worship that once held sway in the area.

As Jerusalem was founded by Pagans (Canaanites) long prior to its Israelite settlement,[2252] and as their founding god Shalim (or Shalem) was identified with the "Evening Star,"[2253] it is apparent that the city, like so many other ancient towns, began as a monument to a female deity; in this case, the Roman goddess of love Venus (in Greece, Aphrodite), known as the "Morning Star" in her dawn aspect.[2254] And, in fact, Pagan temples to Venus were still active in the region as late as the 4th Century A.D.[2255]

Jerusalem's astrological feminine foundation was understood by early Christian mystics such as Paul, which is why he called it "our mother."[2256] (Modern Christians still refer to it as "the mother city of Gentile Christianity," but now without knowing why, since its feminine origins have been ignored and suppressed.)[2257] "Going up to Jerusalem" is an ancient mystical reference to the Soul's growth as it moves ever upward toward at-one-ment with God. Thus Jesus said to the 12 Apostles:

> Behold, *we go up to Jerusalem*, and all things that are written concerning the Son of man shall be accomplished.[2258]

In the mystical Christian Church Jerusalem is viewed as a symbol of the heavenly peace one experiences upon recognizing their Christhood, the Universal Indwelling Christ. This is why Jesus called Jerusalem "the city of the great King."[2259] He is not referring to a human ruler, however, but rather a mystical representation of the Indwelling Christ, the true King of us all. The ancient mystic Origen writes:

> Jerusalem does not lie in a depression, or in a low situation, but is built on a high mountain, and there are mountains round about it, and the participation of it is to the same place, and thither the tribes of *the Lord went up*, a testimony for Israel. But that city also is called Jerusalem, to which none of those upon the earth ascends, nor goes in; but *every soul that possesses by nature some elevation and some acuteness to perceive the things of the mind is a citizen of that city*.[2260]

Augustine writes:

> We ascend Thy ways that be in our heart, and sing a song of degrees; we glow inwardly with Thy fire, with Thy good fire, and we go, because *we go upwards to the peace of Jerusalem*; for glad was I when they said unto me, "Let us go into the house of the Lord." There hath Thy good pleasure placed us, that we may desire no other thing than to dwell there for ever.[2261]

Brooks makes these comments:

> *Every true life has its Jerusalem, to which it is always going up.* A life cannot be really considered as having begun to live until that far-off city in which its destiny awaits it, where its work is to be done, where its problem is to be solved, begins to draw the life towards itself, and the life begins to know and own the summons.
>
> . . . At first far off and dimly seen, laying but light

hold upon our purpose and our will, then gradually taking us more and more into its power, compelling our study, directing the current of our thoughts, arranging our friendships for us, deciding for us what powers we shall bring out into use, deciding for us what we shall be: so every live man's Jerusalem, his sacred city, calls to him from the hill-top where it stands. One man's Jerusalem is his profession. Another man's Jerusalem is his fortune. Another man's Jerusalem is his cause. Another man's Jerusalem is his faith. Another man's Jerusalem is his character. Another man's Jerusalem is his image of purified society and a worthy human life. You stop the student at his books, the philanthropist at his committee, the saint at his prayers. You say to each of them, "What does it all mean? What are you doing? What is it all for?" And the answer is everywhere the same: *"Behold we go up to Jerusalem."* We draw back the vail of history, and everywhere it is the same picture that we see. Companies, great and small, climbing mountains to where sacred cities stand awaiting them with open gates upon the top. The man who is going up to no Jerusalem is but the ghost and relic of a man. He has in him no genuine and healthy human life.[2262]

In fine, Christian mystics view "Jerusalem" as self-realization or spiritual enlightenment: the recognition, acceptance, and embrace of the Universal Indwelling Christ.[2263] See BETHLEHEM, EGYPT, FATHER, GALILEE, GOD, GODDESS, ISRAEL, MOTHER, YAHWEH, ZION.

JESUS: In traditional Christianity Jesus is a supernatural being (part man, part God), the Messiah, the Savior of All Mankind, born of the Virgin Mary, whose death on the cross is humanity's salvation from original sin.[2264]

The mainstream Christian view of Jesus, however, is seriously undermined by the very individuals who sought to glorify Him: the New Testament writers. Not only do the four Evangelists, as well as Paul, Peter, James, Jude, and the Hebraist, each depict a completely different Jesus (Mark's Jesus, for instance, became divine at His baptism,[2265] Matthew's Jesus was divine at birth,[2266] and Hebrews' Jesus was divine before the beginning of time),[2267] but aside from the real historic human Jesus and the false Paganized god Jesus, there are two primary and distinct Jesuses that emerge from a close reading of the New Testament. I call them the "Spiritually Mature Jesus" and the "Spiritually Immature Jesus," of which a few examples will suffice.

• The Jesus who said that those who refer to others as a "fool" are in danger of

- going to Hell[2268] is not the same Jesus who Himself often called others fools.[2269]
- The Jesus who said "my peace I give unto you"[2270] is not the same Jesus who said "I came not to send peace."[2271]
- The Jesus who said "honor thy father and mother"[2272] is not the same Jesus who said that "those who do not hate their parents cannot be my disciple"[2273] or who was known to publicly humiliate His own mother[2274] and father.[2275]
- The Jesus who is portrayed as omniscient (all-knowing)[2276] is not the same Jesus who, on the cross, cried out "My God, my God, why hast thou forsaken me?"[2277] and who did not know when the Parousia would occur.[2278]
- The Jesus who said "resist not evil"[2279] is not the same Jesus who violently drove the money changers from the Temple.[2280]
- The Jesus who said "turn the other cheek"[2281] is not the same Jesus who said "I came not to send peace, but a sword."[2282]
- The Jesus who said "love your enemies"[2283] is not the same Jesus who angrily told the Pharisees they were going to Hell, calling them "vipers"[2284] and the "children of Satan."[2285]

A thousand similar striking contradictions—which, it should be noted, have never been convincingly resolved by conventional Christian scholars—could be presented here.

What these scriptures tell us is that there is something much deeper going on behind the figure of Jesus than the mainstream Church comprehends, or is willing to admit. Christian mysticism, however, acknowledges, understands, and explains these seeming incongruities, so let us begin.

In the mystical Church Jesus is a great and enlightened teacher, healer, and prophet, the human son of Joseph and Mary,[2286] a mortal personification of the Christ, the earthly representative of the perfect man and woman;[2287] the paragon of human perfection; the "Archetypal Man,"[2288] the "prototypical Ideal Man;"[2289] a "model for mankind,"[2290] the "ideal virtuous man" of Luke,[2291] the "pattern for the sons of men"[2292] who "cometh down from heaven, and giveth life unto the world";[2293] that is, to show us, by example, how we too can attain Christhood,[2294] and become like Him and live as a god or goddess on earth.[2295]

Is this shocking? Only to the orthodox. Buddhists, for example, see their master Lord Buddha in precisely the same manner: not as a deity, but as a human embodiment of Spiritual Law and Truth, the "perfect man" who came to earth, took a vow to save us, bore our burdens, and subjected himself to the pain of material life for the salvation of all sentient beings. This makes Buddha, and all other saviors, christs, and messiahs as well, what the East refers to as a Bodhisattva:[2296] a totally enlightened soul who incarnates in order to allay the suffering of humanity and offer redemption and salvation.[2297] In the mystical Christian Church Jesus followed in this same ancient spiritual tradition, taking on the form of the Hebraic "suffering servant"[2298] (as depicted in the fifty-third chapter of Isaiah),[2299] a Jewish Bodhisattva whose trials and pain erased the sins of Mankind.

While Christian mystics believe that our Lord performed many miracles, at the same time they do not believe that He had "supernatural" powers. Jesus merely had a profound understanding of the normal laws of physics, which He was able to control and use according to His will—such as when He utilized this ability to suddenly materialize and dematerialize[2300] or enter a closed room.[2301] Even His healings did not violate natural law. His knowledge of biology allowed Him to alter matter at the cellular level, which resulted in instant cures for those who had enough faith.[2302] Jesus informs us that not only can we perform the same "miracles," but even greater ones than He did.[2303] Indeed, these same feats, and others, are being performed by people all over the world today, and among people of all religions.[2304]

Christian mystics hold that Jesus continued to live on earth long after His so-called "death," possibly for as long as 50 years according to one source.[2305] Only 80 years after John the Evangelist's death, around A.D. 180, in his anti-Gnostic work *Against Heresies*, Irenaeus, basing his testimony on those who knew John personally, noted that many of his own contemporaries at the time claimed that Jesus had never been crucified, and that he had lived on for many years,[2306] not dying until He was an "old man."[2307] This, of course, means that the Crucifixion of Jesus was either a myth, a hoax, or a forgery, which leads us back to the Truth of Christian mysticism!

Here is Church Father Irenaeus, in his own words, writing about Jesus growing into old age:

> Being thirty years old when he came to be baptized, and then possessing the fall age of a Master, he came to Jerusalem, so that he might be properly acknowledged by all as a Master. For he did not seem one thing while he was another, as those affirm who describe him as being a man only in appearance; but what he was, that he also appeared to be. *Being a Master, therefore, he also possessed the age of a Master*, not despising or evading any condition of humanity, nor setting aside in himself that law which he had appointed for the human race, but sanctifying every age, by that period corresponding to it which belonged to himself. For he came to save all through means of himself—all, I say, who through him are born to God—infants, and children, and boys, and youths, and old men.
>
> *He therefore passed through every age*, becoming an infant for infants, thus sanctifying infants; a child for children, thus sanctifying those who are of this age, being at the same time

made to them an example of piety, righteousness and submission; a youth for youths, thus becoming an example to youths, and thus sanctifying them for the Lord. *So, likewise, he was an old man for old men, that he might be a perfect Master for all, not merely as respects the setting forth of the truth, but also as regards age, sanctifying at the same time the aged also, and becoming an example to them likewise.* Then at last he came on to death itself, that he might be the "first born from the dead, and that in all things he might have preeminence," the Prince of life, existing before all and going before all.

They, however, that they might establish their false opinion regarding that which is written, "to proclaim the acceptable year of the Lord," maintain that he preached for one year only, and then suffered in the twelfth month. [In speaking thus] they are forgetful of their own disadvantage, destroying his whole work and robbing him of that age which is both more necessary and more honorable than any other; *that more advanced age of men, I mean, during which, also as a teacher, he excelled all others. For how could he have had disciples if he did not teach? And how could he have taught unless he had reached the age of a Master?*

For when he came to be baptized he had not completed his thirtieth year, but was beginning to be about thirty years of age, (for thus Luke, who has mentioned his years, has expressed it: "Now Jesus was, as it were, beginning to be thirty years old," when he came to receive baptism;) and [according to these men] he preached only one year, reckoning from his baptism. On completing his thirtieth year he suffered, being in fact still a young man, and who had by no means attained to advanced age.

Now that the first stage of early life embraces thirty years, and that this extends onward to the fortieth year, every one will admit; but *from the fortieth and fiftieth year a man begins to decline toward old age, which our Lord possessed, while he still fulfilled the office of a Teacher, even as the Gospel, and all the elders testify; those who were conversant in Asia with John, the disciple of the Lord, [affirming] that John conveyed to them that information. And he [John] remained among them up to the times of Trajan [c. A.D. 53-117]. Some of them, moreover, saw not only John, but the other Apostles also, and heard the very same account from them, and bear testimony as to the [validity of the] statement [that Jesus lived into old age—the age of a Master].*[2308]

Similarly, the *Acts of Pilate* state that Jesus died under Claudius, who ruled between 41 and 54,[2309] while John states that workers had been reconstructing the Jerusalem Temple for 46 years, the same building Jesus said he would tear down and rebuild in three days.[2310]

These are hints that the biblical chronology of our Lord's death at around age 33 is incorrect, which is exactly what ancient tradition held: Jesus lived to at least 50 years of age, and most probably quite longer. The New Testament itself corroborates this. The following revealing conversation took place between Jesus and a group of hostile Jews. Said the Prince of Peace:

> "Your father Abraham rejoiced to see my day: and he saw it, and was glad." Then said the Jews unto him, "Thou art not yet fifty years old, and hast thou seen Abraham?"[2311]

It is more than passing strange that at this time Jesus was supposed to be about 30 years of age, yet His Jewish neighbors assumed that He was nearly 50 years old.

But physical age is hardly relevant when discussing our Lord, whose Indwelling Christ, like yours and mine,[2312] is birthless, ageless, and deathless. Indeed, Jesus, like so many of the ancient religious masters,[2313] is still very much alive and active on earth today, both spiritually and physically, working "unseen by the masses" for the greater good of humanity. Many modern individuals, in fact, have seen and met with Jesus in the flesh, among them Paramahansa Yogananda, Mahavatar Babaji,[2314] and Baird T. Spalding.[2315]

Esoterically Jesus is "the love of God made manifest to men."[2316] Born a "son of man" (that is, a human being), His Transfiguration into a "son of God" (enlightened human being) after His baptism by John[2317] was so that "the men of earth might see the possibilities of man;"[2318] while as the Christ He "came to manifest the power of God."[2319] In *The Aquarian Gospel of Jesus the Christ* Jesus says:

> I come to manifest the Christ to men . . .[2320] What I am, all men will be . . .[2321] What I have done all men can do . . . for every man is God made flesh.[2322]

To those with "the mind of Christ"[2323] such remarks are perfectly understandable.

As the embodiment of the Christ, Jesus is Spiritual Law incarnate. This is why I refer to him, in Greek, as *Iesous Trismegistus*: "Thrice-Greatest Jesus." He was, after all—how ever else one might view him—the most enlightened *teacher*, most powerful *healer*, and most sagacious *prophet* the world has ever known. This, in fact, is exactly how His first followers viewed Him: not as a supernatural godman and the Messiah, but as an extraordinary and fully spiritually enlightened human being, just as the Gospel of Q quite clearly portrays Him.[2324]

Contrary to mainstream Christian belief, Jesus was not a narcissistic deity who intentionally founded the Christian religion in His name and commanded that people worship Him as the King of the Jews or of Christianity. His "divine nature" was not even decided upon until the year 451,[2325] at the Fourth Ecumenical Council at Chalcedon,[2326] where "the West overcame the East" and where, by a "self-contradictory deception," the single nature of Jesus became two, forever dissolving the unity of His person, "thereby cutting off the last possibility of a return to the historical Jesus." To accomplish this, "all justification for, and interest in, the investigation of His life and historical personality were done away with."[2327]

The words of Jesus Himself prove that He did not see Himself as the "Only Begotten Son," or even as being superior to others. He certainly never once openly proclaimed Himself to be the long-awaited Messiah. In many *authentic* New Testament passages, for example, He publicly disclaims this role for Himself, as the following occurrence, recorded in the Gospel of Matthew, reveals:

> While the Pharisees were gathered together, Jesus asked them, saying, "what think ye of Christ? whose son is he?" They say unto him, "the Son of David." He saith unto them, "how then doth David in spirit call him 'Lord,' saying, 'the Lord said unto my Lord, sit thou on my right hand, till I make thine enemies thy footstool?'[2328] If David then call him Lord, how is he his son?" And no man was able to answer him a word, neither durst any man from that day forth ask him any more questions.[2329]

Clearly, as we can see here, Jesus did not associate or connect the Old Testament messianic requirement of Davidic descent with Himself.[2330]

Jesus' focus was *always* on the Father (God) and the Indwelling Christ, not Himself. This is why, though seen as a "miracle worker" by the multitudes,[2331] when the Lord was not healing the sick, mad, deaf, blind, and lame, or preaching His personal Gospel, "the Gospel of the Kingdom"[2332] (that is, our oneness with the Father,[2333] our divine nature,[2334] the Inner Kingdom,[2335] and the various spiritual laws, such as the Law of Attraction),[2336] He often found Himself trying to discourage the growth of a personalty cult in His name.

Thus, when the Pharisees sought to stone Him to death, He appealed for His life by saying that the "doctrine" He preached was not His own, but "his that sent me." Here is the story as it appears in the Gospel of John:

> Now about the midst of the feast Jesus went up into the temple, and taught. And the Jews marvelled, saying, "How knoweth this man letters, having never learned?" Jesus answered them, and said, "*My doctrine is not mine, but his that sent me. If any man will do his will, he shall know of the doctrine, whether it be of God, or*

whether I speak of myself. He that speaketh of himself seeketh his own glory: but he that seeketh his glory that sent him, the same is true, and no unrighteousness is in him.

"Did not Moses give you the law, and yet none of you keepeth the law? Why go ye about to kill me?" . . . Then cried Jesus in the temple as he taught, saying, "Ye both know me, and ye know whence I am: and *I am not come of myself*, but he that sent me is true, whom ye know not. But I know him: for I am from him, and he hath sent me."[2337]

When the Jewish authorities picked up stones and began to threateningly close in on Jesus, He defended Himself even more forcefully, clearly stating that He was not seeking His own glory:

I do nothing of myself; but as my Father hath taught me, I speak these things. And he that sent me is with me: the Father hath not left me alone; for I do always those things that please him. . . . But now ye seek to kill me, a man that hath told you the truth, which I have heard of God. . . . If God were your Father, ye would love me: for I proceeded forth and came from God; *neither came I of myself, but he [that] sent me*. . . . *I seek not mine own glory*: there is [only] one that seeketh and judgeth. . . . *If I honour myself, my honour is nothing* . . .[2338]

If this is not clear enough, Jesus later restates this fact even more glaringly:

. . . *the word which ye hear [me preach] is not mine*, but the Father's which sent me.[2339]

And why does Jesus speak the words of the Father instead of His own? The Master answered this question as well: "My Father is greater than I."[2340] For, as He enigmatically states in The Apocryphon of James:

The Father does not need me, for fathers do not need sons. Instead it is always sons who need fathers.[2341]

During one particular incident in the Gospel of Mark, when the Lord and His Apostles come upon a fig tree that He had cursed earlier, they notice that it has since withered and died. As they look to Him for an explanation, He is quick to reply. But Jesus does not tell them: "See what *I* have done, have faith in *me*." He says: "Have faith in *God*,"[2342] again keeping the attention on the Father rather than on Himself.

In the Gospel of John, Jesus speaks of God and His "sheep" this way:

> *My Father*, which gave them [to] me, *is greater than all*; and no man is able to pluck them out of my Father's hand.[2343]

Jesus makes numerous other self-deflecting statements in John, such as:

> Verily, verily, I say unto you, *the Son can do nothing of himself*, but what he seeth the Father do: for what things soever he doeth, these also doeth the Son likewise.[2344]

> *I can of mine own self do nothing* . . . *because I seek not mine own will, but the will of the Father which hath sent me. If I bear witness of myself, my witness is not true.*[2345]

> . . . the works which the Father hath given me to finish, the same works that I do, bear witness of me, that *the Father hath sent me*.[2346]

> For I came down from heaven, *not to do mine own will*, but the will of him that sent me.[2347]

And, as mentioned:

> *I seek not my own glory* . . .[2348]

What follows are two of the most revealing and little discussed statements the Master makes regarding how He wanted to be perceived by us:

> *I receive not honour from men.*[2349]

> *I am come in my Father's name* . . .[2350]

Think about what Jesus is saying here. "I do not seek out, need, or want human praise. I have come to earth on behalf of God, not on behalf of myself."
From these statements is it not crystal clear that the Lord did not want us to focus on Him, the human Jesus? Is it not apparent that He was not interested in revealing or promoting his own divinity, but rather acquainting each person with their own?[2351] This explains why He wanted our attention centered on God, on the "Father," the Master's occult word for the Divine Mind.[2352] And this is why both early Gnostic-Christians and orthodox Christians referred to the Gospel not as "the Gospel of Jesus," but as "the Gospel of God."[2353] Jesus never claimed superiority

over others, nor did He declare that He was capable of doing anything that an ordinary person could not do.[2354] In fact, He asserted that anyone who believes in the Indwelling Christ would be able to perform "greater works" than He did.[2355]

Our Lord's attitude also explains why, in the Gospel of Thomas, He calls the Inner Kingdom not the "Kingdom of Jesus" or the "Kingdom of Christ," but the "Kingdom of the Father."[2356] And it is why the Essenic flavored Letter to the Hebrews[2357] calls Jesus an "Apostle"—not of Himself (an impossibility), but of God the Father.[2358] Consider the statement Jesus makes in Matthew:

> And call no man your father upon the earth: for one is your Father, which is in heaven.[2359]

The inner mystical (psychological) meaning:

> You only have one true parent, and it is Divine Mind, which is the real you, your Higher Self.[2360]

Understanding this simple doctrine opens up the door to an entirely new spiritual life, which mystic Paul correctly referred to as having "the mind of Christ."[2361]

This advanced high level of spiritual consciousness, called by Hindus and Buddhists "samadhi," was also occultly known to Jesus and the Apostles as the "Upper Room"[2362] (but known to orthodox Christians in the literal manner as the "first synagogue of the Christian community").[2363] The "Upper Room," being but an occult symbol of the top of the human head, is the site of the Crown Chakra (enlightenment), which differentiates our Higher and Lower Selves. Of this doctrine Paul wrote mystically:

> The first man [that is, the Lower Self] is of the earth, earthy: the second man [that is, the Higher Self] is the Lord from heaven. As is the earthy, such are they also that are earthy [unenlightened]: and as is the heavenly, such are they also that are heavenly [enlightened]. And as we have borne the image of the earthy [in body], we shall also bear the image of the heavenly [in spirit].[2364]

Jesus said truly: "My Kingdom is not of this world,"[2365] meaning that it is not physical, but spiritual—that is, it is mental in nature.[2366] For our self-reciprocating Universe, having been created by the mental (Logos) power of the Divine Mind,[2367] operates on thought and thought alone.[2368]

The ancient Hebrew prophets, whose sayings Jesus was so familiar with, also understood that Divine Mind, not human teachers and leaders, was meant to be the true center of religious worship. Hence, they continually referred to the

Father as the one and only "Savior,"[2369] the one and only "Redeemer,"[2370] the one and only "Lord."[2371]

Both the Psalmist and Isaiah believed that our salvation, our savior, is Divine Mind (God)—and they clearly said so,[2372] as did the Virgin Mary.[2373] And as Israelite kings (and in some cases even high priests) were considered deities, and so were called the "anointed"[2374] (that is, "messiahs" or "christs"),[2375] it is not surprising that in many biblical passages Jesus downplays Himself and His kingly role as Messiah and Savior as well, another effort to keep the focus on the Father, Divine Mind.[2376]

Thus in an attempt to discourage the adoration of His followers and put the focus back on "he that sent me,"[2377] Jesus would often make comments such as: "the Son of man came not to be ministered unto, but to minister."[2378] He did not even consider Himself to be inherently good, as Mark relates:

> And when he was gone forth into the way, there came one running, and kneeled to him, and asked him, "Good Master, what shall I do that I may inherit eternal life?" And Jesus said unto him, "*Why callest thou me good? there is none good but one, that is, God.*"[2379]

An unbiased reading of the four canonical Gospels tells us that, like other egoless spiritual teachers from time immemorial, Jesus too shunned personal attention. Once, when a woman in the crowd yelled out to Him, "blessed [happy] is the woman who gave birth to you and nursed you!"[2380] Jesus immediately took the focus off Himself and put it back on Sovereign Mind, Divine Mind, replying:

> Yea rather, blessed [happy] are they that hear the word of God, and keep it.[2381]

After His healing sessions Jesus frequently asked those in attendance *not* to tell anyone that He was involved,[2382] and He would not allow the Apostles to discuss the private experiences and visions they shared with Him with others.[2383] Often He tried to hide both His identity and His whereabouts,[2384] and in some cases He even "charged his disciples that they should tell no man that he was Jesus the Christ."[2385] Once, when Peter observed that Jesus was "the Christ of God," the Lord immediately reprimanded the Apostle, commanding him to "tell no man that thing."[2386] Was all of this simply to conceal His messianic plans from Jewish and Roman authorities until the time was right, as the mainstream Church argues? An honest and objective reading of Jesus' authentic words will prove this theory utterly insufficient.

Let us consider another startling fact: Jesus never once spoke of the Gospel, the "Good News," as being about Himself. Instead He openly referred to it as "the Gospel of the Kingdom (of God),"[2387] avowing that the true Gospel is about "he that sent me,"[2388] that is, the "Father":

> For *I have not spoken of myself*; but the Father which sent me, he gave me a commandment, what I should say, and what I should speak.[2389]

Why this overwhelming emphasis on God?

Again, as Jesus attested, the Father "is greater than I."[2390] And why is the Father "greater"? Because "God is all mind";[2391] He is, as Hermes Trismegistus referred to Him, the "All-Father Mind," the "Mind of All," Divine Mind, the thought-creator of the Universe and all life.[2392]

Neither did the Lord ever claim that it was He who healed the sick, raised the dead, or performed His other miracles ("works").[2393] As always, He attributed all these things to the "Father" that exists within each one of us:[2394]

> ... the words that I speak unto you *I speak not of myself*: but *the Father that dwelleth in me, he doeth the works*.[2395]

In fact, Jesus repeatedly asserted that there was absolutely nothing He did or said that came from Himself. Rather, it was all from the "Father":

> Then said Jesus unto them, "When ye have lifted up the Son of man, then shall ye know that I am he, and that *I do nothing of myself*; but as my Father hath taught me, I speak these things."[2396]

And again:

> *I can of mine own self do nothing*: as I hear, I judge: and my judgment is just; because *I seek not mine own will*, but the will of the Father which hath sent me. *If I bear witness of myself, my witness is not true*.[2397]

At this point we should not be astonished to learn that at times Jesus openly resisted the messianic role that some of His followers ascribed to Him. Mark, for example, relates the following strange event in which Jesus' messiahship is announced for the first time by a group of demoniacs:

> And unclean spirits, when they saw him, fell down before him, and cried, saying, "Thou art the Son of God." And he straitly charged them that they should not make him known.[2398]

Luke tells the story like this:

> Now when the sun was setting, all they that had any sick with divers diseases brought them unto him; and he laid his hands on every one of them, and healed them. And devils also came out of many, crying out, and saying, "Thou art Christ the Son of God." And he rebuking them suffered them not to speak: for they knew that he was Christ.[2399]

John, our most mystical Gospeler, recorded the following emotional outburst, in which Jesus deemphasizes Himself, trying to deflect attention back onto what He believed was most important:

> Jesus cried and said, "*He that believeth on me, believeth not on me, but on him that sent me. And he that seeth me seeth him that sent me.*"[2400]

This declaration is so important that I will repeat it!

> *He that believeth on me, believeth not on me, but on him that sent me.*

The inner meaning:

> If you follow me, trust in me, are committed to me, or believe in me, it is really not me you are following, trusting, committed to, or believe in. It is the one who sent me.[2401]

As I note throughout this book, the "one who sent me" is the "Father," Jesus' occult term for the Universal Divine Mind.[2402]

In the mystical Christian tradition, the key to understanding Jesus and the inner (true) meaning of His teachings is this: in nearly every case, when the Lord uses the words "I," "me," "my," and "mine," He is not referring personally to Himself, Jesus, the *physical* (human) son of Joseph and Mary.[2403] He is speaking of the *spiritual* (divine) Universal Christ,[2404] or God-Self, within all of us, a common practice of all the great spiritual teachers throughout history.

This entity is also called the Indwelling Christ,[2405] the "inner man,"[2406] the "inward man,"[2407] the "hidden man of the heart,"[2408] the "true Light,"[2409] the "Ancient of Days,"[2410] or the Great I AM Presence within;[2411] in other words, it is our Higher Self, the "high priest"[2412] of our own personal God-made "church within"[2413]—the one and only "true tabernacle"[2414]—with its "Twelve Apostles" (that is, our 12 Spiritual Faculties or Mental Powers).[2415] This, the real you, your "divine spark," is what makes you an individualization of God.

It is this, the Immortal Universal Christ Within,[2416] not the man Jesus, which Jesus was referring to when He said:

> All power is given unto me in heaven and in earth . . . and, lo, I AM with you alway[s], even unto the end of the world. Amen.[2417]

Furthermore, when our Lord uses the phrase I AM he is *always* referring, not to Himself, the person named Jesus, but to the all-embracing Christ Within, which, as Paul and John noted, indwells each one of us.[2418] Thus one of Jesus' most famous statements takes on a whole new meaning for those who have eyes to see and ears to hear:

> Jesus saith unto him, *I AM* the way, the truth, and the life: no man cometh unto the Father, but by me.[2419]

Let us bear in mind that Jesus revealed the Great I AM, the Universal Indwelling Christ, in numerous passages, but many of these have been altered by nefarious hands over the centuries to hide the fact. One of the most notorious orthodox redactions can be found in the Gospel of John. The KJV reads:

> And he said unto them [the Jews], "Ye are from beneath; *I AM from above*: ye are of this world; *I AM not of this world*. I said therefore unto you, that ye shall die in your sins: for if ye believe not that I AM *he*, ye shall die in your sins.[2420]

The italicized word "he" in the last sentence is not in the earliest known Gospel texts. Thus, the original read: "for if ye believe not that I AM, ye shall die in your sins."[2421]

The mystical Christian understanding of Jesus is further elucidated by citing several members of the esoteric school of thought. Pfleiderer writes:

> Whoever considers, in open and unprejudiced manner, these actual elements of Jesus's announcement of the kingdom and his ethics according to the first three Gospels, cannot marvel at the further fact that *the object of the faith of the Christian congregation, from its very inception, never was the earthly teacher Jesus, but ever and exclusively it was the heavenly spirit of Christ*—the Son of Man who, according to the apocalyptic expectation, was to come upon the clouds of heaven to set up his kingdom, or the Son of God and Ruling Spirit, who, according to Paul, was sent from heaven in a human body to redeem the sinful world by his death and

resurrection, or the Logos and only-born Son of God, who, according to John, brought life and light to the world through his coming in the flesh.

In the last analysis, all of these are but different shades of expression of the personified ideal of God's humanity, which was from the beginning and is to-day the kernel of the Christian faith. *That this profound idea of God-humanity, which is a universal truth forever realizing itself throughout the whole of human history, was conceived in the mythical form of a one-time and unique supernatural miraculous figure, was certainly a defect, a veiling of the actual truth, but it was in no wise a degeneration, a destruction of some better knowledge that had been; it was, rather, for the first childish stage of development of Christianity, an inevitable form of garment, an essential pictorial envelope of a purely spiritual truth. This envelope was inevitable because the new idea of God-humanity—the indwelling of the divine in the human spirit—stood in entire contradiction to that presupposed crassly dualistic view of the world which was accepted by the entire ancient world, Jewish and heathen.*

To bridge over *this contradiction*, to overcome the ancient dualism, not only practically in the symbols of faith and observance, but also theoretically in the philosophizing on the truth of God-humanity,—that was the task which could not be performed precipitately, but its performance required the entire development of Christianity through milleniums and still requires it.[2422]

During the 13th Century the Medieval Inquisitor Stephen of Borbone investigated a mystical egalitarian Christian sect known as the Waldenses. An enemy of any doctrine that fell outside Church orthodoxy, his resentful, angry description of this group, which he considers "an extreme form of mysticism," sheds more light on the esoteric Christian view of Jesus:

> They absolutely refuse obedience to the Roman Church, which they call the unholy Babylon of the Apocalypse. They hold that all good persons, according to some, even women, are priests, having received direct ordination from God, while ecclesiastics receive it only from men. All good persons, even women, can pronounce absolution, and can consecrate the bread. They teach that it is sufficient to confess sins to God, and that God alone is able to excommunicate. . .
>
> They pretend that every man is a Son of God in the same manner that Christ was. Christ had God or the Holy

Spirit for soul, and they say that other men also have. They believe in the incarnation, the birth, the passion, and the resurrection of Christ, but they mean by it the Spiritual conception, Spiritual birth, Spiritual resurrection of the perfect man.

For them the true passion of Jesus is the martyrdom of a holy man, and the true sacrament is the conversion of a man, for in such a conversion the body of Christ is formed. In the doctrine of the Trinity, the Father is he who converts a stranger to their doctrine. The Son is he who is converted, and the Holy Spirit is the truth by means of which the conversion is accomplished. This is what they mean when they say that they believe in the Father and the Son and the Holy Ghost. They declare that the soul of all men since Adam is the Holy Spirit. . . . It is because God thus dwells in them that all good men are priests. It is God who works through them and gives them power to loose and bind.[2423]

Of the Christian mystic's view of Jesus, Principle Forsyth writes:

[this liberal section of the Church] adopts the modernist view that the ideal content of doctrine is everything, and the historic origin of it nothing. Even a historic Jesus, these extremists say, is indifferent, if only *we trust ourselves to the ideal principles of which He was the symbol rather than the source.* . .[2424]

Kingsford and Maitland write:

Christ Jesus, then, is no other than the hidden and true man of the Spirit, the Perfect Humanity, the Express Image of the Divine Glory. And it is possible to man, by the renunciation—which mystically is the crucifixion—of his outer and lower self, to rise wholly into his inner and higher self, and, becoming suffused or anointed of the Spirit, to "put on Christ," propitiate God, and redeem the earthly and material.

And that which they who, in the outer manifestation, are emphatically called Christs,—whether of Palestine, of India, of Egypt, or of Persia,—have done for man, is but *to teach him what man is able to be in himself by bearing, each for himself, that Cross of renunciation which they have borne.* And inasmuch as these have ministered to the salvation of the world thereby, they are truly said to be saviours of souls, whose doctrine and love and example have redeemed men from death and made them heirs of eternal life. The Wisdom they attained, they kept not secret, but freely gave as they had freely received. And that which thus they gave was their own life, and they gave it knowing that the children of darkness would turn on them and rend them because of the gift. But, with the Christs, Wisdom and Love are one, and the testament of Life is written in the blood of the testator. Herein is the difference between the Christ and the mere adept in knowledge. The Christ gives and dies in giving, because Love constrains him and no fear withholds; the adept is prudent, and keeps his treasure for himself alone. And as the At-one-ment accomplished in and by the Christs, is the result of the unreserved adoption of the Divine Life, and of the unreserved giving of the Love mystically called the Blood of Christ, those who adopt that Life according to their teaching, and who aspire to be one with God, are truly said to be saved by the Precious Blood of the Lamb slain from the foundation of the world. For the Lamb of God is the spiritual Sun in Aries, the spring-tide glory of ascending Light, the symbol of the Pure Heart and the Righteous Life, by which humanity is redeemed. And this Lamb is without spot, white as snow, because white is the sign of Affirmation and of the "Yes;" as black is of Negation and of the devil. It is *Iesous Chrestos*, the *Perfect Yes* of God who is symbolised by this white Lamb, and who, like his sign in heaven, was lifted up on the Cross of Manifestation from the foundation of the world.

. . . For, such of us as know and live the inner life, are saved, not by any Cross on Calvary eighteen hundred years ago, not by any physical blood-shedding, not by any vicarious passion of tears and scourge and spear; but by the Christ-Jesus, the God with us, the Immanuel of the heart, born, working mighty works, and offering oblation in our own lives, in our own persons, redeeming us from the world, and making us sons of God and heirs of everlasting life.

But, if we are thus saved by the love of Christ, it is by love also that we manifest Christ to others. If we have received freely, we also give freely, shining in the midst of night, that is, in the darkness of the world. For so long as this darkness prevails over the earth, Love hangs on his cross; because the darkness is the working of a will at variance with the Divine Will, doing continual violence to the Law of Love.[2425]

Jewish-Christian mystic Paul described with sublime accuracy the difference between the "natural" man Jesus, the "First Adam," and the spiritual entity Christ, the "Last Adam":

> And so it is written, the first man Adam was made a living soul; the last Adam was made a quickening spirit. Howbeit that was not first which is spiritual, but that which is natural; and afterward that which is spiritual. The first man [Jesus] is of the earth, earthy: the second man [Christ] is the Lord from heaven.[2426]

Few individuals ever encapsulated the natural "earthy" Jesus, the mystical Jesus, like U.S. President Thomas Jefferson. He was disgusted by the posthumous violence, perversions, and distortions done to our Lord's figure and teachings by ignorant orthodox hands, as are all Christian mystics to this day. Of the Master Jefferson writes:

> His parentage was obscure; his condition poor; his education null; his natural endowments great; his life correct and innocent; he was meek, benevolent, patient, firm, disinterested, and of the sublimest eloquence. The disadvantages under which his doctrines appear are remarkable.
> 1. Like Socrates and Epictetus, he wrote nothing himself.
> 2. But he had not, like them, a Xenophon or an Arrian to write for him. I name not Plato, who only used the name of Socrates to cover the whimsies of his own brain.
> On the contrary, all the learned of his country, entrenched in its power and riches, were opposed to him, lest his labors should undermine their advantages; and *the committing to writing of his life and doctrines fell on unlettered and ignorant men; who wrote, too, from memory, and not till long after the transactions had passed.*
> 3. According to the ordinary fate of those who attempt to enlighten and reform mankind, he fell an early victim to the jealousy and combination of the altar and the throne, at about 33 years of age, his reason having not yet attained the maximum of its energy, nor the course of his preaching, which was but of three years at most, presented occasions for developing a complete system of morals.
> 4. *Hence the doctrines which he really delivered were defective, as a whole, and fragments only of what he did deliver have come to us mutilated, misstated, and often uninintelligible.*

> 5. They have been still more disfigured by the corruptions of schismatizing followers, who have found an interest in sophisticating and perverting the simple doctrines he taught, by engrafting on them the mysticisms of a Grecian Sophist (Plato), frittering them into subtilties and obscuring them with jargon, until they have caused good men to reject the whole in disgust, and to view Jesus himself as an impostor. Notwithstanding these disadvantages, a system of morals is presented to us which, if filled up in the true style and spirit of the rich fragments he left us, would be the most perfect and sublime that has ever been taught by man. The question of his being a member of the Godhead, or in direct communication with it, claimed for him by some of his followers, and denied by others, is foreign to the present view, which is merely an estimate of the intrinsic merits of his doctrines.
>
> 6. He corrected the Deism of the Jews, confirming them in their belief of one only god, and giving them juster notions of his attributes and government.
>
> 7. His moral doctrines, relating to kindred and friends, were more pure and perfect than those of the most correct of the philosophers, and greatly more so than those of the Jews; and they went far beyond both in inculcating universal philanthropy not only to kindred and friends, to neighbors and country men, but to all mankind, gathering all into one family, under the bonds of love, charity, peace, common wants and common aids. A development of this head will evince the peculiar superiority of the system of Jesus over all others.
>
> 8. The precepts of philosophy and of the Hebrew code laid hold of action only. He pushed his scrutinies into the heart of man; erected his tribunal in the region of his thought, and purified the waters at the fountain head.
>
> 9. He taught emphatically the doctrine of a future state, which was either doubted or disbelieved by the Jews; and wielded it with efficacy as an important incentive, supplementary to the other motives to moral conduct.[2427]

Such insights only further accentuate the lamentable fact that the early orthodox Church (Catholicism) hatched a "Scheme of Salvation" by which the all too human Jesus was deified and apotheosized, and numerous characteristics, motifs, themes, and events from pre-Christian gods were artificially appended to His biography. In 1820 Hone, for example, wrote that the legends of

> Hindoo Mythology are considerably connected with [the New Testament]. . . . Many of the acts and miracles ascribed to the

Indian God, Creeshna [Krishna], during his incarnation, are precisely the same with those attributed to Christ in his infancy, by the Apocryphal Gospels, and are largely particularised by the Reverend Thomas Maurice in his learned *The History of Hindostan*.[2428]

Once known as the "Son of Man," as Jesus referred to Himself, orthodoxy turned Him into a "Son of God" (a title He never once used in any *authentic* biblical passage). Worst of all He was made a Pagan Sun-god for one primary purpose: to attract uneducated and spiritually unenlightened Pagan converts[2429] into the new religion.[2430] Truly, as Frazer notes,

> the Church has skillfully contrived to plant the seeds of the new faith on the old stock of paganism.[2431]

No one better articulated the mystical Christian view of Jesus, as well as the traditional Church's distortion of his figure and teachings, than Victorian Transcendentalist Ralph Waldo Emerson:

> Jesus Christ belonged to the true race of prophets. He saw with open eye the mystery of the soul. Drawn by its severe harmony, ravished with its beauty, he lived in it, and had his being there. *Alone in all history, he estimated the greatness of man. One man was true to what is in you and me. He saw that God incarnates himself in man*, and evermore goes forth anew to take possession of his world. He said, in this jubilee of sublime emotion, "I am divine. Through me, God acts: through me, speaks. Would you see God, see me; or, see thee, when thou also thinkest as I now think." *But what a distortion did his doctrine and memory suffer in the same, in the next, and the following ages!*[2432]

See BUDDHA, CHRIST, CHRISTIANITY, CHRISTMAS, DIVINITY OF JESUS, FISH, GOD, KRISHNA, MITHRA, NATIVITY, OSIRIS, PYTHAGORAS, SON OF MAN, TEACHER OF RIGHTEOUSNESS, WAY OF THE LORD.

JOHN THE BAPTIST: In the traditional Church John the Baptist was a desert-dwelling Jewish prophet who announced the coming of his cousin Jesus Christ. Thus the Gospel of Matthew is literalized:

> In those days came John the Baptist, preaching in the wilderness of Judaea, and saying, "Repent ye: for the kingdom of heaven is at hand. For this is he that was spoken of by the prophet Isaiah,

saying, 'The voice of one crying in the wilderness, prepare ye the way of the Lord, make his paths straight.'"[2433]

In the mystical Church the human John was an Essene mystic[2434] whose baptismal doctrine, according to Josephus, derived from the Qumran community.[2435] More importantly, Christian mystics, like Jesus, view John as an incarnation of Elijah (Hebrew) or Elias (Greek),[2436] while as a biblical figure he is referred to as the "Moral Man," an esoteric symbol of the type of pure morality that is necessary before one can enter into Self-Christhood. As the herald of the Christ, "John" baptizes with water (Truth), while "Jesus" baptizes with fire (Spirit).[2437] Of the baptizing Essene preacher John Kingsford and Maitland write:

> An important factor in the education of the Man Regenerate is that described under the figure of John the Baptist. For he . . . is interior and mystic, inasmuch as he represents that all-compelling summons of the conscience to repentance, renunciation, and purification, which is the indispensable precursor of success in the quest after inward perfection.[2438]

Kingsford writes:

> And [John] the Baptist; how account for his presence in the allegory, and the combination of Christian with "Pagan" ideas? The full explanation was long in coming; but when at length vouchsafed, was absolutely and in the highest degree satisfactory. The revelation of the Christ-idea in interpretation of the Christ—our special task—could be made only through the process whereby Christ Himself is found—the process, that is, whereby Christ becomes Christ; this is to say, that the faculty by means of which man has the apprehension of divine things—namely, the understanding—must first undergo the purification implied in the baptism which is of John. *To say that he who becomes a Christ must be baptized of John, is to say that the first and most essential step to man's realisation of his due divinity is purification of body and mind. Only they who are thus purified can "see"—that is, can realise—God.*[2439]

Of the Moral Man symbolized by John, German Christian mystic Johann Gottlieb Fichte asserts:

> The moral man obeys the command of duty in his breast for no other reason than that it commands; but in doing so he does not

know what duty, to which he is offering up his being, really requires, and what the essence of it is. His acts therefore may be ever so perfect outwardly, in appearance; but inwardly, at the root of his being, there is still division, unclearness, unfreedom, and therefore a want of absolute worth.

It is religion, religion alone, that unfolds to man the one eternal law, which commands the free man and the noble man as the law of duty, the more ignoble tool as a law of nature; religion makes him know it as the living law of development of the one infinite life. *What the moral man called duty and command is to the religious man the highest spiritual blossom of life, his element, in which alone he can breathe.* To him the "shall" of command comes too late; before it commands he wills, and he cannot will otherwise.

As all external law disappears before morality, so even the inner law disappears before religion; the lawgiver in our breast is silent, for our will, our pleasure, our love, our blessedness, have taken the law up into themselves. The pains of self-conquest, for the moral man the speechless sacrifice of blind obedience, are to the religious man no longer his own pains, but the pains of a lower nature in revolt against his true self, the pangs of a new birth, which engenders splendid life far above our expectations. He who is consecrated by religion is raised above time and decay, for his life is rooted in the one fundamental divine life, wherefore he has eternal life with all its blessedness, and possesses it at each moment, immediate and entire. To religion thus understood, morality is related as a preparatory stage: "By morality we are first trained to obedience, and in trained obedience love arises as its sweetest fruit and recompence."

Religion being thus described on its practical or mystical side as a harmonious fundamental disposition of the soul, [we see] . . . how this disposition rests on a terrestrial view of the world, which reckons the world and all life in time to be not the true and real existence, but the divided appearance of the divine being, which in itself is one.[2440]

See BAPTISM, ELIAS, ELISHA, JESUS, JORDAN RIVER, WATER.

JORDAN RIVER: In the mainstream Christian Church the Jordan River is the body of water in Palestine in which Jesus was baptized.[2441] In the mystical Christian Church it is important, in part, because of its symbolism in the various incarnations of Jesus and John Baptist. In their previous respective incarnations as Elisha and

Elijah (Elias), for example, the two were said to have "crossed over" the Jordan, an occult reference to the attainment of spiritual enlightenment or Christhood.[2442]

Christian mystics also view the River Jordan as a symbol of the "River of Life," itself an esoteric emblem of spiritual Involution (the descent of Spirit into Matter) and spiritual Evolution (the ascent of Spirit back into Spirit) as it winds and flows through the progressive upward steps of the human Soul on its path toward self-mastery.[2443] According to the mystical Gnostic-Christian sect, the Naassenes:

> [The Christ] is Ocean—birth-causing of gods and birth-causing of men—flowing and ebbing for ever, now up and now down. When Ocean flows down, it is the birth-causing of men; and when it flows up . . . it is the birth-causing of the gods. . . . For from water alone—that is, spirit—is begotten the spiritual man, not the fleshly. . . . This is the Great Jordan, which, flowing downwards and preventing the sons of Israel [Israel symbolizes the spirit] from going forth out of Egypt [Egypt symbolizes the body], or from the intercourse below was turned back by Jesus and made to flow upwards.[2444]

See BAPTISM, ELIAS, ELISHA, FLOOD OF NOAH, JESUS, JOHN THE BAPTIST, NOAH, WASHING THE FEET, WATER, WAY OF THE LORD, WORD OF GOD.

Jesus and the rich young ruler.

John the Baptist baptizing Jesus in the Jordan River.

Jerusalem.

God and the Sacred Union of the Sun and Moon.

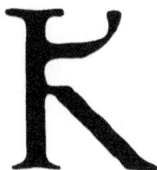

KARMA: In the traditional Church there is no such thing as "karma," and the doctrine, being considered purely Pagan, is not taught. In the mystical Church the ancient doctrine of karma is recognized throughout the Bible in the teachings of not only the Prophets, but also of Jesus and the Apostles. For here it is seen, not as a specifically Pagan concept, but as a universal one, applicable to all people, of all religions, of all nationalities, in all times and places.

The Law of Karma may be summed up simply as cause (the Spirit Plane) and effect (the Material Plane),[2445] similar (on one level) to Newton's Third Law of Motion: for every action there is an equal and opposite reaction. In the esoteric Christian schools karma means that whatever we create through thought, word, and deed returns to us; in some cases double, triple, even 100 fold. As such the inescapable Law of Karma is closely associated with the inescapable Law of Reciprocity, or the Law of Attraction, as it is often called today, for "like attracts like."

In essence, what we think, say, and do projects out into the Universe like a radio signal, then returns to us laden with like energies, be they positive or negative, spiritual or material, godly or evil; it all depends on the original projection. Thus your life is not the product of a random Universe. It is the direct result of your thoughts,[2446] just as Solomon taught: "For as a man thinketh, so is he."[2447] This makes the power of thought "the true savior of humanity."[2448]

Jesus taught the same principle: because thoughts are literal things, "we become that which we worship."[2449] Here is the true meaning of that "faith which moves mountains."[2450] In other words, our lives, our health, our finances, our relationships, our experiences, our circumstances, all are the creation of our most consistent thoughts. It is one of the great tragedies of Christianity that this simple yet life-altering doctrine is no longer preached in the traditional Church. The suffering it would prevent is beyond measure![2451]

Unbeknownst to mainstream Christians the Law of Karma is referenced thousands of times in both the Old and New Testaments. Here is how Paul phrased it in his letter to the Ephesians:

> Knowing that whatsoever good thing any man doeth, the same shall he receive of the Lord, whether he be bond or free.[2452]

In his letter to the Galatians Paul articulated the law even more clearly:

> . . . *every man shall bear his own [karmic] burden. Let him that is taught in the word communicate unto him that teacheth in all good things. Be not deceived; God is not mocked: for whatsoever a man soweth, that shall he also reap. For he that soweth to his flesh [evil] shall of the flesh reap corruption; but he that soweth to the Spirit [good] shall of the Spirit reap life everlasting.*[2453]

We can see why Paul stressed that we work on continually summoning positive feelings, such as "love, joy, peace, longsuffering, gentleness, goodness, faith, meekness, [and] temperance."[2454] If we flood our beings with these types of uplifting emotions, we not only draw more of them to ourselves, but we imbue everyone around us with them as well. This is the Law of Karma in action. Thus the Hindu sage Manu taught that:

> Action, either mental, verbal, or corporeal, bears good or evil fruit, as itself is good or evil; and from the actions of men proceed their various transmigrations in the highest, the mean, and the lowest degree.[2455]

Let us ponder a profound Zen-like fact for a moment: *cause and effect are one and the same.* The thought is the result and the result is the thought; the creator is the creation and the creation is the creator. Once this is understood, we will see that it is for our own good, and for no other reason, that Jesus gave us specific rules or "commandments" to follow. Truly, as Emerson said, "Man is what he thinks all day long." Jesus, the ultimate master of the Law of Karma and Attraction, understood this, and so provided us with a set of simple guidelines on how to think properly "all day long." Let us look at them now.

In the mystical Church "following Jesus' commandments" is not a strict moralistic system forced upon us by a stern intolerant God. It is the Father's way of guiding us toward learning to think positively, constructively, and wisely, for *all is mind and mind is all.* Christianity is not the only religion that embraces this concept. In fact, nearly every faith on earth teaches it. In Hinduism it is said: "Happiness, harmony, and health have their origins in faith and piety."[2456]

You may have been taught otherwise, but the fact is that Jesus was not a sadistic disciplinarian. He did not command that we love our neighbor and constrain ourselves from judging others so that He could punish us when we failed, for as He Himself said:

> . . . *the Son of man is not come to destroy men's lives, but to save them.*[2457]

Jesus' Law of Attraction teachings are eternal; God-formed on Law of Karma principles; impersonal but sacred doctrines that are meant to help us grow spiritually[2458] in our law-governed, reciprocity-based universe.[2459] Put another way: such universal cosmic laws, based on eternal truths, are intended to increase our happiness and allow us to manifest our dreams, our ideal world, our own personal inner "Kingdom of Heaven" here on earth.

Thus when Jesus says that we should forgive others, it is not simply because he said so; so that as good Christians we can avoid spending eternity in Hell. It is because by being forgiving, others will be forgiving toward us, making our lives more enjoyable and our bodies and minds healthier.

Here is how Jesus phrased this particular Law of Karma doctrine in the Gospel of Matthew:

> For if ye forgive men their trespasses, your heavenly Father will also forgive you: but if ye forgive not men their trespasses, neither will your Father forgive your trespasses.[2460]

> So likewise shall my heavenly Father do also unto you, if ye from your hearts forgive not every one his brother their trespasses.[2461]

Jesus in the Gospel of Mark:

> And when ye stand praying, forgive, if ye have ought against any: that your Father also which is in heaven may forgive you your trespasses. But if ye do not forgive, neither will your Father which is in heaven forgive your trespasses.[2462]

In the Gospel of Luke, Jesus gives his simplest yet most complete and understandable exposition on this specific aspect of the Karmic Law:

> Judge not, and ye shall not be judged: condemn not, and ye shall not be condemned: forgive, and ye shall be forgiven.[2463]

Who is it that is going to judge, condemn, and forgive you? It is your "heavenly Father," the Lord, Jehovah, or Yahweh, which is identical to the Universal Divine Mind, the Indwelling Christ,[2464] the Great I AM presence within. And what is the Great I AM? It is the Supreme Self, the Higher Self, your God-Self—for "ye are the temple of the living God"[2465]—named after the image it was created in: the omnific life-force and Source of All, God.[2466] This explains why those who return from near-death experiences nearly always say that in Heaven, during our "Life Review," we are not judged by others, but by ourselves.[2467]

If you harshly and unfairly judge others, your "final judgment" will not be "eternal damnation" in the Afterlife (although it *will* limit which level of the Celestial Realm you will be allowed into). It mainly concerns the suffering you will experience right here on earth as others harshly and unfairly judge you in return. How easy it is to avoid this misery by being nonjudgmental and forgiving toward others.

The Law of Karma is so scientifically accurate that it is actually mathematically exact: we get back precisely what we give out, all the time, no exceptions. Paul said that there is no escape from the karmic Law of Divine Mind,[2468] which explains the occult words of the Proverbist:

> For whom the Lord loveth he correcteth; even as a father the son in whom he delighteth.[2469]

Here is how Jesus articulated this law in the Gospel of Matthew:

> For with what judgment ye judge, ye shall be judged: and with what measure ye mete, it shall be measured to you again.[2470]

Jesus in the Gospel of Mark:

> Take heed what ye hear: with what measure ye mete, it shall be measured to you: and unto you that hear shall more be given.[2471]

Jesus in the Gospel of Luke:

> Give, and it shall be given unto you; good measure, pressed down, and shaken together, and running over, shall men give into your bosom. For with the same measure that ye mete withal it shall be measured to you again.[2472]

In his letter to the Colossians Paul stated the basic Law of Karma and Attraction principle this way:

> Whatsoever ye do, do it heartily, as to the Lord, and not unto men; knowing that of the Lord ye shall receive the reward of the inheritance: for ye serve the Lord Christ. But he that doeth wrong shall receive for the wrong which he hath done: and there is no respect of persons [that is, God or Divine Mind makes no distinction between saint and sinner, and so they are treated the same].[2473]

Emerson, one of many 19th-Century experts on the Law of Karma and the Law of Attraction, wrote:

> All things are moral. . . . Justice is not postponed. A perfect equality adjusts its balance in all parts of life. The dice of God are always loaded [that is, nothing is "random"]. The world looks like a multiplication table, or a mathematical equation, which, turn it how you will, balances itself. Take what figure you will, its exact value, nor more nor less, still returns to you. Every secret is told, every crime is punished, every virtue rewarded, every wrong redressed, in silence and certainty.[2474]

This is what our Lord meant when He said:

> For there is nothing covered, that shall not be revealed; neither hid, that shall not be known.[2475]

To the Christian mystic, understanding and working *with* the Law of Karma in a positive and productive manner means that it will always operate for us, not against us. Not only is this a scientific truth, it is Jesus' guarantee.[2476] Brooks sums up the Christian mystic's approach to karma this way:

> So long as God is in the universe, every soul that is in the universe must feel His power. No space can be so wide, no time so long as to exhaust His influence. *He that obeys must feel the ever present God in joy. He that disobeys must feel Him in pain everywhere and forever. These are the terrible necessities of obedience and disobedience.* We may state it, the Bible often does state it, judicially. We may speak of God's vengeance. It may seem to be the angry revenge of one who has been insulted and ignored. We may picture to ourselves His wrath. With realistic fancy we may imagine to ourselves the flames of His auger consuming the rebellious souls, which yet are so like Him who punishes them that they can never die.
>
> Such pictures have their power, as the crudest, coarsest representations of the essential truth that to the disobedient God must come in suffering, as He comes to the obedient in joy. The essential truth of heaven and hell is ineradicable in the universe. But greater and truer than any picture of angry vengeance, more solemn, more sublime, more impressive to the fear of a reasonable and thoughtful man, *there is the mighty image of God standing in the center of all things. And all*

things have to touch Him. And as all things touch Him, according to their characters, He becomes to them blessing or curse.

He is the happiness of obedience and the misery of disobedience throughout the world. He looks with sympathetic joy or with profoundest pity on the souls He judges, but the judgments both come from Him. The right hand and the left hand are both His. Burning there like the sun of all the world, he must be a comforting and guiding light, or a consuming fire—one of the other—to every soul.[2477]

See DIVINE MIND, FORGIVENESS, GOSPEL, ORIGINAL SIN, REDEMPTION, RIGHTEOUSNESS, SIN, UNION WITH GOD, WAY OF THE LORD.

KEYS OF THE KINGDOM OF HEAVEN: In the traditional Church Jesus gives the "Keys of the Kingdom of Heaven" to Peter, who, in Catholicism, is hence designated the first pope.[2478] Yet, this cannot be historical, for only three sentences later Jesus angrily calls Peter "Satan." Despite this shocking comment by our Lord, institutionalized Christianity goes as far as to claim that believing or rejecting this story is the key to one's personal salvation![2479]

The mystical Church does away with this problematic issue by viewing the entire scenario as an allegory illustrating the conflict between the true Spiritual Church of Jesus (which is "within," that is, mental or invisible) with the Material Church of Peter (which is "without," that is, physical or visible). This is made perfectly understandable when one learns that in the esoteric schools Peter is a symbol of the Lower Self of Man (the Devil, ignorance, selfishness, etc.), as opposed to Jesus, who is the symbol of the Higher Self of Man (the Christ, enlightenment, selflessness, etc.).

The invisible inner "Church" that Jesus formed was the complete opposite of the lavish earthly Church that Catholics formed, and which they patterned on the materialistic ostentatiousness of the Roman Pagan ruling class. From the mystical Christian viewpoint, the two have absolutely nothing in common: the former is of God, the latter is of Man. This same reality dawned on Martin Luther 1,300 years later, sparking the Protestant Reformation, which split the mainstream Church in two. (Note: because the mystical Christian Church accepts all beliefs, it has never experienced a schism.)

In a rare reversal, unlike orthodox Christians, mystical Christians take Jesus' declaration that his "kingdom is not of this world" literally.[2480] Thus no earthly Christian Church, ancient or modern, can be true, for "the most High dwelleth not in temples made with hands."[2481] The one and only *true* Church lies within.[2482] It and only it was made by the hand of God, not Man.[2483] Christian mystics hold that the story of Jesus, Peter, and the keys of the kingdom was fabricated to reveal this precise spiritual truth—perhaps under the auspices of

Constantine the Great,[2484] who ordered the Holy Scriptures to be rewritten around the year A.D. 331.[2485] Any other postulate is both irrational and insulting to the Christian mystic's mind.

It is common knowledge outside mainstream Christianity that the passages in Matthew referring to Jesus handing the "keys of the kingdom of heaven" to Peter are, in fact, late interpolations by orthodox editors who wished to officially establish apostolic succession—even though there is no biblical trace of the apostolate being instituted by Jesus to begin with.[2486] This overt fakery is why, this, the Bible's most honorific passage regarding Peter, was omitted by Mark, Luke, and John.[2487]

The "keys" in this story are, after all, not real keys; nor do they have any connection to the earthly Catholic Church headquartered at the Vatican in Rome. The "keys of the kingdom of heaven" are occult emblems of the intuitive faculty in Man, which, when used properly, can open any locked door, the door itself being an archetypal symbol of the entrance to what Jesus called "the Kingdom Within,"[2488] ruled over by the Great I AM (Om, Aum, Amen) or Indwelling Christ[2489]—which the Essenic Hebraist called the eternal "high priest" who has "neither beginning of days, nor end of life."[2490] In the New Testament the Gnostic Revelator John reminds us that the universal I AM is indeed the bearer of the sacred keys to the kingdom:

> I AM he that liveth, and was dead; and, behold, I AM alive for evermore, Amen; and have the keys of hell and of death.[2491]

In the early Mystery Religions the I AM was embodied in the ancient Egyptian Moon-god Thoth, the patron deity of knowledge.[2492] Thus Mead says:

> It is the power of Thoth that binds and loosens; he holds the keys of heaven and hell, of life and death.[2493]

See GOSPEL, KINGDOM OF GOD, PETER.

KING: In the traditional Church a king is an earthly royal ruler or a religious ruler, such as Jesus.[2494] In the mystical Church the biblical "king," like all of the other so-called "historic" figures in the Good Book, are but personified attributes of Man himself. And here we have the Master Secret of Mysticism: Man is the world in miniature, a microcosm of the Universe.[2495] In the case of the biblical "king" then, he is a symbol of the Higher Self or Indwelling Christ, the "true self," which Hindus equate with the royal Indwelling Brahman.[2496] Thus Peter gave us this esoteric commandment:

> Honour all men. Love the brotherhood. Fear God. Honour

the king.[2497]

Brooks writes:

> God is a truth to you. Your soul is your true self. Christ, the spiritual perfectness of manhood, the true Son of God, is really King of the world.[2498]

Thus when we realize that we are God, we become the divine "King" of our own "Kingdom Within,"[2499] just as Jesus intended for us.[2500] For he that hath recognized the Higher Self or Indwelling Christ hath recognized the Father (God).[2501] Christ is truly king. See CHRIST, CROWN, HIGHER SELF, KINGDOM OF GOD.

KINGDOM OF GOD: In the orthodox branch of the Church the Kingdom of God refers to a future time when God's kingdom will be temporarily instituted on earth, and which will be characterized by peace and harmony.[2502] But because Jesus did not explain what He meant by the "Kingdom of God,"[2503] did not connect Himself with it,[2504] and even acknowledged that He did not know when it was coming,[2505] this definition, like all other traditional ones, can only be speculative—a fact which points us directly to Christian mysticism.

In the mystical Christian school the Kingdom of God is Jesus' arcane term for what I call the "Realm of Divine Mind," an elevated spiritual state of consciousness available to everyone right now,[2506] here on earth—and which carries on into the Afterlife after so-called "death."[2507] This concept, popularly known as Christ Consciousness, is one of Christianity's most potentially powerful, religiously radical, and politically explosive ideas; which is precisely why Jesus never openly and clearly defined the Kingdom of God, except secretly to His closest Disciples—the 120 initiates[2508] of his secret spiritual school,[2509] who gathered together after His crucifixion in the secret "Upper Room" (private temple) at Jerusalem.[2510]

As such, this doctrine was never taught to the masses, and its arcane principles were either not included in the books of the New Testament or, more likely, they were removed and concealed by the Catholic Church in the first few centuries A.D.

Christian mystics know the Kingdom of God as each individual's idea of bliss, harmony, the perfect life on the material plane, while the ancients referred to it as "Divine Mind," or what we now call the Superconscious Mind. Throughout history Christian mystics have given this Cosmic Sense, which Jesus also called "the Kingdom of Heaven,"[2511] a wide variety of other names. Buddha, for example called it "Nirvana," Dante called it "Beatrice," Balzac called it "Seraphita," Whitman called it "My Soul," Saint Teresa of Avila called it the "Interior Castle," and Paul, of course, called it "the Christ,"[2512] or sometimes "the mind of Christ."[2513] Bucke, who refers to it as "Cosmic Consciousness,"[2514] described the Kingdom through the eyes of the Buddhist:

> The whole of Buddhism is simply this: There is a mental state so happy, so glorious, that all the rest of life is worthless compared to it, a pearl of great price to buy which a wise man willingly sells all that he has; this state can be achieved. The object of all Buddhist literature is to convey some idea of this state and to guide aspirants into this glorious country, which is literally the Kingdom of God.[2515]

Studies have shown that those who gain access into the Kingdom of God share a list of similar reactions and (typically) sudden changes, including the loss of the fear of death, a heightened morality, an unaccountable feeling of extreme joy, the knowledge of certain salvation, an indescribable intellectual illumination, an added "charm" or attractiveness to the personality, a new beautiful luminescence radiating from the face, an elevation in character, and a loss of the sense of sin, all which are known collectively to Hindus as the "Brahmic Splendor."[2516]

The Kingdom of God or Christ Consciousness is generally similar to such Eastern concepts as nirvana, satori, wu wei, bodhi, moksha, kensho, Buddhahood, and samadhi, mental states more commonly referred to simply as spiritual enlightenment or self-realization. Whatever name we choose to give it, the Kingdom of God is undoubtedly a special state of mind, one that is ruled over by the Indwelling Christ (Divine Law)[2517] and facilitated by the Father (Divine Mind).[2518] Thus it exists *within* us, which is precisely what Jesus taught:

> The kingdom of God cometh not with observation: neither shall they say "lo here!" or "lo there!" for, behold, *the kingdom of God is within you*.[2519]

We will note here that though conservative Christians like to reinterpret this scripture to mean "the kingdom of God is *among* you" (meaning "Jesus is among us"), this is not what the text says. It says "in you."[2520]

The celebrated spiritual teacher Paramahansa Yogananda called the Kingdom of God the "movable heaven,"[2521] while Jesus declared that "my kingdom is not of this world."[2522] This is why

> God works from within outwards; for God's kingdom is within, being interior, invisible, mystic, spiritual.[2523]

We enter the Inner Kingdom by following Jesus' commandments (that is, by being Christlike), through which we are "born again."[2524] This, in turn, revives and nurtures our "inner child," two of the primary prerequisites for entrance.[2525] This, just one aspect of the authentic Gospel, which the Lord called "the Gospel of the Kingdom"[2526] (not "the Gospel of Jesus Christ"),[2527] was the true focus of His entire ministry—as the Bible explicitly illustrates.[2528]

Tragically, the Master's teachings on the here-and-now Kingdom of God Within were long ago suppressed by the institutional Church, and in the process it was transformed into an arcane, unknowable, unattainable realm relegated strictly to the Afterlife. See CHRIST CONSCIOUSNESS, CROWN, DIVINE MIND, GOLGOTHA, GOSPEL, GOSPEL OF THE KINGDOM OF GOD, UNION WITH GOD, UPPER ROOM, WAY OF THE LORD.

KINGDOM OF HEAVEN: The Kingdom of Heaven is the same as KINGDOM OF GOD. The former expression, however, is found only in Matthew, where it is referenced 32 times.[2529] See also CHRIST, CROWN, HEAVEN.

KRISHNA: This 5,000 year old Indian man-god does not appear by name in the Bible, and so is absent from the doctrines of traditional Christianity. In mystical Christianity, however, like Buddha, Mithra, and Osiris, Krishna, the Hindu Christ, is one of the most important deities in the world Pantheon[2530] due to his many mythological contributions to the figure of the Paganized Jesus.

We can begin with the title-name Christ, which is anciently and occultly linked to Krishna, for *krs* means "universal" and *na* means "self," which gives the definition of the "Universal Self," making it identical to the Indwelling Christ. Thus in colloquial Bengali Krishna is sometimes spelled Krista, meaning "Christ."[2531] But it has also been spelled Khrishna, Chrisna, Cristna, Christna, etc.[2532] As much of Jesus' biography was also patterned on Buddha, all three of these Sun/Son-gods have long been known among mystics as "The Lords of Enlightened Love."[2533]

Other Christian borrowings from the Hindu Christ include the following, all taken directly from Lord Krishna's biography:

- Krishna was born to the Virgin Devaki (also known as Maia, "Mother"); Jesus was born to the Virgin Mary.[2534]
- Krishna was an incarnation of the Father-God Vishnu; Jesus was an incarnation of the Father-God Jehovah.[2535]
- Being virgin-born, Krishna had a foster father, a shepherd named Nanda Baba;[2536] being virgin-born Jesus had a foster father,[2537] a carpenter named Joseph Pandera.[2538]
- Krishna was born in a manger among shepherds, oxen, asses, and angels, at which time "there was great joy in heaven; flowers were thrown down to earth, and celestial music greeted the Incarnated One"; Jesus was born in a manger among shepherds, oxen, asses, and angels, at which time there appeared "a multitude of the heavenly host praising God, saying 'Glory

to God in the highest.'"²⁵³⁹
- Krishna's birth was announced by a star; Jesus' birth was announced by a star.²⁵⁴⁰
- At the time of Krishna's birth, Nanda Baba and his wife Yacoda were staying in a village near Madura, where they had gone to pay their taxes; at the time of Jesus' birth, Joseph and Mary were staying at Bethlehem, where they had traveled to pay their taxes.²⁵⁴¹
- King Kamsa tried to have the infant Krishna killed (the story of the "Massacre of the Innocents"); "King" Herod tried to have the infant Jesus killed.²⁵⁴²
- As a boy Krishna was known for his pranks; as a boy Jesus was known for his pranks.²⁵⁴³
- Krishna's foster father Nanda Baba (God) sent a flood to earth; Jesus' Heavenly Father (God) sent a flood to earth.²⁵⁴⁴
- Krishna battled and defeated Satan (in the form of a serpent named Kaliya); Jesus battled and defeated Satan during the Temptation.²⁵⁴⁵
- Krishna had a female consort named Radha; Jesus had a female consort named Mary (Magdalene).²⁵⁴⁶
- Krishna had a twin brother (named Bala-Rama); Jesus had a twin brother (named Judas Thomas "Didymus").²⁵⁴⁷
- Krishna's followers recognized him as the "highest god"; Jesus' followers recognized Him as the "highest god."²⁵⁴⁸
- Krishna's followers gave him the name Jezeus, meaning "issue of the pure divine essence";²⁵⁴⁹ our Lord was named Jesus,²⁵⁵⁰ meaning to "save," "deliver," or "rescue."²⁵⁵¹
- Krishna performed numerous miracles, including "raising the dead, healing lepers, and the deaf and the blind, and championing the poor and oppressed"; Jesus performed numerous miracles, including "raising the dead, healing lepers, and the deaf and the blind, and championing the poor and oppressed."²⁵⁵²
- Krishna was transfigured before his favorite apostle Arjuna; Jesus was transfigured before His favorite apostle John.²⁵⁵³
- The lance played a role in the myth of Krishna; the lance played a role in The Myth of Christ.²⁵⁵⁴
- Fish played a role in the myth of Krishna; fish played a role in The Myth of Christ.²⁵⁵⁵
- Krishna carried the shepherd's staff; Jesus carried the shepherd's staff.²⁵⁵⁶
- Krishna was only considered divine after his death; Jesus was only considered divine after His death.²⁵⁵⁷
- Krishna's birthday was celebrated on both December 25 and January 6; Jesus' birthday was and still is celebrated on both December 25 and January 6.²⁵⁵⁸
- Krishna was considered a Sun-god; Jesus was considered a Sun-god.²⁵⁵⁹
- Some early myths say Krishna was born in a cave; some early myths say Jesus was

born in a cave.[2560]
- Krishna was crucified on a tree or cross, spilling his blood "for the salvation of men"; Jesus was crucified on a tree or cross, spilling His blood "for the salvation of men."[2561]
- Krishna descended into Hell, then rose from the dead and ascended into Heaven before numerous eyewitnesses; Jesus descended into Hell,[2562] then rose from the dead and ascended into Heaven before numerous eyewitnesses.[2563]
- Krishna is to return to earth one day and lead his followers into glory; Jesus is to return to earth one day and lead His followers into glory.[2564]
- Krishna is "the Alpha and Omega, the beginning, the middle, and the end of all things"; Jesus is "the Alpha and Omega, the beginning, the middle, and the end of all things."[2565]
- Krishna is the second person in the Hindu Trinity; Jesus is the second person in the Christian Trinity.[2566]
- Krishna was called "Savior," "Redeemer," "Preserver," "Comforter," "Mediator," "The Resurrection and the Life," "The Lord of Lords," "The Great God," "The Holy One," and "The Good Shepherd." Jesus went by the same titles.[2567]

This list could be carried on almost indefinitely. Carpenter writes:

> To go into the parallelism of the careers of Krishna, the Sungod, and Jesus would take too long; because indeed the correspondence is so extraordinarily close and elaborate.[2568]

Krishna, then—like Buddha, Bacchus, Hercules, Adonis, Tammuz, Balder, Horus, Osiris, and countless others—was a type of pre-Christian christ or savior. This makes him yet another forerunner of Jesus, whose human life story (courtesy of the New Testament writers, and later the Catholic Church) assimilated the supernatural myths and legends of His messianic predecessors.[2569] See BUDDHA, CHRIST, CHRISTMAS, CRUCIFIXION, JESUS, MITHRA, NATIVITY, OSIRIS, PYTHAGORAS, SAVIOR, TEACHER OF RIGHTEOUSNESS, WAY OF THE LORD.

KYRIOS: In the traditional Church *Kyrios* (also spelled *Kurios*) is the Greek word for "Lord," a uniquely Christian title applied only to Jesus.[2570] In the mystical Church *Kyrios* is understood as an ancient pre-Christian word that was applied not only to human rulers (such as Caesar), but to various Pagan gods (such as Serapis) and goddesses (such as Isis) as well.[2571] It was used by pre-Christian Pagans and Jews alike as both a noun (a title) and as an adjective (meaning authority and power).[2572] Thus, mystically speaking, *Kyrios* or *Kurios* is another word-symbol for the Christ, which indwells all.[2573]

The Pagan origins of both the word *Kyrios* and the accompanying Paganized Christ Myth of the traditional Church are evident when one studies the pre-Christian history behind them. Pike writes:

> *Khri* . . . means white, or an opening; and *Khris*, the orb of the Sun. . . . *Krishna* is the Hindu Sun-God. *Khur*, the Parsi word, is the literal name of the Sun.
>
> From *Kur* or *Khur*, the Sun, comes Khora, a name of Lower Egypt. The Sun, Bryant says in his Mythology, was called *Kur*; and Plutarch says that the Persians called the Sun *Kuros. Kurios*, Lord, in Greek, like *Adonai*, Lord, in Phoenician and Hebrew, was applied to the Sun. Many places were sacred to the Sun, and called *Kura, Kuria, Kuropolis, Kurene, Kureschata, Kuresta*, and *Corusia* in Scythia.
>
> . . . In the Hebrew, *Aoor*, is Light, Fire, or the Sun. *Cyrus*, said Ctesias, was so named from *Kuros*, the Sun. *Kuris*, Hesychius says, was Adonis. Apollo, the Sun-god, was called *Kurraios*, from Kurra, a city in Phocis.
>
> . . . We know, through a precise testimony in the ancient annals of Tsur, that the principal festivity of Mal-karth, the incarnation of the Sun at the winter solstice, held at Tsur, was called his re-birth or his awakening, and that it was celebrated by means of a pyre, on which the god was supposed to regain, through the aid of fire, a new life. This festival was celebrated in the month *Peritius* (*Barith*), the second day of which corresponded to the 25th of December. Khur-um, King of Tyre, . . . first performed this ceremony. These facts we learn from Josephus, Servius on the Aeneid, and the Dionysiacs of Nonnus; and through a coincidence that cannot be fortuitous, the same day was at Rome the *Dies Natalia Solia Invicti*, the festal day of the invincible Sun. Under this title, Hercules, Har-acles, was worshipped at Tsur. Thus, while the temple was being erected, the death and resurrection of a Sun-God was annually represented at Tsur, by Solomon's ally, at the winter solstice, by the pyre of Mal-karth, the Tsurian Haracles.[2574]

The Gnostic Serpent.

See BUDDHA, CHRIST, JESUS, KRISHNA, MESSIAH, MITHRA, OSIRIS, PYTHAGORAS, SAVIOR, TEACHER OF RIGHTEOUSNESS.

Peter and the Keys.

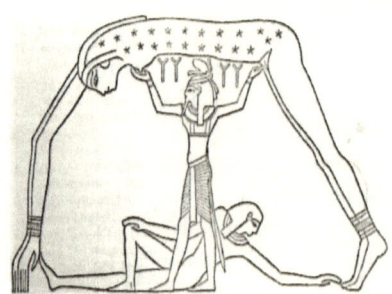
The Egyptian Heaven.

Start of the Exodus.

The Four Horsemen of the Apocalypse.

L

LAMB OF GOD: In the traditional Church the Lamb of God is the name given to Jesus by John the Baptist,[2575] and which signifies Christ's redemptive sacrifice and death on the cross. Here the term derives from the Jewish practice of sacrificing first-born lambs to Yahweh on holy days,[2576] in particular at Passover.[2577]

In the mystical Church the "Lamb of God" is a symbol of sacrifice,[2578] the Just Man, and chaste thoughts; or more generally the purity of the divine life, for the sacrificial lamb is itself an esoteric emblem of sinlessness, innocence, and submissiveness.[2579] The *Agnus Dei*, Latin for "Lamb of God," a Christian Roman figure of a lamb and cross, reveals the inner meaning of the phrase: *agnus* is related to the Greek word *agnos*, "unknown," as well as the Greek word *agni*, "fire," a symbol of Spirit.[2580] This gives the traditional occult meaning of the "invisible God,"[2581] or in Paganism, the "Unknown God,"[2582] otherwise known to Christian mystics as the "Indwelling Christ"[2583] who abides in every human form,[2584] which Paul called "the temple of the living God."[2585]

The origins of the term Lamb of God are, of course, deeply Pagan, for thousands of years prior to the founding of the Church the lamb was closely associated with resurrection. Pre-Christian goddess-worshipers ("witches" or Wiccans), for instance, sacrificed lambs in ceremonies dedicated to raising the souls of the dead.[2586] The ancient Egyptians too utilized the lamb as a symbol of resurrection;[2587] in this case, in connection with the Sun-god Ra and the resurrected Savior-God Osiris, as Budge notes:

> On looking into the boat of the Sun-god we see that this deity has transformed himself, and that he no longer appears as a fiery disk, but as a ram-headed man, who stands within a shrine; in other words, Ra has taken the form of Osiris, in order that he may pass successfully through the kingdom of the dead, whose lord and god is Osiris.[2588]

Jesus Himself was connected to the lamb motif, not because of Christianity or even Judaism, but because He was born in the Age of Aries (which began around 2220 B.C.),[2589] a constellation whose Pagan symbol is the Ram, a male sheep, and whose pre-Christian titles were "the Lamb of God" and the "Savior."[2590] As the Persians were the only ancient people to symbolize what we now call Aries as a lamb, this "Christian" emblem is obviously Iranian in origin.[2591] In this circuitous manner the phrase "Lamb of God" was first attached to Jesus,[2592] becoming the official image of our Lord up to the 7th Century, at which time the 5th Council of Constantinople (the Quinisext Synod in A.D. 692) replaced it with the symbols of the cross and the crucified man.[2593] See BLOOD OF THE LAMB, GOOD SHEPHERD, OSIRIS, WASHED IN THE BLOOD OF THE LAMB.

LAZARUS: In the mainstream Church Lazarus is the brother of Mary and Martha who Jesus raised from the dead.[2594] As the story of Lazarus appears only in the Gospel of John, and since it is the miracle that most stretches the credulity of modern mainstream Christians,[2595] it is apparent that it is not history, but esotery. Thus in the mystical Church the entire story of Lazarus and Jesus is seen as an allegory concealing special knowledge and spiritual truth.

Here, Lazarus represents the human soul that is asleep to the truth of our divine nature (known as psychoma, "soul sleep"). Jesus represents the I AM, the Higher Self, the Universal Indwelling Christ, who, like the Buddha, awakens the somnolent Lower Self to the knowledge of its divinity.[2596] Lazarus' tomb represents the incarceration of Man by the false thoughts of the mass mind. The stone that blocks the entrance to the tomb is a symbol of the human Ego, which hinders spiritual growth by cutting us off from God, Divine Mind, the "Father." Lazarus' sister Martha symbolizes the faith that is necessary to overcome the Ego and mass mind, in order to reawaken the soul from its deathlike slumber back into God Consciousness.[2597]

Kingsford and Maitland note that "the raising from the dead—as of Lazarus—implies resurrection from the condition of spiritual deadness."[2598] See BORN AGAIN, RAISING THE DEAD, RESURRECTION OF JESUS.

LIGHT: In the traditional Church light is a symbol of purity and holiness.[2599] In the mystical Church light is a symbol of spiritual truth, wisdom, and knowledge.[2600] Its opposite, darkness, is a symbol of spiritual error, ignorance, and doubt. Thus Isaiah says mystically:

> Arise, shine; for thy light is come, and the glory of the Lord is risen upon thee. For, behold, the darkness shall cover the earth, and gross darkness the people: but the Lord shall arise upon thee, and his glory shall be seen upon thee.[2601]

Likewise Job declares:

> That he may recall their souls from corruption, and enlighten them with the light of the living.[2602]

The idea of light has long been associated with the Sun, and hence with solar-gods, who themselves are symbols of the Universal Indwelling Christ. Jesus, the "Sun of Righteousness,"[2603] who was portrayed by early Christians as the Sun-god Helios riding across the sky in His fiery chariot,[2604] made the following statement; not as the man Jesus, but as the Great I AM:

> I AM the light of the world: he that followeth me shall not walk in Darkness, but shall have the Light of Life.[2605]

Jones writes:

> Winstanley's central religious idea is the Divine Light within man's soul. He has passed completely and for ever away from the childish and pagan notion, or imagination, as he would call it, of a God who is far off in some distant sphere above the sky, to a Divine Being who is the inward power "by whom every one lives and moves and has his being." "Man," he says, "looks abroad for a God and doth imagine or fancy a God in some particular place of glory beyond the skies. But the Kingdom of Heaven is within you, dwelling and ruling in your flesh." The Spirit within (which he also calls that mighty man Christ Jesus) is to arise, not at a distance from man, but He will rise up in men and manifest Himself to be the Light and Life of every man and woman that is saved by Him. *"The Spirit of reason is not without a man, but within every man; hence he need not run after others to tell him or to teach him, for this Spirit is his Maker, He dwells in him, and if the flesh were subject thereto, he would daily find teaching therefrom."* He tells his little group of "Friends," sometimes calling them "Children of the Light," that they do not look for a God now,
>
>> "as formerly you did, to be in a place of glory beyond the sun, moon, and stars, nor imagine a Divine Being you know not where; but *you see Him ruling within you; and not only in you, but you see and know Him to be the Spirit or Power that dwells in every man and woman, yea, in every creature, according to his orb, within the globe of the Creation.* . . . You rise higher and higher into life and peace as this manifestation of the Father increases and spreads within you."

He speaks of his old unillumined days as a period of darkness and tradition:

> "I worshipped a God, but I neither knew who He was nor where He was, so that I lived in the dark . . . I looked for a God without me, but now *the true worshipper knows who God is and how He is to be worshipped as the Spirit and Power of Light shining within the man himself.*"[2606]

See CHRIST, CHRIST CONSCIOUSNESS, ENLIGHTENMENT, GOOD NEWS, I AM, INDWELLING CHRIST, SUN, SUN OF RIGHTEOUSNESS, THEOSIS, THIRD EYE, TRANSFIGURATION OF JESUS, UNION WITH GOD.

LOGOS: In mainstream Christianity the Logos is a title of Jesus,[2607] one associated with the creative power of God.[2608] Orthodox Christians believe that Logos literally means the "Word," and admit that they do not fully understand the meaning of the term, other than as an abstract "philosophical and theological concept."[2609]

The reason for their confusion is simple enough: Jesus never called Himself "the Word," and he certainly never intended it to be applied to Himself.[2610] The connection between our Lord and the Logos was borrowed by the Gnostic evangelist and mystic John[2611] (who, more than any other New Testament writer, was steeped in Hellenized Gnosticism)[2612] from the first Christians, the Gnostics.[2613] This is why the logos-theology does not appear in any other part of the Gospel tradition.[2614] In the 1851 edition of the *Cyclopedia of Biblical Literature* we find the following:

> "St. John was as far as possible from being the first to apply the term Logos to Christ I suppose him to have found it so universally applied, that he did not attempt to stop the current of popular language, but only kept it to its proper channel, and guarded it from extraneous corruptions." In these few words we have a brief statement of Professor Burton's theory *rejecting the first use of the term Logos by the Christian converts, and its subsequent adoption into the Gospel of St. John*. . . . Professor Burton *considers the term Logos to have been borrowed by the first Christian converts from the Gnostics, and to have been applied by them to Christ, and that it is one of the peculiar objects of St. John's Gospel* to show in what sense the term Logos can be applied properly to Christ.[2615]

It is thus that in mystical Christianity the Logos or Word is perfectly understood as a pre-Christian Pagan notion[2616]—one commonly associated by the ancient Romans with Sun/Son-gods like Mithra,[2617] by Indians with the Hindu creator-god Brahma,[2618] by the Stoics with the World Principle, by early Greek Pagans with the Wisdom-Goddess Sophia, by traditional Jews with "God's agent in creation,"[2619] and by Gnostic Jews with God, not Jesus[2620]—a concept that was eventually popularized by the Hellenistic Jewish writer Philo. Here, according to the Logos doctrine, it is both the Word, that is, the active, creative, mental power of God in Man,[2621] and also a symbol of the Indwelling Christ, which is God. Even the great orthodox Church Father Irenaeus recognized that the Logos is "the Mind of God."[2622]

Pagans imaged the Logos as being associated with the Seven Sacred "Planets" of the ancient Mystery Schools, after which our seven weekdays were named: Sun, Moon, Mercury, Venus, Mars, Jupiter, and Saturn.[2623] Thus Pryse writes:

> As the all-pervading solar Light he [the Logos] walks about among the seven golden lampstands, the seven planetary bodies, holding in his right hand their seven "stars," the light which he confers upon them. The Logos-figure described is a composite picture of the seven sacred planets: he has the snowy-white hair of Kronos [Saturn] ("Father Time"), the blazing eyes of "wide-seeing" Zeus [Jupiter], the sword of Ares [Mars], the shining face of Helios [Sol], and the chiton and girdle of Aphrodite [Venus]; his feet are of mercury, the metal sacred to Hermes [Mercury], and his voice is like the murmur of the ocean's waves (the "many waters"), alluding to Selene [Luna], the Moon-Goddess of the four seasons and of the waters.[2624]

Christian mystics append the term Logos to Jesus as a personification of the perfected (that is, completely enlightened) man/woman; the "prototypical Ideal Man,"[2625] the "Archetypal Man,"[2626] or perfectly virtuous individual.[2627] The Logos thus represents the Conscious Mind, the mental aspect of the Divine Mind. Because our predominate thoughts always manifest as physical reality, we now have the inner meaning of the phrase, "the Word was made flesh."[2628] Word of Faith theology holds that we can alter physical reality through dwelling on and repeating the Word (that is, sacred scripture).[2629]

This accords exactly with Jesus' teachings on the Law of Attraction (what we believe becomes true and real for us), as the Bible itself discloses.[2630] Despite this fact, many mainstream Christian authorities continue to deny the power of the Logos in individual Man, much to the detriment of the laity. Inge writes:

The Logos of Heraclitus is at once world-principle and world-process. It seems to have been a name for the rational self-evolution of the universe, to be apprehended by the human mind which is capable of identifying itself with it. With the Stoics, the "seminal Logos" is God Himself as the organic principle of the universe. *God dwells in our hearts as Logos*; and since He is one, though dwelling in many human beings, we may have communion with each other through the Logos.[2631]

Being the great Judeo-Christian mystic that he was, Paul correctly saw the Word of God as "the mystery which hath been hid from ages and from generations, but now is made manifest to his saints."[2632] The "manifestation" of this "mystery" is the activity of God in the world; or as Clement of Alexandria called the Logos, "the wisdom of God."[2633] See CHRIST, CHRISTMAS, GOOD NEWS, JESUS, MANNA, MOUTH OF GOD, NATIVITY, VOICE OF GOD, WORD OF GOD.

LOWER SELF: The Lower Self is identical to the Ego, but known in the Bible by traditional Christians as "Satan," "Lucifer," or the "Devil." It is part of our human nature and, in the righteous, it dies with our physical body—though it continues on into the Celestial Realm in those who thrive on evil. The Lower Self, false self, or Human Self is opposed by the Higher Self, real self, or Divine Self, also known as the Indwelling Christ.[2634]

Paul referred to the Lower Self as the "outward man,"[2635] as opposed to the "inward man" or Higher Self.[2636] The always mystical Gnostic Apostle John, the most highly spiritually developed of the four Evangelists[2637] (and whose disciple Lucius Charinus later carried on his Gnostic teachings),[2638] called the Lower Self "the beast that was, and is not, and yet is."[2639] See ADVERSARY, ANTICHRIST, BEAST, CHRIST, DEVIL, EGO, EGYPT, EVIL, GODS AND GODDESSES, HELL, HIGHER SELF, KARMA, LUCIFER, MASS MIND, NUMBER OF THE BEAST, ORIGINAL SIN, PHARISEES, PILATE, SATAN, SERPENT, SIN.

LUCIFER: As the first archangel to spring from the depths of chaos, Lucifer was the original Lux ("Light"), making him identical to Satan and the Devil. Like them, Lucifer too is the *Demon est Deus Inversus* (the "Devil is God Inverted"),[2640] as the etymology of his name reveals: the word Lucifer is Latin for "bringer of light," and derives from the bright "Morning Star," which is none other than the figure of the Roman goddess of love, Venus, who, as the brilliantly luminous planet of the same name, appears with the Sun in the morning sky, and who was thus known to the ancients as the "Bringer of Light." The book of Isaiah corroborates this, identifying Lucifer as the "son of the morning,"[2641] while Paul complained that "Satan himself is transformed into an angel of light."[2642] Pike writes:

The true name of Satan, the Kabalists say, is that of Yahveh reversed; for Satan is not a black god, but the negation of God. The Devil is the personification of Atheism or Idolatry.

For the Initiates, this is not a Person, but a Force, created for good, but which may serve for evil. It is the instrument of Liberty or Free Will. They represent this Force, which presides over the physical generation, under the mythologic and horned form of the God Pan; thence came the he-goat of the Sabbat, brother of the Ancient Serpent, and the Light-bearer or Phosphor, of which the poets have made the false Lucifer of the legend.[2643]

In mystical Christianity the word Lucifer is an allusion to the fact that it is through our sins (mistakes) that we become enlightened (that is, "walk in the light").[2644] In other words, through overcoming the worldly "temptations" of Satan/the Devil (the human Ego), we gradually raise our consciousness, bringing ourselves ever closer to realizing our oneness with the Divine Mind, or God—which is enlightenment; or in Eastern parlance, satori, nirvana, bodhi, moksha, wu wei, kensho, or samadhi.[2645]

Furthermore, Jesus is "the light [enlightenment] of the world"[2646] and, as the greatest teacher of the Law of Love,[2647] is Himself love incarnate.[2648] Occultly speaking then, Jesus and the "Bringer of Light"—the love-goddess Venus, the bright "morning star"—are one and the same, as Jesus Himself states in the book of Revelation:

> I am the root and the offspring of David, and the bright and morning star.[2649]

Indeed, this was part of Jesus' great mission here on earth: to reinvest an overly masculinized religion with the Feminine Principle (love), which had been lost over time due to the patriarchal (pharisaic) intellectualization of spirituality.[2650] To this day, what is most needed by humanity is not more sectarian turmoil and formalized religion. It is love. For it is not what we believe or what religion we belong to that counts with God. It is who we are.[2651]

Early orthodox priests, as they nearly always did, misunderstood this simple mystical doctrine. But one thing that is clear was that since Lucifer was the first Light-Bearer (giver of spiritual enlightenment), he was far higher and older than Jehovah, which is why they sacrificed him to orthodox dogma, equating him with "darkness" and "evil."[2652] In this way the figure of Lucifer was rewritten to fit the ecclesiastic needs of the institutional Church.

Besides the Jesuine passage in Revelation, however, they missed at least one other important biblical reference to the "Son of the Morning's" true and original role. In the book of Job, Lucifer and his angels are called the "Sons of God."[2653] This is confirmed by sacred numerology: the occult number of Lucifer is 741, which when added and reduced, equals 3,[2654] the number of God as the Holy Trinity.[2655] All of this accords with historical fact: Satanism was constructed on the same spiritual belief systems as original Christianity, namely, Gnosticism, Kabbalism, and Hermeticism.[2656] See ADVERSARY, BEAST, CHRIST, DEVIL, EGO, EGYPT, EVIL, GODS AND GODDESSES, HELL, HEROD ANTIPAS, KARMA, LOWER SELF, NUMBER OF THE BEAST, ORIGINAL SIN, PHARISEES, PILATE, SATAN, SERPENT, SIN.

Krishna with his lute.

Jesus raising Lazarus.

Lucifer after his fall.

Mystical representation of the Logos.

MANNA: In the traditional Church manna is a strange and unidentifiable food which God miraculously provided for Israel in the desert.[2657] In the mystical Church manna is a symbol of spiritual food, food for the soul; in other words, wisdom. Thus Philo writes:

> Dost thou not see the food of the soul, what is it? It is the Continuing Reason (Logos) of God, like unto dew, encircling the whole of it [the soul] on all sides, and suffering no part of it to be without its share of it [the Logos].[2658]

St. Ambrose says:

> You ask me why the Lord God does not now rain manna as He did on our fathers. If you consider, He does rain manna from heaven on those who serve Him, and that day by day. The earthly manna indeed is to this very day found in many places, but it is not now an event so miraculous because that which is perfect is come. Now that which is perfect is the Bread from heaven, the Body born of the Virgin as to which the Gospel sufficiently instructs us. O how greatly does this excel what went before it! For they who eat that [Old Testament] manna or bread, are dead, but he that eateth of this [New Testament] bread shall live for ever.
>
> *But there is also a spiritual manna, the dew that is of spiritual Wisdom, which descends from heaven upon those who sincerely seek for it,* and which waters the souls of the righteous, and puts sweetness into their mouths. Wherefore he who comprehends this out-pouring of divine wisdom receives pleasure from it, *nor requires any other food, nor lives by bread alone, but by every word of God.*[2659]

See BETHLEHEM, BREAD, FLOOD OF NOAH, LOGOS, MOUTH OF GOD, VOICE OF GOD, WATER, WASHING THE FEET, WORD OF GOD.

MANSIONS: In the Gospel of John Jesus says:

> In my Father's house are many mansions; if it were not so, I would have told you; for I go to prepare a place for you.[2660]

In traditional Christianity this saying is taken to mean that Jesus will never abandon His Disciples or followers. In the mystical Christian Church "mansions" refers to the seven levels of Heaven that are occupied by human souls according to their level of spiritual consciousness.[2661] The purer one's life on earth, the higher the level of Heaven ("mansion") he will be permitted to dwell on in the Afterlife,[2662] the seventh being the highest, the first the lowest. In a trance state or near-death experience of some kind,[2663] Paul said that he visited the "Third Heaven."[2664]

Like most of the aspects, beliefs, rituals, words, and myths of Christianity, the doctrine of the heavenly estates too derives from ancient Egypt.[2665] According to the Egyptian *Book of the Dead*, the Sun-god Osiris possessed seven mansions, which could not be entered "without a knowledge of the names of the doorkeeper, watcher, and herald who belonged to each."[2666] Similarly:

> The Hall of Osiris, wherein the god dwelt with his princes, could only be reached after certain doors, and mansions, and domains, which were guarded by porters in the form of monsters, had been successfully been passed through by the deceased.[2667]

In other words, everyone has a "mansion" waiting for him or her in Heaven, constructed on the level of the First, Second, Third, Fourth, Fifth, Sixth, or Seventh Heaven of the "Sun-god" or "Son-god,"[2668] that is, God. Which one of these we are placed in after death depends on the life we live here on the material plane. We will note that, according to ancient Pagan and Christian tradition, there are also seven levels of Hell.[2669] See HEAVEN, HELL, WAY OF THE LORD.

MARY (VIRGIN): In the traditional Church Mary is the mother of Jesus, the literal mother of God. In Catholicism her devotion and honor are considered "the highest that the Church recognizes possible."[2670] In the mystical Church she is a Judeo-Christian composite of the universal Pagan Virgin-Mother-Goddess, variously known around the world as Aphrodite-Mari, Ishtar-Mari, Ma Ma, Maerin, Maid Marian, Mar, Mara, Marah, Mari, Maria, Mariam, Marie, Marratu, Mary, Maya, and Meri.[2671]

In her *virgin* form specifically she is identical to such pre-Christian virgin-mothers as: Aditi, Arianrhod, Asase Yaa, Atabei, Ataensic, Bugan, Ceto, Dechtere, Diti, the Djanggawul Sisters, Djigonasee, Eurynome, Finchoem, Fu-Pao, Gaea, Henwen, Hera, Kongsim, Ligoapup, Luminu-Ut, Mu Olokukurtilisop, Nana,

Neith, Nessa, Nyx, Parvati, Poza-Mama, Shiwanolia, Tai Yuan, Thalassa, Tiamat, Wari-Ma-Te-Takere, the Wawalag Sisters, and thousands of others.[2672]

The great Goddess was also imaged as a triple-goddess,[2673] the virgin-mother-crone, appearing in different lands and societies as, for example, Parvati-Durga-Uma, Ana-Babd-Macha, Hebe-Hera-Hecate, the Three Gorgons (Stheno, Euryale, and Medusa), the Moerae, the Fates, the Furies, the Three Graeae, the Three Horae, the Norns, the Fortunae, Diana Triformis, the Three Mothers, the Three Grandmothers, the Three Divine Sisters, the Three Damsels, and so on.[2674]

She was sometimes a triple-Moon-goddess called Leucothea: the "White Goddess,"[2675] making her another embodiment of the old Pagan female lunar-deity, some of the better known who were: Arianrhod, Artemis, Britomartis, Candi, Chang-o, Coatlícue, Diana, Europa, Hanwi, Hecate, Helen, Helle, Io, Ishtar, Isis, Juno, Luna, Mawu, Pandia, Perse, Pheraia, Ri, Selene, Tapa, Titania, Tlazoltéotl, Ursula, Yolkai Estan, and Sirna.[2676] The pairing of the Moon with the Virgin Mary is so intuitive that modern Native-Americans, such as the Chamula people, a community of Mayans living in southern Mexico, continue to view the two as a single goddess, one named Hmetik ("Our Mother").[2677] The Christian Church assimilated both the Pagan Goddess' lunar aspect and her triadic form as well, in this case as the "Three Marys" who stood at the foot of Jesus' cross[2678] and the mystical "Mary" who appears on a crescent Moon[2679] wearing a crown of 12 stars (symbols of the 12 astrological Sun-signs).[2680]

Mary took the title "Queen of Heaven"[2681] from her Pagan forerunners Asherah, Astarte, Ishtar,[2682] and Juno,[2683] and the title Stella Maris ("Star of the Sea")[2684] from the goddesses Isis, Aphrodite, and Venus.[2685] The traditional Christian image of Mary holding the infant Son-God Jesus at her breast was borrowed from much earlier images, such as the Egyptian Mother-Goddess Isis nursing the infant savior Horus (*Isis Lactans*),[2686] a Pagan Christ known to the Greeks as the Sun/Son-god Apollo.[2687] To this day Wiccans continue to use statuettes of Isis and Horus and Mary and Jesus interchangeably in their ceremonies.[2688]

For Christian mystics then Mary is the ultimate symbol of the archetypal Divine Feminine, whose primary characteristics are love, gentleness, receptivity, kindness, maternalness, and devotion.[2689] See CHRISTMAS, GODDESS, MOTHER, NATIVITY, STAR OF BETHLEHEM, VIRGIN BIRTH, VIRGO.

MASSACRE OF THE INNOCENTS: The "Massacre of the Innocents," which Herod the Great ordered after the Wise Men lied to him,[2690] claiming that they could not locate the infant Jesus,[2691] is not historical. It is only found in Matthew, who borrowed it from Pagan mythology, particularly that of the far older Sun/Son-god Krishna,[2692] the Hindu Christ also known as Chrisna or Christa.[2693] Schonfield rightly calls it the "Messianic version" of the infancy tales associated with earlier biblical figures, such as Abraham and Moses.[2694] See BETHLEHEM, CHRISTMAS, HEROD ANTIPAS, NATIVITY, VIRGIN BIRTH, WISE MEN.

MASS MIND: The mass mind is not named in the Bible, but it is indirectly referenced thousands of times as the everyday thoughts, concepts, and beliefs of society, of the human race, and so it is also called "race mind." Some of these beliefs are positive (e.g., "the best things in life are free"), but most are negative (e.g., "making money is difficult"), and thus have a destructive impact on the spiritual evolution of humanity. For we become what we think, just as the Proverbist declares.[2695]

    The mass mind is, of course, guided and manipulated by Satan (the atheistic human Ego). Thus the less one follows mass mind (ignorance), and instead follows the Christ Within (knowledge), the faster one will evolve spiritually.[2696] For, as our Lord said, "no man cometh unto the Father but by the Indwelling Christ."[2697] The spiritually enlightened have long understood this doctrine, which is why they stand apart, differing in almost every way, from the mass of humanity.[2698] See ADVERSARY, ANTICHRIST, BEAST, DEVIL, DIVINE MIND, EGO, EGYPT, EVIL, HELL, KARMA, LOWER SELF, LUCIFER, NUMBER OF THE BEAST, ORIGINAL SIN, SATAN, SERPENT, SIN.

MELCHIZEDEK: In the traditional Church Melchizedek is a priest and king of Jerusalem who received war spoils and tithing from Abraham,[2699] and who served as a priest under the Pagan Canaanite god of the city, El Elyon (whose name means "God of the Most High").[2700] He instituted an early primitive form of the Pagans' bread and wine Sacrament.[2701]

    Many mainstream Christians continue to be mystified by the "strange king" Melchizedek, for his name is not a personal one and he was said to have no ancestors. The Bible is not even clear as to why Abraham bestowed plundered goods and money upon him.[2702] Despite these insurmountable issues, the orthodox consider Melchizedek a symbol of the "ideal priest-king."[2703]

    In the mystical Church Melchizedek is not considered either mysterious or unknowable, for his name gives away his true identity. Melchizedek means "my king is righteousness."[2704] Thus, as "king" is always an arcane emblem of Christ Consciousness, he is easily understood as simply another esoteric symbol of the Higher Self,[2705] or Indwelling Christ—the sacred inner meaning of "priest-king." This is why the Hebraist portrays him as a type of Christ, one "without father, without mother, without descent, having neither beginning of days, nor end of life; but made like unto the Son of God."[2706] No better description of the Great I AM, the Universal Christ Within, has ever been penned.

    He is, in other words, the divine spark, made in God's image,[2707] that inhabits every human form as his or her own Soul. Paul referred occultly to Melchizedek as "the mind of Christ,"[2708] yet another name for the Superconscious Mind or Divine Mind.[2709] See CHRIST, CROWN, DIVINE MIND, KING.

MESSIAH: In both traditional Christianity and mystical Christianity the Messiah is one of the many titles of "the Christ." However, there is a massive interpretive difference between the two. In the former the Christ is specifically the man Jesus,[2710] while in the latter the Christ refers to our Higher Self, that "divine spark" that we call the human soul, and which is made in the exact image of God.[2711] Thus John plainly states:

> [Andrew] first findeth his own brother Simon, and saith unto him, "We have found the Messias, which is, being interpreted, the Christ."[2712]

We will note that John does not say "being interpreted, Christ," which is how the mainstream Church reads and interprets it, but rather "being interpreted, *the* Christ," the Christ being the proper form when discussing "the true Light, which lighteth every man that cometh into the world."[2713] We are speaking here of the Universal Christ Within, of which the universalist Paul said: "Christ is all, and in all."[2714]

"Messiah" is not a Christian word, of course, nor is it even Jewish in origin. Indeed, thousands of ancient Pagan priests, kings, and gods were "anointed ones," and were thus known as Messiahs (that is, Christs). One of these was the non-Jewish Persian King Cyrus, who even the Old Testament refers to as a *Moshiach* or Messiah.[2715]

Further proof comes from etymology, which allows us to trace the word back to its Pagan roots. The ancient Egyptian word for an anointed mummy was *mes*, from which derived the related word, *messu*, Egyptian for "to be anointed." When *messu* is added together with the Egyptian *Iah*, "son-god,"[2716] we get the word *Messu-Iah*, which, later, under the Hebrews, became *Messiah*, "Anointed."[2717] Hence, Messiah is identical to the Egyptian word for the risen and eternal human soul, known 5,000 years ago around the Nile as "Karast," the root-word of Christ.[2718] Origen commented on the inner meaning of the Messiah:

> Now the number ten is a sacred one, not a few mysteries being indicated by it; and so we are to understand that the mention of the tenth hour as that at which these disciples turned in with Jesus, is not without significance. Of these disciples, Andrew, the brother of Simon Peter, is one; and he having profited by this day with Jesus and having found his own brother Simon (perhaps he had not found him before), told him that he had found the Messiah, which is, being interpreted, Christ. It is written that "he that seeketh findeth."
>
> Now he had sought where Jesus dwelt, and had followed Him and looked upon His dwelling; he stays with the Lord "at the tenth hour," and finds the Son of God, the Word,

and Wisdom, and is ruled by Him as King. *That is why he says, "We have found the Messiah," and this a thing which every one can say who has found this Word of God and is ruled as by a king, by His Divinity.* As a fruit he at once brings his brother to Christ, and Christ deigned to look upon Simon, that is to say, by looking at him to visit and enlighten his ruling principle; and Simon by Jesus' looking at him was enabled to grow strong, so as to earn a new name from that work of firmness and strength, and to be called Peter.[2719]

Contrary to what we have been taught by the mainstream Church, Jesus never once announced that He was the Messiah,[2720] never once even claimed to be the Messiah,[2721] often discouraged the idea,[2722] and on some occasions even repudiated the notion that He was of Davidic descent[2723]—one of the principal Jewish qualifications for messiahship.[2724] Even many of Christianity's most lettered Bible scholars do not believe that our Lord thought of Himself as the Messiah.[2725] The reasons for holding this view are many, beginning with the following incident, for instance, which was recorded by Matthew:

> While the Pharisees were gathered together, Jesus asked them, saying, "what think ye of Christ? whose son is he?" They say unto him, "the Son of David." He saith unto them, "how then doth David in spirit call him 'Lord,' saying, 'the Lord said unto my Lord, sit thou on my right hand, till I make thine enemies thy footstool?'[2726] If David then call him Lord, how is he his son?" And no man was able to answer him a word, neither durst any man from that day forth ask him any more questions.[2727]

Furthermore, even those passages in which Jesus appears to accept the title of Messiah are highly suspect, since they have long been considered unhistorical additions.[2728] Luke, who traveled and preached with Paul, and who wrote both the Gospel of Luke and the Book of Acts, does not recognize Jesus as "Lord and Christ" until *after* His resurrection and exaltation.[2729] Jesus Himself renounced the belief that he was even omniscient,[2730] saying:

> But of that day and hour no one knows, not even the angels of heaven, nor the Son, but the Father only.[2731]

Obviously, like much else in our Bible that is considered "original Church tradition," the doctrine that Jesus was an all-powerful god, the literal Messiah, was not held by our Lord Himself, but was later interpolated into the New Testament by orthodox hands,[2732] the same ones who authored The Myth of Christ and implemented the Scheme of Salvation. See CHRIST, CHRISTIANITY, GNOSTICISM, GOSPEL, ISRAEL, MYTH OF CHRIST, NATIVITY, SAVIOR.

MITHRA: Since this pre-Christian Pagan god does not appear by name in the Bible, he is not recognized by the traditional Church. Yet the mystical Church recognizes Mithra in the figure, characteristics, and biography of Jesus. Indeed, the first Christians in the city of Rome met in subterranean temples devoted to Mithra.[2733] Due to his deep connection to Christianity this world-honored deity is included here. Without a working knowledge of Mithraism, much of Christianity is nonsensical.

Mithra began as an Indian god named Mitravaruna who is mentioned nearly 200 times in the Vedic Hymns.[2734] Eventually adopted in Persia as Mitra (meaning "contract"),[2735] and then in Greece as Meitras[2736] and at Rome as Mithras, he was imaged as a Sun-god who had been born from a rock or in a cave on December 25.[2737] Since being "born in a cave" (a "feminine" cleft in the earth) was an ancient euphemism for virgin birth, Mithra's mother must have been the great Virgin-Mother-Goddess Aditi or Anahita (the Indo-Persian Virgo,[2738] Venus, or Ishtar)[2739]—a Sun-goddess who wore a crown of 12 stars (symbols of the 12 astrological Sun-signs) and rode through the heavens upon a crescent Moon.[2740] Aditi was later absorbed by the Christian Church, ending up in the book of Revelation as a highly Paganized form of the Virgin Mary.[2741]

Mithra's virgin birth was witnessed by shepherds and Wise Men who brought gifts to the infant deity,[2742] while the solar-child himself was heralded as the intercessor between Man and God, one who would fight against darkness for the salvation of humanity.[2743]

Mithra, who wore a cloak,[2744] rode in a golden chariot drawn by four horses,[2745] and who possessed 12 Apostles and the "Keys to the Kingdom of Heaven,"[2746] served under the great Father-god Ahura Mazda, the god of light, against Angra Mainyu, the god of darkness. After overcoming Satanic forces (symbolized in the slaying of a bull)[2747] Mithra conferred the gift of life (vegetation and animals) on humanity.[2748] His celibate militaristic followers in Rome called themselves "Soldiers for Mithras," while the god himself was variously entitled: "Light of the World," "Helios the Rising Sun," and the "Sun of Righteousness."[2749]

During his life Mithra, also known as the "Logos" or "Word of God,"[2750] did many good deeds, wrought numerous miracles (such as raising the dead, healing the sick, casting out devils), preached ethical doctrines, taught the Final Judgement and the Last Days (in which the forces of light and darkness would battle, destroying the earth), and redeemed Mankind for its sins through baptism in the blood of bulls (in the *Taurobolium*)[2751] and lambs ("washed in the blood of the Lamb"). During the 1st Century A.D. the Sun entered the astrological sign Aries the Ram (known in Persia as the "Lamb") during the sacred season. Thus lambs were often sacrificed in the Mithraic Mystery cults.[2752]

Mithraism included several Holy Trinities, the first made up of Heaven (Jupiter), Earth (Juno), and the Ocean (Neptune); the second, known as the "Triple Mithra," which was comprised of a representation of the double incarnation of Mithra, the two torch-bearing Dadophori (*Cauti* and *Cautopati*), and Mithra the tauroctonous hero himself, imaged as Venus the Morning Star[2753] (a motif later appended by the Church to The Myth of Christ).[2754] A true Sun-god or Son-god, the Greeks calculated his occult number as 365, the number of days in one solar year.[2755]

Mithra's ascetic, dualistic, male-only religion (women worshiped the goddess Cybele) was one of justice, order,[2756] intellectual truth, moral purity, and spiritual righteousness.[2757] It required its members to undergo 12 difficult episodes or challenges, in order to ascend upward through 7 degrees of initiation:

1) Gryphon or Raven (*Corvus*), protected by Mercury.
2) Crow or Bride (*Nymphus*), protected by Venus.
3) Soldier (*Miles*), protected by Mars.
4) Lion (*Leo*), protected by Jupiter.
5) Persian (*Peres*), protected by the Moon.
6) Bull (*Bromios*) or Runner of the Sun (*Heliodromus*), protected by the Sun.
7) Father (*Pater*), protected by Saturn.[2758]

The Catholic Church later patterned its catechumens on the Mithraic initiates who participated in these seven degrees, renaming them "The Seven Sacraments."[2759] Of this and other Mithraic borrowings by the Church, Pike writes:

> The celebration of the Mysteries of Mithras was also styled a *mass*; and the ceremonies used were the same. There were found all the *sacraments* of the Catholic Church, even the breath of *confirmation*. The *Priest* of Mithras promised the initiates *deliverance from sin*, by means of *confession* and *baptism*, and a *future life* of happiness or misery. He celebrated the oblation of *bread*, image of the *resurrection*. The *baptism of newly-born children, extreme unction, confession of sins*,—all belonged to the Mithraic rites. The candidate was *purified by a species of baptism, a mark was impressed upon his forehead*, he offered *bread and water*, pronouncing certain mysterious words.[2760]

After they were baptized in a pool of water[2761] to "wash away their guilty stains,"[2762] the neophytes of Mithra participated in the "Lord's Supper," a sacramental Eucharist or Love Feast[2763] which surrounded the partaking of a cake of bread (with a cross on it) and a consecrated cup of water or wine.[2764] A solar crucifix was then drawn on their foreheads,[2765] and they were given images of the Resurrection, a crown and sword, and Mithra hanging on a tree. Emphasis was placed on living a pure life and Mithra's chief priest was allowed only one marriage (no divorce).[2766]

The pre-Christian Pagan "Christmas," December 25,[2767] was celebrated annually in honor of the Great Virgin-Mother (the constellation Virgo) who gave "birth" to the infant Sun/Son-god Mithra at the Winter Solstice each year.[2768] The various qualities of the Great Mother were long personified in a host of minor goddesses, many who were associated with fertility, children, and home. Thus, it was only natural that, as the Venerable Bede noted, in ancient times Anglo-Saxons referred to Christmas Eve as *Modraniht*, "The Night of the Mothers."[2769]

As a Sun-god or Son-god, Lord Mithra's holy day fell on the first day of the week, which naturally was named after him: the Sun's Day (Sunday), the "Lord's Day." On the final day of his life at the Spring Equinox (Eostre or "Easter," the Pagan symbol of the victory of light over darkness),[2770] he held a "Last Supper" with his followers (where they ate the flesh and blood of the sacred bull),[2771] and was crucified.[2772] The "rock-born" savior was the "living stone" upon which his church was built. Thus after death his body was placed in a rock tomb, from which he resurrected into Heaven[2773] on the third day.[2774]

From his throne in the Afterlife Mithra continues to aid his faithful devotees, promising eternal life to those who live godly lives and eternal punishment for those who do not. The head deity of Mithraism, the most popular religion in the Roman Empire, Mithra was the seen as the Judge, the "Savior of all men," and the "destroyer of the wicked." His followers addressed him as the "Holy Word" and the "Holy One."[2775] Mithra was a member of the Persian Holy Trinity, whose other two members were Ahura Mazda and Apam Napat, a triad that was taken over, like his birthday on December 25,[2776] wholesale by the Church after the 5th Century.[2777] The Persian Trinity derived from the earlier Indian one, comprised of Mitra, Varuna, and Indra (later known in Asia Minor as the Holy Trinity of Zeus, Poseidon, and Hades).[2778]

It has been truly said that if Christianity had not appeared on the scene Mithraism would today be the religion of Europe.[2779] The complete list of similarities between Mithraism and Christianity, not to mention the countless borrowings by the latter of the former, are too numerous to catalog here, proving that, contrary to orthodox thought, Christianity did not replace Mithraism, but instead assimilated it.[2780] Pike writes:

> Mithras was the Sun-God of the Persians; and was fabled to have been born in a grotto or cave, at the winter solstice. His feasts were celebrated at that period, at the moment when the sun commenced to return Northward, and to increase the length of the days. This was the great Feast of the Magian

religion. The Roman Calendar, published in the time of Constantine, at which period his worship began to gain ground in the Occident, fixed his feast-day on the 25th of December. His statues and images were inscribed, *Deo-Soli invicto Mithrae*—to the invincible Sun-God Mithras. *Nomen invictum Sol Mithra. Soli Omnipotenti Mithrae.* To him, gold, incense, and myrrh were consecrated. "Thee," says Martianus Capella, in his hymn to the Sun, "the dwellers on the Nile adore as Serapis, and Memphis worships as Osiris; in the sacred rites of Persia thou art Mithras, in Phrygia, Attis, and Libya bows down to thee as Ammon, and Phoenician Byblos as Adonis; and thus the whole world adores thee under different names."[2781]

Robertson writes:

Now . . . arises the great question, How came such a cultus [like Mithraism] to die out of the Roman and Byzantine empire after making its way so far and holding its ground so long? The answer to that question has never, I think, been fully given, and is for the most part utterly evaded, though part of it has been suggested often enough. The truth is, as aforesaid, that *Mithraism was not overthrown; it was merely transformed.*

It had gone too far to be overthrown: the question was whether it should continue to rival Christianity or be absorbed by it. While [the Pagan Emperor] Julian lived, Mithraism had every prospect of increased vogue and prestige; for the Emperor expressly adopted it as his own cultus. "To thee," he makes Hermes say to him, "I have given to know Mithras, thy Father. Be it thine to follow his precepts, so that he may be unto thee, all thy life long, an assured harbour and refuge; and, when thou must needs go hence, full of good hope, thou mayest take this God as a propitious guide." It is the very tone and spirit of the cult of the Christ; and as we have seen, the Christian Fathers with almost one consent saw in Mithraism the great rival of their own worship. *The spirit of exclusiveness which Christianity had inherited from Judaism—a spirit alien to the older paganism but essential to the building up of an organised and revenue-raising hierarchy in the later Roman empire—made a struggle between the cults inevitable.*

The critical moment in the career alike of Mithraism and of Christianity was the death of Julian, who, though biased in favour of all the older Gods, gave a special adherence to the

War-God Mithra. Had Julian triumphed in the East and reigned thirty years, matters might have gone a good deal differently with Christianity. His death, however, was peculiarly disastrous to Mithraism; for he fell at the hands of the Persian foe, the most formidable enemy of the later empire; and Mithra was "the Persian" par excellence, and the very God of the Persian host. There can be little doubt that [Emperor] Jovian's instant choice of Christianity as his State creed was in large measure due to this circumstance; and that at such a juncture the soldiery would be disposed to acquiesce, seeking a better omen. Yet, even apart from this, we are not entitled to suppose that Mithraism could ever have become the general faith, save by very systematic and prolonged action on the part of the State, to the end of assimilating its organisation with that of the Church.

. . . We may say indeed that the preference for such a God as Jesus over such a one as Mithra was in full keeping with the evolution of æsthetic taste in the Christian period. Some may to-day even find it hard to conceive how the Invincible God of the Sun could ever call forth the love and devotion given to the suffering Christ. As we have seen, *Mithra too was a suffering God, slain and rising again, victorious over death*; so that to him went out in due season all the passion of the weeping worship of Adonis; but it is in his supernal and glorious aspect that the monuments persistently present him; and for the decaying ancient world it was still possible to take some joy in the vision of beauty and strength. Many there must still have been who wondered, not at the adoration given to the mystically figured Persian, beautiful as Apollo, triumphant as Aries, but at the giving of any similar devotion to the gibbeted Jew [Jesus], in whose legend figured tax-gatherers and lepers, epileptics and men blind from birth, domestic traitors and cowardly disciples. Ethical teaching there was in Mithraism; and for the Mithraists it would be none the less moving as coming from an eternal conqueror, the type of dominion.

But even as the best Mithraic monuments themselves tell of the decline of the great art of Greece, so the art of Christism tells of a hastening dissolution in which æsthetic sense and craftsmanship alike sink to the levels of barbarism. In the spheres alike of Byzantium and of papal Rome, the sculptured Mithra would yearly meet fewer eyes that looked lovingly on grace and delightedly on beauty; more and more eyes that recoiled pessimistically from comeliness and turned vacantly from allegorical or esoteric symbols.

The more we study the survival of Christianity, the more clearly do we see that, in spite of the stress of ecclesiastical strife over metaphysical dogmas, the hold of the creed over the people was a matter of concrete and narrative appeal to every-day intelligence. *Byzantines and barbarians alike were held by literalism, not by the unintelligible: for both alike the symbol had to become a fetish; and for the Dark Ages the symbol of the cross was much more plausibly appealing than that of the God slaying the zodiacal bull.*

Other substitutions followed the same law of psychological economy. Thus it was that Christianity turned the mystic rock, Petra, first into the Christ, but later into the chief disciple Petros [Peter]; made an actual tunic of the mystic seamless robe of the Osirian and Mazdean mysteries, the symbol of light and sky; caused to be performed at a wedding-feast, for the convenience of the harder drinkers among the guests, the Dionysiak miracle of turning water into wine; made Jesus walk on the water not merely in poetry and symbol, as did Poseidon, but for the utilitarian purpose of trying Peter's faith and saving him; and put the scourge of Osiris in the Lord's hand for the castigation of those who defiled the temple by unspiritual traffic. There can be little question as to which plane of doctrine was the more popular. *The Christian tales, in a different moral climate, represent exactly the commonplace impulse which built up the bulk of Greek mythology by way of narratives that reduced to an anecdotal basis mystic sculptures and mysterious rites.*

But that was not all. *The fatal weakness of Mithraism, as pitted against Christianity, was that its very organisation was esoteric. For, though an esoteric grade is a useful attraction, and was so employed by the Church, a wholly esoteric institution can never take hold of the ignorant masses. Mithraism was always a sort of freemasonry, never a public organisation. What the Christians did was to start, like Rome herself, from a republican basis, combining the life-elements of the self-supporting religious associations of the Greeks with the connecting organisation of the Jewish synagogues, and then to proceed to build up a great organisation on the model of that of republican and imperial Rome—an organisation so august for an era of twilight that the very tradition of it could serve the later world to live by for a thousand years. The Christian Church renewed the spell of imperial Rome, and brought actual force to make good intellectual* weakness. And so we read that the Mithraic worship was by Christian physical force suppressed in Rome and Alexandria, in the year 376 or 377, at a time when, as the inscriptions show, it was making much headway.

At Rome, the deed was done by the order of the Christian prefect Gracchus; but the proceeding was specifically one of ecclesiastical malice, since even so pious an emperor as Gratian dared not yet decree a direct assault upon an esteemed pagan cult. But, *once begun, the movement of destruction spread, and the Church which still makes capital of the persecution it suffered at pagan hands, outwardly annihilated the rival it could not spiritually defeat. In an old Armenian history of the reign of Tiridates, it is told how St. Gregory destroyed in the town of Pakaiaridj the temple of Mihr [Mithra] "called the son of Aramazd," took its treasure "for the poor," and consecrated the ground to the Church.*

But such acts of piratical violence, which had been made easy by the earlier check to Mithraism in its special field, the army, only *obscured the actual capitulation made by the Church to the Mithraic as to the other cults which it absorbed. Even the usages which it could not conveniently absorb, and therefore repudiated, prevailed within its own fold for centuries, so that in the eighth century we find Church Councils commanding proselytes no more to pay worship to fanes and rocks. And there were other survivals. But all that was a trifle as compared with the actual survival of Mithraic symbols and rites in the very worship of Christ. As to the sacrifice of the lamb we have seen; and though at the end of the seventh century a general Council ventured to resist the general usage of picturing Christ as a lamb, the veto was useless; the symbol survived.*

Some Mithraic items went, but more remained. The Christian bishop went through a ceremony of espousing the Church, following the old mystery in which occurred the formula, "Hail to thee, new spouse; hail, new light." His mitre was called a crown, or tiara, which answered to the headdress of Mithra and the Mithraic priests, as to those of the priests of Egypt; he wore red military boots, now said to be "emblematical of that spiritual warfare on which he had entered," in reality borrowed from the military worship of Mithra, perhaps as early as Jovian. And *the higher mysteries of communion, divine sacrifice, and resurrection, as we have seen, were as much Mithraic as Christist, so that a Mithraist could turn to the Christian worship and find his main rites unimpaired, lightened only of the burden of initiative austerities, stripped of the old obscure* mysticism, and with all things turned to the literal and the concrete, in sympathy with the waning of knowledge and philosophy throughout the world.

The Mithraic Christians actually continued to celebrate Christmas Day as the birthday of the sun, despite the censures of the Pope; and their Sunday had been adopted by the supplanting faith. When they listened to the Roman litany of the holy name of Jesus, they knew they were listening to the very epithets of the Sun-God—God of the skies, purity of the eternal light, king of glory, sun of justice, strong God, father of the ages to come, angel of great counsel. In the epistles of Paul they found Christian didactics tuned to the very key of their mystical militarism. Their priests had been wont to say that "he of the cap" was "himself a Christian." They knew that "the Good Shepherd" was a name of Apollo; that Mithra, like Hermes and Jesus, carried the lamb on his shoulders; that both were mediators, both creators, both judges of the dead.

Like some of their sacred caves, and so many pagan temples, the Christian churches looked toward the east. Their soli-lunar midnight worship was preserved in midnight services, which carried on the purpose of the midnight meetings of the early Christians, who had simply followed Essenian, Egyptian, Asiatic, and Mithraic usage; there being no basis for the orthodox notion that these secret meetings were due to fear of persecution. Their myazd or mizd, or sacred cake, was preserved in the mass, which possibly copied the very name.

Above all, their mystic Rock, Petra, was presented to them in the concrete as the rock Peter, the foundation of the Church. It has been elsewhere shown that the myth of the traitorous Peter connects with those of Proteus and Janus as well as with that of Mithra, inasmuch as Janus also had "two faces," led the twelve months as Mithra presided over the zodiacal signs and Peter over the twelve apostles, and, like Proteus and Peter and the Time-God in the Mithraic cult, bore the heavenly keys. Here again the mythic development of Peter probably follows on that of Jesus; at all events *Jesus too has constructively several of the attributes of Proteus-Janus: as "I am the door"; "I stand at the door and knock"; "I am in the Father and the Father in me" (equals Janus with the two faces, old and young, seated in the midst of the twelve altars); "I have the keys of death and of Hades." The function of Janus as God of War is also associable with the dictum, "I came not to bring peace, but a sword."*

Finally, the epiphany is in January. But there is to be noted the further remarkable coincidence that in the Egyptian Book of the

Dead Petra is the name of the divine doorkeeper of heaven—a circumstance which suggests an ancient connection between the Egyptian and Asiatic cults. On the other hand, the early Christian sculptures which represent the story of Jesus and Peter and the cock-crowing suggest that it originated as an interpretation of some such sculpture; and the frequent presence of the cock, as a symbolic bird of the Sun-God, in Mithraic monuments, raises again a presumption of a Mithraic source. There is even some ground for the view that the legend of St. George is but an adaptation of that of Mithra; and it is not unlikely that St. Michael, who in the Christian east is the bearer of the heavenly keys, is in this aspect an adaptation from the Persian War-God. The dragon-slayer clearly derives from Babylon.

From the Mithraists too, apparently, came the doctrine of purgatory, nowhere set forth in the New Testament save in the spurious epistle of Peter. And though their supreme symbol of Mithra slaying the bull was perforce set aside, being incapable of assimilation, they knew that the Virgin Mother was but a variant of the Goddess-Mothers whose cults had at various times been combined with those of Mithra, and some of whose very statues served as Madonnas; even as the doctrines of the Logos and the Holy Spirit and the Trinity were borrowed from their own and older Asiatic cults and those of Egypt alike.

It has chanced, indeed, that those Christian sects which most fully adopted the theosophies of Paganism have disappeared under the controlling power of the main organisation, which, as we have said, *held by a necessity of its existence to a concrete and literal system, and for the same reason to a rigidly fixed set of dogmas. We know that the Gnostics adopted Mithra, making his name into a mystic charm,* from which (spelling it Μειθρας) they got the number 365, as from the mystic name Abraxas. Manichæism, too, the greatest and most tenacious of all the Christian schisms, carried on its ascetic front the stamp of the Persian environment in which it arose, and visibly stands for a blending of the ascetic and mystic elements of Mithraism and Christianity. For the celebration of the slain Christ it practically substituted that of the slain Manes, at the paschal season; *reducing the crucifixion to a mere allegory of the cult of vegetation, and identifying the power and wisdom of the Saviour-God with the Sun and Moon.*

Neither its adherents nor its opponents avowed that it was thus a fresh variant of Mithraism; but the Mithraists cannot have failed to see and signalise alike the heretical and the orthodox adaptation, and it is clear that Mithraism not only entered into Manichæism but prepared the way for it in the West. *The more reason why Mithras should be tabooed by the organised Church. Thus, then, we can understand why the very name seemed at length to be blotted out. And yet, despite all forcible suppression, not only do the monuments of the faith endure to tell how for centuries it distanced its rival; not only do its rites and ceremonies survive as part of the very kernel of the Christian worship; but its record remains unknowingly graven in the legend on the dome of the great Christian temple of Rome, destined to teach to later times a lesson of human history, and of the unity of human religion, more enduring than the sectarian faith that is proclaimed within.*[2782]

As Robertson alludes to above, in the year A.D. 376 the Catholic Church seized Mithra's cave-temple on the Vatican Hill, then adopted the title of his high priest, Pater Patrum[2783]—which became Papa or Pope.[2784] Even the Mithraic Pagan festival of Epiphany was assimilated by the Church, though it was not officially adopted until 813.[2785] Cumont takes a more conservative though no less penetrating view of the many parallels between Mithraism and Christianity:

> *The struggle between the two rival religions was the more stubborn as their characters were the more alike.* The adepts of both formed secret conventicles, closely united, the members of which gave themselves the name of "*Brothers.*" The rites which they practised offered numerous analogies. The sectaries of the Persian god [Mithra], like the Christians, purified themselves by *baptism*; received, by a species of *confirmation*, the power necessary to combat the spirits of evil; and expected from *a Lord's Supper salvation of body and soul.* Like the latter, they also held Sunday sacred, and *celebrated the birth of the Sun on the 25*[th] *of December*, the same day on which Christmas has been celebrated, since the fourth century at least. They both preached a categorical system of *ethics*, regarded *asceticism* as meritorious, and counted among their principal virtues *abstinence* and *continence, renunciation and self-control.* Their conceptions of the world and of the destiny of man were similar. They both admitted the existence of a *Heaven* inhabited by beatified ones, situate in the upper regions, and of a *Hell* peopled by demons, situate in the bowels of the earth. They both placed a *Flood* at the beginning of history; they both assigned as the source of their traditions a *primitive revelation*; they both, finally, believed in the *immortality of the soul*, in a *last judgment*, and in a

resurrection of the dead, consequent upon a final conflagration of the universe.

We have seen that *the theology of the Mysteries made of Mithra a "mediator" equivalent to the Alexandrian Logos. Like him, Christ also was a [Logos], an intermediary between his celestial father and men, and like him he also was one of a trinity. These resemblances were certainly not the only ones that pagan exegesis established between the two religions, and the figure of the tauroctonous god reluctantly immolating his victim that he might create and save the human race, was certainly compared to the picture of the redeemer sacrificing his own person for the salvation of the world.*

On the other hand, *the ecclesiastical writers, reviving a metaphor of the prophet Malachi, contrasted the "Sun of justice" with the "invincible Sun," and consented to see in the dazzling orb which illuminated men a symbol of Christ, "the light of the world."* Should we be astonished if the multitudes of devotees failed always to observe the subtle distinctions of the [Church] doctors, and if in obedience to a pagan custom they rendered to the radiant star of day the homage which orthodoxy reserved for God? *In the fifth century, not only heretics, but even faithful [Christian] followers, were still wont to bow their heads toward its dazzling disc as it rose above the horizon, and to murmur the prayer, "Have mercy upon us."*

The resemblances between the two hostile churches were so striking as to impress even the minds of antiquity. *From the third century, the Greek [Pagan] philosophers were wont to draw parallels between the Persian Mysteries and Christianity which were evidently entirely in favor of the former. The [Christian] Apologists also dwelt on the analogies between the two religions, and explained them as a Satanic travesty of the holiest rites of their religion. If the polemical works of the Mithraists had been preserved, we should doubtless have heard the same accusation hurled back upon their Christian adversaries.*

We cannot presume to unravel to-day a question which divided contemporaries and which shall doubtless forever remain insoluble. We are too imperfectly acquainted with the dogmas and liturgies of Roman Mazdaism, as well as with the development of primitive Christianity, to say definitely what mutual influences were operative in their simultaneous evolution. But be this as it may, resemblances do not necessarily suppose an imitation. Many correspondences between the Mithraic doctrine and the Catholic faith are explicable by their common Oriental origin. Nevertheless, certain ideas and certain ceremonies must necessarily have passed from the one cult to the other; but in the majority of cases we rather suspect this transference than clearly perceive it.

Apparently the attempt was made to discern in the legend of the Iranian hero [Mithra] the counterpart of the life of Jesus, and the disciples of the Magi probably drew a direct contrast between the Mithraic worship of the shepherds, the Mithraic communion and ascension, and those of the Gospels. The rock of generation, which had given birth to the genius of light, was even compared to the immovable rock, emblem of Christ, upon which the Church was founded; and the crypt in which the bull had perished was made the counterpart of that in which Christ is said to have been born at Bethlehem. But this strained parallelism could result in nothing but a caricature. It was a strong source of inferiority for Mazdaism that it believed in only a mythical redeemer. That unfailing wellspring of religious emotion supplied by the teachings and the passion of the God sacrificed on the cross, never flowed for the disciples of Mithra.

On the other hand, *the orthodox and heretical liturgies of Christianity, which gradually sprang up during the first centuries of our era, could find abundant inspiration in the Mithraic Mysteries, which of all the pagan religions offered the most affinity with Christian institutions.* We do not know whether the ritual of the sacraments and the hopes attaching to them suffered alteration through the influence of Mazdean dogmas and practices. Perhaps the custom of invoking the Sun three times each day,—at dawn, at noon, and at dusk,—was reproduced in the daily prayers of the Church, and *it appears certain that the commemoration of the Nativity was set for the 25th of December, because it was at the winter solstice that the rebirth of the invincible god, the Natalis invicti, was celebrated. In adopting this date, which was universally distinguished by sacred festivities, the ecclesiastical authority purified in some measure the profane usages which it could not suppress.*

The only domain in which we can ascertain in detail the extent to which Christianity imitated Mithraism is that of art. *The Mithraic sculpture, which had been first developed, furnished the ancient Christian marble-cutters with a large number of models, which they adopted or adapted. For example, they drew inspiration from the figure of Mithra causing the living waters to leap forth by the blows of his arrows, to create the figure of Moses smiting with his rod* the rock of Horeb. Faithful to an inveterate tradition, they even reproduced the figures of cosmic divinities, like the Heavens and the Winds, the worship of which the new faith had expressly proscribed; and we find on the sarcophagi, in miniatures, and even on the portals of the Romance Churches, evidences of the influence exerted by the imposing compositions that adorned the sacred grottos of Mithra.

. . . Even the allegorical figures of the cosmic cycle which the devotees of the Persian god had reproduced in great profusion (for nature was for them divine throughout) were adopted by Christianity, although in essence they were diametrically opposed to its spirit. So with the images of the Heavens, the Earth, and the Ocean, of the Sun, the Moon, and the Planets, and of the signs of the Zodiac, of the Winds, the Seasons, and the Elements, so frequent on the Christian sarcophagi, the mosaics, and miniatures.

The mediocre compositions which the artists had conceived to represent the episodes of the legend of Mithra appeared also worthy of imitation to the Christian ages, which were even more powerless than their predecessors to shake off the traditions of the workshops. When, after the triumph of the Church, Christian sculptors were confronted with subjects hitherto unattempted, and found themselves under the embarrassing obligations of depicting on stone the personages and stories of the Bible, they were happy in the opportunity of being able to draw inspiration from the portrayals which the Persian Mysteries had popularized. A few alterations in costume and attitude transformed a pagan scene into a Christian picture. Mithra discharging his arrows against the rock became Moses causing the waters of the mountain of Horeb to gush forth; the Sun, raising his ally out of the Ocean, served to express the ascension of Elijah in the chariot of fire; and to the time of the Middle Ages the type of the tauroctonous god was perpetuated in the images of Samson rending the lion.[2786]

Ghillany writes:

The worship offered to Jesus after His death by the Christian community is . . . not derived from pure Judaism, but from a Judaism influenced by oriental [Pagan] religions. *The influence of the cult of Mithra, for example, is unmistakable. In it, as in Christianity, we find the virgin-birth, the star, the wise men, the cross, and the resurrection.* Were it not for the human sacrifice of the Mithra cult, the idea which is operative in the Supper, of eating and drinking the flesh and blood of the Son of Man, would be inexplicable.[2787]

The remains of ancient Mithraic temples, *Mithraca*, have been found as far away from Rome as England and Germany (the latter country in which they were the most common),[2788] illustrating the popularity of Mithraism.[2789] There is no doubt that this widespread Pagan Faith would have become the dominant religion in Europe had it not been suppressed and finally overshadowed by Christianity in the 4th Century.[2790] Writes Cumont:

> Mithraism reached the apogee of its power toward the middle of the third century, and it appeared for a moment as if the world was on the verge of becoming Mithraic.[2791]

Only the invasions of the Barbarians (3rd Century), the ensuing widespread sacking and burning of Mithraic temples, and the concurrent swift rise of Christianity under Constantine (early 4th Century) and Theodosius (late 4th Century) prevented the world from becoming so.[2792]

Despite being ousted from his ancient throne, this 6,000 year old deity and his Christ-like solar cult have survived into the modern world, worshiped by millions around the globe under the names of both Mithra and Jesus. Mithraism, for example, greatly influenced the 19th-Century secret society known as the Carbonari ("Charcoal Burners"),[2793] while London, England, still has its own Mithraic temple.[2794] See BUDDHA, CHRISTIANITY, JESUS, KRISHNA, OSIRIS, PETER, PYTHAGORAS, ROCK, SAVIOR, TEACHER OF RIGHTEOUSNESS.

MONOTHEISM: Being alien to the ancient Israelite mind, the concept of monotheism (a religion built around the idea of one Supreme God) is not found in the earliest books of the Old Testament, and a clear denial of other father-gods does not appear until the 6th Century B.C., in Second Isaiah (Chapters 40-55).[2795] Nonetheless, according to traditional Christianity the Church absorbed the idea from the late Hebrews (early Jews)—which was only natural since Christianity began as a mystical offshoot of Essenic Judaism (and Pagan Gnosticism).[2796] In mystical Christianity, however, which takes a more pragmatic and scientific approach to this subject, it is acknowledged that monotheism began, as with so many other aspects of Christianity, in ancient Pagan Egypt.

It was around the solar cult of Ra (sometimes confused with, and thus also variously known as, Amon, Amon-Ra, and later Aton or Aten) that the world's first known monotheistic religion began (there were, no doubt, earlier Pagan monotheistic belief systems; however, Egypt's seems to be the first recorded). This occurred under the reign of the Pharaoh Akhenaten (Amenhotep IV),[2797] who ruled from 1375 to 1358 B.C. Amon means "Hidden"; Aton means "Sun disk." It is important to note that Akhenaten did not worship the Sun as a literal celestial object.[2798] Breasted points out that however evident the Heliopolitan origin of the new state religion might be, it was not merely sun-worship; the word Aton was employed in place of the old word for "god" (nuter), and the god is clearly distinguished from the material sun.[2799]

In other words, Akhenaten was venerating the one true God as manifested in every human being under the name the (Indwelling) Christ,[2800] whose symbol has long been the Sun or Son, and whose deification was universally personified as the Sun-God/Son-God.

Though this first monotheistic religion of the Sun-god, known as Atenism,[2801] was later rejected and discarded by the intensely polytheistic Egyptians after Akhenaten's death, the idea of worshiping a single Sun/Son-deity was eagerly adopted by the then henotheistic Israelites.[2802] German atheist Sigmund Freud wrote an entire book on this intriguing subject.[2803] As proof of this Egyptian-to-Israelite appropriation, see Psalm 104 for an almost exact copy of Akhenaten's monotheistic poem to the Sun-god, "Hymn to the Aton."[2804]

From Judaism, where God is called *shemesh tsddhakah*, "the Sun of Righteousness,"[2805] the idea of monotheism passed into mainstream Christianity through 1st-Century Jewish-Gnostic sects, like the Essenes, who were by then referring to God, in the form of Jesus Christ, as *ben tsddhakah*, "the Son of Righteousness."[2806]

Yet, to this day, despite Christianity's professed "monotheism," the Church steadfastly continues to cling to the polytheism of the Old Religion (as Paul did).[2807] Nowhere is this more clearly illustrated than in the Bible itself, which reveals a great Pagan-Judeo-Christian Pantheon of countless gods, goddesses, spirits, demons, beasts, monsters, dragons, devils, and angels.[2808]

Our polytheistic Christian worship is also evident in the following yearly Christianized holidays: Christmas, a Pagan Winter Solstice celebration dedicated to the great Pagan Sun/Son-god;[2809] Halloween (All Soul's Day), a Fall Equinox celebration in which deceased ancestors were (and still are) venerated and appeased through magical rites; Easter, a Spring Equinox celebration ruled by the Pagan Spring-goddess who gave it her name: Eostre; Midsummer or St. John's Day, a Pagan Summer Solstice holy day also dedicated to the Sun-god; and so on.

Evidence for Christian polytheism, that is, "the Paganism in our Christianity," is so vast that it could easily provide material for an entire book. And indeed, one man, Christian author Arthur Weigall, penned a brilliant work with that exact title in 1928.[2810] Like W. Y. Evans-Wentz and countless other religious scholars, in my many years of research (nearly a half century) into traditional Christianity, I have yet to find a single doctrine, idea, belief, ritual, or myth that I consider to be original to our Faith.[2811]

This makes orthodox Christianity the most syncretistic, theocrasiatic, theoxeniatic religion in the history of humanity. This is not surprising, however.

As Saint Augustine wisely observed, Christianity "has existed since the beginning of the human race."[2812] See ASTROLOGY, BUDDHA, CHRIST, CHRISTIANITY, CHRISTMAS, ESSENES, GNOSTICISM, GODS AND GODDESSES, JESUS, KRISHNA, MITHRA, MOSES, PYTHAGORAS, WAY OF THE LORD.

MOSES: In institutional Christianity Moses is the historical Levite son of Amram and Jochebed, and the brother of Aaron and Miriam; a miracle-worker who led the exodus of the Israelites out of Egypt. Sometimes he represents the law of Israel.[2813] In mystical Christianity it is recognized that, like Joshua, David, and Solomon, there is no extra-biblical evidence for Moses.[2814] We have no mention of him, for instance, outside the written traditions of the Jews, and since he was completely unknown to the ancient Egyptians, his legend could have only originated among the early Hebrews.[2815] Thus, his inclusion in the Bible means that he is an esoteric symbol, in this case of the divine laws of God that are always at work within us,[2816] human souls striving for perfection in a law-governed universe.[2817]

Since much of Moses' legend derives from older Pagan gods, such as Oedipus, Karna, Paris, Telephos, Perseus, Hercules, Gilgamesh, Amphion, Zethos, and Bacchus (the latter whose divine rod could transform into a serpent and draw water from stones),[2818] and earlier human leaders, such as Romulus, the co-founder of Rome, and Sargon of Agade, the founder of Babylonia (whose mother laid him in a basket in the Euphrates River),[2819] we must turn to more esoteric sources to unveil his true mystical nature.

The name Moses hints at the symbolism behind the figure: in Hebrew Moses (*Mosheh* or *Mo-Sheh*) is connected to ancient words that are in turn related to words for the Sun, such as *Shemmah, Shammah, Shemesh, Shim, Shem, Sham, Shamas, Shemsi,* etc.[2820] Going further back, however, we find that Moses, or more specifically *mose*, is an Egyptian word meaning "child" or "is born," and was commonly used on monuments in the names of Pagan Egyptian gods, such as Ammon-Mose,[2821] and pharaohs, like Ra-Moses (Ramesses) and Thoth-Moses (Tuthmosis).[2822] Christian mystic Paul wrote the following to the Corinthians:

> Seeing then that we have such hope, we use great plainness of speech: And not as Moses, which put a vail over his face, that the children of Israel could not steadfastly look to the end of that which is abolished: But *their minds were blinded*: for until this day remaineth the same vail untaken away in the reading of the old testament; *which vail is done away in Christ.*
>
> But even unto this day, *when Moses is read, the vail is upon their heart. Nevertheless when it shall turn to the Lord, the vail shall be taken away. Now the Lord is that Spirit: and where the Spirit of the Lord is, there is liberty. But we all, with open face beholding as in a glass the glory of the Lord, are changed into the same image from*

> *glory to glory, even as by the Spirit of the Lord.*[2823]

Moses also represents the earth, the Creative Force, the Procreative Energy, which the Greeks personified as the horned Nature-god Pan, and the Romans personified as the horned Nature-god Faunus.[2824] This is why Christian mystic Michelangelo (and other early artists) depicted Moses with horns,[2825] for the Old Testament Prophet is the Genetic Ram (Aries)[2826] in ancient Hebrew disguise. This makes him, in turn, yet another version of the *Demon est Deus Inversus*,[2827] that is, the "Devil is God Inverted,"[2828] the same image assimilated by early Christians to the figure of Satan or the Devil.[2829] Furthermore, Moses is the "serpent" of Genesis, Lucifer, the "Bringer of Light," whose Gnostic wisdom brought spiritual enlightenment to Adam and Eve, angering the Elohim (mistranslated as "God"),[2830] the seven major deities of the ancient Hebrew and Pagan Pantheon.[2831] All of this is revealed in the book of Exodus. In the King James Version we read:

> When Moses came down from mount Sinai with the two tables of testimony in Moses' hand, when he came down from the mount, that Moses wist not that the skin of his face shone while he talked with him.[2832]

But this is merely the priestly version, which has been heavily tampered with. The original in the Latin Vulgate reads:

> And when Moses came down from Mount Sinai, he held two tables of the testimony, and he did not know that his face was *horned* from conversation with the Lord.[2833]

Orthodox scribes, not comprehending the symbolism of horns (the Vulgate's *facies cornuta*, "horned face"), assumed that the original writer had meant to say that Moses' face was shining like "rays" of sunshine, so they rewrote the passage to correlate with their misunderstanding.[2834] In the process, however, they erased the important esoteric message of the original text, embedded in the story by its mystical author: horns are symbols of divine strength and celestial powers as embodied in Nature.[2835] Moses' horns are thus the same as the horns of the Egyptian cow-goddess Hathor,[2836] Luke's "horn of salvation,"[2837] the seven horns of the Revelator's lamb,[2838] and the ten horns of the Revelator's dragon.[2839]

Along with Moses, many other ancient figures were portrayed with horns, such as Dionysus, Bacchus, Zagreus, Kore, Cernunnos, Persephone, and Alexander the Great. As a symbol the horn appears in scores of early myths, among them Fortuna's "horn of plenty," the horn of the goat Amalthea, and the horn of the river-god Achelous.[2840] Once again we see the universal thread of spiritual truth and knowledge running through and connecting *all* of the world's religions. See

ADVERSARY, DEVIL, HELL, MOUTH OF GOD, SATAN, SERPENT.

MOTHER: In traditional Christianity there is no female equivalent of "God the Father," that is, "Goddess the Mother," and the Church is all the poorer for it. But it was not always so, and even today countless Christian mystics recognize and venerate the Divine Feminine, the archetypal symbol of love, receptivity, maternalness, devotion, and the human Soul.[2841]

Still, orthodox Christians continue to worship Goddess, even though they do not realize it, for their pastors will not reveal the secret to them and most will not question Church teachings. If the Great Virgin-Mother-Goddess still exists within the traditional Christian Church, where is she? Like so many other figures, beliefs, rituals, doctrines, and myths that the Church has borrowed from Paganism, she is hiding in plain sight—if one will but take the time to look for her.

After adopting the Pagan Virgin-Goddess (and her many minor manifestations), the early mainstream Church tore down her temples[2842] and built churches over them, then subsumed her into the figure of both the Virgin Mary[2843] and the Holy Spirit,[2844] along with a host of bogus female saints—after which hagiographers and mythologists heavily embellished their so-called "biographies."

Among them were: the Three Marys (at the foot of Jesus Cross),[2845] Brigid, Marina, Sophia, Eugenia, Irene, Felicity, Lucy, Philomena, Euphrosyne, Margaret, Agape, Faith, Ursula, Thecla of Iconium, Pelagia of Tarsus, Chionia, Tatiana, Agatha, Veronica, Febronia, Barbara, Thais, Ann, Euphemia, Agnes, Viviana, Afra, Christine, and Anastasia. Many if not all of these fabricated Christian figures will be found to have well-known Pagan goddess antecedents around whom they were originally based.[2846]

We can see that despite this transmogrification, this great whitewashing of feminine history, Goddess is still alive and well in Christianity, operating under a host of names and a myriad of functions. Who was the original Virgin-Mother-Goddess? She was the first Supreme Being, worshiped, as the archaeological record shows, around the world thousands of years before the idea of a male Supreme Being arose.[2847] Early peoples considered her the creator of not only the entire Universe and its laws, but the divine ruler of nature, birth, death, time, eternity, fate, truth, wisdom, and love.[2848]

Why was she considered a "virgin mother"? As prehistoric societies had no conception of the biology behind sexual reproduction—that is, of the male's contribution to conception—they believed that all females were parthenogenic: virgin mothers who created life inside their "magical" wombs autonomously and asexually.[2849] The sacrality surrounding the supernatural life-giving powers of the human female thus gave rise to humanity's earliest known religion: the cult of the great Virgin-Mother-Goddess, Divine Creatrix of the Universe and All Life.[2850]

The archetypal Virgin-Mother-Goddess is best known by her astronomical name as the constellation Virgo,[2851] but her more earthly names are also familiar.

These include:

Aditi (Indian)
Arianrhod (Welsh)
Asherah (Canaanite)
Cally Berry (Irish)
Danu (Irish)
Demeter (Greek)
Devi (Indian)
Eriu (Irish)
Eurynome (Greek)
Eve (Hebrew)
Frigg (Scandinavian)
Gaea (Greek)
Hera (Greek)
Ishtar (Babylonian)
Isis (Egyptian)
Juno (Roman)
Kali (Indian)
Kuma (Native-American)
Neith (Egyptian)
Nessa (Irish)
Nyx (Greek)
Parvati (Indian)
Rhea (Greek)
Sarah (Hebrew)
Sarasvati (Indian)
Sela (African)
Shiwanokia (Native-American)
Tai Yuan (Chinese)
Thetis (Greek)
Tiamat (Babylonian)[2852]

Aside from the Virgin Mary and the Holy Spirit, mainstream Christians will also be familiar with the Great Mother-Goddess as the book of Revelation's "woman clothed with the sun, having the moon under her feet, and on her head a crown of twelve stars."[2853] This overtly Pagan depiction of Mary was borrowed by the Revelator from ancient images of the Hindu Sun-goddess Aditi, who rode about the heavens on a lunar crescent tenderly governing her 12 children, the 12 star-signs known as Adityas.[2854] See CHRISTMAS, FATHER, GODDESS, GODS AND GODDESSES, HOLY SPIRIT, HOLY TRINITY, MARY, NATIVITY, THEALOGY, TRINITY, VIRGIN BIRTH, VIRGO.

MOUNTAIN: In the traditional Church a mountain is a literal geophysical feature; that is, a large hill, elevation, or peak.[2855] In the mystical Church a mountain is a symbol of the Higher Self (Christ), the spirit plane (God), or that cosmic state of mind called the "Kingdom of Heaven" or Christ Consciousness (moksha, satori, kensho, bodhi, wu wei, nirvana).[2856] At times mountains represent human problems or difficulties.[2857] The world's greatest mystic, our Lord Jesus, often used it in just this manner.[2858] See CHRIST CONSCIOUSNESS, GOD, VALLEY.

MOUTH OF GOD: In traditional Christianity the word mouth merely means "mouth," while the "mouth of God" is merely the "voice of the Lord."[2859] Mystical Christianity, however, ventures deep beneath the exoteric surface of orthodoxy in order to uncover the real meaning intended by the original mystical authors. In the case of the "mouth of God," we find that it is an occult phrase for the *medulla oblongata*,[2860] a pine cone shaped part of the brain, located at the lower part of the brain stem.

Although it performs a host of involuntary tasks (such as regulating blood pressure and breathing), the *medulla oblongata's* most important job is to transfer messages from the brain to the spinal cord, which is known among Christian mystics as the "Tree of Life." The Tree of Life's seven "fruits" are the seven chakras (or energy stars or light wheels) of Asian religion, up which human consciousness (the "Serpent") must climb in order to reach the top of the tree (the Crown Chakra), and attain enlightenment (Christ Consciousness). The science of "lifting up the serpent"—that is, raising human consciousness from the "Son of Man" to the "Son of God" (Kundalini Yoga)—was well-known to all of the great ancient spiritual leaders, including Moses and Jesus.[2861] In Christian mysticism these same "seven fruits" or chakras are called "the seven churches which are in Asia,"[2862] and are represented, naturally, by "seven stars."[2863]

The sacrality of the "mouth of God" has long been symbolized by the pine cone, which parallels the actual shape of the *medulla oblongata* (the original seat of the "intelligent life energy").[2864] Hence the pine cone, a symbol of immortality (since the "evergreen" tree seems to be constantly "renewing" itself), is often seen in mystical Christian art crowning not only the Tree of Life, but also the Thyrsus: the wooden staff of pre-Christian Sun-gods, saviors, and christs, like Dionysus.[2865] The pine cone itself, which can also be a symbol of the pineal gland,[2866] has ancient associations with deities like Asclepius, Attis, and Mithra.[2867]

The *medulla oblongata* is the main entranceway for the body's supply of cosmic energy, without which it could not long survive. Hence the "mouth of God" is known to Hindus as Aum or Om, to the Persians as Hom,[2868] and to Christians as the Amen,[2869] the great I AM,[2870] the Word,[2871] and the Holy Spirit.[2872] Such knowledge gives an entirely new meaning to the words of Jesus:

> It is written, "Man shall not live by bread alone, but by every word that proceedeth out of the mouth of God."[2873]

See AMEN, CHRIST, CHRIST CONSCIOUSNESS, GOD, MOSES, SERPENT, TEMPLE OF GOD, UNION WITH GOD, VOICE OF GOD, YAHWEH.

MYTH OF CHRIST: The Myth of Christ is unknown to the laity of the traditional Church, a tragedy due almost wholly to orthodox officials, most who are aware of it but choose to disregard it, and for obvious reasons: having invented it they now must continue to subscribe to it.[2874]

In the mystical Church, however, The Myth of Christ is well-known and well described as the paganization, deification, and apotheosization of the man Jesus, the greatest teacher, prophet, and healer the world has ever known; a nefarious plot to attract Pagan converts,[2875] mislead the masses, and consolidate theological, social, political, and economic power at Rome.[2876] It was initiated by

Paul (circa A.D. 40-67), the four Evangelists (circa A.D. 70-100), and countless other early Christian crusaders (all unnamed), and later completed by the Catholic Church (2nd to 12th Centuries).

The principle source for The Myth of Christ came by way of the first true Christians, the Gnostics, whose pre-Christian Messiah was known as *Enos Uthra*. Also known as *Manda da Hayye*, the Mandean legend of this Gnostic-Christian Redeemer tells us that he descended to earth in order to liberate the sparks of light (human souls) entrapped in human bodies. This imprisonment occurred because of the "fall of humanity" in primeval times. Enos Uthra, who declares "I am the Shepherd," takes human form and carries out the work of the Father. He awakens memories in Man and Woman of their true home, the Realm of Light, and under his teachings they come to recognize their divine nature. Both the redeemed and the Redeemer then rise again into the heavenly world of Light and Spirit.[2877]

The Myth of Christ, constructed around the archetypal and all-too familiar "oriental wonder-worker" theme, as well as the standard ancient "suffering servant" motif[2878] of the fifty-third chapter of Isaiah,[2879] then rounded out through back-projecting hundreds of Pagan legends and miracle stories into the biography of the historical Jesus,[2880] is one of the world's greatest and most damaging coverups and the Church's most blatant conspiracy against the people and the Truth. As one early scholar bluntly but correctly put it: "Christianity could not overthrow Paganism, so it Paganized Christianity."[2881]

Proof for what has also been rightly called the "Scheme of Salvation,"[2882] is damning and overwhelming, and this very book contains more than enough evidence to convict it. Of this devilish plot William Ellery Channing writes:

> This corruption of Christianity, alike repugnant to common sense and to the general strain of Scripture, is a remarkable proof of the power of a false philosophy in disfiguring the simple truth of Jesus.[2883]

America's third president, Thomas Jefferson, made these observations:

> *The truth is, that the greatest enemies to the doctrines of Jesus are those, calling themselves the expositors of them, who have perverted them for the structure of a system of fancy absolutely incomprehensible, and without any foundation in his genuine words.* And the day will come, when the mystical generation of Jesus, by the Supreme Being as his father, in the womb of a virgin, will be classed with the fable of the generation of Minerva in the brain of Jupiter. But we may hope that the dawn of reason, and *freedom of thought in these United States*, will do away all *this artificial scaffolding*, and restore to us the primitive and genuine doctrines of this the most

venerated reformer of human errors.[2884]

For those interested in what has been lost due to the orthodox Church's Myth of Christ, here is a mere glimpse: at one time there were over 100 known Gospels and Epistles.[2885] Indeed, the original Greek New Testament contained as least 50 books, yet today's New Testament has only 27. Among those that were discarded: The Shepherd of Hermas and the Essenic Letter of Barnabas,[2886] both once considered canonical by many of the Church Fathers, and which were included in our oldest complete Greek New Testament, the Codex Sinaiticus (written circa A.D. 350). Other important and accepted texts that were later disposed before they could be canonized: The Revelation of Peter, The Letter of Clement of Rome, The Acts of Paul, and The Teaching of the Apostles.[2887]

Once traditional Christians learn about The Myth of Christ, as well as the facts behind the real history of the New Testament and "formal Christianity," many understandably choose to leave the fold, particularly free-thinkers with an esoteric bent. One of these was Massachusetts Transcendentalist and mystic Ralph Waldo Emerson, who, in 1832, resigned his prestigious post as pastor of Boston's Unitarian Church, famously declaring that he had lost his desire to be "suckled by a creed outworn."[2888] Of this event, which rocked the New England Christian community to its foundation, he wrote in his journal:

> I have sometimes thought that in order to be a good minister it was necessary to leave the ministry. The profession is antiquated. In an altered age we worship in the dead forms of our forefathers. Were not a Socratic Paganism better than an effete superannuated Christianity? The whole world holds on to formal Christianity, and nobody teaches the essential truth, the heart of Christianity, for fear of shocking.[2889]

The "essential truth" Emerson speaks of here is Theosis, which he once described this way: "The highest revelation is that God is in every man."[2890] Indeed, the sacred doctrine of Theosis formed the very heart of Jesus' Gospel of the Kingdom of God,[2891] but which was purposefully and violently expunged from conventional Christianity with the creation of the Pagan Myth of Christ. The Church, to this day, has never been completely non-Pagan, and, in fact, owes its very existence to the wholesale Paganization of the human Jesus. Thus, mainstream Christianity is guilty of promoting that which it pretends to condemn.[2892] The mystical Christian Church avoids this heinous spiritual crime altogether, however, by recognizing and embracing our Lord's single greatest teaching: "Ye are gods."[2893]
See BIRTH OF JESUS, BUDDHA, CHRIST, CHRISTIANITY, CHRISTMAS, ESSENES, GNOSTICISM, JESUS, KRISHNA, MITHRA, NATIVITY, OSIRIS, PETER, PYTHAGORAS, TEACHER OF RIGHTEOUSNESS, THEOSIS.

Moses with horns, by Michelangelo.

Mary, Joseph, and Jesus leaving Egypt.

Mithra the Son-God, slaying the bull.

Monotheism began on the Nile.

Melchizedek blessing Abram.

NATIVITY: In traditional Christianity the Nativity of the supernatural birth of Jesus is taken from the Gospels of Matthew and Luke, and is accepted as both literal and historic. But was it?

According to the first and third Evangelists, Jesus was born in a manger in Bethlehem to the Virgin Mary. The miraculous birth was attended by shepherds and angels as the Heavenly Host sang and praised the Lord. Several Wise Men from the East followed the Star of Bethlehem to the site of the stable, and there venerated the baby Jesus with gifts of gold, frankincense, and myrrh. The news of the birth of the Messiah was spread about the countryside and everyone who heard of it glorified God.[2894]

If this quaint tale were unique to Jesus we might be able to consider some or most of it historical. However, as disinterested students of comparative religion and comparative mythology well know, the elements in this story are traditional to nearly all ancient religious and political leaders. Many of the exact same themes, for example, were added to Buddha's nativity after he died around 483 B.C. The same may be said of Moses, Sargon, Krishna, Jason, Apollonius of Tyana, Mithra, Noah, Perseus, Romulus, Alexander the Great, Hercules, Caesar, and thousands of other notable men and deities of antiquity.

But nobody today considers these often jarring additions to be real. Buddhists understand them for what they are, universal legendary motifs. As such they refer to these embedded stories as "Jataka Tales,"[2895] *jataka* being Sanskrit for "birth"; thus literally "Birth Myths." The historicizing of ancient mythological beliefs, particularly concerning the nativities of important gods and men, has been common throughout history. And the figures of Buddha and Jesus were no exception.[2896]

Christian mystics agree, but take it one step further, seeing Jesus' nativity as an occult allegory, one which, therefore, is more illuminating and logical if read mystically rather than literally.

For one thing, there are innumerable serious problems with this story, beginning with the bold fact that our only two Nativities, contained in Matthew and Luke, were not part of the original manuscripts: it is now widely acknowledged that both Gospels originally began with Chapter Three, and that Chapters One and Two were added later,[2897] copied from old Pagan nativities concerning ancient pre-Christian rulers and deities—in particular those from Egypt.[2898] This would certainly explain the abrupt ending of Chapter Two and the unrelated beginning of Chapter Three in both books; not to mention the fact that Mark's Gospel—to which no one thought to append a nativity—begins at the same time and place as Matthew and Luke's Third Chapters: with John the Baptist. This means that all three of the Synoptics originally started not with the birth of Jesus, but with the work of the desert prophet John.

Of this treacherous and obvious copying and interpolating, Sharpe made the following comments:

> Every king of Egypt, even while living, was added to the number of the gods, and declared to be the Son of Ra [that is, "Son of God"], which was the title set over the second oval of his name. He was then sometimes made into the third person of a Trinity, in which case he took the place of the god Chonso. He denied that he owed his birth to the father from whom he inherited the crown; he claimed to be born, like the bull Apis, by a miraculous conception. He styled his mother the wife of Amun-Ra, which explains the mistake of Diodorus Siculus, who calls the tombs of the queens near Thebes the tombs of Jupiter's concubines. Many of the more favourite kings after their death continued to receive the same divine worship.
>
> This opinion of the miraculous birth of the kings is well explained in a series of sculptures on the wall of the temple of Luxor. First, the god Thoth, with the head of an ibis, and with his ink and pen—case in his left hand, as the messenger of the gods, like the Mercury of the Greeks, tells the maiden queen Mautmes that she is to give birth to a son, who is to be king Amunothph III. Secondly, the god Kneph, the spirit, with a ram's head, and the goddess Athor, with the sun and cow's horns upon her head, both take hold of the queen by her hands, and put into her mouth the character for life, which is to be the life of the coming child. Thirdly, the queen, when the child is to be born, is seated on the midwife's stool, as described in Exodus 1:16; two of the attending nurses rub her hands to ease the pains of childbirth, while another of the nurses holds up the baby, over which is written the name of king Amunothph III. He holds his finger to his mouth to mark his infancy; he has not yet learned to speak. Lastly, the several gods or priests attend in adoration upon their knees to present their gifts to this wonderful child, who is seated in the midst of them, and is receiving their homage. In this picture we have the Annunciation, the Conception, the Birth, and the Adoration, as

described in the First and Second Chapters of Luke's Gospel; and as we have historical assurance that the chapters in Matthew's Gospel, which contain the Miraculous Birth of Jesus, are an after addition not in the earliest manuscripts, it seems probable that these two poetical chapters in Luke may also be unhistorical, and be borrowed from the Egyptian accounts of the miraculous birth of their kings.[2899]

There is another egregious problem we encounter with Jesus' birth story. The word "virgin" as applied to Mary in the Nativities is incorrect. The original Greek word *parthenos* means a "marriageable young woman,"[2900] or simply "maiden," a girl.[2901] An understanding of this simple fact would alter the entire foundation of mainline Christianity—which is exactly why it has been suppressed by the traditional Church!

But we encounter many other serious issues as well.

While strangely neither Mark or John even mention the Nativity, the two who do, Matthew and Luke, differ widely in their details. Thus the latter pair are known in scholarly circles as *diptychs*: two different portraits of the same thing that are attached by a "hinge" of commonality.[2902]

For example, Jesus' birth at Nazareth is said to be based on an Old Testament prophecy that "He shall be called a Nazarene."[2903] But no such saying exists, either in the Bible or anywhere else.[2904] And since neither the word "Nazarene"[2905] or the city of Nazareth are mentioned in the Old Testament,[2906] and since no historian from the time period of our Lord refers to it, many modern scholars rightly doubt Nazareth's existence.[2907]

Then there is the so-called "Massacre of the Innocents," in which thousands of baby boys were said to have been slaughtered by Herod. It was only recorded by Matthew, but ignored not only by Mark, Luke, and John, but also by all of the great historians of the day, including Josephus. This tale too was based on an Old Testament prophecy,[2908] which like so many others, was a farfetched misinterpretation by uninformed "Christian" writers, like the overly inventive Matthew,[2909] who consciously sought justification for contemporary messianic events from ancient sources that had no connection to them.[2910] And so on.

Though Jesus' fantastic Nativity, as recorded by Matthew and Luke, may have in fact been a real historic event, in the esoteric Christian schools this is not the point. The focus here is on the numerous profound spiritual truths that are symbolically embedded in it. The evidence for this is overwhelming, and we will examine some of it now.

As we have discussed, revealingly Mark and John do not mention the Nativity, a "mystery" that the mainstream Church still dares not address.[2911] Not even Paul discusses it, another one of the Bible's many indecipherable conundrums.[2912] And why is Jesus' birth story missing from the Gospels of the second and fourth Evangelists? And why are orthodox Christian scholars hesitant to deal with the issue?

In answering the first question we will answer the second. Mark, the author of the earliest and thus the first Gospel, was not aware of the Nativity, because when he was writing, between the years A.D. 50 and 60, it had not yet been invented and incorporated into Jesus' biography. From a historic and scholarly point of view, this is only a theory (as is nearly everything connected with the four Gospels). However, it does itself justice by answering countless previously unanswerable questions, and making sense of heretofore confusing and illogical postulates put forth by conservative Christians and apologists.

One such problem concerns Jesus' birth date: if He was born in the Winter on December 25, as the mainstream Church maintains, why does Luke state that this event took place in the Spring or Summer?[2913] Shepherds do not put their sheep out to pasture in the dead of Winter.

Another problem: if Jesus' birth was announced to the world (or at least to the Roman Empire) and was attended by a myriad of miraculous signs and wonders, why was none of this recorded by a single historian living at the time? Not only this, Jesus' life, miracles, and epochal death on the cross are also missing from the authentic chronicles of early meticulous record keepers, such as Josephus,[2914] Tacitus,[2915] Suetonius,[2916] Pliny the Younger, Philo, and Justus of Tiberias, to name but a few.[2917]

In his 1929 book *The Great Galilean*, English scholar Robert Keable offers the following comments:

> No man knows sufficient of the early life of Jesus to write a biography of him. For that matter, no one knows enough for the normal *Times* obituary notice of a great man. If regard were had to what we should call, in correct speech, definitely historical facts, scarcely three lines could be filled. Moreover, if newspapers had been in existence, and if that obituary notice had had to be written in the year of his death, no editor could have found in the literature of his day so much as his name. Yet few periods of the ancient world were so well documented as the period of Augustus and Tiberius. But no contemporary knew of his existence. Even a generation later, a spurious passage in Josephus, a questionable reference in Suetonius, and the mention of a name that may be his by Tacitus—that is all. His first mention in any surviving document, secular or religious, is twenty years after.[2918]

Even mainstream Christian scholars have been forced to admit that nothing certain is known about Jesus' life, except that His ministry began with His baptism and ended with His crucifixion[2919]—and even these are heavily saturated with archetypal and mythological pre-Christian elements. Hence, contrary to orthodox thought, there is no such thing as a "life of Jesus," for the material to create a true and thorough biographical narrative of our Lord is nonexistent, and in any case is now considered to be unknowable and beyond recovery.[2920] The four canonical Gospels are actually four separate non-historical accounts of Jesus' life,[2921] in many places wildly conflicting, contradicting, and even negating one another.[2922]

In his seminal work, *The Quest of the Historical Jesus*, after reviewing dozens of detailed volumes on "The Life of Jesus" that span several centuries, Schweitzer comes to the same conclusion: based on what we know from meager sources about the Master Healer, Teacher, and Prophet, it is impossible to piece together even a minute sketch of His life.[2923] Writes Schweitzer:

> The Jesus of Nazareth who came forward publicly as the Messiah, who preached the ethic of the Kingdom of God, who founded the Kingdom of Heaven upon earth, and died to give His work its final consecration, never had any existence. He is a figure designed by rationalism, endowed with life by liberalism, and clothed by modern theology in an historical garb.
>
> This image has not been destroyed from without, it has fallen to pieces, cleft and disintegrated by the concrete historical problems which came to the surface one after another, and in spite of all the artifice, art, artificiality, and violence which was applied to them, refused to be planed down to fit the design on which the Jesus of the theology of the last hundred and thirty years had been constructed, and were no sooner covered over than they appeared again in a new form. The thoroughgoing sceptical and the thoroughgoing eschatological school have only completed the work of destruction by linking the problems into a system and so making an end of the *Divide et impera* ["Divide and Conquer"] of modern theology, which undertook to solve each of them separately, that is, in a less difficult form. Henceforth it is no longer permissible to take one problem out of the series and dispose of it by itself, since the weight of the whole hangs upon each.
>
> Whatever the ultimate solution may be, the historical Jesus of whom the criticism of the future, taking as its starting-point the problems which have been recognised and admitted, will draw the portrait, can never render modern theology the services which it claimed from its own half-historical, half-modern, Jesus. *He will be a Jesus, who was*

Messiah, and lived as such, either on the ground of a literary fiction of the earliest Evangelist, or on the ground of a purely eschatological Messianic conception.

In either case, He will not be a Jesus Christ to whom the religion of the present can ascribe, according to its long-cherished custom, its own thoughts and ideas, as it did with the Jesus of its own making. Nor will He be a figure which can be made by a popular historical treatment so sympathetic and universally intelligible to the multitude. *The historical Jesus will be to our time a stranger and an enigma.*[2924]

Another example: Paul (like James, Peter, and John) never quotes Jesus, which is strange since Christians (myself included) have long considered our Lord to be the greatest thinker, teacher, and speaker the Western world has ever produced or known. Just as odd, Paul neglects to make any reference to Jesus' miracles,[2925] His Ascension, the 12 Apostles, the empty tomb,[2926] or even the all-important Jerusalem Council,[2927] as anyone familiar with Paul's *genuine* letters can attest.[2928] And yet Paul lived at the same time as Jesus, and even went on to become both the "Thirteenth Apostle" and the inadvertent founder of Christian theology,[2929] the very man who modern traditional Christian scholars credit with making Christianity a world religion.[2930] Why then Paul's utter silence?

Such uncomfortable issues are handily solved by the theory that though Jesus was a historical figure, the details of His life were unknown to those who came immediately after Him, the so-called "Second Generation"; that is, those who were unaware of the Prince of Peace until *after* His death around A.D. 33. This can only mean that His life story as described in the four Gospels (all written from one to three generations later),[2931] was posthumously developed and written over a period of time, and that the supernatural elements of his biography were added during this process by overly enthusiastic followers and orthodox propagandists. "No sooner is a great man dead," noted Strauss, "than legend is busy with his life."[2932]

Foremost among these early apologists was Mark, who appears to be the first of the important Jesuine mythographers to adopt both ancient Jewish and Hellenistic Pagan myths and append them to the life story of our Lord.[2933] Since he was the first gospeler, he had complete freedom concerning what to include and what to reject,[2934] using his "historical imagination" to great and "dramatic effect."[2935] Thus, according to objective Bible scholars, Mark, who was an editor, redactor, and compiler rather than an author,[2936] must be counted as the "inventor of the Gospel history and the personality of Jesus."[2937]

For example, though he was not and could not have been present at Jesus' passion, including the crucifixion, Mark gives numerous details of the event. Where did he get the material for his version of the crucifixion story if none existed at the time? He "borrowed" it from the Twenty-second Psalm[2938] and from various crucifixion legends regarding pre-Christian Pagan religious leaders (for example, Buddha), gods (for example, Apollo), and saviors (for example, Krishna).[2939]

Orthodox Bible scholars have tried to get around this "problem" by stating that Mark's Gospel is based on the teachings of Peter the Apostle.[2940] But Peter himself was almost certainly fictitious, a legendary figure built around Roman myths of the Pagan rock-god known as Petra or Pater Liber, the gate-keeping deity whose mystical keys (based on the "Key of the Nile," the *ankh* of Osiris) unlocked the doors to Heaven.[2941]

Yet, even if Peter was historical, the four Gospelers, including Mark, portray him as being too naive, uneducated, and spiritually immature to comprehend complex religious themes like "crucifixion,"[2942] which, in the case of mythical deities like the *Paganized Christ* (as opposed to the historical Jesus), was always of an occult nature. At one point Mark actually has Jesus angrily address the dull-witted Peter as "Satan" due to his simplemindedness.[2943]

Now concerning the Nativity specifically, it was clearly invented *after* Mark wrote his Gospel, so he could not have known of it and so did not include it. As for our Gnostic-mystic John, though he wrote late, between A.D. 85 and 100, years after the Nativity had been fabricated, he intentionally left it out of his Gospel because it did not fit with his pantheistic Christology: Jesus as the eternal Gnostic-Pagan *Logos* (a word first used by the Pagan philosopher Heraclitus around 500 B.C.).[2944]

Though all of this is theoretical, a historical search for the truth must inevitably lead to the Pagan legend-obsessed Matthew as the author of the Nativity myth. Since nothing else has come to light, we have no choice but to attribute its creation to him: he was the first ancient writer who mentions it, after which it was later further embellished by others, not the least of which was the orthodox Christian Church itself.

A question that objective Christian scholars have been asking for centuries is why Matthew never once gives any indication that knowledge of Jesus' supernatural birth played a part in His ministry?[2945] To Christian mystics, however, the answer is obvious: since it was a posthumous literary invention, the Nativity did not and could not have any influence on this aspect of our Lord's life.

More importantly, where did Matthew, who penned his Gospel before Luke, sometime between the 50s and the 60s, find the mythological material to develop and write the Nativity? From the world's first and still the most widespread religion: Paganism. And more specifically from Pagan astronomy and astrology.

We have no hard evidence of how Matthew did this.[2946] We only have the Gospels and the words of men like Pope Leo X who, in the 16th Century, admitted that, "It has served us well, this myth of Christ,"[2947] and the early Church Fathers, most who agreed that "these officious lies [about Christ] were devised for a good end."²⁹⁴⁸ Therefore we must use the traditional tools of the detective-historian: deduction and induction.

It has often been repeated that since Jesus the Son-God is a historicized Christian version of Helios the Sun-God, our Lord's life story as laid down in the New Testament can be read and interpreted from beginning to end as an allegory of the Sun's annual regenerational passage through the 12 months,²⁹⁴⁹ representing the 12 astrological signs.²⁹⁵⁰ As Pike states:

> Almost every nation will be found to have had a mythical being, whose strength or weakness, virtues or defects, more or less nearly describe the Sun's career through the seasons.²⁹⁵¹

The various incidents in the four Gospels thus correlate to the changing positions, cycles, and functions of the celestial bodies.²⁹⁵² And if one uses the Third Eye or EYE AM (intuition) as a guide,²⁹⁵³ as Christian mystics do, this becomes absolutely clear, as Kingsford and Maitland intimate:

> . . . the gospel narrative of Jesus' birth is really a presentation, dramatic and symbolical, of the nature of regeneration.²⁹⁵⁴

Likewise, Westbrook writes:

> The very fact that all the apparently historic events in the life of Jesus have an astrological and metaphoric character lifts him out of the category of physical humanity into that of the ideal.²⁹⁵⁵

Even a cursory glance at the seasonal celebrations of the ancient peoples of Europe and the Near and Middle East uncovers the existence of a region-wide solar religion and an accompanying yearly Winter Solstice event that was held in awe by the entire populace. In Rome this festival was known as *Dies Natalis Solis Invicti*: "Birthday of the Unconquered Sun."²⁹⁵⁶ Of this widespread ancient Sun worship and the zodiacal constellations, Pike writes:

> At the vernal equinox, 2455 years before our Era, the Sun was entering the sign and constellation Taurus, or the Bull; having passed through, since he commenced, at the Winter Solstice, to ascend Northward, the Signs Aquarius, Pisces and Aries; on entering the first of which he reached the lowest limit of his journey Southward.
>
> From Taurus, he [the Sun] passed through Gemini and Cancer, and reached Leo when he arrived at the terminus of his journey Northward. Thence, through Leo, Virgo, and Libra,

he entered Scorpio at the Autumnal Equinox, and journeyed Southward through Scorpio, Sagittarius, and Capricornus to Aquarius, the terminus of his journey South.

The path by which he journeyed through these signs became the Ecliptic; and that which passes through the two equinoxes, the Equator.

They knew nothing of the immutable laws of nature; and whenever the Sun commenced to tend Southward, they feared lest he might continue to do so, and by degrees disappear forever, leaving the earth to be ruled forever by darkness, storm, and cold.

Hence they rejoiced when he commenced to re-ascend after the Winter Solstice, struggling against the malign influences of Aquarius and Pisces, and amicably received by the Lamb [Aries]. And when at the Vernal Equinox he entered Taurus, they still more rejoiced at the assurance that the days would again be longer than the nights, that the season of seed-time had come, and the Summer and harvest would follow.

And they lamented when, after the Autumnal Equinox, the malign influence of the venomous Scorpion [Scorpio], and vindictive Archer [Sagittarius], and the filthy and ill-omened He-Goat [Capricorn] dragged him down toward the Winter Solstice.

Arriving there, they said he [the Sun] had been slain, and had gone to the realm of darkness. Remaining there three days, he rose again, and again ascended Northward in the heavens, to redeem the earth from the gloom and darkness of Winter, which soon became emblematical of sin, and evil, and suffering; as the Spring, Summer, and Autumn became emblems of happiness and immortality. Soon they personified the Sun, and [in Egypt, for example,] worshipped him under the name of Osiris, and transmuted the legend of his descent among the Winter Signs, into a fable of his death, his descent into the infernal regions, and his resurrection.

The Moon became Isis, the wife of Osiris; and winter, as well as the desert or the ocean into which the Sun descended, became Typhon, the Spirit or Principle of Evil, warring against and destroying Osiris.[2957]

In order to penetrate the symbolic veil of this annual astronomical occurrence let us imagine that we are living between 2512 B.C. and 360 B.C., the period when the Sun rose precisely in the constellation Capricorn on December 25. This will enable us to look at this magnificent celestial event as an ancient astronomer living then would have seen it.

Why is it necessary to travel back 2,000 years to understand the Nativity of Jesus? Because due to the ongoing expanding forces of the Big Bang, and the resulting "Precession of the Equinoxes," the stars, and hence the constellations, have moved almost a full thirty degrees since the period when astrology first developed. In effect, this means that the Sun is now actually in the sign preceding the sign traditionally assigned to it. Hence, on December 25th today, the Sun no longer actually rises in the constellation Capricorn, but in Sagittarius. It is because of this that we must go back to when it rose in Capricorn.[2958]

In the northern hemisphere, early on the midwinter night of what would have been December 24, in the year 1500 BC, we can observe the constellation of Orion the Hunter rising in the east. We will note here that the Latin word *Orion* is a derivation of the Latin words *oriens*, meaning "rising Sun," and *orior*, meaning "to be born," or "to rise." Most noticeable are the three stars which make up the great hunter's belt, called (from left to right), Alnitak, Alnilam, and Mintaka—three celestial objects that took on profound, divine significance in nearly all ancient cultures, from Africa and South America to Asia and Europe.

As Orion rises higher in the night sky, to the earthly observer these three stars appear to point back to the eastern horizon where the constellation Canis Major (Orion's companion, the "Big Dog") and its brilliant star, Sirius, now begin to emerge. Across from Orion we can see the constellation Scorpio (the "Scorpion") and the constellation of Aquila (Latin for "eagle").[2959]

Around midnight, with Canis Major moving upwards into the sky, the constellation Virgo (the "Virgin") soon appears on the eastern horizon. Nearby, the constellation Aries (the "Ram" or "Lamb") may also be seen rising. At this time, too, the Sun reaches its lowest point in the constellation Capricorn (the "Goat"). Shortly after, at dawn on the following morning (December 25), the Sun rises in the east, still in the sign Capricorn.

Lastly, surrounding Orion, we see the constellations Taurus (the "Bull"), and Ursus Major (known in ancient Egypt, not as the "Big Bear," or "Big Dipper," but as the "Ass of Typhon"). Below Orion is the constellation Columba (the "Dove"), while above Taurus is Auriga (Latin for the "Charioteer"), or, as it was also known in ancient times, the "Augean Stable."

It was this momentous yearly celestial event on December 24 and 25 from which arose one of the earliest known nativity stories.[2960] Remembering that the Pagans of antiquity viewed celestial bodies as living beings, let us now look at this astronomical event through the literalistic eyes of the ancient Egyptians.

The three stars of Orion's belt, Alnitak, Alnilam, and Mintaka, were believed to be of royal birth and so the Egyptians called them the "Three Kings," a name by which they are still known in various parts of Europe. Leading the "Three

Kings" is the bright star Sirius which reached its zenith at midnight on this particular night—December 24, the eve of the birthday of the great Sun-god Ra—and so was considered the messenger who announced the birth of the Supreme Solar-deity. Hence, Sirius was known as the "Herald of the Sun-god" (a title later given to John the Baptist)[2961] or the "Star from the East" (that is, the Star of Bethlehem).

As Sirius rises into the night sky, he is closely followed by the great Mother-Virgin-Goddess (Virgo) who is now preparing to give birth to her son Ra, the Sun-god-savior. The Dove (Columba)—an ancient Pagan symbol of the "Holy Spirit"—now descends on the Virgin while the Eagle (Aquila)—an ancient symbol of the Great Father-God—watches over the proceedings.

The birth of the infant Sun-god at dawn takes place in the Stable of Augeas (Auriga), as the zodiacal ox (Taurus) and ass (Ursus Major) look on. With the lamb (Aries) appearing on the nearby horizon, his mother then lays the newborn Sun-god in a feed trough.

It is this simple astronomical-astrological event from which Matthew drew the material for his Jesuine Nativity: the "Three Kings" (belt of Orion) follow the "Star of Bethlehem" (Sirius, or sometimes Venus) across the sky. The star leads them to the "Virgin Mary" (Virgo), who is "impregnated" by the "Holy Spirit" (Columba), as God (Aquila) governs the event from above. The Virgin then gives birth to the son-god Ra (Jesus) in a "stable" (Auriga). As farm animals, an ox (Taurus) and an ass (Ursus Major), stand by, Mary (Virgo) lays the divine infant in a "manger" (a cluster of stars once known as *Praesepe*), bound on each side by two small stars known as the *Aselli* ("little asses"), while the "Lamb of God" (Aries) looks on.[2962]

Christian mystic William Stainton Moses aptly describes the universality of the great astronomical Gospel Drama that is enacted in the spirit of each person during his or her earthly sojourn:

> The whole course of the typical life of the Pattern [Ideal] Man is emblematic of the progressive development of the life begun on earth, completed in heaven, born of self-denial, and culminating in spiritual ascension. In the Christ-life, as in a story, man may read the tale of the progress of spirit from incarnation to enfranchisement. Thirty years and more of angelic preparation fitted the Christ for His mission: three short years sufficed to discharge so much of it as man could bear.
>
> So man's spirit in its development progresses through the course covered by the Festivals of the Christian Church [Christmas, Epiphany, Lent, Good Friday, Easter, Whitsuntide, the Ascension], from the birth of self-denial to the festival of the completed life. Born in self-denial, progressing through self-sacrifice, developed by perpetual struggles with the

adversaries (the antagonistic principles which must be conquered in daily life, in self, and in the foes), it dies at length to the external, and rises on its Easter morn from the grave of matter, and lives henceforth, baptized by the outpoured spirit of Pentecost, a new and risen life, till it ascends to the place prepared for it by the tendency of its earth life.

This is the Spirit's progress, and it may be said to be a process of regeneration, shortly typified by crucifixion and resurrection. The old man dies, the new man rises from his grave. The old man, with his lusts, is crucified; the new man is raised up to live a spiritual and holy life. It is regeneration of spirit that is the culmination of bodily life, and the process is crucifixion of self, a daily death, as Paul was wont to say.

In the life of spiritual progress, there should be no stagnation, no paralysis. It should be a growth and a daily adaptation of knowledge; a mortification of the earthy and sensual, and a corresponding development of the spiritual and heavenly. In other words, it is a growth in grace, and in the knowledge of the Christ; the purest type of human life presented to your imitation. It is a clearing away of the material, and a development of the spiritual—a purging as by fire, the fire of a consuming zeal; of a life-long struggle with self, and all that self includes; of an ever widening grasp of Divine truth.

By no other means can spirit be purified. The furnace is one of self-sacrifice: the process the same for all. Only in some souls, wherein the Divine flame burns more brightly, the process is rapid and concentrated; while in duller natures the fires smoulder, and vast cycles of purgation are required. Blessed are they who can crush out the earthy, and welcome the fiery trial which shall purge away the dross. To such, progress is rapid and purification sure.[2963]

Of this ancient astronomical-astrological event Carpenter writes:

Let us take Christmas Day first. [The Pagan god] Mithra . . . was reported to have been born on the 25th December (which in the Julian Calendar was reckoned as the day of the Winter Solstice and of the Nativity of the Sun); Plutarch says that Osiris was born on the 361st day of the year, when a Voice rang out proclaiming the Lord of All. Horus, he says, was born on the 362nd day. Apollo on the same.

Why was all this? Why did the Druids at Yule Tide light roaring fires? Why was the cock supposed to crow all Christmas Eve? Why was Apollo born with only one hair (the young Sun with only one feeble ray)? Why did Samson (name derived from Shemesh, the sun) lose all his strength when he lost his hair? Why were so many of these gods—Mithra, Apollo, Krishna, Jesus, and others, born in caves or underground chambers? Why, at the Easter Eve festival of the Holy Sepulchre at Jerusalem is a light brought from the grave and communicated to the candles of thousands who wait outside, and who rush forth rejoicing to carry the new glory over the world? *Why indeed? except that older than all history and all written records has been the fear and wonderment of the children of men over the failure of the Sun's strength in Autumn—the decay of their God; and the anxiety lest by any means he should not revive or reappear?*

Think for a moment of a time far back when there were absolutely no Almanacs or Calendars, either nicely printed or otherwise, when all that timid mortals could see was that their great source of Light and Warmth was daily failing, daily sinking lower in the sky. As everyone now knows there are about three weeks at the fag end of the year [December] when the days are at their shortest and there is very little change. What was happening? Evidently the [Sun] god had fallen upon evil times. Typhon, the prince of darkness, had betrayed him; Delilah, the queen of Night, had shorn his hair; the dreadful Boar had wounded him; Hercules was struggling with Death itself; he had fallen under the influence of those malign constellations—the Serpent and the Scorpion. Would the god grow weaker and weaker, and finally succumb, or would he conquer after all? We can imagine the anxiety with which those early men and women watched for the first indication of a lengthening day; and the universal joy when the Priest (the representative of primitive science) having made some simple observations, announced from the Temple steps that the day was lengthening—that the Sun was really born again to a new and glorious career.

Let us look at the elementary science of those days a little closer. How without Almanacs or Calendars could the day, or probable day, of the Sun's rebirth be fixed? Go out next Christmas Evening, and at midnight you will see the brightest of the fixed stars, Sirius, blazing in the southern sky—not however due south from you, but somewhat to the left of the Meridian line. Some three thousand years ago (owing to the Precession of the Equinoxes) that star at the winter solstice did not stand at midnight where you now see it, but almost exactly on the meridian line. The coming of Sirius therefore to the meridian at midnight became the sign and assurance of the Sun having reached the very lowest point of his course, and therefore of having arrived at the moment of his re-birth. Where then was the Sun at that moment? Obviously in the underworld beneath our feet. Whatever views the ancients may have had about the shape of the earth, it was evident to the mass of people that the Sungod, after illuminating the world during the day, plunged down in the West, and remained there during the hours of darkness in some cavern under the earth. Here he rested and after bathing in the great ocean renewed his garments before reappearing in the East next morning.

But *in this long night of his greatest winter weakness, when all the world was hoping and praying for the renewal of his strength, it is evident that the new birth would come—if it came at all—at midnight.* This then was the sacred hour when in the underworld (the Stable or the Cave or whatever it might be called) *the child was born who was destined to be the Savior of men. At that moment Sirius stood on the southern meridian (and in more southern lands than ours this would be more nearly overhead); and that star—there is little doubt—is the Star in the East mentioned in the Gospels.*

To the right, as the supposed observer looks at Sirius on the midnight of Christmas Eve, stands the magnificent Orion, the mighty hunter. There are *three stars in his belt* which, as is well known, lie in a straight line pointing to Sirius. They are not so bright as Sirius, but they are sufficiently bright to attract attention. *A long tradition gives them the name of the Three Kings.*

. . . *Immediately after Midnight then, on the 25th December, the Beloved Son (or Sungod) is born.* If we go back in thought to the period, some three thousand years ago, when at that moment of the heavenly birth Sirius, coming from the East, did actually stand on the Meridian, we shall come into touch with another curious astronomical coincidence. For *at the same moment we shall see the Zodiacal constellation of the Virgin in the act of rising, and becoming visible in the East divided through the middle by the line of the horizon.*

The constellation Virgo is a Y-shaped group, of which . . . the star at the foot, is the well-known Spica, a star of the first magnitude. The other [three] principle stars . . . are of the second magnitude. The whole resembles more a cup than the human figure; but when we remember the symbolic meaning of the cup [a yonic symbol], that seems to be an obvious explanation of the name Virgo, which the constellation has borne since the earliest times. (The other three principle stars . . . lie very nearly on the Ecliptic, that is, the Sun's path—a fact to which we shall return presently.)

At the moment then when Sirius, the star from the East, by coming to the Meridian at midnight signalled the Sun's new birth, the Virgin was seen just rising on the Eastern sky—the horizon line passing through her centre. And many people think that this astronomical fact is the explanation of the very widespread legend of the Virgin-birth. I do not think that it is the sole explanation—for indeed in all or nearly all these cases the acceptance of a myth seems to depend not upon a single argument but upon the convergence of a number of meanings and reasons in the same symbol. But certainly the fact mentioned above is curious, and its importance is accentuated by the following considerations.

In the Temple of Denderah in Egypt, and on the inside of the dome, there is or was an elaborate circular representation of the Northern hemisphere of the sky and the Zodiac. Here Virgo the constellation is represented, as in our star-maps, by a woman with a spike of corn in her hand (Spica). But on the margin close by there is an annotating and explicatory figure—a figure of *Isis with the infant Horus in her arms*, and quite resembling in style the Christian Madonna and Child, except that she is sitting and the child is on her knee. This seems to show that—whatever other nations may have done in associating Virgo with Demeter, Ceres, Diana, etc.—the Egyptians made no doubt of the constellation's connection with Isis and Horus. But *it is well known as a matter of history that the worship of Isis and Horus descended in the early Christian centuries to Alexandria, where it took the form of the worship of the Virgin Mary and the infant Savior, and so passed into the European ceremonial. We have therefore the Virgin Mary connected by linear succession and descent with that remote Zodiacal cluster in the sky!* Also it may be mentioned that on the Arabian and Persian globes of Abenezra and Abuazar a Virgin and Child are figured in connection with the same constellation.

A curious confirmation of the same astronomical connection is afforded by the Roman Catholic Calendar. For if this be consulted it will be found that the festival of the Assumption of the Virgin is placed on the 15th August, while the festival of the Birth of the Virgin is dated the 8th September. I have already pointed out that the other three principle stars . . . of Virgo are almost exactly on the Ecliptic, or Sun's path through the sky; and a brief reference to the Zodiacal signs and the star-maps will show that the Sun each year enters the sign of Virgo about the first-mentioned date, and leaves it about the second date.

At the present day the Zodiacal signs (owing to precession) have shifted some distance from the constellations of the same name. But at the time when the Zodiac was constituted and these names were given, the first date obviously would signalize the actual disappearance of the cluster Virgo in the Sun's rays—i.e. *the Assumption of the Virgin into the glory of the God*—while the second date would signalize *the reappearance of the constellation or the Birth of the Virgin. The Church of Notre Dame at Paris is supposed to be on the original site of a Temple of Isis; and it is said* (but I have not been able to verify this myself) *that one of the side entrances—that, namely, on the left in entering from the North (cloister) side—is figured with the signs of the Zodiac except that the sign Virgo is replaced by the figure of the Madonna and Child.* So strange is the scripture of the sky![2964]

That the Nativity of Jesus, as described in Matthew, should not be taken literally is thus obvious to Christian mystics. Not only is it pregnant with esoteric symbols and allegories that are meant to convey important spiritual doctrines to the truth seeker, but it is obviously merely a copy of the astrologically based nativities of thousands of earlier saviors, kings, messiahs, and christs, in particular those found in ancient Egypt. See ASTROLOGY, BUDDHA, CHRIST, CHRISTMAS, GOSPEL, JESUS, KRISHNA, MITHRA, OSIRIS, PYTHAGORAS, TEACHER OF RIGHTEOUSNESS, STAR OF BETHLEHEM, WISE MEN, ZODIAC.

NAZARENES: In the traditional Church the Nazarenes were one of several Jewish sects existing during the time of Jesus.[2965] In the mystical Church "Nazarenes" is the New Testament secret codename for the mystical Jewish Gnostic sect known as the Essenes (and also as the Ossenes, the Osim, Esseans, the Jessaeans, the Nozrei ha-Brit, the Nozrim, and the Nasrani),[2966] out of which Palestinian Christianity itself was formed.[2967]

Jesus,[2968] John the Baptist,[2969] and Paul[2970] were all said to be members of the Nazarene community.[2971] The orthodox incorrectly hold that Jesus was only called "the Nazarene" because He was from Nazareth.[2972] But as there was no known ancient city by this name[2973] and as it is not mentioned in the Old Testament,[2974] and since the New Testament prophecy that "he shall be called a Nazarene"[2975] is also not found in the Old Testament,[2976] a mystical element must be assumed.[2977]

Proof that "Nazarenes" was not only the name by which Jews knew the followers of Jesus,[2978] but that it was also, in fact, one of the names of the Essenes, comes from a number of ancient sources,[2979] most famously the anti-Gnostic Church Father Epiphanius, who correctly noted that "the Nazarene sect was before Christ,"[2980] that "at that time all Christians alike were called Nazoraeans [Nazarenes],"[2981] and, most significantly, that the Nazarenes were identical to the Gnostic sect known as the Ebionites[2982]—a group which viewed Jesus as an ordinary man[2983] (virtuous but not divine),[2984] who had been indwelled by God at his baptism.[2985] The Jews themselves were known to have referred to Christians as "Nazarenes,"[2986] as the Bible itself attests.[2987]

According to Epiphanius then, Christianity began as an Essene sect and is thus wholly Gnostic; that is, esoteric or mystical, in origin—a view that forms of one of the very pillars of this work. See BRETHREN, CHRISTIANITY, ENOCH, ESSENES, GNOSIS, GNOSTICISM, GOSPEL, WAY OF THE LORD.

NEIGHBOR: In traditional Christianity a neighbor is a neighbor, and nothing more. In mystical Christianity one's neighbor is a symbol of the universal Self; in other words, *your neighbor is you*, only clothed in a different physical appearance. Thus, our Lord, the greatest Law of Attraction teacher of all time, said that the second greatest commandment (after loving God) is to "love thy neighbor as thyself,"[2988] for "thy neighbor" is thyself.

According to the ancient scientific Law of Reciprocity what we deal out returns to us, whether it is a thought, a word, or a deed. Seeing our neighbor as our self (a spiritual reality), means that we will always be kind and equitable toward him or her. This positive energy (love) will then return to us laden with goodness, helping us to build our ideal life here on earth.[2989] For thoughts are things that shape our lives.[2990] So spoke the Proverbist.[2991] See DIVINE MIND, KARMA.

NOAH: In the traditional Church Noah is the tenth generation from Adam, the son of Lamech, a righteous man commanded by God to build an ark to save himself and his family from the Great Flood.[2992] In the mystical Church Noah is a symbol of the peace and comfort we find in the Christ who indwells us all.[2993] This is revealed in his name: Noah is Hebrew for "rest," "calm," or "tranquility."[2994] Jukes writes:

> Noah is the divinely appointed figure, in whom the whole

course of regeneration is set forth, every secret of this great mystery being here drawn for us as God alone could draw it. . . . Noah then is the spiritual mind,—for he is only the continuation of Seth's line, and figures the form of life which the spiritual mind takes at this stage in its development, when it has come so far as to know the judgment of the old creation, and the way through that judgment to a cleansed and better world. This stage, if we regard it closely, will be seen to embrace several distinct parts; for we may see Noah as in the world to be judged, still in the midst of its sins, though undefiled by them; or as going through the waters, and tossed by them, separated from the old world, and yet not come to the cleansed world; or, as on resurrection ground, coming out of the ark into that sphere where judgment is past, and he in joyful liberty. Each of these are stages of regeneration.

There is, first, the discovery of the sin which is working in the first creation, upon the ground of the old man; then the experience of the judgment of that old man, during which we are tossed about, and the waves and billows of God's judgments are inwardly passed through; and lastly, the rest in resurrection life, when we feel and know ourselves in liberty and redemption beyond those dark waters. And each of these stages has its own parts, for in grace as in nature each general truth comprises many others. The outline may first be seen, then the particulars: first the dark cloud, then the countless rain-drops, full of beauties, if the sun shines. So is the truth, that heavenly rain, which, like its Maker, challenges our wonder on every hand the more we contemplate it.[2995]

See ARK, DOVE, FLOOD OF NOAH, RAINBOW, RIVER, WATER.

NUMBER OF THE BEAST: In traditional Christianity the (second) number of the Beast of Revelation is 666, while the Beast himself is held to be Satan.[2996] This particular number is thought by the orthodox to be a diabolical perversion of three, the number of the Holy Trinity. The mystical Gnostic-Christian writers of the Apocalypse, however, never intended any of these interpretations. To them the "Beast" was Nero Caesar,[2997] whose name in Aramaic is spelled without vowels: *Nron Ksr*.[2998] In Jewish mysticism these Aramaic letters are equivalent to the numbers 50 (n), 200 (r), 6 (o), 50 (n), 100 (k), 60 (s), and 200 (r), which equals 666.[2999]

In mystical Christianity the number 666 is of a completely different derivation, one both positive and spiritual in nature, originating in the ancient worship of the Great Mother-Goddess, variously known around the world as Juno, Hera, Mary, Asherah, Shekinah, Shakti, Hathor, Isis, Nut, Ishtar, Inanna, Astarte, Anat, Aphrodite, *ad infinitum*. Just as God represents men, fatherhood, and the Divine Masculine, Goddess represents women, motherhood, and the Divine Feminine. Thus, 666 also signifies Revelation's Great Pagan-Christian Goddess, or "Woman Clothed with the Sun,"[3000] namely the Virgin Mary, whose sacred number is 1,260—which added together equals nine.[3001]

The key to understanding the mystical meaning of 666 is that in numerology it is a nine number, which we get by reducing it through addition: 6 + 6 + 6 = 18, and 1 + 8 = 9. While nine is magical in part because it is a tripling of the all-powerful number three,[3002] nine itself is the number of months of human pregnancy and the number of holes in the body (two eyes, two nostrils, two ears, the mouth, and two "vents" below the naval).[3003] These associations gave rise to the ancients' Nine Muses, the nine orders of angels, the nine cosmic spheres, the nine Divine Powers of the Ennead (at Heliopolis), etc.

The Gnostic-Christian mystic who wrote Revelation ("John")[3004] incorporated the Number of the Beast, nine, into countless other elements of his prophecies, including:

- The glorified saints, who numbered 144,000 (numerologically which equals nine: 1 + 4 + 4 = 9).[3005]
- The first Beast (Emporer Domitian), who was given the power to rule for 42 months, or 504 days (which equals nine).[3006]
- The length of time Gentiles would "tread under foot" the holy city: 42 months (504 days, which equals nine).[3007]
- The length of time the "two witnesses" would prophecy: 1,260 days (which equals nine).[3008]
- The woman ("clothed with the sun") who fled to the wilderness for 1,260 days (which equals nine).[3009]
- The dimensions of the New Jerusalem, which were 144 cubits (which equals nine).[3010]

As three squared, the sacred number 666 is a triple empowerment of the divine number three, the archetypal number of perfection and completion as embodied in humanity's first and original Trinity: Father, Mother, and Child. In Paganism this sacred threesome was personified in countless trinities of deities, representing heaven (male), earth (female), and air (the child that unites them). The Holy Trinity in ancient Egypt, for example, was Osiris, Isis, and Horus,[3011] in Greece Zeus, Athene, and Apollo, in India Brahma, Shiva, and Vishnu,[3012] and in Scandinavia Odin, Frea, and Thor.[3013] In traditional Christianity these were personified as God, the Holy Spirit, and Jesus.

The sacrality of the number nine, and its corollary 666, can also be seen in the fact that they symbolize a tripling of the three stages of life (childhood, adulthood, seniorhood), the three bodies (physical, mental, spiritual), the three minds (conscious, subconscious, superconscious), the three phases of human existence (birth, life, and death; or life, death, and rebirth), the three mystical languages (exoteric, mesoteric, esoteric), the three primary symbols of the alchemists (salt, sulphur, mercury), and so on.

Since Solomon worshiped the Great Mother (in the form of the Hebrew mother-goddess Asherah or Ashtoreth),[3014] he symbolically possessed 666 talents of gold,[3015] for as Solomon's name reveals (Sol-Om-On means "Sun-God of On"),[3016] he is none other than the Sun or Sol himself, whose sacred number is 666.[3017] The hexagram or Star of David contains six points, considered the perfect number by Pythagoreans since it lies midway between two and ten (one was not then viewed as a number).[3018]

Contrary to what conservative Christianity teaches about the Number of the Beast, the Bible states that ultimately 666 is the number of Man.[3019] And who is this "Man"? It is you and I, individuations of God, who both indwells and outdwells us.[3020] We are, in other words, thoughts from the mind of God, for as the Gnostic-Christians taught, "God is all mind and mind is all God."[3021] And indeed, the word man derives from the same root as the Sanskrit word *manas*, meaning "mind"; which is why in Hinduism the Self (Indwelling Christ) is known as "At-Man."[3022] Of the number of the Beast and its associations, Heindel writes:

> [The] number nine is the root-number of our present stage of evolution. It bears a significance in our system that no other number does. It is the number of Adam, the life which commenced its evolution as Man, which reached the human stage during the Earth Period. In the Hebrew, as in the Greek, there are no numerals, but each letter has a numerical value. In Hebrew "Adam" is called "ADM." The value of "A" is 1; of "D," 4; and of "M," 40. If we add these figures, we get 1 + 4 + 4 + 0 = 9—the number of Adam, or humanity.
>
> If we turn from the Book of Genesis, which deals with the creation of man in the hoary past, to the Book of Revelation, which deals with his future attainment, we find that the number of the beast which hinders is 666. Adding these figures, 6 + 6 + 6 = 18; and further, 1 + 8 = 9—we have again the number of humanity, which is itself the cause of all the evil which hinders its own progress.
>
> Going further, to the point where the number of those who are to be saved is stated, we find it to be 144,000. Adding as before, 1 + 4 + 4 + 000 = 9—again the number of humanity, showing that practically it will be saved in its totality,

the number incapable of progress in our present evolution being negligible in comparison to the grand total, and even the few who fail are not lost, but will progress in a later scheme.

The consciousness of the mineral and the plant is really unconsciousness. The first glimmering dawn of consciousness begins with the animal kingdom. We have seen also that according to the most modern classification, there are thirteen steps in the animal kingdom: three classes of Radiates; three classes of Mollusks; three classes of Articulates; and four classes of Vertebrates. If we regard ordinary man as a step by himself, and remember that there are thirteen Initiations from man to God, or from the time he commenced to qualify himself for becoming a self-conscious Creative Intelligence, we have again the same number, Nine—13 + 1 + 13 = 27; 2 + 7 = 9. The number 9 is also hidden in the age of Christ Jesus, 33; 3 x 3 = 9, and in a similar manner in the 33 degrees of Masonry.[3023]

See BEAST, DEVIL, EGYPT, HEROD ANTIPAS, NUMBERS, SATAN.

NUMBERS: In the traditional Church biblical numbers are typically viewed as merely literal numerical qualities, rarely as symbols. In the mystical Church biblical numbers—like people, events, and things—are nearly always seen as symbols, metaphors, or emblems concealing profound spiritual concepts and truths.

Behind this idea lie the occult pre-Christian arts of numerology[3024] and gematria,[3025] the former which is a study of the esoteric significance of numbers, the latter in which scripture is interpreted based on the numerical value of letters (and thus words). Some trace the origin of the idea of mystical and symbolical numerology to Pythagoras and his followers. There is evidence that the Babylonians and the ancient Greeks were using gematria thousands of years ago.[3026]

All of the great Christian mystics were aware of numerology and gematria in one form or another. Christopher Wordsworth, for example, writes:

> The symbolical meaning of Numbers in Holy Scripture deserves more study and attention than it has received in recent times. "God doeth all things in number and measure and weight."[3027] From an induction of particulars it would appear that 3 is an arithmetical Symbol of what is Divine, and 4 of what is Created. 3 + 4 = 7 is the union of the Two; hence signifying Rest, a Sabbath; 3 x 4 = 12 is the blending and indwelling of what is Divine with what is created: e.g., as in Israel, the people of God: and in the heavenly Jerusalem.[3028]

Swedenborg writes:

> "John to the seven churches," signifies to all who are in the Christian world where the Word is, and by it the Lord is known, and who accede to the church. By the seven churches are not to be understood seven churches, but all who are of the church in the Christian world; *for numbers, in the Word, signify things*, and seven, all things and all, and thence, also, what is full and perfect, and it occurs in the Word where any thing holy is treated of, and, in an opposite sense, where it treats of any thing profane; consequently, this number involves what is holy, and, in an opposite sense, what is profane.
>
> *The reason why numbers signify things, or rather resemble certain adjectives to substantives denoting some quality in things, is, because number is, in itself, natural; for natural things are determined by numbers, but spiritual things by things and their states: therefore, he who is ignorant of the signification of numbers in the Word, and especially in the Apocalypse, must be ignorant of many arcana which are contained therein.* Now, since seven signifies all things and all, it may appear that by seven churches are meant all who are in the Christian world where the Word is, and where consequently the Lord is known: these, if they live according to the Lord's precepts in the Word, constitute the true church. For this reason the sabbath was instituted on the seventh day, and the seventh year was called the Sabbatarian year; and the seven times seventh year the jubilee, by which was signified every thing holy in the church . . .[3029]

Though many of the early Christian Fathers, such as Irenaeus, rejected the idea of mystical biblical numerology as a "fictitious system untenable"[3030]—considering it a diabolical ruse invented by enemies of the Church to lead the faithful astray—there were others who not only accepted it, but encouraged its study. One of these was the great Church Father Augustine, who writes:

> *Ignorance of numbers, too, prevents us from understanding things that are set down in Scripture in a figurative and mystical way.* A candid mind, if I may so speak, cannot but be anxious, for example, to ascertain what is meant by the fact that Moses and Elijah, and our Lord Himself, all fasted for forty days. And except by knowledge of and reflection upon the number, the difficulty of explaining the figure involved in this action cannot be got over.

For the number contains ten four times, indicating the knowledge of all things, and that knowledge interwoven with time. For both the diurnal and the annual revolutions are accomplished in periods numbering four each; the diurnal in the hours of the morning, the noontide, the evening, and the night; the annual in the spring, summer, autumn, and winter months.

Now while we live in time, we must abstain and fast from all joy in time, for the sake of that eternity in which we wish to live; although by the passage of time we are taught this very lesson of despising time and seeking eternity. Further, the number ten signifies the knowledge of the Creator and the creature, for there is a trinity in the Creator; and the number seven indicates the creature, because of the life and the body. For the life consists of three parts, whence also God is to be loved with the whole heart, the whole soul, and the whole mind; and it is very clear that in the body there are four elements of which it is made up. In this number ten, therefore, when it is placed before us in connection with time, that is, when it is taken four times, we are admonished to live unstained by, and not partaking of, any delight in time, that is, to fast for forty days. Of this we are admonished by the law personified in Moses, by prophecy personified in Elijah, and by our Lord Himself, who, as if receiving the witness both of the law and the prophets, appeared on the mount between the other two, while His three disciples looked on in amazement.

Next, we have to inquire in the same way, how out of the number forty springs the number fifty, which in our religion has no ordinary sacredness attached to it on account of the Pentecost, and how this number taken thrice on account of the three divisions of time, before the law, under the law, and under grace, or perhaps on account of the name of the Father, Son, and Holy Spirit, and the Trinity itself being added over and above, has reference to the mystery of the most Holy Church, and reaches to the number of the one hundred and fifty-three fishes which were taken after the resurrection of our Lord, when the nets were cast out on the right-hand side of the boat. And *in the same way, many other numbers and combinations of numbers are used in the sacred writings, to convey instruction under a figurative guise, and ignorance of numbers often shuts out the reader from this instruction.*[3031]

Saint Methodius writes:

For a thousand, consisting of a hundred multiplied by ten, embraces a full and perfect number, and is a symbol of the Father Himself, who made the universe by Himself, and rules all things for Himself. Two hundred embraces two perfect numbers united together, and is the symbol of the Holy Spirit, since He is the Author of our knowledge of the Son and the Father. But sixty has the number six multiplied by ten, and is a symbol of Christ, because the number six proceeding from unity is composed of its proper parts, so that nothing in it is wanting or redundant, and is complete when resolved into its parts.

Thus it is necessary that the number six, when it is divided into even parts by even parts, should again make up the same quantity from its separated segments. For, first, if divided equally, it makes three; then, if divided into three parts, it makes two; and again, if divided by six, it makes one, and is again collected into itself. For when divided into twice three, and three times two, and six times one, when the three and the two and the one are put together, they complete the six again. But everything is of necessity perfect which neither needs anything else in order to its completion, nor has anything over.

Of the other numbers, some are more than perfect, as twelve. For the half of it is six, and the third four, and the fourth three, and the sixth two, and the twelfth one. The numbers into which it can be divided, when put together, exceed twelve, this number not having preserved itself equal to its parts, like the number six. And those which are imperfect, are numbers like eight. For the half of it is four, and the fourth two, and the eighth one. Now the numbers into which it is divided, when put together, make seven, and one is wanting to its completion, not being in all points harmonious with itself, like six, which has reference to the Son of God, who came from the fulness of the Godhead into a human life. For having emptied Himself, and taken upon Him the form of a slave, He was restored again to His former perfection and dignity. For He being humbled, and apparently degraded, was restored again from His humiliation and degradation to His former completeness and greatness, having never been diminished from His essential perfection.[3032]

Pike writes of the importance of sacred numbers in Freemasonry, and how they are connected to ancient Judaism and the Bible:

The Temple of Solomon presented a symbolic image of the universe; and resembled, in its arrangements and furniture, all the temples of the ancient nations that practised the mysteries. The system of numbers was intimately connected with their religions and worship, and has come down to us in Masonry; though the esoteric meaning with which the numbers used by us are pregnant is unknown to the vast majority of those who use them. Those numbers were especially employed that had a reference to the Deity, represented his attributes, or figured in the frame-work of the world, in time and space, and formed more or less the bases of that frame-work. These were universally regarded as sacred, being the expression of order and intelligence, the utterances of Divinity himself.

The Holy of holies of the temple formed a cube; in which, drawn on a plane surface, there are $4 + 3 + 2 = 9$ lines visible, and three sides or faces. It corresponded with the number four, by which the ancients represented Nature, it being the number of substances or corporeal forms, and of the elements, the cardinal points and seasons, and the secondary colors. The number three everywhere represented the Supreme Being. Hence the name of the Deity, engraven upon the triangular plate, and that sunken into the cube of agate, taught the ancient Mason, and teaches us, that the true knowledge of God, of His nature and His attributes, is written by Him upon the leaves of the great Book of Universal Nature, and may be read there by all who are endowed with the requisite amount of intellect and intelligence. This knowledge of God, so written there, and of which Masonry has in all ages been the interpreter, is the Master Mason's Word.

Within the Temple, all the arrangements were mystically and symbolically connected with the same system. The vault or ceiling, starred like the firmament, was supported by twelve columns, representing the twelve months of the year. The border that ran around the columns represented the zodiac, and one of the twelve celestial signs was appropriated to each column. The brazen sea was supported by twelve oxen, three looking to each cardinal point of the compass.[3033]

See APOSTLES, ASTROLOGY, NUMBER OF THE BEAST, SEVEN STARS, TWELVE, ZODIAC.

Jesus takes leave of His mother.

Egyptian temple.

Pre-Christian Mithraic sacrament of bread and water.

Bethlehem.

OIL: In traditional Christianity the use of oil in the Bible is either for food or for the ritual of anointing,[3034] such as in baptism, confirmation, ordination, and unction.[3035] In mystical Christianity oil is a symbol of love, and more specifically of God's love for all humanity.[3036] This gives it a dual meaning, one spiritual, one carnal, two doctrines that were not mutually exclusive in antiquity.

First let us look at the mystical religious manner in which oil was used in the days of the Bible.

Shiny oil, in particular olive oil, is an occult symbol of the Sun, which in turn is a symbol of the Indwelling Christ.[3037] Thus consecrating the top of the human head (site of the Crown Chakra) with oil was an arcane representation of attaining Christhood or enlightenment, or what is variously known in different religions and societies as: Abraham Consciousness, ananda, apavarga, bodhi, Buddha Consciousness, Buddhahood, Christ Consciousness, Christhood, christophany, Cosmic Consciousness, darshan, epiphany, fana, hazon, hierophany, illumination, kaivalya, kensho, Krishna Consciousness, Krishnahood, mar'eh, moksha, Moses Consciousness, mukti, nirvana, salvation, samadhi, sat-chit-ananda, satori, self-realization, sukha, tapas, theaphany, theophany, turiya, wu wei, and yogasema.[3038]

Because ancient people considered *all* kings, queens, and leaders in general to be deities or "Christs," they were christed by anointing the head with a sacred oil known as *chrism*.[3039] Thus the Psalmist says:

> Thou lovest righteousness, and hatest wickedness: therefore God, thy God, hath anointed thee with the oil of gladness above thy fellows.[3040]

The "oil of gladness" is a symbol of the Sun or Son (that is, Christhood), while "above thy fellows" is yet another occult Bible expression for spiritual enlightenment. Thus a heavily allegorical prayer from an ancient Egyptian ceremony reads:

> Thou receivest the oil of the cedar in Amentet [entrance to the Underworld], and the cedar which came forth from Osiris [Christ] cometh unto thee; it delivereth thee from thy enemies. . . . Thy soul alighteth upon the venerable sycamores. Thou

criest to Isis [Virgin Mary], and Osiris heareth thy voice, and
Anubis [transfiguration] cometh unto thee to invoke thee. Thou
receivest the oil of the country of Manu [the first man, Adam]
which hath come from the East [entrance to Heaven], and Ra
[the Sun] riseth upon thee at the gates of the horizon, at the holy
doors of Neith [power]. Thou goest therein, thy soul is in the
upper heaven [enlightenment].[3041]

Swedenborg writes:

. . . oil signifies the good of love which sanctifies, and every
thing that is sanctified has relation to truth.[3042]

Secondly, we have the religiosexual context in which oil was used. In the Goddess-worshiping Matriarchal Age, before paternity was understood (pre-6000 B.C.), the ancients held that women were reproductively superior to men. It was thought that the male lacked the female's ability to generate the life force (Shakti), which could only be transferred to a man from a woman by way of the sex act. From this idea grew the Pagan and Hebrew practice of religious harlotry or Sacred Prostitution: Temple-priestesses known as the *Horae*, "Holy Whores," would perform a magic ceremony, then anoint a man's phallus (euphemistically called the "head") with sacred sexual oil (chrism), and mount him to orgasm. This sacred act, known as the Hieros Gamos ("Holy Union"), allowed for the male's participation in the procreative act, aided in assuring the fertility of the community, and propitiated the gods and goddesses in the hopes of an abundant harvest in the Fall.[3043]

In addition, this feminine christing ceremony was part of the Bible's Pagan-Hebrew ritual known as *Yada* (Hebrew), *Ginosko* (Greek), or *Horasis* (Greek): the Tantric-like attainment of spiritual enlightenment or Christhood through sex[3044]—via the secret Whore-Wisdom of the Great Mother-Goddess.[3045] The Old Testament refers to a female temple prostitute as a *Kadeshah* ("Holy One"), a male temple prostitute as a *Kadesh*.[3046] The notion of the holy whore, the practice of the Yada or Ginosko rite, and the doctrine of whore wisdom were deeply entrenched in early societies. The ancient Semitic clan the Horites,[3047] for instance claimed descent from the Great Whore-Goddess Hora,[3048] while Jewish sacred whores are shown living next to the Jerusalem Temple, where they wove hangings for the Goddess' sacred tree groves.[3049]

Why is this knowledge virtually unknown to modern day Christians? Because the words *yada* and *ginosko* were disguised in the Old and New Testaments by early English scribes, who intentionally mistranslated them as the words "know," "knew," and "knowing," to this day still codewords for sexual congress.[3050] As the Pagan-Christian word for spiritually revealed self-knowledge is *gnosis* (that is, "knowledge" obtained by intuition), the connection between anointing oil and these various Christian schools, doctrines, and rituals becomes clear.

Religious and religiosexual oil-christing rituals predate Christianity by thousands of years. Thus, we should not be surprised to learn that they were commonly used by the Israelites,[3051] as well in what some scholars consider ancient Hebrew male homosexual rites.[3052] Jacob, the son of Isaac and Rebecca and the eponymous ancestor of the 12 Tribes of Israel, for example, is shown performing christing ceremonies using chrism oil and a "pillar of stone," or what archaeologists know as a menhir and what Jews know as a *massebah*: a phallus-shaped standing stone. Revealingly, the second ritual listed below took place after God, then called El Shaddai (a Mesopotamian mountain-god),[3053] renamed Jacob "Israel," a composite title made up of the names of the three popular ancient Pagan deities, Isis, Ra, and El:

> And Jacob rose up early in the morning, and took the stone that he had put for his pillows, and set it up for a pillar, and poured oil upon the top of it. . . [saying] "And this stone, which I have set for a pillar, shall be God's house."[3054]

> And Jacob set up a pillar in the place where he talked with him [El Shaddai, God], even a pillar of stone: and he poured a drink offering thereon, and he poured oil thereon.[3055]

The "pillar" or *massebah* used in ancient Hebrew phallic worship was occultly entitled the "House of God" because as a lingam symbol it represented the generative power of the Father. The Bible openly confirms this, calling God "the rock that begat thee."[3056]

It is through the Hieros Gamos that we uncover the occultic secret behind Jacob's "oil," a word often used in the Bible as a euphemism for the male reproductive fluid, *semen*: the original Hebrew word for this christing oil is *shemen*, which appears 176 times in the Old Testament.[3057] Unhappily, these facts have been obscured by misunderstanding, fear, ignorance, and mistranslation, preventing millions of Christians from advancing in biblical literacy and spiritual wisdom.[3058]

Nonetheless, the connection between the Virgin-Mother-Whore-Goddess, her christing-oil rituals, phallic worship (or Priapism),[3059] and the Goddess' holy child, the Sun/Son-God, is patently obvious when we use etymology to further explore the hidden or esoteric meaning of the word chrism. Chrism derives from the ancient Chaldean word *chrs* or—with vowels—*chris* (in Hebrew written *heres* or *hrs*), meaning the "Sun"; in nearly every society a symbol of the universal Savior-Son-God and his role as a solar deity or Sun-god.[3060]

Naturally, as an enlightened spiritual leader and teacher, that is, a spiritual "king" or Sun/Son-god, Jesus too underwent the christing ritual of the Holy

Whore. But this momentous event is not recognized by the mainstream Church as such—though all four of the Evangelists mention it. We cannot altogether blame mainstream Christians for glossing over it, for the event is written esoterically, in a language that is not taught in the institutional Church. Matthew recorded it like this:

> Now when Jesus was in Bethany, in the house of Simon the leper, there came unto him a woman [the Temple prostitute Mary Magdalene] having an alabaster box of very precious ointment, and poured it on his head, as he sat at meat.[3061]

Luke moves the location of the anointing to our Lord's feet (possibly to conceal the carnal aspect), but this does not alter the secret meaning of the rite:

> And one of the Pharisees desired Him [Jesus] that He would eat with him. And He went into the Pharisee's house and sat down to meat. And behold, a woman in the city, who was a sinner, when she learned that Jesus sat at meat in the Pharisee's house, brought an alabaster box of ointment, and stood at His feet behind Him weeping; and began to wash His feet with tears and wiped them with the hair of her head, and kissed His feet and anointed them with the ointment.[3062]

Based on a scripture in Matthew, orthodox Christians explain this incident away as nothing more than a symbolic preparation for Jesus' impending death and burial.[3063] But the Matthean passage in question is also esoterically written, and so Bible literalists and exoteric scholars get no closer to the truth by relying on it.

In the mystical Church the anointing of the Master's head by a "sinful" woman (a temple prostitute) takes on an entirely new and profound meaning. It is, in fact, a Christian copy of the pre-Christian rite of Pagan Christing or Christening, wherein the Mother-Goddess (sometimes depicted as the great Holy Whore[3064] or Triple-Goddess)[3065] anoints her son the Sun-god as a sacred king, then laments his sacrificial but necessary death on the tree. Just as early Hebrew women lamented the death of the Mesopotamian dying and rising savior-god Tammuz,[3066] the pre-biblical Epic of Gilgamesh tells of the christening of the hero-god Enkidu by a harlot.[3067] This same story is told of the Triadic Mother-Goddess Mari-Anna-Ishtar, who anoints her son before he dies and enters the Underworld, from which he later rises up in glory.[3068] And so this theme occultly entered Christianity as well, in this case as the "Three Marys" who "stood by the cross of Jesus" during His crucifixion.[3069]

Why is it nearly always the male and not the female who is sacrificed in ancient myth? As discussed, in the period before the male's role in reproduction was recognized, women were believed to be parthenogenic (self-reproducing).[3070] Hence, the blood of childbirth was considered to be the sacred life-bearing fluid of the Supreme Being (imaged then as a female, "Goddess").[3071] In order for the male to participate in the creative process, his own blood was needed to replace what the goddess had lost giving birth. Such males were commonly deified after their deaths as a reward.[3072]

As a vestige of the ancient Pagan christening myth of the Mother-Goddess and her divine Sun/Son-King, to this day the ointment jar or vase of holy oil remains a Christian womb or yonic symbol of the Sacred Prostitute Mary Magdalene,[3073] who Mark mystically portrays visiting Jesus' tomb in order to "anoint" His body a second time.[3074] Jesus Himself is listed in the New Testament as descending from a number of Horae ("whores"), including Thamar, Rachab, Ruth, and Bathsheba.[3075] Our Lord, a hierophantic adept deeply schooled in the Ancient Mysteries, well understood the divine import of the sacred Whore Wisdom, cryptically saying in the Gospel of Matthew:

> I tell you truthfully that . . . prostitutes will enter the Kingdom of God before most of those who call themselves "Christians."[3076]

These facts alone make it plain that our Lord's entire life story as recorded in the four canonical Gospels is pregnant with vital "hidden wisdom."[3077] Let those who have eyes to see and ears to hear freely partake of the sacred knowledge contained herein. See ANOINTING, ENLIGHTENMENT, GNOSIS, ISRAEL, MYTH OF CHRIST, PETER, ROCK, TEMPLE OF GOD, TRIBES OF ISRAEL.

ONLY BEGOTTEN SON: In traditional Christianity the phrase "Only Begotten Son" means "the sole son, born of God." As such, it is used as a title of Jesus, depicted as God's "first and only son."[3078] "Only begotten" is a mistranslation, however, of the original Greek word here, *monogenes*, which means "unique," not "born of God." Indeed, according to the ancient usage of the word *monogenes*, it was more often used as a synonym for *agapetos*, "beloved." Proof that this is the intended meaning of the phrase comes from the esoteric Essenic book of Hebrews, wherein Isaac is called Abraham's *monogenes* son, translated as "only begotten son,"[3079] an impossibility if taken literally since Abraham had a number of sons. What the writer is actually telling us is that Isaac was a special son to Abraham, *unique* because, perhaps, he was more *loved* than the others.[3080]

As we will now see, the Only Begotten Son *is* truly unique; but in a way that the mainstream Church does not recognize or teach.

In mystical Christianity any of the traditional Christian meanings is acceptable because the term Only Begotten Son does not concern only the historic Jesus, but *all* men and women, for it is a symbol of Christ Consciousness,[3081] or what Paul called "the mind of Christ."[3082] It is, in other words, the Higher Self,[3083] created in the image of God,[3084] indwelling every human being.[3085] And there is indeed only *one*, though split into an infinite number of "divine sparks" which God has implanted in us one at a time. We call this *divinity within*, the "human Soul," or more correctly, the "human Spirit."

The universality of the concept of the "Only Begotten Son" or "Firstborn" means that it is not specifically biblical, or even Christian, for we find it in nearly every faith dating back to one of the world's oldest religions: Hinduism.

Here, however, we discover the same problem: the inability to understand the mystical (inner or hidden) meaning of the doctrine of the Only Begotten Son. Deussen notes, for instance, that, just as mainstream Christianity has done with Jesus, some in the East have misinterpreted Indian scripture to mean that the founder of the Sankhya system was himself the "Only Begotten Son" or "Firstborn" of God:

> Hiranyagarbha came forth as the first-born of creation from the primeval waters which were created by the first principle. Because it is the first principle itself which appears in its creation as first-born, therefore, the latter also is denoted by Brahman [the creative principle or world-soul] with change of gender and accent, as though it were Brahman personified.
> ... This conception of the first-born of creation as the original source of all wisdom is carried further first in the S'vetasvatara Upanishad (which in general inclines towards a personification of the divine), and here it is described as the *Brahman, Hiranyagarbha* the "golden germ," or even in one passage with a poetic and metaphorical use of the word as the "red wizard," *kapila rishi*, an expression that has led many into the mistaken belief that here, in a Vedic Upanishad, Kapila the founder of the Sankhya system was named as the first-born of creation! Had the author of our Upanishad, so strongly opposed to all dualism and atheism, known him (which we do not believe), he would have assuredly characterised him with altogether different epithets.[3086]

The great Judeo-Christian mystic Paul understood that the Only Begotten Son is not the human being Jesus. It is "the firstborn of every creature":

> Giving thanks unto the Father, which hath made us meet to be partakers of the inheritance of the saints in *light* [spiritual enlightenment]: Who hath delivered us from the power of darkness [spiritual ignorance], and hath translated us into the

kingdom [consciousness] of his dear *Son* [the Indwelling Christ]: In whom we have redemption through his blood [divine truth], even the forgiveness of sins [errors]: Who is the image of the invisible God, *the firstborn of every creature*: For by him were all things created, that are in heaven, and that are in earth, visible and invisible . . .³⁰⁸⁷

Tellingly, the term Only Begotten Son is used only for "Jesus" (that is, a human symbol of the Indwelling Christ) by the most mystical of the four Evangelists, the Gnostic-occultist John³⁰⁸⁸ (whose Christian disciple Lucius Charinus passed on his Gnostic teachings to another generation.)³⁰⁸⁹ It is from John's esoteric point of view that we see that there was and is only *one* "Only Begotten Son." And that "Son" is the Universal Christ of the One Living Father/Mother, also known as the One, the Source of All. Truly, Jesus, speaking as the great I AM or EYE AM, the Aum, the Om, the Hum, the Amen, the Yes, the Divine Spark in every man and woman, said:

> I AM the way, the truth, and the life: no man cometh unto the Father, but by me.³⁰⁹⁰

In occultic terms our Lord is declaring one of the greatest of all eternal truths: no one can attain at-one-ment (atonement) with God without first acknowledging and attuning himself or herself to the one and "Only Begotten Son," which is the Higher Self, the Divine Self, the "immaculately conceived," "virgin-born" Universal Inner Christ,³⁰⁹¹ which the ancient Egyptians (and later Gnostic John the Evangelist)³⁰⁹² referred to as "the true Light, which lighteth *every* man that cometh into the world."³⁰⁹³ See CHRIST, CHRIST CONSCIOUSNESS, GOD, JESUS, MESSIAH, SAVIOR, SON OF GOD, WAY OF THE LORD.

ORIGINAL SIN: In traditional Christianity the doctrine of original sin states that every human being is born in a state of sin due to the fall of Adam and Eve in the Garden of Eden.³⁰⁹⁴ It is allegedly based on Paul's statement that "sin entered into the world by one man."³⁰⁹⁵ But this does not reflect the true idea of original sin, which holds that we all share in the *personal* sinful act of Adam and Eve.³⁰⁹⁶ Indeed, Paul's words have been greatly misunderstood by the orthodox, and thus greatly perverted over the centuries.

What he is saying in this particular passage is merely that because "sin is death,"³⁰⁹⁷ and because both sin³⁰⁹⁸ and death are universal,³⁰⁹⁹ then all people must be sinners, nothing more.³¹⁰⁰ In fact, in his same letter to the Romans, Paul wholly contradicts what would later become the idea of "original sin," which, as noted, states that we must "pay" for the sins of Adam and Eve. Says Paul:

> For if, when we were enemies, we were reconciled to God by the death of his Son, much more, being reconciled, we shall be saved by his life.[3101]

In mystical Christianity there is no such belief as original sin,[3102] for, as just mentioned, the idea does not appear anywhere in the Bible, and is thus manmade.[3103] This has momentous ramifications for traditional Christianity and the doctrine of atonement or at-one-ment. Dupuis writes:

> These two dogmas cannot be separated from each other: if there is no sin, there is no atonement; if there is no tresspasser, then no redeemer is required.[3104]

This means, of course, that Jesus did not need to be born of a virgin or die on the cross, rendering these two orthodox Christian doctrines meaningless, which is precisely what a close reading of the Bible reveals to many truth seekers.

Furthermore, Christian mystics view the story of Adam and Eve as an allegory, the word sin as meaning merely a "mistake,"[3105] and the perfection and salvation of all people[3106] as being assured by the perfection we possess being born "in the image of God."[3107] Jesus commented on our innate flawlessness when He said:

> Be ye therefore perfect, as your Father which is in heaven is perfect.[3108]

Obviously, we cannot strive for the perfection of God if we do not already possess the potential for this perfection within us.[3109] Like the oak tree which creates acorns rather than pine cones, we can only produce that which is already within us.[3110] Indeed, our Lord is telling us here that we *can* and we *must* come to realize our inner divinity here and now[3111]—a doctrine (known as Theosis) which forms the very foundation of all of the great religions.

Thus, traditional Christian doctrines which state that Man is inherently depraved and that Jesus' death was necessary to appease a furious, overly judgmental Supreme Being, are erroneous, irrational, unethical, and unscriptural, not to mention a dishonor to the God of love himself.[3112]

The concept of original sin is not even Christian in origin. It was taught, for example, in the ancient Greek religion Orphism some 500 years before the birth of Jesus.[3113] Here, early Pagans believed that the Soul had been condemned to earthly existence as a form of punishment for the sin of the 12 Titans, the ancestors of humanity, who had "treacherously slain the young god Zagreus."[3114]

As with all religious and spiritual notions, Christian mystics see the non-Christian, un-Christian, and anti-Christian idea of original sin as a metaphor. In this case, as Kingsford and Maitland write,

> Original sin is . . . precisely the condition of blindness which—owing to the soul's immergence in materiality—hinders the perception of divine things. By no possibility can the Divine Life be generated in any soul afflicted with this blindness.[3115]

The only real "original sin" is the literalization, adoption, and promotion of this Pagan idea by the traditional Church to begin with. For in doing so, it has blinded millions to their unity with the Divine,[3116] the Christ,[3117] and the Holy Spirit,[3118] thereby preventing true at-one-ment with God—the very problem this doctrine is meant to resolve! To borrow an apt phrase from Strauss, it is my view that the Christian idea of original sin is the "offspring of a legitimate marriage between theological ignorance and religious intolerance, blessed by a sleep-walking philosophy."[3119] See DEVIL, KARMA, LUCIFER, MESSIAH, REDEEMER, REDEMPTION, SALVATION, SATAN, SAVIOR, SIN, THEOSIS.

OSIRIS: Although the ancient Egyptian god Osiris does not appear by name in the Bible, his essence certainly does, for dozens if not hundreds of elements of his figure and life story were adopted by the early theocrasiatic Christian Church and assimilated to Jesus. Thus the importance of his inclusion here.

Ancient Egypt herself has contributed more to the doctrines, rituals, names, myths, ideas, and figures of Christianity than any other religion or source.[3120] Such donations include: the word "Christ,"[3121] the rite of anointing,[3122] the idea of the "Last Supper,"[3123] the concept of the resurrection of the dead (in association with the 6,000 year old doctrine of the dying and rising god),[3124] the use of the crucifix or cross (ankh), the ritual of baptism, communion, and the Eucharist or Sacrament of bread and wine, the use of holy water, sacred iconography, the *Agnus Dei* and shepherd's crook, incantations, the rosary, unction, invocations, exorcism, the belief in saints' relics,[3125] the *Agape* (love feast),[3126] Lent,[3127] Christmas, the Christmas tree,[3128] and countless others.

As ancient Egypt's most popular deity,[3129] and as one who ruled the land for some 4,000 years,[3130] it is thus little wonder that Osiris has gifted more to the figure of Jesus than any other Pagan god.[3131] It would be perfectly correct, in fact, to say that the early Christian Church was overly excessive in borrowing from the great African deity. Of him Budge writes:

> . . . it is clear that in Plutarch's time the Egyptians believed that Osiris was the *son of a god*, that *he lived a good life upon earth and ruled as a wise and just king*, that *he was slain by the malice of evil men*, that *his body was mutilated*, and that his wife Isis collected

his limbs which had been scattered throughout Egypt by Set [later to appear in the Bible as "Seth"], or Typhon [later to appear in the Bible as the "serpent"], and that *Osiris by some means obtained a new life in the next world, where he reigned as god and king.* The hieroglyphic texts contain abundant testimony that the statements of Plutarch are substantially correct, and *from first to last Osiris was to the Egyptians the god-man who suffered, and died, and rose again, and reigned eternally in heaven. They believed that they would inherit eternal life, just as he had done*, provided that what was done for him by the gods was done for them, and they made use of amulets, and magical texts of all kind, and performed ceremonies connected with sympathetic magic in order that they might compel Osiris and the gods who had brought about his resurrection . . .[3132]

Just as ancient Christian texts asserted of Jesus, far older Egyptian texts stated of the North African Christ:

As truly as Osiris lives, so truly shall his followers live; as truly as Osiris is not dead he shall die no more; as truly as Osiris is not annihilated he shall not be annihilated.[3133]

The contributions of Osiris to the myth and figure of Jesus could fill a large volume, so we will only touch on a fraction of them here. In the following partial list I have itemized a few of the characteristics and elements of the great Nile Savior that were later appended to Jesus by the mainstream Christian Church. Where germane I have noted the similarities to Jesus in the endnote after the entry:

- Osiris was the original "Christ," a name which derives from the name and functions of the ancient Egyptian mummy-image known as *Karast*, "mummy"[3134] (in Egyptian, without vowels, written *Krst*, and meaning to "make a mummy," to "embalm," to "bandage").[3135] Egyptian mummies were first embalmed, making them *karast*; that is, they were imbued with immortality. Second, mummies were "anointed," *mes* in Egyptian. "To be anointed" was *messu*. This word, combined with the Egyptian word *Iah*, "son-god,"[3136] created the Hebrew *Messu-Iah*, or *Messiah*, the Jewish word for "Anointed"[3137]—which is identical to the Egyptian word for the resurrected and immortal human soul called "Karast." In Rome *Karast* or *Krst* became *Chrestus*; in Greece, *Christos*; in England, *Christ*.[3138]
- Osiris was thus the resurrected Egyptian Savior or Messiah,[3139] and was himself a symbol of resurrection[3140] and of death and rebirth.[3141]
- The resurrected Osiris promised personal salvation and spiritual bliss in the

Hereafter to faithful followers.[3142]
- Osiris, whose name means "many-eyed,"[3143] was the son and avatar of the primary Egyptian Sun-god or "Heavenly Father," Ra[3144] (in Greece, Zeus; in Rome, Jupiter; in Norway, Odin; in Ireland, Dagda; in Israel, Yahweh).[3145]
- At one time Osiris was considered a type of Sun/Son-god, a "twin-soul" of his father Ra.[3146]
- Osiris' birth was announced by "Three Wise Men," the three stars in the belt of Orion: Mintaka, Anilam, and Alnitak.[3147]
- These Three Wise Men (stars) pointed to the "Star in the East," Sirius, the heavenly body that heralded the birth of Osiris.[3148]
- In ancient Near Eastern myth the star Sirius is called the "Messiah."[3149]
- A heavenly choir accompanied the birth of Osiris.[3150]
- Osiris made up one-third of one of the ancient world's most popular pre-Christian Holy Trinities: Osiris, the Father-god; Isis, the Virgin-Mother-goddess; and Horus, the Divine Son-god.[3151]
- Osiris was also part of a second Egyptian triad, this one comprised of himself, as well as the gods Ptah and Socharis.[3152]
- Osiris had over 200 divine names and titles.[3153]
- Osiris' many sacred titles included: "Savior,"[3154] "Son of God," the "Word of God," the "Anointed One," "Osiris in the Monstrance,"[3155] "Lord of Lords," "King of Kings," "God of Gods,"[3156] the "Great One God," "All-One God," "Lord Over All,"[3157] the "Prince,"[3158] the "Perfect One,"[3159] "Lord of Eternity,"[3160] "Eternally Incorruptible,"[3161] "King of Eternity," and "Ruler of Everlastingness."[3162]
- Osiris was also known as "The Resurrection and the Life," the "Good Shepherd,"[3163] and the "Good One."[3164]
- Two additional meanings of Osiris' name are "Mighty One" and "Great One."[3165]
- Osiris was a prototypical dying and rising god,[3166] who was born in the Spring (Equinox), exalted in the Summer (Solstice), died in the Fall (Equinox), was reborn in the Winter (Solstice),[3167] and who was resurrected in the Spring (Equinox).[3168]
- During the Osirian Mystery rites the god's priests mourned over his death for 40 days (Lent).[3169]
- Osiris battled his brother, the Evil One, Set,[3170] eventually absorbed by the Hebrews as Seth, and also Satan, the "serpent" of Genesis, and later by Christians as "Judas."[3171]
- Osiris sat on a throne in Heaven.[3172]
- Osiris was a peace-loving divinity who conquered his enemies through gentleness and nonviolence.[3173]
- Osiris was known for being democratic,[3174] good, wise,[3175] humane, righteous, just, truthful, merciful, and charitable.[3176]

- Just as one who followed Christ became a "Christian," one who followed Osiris became an "Osirian," literally adding his personal name to their own after death.[3177]
- The worship of Osiris included a type of communion in which cakes of bread, representing his flesh, were eaten.[3178]
- The Osirian Eucharist also employed grape juice, which represented the blood of the god, and which was drunk from a sacramental cup.[3179]
- Osiris was considered a "universal god," one for *all* people.[3180]
- Osiris was a vegetation-god or grain-god who, like grains of wheat or barely, was "born again" out of "death" each year.[3181]
- A ram-headed god,[3182] Osiris was an incarnation of the Ram of Mendes,[3183] and wore a crown with ram's horns (known as the *Atef*),[3184] framed with tall feather plumes.[3185]
- Osiris was known as the "king of the gods"[3186] and the "Lord of Light."[3187]
- Osiris was also entitled "Lord of the Living," "Lord of the Universe," and "Ruler of Eternity."[3188]
- Osiris was known to be "sagacious and beneficent."[3189]
- As a grain- or vegetation-god,[3190] Osiris' doctrines included the beliefs that human death is similar to dying grain[3191] and that the land of Osiris contains "many mansions."[3192]
- Osirian stories included a tale of the healing of a princess by one of the god's priests.[3193]
- Osiris was enthusiastically worshiped at shrines, monuments, and temples across the Near and Middle East.[3194]
- Osiris had a sanctuary at Djedu, a town whose name means "House of Osiris."[3195]
- Yearly pilgrimages were made to Osiris' sacred city Abydos, to venerate him and obtain his guarantee of protection and eternal life.[3196]
- Osiris was associated with "Truth,"[3197] and indeed his figure was part of the Egyptian hieroglyph for "Truth."[3198]
- Osiris was the king and judge of the dead.[3199]
- Osiris was "the typical god-man who died and rose again."[3200]
- Osiris carried the shepherd's staff[3201] or crook,[3202] known as the *heka*.[3203]
- The worship of Osiris contained numerous "mysteries."[3204]
- Osiris was considered a "culture hero"[3205] and a "protective deity."[3206]
- Osiris was accompanied by a "Comforter" or "paraclete" known as the *Ka*.[3207]
- As the Egyptian Christ, all those who lived a life of purity in Osiris' name were given everlasting salvation,[3208] as well as the promise of an "eternally happy life" in Heaven (*Annu*),[3209] where they would be ruled over by the virtuous god himself.[3210]
- The Greeks associated Osiris with their savior-god Dionysus[3211] (who changed water into wine)[3212] and with their Sun/Son-god Hercules[3213] (who walked on water);[3214] the Phrygians connected him with their savior-god

Attis, the Sumerians with their savior-god Tammuz,[3215] the Romans with their savior-god Bacchus,[3216] the Pelasgians with their savior-god Proteus,[3217] and the Babylonians with their savior-god Adonis[3218]—the latter from whom Jesus derived one of his many titles: *adon*, "lord."

- "The Mysteries of Osiris" was the greatest and most popular festival in ancient Egypt,[3219] held chiefly at his holy city Abydos. The annual drama, an eight-act passion play,[3220] featured Osiris' "Last Supper" and the miming of his life, death, mummification, resurrection, and enthronement.[3221] The actors were chosen by the pharaoh, with the re-enactment being performed in additional cities such as Heliopolis, Buto, Bubastis, Letopolis, and Busiris.[3222]
- Osiris commanded a group of messengers known as the *weputiu*, who assisted him in the judgement of the wicked after death.[3223]
- After his earthly death Osiris retired to the Elysian Fields (Heaven), where he lovingly welcomed the souls of the righteous as they departed earth.[3224]
- As the Egyptian Universal Indwelling Christ, Osiris was believed to be present in every Egyptian at his or her death.[3225]
- Osiris was associated with various sacred trees, such as the persea, the Erica,[3226] the heath,[3227] the acacia, and the fir.[3228]
- Osiris was executed by his enemies and his sacred blood was spilled.[3229]
- Part of Osiris' body was consumed by fishes.[3230]
- Osiris was a scapegoat figure,[3231] someone who is punished for the sins of others.[3232]
- After death Osiris was "resurrected" and "reborn," becoming Lord of the "Other Land."[3233]
- Thus a prayer to Osiris went as follows: "Hail Osiris! Thou art born twice!"[3234]
- Twice-born Osiris was captured and murdered in a wooden "ark" or box made of shittim wood from cypress.[3235]
- As an immortal dying and rising god of grain and vegetation,[3236] Osiris was "ceaselessly reborn."[3237]
- As a god of vegetation Osiris is associated with the vine[3238] and with wine.[3239]
- Besides his "Mysteries," Osiris had numerous other yearly festivals (marking significant events in his life) at which he was venerated.[3240]
- Osiris was "reborn" each year during the annual Summer flooding of the Nile,[3241] the "River [Water] of Life."
- Osiris' resurrection was the foundation of the faith for everyday Egyptians, who hoped for life beyond the death of the earthly body[3242] as a reward for living righteously.[3243] As part of the Osirian Cult, the god's initiates would read aloud the following verse: "As truly as Osiris lives shall I live; as truly as Osiris is not dead I shall not die."[3244]

It is clear that Osiris and his widespread religious cult Osirianism donated much to both Jesus and the Church, even lending material to the Old Testament writers in regards to Moses, the Garden of Eden, and numerous other early Hebrew figures and myths.[3245] We know for a fact that the pre-Christian Gnostics continued the Egyptian Mysteries surrounding the Osiris-Karast (Krst), the original Oriental Christ, well into the 1st Century A.D., after which they were Christianized at Rome becoming what we now know as "Christian traditions,"[3246] but which Paul more honestly referred to as "the Mysteries of God"[3247] "the Hidden Wisdom,"[3248] and "the Mystery which was kept secret since the world began."[3249]

Carl Jung understood the connection between the two Christs, asserting that Christianity owes both its name and its significance to the archetypal myth of the dying and rising god-man (a concept dating from at least 4000 B.C.),[3250] personified in the ancient figure of the Egyptian deity Osiris,[3251] as well as in his own "divine child," the Sun/Son-god Horus.[3252]

In short, the ancient Egyptian mummy was the original Christ (*Karast*), which after death was resurrected into Heaven to live as one with the Heavenly Father, Osiris. Writes Massey:

> Say what you will or believe what you may, there is no other origin for Christ the anointed than for Horus the *karast* [*krst*] or anointed son of god the father. There is no other origin for a Messiah as the anointed than for the *Masu* [*Messu*] or anointed. Finally, then, the mystery of the mummy is the mystery of the Christ. As Christian, it is allowed to be for ever inexplicable. As Osirian, the mystery can be explained.[3253]

In the opinion of Christian mystics, the obviously legendary aspects of Jesus' biography are, in great part, those of Osiris: the Egyptian Messiah, symbol of spiritual rebirth and a pre-Christian personification of the Universal Indwelling Christ. See BUDDHA, CHRIST, JESUS, KRISHNA, MESSIAH, MITHRA, PYTHAGORAS, SAVIOR, TEACHER OF RIGHTEOUSNESS.

OUTWARD MAN: In traditional Christianity the "outward man" is Paul's term for the physical body.[3254] In mystical Christianity it refers to the Lower Self. See ADVERSARY, ANTICHRIST, BEAST, DEVIL, EGO, EGYPT, EVIL, GODS AND GODDESSES, HELL, HIGHER SELF, INWARD MAN, LOWER SELF, LUCIFER, MASS MIND, NUMBER OF THE BEAST, SATAN, SERPENT, SIN.

Ancient menhirs, or upright stones.

Osiris and Isis.

Egyptian obelisk.

Nativity of Jesus.

PARABLE: In traditional Christianity a parable is simply a story contrasting two objects for the purpose of teaching.[3255] In mystical Christianity a parable is a symbolic narrative used for the purpose of revealing profound spiritual truths or "hidden wisdom"[3256] to those "who have ears to hear";[3257] that is, those who are spiritually evolved and have learned how to read and perceive scripture mystically and intuitively rather than literally and intellectually. See GOSPEL, JESUS.

PARACLETE: The Paraclete is identical to the COMFORTER.

PASSION OF JESUS: In traditional Christianity the Passion of Jesus entails the events surrounding the final sufferings and execution of Jesus.[3258] In mystical Christianity the Passion is a symbol of the undeveloped soul as it moves inevitably toward perfection, enlightenment, and at-one-ment with God.[3259] We will note here that the "Passion" was not part of the earliest records of the historical earthly Jesus: The Gospel of Q and The Gospel of Thomas. This is because it is a purely Pagan motif, one that was only appended to the Lord's biography after His death, during the sweeping Paganization of His figure known as the "Scheme of Salvation."[3260] See ASCENSION, ASTROLOGY, CHRIST, CROSS, CROWN, DEATH OF JESUS, GOOD NEWS, GOSPEL, GOSPEL OF Q, GOSPEL OF THOMAS, JESUS, MYTH OF CHRIST, TRANSFIGURATION OF JESUS.

PAUL: In the traditional Church Paul of Tarsus is the "Thirteenth Apostle," the orthodox author of the Pauline Epistles,[3261] and a former Pharisee and enemy of Christianity who was converted by the appearance of the risen Jesus on the road to Damascus.[3262] In the mystical Church Paul is seen as one of Christianity's greatest mystics;[3263] both an ecstatic and a pneumatic who derived much of his material from Jewish Gnosticism;[3264] a man who viewed Christ, not in the flesh, as a person, but rather in the Gnostic manner, as a spiritual symbol or concept (or even as a type of ghost known to mystics as a "phantasm"); that is, as the fully spiritually realized human being or "prototypical Ideal Man,"[3265] an ideal which all can attain.[3266]

His occultic view of the Christ, as an enigmatic mental state or unknowable and mysterious presence that one must unite with,[3267] was set down in his famous statement: "I live; yet not I, but Christ liveth in me."[3268] And in one of his letters he quotes a portion of not a Jewish or Christian hymn but a Gnostic one,[3269] and in another he cites a well-known Gnostic phrase, the "cross the power of God."[3270] Such things make him not just a Gnostic,[3271] as even the Gnostics themselves seemed to believe,[3272] but as German scholar Richard A. Reitzenstein declared, "the greatest Gnostic,"[3273] and the only Jew of the 1st Century A.D. to have left us chronicles of personal mystical experiences.[3274]

Paul's enigmatic doctrines (many which were not understandable to Christians in ancient times,[3275] and continue to baffle modern mainstream Christian scholars)[3276] also link him to the mystical Jewish Essenes, of whom he may have been a member, student, or admirer.[3277] The Bible seems to corroborate this: Ananias, the man who rescued Paul and restored his eyesight after the Jewish convert's mystical experience with Christ Consciousness,[3278] was almost certainly an Essene, for he makes reference to Essenic rituals (for example, baptism for sin) and Essenic terms (for example, the "Just One").[3279]

Even mainstream Jewish and Christian scholars have had to acknowledge that Paul was a pneumatic[3280] who often relied on Jewish occult lore, as well as on the theological language of Plato[3281] and the Pagan mystery cults.[3282] Not surprisingly, it is Paul who gives us one of the most mystical, arcane, and docetic statements ever recorded about Jesus and the Universal Indwelling Christ:

> Wherefore henceforth know we no man after the flesh: yea, though we have known Christ after the flesh, yet now henceforth know we him no more. Therefore if any man be in Christ, he is a new creature: old things are passed away; behold, all things are become new.[3283]

And again:

> But the righteousness which is of faith speaketh on this wise, "Say not in thine heart, who shall ascend into heaven?" (that is, to bring Christ down from above:) Or, "Who shall descend into the deep?" (that is, to bring up Christ again from the dead.) But what saith it? *The word [of God, the Logos] is nigh thee, even in thy mouth, and in thy heart:* that is, the word of faith, which we preach . . .[3284]

It was also Paul who not only often used the enigmatic Gnostic term *Plemora* ("Fullness"),[3285] but who uttered one of the most spectacularly occultic, most profoundly mystical, and most accurate spiritual statements of all time: "Christ is all, and in all,"[3286] an arcane Theosistic doctrine that is still repudiated, disregarded, and suppressed by many orthodox Christians. Indeed, few traditional Churches today will admit that Paul developed this concept, one of Christianity's most important tenets, purely on "mystical lines."[3287] The Unitarian Universalist

Church was literally founded on this doctrine, a body which, of course—in the mystic tradition—assumes a human Jesus rather than a deified Pagan one.[3288]

Paul's mystical experience in traveling to the Gnostic's "Third Heaven," something seemingly akin to a Near Death Experience or Out of Body Experience, is pertinent. Even his description of the event is given in arcane language using the third person:

> It is not expedient for me doubtless to glory. I will come to visions and revelations of the Lord. I knew a man in Christ above fourteen years ago, (whether in the body, I cannot tell; or whether out of the body, I cannot tell: God knoweth;) such an one *caught up to the third heaven.* And I knew such a man, (whether in the body, or out of the body, I cannot tell: God knoweth;) how that *he was caught up into paradise, and heard unspeakable words, which it is not lawful for a man to utter. Of such an one will I glory*: yet of myself I will not glory, but in mine infirmities.[3289]

If Paul was not a mystic, an Essene, or a Gnostic, but an orthodox, traditional Christian, as the organized Church maintains, a myriad of unsolvable problems arise. We have, for example, his silence on, not to mention his complete indifference toward, some of Christianity's most significant doctrines, ideas, beliefs, institutions, and figures (such as the 12 Apostles[3290]), as well as various so-called "historical" events (such as the empty tomb,[3291] Jesus' supernatural birth,[3292] Jesus' miracles,[3293] Peter's mission to Rome, and John and the Virgin Mary's presence in Ephesus).[3294] Such facts add weight to the Christian mystic's image of Paul;[3295] namely, that he viewed Jesus and the Church through esoteric even Gnostic eyes;[3296] that is, intuitively, through the Third Eye or EYE AM, the same occult organ of which Jesus spoke:

> The light of the body is the [Third] eye: if therefore your [Third] eye be single, your whole body shall be full of light. But if your [Third] eye be evil, your whole body shall be full of darkness. If therefore the light that is in you be darkness, how great is that darkness![3297]

On the topic of Paul's silence Westbrook writes:

> It is a well-known fact that many early Christian sects [known generally as Docetists] absolutely denied the existence of Christ in the flesh, regarding him as a phantom [or phantasm]. It is very difficult to decide whether the apostle Paul believed in a

real or an ideal Christ. He wrote his Epistles before the Gospels were written, and therefore could have learned nothing from that source. Concerning the various appearances of Jesus after the resurrection, he says: "Last of all, he was seen of me, as by one born out of due time;" and this seems to bear out the conjecture that *Jesus was an ideal, inasmuch as it was not in the flesh that he saw him, and his refusal to know him after the flesh indicates his strong preference for him as an idea, and not as a person.*

Paul makes no mention of any miracle but that of the resurrection, and that was manifestly a spiritual rather than a physical fact. Moreover, he was a Pharisee, and it is difficult to see how he could have "gloried in the cross" had he taken the cross in a literal sense. He casts no reproach on the Jews for causing Jesus to suffer, and never speaks of the crucifixion as a crime, nor shows a particle of sympathy or compassion with the sufferer. He seems to have been the real founder of Christianity, and might have had in view the direct action of the solar divinity [Helios, Osiris, Apollo, etc.] with whom Christ had become associated.

A careful analysis of the Pauline Epistles will show, we think, that *the Christ of Paul was an idea. And here it is important to bear in mind that those who attributed to him at least ten Epistles he never wrote would not scruple to alter, amend, interpolate, and change portions of the Epistles he actually did write. Those who formed the system of Christian ecclesiasticism never could afford to have a conscience. Those Fathers of the second century who formed the foundations of the Catholic hierarchy were most unscrupulous men.*[3298]

Robertson notes the many difficulties that Paul's silence (on so many important aspects of Jesus' earthly life and ministry)[3299] has created for those trying to understand our Lord and the origins of the Bible and Christianity. Of German theologian Paul W. Schmiedel, for example, Robertson writes:

> . . . he has not recognised (1) the primary reason for doubting the genuineness of every detail of teaching set forth in *the gospels*—namely, *the total ignorance of those teachings shown in the Pauline epistles*. He takes as genuine the plainly interpolated passage in 1 Cor. 11 [23-29] as to the institution of the Eucharist, then concludes that "*the details of the life of Jesus had so little interest for Paul that*" he fails to quote him when he effectively might. To reason thus is to ignore a far greater difficulty than many which the exegete admits to be insuperable. (2) Schmiedel makes his arguments at some points

turn on the assumption of the general certainty of the whole narrative as to Jesus being a teacher with disciples, who established his cult; whereas the existence of the disciples is no better proved than many of the data already surrendered. (3) He is evidently biased to his illicit inference (that Jesus really existed) by other inferences which, on his own showing, he was not entitled to draw. For instance, he decides that Jesus probably accomplished faith-healing as distinguished from miracles, because "this power is so strongly attested throughout the first and second centuries that, in view of the spiritual greatness of Jesus and the imposing character of his personality, it would be indeed difficult to deny it to him."

What then proved the spiritual greatness and the imposing character of Jesus? The nine credible texts [said to have been the only authentic sayings of Jesus in the New Testament]? Clearly they amount to no such proof, even if they were genuine: a thousand rabbis might have uttered them. What, again, is the value of the "strong attestation" of the first and second centuries *in the face of the silence of Paul*, ostensibly the first witness? The first and second centuries, that is to say the gospels (which certainly did not exist within thirty years of the date alleged for Jesus' death), and the people who believed them, equally attest the prodigies which Professor Schmiedel rejects. Is a witness who solemnly affirms twenty impossibilities to be believed whenever he happens to assert something that might be true, while a more important witness, who in the terms of the case ought to have heard of it if it happened, has evidently never heard of it at all?

. . . Once more, *if the synoptic discourses are records of commonly remembered passages from Jesuine discourses, how comes it that Paul never cites a word of them?* To miss that crux is to make as great an oversight as that of the critics who regarded the so-called Sermon on the Mount as the full report of a real sermon.

. . . *an intelligent perusal of the epistles of Paul can suffice to show that the preaching Jesus was created after they were written.*

It does not indeed follow that Paul's period was what the tradition represents. The reasonable inference from his doctrine is that his *Jesus was either a mythic construction or a mere tradition, a remote figure said to have been crucified, but no longer historically traceable.* If then *Paul's Jesus, as is conceivable, be merely a nominal memory of the slain Jesus ben Pandira of the Talmud* (about

100 B.C.), Paul himself may belong to an earlier period than that traditionally assigned to him. Certainly the most genuine-looking epistles in themselves give no decisive chronological clue. But such a shifting of his date would not finally help the case for "Jesus of Nazareth." Escape the argument from the silence of Paul by putting Paul a generation or more earlier, and you are faced by the fresh incredibility of a second crucified Jesus, a second sacrificed Son of God, vouched for by records for the most part visibly false, and containing but a fraction of plausible narrative. The only conclusion open is that the teaching Jesus of the gospels is wholly a construction of the propagandists of the cult, even as is the wonder-working God.[3300]

Of the origins of Paul's esoteric approach to Christianity, Angus offers the following opinions:

> Unlike Philo, faith, in Paul's view, is not something inferior to the ecstatic or mystic condition which gives a superior Knowledge [Gnosis], but the mystic state depends wholly on faith as its source. Perhaps it might be more truly said that in Paul these two functions of the psychic life are one: *his mysticism is "faith-mysticism," or "Christ-mysticism."* To be "in faith," "in Christ," "in the Spirit" are synonymous. Paul himself, as a "pneumatic," enjoyed revelations, visions, ecstasis, pneumatic charismata, but while he prized these as spiritual phenomena he held them secondary to the more normal experiences of Christian living.
>
> To be "in Christ" or to have "Christ in you," it was unnecessary for a man to be transported into that ecstatic condition described by Philo, in which personality is for the time being in abeyance, or by Paul himself in the experience of being caught up into the third heaven. Whence came this faith-mysticism of Paul which laid hold of the Graeco-Roman world and attracted initiates from the gods of the Mystery-Religions to Christ? Hatch answers:
>
>> "Paul's mysticism seems to have been derived from no one source in particular, as from Philo or some one of the Mystery-cults. It was rather absorbed, in a perfectly natural and partly unconscious way, from his Graeco-Roman environment,

in which mysticism was a very prominent and important factor."

This answer recognizes the fact that *Paul's converts were steeped in mystic ideas* and that they could without difficulty put themselves *en rapport* with Paul's teaching; also, that *Paul himself, as a son of the Diaspora, must have been familiar with the main religious ideas of the Mystery-cults and touched by the mysticism that was "in the air"* but it hardly does justice to the fact that one who had "seen the Lord" did not need to absorb a mystery-atmosphere, and that Paul's mysticism was first-hand and can be shown to date only from that moment when "it pleased God to reveal His Son in me," which the three narratives of his conversion in Acts bear out; nor does it do justice to the distance between Paul's "Christ-mysticism" and that mysticism which clung round the Mysteries.

Paul, as a Hebrew of Hebrews, was prior to his conversion too conservative a Jew to welcome mystic ideas, for, though the Jewish race produced the three great mystics, Philo and Paul and the author of the Fourth Gospel, "the Jewish mind and character, in spite of its deeply religious bent, was alien to mysticism." It would be difficult to detect the affinity between the Faith-mysticism of Paul and the surrounding Graeco-Roman mysticism: the differences far outweigh the faint resemblances.

In Paul there is a type of mysticism which stands by itself and which differs from the mysticism of the Mystery-Religions and from that of Philo in two important aspects: first, as regards the human factor, there is a conspicuous absence of any idea of absorption in the deity. Paul valued too highly his own personality and individuality. The will is a factor as potent as emotion. Paul's "life hid with Christ in God" is a life of active fellowship with Christ, but never absorption into Christ.

Secondly, as regards the Divine factor, in the mystic fellowship the faith-mysticism of Paul is faith grounded on an historic Personality to whose love faith is the necessary response. The Christian who is "in Christ" finds himself in fellowship with a Person, and is not lost, as in the mysticism of Philo or Neo-Platonism, in the ocean of the Absolute, nor, as in the Mysteries, does he undergo divinization. He becomes like Christ, but never Christ.[3301]

Paul's mystical Gnostic approach to Jesus and to Christianity as a whole is also evident in other biblical passages. For instance:

> Know ye not that ye are the temple of God, and that the Spirit of God dwelleth in you?[3302]

Christian mystics are honored to be cataloged alongside one of the greatest Christian mystics of all time; the man who was the literal founder of both Christian theology[3303] and the organized Christian Church;[3304] the Christian occultist who favored a mystical soteriology over the Mosaic Law[3305] and made Christianity more Pauline than Jesuine;[3306] and whose theological influence sometimes overshadows even that of Jesus (much to the consternation of many mainline Christians).[3307]

But what proof do we have of his mysticism beyond theories and opinions? many ask.

For one thing, like most ancient mystical spiritual teachers Paul possessed his own cult[3308] and preached his own gospel.[3309] In the fashion of Pagan Rome, he often refers to Jesus' teachings (as did our Lord Himself)[3310] as "mysteries,"[3311] and even describes himself as having been initiated into these mysteries by being mystically "crucified with Christ."[3312] He borrowed freely from other mystical religions, including Buddhism, patterning his famous sermon on love (to the Corinthians)[3313] on passages from the ancient pre-Christian Buddhist hymn known as the Sutta-Nipata.[3314] During his Mars Hill Sermon Paul nonchalantly cites several Pagan poems (by the Greek writers Epimenides and Cleanthes)[3315] that center on the great Grecian Father-God Zeus.[3316]

Above all our "Christian rabbi" speaks of "the mystery, which from the beginning of the world hath been hid in God."[3317] Even the most conservative, anti-mystic Christian theologians have had to admit that the revelation of this "mystery" is the real subject of Paul's gospel, as well as the entire purpose of his ministry.[3318] But what is this "mystery," that great secret teaching of Jesus, "which hath been hid from ages and generations, but now is made manifest in his saints"?[3319] Paul does not try to hide it from his readers. Instead he declares it in the clearest possible terms: this mystery, he says, "is Christ *in* you"![3320] Not "*near* you," "*close* to you," "*among* you," or the traditional Christian's most infamous biblical mistranslation, "in the *midst* of you." Paul means just what he says: "Christ *in* you."

This is *not* the concretized Pagan "Christ" of traditional Christianity, of institutional Churchianity, who was executed and rose once into heaven on the third day. It is an esoteric Christ, the Gnostic Christ, the Christ of mystical Christianity, whose resurrection is not physical but spiritual;[3321] whose resurrection is an ever present, ongoing reality in our personal lives.[3322] It is the "Son in you,"[3323] by whom each one of us can "die daily,"[3324] and in this mysterious "crucifixion"[3325] of the Ego or Lower Nature (the "old man"),[3326] we are "raised up,"[3327] becoming a "new creature."³³²⁸

One explanation for Paul's deep Paganistic mysticism comes from Epiphanius, who wrote of a tradition in which it is claimed that the Apostle was actually a Greek Pagan who converted to Judaism in order to win the hand of the daughter of a Jewish High Priest. When the father rejected him, Paul turned against the Jews and the Law of Moses.³³²⁹ Even if this story is untrue, a Jewish Paul, born in Cilicia, would have been very familiar with the local Cilician savior-god known as Sandan, an ancient Turkish personification of the equally well-known Babylonian christ named Tammuz, the Syrian christ Adonis, the Phrygian christ Attis, the Roman christ Mithra, the Greek christ Hercules, and the Egyptian christ Osiris.³³³⁰ When it came to designing his gospel for a Pagan audience, Paul would have quite naturally transposed the Mysteries of the Sun-god or Son-god Sandan (which involved his yearly death and resurrection) to the figure of the historical Jesus and the Indwelling Christ³³³¹—as was the syncretistic custom at the time.³³³²

Being a mystic, Paul could not and did not view the death and resurrection of Jesus literally. If he had, certainly he would have mentioned this momentous occurrence, the pivotal point in traditional Christian history, in his letters, for he was raised in Jerusalem, and would have witnessed the Passion of our Lord firsthand around the year 33.³³³³ Instead, for him, as for all mystics, the crucifixion and death of the Master was a symbolic mystical event; one he says that we can all participate in on a daily basis³³³⁴ in order to "liveth with God"; that is, to attain at-one-ment with the Father. Writes the Gnostic-Essenic Paul:

> Know ye not, that so many of us as were baptized into Jesus Christ were baptized into his death? Therefore we are buried with him by baptism into death: that like as Christ was raised up from the dead by the glory of the Father, even so we also should walk in newness of life.
>
> For if we have been planted together in the likeness of his death, we shall be also in the likeness of his resurrection: Knowing this, that our old man [Lower Self] is crucified with him, that the body of sin might be destroyed, that henceforth we should not serve sin. For he that is dead is freed from sin.
>
> Now if we be dead with Christ, we believe that we shall also live with him: Knowing that Christ being raised from the dead dieth no more; death hath no more dominion over him. For in that he died, he died unto sin once: but in that he liveth, he liveth unto God.³³³⁵

Having established Paul's mystical credentials, let us now look at a partial list of his mystical views. Paul believed in, embraced, and espoused the following doctrines:

- the Indwelling Christ.[3336]
- the Gnostic Christ.[3337]
- mystical baptism.[3338]
- mystical marriage to the Indwelling Christ.[3339]
- the mystical death of the Ego.[3340]
- the mystical Law of Attraction or Reciprocity.[3341]
- the mystical Universal Son of God.[3342]
- the mystical Divine Mind.[3343]
- mystical Divine Love.[3344]
- the mystical Indwelling Divine Logos.[3345]
- the mystical Third Eye (EYE AM)[3346] and Third Ear (intuition).[3347]
- mystical pantheism.[3348]
- the mystical Gnosis (*inner* "knowledge").[3349]
- the mystical Sophia (*inner* "wisdom").[3350]
- the mystical transformation of the mind, that is, the Christ.[3351]
- the mystical Egyptian and Essenic Sacrament.[3352]
- a Pagan mystical view of the Lord's Supper.[3353]
- the Church, or body of believers, as the Gnostic Plemora ("Fullness").[3354]
- the mystical White Light of God.[3355]
- the mystical Kingdom of God.[3356]
- mystical Judaism, "for Paul had studied the Kabalah [Hermeticism] at the feet of Gamaliel the Rabbi."[3357]
- the standard mystical educational method of teaching to individuals divided into three degrees or stages (the Perfect, the Progressing, and the Beginners).[3358]
- the mystical use of intuition (spirit) as opposed to tuition (intellect).[3359]
- the mystical Divine Mind, the Nous, or "Mind of Christ."[3360]
- the mystical body-temple.[3361]
- the occult "Mysteries of God."[3362]
- the mystical doctrine that we will "judge angels."[3363]
- mystical antinomianism (salvation by faith alone).[3364]
- the mystical Indwelling Holy Ghost, Comforter, or Paraclete.[3365]
- mystical Essenic and Stoic celibacy.[3366]
- mystical henotheism.[3367]
- the mystical Crown Chakra (Paul's "Incorruptible Crown" or "Helmet of Salvation").[3368]
- the mystical Rock of (not Peter) but the Indwelling Christ.[3369]
- the mystical Androgyne,[3370] known to the first Christians as Metropator ("Mother-Father");[3371] that is, the "Earthly Mother" and the "Heavenly Father").[3372]
- mystical angel worship.[3373]
- the mystical Pagan doctrine of the Seven Heavens[3374] (one for each of the then

seven gods: Sun, Moon, Mercury, Venus, Mars, Jupiter, Saturn—after which the seven days of our week are named).[3375]
- the mystical I AM or EYE AM.[3376]
- the Pagan mystical doctrine of being "sealed," that is, passing a test.[3377]
- the mystical "daily death."[3378]
- the mystical birth, death, and resurrection of the vegetation-god.[3379]
- the mystical Gnostic "materiality is corrupt" doctrine.[3380]
- mystical Gnostic dualism (spirit vs. physical).[3381]
- the mystical death curse of the Ugarit goddess Anath-Ma.[3382]
- the mystical anti-literalization doctrine.[3383]
- the mystical "god of this world" doctrine—a deity known to the Gnostics as the Demiurge or Yaldabaoth[3384] ("he who blasphemes against the Divine")[3385] and to Christians as Jehovah—who is different than the real Father in Heaven,[3386] which Gnostics call Bythus, the one true God.[3387]
- mystical Docetism (the Christ is a "phantasm" not a real person).[3388]
- the mystical Essene doctrine of spiritual segregation.[3389]
- the mystical doctrine of Theosis (God in Man).[3390]
- the mystical belief in the Pagan Father-God known as Pantokrator (a title of the Greek messenger-god Hermes)[3391] or El Shaddai[3392] (the name of a pre-Mosaic Mesopotamian mountain-god).[3393]
- the mystical doctrine of "working out our own salvation"[3394] (which Paul borrowed from Buddha).[3395]
- the mystical Essene doctrine of physical and spiritual "cleanliness."[3396]
- the mystical Gnostic Devil.[3397]
- having Gnostic mystical experiences.[3398]
- the Inner Gospel or Gospel Within.[3399]
- the mystical Gnosis (self-revealed knowledge).[3400]
- the ardent anti-formalism of the mystical Church.[3401]
- the mystical doctrine that Jesus was a normal human being (who, like all people, possessed the Indwelling Christ).[3402]
- the mystical allegorical interpretation of scripture.[3403]
- the Divine Feminine as embodied in the city of Jerusalem, which originally had been dedicated to the Pagan Roman goddess Venus.[3404]
- the Pagan mystical concept that baptism is a symbol of spiritual enlightenment.[3405]
- the Pagans' mystical Golden Rule, first espoused by Confucius.[3406]
- the mystical initiation into the Divine Logos.[3407]
- the ancient Pagan (Hindu-Buddhist) mystical Law of Karma.[3408]
- the ancient Pagan (Hindu) Law of Reincarnation.[3409]
- the ancient Buddhist doctrine of learning by way of self-teaching[3410] or intuition.[3411]
- the mystical Theosistic Pagan doctrine of Recapitulation, wherein all are made divine under the unifying principle of the Indwelling Christ.[3412]

- the mystical doctrine of spiritual enlightenment via the Third Eye.[3413]
- the mystical "Gnosis in the mystery of the Indwelling Christ."[3414]
- the mystical "mystery which from the beginning of the world hath been hid in God."[3415]
- the mystical Universal Indwelling God.[3416]
- the mystical "Gnosis of the Son of God" doctrine.[3417]
- the mystical doctrine of the Indwelling Christ as the "Perfect Man."[3418]
- the mystical doctrine of the "Children of Light" (that is, spiritual enlightenment).[3419]
- the mystical doctrine of spiritual enlightenment through the Indwelling Christ.[3420]
- the "Great Mystery" of the Indwelling Christ: the *Hieros Gamos*[3421] or spiritual "Sacred Union" of the Male and Female Principles[3422]—the Superconscious Mind (Sun) and Subconscious Mind (Moon) respectively,[3423] otherwise known as the "Marriage Between Heaven and Earth,"[3424] which Plutarch called "the basis of all the Mysteries."[3425]
- the mystical doctrine of the "Invisible God" (God is not an anthropomorphic being, but rather he is pure Spirit, "invisible").[3426]
- mystical polytheism.[3427]
- the mystical doctrine that during his 18 "silent years" (between the ages of 12 and 30) Jesus traveled throughout numerous countries across the East and in Europe[3428] to study and teach (for example, India, Tibet, Persia, Egypt, Greece, Cyprus, Nepal, Ladakh, etc.).[3429]
- the Indwelling Holy Spirit.[3430]

For embracing, espousing, and practicing these Hellenistic, Oriental esoteric beliefs, as well as many more involving the Pagan Mystery Religions, Paul has been rightfully called "the greatest of all the Gnostics,"[3431] and one of the three most important mystics produced by Judaism (along with Philo and John the Evangelist).[3432]

Many mainstream Christians will read the above list with skepticism, citing scriptures in which Paul is shown being against mystical and Gnostic doctrines like docetism,[3433] the Inner Resurrection,[3434] angel worship,[3435] and even mysticism itself.[3436] This confusion is cleared away, however, with the realization that *all* 27 books of the New Testament have been tampered with by later orthodox (mainly Catholic) Christian hands.[3437] Thus, not only do we now have two Jesuses depicted in the Bible—the first, a human and very Jewish spiritual teacher; the second, a symbolic and very Pagan dying and rising savior-god[3438]—we now also have two very different and distinct Pauls:[3439] a liberal mystical Christian and a conservative conventional Christian. For example:

- The "Paul" who said this: "Wives submit yourselves unto your husbands,"[3440] is not the same "Paul" who said this: "There is neither male nor female in

Christ."[3441]
- The "Paul" who encouraged Christians to avoid marriage and practice celibacy[3442] is not the same "Paul" who said that the "women should marry and bear children."[3443]
- The "Paul" who was proud of being Jewish[3444] is not the same "Paul" who scoffed at "Jewish fables"[3445] and condemned the Jews for killing both Jesus and the prophets.[3446]
- The "Paul" who said that he felt "weakness, fear, and much trembling" at Corinth[3447] is not the same "Paul" who taught that God "hath not given us the spirit of fear."[3448]

Obviously, as the organized institutional Church began to form in the centuries following Jesus' death, many of the mystical elements of Jesus' and Paul's teachings were removed or rewritten to bring them more in line with what were by then considered orthodox beliefs (as opposed to the "heterodox," that is, Gnostic and Essenic beliefs of the first Christians).[3449] This explains, for instance, the enormous difference in tone between Paul's highly mystical letter to the Galatians and his highly orthodox letter to the Colossians, the latter which is clearly a forgery in Paul's name (hence, scholars refer to its anonymous author as "deutero-Paul").

Indeed, it is widely understood and accepted by most Bible scholars that Paul did not write all of the letters conventionally attributed to him. Some go as far as to claim that he did not write any of the epistles, and that he did not even exist as a historic figure.[3450] In either case, most Christian mystics accept Paul as a real person, the accidental founder of orthodox Christian theology, and, second only to Jesus and John, the Church's greatest mystic.[3451] Most notably, it is the teachings of Paul, not Jesus, on which the whole of the Christian philosophy has been constructed.[3452] See APOSTLES, CHRIST CONSCIOUSNESS, CHRISTIANITY, ESSENES, GNOSTICISM, JESUS, PETER, TWELVE.

PEACE & SWORD: The "peace and sword" motif that appears in the life story of our Lord is best known for its appearance in the Gospel of Matthew, where Jesus says:

> Think not that I am come to send peace on earth: I came not to send peace, but a sword. For I am come to set a man at variance against his father, and the daughter against her mother, and the daughter in law against her mother in law. And a man's foes shall be they of his own household.[3453]

In the traditional Church the peace and sword Jesus speaks of here are literal references to the so-called "Rapture" which will occur at Jesus' Second Coming.[3454] One result, we are told, will be tremendous upheaval, division, and even separation within those families that are comprised of believers and nonbelievers.[3455] In the mystical Church the peace and the sword are symbols of profound spiritual truths having to do with the Heavenly Plane (the soul) and the Earthly Plane (the body). Of this view Origen writes:

> And indeed Jesus came not to bring peace on the earth, that is, to corporeal and sensible things, but a sword, and to cut through, if I may say so, the disastrous friendship of soul and body, so that the soul, committing herself to the spirit which was against the flesh, may enter into friendship with God.[3456]

Likewise Brooke writes:

> The only way in this world to get peace is to make it out of pain. And, after all, did you come into this world to find happiness? Was it for your own sake alone that you were created into the midst of this vast humanity? What are you that you should pay so much attention to yourself, and lose in that attention the thought of others?
>
> You are not here to find happiness directly as the first thing. You are here to discover truth; and the way is dark, and leads to the Cross before it finds the Resurrection. You are here to consecrate your life to the discovery of a portion of the Divine Law, to practise it, and to diffuse the knowledge and love of it among your brethren; and it is a work which will call upon you to go through much darkness, and to make sacrifices which will seem at first to rend your heart in sunder. You are here to help to build up the Temple of Humanity, to give your life for the welfare of the race; and it is not possible to do that work and at first to have an easy life of it.
>
> Happiness, indeed! What business have we yet with happiness? We must win it before we wear it. Only toil can give us the power of enjoying. And God knows this, and he puts us through this long and painful process. He saves us; but we must work out our own salvation. He gives light; but we must conquer darkness.
>
> . . . In this world, we cannot yet have peace, without previous war in matters pertaining to truth. Every truth or form of truth calls up its opponent falsehood. Every good insisted on evokes its own special adversary, and war is inevitable. I came not, said Christ, to send peace on earth, but a sword.[3457]

See CHRIST, CHRISTMAS, GOSPEL, JESUS, NATIVITY.

PEARL OF GREAT PRICE: In traditional Christianity the Pearl of Great Price is a symbol of a spiritual truth.[3458] In mystical Christianity it is a symbol of the Higher Self.[3459] Sometimes the Pearl of Great Price is spiritual understanding, in which case the truth-seeker is a "pearl-fisher."[3460] See GOSPEL, JESUS, PARABLE.

PETER: In traditional Christianity Peter is one of the 12 Apostles, and the individual to whom Jesus gave the keys to the Kingdom of God. In Catholicism Peter is considered the first pope and the founder of the Roman Church.[3461] Thus the Catholic declaration, *Ubi Petrus ibi ecclesia*: "Where there is Peter there is the Church."

In mystical Christianity Peter has nearly the opposite image. Here he is a symbol of the Lower Self[3462] or "natural man" of Paul,[3463] which explains why Jesus once said to Peter:

> Get thee behind me, Satan: thou art a stumbling block unto me: for thou mindest not the things of God, but the things of men.[3464]

While expounding on a passage in the book of Job,[3465] Saint Gregory the Great writes:

> What then is designated by the "air," but the minds of worldly men, which, given up to the countless desires of this life, are, being fluid, scattered hither and thither like the air? But the air is collected into clouds, when unstable minds are, by the grace of the Divine regard, strengthened with the solidity of virtue, in order that, by thinking of what is right, they may gather themselves within the bosom of their heart, and may not melt away in empty thoughts.
> Peter had been air, when the occupation of fishing for the life of the flesh used, as a transient breeze to agitate him, distracted still with earthly desires.[3466]

The Catholic Church is supposed to have been founded on Jesus' statement that he would build His church on Peter the "rock,"[3467] and it is said that this occurred when Peter traveled to Rome in A.D. 42, at which time he became the first pope until his martyrdom in A.D. 67.[3468] But there is no evidence Peter was ever in Rome,[3469] and indeed this passage was a 3rd-Century forgery, intentionally inserted into the Gospel of Matthew as a political ploy to establish the superiority of the Roman Church over its Eastern rivals.[3470]

Not even Protestant and Roman Catholic scholars still subscribe to the "Peter as the Rock" doctrine, and for several good reasons: Peter was not the first to bring the Gospel to Rome, he was not the first pope, and he did not found the Christian Church there or anywhere else.[3471] Indeed, the Church at Rome had already been established by an anonymous founder by the time Paul began writing (around the year 51).[3472] Thus the person who first took the Gospel to the Eternal City is unknown.[3473]

Either way, fabricating this scripture and inserting it into the Gospel of Matthew was pointless since Jesus stated that He had no desire to found a new religion.[3474] In any case, Christianity itself was said by the Church Fathers to have existed since before the beginning of time.[3475] It was not until five centuries after Jesus' death, in fact, that the doctrine of the primacy of the Roman See was developed, and with it the myth of Saint Peter, the key-holding "Rock" upon which the Church was allegedly constructed.[3476]

There are other problems with viewing Peter as a historic person. For one thing, his authorship of his two biblical epistles[3477]—along with all of the noncanonical works attributed to him[3478]—as well as his reverse crucifixion and burial at the foot of Vatican Hill, are now seen by Catholic academicians as fabrications,[3479] based on nothing more than "very early tradition."[3480] Not even the relics discovered under St. Peter's Basilica belong to the Apostle. And since neither his apostolate or his martyrdom at Rome are affirmed in the New Testament (for they were invented later),[3481] Christian mystics turn to the great "Book of Esoteria" (spiritual intuition) to uncover the real "Peter."

The devices that unscramble the mystery of the "universal saint" are an understanding of lithology (stone worship), as well as his name and his special attribute, one for which he has long been invoked as the "heavenly doorkeeper":[3482] a set of keys.[3483] Though on account of his gross misunderstanding of Jesus' teachings[3484] Peter is typically viewed by mystics as a symbol of the Lower Self, he began as a Christian composite of the ancient Roman city-god variously known to Pagans as Petra, Pater Liber, Pater Patrum, Patriarch, Pompeius, or Patricius, the "Father-Rock" who guarded the gates of the dead and whose keys unlocked the doors of Heaven. Peter's "keys" then were based on the "Key of the Nile" (the ankh of Osiris), the Trident of Shiva, and other similar magic keys possessed by Pagan key-holding and door-guarding gods and goddesses.[3485]

Another early model for Peter was the Roman two-faced deity Janus, "god of doors and gateways,"[3486] who guarded the Temple of Wisdom[3487] as well as the gates of the year, and required the correct password before using his keys to open the "pearly gates" of Heaven. His holy day fell on or around January 20, when the Sun enters the astrological sign Aquarius, a symbol of the "Gate of the Year," which is why the Church placed the festival of Saint Peter on the same day.[3488] Of this particular aspect of Peter, Robertson writes of early Christians:

Above all, their mystic Rock, Petra, was presented to them in the concrete as the rock Peter, the foundation of the Church. It has been elsewhere shown that the myth of the traitorous Peter connects with those of Proteus and Janus as well as with that of Mithra, inasmuch as Janus also had "two faces," led the twelve months as Mithra presided over the zodiacal signs and Peter over the twelve apostles, and, like Proteus and Peter and the Time-God in the Mithraic cult, bore the heavenly keys.

Here again the mythic development of Peter probably follows on that of Jesus; at all events Jesus too has constructively several of the attributes of Proteus-Janus: as "I am the door"; "I stand at the door and knock"; "I am in the Father and the Father in me" (= Janus with the two faces, old and young, seated in the midst of the twelve altars); "I have the keys of death and of Hades." The function of Janus as God of War is also associable with the dictum, "I came not to bring peace, but a sword."

Finally, the epiphany is in January. But there is to be noted the further remarkable coincidence that in the Egyptian *Book of the Dead* Petra is the name of the divine doorkeeper of heaven—a circumstance which suggests an ancient connection between the Egyptian and Asiatic cults. On the other hand, the early Christian sculptures which represent the story of Jesus and Peter and the cock-crowing suggest that it originated as an interpretation of some such sculpture; and the frequent presence of the cock, as a symbolic bird of the Sun-God, in Mithraic monuments, raises again a presumption of a Mithraic source.[3489]

The Mithraic aspects of "Peter" are due to the fact that the Pagan Sun-god Mithra was said to have been virgin-born out of the "Generative Rock" on the bank of a river, "under the shade of a sacred tree," as shepherds watched from the surrounding countryside.[3490]

As a rock-god Petra also represents the fertilizing spirit of the Masculine Principle, and so he was often portrayed as a menhir or phallic standing stone, most familiar to us as the obelisk of the ancient Egyptians, whose rock-god was called Petra or Par.[3491] *Cephas* ("rock") or "Saint Peter" was, in other words, a Christianized version of the ancient regenerative Pagan Father-Rock-God, the same one referred to in the Old Testament as "the Rock that begat thee."[3492] See ANOINTING, APOSTLES, CHRIST, CHRISTIANITY, GOSPEL, JESUS, MITHRA, OIL, ROCK.

PHARISEES: In the traditional Church the Pharisees were a strict Jewish sect that opposed Jesus and plotted his death for blasphemy.[3493] In mystical Christianity they are a symbol of formalism, dogmatism, and literalism,[3494] all which prevent one from understanding the inner truths of Jesus' teachings, *which were mystical*.[3495] See EGYPT, HEROD ANTIPAS, LOWER SELF, MASS MIND, PILATE, SATAN.

PILATE (PONTIUS): In the traditional Church Pontius Pilate was the fifth procurator of Judea and the man who put Jesus to death to appease the wishes of the Jews.[3496] In the mystical Church he represents the Mass Mind, or everyday mundane (and often dark, negative) thoughts of humanity.[3497] See DEVIL, EGYPT, HEROD ANTIPAS, LOWER SELF, MASS MIND, PHARISEES, SATAN.

POOL OF BETHESDA: According to the mainstream Church the Pool of Bethesda was the place at Jerusalem where Jesus performed one of His greatest miracles.[3498] In the esoteric Church it is a symbol of spiritual enlightenment by way of intuition.[3499] See BAPTISM, CHRIST CONSCIOUSNESS, FLOOD OF NOAH, THIRD EAR, THIRD EYE, WASHING THE FEET, WATER, WORD OF GOD.

PRAYER: In the traditional branch of Christianity prayer is a conversation between God and the supplicant.[3500] In the mystical branch of Christianity it is a symbol of the Soul's yearning to progress up the ladder of spiritual evolution.[3501] Thus Bushnell writes:

> *God dispenses the Holy Spirit by fixed laws. Prayer, also, is heard by laws as definite as the laws of equilibrium in forces.* And what is called the doctrine of the Spirit and the doctrine of prayer, as given in the Scriptures, is, in fact, nothing more nor less than the unfolding to us, if we could so regard it, of the laws of the Spirit and the laws of prayer, as pertaining to the supernatural kingdom of God. These two great powers, the hearing of prayer and the dispensing of the Spirit, are like the waterfalls and winds of nature, to which we set our wheels and lift our sails, and so by their known laws take advantage of their efficacy. A crystal or gem that is being distilled and shaped in the secret depths of the world, is not shaped by laws as well understood as the law of the Spirit of life when it moulds the secret order and beauty of a soul.[3502]

God and Jesus both promise us that every prayer will be answered,[3503] for God *always* says yes![3504] In Jeremiah we find this wonderful passage, straight from the mouth of the Father:

> *Call unto me, and I will answer thee,* and shew thee great and mighty things, which thou knowest not.[3505]

From the book of Job:

> Thou shalt make thy prayer unto him, and *he shall hear thee.*[3506]

Jesus had this to say about prayer:

> For *everyone* that asketh receiveth; and he that seeketh findeth; and to him that knocketh it shall be opened.[3507]

Following the teachings of our Lord (to pray unceasingly),[3508] Christian mystics believe that daily constant prayer is essential, for prayer has the power to "to divert the stream of fate" and change one's destiny.[3509] See DIVINE MIND, JESUS, LOGOS, VOICE OF GOD, WAY OF THE LORD, WORD OF GOD.

PRECIOUS STONES: In the traditional Church precious stones are usually just precious stones, or more rarely representations of God's richness.[3510] In the mystical Church they are symbols of spiritual virtues, or more specifically, the "fruit of the Spirit": love, joy, peace, longsuffering, gentleness, faith, meekness, and temperance.[3511] Of them Swedenborg writes:

> A stone, in the Word, signifies truth in ultimates, and a precious stone, truth transparent from good. There are two colours fundamental of the rest in the spiritual world, red and white; white derives its origin from the light of the sun in heaven, thus from spiritual light, which is white; and red derives its origin from the fire of the sun there, thus from celestial light, which is flame-coloured.
>
> The spiritual angels, being in truths of wisdom from the Lord, are in that white light, therefore they are clothed in white; and the celestial angels, being in the good of love from the Lord, are in that flame-coloured light, therefore they are clothed in red; thence those two colours obtain also in precious stones in heaven, where they are in great abundance.
>
> This is the reason why precious stones, in the Word, signify such things as are of the truth of wisdom, or of the good of love, and that a jasper, because it is white, signifies the things which are of the truth of wisdom, and a sardine stone, because it is red, the things which are of the good of love. These stones signify the appearance of the divine wisdom and the divine love

in ultimates, because all precious stones in heaven derive their origin from the ultimates of the Word, and their transparency from the spiritual sense within those ultimates.

The ultimates of the Word are the truths and goods of its literal sense. That this is the origin of precious stones in heaven is difficult to be believed by any one in our world, because he does not know that all the things which exist in the spiritual world are correspondences, and that from thence all the things which exist in the natural world derive their spiritual origin. That this is the origin of precious stones in heaven has been permitted me to know from discourse with angels, and also to see it with my eyes, but the formation of them is from the Lord alone.[3512]

The 12 precious stones of Revelation's "New Jerusalem" are, of course, mystical Judeo-Christian symbols of the 12 astrological Sun-signs,[3513] which are, in turn, representations of the 12 divine faculties of the human Soul or Indwelling Christ: 1) love, 2) faith, 3) strength, 4) judgement, 5) understanding, 6) self-control, 7) power, 8) the will, 9) imagination, 10) fervor, 11) orderliness, and 12) acquisitiveness.[3514] See ASTROLOGY, TWELVE, ZODIAC.

PURPLE: In the mainstream Church purple is the color of the robe the Romans placed on Jesus during his march to the site of the crucifixion,[3515] no accident! In the mystical Church it is the color of celestial wisdom.[3516] Swedenborg writes that "by purple and scarlet is signified divine good and truth celestial."[3517] See JESUS.

PYTHAGORAS: The famed ancient Greek philosopher Pythagoras, who lived nearly 600 years before Jesus, does not appear by name in the Bible. But many elements of his life do, namely in the biography of our Lord. Thus Pythagoras is included here. On this crucial topic Higgins writes:

> The early [Church] fathers travelling for information, which was the case with Papias, Hegesippus, Justin, etc., mixed the traditions relating to Pythagoras, which they found spread all over the East, with those relating to the Indian Cristna [Krishna], and from the two formed their own system. Pythagoras himself having drawn many of his doctrines, etc., from the Indian school, the commixture could scarcely be avoided. Thus we find the few peculiarities respecting *the birth of Jesus,* such as the immaculate conception, wherein the history of Jesus differs from that of Cristna, *exactly copied from the life of Pythagoras.* And the circumstances relating to the immaculate conception by the mother of Pythagoras, I have no doubt were taken

from the history of Buddha, and from the virgin of the celestial sphere—herself of Oriental origin. Thus from a number of loose traditions at last came to be formed, by very ignorant and credulous persons, the complete history of the Jesus Christ of the Romish Church, as we now have it.

I think no person, however great his credulity may be, will believe that *the identity of the immaculate conceptions of Jesus and Pythagoras can he attributed to accident. The circumstances are of so peculiar a nature that it is absolutely impossible. With this system the fact pointed out by the Unitarians is perfectly consistent, that the first two chapters of Matthew and of Luke, which contain the history of the immaculate conception, are of a different school from the remainder of the history.*

The first striking circumstance in which the history of Pythagoras agrees with the history of Jesus is, that *they were natives of nearly the same country; the former being born at Sidon, the latter at Bethlehem, both in Syria. The father of Pythagoras, as well as the father of Jesus, was prophetically informed that his wife should bring forth a son, who should be a benefactor to mankind. They were both born when their mothers were [far] from home on journeys: Joseph and his wife having gone up to Bethlehem to be taxed, and the father of Pythagoras having travelled from Samos, his residence, to Sidon, about his mercantile concerns. Pythais, the mother of Pythagoras, had a connexion with an Apolloniacal spectre, or ghost, of the [Son] God Apollo, or [Sun] God Sol, (of course this must have been a holy ghost, and here we have* The Holy Ghost,*) which afterward appeared to her husband, and told him that he must have no connexion with his wife during her pregnancy*—*a story evidently the same as that relating to Joseph and Mary. From these peculiar circumstances, Pythagoras was known by the same identical title as Jesus, namely, the* Son of God; *and was supposed by the multitude to be under the influence of Divine inspiration.*

When young, he *[Pythagoras] was of a very grave deportment, and was celebrated for his philosophical appearance and wisdom. He wore his hair long, after the manner of the Nazarites, whence he was called the long-haired Samian. And I have no doubt that he was a Nazarite for the term of his natural life,* and the person called his daughter was only a person figuratively so called.

He spent many years of his youth in Egypt, where he was instructed in the secret learning of the priests, as Jesus, in the Apocryphal Gospels, is said to have been, and was carried thence to Babylon by Cambyses, the iconoclast and restorer of the Jewish religion and temple, where he was initiated into the doctrines of the Persian Magi. Thence he went to India, where he learned the doctrines of the Brahmins. Before he went to Egypt he spent some time at Sidon, Tyre, and Biblos, learning the secret mysteries of all these places. Whilst in this country he chiefly dwelt in a temple on Mount Carmel; probably in the temple of Jove, in which there was no image. After his return from India, he [Pythagoras] is stated to have travelled about the world, to Egypt, Syria, Greece, Italy, etc., preaching reformation of manners to these different nations, and leaving among them numbers of proselytes. He was generally favoured by the people, but as generally persecuted by the governments; which almost always persecute real philanthropists. *Here are certainly some circumstances in this history very like those in the histories of Jesus.*

The stories told of the mother of Pythagoras having had connexion with an Apolloniacal spectre, is not the only one of the kind: *the same story is told of Plato*, who was said to be born of Parectonia, without connexion with his father Ariston, but by a connexion with Apollo. On this ground the really very learned Origen defends the immaculate conception, assigning, also, in confirmation of the fact, the example of Vultures, (Vautours,) who propagate without the male. What a striking proof that a person may possess the greatest learning, and yet be in understanding the weakest of mankind!

It seems to be quite impossible for any person of understanding to believe, that the coincidence of these histories of Plato and Pythagoras, with that of Jesus, can be the effect of accident. Then how can they be accounted for otherwise than by supposing that in their respective orders of time they were all copies of one another? How the priests are to explain away these circumstances I cannot imagine, ingenious as they are. They cannot say that Jamblicus, knowing the history of Christ, attributed it to the philosophers, because he quotes for his authorities Epimenides, Xenocrates, and Olimpiodorus, who all lived long previous to the birth of Christ.[3518]

Let us now summarize these amazing "coincidences," while adding a few new ones:

- Both Pythagoras and Jesus traveled throughout Europe and the Middle East (Egypt, India, Persia, Crete, Palestine, etc.) to study the mystical teachings of other faiths.

- Both established occult schools.
- Both had disciples and students.
- Both taught the Secret Wisdom to special initiates.
- Both were known as "the Master."
- Both taught monotheism and prayer.
- Both promoted vegetarianism (as did Jesus and his brother James and the Nazarenes or Essenes).
- Both taught various healing methods.
- Both taught the Law of the Triangle.
- Both taught the doctrine of Theosis (God in Man).
- Both taught the doctrine of reincarnation.
- Both performed miracles.
- Both taught the doctrine of solitude.
- Both taught the doctrine of love for God.
- Both taught non-materialism.
- Both married and had children (Jesus to Mary Magdalene, with whom He bore a daughter named Sarah).
- Both incurred the wrath of political and personal foes by whom they were later killed.
- After their deaths both came to be known as gods.[3519]

See BUDDHA, CHRIST, JESUS, KRISHNA, MESSIAH, MITHRA, OSIRIS, REINCARNATION, SAVIOR, TEACHER OF RIGHTEOUSNESS, THEOSIS, WAY OF THE LORD.

Pyramids of Egypt.

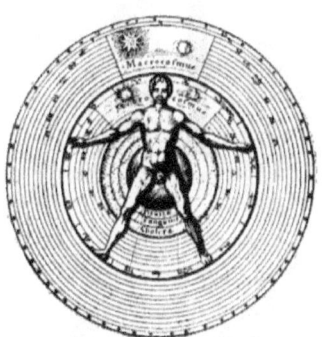

Microcosmic Man:
The Universe in miniature.

Mount Horeb.

Saint Paul.

Samuel anointing Saul.

RAINBOW: In the traditional Church the rainbow is a symbol of God's promise to Noah that He would never again flood the entire earth.[3520] As the story of the Universal Deluge, or something similar to it, is found in the mythologies of pre-Christian civilizations around the globe (from India and Polynesia, to Scandinavia and Palestine),[3521] it is obvious that the many individual elements within this tale, such as the rainbow, possess deep occult meanings; mystical arcana wholly overlooked by the literalizing tendencies of mainstream Christianity.

In the mystical Church the rainbow, delightfully known in ancient times as "the scarf of Isis,"[3522] signifies a bridge that spans and connects the Higher Nature (heaven) with the Lower Nature (earth). In the mystical language of Genesis, God says:

> And it shall come to pass, when I bring a cloud over the earth, that the bow shall be seen in the cloud.[3523]

Jukes writes:

> [The] token is "the bow set in the cloud." Before the flood, the elect, though not so fully instructed, yet had "the covenant." But of its "token" nothing had been heard: for this is only learnt experimentally, when we have known and in spirit passed the deep waters. This token now appears "in the cloud." The cloud, brought over the earth, was not only a remembrance, but something like a remnant, of the judgment. We therefore sometimes "fear to enter the cloud." If it might be so, we would have "tokens" of the covenant without the dark waters. But it cannot be.
>
> Only in dark and cloudy days can the bow of heaven be seen spanning the lower earth. Then, mid dark waters, when the sun breaks out, though the cloud may be dark, a bow appears amid the darkness; half a ring—half *that ring with which the regenerate soul is now married to the Lord, and assured of endless rest with Him.* The lower world yet hides the rest of the ring; but on high "a rainbow" shall be seen "in a circle round the

throne." Such are the joys to which we are called by the power of Christ's resurrection and the fellowship of His sufferings.[3524]

Swedenborg writes:

> That "I have given my bow in the cloud," signifies the state of the regenerate spiritual man, which is like the rainbow. It may appear surprising that a token of the covenant in the Word should be a bow in the cloud, or rainbow, since this is produced by the modification of the solar rays when falling upon drops of rain, and,—unlike the other signs of the covenant in the church,—is a purely natural phenomenon. That *it does, however, represent regeneration, and denote the state of the regenerated spiritual man, can only be known by those who are permitted to see, and thereby to know the reason of it.*
>
> *The spiritual angels, who have all been regenerate men of the spiritual church,—when presented to view in the other life, have an appearance like the rainbow about the head*; and as these rainbows agree perfectly with the state of the angels, their quality is hence discernible in heaven and in the world of spirits. The reason why the likeness of a rainbow appears, is, that their natural things, corresponding to their spiritual, present such an appearance; it is a modification of spiritual light from the Lord in their natural things.[3525]

The German Christian mystic Jakob Böhme writes:

> *For the rainbow is the sign and token of this covenant . . . that man was created out of Three Principles into an Image, and that he should live in all three. . . . For the rainbow has the colour of all the three principles*: the colour of the first principle is *red*, and *darkish-brown*; which betokens the dark and fire-world, that is, the first principle, the Kingdom of God's *Anger*; the colour of the second principle is *white*, and *yellow*; this is the majestatical colour, signifying as a type of the holy world, God's *Love*.
>
> The third principle colour is *green* and *blue*; blue from the chaos, and green from the water or saltpeter; wherein the crack of the fire the sulphur and mercury do sever themselves, and produce distinct various and several colours which betoken unto us the inward spiritual worlds, which are hidden in the Four Elements. *This rainbow is a figure of the last judgement showing how the inward Spiritual World will again manifest itself and*

> *swallow up . . . into itself this outward world of four Elements.*[3526]

Kingsford and Maitland write:

> Over and around the seat or car of Adonai, as described by the seers of both Old and New Testaments, is a Rainbow, or Arch. This, *the symbol of the Cup of the Heavens encircling and enclosing the Kosmos, is in the Scriptures termed Mount Sion [Zion] and the Mount of the Lord; by the Hindus it is called Mount Meru, and by the Greeks Olympus, the home of the Gods. And with all it is the symbol of the Celestial Kingdom*, the Uncreate, which "was, and is, and is to come;" wherein dwell the Seven Spirits of Light, the Elohim of the Godhead.[3527]

See ARK, DOVE, FLOOD OF NOAH, NOAH, WATER.

RAISING THE DEAD: In the traditional Church raising the dead is a miracle consigned solely to Jesus. However, since pre-Christian Pagans were also known to have raised the dead, and since numerous other biblical figures also performed this feat,[3528] we must seek a deeper meaning than the one customarily assigned to it by institutional Christianity.

In the mystical Church "raising the dead" is a metaphor signifying the rebirth of the Higher Self; that is, it is the act of being "born again,"[3529] in which one is reawakened to spiritual truth from the deathlike slumber of the Lower Self. See BORN AGAIN, LAZARUS, REINCARNATION, RESURRECTION OF JESUS.

REBIRTH: In the traditional Church Christian rebirth is accomplished through baptism by water and the Spirit. In the mystical Church rebirth is entirely interior (that is, spiritual, mental, or psychological), and has nothing to do with external trappings or rituals. Here the Ego is purified by truth (water)[3530] and the Spirit is allowed to take control of the mind, forming a "new creature in Christ."[3531] See BAPTISM, BORN AGAIN, SECOND COMING OF CHRIST, WATER.

REDEEMER: In the traditional Church the Redeemer is Jesus Christ, whose suffering and death delivered humanity from sin.[3532] In the mystical Church the Redeemer is the Higher Self or Indwelling Christ of each individual,[3533] which must sacrifice itself in order to raise up the Lower Self, allowing entrance into the Kingdom of Heaven.[3534] It is this alone, the Christ Within, which "saves" us by releasing us from the Law of Karma.[3535] Seen through the eyes of the Christian mystic, the occultic words of Job are now perfectly comprehensible:

> For I know that my redeemer liveth, and that he shall stand at

the latter day upon the earth: And though after my skin worms destroy this body, yet in my flesh shall I see God: Whom I shall see for myself, and mine eyes shall behold, and not another.[3536]

Strauss writes:

> Man being once mature enough to receive as his religion the truth that *God is man, and man of a divine race*; it necessarily follows, since religion is the form in which the truth presents itself to the popular mind, that this truth must appear in a guise intelligible to all, as a fact obvious to the senses: in other words, there must appear a human individual who is recognised as the visible God. This God-man uniting in a single being the Divine essence and the human personality, it may be said of him that he has the Divine Spirit for a father, and a woman for his mother. His personality reflecting itself, not in himself, but in the absolute substance, having the will to exist only for God, and not at all for himself, he is sinless and perfect. As a man of Divine essence, he is the power that subdues nature—a worker of miracles; but as God in a human manifestation he is dependent on nature, subject to its necessities and sufferings—is in a state of abasement. Must he even pay the last tribute to nature? Does not the fact that human nature is subject to death preclude the idea that that nature is one with the Divine?
>
> No: the God-man dies, and thus proves that the incarnation of God is real, that the infinite Spirit does not scorn to descend into the lowest depths of the finite, because he knows how to find a way of return into himself,—because in the most entire alienation of himself, he can retain his identity. Further, the God-man, in so far as he is a spirit reflected in his infinity, stands contrasted with men, in so far as they are limited to their finiteness; hence opposition and contest result, and the death of the God-man becomes a violent one, inflicted by the hands of sinners; so that to physical degradation is added the moral degradation of ignominy and accusation of crime.
>
> *If God, then, finds a passage from heaven to the grave, so must a passage be discoverable for man from the grave to heaven: the death of the prince of life is the life of mortals. By his entrance into the world as God-man, God showed himself reconciled to man; by his dying, in which act he cast off the limitations of mortality, he showed, moreover, the way in which he perpetually effects that reconciliation:*

namely, by remaining, throughout his manifestation of himself, under the limitations of a natural existence, and his suppression of that existence, identical with himself. Inasmuch as the death of the God-man is merely the cessation of his state of alienation from the infinite, it is, in fact, an exaltation and return to God; and thus the death is necessarily followed by the resurrection and ascension.[3537]

Kerr Cranston Anderson writes:

> To know the cross from this higher standpoint is to know all there is to know; there is nothing beyond this. The cross was the symbol of a profound mystery which opened up the heart of Deity himself to the gaze of the world. The divine sufferer was God himself, who in creating the universe sacrificed himself for it. The cross, therefore, represents the greatest of all sacrifices, not something that happened once and once for all, but something that is eternal and timeless—the sacrifice of God in and for his own creation that could not be unless he poured his own life into it and restricted himself within the forms of matter. "Confessedly great is the mystery of godliness."
>
> Unthinkable in its magnitude is this sacrifice, for it means nothing less than the identification of the infinite with the finite in its lowest forms. *Here is the profoundest mystery open to human contemplation to speak of which is possible only in forms of symbol and parable. The literal truth is too vast, too mysterious, too sublime, to be made known to human comprehension.* It is the mystery before which angels, we are told, veil their faces; and to gain a single glimpse of it one may well surrender all other knowledge and determine, as Paul did, to know nothing else.
>
> Here is the oldest form of the Christian faith. The story of Jesus is the parable of this infinitely larger truth. It is the symbol of the Lamb slain from the foundation of the world, that is, prior to human history, the emblem of divine body and blood voluntarily sacrificed in outward physical nature and entombed in the lower consciousness of man. *It was the claim of the second century Gnostics that Christianity was none other than the consummation of the inner doctrine of the mystery institutions of all the nations; and it is this interpretation of the Gospel story which is set forth in the apocryphal Gospels and Acts. The end of them all was the revelation of the mystery of man which is none other than the mystery of Christ.*[3538]

See ADAM, CHRIST, CHRIST CONSCIOUSNESS, CROSS, CRUCIFIXION, JESUS, KARMA, MESSIAH, MYTH OF CHRIST, ORIGINAL SIN, REDEMPTION, SALVATION, SAVIOR, SIN, THEOSIS, WAY OF THE LORD.

REDEMPTION: In the traditional Church redemption is our emancipation from the enslavement of sin, and it comes through and only through the sacrificial blood of Jesus.[3539] In the mystical Church, because as Emerson said, "the highest revelation is that God is in every man,"[3540] we each contain all that is necessary for our salvation, including our own redemption.[3541] When the fear of death is destroyed by understanding the immortality of the Soul, we are redeemed.[3542] See DEVIL, EVIL, GOOD NEWS, KARMA, MESSIAH, ORIGINAL SIN, REDEEMER, SALVATION, SATAN, SAVIOR, SIN, THEOSIS.

REINCARNATION: In the traditional Church there is no such thing as reincarnation, for it is not mentioned in the Bible. In the mystical Church, however, reincarnation is not only recognized throughout the Bible, it is an important aspect of the spiritual journey of the human Soul or Indwelling Christ as it progresses along its path to spiritual perfection. Little wonder: reincarnation was accepted not only among early Jews,[3543] Hindus, Buddhists, and Druids, but also among the Essenes and Gnostics,[3544] the two mystical sects who gave birth to the original Christian Church.[3545]

At the center of every religion is the doctrine of repeated involution and evolution: the fall of the Soul into the physical plane (known in the ancient mysteries as the *Aphanism* or "Disappearance"), and the rise of the Soul back up into the spiritual plane (known in the ancient mysteries as the *Euresis* or "Finding").[3546] Repetition is necessary to "burn off" (that is, pay off or work off) the dross of "sin" created and accumulated during each lifetime on earth until perfection is attained. According to this view, like raw metal, the human Soul must be cleansed of impurities through the refining process of reincarnation, whose law requires the "redemptive sacrifice" of the Higher Self (the Indwelling Christ) upon the "Cross" (the human body) in order to "Resurrect" the Lower Self back upward into Spirit.

The goal? To realize our divinity while in the body.[3547] "It is not enough to be sinless," wrote Plotinus, "one must become God."[3548] This at-one-ment with the Father comes through a desire for self-harmony, the use of self-control (over thought, speech, and action), and the final achievement of total self-mastery (over the mind and body), an idea emphasized over and over again in Eastern works, such as the Bhagavad Gita.[3549] Mead writes:

> Together with all the adherents of the Mysteries in every land the Orphics believed in reincarnation. Now Plato in the *Cratylus* gives the following mystical word-play of the term body:

"According to some *the body is the sepulchre of the soul*, which they consider as buried in the present life; and also because whatever the soul signifies it signifies by *the body*; so that on this account it is properly *called a sepulchre*. And indeed the followers of Orpheus seem to me to have established this name, principally because *the soul suffers in body the punishment of its guilt, and is surrounded with this enclosure that it may preserve the image of a prison.*"

The Phrygians in their Mysteries *called the soul imprisoned in the body the "dead."* The writer of the Naasenian School of Gnosticism, quoted by Hippolytus, tells us:

"The Phrygians also call it the 'dead,' inasmuch as it is in a tomb and sepulchre buried in the body. This, he says, is what is written [in the New Testament]: 'Ye are whited sepulchres, filled within with the bones of the dead'[3550]—for the 'living man' is not in you. And again [in the New Testament]: 'The "dead" shall leap forth from the tombs.'[3551] That is to say, *from their earthly bodies regenerated spiritual men, not fleshly*. For this (he says) is the resurrection which takes place through the Gate of the Heavens, and *they who pass not through it all remain dead.*"

On the above passage of Plato, Taylor adds an interesting note, from which we learn that Heraclitus, speaking of unembodied souls, says: *"We live their death, and we die their life."* And Empedocles, speaking of "generation," the equivalent of the Brahmanical and Buddhist *Sansara*, or the Wheel of Rebirth, writes: "She makes the 'living' pass into the 'dead'"; and again, lamenting his imprisonment in the corporeal world, he calls it an "unaccustomed realm."

[Of this, the ancient idea that the soul is punished in the body,] . . . the Pythagorean Philolaus writes: "The ancient theologians and initiates also testify that the soul is united with body for the sake of suffering punishment; and that it is buried in body, as in a sepulchre." And Pythagoras himself assures us that: "Whatever we see when awake is death, and when asleep a dream." Real life is in neither of these states. And so Taylor in his *Eleusinian and Bacchic Mysteries* shows us that:

> "The ancients by Hades signified nothing more than the profound union of the soul with the present body [Hieros Gamos]; and consequently, that till *the soul* separated herself by philosophy from such a ruinous conjunction, *she subsisted in Hades even in the present life; her punishment hereafter being nothing more than a continuation of her state upon earth, and a transmigration, as it were, from sleep to sleep, and from dream to dream*: and this, too, was occultly signified by the shows of the lesser mysteries."

Cicero also, referring to Orpheus and his successors, says: "The ancients, whether they were seers or interpreters of the divine mind in the tradition of the sacred initiations, seem to have known the truth, when they affirmed that *we were born into the body to pay the penalty for sins committed in a former life*." Augustine also writes:

> "Certain of the gentiles [Pagans] have asserted that in the rebirth of men there is what the Greeks call *palingenesis*." He further adds that "they taught that there was a conjunction of the same soul and [subtle?] body in four hundred and forty years."

But according to Plato the average time that elapsed between two births was a thousand years. Virgil gives the same period. Olympiodorus in his Scholion on Plato's *Phaedo* says that: "There is an archaic teaching of the Orphic and Pythagorean tradition which *brings souls into bodies and takes them out of bodies, and this repeatedly and in a cycle*."

. . . curiously enough *we find the story of the resurrection of Dionysus, after his dismemberment by the Titans, compared by the most learned of the Christian Fathers with the resurrection of the Christ.*

Thus Origen, after making the comparison, remarks apologetically and somewhat bitterly: "Or, forsooth, are the Greeks to be allowed to use such words with regard to the soul and speak in allegorical fashion, and we forbidden to do so?"—thus clearly declaring that *the "resurrection" was an allegory of the soul, and not historical.* And so Damascius, speaking of the dismemberment and resurrection of Osiris, remarks, "this should be a mingling with God, an all-perfect at-one-ment, a return upwards of our souls to the divine.[3552]

The Soul's journey through multiple incarnations on the earth plane has been allegorized countless times in holy scriptures, legends, and myths around the globe, chiefly in the annual procession of the Sun (symbol of the Soul or Higher Self, that is, the "Christ") through the 12 astrological signs (the 12 spiritual faculties of the Soul).[3553] It was this very story which gave rise, at least 6,000 years ago, to the idea and celebration of the dying and rising son of God (or Goddess),[3554] who is born at the Spring Equinox (Easter), attains adulthood at the Summer Solstice (Midsummer), begins to age at the Fall Equinox (Halloween), and dies and is reborn (reincarnated) at the Winter Solstice (Christmas).

The world's great Christian thinkers have penned thousands of works on the topic of the Law of Reincarnation. R. J. Campbell writes:

> *The soul, like the body, has to go through various stages of development, and change very greatly at one phase of experience as compared with another, before it is ready to enter upon its full inheritance.* I feel moved to add that I am not at all prepared to say that it is the persons of religious temperament who are in every case the most highly developed of their kind; on the contrary, it is highly probable that, here or here after, many of these will have to go back and learn some of the lessons which their fellows are learning now.[3555]

Schopenhauer writes:

> So long as no denial of the will takes place, what death leaves untouched is the germ and kernel of quite another existence, in which a new individual finds itself again, so fresh and original that it broods over itself in astonishment. What sleep is for the individual, death is for the will as [a] thing in itself. It would not endure to continue the same actions and sufferings throughout an eternity without true gain, if memory and individuality remained to it. It flings them off, and this is lethe

[forgetfulness]; and through this sleep of death it reappears refreshed and fitted out with another intellect, as a new being—"a new day tempts to new shores."

. . . In accordance with this, this doctrine is more correctly denoted by the word palingenesis than by metempsychosis. These constant new births, then, constitute the succession of the life-dreams of a will which in itself is indestructible, until, instructed and improved by so much and such various successive knowledge in a constantly new form, it abolishes or abrogates itself.[3556]

J. G. Fichte writes:

> These two systems, the purely spiritual [heaven] and the sensuous [earth]—which last may consist of an immeasurable series of particular lives—exist in me from the moment when my active reason is developed, and pursue their parallel course. The former alone gives to the latter meaning and purpose and value. I am immortal, imperishable, eternal, so soon as I form the resolution to obey the law of reason. After an existence of myriad lives the super-sensuous world cannot be more present than at this moment. Other conditions of my sensuous existence are to come, but these are no more the true life than the present condition is.[3557]

Why, the mainstream Christian asks, if reincarnation is genuine is it not discussed in the Bible? Why does the word reincarnation appear nowhere in the Good Book? In part, as we will see, because most of the overt references to it were later edited out by orthodox hands. But there is another reason, and it is the same reason that the right of secession is not specifically mentioned in the U.S. Constitution: it was so taken for granted by the Founding Fathers and the American people that it was not thought necessary. The U.S. itself had, of course, been formed on the basis of secession (from England), which is why secession was the most discussed topic in America in the 1700s and 1800s.[3558]

Likewise, the biblical authors considered reincarnation an ordinary aspect of the spiritual life, a doctrine so well-known to the populace at the time that there was no need to mention it or discuss it in detail. However, this does not mean that they completely ignored it. In fact, there are hundreds of subtle and even overt references to reincarnation throughout the Bible.

Jesus, for instance, was well versed in the concept of rebirth, or the Law of Metempsychosis, or more correctly Metensomatosis (at death the transmigration of the Soul into another body),[3559] as it was known during the Graeco-Roman period.³⁵⁶⁰ Here are a few examples from the New Testament:

> When Jesus came into the coasts of Caesarea Philippi, he asked his disciples, saying, "Whom do men say that I the Son of man am?" And they said, *"Some say that thou art John the Baptist: some, Elias; and others, Jeremias, or one of the prophets."*³⁵⁶¹

> Then said Jesus unto him, "Put up again thy sword into his place: for all they that take the sword shall perish with the sword."³⁵⁶²

> Jesus answered and said unto him, "Verily, verily, I say unto thee, except a man be *born again*, he cannot see the kingdom of God." Nicodemus saith unto him, "How can a man be born when he is old? can he enter the second time into his mother's womb, and be born?" Jesus answered, "Verily, verily, I say unto thee, except a man be born of water and of the Spirit, he cannot enter into the kingdom of God. That which is born of the flesh is flesh; and that which is born of the Spirit is spirit. Marvel not that I said unto thee, *ye must be born again*. The wind bloweth where it listeth, and thou hearest the sound thereof, but canst not tell whence it cometh, and whither it goeth: so is every one that is born of the Spirit."³⁵⁶³

> Jesus said, "Your father Abraham rejoiced to see my day: and he saw it, and was glad." Then said the Jews unto him, "Thou art not yet fifty years old, and hast thou seen Abraham?" Jesus said unto them, "Verily, verily, I say unto you, *Before Abraham was, I AM*."³⁵⁶⁴

> And as Jesus passed by, he saw a man which was blind from his birth. And his disciples asked him, saying, "Master, who did sin, this man, or his parents, that he was born blind?" Jesus answered, "Neither hath this man sinned, nor his parents: but that the works of God should be made manifest in him."³⁵⁶⁵

> I am *the door*: by me if any man enter in, he shall be saved, and shall *go in and out*, and find pasture.³⁵⁶⁶

> Let not your heart be troubled: ye believe in God, believe also in me [the Indwelling Christ]. *In my Father's house are many mansions*: if it were not so, I would have told you. I go to

prepare a place for you. And if I go and prepare a place for you, *I will come again*, and receive you unto myself; *that where I am, there ye may be also.*[3567]

One of our Lord's most obvious teachings on reincarnation is related to John the Baptist and his former incarnation as Elijah (Elias in New Testament Greek). The Old Testament openly states that Elijah will reincarnate around the same time as Jesus (the reincarnation of Elisha) in order to herald the coming of the Messiah:

> Behold I will send you Elijah the prophet, before the coming of the great and dreadful day of the Lord.[3568]

With this key from Malachi in mind, the inner meaning of Jesus's words some 500 years later are fully revealed:

> Verily I say unto you, among them that are born of women there hath not risen a greater than John the Baptist: notwithstanding he that is least in the kingdom of heaven is greater than he. And from the days of John the Baptist until now the kingdom of heaven suffereth violence, and the violent take it by force. For all the prophets and the law prophesied until John. *And if ye will receive it, this is Elias, which was for to come.* He that hath ears to hear, let him hear [indicating an occult or mystical doctrine].[3569]

> And his disciples asked him, saying, "Why then say the scribes that Elias must first come?" And Jesus answered and said unto them, "Elias truly shall first come, and restore all things. But I say unto you, that *Elias is come already*, and they knew him not, but have done unto him whatsoever they listed. Likewise shall also the Son of man suffer of them." *Then the disciples understood that he spake unto them of John the Baptist.*[3570]

Just as Jesus taught, Luke also depicts John the Baptist as the reincarnation of Elijah (Elias), as is plain in the story of John's birth:

> But the angel said unto him [John's earthly father], "Fear not, Zacharias: for thy prayer is heard; and thy wife Elisabeth shall bear thee a son, *and thou shalt call his name John*. And thou shalt have joy and gladness; and many shall rejoice at his birth. For he shall be great in the sight of the Lord, and shall drink neither

wine nor strong drink; and he shall be filled with the Holy Ghost, even from his mother's womb. And many of the children of Israel shall he turn to the Lord their God. *And he shall go before him in the spirit and power of Elias*, to turn the hearts of the fathers to the children, and the disobedient to the wisdom of the just; to make ready a people prepared for the Lord."[3571]

Paul the great Christian mystic also taught reincarnation. Here are a few samples:

And not only this; but when Rebecca also had conceived by one, even by our father Isaac; *(for the children being not yet born, neither having done any good or evil, that the purpose of God according to election might stand*, not of works, but of him that calleth;) It was said unto her, The elder shall serve the younger. As it is written, Jacob have I loved, but Esau have I hated. What shall we say then? Is there unrighteousness with God? God forbid.[3572]

According as *he hath chosen us in him before the foundation of the world*, that we should be holy and without blame before him in love.[3573]

The Essenic Hebraist speaks of reincarnation in the following passage:

For *if the word spoken by angels was stedfast, and every transgression and disobedience received a just recompence of reward; How shall we escape*, if we neglect so great salvation; which at the first began to be spoken by the Lord, and was confirmed unto us by them that heard him.[3574]

One of the New Testament's most powerful and clear statements on reincarnation comes from the Gnostic-tinged Revelation of John the Evangelist:[3575]

Him that overcometh will *I make a pillar* in the temple of my God, and *he shall go no more out*: and I will write upon him the name of my God, and the name of the city of my God, which is new Jerusalem, which cometh down out of heaven from my God: and I will write upon him my new name.[3576]

Here is the mystical meaning of this scripture:

Those who pass the test of self-mastery on the material plane will be allowed to stay permanently in Heaven, and will not have to reincarnate on earth ever again.[3577]

The Old Testament too brims with passages that can only be interpreted as palingenetic or reincarnational doctrines, again all closely tied to the Law of Karma:

> *Whoso sheddeth man's blood, by man shall his blood be shed*: for in the image of God made he man.[3578]

> And he said unto them, "I am an hundred and twenty years old this day; *I can no more go out and come in*": also the Lord hath said unto me, "*Thou shalt not go over this Jordan.*"[3579]

> God said: "*Before I formed thee in the belly I knew thee*; and before thou camest forth out of the womb I sanctified thee, and I ordained thee a prophet unto the nations." Then said I, *"Ah, Lord God! behold, I cannot speak: for I am a child."*[3580]

> He looketh upon men, and if any say, "I have sinned," and perverted that which was right, and it profited me not; He will *deliver his soul from going* [reincarnating] into *the pit* [earth], and his life shall see *the light* [stay in Heaven]. Lo, all these things worketh God oftentimes with man, to *bring back his soul* from *the pit*, to be enlightened with *the light* of the living.[3581]

> The Lord possessed me in the beginning of his way, before his works of old. *I was set up from everlasting, from the beginning, or ever the earth was*. When there were no depths, I was brought forth; when there were no fountains abounding with water. Before the mountains were settled, before the hills was I brought forth: While as yet he had not made the earth, nor the fields, nor the highest part of the dust of the world. When he prepared the heavens, I was there: when he set a compass upon the face of the depth: When he established the clouds above: when he strengthened the fountains of the deep: When he gave to the sea his decree, that the waters should not pass his commandment: when he appointed the foundations of the earth: Then I was by him, as one brought up with him: and I was daily his delight, rejoicing always before him; Rejoicing in the habitable part of his earth; and my delights were with the sons of men.[3582]

For the day of the Lord is near upon all the heathen: *as thou hast done, it shall be done unto thee: thy reward shall return upon thine own head.*[3583]

Naturally many mainstream Christian authorities today, not understanding the mystical and allegorical nature of biblical writing, refute the claim that Jesus and the prophets taught reincarnation. Yet, I invite my readers to study the above scriptures and decide for themselves, with this one important caveat: according to the ancient Law of Attraction, *what we believe becomes true for us.*[3584]

One must also consider the extrabiblical evidence. Many Gnostic-Christian groups, the original Christians, are known to have taught the preexistence of the soul and reincarnation, evidence for which may be found in such sacred Gnostic texts as Pistis Sophia ("Faith Wisdom").

Not only did many early Christian sects (for example, the Priscillians, Simonists, Manicheans, Marcionists, Basilidians, Valentinians, Cathari, Albigenses, Waldensians, Bogomiles, and Paulicians) formally embrace these doctrines, but for at least 500 years the institutional Church (mainly in the Alexandrian school) did as well, for, as the above passages surely reveal, they were taught by our Lord Himself.[3585] And based on their writings, a number of Church Fathers and authorities—men such as Saint Augustine, Bishop Synesius, Justin Martyr, Saint Gregory, Arnobius, Basilides, and Lactantius—also accepted these concepts, and in some cases even taught them.[3586] Among the latter was Clement of Alexandria, Jerome, and Origen,[3587] the last who developed a detailed Christian reincarnational belief system.[3588]

Eventually, of course, because the idea of palingenesis or metempsychosis did not suit the "ecclesiastical necessity" of the Catholic Church,[3589] it (and by implication, reincarnation) was condemned, and attempts began to be made to rid the canonical books of all traces of it. While Constantine the Great had the Bible rewritten around A.D. 331,[3590] the chief orthodox cleansing of the canon seems to have occurred in the year 553 after the Second Ecumenical Council at Constantinople. It was here that the Byzantine Christian Emperor Justinian I (the Great) decided that the idea of the preexistence of the soul was a threat to the institutional Church (since it undermined the doctrine of the Resurrection), and that it therefore must be declared a "heresy" and struck from the Bible.[3591] His famous anti-metempsychosis edict reads:

> If anyone asserts the fabulous preexistence of souls, and shall assert the monstrous restoration [that is, reincarnation] which follows from it: let him be anathema.[3592]

The doctrine of metempsychosis itself, or what we now call reincarnation, was not officially banned until the Church Council of Lyons in 1274, when Papal authorities condemned it as a pernicious teaching of the mystical Gnostic-Christian sect known as the Cathars (one of the most fascinating Christian groups to have ever existed). The final blow came between 1439 and 1441, at the Council of Florence, where reincarnation was condemned a second and final time.[3593]

Despite the Church's issuance of execrations against the doctrine of the transmigration of souls, numerous Catholic authorities have supported the idea of reincarnation right into modern times, among them Belgian Cardinal Mercier, Archbishop Passavalli, and the noted European priest Edward Dunski.[3594] In the 1930s at least 75 percent of the world's literate population believed in reincarnation, and at one time it is even said that the doctrine of reembodiment was taught by the Catholic Church herself.[3595] During the 20th Century famed American Christian seer Edgar Cayce discussed and taught reincarnation and its principles.[3596]

Concerning reincarnation, the 18th-Century German Christian mystic Gotthold Ephraim Lessing offered the following comments:

> The very same way by which the race reaches its perfection, must every individual man, one sooner, another later, have traveled over. Have traveled over in one and the same life? Can he have been, in one and the selfsame life, a sensualist and a spiritual Christian? Can he in the selfsame life have overtaken both?
>
> Surely not that! But why should not every individual man have existed more than once upon this world?
>
> Is this hypothesis so laughable merely because it is the oldest? Because the human understanding, before the sophistries of the schools had dissipated and debilitated it, lighted upon it at once?
>
> Why may not even I have already performed those steps of my perfecting which bring to man only temporal punishments and rewards?
>
> And once more, why not another time all those steps, to perform which the views of eternal rewards so powerfully assist us?
>
> Why should I not come back as often as I am capable of acquiring fresh knowledge, fresh expertness? Do I bring away so much from once, that there is nothing to repay the trouble of coming back?
>
> Is this a reason against it? Or because I forget that I have been here already? Happy it is for me that I do forget. The recollection of my former condition would permit me to make only a bad use of the present. And that which even I must forget now, is that necessarily forgotten for ever?

Or is it a reason against the hypothesis that so much time would have been lost to me? Lost? And how much then should I miss? Is not a whole eternity mine?[3597]

Despite the Bible's emphasis on reincarnation, Christian mystics do not believe that one must necessarily reincarnate in order to attain spiritual perfection. In other words, it can be avoided by simply recognizing and accepting that our divine nature is already perfect,[3598] that the Christ indwells us, and that this, "the true Light which lighteth every man that cometh into the world,"[3599] is God.[3600]

From this standpoint many mystics believe that the doctrine of reincarnation is, after all, not real but merely symbolic; an arcane representation of the psychological, moment-by-moment "crucifixion and rebirth" process that is necessary if one wishes to detach from the personal Ego and find at-one-ment with the impersonal Divine.[3601] This is certainly what Paul meant when he said "in Christ Jesus our Lord, I die daily."[3602] See BORN AGAIN, GOOD NEWS, GOSPEL, KARMA, REBIRTH, RESURRECTION OF JESUS, SOUL, SPIRIT, THEOSIS.

RESURRECTION OF JESUS: In the traditional Church the Resurrection of Jesus was the historical death of Christ on the cross and His subsequent return to earth in the body. This established Him as the "Son of God," turning the atoning cross into the great redemptive act which guarantees that life continues after so-called "death."[3603]

Because this is a literalization of the Resurrection, it has long created a massive misunderstanding of this important and deeply mystical "event."[3604]

As the Virgin Birth, the Passion, the Crucifixion, the Resurrection, and the Ascension have all been attributed to thousands of pre-Christian deities and religious founders throughout the ages—for example, Osiris, Mithra, Bacchus, Iacchos, Attis, Balder, Tammuz, Odin, Zoroaster, Apollo, Krishna, Acmon, Adonis, Soura-Parama, Buddha, etc.[3605]—it is clear that these aspects of the life of Jesus are worldwide archetypes (universal concepts), not strictly Christian ones. Thus, in the mystical Church the Resurrection of Jesus is more properly called the "Resurrection of the Indwelling Christ," for here it is seen as a spiritual process that occurs within every human being, not just Jesus. This gives new meaning to the oft repeated phrase of the Christian mystic that "the Resurrection was not something that happened to Jesus, but something that happened to the faith of His disciples."[3606]

To take this one step further, because every cell in our physical frame is regenerated annually, the Resurrection takes place in our bodies every year as well. This is one of the great secrets of the Christian Mysteries, one with which every mystic is familiar.[3607] Freemasons (the modern descendants of ancient Gnostic-Essenic Christianity) thus speak of the Resurrection as the simple fact of a progressive advancement from a lower to a higher sphere, and the raising of the soul from the bondage of death to its inheritance of eternal life.³⁶⁰⁸

This leads us unerringly into the doctrine of the *philosophic death* and the *philosophic resurrection*, known to mystics respectively as the "Lesser Mysteries" and the "Greater Mysteries." Taken together, "death" and "resurrection" give us the key to the doctrine of universal equilibrium. Just as Nature can only produce by way of polarity, understanding only comes through balance, personified in mystical Christianity as the "two thieves" who were crucified on either side of Jesus. This balance of polar opposites leads to individual redemption, long occultly symbolized in the world's religions in the figure of the dying and rising god.³⁶⁰⁹ Thus Liddon writes of the phrase "risen with Christ":

> *This Resurrection, then, is a moral change; it is a spiritual movement.* But observe that it is not merely a movement, a shifting of spiritual position from a lower to a higher point in the same sphere. That would be an elevation. It would not be a resurrection. *A resurrection is a transfer from one state to another.* It is a passage from the darkness of the tomb to the sunshine of the upper air. It is an exchange of the coldness, stillness, corruption of death for the warmth, and movement, and undecayed energies of life. It is necessary to remark this distinction, because an elevation, whether in thought or in morals, is sometimes described as if it were equivalent to a resurrection of faith and life.
>
> . . . The spiritual resurrection of a soul belongs to nature just as little as does the bodily raising of a corpse. It is the evidence of a real introduction of a Higher Power into humanity. It is, in short, simply and emphatically, the work of the quickening grace of God. It is essentially supernatural.³⁶¹⁰

Also speaking of the resurrection from a mystical viewpoint, Jones writes:

> [Gerrard Winstanley] . . . does not set up some vague, undifferentiated, abstract "principle" to take the place of the God above the stars; he makes Christ the type and goal of the manifestation of God in the flesh, and he calls his "Friends" to an experience of this Christ rising up within themselves:
>
>> "Friends, do not mistake the resurrection of Christ. You expect that He shall come in one

single person as He did when He came to *suffer and die, and thereby to answer the types of Moses' Law*. Let me tell you that *if you look for Him under the notion of one single man after the flesh, to be your Saviour, you shall never, never taste Salvation by him. . . . If you expect or look for the resurrection of Jesus Christ, you must know that the spirit within the flesh is the Jesus Christ, and you must see, feel, and know from Himself His own resurrection within you, if you expect life and peace by Him*. For He is the Life of the World, that is, of every particular son and daughter of the Father . . . for *every one hath the Light of the Father within himself, which is the mighty man Christ Jesus*. And He is now rising and spreading Himself in these His sons and daughters, and so rising from one to many persons till He enlightens the whole creation (mankind) in every branch of it, and covers this earth with knowledge as the waters cover the sea. . . . And this is to be saved by Jesus Christ; for that mighty Man of spirit hath taken up His habitation within your body; and your body is His body, and now His spirit is your spirit, and so you are become one with Him and with the Father. This is the faith of Christ, when your flesh is subject to the Spirit of Righteousness, as the flesh of Christ was subject. *And this is to believe in Christ, when the actings and breathings of your soul are within the centre of the same spirit in which the man Jesus Christ lived, acted, and breathed*."[3611]

In a word, to the Christian mystic then, resurrection implies a raising up "from the condition of spiritual deadness."[3612] R. J. Campbell writes:

The true resurrection, the resurrection to newness of life, is the rising of the Christ in human nature and human society into higher, fuller, and richer modes of expression. That resurrection is continually going on, and it correlative is the ascension of human consciousness into perfect oneness with the all-embracing mind of God in the sacred fellowship of love.[3613]

Mead writes:

> Curiously enough *we find the story of the resurrection of Dionysus*, after his dismemberment by the Titans, *compared by the most learned of the Christian Fathers with the resurrection of the Christ.* Thus Origen, after making the comparison, remarks apologetically and somewhat bitterly: "Or, forsooth, are the Greeks to be allowed to use such words with regard to the soul and speak in allegorical fashion, and we forbidden to do so?"—thus *clearly declaring that the "resurrection" was an allegory of the soul, and not historical.* And so Damascius, speaking of the dismemberment and resurrection of Osiris, remarks, "this should be a mingling with God, an all-perfect at-one-ment, a return upwards of our souls to the divine."[3614]

Bunyan writes:

> Now in all this, considering what has been said before, we that are of the elect are privileged, for that we also are raised up by the rising of the body of Christ from the dead. And thus the apostle bids us reckon: "Likewise (saith he) reckon also yourselves to be dead indeed unto sin, but alive unto God through Jesus Christ."
>
> Hence Christ says, "He is the resurrection and the life," for that all his are safe in him, suffering, dying, and rising. He is the life, our life; yea, so our life that by him the elect do live before God, even then when, as to themselves, they yet are dead in their sins. Wherefore, hence it is that in time they partake of quickening grace from this their Head, to the making of them also live by faith, in order to their living hereafter with him in glory. For if Christ lives they cannot die that were sharers with him in his resurrection. Hence they are said to live, being quickened together with him.
>
> Also, as sure as at his resurrection they lived by him, so sure at his coming shall they be gathered to him. Nay, from that day to this all that, as aforesaid, were in him at his death and resurrection are already in the fulness of the dispensation of time daily gathering to him. For this he hath proposed, wherefore none can disannul it: "In the fulness of the dispensation of time to gather together in one all things in Christ, both which are in heaven and which are in earth, even in him."[3615]

As with all things Christian and mystical, the Resurrection of the Sun/Son-God is a universal symbol, one that dates back to prehistoric Pagan religions. Sayce notes, for instance, that the Babylonian Osiris, known as Asari,

> was the sun-god of Evidu, the ancient seaport of Babylonia on the Persian Gulf. He was the son of Ea, the chief god of the city, of whose will and wisdom he was the interpreter. It was he who communicated to men the lessons in culture and the art of healing, which Ea was willing they should learn. Just as Osiris spent his life in doing good, according to the Egyptian legend, so Asari was he "who does good to man." He was ever on the watch to help his worshippers, to convey to them the magic formula; which could ward off sickness or evil, and, as it is often expressed, to "raise the dead to life."
>
> In this last expression we have the key to the part played by Osiris. Osiris died, and was buried, like Asari or [the Semitic god] Merodach, whose temple at Babylon was also his tomb; but it was that he might rise again in the morning with renewed strength and brilliancy. And through the spells he had received from his father all those who trusted in him, and shared in his death and entombment, were also "raised to life." Both in Egypt and in Babylonia *he was the god of the resurrection*, whether that took place in this visible world or in the heavenly paradise, which was a purified reflection of the earth.[3616]

The "Resurrection," in fact, takes place in every person in a myriad of ways, even at so-called "death," when the spirit of all individuals automatically transits into the Spirit Plane. In other words, "resurrection" has always been part of Man and Woman's life cycle, and has nothing to do specifically with the Resurrection of our Lord, which mystics view as an allegory to begin with. This is why ancient Gnostic-Christians referred to the literalization of the Resurrection as "the faith of fools."[3617]

This truth becomes even more apparent when we consider the origins of the concept of resurrection. In simplest terms, as Pike explains, in ancient times

> the struggle between the Good and Evil Principles was personified, as was that between life and death, destruction and re-creation, in allegories and fables which poetically represented the apparent course of the Sun; who, descending toward the Southern Hemisphere, was figuratively said to be conquered and put to death by darkness, or the genius of Evil; but, returning again toward the Northern Hemisphere, he

seemed to be victorious, and to arise from the tomb. This death and resurrection were also figurative of the succession of day and night, of death, which is a necessity of life, and of life which is born of death; and everywhere the ancients still saw the combat between the two Principles that ruled the world.

Everywhere this contest was embodied in allegories and fictitious histories: into which were ingeniously woven all the astronomical phenomena that accompanied, preceded, or followed the different movements of the Sun, and the changes of Seasons, the approach or withdrawal of inundation. And thus grew into stature and strange proportions the histories of the contests between Typhon and Osiris, Hercules and Juno, the Titans and Jupiter, Ormuzd and Ahriman, the rebellious Angels and the Deity, the Evil Genii and the Good; and the other like fables, found not only in Asia, but in the North of Europe, and even among the Mexicans and Peruvians of the New World; carried thither, in all probability, by those Phoenician voyagers who bore thither civilization and the arts. The Scythians lamented the death of Acmon, the Persians that of Zohak conquered by Pheridoun, the Hindus that of Soura-Parama slain by Soupra-Muni, as the Scandinavians did that of Balder, torn to pieces by the blind Hother.[3618]

Those who cling to a literal physical resurrection of Jesus must consider the following. The original pre-organized Church view of Jesus' "Resurrection" was eschatological, that is, philosophical, which is why none of the canonical Gospels describe it or mention any eyewitnesses. This is also why Paul never mentions the empty tomb.[3619] Being a mystical (that is, psychological) event, Jesus' resurrection was not visible to the human eye! Mark retains this occult tradition by having the angel at the tomb say simply: "He is risen; he is not here."[3620] Later writers embellished this truth with Pagan and institutional Christian ideas. But this does not change the original mystical meaning. See BORN AGAIN, DEATH OF JESUS, GOOD NEWS, GOSPEL, NATIVITY, REBIRTH, REINCARNATION.

REVELATION: In the traditional Church a revelation is an act in which God makes Himself and His truths known to humanity. According to mainstream Christianity, anyone can receive a "general" revelation. However, a "special" revelation can only come through the Bible and Jesus Christ.[3621]

In the mystical Church a revelation is a communication of special knowledge (Gnosis) from the Higher Self, the Indwelling Christ, to the Lower Self, Ego/Satan; one that can transpire within any individual. Among Christian mystics, going back to at least the pre-Christian Gnostic Church, this has been known as "revealed truth."³⁶²² Jesus commented on this type of revelation during an exchange with the Apostle Peter:

> When Jesus came into the coasts of Caesarea Philippi, he asked his disciples, saying, "Whom do men say that I the Son of man am?" And they said, "Some [say that thou art] John the Baptist: some, Elias; and others, Jeremias, or one of the prophets." He saith unto them, "But whom say ye that I am?" And Simon Peter answered and said, "Thou art the Christ, the Son of the living God." And Jesus answered and said unto him, "Blessed art thou, Simon Barjona: *for flesh and blood hath not revealed [it] unto thee, but my Father which is in heaven.*"³⁶²³

Paul declared that his knowledge of the Gospel, of God, and of "his Son in me" (the Indwelling Christ), came not from teachers or books:

> But I certify you, brethren, that *the gospel which was preached of me is not after man. For I neither received it of man, neither was I taught [it], but by the revelation of Jesus Christ.*
>
> For ye have heard of my conversation in time past in the Jews' religion, how that beyond measure I persecuted the church of God, and wasted it: And profited in the Jews' religion above many my equals in mine own nation, being more exceedingly zealous of the traditions of my fathers.
>
> But when it pleased God, who separated me from my mother's womb, and called [me] by his grace, *to reveal his Son in me*, that I might preach him among the heathen; immediately I conferred not with flesh and blood.³⁶²⁴

Ladd writes:

> In the religious history of humanity it is human thought and human speech which are the most distinctive and effective media of the Self-revelation of God; and yet more especially, the thought and speech of the divinely selected and inspired men of revelation.
>
> . . . This voice of God to man, through man, has been variously expressed. In the creeds of these different religions, the avatars of Vishnu, the various incarnations of the Buddha, the demi-gods that descended from the Scandinavian Heimdallr, the prophets and seers of Old Testament religion, and Jesus and his Apostles in the New Dispensation, all have the office of

revealing God to man. . . . *Spiritual truth is made known by communion of human spirits with the Spirit of God.*[3625]

De Bunsen writes of Paul's concept of universal revelation:

With the remarkable exception of the death of Jesus on the cross, and of the doctrine of atonement by vicarious suffering, which is absolutely excluded by Buddhism, *the most ancient of the Buddhistic records known to us contain statements about the life and the doctrines of Gautama-Buddha which correspond in a remarkable manner, and impossibly by mere chance, with the traditions recorded in the Gospels about the life and doctrines of Jesus Christ. It is still more strange that these Buddhistic legends about Gautama as the Angel-Messiah refer to a doctrine which we find only in the Epistles of Paul and in the fourth Gospel.*

This can be explained by the assumption of a common source of revelation; but then the serious question must be considered, why the doctrine of the Angel-Messiah, supposing it to have been revealed, and which we find in the East and in the West, is not contained in any of the Scriptures of the Old Testament which can possibly have been written before the Babylonian Captivity, nor in the first three Gospels. Can the systematic keeping back of essential truth be attributed to God or to man?

Had we only to consider the statements of Paul, we should be led to believe in the gradual revelation or publication of the mystery kept in secret. For he declares that he preached "the hidden wisdom," after that he had "renounced the hidden things of dishonesty," or, rather, "the shameful hiding," which Moses had first introduced, and which had led to a "deceitful handling," or, rather, to a falsifying, of God's Word.[3626] According to the theory we are considering, it would have been Paul who, not doing like Moses, had first "commended himself to every man's conscience in the sight of God" by "manifestation," or, rather, "revelation of the truth."

In this case it might not have been before the second century that, by the publication of the Gospel after John, the preaching of Jesus Christ was revealed in its absolute fulness and purity. The first Evangelists, according to this theory, had to consider the opposition of the Jewish authorities, who had forbidden the public preaching of this secret doctrine, whilst Jesus is implied to have forbidden the Apostles forthwith to preach from the roofs the mysteries which—so we are told—he had made known to them alone, whilst speaking only in parables to the people. According to this explanation of the problem presented to us, *Jesus must have been an Essene.*

The theory of an essentially similar revelation in East and West would harmonise with the conceptions of Paul. He writes that *God had never left himself without witness, that man's conscience is the witness of God, and that a "mystery" was hid in God from the beginning of the world, which "eternal purpose" was in his time made known as it had in former times not been made known. According to this universalist conception, held by Origen and Augustine, Christian revelation is directly connected with Divine revelations at all times and in all places, with a continuity of Divine influences.* [3627]

How does self-revelation work? According to God, He imbues our minds with Divine Gnosis (knowledge) before we are born, so that we can access this information, through self-revelation, during our sojourn on the earth plane:

> "But this shall be the covenant that I will make with the house of Israel; After those days," saith the Lord, "*I will put my law in their inward parts, and write it in their hearts*; and will be their God, and they shall be my people."[3628]

Thus we are all born with the Sacred Knowledge permanently engraved in our "inward parts" or "hearts"; that is, our Indwelling Christ, the Higher Self.

Naturally, orthodox Christianity opposes "special" revelation outside Church officials (the clergy, etc.), for it renders the priesthood, and even the Church itself, unnecessary—which accords with the teachings of our Lord, who never said anything regarding a priesthood, or even a church.[3629] And herein lies the crux of the ageless battle between the literal Church (conservative Christianity) and the mystical Church (liberal Christianity). See GNOSIS, GNOSTICISM, LOGOS, VOICE OF GOD, WAY OF THE LORD, WORD OF GOD.

RIGHTEOUSNESS: In the traditional Church righteousness simply means following God's commandments, living a pure life as a Christian.[3630] In the mystical Church righteousness has to do with thought, for as the ancient Gnostic-Christians once said: "God is all mind and mind is all God."[3631] Because we live in a law-governed, reciprocal universe,[3632] and since the Christian Laws of Karma, Reciprocity, and Attraction are scientifically precise, it is important to understand that there is a right and a wrong way of thinking. For as the Old Testament declares, what we think is what our lives become—now and in the Hereafter.[3633] Thus, when the Christian mystic speaks of righteousness, he means right-thinking (which includes right-speaking and right-acting) as opposed to wrong-thinking ("sin").³⁶³⁴ See KARMA, SALVATION, SIN, UNRIGHTEOUSNESS.

RIVER: In the traditional Church the biblical river is merely a physical body of water, usually connected to the Old Testament prophets or New Testament figures and events, such as the baptism of Jesus in the River Jordan.³⁶³⁵ In the mystical Church the rivers mentioned in the Bible are symbols of Divine Truth, the fountain of the Divine Life in Christ. This is the energy of God pouring down upon Mankind on the earth plane. Budge refers to this doctrine in the following description of the Egyptian savior-god Osiris:

> In return for the lands which were given them [the gods] by Osiris, in the possession of which they were confirmed by Afura, these gods have certain duties to perform, viz., to take vengeance upon the fiend Seba, to make Nu to come into being, and to cause Hapi to flow. From this it appears that Seba possessed at times power over Nu, that is to say, *the great celestial watery mass which was the source of the river Nile in Egypt*; to destroy this fiend was all-important, for without water the inhabitants of the Tuat could not live, and the cessation of the flow of the Nile would cause the ruin and death of the people of Egypt. It is interesting to note the connexion of the Nile with the chief domain of Osiris, and it is, no doubt, a reminiscence of the period in the history of the god when he was a water-god.³⁶³⁶

In the book of Genesis we read:

> And out of the ground made the Lord God to grow every tree that is pleasant to the sight, and good for food; the tree of life also in the midst of the garden, and the tree of knowledge of good and evil. And a river went out of Eden to water the garden; and from thence it was parted, and became into four heads.³⁶³⁷

Here the river signifies divine truth being transmitted to the Indwelling Christ (spirituality or "Heavenly Father"), while the number four is—as represented in the four-pointed crucifix—a symbol of the earth plane (materiality or "Earthly Mother"), which equals spiritual involution and evolution: God in physical Nature, ordering the laws of the Universe. This is the same invisible cosmic "river of God" mentioned by the Psalmist:

> Thou visitest the earth, and waterest it: thou greatly enrichest

it with *the river of God*, which is full of water: thou preparest them corn, when thou hast so provided for it.[3638] ... *There is a river*, the streams whereof shall *make glad the city of God, the holy place* of the tabernacles of the most High.[3639]

Here the "City of God" or "Holy Place of the Tabernacles" is an esoteric symbol of the human skull, the location of the Crown Chakra or Indwelling Christ. It is being "watered" by the "River of God": spiritual truth. Of this arcane symbolism Maclaren writes:

> First, we have the gladdening River—an emblem of many great and joyous truths. The figure is occasioned by, or at all events derives much of its significance from, a geographical peculiarity of Jerusalem. Alone among the great cities and historical centres of the world, it stood upon no broad river. One little perennial stream, or rather rill of living water was all which it had; but Siloam was mightier and more blessed for the dwellers in the rocky fortress of the Jebusites than the Euphrates, Nile, or Tiber for the historical cities which stood upon their banks.
>
> One can see the psalmist looking over the plain eastward and beholding in vision the mighty forces which came against them, symbolised and expressed by the breadth and depth and swiftness of the great river upon which Nineveh sat as a queen, and then thinking upon the little tiny thread of living water that flowed past the base of the rock upon which the temple was perched. It seems small and unconspicuous, nothing compared to the dash of the waves and the rise of the floods of those mighty secular empires; still "There is a river the streams whereof shall make glad the city of God." Its waters shall never fail, and thirst shall flee whithersoever this river comes.
>
> It is also to be remembered that *the psalm is running in the track of a certain constant symbolism that pervades all scripture*. From the first book of Genesis down to the last chapter of Revelations, you can hear the dashing of the waters of the river. "It went out from the garden and parted into "four heads." "Thou makest them drink of the river of Thy pleasures." "Behold, waters issued out from under the threshold of the house eastward," and everything shall live whithersoever the river cometh. "He that believeth on me, out of his belly shall flow rivers of living water." "And he shewed me a pure river of water of life, clear as crystal, proceeding out of the throne of

God and of the Lamb."

Isaiah, who has already afforded some remarkable parallels to the words of our psalm, gives another very striking one to the image now under consideration, when he says "The glorious Lord will be unto us a place of broad rivers and streams wherein shall go no galley with oars." The picture in that *metaphor* is of a stream lying round Jerusalem, like the moated rivers which girdle some of the cities in the plains of Italy, and are the defence of those who dwell enclosed in their flashing links.

Guided then by the physical peculiarity of situation which I have referred to, and by *the constant meaning of scriptural symbolism*, I think we must conclude that this river, "the streams whereof make glad the city of God," is God himself in the outflow and self-communication of His own grace to the soul. *The stream is the fountain in flow. The gift of God, which is living water, is God himself, considered as the ever-imparting source of all refreshment, of all strength, of all blessedness.* "This spake He of the Spirit, which they that believe should receive."[3640]

See ARK, DOVE, NOAH, NOAH'S FLOOD, WATER, WORD OF GOD.

ROCK: In traditional Christianity rock is often used figuratively to mean a mountain, a natural fortress, or sometimes God. Most often, however, the "Rock" is the Apostle Peter,[3641] upon whom "Jesus built His Church."[3642] But since the Matthean scripture in which this doctrine is cited is a late interpolation by orthodox priests, the truth behind the "Rock" must be found elsewhere.[3643] And indeed, on the surface the Bible is quite clear that it was Jesus, not Peter, upon whom the Church would be founded.[3644]

Mystical Christianity resolves these conflicting issues (brought about by the bad orthodox habits of both textual literalization and textual tampering) by digging deep into the esoteric (secret) teachings of our Lord. Here we discover that the "Rock" is not the man Jesus, but the spirit Christ, the Higher Self, and that Jesus' "Church" is not a physical building or even a group of believers, but the "Church" that resides within each individual,[3645] made by the hands of God, not man.[3646] The mystical Christ-Rock then is an occult symbol of living the Holy Life, which naturally expresses itself as love, joy, peace, longsuffering, gentleness, faith, meekness, and temperance; in other words, the "fruit of the Spirit."[3647] Robertson writes of the Pagan origins and inner meanings of the Bible's rock motif:

> When . . . [the Church Father] Justin asserts that the Mithraists in their initiation imitate not only Daniel's utterance "that a

stone without hands was cut out of a great mountain," but "the whole of [Isaiah's] words,"[3648] he merely helps us to realise *how much older than Christianity is that particular element of Christian symbolism which connects alike Jesus and Peter with the mystic Rock.* That Mazdeism or Mithraism borrowed this symbol from Judaism, where it is either an excrescence or a totemistic survival, is as unlikely as it is likely that the Hebrews borrowed it from Babylonia or Persia. In Polynesian mythology, where (as also in the rites of human sacrifice) there are so many close coincidences with Asiatic ideas, it was told that the God Taaroa "embraced a rock, the imagined foundation of all things, which afterwards brought forth the earth and sea."

Here again we are in touch with the Græcised but probably Semitic myth of the rock-born Agdestis, son of Jupiter. Even the remarkable parallel between the myth of Moses striking the rock for water and a scene on one of the Mithraic monuments suggests rather a common source for both myths than a Persian borrowing from the Bible. In the monument, Mithra shoots an arrow at a rock, and water gushes forth where the arrow strikes. As the story of the babe Moses is found long before in that of Sargon, so probably does the rock-story come from Central Asia.

The passage in Isaiah, which strongly suggests the Mithraic initiation, seems to have been tampered with by the Jewish scribes; and corruption is similarly suspected in the [Genesaic] passage[3649] where "the Shepherd, the Stone of Israel," points to some credence latterly thrust out of Judaism. Above all, the so-called Song of Moses (in which both Israel and his enemies figure as putting their faith in a divine "Rock," and the hostile "Rock" is associated with a wine-sacrament)[3650] points to the presence of such a God-symbol in Hebrew religion long before our era.

There is a clear Mazdean element, finally, in the allusion to the mystic stone in Zechariah,[3651] the "seven eyes" being certainly connected with the Seven Amesha-Spentas, of whom Mithra on one view, and Ormazd on another, was chief. And when we find in the epistles[3652] phrases as to Jesus being a "living stone" and a "spiritual rock," and read in the gospels how Jesus said, "Thou art Peter, and upon this rock I will build my church,"[3653] we turn from the latter utterance, *so obviously unhistorical*, back to the Mithraic rite, and see in the mystic rock of Mithra, the rock from which the God comes—be it the earth or the cloud—the probable source alike of the Roman legend and the doctrine of the pseudo-Petrine and Pauline epistles.

The Mithraic mysteries, then, of the burial and resurrection of the Lord, the Mediator and Saviour; burial in a rock tomb and resurrection from that tomb; the sacrament of bread and water, the marking on the forehead with a mystic mark—*all these were in practice, like the Egyptian search for the lost corpse of Osiris, and the representation of his entombment and resurrection, before the publication of the Christian Gospel of a Lord who was buried in a rock tomb, and rose from that tomb on the day of the sun, or of the Christian mystery of Divine communion, with bread and water or bread and wine, which last were before employed also in the mysteries of Dionysus, Sun-God and Wine-God, doubtless as representing his body and blood.*[3654]

Mystic Paul too commented on the occult symbolism of the "Rock," referring to it as a "spiritual" one, not a physical one:

Moreover, brethren, I would not that ye should be ignorant, how that all our fathers were under the cloud, and all passed through the sea; And were all baptized unto Moses in the cloud and in the sea; And did all eat the same *spiritual meat*; And did all drink the same *spiritual drink*: for they drank of that *spiritual Rock* that followed them: and *that Rock was Christ*.[3655]

The biblical "Rock" then is not Peter or even Jesus. As Paul clearly states, it is our Indwelling Christ, the Higher Self, the Divine Spark or Light in all of us[3656] that was made in the exact image of God,[3657] whom Moses mystically and correctly calls "the rock that begat thee."[3658] This is the true "Rock" upon which the authentic (inner) Church was built. See ANOINTING, APOSTLES, ASTROLOGY, CHURCH, OIL, PETER, WAY OF THE LORD, ZODIAC.

The Resurrection of Jesus.

"Strictly speaking, it is difficult to view the Jewish Book of Genesis otherwise than a chip from the trunk of the mundane tree of universal Cosmogony rendered in Oriental allegories. . . . The parent cult was none other than the primitive Wisdom-Religion. The Israelitish Scriptures are no exception."
— MADAME H. P. BLAVATSKY, 1892

S

SACRAMENT: According to traditional Christianity there were a number of sacraments instituted by Jesus (resulting in two in the Protestant Church, seven in the Catholic Church), establishing the foundation of the Christian Church on the suffering and redemptive death of Jesus for all humanity.[3659] In mystical Christianity the Sacrament is a metaphor of the union of the body or Lower Self (symbolized by bread) with the spirit or Higher Self (symbolized by wine), which produces the Christ, which indwells us all.[3660] This is also known as the Hieros Gamos, or "Sacred Union,"[3661] which "marries" the Divine Feminine (earth, Moon, darkness, negative polarity) with the Divine Masculine (heaven, Sun, light, positive polarity), and produces the god-man and god-woman known as a human being.[3662] This, the original and only true "Sacrament," the Hieros Gamos, Plutarch called "the basis of all the Mysteries."[3663]

Christian mystics not only recognize, with John, that Jesus did not institute a Eucharistic sacrament,[3664] but that the "Christian" sacrament itself is both Pagan and pre-Christian,[3665] dating back to the edge of history and some of humanity's most primitive Pagan societies, which held that wine could be transformed into blood and bread could be transformed into flesh.[3666] Thus, the actual body and blood of sacrificial victims were consumed in order to appease the gods, achieve immortality, and expiate sin. Gilbert Murray, for example, notes that:

> The [pre-Christian] Orphic congregations of later times, in their most holy gatherings, solemnly partook of the blood of a bull, which was, by a mystery, the blood of Dionysus-Zagreus himself, the "Bull of God," slain in sacrifice for the purification of man. And the Maenads of poetry and myth, among more beautiful proofs of their superhuman or infra-human character, have always to tear bulls in pieces and taste of the blood.[3667]

The Cretans too venerated the bull as a savior-god, and so ritually sacrificed and consumed it, always with the prayer: "I eat of his body, I drink of his blood."[3668]

In ancient Rome and Greece such customs naturally found their way into the Mystery Religions, whose central focus was the worship of the great gods, goddesses, saviors, christs, and virgin-mothers of the Pagan Pantheon. Chief among these pre-Christian faiths was, as just noted, Orphism, which, by 500 B.C., was already practicing a "cathartic rite of sacramental efficacy for sin."[3669] Thus, Winston Churchill once wrote:

> The mysteries of Eleusis, of Attis, Mithras, Magna Mater, and Isis developed into Christian sacraments—*the symbol became the thing itself.*[3670]

According to Carpenter,

> the Pagan cults generally appear to have included rites—sometimes half-savage, sometimes more aesthetic—in which a dismembered animal was eaten, or bread and wine (the spirits of the Corn and the Vine) were consumed, representing the body of the god whom his devotees desired to honor.[3671]

One of the best examples of the pre-Christian Pagan sacrament, says Carpenter, is to be found in the rites of the Greek god Dionysus, who turned water into wine:[3672]

> Dionysus, like other Sun or Nature deities, was born of a Virgin (Semele or Demeter) untainted by any earthly husband; and born on the 25th December. He was nurtured in a Cave, and even at that early age was identified with the Ram or Lamb [Aries], into whose form he was for the time being changed. At times also he was worshiped in the form of a Bull [Taurus]. He travelled far and wide; and brought the great gift of wine to mankind. He was called Liberator, and Saviour. His grave "was shown at Delphi in the inmost shrine of the temple of Apollo. Secret offerings were brought thither, while the women who were celebrating the feast woke up the new-born god. . . . Festivals of this kind in celebration of the extinction and resurrection of the deity were held (by women and girls only) amid the mountains at night, every third year, about the time of the shortest day. The rites, intended to express the excess of grief and joy at the death and reappearance of the god, were wild even to savagery, and the women who performed them were hence known by the expressive names of *Bacchae*, *Mœnads*, and *Thyiades*. They wandered through woods and mountains, their flying locks crowned with ivy or snakes, brandishing wands and torches, to the hollow sounds of the drum, or the shrill notes of the flute, with wild dances and insane cries and jubilation. The victims of the sacrifice, oxen, goats, even fawns

and roes from the forest, were killed, torn to pieces, and eaten raw. This in imitation of the treatment of Dionysus by the Titans"—who it was supposed had torn the god in pieces when a child.

Dupuis, one of the earliest writers (at the beginning of last century) on this subject, says, describing the mystic rites of Dionysus:

> "The sacred doors of the Temple in which the initiation took place were opened only once a year, and no stranger might ever enter. Night lent to these august mysteries a veil which was forbidden to be drawn aside—for whoever it might be. It was the sole occasion for the representation of the passion of Bacchus [Dionysus] dead, descended into hell, and rearisen—in imitation of the representation of the sufferings of Osiris which, according to Herodotus, were commemorated at Sais in Egypt. It was in that place that the partition took place of *the body of the god*, which was then eaten—the ceremony, in fact, of which our Eucharist is only a reflection; whereas in the mysteries of Bacchus actual raw flesh was distributed, which each of those present had to consume in commemoration of the death of Bacchus dismembered by the Titans, and whose passion, in Chios and Tenedos, was renewed each year by the sacrifice of a man who represented the god. Possibly it is this last fact which made people believe that the Christians (whose *hoc est corpus meum* ["this is my body"] and sharing of an Eucharistic meal were no more than a shadow of a more ancient rite) did really sacrifice a child and devour its limbs."3673

Pfleiderer notes that the Christian sacrament has numerous pre-Christian antecedents, such as the Mithraic religion, in which wine was imbibed and small bread loaves with crosses etched into them were eaten:

To the mysteries of Mithras, . . . besides the holy ablutions and the signing of the forehead with a covenant sign, there belonged a sacred banquet of which only the initiated of the higher degrees might partake. This was regarded as an imitation of the meal by which Mithras himself, according to the legend, had sealed his covenant with the sun-god Helios. In a relief which has come down to us, we see the two gods sitting side by side on cushions, each with a cup in his right hand, while before them is set a small dish containing four small loaves, each marked with crossed lines. On either side stand the initiated wearing masks which represent the nature of Mithras under different attributes; they have thus "put on" the god in order to place themselves in mystic communion with him (see Galatians 4:37: "ye have put on Christ").

Justin relates of the banquet of Mithras that "Bread and a cup full of water were brought forward with some words of blessing"; and Tertullian speaks of an offering of bread and a symbol of the resurrection. *Both apologists regarded this [Mithraic] rite as a diabolical aping of the Christian Sacrament; and in forming this opinion of theirs they partly ignored the unquestionable priority of the heathen to the Christian Sacrament in point of time, and partly explained it by assuming a prophetic anticipation on the part of the demons.*

A noteworthy point of coincidence is found in the fact that in both cases the same uncertainty exists concerning the content of the cup, whether it contained only water or also wine, for the original cup of the Christian Sacrament did not always at all events contain wine, for *in the primitive Christian love-feasts of the Acts of the Apostles no mention is ever made of wine.* In the Corinthian community however according to 1 Corinthians 11:21, celebration with wine had become the custom, and had afforded the Apostle Paul (who besides speaks never of "the wine," but only of "the cup") a welcome occasion for the mystical explanation of the Lord's Supper as a communion not only with the body but also with the blood of Christ (1 Corinthians 10:16).

Though there is no parallel in the banquet of Mithras to this blood-symbolism of the Christian Sacrament, one is certainly found in the blood-baptism of the Taurobolians and the Criobolians which belongs to the mysteries of Cybele, and perhaps also of Mithras. These sacrifices of bulls and rams, when adopted into the cult of Mithras, were evidently regarded as a sacramental imitation of the sacrifice of the bull which Mithras himself once offered for the salvation of the world—a sacrifice which is represented in all pictorial monuments of the cult of Mithras, wherein the bull may be conceived as an incarnation of the god himself, as is the case at all events in the cult of Dionysus.

As now the postulant for initiation was sprinkled with the blood of the slain bull or ram, this blood-baptism served him as a sacramental means of communion with the death and life of the god; and the thought of purification and new birth by means of the sacramental death-symbol, which according to the liturgy quoted above was a fundamental conception in the religion of Mithras, came in this blood-baptism to very drastic expression. *In this connection we may call to mind the Christian doctrine concerning cleansing and purification "by the blood of the Lamb"* (Revelation 7:14).[3674]

For modern Christians the mystical implications of the Christian Sacrament are clear, as Jones notes concerning the opinions of John the Scot:

"There is nothing in the visible and material world which does not signify something immaterial and reasonable," so that everything is a symbol, and has a sacramental significance. Matter is only a concourse of accidents or qualities, no real being. It is wholly dependent on thought for its existence, and therefore it would be absurd to say that the "material" Bread and Wine are more than symbols. The value of a sacrament for John [the Scot] could only be an inward and spiritual value—a value for faith.

There is a striking passage in his Exposition of the Celestial Hierarchy of Dionysius in which he expresses the view, now so familiar among English Protestants, that the sacrament of the bread and wine is an outward and visible sign of an inward and spiritual grace, which grace is a direct participation in spirit with Christ, Whom we taste with our minds and Whom we receive in the inner man for our salvation and spiritual increase, until we come through His presence to an unspeakable deification; this idea of deification being, of course, an inheritance from his [Pagan] Greek masters.

This position that a sacrament is only an outward sign of an inward event, plainly comes out in what he says on Baptism: "When any faithful persons receive the sacrament of baptism, what happens but the conception and birth in their hearts of God the word, of and through the Holy Ghost? Thus every day Christ is conceived in the womb of faith as in that of a pure mother, and is born and nourished."

He says elsewhere: "We who do believe in Him (the Christ), do in our spirits sacrifice Him and in our minds—not with our teeth—eat of Him." "The pious mind tastes inwardly the body of Christ, the stream of sacred blood, and the ransom price of the world."[3675]

This exact rite was in use thousands of years prior to the rise of Christianity. An ancient Egyptian inscription reads:

O ye who give *cakes and ale* to perfected souls in the Temple of Osiris, give ye *cakes and ale* at the two seasons [sunrise and sunset] to the soul of Osiris Ani, who is victorious before all the gods of Abtu [Abydos] and who is victorious with you.[3676]

Pfleiderer writes that in the early Christian Church the sacraments

served to abolish the time-form of the redemption myth, in that they represented under symbolic signs the eternal spiritual truth that lay hidden in the myth—*the truth of the continuous incarnation of God in the hearts of good men.*[3677]

As Freud pointed out, all of this makes the traditional Christian's modern sacrament of Holy Communion little more than a repeat of the old Pagan totem feast.[3678] See BETHLEHEM, BREAD, EUCHARIST, WATER, WAY OF THE LORD, WINE.

SALVATION: As is the custom of the traditional Church, over the millennia the doctrine of salvation has been developed into an extremely complex theological system, one comprised primarily of manmade tenets that are based on a narrow and literal interpretation of scripture. In simplest terms, however, the orthodox view of salvation concerns the saving grace of Jesus and only Jesus, who died on the cross to atone for the sins of Mankind, created by the Fall of Adam and Eve in the Garden of Eden (the "original sin").[3679]

In the mystical Church salvation is a much simpler affair: because there is no such thing as "original sin,"[3680] the perfection and salvation of all people[3681] is assured by the perfection we possess being born "in the image of God."[3682] For one thing, contrary to what many have been taught, Jesus never once mentions anything about "original sin." For another, not only does the phrase "original sin" itself appear nowhere in the Bible, but, from a mystical Christian standpoint, all of the scriptures that allegedly "refer to it" have been grossly misinterpreted by ecclesiastical apologists,[3683] as well as heavily reshaped by the absorption of Oriental and Greek Pagan influences.[3684]

Jesus also never uses the word "atonement" (the mainstream Christian idea that we are reconciled with God by the redemptive life and death of Jesus, who died due to our inherently sinful nature). The word appears only once in the New Testament, in Paul's letter to the Romans.[3685] As for the doctrine of Christian salvation itself, Jesus taught neither salvation of the physical body or of the human Soul.[3686]

Our Lord did not speak of atonement for the same reason He did not speak of original sin or salvation: according to mystical Christian tradition, since we are of divine origin, our real selves, our souls or Higher Selves, are beyond sinfulness.[3687] Thus, "no special 'salvation' is needed,"[3688] and like every mystic who came before Him, Jesus taught that the human Soul is perfect, immortal, and divine, made in the exact image of God[3689]—unsullied by corruption and decay, wholly out of reach of celestial judgment.[3690] This, the unstained Soul, is what Peter referred to as "the hidden man of the heart . . . which is not corruptible."[3691]

To put it another way, because our incorporeal true Self, the Indwelling Christ, is inherently pure, we are inherently pure. This has always been true and it will always be true. This secret knowledge is built into the name of our Lord: Jesus means "God is salvation," or in mystical parlance, "the Indwelling Christ automatically redeems you from sin." Victorian Christian Liberals, like Channing, rightly noted that if we are *innately* sinful at birth, we are not truly sinners, for we have no choice in the matter, making any form of punishment an "unspeakable cruelty" and "the most merciless despotism."[3692]

These doctrines being true, the earliest Christians, the Gnostics, taught that we need not be "saved" from anything. Indeed, to the contrary, they taught, like Buddha,[3693] the doctrine of Universal Salvation, just as Jesus' Disciples did. Here is how one of them, Luke, put it:

> *All* flesh shall see the salvation of God.[3694]

The reason for this is, as Paul declared, the Father wants each and every one of His children to be delivered:

> God will have *all* men to be saved, and to come unto the knowledge of the truth.[3695]

The Father Himself said, in the end I will bestow my Spirit on *all* people,[3696] for I am

> not willing that any should perish, but that *all* should come to repentance [that is, see the error of wrong-thinking and be

saved].[3697]

Yes, according to Jesus, the Apostles, and God himself, the doctrine of Universalism is true, and thus each one of us will be saved. How could it be otherwise? As our Lord revealed to the world, we are endowed with all of the power, perfection, and divinity of the Almighty, as his great and irrevocable gifts[3698] to humanity, the Laws of Karma and Reciprocity, amply confirm.[3699]

God tells us that we were made in his image[3700] (not his "physical" image, but his spiritual one).[3701] Was God "born in sin"? Of course not. And because of this neither are we, for our true self is our Higher Self, the Indwelling Christ.[3702] Yes, we all make mistakes, and indeed figuratively, as Isaiah wrote, "we are all as an unclean thing, and all our righteousnesses [that is, even our so-called "righteous acts"] are as filthy rags."[3703] But this is only because we have a *human nature* (the Lower Self)—something God the Father does not possess. But the Lower Self is not the real you. It is a temporary fleshly garment we put on for our temporary journey here to Earth School.

Let us look at salvation from Jesus' point of view: if we are one with God (as He taught),[3704] we are each a god in our own right (as He also taught).[3705] If original sin and salvation are to be accepted as real in the literal sense then, in condemning and punishing us, God would also need to condemn, punish, and save Himself. Obviously, God, who is universal love,[3706] is beyond such things, for as Christian mystics and Christian pantheists hold, he *is* all things![3707] Furthermore, Jesus showed us that both God and the human entity He created in His own image[3708] are both already spiritually perfect.[3709]

Another problem for the institutional Church: Jesus uses the word "salvation" (according to the mainstream definition: deliverance from the power and effects of sin through Jesus' crucifixion) only once in the entire New Testament (in Luke); and even then He does not in any way connect the word to his own execution or resurrection.[3710] This is odd considering that the mainstream Church, the Ecclesia,[3711] teaches that Jesus' salvific death on the cross was the "central theme of His life's mission" on earth, and hence the "foundational doctrine of the entire Church." Furthermore, the word here is more accurately translated from Aramaic (the daily language Jesus used) as "life," not "salvation," completely altering the meaning of this particular Lucan passage.[3712] Maclaren writes:

> *The gift and blessing of salvation is primarily a spiritual gift, and only involving outward consequences secondarily and subordinately. It mainly consists in the heart being at peace with God, in the whole soul being filled with Divine affections, in the weight and bondage of transgression being taken away, and substituted by the impulse and the life of the new love.* Therefore, neither God can give, nor man can receive, that gift upon any other terms, than just this, that

the heart and nature be fitted and adapted for it. Spiritual blessings require a spiritual capacity for the reception of them; or, as my [Bible] text says, you cannot have the inheritance unless you are sons. If salvation consisted simply in a change of place; if it were merely that by some expedient or arrangement, an outward penalty, which was to fall or not to fall at the will of an arbitrary judge, were prevented from coming down, why then, it would be open to Him who held the power of letting the sword fall, to decide on what terms He might choose to suspend its infliction.

But inasmuch as God's deliverance is not a deliverance from a mere arbitrary and outward punishment: inasmuch as God's salvation, though it be deliverance from the penalty as well as from the guilt of sin, is by no means chiefly a deliverance from outward consequences, but a *removal of the nature and disposition* that makes these outward consequences certain,—therefore a man cannot be saved, God's love cannot save him, God's justice will not save him, God's power stands back from saving him, upon any other condition than this, that his soul shall be adapted and prepared for the reception and enjoyment of the blessing of a spiritual salvation.[3713]

For Christian mystics ultimately salvation is a personal, inner, mystical experience,[3714] one that symbolizes the emancipation of the human Soul (Christ) from its Lower Self (Satan), after it has suffered and has been purified on its journey through involution (incarnation on the material plane) and evolution (return to the realm of Spirit).[3715] As Mascaró remarks, this knowledge does not lead to salvation. This knowledge *is* salvation.[3716] And this is why the Gnostic-Christians portrayed the world-honored, all-knowing Jesus, not lamenting (as in the canonical Gospel of Matthew),[3717] but singing and dancing at the Last Supper (as in the noncanonical Hymn of Jesus),[3718] and later laughing as He hung on the cross (as in the noncanonical Apocalypse of Peter)![3719] Theodore Parker wonderfully encapsulated the Christian mystic's view of salvation:

> For it is not so much by the Christ who lived so blameless and beautiful eighteen centuries ago, that we are saved directly, but by the Christ we form in our hearts and live out in our daily life, that *we save ourselves*, God working with us, both to will and to do.[3720]

Jesus never forgave anyone "in the name of Jesus Christ." Instead He taught that since we are constantly living in God's grace, we are already "saved" by the Father's justice and mercy,[3721] making original sin meaningless, salvation superfluous, and universal forgiveness a fact. See BAPTISM, FORGIVENESS, KARMA, REDEEMER, REDEMPTION SACRAMENT, SAVIOR, SIN.

SATAN: In the traditional Church Satan is the evil god of Judeo-Christian mythology, the "chief of the fallen spirits."[3722] He goes by a myriad of epithets: "Devil,"[3723] "Accuser,"[3724] "Adversary,"[3725] "Beelzebub,"[3726] "Belial,"[3727] "Deceiver,"[3728] "Great Dragon,"[3729] "Evil One,"[3730] "Father of Lies,"[3731] "god of this world,"[3732] "Murderer,"[3733] "Old Serpent,"[3734] "Prince of the Powers of the Air,"[3735] "Prince of this World,"[3736] and the "Tempter."[3737]

In the mystical Church Satan's many negative names actually reveal his true identity: he is, along with the Devil and Lucifer, an arcane symbol of the atheistic, ever self-serving human Ego or rational brain,[3738] which can never understand that which is spiritual, for these things are unknowable to the reasoning analytical mind (this is why one of Buddha's goals was stop his followers from relying on the rational mind).[3739] Thus mystic Paul calls Satan "the god of this [earthly] world,"[3740] which is a Gnostic phrase for the evil Demiurge[3741] known as Yaldabaoth or Ialdabaoth[3742] (his name means "he who blasphemes against the Divine"),[3743] another arcane symbol of the Ego. This is supported by the Aramaic meaning of the word Satan itself: "to slide," "to mislead," or "to slip," making it identical in meaning to the word sin, or in Old English, *synne* (the biblical Greek *anomia*): "to miss the mark" (an old archer's term).[3744]

Satan's name and figure were borrowed from the ancient Egyptian serpent-god Sata (identical to the Greek Saturn),[3745] an underworld expression of the Egyptian father-god Ra, whose Jewish equivalent was the Father-God Yahweh, in English, Jehovah (the Father, the Lord, God)[3746]—that is, Yaldabaoth. This good/light, evil/dark dualism is found in countless other religions, including Zoroastrianism, whose Father-God Ahura Mazda has a dark side known as Angra Mainyu, Ahriman, or Shaitin (Satan).[3747]

Indeed, to this day most mystery schools view God and Satan not as two separate, opposing beings, but rather as two sides of the same coin, one known as the *Demon est Deus Inversus*,[3748] Latin for the "Devil is God Inverted."[3749] Thus Mormons believe that Satan and Jesus (God) are brothers,[3750] while Kabbalists maintain that the true name of Satan is (numerologically speaking) God's name in reverse.[3751] The Old Testament mystics were certainly aware of this occult doctrine. In the book of Isaiah, for example, God says:

> I form the light, and create darkness: I make peace, and create evil: I the Lord do all these things.[3752]

Satanists have known this fact for centuries, which is why, after all, they harmonize a number of the very spiritual belief systems out of which Christianity first grew:

Gnosticism, Kabbalism, and Hermeticism.[3753]

According to the ancient Law of Attraction, God is Divine Mind, individualized in each one of us as our Superconscious, Conscious, and Subconscious Minds (our inner "Holy Trinity").[3754] The most powerful force in the Universe, Divine Mind is equally capable of creating both good and evil, as we have all repeatedly proven to ourselves.[3755] Only when we learn to think positive thoughts can we use Divine Mind constructively, for good (God), instead of destructively, for evil (Devil).[3756]

Jesus taught that Satan, the evil aspect of God or Divine Mind, is an illusion, and so should be ignored and denied. For if we respond to it, we not only energize it, we become one with it. By the Law of Attraction, reacting to something—either positively or negatively—activates, stimulates, enlarges, and attracts it.[3757] Thus our Lord said: "Resist not evil."[3758]

In his guise as Lucifer, Satan is the archetypal "Bringer of Light" (spiritual enlightenment), making him the same as the serpent who gave the Gnosis (sacred knowledge) to Adam and Eve in the Garden of Eden. What was this knowledge? It was the awareness of Theosis, "God in Man," which gives humanity the same divine power as God: the free will to create righteousness or wickedness; the limitless power to make of one's life whatever one wishes. Thus to Christian mystics Satan is not a living entity, as Christian orthodoxy teaches. It is the Law of Free Will,[3759] also known as the *Demon-Deus*, available to all, to be used for good or evil.[3760] See ADVERSARY, ANTICHRIST, BEAST, CHRIST, DEVIL, EGO, EGYPT, EVIL, GODS AND GODDESSES, HELL, KARMA, LOWER SELF, LUCIFER, MASS MIND, NUMBER OF THE BEAST, SERPENT, SIN.

SAVIOR: In traditional Christianity the Savior is our Lord Jesus, given this title because he saves, preserves, and delivers us from the powers of evil,[3761] embodied in Satan.[3762] But this was not the original savior of Christianity. It was God, as the Old Testament clearly states,[3763] and as Jesus Himself taught during his brief earthly ministry.[3764] And unlike today's mainstream Church, the early Hebrews used the title "savior" for everyday men.[3765]

But as God is identical to the Christ and the Christ is identical to the Savior, in the mystical Christian Church the Savior represents the Higher Self, or what is best known as the Indwelling Christ,[3766] symbolized in the Bible as the Sun or Solar-god[3767]—which is why the initials IHS (the first three letters of Jesus' name in Greek, *Ihsus*) are typically inscribed inside of an image of the Sun.[3768] Thus the Savior is not external. It lives and breathes in each one of us, for it is our very soul, our True Self.[3769] In this sense, we carry our own salvation within us: immortality, for *we "conquer death" by recognizing that life is eternal*.[3770]

Becoming one with the Christ Within is enlightenment or nirvana, satori or kensho, bodhi, wu wei, or moksha, a cosmic state of mind which Jesus called "the Kingdom of Heaven,"[3771] and which Christian mystics have long referred to as

Christ Consciousness or Cosmic Consciousness. Of this illuminated mental state Bucke provides the mystical key of understanding that is wholly missing from traditional Christianity:

> *The Saviour of man is Cosmic Consciousness*—in Paul's language—*the Christ. The cosmic sense (in whatever mind it appears) crushes the serpent's head—destroys sin, shame, the sense of good and evil as contrasted one with the other* . . .[3772]

For Christian mystics, this is the true Good News: our mortal birthday is our true spiritual death day, while our mortal death day is our true spiritual birthday;[3773] hence physical death has long been known as the "Second Birth,"[3774] and those who have transited into spirit ("died") are "twice-born."[3775] This is Truth, and this is precisely what all saviors, whether Pagan, Jewish, or Christian have always ultimately symbolized,[3776] dating back to the earliest representations of the fabled Green Man, a primitive death and renewal "son" archetype (born of the Sky-Father and the Earth-Mother), who is perpetually sacrificed and reborn.[3777]

In some ancient Christian texts Jesus' 12 Apostles are said to be indwelled with 12 powers called the "Twelve Saviors of the Treasure of Light." One example comes from the Gnostic-Christian document called Pistis Sophia ("Faith Wisdom"), in which Jesus addresses these 12 men with the following words:

> . . . I chose you from the beginning through the first mystery. Rejoice, therefore, and be glad, in that when I came into the world, from the beginning, I brought with me *twelve powers*, as I told you from the beginning. I took them from the hands of the *twelve saviours of the treasure of light*, according to the command of the first mystery. These powers, therefore, I cast into the wombs of your mothers, when I came into the world, and they are those which are in your bodies this day.
>
> For these powers have been given unto you before the whole world, for it is ye who are to save the whole world, and that ye may be able to bear the threat of the rulers of the world, and the calamities of the world, and their dangers, and all the persecutions which the rulers of the height must bring upon you. Many times have I said unto you, the power which is in you, I have brought it from the *twelve saviours which are in the treasure of light*. For which cause I said unto you from the beginning that ye were not of this world.
>
> And I also am not of this world, for all men who are of this world have taken their soul from the rulers of the aeons. But the power which is in you is from me. Ye are souls which

pertain to the height, which I have brought from the *twelve saviours of the treasure of light*, and which I have received as a share of my power, which I received from the beginning.[3778]

While traditional Christianity teaches that there was, is, and always will be only one Savior, mystical Christians recognize that the Savior-Christ motif itself is both archetypal and universal in nature, and that this is why there have been untold thousands of savior-christs who have periodically appeared, and who continue to appear, throughout history. In Eastern religions the archetypal messiah is know as a Bodhisattva:[3779] a self-realized man or woman who comes to earth for the sole purpose of relieving the suffering of Mankind, with the offer of redemption and eternal salvation.[3780] In the Bhagavad Gita the great Hindu Bodhisattva, Lord Krishna (Chrishna), speaking as the Eternal One, explains why this is so:

> As often as there is a decline of dharma (righteousness) and an exaltation of adharma (evil) in the world, I produce myself. Thus I am born, from age to age, for the preservation of the good, the destruction of the wicked, and the reestablishment of dharma.[3781]

Now each incarnation of the Savior mystically represents the same savior-symbol—including our Christian Bodhisattva, Jesus. He is an occult emblem, whatever name we give Him, of the Higher Self,[3782] the Universal Indwelling Christ,[3783] made perfect in the image of God.[3784] This is evident from the following partial list of some of the better known pre-Christian Pagan and Jewish saviors and christs.

In keeping with the universality of the savior theme, let us note that many of these figures were Sun-gods or sky-gods, born of a virgin at the Winter Solstice (Christmas), performed miracles, had 12 disciples, promised salvation to true believers, were attacked by critics, were crucified on a cross (or hung on a tree) at the Spring Equinox (Easter-Passover), and were reborn three days later (correlating with the ancient belief that the infant Sun-god was born on December 25, three days after the Winter Solstice on December 22):[3785]

Adad, the Assyrian Christ
Adonis, the Greek Christ
Apollo, the Greek Christ
Attis, the Phrygian Christ
Baal, the Phoenician Christ
Baili, the Orissan Christ
Balder, the Scandinavian Christ
Bali, the Afghan Christ

Beddru, the Japanese Christ
Belenus, the Celtic Christ
Buddha, the Indian Christ
Bunjil, the Australian Aboriginal Christ
Chrishna (Krishna or Krista), the Hindu Christ
Christ, the Gnostic Christ
Criti, the Chaldean Christ
Cyrus, the Jewish Christ
Dhouvanai, the Chaldean Christ
Dionysus, the Greek Christ
Eros, the Druidic Christ
Glooskap, the Abnkaian Christ
Hesus, the Druidic Christ
Horus, the Egyptian Christ
Hyacinth, the Spartan Christ
Indra, the Tibetan Christ
Iao, the Chaldean Christ
Ieoud, the Greek Christ
Iu, the Egyptian Christ
Iva, the Nepalese Christ
Jao, the Nepalese Christ
Jason, the Greek Christ
Jesus ben Pandira, the Jewish Christ
Joshua, the Jewish Christ
Karast, the Egyptian Christ
Kiountse, the Chinese Christ
Kukulcan, the Mayan Christ
Lleu Llaw Gyffes, the Welsh Christ
Lugh, the Irish Christ
Mahavira, the Jainist Christ
Marduk, the Babylonian Christ
Mikado, the Shintosian Christ
Mitra, the (East) Indian Christ
Mithra, the Persian Christ
Mithras, the Graceo-Roman Christ
Odin, the Germanic Christ
Orontes, the Egyptian Christ
Orpheus, the Greek Christ
Osiris, the Egyptian Christ
Prometheus, the Graceo-Roman Christ
Quetzalcoatl, the Aztec Christ
Rama, the Northern European Christ

Sakia, the Indian Christ
Sandan, the Cilician (Turkish) Christ
Saoshyant, the Zoroastrian Christ
Shemesh, the Hebrew Christ
Son of Man, the Essenic Christ
Son of Righteousness, the Gnostic-Jewish Christ
Sosiosch, the Persian Christ
Tammuz, the Babylonian Christ
Thor, the Scandinavian Christ
Thules, the Egyptian Christ
Witoba, the Telingoneseian Christ
Woden, the Scandinavian Christ
Zoroastra, the Persian Christ[3786]

I use the phrase "Savior-Christ motif" here, not to diminish my Christian religion in any way, but in a factual and historical sense, as there were, historically speaking, countless numbers of Christs in those Pagan religions that existed before the Christian Era. For those who have "eyes to see" and "ears to hear,"[3787] this can only aid us in better understanding and appreciating our Lord, the one and only true "Christ" of the "Church." For just as Jesus taught the Masters of the Far East, "we are our own saviors."[3788] See BUDDHA, CHRIST, CHRISTIANITY, CHURCH, JESUS, KRISHNA, MESSIAH, MITHRA, MYTH OF CHRIST, OSIRIS, PYTHAGORAS, TEACHER OF RIGHTEOUSNESS, THREE DAYS.

SCHEME OF SALVATION: The Scheme of Salvation was a massive and villainous rewriting and Paganization of the figure of the historical Jesus by the orthodox Church that began within a few decades after the Lord's death. In essence, it transformed Him from a great human prophet, teacher, and healer (the "Son of Man") into a supernatural deity (the "Son of God"). I consider the Scheme of Salvation to be the largest and most notorious coverup in Western history. See CHRISTIANITY, GOSPEL, GNOSTICISM, MYTH OF CHRIST, NATIVITY.

SECOND COMING OF CHRIST: In traditional Christianity the Second Coming of Christ is Jesus' return to earth to usher in the Kingdom of God,[3789] completing the "Age of the Holy Spirit."[3790] In the process Jesus will bestow sanctification,[3791] resurrect all dead believers,[3792] and transform the bodies of believers to accord with His own resurrected body.[3793] It is not known when this will take place, but mainstream Christians have been awaiting the return of Jesus for several millennia now—with disappointing results.

Early Christians, for example, believed that Jesus would return in their own lifetimes.[3794] Our Lord Himself promised that He would come back during the generation in which He lived[3795]—creating a problem for *conservative* Christian scholars, one they still have not satisfactory addressed. In any event, when this prophecy did not come to pass, it forced a bitter division between mainstream believers and mystical believers in the 2nd, 3rd, and 4th Centuries that led to the formation of the Catholic Church and the canonical New Testament. Accompanying this schism came the inevitable violent persecution and suppression of so-called "heterodox" Christians, primarily mystical Christians such as the Gnostics—the first and original Christians.[3796]

In mystical Christianity there are no such issues, for just as Jesus said his Kingdom is not physical,[3797] the Second Coming cannot be physical either. It is mental or psychological, that is, spiritual;[3798] and thus it is not connected to Jesus the man, but to Christ the spirit: the "First Coming of Christ" is our acceptance of the reality of the Christ (conversion to Christianity), while the "Second Coming of Christ" is the realization that the Christ indwells each one of us,[3799] making the Christ of Jesus our own personal Christ[3800] (a doctrine known as Theosis, "God in Man").[3801] Some mystics hold that to believe or say otherwise, as Bible literalists do, is to denigrate Holy Scripture and pronounce our Lord a liar. See CHRIST, CHRIST CONSCIOUSNESS, CHURCH, KINGDOM OF GOD, THEOSIS.

SERPENT: In the traditional Church the biblical serpent is a version of Satan.[3802] In the mystical Church it is a symbol of wisdom and of the Creative Principle; or, in psychological terms, the unfolding human consciousness that is seeking individuation.[3803] Mystically it is also the descent of spirit into matter; that is to say, it is the *Demon est Deus inversus* ("the Devil is God inverted").[3804] This doctrine was taught in ancient Rome, and is still found in Kabbalah (modern Hermeticism[3805] or Jewish Gnosticism),[3806] which states that "the name Satan is Yahweh reversed."[3807]

Evidence that the Serpent (Satan) is merely the other side of the Christ (God) comes from the Bible itself. In the book of Isaiah, for instance, Lucifer, whose name means "Bringer of Light" (that is, spiritual wisdom), is called the "morning star,"[3808] the same name that Jesus later applies to Himself. "I AM the bright and morning star," He declares in the book of Revelation[3809]—I AM being another arcane name for the Indwelling Christ that resides in every human being.[3810] Job calls Satan and God "the Sons of God," referring to them mystically as the two "morning stars" who sang together as one:

> When the morning stars sang together, and all the sons of God shouted for joy.[3811]

If more proof is needed that the Serpent and God are one, let us read the words of God himself as recorded in Isaiah:

> I form the light, and create darkness: I make peace, and create evil: I the Lord do all these things.[3812]

Paul too makes reference to the dualistic *Demon est Deus inversus* doctrine, saying that "Satan himself is transformed into an angel of light."[3813] The "light" referenced here is the inner light of the Christ, which the ancient Egyptians and the mystical Bible writers knew as the "true Light, which lighteth every man that cometh into the world."[3814] This is none other than the spiritual wisdom of the Great Mother-Goddess in her role as a snake deity. The Serpent-Goddess wore many guises and had a thousand names, among them: Ananta, Mat Kadru, Chinoi, Kadi, Buto, Anqet, and Ninhursag.[3815] Thus Paul's "angel of light" is the same as the "Bringer of Light," who offered to reveal the secrets of immortality and Theosis to Adam and Eve in the Garden of Eden[3816]—before the legend was distorted and rewritten by the patriarchal authors of Genesis.[3817] Thus, one of the first Christian branches, the Gnostic-Essenic Ophites, taught that the serpent who "tempted" Eve was merely bringing knowledge into the world.[3818]

The "Old Serpent" is an archetype, and thus it is found among nearly every people and in every region on earth. In ancient Egypt it was Kneph, a symbol of the creator. In the Orient it was Narayana, a symbol of the Creative Principle. Ancient Greeks portrayed it as the double-snaked Caduceus, spiraling up and down the staff of the god of healing, Aesculapius—the symbol of medicine to this day. Among the Mayans it was Naga, a symbol of the Life Force. Early Buddhists also called it Naga, revealing the universality of this profoundly esoteric emblem.[3819]

Scandinavians had their Serpent of Midgard, while the Hindus have their Kundalini serpent,[3820] a symbol of the spine and its seven chakras[3821] (the "Seven Churches of Asia" in Revelation).[3822] Moses worshiped the Serpent-God as Nehushtan,[3823] an Israelite copy of the Vedic "Supreme Ruler of Heaven," the serpent-king Nahusa, who was cast down to Hell by his rival.[3824] Our Christian mystic John the Apostle-Evangelist,[3825] some who say lived on into the Middle Ages in a wondrous kingdom in the East under the name "Prester John,"[3826] identifies Jesus with this same creature, revealing the true twofold character of the Divine Serpent:[3827]

> As Moses lifted up the serpent in the wilderness, even so must the Son of Man be lifted up.[3828]

The dual God-Satan, Jesus-Lucifer, Christ-Devil, Good-Evil, Light-Darkness nature of the serpent was wonderfully captured by the first Christians, the mystical Gnostics, in their symbol known as the Ouroboros, which shows a snake swallowing its own tail (itself a symbol of infinity or immortality). Half of it is black, half of it is white, just like the Chinese Yin-Yang symbol. Both represent the two-sided nature of life: birth and rebirth, the active and the passive, the positive and the negative, the constructive and the destructive, transformation and renovation, death and reincarnation. One Gnostic group, the Naassene sect, took its name from the word *nass*, "snake." They taught that the divine serpent "lives in all objects and in all beings." As the snake signifies the primordial Life Force, they were correct.[3829]

As the ultimate symbol of the two sides of the Creative Principle, the serpentine Yahweh-Lucifer, the "Bringer of Light" who sheds its skin and is thus "born again," gives enlightenment to humans through both pain and suffering and pleasure and joy. Christian Gnostics represented this aspect of the serpent as well, in the twin snakes called Agathodaemon and Kakodaemon.[3830]

Our Lord Jesus, educated in the Far East under the tutelage of the great spiritual masters of Tibet, India, Persia, Greece, Syria, Nepal, Cyprus, Ladakh, and Egypt,[3831] well understood the arcane meaning of the Serpent who bestowed wisdom (sophia) and knowledge (gnosis) on all faithful believers:

> Behold, I send you forth as sheep in the midst of wolves: be ye therefore *wise as serpents*, and harmless as doves.[3832]

The Serpent Wisdom-god, the God-Devil who creates good and evil and light and darkness,[3833] reveals its sacred dualism in the Sanskrit word *deva*, from which the positive words divine and divinity derive, as well as the negative words devil and demon derive.

Thus, however we choose to look at it, the Serpent remains the *Demon est Deus inversus*, a two-sided coin with Satan-Lucifer-Darkness-Evil on one side and God-Christ-Light-Goodness on the other. The former is involution or the *Aphanism* (Spirit fallen into Matter), the latter is evolution or the *Euresis* (Matter returning upward to Spirit).[3834] Jesus spoke of the *Demon est Deus inversus*, calling the evil side "the prince of this world," and the righteous side "the Indwelling Christ":

> Now is the judgment of this world: now shall the prince of this world be cast out. And I [the Indwelling Christ], if I be lifted up from the earth, will draw all men unto me.[3835]

Our Gnostic Gospeler John the Divine recorded the above passage, and so it is clear that he understood the true meaning of the *Demon est Deus inversus*, which he describes mystically as the "two angels in white" sitting in Jesus' empty tomb. According to the Evangelist, one sat where our Lord's feet had rested, the other where His head had lain.[3836] Since the feet are symbols of the earth plane (materiality), the former entity represents the angel of death (involution into matter); because the head is a symbol of the heavenly plane (spirituality), the latter entity represents the angel of life (evolution into spirit).

This double-angel is the same as the "serpent" in the Garden of Eden,[3837] the "old serpent" of Revelation,[3838] the "bright and morning star" of Revelation,[3839] Jesus' "prince of this world,"[3840] Isaiah's "Lucifer, son of the morning (star),"[3841] Job's "Son of God,"[3842] and Isaiah's Yahweh-Jehovah, who creates both "light and darkness."[3843]

As a Gnostic oriented Christian, John the Evangelist,[3844] whose Gospel brims over with occult mysticism[3845] and symbolism,[3846] was thus later assigned a cup with a snake in it as one of his symbols,[3847] the "cup" being a chalice,[3848] a symbol of the "Holy Grail"—the vessel from which our Lord (a symbol of the light side of the Serpent) drank at the Last Supper. The Grail itself is thus a symbol of the "wine" of enlightenment,[3849] that is, of spiritual wisdom ("light").

Most of the world's Sun/Son-gods, saviors, christs, and messiahs are shown wrestling with the dark side of the Serpent (the human Ego) at some point in their ministries, as they battled worldly temptations. Among these are Krishna, Apollo, Buddha, and of course Jesus. See ADAM, ADVERSARY, ANTICHRIST, BEAST, DEVIL, EDEN, EGO, EGYPT, EVE, EVIL, FALL OF MAN, GARDEN OF EDEN, GODS AND GODDESSES, HELL, HEROD ANTIPAS, KARMA, LOWER SELF, LUCIFER, MASS MIND, MOSES, MOUTH OF GOD, NUMBER OF THE BEAST, ORIGINAL SIN, OUTWARD MAN, PHARISEES, PILATE, SATAN, SIN, TREE OF LIFE.

SEVEN STARS: In traditional Christianity the "seven stars" of the book of Revelation[3850] are symbols of the seven Churches of Asia.[3851] In mystical Christianity both the seven stars and the seven churches are symbols of the seven chakras,[3852] the nerve ganglia[3853] or "energy centers" located along the human spine,[3854] referred to in Eastern literature as the "seven lotuses of light."[3855]

In mystical Christianity the seven "flowers" or chakras (literally "wheels"), from lowest to highest, are:

1) Root Chakra, tailbone area (four-petaled lotus).
2) Sacral Chakra, lower abdomen (six-petaled lotus).
3) Solar Plexus Chakra, upper abdomen (ten-petaled lotus).
4) Heart Chakra, center of chest (12-petaled lotus).
5) Throat Chakra, throat area (16-petaled lotus).
6) Third Eye Chakra, forehead (22-petaled lotus).
7) Crown Chakra, top of head (thousand-petaled lotus), which is often symbolized by the royal crown, or the "crown of glory" as Peter called it,[3856] or the "incorruptible crown," as Paul referred to it.[3857]

The seven chakras are aligned along the human spine—in the Bible occultly symbolized as, for example, Aaron's "rod,"[3858] Moses' "staff"[3859] (originally the Rod of Bacchus),[3860] and the "Tree of Life"[3861]—which contains 33 segments.[3862] Numerologically, 33 is 6 (3 + 3 = 6), which Pythagoras called the "perfect number,"[3863] or "The Mother,"[3864] and which was incorporated into the six-pointed Pagan hexagram, more recently known in Judaism as "Solomon's Seal"[3865] or the "Star of David."[3866]

Also sometimes written in triplicate form as 666, the number 6 is the occult number of humanity. What is a human being? It is a combination of a body, a soul, and a spirit;[3867] in other words, Man and Woman are themselves symbols of spiritual involution and spiritual evolution. Thus the number 33 entered mysticism, religion, and mythology as a sacred number. For example, Solomon's first temple stood for 33 years; King David ruled for 33 years in Jerusalem; Jesus died in His 33rd year; the word God appears 33 times in the first chapter of Genesis; the Masonic Order is divided into 33 "degrees"; etc.[3868]

The seven chakras overlay the 33 segments of the human spine (the "Tree of Life"), up which must climb the Kundalini "Serpent" (human consciousness), in order to reach the "crown" of the tree (the skull, "Golgatha"), the Crown Chakra or "Temple of Wisdom," resulting in enlightenment, nirvana, satori, or Christ Consciousness, symbolized by the Sun.

The seven chakras are in turn related to our seven bodies, which from the densest to the lightest, are:

1) The Physical Body.
2) The Ethereal Body.
3) The Astral Body.
4) The Mental Body.
5) The Casual Body.
6) The Spiritual Body.
7) The Divine Body.

Mystically speaking there are also seven degrees or levels of Heaven[3869] and Hell[3870] (as Paul noted),[3871] the four seven-day phases of the Moon each month,[3872] the Seven Wonders of the World,[3873] the seven deadly sins,[3874] the seven virtues,[3875] the seven days of Creation,[3876] as mentioned, the "seven churches" in the book of Revelation,[3877] and so on.[3878]

These accord with the seven planets of the ancient world, for at that time the furthermost outer planets had not been discovered yet, while the Sun and the Moon were considered planets. Thus, the seven known "planets" then were: the Sun, the Moon, Mercury, Mars, Jupiter, Venus, and Saturn.[3879] These names, in turn, came to be appended to our seven weekdays (in the same order, Sunday through Saturday):

1) Sunday was named after the Pagan Sun-god (Sol/Helios): the Sun's day.
2) Monday was named after the Pagan Moon-goddess (Luna/Selene): the Moon's Day.
3) Tuesday was named after the Pagan god Tiw (Mercury/Hermes): Tiw's Day.
4) Wednesday was named after the Pagan god Woden (Mars/Aries): Woden's Day.

5) Thursday was named after the Pagan god Thor (Jupiter/Zeus): Thor's Day.
6) Friday was named after the Pagan goddess Fri, Frey, or Frigg (Venus/Aphrodite): Fri's Day.
7) Saturday was named after the Pagan god Saturn (Kronos): Saturn's Day.

Most significantly, according to Christian numerology, seven is the mystical number of physical manifestation through thought, which is the Law of Attraction, one of Jesus' secret Gospel of the Kingdom teachings.[3880] Why is this so? The number three symbolizes Spirit and the Divine Masculine (Yang, Sun), while the number four symbolizes Matter and the Divine Feminine (Yin, Moon). Added together, three and four equal seven, the number of the Hieros Gamos.[3881] This is the "Holy Marriage" between the spirit (positive polarity, the Higher Self, Heaven, superconscious mind),[3882] and the body (negative polarity, the Lower Self, Earth, subconscious mind), which creates human life. This occult doctrine Plutarch called "the basis of all the Mysteries."[3883]

It is my theory that the sacrality of the number seven began with the realization that the head contains seven holes (two eyes, two nostrils, two ears, and the mouth). The head, of course, is the site of the Crown Chakra, the occult location of Christ Consciousness,[3884] spiritual enlightenment, or atonement (at-one-ment) with God. See APOSTLES, ASTROLOGY, CHRIST, JESUS, NUMBER OF THE BEAST, NUMBERS, SUN, TWELVE, ZODIAC.

SILENT YEARS (THE): Because it is not mentioned in the Bible, in the traditional Church the 18 year period of Jesus' life, between the ages of 12 and 30, is glossed over without thought. In the mystical Church, however, this period, known as our Lord's "Silent Years," is all important, for it was during this time that He received His education in the spiritual mysteries,[3885] later which became known as His "Gospel of the Kingdom of God."[3886]

We must remember that Jesus was a Jew born in the East (the "Orient"), and was thus an Oriental Christ, making both the Bible and Christianity themselves Eastern or Oriental in origin and character.[3887] It is not surprising then to discover that there is an ancient and well documented tradition that during His "Silent Years," our Lord not only studied (and perhaps lived) in the great Essene Community at Qumran near the Dead Sea,[3888] but that He also journeyed throughout the Mideast, primarily India, Tibet, Nepal, Persia, Ladakh, and Arabia,[3889] learning and teaching under the tutelage of various spiritual masters,[3890] including the Pythagoreans, the Essenes, and the Gnostics.[3891] As an Oriental familiar with His region of the world, He no doubt used the popular trade route that connected the Mediterranean with India and China.[3892]

There is ample and even ironclad evidence to back up this view: a Buddhist monastery on the island of Sri Lanka (earlier known as Ceylon) possesses documents recording Jesus' visit 2,000 years ago; early Christian texts have been found among ancient Tibetan chronicles;[3893] and in India a 1st-Century coin was discovered bearing the image of Jesus.[3894] In Tibet, in particular, we find authenticated records of a man known as "Saint Issa from Israel," who, from the ages of 14 to 28, studied and taught among the saints and monks of not only Tibet, but also of India and Nepal, then returned to his homeland, where he was persecuted, arrested, and murdered.[3895]

While traveling in India in 1887, a Russian tourist named Nicholas Notovich began hearing about the legend of Issa, and soon discovered that there were ancient manuscripts at the Himis Monastery near Leh (the capital city of Ladakh, Tibet) to support it. Journeying there he pleaded for permission to review the invaluable papers. After a lengthy negotiation permission was granted and he studiously copied out the entire work by hand with the help of the head lama.[3896] Back in Europe he found that no publisher would touch his manuscript. Thus in 1894 he published it himself under the title, *The Unknown Life of Jesus Christ*.[3897]

Subsequently, a number of recognized scholars, such as Swami Abhedananda and Nicholas Roerich, traveled to the monastery to check on Notovish's claims. Each came away convinced of the authenticity of both the legend of Jesus in the Mideast and the monastery's manuscripts. Roerich published his own book citing a number of the Tibetan verses regarding Issa, which he published in 1929 under the title, *Journey in Kashmir and Tibet*. The Russian archaeologist and explorer was stunned to find that though most of the native people of Ladakh, India, and Central Asia had never heard of Notivich or his book, they were very familiar with the stories of "Saint Issa," whose memory they treated with deep reverence. This was, they declared solemnly, none other than the "Jewish Christ" as a young man, who spent the Bible's unaccounted 18 years in the East, a journey first undertaken (accompanying a caravan to India) to avoid a prearranged Israelite marriage that He was to undergo at the age of 13.[3898]

Notovitch's book records the following description of Saint Issa by a lama he met at a monastery near Wakkha, Tibet:

> Issa is a great prophet, one of the first after the twenty-two Buddhas; he is greater than any of the Dalai-Lamas, for he constitutes a part of the spirituality of the Lord. It is he who has instructed you, who has brought back frivolous souls to God, who has rendered you worthy of the blessings of the Creator, who has endowed each creature with the knowledge of good and evil. His name and his deeds have been recorded in our sacred writings, and, whilst reading of his great existence spent in the midst of erring people, we weep over the horrible sin of the pagans [Romans], who assassinated him after putting him to the most cruel tortures.[3899]

What follows is an excerpt from Notovitch's own translation of one of the books containing the Tibetan story of Issa (Jesus) in the Middle East. It begins with Moses in Egypt. We will start off, however, from the point of most interest to us, Jesus' thirteenth birthday:

> When Issa had attained the age of thirteen, when an Israelite should take a wife, the house in which his parents dwelt and earned their livelihood in modest labor, became a meeting place for the rich and noble, who desired to gain for a son-in-law the young Issa, already celebrated for his edifying discourses in the name of the Almighty. It was then that Issa clandestinely left his father's house, went out of Jerusalem, and, in company with some merchants, traveled toward Sindh that he might perfect himself in the divine word and study the laws of the great Buddhas.
>
> In the course of his fourteenth year, young Issa, blessed by God, journeyed beyond the Sindh and settled among the Aryas in the beloved country of God. The fame of his name spread along the Northern Sindh. When he passed through the country of the five rivers and the Radjipoutan, the worshipers of the god Djaine begged him to remain in their midst. But he left the misguided admirers of Djaine and visited Juggernaut, in the province of Orsis, where the remains of Viassa-Kriehna rest, and where he received a joyous welcome from the white priests of Brahma. They taught him to read and understand the Vedas, to heal by prayer, to teach and explain the Holy Scripture, to cast out evil spirits from the body of man and give him back human semblance. He spent six years in Juggernaut, Rajegriha, Benares, and the other holy cities; all loved him, for Issa lived in peace with the Vaisyas and the Soudras, to whom he taught the Holy Scripture.
>
> But the Brahmans and the Kshatriyas declared that the Great Para-Brahma forbade them to approach those whom he had created from his entrails and from his feet: That the Vaisyas were authorized to listen only to the reading of the Vedas, and that never save on feast days. That the Soudras were not only forbidden to attend the reading of the Vedas, but to gaze upon them even; for their condition was to perpetually serve and act as slaves to the Brahmans, the Kshatriyas, and even to the Vaisyas. "Death alone can free them from servitude," said Para-Brahma. "Leave them, therefore, and worship with us the gods who will show their anger against you if you disobey

them."

But Issa would not heed them; and going to the Soudras, preached against the Brahmans and the Kshatriyas. He strongly denounced the men who robbed their fellow-beings of their rights as men, saying: "God the Father establishes no difference between his children, who are all equally dear to him." Issa denied the divine origin of the Vedas and the Pouranas, declaring to his followers that one law had been given to men to guide them in their actions. "Fear thy God, bow down the knee before Him only, and to Him only must thy offerings be made."

Issa denied the Trimourti [Trimurti, the Hindu Holy Trinity] and the incarnation of Para-Brahma in Vishnou, Siva, and other gods, saying: "The Eternal Judge, the Eternal Spirit, composes the one and indivisible soul of the universe, which alone creates, contains, and animates the whole. He alone has willed and created, he alone has existed from eternity and will exist without end; he has no equal neither in the heavens nor on this earth. The Great Creator shares his power with no one, still less with inanimate objects as you have been taught, for he alone possesses supreme power. He willed it, and the world appeared; by one divine thought, he united the waters and separated them from the dry portion of the globe. He is the cause of the mysterious life of man, in whom he has breathed a part of his being. And he has subordinated to man, the land, the waters, the animals, and all that he has created, and which he maintains in immutable order by fixing the duration of each. The wrath of God shall soon be let loose on man, for he has forgotten his Creator and filled his temples with abominations, and he adores a host of creatures which God has subordinated to him.

"For, to be pleasing to stones and metals, he sacrifices human beings in whom dwells a part of the spirit of the Most High. For he humiliates them that labor by the sweat of their brow to gain the favor of an idler who is seated at a sumptuously spread table. They that deprive their brothers of divine happiness shall themselves be deprived of it, and the Brahmans and the Kshatriyas shall become the Soudras of the Soudras with whom the Eternal shall dwell eternally. For on the clay of the Last Judgment, the Soudras and the Vaisyas shall be forgiven because of their ignorance, while God shall visit his wrath on them that have arrogated his rights."

The Vaisyas and the Soudras were struck with admiration, and demanded of Issa how they should pray to secure in their happiness. "Do not worship idols, for they do not hear you; do not listen to the Vedas, where the truth is perverted; do not believe yourself first in all things, and do not humiliate your neighbor. Help the poor, assist the weak, harm no one, do not covet what you have not and what you see in the possession of others."

The white priests and the warriors becoming cognizant of the discourse addressed by Issa to the Soudras, resolved upon his death and sent their servants for this purpose in search of the young prophet. But Issa, warned of this danger by the Soudras, fled in the night from Juggernaut, gained the mountains, and took refuge in the Gothamide Country, the birth-place of the great Buddha Cakya-Mouni, among the people who adored the only and sublime Brahma. Having perfectly learned the Pali tongue, the just Issa applied himself to the study of the sacred rolls of Soutras.

Six years later, Issa, whom the Buddha had chosen to spread his holy word, could perfectly explain the sacred rolls. He then left Nepal and the Himalaya Mountains, descended into the valley of Rajipoutan and went westward, preaching to divers people of the supreme perfection of man, and of the good we must do unto others, which is the surest means of quickly merging ourselves in the Eternal Spirit. "He who shall have recovered his primitive purity at death," said Issa, "shall have obtained the forgiveness of his sins, and shall have the right to contemplate the majestic figure of God."

In traversing the pagan territories, the divine Issa taught the people that the adoration of visible gods was contrary to the laws of nature. "For man," said he, "has not been favored with the sight of the image of God nor the ability to construct a host of divinities resembling the Eternal. Furthermore, it is incompatible with the human conscience to think less of the grandeur of divine purity than of animals; or of works made by the hand of man from stone or metal. The Eternal Legislator is one; there is no God but him; he has shared the world with no one, neither has he confided his intentions to anyone. Just as a father may deal toward his children, so shall God judge men after death according to his merciful laws; never will he humiliate his child by causing his soul to emigrate, as in a purgatory, into the body of an animal."

"The heavenly law," said the Creator through the lips of Issa, "is averse to the sacrifice of human victims to a statue or animal; for I have sacrificed to man all the animals and every thing the world contains. Everything has been sacrificed to man, who is directly and closely linked to Me, his Father; therefore, he that shall have robbed Me of My child shall be severely judged and punished according to the divine law.

"Man is as nothing before the Eternal Judge, to the same degree that the animal is before man. Therefore, I say to you, abandon your idols and perform no ceremonies that separate you from your Father and bind you to priests from whom the face of heaven is turned away. For it is they who have allured you from the true God, and whose superstitions and cruelty are leading you to perversion of the intellect and the loss of all moral sense."

The words of Issa spread among the pagans, in the countries through which he traveled, and the inhabitants abandoned their idols. Seeing which, the priests demanded from him who glorified the name of the true God, proofs of the accusations he brought against them and demonstration of the worthlessness of idols in the presence of the people. And Issa replied to them: "If your idols and your animals are mighty, and really possess a supernatural power, let them annihilate me on the spot!"

"Perform a miracle," retorted the priests, and let thy God confound our own, if they are loathsome to him."

But Issa then said: "The miracles of our God began when the universe was created; they occur each day, each instant; whosoever does not see them is deprived of one of the most beautiful gifts of life. And it is not against pieces of inanimate stone, metal, or wood, that the wrath of God shall find free vent, but it shall fall upon man, who, in order to be saved, should destroy all the idols they have raised. Just as a stone and a grain of sand, worthless in themselves to man, await with resignation the moment when he shall take and make them into something useful. So should man await the great favor to be granted him by God in honoring him with a decision.

"But woe be to you, adversary of man, if it be not a favor that you await, but rather the wrath of Divinity; woe be to you if you await until it attests its power through miracles! For it is not the idols that shall be annihilated in His wrath, but those that have raised them; their hearts shall be the prey of everlasting fire, and their lacerated bodies shall serve as food for wild beasts. God shall drive away the contaminated ones of his flocks, but shall take back to himself those that have strayed because they misconceived the heavenly atom which dwelt in them."

Seeing the powerlessness of their priests, the pagans believed the words of Issa, and fearing the wrath of the Divinity, broke their idols into fragments; as to the priests, they fled to escape the vengeance of the people. And Issa also taught the pagans not to strive to see the Eternal Spirit with their own eyes, but to endeavor to feel it in their hearts, and, by a truly pure soul, to make themselves worthy of its favors. "Not only must you desist from offering human sacrifices," said he, "but you must immolate no animal to which life has been given, for all things have been created for the benefit of man. Do not take what belongs to others, for it would be robbing your neighbor of the goods he has acquired by the sweat of his brow. Deceive no one, that you may not yourself be deceived; strive to justify yourself before the last judgment, for it will then be too late. Do not give yourself up to debauchery, for it is a violation of the laws of God. You shall attain supreme beatitude, not only by purifying yourself, but also by leading others into the path that shall permit them to regain primitive perfection."

The fame of Issa's sermons spread to the neighboring countries, and, when he reached Persia, the priests were terrified and forbade the inhabitants to listen to him. But when they saw that all the villages welcomed him with joy, and eagerly listened to his preaching, they caused his arrest and brought him before the high-priest, where he was submitted to the following interrogatory: "Who is this new God of whom thou speaketh? Dost thou not know, unhappy man that thou art, that Saint Zoroaster is the only just one admitted to the honor of receiving communications from the Supreme Being, who has commanded the angels to draw up in writing the word of God, laws that were given to Zoroaster in paradise? Who then art thou that darest to blaspheme our God and sow doubt in the hearts of believers?"

And Issa replied: "It is not of a new god that I speak, but of our heavenly Father, who existed before the beginning and will still be after the eternal end. It was of him I spoke to the people, who, even as an innocent child, can not yet understand God by the mere strength of their intelligence and penetrate his spiritual and divine sublimity. But, as a new-born child recognizes the maternal breast even in obscurity, so your people, induced in error by your erroneous doctrines and religious ceremonies, have instinctively recognized their Father in the Father of whom I am the prophet. The Eternal Being says to your people through the intermediary of my mouth:

> 'You shall not adore the sun, for it is only a part of the world I have created for man. The sun rises that it may warm you during your labor; it sets that it may give you the hours of rest I have myself fixed. It is to Me, and to Me only, that you owe all you possess, all that is around you, whether above or beneath you.'

"But," interjected the priests, "how could a nation live according to the laws of justice, if it possessed no preceptors?"

Then Issa replied: "As long as the people had no priests, they were governed by the law of nature and retained their candor of soul. Their souls were in God, and to communicate with the Father, they had recourse to the intermediary of no idol or animal, nor to fire, as you practice here. You claim that we must worship the sun, the genius of Good and that of Evil; well, your doctrine is an abomination, I say to you, the sun acts not spontaneously, but by the will of the Invisible Creator who has given it existence, and who has willed that this orb should light the day and warm the labor and the crops of man.

"The Eternal Spirit is the soul of all that is animated; you commit a grievous sin in dividing it into the spirit of Evil and the spirit of Good, for there is no God save that of good, who, like the father of a family, does good only to his children, forgiving all their faults if they repent of them. And the spirit of Evil dwells on this earth, in the heart of men who turn the children of God from the right path, therefore I say to you, beware of the day of judgment, for God will inflict a terrible punishment on all who have turned his children from the right path and filled them with superstitions and prejudices, on them that have blinded the seeing, transmitted contagion to the sound of health, and taught the adoration of things which God has subjected to man for his own good and to aid him in his labor.

Your doctrine is therefore the fruit of your errors, for, in desiring to approach the God of Truth, you have created false gods."

After listening to him, the wise men resolved to do him no harm. In the night, while the city was wrapped in slumber, they conducted him outside the walls and left him on the highway, hoping that he might soon become the prey of wild beasts. But, being protected by the Lord our God, Saint Issa continued his way unmolested.

Issa, whom the Creator had chosen to recall the true God to the people that were plunged in depravities, was twenty-nine years of age when he arrived in the land of Israel.[3900]

Here the story continues from Issa's (Jesus') return to his native land and on to his execution on the cross at Cavalry, which all Christians are familiar with from the canonical Gospels.

The original Eastern documents were written in Pali script only a few years after Jesus' death, undergoing various translations into different languages over the following centuries. Notovitch's own version was originally in French, after which it was translated into English.[3901] We must add to this striking evidence one of the many names for the Essenes (one of the pre-Christian sects from which Christianity was formed), who sometimes called themselves "The Men of Essa."[3902]

According to ancient sacred lore, Jesus also ventured through Egypt, Iran, Greece, and even Britain, for the same educational purposes.[3903] The Bible seems to support such claims. Some of Jesus' own biblical words, for example, suggest that at one time He traveled and sermonized around the globe:

> And this gospel of the kingdom shall be *preached in all the world for a witness unto all nations*; and then shall the end come.[3904]

> And the gospel must first be published *among all nations*.[3905]

> [Quoting Himself:] And that repentance and remission of sins should be preached in his name *among all nations*, beginning at Jerusalem.[3906]

> As long as I am in *the world*, I am the light of *the world*.[3907]

Paul hints at the same thing:

> And without controversy great is the mystery of godliness: God

was manifest in the flesh, justified in the Spirit, seen of angels, *preached unto the Gentiles, believed on in the world*, received up into glory.[3908]

Lastly, we must consider the fact that many of Jesus' teachings and doctrines, if not His exact wording in numerous instances, come from Eastern Pagan texts, an intriguing example being the Hindu's Khandogya-Upanishad. One of its passages concerns mystical doctrines, which cannot be directly transmitted to the rational literalistic mind, but which must instead come from the God Within (intuition),[3909] which Jesus called the "Heavenly Father."[3910] This is a type of occult (inner) instruction, the Upanishad states,

> by which we hear what cannot be heard, by which we perceive what cannot be perceived, by which we know what cannot be known.[3911]

Centuries later Jesus made this comment to His initiates (the Apostles) when they asked Him why He taught His ordinary followers using mystical concepts (for example, parables) instead of openly and concretely. He answered:

> That seeing they may see and not perceive; and hearing they may hear and not understand.[3912]

Another one of Jesus' favorite sacred Eastern texts was the Bhagavad Gita (the "Song of the Lord"), which contains a conversation between the Hindu Christ Chrishna or Krishna and his devotee Arjuna. In studying the Gita over the years I have discovered a striking number of comparisons between the words and doctrines of Chrishna and Jesus, a partial list which follows. For instance:

Chrishna: "Those who worship me devoutly dwell in me and I in them."[3913]
Christ: "I am in my Father, and ye in me, and I in you."[3914]

Chrishna: "Rest assured that they who worship me never perish."[3915]
Christ: "Verily, verily I say unto you, he that believeth on me hath everlasting life."[3916]

Chrishna: "By knowing . . . thou wilt be delivered from misfortune."[3917]
Christ: "And ye shall know the truth, and the truth shall make you free."[3918]

Chrishna: "The Yogi of a subdued mind, thus employed in the exercise of his devotion, is compared to a lamp, standing in a place without wind, which flickereth not."[3919]

Christ: "Let your light so shine before men, that they may see your good works, and glorify your Father which is in heaven."[3920]

Chrishna: "I AM the producer and the destroyer of the whole universe. . . . I AM the beginning, the middle, and also the end of all beings."[3921]
Christ: "I AM Alpha and Om-ega, the beginning and the end, the first and last."[3922]

Chrishna: "I AM [the] taste in the [living] waters."[3923]
Christ: "He that believeth on me [that is, the universal I AM] . . . out of his belly shall flow rivers of living water."[3924]

Chrishna: "I AM distinct from [material delusions] and eternal."[3925]
Christ: "I AM with you alway, even unto the end of the world."[3926]

Chrishna: Speaking of the Third Eye in the middle of the forehead: "The man who shall in his last hour meditate on the ancient sage, the Ruler, smaller than an atom, the Preserver of all, unimaginable in form, shining like the sun above the darkness, with unwavering heart, and by the force of Yoga draweth his breath together between his eyebrows, that man goeth to this Supreme Divine Being."[3927]
Christ: "The light of the body is the [Third] eye: if therefore thine eye be single [spiritual], thy whole body shall be full of light [enlightenment]. But if thine eye be evil [double, physical], thy whole body shall be full of darkness [spiritual ignorance]. If therefore the light that is in thee be darkness, how great is that darkness!"[3928]

Chrishna: Concerning "that most mysterious secret": "It is a royal knowledge, a royal mystery, sublime and immaculate; clear unto the sight, virtuous, eternal and easy to be performed."[3929]
Christ: "Come unto me, all ye that labour and are heavy laden, and I will give you rest. Take my yoke upon you, and learn of me; for I am meek and lowly in heart: and ye shall find rest unto your souls. For my yoke is easy, and my burden is light."[3930]

Chrishna: "I AM the way, the sustainer, the Lord, the witness, dwelling, refuge and friend, the origin and destroyer (of life), the place, the receptacle, and the inexhaustible seed. I cause heat; I withhold and send forth the rain; I AM immortality and death ; I AM *sat* (that which is) and *asat* (that which is not)."[3931]
Christ: "I AM the way, the truth, and the life: no man cometh unto the Father, but by me."[3932]

Chrishna: "I accept and enjoy the holy offerings of the humble soul, who in his worship presenteth leaves and flowers, and fruit and water unto me."[3933]

Christ: After watching the rich give thousands of dollars to the treasury while a poor widow donates her last penny: "Verily I say unto you, that this poor widow hath cast more in, than all they which have cast into the treasury: For all they did cast in of their abundance; but she of her want did cast in all that she had, even all her living."[3934]

Chrishna: "Among the trees I AM aswattha [the Tree of life]."[3935]

Christ: "To him that overcometh will I give to eat of the Tree of Life."[3936]

Chrishna: "Of secret things I AM silence, and knowledge of those who know [Gnosis]."[3937]

Christ: "Unto you is given to know [Gnosis] the mystery of the Kingdom of God."[3938]

Chrishna: "Freedom from attachment, indifference toward son, wife, home and the rest... this is called knowledge [Gnosis]."[3939]

Christ: "If any man come to me, and hate not his father, and mother, and wife, and children, and brethren, and sisters, yea, and his own life also, he cannot be my disciple."[3940]

Chrishna: "[God is] without and within all beings; motionless and yet moving; undiscernible through its subtlety; afar and yet near."[3941]

Christ: "God is Spirit: and they that worship him must worship him in Spirit."[3942]

Chrishna: "For he who seeth the Lord abiding everywhere alike doth not destroy himself by himself, and thus goeth to the supreme Self."[3943]

Christ: "Is it not written in your law, I said 'Ye are gods'?"[3944]

    That Jesus relied heavily on the doctrines of the Bhagavad Gita is certainly not surprising. The ethical and moral principles found in the Gita are universal, and were thus not only adopted by both our Lord and most of the New Testament writers, but by scores of other great spiritual teachers throughout history.[3945]

    In light of the facts regarding Jesus' Silent Years, the questions traditional Christians must ask themselves are:

- Why did Matthew, Mark, and John stop writing about our Lord immediately after His birth?
- Why did Luke ignore Jesus' life after He turned 12? (Note: the Gospel of Luke originally began with Chapter Three; thus, even the story about the 12 year old Jesus at the Temple—in Chapter Two—is now recognized as a

late interpolated fiction,[3946] one which Luke "borrowed" from the autobiography of the Romanized Jewish historian Josephus).[3947]
- Why does the Bible as a whole skip over Jesus' all-important 18 formative years between 12 and 30?

The Evangelists claim to be either eyewitnesses or to have gotten their information from those who were.[3948] If so, all four would certainly have known minute details about the events leading up to Jesus' birth, as well as the birth itself. How then could they not have known anything about the Master's life during the period which lay closer to their own, namely the years A.D. 12 to 30? Are we really expected to believe that nothing of interest occurred during this time, a period covering nearly a generation in the life of a man we Christians view as the most fascinating individual and most spiritually evolved soul to have ever walked the earth?

As the evidence in this entry makes abundantly clear, the answer to these questions is elementary: the 18 Silent Years, which Catholic theologians disingenuously refer to as the "hidden life" of Jesus,[3949] represent a purposeful omission, an intentional suppression, for His teachings must be made to look original to him so that orthodox Christianity retains its "uniqueness," the New Testament its "infallibility," the Old Testament its "inerrantness."

That our Lord spent these 18 Lost or Missing Years, as they are also called, traveling, studying, and teaching in places like Egypt, Greece, Tibet, Persia, Arabia, Nepal, and India under countless Pagan and Jewish spiritual masters, is not an issue for mystical Christians, however. Jesus' Pythagorean, Essenic, Gnostic, Egyptian, Hellenistic, Hinduistic, and Buddhistic doctrines had to derive from somewhere, and the many traditions, records, and proofs of His journeys throughout the ancient world offer the only rational and understandable explanation. And the complete cleansing of these facts from the Bible by orthodox hands only helps reinforce their truthfulness!

Due to the massive evidence from within Jesus' teachings themselves, even many mainstream Christian literalists have now accepted the very real possibility that Jesus was "exposed" to religions like Zoroastrianism, Hinduism, and Buddhism.[3950] Our most mystical Evangelist John ends his Gospel with these cryptic words:

> And there are also many other things which Jesus did, the which, if they should be written every one, I suppose that even the world itself could not contain the books that should be written. Amen.[3951]

Thus, according to one of Christianity's most respected Gospel authorities, not only were there "many other things which Jesus did" that were *not* recorded in the

Bible, they were *purposefully* omitted. Among these were most assuredly our Lord's 18 Silent Years. See CHRIST, CHRISTIANITY, GNOSTICISM, GOSPEL, JESUS.

SIN: From the Old English archer's word, *synne*, meaning "to miss the mark,"[3952] that is, "miss the bull's-eye." Identical to the New Testament Greek word *anomia*: "to miss the point."[3953] In other words, originally a sin was a "mistake," an "error against the Spirit,"[3954] a feeling or act that is out of harmony with God,[3955] an unspiritual thought, word, or deed, which, as Jesus taught, could be canceled by simply asking God for forgiveness;[3956] that is, by renewing one's faith in God.[3957]

Jesus indeed spent little time discussing the cause and nature of sin,[3958] but focused almost exclusively on the forgiveness of sin, most poignantly illustrated in the wonderful parable of the Prodigal Son[3959] and the story of the "sinful" Samaritan woman at Jacob's Well.[3960]

Unfortunately, the true meaning of the word sin was recast by the early Catholic Church, in part, into the regrettable manmade concept of "original sin,"[3961] which appears nowhere in the Bible, and which was, in fact, repudiated by Paul.[3962] Since there was no original sin, and since we were made in the image of the perfect God,[3963] our Higher Self, the Indwelling Christ,[3964] is sinless.[3965] Luke certainly understood this, which is why he said: "*All* flesh shall see the salvation of God."[3966]

Thus the Bible itself renders the doctrine of "divine punishment for sin" both illogical and self-defeating.[3967] "Be ye therefore perfect, even as your Father which is in heaven is perfect," saith the Master.[3968] See BAPTISM, FORGIVENESS, KARMA, ORIGINAL SIN, REDEMPTION, SACRAMENT, SALVATION.

SOLOMON: In the traditional Church Solomon is the son of David and Bathsheba, a worshiper of Pagan deities, and one of the most famous of all the Israelite kings.[3969] In the mystical Church Solomon is a mythical figure who symbolizes the Sun:[3970] his name, Sol-Om-On, means "Sun-God of On,"[3971] thus he is often symbolized as a lion (the Sun-sign Leo),[3972] making him a Jewish version of the Egyptian Sun-God Ra of Heliopolis.[3973]

Solomon's sacred number is the same as the Sun or Sol: 666, known as *Sorath*.[3974] His triadic three-part name mystically equates to "Light, Glory, Truth."[3975] Solomon the Sun/Son is thus another esoteric emblem of the Indwelling Christ, represented in thousands of religions throughout history as the "Sun of God" or "Son of God." See CHRIST, CROWN, MYTH OF CHRIST, NUMBER OF THE BEAST, SON OF GOD, SUN, SUN OF RIGHTEOUSNESS.

SON OF GOD: In traditional Christianity Jesus was the Son of God from birth.[3976] In mystical Christianity, however, He adopted this title only *after* His baptism in the Holy Spirit.[3977] Now enlightened, He became the true Son of God, the Father's "Only Begotten Son."[3978]

As thoroughly discussed in the next entry under "Son of Man," the truth is that the historical Jesus never thought of Himself as the "Son of God,"[3979] nor did He ever refer to Himself by this title.[3980] Even though the term appears in the writings of the mystical pre-New Testament Essenes,[3981] mainstream Judaism considered it to be a thoroughly un-Jewish Pagan concept (one of the main reasons Jews today continue to reject the idea of Jesus' Messiahship).[3982] This phrase then was appended to His biblical biography by the orthodox Church (Ecclesia) long after His death. But since we are all Sons of God, this fact is not spiritually important (though it is theologically important). Indeed, the Bible tells us that whoever "receives Jesus," whoever is "led by the spirit of God," becomes and is to be called a "Son of God," just as Jesus was,[3983] for we are all born with the "Son in me," as Paul put it.[3984] Thus, Jesus told Mary that His Father was her Father, and that His God was her God.[3985]

Esoterically, the Son of God is yet another of many names for our Higher Self, the Indwelling Christ,[3986] the perfect, that is, "only begotten," soul of each individual.[3987] The outer meaning of the Son of God is "Child of God"; the inner meaning is "One with God."

While the spelling "Son" is used in institutional Christianity, in the Mystery Religions, including the occult branches of Paganism, Christianity, and Judaism, it is spelled "Sun." Hence, in the book of Malachi, Jesus, or more correctly the Christ, is referred to as the "Sun of Righteousness";[3988] His birthday was placed on December 25,[3989] the Winter Solstice birthday of the Pagan Sun- and savior-gods Mithras, Attis, Adonis, and Sol;[3990] the Christian Sabbath was moved from the Jewish Sabbath on Saturn's Day (Saturday) to Sun's Day (Sunday);[3991] and early mystical Christians artistically portrayed the Lord as a literal Sun-god, identical to the Greek solar-deity Helios.[3992]

To this day it is a Christian tradition to inscribe IHS (the sacred monogram of the Pagan Greek god Bacchus[3993] and the first three letters of Jesus' name in Greek, *Ihsus*) inside an image of the Sun.[3994] Now Bacchus was nursed by panthers, and, according to the Talmud, Jesus' family name was said to be *Panthera* or *Pandira* ("Panther"),[3995] the name of a Roman soldier who, according to "slanderous" early tradition, was the lover of the Virgin Mary—and thus Jesus' real (biological) father.[3996] This would have made the Master's full name, Jesus Ben-Panthera,[3997] revealing more mysterious pre-Christian links between our Lord and Paganism.[3998]

In sacred numerology IHS equals 608, the time period of the solar-lunar cycle; that is, the number of years that elapse before the Sun and Moon are again in the same relative position in the sky.[3999] Thus Doane writes:

> These three letters, the monogram of the Sun, are the celebrated I.S.H., which are to be seen in the Roman Catholic churches at the present day, and which are now the monogram of the Sun-god Christ Jesus.[4000]

We all possess an inner IHS monogram permanently branded by God on our "inward parts."[4001] This sacred "monogram" is the Sun-God Within, the Indwelling Christ, for it is none other than God himself, in whose image we are made.[4002] Thus, since the Buddha and the Christ are identical, those who followed our Lord were called "Sons of God"[4003] or "Christians,"[4004] while those who followed Buddha were referred to as "Buddha-sons," "Sons of Buddha" or "Buddhists."[4005] Pfleiderer writes:

> Without creatures God were not God. He can do as little without us as without Himself. What creatures are in truth, that they are in God, through the existence which God Himself has imparted to them. It is the goodness of God that He imparts Himself to all, but *only in the human soul is God present in Godlike fashion*. The soul is, therefore, God's resting-place in which the temporal and the eternal are allied.
>
> *Our spirit is the divine spark within us, wherein is completed the alliance of God and the soul. As God contains all things in Himself, so it is in our soul; the soul is the micro-cosmos in which all things are contained and are led back to God. Therefore, there is no difference between the Son of God and the [human] soul. Humanity itself is the one Son whom the Father eternally bore, but the individual man is only a limited phenomenon of all human being[s]*.[4006]

Underhill writes:

> All great spiritual literature is full of invitations to a newnness of life, a great change of direction; which shall at last give our human faculties a worthy objective and redeem our consciousness from its present concentration upon unreal interests. It urges us perpetually, as a practical counsel, as something which is within human power and has already been achieved by the heroes of the race, to "put on the new man"; to "bring to birth the Son of God in the soul."
>
> But humanity as a whole has never responded to that invitation, and therefore its greatest possibilities are still latent. We, the guardians of the future, by furnishing to each emerging consciousness committed to our care such an apperceiving mass as shall enable it to discern the messages of reality, may do something to bring those possibilities into manifestation.[4007]

In other words, the Son of God signifies spiritual evolution (spirit rising back into spirit), while the Son of Man signifies spiritual involution (spirit falling into matter).

In my book *Christmas Before Christianity: How the Birthday of the "Sun" Became the Birthday of the "Son,"* I detail the development of the ecclesiastical Christian concept of the Son-god from out of the pre-Christian Pagan idea of the Sun-god. This is not anti-Christian fiction. It is pro-Christian history; authentic spiritual allegory long ago historicized for the masses by the orthodox Church. See CHRIST, CHRISTIANITY, GNOSTICISM, GOSPEL, JESUS, MESSIAH, MYTH OF CHRIST, SAVIOR, SON OF MAN, SUN, SUN OF RIGHTEOUSNESS.

SON OF MAN: In the traditional Church the Son of Man is just another one of Jesus' many titles,[4008] a title that is not at all understood,[4009] but which, orthodox authorities hold, is mysteriously connected to His role as the Messiah.[4010] But since Buddha was referred to as the "Son of Man,"[4011] and as even other biblical figures, such as Ezekiel, were as well,[4012] and since Jesus Himself sometimes differentiates His person from the Son of Man,[4013] it is obvious that this phrase means far more than this.

The mystical Church perceives profound spiritual mysteries in it, as the Psalmist intimates:

> What is man, that thou art mindful of him? and the son of man, that thou visitest him? For thou hast made him a little lower than the angels, and hast crowned him with glory and honour. Thou madest him to have dominion over the works of thy hands; thou hast put all things under his feet.[4014]

The Son of Man or *Bar Nash*a, in fact, was an ancient everyday Aramaic expression meaning "a man,"[4015] "the Man,"[4016] or simply "anyone,"[4017] that is, a mortal human.[4018] Thus this phrase was also written the "son of adam,"[4019] the word "man" in Hebrew being *adam*. In fact, the standard use of the word *adam* as a proper name for the "First Man" is incorrect. Up until Genesis 4:25 Adam is called simply "the man" (*adam*), which spiritually ignorant priests have mistranslated as the proper name "Adam."[4020]

As is clear from the Gospel of Q (the earliest known record of Jesus' teachings,[4021] and mentioned by both Bishop Papias of Hierapolis[4022] and Paul),[4023] the historical Jesus never once used the phrase "Son of God" in regard to Himself;[4024] only the "Son of Man," that is, the "son of a man."[4025] This was due to the fact that He wanted to stress the divinity of *all* human beings, not just Himself—for we all possess the Universal Inner Christ,[4026] the Indwelling Christ (Divine Law).[4027] This fact has been common knowledge among Church officials for centuries. In 1597, for instance, Archbishop of Aix, Gilbert Génébrard,

> emphasised the point that the term Son of Man should not be interpreted with the reference solely to Christ, but to the race

of mankind.[4028]

The Old Testament writers also used the phrase "Son of Man," which when stripped of its Orientalism ("Son of"), simply means "the Man," that is, an ordinary human being,[4029] as is clear in Isaiah,[4030] Ezekiel,[4031] and Daniel.[4032] In the Gospel of Thomas we find the term "Son of Man" being used correctly to indicate the "earthly Jesus."[4033] Our Lord Himself, though He never openly defined the term,[4034] used it to mean "humanity," as the Gospel of Mark clearly shows.[4035] Even the orthodox are finally beginning to come around to the fact that Son of Man means nothing more than one who is "a member of the order of humanity."[4036]

According to objective scholarly studies of the development of the New Testament and the Church, it is obvious that during the Paganization and apotheosization process of Jesus (late 1st Century to the 5th Century), during its nefarious "Scheme of Salvation,"[4037] the Church gave Him the title "Son of God" in order to deemphasize His humanity and emphasize His divinity. Indeed, He was not formally made a Savior-God until the year 325, at the Council of Nicaea,[4038] where it was declared heresy to refer to Jesus as a mortal man.[4039] Then, at the Council of Chalcedon in A.D. 451,[4040] the Church further deified our Lord by pronouncing him a result of the union of divinity (God) and humanity (the Virgin Mary).[4041] Up until this period, Jesus' many Pagan and Jewish followers considered Him nothing more than a great teacher, healer, and prophet, just as Pagans and Jews do to this very day.[4042]

In contrast to the orthodox Church, Paul, who, like our Lord, understood that the Christ was not only in Jesus,[4043] but in all men and women,[4044] never hesitated to focus on the human Jesus, stating that He

> took upon him the form of a *servant*, and was *made in the likeness of men*; and being found in fashion *as a man*, he humbled himself, and became obedient unto death, even the death of the cross.[4045]

In his letter to his followers at Rome, Paul wrote:

> For what the law could not do, in that it was weak through the flesh, *God sending his own Son in the likeness of sinful flesh*, and for sin, condemned sin in the flesh.[4046]

In his letter to the Corinthians, Paul calls Jesus "the last Adam,"[4047] another overt reference to Jesus' humanity; for, as noted, *adam* is Hebrew for "man," or more precisely, a "human being."[4048]

All of this ties in perfectly with the authentic (that is, the earliest undoctored) New Testament scriptures, which portray Jesus as a human (though extraordinary) child of a human father and a human mother, with at least six human brothers and sisters. Mark and Matthew, for instance, record the following revealing incident. While Jesus was teaching at the synagogue one day, the people began asking one another questions:

> Is not this the carpenter's son [Joseph]? is not his mother called Mary? and his brethren, James, and Joses, and Simon, and Judas? . . . And are not his sisters here with us?[4049]

Just how *human* was our Lord Jesus? Human enough to own His own house at Capernaum,[4050] where He and the Apostles stayed on occasion,[4051] and where He ran a secret spiritual academy known as "The School of Christ."[4052] *The Aquarian Gospel of Jesus the Christ* corroborates this view:

> In Cana Jesus tarried not; he went his way with his disciples to Capernaum, where *he secured a spacious house* where, with his mother, he could live; where his disciples might repair to hear the Word. He called the men who had confessed their faith in him to meet him *in his home*, which *his disciples called, 'The school of Christ'* . . . *[where they] were taught the secret things of God.*"[4053]

Mark goes as far as to say that after His Galilean ministry Jesus returned to Capernaum, where it was reported that He was "at home."[4054]

Owing to His obvious humanity, many have seen biblical hints of marriage and children in the life of Jesus. And this is only natural, for the expectancy of a Jewish male to marry was so strong in early Judaism that it lacked a word for "bachelor."[4055] Thus many believe that the wedding at Cana,[4056] for instance, was our Lord's own marriage,[4057] that the "lad" mentioned by John was His son,[4058] and that His wife was Mary Magdalene, of whom the Gospel of Philip says Jesus "kissed her often on the mouth."[4059] Ancient stories, some well attested, persist into the present day that Jesus and Mary also had a daughter named Sarah ("Princess"), and that Mary and Sarah later traveled to France, where one of Sarah's descendants married into Frankish royalty, producing the Merovingian family, the "Long-Haired Kings" of France (a line from which I myself descend).[4060]

Just as the Hebraist, the unknown Essene who wrote the Letter to Hebrews,[4061] repeatedly refers to Jesus as "this man,"[4062] Mark—who "chose" to leave out the Master's supernatural nativity story and resurrection appearances—also emphasized Jesus' humanity,[4063] depicting Him as a repentant human sinner who became the Son of God only *after* His baptism by John,[4064] or perhaps *after* His resurrection,[4065] after which He was adopted by God—a "problem" (known as Adoptionism) that was later "corrected" by unknown scribal hands in the books of Matthew,[4066] Luke,[4067] and John (the latter who avoids the issue by eliminating Jesus' baptism altogether).[4068]

Luke shows Jesus openly calling Himself the "Son of Man" (as discussed, a common Aramaic term for a mortal human being)[4069] before the Jewish authorities, while simultaneously spurning the title "Son of God."[4070] Mark even has Jesus denying that He descends from David,[4071] contravening one of the Old Testament requirements for Messiahship.[4072] This "difficulty" too was later remedied in other New Testament books, with mixed, confusing, contradictory, and often irreconcilable results.[4073]

The Ecclesia (the orthodox Church),[4074] of course, wanting to present Jesus purely as a god, or as God the Father himself, fought back against Adoptionism. Church officials, like the 3rd-Century Antioch Bishop Paul of Samosata,[4075] who held that Jesus was a man, the human son of Joseph and Mary[4076]—who later had become God only after He was "instilled" with the Indwelling Christ[4077]—were summarily deposed or even excommunicated,[4078] and their teachings pronounced "heretical."[4079]

Yet, what is revealing is that Adoptionism (also known as Dynamic Monarchianism) was the doctrine embraced by Jesus' earliest followers, not its opposite, Tritheism, the tenet developed and held much later by the orthodox Church.[4080] Hence, the Lucan passage found in current Bibles, "Thou art my beloved Son; in thee I am well pleased,"[4081] is missing from a number of ancient New Testament manuscripts, such as the Codex Bezae (written perhaps about the year 400). In its place we find this scripture: "Thou art my Son; today I have begotten thee,"[4082] confirming the original Adoptionist stance of Jesus' first followers who, according to the Bible, viewed the Lord as "a man," albeit a great one, but still "a man," one who became a Son of God only after his baptism,[4083] the same appellation to which every sincere believer is also entitled.[4084]

If this evidence is not convincing enough, we need only look to Jesus, who, as mentioned, often referred to Himself as the "Son of Adam," or in modern English, the "Son of Man" (from the Greek *anthropos*, "man," a human being),[4085] a Hebraism indicating one who is a member of the human race.[4086] On at least one occasion He very straightforwardly refers to Himself simply as "a man."[4087]

Was this the only time Jesus used this phrase? It is highly doubtful. What happened to the other occurrences then? Only the discovery of a *complete* copy of the *original* New Testament will reveal the answer. The present version of the New Testament assures us, however, that Jesus was fully human; that is, the *human* son of two *human* parents.[4088] Mark, for instance, refers to our Lord's siblings not as "half brothers" and "half sisters" (as the organized Church does), but as *full* "brothers" and *full* "sisters."[4089]

That early on Jesus was known to Church authorities not as God but as a mortal man, is authenticated by one of Christianity's greatest apologists, Justin Martyr. During his dialogue with Trypho the Jew, Justin defended the Faith by citing several Old Testament prophecies concerning Jesus. Then, said the great 2nd-Century Christian theologian to his Jewish nemesis:

Of these and several other such like words which were spoken by the prophets, some of them relate to the first coming of Christ, in which it is foretold that he was to appear in an inglorious, dishonourable, and *mortal state*.[4090]

As for the Paganization and apotheosis of Jesus "the man," the evidence is abundant.[4091] Not only are all references to our Lord as the "Son of God" completely absent from the Gospel of Q, we have canonical proof as well. Acts 8:37 (in which Jesus is referred to as the "Son of God"), for example, is an obvious interpolation, since it is not found in the earliest known complete New Testament texts (such as the Codex Sinaiticus).

Thus in mystical Christianity the "Son of Man" is exemplified in the pre-baptized Jesus, who had not yet realized His own divinity, that is, His oneness with God (Divine Mind), until the Holy Spirit descended on Him in the form of a dove (enlightenment).

Revealingly, throughout the entire New Testament the phrase Son of Man is never used by anyone but Jesus, and in authentic passages our Lord only refers to the Son of Man as a future figure who is separate and distinct from Himself.[4092] Also revealing is the fact that the Son of Man sayings never mention the Kingdom of God, nor do the Kingdom of God sayings ever refer to the Son of Man.[4093] We are dealing here with mysticism, with pure spirituality, not history, or even theology, and this has always been something that the traditional Church cannot abide. This is why, by the time of Ignatius of Antioch (2nd Century), the title Son of Man (which described Jesus' human nature) was supplanted by the title Son of God.[4094]

Mystically, the Son of Man is the Conscious Mind, the unperfected soul. Hence, we are all "Sons of Man" until we understand and accept our oneness with the Universal Divine Mind, after which we become "Sons of God."[4095] In other words, the Son of Man signifies spiritual involution or the *Aphanism* (spirit falling into matter), while the Son of God signifies spiritual evolution or the *Euresis* (spirit rising back into spirit).[4096]

The outer meaning of the Son of Man is "Child of Humanity," that is, one born of mortal parents, as the Bible clearly states Jesus was.[4097] The inner meaning then is "a mortal human being."

In the Gnostic-Christian Gospel of Mary (Magdalene), Jesus tells the Apostles that:

> *The Son of Man is inside of you.* Those who earnestly seek oneness with him shall locate him.[4098]

This means that in order to discover and live in the here-and-now Kingdom Within,[4099] we must seek to have a "pure" Conscious Mind. Indeed, another meaning of the Son of Man is "Son of Mind,"[4100] for the word man derives from the same root as the Sanskrit word *manas*, meaning "mind."[4101] That "Mind" is the Divine Mind, also known variously as God, Nature, the Unified Field, and physics.

Biblically speaking then, the term "Son of Man" was merely Jesus' mystical way of differentiating between the body and the spirit, or the Indwelling Christ, which was known among ancient mystics as the "Son of God."[4102] Thus, to this day secret Christian societies, such as the Freemasons, teach that "Jesus of Nazareth was but a man like us" and that "His history is but the unreal revival of an older legend." With this view Christian mysticism wholeheartedly agrees.[4103] See CHRIST, CROWN, DIVINITY OF JESUS, GOD, GOOD NEWS, GOSPEL, JESUS, MESSIAH, MYTH OF CHRIST, REDEEMER, SAVIOR, SON OF GOD.

SOUL: In the traditional Church the Soul is "the immortal part of man."[4104] In the mystical Church the Soul is identical to the mind. Though normally invisible to the physical eyes, the Soul is a real thing, for it has been measured scientifically. When terminal patients are weighed immediately before and immediately after death, the scale records a loss of exactly 11 ounces.[4105] And it is this aspect, also known as the Astral Body, which is so often experienced as the "ghosts" that haunt our homes.[4106]

Further evidence of the Soul comes from dreams: when we dream our senses of taste, touch, hearing, and smell are actually heightened, even though our conscious mind is dormant and inactive. More revealing is the fact that during our dreams we can see exceptionally well, even if we wear glasses in our waking life, and even if it is "night" in the dream. And this while our physical eyes are closed. What is it that is able to sense all of these experiences while we are fast asleep? It is the Soul.[4107]

During seances, in nearly every case, the main message of the dead is that *life and love continue after so-called "death," and that the Soul is immortal*.[4108] Emerson writes of the Soul:

> The doctrine of this Supreme Presence is a cry of joy and exultation. Who shall dare think he has come late into nature, or has missed anything excellent in the past, who seeth the admirable stars of possibility, and the yet untouched continent of hope glittering with all its mountains in the vast West? I praise with wonder this great reality, which seems to drown all things in the deluge of its light. What man, seeing this, can lose it from his thoughts, or entertain a meaner subject? The entrance of this into his mind seems to be the birth of man.
>
> We cannot describe the natural history of the soul, but *we know that it is divine*. I cannot tell if these wonderful qualities which house today in this mortal frame, shall ever reassemble in equal activity in a similar frame, or whether they have before

had a natural history like that of this body you see before you; but *this one thing I know, that these qualities did not now begin to exist, cannot be sick with my sickness, nor buried in any grave; but that they circulate through the Universe: before the world was, they were. Nothing can bar them out, or shut them in, they penetrate the ocean and land, space and time, form and essence, and hold the key to universal nature.*

I draw from this faith courage and hope. All things are known to the soul. It is not to be surprised by any communication. Nothing can be greater than it. Let those fear and those fawn who will. The soul is in her native realm, and it is wider than space, older than time, wide as hope, rich as love. Pusillanimity and fear she refuses with a beautiful scorn: they are not for her who putteth on her coronation robes, and goes out through universal love to universal power.[4109]

In mystical Christianity the physical body is the vehicle that carries the soul, while the soul is the vehicle that carries the spirit,[4110] the spirit being the Indwelling Christ or Divine God-Spark found in every man and woman.[4111] To put it another way, while the body signifies spiritual involution (spirit falling into matter), the soul signifies spiritual evolution (spirit returning to spirit). In this sense some Christian mystics hold that the soul has three parts: physical, mental, and spiritual. Mead writes:

> The kinds of Souls are three:—divine, human, irrational. Now the divine [is that] of its divine body, in which there is the making active of itself. For it is moved in it, and moves itself. For when it is set free from mortal lives, it separates itself from the irrational portions of itself, departs unto the godlike body, and as 'tis in perpetual motion, is moved in its own self, with the same motion as the universe.
>
> The human [kind] has also something of the godlike [body], but it has joined to it as well the [parts] irrational,—the appetite and heart. These latter also are immortal, in that they happen also in themselves to be activities; but [they are] the activities of mortal bodies. Wherefore, they are removed far from the godlike portion of the Soul, when it is in its godlike body; but when this enters in a mortal frame, they also cling to it, and by the presence [of these elements] it keeps on being a human Soul.
>
> But that of the irrationals consists of heart and appetite. And for this cause these lives are also called irrational, through deprivation of the reason of the Soul.[4112]

Thus mystic Paul writes:

> And the very God of peace sanctify you wholly; and I pray God your whole spirit and soul and body be preserved blameless unto the coming of our Lord Jesus Christ.[4113]

The human Soul is indeed designed by God to be "blameless." Pike writes that

> the soul of man is formed by Him for a purpose; that, built up in its proportions, and fashioned in every part, by infinite skill, an emanation from His spirit, its nature, necessity, and design is virtue. It is so formed, so moulded, so fashioned, so exactly balanced, so exquisitely proportioned in every part, that sin introduced into it is misery; that vicious thoughts fall upon it like drops of poison; and guilty desires, breathing on its delicate fibres, make plague-spots there, deadly as those of pestilence upon the body. It is made for virtue, and not for vice; for purity, as its end, rest, and happiness.[4114]

Honoré de Balzac summarized the Christian mystic's viewpoint, saying that "all we are is in the soul."[4115] See CHRIST, CROWN, DIVINE MIND, GOD, SPIRIT.

SPIRIT: In the traditional Church the human Spirit is considered identical to the Soul.[4116] In the mystical Church (as Paul notes in the previous entry)[4117] the Spirit is different from and separate from the Soul. The Spirit is the real you, your Higher Self or Mind, identical to the Logos, which Irenaeus called "the Mind of God."[4118] It is a literal piece of God, the divine spark "which lighteth every man that cometh into the world."[4119] Here the Soul is the vehicle which sheaths the Spirit, while the physical body is the vehicle that sheaths the Soul. In Hinduism these three bodies are called the causal body (that is, the Spirit, also known as the mental body, the seed body, or *Karan Sharir*), the astral body (that is, the Soul, also known as the subtle body, the light body, the rainbow body, or *Sukhsham Sharir*), and the physical body (that is, the material body, also known as the desire body, the gross body, or *Isthul Sharir*).[4120]

As the Rosicrucians have long taught,[4121] in ancient alchemy, which symbolized the *spiritual* transmutation of base metals (spiritual "ignorance") into precious metals (spiritual "illumination"),[4122] the world was divided into these same three parts as *corpus* (body), *anima* (soul), and *spiritus* (spirit or mind), and, as emblems of salt (physical body), sulfur (soul), and mercury (spirit or mind),[4123] they were often disguised as the Holy Trinity.[4124]

In ancient times the human Spirit was depicted as the Sun (heavenly, masculine, positive polarity). Hence it eventually came to be seen as a god, a Sun-god, Son-god, or Son of God; while the body was personified as the Moon (earthly, feminine, negative polarity), eventually seen as a Moon-goddess or Daughter of Goddess. Thus the Spirit is the Universal Indwelling Christ, of which Jesus[4125] and Paul taught.[4126]

  The Sun of mystical Christianity is triadic in form as well: the Spiritual Sun represents the power of the Father; the Solar (Soul-ar) Sun represents the life of the Son; and the Material Sun represents the manifestation of the Holy Spirit. This describes not only the esoteric symbolism of the Sun/Son-God, but the life process of each individual human as well: the physical nature is birthed and energized by the Material Sun; our divine nature is enlightened by the Spiritual Sun; and our intellectual nature is saved by the Solar Sun.[4127] See ASTROLOGY, CHRIST, DIVINE MIND, HOLY TRINITY, SOUL, SUN, ZODIAC.

STAR OF BETHLEHEM: In traditional Christianity the Star of Bethlehem, or "Star in the East," is simply a star that was followed by the Wise Men or Magi to the manger of the baby Jesus. But as single stars do not move across the sky and stop over specific locations, a deeper more occult meaning was obviously intended by Matthew (the only one to include this popular Pagan motif in the nativity of our Lord).[4128]

  Indeed, even the most conservative Christian scholars today admit that the Star of Bethlehem is one of the great "unsolved astronomical problems" of the Bible.[4129] Though some fundamentalists surmise that it may have been Venus, Sirius,[4130] a meteor, a nova,[4131] or Halley's comet,[4132] diligent searches for astronomical events (such as a conjunction of stars, or planets[4133] like Jupiter, Saturn, and Venus)[4134] around the time and place of Jesus' birth, which might explain the "Star of Bethlehem," have come to naught. Some have tried to interpret the story of the mysterious celestial body as a midrash (an ancient Hebrew commentary) formed around a lone passage in the book of Numbers.[4135] But this too is quite unsatisfactory to the rational mind, and must be rejected as a violation of Occam's Razor.[4136]

  In the mystical Christian tradition there are no such problems or issues. Here, occultically, stars symbolize the divine light of Spirit piercing the darkness of ignorance and materiality. Stars can also represent angels,[4137] which are symbols of spiritual protection and guidance.[4138] But we have many other clues, most which derive from the Bible itself.

  The Star of Bethlehem came from "the East," a direction that symbolizes the rising Sun, the archetypal symbol of the Christ (of the tribe of Judah, governed by the astrological sign Leo the Lion, which is ruled by the Sun)[4139] that indwells every individual.[4140] Additionally, since the "East" is a pre-Christian emblem of the human forehead, the Star of Bethlehem is unquestionably an occult symbol of the Third Eye, widely known among mystics as "the Sun (Son) of God" and "the gateway to the Kingdom Within."[4141] Read mystically rather than literally, the following passages from the book of Ezekiel are now intelligible:

> Afterward he brought me to the gate, *the gate that faces toward the east.* And behold, *the glory of the God of Israel came from the way of the east.* His voice was like the sound of many waters; and the earth shone with His glory.[4142]

Christian mysticism also views the Star of Bethlehem as the "Sacred Pentagram," an initiatory symbol of Divine Truth, Wisdom, and Knowledge. For

> when truth comes into the world, the Star of Knowledge advises the Magi of it, and they hasten to adore the Infant who creates the future.[4143]

In summation the story of the Star of the East is mystically referring to the emergence in the human mind of the enlightened knowledge[4144] that the birth of the Universal Christ takes place in the "manger" of the human soul. See BIRTH OF JESUS, CHRISTMAS, GODDESS, GOOD NEWS, GOSPEL, ENLIGHTENMENT, NATIVITY, VIRGIN BIRTH, VIRGO, WISE MEN.

SUBCONSCIOUS MIND: The Subconscious Mind does not appear by this name in the Bible, of course, but it does appear nonetheless, in this case in the mystical guise of the "Holy Spirit," "Holy Ghost," "Comforter," or "Paraclete," thus its inclusion here. I call the Subconscious Mind "the Communicator." It is a symbol of love, the soul, and all that is spiritual. The Subconscious Mind (female) receives thoughts and ideas from the Conscious Mind (male, personified in the Bible as "Jesus"), which it communicates to the Superconscious Mind (androgynous, personified in the Bible as "God") as beliefs.

In patriarchal religions the Subconscious is identical to, as noted, the "Holy Spirit." In matriarchal religions it is identical to the "Moon."

The Subconscious Mind never tires, never sleeps, and never dies. It is the spiritual aspect of our mental system, passing with us into the World Beyond after so-called "death." While we are here on earth, it acts as our obedient personal assistant and attendant, always ready to help turn our dominant thoughts and beliefs into physical reality. Thus, it is also occultly known as "the Servant," unquestioningly operating under the auspices of "the Master," the Conscious Mind (Jesus).[4145]

The Subconscious not only regulates many of our body's involuntary functions and cellular processes (such as our circulation, digestion, breathing, and immune system), but it also records and stores all of our thoughts, beliefs, experiences, and memories. Proof of the Subconscious Mind's tremendous spiritual and physical powers can be seen in, for example, the commonplace healing of cuts, burns, and broken bones, the unassisted "miraculous" curing of nearly every known disease, the placebo effect, hypnosis, and the creation of different fingerprints in identical twins (who share identical DNA).[4146]

Additional evidence comes from the so-called "occult arts," such as divination, telepathy, clairaudience, levitation, intuition, remote viewing, clairvoyance, retrocognition, clairsentience, bilocation, automatic writing, and channeling, all which take place in and through the Subconscious Mind.

It is also via the Subconscious that we experience night "dreams," during which time our spirits temporarily return to the world of Spirit to rest and reenergize themselves. This is only possible because the Subconscious is a spiritual instrument that links the earthly to the heavenly. Learning how to work with Jesus' teachings (such as the Law of Attraction) and the Subconscious Mind to establish health, wealth, and happiness in our lives is to truly possess one of the Keys to the Kingdom of Heaven.[4147]

The Subconscious Mind correlates with the right side of the brain, which operates the left (female) side of the body. Its keywords are: emotional, random, intuitive, subjective, feminine, nighttime, belief, heavenly, expression, symbols, spirituality.[4148] See CONSCIOUS MIND, DIVINE MIND, GOD, HOLY SPIRIT, JESUS, KEYS OF THE KINGDOM OF HEAVEN, SUPERCONSCIOUS MIND.

SUN: In modern traditional Christianity the Sun is a scriptural symbol of faithfulness and constancy.[4149] In mystical Christianity the sun is a symbol of Christ, the human Soul,[4150] whose inner meaning is "revealed knowledge of Divine Law." Thus Neander writes:

> [The Gnostic Christian] Manicheans taught expressly that Mani, Buddas [Buddha], Zoroaster, Christ, and the Sun, are the same.[4151]

This doctrine is so obvious that it is found even among modern native peoples, such as the Chamulas, a Tzotzil-speaking community of Mayan Indians living in southern Mexico. In their religion the Sun-god Htotik ("Our Father") is identical to Jesus, whom they image as the "Sun-Christ," ruler of Chamula agriculture and ritual.[4152]

The Sun is a common solar symbol in ancient Pagan and Christian literature and art, one representing enlightenment, the lucent Higher Self, the incandescent Divine Self, the luminescent Indwelling Christ[4153] that resides in each human being,[4154] which Paul called "the temple of the living God."[4155] A modern remnant of the early Christian connection between the *Son* of God and the *Sun* of God is found in the German word for the Sun: *sonne*, in English "son."[4156] Of solar-worship in general, Mackey remarks:

> A recent writer eloquently refers to the universality, in ancient

times, of sun-worship: "Sabaism, the worship of light, prevailed amongst all the leading nations of the early world. By the rivers of India, on the mountains of Persia, in the plains of Assyria, early mankind thus adored, the higher spirits in each country rising in spiritual thought from the solar orb up to Him whose vicegerent it seems—to the Sun of all being, whose divine light irradiates and purifies the world of soul, as the solar radiance does the world of sense.

"Egypt, too, though its faith be but dimly known to us, joined in this worship; Syria raised her grand temples to the sun; the joyous Greeks sported with the thought while feeling it, almost hiding it under the mythic individuality which their lively fancy superimposed upon it. Even prosaic China makes offerings to the yellow orb of day; the wandering Celts and Teutons held feasts to it, amidst the primeval forests of Northern Europe; and, with a savagery characteristic of the American aborigines, the sun temples of Mexico streamed with human blood in honor of the beneficent orb."

"There is no people whose religion is known to us," says the Abbé Banier, "neither in our own continent nor in that of America, that has not paid the sun a religious worship, if we except some inhabitants of the torrid zone, who are continually cursing the sun for scorching them with his beams." Macrobius, in his *Saturnalia*, undertakes to prove that all the gods of Paganism may be reduced to the sun.[4157]

Not surprisingly, the book of Malachi refers to Jesus, the Christian Sun (that is, Son), as the "Sun of Righteousness."[4158] John asserted of the Master that "his countenance was as the sun,"[4159] while Jesus referred to Himself as "the Light of the world."[4160] Speaking as the Christ Within, our Lord describes His mission this way:

> I am come a light [spiritual enlightenment] into the world, that whosoever believeth on me should not abide in darkness [spiritual ignorance].[4161]

Thus, all those who believe in Him, that is, who recognize the Indwelling Christ, become "children of light."[4162] This is why:

- Ancient Christian writers associated Jesus with the astrological star-sign Leo the Lion, ruled by the Sun.[4163]
- Early Christian artists portrayed Jesus as the Greek solar-gods Helios or Apollo

(or the Roman Sun-gods Sol or Mithra),[4164] riding across the sky each day in his fiery chariot, pulled by four white horses.[4165]
- The Lord's birthday was assigned to the birthday of the Roman Sun-god Mithra on December 25.[4166]
- The Christian Sabbath was changed from Saturday (Saturn's Day, the Jewish Sabbath) to Sunday (the Sun's Day, the Pagan Sabbath).[4167]
- The Church gave Jesus the Pagan title *Sol Justitiae*, the "Just Sun."[4168]
- The 12 Apostles were identified with the 12 astrological Sun-signs (orbiting Jesus "the Sun").[4169]
- Jesus' mother, the Virgin Mary, was portrayed as being "clothed with the sun . . . and upon her head a crown of twelve stars," representing the 12 Sun-signs (or "Apostles") of the Zodiac.[4170]
- Under Constantine the Great,[4171] 4th-Century Christians famously worshiped Jesus as the Roman solar-deity *Sol Invictus*,[4172] the "Unconquered Sun."[4173]
- In Greek Jesus' name is spelled *Ihsus*. The first three letters, IHS, are, by Christian tradition, always placed inside an image of the Sun.[4174]

Saint Francis of Assisi plainly understood the mystical meaning of the Sun-Christ, for writing in the year 1225, he devoted an entire poem to it, which he called, *The Canticle to the Sun*, referring to Jesus, that is, the Indwelling Christ, as "brother sun." Here is a portion:

> Most high, omnipotent, good Lord,
> Praise, glory and honor and benediction all, are Thine.
> To Thee alone do they belong, most High,
> And there is no man fit to mention Thee.
>
> Praise be to Thee, my Lord, with all Thy creatures,
> Especially to my worshipful brother sun,
> The which lights up the day, and through him dost Thou
>   brightness give;
> And beautiful is he and radiant with splendor great;
> Of Thee, most High, signification gives.[4175]

From the mystical Christian point of view, Jesus the Son-God is a historicized Christian version of the Universal Sun-God,[4176] who is born at the Spring Equinox ("Easter"), matures at the Summer Solstice ("Midsummer"), becomes aged at the Fall Equinox ("Halloween"), and dies and is reborn at the Winter Solstice ("Christmas"). Thus, Jesus' biography (as put forth in the four canonical Gospels) can only truly be understood as an allegory of the Sun's yearly passage through the 12 months, representing the 12 astrological Sun-signs—occultically known in Christianity as the "12 Apostles," who "encircle" the

Sun-God Jesus.

  The first Christians, the Essenes and the Gnostics, understood this, which is why they venerated the Sun as the Christ,[4177] a custom that passed on into the 2nd-Century Church, at which time Christians were still praying each morning while facing the East in order to greet the "rising Sun/Son."[4178] Thus ancient Pagans, like Emperor Hadrian, saw no difference between Roman Christians and the followers of the Egyptian Sun-god Serapis.[4179]

  Many of today's mainstream Christians refuse to accept the overt and inescapable correlation between ancient Pagan Sun worship and modern Christian Son worship. Of this issue Dupius writes that the "fable of Christ" is doubtless

> really dedicated to the worship of the Sun. The hatred, which the sectarians of that religion [today's orthodox Christians],—jealous to make their form of worship dominant over all others,—have shown against those, who worshipped Nature, the Sun, the Moon and the Stars, against the Roman Deities, whose temples and altars they have upset,—would suscitate the idea, that their worship did not form a part of that otherwise universal religion. But *the error of a people about the true object of its worship has never proved anything else but its own ignorance. Because, if in the opinion of the Greeks, Hercules and Bacchus were men, who had been raised to the ranks of Gods; and if in the opinion of the people of Egypt, Isis was a benevolent Queen, who had formerly reigned over Egypt, the worship of Bacchus, of Hercules and of Isis would be nevertheless the worship of the Sun and the Moon.*

>   *The Romans ridiculed the Deities, which were worshipped on the shores of the Nile; they proscribed Annubis, Isis and Serapis, and yet they worshipped themselves Mercury, Diana, Ceres and Pluto, in other words, absolutely the same Gods under other names and under different forms; so much is the ignorant vulgar swayed by names. Pluto said, that the Greeks had worshipped since the remotest antiquity, the Sun, the Moon and the Stars, and yet the same Pluto was not aware, that they had still preserved at his time the same Gods under the names of Hercules and Bacchus, of Apollo, Diana and Aesculapius, etc. . . .*

>   Convinced of this truth, that the opinions, which a nation has of the character of its religion, proves nothing else but its faith, and does not change its nature, we shall carry our investigations even into the very sanctuaries of modern Rome, and we shall find that the God Lamb, which they worship there, is the ancient Jupiter of the Romans, who frequently takes the same forms under the name of Amnion, in other words, those of the "Ram" or of the "vernal Lamb;" that the conqueror of the

Prince of Darkness at Easter, is the same God, who triumphs in the poem of the Dionysiacs over Typhon at the same epoch, who redeems the evil, which the Chief of Darkness had introduced into the World under the form of a serpent, with which form Typhon was invested.

We shall also recognize there under the name of [the Apostle] Peter, old Janus with his keys and his bark [boat], at the head of the twelve Deities of the twelve months, the altars of which are at his feet. *We feel, that we shall have to overcome a great many prejudices, and that those, who agree with us, that Bacchus and Hercules are nothing else, but the Sun, will not easily agree, that the worship of Christ is nothing more, than the worship of the Sun.* But let them reflect, that the Greeks and the Romans would have willingly yielded their opinion on the evidences, which we shall produce, when they would not have so easily consented to the point, of not recognizing in Hercules and Bacchus Heroes and Princes, who had merited by their achievements, to be raised to the rank of the Gods.

Every one takes good care, to guard against anything, which might destroy the illusion of an ancient prejudice, which education, example and the habit of believing have fortified. Thus, *notwithstanding the clearest evidence, with which we shall support our assertions, we only hope to convince the wise man, who reflects; the sincere friend of truth, disposed to sacrifice to it his prejudices, whenever it shall become evident to him. It is but too true, that we write only for him; the rest is devoted to ignorance and to the priests, who live at the expense of the credulity of the people, which they lead like a vile drove.*

. . . *the pretended history of a God, born of a virgin at the winter solstice, who resuscitates at Easter or at the equinox of spring, after having descended into hell; of a God who has twelve apostles in his train, whose leader [Peter] has all the attributes of [the Pagan god] Janus; of a god-conqueror of the Prince of Darkness, who restores to mankind the dominion of Light, and who redeems the evils of Nature*—*is merely a solar fable.* . . . *the being, consecrated by worship under the name of Christ, is the Sun, and* . . . *the marvelousness of the legend* . . . *has that luminary for its object; because it would seem proved that the Christians are mere worshippers of the Sun, and that their priests have the same religion as those [Native-Americans] of Peru, whom they have caused to be put to death.*[4180]

Just as the story of Jesus and the 12 Apostles is an allegory of the Sun's journey through the 12 astrological signs, the same is true of the Graeco-Roman legend of the 12 Labors of Hercules, who was the divine son of Zeus (the "Father"). This is a standard element in the myths of nearly *all* Sun/Son-gods, including Krishna or Krista, the Hindu Christ, son of the Father-god Vishnu. Volney writes that according to the sacred books of the Persians and the Chaldeans,

> the first authors had understood the annual revolution of the great celestial orb, called the world (a revolution composed of twelve months or signs, divided each into a thousand parts); and the two systematic periods of winter and summer, composed each of six thousand. These expressions, wholly equivocal and badly explained, having received an absolute and moral, instead of a physical and astrological sense, it happened that the annual world was taken for the secular world, the thousand of the zodiacal divisions for a thousand of years; and supposing, from the state of things, that they lived in the age of evil, they inferred that it would end with the six thousand pretended years.
>
> Now, according to calculations admitted by the Jews, they began to reckon near six thousand years since the (supposed) creation of the world. This coincidence caused a fermentation in the public mind. Nothing was thought of but the approaching end; they consulted the hierophants and the mystical books, which differed as to the term. The great restorer [the Savior or Messiah] was expected and desired; he was so much spoken of that some person finally was said to have seen him, or some one of a heated imagination fancied himself such and acquired proselytes, who, deprived of their leader by an incident true no doubt, but obscurely recorded, gave rise by their reports to a rumor which was gradually converted into an historical fact. Upon this first basis, all the circumstances of mythological traditions took their stand, and produced an authentic and entire system, which it was no longer permitted to call in question.
>
> These mythological traditions recounted that, "in the beginning, a woman and a man had, by their fall, introduced into the world sin and misery." By this was denoted the astronomical fact that the celestial virgin [Virgo] and the herdsman (Bootes), by setting heliacally at the autumnal equinox, delivered the world to the wintry constellations, and seemed, on falling below the horizon, to introduce into the world the genius of evil [the Persian Ahrimanes], represented

by the constellation of the serpent [the snake of Genesis].

These traditions related, that the woman had decoyed and seduced the man. And, in fact, the virgin setting first seems to draw the herdsman after her. That the woman tempted him by offering him fruit fair to the sight, and good to eat, which gave the knowledge of good and evil.

And, in fact, the virgin holds in her hand a branch of fruit which she seems to offer to the herdsman; and the branch, emblem of autumn, placed in the picture of Mithra between winter and summer, seems to open the door and give knowledge, the key of good and evil.

That this couple had been driven from the celestial garden, and that a cherub with a flaming sword had been placed at the gate to guard it. And, in fact, when the virgin and the herdsman fall beneath the western horizon, Perseus rises on the other side; and this genius, with a sword in his hand, seems to drive them from the summer heaven, the garden and dominion of fruits and flowers.

That of this virgin should be born, spring up, an offspring, a child, who should bruise the head of the serpent, and deliver the world from sin.

This denotes the sun, which, at the moment of the winter solstice, precisely when the Persian magi drew the horoscope of the new year, was placed on the bosom of the virgin, rising heliacally in the eastern horizon. On this account he was figured in their astrological pictures under the form of a child suckled by a chaste virgin, and became afterward, at the vernal equinox, the ram, or lamb, triumphant over the constellation of the serpent, which disappeared from the skies.

That, in his infancy, this restorer of divine and celestial nature would live abased, humble, obscure and indigent.

And this, because the winter sun is abased below the horizon, and that this first period of his four ages or seasons is a time of obscurity, scarcity, fasting, and want.

That, being put to death by the wicked, he had risen gloriously; that he had reascended from hell to heaven, where he would reign for ever.

This is a sketch of the life of the sun, who, finishing his career at the winter solstice, when Typhon and the rebel angels gain the dominion, seem to be put to death by them; but who soon after is born again, and rises into the vault of heaven, where he reigns.

Finally, these traditions went so far as to mention even Krishna's astrological and mysterious names, and inform us that he was called sometimes Chris, that is to say, preserver; and from that ye Indians have made your god Chris-en or Chris-na; and ye Greek and Western Christians, your Chris-tos, son of Mary, is the same: sometimes he is called Yes, by the union of three letters, which by their numerical value form the number 608, one of the solar periods: and this, Europeans, is the name which, with the Latin termination, is become your *Iesus, or Jesus*, the ancient and cabalistic name attributed to young Bacchus, the clandestine (nocturnal) son of the virgin Minerva, who, in the history of his whole life, and even of his death, brings to mind the history of the God of the Christians, that is, of the star of day [the Morning Star, Venus], of which they are each of them the emblems.[4181]

The solar mythology that the Church assimilated to Jesus is thus thousands of years older than our Lord, having its earliest known historic origins in the Hindu Sun/Son-god Krishna, but no doubt originating in prehistoric religion.

Revealingly, while Matthew identifies Jesus' paternal grandfather as Jacob,[4182] Luke (contradictorily) gives his name as Heli,[4183] a variation of the name Helios—yet another mystical allusion to Jesus' association with the Sun, the ever effulgent Indwelling Christ.[4184] Thus in mystical Christianity, Jesus' cry from the cross, "*Eli, Eli, lema sabachthani*,"[4185] is addressed not to "God," as in traditional Christianity, but to His Father Eli/Heli/Helios, the Sun, from whom He Himself descends. This makes Jesus a true Sun/Son of God. See ASTROLOGY, CHRIST, CHRIST CONSCIOUSNESS, CHRISTIANITY, DIVINITY OF JESUS, HIGHER SELF, JESUS, MYTH OF CHRIST, NATIVITY, SON OF GOD, ZODIAC.

SUN OF RIGHTEOUSNESS: It is well-known in the traditional Church that Malachi's phrase "Sun of Righteousness" applies to Jesus.[4186] Yet, this truth is barely discussed from the pulpit and few mainline Christian Bible dictionaries contain an entry on this subject—no doubt due to its many Pagan associations.[4187] But ignoring this fact does not alter or obliterate it. It only highlights it.

In the mystical Church the title Sun of Righteousness is fully embraced and discussed, although here it stands not for the man Jesus but for the spirit Christ, two separate entities.[4188] Thus this term is another name for the Higher Self, more commonly known in mystical circles as the Universal Indwelling Christ.[4189] It is for this same reason that a spiritually illuminated Buddhist is referred to as the "Son of Enlightenment"[4190] (that is, "Sun of Light"), for occultly the words righteousness and light, Sun and Son, and the Buddha and the Christ, are all identical. See ASTROLOGY, BUDDHA, CHRIST, CHRIST CONSCIOUSNESS, CROWN, DIVINITY OF JESUS, HIGHER SELF, I AM, INDWELLING CHRIST, JESUS, KRISHNA, LIGHT, LOGOS, MESSIAH, MITHRA, OSIRIS, PYTHAGORAS, SAVIOR, SON OF GOD, SUN, TEACHER OF RIGHTEOUSNESS, ZODIAC.

SUPERCONSCIOUS MIND: In the traditional Church there is no doctrine concerning the Superconscious Mind, or what I call "the Creator," for it is not mentioned anywhere in the Bible by that name. This does not mean, however, that it is not in the Good Book. In the mystical Church the Superconscious Mind is the Source, the Divine One, the Ultimate Mind, and is related to the mental plane and all-encompassing universal power. It receives beliefs (strong predominant thoughts) from the Subconscious Mind, which it then manifests as physical reality.

In patriarchal religions, like traditional Christianity, the Superconscious Mind is the "Father" or "God." In matriarchal religions it is the "Mother" or "Goddess." In mystical religions it is the "I AM,"[4191] the Great Aum or Om, "Divine Mind," the "Akashic Record," and the "Book of Life."[4192] In science it is the "Unified Field," "Nature," or the "laws of physics."

Along with the Conscious Mind (the Son, "Jesus" of the Bible) and the Subconscious Mind (the Servant, the "Holy Spirit" of the Bible), the Superconscious Mind (the Creator, the "Father" of the Bible) forms our Inner Holy Trinity.[4193] The keywords associated with the Superconscious Mind are: androgynous, light, perfection, omnipresent, omnipotent, omniscient, omniactive, manifestation, materialization, universal, infinite, eternal.[4194] See CONSCIOUS MIND, DIVINE MIND, FATHER, GOD, GODDESS, HOLY SPIRIT, JESUS, KEYS OF THE KINGDOM OF HEAVEN, MOTHER, SUBCONSCIOUS MIND, SUN.

Pagan Sun worship.

The Sun/Son-god Apollo and his solar chariot.

The Greek nature-god Pan.

Orpheus, founder of Orphism.

Pagan serpent worship.

TEACHER OF RIGHTEOUSNESS: In the traditional Church there is no Teacher of Righteousness, for he is not mentioned in the Bible. In the mystical Church, however, the Teacher of Righteousness is an important figure in the doctrines of the Nazarenes, or Jewish-Gnostic Essenes, the sect once centered at Qumran (in modern Israel's West Bank) and which gave rise to the authentic and first form of Christianity in Palestine.[4195] The Teacher of Righteousness, in fact, shares numerous similarities with Jesus, the "Sun of Righteousness."[4196]

Both were important Jewish teachers who were worshiped as messiah-like leaders by their followers,[4197] and who were persecuted and executed by orthodox Jewish authorities: the Teacher by the Jewish King Alexander Jannaeus around 65 B.C.,[4198] Jesus by the Roman Prefect Pontius Pilate around A.D. 33. Both men lived in the same country and their homes were only miles apart. There is a preponderance of evidence that Jesus was an Essene who lived at the Qumran Community near the Dead Sea (or at least that he often visited and studied there during His 18 "Silent Years" between the ages of 12 and 30).[4199]

Thus many believe that Jesus may have patterned His career and teachings on that of the earlier Essene leader (as our Lord's Essene-flavored Sermon on the Mount suggests).[4200] Some have even surmised that the two were one and the same man,[4201] namely the Teacher of Righteousness, who the early orthodox Church simply renamed Jesus in order to make Him appear uniquely Christian; or perhaps the Church combined two real historical figures for the same reason. Either way, if the two were separate individuals (as I believe) then the ruse was completely exposed 2,000 years later by the discovery of the Dead Sea Scrolls in 1947, which make frequent references to the Qumran spiritual leader, a separate but similar Jewish prophet who lived nearly a century before Jesus[4202] This exact thing occurred with the great spiritual leader Zoroaster, of whom it is said there were three individuals by this name living many years apart, who subsequent historians superimposed upon one another.[4203] Why then, many ask, could this not have happened with Jesus and the Teacher of Righteousness?

Springett provides the following details about the 1st-Century B.C. Essenes and their great "Teacher" Joshua, a name identical to "Jesus" (which is a late Greek form of the Hebrew Joshua):[4204]

Yet, though they lived in great purity of body and soul, they were evilly slandered by the people round about them on every side. But Jehovah prospered the seed of the Essenians, in holiness and love, for many generations. Then came the chief of the angels, according to the commandment of God, to raise up an heir to the Voice of Jehovah. And, in four generations more, an heir was born, and named Joshua, and he was the child of Joseph and Mara, devout worshippers of Jehovah, who stood aloof from all other people save the Essenians. And this Joshua, in Nazareth, re-established Jehovah, and restored many of the lost rites and ceremonies. In the thirty-sixth year of his age he was stoned to death in Jerusalem, by the Jews that worshipped the heathen gods.[4205]

If this view is correct, the Teacher of Righteousness, the "begotten Son of God" of the Qumran Essenes, was a prototype of Jesus,[4206] and the apotheosized miracle-working "Son of God"—who was created by Mark and the other three Evangelists from a variety of Pagan Sun/Son-gods (and later amplified and authorized by the theologically obsessed, creed-making Catholic Church)—was nothing more than a mythological character fabricated by His followers for the purpose of winning new Pagan converts.[4207]

In this way the gentle pacifist and human teacher Jesus (the "Son of Man"), whose focus was love and whose preaching centered on the "Gospel of the Kingdom of God,"[4208] was transformed into an all-powerful deity (the "Son of God"), whose focus was moral judgment and whose teaching centered on the "Gospel of Jesus Christ."[4209] And this despite our Lord's earnest protest: "Why callest thou me good? There is none good but one, that is, God."[4210] See BUDDHA, BRETHREN, CHRIST, CHRISTIANITY, DIVINITY OF JESUS, ENOCH, ESSENES, GNOSIS, GNOSTICISM, JESUS, KRISHNA, MESSIAH, MITHRA, MYTH OF CHRIST, OSIRIS, PYTHAGORAS, SAVIOR, SILENT YEARS, WAY OF THE LORD.

TEMPLE OF GOD: In the traditional Church the doctrine of the Temple of God is rarely considered, discussed, or even acknowledged. Hence, there are few if any mainstream Bible dictionaries with an entry under this phrase. In the mystical Church, where it is an important element of the esoteric Gospel, the Temple of God is the human mind, the invisible abode of the Indwelling Christ.[4211] More specifically, it is the "heart" or Subconscious Mind, the biblical "Holy Spirit," that piece of divinity which God has implanted in us.[4212] Thus Augustine could say:

> A pure mind is a holy temple for God, and a clean heart without sin is His best altar.[4213]

Paul writes:

Know ye not that *ye are the temple of God*, and that *the Spirit of God dwelleth in you?* If any man defile the temple of God, him shall God destroy; for *the temple of God is holy, which temple ye are.*[4214]

Emerson commented:

God builds his temple in the heart on the ruins of churches and religions.[4215]

Epictetus says:

If you always remember that in all you do, in soul or body, God stands by as a witness, in all your prayers and your actions you will not err; and you shall have God dwelling with you.[4216]

Ignatius writes:

The true temple are men in whom God dwells; the true place of promise is Jesus, who is manifested in the flesh. . . . Christ worked that we might obtain another type—might become in soul as children; He transforms us. The last formation, however, must be as the first: *a holy temple for the Lord shall the house of our heart be*; though the dominion over the world, which man has, shall be complete only in the future. How can God dwell in us? By His word that calls to faith, through His call to promise. He Himself predicts, *He Himself dwells in us, opening the door of the temple*, which we are, i.e., the mouth; granting us repentance, He carries us into the everlasting temple (by which he understands the inner man, to which also he ascribes self-legislation and self-counsel).[4217]

Seneca writes:

Temples are not to be built for God with stones piled on high. He is to be consecrated in the breast of each.[4218]

See CHRISTIANITY, CHURCH, THEOSIS, WORD OF GOD.

TETRAMORPH (CHRISTIAN): Though the Bible does not contain the word tetramorph, the object itself appears numerous times in the Good Book, and is integral to an understanding of both traditional and mystical Christianity.

Therefore it is included here.

    Tetramorph literally means "four bodies," and is not specifically Christian. The tetramorph, in one form or another, has existed since time immemorial. It is found in the cultural and religious remains of numerous Megalithic societies such as Mesopotamia, China, Egypt, and Sumeria,[4219] and ancient Ireland was once called the "Island of the Four Kings."[4220]

    The mystical symbolism of the tetramorph is elegant in its simplicity: as its name suggests, it is an archetypal emblem of all things related to the number four, and in particular all earthly and heavenly things connected to this number.[4221] These would include, above and foremost, the four fixed directions (east, west, north, south), the four fixed elements (fire, air, water, earth), and the four fixed seasons (Spring, Summer, Fall, Winter). The foundation of the Gnostics' entire belief system rested on a Divine Square whose four angles were "Silence," "Profundity," "Intelligence," and "Truth."[4222]

    As a *horizontal* symbol the tetramorph reflects those things that are material; as a *vertical* one it represents those things that are spiritual.[4223] Hence the importance of the cross, which possesses both of these tetramorphic elements, in mystical Christianity. Not surprisingly, during the time of Jesus the cross was a common symbol among both Pagans and Jews, the latter who enigmatically symbolized it in the obscure design known as the "Holy of Holies."[4224] What is the true significance of this, the cryptic *Sanctum Sanctorum*, the cross, and the Christian Tetramorph?

    The Holy of Holies, sometimes called the Oracle,[4225] was a six-sided cube, in ancient times often idealized as a perfectly square temple.[4226] Of its internal mystical qualities, Pike writes:

> If we delineate a cube on a plane surface thus: we have visible three faces, and nine external lines, drawn between seven points. The complete cube has three more faces, making six; three more lines, making twelve; and one more point, making eight. As the number 12 includes the sacred numbers 3, 5, 7, and 3 times 3, or 9, and is produced by adding the sacred number 3 to 9; while its own two figures, 1, 2, the unit or monad, and duad, added together, make the same sacred number 3; it was called the perfect number; and the cube became the symbol of perfection.[4227]

    When cut open and laid flat the cube presents a crucifix with *four arms*[4228] (which, along with the "fours" just listed, are also symbols of the four ages of the world, the four suits in a deck of cards, the four parts of Jesus' garments divided by the Roman soldiers, the four horns, angels, and beasts of Revelation, the four corners of the earth, the four Gospels, etc.) and *12 lines* and *12 intersecting points* (symbols of the 12 Sun-signs, the 12 months of the year, the 12 hours each of daytime and nighttime, the 12 years of Jesus' childhood, the 12 Tribes of Israel, the 12 Patriarchs, the 12 gates, foundations, angels, fruits, and pearls of Revelation, the 12 Apostles, etc.).[4229]

The chief object with which the tetramorph has long been associated, however, is the celebrated four compass gods of Pagan astrology,[4230] from whom it almost certainly derived. In the ancient Graeco-Roman world these were:

1) Aquila the Eagle (later Scorpio the Scorpion)
2) Leo the Lion
3) Aquarius the Water Bearer
4) Taurus the Bull

In astrology these four points are imaged as the Ascendant or rising sign (first house), the Nadir (fourth house), the Descendant (seventh house), and the Midheaven (tenth house). Though the placement of one's Sun-signs (and other astrological elements) in a horoscope are different depending on where and when one is born, these four points themselves are stationary and are thus considered one of the most important aspects of a natal chart. Hence their name: "fixed points."

In ancient societies the four compass gods were frequently depicted artistically on pottery, in temples, and in literature. In ancient China four animals were said to serve the nation's saints: the first was covered with feathers and the second with hair, both originating out of the Divine Feminine or Yin Principle. The third wore an animal skin and the fourth possessed scales, these two being birthed from the Divine Masculine or Yang Principle. In Sumeria archaeologists discovered another early tetramorph: a rendition of a peacock, eagle, and lion riding on the back of an ox.[4231] The ancient Roman Cult of Mithras possessed a "Cosmic Quadriga," comprised of four horses representing the four elements: fire, air, water, and earth.[4232]

In the ancient Egyptian *Book of the Dead* the "four gods" of the fixed compass points are named Mestha (with the head of a man), Hapi (with the head of an ape), Tuamautef (with the head of a jackal), and Qebhsennuf (with the head of a hawk).[4233] Here they were known variously as the "Fathers,"[4234] the "Children of Horus," the "Children of Osiris,"[4235] the "Friends of the King," and the "Souls of Horus."[4236] Of them Budge writes:

> The four children of Horus, or the gods of the four cardinal points, were called Mestha, Hapi, Tuamutef, and Qebhsennuf, and with them were associated the goddesses Isis, Nephthys, Neith, and Serqet respectively. Mestha was man-headed, and represented the south, and protected the stomach and large intestines; Hapi was dog-headed, and represented the north,

and protected the small intestines; Tuamutef was jackal-headed, and represented the east, and protected the lungs and the heart; and Qebhsennuf was hawk-headed, and represented the west, and protected the liver and the gall-bladder.

The various internal organs of men were removed from the body before it was mummified, and having been steeped in certain astringent substances and bitumen were wrapped up in bandages, and laid in four jars made of stone, marble, porcelain, earthenware, or wood. Each jar was placed under the protection of one of the four children of Horus, and as it was hollow, and its cover was made in the form of the head of the god who was represented by it, and as the jar by means of the inscription upon it became an abode of the god, it might well be said that the organ of the deceased which was put in it was actually placed inside the god.

. . . They originally represented the four supports of heaven, but very soon each was regarded as the god of one of the four quarters of the earth, and also of that quarter of the heavens which was above it. As the constant prayer of the deceased was that he should be able to go about wherever he pleased, both on earth and in heaven, it was absolutely necessary for his welfare that he should propitiate these gods and place himself under their protection, which could only be secured by the recital of certain words of power over figures of them, or over jars made to represent them.[4237]

In early India these same four fixed compass gods were known as the "Winged Globes" or the Maharajahs, who guard the four corners of Creation.[4238]

Naturally, as the great assimilators of Pagan myths, symbols, and rituals, Judaism and Christianity eventually adopted the idea of the astrological tetramorph. One of the earliest was the author of the book of Ezekiel, who wrote of "four living creatures":

And I looked, and, behold, a whirlwind came out of the north, a great cloud, and a fire infolding itself, and a brightness was about it, and out of the midst thereof as the colour of amber, out of the midst of the fire. Also out of the midst thereof came the likeness of *four living creatures*. And this was their appearance; they had the likeness of a man. And every one had four faces, and every one had four wings. And their feet were straight feet; and the sole of their feet was like the sole of a calf's foot: and they sparkled like the colour of burnished brass.

And they had the hands of a man under their wings on their four sides; and they four had their faces and their wings.

Their wings were joined one to another; they turned not when they went; they went every one straight forward. As for the likeness of their faces, *they four had the face of a man [Aquarius], and the face of a lion [Leo], on the right side: and they four had the face of an ox [Taurus] on the left side; they four also had the face of an eagle [Aquila-Scorpio].*[4239]

Contrary to popular opinion, as well as that of the mainstream Church, it is plain that the early Hebrews were practitioners of astrology, for here, from around 600 B.C., we have the perfect description of the four fixed compass gods or Sun-signs of the Pagan Zodiac.

In early Judaism these were sometimes known as the Cherubim. Mystical symbols of arcane wisdom, they were said to be the spiritual guardians of the four rivers of life flowing from God:[4240] the Pishon, the Gihon, the Tigris, and the Euphrates.[4241] Later, as the Jewish Tetramorph, these were mystically personified as Reuben (Aquarius), Judah (Leo), Ephraim (Taurus), and Dan (Aquila/Scorpio).[4242]

Ezekiel's four beasts also represent the four basic elements. In the Hebrew of mystical Judaism these are spelled out as: *Iammin*, "water"; *Nour*, "fire"; *Rouach*, "air"; and *Iebeschah*, "earth."[4243] The first letter of each Hebrew word spells INRI, an acronym, according to mainstream Christianity, representing the Latin: *Iesus Nazarenus, Rex Iudaeorum* ("Jesus of Nazareth, King of the Jews"),[4244] the sign on Jesus' cross.[4245] Mystically speaking, however, it is my theory that INRI is an acronym for the Latin: *In Nobis Regnat Iesus* ("Within Us Jesus Reigns"),[4246] for as mystic Paul noted: "Christ is all, and in all."[4247] Of these topics Pike writes:

> Hermes calls the Zodiac, the Great Tent,—Tabernaculum. In the [Freemasons'] Royal Arch Degree of the American Rite, the Tabernacle has four veils, of different colors, to each of which belongs a banner. The colors of the four are White, Blue, Crimson, and Purple, and the banners bear the images of the Bull, the Lion, the Man, and the Eagle, the Constellations answering 2500 years before our era to the Equinoctial and Solstitial points: to which belong four stars, Aldebaran, Regulus, Fomalhaut, and Antares. At each of these veils there are three words: and to each division of the Zodiac, belonging to each of these Stars, are three Signs. The four signs, Taurus, Leo, Scorpio, and Aquarius, were termed the fixed signs, and are appropriately assigned to the four veils.
>
> So the Cherubim, according to Clemens and Philo,

represented the two hemispheres; their wings, the rapid course of the firmament, and of time which revolves in the zodiac. "For the Heavens fly," says Philo, speaking of the wings of the Cherubim: which were winged representations of the Lion, the Bull, the Eagle, and the Man; of two of which, the human-headed, winged bulls and lions, so many have been found at Nimroud; adopted as beneficent symbols, when the Sun entered Taurus at the vernal equinox and Leo at the summer solstice: and when, also, he entered Scorpio, for which, on account of its malignant influences, Aquila, the eagle was substituted, at the autumnal equinox; and Aquarius (the water-bearer) at the winter solstice.[4248]

Some 700 years after Ezekiel, around A.D. 100, "John" (or more likely the Pagan philosopher Cerinthus),[4249] the Gnostic-Christian author of the book of Revelation (which was patterned on the Essenes' "War Scroll"),[4250] penned his own description of the Pagan tetramorph during his vision of God's Throne:

> After this I looked, and, behold, a door was opened in heaven: and the first voice which I heard was as it were of a trumpet talking with me; which said, "Come up hither, and I will shew thee things which must be hereafter." And immediately I was in the spirit: and, behold, a throne was set in heaven, and one sat on the throne. And he that sat was to look upon like a jasper and a sardine stone: and there was a rainbow round about the throne, in sight like unto an emerald.
> . . . And before the throne there was a sea of glass like unto crystal: and in the midst of the throne, and round about the throne, were *four beasts* full of eyes before and behind. And *the first beast was like a lion [Leo], and the second beast like a calf [Taurus], and the third beast had a face as a man [Aquarius], and the fourth beast was like a flying eagle [Aquila-Scorpio].*[4251]

By the end of the 1ˢᵗ Century A.D., the budding orthodox branch of the Church began to feel enormous pressure from several directions:

1) The enormous growth and popularity of Gnostic Christianity (the original form of Christianity, and thus the sworn enemy of the newly developing orthodox branch).[4252]
2) The writing of countless Gospels (currently scholars know of over 100 Gospels).[4253]
3) The "heretical challenge" thrown down by great Gnostic Marcion, who created

and compiled the first New Testament.[4254]

In response to these "pressures," the orthodox Church began to formulate its own New Testament.

By the beginning of the 2nd Century A.D., four specific Jewish-Christian Gospels had begun to circulate together: the Gospels of Matthew, Mark, Luke, and John.[4255] Because of their doctrinal conservatism, as well as their popularity in the mainstream churches, this "fourfold codex" began to be considered "canonical," and by the end of the 2nd Century the renowned Church Father Irenaeus declared them the "true Gospels," being exactly four in number, "no more, no less."[4256] (We will note that the final compilation of the New Testament, as we know it today, did not occur until A.D. 367).[4257]

Irenaeus' authorization of *four* books specifically, rather than three or five, was not an accident. Besides the fact that they were already coming into general acceptance, conventional Christianity maintains that his decision was based on the existence of the "four quarters of the earth," which allegedly correlate with the "fact" that Mark's Gospel was associated with Italy, Matthew's with Egypt, Luke's with Greece, and John's with Asia Minor (modern Turkey).[4258]

The truth, according to Irenaeus' own words however, is that he selected *four* Gospels because he correlated them with the "four angelic creatures of Ezekiel," the Jewish Tetramorph.[4259] This can only mean that he understood that the names "Matthew," "Mark," "Luke," and "John" were mystically associated with the cherubim (Ezekiel's four entities)—and probably Revelation's "four beasts" as well.[4260] But being orthodox, he could not let it be known that these creatures had been borrowed from the Pagans' four astrological compass gods: Aquarius, Leo, Taurus, and Aquila-Scorpio. And so by duplicity the four "Sons of Horus," the four corner constellations of the Zodiac, were duplicated in the four Evangelists, Pagan elements which entered the New Testament masquerading as Christian ones.[4261]

Thus, while the traditional Christian views the titles of the four canonical Gospels as "Christian," the mystical Christian reads them for what they really are: Pagan-Christian names permeated with mystical symbols, founded on occult doctrines taken straight from the ancient Egyptian Mysteries:

- "Matthew" is the Egyptian god Amset; thus his Gospel became astrologically associated with Aquarius the Winged Water Bearer, the direction east, the element air, the Divine Masculine, the Spring Equinox, childhood, birth, and the Spirit.[4262]
- "Mark" is the Egyptian god Hapi; thus his Gospel came to be astrologically connected with Leo the Lion, the direction south, the element fire, the Divine Feminine, the Summer Solstice, youth, growth, and the Soul.[4263]
- "John" is the Egyptian god Gebhsennuf; thus his Gospel was astrologically linked with Aquila the Eagle (later Scorpio), the direction west, the element

water, the Divine Feminine, the Autumnal Equinox, middle age, maturity, and the Mind.[4264]
- "Luke" is the Egyptian god Tuamutef; thus his Gospel became astrologically associated with Taurus the Bull, the direction north, the element earth, the Divine Masculine, the Winter Solstice, old age, decay, and the Body.[4265]

Being exoteric in nature, the traditional Church calls this group the "Christian Tetramorph." Being esoteric in nature, the mystical Church understands it as the four fixed astrological Sun-signs which form the Galactic Cross in the natal horoscope. Nonetheless, the traditional version held sway, which is why it can still be seen in the iconography of ancient Christian structures all over Europe, most notably France's famous Chartres Cathedral.[4266] In the apse of the Santa Pudenziana basilica in Rome, as another example, there is a 4th-Century mosaic portraying the Pagan-Jewish-Christian Tetramorph in pairs, one on each side of the crucifix.[4267]

Despite the massive and overt evidence of its Pagan origins, the majority of mainstream Christian scholars, educators, and clergymen and women continue to believe that the Christian Tetramorph is nothing more than an overly ornate Medieval representation of the Four Evangelists,[4268] whose symbolism was taken from the vision of Ezekiel.[4269] Christian mystics understand its deeper history and meanings. See APOSTLES, ASTROLOGY, FOUR HORSEMEN, GOSPEL, NUMBERS, TWELVE, ZODIAC.

THEALOGY: The word thealogy derives from the Greek word *thea* ("goddess") and the Latin word *logia* ("sayings"), thus meaning the "study of Goddess," or more generally, the study of female-based religions and spiritual practices. In other words, goddess-worship. While the orthodox deny the existence of goddess-worship within the Church, mystics accept that it has existed from the very beginning of Christianity, particularly in the recognition of the Virgin Mary, the Holy Spirit, Mary Magdalene, and a host of fake female saints that were patterned on various Pagan goddesses. Thus Christianity, which was born of a female-oriented Gnosticism, was at first essentially thealogical rather than theological.[4270] See CHRISTIANITY, FATHER, GNOSIS, GNOSTICISM, GODDESS, GODS AND GODDESSES, MARY, MOTHER, MYTH OF CHRIST, THEOLOGY, VIRGIN BIRTH, VIRGO.

THEOLOGY: The word theology derives from the Greek word *theo* ("god") and the Latin word *logia* ("sayings"), thus meaning the "study of God," or more generally the study of male-based religions and spiritual practices. In other words, god-worship. Though institutional Christianity is essentially patriarchal, from the beginning mystical Christianity has embraced matriarchal elements as well, and was, in fact, feministic in nature.[4271] See CHRISTIANITY, FATHER, GNOSIS,

GNOSTICISM, GOD, GODDESS, GODS AND GODDESSES, JESUS, MOTHER, MYTH OF CHRIST, PETER, THEALOGY.

THEOSIS: The word Theosis does not appear in the Bible, but it was taught by the Prophets, by our Lord and the Apostles, and later by *all* of the early Church Fathers. And because Christian mystics consider it the most important of all the spiritual concepts, it is included here.

The doctrine of Theosis, which means "God in Man," is not peculiar to Christianity. In fact, it is preached around the world in every major faith and philosophical school. Here, for example, is a partial list of some of them (I have included Christianity for context), along with their primary Theosistic doctrine:

Taoism: "Man consisting of a trinity of spirit, mind and body, cometh forth from the Eternal, and after putting off desire re-enters the glory of Tao."[4272]
Brahmanism: "Man's inner self is one with the self of the Universe, and to that Universe and to that Unity it must return in the fullness of time."[4273]
Buddhism: "Man, fundamentally Divine, is held in the three worlds by desire. Purification from desire leads the man to Nirvana."[4274]
Hebrewism: "Man came into being through emanation from the will of the King, therefore is divine."[4275]
Egyptianism (ancient): "Teaches the divinity of man, Osiris as his source."[4276]
Zoroastrianism: "Man is a spark of the universal flame to be ultimately united with its source."[4277]
Orphism: "Man has in him potentially the sum and substance of the Universe."[4278]
Jesusism: "Ye are gods."[4279]
Christianity: "Man made in the image of God—Body, Soul and Spirit—a Trinity."[4280]
Paulism: "Ye are the temple of the living God."[4281]
Johnism: "The true Light, which lighteth every man that cometh into the world."[4282]
Peterism: We are all "partakers of the divine nature."[4283]
Quakerism: "Every man is enlightened by the divine Light of Christ, and it shines through all."[4284]
Blakeism: "Jesus Christ is the only God, and so am I, and so are you."[4285]
Whitmanism: "Divine am I inside and out, and I make holy whatever I touch."[4286]
Emersonism: "The highest revelation is that God is in every man."[4287]
Böhmeism: "I am not collecting my knowledge from letters and books, but I have it within my own Self; because heaven and earth with all their inhabitants, and moreover God himself, is in man."[4288]

When we add all of these spiritual expressions into one doctrine, in essence we get, as Trine writes, the fact that the life of God and the life of man are identically the same, and so are one.[4289]

This is due to the fact that in order to experience his earthly creations and spread spiritual light across the darkness of the physical Universe, God had to become human; or rather, needed to implant a piece of himself within Man and Woman.[4290] This "divine spark" (God's "image" created in Mankind)[4291] is known as "the Christ" by mystical Christians, "Buddha" by Buddhists, "Krishna" by Hindus, and so on.[4292] Thus all human beings are born with a "divine ray" of light in them, making us literal gods and goddesses in our own right—just as Jesus,[4293] Paul,[4294] John,[4295] Peter,[4296] and the rest of the first Christians, the Essenes and Gnostics, taught. In psychological terms one could say that the Divine is always endeavoring to come to consciousness in us.[4297] This is why, for the Christian mystic, spiritual growth should always be "in the direction of a practical, working realization of the immanence of God and the Divinity of man's true, inner self."[4298]

Let us look at some of the primary Theosis traditions more closely.

Just as the Old Testament prophets said we are all deities,[4299] just as Jesus said we are all gods,[4300] just as Paul said we are all "sons of Gods,"[4301] "one in Christ,"[4302] and just as God Himself said that we are all immortal supernatural beings,[4303] the Hindus too teach that we are each what they refer to as "avatars": sparks of divinity that have descended from Heaven to incarnate into mortal bodies. God is not just inside of us. He is our very self.[4304]

Why are we individuations of God, pieces of humanity implanted with the Divine Essence?

Jesus phrased it this way: "He that hath seen me hath seen the Father."[4305] The inner meaning: "He that has realized his union with the Indwelling Christ-Self has realized his oneness with the Divine Mind."[4306] Paul referred to this mystically as "winning Christ,"[4307] while the Essenic Hebraist asserted that the spiritually mature will become "partakers of his holiness."[4308] This makes clear the true significance of this statement by God, the Divine Mind: "I AM holy."[4309]

Thus all can say, along with the Psalmist, "I AM holy,"[4310] for the real you is the I AM, which is a piece of the Father, and he is truly holy. This means that we too, not just Jesus, possess a hypostatic nature in which both our human and divine aspects are one.[4311] For like the Lord, in each of us "dwelleth all the fulness of the Godhead bodily," making us *complete in Him.*[4312]

We are all one within, one with the Cosmos, and one with each other, for God himself is one.[4313] Being birthless, ageless, deathless, timeless, and boundless, however, he could not know himself. In order to do so, he had to individuate himself as finite matter. This he did by creating earthly life, which means that each one of us is a thought of the Divine Mind, or in biblical terminology, a "child of God." We are all an aspect of the immeasurable, inexhaustible, everlasting Father, who is expressing himself through us. You are, in other words, the infinite consciousness of God, the Great and Limitless I AM.[4314]

The Victorian English biologist Herbert Spencer described God and our relationship to him this way:

> God is infinite intelligence, infinitely diversified through infinite time and infinite space, manifesting through an infinitude of ever-lasting individualities.

Here is this same concept in the words of Jesus as recorded by John:

> I am in my Father, and ye in me, and I in you.[4315]

Here is another one of our Lord's comments on Theosis, this one from Matthew:

> Be ye therefore perfect, even as your Father which is in heaven is perfect.[4316]

Jesus is telling us that the ideal of realizing the nature of God within us is not just possible, it is a commandment.[4317]

Though many modern Christian authorities reject Jesus' doctrine of Theosis—that is, God's deification of humanity—the early Church Fathers heartily embraced this, the great Master Secret, imparted by our Lord some 2,000 years ago. Here is what one of them, the 3rd-Century theologian Hippolytus of Rome, says about it:

> For *thou hast become God*: for whatever sufferings thou didst undergo while being a man, these He gave to thee, because thou wast of mortal mould, but whatever it is consistent with God to impart, these God has promised to bestow upon thee, because *thou hast been deified, and begotten unto immortality*. This constitutes the import of the proverb, "Know thyself"; that is, *discover God within thyself, for He has formed thee after His own image*. For with the knowledge of self is conjoined the being an object of God's knowledge, for *thou art called by the Deity Himself*.[4318]

Likewise, Saint Augustine writes:

> And *we indeed recognize in ourselves the image of God*, that is, of the supreme Trinity, an image which, though it be not equal to God, or rather, though it be very far removed from Him,—being neither co-eternal, nor, to say all in a word,

> consubstantial with Him,—*is yet nearer to Him in nature than any other of His works, and is destined to be yet restored, that it may bear a still closer resemblance. For we both are, and know that we are, and delight in our being, and our knowledge of it.*[4319]

The estimable 4th-Century theologian also stated that

> man is most properly understood . . . to be *made in God's image.*[4320]

Citing 2 Peter 1:4, Athanasius, the 4th-Century Bishop of Alexandria, said this about the divinization of human beings:

> He [Jesus] has become Man, *that He might deify us in Himself*, and He has been born of a woman, and begotten of a Virgin, in order to transfer to Himself our erring generation, and *that we may become henceforth a holy race*, and *"partakers of the Divine Nature,"* as blessed Peter wrote.[4321]

The 4th-Century Archbishop of Constantinople, Gregory of Nazianzus, explained Theosis this way:

> For He [Jesus] whom you now treat with contempt was once above you. He who is now Man was once the Uncompounded. What He was He continued to be; what He was not He took to Himself. In the beginning He was uncaused; for what is the Cause of God? But afterwards for a cause He was born. And that cause was that you might be saved, who insult Him and despise His Godhead, because of this, that He took upon Him your denser nature, having converse with flesh by means of Mind. While *His inferior Nature, the Humanity, became God, because it was united to God*, and became One Person because the Higher Nature prevailed . . . *in order that I too might be made God so far as He is made Man.*[4322]

Based on Jesus' teaching that we are gods,[4323] the 2nd-Century theologian, Clement of Alexandria, left us this instruction on Divine Man:

> . . . and they [humans] are called by the appellation of gods, being *destined to sit on thrones with the other gods* that have been first put in their places by the Savior.[4324]

The 4th-Century Bishop of Nyssa, Saint Gregory, wrote:

> This is the safest way to protect the good things you enjoy: realize how much your Creator has honored you above all other creatures. He did not make the heavens in His image, nor the moon, the sun, the beauty of the stars, nor anything else which surpasses all understanding. *You alone are a similitude of eternal beauty, a vessel of happiness, a mirror image of the True Light. And if you look at Him, you will become what He is, imitating Him who shines within you, whose glory is reflected in your purity.* Nothing in all of creation can equal your grandeur. All the heavens can fit in the palm of God's hand. . . . And though He is so great, *you can wholly embrace Him: He dwells within you. He pervades your entire being.*[4325]

In his massive work, *Summa Theologica*, the 13th-Century Italian saint and theologian Thomas Aquinas made this comment:

> . . . when it is said that "God was made Man," the making is taken to be terminated in the human nature. Hence, *properly speaking, this is true: "God was made Man."*[4326]

Ancient Pagan intellectuals also embraced the doctrine of Theosis. The last words of Plotinus are nearly as famous as he is:

> Strive to bring back the god in yourselves to the divine in the universe.[4327]

Paul commented on the mental attitude we should take in understanding Theosis, for it is the same one promulgated by Jesus' Indwelling Christ:

> Let this mind be in you, which was also in Christ Jesus: Who, being in the form of God, thought it not robbery to be equal with God.[4328]

Even though our souls are temporarily encased in physical bodies, "it is not robbery to believe that we are actually equal to God," saith Paul!

The Gospel of Barnabas (named after the Apostle and traveling companion of Paul) contains the following passage:

> Now do this in the service of God, with the law that God hath given you through Moses, for in such wise shall ye find God that

in every time and place ye shall feel that *ye are in God and God in you*.[4329]

Can Jesus, the Apostles, the Old Testament prophets, and the Church Fathers, educated Pagans, and even God Himself, all be wrong about a spiritual doctrine that has been in place since the beginning of historical records, among all people, in all societies, in all religions, right up and into modern times? Here is what the 19th-Century American poet Walt Whitman says about God in Man:

> What do you suppose I would intimate to you in a hundred ways but that man or woman is as good as God? And there is no God any more divine than yourself.[4330]

Saint John of the Cross writes:

> *God is always in every soul.* . . . *O how blessed is that soul which is ever conscious of God reposing and resting within it.* . . . He is there, as it were, asleep in the embraces of the soul and the soul is in general conscious of His presence and in general delights exceedingly in it. If He were always awake in the soul the communications of knowledge and love would be unceasing, and that would be a state of glory. If He awakes but once, merely opening his eyes, and affects the soul so profoundly, what would become of it if He were continually awake within it?[4331]

It is apparent that, despite all the tortured scripture twisting that John 10:34 has undergone by the unenlightened, Jesus meant exactly what he said: we are all divine beings, possessing all of the qualities and powers of a supernatural deity, of the Creator himself, in fact. Speaking as the Indwelling Christ, this is precisely what Jesus meant when He said to God (Divine Mind) that "everything I have is yours and everything you have is mine."[4332] Or as Paul put it:

> The Spirit itself beareth witness with our spirit, that we are the children of God: and if children, then heirs; heirs of God, and joint-heirs with Christ; if so be that we suffer with him, that we may be also *glorified together*.[4333]

This is Paul's way of expressing what Emerson said nearly 2,000 years later: "The highest revelation is that God is in every man,"[4334] and which Jesus declared only decades earlier: "You are gods."[4335] This is the selfsame doctrine promulgated by the enlightened in every part of the globe, and in every faith, under every Supreme

Being, whatever his or her name.[4336] According to the Father himself, Theosis is an absolute reality:

> I will dwell in them, and walk in them; and I will be their God, and they shall be my people.[4337]

Hindus daily acknowledge the Indwelling God using the customary greeting *namaste*, a Sanskrit word meaning "I bow to you." But the "I" and the "you" here do not refer to the personal ego, but to the Interior Deity. Therefore the inferred (mystical) meaning is "the divinity within me salutes the divinity within you."[4338] Christian mystics believe that recognizing, accepting, and actuating this Eternal Truth is the very purpose of incarnating on earth.[4339] See CHRIST, CHRIST CONSCIOUSNESS, CHRISTIANITY, DIVINITY OF JESUS, GOSPEL, JESUS, KARMA, MESSIAH, NATIVITY, ORIGINAL SIN, REDEEMER, REDEMPTION, SIN, SOUL, SPIRIT, WAY OF THE LORD.

THIRD EAR: Belief in the Third Ear is not found in traditional Christianity. But because it is so often referenced in the Bible, particularly by Jesus, it is accepted and taught in mystical Christianity, where it alludes to intuition. See EARS, EYES, GNOSIS, I AM, THIRD EYE.

THIRD EYE: Belief in the Third Eye, located in the center of the forehead, is not found in traditional Christianity. Yet, the Bible writers often mystically reference it, as does our Lord and Savior Jesus. Thus it is accepted and taught in mystical Christianity.

The Third Eye is depicted esoterically throughout all mythology. For example, the giant Greek Cyclops, a member of the folkloric "one-eyed race," is the most obvious personification of this occult organ.[4340] The Old Testament authors, like the mystical writers of fairy tales, however, knew it as the unicorn,[4341] which was believed by them to have great strength and a single magical horn growing from its forehead.[4342] Paul knew the Third Eye as "the eyes of your understanding."[4343] Jesus liked to contrast two-eyed physical vision (intellectual perception) with single-eyed spiritual vision (intuitive perception); meaning that the "Third Eye" is identical to the great I AM or EYE AM.[4344] Saith our Lord:

> The light of the body is the [Third] eye [intuition]: if therefore thine eye be *single* [spiritual], thy whole body shall be full of light [enlightenment]. But if thine eye be evil [*double*, the two physical eyes, tuition], thy whole body shall be full of darkness [spiritual ignorance]. If therefore the light that is in thee be darkness, how great is that darkness![4345]

The following mystical passage from Ephesians is now understandable:

> For ye were sometimes darkness, but now are ye light in the Lord: walk as children of light.[4346]

The Third Eye, which is also associated by mystics with the pineal gland,[4347] goes by many other names as well, depending on the religion. For example: the Eye of Shiva, the Inner Eye, the Star of the East, the Star of Bethlehem, Ajna, the Dove Descending From Heaven, and the Eye of Intuition. The Third Eye is associated with the Brow (sixth) Chakra and sometimes the Crown (seventh) Chakra, as well as shamanic sight or clairvoyance.

Where did Jesus learn about the Third Eye (not to mention hundreds of other esoteric doctrines) if it is not mentioned by that name in the Old Testament? This same question was asked of the Master by His own followers.[4348] According to mystical Christian tradition, Jesus picked it up during His 18 "Silent Years" (between ages 12 and 30), during which time He was traveling throughout the Near and Middle East studying under the great Pagan teachers of His Day.[4349] See CHRISTIANITY, EARS, EYES, GNOSIS, GNOSTICISM, I AM, SILENT YEARS.

THREE DAYS: In traditional Christianity the three days motif is linked with Jesus, who is said to have risen from His burial tomb after "three days."[4350] Here it is, as one mainstream Christian scholar simplistically put it, merely the Bible writer's way of "describing a decisive change"![4351] In early Palestinian Judaism the third day after death was significant because it was believed that this was the moment the soul finally left the body (which is why mourning for the deceased reached its peak on the third day).[4352] In mystical Christianity, however, the three day motif is recognized as an important occultly loaded theme that is found in all religions.

The 1st-Century, virgin-born Pagan philosopher Apollonius of Tyana, for instance, was said to have "died" on a cross and come back to life after three days in a rock tomb.[4353] As part of the ancient Mystery Religions aspirants were "kept in terror and darkness to perform the Three Days and Nights."[4354] The Passion Feast of the pre-Christan Savior Attis "continued three days; the first of which was passed in mourning and tears; to which afterward clamorous rejoicings succeeded."[4355] In the *Tibetan Book of the Dead* we are told that at "death," after the spirit separates from the physical body, we enter Heaven where there is an immediate life review, and then a three-day period of rest or "sleep," after which one is met by deceased family members and friends.[4356] Jesus' mother, the Virgin Mary, is said to have risen bodily into Heaven "three days" after her burial,[4357] while her 12 year old son was lost for "three days" before being discovered at the Jerusalem Temple.[4358] The question is, why *three* days specifically?

Esoterically, "Jesus" is the Sun, His burial "tomb" is Winter, and the "three days" is an astronomical peculiarity that occurs at the Winter Solstice, the "birthday of the Sun." When the Sun reaches its nadir beginning on or around the Winter Solstice (approximately December 22), it takes three days before its "rebirth" is visibly apparent in the sky. Though one would expect the Sun to begin noticeably rising earlier beginning on the Winter Solstice, there is actually a brief three-day delay before it *appears* to do so.[4359]

This lag event falls, of course, on December 25, which is why most of the pre-scientific, pre-Christian christs, saviors, and Sun-gods were said to have been born on that day rather than precisely on the day of the Winter Solstice three days earlier. It was for this same reason as well that the ancient Egyptian Phoenix, another manifestation of the Sun, was said to have risen from the ashes at Heliopolis after three days,[4360] and that the Egyptian Savior/Sun-god Horus was "buried three days, was regenerated, and triumphed over the evil principle."[4361]

This astronomical-astrological phenomenon is linked to another curious three day event in the heavens, one that is also celebrated in the religions, doctrines, legends, and myths of every known people and civilization:[4362] the three "dark days" of the Moon.[4363] Here, at the end of the 28-day lunar cycle, there are three days in which the Moon is invisible (called the "Dark of the Moon"), before it begins its cycle over as the "New Moon." As with its solar partner, to make sense of this the ancients held that the Moon was a deity (usually a goddess), who was "born" at the New Moon, "matured" at the Full Moon, "grew old" at the Waning Moon, and finally "died" at the Dark of the Moon. Following her "death," so they believed, the Moon-goddess visited the Underworld (Hell) for three days, where she was renewed and "born again" as the New Moon.[4364]

Early on these two three day Pagan motifs, the solar and the lunar, were assimilated by Old Testament mythographers and scribes, and are still well-known to this day in the tales of individuals like Moses (who cast a "thick darkness" on Egypt for three days),[4365] Jonah (who "was in the belly of the fish three days and three nights"),[4366] and Hosea (who declared that "in the third day God will raise us up").[4367] It was only natural that this three day theme was later adopted by New Testament writers as well, appearing most notably in our Lord's biography as the three days and nights which the Son of Man was to spend in "the heart of the earth" (Hell),[4368] the three days in which He would destroy and rebuild the "temple of God,"[4369] and the three days between His death and resurrection.[4370] Today the Bible as a whole contains over 100 references to this mystical concept, one deeply connected to the Trinity, or three bodies of man: spirit, soul, and body.[4371]

The three day source myth was appended to the figure of the Master during the Catholic Church's tragic Paganization process known as the "Scheme of Salvation."[4372] Here, the very human Jesus was apotheosized, transformed into a Pagan Sun-god for the uneducated, literalistic, formalistic, dogmatic masses, who could not hope to understand the nuances of Jesus' true and all too esoteric teachings.[4373] In this way the mystical became the literal, "the spirit which giveth life" was replaced by "the letter which killeth,"[4374] and the "gross superstitions" of the Church,[4375] the countless "fictions of theologians,"[4376] the great "theological lie" of the New Testament, the "web of deceit" spun by the four Evangelists,[4377] and the "regrettable accretions foisted on by superstition to the pure morality of the original Gospel,"[4378] entered orthodox Christian doctrine as "historical tradition." See CHRIST, CHRISTIANITY, CHRISTMAS, DIVINITY OF JESUS, GNOSTICISM, GOSPEL, JESUS, MYTH OF CHRIST, SON OF GOD, SON OF MAN.

TRANSFIGURATION OF JESUS: In the traditional Church the Transfiguration of Jesus is the moment our Lord was visibly glorified.[4379] This occurred before three eyewitnesses: the Apostles Peter, James, and John.[4380] According to Matthew:

> And after six days Jesus taketh *Peter, James, and John* his brother, and bringeth them up into an high mountain apart, and was transfigured before them: and *his face did shine as the sun, and his raiment was white as the light*. And, behold, there appeared unto them *Moses and Elias* talking with him. Then answered Peter, and said unto Jesus, "Lord, it is good for us to be here: if thou wilt, let us make here three tabernacles; one for thee, and one for Moses, and one for Elias." While he yet spake, behold, a bright cloud overshadowed them: and behold a voice out of the cloud, which said, "This is my beloved Son, in whom I am well pleased; hear ye him." And when the disciples heard [it], they fell on their face, and were sore afraid. And Jesus came and touched them, and said, "Arise, and be not afraid." And when they had lifted up their eyes, they saw no man, save Jesus only.[4381]

The orthodox assert that the "Evangelists describe it as a historical event."[4382] Revealingly, however, though John was said to be present at the Transfiguration, he neglected to mention this important incident in his Gospel. And in the Synoptic Gospels the name of the mountain on which this event takes place is not given, a staggering omission.[4383] These are but a few clues that the entire event was allegorical in nature. Indeed, this is the reason orthodox Bible scholars are still confused by the Transfiguration, to this day maintaining that "it is impossible to reconstruct it completely." At the same time they grudgingly admit that it was "ecstatic in character";[4384] that is, it was a mystical experience, not a real one!

Christian mystics have no such difficulties with the Transfiguration, for according to the ancient arcana:

> *The Spiritual meaning of anything is its real meaning. Physical things*

are but shadows or symbols of Spiritual realities. When Jesus spoke of physical bread it was really Spiritual bread he meant. *It is impossible for a deeply Spiritual being, such as He is represented to be, to speak of physical things without having in his mind their Spiritual equivalents.*[4385]

Transfiguration is a pre-Christian concept known as "metamorphosis," a divine power which gods and goddesses used to alter their form and appearance.[4386] Hence, this notion, along with "salvation" and "rebirth," was a common theme in the Pagan Mystery Religions,[4387] with numerous examples to be found in ancient mythology. Krishna (Chrishna), for example, experienced transfiguration,[4388] as did Buddha, both from whom the Transfiguration of Jesus was later copied. This is why, since time immemorial, all three have been known by the same titles, such as "The Lords of Enlightened Love."[4389] Writes Titcomb:

> It is said that towards the end of his life *Buddha was transfigured on Mount Pandava*, in Ceylon. Suddenly *a flame of light descended upon him*, and *encircled the crown of his head with a circle of light*. His body became *"glorious as a bright, golden image,"* and shone as the brightness of the Sun and moon. *"His body was divided into three parts [the three 'Apostles' of Jesus], from each of which a ray of light issued forth."* It is recorded, in the sacred canon of the Buddhists, that the multitude required a sign from Buddha, that they might believe.[4390]

Likewise Evans writes:

> The Transfiguration [of Jesus] finds a parallel in the light which streamed from Buddha's body as he lay dying under a tree—a light so brilliant as to outshine the glitter of a gold-embroidered robe in which a pious disciple had just enveloped him. In the case of Jesus, as in that of Buddha, the illumination occurred in connection with the announcement of approaching death.[4391]

But this is all metaphoric. Thus in mystical Christianity the entire Transfiguration-of-Jesus allegory is unveiled by the description of our Lord as the "shining Sun" whose clothing "was white as the light." As the Sun is always a mystical symbol of the Higher Self or Indwelling Christ, this story is an illustration of the raising up of the Lower Self (Jesus) by the Higher Self (Christ), a spiritual paradigm that is meant to apply to everyone.

Likewise, Moses here represents Man's ethical nature, while Elijah (later to reincarnate as John the Baptist)[4392] represents our psychic nature.[4393] The three

Apostles on the scene, who are also esoteric symbols (otherwise John, an eyewitness, would have mentioned the event), signify the Holy Trinity of body (Peter), heart (James), and mind (John). On this topic Kingsford and Maitland write:

> [The relation of Buddha and Pythagoras] to the system of Jesus, as its necessary pioneers and forerunners, finds recognition in the Gospels under the allegory of the Transfiguration. For the forms beheld in this—of Moses and Elias—are the Hebrew correspondences of Buddha and Pythagoras. And they are described as beheld by the three Apostles in whom respectively are typified the functions severally fulfilled by Pythagoras, Buddha, and Jesus; namely, Works, Understanding, and Love, or Body, Mind, and Heart. And by their association on the Mount is denoted the junction of all three elements, and the completion of the whole system comprising them, in Jesus as the representative of the Heart or Innermost, and as in a special sense the "beloved Son of God."[4394]

Channing writes:

> True Christians give a sanctifying power, a glory to the place of worship where they come together. In them Christ is present and manifested in a far higher sense than if he were revealed to the bodily eye. We are apt, indeed, to think differently. Were there a place of worship in which a glory like that which clothed Jesus on the Mount of Transfiguration were to shine forth, how should we throng to it as the chosen spot on earth! How should we honour this as eminently [as] his church! But there is a more glorious presence of Christ than this. It is Christ formed in the souls of his disciples.[4395]

See BUDDHA, CHRIST, JESUS, JOHN THE BAPTIST, KRISHNA, MESSIAH, MITHRA, MOSES, OSIRIS, PYTHAGORAS, TEACHER OF RIGHTEOUSNESS.

TREE OF LIFE: As is its custom, in the traditional Church the Tree of Life is literalized, and it is thus seen as a "special"[4396] but "unidentifiable" *real* tree that grew in the midst of the Garden of Eden,[4397] of which, when partaken, the gift of immortality was given.[4398] But the fact that the Tree of Life also grows in the Heavenly City, the "New Jerusalem,"[4399] gives its occult identity away, as even St. Ambrose understood.[4400] Thus in the mystical Church, just as trees are symbols of Man (both exist halfway between two worlds, above in heaven and below on earth),[4401] the Tree of Life is a symbol of the perfect human being,[4402] that is of God; or more specifically, the Word or Wisdom of God.[4403]

In the Mystery Schools wisdom is always feminine, and so among the ancient Greeks she was personified as the goddess Sophia[4404] (who some assert gave her name to the Sufis, or "Wise Ones");[4405] among the Romans she was Sapientia;[4406] among the Estruscans she was Vegoia; among the Scandinavians she was Snotra; among the Iroquois she was Genetaska; among the Hindus she is Saranya; among the early Irish she was Ceibhfhionn;[4407] and among the Hebrews she was Shekinah.[4408] Using the pronoun "she," the Bible itself openly states that the Tree of Life is the Wisdom of the Goddess:

> Happy is the man that findeth wisdom, and the man that getteth understanding. For the merchandise of it is better than the merchandise of silver, and the gain thereof than fine gold. *She* [Shekinah] is more precious than rubies: and all the things thou canst desire are not to be compared unto *her*. Length of days is in *her* right hand; and in *her* left hand riches and honour.
>
> *Her* ways are ways of pleasantness, and all her paths are peace. *She is a tree of life to them that lay hold upon her: and happy is every one that retaineth her.* The Lord by wisdom [Sophia] hath founded the earth; by understanding hath he established the heavens. By his knowledge [Gnosis] the depths are broken up, and the clouds drop down the dew.[4409]

Augustine understood, writing:

> The Tree of Life would seem to have been in the terrestrial Paradise what the wisdom of God is in the spiritual, of which it is written [in the Bible], "She is a tree of life to them that lay hold upon her."[4410]

The Tree of Life also represents not only the Creative Life Force,[4411] but also the primordial paradise or perfect world,[4412] and is thus sometimes viewed as the *Axis Mundi*, or "World Axis," a symbol of an orderly Universe under the guidance and protection of God. For Christian mystics it also signifies both the wisdom of the Holy Spirit and Christ (the Indwelling Christ), the "true tree of life," whose spiritual fruit nourishes believers but which is inedible to the Devil (Ego).[4413] Jewish mystics image the ten Sefiroth (or emanations of the Godhead)[4414] of the Kabbalah as the Tree of Life,"[4415] each emanation which also exists in Man[4416]—which is why the Sefiroth is also sometimes portrayed as a human body.[4417] For man is a microcosm of the world; a universe in miniature.

As dendrolatry (tree worship and tree cults) predate even human history, it is not surprising that variations of the Judeo-Christian "Tree of Life" were appearing in the myths of various religions and peoples thousands of years prior to the writing of the Bible, from places as far apart as India, Syria, and Germany.[4418] For example, Osiris was born out of a tree, Attis was sacrificed on a pine tree, Odin was hanged on the Yggdrasil tree, and Buddha attained enlightenment under the Bodhi tree.[4419] Our Christmas tree—in mystical Christianity a symbol of Jesus as the Tree of Life[4420]—is a descendant of this same common and universal vegetation motif,[4421] most all which date, of course, from ancient Egypt. Barlow writes:

> . . . Sacred Trees are met with among all ancient nations, from China to Scandinavia—the palm, the sycamore, the fig tree, the oak, the ash, and some others which might be mentioned; a divine influence was believed to be present about them; in some instances God himself was imagined to inhabit them, and they were held in devout veneration, or worshipped with religious awe.
>
> In the "Tree of Life" of the Egyptians, we have perhaps the earliest, certainly the most complete and consistent representation of this most ancient and seemingly universal symbol—the "Tree of Life," in the midst of Paradise, *furnishing the divine support of immortality*.
>
> And what does this tree mean? In the Scriptures we read that "man doth not live by bread alone, but by every word that proceedeth out of the mouth of God." Here we have a key to the symbolical teaching, itself symbolically explained. *The divine word is the support of the divine life; they who live by it shall never die*. "Whoso receiveth me and my word," saith our Lord, "I will raise him up again at the last day." We have the authority of St. Augustine, that the Egyptians firmly believed in a resurrection from the dead, and their sacred monuments show that they did so, at least during one period of their highly-civilized history.
>
> The "Bread of Life," and the fruit of the "Tree of Life," and the "Water of Life," are all significant of one and the same thing—*the divine nourishment of the soul unto everlasting life*. And this primitive doctrine, which has never changed, is, it would seem, dimly, yet not obscurely, traceable among the Gentile nations in the religious associations of ideas symbolized by their sacred trees.[4422]

The Tree of Life is also a symbol of the "spinal fire," or human spine,[4423] up which the human consciousness (the Kundalini "Serpent" of Genesis) must ascend through the seven tree blossoms (chakras, John's "seven churches of Asia") to reach the "crown" of the tree (Christ Consciousness).[4424]

In short, the Tree of Life is a mystical symbol of the "birth," "life," "death," and "resurrection" of the human spirit as it progresses by self-mastery through involution (the earth plane) and evolution (the heavenly plane). Knowledge of this great eternal truth brings the realization that our real Self, the Indwelling Christ, is immortal. And it is this knowledge of the Self that is salvation![4425] This is the true meaning and "fruit" of the Tree of Life—before it was perverted by the unenlightened scribes of Genesis. See ADAM, BETHLEHEM, BREAD, CROSS, EDEN, EVE, GARDEN OF EDEN, SATAN, SERPENT, WATER.

TRIBES OF ISRAEL (12): In the traditional Church the 12 Tribes of Israel are descendants of one of the 12 sons of the patriarch Jacob: Gad, Joseph, Benjamin, Issachar, Judah, Zebulon, Levi, Dan, Asher, Naphtali, Reuben, and Simeon.[4426] In the mystical Church the 12 Tribes of Israel are symbols of the 12 Sun-signs of the Zodiac, which are, in turn, symbols of profound esoteric truths and hidden wisdom related to spiritual involution and evolution:

1) Gad, Aries the Ram.
2) Joseph, Taurus the Bull.
3) Benjamin, Gemini the Twins.
4) Issachar, Cancer the Crab.
5) Judah, Leo the Lion.
6) Zebulon, Virgo the Virgin.
7) Levi, Libra the Scales.
8) Dan, Scorpio the Scorpion.
9) Asher, Sagittarius the Archer.
10) Naphtali, Capricorn the Goat.
11) Reuben, Aquarius the Water Bearer.
12) Simeon, Pisces the Two Fishes.[4427]

Jukes writes:

> Without, our eyes can see the immense variety of tribes which have come forth from Adam, all of which are but various forms or manifestations of man or human nature. But within, though secret and hidden, the outcome is the same. Old Adam in us brings forth as many different minds, each of which throughout the book of Genesis is figured and set before us in some son of Adam, or Noah, or Shem, or Ham, or Japhet; some outward, some inward, some sensual, some natural, some spiritual, and this in different measures; the elect all representing some form

of the spiritual mind in us; the non-elect, some form of that mind which is earthly, sensual, devilish.[4428]

De Bunsen comments:

> The temptations come from within, and they can be resisted. For "of his own will" the Father of Lights, the source of every good and perfect gift, has begotten "us," the Israel of the twelve tribes, including the Christians as in the Apocalypse, "with the word of truth, that we should be a kind of first-fruit of his creatures."[4429]

Swedenborg notes:

> Of all the tribes of the children of Israel, signifies the Lord's heaven and church composed of them. By a tribe is signified religion as to good of life, and by every tribe is signified the church as to every good of love and as to every truth from that good in which good of life originates; for there are two things which constitute a church—good of life, and truth of doctrine; the marriage of these is the church. The twelve tribes of Israel represented, and thence signified the church as to that marriage, and *each tribe some universal truth of good or good of truth therein*.
> But what each tribe signifies has not been revealed to any one, nor could be revealed, lest, by an ill-connected explanation, the sanctity which lies concealed in their several conjunctions into one, should be profaned, for their signification is determined by their conjunction. They have one signification in the series in which they are named according to their nativities.[4430]

Dunlap writes:

> [The number] twelve points to the twelve signs of the Zodiac or to the twelve months.[4431]

Higgins elucidates:

> The observation made respecting the twelve Caesars only applies to a part of a universal mythos. There were twelve tribes of Israel, who all assembled to worship at one temple. There were twelve tribes of Ionians, who all assembled in like

manner at one temple. There were twelve tribes of Etruscans, who all assembled at one temple; and who, by colonies, founded twelve tribes in Campania, and twelve more in the Apennine mountains. There were twelve Caesars, and twelve Imaums of Persia, followers of Ali, all believed to be foretold by Esdras.[4432]

When Moses built a Druidical temple near to Sinai, he set up twelve stones; at Gil-Gal again twelve unhewn stones, and on Gerizim, again, twelve stones in circles. I need not point out the circles of twelves so often found in the remaining Druidical temples—all Pythagorean and Masonic—still intelligible in many of our chapter-houses, for the builders of these were the oldest monks (probably Carmelites) and masons.[4433]

The Gnostic-Christian sect known as the Naassenes made these comments on the 12 Tribes of Israel:

Jesus knew of which nature each of His disciples is, and that it needs must be that each of them should go to his own nature. For from the twelve tribes He chose twelve disciples, and through them He spake to every tribe. On this account all have not heard the preachings of the twelve disciples; and even if they hear, they cannot receive them. For the [preachings] which are not according to their nature are contrary to it.[4434]

See APOSTLES, ASTROLOGY, ISRAEL, TWELVE, ZODIAC.

TRINITY: The doctrine of the Trinity is a pre-Christian Pagan concept that does not appear in the Bible.[4435] Thus the Christian version is a post-Jesus manmade fabrication.[4436] Yet, it is its universality which makes it one of the most important doctrines in the mystical Church. See DIVINE MIND, HOLY TRINITY.

TWELVE: In the traditional branch of the Christian Church the number Twelve is the number of the 12 Tribes of Israel and, more importantly, the 12 Apostles of Jesus.[4437] In the mystical branch of the Church 12 is a number of great and universal sacrality, for as Thomas Carlyle wrote in 1841:

The number Twelve, divisiblest of all, which could be halved, quartered, parted into three, into six, the most remarkable number,—this was enough to determine the Signs of the Zodiac, the number of Odin's Sons, and innumerable other

Twelves. Any vague rumour of number had a tendency to settle itself into Twelve. So with regard to every other matter.[4438]

More importantly, as a number of completeness,[4439] for 12 times 30 degrees creates a perfect circle of 360 degrees,[4440] 12 symbolizes the 12 faculties of the human mind,[4441] as well as the 12 stages of spiritual evolution through which the human soul must travel on its way toward at-one-ment with Divine Mind or God.

Thus 12 has permeated myth and legend for millennia, both Pagan and Christian. In Celtic mythology, for example, we have King Arthur and his 12 Knights; in Scandinavian mythology we have Balder and his 12 Judges, Odin and his 12 Sons, and Forseti and his 12 Representatives;[4442] in Greek mythology we have Odysseus and his 12 Companions and Zeus and the 12 Titans; in Roman mythology we have Romulus and his 12 Shepherds; in French mythology we have Roland and his 12 Peers; in Jewish mythology we have Jacob and his 12 Sons (the 12 Tribes of Israel); in Danish mythology we have Hrolf and his 12 Berserks;[4443] in Hermetic mythology we have Alexander the Great and his 12 Princes;[4444] in Gnostic history we have Mani and his 12 Apostles; in Etrurian mythology we have the 12 Lucumones of Razena;[4445] in Persian mythology we have Mithra and his 12 Apostles;[4446] in Hindu mythology we have Aditi and her 12 Sons;[4447] in ancient Egyptian mythology we have Ra and his 12 Disciples; in Asian mythology we have Buddha and his 12 Apostles;[4448] and so on.

In Egyptian mythology we also have Osiris and his 12 Apostles, as well as the 12 parts of his torn body,[4449] and in Greek myth there is Hercules and his 12 Labors. There are also the 12 hours of day and 12 hours of night; the 12 Moons of the lunar year; the 12 Altars of James; the 12 Caesars of Rome; the 12 Shields of Mars; the 12 brothers of Arvaux; the 12 Governors in the Manichean system; the 12 Adityas of India; the 12 Asses of Scandinavia; the Holy City with 12 Gates in Revelation; the 12 Wards of the City; the 12 Sacred Cushions of Japanese myth;[4450] the "12 Grand Points of Masonry"; the 12 Court Cards found in playing cards; the "12 names of Odin"; the "12 Permutations of the Tetragrammaton" of the Kabbalists; the 12 recorded Appearances of Jesus after His death;[4451] *ad infinitum*.

And let us not forget the 12 primary deities of the ancient Graeco-Roman world, a "12-god theology" founded even earlier, according to Herodotus, by the ancient Egyptians:

1. Pallas/Minerva (symbolized by the owl).
2. Aphrodite/Venus (symbolized by the dove).
3. Helios/Sol (symbolized by the rooster).
4. Hermes/Mercury (symbolized by the ibis).
5. Zeus/Jupiter (symbolized by the eagle).
6. Demeter/Ceres (symbolized by the sparrow).

7. Hephaistos/Vulcan (symbolized by the goose).
8. Aries/Mars (symbolized by the magpie).
9. Artemis/Diana (symbolized by the crow).
10. Hestia/Vesta (symbolized by the heron).
11. Hera/Juno (symbolized by the peacock).
12. Poseidon/Neptune (symbolized by the swan).[4452]

In the early Gnostic-Christian Church, the archetypal 12 became the "12 Aeons":[4453] six, which were ruled by the Gnostic "first man" Adamas (that is, Adam), and six that were ruled by the Gnostic Creator-God Yaldabaoth (meaning "he who blasphemes against the Divine")[4454]—the Supreme Being known in the orthodox Judeo-Christian heritage as Yahweh or Jehovah.[4455] All 12 Aeons were headed by the Thirteenth Aeon,[4456] Jesus, who here symbolizes the Christ-Soul's completion of its journey through the 12 lower Aeons.[4457] These, in turn, signify the 12 main compartments of human experience,[4458] the 12 highest qualities of the soul,[4459] and the 12 primary archetypes that dwell in the human psyche.[4460] Thus the young Jesus was exactly 12 years old when, after "three days," he was found studying at the Jerusalem Temple.[4461] See APOSTLES, ASTROLOGY, CHRIST, JESUS, NUMBER OF THE BEAST, NUMBERS, SEVEN STARS, SUN, THREE DAYS, TRIBES OF ISRAEL, WAY OF THE LORD, ZODIAC.

The Assyrian Tree of Life.

The Babylonian Tree of Life.

The Greek Tree of Life.

Church windows with Matthew, Mark, Luke, and John as the astrological Pagan-Christian Tetramorph.

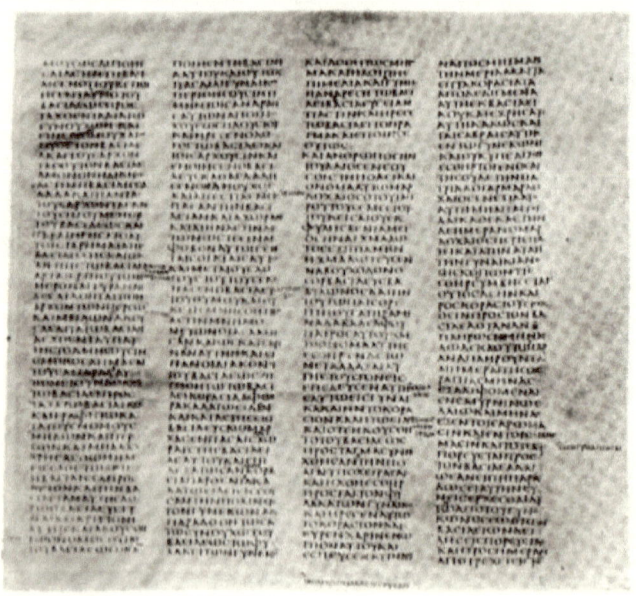

A page from the Codex Sinaiticus, showing a portion of the book of Esther.

UNDERWORLD: The biblical Underworld is the same as Hades or HELL.

UNION WITH GOD: In the traditional Christian Church union with God can only be accomplished through Jesus, and through Jesus only by baptism.[4462] In the mystical Christian Church anyone can be unified with God, Christian or non-Christian, for at-one-ment with the "Father" or Divine Mind only requires the realization that *you are your Higher Self* (as opposed to your Lower Self, Ego/body), and that your Higher Self *is* the Indwelling Christ and that the Indwelling Christ *is* our "ground of being":[4463] Nature, matter, energy, the Laws of Physics, the Unified Field, or whatever name one chooses to call God.[4464] In other words, self-realization is enlightenment and enlightenment is salvation. Macarius writes:

> If a man surrender his hidden being, that is his spirit and his thoughts, to God, occupied with nothing else, and moved by nothing else, but restraining himself, then the Lord holds him worthy of the mysteries in much holiness and purity, nay, He offers Himself to him as divine bread and spiritual drink.[4465]

Fichte writes:

> Just as this faith disappears by means of the highest crowning act of Freedom, does the previously existing Ego likewise disappear in the pure Divine Ex-istence; and we can no longer say, strictly speaking, that the Affection, the Love, and the Will of this Divine Ex-istence is ours, since there are no longer two Ex-istences and two Wills; but now one Ex-istence, and one and the same Will, is all in all. So long as man cherishes the desire of being himself something, God comes not to him, for no man can become God. But so soon as he renounces himself sincerely, wholly, and, radically, then God alone remains, and is all in all. Man can create no God for himself; but he can renounce himself as the true negation,—and then he is wholly absorbed in God.
>
> This self-renunciation is the entrance into the Higher

Life which is wholly opposed to the lower life,—the latter taking its distinctive character from the existence of a self; and it is, according to our former mode of computation, the attainment of the Third standpoint in the view of the World;—that of the pure and Higher Morality.[4466]

One of the finest explanations of at-one-ment or union with God comes from the mind of the great Christian mystic Meister Eckhart. Of his spiritual philosophy on this topic, Ueberweg writes:

> Thou mayst by faith arrive at the state in which *thou shalt have God essentially dwelling in thee, and thou shalt be in God and God in thee.*
>
> Since God accomplishes the process of his own redintegration from a state of self-alienation by means of the soul, it follows that *God needs the [human] soul.* He lies constantly in wait for us, that he may draw us into himself. For this end he works all his works. *God can as little do without us as we without him.* This eternal process in God is his grace. God's grace works supernaturally and in a manner that transcends reason; it is unmerited, eternally predestined, but does not destroy our freedom of will.
>
> Nature makes no leaps; she commences with the least, and works steadily forward till she reaches the highest. God's action does not conflict with man's free-will. The work of grace is nothing else than a revelation of God, a revelation of himself for himself in the soul. Grace begins with the conversion of the will, which conversion is at once a new creation out of nothing. It effects in man, not a course of action, but a condition, an indwelling of the soul in God. Concerning the relation of grace to free will, Eckhart expresses himself in an uncertain manner.
>
> *By grace man regains the complete union with God, which he had originally. The soul, like all things, pre-existed in God. Then I was in God, not as this individual man, but as God, free and unconditioned like him. Then there were no real differences in God. Immanent in the divine essence, I created the world and myself. By my emanation from him into individual existence I gave God his divine nature (his Godship), and do give it him constantly; for I give him that possibility of communicating himself which constitutes his essence. God can only understand himself through the human soul; in so far as I am immanent in the essence of the Deity,*

he works all his works through me, and whatever is an object of the divine understanding, that am I.

If I return out of my finite form of existence into God, I receive an impulse that bears me above the angels and makes me one with God. Then I am again what I was; I neither increase nor decrease, but remain an immovable cause, that moves all things. This breaking through and out from the limitations of creatureship is the end of all existence and of all change. *God became man that I might become God. I become one body with Christ and one spirit with God. I comprehend myself no otherwise than as a son of God, and draw all things after me into the uncreated good.*[4467]

See ATONEMENT, CHRIST, CHRIST CONSCIOUSNESS, GOD, HEAVEN, KINGDOM OF GOD, SALVATION, THEOSIS, WORD OF GOD.

UNRIGHTEOUSNESS: In the traditional Church unrighteousness means disobeying God's commandments, living a sin-filled life. In the mystical Church unrighteousness, like righteousness, concerns thought, for it is an ancient Gnostic-Christian tradition that "God is all mind and mind is all God." Because we live in a law-governed universe,[4468] and since the Christian Laws of Karma, Reciprocity, and Attraction are scientifically precise, it is important to understand that there is a right and a wrong way of thinking. The Old Testament declares that we become what we think.[4469] This wholly accords with modern psychology, which states that whatever we focus on most persistently will eventually become a part of us.[4470] Thus, to the Christian mystic unrighteousness is wrong-thinking ("sin"), as opposed to right-thinking (righteousness).[4471] See DIVINE MIND, RIGHTEOUSNESS, SIN.

UPPER ROOM: In traditional Christianity the "Upper Room" is nothing more than the "place" where Jesus held the Last Supper with His Apostles,[4472] and is thus called by orthodox Christians—in the usual literal manner—the "first synagogue of the Christian community."[4473]

In mystical Christianity the Upper Room[4474] (also known secretly to our Lord and His 120 initiates as their private "temple")[4475] is, like the "high mountain" on which the Transfiguration took place, and like the top of the human head (the site of the Crown Chakra or Christ Consciousness): an esoteric symbol of spiritual enlightenment.[4476] Hence Christian mystics refer to the human skull as the "Temple of Wisdom"[4477] or "Holy of Holies,"[4478] occultly referenced in the New Testament as Golgotha[4479] or Mount Calvary.[4480] See ASCENSION, CHRIST CONSCIOUSNESS, CROWN, CRUCIFIXION, DEATH OF JESUS, GOLGOTHA, KINGDOM OF GOD, UNION WITH GOD.

Norse Queen of the Underworld, the Goddess Hel, after whom the Christian "Hell" was named. She also gave her name to Helsinki, Holstein, and Holland.

The astrological Jesus.

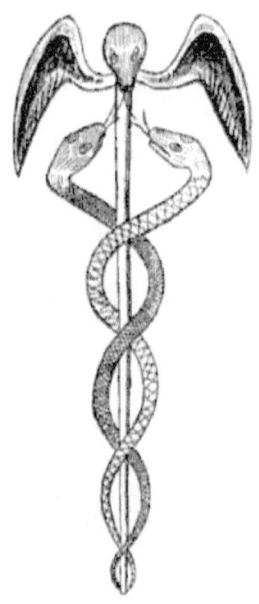

The Caduceus of Hermes.

Christianity began in ancient Egypt.

VALLEY: In the traditional Church a valley is a literal geophysical feature; that is, a low-lying ground, ravine, or gorge.[4481] In the mystical Church a valley is a symbol of the Lower Self (Ego) or the material plane (Satan), or sometimes worldly troubles. See ADVERSARY, DEVIL, MOUNTAIN, SATAN, SERPENT.

VIRGIN BIRTH: In traditional Christianity the virgin birth relates only to Jesus and His mother the Virgin Mary. In mystical Christianity the "Virgin Birth" has nothing directly to do with the historical figures of Mary or Jesus. For countless pre-Christian gods, saviors, messiahs, spiritual teachers, and religious founders were also born of virgins—mythologically *de rigueur*. According to the ancient Buddhist scripture Jataka, for example, 500 years before Jesus, Lord Buddha was born "immaculately" to the virgin-mother Maia.[4482]

Graves notes that in ancient Greece unwed girls often attributed their out-of-wedlock births to various male deities. The problem

> became so common that the reigning king issued an edict, decreeing the death of all young women who should offer such an insult to deity as to lay to him the charge of begetting their children. The virgin Alcmene furnishes a case of a young woman claiming God as the father of her offspring, when she brought forth the divine Redeemer Alcides, 1280 years B.C. And Ceres, the virgin mother of Osiris, claimed that he was begotten by the "father of all Gods." Mr. Kenrick tells us the likeness of this virgin mother, with the divine child in her arms, may now be seen represented in sculpture on some of the ancient, ruined temples of that ruined empire. And Mr. Higgins makes the broad declaration that "the worship of this virgin mother, with her God-begotten child, prevailed everywhere." This author also quotes Mr. Riquord as saying, this son of God "was exhibited in effigy, lying in a manger, in the same manner the infant Jesus was afterward laid in the cave at Bethlehem." Mr. Higgins further testifies that the worship of this virgin God-mother (that is, the God and the mother) is of very ancient date and universal prevalence in all the eastern

countries, as is proved by sculptured figures bearing the marks of great age.

In corroboration of this statement we might cite many cases, if our space would permit, from the religious records of India, Egypt, Persia, Greece, Rome, Mexico, Tibet, etc. Maia, mother of Sakia and Yasoda of Chrishna; Celestine, mother of the crucified Zulis; Chimalman, mother of Quexalcote; Semele, mother of the Egyptian Bacchus, and Minerva, mother of the Grecian Bacchus; Prudence, mother of Hercules; Alcmene, mother of Alcides; Shing-Mon, mother-of Yu, and Mayence, mother of Hesus, were all as confidently believed to be pure, holy and chaste virgins, while giving birth to these Gods, sons of God, Saviors and sin-atoning Mediators, as was Mary, mother of Jesus, and long before her time.

Mr. Higgins remarks that the mother was still held to be a virgin, even after she had given birth to other children besides the deity-begotten bantling, which furnishes another striking parallel to the history of Mary, as she was still called a virgin after she had given birth to Jesus and his brothers James and John. And it is an incident worth noticing here, that, in the case of Mayence, virgin-mother of the God-sired Hesus of the Druids, the ancient traditions of the country, more than two thousand years old, represent her body as being enveloped in light, and a crown of twelve stars upon her head, corresponding exactly to the apocalyptic figure described by the mystagogue, St. John, in the twelfth chapter of his Revelation. She is also represented with her foot on the head of a serpent, according to Davie's *Universal Etymology*.[4483]

Auguste Nichols tells us, in his *Philosophical Essays on Christianity*, that Io is called, in Eschylus, "the Chaste Virgin," and her son "the Son of God." (For other similar cases, see Guigne's *History of the Huns*.) Gonzales informs us he found on an ancient temple in India the Latin inscription *Partura virginis*, "the virgin about to bring forth." And similar inscriptions have been found on pagan temples in the country of the ancient Gauls. (For proof, see Riquord's *Theology of the Ancient Gauls*, Chapter 10).... According to Chinese history there were two beings, Tien and Chang-Ti, worshiped in that country as Gods more than twenty-five hundred years ago, born of virgins "who knew no man." The mother of the mighty and the almighty God Hercules, we are told, "knew only love."

If history and tradition, then, are to be credited, God

had many "well beloved sons," born of pious and holy virgins, besides Jesus Christ. And some of them are represented as being his "only begotten," and others his "first begotten," sons. And all these cases appear to be equally as well authenticated as the story of Jesus Christ. All stand upon a level, the same kind and the same amount of evidence being offered in each case.[4484]

With this background in mind, Christian mystics turn to the ancient arcana to find the true meaning of the "Virgin Birth."

Here it is a symbol of the pure and perfect "birth" of each human soul from the "womb" of God, made in the exact image of God—often portrayed in the Bible as female.[4485] For as all religions teach, everything created by God, as all human souls are, is by its very nature immaculate.[4486] Of the concept of the Virgin Birth Kingsford and Maitland write:

> The object set before the saint is so to live as to render the soul luminous and consolidate with the spirit, that thereby the spirit may be perpetually one with the soul, and thus eternise its individuality. For individuality appertains to the soul, inasmuch as it consists in separateness, which it is the function of soul-substance to accomplish in respect of spirit. Thus, though *eternal and immaculate in her substance, the soul acquires individuality by being born in matter and time*; and within her is conceived the divine element which, divided from God, is yet God and man. Wherefore Catholic dogma and tradition, while making Mary the "mother of God," represent her as born of [her mother] Anna, the year, or time.
>
> *The . . . Immaculate Conception . . . concerns the generation of the soul, presenting her as begotten in the womb of matter, and by means of matter brought into the world, and yet not of matter, but from the first moment of her being, pure and incorrupt.* Otherwise she could not be "Mother of God." In her bosom, as Nucleus, is conceived the bright and holy Light, the Nucleolus, which—without participation of matter—germinates in her and manifests itself as the express image of the Eternal and Ineffable Selfhood. To this image she gives individuality; and through and in her it is focused and polarised into a perpetual and self-subsistent Person, *at once human and Divine, Son of God and of man.* Thus is the soul at once Daughter, Spouse, and Mother of God. By her is crushed the head of the Serpent. And from her triumphant springs the Man Regenerate, who, as the product of a pure soul and divine spirit, is said to be born of

water (Maria) and the Holy Ghost.[4487]

... The history of the Virgin Mary and her functions in regard to her Son, as presented alike in the Gospels and in Catholic tradition and ritual, are in every particular those of the soul to whom it is given to be *"Mother of God" in man. Her acts and graces, as well as his life and passion, belong to the experience of every redeemed man.* As the Christ in him delivers him from the curse of Adam, so the Virgin Mary in him delivers him from the curse of Eve, and secures the fulfilment of the promise of the conquest over the serpent of Matter. *And, whereas, as sinner, he has seen enacted in his own interior experience the drama of the Fall; so, as saint, he enacts the mysteries represented in the Rosary of the Virgin, his soul passing in turn through every stage of her joys, her sorrows, and her glories. Wherefore the part assigned to Mary in the Christian Evangel is the part borne by the soul in all mystical experience.*

That which first beguiles and leads astray the soul is the attraction of the illusory world of mere phenomena, which is aptly represented under the figure of the Serpent with glittering coils, insinuating mien, and eyes full of fascination. Yielding to this attraction, through directing her gaze outwards and downwards instead of inwards and upwards, the soul—as Eve—has abandoned celestial realities for mundane shadows, and entangled in her fall the mind, or Adam. Thus mind and soul fall together and lose the power of desiring and apprehending the divine things which alone make for life, and, so, become cast out of divine conditions, and conscious only of material environments and liable to material limitations.

This substitution of the illusory for the real, of the material for the spiritual, of the phenomenal for the substantial, constitutes the whole sin and loss of the Fall. Redemption consists in the recovery of the power once more to apprehend, to love, and to grasp the real. *"Original sin," from which Mary is exempt, is precisely the condition of blindness which—owing to the soul's immergence in materiality—* hinders the perception of divine things. By no possibility can the Divine Life be generated in any soul afflicted with this blindness. Christ cannot be conceived save of a soul immaculate and virgin as to matter, and meet to become the spouse of the Divine Spirit.

Therefore, as the soul as Eve gives consent to the annunciation of the Serpent, so, as Mary, become virgin, she gives consent to the annunciation of the Angel, and understands the mystery of the Motherhood of the man regenerate. She has no acts of her own, all the acts of her Son are hers also. She participates in his nativity, in his manifestation, in his passion, in his resurrection, in his ascension, in his pentecostal gift. He himself is her gift to the world. But it is always he who operates; she who asks, acquiesces, consents, responds. Through her he outflows into the mind and external man, and, so, into life and conduct . As Augustine says, *"All graces pass to us through the hands of Mary."* For the purified soul is the mediatrix, as she is the genetrix, of the Divine presence.[4488]

Of Eckhart's view of the Virgin Birth, Pfleiderer writes:

> If I put aside the limitations of self, which separate me from others, and return to the simplicity of my spiritual being, then all that remains is *the pure nature of the soul which is so one with the nature of God that the soul might almost be called God itself and the creator of all things*. Whatever separates us from God is but the deceptive semblance of self which chains our volition. Hence, man must release himself from the fetters of self and creature love, must have nothing and desire nothing excepting God, and experience God in the solitude of his spirit. [Eckhart said:]
>
>> "Shall I make God with thee? Then must thou first become as nothing, must give up all thy willing and thinking and offer up thy soul pure to God, must not will anything excepting what He wills; then hast thou no need to care for righteousness, but let God be active in thee, and then in thy love of God art thou certain of thy bliss which can never again be destroyed by the evils of the age. *Ever and ever therein goes on the incarnation of God as in Christ, for the Father did not bear the Son only in eternity, but ever and ever does He give birth to Him in the soul of him who offers himself to Him, and what the Son has taught us in Christ is merely this, that we are the selfsame sons of God.*"[4489]

Jukes offers the following:

I cannot write what crowds upon me here, as to the "woman," and her "Seed," who shall destroy and bruise the serpent; or *how Christ, if He be "formed within," is made of the woman in us, that is the human will; growing thence, out of the womb of human affections, not by man, but by the Holy Ghost, who begets that new life, to be in due time born amidst beasts, out of a pure virgin affection, like Mary, in us; which is itself the fruit of numberless other affections*, some grievously defiled, as Rahab and Thamar, which have gone before.

For from Adam to Christ are seventy-two generations, as from Abraham to Christ are forty-two; that is, many a form of life is produced, and many an inward travail and death is known by us, before the will brings forth that life of faith, of which Abraham is the appointed figure. And after Abraham, or faith, more births will there yet be, in which the energy of nature is more or less manifest, before that form of life appears, which is of the Holy Ghost, and is the "perfect man."

Some of these, as David and Solomon, are like, but yet are not, the perfect man, but only carnal forms or copies of Him; as we know, that, before *God's image comes in us*, certain outward likenesses, and carnal prefigurings or preludings of it, in different measures will appear in us. Many a form of life grows, toils, withers, and dies, having produced another to succeed it, which again dies out, and this many times, before the image of God, the perfect man, the true Seed, comes. But it comes at last, and the serpent's head is bruised. She, by whom came death, brings forth the Life-giver.[4490]

The Gnostic-Christian sect known as the Naassenes believed that the "Virgin Birth" signifies

"the Gate of Heaven, and this is the House of God, where the Good God dwells alone, into which no impure man shall come, no psychic, no fleshly man; but it is kept under watch for the spiritual alone, where they must come, and, casting away their garments, all become bridegrooms made virgin by the Virginal Spirit. For such a man is the virgin with child, who conceives and brings forth a son, which is neither psychic, animal, nor fleshly, but a blessed teen of teens."

This is the Kingdom of the Heavens, the "grain of mustard seed, the indivisible point, which is the primeval spark in the body, and which no man knoweth save only the spiritual." The school of the Naasseni, it is said, were all initiated into the

Mysteries of the Great Mother because they found that the whole mystery of the Great of rebirth was taught in these rites.[4491]

Eckhart believed that

> Mary is blessed, not because she bore Christ bodily, but because she bore him spiritually, and in this everyone can become like her.[4492]

In essence, we are all "virgin-born," for all mothers are spiritual virgins. This is because we are not human bodies with spirits, but spirits with human bodies; and our spirits, the pure and undefiled Indwelling Christ, is unsulliable and therefore forever immaculate. See CHRISTMAS, GODDESS, GOSPEL, MARY, MOTHER, MYTH OF CHRIST, NATIVITY, THEALOGY, VIRGO.

VIRGO: In the traditional Christian Church there is no such thing as Virgo, for since this is merely the name of one of the astrological Sun-signs, she does not appear in the Bible and does not figure in any way in Christian doctrine. In the mystical Christian Church, however, Virgo (the "Virgin") is all important: she is the original Pagan "Virgin-Mother" (the constellation)[4493] who gives "birth" to the new "Christ Child" (the Sun) on December 25, *three days* after the Winter Solstice on December 22.[4494]

Thus, the Pagan Virgo is none other than the Christian Mary, the Virgin-Mother who bore Jesus,[4495] the "Sun of Righteousness,"[4496] on the universal birthday of all saviors, christs, and messiahs.[4497] Virgo also appears in the book of Revelation, where the great Gnostic-Christian mystic John the Evangelist[4498] (or the Gnostic teacher Cerinthus)[4499] portrays her as "the woman arrayed with the sun, and the moon under her feet, and upon her head a crown of twelve stars."[4500] Virgo-Mary's crown is, of course, the Zodiacal crown, signifying the 12 Sun-signs of the astrological year. See ASTROLOGY, CHRISTMAS, GODDESS, MARY, MOTHER, MYTH OF CHRIST, NATIVITY, THREE DAYS, VIRGIN BIRTH, ZODIAC.

VOICE OF GOD: In the traditional Church the voice of God is the literal "voice" of the Father. But this presupposes that God is a visible, physical, anthropomorphic being with a mouth and vocal cords—an idea that is wholly contrary to the teachings of our Lord Jesus[4501] and the Apostle Paul.[4502] In the mystical Church the voice of God is the Higher Self (Christ) speaking to the Lower Self (Satan).[4503] Thus Gnostic-Christian John has Jesus say:

> Behold, I stand at the door, and knock: if any man hear my

voice, and open the door, I will come in to him, and will sup with him, and he with me. To him that overcometh will I grant to sit with me in my throne, even as I also overcame, and am set down with my Father in his throne.[4504]

See CHRIST, FATHER, GOD, GOSPEL OF THE KINGDOM OF GOD, JESUS, KINGDOM OF GOD, LAMB OF GOD, MOUTH OF GOD, SON OF GOD, TEMPLE OF GOD, UNION WITH GOD, WAY OF THE LORD, WORD OF GOD, YAHWEH.

The Greek goddess Athena.

The original Holy Trinity: Father, Mother, and Child, the foundation of civilization.

Reign of the Antichrist.

Jesus washing the feet of the Apostles.

Virgin Mary and the Vesica Piscis.

Jacob pouring oil on the stone.

WALKING ON WATER: In the traditional Church Jesus performed the miracle of walking on water when he stepped across the surface of the Sea of Galilee.[4505] While Christian mystics do not doubt that our all-powerful Lord possessed this ability, this same story appears in the biographies of countless pre-Christian saviors, messiahs, and christs as well (Poseidon, Dionysus, and Hercules, for example, all walked on water).[4506] So a deeper meaning beyond the mere literal appearance must be sought. Thus, in the mystical Church walking on water is a symbol of the Higher Self (Christ) subduing the earthly passions of the Lower Self (Satan). See BUDDHA, CHRIST, JESUS, KRISHNA, MESSIAH, MITHRA, OSIRIS, PYTHAGORAS, SAVIOR, TEACHER OF RIGHTEOUSNESS.

WASHED IN THE BLOOD OF THE LAMB: In the traditional Church being washed in the blood of the Lamb means that one is "washed clean" of sin by the saving grace of the "Lamb of God";[4507] that is, Jesus' death and resurrection on the cross.[4508] However, being "washed in the blood" is a pre-Christian Pagan doctrine, found in the Mysteries, for example, of the god Mithra, the goddess Cybele, and many others,[4509] while the "Lamb of God" was a popular title for scores of pre-Christian saviors, such as Osiris.[4510] Therefore, because it is a universal theme rather than specifically Christian, the Christian mystic seeks the esoteric meaning that lies beneath the merely exoteric.

In the mystical Church being "washed in the blood of the Lamb" is a doctrine having to do with the purification of the human soul through spiritual involution (spirit falling into matter) and spiritual evolution (spirit rising back into spirit). Hislop writes:

> [The universal] . . . son, thus worshipped in his mother's arms, was looked upon as invested with all the attributes, and called by almost all the names of the promised Messiah. As Christ, in the Hebrew of the Old Testament, was called Adonai, The Lord, so Tammuz was called Adon or Adonis. Under the name of Mithras, he was worshipped as the "Mediator." As Mediator and head of the covenant of grace, he was styled Baal-berith, Lord of the Covenant.[4511] In this character he is represented in Persian monuments as seated on the rainbow, the well-known

symbol of the covenant. In India, under the name of Vishnu, the Preserver, or Saviour of men, though a god, he was worshipped as the great "Victim-Man," who before the worlds were, because there was nothing else to offer, offered himself as a sacrifice. The Hindu sacred writings teach that this mysterious offering before all creation is the foundation of all the sacrifices that have ever been offered since.

Do any marvel at such a statement being found in the sacred books of a Pagan mythology? Why should they?

Since sin entered the world there has been only one way of salvation, and that through the blood of the everlasting covenant—a way that all mankind once knew, from the days of righteous Abel downwards. When Abel, "by faith," offered unto God his more excellent sacrifice than that of Cain, it was his faith "in the blood of the Lamb slain" in the purpose of God "from the foundation of the world," and in due time to be actually offered up on Calvary, that gave all the "excellence" to his offering. *If Abel knew of "the blood of the Lamb," why should Hindoos not have known of it?*

One little word shows that even in Greece the virtue of "the blood of God," had once been known, though that virtue, as exhibited in its poets, was utterly obscured and degraded. That word is *Ichor*. Every reader of the bards of classic Greece knows that *Ichor is the term peculiarly appropriated to the blood of a divinity*. Thus Homer refers to it:

> From the clear vein the immortal Ichor flowed,
> Such stream as issues from a wounded god,
> Pure emanation, uncorrupted flood,
> Unlike our gross, diseased terrestrial blood.

Now, what is the proper meaning of the term Ichor? In Greek it has no etymological meaning whatever; but in Chaldee, Ichor signifies "The precious thing." Such a name, applied to the blood of a divinity, could have only one origin. It bears its evidence on the very face of it, as coming from that grand patriarchal tradition, that led Abel to look forward to the "precious blood" of Christ, the most "precious" gift that love divine could give to a guilty world, and which, while the blood of the only genuine "Victim-Man," is at the same time, in deed and in truth, "The blood of God."[4512]

Even in Greece itself, though the doctrine was utterly

perverted, it was not entirely lost. It was mingled with falsehood and fable, it was hid from the multitude; but yet, in the secret mystic system, it necessarily occupied an important place. As Servius tells us that *the grand purpose of the Bacchic orgies "was the purification of souls," and as in these orgies there was regularly the tearing asunder and the shedding of the blood of an animal, in memory of the shedding of the life's blood of the great divinity commemorated in them, could this symbolical shedding of the blood of that divinity have no bearing on the "purification" from sin, these mystic rites were intended to effect?*

 . . . *The sufferings of the Babylonian Zoroaster and Belus were expressly represented as voluntary, and as submitted to for the benefit of the world, and that in connection with crushing the great serpent's head, which implied the removal of sin and the curse. If the Grecian Bacchus was just another form of the Babylonian divinity, then his sufferings and bloodshedding must have been represented as having been undergone for the same purpose, viz., for "the purification of souls."*

Now from this point of view, let the well-known name of Bacchus in Greece be looked at. That name was Dionusos [Dionysus]. What is the meaning of that name? Hitherto it has defied all interpretation. But deal with it as belonging to the language of that land from which the god himself originally came, and the meaning is very plain. *D'ion-nuso-s signifies "The Sin-Bearer," a name entirely appropriate to the character of him whose sufferings were represented as so mysterious, and who was looked up to as the great "purifier of souls."*

Now this Babylonian god known in Greece as "The Sin-Bearer," and in India as the "Victim-Man," among the Buddhists of the east, the original elements of whose system are clearly Babylonian, *was commonly addressed as "The Saviour of the world."* It has been all along well enough known that the Greeks *occasionally worshipped the supreme god, under the title of "Zeus the Saviour;"* but this title was thought to have reference only to deliverance in battle, or some such-like temporal deliverance. But *when it is known that "Zeus the Saviour" was only a title of Dionusos, the "sin-bearing" Bacchus, his character, as "The Saviour," appears in quite a different light.*

In Egypt, the Chaldean god was held up as the great object of love and adoration, as the god through whom "goodness and truth were revealed to mankind." He was regarded as the predestined heir of all things; and, on the day of his birth, it was believed that a voice was heard to proclaim, "The Lord of all the earth is born." In this character he was styled "King of kings, and Lord of lords," it being as a professed representative of this hero-god that the celebrated Sesostris caused this very title to be added to his name on the monuments which he erected to perpetuate the fame of his victories. Not only was he honoured as the great "World-King," he was regarded as Lord of the invisible world, and "Judge of the dead;" and it was taught that, in the world of spirits, all must appear before his dread tribunal, to have their destiny assigned them.

As the true Messiah was prophesied of under the title of the "Man whose name was the branch," he was celebrated not only as the "Branch of Cush," but as the "Branch of God," graciously given to the earth for healing all the ills that flesh is heir to. He was worshipped in Babylon under the name of El-Bar, or *"God the Son."* Under this very name he is introduced by Berosus, the Chaldean historian, as the second in the list of Babylonian sovereigns.

Under this name he has been found in the sculptures of Nineveh by Layard, the name Bar "the Son," having the sign denoting El or "God" prefixed to it. Under the same name he has been found by Sir H. Rawlinson, the names "Beltis" and the "Shining Bar" being in immediate juxtaposition. Under the name of Bar he was worshipped in Egypt in the earliest times, though in later times the god Bar was degraded in the popular Pantheon, to make way for another more popular divinity. In Pagan Rome itself, as Ovid testifies, he was worshipped under the name of the "Eternal Boy." Thus daringly and directly was a mere mortal set up in Babylon in opposition to the "Son of the Blessed."[4513]

Hence, in the mystical Christian Church all true believers are "washed in the blood of the Lamb." For it is faith and righteousness that cleanse sin. And herein lies the Master Secret: the unsullied Soul or Universal Christ,[4514] made in the image of God,[4515] is already stainless *and* unstainable. Realizing this is enlightenment, the Mind of Christ,[4516] nirvana, satori, the Kingdom of God.[4517] See BAPTISM, BLOOD OF THE LAMB, CHRIST CONSCIOUSNESS, CRUCIFIXION, DEATH OF JESUS, GOOD SHEPHERD, LAMB OF GOD.

WASHING THE FEET: In the traditional Church Jesus is shown washing the feet of the Apostles after the Last Supper, his method of teaching them about humility.

This is merely the outer or exoteric meaning, however. Mystical Christianity reveals to us a much more profound and important one.

Feet are the lowest parts of our bodies. Because they come in contact with dirt (that is, the material plane), they symbolize the Lower Self. Water symbolizes truth. As always, Jesus here symbolizes the Universal Indwelling Christ. Thus, in mystical terms this event actually depicts the cleansing of the Lower Self with the Living Waters (truth) of the God Within.

When the Lower Self is "washed," the purification of our entire being is finally complete, for our Higher Self is already perfect. We are then made whole, freed from our past, freed from sin, freed from the fetters of the material world. This is why Jesus made this arcane statement to Peter:

> He that is washed needeth not save to wash his feet, but is clean every whit.[4518]

Saint Augustine mystically refers to this occult practice as "ordering aright the path of our spiritual footsteps."[4519]

What does the symbolic "washing of our feet" mean for humanity on a personal level?

After finishing the foot cleansing ritual, Jesus tells the Apostles: "I have given you an example, that ye should do as I have done to you." The inner meaning here is that we are to strive to be Christlike; that is, obey Divine Law.[4520] This purifies the Lower Self, bringing it into alignment with the Higher Self. This mystical "marriage of Cana," the merging of the masculine Lower Self with the feminine Higher Self, or what the ancients called the *Hieros Gamos*[4521] (the "Sacred Union"—mystically, of the Sun-god Sol and the Moon-goddess Luna), is the true wedding of the "bride" (human Ego) and the "bridegroom" (Indwelling Christ) that John the Baptist spoke of, and it is what Jesus meant by the statement: "The Father is in me, and I in him."

Why was this doctrine so important to our Lord?

"Washing our feet" at the doorway to the Kingdom of Heaven allows us entrance. Here, in this sacred Holy of Holies, mystically symbolized as the human head or skull (in the Bible, "Golgotha," "Calvary," the "Upper Room," etc.),[4522] and viewed as a psychological state known as Christ Consciousness, or what Paul called "the Mind of Christ,"[4523] we may use Spiritual Law positively and productively to alter our lives and improve our conditions, health, and finances.[4524] See CHRIST, CHRIST CONSCIOUSNESS, KINGDOM OF GOD, WATER.

WATER: In the traditional Church water is viewed both as an ordinary liquid and as a symbol of cleansing the soul of sin.[4525] In the mystical Church water is a symbol of the "vital energy" of life;[4526] in other words, spiritual truth.[4527] Thus in the Essene and Gnostic inspired book of Revelation[4528] we read:

And the Spirit and the bride say, "Come." And let him that heareth say, "Come." And let him that is athirst come. And whosoever will, let him take the water of life freely.[4529]

Surely, says Kingsley, this biblical

> text speaks not of earthly water. No doubt the words "Water of Life" have a spiritual and mystic meaning. Yet that alone does not prove the inspiration of the text. They had a spiritual and mystic meaning already among the heathens of the East—Greeks and barbarians alike.
>
> The East—and indeed the West likewise—was haunted by dreams of a Water of Life, a Fount of Perpetual Youth, a Cup of Immortality: dreams at which only the shallow and the ignorant will smile; for what are they but tokens of man's right to Immortality,—of his instinct that he is not as the beasts,—that there is somewhat in him which ought not to die, which need not die, and yet which may die, and which perhaps deserves to die? How could it be kept alive? How strengthened and refreshed into perpetual youth?
>
> And water—with its life-giving and refreshing powers, often with medicinal properties seemingly miraculous—what better symbol could be found for that which would keep off death? Perhaps there was some reality which answered the symbol, some actual Cup of Immortality, some actual Fount of Youth. But who could attain to them? Surely the gods hid their own special treasure from the grasp of man. Surely that Water of Life was to be sought for far away, amid trackless mountain-peaks, guarded by dragons and demons. That Fount of Youth must be hidden in the rich glades of some tropic forest. That Cup of Immortality must be earned by years, by ages, of superhuman penance and self torture.
>
> Certain of the old Jews, it is true, had had deeper and truer thoughts. Here and there a psalmist had said, "With God is the well of Life;" or a prophet had cried, "Ho, every one that thirsteth, come ye to the waters, and buy without money and without price!"
>
> But *the Jews had utterly forgotten (if the mass of them ever understood) the meaning of the old revelations; and, above all, the Pharisees, the most religious among them. To their minds, it was only by a proud asceticism,—by being not as other men were; only by doing some good thing—by performing some extraordinary religious*

feat,—*that man could earn eternal life. And bitter and deadly was their selfish wrath when they heard that the Water of Life was within all men's reach, then and for ever; that The Eternal Life was in that Christ who spoke to them; that He gave it freely to whomsoever He would;*—*bitter their wrath when they heard His disciples declare that God had given to men Eternal Life; that the Spirit and the Bride said, "Come."*[530]

Barlow writes:

Rosellini, in his great work on Egypt, has a scene in Paradise, taken from a tomb at Thebes, in which several generations of an Egyptian family which flourished under the eighteenth dynasty up to the time of Rameses III, or from the sixteenth century B.C., to the thirteenth, are represented *partaking of this immortal nourishment,* the fruit of the Tree of Life, and *receiving also the living water of life proceeding from the same divine source.*

The paradise here intended is the state or place of departed righteous souls, who, according to Egyptian theology, as explained in the works of Rosellini, Wilkinson, Lepsius, Brugsch, Birch, and Emmanuel de Rouge, have triumphed over evil through the power of Osiris, whose name they bear, and are now set down for ever in his heavenly kingdom. *Osiris was venerated as the incarnation of the goodness of the Deity, and according to the last-mentioned authority, was universally worshipped in Egypt, as the Redeemer of souls, two thousand years before Christ.*

The head of this family was named Poèr, and the members of it are shown seated in two rows on thrones, one below the other; each is receiving from the Tree of Life, or rather from the divine influence residing in the tree, and personified as a vivifying agent under the figure of the goddess Nutpe or Netpe, *a stream of the life-giving water,* and at the same time an offering of its fruit.

The tree is the *ficus-sycamorus,* the sycamore tree of the Bible, and it stands on a sort of aquarium, symbolical of the sacred Nile, the life-supporting agent in the land of Egypt. Within this are various fishes that inhabit its waters, certain plants that grow on the surface, and birds that fly above, while the lotus is seen on its banks, and a heron, the symbol of the first transformation of the soul in the paradise of Osiris, stands on each side.

The tree is abundantly productive, and from the upper

part of it, among the branches, the goddess Netpe rises with a tray of its fruit in one hand, and with the other *pours from a vase streams of its life-giving water.*

This water is represented by parallel zigzag lines, similar to a well-known architectural moulding frequently seen over the door-heads of Saxon and early Norman churches, and which was no doubt originally there introduced as symbolical of the water of baptism, the initiatory sacrament of the Church, and at one time figuratively called its gate or door, janua ecclesize.

The Egyptians had also a baptism by water, or a sacred function of a similar kind, administered to adults; it is occasionally seen represented on tablets where two priests, or divine personifications, standing one on each side of a royal personage, *pour over his head streams of water from vases held in their hands*: there is a fragment of a large tablet in the Egyptian Museum of the Vatican, on which this is seen, and *where the water is not represented by parallel zigzag lines merely, but by a series of the crux ansata joined together in a zigzag manner.*

The *crux ansata*, as is well known, was the symbol of life among the Egyptians, and is here introduced, (the subject being on a scale sufficiently large to admit of it) to *signify the life-giving properties of this water.* In the great work of Lepsius will be found a similar representation. The parallel zigzag lines are an abbreviation of the larger and more complete symbol.

In the gospel of St. John we read of our Lord making a distinction between ordinary water and the water which he should give of eternal life.

Thus in reference to the water of the well of Samaria, Jesus says, *"Whosoever drinketh of this water shall thirst again: but whosoever drinketh of the water that I shall give him shall never thirst: but the water that I shall give him shall be in him a well of water springing up into everlasting life."*[531]

What our Lord meant by this water of everlasting life is obvious from various passages of Scripture. Thus in John 7:37, we read:—*"In the last day, that great day of the feast, Jesus stood and cried, saying, If any man thirst, let him come unto me and drink."* When Christ said to Peter, *"Will ye also go away?"* that apostle replied, *"Lord, to whom shall we go? Thou hast the words of eternal life."*[532]

So that *the living water was the doctrine of eternal life*, which they who believed in Christ should receive.

The living water in the Egyptian theology would appear to

have signified the same thing; it was, in their doctrine, the symbolical support of eternal life to all who received it, along with the fruit of the Tree of Life which grew in the paradise of Osiris.[4533]

In essence, mystical Christianity views water as a symbol of Jesus' secret teachings, known collectively as "the Gospel of the Kingdom of God."[4534] These esoteric doctrines are the "waters of life" which cure the disease of spiritual ignorance.[4535] Again, here is how our Lord described this divine liquid:

> But whosoever drinketh of the water that I shall give him shall never thirst; but the water that I shall give him shall be in him a well of water springing up into everlasting life.[4536]

See ARK, BETHLEHEM, BREAD, DOVE, EUCHARIST, NOAH, NOAH'S FLOOD, RAINBOW, RIVER, SACRAMENT, WINE.

WAY OF THE LORD: In the traditional Church the "Way of the Lord" is Jesus Christ, through whom can be found "the only path to Heaven."[4537] In other words, "the Way" is the mainstream conservative Church, and only the mainstream conservative Church. In the mystical Church, however, it is held that Jesus founded no religion, and never had any intention of doing so[4538]—a view, incidentally, held even by many mainstream Bible scholars and theologians,[4539] one of them who states:

> To all unprejudiced persons it is manifest that Jesus had not the slightest intention of doing away with the Jewish religion and putting another in its place.[4540]

This view is not only proven by our Lord's own words,[4541] but by the many writings of the Church Fathers as well, most who maintained that Christianity existed far prior to the birth of Jesus, in fact, from the beginning of time.[4542]

Contrarily, and unbeknownst to the masses, mainline Christian authorities have long taught the opposite; namely that the Christian religion began with the empty tomb,[4543] that the organized Church (the Ecclesia) began with Peter,[4544] and that Christian theology began with Paul,[4545] all which came after the earthly life of our Lord. But is this true? Certainly the 12 Apostles did not consider themselves to be part of a new religion, or even a new sect within Judaism. In their minds they were merely announcing what Israel had already long been awaiting: the appearance of the Messiah.[4546]

Jesus did have a "faith." But it was neither Judaism or Christianity. It was an informal mystical spirituality that was identical to what Hindus call *Sanatana Dharma*, or the "Eternal Way." This is the One Universal Religion that is known by hundreds of thousands of different names around the world. For at the core of *Sanatana Dharma* lies those three immortal and timeless spiritual truths upon which all religions are ultimately founded: *love, compassion,* and *wisdom.* Thus, if we were to give a name to Jesus' so-called "religion," it would be "The Way"—which is exactly what He[4547] and His followers called it.[4548]

The name is not original to Jesus, however. He was simply borrowing a title that was commonplace among the great spiritual teachers throughout pre-Christian history, from the Old Testament authors, such as Moses,[4549] Jeremiah,[4550] Job,[4551] and the Psalmist,[4552] to the ancient philosopher-priest Hermes Trismegistus,[4553] celebrated Asian spiritual leader Buddha (whose gospel was known as "The Way of Truth"),[4554] and the famed Chinese teacher Lao Tzu, the founder of the religion literally known as "The Way": Tao (that is, Taoism).[4555]

In short, Jesus' "religion" is nothing more than charity, forgiveness, humility, prayer, and love of God, a spiritual belief system which, in its elegant simplicity, can be understood even by "little children,"[4556] just as our Lord intended.[4557] See CHRISTIANITY, GOOD NEWS, JESUS, WORD OF GOD.

WINE: In the traditional Christian Church wine is usually merely a beverage frequently used in the Old and New Testaments,[4558] but it is also the Eucharistic liquid Jesus employs at the Last Supper as a representation of His blood.[4559] Since wine was the standard symbol of blood in pre-Christian Paganism (the Greeks, for example, saw it as the blood of their Savior Dionysus, who often turned water into wine),[4560] the mystical Christian Church does not directly associate wine with Jesus. Rather it is viewed as a symbol of spiritual drink, that is, spiritual knowledge[4561] attained through intuition,[4562] which can come only by way of the Christ[4563] which indwells us all.[4564] See BETHLEHEM, BREAD, EUCHARIST, RIVER, SACRAMENT, WATER.

WISE MEN: In traditional Christianity the Wise Men (their precise number is never mentioned in scripture) from the East were philosopher-astrologers (viewed as "magicians" in the 1st Century), who followed the Star of Bethlehem, which led them to the newly born Messiah, the baby Jesus.[4565] With them they brought "treasures," gifts of gold, frankincense, and myrrh.[4566] While the orthodox assume they were Chaldean, there is much evidence showing that they may have been from India, a view which has been supported by scores of Christian mystics (Therese Neumann among them).[4567] Pliny the Elder even associated them with the Druids of Britain.[4568]

The canonical story of the Wise Men appears only in Matthew, and was obviously not known to the other Gospel writers, nor to Paul and the other Apostles—otherwise they too would have recorded it, or at least mentioned it. That they did not speaks volumes to the mystically oriented.

History has shown that the Star of Bethlehem motif was a mythological

Pagan element appended to Jesus' biography several generations after His death. It does not appear in the earliest known Gospels, the Gospel of Q and the Gospel of Thomas. Indeed, the heraldic heavenly body (star, comet, nova, meteor, etc.), along with the numerous other standard trappings of mythology, are common in the biographies of ancient gods and historic royals and spiritual leaders, one intended to invest their births with awe and wonderment. For example:

- At the birth of Socrates in 469 B.C. magi came from the East bearing gifts of gold, frankincense, and myrrh.[4569]
- At the birth of Confucius in 598 B.C. five wise men paid him a visit, as celestial music played and angels lovingly surrounded his crib.[4570]
- At the birth of Buddha in 624 B.C., born of the Virgin Mother Maya or Maia, he was attended by heavenly beings, the "universe blossomed like a garden," and divine music was heard.[4571]
- At the birth of Krishna (Chrishna, the Hindu Christ) around 1200 B.C., angels, shepherds, and prophets sought him out in order to bring him gold, frankincense, and myrrh. It is recorded in the Vishnu Purana that

> while the virgin Devaki bore Krishna, "the protector of the world," in her womb, she was eulogized by the gods, and on the day of Krishna's birth, "the quarters of the horizon were irradiate with joy, as if moonlight was diffused over the whole earth." "The spirits and the nymphs of heaven danced and sang," and, "at midnight, when the support of all was born, the clouds emitted low pleasing sounds, and poured down [a] rain of flowers."[4572]

The births of Caesar, Zoroaster, Osiris, and Mithra, among thousands of others, were also accompanied by a myriad of similar supernatural signs and events. We are dealing here with symbols, emblems, metaphors, allegories, parables, key words, similes, and archetypes. This is the "language of mythology" after all.[4573]

Revealingly, Matthew gives no specific reason for the Wise Men's visit, other than the fact that King Herod ordered them to locate the infant "King of the Jews," so that he might come and worship him.[4574] And one is certainly entitled to wonder why Pagan astrologers from the East would know or care about such a child, one to whom they owed no allegiance and who was born in an insignificant desert town 1,000 miles away.[4575]

All of this must inspire the objective Bible reader to dig deeper into this particular aspect of our Lord's history. And the occultic view allows us to do just that.

In mystical Christianity these astrologers (as mentioned, Chaldeans, Indians, or Persians)[4576] were three in number, to accord with the three gifts they bore: gold, frankincense, and myrrh. In later legends their names were given as Gaspar, Melchior, and Belthazar. Christian mystics view these three men as kings in their own right, royal Pagan astrologers who symbolize the Holy Trinity of mind, body, and spirit, personified in Greece as Zeus (male), Apollo (male), and Athene (female), and in the Christian Church as God (male), Jesus (male), and the Holy Ghost (female).

The inner meaning of the Star of Bethlehem, that is, the star Sirius, comes from Hinduism, where it is a symbol of the Third Eye (spiritual intuition),[4577] which correlates perfectly with Sirius' ancient Middle Eastern name: *Massaeil*, "Messiah."[4578] Herod symbolizes the Ego, the Lower Self, or Satan,[4579] while the three Wise Men represent belief in the divinity of the Christ; or, in the orthodox Church, the conversion of Pagans to Christianity.[4580] Mystically the three gifts of the kings symbolize the abundance of Spirit (gold), the charm of Spirit (frankincense), and the immortality of Spirit (myrrh),[4581] while the "East" (the Orient, the direction of the rising Sun) symbolizes light, that is, spiritual enlightenment.[4582]

In some esoteric Christian schools the Star of Bethlehem (again, scientifically speaking, the star Sirius)[4583] represents intuition,[4584] gold represents "perfection,"[4585] frankincense represents "worship,"[4586] and myrrh represents "protection."[4587] Sometimes the "three gifts" are emblems of Jesus' divinity, royalty, and humanity, respectively.[4588] Kingsford and Maitland write of the Magi:

> According to Catholic tradition, they were three in number, and were royal personages, a description which seems to identify them with the "kings of the East" of the Apocalyptic visions, whose habitat lies beyond the "great river Euphrates," and the way for whose coming requires to be specially prepared by the making of a ford across that river. Now the Euphrates is one of the "four rivers" of Genesis . . . as denoting the four constituent principles of the human kosmos. It is the Will; in man unfallen, the Divine Will; in man fallen, the human will. The East is the mystical term for the source of heavenly light "The glory of God came from the way of the East," says Ezekiel. Wherefore the "Kings of the East" are they who hold sway in a region lying beyond and above the "river" of the human Will, and only when that river is "dried up" can they approach man as heralds of the Divine Glory. Their function it is to announce the Epiphany of the Divine Life, to be the Sponsors for the Christ, the Godfathers of the heavenly Babe. To them it is

appointed to discern him from afar off, and to hasten to affirm and declare him while yet in his cradle. *Their offerings of gold, frankincense, and myrrh denote the recognition of the indwelling divinity by the prophetic, priestly, and regal attributes of man. Representing, respectively, the spirit, the soul, and the mind, they are symbolised as an angel, a queen, and a king; and they are, actually, Right Aspiration, Right Perception, and Right Judgment.* The first implies enthusiasm for the glory of God and the advancement of souls, unalloyed by any selfish end. The second implies a vision for things spiritual, undimmed and undistorted by intrusion of elements material or astral. And the third implies the ability to "compare like with like and preserve the affinity of similars," so that things spiritual may not be confounded with things physical, but "to God shall be rendered the things of God, and to Caesar the things of Caesar."[4589]

My mystical summation of the entire story of the Wise Men is as follows. A human being is made up of three divine aspects: spirit, soul, and body, and these are symbolized here, in order, as gold, frankincense, and myrrh. The infant Jesus represents the Universal Indwelling Christ awakening to its temporary life on the material plane (the "manger"). Joseph and Mary are emblems of the Hieros Gamos or "Holy Marriage" between the Divine Masculine (the Sun, spirit) and the Divine Feminine (the Moon, earth), a union which procreates the Indwelling Christ in each human body. The animals at the scene (not mentioned in the Bible, but astrologically inferred by Christian mystics) are symbols of humanity's base instincts, which must be "domesticated" (by the Christ) before we can experience at-one-ment with God. As "crowned kings" the Wise Men themselves represent spiritual enlightenment or Cosmic Consciousness (the head being the site of the Crown Chakra). They follow the Star of Bethlehem (the "Messiah" or "Third Eye") to its source (the Holy city, Jerusalem; a symbol of God), and there recognize and pay homage to the divinity, the Christ,[4590] within every man and woman (Theosis). See BIRTH OF JESUS, CHRIST, CHRISTMAS, GOOD NEWS, GOLD, FRANKINCENSE, AND MYRRH, GOSPEL, JESUS, MARY, NATIVITY, STAR OF BETHLEHEM, THEOSIS, VIRGIN BIRTH, VIRGO.

WORD (THE): The Word is identical to the LOGOS.

WORD OF GOD (THE): In traditional Christianity the Word of God includes only the canonical scriptures: the Old and New Testaments. In mystical Christianity the Word of God means any expression of Divine Truth, no matter where it derives from.[4591] This includes, of course, the sacred books, texts, documents, and doctrines of *all* religions, both Christian and non-Christian, both major and minor, both popular and unpopular, both well-known and obscure.

To the Christian mystic it is unthinkable that God would speak only to one select group. He/She/It is the God of all people, the entire human family, and, in fact, the hundreds of thousands of religions and names for God (and Goddess) that humanity has produced over the millennia is living proof. Christianity alone possesses some 50,000 denominations, sects, factions, schisms, and cults.

There is only one race: the human race, and every member of it is a child of God,[4592] made in His exact image and glory.[4593] As Paul states, God "hath made of one blood all nations of men for to dwell on all the face of the earth."[4594] See BIBLE, CHRISTMAS, FATHER, GOOD NEWS, GOSPEL, LOGOS, MOTHER, MOUTH OF GOD, UNION WITH GOD, VOICE OF GOD, WATER, WAY OF THE LORD.

A Buddhist monk walking on water.

A Greek triple-goddess: Clio, Ourania, and Thalia.

Seti I offering an image of Truth to Osiris.

Pagan Nativity with the Three Wise Men or Magi.

YAHWEH: In both the traditional and mystical Churches Yahweh is the same as God, though the latter finds additional esoteric symbolism in the word. The name Yahweh (or without vowels, YHWH, JHVH, or YHVH) is a Hebrew word whose meaning is much disputed by traditional Christians, the original meaning and pronunciation having been long ago lost (due, in great part, to the ancient Hebrew prohibition against uttering or writing the divine name). In the King James Bible Yahweh is often rendered "Lord" (a guess), though some conventional scholars speculate that the word derives from an archaic form of the verb *hawah*, "to be."[4595]

The Bible clearly shows that the name Yahweh was not used among the earliest Israelitish people. Moses himself did not know God's name,[4596] and God admits to the prophet that his name was not known to the Patriarchs Abraham, Isaac, and Jacob.[4597] Pre-Mosaic Semites, however, venerated their father-god as El Shaddai (traditionally translated in English as "God Almighty"), which is the name by which Abraham knew God.[4598]

Shaddai is a Hebracized version of the Greek word *Pantokrator*, meaning "All Power," "All Ruler," or "Almighty," Pantokrator itself being a title of the Greek messenger-god Hermes (in Rome, Mercury).[4599] As a proper name rather than a title, Shaddai was the name of an ancient Mesopotamian mountain-god,[4600] for El Shaddai literally means the "god of the mountain"; though it may have also referred to a double deity, such as a father-god (El) and his son (Shaddai).[4601]

In Genesis, the first book of the Bible, the Hebrew "God" is neither specifically male or even singular. He, She, It, or They was imaged as a group of deities that went by the pantheistic, polytheistic, Pagan noun-title, Elohim (El-Lohim)—El being the personal name of the father-god of the Ugaritic Pantheon.[4602]

In the earliest records, however, Yahweh is a supreme androgyne (half-god, half-goddess);[4603] that is, a hermaphrodite,[4604] complete with sewing[4605] and nursing skills,[4606] and a womb (*rechem*)[4607] by which She/He experienced labor pains (*meholeleka*)[4608] and gave birth (*yalad*).[4609] It is only later that Yahweh was transformed into the multi-god Elohim (the divine "us" of Genesis),[4610] comprised of the seven (some say 12, patterned on the 12 Greek Titans) deities who made up the ancient Jewish godhead.[4611]

Whatever its exact delineation, at the very least the later evolving "Yahweh" indeed consisted of a multiplicity of male and female deities, for the Bible itself says as much:

So God created man *in his own image*, in the image of God created he him; *male and female created he them*.[4612]

Tellingly, at one period Yahweh was also known as Baal,[4613] meaning "Lord,"[4614] the name of a Western Semitic (Canaanite) weather-god whose seven storm-god children[4615] were probably the Pagan models for the seven Israelite gods known collectively as the Elohim.[4616]

To complicate matters further, the English name for Yahweh is Jehovah, fabricated from combining a, o, a, the vowels of a Pagan god-name (Adonai, that is Adon or Adonis),[4617] and the sacred Tetragrammaton, JHVH, thus giving JaHoVaH. As noted, King James' 54 scribes routinely translated the Tetragrammaton as "Lord,"[4618] though "Jehovah" is used four times in the Old Testament.[4619]

While traditional Christians continue to wrangle with such historical minutia, in mystical Christianity the true identity of Yahweh is easily obtained from the narrative of the first meeting between God and Moses. Perplexed by a deity that was completely unknown to him, the prophet asked God's name. "I AM," the Heavenly Father replied.[4620]

I AM (rendered *EHYEH* in Hebrew)[4621] is an ancient spiritual code-phrase for the Universal Immanent God, revealed to Moses by his Third Eye (intuition) or EYE AM (I AM).[4622] It is identical to the Hindu Om or Aum, later known in Christianity as "the Amen,"[4623] another mystical expression for the Christ, the Higher Self that indwells all;[4624] that unchanging, unborn, unmade, unformed, imperishable, immortal portion of our being that was made in the image of God.[4625]

As the ultimate symbol of the sacred Hieros Gamos, or Sacred Union, between Heaven (man) and Earth (woman), in mystical Christianity another meaning for Yahweh is the "Immortal Masculine and Feminine Principles." This is why, from an arcane viewpoint, God can be an androgyne made up of both male and female energies,[4626] a common motif (Osiris and Isis, Ra and Hathor, Bilit and Bel) in pre-Christian Pagan religions.[4627] The first Christians, the Gnostics, viewed God in just this manner,[4628] calling him/her by the name Metropator: "Mother-Father,"[4629] the "two immortal parents."[4630] For, as they taught, we are born of two substances, which they mystically called the "Earthly Mother" (materiality, the conceptive force) and the "Heavenly Father" (spirituality, the generative force).[4631]

A deeper look into Yahweh's origins is instructive.

According to one school of thought Yahweh was first discovered by the Israelites during their stay at Meribat-Qades, an oasis located south of Palestine between the east end of the Sinai peninsula and western Arabia. Here they encountered an Arabic tribe of Midianites who were worshiping a god named Yahve or Jahve (later Hebracized as "Yahweh"), a demonic volcano-god. Though there are no volcanos in the area today, there were once active volcanos on Arabia's western border,[4632] one of these possibly being Mount Sinai[4633] or Mount Horeb,[4634] as it is also called, where Moses is said to have encountered Yahweh in a burning bush.[4635]

As Mount Sinai, literally the "Mountain of the Moon," takes its name from the Moon-god Sin—one-third of the ancient Babylonian Holy Trinity (along with the Sun-god Shamash and the Star-goddess Ishtar)—we can be sure that the "God" Moses spoke with was none other than Sin, that Jahve was a Midianite name for Sin,[4636] and that Yahweh took his name and identity from Jahve, and was thus yet another personification of this monstrous, pre-Israelite lunar deity.[4637] It was Sin after all, under the Chaldean name Kingu, who was born of the Mother-Goddess Inanna (Anna) and who received the "Tablets of Law" from the great Mother-Goddess Tiamat.[4638] This ties in exactly with the Gnostic-Christian doctrine that Yahweh is not the authentic Supreme God at all. Rather he is Satan, the evil misbegotten god of earth known to Gnostics as the Demiurge[4639] (from the Greek *demiourgos*, "public laborer" or "worker of the people").[4640] Thus orthodox Christians call the Demiurge "Jehovah," but Gnostic-Christians call him by his proper name: Yaldabaoth,[4641] whose name means "he who blasphemes against the Divine."[4642] Yaldabaoth (Yahweh) is thus the adversary of the authentic "Father in Heaven,"[4643] known to Gnostic-Christians as Bythus, the "one true God."[4644]

Jahve-Kingu-Sin-Yahweh's mother, the Goddess Inanna or Anna, was later assimilated by the Christian Church as "Saint Anne," the mother of the Virgin Mary and the wife of Joachim.[4645] Saint Anne's fabulous biography, taken from the apocryphal Protevangelium of James, bears a close resemblance to the Bible story of the childless Hannah (Anna, Anne) on which it was obviously patterned.[4646] In fact, Hannah, Inanna, and Anne are all personifications of the Canaanite goddess Ana, in Syria known as Anatha, in Sumeria as Anna-Nin, in Rome as Di-Ana, in Ireland as Morg-Ana, and in England as Black Annis. She was the Pagan "Grandmother of God," worshiped at Rome as Anna Perenna ("Eternal Anna") and also as Jana or Juno.[4647]

As Anne's early Syrian name was Anat and as many of her bloodthirsty attributes were passed onto Yahweh,[4648] it is possible that the word-name Yahweh may have originally evolved out of one of her ancient Near Eastern titles: Iahu Anat,[4649] Iahu, like IAOOUE and IEVOA, being an early magical sacred spelling of Yahweh.[4650] This is perfectly plausible, for as objective archaeology has proven, belief in a female supreme being ("Goddess") came long before belief in a male one ("God"). The name Iahu is no doubt then a variation of Jove (Jovis, Jupiter, Zeus), the male deity who would have replaced Iahu after the Patriarchal Takeover,[4651] which began in various parts of the world between 10,000 and 6,000 B.C.[4652]

Now Anat was the sister of the Pagan god Baal (one of Yahweh's original names), who was later known variously around Europe and the Middle East as Zeus,[4653] Jupiter,[4654] El, Cronos, Saturn, Bran, Dis, and Dionysus.[4655] Thus it is clear that from whatever angle we view him, Yahweh was a Jewish composite deity, patterned on hundreds of Pagan gods (and even many goddesses) who came before him. See FATHER, GOD, JEHOVAH, KINGDOM OF GOD, MOTHER,

MOUTH OF GOD, SON OF GOD, TEMPLE OF GOD, THEOSIS, UNION WITH GOD, VOICE OF GOD, WORD OF GOD.

YOKE OF JESUS: In traditional Christianity the *true inner* (that is esoteric) meaning of the "yoke of Jesus" is completely disregarded, many of the orthodox apparently viewing the topic with little interest beyond the superficial.[4656] Our Lord Himself describes His "yoke" this way:

> Come unto me, all ye that labour and are heavy laden, and I will give you rest. Take my yoke upon you, and learn of me; for I am meek and lowly in heart: and ye shall find rest unto your souls. For my yoke is easy, and my burden is light.[4657]

When the mainstream Church does comment on this subject it maintains that Jesus' yoke implies a type of "submission"[4658] in which good Christians must serve as a sort of slave under Him, their "slave master." Here, in turn, the removal of His yoke represents freedom, emancipation, or deliverance.[4659]

In mystical Christianity the inner meaning of the Greek word *zeugos* ("yoke"), as used by Jesus, has far deeper implications. In English *zeugos* can be spelled either "yoke" or "yoga," and esoterically both of these words mean the same thing: "balance,"[4660] "union,"[4661] "joining,"[4662] "to bind together,"[4663] or "conjunction" (that is, "conjugal").[4664] Yoke and yoga derive from the Indo-European root-word *jog*, *yuj*, or *yug*, symbolizing subordination to spiritual principles that entail both body and spirit.[4665] That is, one yokes himself to a particular spiritual objective in order to achieve it.[4666] Here, at-one-ment with the divine essence, that is, union with the Supreme Being,[4667] is attained by withdrawal from the world and mental suspension, which ultimately leads to the goal of samadhi,[4668] also known as self-realization, satori, kensho, moksha, nirvana, wu wei, enlightenment, or Christhood (acknowledging and embracing the Indwelling Christ).[4669]

Thus Jesus is actually saying "my yoga is easy"; that is, Union with the Universal I AM is simple and undemanding. For the Way of Christ is the balanced path to Oneness (at-one-ment) with God. Here is how our Lord's words read to the Christian mystic:

> Discover the Indwelling Christ, all those who seek at-one-ment, and it, the I AM, will give you rest. Take its yoga upon you, and learn of it; for the I AM is meek and lowly in heart: and in it you will find spiritual rest. For the yoga of the I AM is comfortable and gentle, and its weight is easily borne by anyone.[4670]

It is no accident that the body of the crucified Christ exhibits all of the elements of the Kundalini system of Indian Yoga, with the "Serpent" (human consciousness) ascending the "Tree of Life" (the spine),[4671] up the seven tree blossoms (chakras) to the "Sun" (the "crown"), where it realizes its divinity (Buddha or Christ Consciousness).[4672] Here unity with Spirit is the sole goal of the yogi, who is defined as a disciple of the Yoke of Christ-Buddha.[4673]

This doctrine, which began with the worship of the Indian god Shiva (the "Lord of Yoga") millennia ago,[4674] is found in all religions in one form or another. One of the many Buddhist "my-yoke-is-easy" formulas, for instance, goes as follows:

> To Buddha will I look in faith: he, the Exalted, is the holy, supreme Buddha, the Knowing, the instructed, the blessed, who knows the worlds, the Supreme One, who yoketh men like an ox, the Teacher of gods and men, the Exalted Buddha.[4675]

Whether Buddhist, Christian, Hindu, Shintoist, Jainist, Wiccan, Confucianist, or Jew, if we harness ourselves to the Christ Within (whatever name we choose to give it), we will be led to the ultimate reality, where perpetual happiness reigns supreme.[4676] In this sense, yoke or yoga has a further meaning: love.[4677]

It is not surprising that Jesus used the word yoga. It is clear from various passages in both the Gospels and the book of Revelation that He was well versed in the yoga sciences, and that He taught various yogic disciplines, such as meditation.[4678] Where would our Lord have learned such things? There is a long, ancient, and highly credible tradition that during his eighteen "silent years" (approximately ages 12-30), Jesus spent some of His time studying with various Hindu and Buddhist masters in the East.[4679] See JESUS, SILENT YEARS, WAY OF THE LORD.

Yahweh blessing his world.

The Virgin-Mother Isis nursing the Egyptian Christ-child, the Son-god Horus.

Emperor Nero, the "Beast" of Revelation.

The Greek Father-God Zeus.

The New Jerusalem.

Z

ZION: In the mainstream Church Zion is the name of a fortified hill in pre-Israelite Jerusalem. Later it became a poetic name for Jerusalem itself, as well as for the future religious capital of Israel.[4680] It is also used figuratively for both heaven and for the Jewish-Christian Church.[4681]

In the mystical Christian tradition Zion is a symbol of the Higher Self, the Indwelling Christ,[4682] which resides in "the temple of the living God": each human being.[4683] EGYPT, HEAVEN, HIGHER SELF, ISRAEL, JERUSALEM, THEOSIS.

ZODIAC: Traditional Christianity rejects astrology, claiming it does not appear in the Bible and is nothing more than a meaningless Pagan "pseudo-science," one that is both opposed by Christianity and condemned by the Good Book.[4684]

In mystical Christianity, however, astrology is completely accepted. Not only because the Zodiac (a word distantly related to the Hebrew *zedek*, "righteous")[4685] and its associated astrological elements appear countless times throughout the Bible, but because this important scientific art was taught by the early Israelites, as well as 1st-Century Jews, Essenes, Gnostics, and Christians. One scholar who carefully studied the history of astrology for several decades reckons that humanity has had an understanding of the Zodiac for at least 5 million years.[4686]

What is the Zodiac? Deriving from the Greek word *zoidiakos* ("carved figures"),[4687] it is an imaginary "circle" of figures (constellations) in the night sky. Hence the author of the book of Proverbs writes:

> When he prepared the heavens I was there: when he set a circle upon the face of the depth.[4688]

Ward writes of the Zodiac's mystical significance:

> In the [human] soul . . . is the spiritual Circle or Zodiac, wherein is fulfilled what the Twelve [Sun] signs represent in the natural Zodiacal system of the Universe or Macrocosm.[4689]

Pike explains how the annual passage of the Sun through the sky, particularly around the Mediterranean, gave birth to some of the 12 zodiacal constellations:

... the Ethiopian of Thebes or Saba styled those Stars under which the Nile commenced to overflow, Stars of Inundation, or that *poured out water* (Aquarius).

Those Stars among which the Sun was, when he had reached the Northern Tropic and began to *retreat* Southward, were termed, from his retrograde motion, the Crab (Cancer).

As he [the Sun] approached, in Autumn, the middle point between the Northern and Southern extremes of his journeying, the days and nights became *equal*; and the Stars among which he was then found were called Stars of the Balance (Libra).

Those stars among which the Sun was, when the *Lion*, driven from the Desert by thirst, came to slake it at the Nile, were called Stars of the Lion (Leo).

Those among which the Sun was at harvest, were called those of the Gleaning *Virgin*, holding a Sheaf of Wheat (Virgo).

Those among which he was found in February, when the *Ewes* brought their young, were called Stars of the Lamb (Aries).

Those in March, when it was time to *plough*, were called Stars of the Ox (Taurus).

Those under which hot and burning winds came from the desert, venomous like *poisonous reptiles*, were called Stars of the Scorpion (Scorpio).

Observing that the annual return of the rising of the Nile was always accompanied by the appearance of a beautiful Star [the future "Star of Bethlehem"], which at that period showed itself in the direction of the sources of that river, and seemed to warn the husbandman to be careful not to be surprised by the inundation, the Ethiopian compared this act of that Star to that of the Animal which by *barking* gives warning of danger, and styled it the Dog (Sirius).

Thus commencing, and as astronomy came to be more studied, imaginary figures were traced all over the Heavens, to which the different Stars were assigned. Chief among them were those that lay along the path which the Sun travelled as he climbed toward the North and descended to the South: lying within certain limits and extending to an equal distance on each side of the line of equal nights and days. This belt, curving like a Serpent, was termed the Zodiac, and divided into twelve Signs.[4690]

Among the more significant mystical Christian astrological doctrines there is the Cancer-Capricorn Polarity, or "Gates of the Sun," which have to do with spiritual involution, evolution, and reincarnation. Cancer, ruled by the Moon-Goddess Luna or Diana, is the "entrance gate" or "Gate of Men," where souls enter the earth plane. Capricorn, ruled by the Father-God Saturn or Kronos, is the "exit gate" or "Gate of the Gods," where souls leave and reenter the spirit plane.[4691] Cancer falls at the beginning of Summer (the Summer Solstice), where, according to the ancient universal pre-Christian Solar Passion Play, the Sun-God reaches its peak physical strength. Capricorn falls at the start of Winter (the Winter Solstice), where the Sun-God "dies," but is "reborn" of the Virgin-Mother (Virgo) in the Stable of Augeas (Auriga the Shepherd). Both of these Pagan holy days were taken over by the orthodox Church, the former becoming Midsummer or John the Baptist's Feast Day, the latter becoming Christmas, the Mass of the Indwelling Christ.[4692]

This same Zodiacal creed was once taught by some of our earliest and most enlightened Christian authorities. Müller writes:

> [The] cave of the nymphs, mentioned by Homer, was taken by Porphyrius and other philosophers, such as Numenius and Cronius, as *a symbol of the earth with its two doors.* . . . These doors of the cave have been explained as the *gates leading from and to the earth.* Thus Porphyrius says that there are two extremities in the heavens, viz. the *winter solstice,* than which no part is nearer to the South, and the *summer solstice* which is situated next to the North. But the summer tropic, that is the solstitial circle, is in Cancer, and the winter tropic in Capricorn. And since Cancer is the nearest to the earth, it is deservedly attributed to the *Moon,* which is itself proximate to the earth. But since the southern pole by its greatest distance is inconspicuous to us, Capricorn is ascribed to *Saturn,* who is the highest and most remote of all the planets.
>
> . . . *Theologians admitted therefore two gates,* Cancer *and* Capricorn, and Plato also meant these by what he calls the two mouths. *Of these they affirm that Cancer is the gate through which souls descend, but Capricorn that through which they ascend (and exchange a material for a divine condition of being).* And indeed the gates of the cave which look to the North are with great propriety said to be pervious to *the descent of men:* but the northern gates are not the avenues of the gods, but of *souls ascending to the gods.* On this account the poet does not say it is the passage of the gods, but of immortals, which appellation is also common to *our souls, which by themselves or by their essence are*

immortal.

The idea that the place to which the sun returns, whether in its northward or southward progress, is a door by which the souls may ascend to heaven, is at least conceivable, quite as much as the idea which Macrobius in the twelfth chapter of his comment on Scipio's dream ascribed to Pythagoras, who, as he tells us, thought that the empire of Pluto began downwards with the Milky Way, because souls falling from thence appear already to have receded from the gods.[4693]

In Judaism the Zodiac is best known as the "12 Tribes of Israel," while in Christianity it is best known as the "12 Apostles." Both are mystical symbols of the 12 Sun-signs, which are, in turn, occult representations of Man's 12 faculties or spiritual powers.[4694] The 2nd-Century synagogue at Beth Shan was decorated with Zodiacal features,[4695] and astrological emblems can still be seen in Christian Cathedrals, like Chartres in Paris, France.[4696] See APOSTLES, ASTROLOGY, CHRISTMAS, GOOD NEWS, GOSPEL, NATIVITY, REINCARNATION, TETRAMORPH, TRIBES OF ISRAEL, TWELVE.

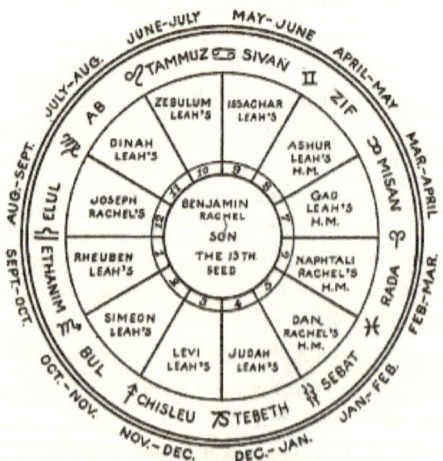

The Zodiac and the 12 Tribes of Israel.

Jesus blessing the children.

Jesus and the woman of Samaria.

Jesus' triumphant entry into Jerusalem.

The Sermon on the Mount.

Appendix A: A List of Christian Mystics

Notable Mystical Christians Through History

Abraham von Franckenberg
Agnes Blannbekin
Albertus Magnus
Aldebert
Alexandrina Maria da Costa
Alice Auma
Amalric of Bena
Anna Kingsford
Anne Catherine Emmerich
Ann Lee
Antoine Arnauld
Antoinette Bourignon
Athenagoras of Athens
Augustine of Hippo
Basil the Great
Beatrice of Nazareth
Benedetta Carlini
Bernadette Soubirous
Bernard of Clairvaux
Blaise Pascal
Brother Lawrence
Bruno of Cologne
Carmella Carabelli
Charles Fillmore
Charles Marshall
Christian Markyate
Conrad Beissel
Consolata Betrone
Cora Evans
Corinne Heline
Dag Hammarskjöld
David of Augsburg
Denis the Carthusian
Edgar Cayce
Edmund H. Broadbent
Elisabeth of Schönau
Emma Curtis Hopkins
Emmet Fox
Emanuel Swedenborg
Evagrius Ponticus
Evelyn Underhill
Flower A. Newhouse
Gabrielle Bossis
George Fox
George Herbert
George MacDonald
George Rapp
Gerard Appelmans
Giordano Bruno
Gottfried Arnold
Grace Mann Brown

Gregory of Nazianzus
Gregory of Nyssa
Gundolfo
Guy Finley
Hadewijch
Henry Suso
Henry Vaughan
Hildegard of Bingen
Hugh of St. Victor
Ignatius of Antioch
Irenaeus
Jakob Böhme
James Nayler
Jan van Ruysbroeck
Jeanne Guyon
Jeremy Taylor
Jesus of Nazareth (Essene-Gnostic)
Joachim of Fiore
Joan of Arc
Johannes Tauler
John A. Sanford
John Chrysostom
John O'Donohue
John of Patmos
John Philip Newell
John Scotus
Julian of Norwich
Justin Martyr
Kathleen Norris
Lilian Staveley
Lilias Trotter
Lochlainn Seabrook
Lucy Brocadelli
Macarius of Egypt
Madam Guyon
Margaret Prescott Montague
Margery Kemp
Marguerite Porete
Maria Grazia Tarallo
Maria Orsola Bussone
Maria Theresa Chiramel
Martin Luther
Martin Moller
Max Heindel
Maximus the Confessor
Mechthild of Magdeburg
Meister Eckhart
Mother Shipton
Mother Teresa
Nicholas Ferrar
Origen

Osanna of Cattaro
Paracelsus
Paul the Apostle
Peter of Bruys
Peter Lombard
Peter Waldo
Phineas Quimby
Pierre Teilhard de Chardin
Pope Gregory I the Great
Priscillian
Pseudo-Dionysius the Aeropagite
Richard Crashaw
Richard Rolle
Richard of St. Victor
Saint Angela of Foligno
Saint Antony
Saint Bonaventure
Saint Bridget of Sweden
Saint Catherine of Genoa
Saint Catherine Labouré
Saint Catherine of Siena
Saint Claire of Assisi
Saint Faustina
Saint Francis de Sales
Saint Francis of Assisi
Saint Gertrude
Saint Ignatius Loyola
Saint John of the Cross
Saint Pio
Saint Polycarp
Saint Teresa of Avila
Saint Thomas Aquinas
Seraphim Rose
Simone Weil
Sophie Swetchine
Tertullian
Therese Neumann
Thérèse of Lisieux
Thomas Merton
Venerable Luis de Lapuente
Walter Hilton
William Blake
William Flete
William Inge
William Law
William M. Branham
William of Saint-Thierry
William Walker Atkinson
William Wordsworth
Yvette of Huy
Zosimas of Palestine

Appendix B: The Mystic's Creed

A Brief Summary of Mystical Christian Beliefs

† The Bible is a mystical work and so is best read and understood mystically.
† The Jesus of the Bible was a historical person, a real teacher, mystic, and healer.[4697]
† Jesus' *authentic* teachings are true.[4698]
† The many Pagan elements that have been appended to Jesus are not literally true. They are allegorical, concealing profound spiritual truths.[4699]
† Jesus taught "The Gospel of the Kingdom of God";[4700] the Church teaches its own invention, "The Gospel of Jesus Christ."[4701]
† Jesus came to earth as a "model for mankind,"[4702] an example of what all men and women can be.[4703]
† The salvation of every person is guaranteed.[4704]
† Jesus chose us[4705]—and we chose Him.[4706]
† Jesus is divine—and so are we.[4707]
† Jesus is the Christ—and so are we.[4708]
† Jesus performed miracles—and so can we.[4709]
† Our experiences, health, life, and "fate" are determined by our thoughts.[4710]
† This amazing spiritual gift (total free will) makes us, not God or Satan, responsible for everything that happens to us.[4711]
† As mystically portrayed in the Gospels, every human being is "immaculately conceived," "virgin-born," "bears a cross" (the body), has "12 Apostles" (12 mental faculties), and experiences the "Temptation," the "Transfiguration," "Crucifixion," "Resurrection," "Ascension," and finally "Exaltation."[4712]
† Jesus' name is all powerful and praying in His name (with total faith) can bring about any positive result that is sincerely desired.[4713]
† Jesus said, did, and taught many things that have been perverted, suppressed, and forgotten.[4714]
† Jesus is unique.[4715]
† Jesus' Kingdom is within us.[4716]
† Jesus is still very much alive and is at work on earth right now.[4717]
† Jesus is a Bodhisattva, one of many who have appeared periodically throughout history in order to restore spirituality to religion[4718] and save mankind.[4719]
† Jesus is a numenistic mystery that cannot be understood by the rational mind.[4720]
† The more we try to literally define and explain Jesus the further away we get from understanding Him.[4721]
† Jesus' life story, as recorded in the New Testament, contains so many mistranslations, redactions, contradictions, and lacunae, that it can never be fully pieced together.[4722] Thus the importance of faith.[4723]
† Jesus centered His worship on God the Father—and so must we.[4724]
† If read and understood mystically (rather than literally) the Bible is the world's most complete and useful guidebook to living the Good Life.[4725]
† Jesus taught many Spiritual Laws and Doctrines, but His most important are the Laws of Universal Love,[4726] Forgiveness,[4727] and Tolerance.[4728]

NOTES

1. Van Etten, pp. 122, 137.
2. Matthew 19:26.
3. M. P. Hall, p. 126.
4. See Akerley, passim.
5. For more on this topic, see e.g., Schonfield, TJP, pp. 10-11.
6. Freud, MAM, p. 52.
7. I. M. Price, p. 293.
8. Szekeley, TDOTEGOP, p. 17.
9. Kee, p. 2.
10. Strauss, TLOJCE, Vol. 1, p. 77.
11. Baigent and Leigh, p. xiii.
12. Layton, p. 382. (From The Gospel of Thomas.)
13. See H. Smith, p. 323.
14. James, p. 379.
15. A. Pike, pp. 512-513.
16. Krishna, TRNOME, p. 41.
17. A. Pike, p. 593.
18. Inge, CM, p. 250.
19. M. P. Hall, p. 20.
20. Spong, p. 64.
21. A. Pike, p. 371.
22. Potter, pp. 153-154.
23. Schonfield, TPP, p. 59.
24. Hoeller, pp. 187-201.
25. May, p. 73.
26. See A. Pike, p. 375.
27. H. S. Lewis, TSDOJ, pp. 75, 82-84, 199.
28. See e.g., Mascaró, p. 23.
29. M. P. Hall, p. 76.
30. M. P. Hall, p. 155.
31. See Lundy, passim.
32. Matthew 15:6-9.
33. Potter, pp. 81-84.
34. See Luke 21:32.
35. See 1 Thessalonians 4:16-17.
36. Hoffman, p. 26.
37. Zechariah 4:14.
38. See Potter, passim.
39. See Acts 15.
40. Lamsa, IITBE, p. 75; Neill, WWKAJ, p. 77.
41. Filson, pp. 153-154; Potter, pp. 77-78, 138-139, 155; Lamsa, IITBE, p. 86; Spivey and Smith, p. 498.
42. Schonfield, TPP, p. 211.
43. Brewster, p. 39.
44. Schweitzer, TQOTHJ, p. 172.
45. Feuerbach, p. 148.
46. Schweitzer, TQOTHJ, p. 3.
47. M. P. Hall, p. 50.
48. Frazer, AAO, p. 156.
49. See J. M. Robertson, PC, passim.
50. J. E. M. White, AE, p. 45.
51. Neil, TIOTNT, pp. 154-155.

52. M. P. Hall, p. 35.
53. Thus in ancient Egypt the Greek god Zeus was adopted and renamed Zeus-Amon-Re, in Italy Zeus-Jupiter, and Zeus-Hypsistos, etc. See F. C. Grant, p. xiii, passim.
54. Gordon, s.v. "Christianity."
55. See e.g., M. Grant, CTG, pp. 135-136.
56. Mark 1:14.
57. Schweitzer, TQOTHJ, p. 102.
58. Mark 1:1.
59. Schonfield, TPP, pp. 220-221, 236.
60. Link, pp. 40-41. For other biblical examples of purposeful exaggeration that is not meant to be taken literally, see Genesis 5:1-32; 24:60; Judges 15:15; Mark 1:33; John 2:19.
61. See Matthew 26:69-75; Luke 22:55-62; John 18:15-27.
62. Schonfield, TPP, p. 135.
63. Potter, pp. 82-84, 129; H. S. Lewis, TSDOJ, pp. 220-221.
64. Filson, p. 44.
65. Freud, MAM, p. 115.
66. Wheeler, pp. 1-2. Emphasis added.
67. Wheeler, p. 2. Emphasis added.
68. Wheeler, p. 2. Emphasis added.
69. Wheeler, p. 2. Emphasis added.
70. Wheeler, pp. 2-3. Emphasis added.
71. Emerson, p. 575. Emphasis added.
72. A. Pike, p. 516. Emphasis added.
73. Channing, p. 306. Emphasis added.
74. For more on the topic of the American "Civil War" as seen from the South's point of view, see Seabrook, EYWTATCWIW, passim; Seabrook, TGYC, passim; Seabrook, C101, passim; Seabrook, EYWTAASIW, passim.
75. A. Pike, pp. 22, 161, 205, 732, 818. Emphasis added.
76. A. Pike, p. 210. Emphasis added.
77. Parker, pp. 13-17. Emphasis added.
78. Angus, p. 244.
79. Schweitzer, TQOTHJ, p. 309.
80. Schonfield, TPP, pp. 13-14.
81. See e.g., Weigall, passim.
82. H. S. Lewis, TSDOJ, pp. 195, 217, 219, 224, 226-227.
83. Van Etten, pp. 145, 149, 151.
84. John 18:36.
85. A. Pike, pp. 295-296. Emphasis added.
86. Neill, WWKAJ, p. 68.
87. M. Grant, CTG, pp. 160, 184.
88. The three Pastorals are: 1 Timothy, 2 Timothy, and Titus.
89. Spivey and Smith, pp. 404, 413.
90. H. S. Lewis, TSDOJ, pp. 215-219.
91. Hefele, passim.
92. See Schweitzer, TQOTHJ, passim.
93. John 10:34.
94. John 14:12.
95. Luke 17:21.
96. Schonfield, TPP, p. 196.
97. Schonfield, TPP, p. 92.
98. A. Pike, pp. 62-63. Emphasis added.
99. Parker, pp. 25-26. Emphasis added.
100. H. S. Lewis, TSDOJ, pp. 220-221.

101. In order to buttress the official authority of the priesthood over personal intuition the Catholic Church's "Norms of Orthodoxy" goes as far as to declare: "We must put aside all judgment of our own and keep the mind ever ready and prompt to obey in all things the true Spouse of Christ our Lord, and Holy Mother, the hierarchical Church." Hardon, s.v. "Norms of Orthodoxy."
102. Grusin, p. 20.
103. See Channing, p. 302.
104. Schweitzer, TQOTHJ, p. 153.
105. Schweitzer, TQOTHJ, p. ix.
106. Hodson, Vol. 1, p. i.
107. Filson, p. 44.
108. J. G. Jackson, CBC, p. 122; H. S. Lewis, TSDOJ, p. 219. See also Gaskell, s.v. "Three Days."
109. See M. Grant, CTG, passim.
110. Schonfield, TPP, p. 61.
111. Herrmann, p. 53. See also Baigent, Leigh, and Lincoln, TML, p. 367, who attribute this quote to Pope Alexander VI.
112. Titcomb, p. 105.
113. The immense debt Christianity owes to mysticism and especially to the Pagan Mystery Cults can be proven not only from a careful reading of the New Testament, as this very book shows, but by the inscriptions on ancient Graeco-Roman sepulchers. Of them Angus writes: "The language would sometimes point equally to membership in the Christian Church or in a [Pagan] mystery-cult." Angus, p. 20.
114. Kingsford and Maitland, p. 188.
115. Matthew 2:11.
116. Matthew 1:25.
117. Matthew 1:20.
118. Matthew 1:18.
119. Matthew 3:16.
120. Luke 9:23; 14:27.
121. Matthew 1:23.
122. Luke 2:40-49.
123. Luke 2:52.
124. Matthew 4:1-11.
125. Matthew 17:1-13.
126. Matthew 26:1-75; 27:1-50.
127. Matthew 27:35-50.
128. Luke 24:1-6.
129. Luke 24:51.
130. Revelation 3:12.
131. John 3:7.
132. 2 Corinthians 12:2.
133. Luke 22:69.
134. Hoeller, p. 130.
135. Luke 3:6; Romans 10:13; Acts 2:17; 2 Peter 3:9.
136. For more on this topic, see Seabrook, JATLOA, passim.
137. M. P. Hall, p. 202.
138. Proverbs 23:7.
139. Steiger, IMSIAF, p. 125.
140. Evans-Wentz, p. 82. My paraphrasal.
141. Lieberman, p. xxiv.
142. Evans-Wentz, p. 99.
143. Burtt, pp. 139, 213.
144. See Martin and Romanowski, p. 61.
145. Curtiss and Curtiss, TKTTU, p. 371.
146. Elder, pp. 10, 20.
147. Hartmann, ITPOTTOW, p. 133.
148. A. Pike, p. 436. Emphasis added.

149. Heckethorne, Vol. 1, p. 16.
150. Baba, pp. 18-19. My paraphrasal.
151. Maharshi, p. 106.
152. Lasne and Gaultier, p. 220.
153. See Seabrook, JATLOA, pp. 15, 61, 285.
154. Grusin, p. 52.
155. Hoeller, p. 187.
156. See Grusin, p. 71.
157. E. D. Cohen, p. 409.
158. See e.g., Ramm, p. 94.
159. See, e.g., James, p. 7. This same intolerant unenlightened group refers to Paul's vision on the road to Damascus as a "discharging lesion of the occipital cortex, he being an epileptic." James, p. 13. In turn, some from the more liberal Christian school might be inclined to see conservative Christianity as theopathological and even Christopathological.
160. Mascaró, p. 27. My paraphrasal.
161. Szekely, TDOTEGOP, p. 29.
162. Neill, TIOTNT, p. 179.
163. Spivey and Smith, p. 496.
164. See e.g., 1 Corinthians 1:10-13. Among the many types of early Christianity, there was Gnostic-Christianity, Essenic-Christianity, Jewish-Christianity, Hellenistic-Christianity, Apocalyptic-Christianity, Enthusiastic-Christianity, and Catholic-Christianity, among others. See Dunn, passim.
165. Ross and Hills, p. 149.
166. Philippians 2:12. See also Dowling, 100:17. Buddha made a similar comment: "Work out your own salvation with diligence." Burtt, pp. 22, 49, 80.
167. Burtt, p. 22.
168. M. P. Hall, p. 132 b.
169. J. N. D. Anderson, p. 25.
170. 1 Corinthians 2:16; Philippians 2:5.
171. Matthew 18:3; Mark 10:15.
172. See Suzuki, passim.
173. Luke 17:21.
174. A. Pike, p. 252.
175. M. P. Hall, p. 58.
176. Ramm, p. 23.
177. Sewall, p. 132.
178. From the sermon "The Spiritual Meaning of Childhood," by John Reginald Campbell.
179. R. J. Campbell, p. 255.
180. Strauss, TLOJCE, Vol. 1, p. 12.
181. Hoeller, pp. 8-9.
182. Keck, pp. 168-169.
183. Spong, p. 6.
184. Deuteronomy 13:6-10.
185. Exodus 31:14-15.
186. Numbers 11:32-36; Exodus 35:2-3.
187. Exodus 12:15, 19.
188. Leviticus 7:22-25.
189. Deuteronomy 22:21; Leviticus 21:9.
190. Deuteronomy 22:22-24.
191. Leviticus 20:27; Exodus 22:18.
192. Exodus 22:20.
193. For more on this view, see Hoeller, pp. 4-5.
194. Rich, p. 19.
195. See Van Etten, p. 14.
196. Bucke, p. 124.
197. Bucke, p. 124.

198. Job 42:5.
199. James, p. 383.
200. See Goring, s.v. "hermeneutics, Christian."
201. Note that hermeneutics can be applied to any text, not just the Bible.
202. Ramm, p. 7. Hermes was known in ancient Egypt as the god Thoth and in Rome as the god Mercury.
203. See Carlyon, s.v. "Hermes"; R. Graves, TWG, pp. 99, 126, 159, 174, 191, 229, 230, 233, 288, 331, 355, 357; B. Evans, s.v. "Hermes"; Grimal, s.v. "Hermes"; Zimmerman, s.v. "Hermes"; Bently, s.v. "Hermes"; Tripp, s.v. "Hermes"; Lurker, TGASOAE, s.v. "Thoth"; Jung, MAHS, pp. 154, 154; Leeming, s.v. "Hermes" (pp. 163-165); M. Jordan, s.v. "Hermes"; Goring, s.v. "Hermetica"; Spence, s.v. "Hermes Trismegistus"; Grant and Hazel, s.v. "Hermes"; L. M. Graham, p. 251; B. G. Walker, TWEOMAS, s.v. "Hermes"; Biedermann, s.v. "Mercury"; Sykes, s.v. "Thoth"; Butler, s.v. "Hermes"; A. T. White, pp. 21, 28, 30; Cotterell, TMIEOMAL, s.v. "Hermes"; Guirand, pp. 123-124; Neumann, pp. 324, 328; Littleton, M, pp. 188-195; Lurker, DOGAGDAD, s.v. "Hermes"; Hinnels, s.v. "Hermetica"; "Hermetism"; Perowne, pp. 51, 53, 54, 67; B. G. Walker, TWDOSASO, pp. 204-205; Layton, pp. 447-448, Hart, s.v. "Hermes"; Cotterell, ADOWM, s.v. "Hermes" (p. 163); Baumgartner, s.v. "Hermes."
204. Swedenborg, TTCR, p. 291. Emphasis added.
205. A. Pike, p. 434. Emphasis added.
206. J. Campbell, TOMTT, p. 94.
207. Kingsford, and Maitland, p. 149. Emphasis added.
208. 1 Corinthians 2:7.
209. Daraul, pp. 138-139.
210. Matthew 13:11.
211. Daraul, p. 139.
212. Stirling, p. 45. Emphasis added.
213. Stirling, p. 45. Emphasis added.
214. Ephesians 3:3. See also Acts 2:28.
215. Stirling, p. 47. Emphasis added.
216. A. Pike, pp. 265-266. Emphasis added.
217. Galatians 4:22-26. Emphasis added.
218. Dentan, p. 161.
219. Galatians 2:20. Emphasis added.
220. Channing, p. lxi. Emphasis added.
221. Shinn, p. 11.
222. M. Fox, WS, p. 389.
223. Yogananda, TSCOC, Vol. 1, pp. 240, 257. My paraphrasal.
224. Neill, WWKAJ, p. 40.
225. A. Pike, p. 250. Emphasis added.
226. Clymer, p. 124. Emphasis added.
227. See e.g., Matthew 13:11; Mark 4:11; Luke 8:10; Romans 11:25, 16:25; 1 Corinthians 2:7, 4:1, 13:2, 14:2, 15:51; Ephesians 1:9, 3:3-9, 5:32; Colossians 1:26-27, 2:2, 4:3; 2 Thessalonians 2:7; 1 Timothy 3:9-16; Revelation 1:20, 10:7, 17:5, 17:7.
228. H. S. Lewis, TSDOJ, p. 192.
229. Schweitzer, TQOTHJ, pp. 162, 174, 178. My paraphrasal.
230. Neill, WWKAJ, p. 71.
231. Schweitzer, TQOTHJ, p. ix.
232. Matthew 7:6.
233. See Schweitzer, TQOTHJ, p. 246.
234. See Schweitzer, TQOTHJ, pp. 263, 354.
235. Mark 4:1-12, 33-34.
236. Mark 4:9.
237. See Schweitzer, TQOTHJ, pp. 266, 358.
238. Schonfield, TPP, p. 74.
239. See e.g., Mark 4:10-23.
240. John 4:24. The KJV uses "God is *a* Spirit," a mistranslation. The original is: "God is Spirit." Spalding, Vol. 4, p. 24; Neill, WWKAJ, p. 78. See also Romans 1:20; 1 Timothy 1:17.

241. John 4:24.
242. Baba, pp. 37-38.
243. Matthew 16:17.
244. Ramm, p. 18.
245. Ramm, p. 82. Emphasis added.
246. Knox, p. 236.
247. Wright, Ballantine, and Foster, pp. 375-376. Emphasis added.
248. 2 Corinthians 3:6.
249. A. Pike, p. 237.
250. Cooper-Oakley, pp. 45-46.
251. John 6:35.
252. Mark 4:23.
253. Colossians 3:11.
254. Psalm 18:28.
255. See Keck, pp. 49-50.
256. Luke 8:50.
257. A. Pike, p. 819.
258. See Keck, pp. 8, 16.
259. Steiger, IMSIAF, p. 72.
260. Yoder, TPOJ, p. 17.
261. Leishman, TCOTB, pp. 86, 89.
262. See Galatians 3:24-25.
263. Ramm, pp. 21-23.
264. Burtt, p. 226.
265. A. Pike, p. 771.
266. Ramm, pp. 23-24.
267. The battle between liberal esotericism and conservative exotericism can be found in nearly every religion. See e.g., Evans-Wentz, pp. 32-33.
268. Evans-Wentz, p. 122.
269. Eavns-Wentz, p. 148.
270. Romans 16:25.
271. Dowling, 145:31.
272. See M. Smith, passim.
273. Canonical Mark appears to be the "public" version of the original, Secret Mark, which was reserved for Jesus' most advanced students, the 12 Apostles.
274. Clement referred to Jesus' mysterious teachings in the Secret Gospel of Mark as "that truth hidden by seven veils."
275. Hoeller, p. 202.
276. H. S. Lewis, TSDOJ, pp. 97-100, 110-112, 149.
277. Luke 8:10.
278. H. S. Lewis, TSDOJ, pp. 85-95.
279. Clement's comment is from his work *Stromata*.
280. A. Pike, p. 103. Emphasis added.
281. A. Pike, pp. 104-105. Emphasis added.
282. Daraul, p. 35.
283. A. Pike, pp. 815-816. Emphasis added.
284. See e.g., John 7:10.
285. Acts 1:15.
286. Jesus' secret academy, the "School of Christ," offered a curriculum that included private lectures and demonstrations of His teachings and doctrines at various secret meeting places. See H. S. Lewis, TSDOJ, pp. 97-100, 110-112, 149, 172.
287. Cox, Vol. 2, p. 125.
288. Mark 4:34.
289. Dowling, 115:10-14.
290. John 16:12.

291. F. M. Müller, TSBOTE, Vol. 15, pp. 41-42. (Mundaka Upanishad 3:2:10.) Emphasis added.
292. See Mark 4:1-9.
293. Burtt, pp. 121-122, 126-127, 154.
294. Matthew 24:14. See also Matthew 4:23; 9:35; Luke 4:43.
295. Mark 1:1.
296. Luke 8:10.
297. See Shinn, p. 30.
298. The belief that "Christ" is Jesus' surname is still current in many parts of the world.
299. James, p. 6.
300. See Matthew 13:55; Luke 2:41, 48; 3:23; 4:22; John 1:45; 6:42; Hebrews 3:3; 7:24; 10:12.
301. Matthew 16:20.
302. John 12:32; 14:20; 15:4; 17:21-23, 26; Colossians 1:27; 3:10-11; Romans 8:10; 1 Corinthians 6:15, 17; 2 Corinthians 5:16; 13:3, 5; Galatians 1:16; 2:20; 4:19; Ephesians 3:14-17; Philippians 1:20; 2:5; 1 Peter 1:11; 1 John 2:27; 3:24; 4:4.
303. 1 Corinthians 3:16.
304. Matthew 3:2; 4:17; 5:3, 10; 10:7.
305. Colossians 1:27. See also Ephesians 2:13-18.
306. Matthew 5:48.
307. Colossians 2:10.
308. Genesis 1:27. See also A. Pike, p. 252.
309. Yogananda, TSCOC, Vol. 1, p. 148.
310. Schweitzer, TQOTHJ, p. 318.
311. Schonfield, TANT, p. 139.
312. A. Pike, p. 308.
313. M. P. Hall, p. 178. See Ephesians 4:13.
314. Schonfield, TPP, pp. 192-193.
315. Dowling, 127:6.
316. 2 Peter 1:4.
317. John 17:21.
318. See John 14:12.
319. John 12:32; 14:20; 15:4; 17:21-23, 26; Colossians 1:27; 3:10-11; Romans 8:10; 1 Corinthians 6:15, 17; 2 Corinthians 5:16; 13:3, 5; Galatians 1:16; 2:20; 4:19; Ephesians 3:14-17; Philippians 1:20; 2:5; 1 Peter 1:11; 1 John 2:27; 3:24; 4:4.
320. Romans 8:14; John 1:12.
321. See e.g., Galatians 4:19; 2 Corinthians 1:21.
322. Daniel 7:13-14.
323. 2 Corinthians 6:16.
324. See the Gnostic text entitled, The Prayer of the Apostle Paul.
325. See Psalms 110:1.
326. Matthew 22:41-46. See also Daniel 7:13-14; Micah 5:2; Matthew 28:20; John 8:58; Hebrews 7:3; Revelation 22:13.
327. One of the Hindu prayers goes like this: "They call you by so many names. They divide you, as it were, by different names; yet in each one of these is to be found your omnipotence. You can be reached through any of these."
328. Note: The three grades I have listed here are not meant to be prejudicial. For example, in our earthly schools the second grade is not inferior to the ninth grade merely because it is lower on the educational scale. All men and women are equal in the sight of God, though he recognizes that we are each at a different level of spiritual evolution.
329. M. L. Prophet and E. C. Prophet, p. 93.
330. See Yogananda, TSCOC, Vol. 1, pp. xxiii-xxiv.
331. Pertaining to religion, Jung also divided humanity into three types. See Jung, MAHS, pp. 250-251.
332. H. S. Lewis, TSDOJ, pp. 20-21.
333. See Watts, MARIC, pp. 160-161; Guignebert, pp. 270-271. These three "essential types of mankind" are also discussed at length in numerous Gnostic-Christian texts. See e.g., the document known as the Tripartite Tractate, Part 3, Chapter 14. See also Kelly, p. 5.

334. The orthodox Church was not the only branch that divided its members into three classes. The so-called "heterodox" branch did as well, including the following Christian sects: the Basilideans, the Simonians, the Valentinians, the Marcosians, Manicheans, and the Ophites. As illustrated in the Bhagavad-Gita, Hinduism also teaches that Man must go through three distinct stages of spiritual development before attaining the ultimate goal of self-realization or enlightenment.
335. A. Pike, p. 541. Emphasis added.
336. Eusebius, *The History of the Church*, 2.1.4.
337. See A. Pike, pp. 542-548.
338. 1 Corinthians 4:1.
339. M. L. Prophet and E. C. Prophet, p. xlviii.
340. 1 Corinthians 15:41.
341. 1 Corinthians 2:7.
342. 1 Corinthians 2:10.
343. 1 Corinthians 14:2. What was this "hidden wisdom," in Greek, literally the "*Mistikos Sophia*"? From the name itself we know that it was related, in part, to the mysteries of the Sacred Feminine, for Sophia was the great Greek wisdom-goddess (known as Sapientia in Rome, and as Shekina in mystical Judaism), worshiped widely across the Roman world.
344. 1 Corinthians 4:1.
345. 1 Corinthians 2:6-16; 3:1-3. Emphasis added.
346. See Watts, MARIC, pp. 160-161.
347. 1 Corinthians 4:8, 14-21.
348. Matthew 5:48. Emphasis added.
349. Matthew 19:21. Emphasis added.
350. John 17:23. Emphasis added.
351. Luke 6:40. Emphasis added.
352. My paraphrasal.
353. The Gospel of Thomas, Logion 114. Paul often used this same occult symbolism to denote spiritual immaturity (females) and spiritual maturity (males). See e.g., 1 Corinthians 14:34; 1 Timothy 2:11-12.
354. The Gospel of Thomas the Contender, 140:9-11. My paraphrasal. (Some translations have "for" instead of "of.")
355. 2 Corinthians 13:9, 11. Emphasis added.
356. Ephesians 4:13. Emphasis added.
357. Philippians 3:12. Emphasis added.
358. Philippians 3:15. Emphasis added.
359. Colossians 1:28. Emphasis added.
360. Colossians 4:12. Emphasis added.
361. 2 Timothy 3:17. Emphasis added.
362. Hebrews 11:40. Emphasis added.
363. James 1:4. Emphasis added.
364. James 3:2. Emphasis added.
365. 1 Peter 5:10. Emphasis added.
366. Potter, p. 130.
367. Hebrews 6:1-6. Emphasis added.
368. 1 Corinthians 2:7.
369. Colossians 2:2-3.
370. Romans 1:16-17.
371. Colossians 1:26.
372. The Genesaic cosmogony, or Hebrew creation story, is an obvious apologue: not only are there two separate versions in Genesis (the first, the Priestly Account—which contains no Adam and Eve / Garden of Eden legend—runs from Genesis 1:1-31 through 2:1-3; while the much older second version, the Jehovistic Account, runs from Genesis 2:4-25 through 3:1-24), but earth scientists can find no trace of a worldwide flood during the period it was supposed to have occurred, or at any other time in our planet's history for that matter. Additionally, numerous nearly identical Creation myths were in existence long before the writing of Genesis. Other elements were borrowed from older creation myths as well: the Pagans' "First Man" Adamu or Adapa became "Adam," while the Pagans' "First Woman" Hawwah, Hebat, Heba, or Hebe was transformed into "Eve." Notable examples of pre-biblical cosmologies include the Babylonian creation story, the Sumerian creation

story, and the Mesopotamian creation story, all which heavily influenced the writer(s) of Genesis. Frazer records Creation Myths, many with similar and even identical figures, events, and themes, in ancient Egypt, New Zealand, Tahiti, Burma, Melanesia, the Philippines, India, Russia, Africa, Native America, Mexico, Peru, and Paraguay. See Frazer, FITOT, pp. 3-15.
373. Titus 1:14.
374. See e.g., Galatians 4:21-24.
375. 1 Peter 3:20-21.
376. 1 Corinthians 1:10-12; 4:6, 16.
377. Romans 2:16; 16:25; 2 Timothy 2:8.
378. 2 Corinthians 3:6.
379. Romans 2:29.
380. Romans 7:6.
381. Schweitzer, TQOTHJ, p. 26.
382. Acts 1:15. For more on the 120 secret Disciples, see H. S. Lewis, TSDOJ, pp. 27-28, 49, 51-52, 55, 58-59, 84, 88, 99, 112, 138, 149, 154-155, 163, 170-173, 205, 228-229.
383. H. S. Lewis, TSDOJ, pp. 20-21. See e.g., Matthew 13:3, 34; Mark 4:33; 12:1.
384. See Matthew 5:1-2.
385. Matthew 13:38.
386. Mark 4:33.
387. See Romans 3:2; Hebrews 5:12; 1 Peter 4:11.
388. Ephesians 2:18; Romans 5:1-2; 8:10; 1 Corinthians 6:15, 17; 2 Corinthians 5:16; 13:3, 5.
389. See Ephesians 2:18. Emphasis added.
390. Hebrews 5:11-14; 6:1.
391. See Schweitzer, TQOTHJ, pp. 41-42.
392. Mark 4:10-12.
393. See Isaiah 6:9-10.
394. Matthew 13:10-17.
395. See Burtt, pp. 121-122, 126-127, 154.
396. Matthew 13:18-23.
397. My paraphrasal.
398. See John 19:38.
399. H. S. Lewis, TSDOJ, pp. 29-31; Schweitzer, TQOTHJ, pp. 39-41, 162-163, 327-329; M. P. Hall, p. 179; A. Pike, pp. 260-266.
400. Note: Some scholars believe that The Thunder: Perfect Mind is Gnostic, while others do not. I fall in with the former group.
401. Matthew 24:14. See also Matthew 4:23; 9:35; Luke 4:43.
402. 1 Peter 1:12.
403. See e.g., Matthew 17:1; Mark 9:2; 14:33; Luke 8:51; 9:28.
404. 1 Corinthians 2:7.
405. Mackay, pp. 195-196. Emphasis added.
406. Dowling, 58:6-9.
407. Matthew 5:48.
408. Hebrews 8:10; 10:16.
409. Romans 1:17; Galatians 3:11; Hebrews 10:38.
410. John 7:24; 2 Corinthians 10:7.
411. John 1:18; 5:57; 1 Timothy 1:17.
412. Paul repeatedly preached against the anthropomorphic Paganesque God that is embraced in so many Christian churches today. See e.g., 2 Corinthians 6:16; 1 Thessalonians 1:9. See also 1 Corinthians 12:2; Revelation 9:20.
413. Matthew 19:28; Luke 22:30; 2 Timothy 2:12; Revelation 3:12, 21; 5:10; 20:6; 22:5.
414. Luke 17:20-21.
415. Matthew 24:14. See also Matthew 4:23; 9:35; Luke 4:43.
416. John 10:34.
417. The Gospel of Philip, Logion 59. For the text, see A. P. Smith, p. 63.
418. Matthew 16:17.

419. Hardon, s.v. "Abraham."
420. Comay, s.v. "Abraham."
421. Runes, s.v. "Abraham."
422. Calvocoressi, s.v. "Abraham."
423. Goring, s.v. "Abraham."
424. Tenney, s.v. "Abraham." See Genesis 17:5-8.
425. Metzger and Coogan, s.v. "Abraham"; J. L. McKenzie, s.v. "Abraham"; B. G. Walker, TWDOSASO, p. 303.
426. Meissner, p. 116.
427. Butler, s.v. "Abraham."
428. Dowley, p. 126.
429. See Genesis 22.
430. Genesis 14:18-19.
431. Livingstone, s.v. "Abraham."
432. Metford, s.v. "Abraham."
433. G. D. Young, s.v. "Abraham."
434. Brownrigg, s.v. "Mary, Mother of Jesus."
435. Schwartz, p. 60.
436. B. G. Walker, TWDOSASO, pp. 335-336.
437. Patai, pp. 34-53; Finegan, Vol. 1, pp. 167-168, 173. See also Pritchard, passim.
438. Nelson's s.v. "Abraham." See Genesis 11:27-25:8.
439. B. G. Walker, TWEOMAS, s.v. "Abraham." See Genesis 21:33.
440. Budge, AAT, p. 466.
441. R. Graves, TWG, p. 160. See Genesis 23:9; 25:9.
442. Learsi, pp. 3-7.
443. Chetwynd, pp. 36-37.
444. Biedermann, s.v. "Abraham, Bosom of."
445. Farrell and Presser, s.v. "Abraham."
446. Ferguson, pp. 23-24.
447. Genesis 25:7.
448. Gaskell, s.v. "Abraham."
449. B. G. Walker, TWEOMAS, s.v. "Circumcision."
450. Daraul, p. 149.
451. Freud, MAM, pp. 29-35.
452. Watts, MARIC, p. 91.
453. L. M. Graham, p. 109.
454. Fillmore, s.v. "Abraham."
455. John 10:34.
456. My theory. The Gospel of Thomas, Logion 13. For the text, see Zinner, p. 293.
457. Colossians 3:11.
458. Matthew 22:41-46. See also Daniel 7:13-14; Micah 5:2; Matthew 28:20; John 8:58; Colossians 1:17; Hebrews 7:3; Revelation 22:13.
459. John 8:58.
460. Genesis 11:26.
461. M. P. Hall, pp. 58-59.
462. See Spalding, Vol. 3, p. 164.
463. Genesis 17:5.
464. Ephesians 4:6.
465. W. W. Westcott, p. 29.
466. Potter, pp. 24, 90, 127; Kümmel, pp. 197-199.
467. John 8:23-24; 27-28. Emphasis added.
468. My paraphrasal.
469. Daniel 7:13-14.
470. Genesis 17:1; Exodus 3:14-15; Psalms 46:10; Mark 8:29; 14:61-62; Luke 22:70; John 6:35; 8:12, 23, 58; 9:5; 10:7-11, 30-39; 11:25; 12:26, 46; 13:13; 14:3, 6, 10-11, 20; 15:1; 17:10, 16.

471. John 13:19.
472. Colossians 1:19; 2:9.
473. John 10:30. Zen Buddhists have a similar saying. *Namu Dai Butsu*: "I am one with the great Buddha."
474. John 17:23; Galatians 3:28.
475. Colossians 1:27.
476. Ephesians 2:6, 13.
477. John 17:11.
478. John 17:21-22.
479. See e.g., Isaiah 9:6; Matthew 22:41-45; John 1:1; 14:9; 1 Timothy 3:16; Titus 1:3. Indeed, many mainstream Christian churches today teach that the Jehovah of the Old Testament "became" the man known as Jesus in the New Testament, and even translate the name of Jesus (meaning "Jehovah the Savior") as "He is Jehovah the Savior."
480. Romans 3:29-30.
481. Deuteronomy 6:4; Mark 12:29. See also Dowling, 96:3-7.
482. Isaiah 42:8.
483. Romans 9:26; 2 Corinthians 6:16.
484. John 12:32; 14:20; 15:4; 17:21-23, 26; Colossians 1:27; 3:10-11; Romans 8:10; 1 Corinthians 6:15, 17; 2 Corinthians 5:16; 13:3, 5; Galatians 1:16; 2:20; 4:19; Ephesians 3:14-17; Philippians 1:20; 2:5; 1 Peter 1:11; 1 John 2:27; 3:24; 4:4.
485. Colossians 1:15-17. Emphasis added.
486. L. S. Das, pp. 3-23, 45.
487. John 1:1-14. See also John 8:58; Psalms 90:2; 1 Timothy 1:17; Colossians 1:17; Hebrews 9:14; Matthew 22:41-46; Mark 12:35-37.
488. Farrell and Presser, s.v. "Adam."
489. Calvocoressi, s.v. "Adam."
490. Genesis 5:5.
491. 1 Corinthians 15:45. Ferguson, p. 28.
492. Comay, s.v. "Adam."
493. Butler, s.v. "Adam."
494. Watts, MARIC, p. 167.
495. Tenney, s.v. "Adam."
496. Arieti, pp. 340-342.
497. See Pagels, AEATS, p. xix, passim.
498. Spence, s.v. "Adam, Book of the Penitence of." See also Chetwynd, p. 215.
499. See Genesis 1:1-31.
500. Runes, s.v. "Adam."
501. M. P. Hall, p. 126.
502. See e.g., Learsi, passim.
503. See e.g. Romans 5:14.
504. See Gaskell, s.v. "Adam (Lower Aspect)"; "Adam (Higher Aspect)."
505. Metzger and Coogan, s.v. "Adam."
506. Metford, s.v. "Adam."
507. Comay, s.v. "Adam."
508. Genesis 2:7. Emphasis added.
509. Fillmore, s.v. "Adam."
510. L. M. Graham, pp. 36-37.
511. Farrell and Presser, s.v. "Adam."
512. Budge, AAT, pp. 224, 226, 227.
513. Dowley, p. 97.
514. Schwartz, p. 59
515. G. D. Young, s.v. "Devil."
516. See Seabrook, JATLOA, passim.
517. See e.g., Proverbs 23:7.
518. M. P. Hall, pp. 117-120.
519. Genesis 1:27; John 10:34; Colossians 3:11.

520. John 10:34.
521. Livingstone, s.v. "Alpha and Omega."
522. Potter, pp. 24, 90, 127.
523. Yogananda, TSCOC, Vol. 1, p. 6.
524. Revelation 1:10-13.
525. Colossians 3:11.
526. See Gaskell, s.v. "Alpha and Omega."
527. Revelation 1:13.
528. L. M. Graham, p. 389.
529. John 1:9.
530. Colossians 3:11.
531. Genesis 1:27. See also A. Pike, p. 252.
532. Cotterell, TMIEOMAL, s.v. "Osiris."
533. Spalding, Vol. 3, p. 116.
534. Cirlot, s.v. "Phonetics."
535. L. M. Graham, p. 390.
536. G. D. Young, s.v. "amen."
537. See e.g., John 5:24.
538. Spalding, Vol. 3, p. 116.
539. A. Pike, pp. 204-205.
540. Evans-Wentz, p. 132.
541. Yogananda, TSCOC, Vol. 1, p. 11.
542. Colossians 3:11.
543. Revelation 3:14. For John's corresponding Gospel text, see John 1:1-3.
544. Young, s.v. "Ancient of Days"; Zondervan, s.v. "Ancient of Days." See Daniel 7:9, 13, 22.
545. Colossians 3:11.
546. Genesis 1:27.
547. 1 Corinthians 12:7.
548. Doyle, TEOTU, p. 61.
549. Strauss, TLOJCE, Vol. 1, p. 78.
550. Finegan, Vol. 1, pp. 50-51.
551. See B. Graham, A, passim.
552. G. D. Young, s.v. "angel."
553. See Daniel, Wyllie, and Ramer, passim.
554. Curtiss and Curtiss, TKTTU, pp. 142-143.
555. See e.g., Revelation 7:1-3; 14:18; 16:5.
556. A. Pike, p. 21.
557. A. Pike, p. 440.
558. Aquarius the Water-Bearer appears esoterically numerous times in the Bible. See e.g., Mark 14:13.
559. Seabrook, JATLOA, p. 404.
560. Gaskell, s.v. "Angels."
561. Tenney, s.v. "Anoint."
562. See Seabrook, AT, pp. 41, 55.
563. Gaskell, s.v. "Anointing With Oil."
564. Psalm 23:5.
565. Tenney, s.v. "Antichrist." See 2 Thessalonians 2:1-12.
566. 1 John 2:18,22; 4:3.
567. 2 John 7.
568. Gaskell, s.v. "Antichrist."
569. Fillmore, s.v. "Antichrist."
570. Tenney, s.v. "Apostle."
571. Metzger and Coogan, s.v. "Twelve, The."
572. Hebrews 3:1.
573. Gaskell, s.v. "Apostles, The Twelve"; "Twelve."
574. See Galatians 2:9.

575. Graves and Patai, p. 111.
576. Tenney, s.v. "Noah."
577. Cotterell, TMIEOMAL, p. 147.
578. Cotterell, TMIEOMAL, p. 125.
579. Cotterell, TMIEOMAL, p. 139.
580. Cotterell, TMIEOMAL, p. 86.
581. Guirand, p. 54.
582. W. Smith, s.v. "Noah."
583. Gaskell, s.v. "Ark of Noah."
584. Fillmore, s.v. "Noah."
585. Genesis 1:27.
586. Baba, p. 17; Yogananda, TSCOC, Vol. 1, p. 14; Steiger, IMSIAF, pp. 129-130; S. Smith, pp. 56-66.
587. Farrell and Presser, s.v. "Seven."
588. See Biedermann, s.v. "Ark."
589. Farrell and Presser, s.v. "Ark."
590. Graves, TWG, pp. 321, 480.
591. Tenney, s.v. "Ascension of Christ."
592. Cirlot, s.v. "Ascension."
593. Bently, s.v. "Herakles."
594. Only Mark (16:19) and Luke (24:51) mention the Ascension. But both of these passages are late interpolations, for neither of them are found in our earliest known New Testament copies, such as the Codex Sinaiticus. See M. L. Prophet and E. C. Prophet, p. liv; Sheehan, p. 117.
595. See J. G. Jackson, CBC, p. 122.
596. Matthew 13:16.
597. D. Lee, p. 25.
598. See D. Lee, p. 163.
599. Luke 21:25.
600. Luke 21:11.
601. Houvet, p. 73.
602. Riedel, Tracy, and Moskowitz, p. 272.
603. See Revelation 21:21.
604. See Revelation 21:19-20.
605. M. P. Hall, p. 56.
606. See Revelation 21:19.
607. Gaskell, s.v. "Zodiac."
608. Proverbs 7:27.
609. Chetwynd, pp. 110-111.
610. M. P. Hall, p. 54.
611. John 1:29, 36; Revelation 5:6.
612. Romer, p. 231.
613. There are many alternate configurations of this list. See e.g., Biedermann, s.v. "Stars."
614. See Fillmore, s.v. "Faculties"; T. Andrews, pp. 59-60, 145-148; Gaskell, s.v. "Disciples, The Twelve, of Jesus."
615. M. P. Hall, p. 121.
616. M. P. Hall, p. 135.
617. See Matthew 27:3; Mark 15:22; John 19:17.
618. See Luke 23:33.
619. J. L. McKenzie, s.v. "Golgotha."
620. Seabrook, JATLOA, pp. 517-518.
621. Frazer, TGB, Vol. 2, p. 119.
622. B. G. Walker, TWEOMAS, s.v. "Aphrodite."
623. Revelation 22:16.
624. See 1 Kings 11:5.
625. B. G. Walker, TWEOMAS, s.v. "Astarte."
626. B. G. Walker, TWEOMAS, s.v. "Astrology."

627. See Drexel, passim.
628. Zondervan, s.v. "Atonement."
629. Romans 5:11.
630. John 14:20.
631. 1 Timothy 3:16.
632. Fillmore, s.v. "Babylon." Bel was the supreme god of the Babylonian Pantheon.
633. Zondervan, s.v. "Babylon."
634. Nelson's, s.v. "Babel, Babylon."
635. Genesis 11:9.
636. Tenney, s.v. "Babylon."
637. Biedermann, s.v. "Babylon."
638. Metzger and Coogan, s.v. "Babylon"; W. Smith, s.v. "Babylon"; G. D. Young, s.v. "Babylon."
639. Revelation 17:5.
640. Farrell and Presser, s.v. "Babylon."
641. L. M. Graham, p. 381.
642. Fillmore, s.v. "Babylon." Bel was the supreme god of the Babylonian Pantheon.
643. Gaskell, s.v. "Babylon."
644. J. L. McKenzie, s.v. "Babylon, Babylonia."
645. W. Smith, s.v. "Baptism."
646. Yogananda, TSCOC, Vol. 1, pp. 104, 106. See also A. Pike, p. 362.
647. Neill, TIOTNT, p. 172.
648. Angus, p. 46; Cumont, TMOM, p. 86.
649. H. S. Lewis, TSDOJ, pp. 29-31; Leishman, OAB, pp. 148-149; Schweitzer, TQOTHJ, pp. 162-163, 327; Yogananda, TSCOC, Vol. 1, p. 100; Neill, TIOTNT, p. 305; Neill, WWKAJ, p. 14.
650. See J. L. McKenzie, s.v. "Baptism."
651. Yogananda, TSCOC, Vol. 1, p. 245.
652. See John 3:22, and also John 4:1-2.
653. Schweitzer, TQOTHJ, p. 18.
654. Luke 23:39-43. See also E. D. Cohen, p. 78.
655. Roberts and Donaldson, Vol. 1, p. 345.
656. Strauss, TLOJCE, Vol. 1, pp. 216-217.
657. Goring, s.v. "Baptism."
658. Livingstone, s.v. "Baptism."
659. See Matthew 28:19.
660. J. L. McKenzie, s.v. "Trinity."
661. Schweitzer, TQOTHJ, p. 18.
662. Goguel, Vol. 2, p. 315.
663. Roberts and Donaldson, Vol. 1, p. 345.
664. Matthew 3:11. The orthodox will mention Matthew 28:19-20 in this regard. But even a superficial reading of these passages reveals that Jesus is not referring to water baptism. He commands an esoteric rebirth "in the name of the Father, and of the Son, and of the Holy Ghost"; that is, a spiritual or psychological "born again" experience involving the Inner Holy Trinity: Divine Mind, the Indwelling Christ, and the Spirit.
665. Matthew 28:19.
666. Eusebius, TPOTG, Vol. 1, p. 157.
667. Matthew 24:14.
668. See Acts 2:38; 8:16; 10:48.
669. Zondervan, s.v. "Beast."
670. G. D. Young, s.v. "Beast, The."
671. Moses Stuart, Vol. 2, p. 232.
672. Lamsa, IITBE, p. 70.
673. J. L. McKenzie, s.v. "Bethlehem." See Matthew 2:1.
674. W. Smith, s.v. "Bethlehem."
675. Gaskell, s.v. "Bread."
676. Fillmore, s.v. "Bethlehem."
677. Gaskell, s.v. "Bethlehem."

678. 1 Corinthians 10:17.
679. Ambrose, p. 416.
680. Schonfield, TPP, p. 212.
681. John 10:11.
682. Ramm, pp. 55-56.
683. For more on the growth of the Soul, the purpose of life, and aids to living the good life as Jesus taught them, see Seabrook, JATLOA, passim; Seabrook, TBATLOA, passim.
684. Paraphrased from Parker. See Parker, p. 32.
685. Kingsford and Maitland, pp. 240-241. Emphasis added.
686. Genesis 1:27.
687. Matthew 13:16.
688. Revelation 7:14.
689. Cooper, s.v. "Blood."
690. Cooper, s.v. "Lamb."
691. Swedenborg, TAR, Vol. 1, p. 379.
692. Kingsford and Maitland, p. 108.
693. M. P. Hall, p. 91.
694. Chetwynd, pp. 110-111.
695. Van Etten, p. 159.
696. John 1:9.
697. G. D. Young, s.v. "Born Again."
698. 1 Corinthians 2:16; Philippians 2:5.
699. See e.g., Geddes MacGregor, passim; E. D. Walker, passim; E. C. Prophet and E. L. Prophet, passim.
700. In some schools the second "birth" of the twice-born experience can refer to spiritual rebirth, the psychological transformation that one goes through upon achieving Cosmic Consciousness or Christ Consciousness, which Jesus called being "born again." See Eliade, Y, pp. 6, 145, 272-273.
701. John 3:3.
702. G. D. Young, s.v. "Bread."
703. Tenney, s.v. "Bread."
704. Gaskell, s.v. "Bread, or Bread of Heaven."
705. John 6:35.
706. See Acts 15.
707. Acts 24:5. See Lemesurier, passim.
708. Potter, p. 12.
709. Titcomb, pp. 95-96. In the 2nd Century A.D., the mainstream Church put out its own redacted version of the works of Josephus, "an edition corrected according to Christian ideas." Renan, p. 5.
710. For a full and wonderful treatment of this topic, see Potter, passim.
711. H. S. Lewis, TSDOJ, pp. 29-31; Schweitzer, TQOTHJ, pp. 39-41, 162-163, 327-329; M. P. Hall, p. 179; A. Pike, pp. 260-266.
712. Spivey and Smith, p. 227.
713. Acts 11:26; 26:28; 1 Peter 4:16.
714. Potter, p. 154.
715. See Leeming, pp. 262-267.
716. See Potter, pp. 81-84.
717. A. Pike, pp. 258-266.
718. Schweitzer, TQOTHJ, pp. 292-293, 320.
719. Compare, e.g., Buddha: "Work out your own salvation with diligence" (Burtt, pp. 22, 49, 80) with Paul: "Work out your own salvation with fear and trembling." Philippians 2:12.
720. In particular see Berry, passim.
721. K. Graves, pp. 116-120.
722. Schweitzer, TQOTHJ, p. 291.
723. See Cotterell, ADOWM, s.v. "Buddha"; Evans-Wentz, p. xxxix.
724. Sykes, s.v. "Buddha."
725. See e.g., Mark 3:26.
726. Spivey and Smith, p. 152. For Buddha's earlier version, see Burtt, pp. 150-154.

727. Mark 4:31; Burtt, pp. 43-46.
728. Luke 11:33; Burtt, p. 43.
729. Burtt, pp. 51-52.
730. Titcomb, p. 56.
731. See John 14:6.
732. Burtt, p. 140.
733. Mark 12:31.
734. Burtt, pp. 121-122.
735. Mark 4:1-9.
736. Some 500 years before Jesus, Buddha laid out his eight-part guideline for attaining Self-Godhood. It is known as the Noble Eightfold Path: 1) Right View; 2) Right Intention; 3) Right Speech; 4) Right Action; 5) Right Livelihood; 6) Right Effort; 7) Right Mindfulness; and 8) Right Concentration. As Jesus studied in the East during His 18 "Silent Years," and as all of the world's most enlightened individuals tap into the same universal consciousness, it is plain that Jesus' eight Beatitudes are loosely based on Buddha's eight "Beatitudes." See Matthew 5:3-10.
737. Seabrook, JATLOA, p. 218.
738. Sykes, s.v. "Buddha."
739. Luke 3:23.
740. Bucke, p. 60.
741. See Lillie, TIOBOPC, passim.
742. See Psalms 106:18-19.
743. Gaskell, s.v. "Calf, the Molten."
744. Hodson, Vol. 1, p. 106.
745. John 2-4.
746. See e.g., Eyerly, pp. 120-126; Schaberg, pp. 154-155.
747. B. G. Walker, TWEOMAS, s.v. "Hieros Gamos."
748. McGovern, p. 237.
749. Goring, s.v. "Sacred Marriage."
750. Shinn, p. 26.
751. A. Pike, p. 404.
752. See e.g., Matthew 1:1.
753. J. M. Robertson, p. 237.
754. See e.g. Matthew 16:20; Mark 14:61-62.
755. See e.g., Matthew 16:16; Luke 9:20; John 1:41; 1 John 2:22; 5:1.
756. Legge, Vol. 1 and Vol. 2, passim.
757. Spivey and Smith, p. 438.
758. M. P. Hall, p. 185.
759. See Potter, pp. 24, 90.
760. Revelation 11:15. Emphasis added.
761. Roberts and Donaldson, Vol. 1, p. 345. Emphasis added.
762. Frothingham, p. 185. Emphasis added.
763. Doyle, TEOTU, p. 93. Slightly paraphrased from the original.
764. Farrell and Presser, s.v. "Chrism."
765. John 1:14.
766. Condon, pp. 12-13.
767. J. L. McKenzie, s.v. "Anoint."
768. See e.g., Mark 15:32; Luke 23:2; John 19:19; Acts 17:7.
769. Massey, Vol. 1, p. 213.
770. Westbrook, p. 288.
771. See e.g., Acts 17:7, where both Caesar and Jesus are referred to as a "king." In Acts 26:28, during his conversation with Paul, the Tetrarch Herod Agrippa (grandson of Herod the Great) uses the word "Christian" derogatorily, for as a royal he has been christed ("anointed") and is therefore already a "Christ."
772. See e.g., Leviticus 4:3; 1 Samuel 2:10; 2 Samuel 1:21; 1 Chronicles 16:22; Psalms 18:50; Isaiah 45:1; Lamentations 4:20; Daniel 9:25-26; Habakkuk 3:13.
773. Seabrook, CBC, passim.

774. M. P. Hall, p. 179.
775. Meyer, TSTOJ, p. xvi.
776. Schonfield, TANT, p. 139.
777. Bucke, p. 103.
778. Yogananda, TSCOC, Vol. 1, p. 188.
779. Chetwynd, p. 113.
780. Eavns-Wentz, p. 134.
781. 1 John 2:20.
782. 2 Corinthians 1:21.
783. Galatians 1:16.
784. Matthew 24:23.
785. Luke 17:20-21.
786. Bucke, p. 155. Emphasis added.
787. See e.g., Romans 8:9.
788. John 12:32; 14:20; 15:4; 17:21-23, 26; Colossians 1:27; 3:10-11; Romans 8:10; 1 Corinthians 6:15, 17; 2 Corinthians 5:16; 13:3, 5; Galatians 1:16; 2:20; 4:19; Ephesians 3:14-17; Philippians 1:20; 2:5; 1 Peter 1:11; 1 John 2:27; 3:24; 4:4.
789. 2 Corinthians 6:16.
790. Colossians 3:11.
791. Proverbs 20:27.
792. Genesis 1:27.
793. Kingsford and Maitland, p. 188. Emphasis added.
794. Kingsford and Maitland, p. 245. Emphasis added.
795. Daniel 7:13-14. See also John 17:5, 24; Revelation 22:13.
796. Hebrews 7:3.
797. Matthew 22:41-46. See also Micah 5:2; Matthew 28:20; John 8:58; Hebrews 7:3.
798. Burtt, pp. 17-18.
799. Evans-Wentz, p. 121.
800. Emerson, WORWE, pp. 59-66.
801. Irving, Vol. 1, pp. 80-81.
802. Micah 5:2.
803. John 12:34.
804. John 8:58.
805. Matthew 28:20.
806. Spalding, Vol. 4, p. 81.
807. 1 Corinthians 2:16; Philippians 2:5.
808. Gaskell, s.v. "Pleroma."
809. Philippians 2:5.
810. John 14:21.
811. Matthew 11:28-30.
812. Ponder, p. 183.
813. M. P. Hall, pp. 78, 80.
814. Eavns-Wentz, p. 147.
815. John 14:23.
816. James 4:8.
817. Zechariah 2:8.
818. Joshua 1:9.
819. Zechariah 2:10.
820. A. Pike, p. 603.
821. Shinn, p. 40.
822. Matthew 7:7-8.
823. Colossians 1:27.
824. Curtiss and Curtiss, TKOD, p. 18.
825. See e.g., Matthew 13:55; Luke 2:41, 48; 3:23; 4:22; John 1:45; 6:42; Hebrews 3:3; 7:24; 10:12.
826. Matthew 23:8-10.

827. Hinnells, s.v. "Buddha."
828. Bently, s.v. "Buddhism."
829. M. Jordan, s.v. "Buddha."
830. See Seabrook, CBC, passim; Doane, passim; E. E. Evans, passim; J. M. Robertson, PC, passim.
831. John 14:20. See also John 17:23.
832. See John 1:12; Romans 8:14; 1 John 3:1-2.
833. Besant and Leadbetter, p. 295.
834. John 1:9.
835. Sheehan, p. 81. See also Mark 8:32-33.
836. Sheehan, p. 76.
837. 1 Corinthians 2:16; Philippians 2:5.
838. Watts, TWOZ, p. 46.
839. Bucke, pp. 51-52, 155.
840. Watts, G, p. 59.
841. Matthew 6:6; Mark 1:15; John 18:36.
842. Luke 23:2.
843. Genesis 1:27.
844. Jukes, p. 38.
845. Bucke, pp. 8, 14, 148, 194, 228, 237, 238, 240, 250, 257, 270, 283, 285.
846. Yogananda, TSCOC, Vol. 1, pp. 4, 187.
847. Goring, s.v. "Buddha Nature."
848. Colossians 3:11.
849. Genesis 1:27.
850. Zen Buddhists hold that we are born with Buddha (or Christ) Consciousness: perfect enlightenment. We must merely recognize this fact. Thus there is nothing to strive for or "attain." See Watts, TWOZ, passim.
851. See Bucke, passim.
852. See 1 Corinthians 13.
853. See Bucke, passim.
854. Maharshi, p. 81.
855. John 10:34.
856. 2 Peter 1:4.
857. Yogananda, TSCOC, Vol. 1, p. 15.
858. Among the many types of early Christianity, there was Gnostic-Christianity, Essenic-Christianity, Jewish-Christianity, Hellenistic-Christianity, Apocalyptic-Christianity, Enthusiastic-Christianity, and Catholic-Christianity, among others. See Dunn, passim.
859. Ross and Hills, p. 149.
860. Spivey and Smith, p. 496.
861. Calvocoressi, s.v. "Jesus." See also Spivey and Smith, pp. 199, 465.
862. Schonfield, TANT, p. 192.
863. M. Grant, CTG, pp. 121-186.
864. Yogananda, TSCOC, Vol. 1, p. 58.
865. See e.g., John 1:1; Ephesians 3:9; 1 John 1:1.
866. Hebrews 13:8.
867. M. P. Hall, p. 179. My paraphrasal.
868. Goguel, Vol. 2, p. 585; Schweitzer, TQOTHJ, p. 17; Dunn, p. 105; Hoffman, p. 9, passim.
869. Matthew 5:17. Few great religious leaders have ever set out to intentionally found a religion or even a sect of a religion. George Fox, for example, never evinced the slightest desire to establish a new Christian denomination. Despite this, as with Jesus, one later grew up around his teachings and its founding was falsely attributed to him. In Fox's case "his" new sect was The Religious Society of Friends, or Quakers. Van Etten, p. 77.
870. Parsons, pp. 276-277. Emphasis added.
871. Titcomb, pp. 100, 102. Emphasis added.
872. The Tripartite Tractate, 3:34-35. My paraphrasal. Emphasis added.
873. Richardson, pp. 188-189.
874. J. N. D. Kelly, p. 191.

875. 1 Corinthians 10:1-4. Emphasis added.
876. Ephesians 1:4-5. Emphasis added. See also Philippians 2:13.
877. Colossians 1:15-17. Emphasis added.
878. Colossians 1:23. Emphasis added.
879. 1 Peter 1:20. Emphasis added.
880. Daniel 7:13-14. Emphasis added.
881. Hebrews 7:24. My paraphrasal.
882. Revelation 1:8. Emphasis added.
883. John 17:5. Emphasis added.
884. John 8:58. Emphasis added.
885. The Gospel of Thomas, Logion 77. My paraphrasal.
886. Evans-Wentz, pp. 1, 3.
887. See Psalms 110:1.
888. Matthew 22:41-46. See also Daniel 7:13-14; Micah 5:2; Matthew 28:20; John 8:58; Hebrews 7:3; Revelation 22:13.
889. Titcomb, p. 100.
890. Titcomb, pp. 100-101. Emphasis added.
891. Titcomb, p. 102.
892. Titcomb, p. 105.
893. Titcomb, p. 105. Emphasis added.
894. Titcomb, pp. 105-106. Emphasis added.
895. Titcomb, p. 106. Emphasis added.
896. Titcomb, pp. 106-107.
897. See Potter, passim.
898. Titcomb, p. 107.
899. C. W. King, pp. 48-50, 68.
900. Bonwick, p. 283.
901. Titcomb, pp. 108-110.
902. Roberts and Donaldson, p. 170. Emphasis added.
903. Westbrook, pp. 290-294. Emphasis added.
904. Westbrook, pp. 294-298. Emphasis added.
905. J. G. Jackson, CBC, p. 2. For more on how Orphism influenced Christianity, see Angus, pp. 150-156.
906. Dentan, p. 138.
907. A. Pike, p. 415.
908. James, p. 32.
909. See Yogananda, TSCOC, Vol. 1, pp. xxiii, 242.
910. John 8:32.
911. See e.g., John 8:1-15.
912. Matthew 6:6.
913. See e.g., Matthew 6:1-6; 23:9.
914. See e.g., Matthew 22:37-39.
915. See e.g., Jeremiah 31:34; Matthew 6:14-15; Mark 11:25-26; Luke 17:3-4; 24:57; 1 John 1:9.
916. John 14:20.
917. Romans 12:5; Hebrews 9:24. See also Dowling, 15:22.
918. Hebrews 8:2. See also Hebrews 9:11.
919. Hebrews 5:5; 6:20; 1 Peter 2:9.
920. See e.g., Matthew 12:48-50; Luke 8:19-21; Romans 10:12; 15:7; Colossians 3:11; 1 Timothy 2:1-5; 1 Peter 2:17. See also Dowling, 24:27. Paul rightly said: "There is neither Jew nor Greek, there is neither bond nor free, there is neither male nor female: for ye are all one in Christ Jesus." Galatians 3:28. Truly, God "hath made of one blood all nations of men for to dwell on all the face of the earth." Acts 17:26.
921. 2 Corinthians 12:9; Ephesians 2:4, 8.
922. See e.g., Matthew 17:20; Mark 11:22; Luke 22:32.
923. Romans 10:1-4.
924. Genesis 17:1; Exodus 3:14-15; Psalms 46:10; Mark 8:29; 14:61-62; Luke 22:70; John 6:35; 8:12, 23, 58; 9:5; 10:7-11, 30-39; 11:25; 12:26, 46; 13:13; 14:3, 6, 10-11, 20; 15:1; 17:10, 16.

925. Exodus 3:14; Ezekiel 37:14; John 14:10-11; Romans 8:9, 11; 1 Corinthians 6:17; 2 Corinthians 6:16; Ephesians 2:22; 4:6.
926. John 12:32; 14:20; 15:4; 17:21-23, 26; Colossians 1:27; 3:10-11; Romans 8:10; 1 Corinthians 6:15, 17; 2 Corinthians 5:16; 13:3, 5; Galatians 1:16; 2:20; 4:19; Ephesians 3:14-17; Philippians 1:20; 2:5; 1 Peter 1:11; 1 John 2:27; 3:24; 4:4.
927. John 14:16-17; 1 Corinthians 6:19; 2 Timothy 1:14.
928. The Great I AM has always existed: John 8:58. The Inner God has always existed: Psalms 90:2; 1 Timothy 1:17. The Indwelling Christ has always existed: John 1:1-14. The Holy Spirit has always existed: Hebrews 9:14. Thus all four predate Jesus, as the Master Himself acknowledged: Matthew 22:41-46; Mark 12:35-37. See also Daniel 7:13-14; Micah 5:2; Matthew 28:20; Hebrews 7:3; Revelation 22:13.
929. A. Pike, p. 219.
930. A. Pike, pp. 168-170.
931. Luke 9:50. See also Romans 8:31.
932. Dowling, 131:31-40. For the canonical version of this account, see Mark 9:38-41.
933. Religio-facism and spiritual intolerance began early among the Israelites. See e.g., 2 Kings 5:15; Isaiah 45:5; Psalms 135:5.
934. See e.g., Acts 4:10-12.
935. Angus, p. 278.
936. Jesus, like all enlightened souls, understood that it is not religion but spirituality that is important, and spirituality, by its very nature, cannot be categorized, collectivized, or organized. It is an individual journey, which is why Paul enjoined religious tolerance to his followers in Rome. See Romans 14:1-10. It is interesting to note that amid the narrow-mindedness of many of the ancient Jews, there were also signs of religious tolerance. See e.g., the words of Trito-Isaiah in Isaiah 56:1-8.
937. Matthew 24:14. See also Matthew 4:23; 9:35; Luke 4:43.
938. Matthew 18:3.
939. See Suzuki, passim.
940. 1 Corinthians 3:8.
941. Szekely, TETOZ, pp. 22, 25.
942. See e.g., Matthew 7:16-24.
943. James 1:27. Emphasis added.
944. Szekeley, TDOTEGOP, p. 27. My paraphrasal.
945. See e.g., Ephesians 4 and 5.
946. Mark 14:64; John 10:33.
947. Proverbs 12:5.
948. Parker, p. 53.
949. Parker, pp. 28-29. Emphasis added.
950. A. Pike, pp. 540-541. Emphasis added.
951. John 3:16.
952. Hopfe, pp. 430-433.
953. See e.g., Burtt, passim.
954. See e.g., Leek, passim.
955. Hopfe, pp. 262-267.
956. Bruce, p. 7.
957. See e.g., Matthew 7:13-14; 21:32; John 14:6.
958. See e.g., Mark 1:3; 10:52; Luke 3:4; John 1:23; 14:4; Acts 9:2; 18:25-26; 19:9, 23; 22:4; 24:14, 22. Barnabas, an early disciple and a companion of Paul (Acts 13:43), more aptly called Jesus' "religion" the "Way of the Light." The Epistle of Barnabas 14:5.
959. See e.g., Genesis 18:19; Exodus 32:8; Deuteronomy 9:16.
960. See e.g., 2 Kings 21:22.
961. See e.g., Job 31:7.
962. See e.g., Psalms 25:8.
963. Hermes Trismegistus, a mysterious ancient figure, is said to have founded the religion of Hermeticism and authored the extraordinary mystic writings known as the *Corpus Hermeticum*.
964. Lao Tzu is the probable author of the ancient Chinese work entitled *Tao Te Ching*, "The Way of Virtue."
965. Micah 6:8. See also Deuteronomy 10:12.

966. Stewart, pp. 4-5.
967. A. Pike, p. 309.
968. T. Paine, p. 5.
969. Jefferson, p. 10.
970. A. Pike, p. 333.
971. A. Pike, p. 333.
972. Tichenor, p. 491.
973. Hartmann, MWAB, pp. 45-46. Emphasis added.
974. See e.g., Mark 7:17-18; Luke 2:50; John 10:6.
975. Yogananda, TSCOC, Vol. 1, p. 380.
976. Parker, pp. 29-31. Emphasis added.
977. Dowley, p. 31; H. S. Lewis, TSDOJ, p. 218.
978. J. G. Jackson, CBC, pp. 192, 193, 199, 200; Gordon, s.v. "Christianity."
979. Cumont, TORIRP, p. 228.
980. Lasne and Gaultier, p. 152; Goring, s.v. "Christmas."
981. Goring, s.v. "Sol Invictus."
982. Cumont, TORIRP, p. 228.
983. Romer, p. 231; M. P. Hall, pp. 49-52.
984. Hampson, Vol. 2, pp. 45-46.
985. Carpenter, pp. 50-51. Emphasis added.
986. Brewster, pp. 38-40.
987. Ramm, p. 137.
988. Angus, p. 244.
989. Potter, pp. 81-84.
990. For more on this topic, see my book *Jesus and the Gospel of Q*.
991. For more on the topic of Jesus and Christmas, see my book *Christmas Before Christianity*.
992. 1 Corinthians 12:12-27.
993. Acts 7:48. See also Acts 17:24.
994. 1 Corinthians 3:16-19; 2 Corinthians 6:16.
995. Hebrews 5:5-6; 6:20. See also Hebrews 7:3. We believers are all members of a very special spiritual community, "a royal priesthood," as Peter called it. 1 Peter 2:9.
996. Dowling, 15:22. See also Hebrews 9:24.
997. Hebrews 8:2. My paraphrasal. See also Hebrews 9:11.
998. Channing, pp. 355-356. Emphasis added.
999. Matthew 6:6.
1000. 1 Kings 19:11-13.
1001. 1 Corinthians 6:17; 2 Corinthians 6:16; Ephesians 4:6.
1002. Seabrook, JATLOA, p. 171. My paraphrasal.
1003. John 14:26.
1004. John 14:16; 15:26; 16:7.
1005. John 12:32; 14:20; 15:4; 17:21-23, 26; Colossians 1:27; 3:10-11; Romans 8:10; 1 Corinthians 6:15, 17; 2 Corinthians 5:16; 13:3, 5; Galatians 1:16; 2:20; 4:19; Ephesians 3:14-17; Philippians 1:20; 2:5; 1 Peter 1:11; 1 John 2:27; 3:24; 4:4.
1006. Exodus 3:14; Ezekiel 37:14; John 14:10-11; Romans 8:9, 11; 1 Corinthians 3:16; 6:17; 14:25; 2 Corinthians 6:16; 9:14; Ephesians 2:22; 4:6; Philemon 2:13; 1 John 3:24; 4:4, 12-13, 16; Zechariah 2:10.
1007. Romans 1:25.
1008. John 14:16-17, 26.
1009. Exodus 3:14; Ezekiel 37:14; Zechariah 2:10; John 10:30; 14:10-11; 17:22; Romans 8:9, 11; 1 Corinthians 3:16; 6:17; 12:12; 14:25; 2 Corinthians 6:16; 9:14; Ephesians 2:22; 4:6; Philemon 2:13; 1 John 3:24; 4:4, 12-13, 16.
1010. John 12:32; 14:20; 15:4; 17:21-23, 26; Colossians 1:27; 3:10-11; Romans 8:10; 1 Corinthians 6:15, 17; 2 Corinthians 5:16; 13:3, 5; Galatians 1:16; 2:20; 4:19; Ephesians 3:14-17; Philippians 1:20; 2:5; 4:13; 1 Peter 1:11; 1 John 2:27; 3:24; 4:4.
1011. John 14:16-17, 20; 1 Corinthians 6:19; 2 Corinthians 1:22; 2 Timothy 1:14.
1012. John 14:17; 1 Corinthians 6:19.

1013. Dods, Vol. 11, p. 357. Emphasis added.
1014. Gaskell, s.v. "Paraclete, Comforter, or Intercessor"; Hoeller, p. 69.
1015. Burkitt, pp. 88-90. Some emphasis added.
1016. My theory.
1017. See e.g., Matthew 13:55; Luke 2:41, 48; 3:23; 4:22; John 1:45; 6:42; Hebrews 3:3; 7:24; 10:12.
1018. My theory.
1019. Proverbs 23:7.
1020. See Ponder, pp. 3-11, passim; Krippner and Rubin, p. 145, passim.
1021. Seabrook, JATLOA, p. 15.
1022. Tenney, s.v. "Cross."
1023. Butler, s.v. "Cross, Crucifixion."
1024. Zondervan, s.v. "Cross."
1025. Hardon, s.v. "Cross."
1026. G. D. Young, s.v. "Cross."
1027. See Matthew 10:38; 16:24; Mark 8:34; Luke 9:23; 14:27. J. L. McKenzie, s.v. "Cross."
1028. Livingstone, s.v. "Veneration of the Cross."
1029. B. G. Walker, TWDOSASO, p. 54.
1030. Biedermann, s.v. "Cross."
1031. Curtiss and Curtiss, TKTTU, p. 138.
1032. B. G. Walker, TWDOSASO, p. 50.
1033. M. P. Hall, p. 182.
1034. Watts, MARIC, pp. 138-169.
1035. See e.g., Gimbutas, TCOTG, pp. 235, 316, 370; Streep, passim.
1036. Romer, p. 195.
1037. Biedermann, s.v. "Cross."
1038. Gordon, s.v. "Cross."
1039. M. P. Hall, p. 182.
1040. Doane, p. 339. Emphasis added.
1041. Chetwynd, p. 160; A. Pike, pp. 21, 440.
1042. Curtiss and Curtiss, TKTTU, p. 181.
1043. M. P. Hall, pp. 103-104.
1044. Farrell and Presser, s.v. "Cross."
1045. See Shinn, p. 26.
1046. B. G. Walker, TWDOSASO, p. 69.
1047. M. P. Hall, p. 182.
1048. Watts, MARIC, p. 161.
1049. Cirlot, s.v. "Cross."
1050. Gaskell, s.v. "Cross."
1051. Maharshi, p. 71.
1052. A. Pike, p. 473.
1053. See Angus, pp. 172-173.
1054. B. G. Walker, TWDOSASO, p. 54.
1055. Watts, MARIC, pp. 158-159.
1056. See e.g., Acts 5:30; 1 Peter 2:24.
1057. B. G. Walker, TWDOSASO, p. 54.
1058. Metford, s.v. "Cross."
1059. Nelson's, s.v. "Cross."
1060. There is still much confusion over this detail, a result, in part, of the following scriptures: Acts 5:30; 1 Peter 2:24.
1061. W. Smith, s.v. "Cross"; Gordon, s.v. "Cross."
1062. Gordon, s.v. "Cross."
1063. Biedermann, s.v. "Cross."
1064. J. L. McKenzie, s.v. "Crown."
1065. G. D. Young, s.v. "Crown."
1066. Spalding, Vol. 4, p. 81.

1067. 1 Thessalonians 2:19.
1068. 2 Timothy 4:8.
1069. James 1:12; Revelation 2:10.
1070. 1 Peter 5:4.
1071. Revelation 14:14.
1072. 1 Peter 5:4.
1073. 1 Corinthians 9:25.
1074. M. P. Hall, p. 121.
1075. M. P. Hall, p. 135.
1076. Matthew 27:33; Mark 15:22; John 19:17.
1077. Mark 14:15; Luke 22:12; Acts 1:13.
1078. See J. M. Robertson, PC, p. 5; Goguel, Vol. 2, pp. 528-529; Sheehan, pp. 129-130.
1079. See e.g., Mark 15:17, and also Matthew 27:29; John 19:2, 5. For more on this topic, see my book *Christmas Before Christianity*.
1080. Revelation 12:1.
1081. B. G. Walker, TWEOMAS, s.v. "Aditi."
1082. Balfour, Vol. 3, s.v. "Surya."
1083. W. Smith, s.v. "Crucifixion."
1084. Baba, p. 53.
1085. Revelation 11:15. Emphasis added.
1086. Malachi 4:2.
1087. Galatians 1:16.
1088. See e.g., Cotterell, ADOWM, s.v. "Buddha."
1089. Neander, Vol. 1, p. 500. Emphasis added.
1090. M. P. Hall, pp. 183, 194.
1091. Lange, Vol. 1, pp. 44-47.
1092. See Evans-Wentz, p. xxxix.
1093. Evans-Wentz, p. 75.
1094. 1 Corinthians 15:31. See also Philippians 1:21.
1095. Galatians 6:14.
1096. G. D. Young, s.v. "Death."
1097. Matthew 27:45-53.
1098. Luke 23:44-56.
1099. Luke 24.
1100. Gibbon, Vol. 2, pp. 109-110. Emphasis added.
1101. Revelation 5:5.
1102. Malachi 4:2.
1103. Luke 4:23.
1104. John 3:16.
1105. John 1:1.
1106. 1 Corinthians 1:25.
1107. 1 Corinthians 3:10.
1108. John 14:6.
1109. John 14:6.
1110. John 14:6.
1111. Isaiah 9:6.
1112. John 10:11.
1113. John 8:12.
1114. 1 Samuel 2:35.
1115. 1 John 5:1.
1116. Daniel 9:26.
1117. John 4:42.
1118. Isaiah 35:8.
1119. 1 John 1:2. For more on the orthodox names and titles of Jesus, see Towns, passim; Derk, passim.
1120. Titcomb, pp. 54-57.

1121. Dunn, p. 18.
1122. A. Pike, p. 377.
1123. See Gaskell, s.v. "Death of Balder"; "Death of Osiris."
1124. M. L. Prophet and E. C. Prophet, p. 174.
1125. Cumont, TORIRP, p. 228.
1126. W. Smith, s.v. "Devil."
1127. Tenney, s.v. "Devil."
1128. Modi, pp. 12-14.
1129. Mish, s.v. "Devanagari"; "devil."
1130. Baumgartner, s.v. "Pan"; J. M. Robertson, CAM, pp. 343-356.
1131. Tripp, s.v. "Faunus"; "Pan."
1132. Matthew 5:39.
1133. Proverbs 23:7.
1134. For more on this topic, see Seabrook, JATLOA, passim.
1135. See Carus, THOTD, p. 468.
1136. Luke 8:2.
1137. See Lamsa, IITBE, p. 57.
1138. Blavatsky, p. 99.
1139. Isaiah 45:7.
1140. A. Pike, p. 102.
1141. Matthew 4:1-11.
1142. Spalding, Vol. 2, p. 67.
1143. See e.g., Proverbs 23:7.
1144. See e.g., Spalding, Vol. 2, pp. 69-71.
1145. Yogananda, TSCOC, Vol. 1, p. 274.
1146. Meyer, TSTOJ, pp. xx-xxi.
1147. M. P. Hall, p. 101.
1148. Luke 11:2.
1149. My paraphrasal.
1150. Matthew 18:18-19.
1151. Matthew 16:19.
1152. M. P. Hall, p. 19.
1153. See Seabrook, JATLOA, passim.
1154. Baba, p. 38.
1155. See e.g., Matthew 9:22; Mark 5:34; Luke 8:48; 17:19.
1156. G. D. Young, s.v. "Christ, Life and Teachings."
1157. Matthew 13:55. Emphasis added.
1158. Luke 2:41. Emphasis added.
1159. Luke 2:48. Emphasis added.
1160. Luke 3:23. Emphasis added. Let us note here that the original Greek word *nomizo*, which has been translated as "supposed," actually means "by tradition," or "by custom."
1161. Luke 4:22. Emphasis added.
1162. Evans-Wentz, pp. 4, 217-218.
1163. John 1:45. Emphasis added.
1164. John 6:42. Emphasis added.
1165. Mark 6:3.
1166. Hebrews 3:3. Emphasis added.
1167. Hebrews 7:24. Emphasis added.
1168. Hebrews 10:12. Emphasis added.
1169. Colossians 3:11. Emphasis added.
1170. John 1:12. Emphasis added.
1171. 1 John 3:1-2. Emphasis added.
1172. Romans 8:14. Emphasis added.
1173. John 10:34. Emphasis added.
1174. John 14:12. Emphasis added.

1175. Kee, p. 90.
1176. John 10:34; 14:12.
1177. Dowling, 129:13-14.
1178. Dowling, 135:15.
1179. Dowling, 176:30.
1180. Dowling, 163:36, 37. Emphasis added.
1181. Zondervan, s.v. "Door."
1182. John 10:7-9.
1183. Colossians 3:11.
1184. John 1:9.
1185. A. Pike, pp. 204-205.
1186. Evans-Wentz, p. 132.
1187. Yogananda, TSCOC, Vol. 1, p. 11.
1188. Spalding, Vol. 4, p. 81.
1189. 1 Corinthians 2:16; Philippians 2:5.
1190. See e.g., Job 32:8; Ezekiel 36:27.
1191. Matthew 3:16. See J. L. McKenzie, s.v. "Dove."
1192. John 1:32-33.
1193. Mark 1:4.
1194. 1 John 3:5.
1195. The Gospel of the Nazoreans, 2:2. My paraphrasal. See Seabrook, JATLOA, p. 418.
1196. See Gaskell, s.v. "Dove."
1197. Farrell and Presser, s.v. "Dove."
1198. B. G. Walker, TWDOSASO, pp. 108, 400. See also Attwater, s.v. "St. Columba of Sens."
1199. B. G. Walker, TWDOSASO, p. 399.
1200. B. G. Walker, TWEOMAS, s.v. "Sophia, Saint."
1201. B. G. Walker, TWDOSASO, p. 400.
1202. Matthew 10:16.
1203. B. G. Walker, TWEOMAS, s.v. "Dove."
1204. Matthew 6:22-23.
1205. John 14:20.
1206. Luke 3:22.
1207. 1 Corinthians 2:16. See also Philippians 2:5.
1208. Yogananda, TSCOC, Vol. 1, pp. 109-110.
1209. Hodson, Vol. 1, p. 105; Bucke, passim.
1210. Jung, PAR, p. 89.
1211. Mark 4:9.
1212. See e.g., Matthew 11:15; 13:9, 15-16, 43; Mark 4:9, 23; 7:16; 8:18; Luke 8:8; 9:44; 14:35; 1 Corinthians 1:17-31; 2:1-16.
1213. Dods, Vol. 1, pp. 437-438. Emphasis added.
1214. Tenney, s.v. "East."
1215. Genesis 1:26-27. See also A. Pike, p. 252.
1216. Malachi 4:2.
1217. See Gaskell, s.v. "East, The Sun-rise."
1218. See e.g., Matthew 16:18; Acts 11:26.
1219. See e.g., J. G. Jackson, CBC, p. 122.
1220. Matthew 24:14. See also Matthew 4:23; 9:35; Luke 4:43.
1221. Mark 1:1.
1222. Acts 24:14.
1223. John 10:34; 14:20.
1224. See Matthew 26:65; Mark 14:63-64; John 5:18; 10:30-40.
1225. Philippians 2:6.
1226. Exodus 20:3.
1227. The manner of execution was stoning. Leviticus 24:16.
1228. Neill, WWKAJ, p. 81.

1229. John 7:16. Further evidence that Jesus did not invent a new religion is that He left no detailed instructions on how to organize his followers into a fully operational church. He did not even once clearly define "the Kingdom of God (or Heaven)", the very foundation of His life teachings. See Neill, WWKAJ, p. 82; Schweitzer, TQOTHJ, p. 17.
1230. Matthew 5:17.
1231. See Matthew 5:1-11.
1232. See e.g., Matthew 3:7; 23:27; Luke 11:39.
1233. See e.g., Matthew 22:15-22; Mark 3:6; 12:13-17.
1234. See e.g., Matthew 3:7; 16:1-12; 22:23-34.
1235. See e.g., Matthew 23:1-39.
1236. W. Smith, s.v. "Eden."
1237. Swedenborg, AC, Vol. 1, p. 40.
1238. Myer, pp. 205, 369.
1239. Berens, p. 44.
1240. Maharshi, p. 120.
1241. Baba, p. 53.
1242. Romans 6:6; Galatians 2:20.
1243. John 12:32; 14:20; 15:4; 17:21-23, 26; Colossians 1:27; 3:10-11; Romans 8:10; 1 Corinthians 6:15, 17; 2 Corinthians 5:16; 13:3, 5; Galatians 1:16; 2:20; 4:19; Ephesians 3:14-17; Philippians 1:20; 2:5; 1 Peter 1:11; 1 John 2:27; 3:24; 4:4.
1244. Genesis 17:1; Exodus 3:14-15; Psalms 46:10; Mark 8:29; 14:61-62; Luke 22:70; John 6:35; 8:12, 23, 58; 9:5; 10:7-11, 30-39; 11:25; 12:26, 46; 13:13; 14:3, 6, 10-11, 20; 15:1; 17:10, 16.
1245. Psalms 122:7.
1246. Evans-Wentz, p. xxxix.
1247. See e.g., Cotterell, ADOWM, s.v. "Buddha."
1248. See the books of Exodus and Leviticus.
1249. Matthew 2:13-15, 19-21.
1250. Fillmore, s.v. "Egypt."
1251. Spalding, Vol. 1, p. 103.
1252. Hoeller, p. 160.
1253. Metzger and Coogan, s.v. "Egypt."
1254. Kingsford and Maitland, p. 232.
1255. Swedenborg, TAR, Vol. 1, pp. 216, 375.
1256. See Gaskell, s.v. "Egypt."
1257. Matthew 2:15.
1258. Comay, s.v. "Elijah."
1259. G. D. Young, s.v. "Elijah." See e.g., 1 Kings 18:17-19, 2 Kings 1:1-8; 2 Chronicles 21:12-15.
1260. See e.g., Malachi 3:1; 4:5.
1261. Matthew 17:10-13. Emphasis added. See also Matthew 11:12-15.
1262. G. R. S. Mead, PS, pp. 11-13.
1263. In sheer number and variety alone Elisha's miracles far surpassed those of his later incarnation as Jesus. See e.g., 2 Kings 3:14; 4:1-44; 5:1-27; 6:1-26; 8:1-15; 13:14-20.
1264. Nelson's, s.v. "Elisha."
1265. 1 Kings 19:19.
1266. Yogananda, TSCOC, Vol. 1, pp. 38-40.
1267. 2 Kings 2:1, 9-15.
1268. H. S. Lewis, TSDOJ, pp. 29-31; Leishman, OAB, pp. 148-149.
1269. Luke 7:28.
1270. Matthew 11:14.
1271. Matthew 17:1-3.
1272. Mark 14:15; Luke 22:12; Acts 1:13.
1273. Spalding, Vol. 4, p. 81.
1274. Comay, s.v. "Elisha."
1275. J. L. McKenzie, s.v. "Elisha."
1276. See Yogananda, TSCOC, Vol. 1, pp. 38-40.

1277. Luke 4:27.
1278. See e.g., Matthew 17:10-12; Mark 9:11-13; Luke 4:25.
1279. John 12:32; 14:20; 15:4; 17:21-23, 26; Colossians 1:27; 3:10-11; Romans 8:10; 1 Corinthians 6:15, 17; 2 Corinthians 5:16; 13:3, 5; Galatians 1:16; 2:20; 4:19; Ephesians 3:14-17; Philippians 1:20; 2:5; 1 Peter 1:11; 1 John 2:27; 3:24; 4:4.
1280. See e.g., Isaiah 9:6; Matthew 22:41-45; John 1:1; 14:9; 1 Timothy 3:16; Titus 1:3. We will note that a number of modern mainstream Christian churches believe that the Jehovah of the Old Testament "became" the man known as Jesus in the New Testament. Thus they translate the name of Jesus (meaning "Jehovah the Savior") as "He is Jehovah the Savior."
1281. John 10:34.
1282. Potter, pp. 24, 90, 127.
1283. Besant and Leadbetter, p. 295.
1284. John 1:9.
1285. Psalms 27:1.
1286. Malachi 4:2.
1287. Psalms 18:28.
1288. Early Christians had their own names for the Crown Chakra, including the "Incorruptible Crown" (1 Corinthians 9:25), "Crown of Rejoicing" (1 Thessalonians 2:19), "Crown of Righteousness" (2 Timothy 4:8), "Crown of Life" (James 1:12; Revelation 2:10), "Crown of Glory" (1 Peter 5:4), and the "Golden Crown" (Revelation 14:14).
1289. M. P. Hall, p. 121.
1290. 1 Peter 5:4.
1291. 1 Corinthians 2:16. See also Philippians 2:5.
1292. Ephesians 6:17.
1293. See e.g., Matthew 16:17; Luke 2:26; 10:21; 1 Corinthians 2:10; Galatians 1:11-12; Ephesians 3:1-5; 1 Peter 1:12.
1294. John 14:20.
1295. John 10:34. See also Psalms 82:6.
1296. W. Smith, s.v. "Apocrypha."
1297. See Jude 1:14-15, which is from Enoch 2:1.
1298. Potter, pp. 93-94.
1299. John 4:14.
1300. Enoch 48:1.
1301. John 12:36.
1302. Enoch 105:25.
1303. Matthew 19:28.
1304. Enoch 105:26.
1305. Matthew 26:24.
1306. Enoch 38:2.
1307. John 5:22.
1308. Enoch 68:39.
1309. Luke 16:26.
1310. Enoch 22:10-13.
1311. Matthew 19:29.
1312. Enoch 40:9.
1313. John 14:2.
1314. Enoch 45:3.
1315. Matthew 5:5.
1316. Enoch 6:9.
1317. Luke 6:24.
1318. Enoch 93:7.
1319. See Potter, passim.
1320. H. S. Lewis, TSDOJ, p. 31.
1321. Potter, p. 154.
1322. Hoeller, p. xviii. Note: Essenism was, in fact, a form of Jewish Gnosticism.

1323. Potter, pp. 93-94.
1324. Barnstone, TOB, p. 485.
1325. Dupuis, pp. 215-299; Spalding, Vol. 3, pp. 64-65. See also Malachi 4:2.
1326. Andrews, pp. 59-60, 145-148.
1327. See Potter, pp. 27, 38-39.
1328. See Potter, passim.
1329. Baigent and Leigh, p. 63.
1330. Goring, s.v. "Essenes."
1331. See Potter, pp. 27, 38-39.
1332. Schonfield, TPP, p. 205.
1333. H. S. Lewis, TSDOJ, pp. 29-31; Ramm, pp. 78-79; Schweitzer, TQOTHJ, pp. 162-163, 327; Neill, TIOTNT, p. 305; Neill, WWKAJ, p. 14; M. P. Hall, p, 179; A. Pike, pp. 260-266.
1334. Potter, pp. 12-13, 154, passim; Yogananda, TSCOC, Vol. 1, p. 100.
1335. Westbrook, p. 291.
1336. Potter, p. 22.
1337. Acts 24:5. See Lemesurier, passim.
1338. Schonfield, TPP, p. 199.
1339. See e.g., Matthew 2:23.
1340. Szekely, TDOTEGOP, p. 50, passim.
1341. Szekely, TEGOP, Vol. 1, pp. 48-49, passim.
1342. See e.g., Acts 15:13-21.
1343. Schonfield, TPP, p. 204.
1344. Mark 6:3.
1345. Matthew 13:55.
1346. M. P. Hall, 178.
1347. See Terapeut, passim.
1348. Potter, p. 12.
1349. Dunlap, p. 488.
1350. Epiphanius, *Panarion*, 29, 1:3.
1351. Epiphanius, *Panarion*, 20, 3:2. See also Potter, p. 118.
1352. Livingstone, s.v. "Ebionites."
1353. Goring, s.v. "Ebionites."
1354. See e.g., Acts 9:2.
1355. Baigent and Leigh, p. 174.
1356. A. Pike, p. 265.
1357. Titcomb, pp. 96-97.
1358. Evans-Wentz, p. 84.
1359. See e.g., Matthew 8:19; Mark 9:5; Luke 8:24; John 9:2.
1360. Seabrook, JATLOA, p. 429.
1361. Schonfield, TJP, p. 284.
1362. See e.g., Matthew 8:14-18; 9:1-8, 35; Luke 4:23.
1363. Potter, p. 21.
1364. M. P. Hall, p. 178.
1365. Titcomb, p. 97.
1366. See Matthew 1:1-17; Luke 3:23-38.
1367. See Isaiah 11:10; Romans 15:12.
1368. Titcomb, pp. 97-98. Emphasis added.
1369. Titcomb, p. 98. Emphasis added.
1370. See Colossians 1:23.
1371. Titcomb, pp. 98-99.
1372. Schweitzer, TQOTHJ, p. 158. Emphasis added.
1373. Schweitzer, TQOTHJ, p. 166. Emphasis added.
1374. Titcomb, p. 99. Emphasis added.
1375. Titcomb, pp. 99-100. Emphasis added.
1376. Schweitzer, TQOTHJ, p. 162.

1377. Doane, pp. 442-443. Emphasis added.
1378. Potter, p. 130.
1379. Sanders, p. 241.
1380. See Hebrews 7:1-28.
1381. See e.g., Acts 6:2, 5; 13:30; 15:12.
1382. Baigent and Leigh, p. 133.
1383. See e.g. Mark 14:25, Luke 22:14-19; 1 Corinthians 11:26. J. L. McKenzie, s.v. "Qumran Scrolls."
1384. Baigent and Leigh, p. 63.
1385. M. Grant, p. 25.
1386. Ramm, p. 65; Baigent and Leigh, p. 65.
1387. Potter, pp. 12-13.
1388. M. Grant, J, p. 10.
1389. See Luke 16:16.
1390. Matthew 7:12.
1391. Lord, p. 173; Windle, p. 23.
1392. See R. L. Fox, TUV, pp. 205-206; Schweitzer, TQOTHJ, pp. 126-127.
1393. Neill, TIOTNT, p. 323.
1394. See John 1:4-5.
1395. See Hoeller, pp. 32-33.
1396. Neill, TIOTNT, pp. 308-318.
1397. Angus, p. 57; Schweitzer, TQOTHJ, pp. xv, xxviii, 113, 183, 344. Yes, the Gospel of John also contains anti-Gnostic elements. However, as Strauss has pointed out, John was "fighting the Gnostics as a Gnostic of another kind." See Schweitzer, TQOTHJ, p. 86.
1398. See Lemesurier, passim.
1399. Leishman, OAB, pp. 148-149; Yogananda, TSCOC, Vol. 1, p. 100; Neill, TIOTNT, p. 305.
1400. See Matthew 2:23.
1401. See Acts 24:5.
1402. Baigent and Leigh, p. 66.
1403. See Dowley, pp. 140-142.
1404. Potter, p. 21.
1405. See e.g., Romans 16:14; 1 Corinthians 8:12; 9:5; 16:11, 12, 20; 2 Corinthians 9:3, 5; 11:9; Galatians 1:2; Ephesians 6:23; Philippians 1:14; 4:21; Colossians 4:15; 1 Thessalonians 4:10; 5:26; 1 Timothy 4:6; 2 Timothy 4:21; 1 Peter 1:22; 1 John 3:14, 16; 3 John 1:3, 5, 10.
1406. Schonfield, TPP, p. 31.
1407. Malachi 4:2.
1408. Bilde, pp. 183-188.
1409. Hoeller, p. 23.
1410. Baigent and Leigh, p. 44.
1411. Potter, pp. 16, 21.
1412. See Jude 1:14-15. The original text for Jude's quote, confirmed by the finding of the book of Enoch among Qumran's Essenic Dead Sea Scrolls, is 1 Enoch 1:9.
1413. Potter, p. 76.
1414. Potter, pp. 17, 22-23, 33-37.
1415. Josephus, Vol. 5, pp. 137-138.
1416. Potter, p. 19.
1417. See Potter, pp. 77-78.
1418. Seabrook, JATLOA, pp. 412, 509.
1419. Zondervan, s.v. "Eve."
1420. Kingsford and Maitland, pp. 185, 242.
1421. See Frazer, FITOT, pp. 1-33; Graves and Patai, p. 15.
1422. Butler, s.v. "Evil."
1423. See Proverbs 23:7.
1424. Bucke, p. 194.
1425. See Proverbs 15:26.
1426. See e.g., Romans 2:6-7.

1427. Matthew 5:39.
1428. See Ponder, pp. 80-83.
1429. See A. Pike, p. 307.
1430. Chernin, p. 162.
1431. For more on how to create your ideal life, see Seabrook, JATLOA, passim.
1432. A. Pike, p. 435.
1433. Butler, s.v. "Exodus."
1434. Romer, pp. 57-58.
1435. Freud, MAM, p. 38.
1436. Graves and Patai, pp. 18-19.
1437. L. M. Graham, p. 147.
1438. Alighieri, p. 49.
1439. Wordsworth, Vol. 4, p. 97.
1440. Dods, Vol. 1, pp. 398-399.
1441. Lasne and Gaultier, p. 203.
1442. See e.g., Matthew 13:15-16; Mark 8:18; Luke 10:23; 19:42; 24:16, 31; John 12:40; 1 Corinthians 1:17-31; 2:1-16.
1443. Tenney, s.v. "The Fall."
1444. Frazer, FITOT, pp. 15-19.
1445. Gaskell, s.v. "Fall of Man."
1446. Gardner, pp. 108-109. Emphasis added.
1447. Kingsford and Maitland, p. 160.
1448. The Divine Mind works via human thought. See e.g., Matthew 6:8; 18:19; John 14:13; 15:16; 16:23, 26.
1449. See M. P. Hall, p. 126.
1450. Genesis 1:26.
1451. Hoeller, p. xviii.
1452. Szekeley, TDOTEGOP, p. 9.
1453. Ferguson, p. 18.
1454. Chetwynd, pp. 110-111.
1455. M. P. Hall, p. 54.
1456. John 1:29, 36; Revelation 5:6.
1457. Prophet, pp. 391-392; E. R. Smith, p. 18.
1458. Seabrook, AT, p. 40.
1459. Seabrook, BR, pp. 68, 91, 100; Seabrook, CBC, p. 52.
1460. Graves, TWG, p. 395.
1461. Tate, p. 35.
1462. Frazer, TGB, Vol. 2, p. 119.
1463. Hampson, Vol. 2, pp. 155-156.
1464. Seabrook, BR, p. 74.
1465. See Seabrook, TBOK, passim.
1466. Henry, p. 17.
1467. Matthew 12:40; Luke 11:30.
1468. Matthew 4:19; Mark 1:17.
1469. Matthew 4:18-22.
1470. Sykes, s.v. "Freyja"; "Frigg."
1471. Walker, TWEOMAS, s.v. "Fish."
1472. Tchakirides, p. 91.
1473. Doane, p. 328.
1474. B. G. Walker, TWEOMAS, s.v. "Aditi."
1475. See e.g., Revelation 12:1.
1476. Zondervan, s.v. "Flood, Deluge." See Genesis 6:5-7.
1477. See Romer, pp. 29-33; R. L. Fox, TUV, p. 218.
1478. See e.g., Ramm, pp. 58-59.
1479. See Frazer, FITOT, pp. 46-143.

1480. Swedenborg, THA, Vol. 1, p. 313.
1481. Philo, Vol. 4, pp. 356, 365.
1482. J. L. McKenzie, s.v. "Babylon, Babylonia."
1483. Metzger and Coogan, s.v. "Flood, The."
1484. Romer, pp. 30-31.
1485. Doane, p. 22.
1486. Doane, p. 24.
1487. See e.g., Hodson, Vol. 2, pp. 172-178.
1488. Zondervan, s.v. "Tree of Knowledge."
1489. Gaskell, s.v. "Fruit of the Tree of Knowledge of Good and Evil."
1490. See e.g., Genesis 3:5; 4:1. See also 1 Kings 1:4.
1491. See e.g., Matthew 1:25.
1492. G. D. Young, s.v. "Forgiveness."
1493. H. S. Lewis, TSDOJ, pp. 220-222.
1494. Exodus 3:14; Ezekiel 37:14; John 14:10-11; Romans 8:9, 11; 1 Corinthians 3:16; 6:17; 14:25; 2 Corinthians 6:16; 9:14; Ephesians 2:22; 4:6; Philemon 2:13; 1 John 3:24; 4:4, 12-13, 16; Zechariah 2:10.
1495. Genesis 1:27.
1496. Romans 8:9, 11.
1497. Colossians 3:13.
1498. Also see Philippians 3:13-14.
1499. For a full Evangelical discussion of the Four Horsemen, see B. Graham, AH, passim.
1500. Matthew 16:28. See Schweitzer, TQOTHJ, p. 20. In the traditional Church the problem of the delay of the Parousia has never been satisfactorily addressed or resolved. This is not an issue in the mystical Church, however, which sees this scripture as a jarring interpolation which seeks to attribute words to our Lord that He never uttered and would never have uttered.
1501. A. Pike, p. 235.
1502. Revelation 6:1-2.
1503. M. P. Hall, p. 187.
1504. Revelation 6:4.
1505. M. P. Hall, p. 187.
1506. Revelation 6:5.
1507. M. P. Hall, p. 187.
1508. Revelation 6:8. See also J. G. Jackson, CBC, p. 150.
1509. M. P. Hall, p. 187.
1510. Cumont, TMOM, pp. 116-118.
1511. Tenney, s.v. "Galilee"; Zondervan, s.v. "Galilee."
1512. Matthew 26:32.
1513. Matthew 28:3.
1514. Alighieri, p. 248.
1515. G. D. Young, s.v. "Galilee."
1516. See Gaskell, s.v. "Galilee."
1517. Metzger and Coogan, s.v. "Eden, The Garden of."
1518. G. D. Young, s.v. "Eden."
1519. Frazer, FITOT, pp. 1-33.
1520. G. D. Young, s.v. "Eden."
1521. Genesis 1:27.
1522. A. Pike, p. 771.
1523. Hoeller, p. 6.
1524. Watts, TWOZ, p. 46.
1525. See e.g., John 5:39.
1526. 1 Corinthians 1:17-31; 2:1-16.
1527. 1 Corinthians 1:30.
1528. 1 Corinthians 2:5; 1 Corinthians 6:17; 2 Corinthians 6:16; Ephesians 4:6; Zechariah 2:10.

1529. Galatians 3:23-25. Emphasis added. Hence, Christian mystics generally eschew organized religion, with its unbiblical priesthood and doctrines. Starbuck cites what I consider a typical "case" of Christian mysticism, in which a woman who had ceased attending church "related how the Spirit had said to her, 'Stop going to church. Stop going to holiness meetings. Go to your own room and I will teach you.'" Starbuck, p. 389.
1530. See Bucke, passim.
1531. 1 Corinthians 2:16; Philippians 2:5.
1532. 2 Samuel 22:22; Hosea 14:9; Acts 13:10.
1533. Matthew 13:11.
1534. John 14:16-17; 1 Corinthians 6:19; 2 Timothy 1:14.
1535. 1 Corinthians 2:14.
1536. Watts, TWOZ, p. 39.
1537. Albertson, pp. 21-22.
1538. Bucke, p. 160.
1539. Bucke, p. 160.
1540. Bucke, p. 160.
1541. Bucke, p. 160.
1542. See Matthew 16:17.
1543. John 12:50.
1544. Kümmel, pp. 223-224.
1545. Legge, Vol. 1 and Vol. 2, passim.
1546. Matthew 24:14. See also Matthew 4:23; 9:35; Luke 4:43.
1547. Mark 1:14.
1548. John 12:32; 14:20; 15:4; 17:21-23, 26; Colossians 1:27; 3:10-11; Romans 8:10; 1 Corinthians 6:15, 17; 2 Corinthians 5:16; 13:3, 5; Galatians 1:16; 2:20; 4:19; Ephesians 3:14-17; Philippians 1:20; 2:5; 1 Peter 1:11; 1 John 2:27; 3:24; 4:4.
1549. John 14:20.
1550. Mark 11:24.
1551. The Gospel of Philip, Logion 48.
1552. Meyer, TSTOJ, p. xvii.
1553. Hoeller, p. 73.
1554. See e.g., Matthew 16:17; Luke 2:26; 10:21; 1 Corinthians 2:10; Galatians 1:11-12; Ephesians 3:1-5; 1 Peter 1:12.
1555. See e.g., The Gospel of Thomas.
1556. Goring, s.v. "Gnosticism."
1557. J. L. McKenzie, s.v. "Know, Knowledge."
1558. Legge, Vol. 1 and Vol. 2, passim.
1559. Daraul, p. 89.
1560. See Potter, p. 154.
1561. Romer, pp. 195-196.
1562. Stirling, pp. 44-45.
1563. Mish, s.v. "cabal"; "cabala."
1564. John 14:16-17; 1 Corinthians 6:19; 2 Timothy 1:14.
1565. Romans 16:25.
1566. Stirling, p. 45. Emphasis added.
1567. Stirling, pp. 45-46.
1568. J. M. Robinson, p. 6.
1569. Parker, p. 18. Emphasis added.
1570. See Layton, passim; Barnstone, TOB, passim; R. J. Miller, passim; J. M. Robinson, passim; Pagels, TGG, passim.
1571. Schweitzer, TQOTHJ, p. 167. This is Schweitzer's paraphrasal of Ghillany. Emphasis added.
1572. A. Pike, pp. 247-248. Emphasis added.
1573. Paine, p. 134.
1574. Meyer, TSTOJ, p. xvii.
1575. For more on pre-Christian Gnosticism, see Neill, TIOTNT, pp. 137-190. See also Doresse, passim; Jonas, passim.

1576. Doane, p. 438.
1577. M. P. Hall, p. 50.
1578. Brewster, p. 39.
1579. Filson, pp. 153-154; Potter, pp. 77-78, 138-139, 155; Lamsa, IITBE, p. 86; Spivey and Smith, p. 498.
1580. Sheehan, p. 12.
1581. See Sheehan, p. 92.
1582. Feuerbach, p. 148. My paraphrasal.
1583. For more on Leo X, see Ide, U, p. 161.
1584. Doane, p. 438. Emphasis added.
1585. Doane, pp. 407-408. Emphasis added.
1586. Doane, pp. 438-443. Emphasis added.
1587. In truth, these were neither "errors" or "fictions," but merely mystical symbols of various spiritual principles. It is surprising that Pike does not recognize this.
1588. A. Pike, pp. 542-548. Emphasis added.
1589. H. S. Lewis, TSDOJ, pp. 29-31.
1590. Spivey and Smith, p. 497.
1591. Luke 8:10.
1592. Temple, p. 35.
1593. Dunlap, p. 488.
1594. Epiphanius, *Panarion*, 29, 1:3.
1595. Epiphanius, *Panarion*, 20, 3:2; 40, 1:5.
1596. Potter, p. 154.
1597. Hoeller, p. xviii.
1598. Romer, pp. 194, 195.
1599. Neill, TIOTNT, p. 173.
1600. Colossians 3:11.
1601. Hoeller, p. 73.
1602. See Sewall, p. 75.
1603. Matthew 16:20. John used the same mystical language. See e.g., John 1:41.
1604. See e.g., Leviticus 4:3; 1 Samuel 2:10; 2 Samuel 1:21; 1 Chronicles 16:22; Psalms 18:50; Isaiah 45:1; Lamentations 4:20; Daniel 9:25-26; Habakkuk 3:13.
1605. John 12:32; 14:20; 15:4; 17:21-23, 26; Colossians 1:27; 3:10-11; Romans 8:10; 1 Corinthians 6:15, 17; 2 Corinthians 5:16; 13:3, 5; Galatians 1:16; 2:20; 4:19; Ephesians 3:14-17; Philippians 1:20; 2:5; 1 Peter 1:11; 1 John 2:27; 3:24; 4:4.
1606. Genesis 1:27.
1607. Daraul, p. 90.
1608. John 4:24.
1609. Exodus 3:14; Ezekiel 37:14; John 14:10-11; Romans 8:9, 11; 1 Corinthians 6:17; 2 Corinthians 6:16; Ephesians 2:22; 4:6.
1610. Luke 11:9; Mark 11:24.
1611. Colossians 1:15.
1612. Romans 8:9. Compare with Job 32:8: "There is a spirit in man."
1613. J. L. McKenzie, s.v. "Know, Knowledge."
1614. See Kuhn, WITKOG, passim.
1615. J. M. Robinson, p. 5.
1616. Leishman, OAB, pp. 148-149; H. S. Lewis, TSDOJ, pp. 29-31; Neill, TIOTNT, p. 305; Yogananda, TSCOC, Vol. 1, p. 100; M. P. Hall, pp. 178-179. Jesus was often called an Essene ("Nazarene"). See e.g. Matthew 2:23. See also Lemesurier, passim.
1617. See Lemesurier, passim.
1618. Epiphanius, *Panarion*, 20, 3:2; 40, 1:5.
1619. Acts 11:26.
1620. Sewall, pp. 61-62.
1621. See Acts 8:9-24; 2 Timothy 2:16-18.

1622. Examples of Gnosticism in Jesus: Matthew 11:25, 27; 13:9-17; 16:17; 24:23-27; Mark 7:14-16; Luke 8:10; 10:21; 11:34-35; 12:2; 17:21; 24:45; John 3:5; 7:15-17; 8:58; 9:5; 10:30-36; 12:31, 36, 46; 14:20; 17:21-22, 30; 18:36.
1623. Examples of Gnosticism in Paul: Romans 6:6; 11:33; 15:14; 1 Corinthians 1:5; 2:14; 12:8; 14:6; 2 Corinthians 8:7; Galatians 3:7; Ephesians 1:17; 3:19; 4:13; 5:14; Philippians 3:8-10; Colossians 2:2; 3:3; Philemon 1:9.
1624. Examples of Gnosticism in James: James 2:20.
1625. Examples of Gnosticism in John: John 7:17; 8:43; 17:7; 1 John 2:13, 21; 5:20.
1626. Acts 24:14.
1627. Acts 24:5. See Lemesurier, passim.
1628. Acts 21:23-26.
1629. See e.g., Matthew 2:23.
1630. Dunlap, p. 488.
1631. Examples of anti-Gnostic sentiment: 1 Corinthians 1:17; 2:6; 8:1, 7, 10; 13:8; 1 Timothy 6:20; Revelation 2:24.
1632. H. S. Lewis, TSDOJ, p. 219.
1633. Seabrook, JATLOA, p. 174.
1634. Pagels, TGG, pp. 172-175, passim.
1635. Filson, p. 44.
1636. J. M. Robinson, p. 4.
1637. Pagels, TGG, p. 22.
1638. See Christie-Murray, passim.
1639. J. M. Robinson, pp. 373-378. My paraphrasal. Emphasis added.
1640. Matthew 23:13-38.
1641. 1 Corinthians 2:14.
1642. Colossians 3:3.
1643. Ephesians 5:14.
1644. Genesis 1:27; Colossians 3:11.
1645. John 1:9.
1646. Colossians 1:26.
1647. 1 Corinthians 1:18.
1648. Carus, TM, pp. 608-615. Emphasis added.
1649. Barnstone, TOB, p. xxv.
1650. Daraul, p. 95.
1651. J. M. Robinson, p. 6.
1652. Daraul, p. 96. See also A. Pike, passim.
1653. Kümmel, pp. 222-223.
1654. M. P. Hall, p. 35.
1655. Neil, TIOTNT, pp. 162-163, 179.
1656. Schonfield, TJP, pp. 98, 282.
1657. See Zondervan, s.v. "God."
1658. See e.g., 2 Samuel 22:7-16.
1659. Hosea 2:16. The name Baal means "Father" or "Lord."
1660. Genesis 14:18-20. In these passages El Elyon's name has been mistranslated as the "most high."
1661. Genesis 17:1; Ruth 1:20. The name Israel itself comes from Paganism: *Is* derives from the name of the Egyptian Mother-Goddess Isis; *Ra* derives from the name of the Egyptian Father-God Ra; and *El* derives from the Canaanite Father-God El. Thus Isis-Ra-El, or Is-Ra-El.
1662. Meissner, p. 116.
1663. See e.g., Psalms 2:4-12.
1664. Exodus 15:3.
1665. Numbers 11:32-36.
1666. Exodus 35:2-3.
1667. Exodus 12:15.
1668. Deuteronomy 22:20-21; Leviticus 21:9.
1669. Leviticus 24:16.

1670. Deuteronomy 18:20.
1671. See e.g., Numbers 31:1-18; Deuteronomy 2:30-34; 3:6; 7:1-6; 20:16-17; Joshua 6:17-21; 7:10-26; 8:26; 10:28-40; 11:10-21; Judges 18:6, 27; 1 Samuel 6:19; 15:1-8, 33; 18:27; 2 Samuel 8:4; 1 Chronicles 21:1-15; 1 Kings 18:40; 2 Kings 19:35.
1672. Exodus 34:14.
1673. There are numerous other biblical scriptures illustrating the capricious barbarity of the Paganized Old Testament "Lord of Lords," the Pagan-styled Hebrew sky-god that Jesus did away with. See e.g., Lamentations 2:21; 3:10-11; Hosea 13:7-8; Ezekiel 6:12-13; 8:17-18; Isaiah 13:6-18; Micah 6:9-16; Nahum 1:2-6; Habakkuk 3:5; Zephaniah 1:2-3.
1674. See e.g., 2 Maccabees 6:2.
1675. John 4:24. The KJV has "God is *a* Spirit," a mistranslation. The original is: "God is Spirit." Spalding, Vol. 4, p. 24; Neill, WWKAJ, p. 78. See also Romans 1:20; 1 Timothy 1:17.
1676. John 5:37.
1677. John 1:18.
1678. Genesis 1:27.
1679. Barbanell, p. 152.
1680. See Bucke, passim.
1681. John 6:46.
1682. 1 John 4:12.
1683. The Apocryphon of John, 2:34. My paraphrasal.
1684. Colossians 3:11.
1685. John 10:34.
1686. My theory. See The Gospel of Thomas, Logion 13. For the text, see Zinner, p. 293.
1687. John 10:30-33.
1688. A. Pike, p. 643.
1689. See Gaskell, s.v. "Gods, Deities."
1690. Deuteronomy 5:8.
1691. Dowling, 8:19-20.
1692. Luke 20:38.
1693. Mark 12:18-27.
1694. John 4:24. The KJV has "God is *a* Spirit." This is a mistranslation. The original text is: "God is Spirit." Spalding, Vol. 4, p. 24; Neill, WWKAJ, p. 78. See also Romans 1:20; 1 Timothy 1:17.
1695. Romans 8:9, 11; Ezekiel 36:27.
1696. 1 Kings 19:11-13.
1697. Job 32:8.
1698. See e.g., Fenwick and Fenwick, p. 114, passim; Ritchie, passim.
1699. Colossians 1:15. See also 1 Timothy 1:17.
1700. 1 Timothy 6:16.
1701. Acts 7:48. See also Acts 17:24.
1702. Dowling, 15:22.
1703. Hebrews 8:2. My paraphrasal. See also Hebrews 9:11.
1704. Baba, p. 3.
1705. C. Johnston, p. 70. (Bhagavad Gita 4:11.) My paraphrasal. See also Howells, passim.
1706. John 4:24. The KJV has "God is *a* Spirit," which is a mistranslation. The original is: "God is Spirit." Spalding, Vol. 4, p. 24; Neill, WWKAJ, p. 78. See also Romans 1:20; 1 Timothy 1:17.
1707. John 12:32; 14:20; 15:4; 17:21-23, 26; Colossians 1:27; 3:10-11; Romans 8:10; 1 Corinthians 6:15, 17; 2 Corinthians 5:16; 13:3, 5; Galatians 1:16; 2:20; 4:19; Ephesians 3:14-17; Philippians 1:20; 2:5; 1 Peter 1:11; 1 John 2:27; 3:24; 4:4.
1708. Matthew 24:24; Mark 13:22.
1709. Luke 17:21.
1710. Dowling, 61:15.
1711. John 17:21; Hebrews 12:10; 2 Peter 1:4.
1712. John 4:23.
1713. Spalding, Vol. 5, pp. 79, 100-101.
1714. Spalding, Vol. 5, pp. 27-31.

1715. M. P. Hall, p. 15.
1716. 1 Corinthians 10:26.
1717. See e.g., Psalms 48:3.
1718. The feminine singular of the plural Elohim is Eloah, "Goddess," from El, "God."
1719. Genesis 1:27; 5:2.
1720. Hoeller, p. xviii.
1721. See e.g., The Apocryphon of John. Also, as just one of thousands of biblical examples, see e.g., the Hebrew word for "God" (Elohim) in Genesis 1:1. See also Galatians 3:28.
1722. See e.g., The Gospel of the Egyptians, 3:10-11.
1723. Fillmore, s.v. "Jehovah."
1724. Szekeley, TDOTEGOP, p. 9.
1725. Spalding, Vol. 5, p. 143.
1726. See Baba, p. 13.
1727. Acts 17:28.
1728. John 12:32; 14:20; 15:4; 17:21-23, 26; Colossians 1:27; 3:10-11; Romans 8:10; 1 Corinthians 6:15, 17; 2 Corinthians 5:16; 13:3, 5; Galatians 1:16; 2:20; 4:19; Ephesians 3:14-17; Philippians 1:20; 2:5; 1 Peter 1:11; 1 John 2:27; 3:24; 4:4.
1729. John 14:16-17; 1 Corinthians 6:19; 2 Timothy 1:14.
1730. See John 14:16-17.
1731. Exodus 3:14; Ezekiel 37:14; John 14:10-11; Romans 8:9, 11; 1 Corinthians 3:16; 6:17; 14:25; 2 Corinthians 6:16; 9:14; Ephesians 2:22; 4:6; Philemon 2:13; 1 John 3:24; 4:4, 12-13, 16; Zechariah 2:10.
1732. 1 John 5:7; 2 Corinthians 13:14.
1733. MacCulloch, pp. 93-95.
1734. John 10:34.
1735. Proverbs 23:7.
1736. Gardner, pp. 33-34. Emphasis added.
1737. Swedenborg, TAR, Vol. 1, p. 160. Emphasis added.
1738. Channing, p. xxii. Emphasis added.
1739. Luke 17:21.
1740. John 10:34.
1741. John 1:9.
1742. Colossians 3:11.
1743. 2 Peter 1:4.
1744. Hebrews 12:10.
1745. See e.g., Matthew 19:17; John 5:30; 8:28, 42, 54; 12:19; 14:10.
1746. John 1:9.
1747. Genesis 1:27. See also A. Pike, p. 252.
1748. Spalding, Vol. 4, p. 112.
1749. Spalding, Vol. 4, p. 169.
1750. John 10:30.
1751. John 14:9.
1752. Meyer, TSTOJ, p. xvi.
1753. John 10:34.
1754. The Christian mystic repeats the following scriptures aloud: Psalm 46:10a; Exodus 3:14a.
1755. Spalding, Vol. 4, p. 91.
1756. Luke 17:21.
1757. Testimonies, p. 17.
1758. Ludlow, s.v. "Mother in Heaven."
1759. See Mollenkott, passim.
1760. Matthew 6:14.
1761. Genesis 1:27.
1762. Hoeller, p. xviii.
1763. Curtiss and Curtiss, TKTTU, pp. 219-221.
1764. Genesis 1:26; 3:22. See A. Pike, p. 727.
1765. See e.g., Psalms 48:3; Job 38:29; Isaiah 42:14; 46:3; 49:15; 66:13; Luke 15:8-10; Matthew 23:37.

1766. Seabrook, BR, p. 16.
1767. See Gimbutas, TCOTG, passim; Gimbutas, TGAGOOE, passim; Streep, passim.
1768. See e.g., Graves and Patai, pp. 26, 27, 43, 208, 218, 219.
1769. Metzger and Coogan, s.v. "Astarte."
1770. See e.g., Judges 2:13-14; 10:6-7; 1 Kings 11:5, 33; Jeremiah 7:16-20; 44:15-28.
1771. Acts 19:27.
1772. 1 Kings 11:5, 33; 2 Kings 23:13. See Finegan, Vol. 1, pp. 167-168, 173; Pritchard, passim.
1773. Hart, s.v. "Astarte."
1774. Metzger and Coogan, s.v. "Queen of Heaven."
1775. See Gimbutas, TCOTG, pp. 222, 266, 267; Streep, passim.
1776. Revelation 12:1.
1777. B. G. Walker, TWEOMAS, s.v. "Aditi."
1778. Balfour, Vol. 3, s.v. "Surya."
1779. Kingsford and Maitland, p. 188.
1780. Pritchard, passim; Finegan, Vol. 1, pp. 167-168, 173; R. L. Fox, TUV, p. 243.
1781. Hart, s.v. "Astarte."
1782. See e.g., 1 Kings 11:5, 33; 2 Kings 23:13.
1783. See e.g., Exodus 34:13; Deuteronomy 7:5; 12:3; Judges 3:7; 1 Kings 14:15; 18:19; 2 Kings 17:10; 18:4; 23:14; 2 Chronicles 14:3; 17:6; 19:3; 24:18; 31:1; 33:3, 19; 34:3, 4, 7; Isaiah 27:9; Jeremiah 17:2.
1784. Aphrodite's name means "born of sea-foam." She is the Greek version of the Roman love-goddess Venus. See Cox, Vol. 2, pp. 1-9.
1785. Frazer, TGB, Vol. 2, p. 119.
1786. Graves, TWG, p. 395.
1787. For more information on Goddess, thealogy, and the Divine Feminine, see my books, *Christmas Before Christianity: How the Birthday of the "Sun" Became the Birthday of the "Son"*; *Britannia Rules: Goddess-worship in Ancient Anglo-Celtic Society*; *The Book of Kelle: An Introduction to Goddess-worship and the Great Celtic Mother-Goddess Kelle*; and *The Goddess Dictionary of Words and Phrases*.
1788. Eliade, IAS, pp. 131-132.
1789. B. G. Walker, TWEOMAS, s.v. "Vesica Piscis"; "Sheila-na-gig"; Monaghan, s.v. "Sheila-na-Gig."
1790. Eliade, IAS, pp. 131-132.
1791. B. G. Walker, TWEOMAS, s.v. "Mary."
1792. F. M. Müller, R, p. viii.
1793. Ancient Egypt possessed some 2,000 deities alone. J. E. M. White, AE, p. 21.
1794. Angus, p. 12.
1795. Freud, MAM, pp. 18-19.
1796. M. P. Hall, p. 184. See also James, pp. 57-58.
1797. M. P. Hall, p. 75.
1798. Swedenborg, TAR, Vol. 1, p. 45.
1799. G. R. S. Mead, O, p. 53.
1800. Dods, Vol. 1, p. 324.
1801. Plutarch's Morals, p. 57. Emphasis added.
1802. See e.g., 1 Corinthians 8:5-6.
1803. The Bhagavad Gita 4:11; 9:22-23.
1804. A. Pike, p. 387. Emphasis added.
1805. Cumont, TMOM, p. 188.
1806. Cumont, TMOM, p. 187. Emphasis added.
1807. See e.g., 1 Corinthians 8:5. See also Romans 8:38-39.
1808. For biblical examples of polytheistic references to the Judeo-Christian Pantheon, see e.g., Matthew 4:6, 11; 8:16, 31; 9:34; 12:24, 28; 13:41, 49; 16:27; 24:31; 25:31, 41; 26:53; Mark 1:13, 34; 3:22; 5:9, 12; 8:38; 13:27; 16:9; Luke 4:41; 8:2, 27, 30, 33; 9:1; 10:17; 11:15; 12:9; John 1:51; 10:34-35; Acts 19:27-28; 34-35; 1 Corinthians 6:3; 8:5; Hebrews 1:6-7; 12:22; 1 Peter 3:22; Jude 1:6; James 2:19; Revelation 5:11; 7:1; 8:2; 12:7; 16:4; 21:12.
1809. H. S. Lewis, TSDOJ, p. 223.
1810. See Attwater, passim; Delaney, passim; Farmer, passim; Kelly and Rogers, passim.
1811. Freud, MAM, p. 117.

1812. Matthew 2:11.
1813. Fillmore, s.v. "Wise-men"; Gaskell, s.v. "Magi from the East."
1814. Swedenborg, TAR, Vol. 1, p. 239.
1815. Matthew 27:33; Mark 15:22; John 19:17.
1816. Bruce, p. 94.
1817. J. L. McKenzie, s.v. "Golgotha."
1818. James 1:12.
1819. M. P. Hall, pp. 121, 135.
1820. Seabrook, JATLOA, pp. 517-518.
1821. Colossians 3:11.
1822. Genesis 1:27. See also A. Pike, p. 252.
1823. John 1:9.
1824. J. L. McKenzie, s.v. "Gospel."
1825. Kümmel, p. 35; Spivey and Smith, p. 61.
1826. Compare with Jesus' statement, speaking as the Universal Indwelling Christ, in John 14:6.
1827. Burtt, pp. 51-52.
1828. Matthew 24:14. See also Matthew 4:23; 9:35; Mark 1:14; Luke 4:43.
1829. Dunn, p. 204. See e.g., John 5:30; 8:50-54.
1830. John 10:34.
1831. John 14:12. In the Gnostic-Christian work, The Apocryphon of James (also known as The Secret Book of James), 6:17-20, Jesus tells His 12 Apostles: "Become better than I; make yourselves like the son of the Holy Spirit."
1832. For more on the authentic Good News of Jesus, see Seabrook, JATLOA, passim; Seabrook, TBATLOA, passim.
1833. M. Grant, CTG, pp. 121-186.
1834. See Layton, passim; Barnstone, TOB, passim; R. J. Miller, passim; J. M. Robinson, passim; Pagels, TGG, passim.
1835. John 10:34.
1836. John 14:20.
1837. Colossians 3:11.
1838. John 14:12. For more on these topics, see Seabrook, JATLOA, passim; Seabrook, TBATLOA, passim.
1839. Gaskell, s.v. "Shepherd, Good."
1840. John 10:7-17.
1841. Colossians 3:11.
1842. 2 Corinthians 6:16.
1843. Schonfield, TPP, p. 211.
1844. B. G. Walker, TWDOSASO, p. 204.
1845. Guirand, p. 88.
1846. C. O. Müller, p. 77.
1847. Farrell and Presser, s.v. "Shepherd."
1848. Gaskell, s.v. "Osiris."
1849. B. G. Walker, TWDOSASO, pp. 104-105.
1850. Biedermann, s.v. "shepherd."
1851. Tripp, s.v. "Pan."
1852. Collignon, pp. 107, 111-112, 255-256.
1853. J. M. Robertson, CAM, pp. 343-356.
1854. Blavatsky, p. 99.
1855. Butler, s.v. "Gospel."
1856. For the many problems and issues theologians have found in the Gospel of Mark alone, see Schweitzer, TQOTHJ, pp. 334-347, passim.
1857. Spivey and Smith, p. 84.
1858. Mark 6:14.
1859. Luke 3:19.
1860. See John 19:25-27.
1861. Strauss, TLOJCE, Vol. 1, pp. 119-120.

1862. Matthew 5.
1863. See Goguel, Vol. 2, pp. 460-462.
1864. Matthew 17.
1865. Matthew 28:16-20.
1866. Luke 24:33-41, 51.
1867. Conservative Bible scholars like to say that John did not mention these events because "he did not think it necessary to repeat what had already been presented in the Synoptics." However, since there are no irrefutable connecting links between John and the Synoptics, we cannot know that he was aware of them, and it is therefore entirely logical to assume that he did not. While John *did* mention some things that are also found in the Synoptics, this could merely be because these particular items were by then widely known and well established elements of Jesus' ever growing "biography" (e.g., Mary and Martha of Bethany, Jesus at the lake, Peter's confession, the feeding of the multitudes, etc., all of which are found in John *and* the Synoptics). Either way, John neglects to refer to what Matthew, Mark, and Luke portray as some of the most significant events in the history of Christianity; *events at which John himself was said to be an eyewitness*—ultimately an irreconcilable problem for Bible literalists.
1868. Spivey and Smith, p. 85.
1869. Matthew 24:34. See Spivey and Smith, p. 461. Paul too mistakenly predicted a literal Second Coming within his own lifetime. See e.g., 1 Thessalonians 4:16-17.
1870. See e.g., Matthew 14:33.
1871. See e.g., John 1:1.
1872. See e.g., Jude 1:25.
1873. Strauss, TLOJCE, Vol. 1, p. 120.
1874. See Matthew 1:1-16; Luke 3:23-38.
1875. Leishman, TCOTB, p. 22.
1876. Matthew 1:20-25.
1877. Concerning Matthew and Luke's contradictory genealogies for Jesus through his biological father Joseph: why include them if not "to prove Jesus to be of the lineage of David through Joseph?" Strauss, TLOJCE, Vol. 1, pp. 121-122. Since early Jews reckoned descent through the father not the mother, we do not know if Mary was descended from David. However, Luke hints that she was a descendant of a different line, that of Levi, an ancestor of Aaron and Moses. Here Elizabeth, the mother of John the Baptist and a supposed "cousin" of Mary, is said to be a "daughter of Aaron." See Luke 1:5, 36.
1878. Strauss, TLOJCE, Vol. 1, p. 109.
1879. Luke 2:41-52.
1880. Matthew 10:2-4; Mark 3:6-10; Luke 6:14-16; Acts 1:13.
1881. Strauss, TLOJCE, Vol. 1, pp. 348-353.
1882. See Kümmel, pp. 43-44.
1883. See e.g., Matthew 28:19, an overt orthodox addition, for not only was the Trinity not taught by Jesus or anyone else in the 1st Century A.D., but Jesus never once discusses baptism by immersion (until this abrupt scripture appears at the end of Matthew), never shows any interest in it, and never commands it.
1884. Mark 16:9-20, all interpolated.
1885. Luke originally began with Chapter 3. Chapters 1 and 2 are late additions. See Strauss, TLOJCE, Vol. 1, p. 77.
1886. The last part of John, Chapter 21, was added to this Gospel later to make the author look like an eyewitness.
1887. Dentan, pp. 121-122; Kümmel, pp. 46-47.
1888. Luke 22:44.
1889. Matthew 26:36-46.
1890. John 18:1-3.
1891. Schonfield, TPP, pp. 136-137, 220-221.
1892. Matthew 6:13.
1893. See Hoeller, p. 170.
1894. 1 John 4:8.
1895. See e.g., Strauss, TLOJCE, Vol. 1, pp. 115-118, 235-236, passim; Hoffman, pp. 24-25; Spivey and Smith, pp. 102, 283-285. The same may be said of Paul concerning both the Old Testament and the words of Jesus (the latter which, because there was as yet no New Testament, Paul apparently drew from faulty Church tradition). See e.g., Spivey and Smith, pp. 312-313, 320-321. For a fuller treatment of the actual Old

Testament prophecies used to flesh out Jesus' biography, see Schonfield, TPP, pp. 86-90.
1896. Kümmel, pp. 52-53.
1897. Keck, p. 55; Kümmel, p. 513.
1898. Keck, p. 55.
1899. John 3:1, 4, 9; 7:50; 19:39.
1900. John 19:38.
1901. See Schonfield, TPP, p. 161.
1902. Burr, pp. 353-354.
1903. See e.g., Mark 16:1-2.
1904. Schonfield, TPP, p. 161.
1905. D. A. Carson, pp. 18, 70-72.
1906. Keck, p. 57.
1907. Schonfield, TJP, p. 11.
1908. Schonfield, TPP, p. 221.
1909. Spong, pp. 83-85.
1910. Sanders, pp. 153-154.
1911. See e.g., Matthew 5:38-48. Compare with Exodus 21:24; Leviticus 19:18; 24:20; Deuteronomy 19:21.
1912. Compare e.g., John 4:14 with Enoch 48:1.
1913. John 11:1-57.
1914. Schonfield, TPP, p. 261.
1915. J. L. McKenzie, s.v. "Lazarus."
1916. Matthew 28:4.
1917. Matthew 28:11.
1918. See Luke 24:13.
1919. Graves and Podro, p. 763; Schonfield, TPP, p. 170.
1920. Luke 2:41-52.
1921. Schonfield, TPP, pp. 46-47.
1922. Matthew 3:13-17.
1923. Matthew 11:1-4. What we have here are two separate and contradictory stories which Matthew unwittingly wove into his Gospel.
1924. See Seabrook, JATGOQ, passim.
1925. Mark, 1:9-11.
1926. Matthew 1:16; Luke 2:11.
1927. John 1:1-14.
1928. Schonfield, TPP, p. 120.
1929. Schweitzer, TQOTHJ, pp. 7-9. For more examples of New Testament issues, see Spivey and Smith, pp. 259-263, passim.
1930. Matthew 22:41-46. See also Daniel 7:13-14; Micah 5:2; Matthew 28:20; John 8:58; Hebrews 7:3; Revelation 22:13.
1931. Strauss, TLOJCE, Vol. 1, pp. 274-293.
1932. Parker, pp. 16-17. For an in-depth examination of the Gospelers' many disagreements, see Strauss, passim.
1933. See e.g. Matthew 15:1-20; Mark 8:31-33; 9:31-32; Luke 24:21; John 6:32-66; 16:5-6, 17-18.
1934. See e.g., Mark 8:14-21.
1935. Mark 14:50.
1936. See e.g., Matthew 28:17; Luke 24:25, 36-41; John 12:16.
1937. For more on the topic of Bible criticism, I recommend the works of the great 18th- and 19th-Century German scholars.
1938. M. D. Roberts, p. 49.
1939. Spivey and Smith, pp. 82, 206.
1940. Spivey and Smith, p. 464.
1941. See Akerley, passim.
1942. See Schweitzer, TQOTHJ, p. 395.
1943. M. L. Prophet and E. C. Prophet, pp. lii, lvi.
1944. See A. Pike, p. 377.

1945. See Gaskell, s.v. "Gospel Story of Jesus Christ."
1946. Kingsford and Maitland, p. 188.
1947. Matthew 2:11.
1948. Matthew 1:25.
1949. Matthew 1:20.
1950. Matthew 1:18.
1951. Matthew 3:16.
1952. Luke 9:23; 14:27.
1953. Matthew 1:23.
1954. Luke 2:40-49.
1955. Luke 2:52.
1956. Matthew 4:1-11.
1957. Matthew 17:1-13.
1958. Matthew 26:1-75; 27:1-50.
1959. Matthew 27:35-50.
1960. Luke 24:1-6.
1961. Luke 24:51.
1962. Revelation 3:12.
1963. John 3:7.
1964. 2 Corinthians 12:2.
1965. Luke 22:69.
1966. Martin and Romanowski, p. 61.
1967. Baba, pp. 18-19.
1968. Kingsford and Maitland, p. 228. Emphasis added.
1969. Strauss, TLOJCE, Vol. 1, pp. 890-891. Emphasis added.
1970. Inge, PIAM, pp. 54-55, 62. Emphasis added.
1971. Bunsen, Vol. 1, p. 120.
1972. Bucke, pp. 270, 271.
1973. Burtt, pp. 202-203.
1974. Watts, G, p. 39.
1975. 2 Corinthians 3:6.
1976. John 5:39-40.
1977. Mark 1:1.
1978. Matthew 24:14. See also Matthew 4:23; 9:35; Luke 4:43.
1979. See Seabrook, JATLOA, pp. 405-446. See also A. Pike, pp. 508-509; Sheehan, pp. 125-126.
1980. Freud, MAM, p. 111.
1981. Hoffman, p. 13.
1982. A. Pike, pp. 508, 516, 522, 558.
1983. See e.g., Goguel, Vol. 2, pp. 280, 331; Spivey and Smith, p. 472.
1984. Neill, WWKAJ, p. 68.
1985. Kloppenborg, TFOQ, p. 5.
1986. Kloppenborg, TFOQ, p. 23.
1987. About 90 percent of Mark is found in Matthew, about 50 percent of Mark is found in Luke. Boer, p. 54.
1988. Mack, pp. 3-4.
1989. See Mack, pp. 172, 178-180; Harrington, p. 97.
1990. Kloppenborg, TFOQ, p. 16.
1991. See my book, *Jesus and the Gospel of Q: Christ's Pre-Christian Teachings as Recorded in the New Testament*. Bernhard Weiss also maintained that Mark used Q. See Kloppenborg, TFOQ, p. 9.
1992. See Kloppenborg, QP, p. 3; Kloppenborg, TFOQ, pp. 28-29.
1993. Kloppenborg, TFOQ, p. 32.
1994. Hoeller, pp. 186-187.
1995. Harrington, pp. 62-63.
1996. See Eusebius' *History of the Church*, 3:39. See also Neil, TIOTNT, p. 126; Filson, p. 48; Kümmel, p. 55.
1997. For Paul's reference, see Acts 20:35, where he cites a saying by Jesus that is not found in the canonical Bible.

1998. Examples of the Gospel of Q that were used in the Gospel of Matthew: 5:3-4, 6, 39, 42, 44-47; 6:9-13; 7:7-11, 12; 10:26-31, 39; 8:20-22; 16:25.
1999. See Kloppenborg, TFOQ, p. 81.
2000. Sheehan, pp. 20-21.
2001. My theories. But see Mack, pp. 44-49, 107-108, 259.
2002. Dunn, pp. 70-76.
2003. Kümmel, p. 76.
2004. See Mack, p. 42.
2005. Matthew 24:14. See also Matthew 4:23; 9:35; Luke 4:43.
2006. For more on our Lord's true Gospel (of the Kingdom), see Seabrook, JATLOA, passim.
2007. Harnack, p. 171.
2008. Kloppenborg, TFOQ, p. 21.
2009. See Seabrook, JATGOQ, passim.
2010. Yogananda, TSCOC, Vol. 1, p. 378.
2011. See Miller, passim.
2012. Matthew 24:14. See also Matthew 4:23; 9:35; Luke 4:43.
2013. Mark 1:1.
2014. Spivey and Smith, p. 85.
2015. Matthew 22:36-40.
2016. Calvocoressi, s.v. "Jesus."
2017. John 17:21; Hebrews 12:10; 2 Peter 1:4.
2018. Luke 8:50.
2019. See e.g., Matthew 11:12-15; 17:10-13.
2020. Szekely, TEGOP, Vol. 1, pp. 48-49, passim. The Nazarenes or Essenes advocated vegetarianism as well. See Schonfield, TPP, pp. 199-200.
2021. Luke 11:34.
2022. John 14:6.
2023. See e.g., Luke 24:15, 31, 36.
2024. Matthew 7:12; Luke 6:31.
2025. Mark 4:20; Matthew 7:7-11.
2026. For more on the aura, see Kul, passim; Krippner and Rubin, passim.
2027. Luke 6:38.
2028. Luke 8:50. Later, individuals like Paracelsus continued teaching the doctrine of faith, maintaining that total belief can cure any and all ailments. See M. P. Hall, p. 111.
2029. Matthew 6:9-13.
2030. Matthew 12:37.
2031. Matthew 5:39.
2032. Matthew 18:21-22.
2033. See e.g., Luke 24:31.
2034. H. S. Lewis, TSDOJ, pp. 52-53, 103-104, 131, 138, 141-143, 146, 176-178, 184, 187, 189-191, 208-210.
2035. Mark 11:24.
2036. John 14:20.
2037. Seabrook, JATLOA, pp. 61, 170, 261, 322, 334, 365-369.
2038. See Seabrook, JATGOQ, passim. See also Kümmel, pp. 72-73.
2039. Luke 2:11; John 4:42.
2040. Schweitzer, TQOTHJ, pp. 226-229.
2041. J. L. McKenzie, s.v. "Gospel."
2042. Mark 1:14.
2043. Mark 1:1.
2044. J. L. McKenzie, s.v. "Gospel."
2045. R. Kirk, p. 56.
2046. Kingsford and Maitland, pp. 222-225. Emphasis added.
2047. Menzies, Vol. 9, p. 301. Emphasis added.
2048. 1 Peter 1:12.

2049. See Patterson and Robinson, passim.
2050. See Kloppenborg, QP, p. 3.
2051. Mack, p. 34.
2052. 1 Corinthians 2:7.
2053. Meyer, TSTOJ, p. xviii.
2054. J. M. Robinson, pp. 124-126.
2055. Meyer, TSTOJ, pp. xviii, xix, xx.
2056. R. J. Miller, pp. 301-304.
2057. My theories. But see Layton, pp. 376-379; R. J. Miller, pp. 301-304.
2058. For more on The Gospel of Q and The Gospel of Thomas, see Seabrook, JATGOQ, passim.
2059. W. Smith, s.v. "Heaven."
2060. Malachi 3:8-10. Also known as "the Law of Attraction."
2061. Proverbs 23:7.
2062. Luke 17:20-21.
2063. See Spalding, Vol. 1, p. 71; M. P. Hall, p. 117. See also Greaves, pp. 96-97.
2064. The outer planets had not yet been discovered and the Sun and Moon were considered planets at the time.
2065. M. P. Hall, p. 83.
2066. 2 Corinthians 12:2-4. See also Ephesians 1:20; 2:6; 3:10; 4:9-10.
2067. Revelation 21:1.
2068. Revelation 12:12.
2069. Matthew 5:19. Emphasis added.
2070. John 14:2. Emphasis added.
2071. B. Evans, s.v. "Elysium."
2072. B. Evans, s.v. "Valhalla."
2073. Kawaguchi, pp. 498-499.
2074. Dasgupta and Seabrook, p. 191.
2075. See Barbanell, pp. 18-23.
2076. See Wong, passim.
2077. Burtt, pp. 207-211.
2078. See e.g., Yogananda, AOAY, pp. 316, 361.
2079. Barbanell, p. 20.
2080. See Ecclesiastes 12:6.
2081. Seabrook, JATLOA, pp. 157, 401, 466.
2082. W. Smith, s.v. "Hell."
2083. Lamsa, IITBE, p. 57; Watts, G, p. 33.
2084. See e.g., Luke 16:23.
2085. See e.g., Matthew 23:15. According to the Old Testament, early Jews performed human sacrifice (including children) in the Valley of Gehenna, adding to its "hellish" ambiance and reputation. The site, then known as Tophet ("place of fire"), was the location of the Shrine of Molech, a Tyrian fire-god. See e.g., Leviticus 18:21; 20:2-5; 1 Kings 11:7; 2 Kings 23:10; 2 Chronicles 28:3; 33:6; Jeremiah 7:31-32; 19:2-14; 32:35. See also Isaiah 30:33.
2086. See e.g., 2 Peter 2:4.
2087. See The Book of the Resurrection of Christ.
2088. See the Apostles' Creed.
2089. See Ephesians 4:9.
2090. See Proverbs 23:7; Seabrook, JATLOA, passim; Seabrook, TBATLOA, passim.
2091. Matthew 14:1-12.
2092. Luke 13:32.
2093. Mark 6:14. See Luke 9:7 for comparison, where this mistake has been corrected.
2094. Goguel, Vol. 2, p. 350.
2095. Gaskell, s.v. "Herod the King."
2096. Eddy, p. 516.
2097. 1 Peter 3:4.
2098. John 1:9.

2099. Romans 7:22.
2100. 2 Corinthians 4:16.
2101. Romans 8:26.
2102. John 16:8.
2103. Acts 1:16.
2104. 1 Corinthians 12:11.
2105. Romans 8:27.
2106. 1 Corinthians 2:10-13.
2107. Romans 15:30. See Tenney, s.v. "Holy Spirit."
2108. Küng and Moltmann, p. xi.
2109. Yogananda, TSCOC, Vol. 1, p. 136.
2110. Gaskell, s.v. "Holy Ghost, or Spirit."
2111. Jung, PAR, p. 89.
2112. R. Graves, TWG, p. 160.
2113. Yogananda, TSCOC, Vol. 1, p. 11.
2114. Matthew 3:16.
2115. K. L. King, p. 117.
2116. *Theacrasia*. I have coined this much needed word, as it did not exist before. Definition: The combining of the traits of multiple goddesses into one goddess.
2117. 1 John 5:7; 2 Corinthians 13:14.
2118. John 20:19-22.
2119. John 1:1.
2120. Genesis 2:7.
2121. See John 14:16-17.
2122. Nicholson, p. 76. See also Runes, s.v. "Ruach ha-Kodesh."
2123. 1 Thessalonians 4:8.
2124. 1 Corinthians 6:19; 2 Corinthians 1:22.
2125. Exodus 3:14; Ezekiel 37:14; John 14:10-11; Romans 8:9, 11; 1 Corinthians 3:16; 6:17; 14:25; 2 Corinthians 6:16; 9:14; Ephesians 2:22; 4:6; Philemon 2:13; 1 John 3:24; 4:4, 12-13, 16; Zechariah 2:10.
2126. John 12:32; 14:20; 15:4; 17:21-23, 26; Colossians 1:27; 3:10-11; Romans 8:10; 1 Corinthians 6:15, 17; 2 Corinthians 5:16; 13:3, 5; Galatians 1:16; 2:20; 4:19; Ephesians 3:14-17; Philippians 1:20; 2:5; 1 Peter 1:11; 1 John 2:27; 3:24; 4:4.
2127. See John 14:16-17.
2128. 1 Corinthians 6:19; 2 Timothy 1:14.
2129. Spalding, Vol. 5, p. 46.
2130. Yogananda, TSCOC, Vol. 1, p. 16.
2131. A. Pike, p. 82.
2132. Mascaró, p. 14.
2133. Matthew 28:19.
2134. Seabrook, JATLOA, passim.
2135. Keck, p. 77.
2136. Metzger and Coogan, s.v. "Trinity"; L. M. Graham, p. 452; Potter, p. 16.
2137. This fabricated passage reads: "Therefore go and make disciples of all nations, baptizing them in the name of the Father and of the Son and of the Holy Spirit."
2138. Eusebius, TPOTG, Vol. 1, p. 157.
2139. Romans 1:7.
2140. John 20:28.
2141. Acts 5:3-4.
2142. Deuteronomy 6:4.
2143. B. G. Walker, TWEOMAS, s.v. "Trinity."
2144. L. M. Graham, p. 452.
2145. Boer, p. 22.
2146. See e.g., The Apocryphon of John.
2147. 1 John 5:7.
2148. Meyer, TSTOJ, pp. xvii, 95, 112.

2149. Guirand, p. 378.
2150. M. P. Hall, p. 19.
2151. Hone, AMD, p. 86.
2152. A. Pike, p. 87.
2153. See R. Graves, TWG, passim.
2154. See e.g., J. E. M. White, AE, p. 122; Lasne and Gaultier, p. 251.
2155. See Briffault, passim.
2156. Rozak and Rozak, p. 30.
2157. See Gimbutas, TCOTG, p. x, passim; Streep, passim.
2158. See Briffault, passim.
2159. In Ireland the Triple-Goddess is known as the Morrigan, and is made up of the goddesses Éire (from whom the name Ireland, "Éire's Land," derives), Banba, and Fódla.
2160. In Norse mythology the Triple-Goddess is called the Norns, and is made up of the goddesses Urðr, Verðandi, and Skuld (known in the British Isles as Scotia, she gave her name to Scotland).
2161. The ancient Romans called their Triple-Goddess the Matres, "the [three] Mothers."
2162. The ancient Greeks referred to their Triple-Goddess as the Moirai, made up of the goddesses Clotho, Lachesis, and Atropos.
2163. C. Wilson, p. 66.
2164. Aphrodite's name means "born of sea-foam." She is the Greek version of the Roman love-goddess Venus.
2165. Frazer, TGB, Vol. 2, p. 119.
2166. By the use of the word myth here I do not mean "imaginary" or "fictitious," but rather "the collective traditional stories of the Christian Church."
2167. John 19:25. The "Three Marys" were the Virgin Mary (Jesus' mother), Mary Magdalene (according to many early traditions, Jesus' wife), and Mary the wife of Cleophas (Jesus' aunt).
2168. Gimbutas, TCOTG, pp. 297-302, passim; Streep, passim.
2169. G. D. Young, s.v. "I am."
2170. Exodus 3:14.
2171. Spalding, Vol. 4, p. 33.
2172. Romans 8:9, 11.
2173. See Genesis 17:1; Exodus 3:14-15; Psalms 46:10; Mark 8:29; 14:61-62; Luke 22:70; John 6:35; 8:12, 23, 58; 9:5; 10:7-11, 30-39; 11:25; 12:26, 46; 13:13; 14:3, 6, 10-11, 20; 15:1; 17:10, 16.
2174. John 12:32; 14:20; 15:4; 17:21-23, 26; Colossians 1:27; 3:10-11; Romans 8:10; 1 Corinthians 6:15, 17; 2 Corinthians 5:16; 13:3, 5; Galatians 1:16; 2:20; 4:19; Ephesians 3:14-17; Philippians 1:20; 2:5; 1 Peter 1:11; 1 John 2:27; 3:24; 4:4.
2175. Krishna, TRNOME, p. 18; Maharshi, p. 104.
2176. Spalding, Vol. 1, pp. 136-137.
2177. Maharshi, p. 21.
2178. Luke 19:9.
2179. Mascaró, p. 14.
2180. Matthew 6:13.
2181. John 1:1.
2182. Hinduism teaches that God is the Aum or Om, the "Creative Word," while Christianity teaches that Jesus is the Word or the Logos.
2183. Revelation 1:8, 11; 21:6.
2184. Revelation 3:14. For John's corresponding Gospel text, see John 1:1-3.
2185. Exodus 3:14.
2186. John 8:58.
2187. Revelation 14:2; 19:6.
2188. Maharshi, p. 76.
2189. Watts, G, p. 19.
2190. Acts 17:28.
2191. Psalms 46:10.
2192. See Seabrook, JATLOA, passim.
2193. Daniel 7:13-14.
2194. Spivey and Smith, p. 381.

2195. John 14:6.
2196. My paraphrasal. See John 12:32; 14:20; 15:4; 17:21-23, 26; Colossians 1:27; 3:10-11; Romans 8:10; 1 Corinthians 6:15, 17; 2 Corinthians 5:16; 13:3, 5; Galatians 1:16; 2:20; 4:19; Ephesians 3:14-17; Philippians 1:20; 2:5; 1 Peter 1:11; 1 John 2:27; 3:24; 4:4.
2197. Matthew 28:20.
2198. Isaiah 40:6.
2199. Galatians 4:19.
2200. Colossians 3:11.
2201. Genesis 1:27.
2202. Ephesians 3:16.
2203. Romans 7:22.
2204. 1 Peter 3:4.
2205. Acts 3:14.
2206. Daniel 7:9, 13, 22.
2207. Hebrews 13:8.
2208. Hebrews 7:3.
2209. John 12:34.
2210. John 1:9.
2211. John 12:32; 14:20; 15:4; 17:21-23, 26; Colossians 1:27; 3:10-11; Romans 8:10; 1 Corinthians 6:15, 17; 2 Corinthians 5:16; 13:3, 5; Galatians 1:16; 2:20; 4:19; Ephesians 3:14-17; Philippians 1:20; 2:5; 1 Peter 1:11; 1 John 2:27; 3:24; 4:4.
2212. John 18:5-6.
2213. Mark 14:61-62. Emphasis added.
2214. John 8:23.
2215. John 6:35.
2216. John 10:7. In Hinduism, this cosmic "door" is viewed as a spiritual portal through which trained yogis can leave and reenter their physical bodies at will. Thus Jesus, speaking as the Indwelling Christ, said: " I am the door: by me if any man enter in, he shall be saved, and shall go in and out, and find pasture." John 10:9.
2217. John 10:11.
2218. John 8:12.
2219. Revelation 1:18.
2220. John 13:13.
2221. Matthew 11:29.
2222. John 18:37.
2223. John 14:6.
2224. John 15:1.
2225. Mark 14:61-62.
2226. Grenfell and Hunt, p. 36. (From The Gospel of Thomas.)
2227. John 1:14.
2228. Budge, TBOTD, Vol. 1, pp. 93, 102, 209, 211-212. Emphasis added.
2229. A. Pike, p. 380.
2230. Daniel 7:13-14.
2231. Colossians 3:11.
2232. Exodus 3:14; Ezekiel 37:14; John 14:10-11; Romans 8:9, 11; 1 Corinthians 3:16; 6:17; 14:25; 2 Corinthians 6:16; 9:14; Ephesians 2:22; 4:6; Philemon 2:13; 1 John 3:24; 4:4, 12-13, 16; Zechariah 2:10.
2233. See Mark 14:63-64; John 10:30-34.
2234. Acts 24:14.
2235. John 10:34.
2236. John 12:32; 14:20; 15:4; 17:21-23, 26; Colossians 1:27; 3:10-11; Romans 8:10; 1 Corinthians 6:15, 17; 2 Corinthians 5:16; 13:3, 5; Galatians 1:16; 2:20; 4:19; Ephesians 3:14-17; Philippians 1:20; 2:5; 1 Peter 1:11; 1 John 2:27; 3:24; 4:4.
2237. Ephesians 3:16.
2238. Romans 7:22; 2 Corinthians 4:16.
2239. Genesis 32:28; 35:10.
2240. See Fillmore, s.v. "Israel."

2241. Seabrook, CBC, p. 87.
2242. G. D. Young, s.v. "Israel."
2243. Fillmore, s.v. "Egypt."
2244. Mish, s.v. "Jehovah."
2245. M. P. Hall, p. 124.
2246. Exodus 6:3; Psalms 83:13; Isaiah 12:2; 26:4.
2247. Spence, s.v. "Adonai."
2248. Gaskell, s.v. "Yedud."
2249. Blunt, s.v. "Gnosticism."
2250. M. P. Hall, p. 133; Evans-Wentz, p. 128.
2251. Metzger and Coogan, s.v. "Jerusalem;" G. D. Young, s.v. "Jerusalem."
2252. See Exodus 16:3.
2253. Murdock, DME, p. 154. See Exodus 16:3.
2254. Farrell and Presser, s.v. "Evening Star."
2255. G. D. Young, s.v. "Jerusalem."
2256. Galatians 4:25-26.
2257. Dentan, p. 152.
2258. Luke 18:30. Emphasis added.
2259. Matthew 5:35.
2260. Menzies, Vol. 9, p. 393. Emphasis added.
2261. Augustine, TCOSA, p. 358. Emphasis added.
2262. Brooks, VATAOS, pp. 316-317. Emphasis added.
2263. Yogananda, TSCOC, Vol. 1, p. 305. See also Colossians 3:11.
2264. See Moltmann, passim.
2265. Mark 1:9-11.
2266. Matthew 1:18-25.
2267. Hebrews 7:1-3.
2268. Matthew 5:22.
2269. Matthew 23:17, 19.
2270. John 14:27.
2271. Matthew 10:34.
2272. Matthew 15:4.
2273. Luke 14:26. My paraphrasal.
2274. Mark 3:31-34.
2275. Matthew 23:9.
2276. Jude 1:25.
2277. Matthew 27:46.
2278. Matthew 24:36.
2279. Matthew 5:39.
2280. Matthew 21:12.
2281. Matthew 5:39.
2282. Matthew 10:34. See also Luke 22:36.
2283. Luke 6:27.
2284. Matthew 23:33.
2285. John 8:44.
2286. See e.g., Matthew 13:55; Luke 2:41, 48; 3:23; 4:22; John 1:45; 6:42; Hebrews 3:3; 7:24; 10:12.
2287. M. P. Hall, p. 178. See Ephesians 4:13.
2288. Schonfield, TPP, pp. 192-193.
2289. Schweitzer, TQOTHJ, p. 318.
2290. A. Pike, p. 308.
2291. Schonfield, TANT, p. 139.
2292. Dowling, 127:6, 26.
2293. John 6:33.
2294. Colossians 1:27.
2295. See Yogananda, TSCOC, Vol. 1, pp. xxvi, 3. See also John 10:34.

2296. To this day Buddhists consider Jesus a great yogi and Bodhisattva. See Evans-Wentz, p. 26.
2297. Burtt, pp. 125, 133-134.
2298. Zaehner, p. 43; M. Grant, J, pp. 136-138.
2299. Dentan, pp. 131, 140, 147.
2300. See e.g., Luke 24:15, 31, 36.
2301. See e.g., John 20:19.
2302. For more on Jesus' so-called "supernatural" powers, see Seabrook, JATLOA, passim.
2303. John 14:12. In the Gnostic-Christian work, The Apocryphon of James (also known as The Secret Book of James), 6:17-20, Jesus tells His 12 Apostles: "Become better than I; make yourselves like the son of the Holy Spirit."
2304. See e.g., Spalding, passim; Yogananda, AOAY, passim; Yogananda, TSCOC, passim.
2305. See Spalding, Vol. 2, pp. 55-56.
2306. M. P. Hall, p. 177.
2307. J. G. Jackson, CBC, p. 207.
2308. Burr, pp. 353-354. Emphasis added.
2309. Goguel, Vol. 2, p. 230.
2310. John 2:18-22.
2311. John 8:56-57.
2312. Colossians 3:11.
2313. Steiger, IMSIAF, p. 142.
2314. See Yogananda, TSCOC, Vol. 1, pp. xxvii-xxix, xxxi-xxxii.
2315. Spalding, all five volumes, passim.
2316. Dowling, 128:31.
2317. See e.g., Mark 1:4-11.
2318. Dowling, 129:13-14.
2319. Dowling, 138:41.
2320. Dowling, 135:15.
2321. Dowling, 176:30.
2322. Dowling, 163:36, 37.
2323. 1 Corinthians 2:16; Philippians 2:5.
2324. See my book *Jesus and the Gospel of Q*.
2325. G. E. Kirk, p. 8.
2326. Boer, p. 43.
2327. Schweitzer, TQOTHJ, p. 3.
2328. See Psalms 110:1.
2329. Matthew 22:41-46. See also Daniel 7:13-14; Micah 5:2; Matthew 28:20; John 8:58; Hebrews 7:3; Revelation 22:13.
2330. Schweitzer, TQOTHJ, pp. 254-261.
2331. See e.g., John 2:23; 6:2, 26; 7:31; 9:16; 11:47; Acts 2:22.
2332. Matthew 24:14. See also Matthew 4:23; 9:35; Luke 4:43.
2333. John 14:20.
2334. John 17:21.
2335. Luke 17:20-21.
2336. Mark 11:24.
2337. John 7:14-19, 28-29. Emphasis added. Paul held the same belief. See 1 Corinthians 4:4.
2338. John 8:28-29, 40, 42, 50, 54. Emphasis added.
2339. John 14:24. Emphasis added.
2340. John 14:28.
2341. My paraphrasal.
2342. Mark 11:22.
2343. John 10:29. Emphasis added.
2344. John 5:19. Emphasis added.
2345. John 5:30-31. Emphasis added.
2346. John 5:36. Emphasis added.
2347. John 6:38. Emphasis added.

2348. John 8:50. Emphasis added.
2349. John 5:41. Emphasis added.
2350. John 5:43. Emphasis added.
2351. Spalding, Vol. 4, p. 121.
2352. Spalding, Vol. 3, pp. 18-20.
2353. See e.g., the Sophia of Jesus Christ, 119:15, and also Romans 1:1; 15:16; 2 Corinthians 11:7; 1 Thessalonians 2:2, 8-9; 1 Peter 4:17.
2354. Spalding, Vol. 5, p. 19.
2355. John 14:12.
2356. The Gospel of Thomas, Logion 57.
2357. Potter, p. 130.
2358. Hebrews 3:1.
2359. Matthew 23:9.
2360. My paraphrasal.
2361. 1 Corinthians 2:16; Philippians 2:5.
2362. See e.g., Mark 14:15; Luke 22:12; Acts 1:13.
2363. Brownrigg, s.v. "Mary, Mother of Jesus."
2364. 1 Corinthians 15:47-49. Emphasis added.
2365. John 18:36.
2366. Luke 17:20-21.
2367. Hebrews 11:3.
2368. John 1:1-4.
2369. See e.g., Hosea 13:4; Isaiah 43:3, 11; 45:15, 21; Psalms 106:21.
2370. See e.g., Isaiah 47:4; 49:26; 54:8; 60:16; Jeremiah 50:34.
2371. See e.g., Psalms 118:27; 140:6; Isaiah 36:7; Ezekiel 28:26; Haggai 1:12.
2372. See e.g., Psalms 62:7; Isaiah 12:2.
2373. See e.g., Luke 1:46-47.
2374. Potter, p. 31.
2375. See e.g., Leviticus 4:3; 6:22; 1 Samuel 2:10; 12:3; 2 Samuel 1:14; 22:51; 1 Chronicles 16:22; Psalms 18:50; 20:6; 28:8; 84:9; Isaiah 45:1; Lamentations 4:20.
2376. See e.g., Matthew 26:63-64; John 18:37.
2377. John 7:28; 8:26, 29.
2378. Mark 10:45.
2379. Mark 10:17-18. Emphasis added.
2380. Luke 11:27.
2381. Luke 11:28.
2382. See e.g., Matthew 8:4; 9:30; 12:15-16; Mark 3:12; 5:43; 7:36; 8:30; Luke 5:14; 8:56.
2383. Matthew 17:9; Mark 9:9; Luke 9:36.
2384. Mark 7:24.
2385. Matthew 16:20.
2386. Luke 9:20-21.
2387. Matthew 24:14. See also Mark 1:14.
2388. John 7:28; 8:26, 29.
2389. John 12:49. Emphasis added.
2390. John 14:28.
2391. The Sophia of Jesus Christ, 96:3-4.
2392. Ephesians 3:9.
2393. See e.g., Mark 10:52; Luke 8:48; 17:19.
2394. Exodus 3:14; Ezekiel 37:14; John 14:10-11; Romans 8:9, 11; 1 Corinthians 3:16; 6:17; 14:25; 2 Corinthians 6:16; 9:14; Ephesians 2:22; 4:6; Philemon 2:13; 1 John 3:24; 4:4, 12-13, 16; Zechariah 2:10.
2395. John 14:10. Emphasis added.
2396. John 8:28. Emphasis added.
2397. John 5:30-31. Emphasis added.

2398. Mark 3:11-12. Note: Why God would make a group of demons be the first to announce the messiahship of Jesus is only one of the many problems in the New Testament that has never been satisfactorily answered by traditional (conservative) Bible scholars.
2399. Luke 4:40-41.
2400. John 12:44-45. Emphasis added.
2401. My paraphrasal.
2402. Psalms 30:10; 1 Corinthians 3:9; 2 Corinthians 6:1; Ephesians 2:19-22; Hebrews 13:6.
2403. See e.g., Matthew 13:55; Luke 2:41, 48; 3:23; 4:22; John 1:45; 6:42; Hebrews 3:3; 7:24; 10:12.
2404. Daniel 7:13-14.
2405. John 12:32; 14:20; 15:4; 17:21-23, 26; Colossians 1:27; 3:10-11; Romans 8:10; 1 Corinthians 6:15, 17; 2 Corinthians 5:16; 13:3, 5; Galatians 1:16; 2:20; 4:19; Ephesians 3:14-17; Philippians 1:20; 2:5; 1 Peter 1:11; 1 John 2:27; 3:24; 4:4.
2406. Ephesians 3:16.
2407. Romans 7:22.
2408. 1 Peter 3:4.
2409. John 1:9.
2410. Daniel 7:9, 13, 22.
2411. Genesis 17:1; Exodus 3:14-15; Psalms 46:10; Mark 8:29; 14:61-62; Luke 22:70; John 6:35; 8:12, 23, 58; 9:5; 10:7-11, 30-39; 11:25; 12:26, 46; 13:13; 14:3, 6, 10-11, 20; 15:1; 17:10, 16.
2412. Hebrews 5:5-6; 6:20. See also Hebrews 7:3; 1 Peter 2:9.
2413. Dowling, 15:22; Hebrews 9:24.
2414. Hebrews 8:2. See also Hebrews 9:11.
2415. These are: 1) love, 2) faith, 3) strength, 4) judgement, 5) understanding, 6) self-control, 7) power, 8) the will, 9) imagination, 10) fervor, 11) orderliness, and 12) acquisitiveness.
2416. Daniel 7:13-14.
2417. Matthew 28:18, 20.
2418. Colossians 3:11; John 1:9.
2419. John 14:6. Emphasis added.
2420. John 8:23-24. Emphasis added.
2421. In the KJV the word "he" in John 8:24 is italicized, meaning that this word was not in the original text, but was added by King James' translators in 1611.
2422. Pfleiderer, TDOC, pp. 25-26. Emphasis added.
2423. R. M. Jones, p. 191.
2424. McBee, p. 499. Emphasis added.
2425. Kingsford and Maitland, pp. 112-113. Emphasis added.
2426. 1 Corinthians 15:45-47.
2427. Jefferson, pp. 15-17.
2428. Hone, TANT, p. xii. See also Maurice, passim.
2429. Filson, pp. 153-154; Potter, pp. 77-78, 138-139, 155; Lamsa, IITBE, p. 86.
2430. Potter, pp. 81-83; Seabrook, CBC, passim; Brewster, p. 39; J. M. Robertson, PC, passim; J. G. Jackson, CBC, passim.
2431. AAO, p. 156.
2432. Emerson, p. 575. Emphasis added.
2433. Matthew 3:1-3.
2434. Leishman, OAB, pp. 148-149; Yogananda, TSCOC, Vol. 1, p. 100; Neill, TIOTNT, p. 305; Roddy and Sellier, p. 60; Sheehan, pp. 49-50.
2435. Bruce, p. 107.
2436. See G. R. S. Mead, PS, pp. 11-13.
2437. Gaskell, s.v. "John the Baptist."
2438. Kingsford and Maitland, pp. 238-239.
2439. Maitland, Vol. 1, p. 151. Emphasis added.
2440. Pfleiderer, TPOR, pp. 287-288. Emphasis added.
2441. Nelson's s.v. "Jordan."
2442. See 2 Kings 2:6-14.
2443. Gaskell, s.v. "Jordan."

2444. G. R. S. Mead, TGH, Vol. 1, pp. 163-164.
2445. Holroyd, s.v. "Karma" (p. 92); M. P. Hall, p. 51.
2446. Doyle, TEOTU, p. 72.
2447. Proverbs 23:7.
2448. M. P. Hall, p. 202.
2449. Spalding, Vol. 5, pp. 114, 149.
2450. Doyle, TEOTU, p. 37.
2451. For more on the Law of Attraction, see Seabrook, JATLOA, passim; Seabrook, TBATLOA, passim.
2452. Ephesians 6:8.
2453. Galatians 6:5-8. Emphasis added.
2454. Galatians 5:22-23.
2455. W. Jones, p. 327.
2456. My paraphrasal.
2457. Luke 9:56.
2458. Romans 15:4.
2459. Barbanell, p. 152.
2460. Matthew 6:14-15.
2461. Matthew 18:35.
2462. Mark 11:25-26.
2463. Luke 6:37.
2464. Daniel 7:13-14.
2465. 2 Corinthians 6:16.
2466. Genesis 17:1; Exodus 3:14-15; Psalms 46:10; Mark 8:29; 14:61-62; Luke 22:70; John 6:35; 8:12, 23, 58; 9:5; 10:7-11, 30-39; 11:25; 12:26, 46; 13:13; 14:3, 6, 10-11, 20; 15:1; 17:10, 16.
2467. See e.g., Fenwick and Fenwick, p. 114, passim; Ritchie, passim.
2468. 1 Thessalonians 5:3.
2469. Proverbs 3:12.
2470. Matthew 7:2.
2471. Mark 4:24.
2472. Luke 6:38.
2473. Colossians 3:23-25.
2474. Emerson, TWORWE, pp. 23-24.
2475. Luke 12:2.
2476. For more on the Law of Attraction (as well as the Law of Karma), see Seabrook, JATLOA, passim; Seabrook, TBATLOA, passim.
2477. Brooks, VATAOS, pp. 308-309. Emphasis added.
2478. See Matthew 16:15-19.
2479. See e.g., G. D. Young, s.v. "Key, Key of the Kingdom."
2480. John 18:36.
2481. Acts 7:48. See also Acts 17:24.
2482. Dowling, 15:22. See also Hebrews 9:24.
2483. Hebrews 8:2. My paraphrasal. See also Hebrews 9:11.
2484. M. Grant, CTG, pp. 121-186.
2485. The 50 Bibles that Constantine ordered to be "prepared" are long lost to history—though some believe that two copies remain: the Codex Sinaiticus and the Codex Vaticanus. See Leishman, OAB, pp. 46-47.
2486. Goguel, Vol. 2, p. 340.
2487. See Gaskell, s.v. "Keys of Heaven and Hell."
2488. Luke 17:21.
2489. John 10:7-9.
2490. Hebrews 5:5-6; 6:20; 7:3; 1 Peter 2:9.
2491. Revelation 1:18.
2492. Hart, s.v. "Thoth."
2493. G. R. S. Mead, TGH, Vol. 1, p. 61.
2494. See e.g. 1 Corinthians 15:24; Revelation 1:5; 15:3; 17:14.
2495. M. P. Hall, pp. 117-120, 154.

2496. Burtt, pp. 17-18.
2497. 1 Peter 2:17.
2498. Brooks, VATAOS, p. 102.
2499. Spalding, Vol. 4, pp. 100-101.
2500. Spalding, Vol. 5, p. 61.
2501. John 14:9.
2502. Tenney, s.v. "Kingdom of God."
2503. Schweitzer, TQOTHJ, p. 16; Goguel, Vol. 2, pp. 282, 312; Strauss, TLOJCE, Vol. 1, p. 308.
2504. Spivey and Smith, p. 85.
2505. Mark 13:32. See also Schweitzer, TQOTHJ, pp. 239, 246; Calvocoressi, s.v. "Jesus."
2506. Neill, TIOTNT, p. 111.
2507. Matthew 3:2; 4:17; 5:3, 10; 10:7.
2508. Acts 1:15.
2509. See H. S. Lewis, TSDOJ, pp. 27-28, 49, 51-52, 55, 58-59, 84, 88, 99, 112, 138, 149, 154-155, 163, 170-173, 205, 228-229.
2510. See Mark 14:15; Luke 22:12; Acts 1:12-15.
2511. Matthew 5:20.
2512. Bucke, pp. 51-52, 155.
2513. 1 Corinthians 2:16; Philippians 2:5.
2514. See Bucke, passim.
2515. Bucke, p. 80.
2516. Bucke, pp. 60-63.
2517. John 12:32; 14:20; 15:4; 17:21-23, 26; Colossians 1:27; 3:10-11; Romans 8:10; 1 Corinthians 6:15, 17; 2 Corinthians 5:16; 13:3, 5; Galatians 1:16; 2:20; 4:19; Ephesians 3:14-17; Philippians 1:20; 2:5; 1 Peter 1:11; 1 John 2:27; 3:24; 4:4.
2518. John 10:38; 14:6, 10-13.
2519. Luke 17:20-21. Emphasis added.
2520. Goguel, Vol. 2, p. 567.
2521. Yogananda, AOAY, p. 524. My paraphrasal.
2522. John 18:36.
2523. Kingsford and Maitland, p. 53.
2524. John 3:3.
2525. Matthew 18:3; 19:14.
2526. Matthew 24:14. See also Matthew 4:23; 9:35; Luke 4:43.
2527. Mark 1:14-15.
2528. See e.g., Luke 4:43; 8:1; Acts 1:1-3.
2529. See e.g., Matthew 5:3, 19-21; 8:11; 10:7; 11:11; 19:14; 20:1; 22:2.
2530. See Leeming, pp. 125-129, 163, 165-169.
2531. Yogananda, TSCOC, Vol. 1, p. 188.
2532. Doane, pp. 112-113; M. P. Hall, p. 55.
2533. Chetwynd, p. 113.
2534. Luke 1:26-31.
2535. John 1:1, 14.
2536. Moor, p. 123.
2537. Matthew 1:16.
2538. Suarès, p. 208; M. P. Hall, p. 178.
2539. Luke 2:7-18.
2540. Matthew 2:2.
2541. Luke 2:1-6.
2542. Matthew 2:16. Herod Antipas was not a true king (as Mark mistakenly calls him—see Mark 6:14), but a tetrarch.
2543. For more on the boyhood of Jesus, see the non-canonical infancy Gospels; e.g.: The Infancy Gospel of James; The Infancy Gospel of Pseudo-Matthew; The Infancy Gospel of Thomas; The Latin Infancy Gospel; and The Arabic Infancy Gospel. Barnstone, TOB, pp. 383-410; Meyer, TSTOJ, p. xvii.
2544. Genesis 6:13; 7:4-10.

2545. Matthew 4:1-11.
2546. Mark 16:9. Many believe that the Cana wedding was between Jesus and the Magdalene. See John 2:1-12.
2547. See John 11:16; 14:5; Mark 6:3. *Didymos* is Greek for "twin"; *Thomas* is the Semitic word for "twin."
2548. John 10:30.
2549. Jacolliot, p. 247.
2550. See Matthew 1:21.
2551. J. L. McKenzie, s.v. "Jesus Christ."
2552. Luke 7:22.
2553. Matthew 17:1-8.
2554. John 19:34.
2555. Matthew 4:19; 17:27; John 21:10-13.
2556. Farrell and Presser, s.v. "Staff." See also Mark 6:8.
2557. Mark 15:39.
2558. Seabrook, CBC, pp. 17, 44, 64, 111, 114, 121, 192, 195 (January 6); pp. 17, 26, 45, 57, 58, 60, 63, 73, 105, 111, 122, 145, 177, 181, 188-190 (December 25).
2559. Malachi 4:2.
2560. D. M. Bennett, Vol. 2, p. 582.
2561. Acts 5:30; 10:39.
2562. Townsend, passim.
2563. Acts 1:9-12.
2564. Mark 13:26.
2565. Revelation 22:13.
2566. Matthew 28:19.
2567. For more on both Jesus and Krishna, see Jacolliot, passim; Moor, pp. 123-150; E. E. Evans, pp. 28-39; Doane, pp. 143, 147, 280, 408, 499-500, 546; Carpenter, pp. 10, 24, 27, 129, 183; Bently, s.v. "Krishna"; M. Jordan, s.v. "Krsna"; Brownrigg, s.v. "Mary, Mother of Jesus"; Sykes, s.v. "Krisna"; Patterson and Robinson, pp. 37-38; Carlyon, s.v. "Krishna" (p. 129); Pagels, TGG, pp. 21-22.
2568. Carpenter, p. 51.
2569. Doane, p. 408.
2570. Neill, WWKAJ, p. 43.
2571. Dunn, p. 52.
2572. J. L. McKenzie, s.v. "Lord."
2573. Colossians 3:11.
2574. A. Pike, pp. 78-79.
2575. John 1:29, 36.
2576. B. G. Walker, TWEOMAS, s.v. "Lamb." See Exodus 13:2, 13.
2577. G. D. Young, s.v. "Lamb"; "Lamb of God." See 1 Corinthians 5:7; Revelation 7:9-17.
2578. Gaskell, s.v. "Lamb of God."
2579. Fillmore, s.v. "Lamb of God."
2580. Cirlot, s.v. "Lamb."
2581. Colossians 1:15.
2582. See Acts 17:23.
2583. John 12:32; 14:20; 15:4; 17:21-23, 26; Colossians 1:27; 3:10-11; Romans 8:10; 1 Corinthians 6:15, 17; 2 Corinthians 5:16; 13:3, 5; Galatians 1:16; 2:20; 4:19; Ephesians 3:14-17; Philippians 1:20; 2:5; 1 Peter 1:11; 1 John 2:27; 3:24; 4:4.
2584. Colossians 3:11.
2585. 2 Corinthians 6:16.
2586. Frazer, FITOT, Vol. 2, p. 532.
2587. A. Pike, p. 431.
2588. Budge, TEHAH, Vol. 3, pp. 105-106.
2589. Chetwynd, pp. 110-111.
2590. M. P. Hall, p. 54.
2591. M. P. Hall, p. 186.
2592. John 1:29, 36; Revelation 5:6.

2593. B. G. Walker, TWDOSASO, pp. 380-381.
2594. John 11:5, 43.
2595. Calvocoressi, s.v. "Lazarus (2)."
2596. See Evans-Wentz, p. 45.
2597. Seabrook, JATLOA, p. 282.
2598. Kingsford and Maitland, p. 227.
2599. G. D. Young, s.v. "Light and Darkness."
2600. Gaskell, s.v. "Light"; "Light, Primordial."
2601. Isaiah 60:1-2.
2602. Job 33:30.
2603. Malachi 4:2.
2604. Seabrook, CBC, p. 68; Dowley, pp. 139-142.
2605. John 8:12.
2606. R. M. Jones, pp. 495-496. Emphasis added.
2607. John 1:1.
2608. See e.g., Genesis 1:3. G. D. Young, s.v. "Logos."
2609. See e.g., Zondervan, s.v. "Logos."
2610. Yogananda, TSCOC, Vol. 1, pp. 9-10.
2611. Köstenberger, pp. 26-29; Kuehl, p. 45.
2612. Barnstone, TRNT, p. 448; Barnstone and Meyer, pp. 70-71; Spivey and Smith, p. 497; M. P. Hall, pp. 185-188.
2613. Legge, Vol. 1 and Vol. 2, passim.
2614. Neill, WWKAJ, p. 59.
2615. Kitto, ACOBL, Vol. 2, s.v. "Logos." Emphasis added.
2616. Neill, TIOTNT, p. 320.
2617. Cumont, TMOM, p. 140; J. M. Robertson, PC, p. 292.
2618. A. Pike, p. 604.
2619. Spivey and Smith, p. 1572.
2620. John 1:1.
2621. Exodus 3:14; Ezekiel 37:14; John 14:10-11; Romans 8:9, 11; 1 Corinthians 3:16; 6:17; 14:25; 2 Corinthians 6:16; 9:14; Ephesians 2:22; 4:6; Philemon 2:13; 1 John 3:24; 4:4, 12-13, 16; Zechariah 2:10.
2622. Christie-Murray, p. 39.
2623. Seabrook, CBC, passim.
2624. Pryse, p. 296.
2625. Schweitzer, TQOTHJ, p. 318.
2626. Schonfield, TPP, pp. 192-193.
2627. Schonfield, TANT, p. 139.
2628. John 1:14.
2629. See Seabrook, JATLOA, passim.
2630. See e.g., Matthew 8:8, 16; Mark 2:2; Luke 4:32; 8:11; John 2:22; 15:3; 1 John 2:5.
2631. Inge, PIAM, p. 274. Emphasis added.
2632. Colossians 1:26. See J. L. McKenzie, s.v. "Word."
2633. Yogananda, TSCOC, Vol. 1, p. 10.
2634. John 12:32; 14:20; 15:4; 17:21-23, 26; Colossians 1:27; 3:10-11; Romans 8:10; 1 Corinthians 6:15, 17; 2 Corinthians 5:16; 13:3, 5; Galatians 1:16; 2:20; 4:19; Ephesians 3:14-17; Philippians 1:20; 2:5; 1 Peter 1:11; 1 John 2:27; 3:24; 4:4.
2635. 2 Corinthians 4:16.
2636. See Romans, 7:22.
2637. Yogananda, TSCOC, Vol. 1, p. 6.
2638. Hoeller, p. 80.
2639. Revelation 17:8.
2640. Blavatsky, p. 99.
2641. Isaiah 14:12.
2642. 2 Corinthians 11:14.
2643. A. Pike, p. 102.

2644. Isaiah 2:5; 1 John 1:7; Revelation 21:24.
2645. Bhaktivedanta, passim.
2646. John 8:12; 9:5.
2647. Matthew 5:43-44; 22:36-40.
2648. 1 John 4:7-8.
2649. Revelation 22:16.
2650. Paul complained about this same problem in his day. See e.g., 1 Corinthians 1:17-31; 2:1-16.
2651. See Baba, pp. 45, 60.
2652. Blavatsky, pp. 99-100.
2653. Job 38:7.
2654. $7 + 4 + 1 = 12; 1 + 2 = 3$.
2655. M. P. Hall, p. 145.
2656. LaVey, TSR, p. 21.
2657. Tenney, s.v. "Manna."
2658. G. R. S. Mead, TGH, Vol. 1, p. 247.
2659. Ambrose, p. 395. Emphasis added.
2660. John 14:2.
2661. See Gaskell, s.v. "Mansions."
2662. See Cerminara, MM, passim.
2663. For more on NDEs, see Fenwick and Fenwick, p. 114, passim; Ritchie, passim.
2664. 2 Corinthians 12:2.
2665. See Kuhn, WITKOG, passim.
2666. Budge, TBOTD, Vol. 1, pp. lxxxi, lxxxii.
2667. Budge, TBOTD, Vol. 1, p. xcii.
2668. See e.g., Spalding, Vol. 1, p. 149.
2669. See Seabrook, JATLOA, p. 304.
2670. Brantl, p. 74.
2671. B. G. Walker, TWEOMAS, s.v. "Mary."
2672. Monaghan, p. 388.
2673. See R. Graves, TWG, passim.
2674. Biedermann, s.v. "Triads"; B. G. Walker, TWEOMAS, s.v. "Trinity."
2675. C. Wilson, p. 66.
2676. Monaghan, p. 373.
2677. Lessa and Vogt, p. 118.
2678. See John 19:25.
2679. Doane, p. 328.
2680. See Revelation 12:1.
2681. Metford, s.v. "Mary the Virgin, St."
2682. Finegan, Vol. 1, pp. 167-168, 173; Metzger and Coogan, s.v. "Queen of Heaven"; Pritchard, passim.
2683. Bell, s.v. "Juno."
2684. Frazer, TGB, Vol. 2, p. 119.
2685. B. G. Walker, TWEOMAS, s.v. "Stella Maris."
2686. Romer, p. 231.
2687. Goring, s.v. "Horus."
2688. J. Johns, p. 87.
2689. Gaskell, s.v. "Mother, Divine."
2690. Matthew 2:3-19.
2691. Calvocoressi, s.v. "Herod the Great."
2692. Doane, pp. 172-174; Carpenter, pp. 50-51.
2693. Yogananda, TSCOC, Vol. 1, p. 188; Doane, pp. 112-113.
2694. Schonfield, TJP, p. 30.
2695. Proverbs 23:7.
2696. Spalding, Vol. 4, pp. 190, 198, 203.
2697. John 14:6.
2698. Evans-Wentz, p. 44.

2699. W. Smith, s.v. "Melchizedek"; Tenney, s.v. "Melchizedek."
2700. J. L. McKenzie, s.v. "Melchizedek."
2701. Butler, s.v. "Melchizedek."
2702. Calvocoressi, s.v. "Melchizedek."
2703. Comay, s.v. "Melchizedek."
2704. J. L. McKenzie, s.v. "Melchizedek."
2705. Gaskell, s.v. "Melchizedek."
2706. Hebrews 7:3.
2707. Genesis 1:27.
2708. 1 Corinthians 2:16; Philippians 2:5.
2709. Fillmore, s.v. "Melchizedek."
2710. Tenney, s.v. "Messiah."
2711. Genesis 1:27.
2712. John 1:41. Emphasis added.
2713. John 1:9.
2714. Colossians 3:11. For more on this topic, see my book *Christ Is All and In All*.
2715. Isaiah 45:1.
2716. Massey, Vol. 1, pp. 500, 519.
2717. Massey, Vol. 1, p. 217.
2718. Massey, Vol. 1, p. 218.
2719. Menzies, Vol. 9, p. 344. Emphasis added.
2720. Spivey and Smith, p. 244.
2721. Goguel, Vol. 2, p. 271; Neill, WWKAJ, pp. 21, 69.
2722. Goguel, Vol. 2, p. 366.
2723. See Goguel, Vol. 2, pp. 256-258.
2724. 2 Samuel 7:12-13; Isaiah 9:7. See also Luke 1:32-33; Romans 1:3.
2725. Sanders, pp. 241-242.
2726. See Psalms 110:1.
2727. Matthew 22:41-46. See also Daniel 7:13-14; Micah 5:2; Matthew 28:20; John 8:58; Hebrews 7:3; Revelation 22:13.
2728. Spivey and Smith, p. 243.
2729. Spivey and Smith, p. 285.
2730. Boer, p. 95.
2731. Matthew 24:36.
2732. Lamsa, IITBE, pp. 85-86.
2733. M. P. Hall, p. 21.
2734. Sykes, s.v. "Mithra."
2735. Bently, s.v. "Mithra."
2736. Daraul, p. 85.
2737. Leeming, p. 197.
2738. M. P. Hall, p. 47.
2739. J. M. Robertson, PC, pp. 321-322.
2740. Doane, p. 328.
2741. See Revelation 12:1.
2742. B. G. Walker, TWEOMAS, s.v. "Mithra."
2743. M. Jordan, s.v. "Mithra."
2744. Cirlot, s.v. "Cloak."
2745. Bently, s.v. "Mithra." These four horses have affinities with the Four Horses of the book of Revelation.
2746. B. G. Walker, TWEOMAS, s.v. "Mithra."
2747. Cirlot, s.v. "Bull." This bull-slaying was an allegory of the Creation, illustrating the idea that "there is no life without death." See Cirlot, s.v. "Cosmogony."
2748. Butler, s.v. "Mithra."
2749. B. G. Walker, TWEOMAS, s.v. "Mithra."
2750. J. M. Robertson, PC, p. 292.
2751. Cumont, TMOM, p. 86.

2752. J. M. Robertson, PC, pp. 301-303.
2753. Cumont, TMOM, pp. 109-111, 128-130.
2754. See Revelation 2:28; 22:16.
2755. Daraul, p. 85.
2756. Bently, s.v. "Mithra."
2757. Sykes, s.v. "Mithra."
2758. J. M. Robertson, PC, p. 309; Hinnells, s.v. "Mithras."
2759. Cumont, TMOM, pp. 155-157.
2760. A. Pike, pp. 541-542. Emphasis added.
2761. Goring, s.v. "Mithra."
2762. Cumont, TMOM, p. 157.
2763. Cumont, TMOM, p. 138.
2764. L. M. Graham, p. 336; Cumont, TMOM, p. 158; Daraul, p. 83.
2765. Daraul, p. 84.
2766. J. M. Robertson, PC, pp. 307-310, 317-318.
2767. Dowley, p. 31; Cumont, TMOM, p. 167; H. S. Lewis, TSDOJ, p. 218.
2768. R. Graves, TWG, pp. 319, 469.
2769. Davidson, p. 113.
2770. A. Pike, p. 473.
2771. R. Graves, TWG, pp. 142, 219. The bull's flesh represented Mithra's flesh, while the bull's blood represented Mithra's blood.
2772. M. P. Hall, p. 24.
2773. J. M. Robertson, PC, pp. 305-306, 316-318.
2774. M. P. Hall, p. 24.
2775. J. M. Robertson, PC, pp. 314-315. See also Butler, s.v. "Mithra, Mithraism."
2776. Daraul, p. 87.
2777. L. M. Graham, pp. 452-453.
2778. R. Graves, TWG, p. 62.
2779. Sykes, s.v. "Mithra."
2780. Daraul, p. 87.
2781. A. Pike, p. 587.
2782. J. M. Robertson, PC, pp. 327-334.
2783. Angus, p. 205; Cumont, TMOM, p. 155.
2784. B. G. Walker, TWEOMAS, s.v. "Mithra."
2785. Brewster, p. 55.
2786. Cumont, TMOM, pp. 190-197, 227-228. Emphasis added.
2787. Schweitzer, TQOTHJ, p. 167. This is Schweitzer's paraphrasal of Ghillany. Emphasis added.
2788. Cumont, TMOM, p. 52.
2789. Goring, s.v. "Mithraism."
2790. Neil, TIOTNT, p. 156.
2791. Cumont, TMOM, p. 199.
2792. Hopfe, pp. 275-276.
2793. Daraul, pp. 120-121.
2794. Daraul, pp. 80-81.
2795. J. L. McKenzie, s.v. "God."
2796. See Potter, p. 154.
2797. H. S. Lewis, TSDOJ, pp. 40-41, 69.
2798. Freud, MAM, p. 23.
2799. Breasted, p. 360.
2800. John 1:9.
2801. Goring, s.v. "Atenism."
2802. Exodus 20:3.
2803. See Freud, MAM, passim.
2804. Romer, pp. 51-52.
2805. Malachi 4:2.

2806. Celeste, pp. 86, 206.
2807. See e.g., 1 Corinthians 8:5.
2808. For biblical examples of polytheistic references to the Judeo-Christian Pantheon, see e.g., Matthew 4:6, 11; 8:16, 31; 9:34; 12:24, 28; 13:41, 49; 16:27; 24:31; 25:31, 41; 26:53; Mark 1:13, 34; 3:22; 5:9, 12; 8:38; 13:27; 16:9; Luke 4:41; 8:2, 27, 30, 33; 9:1; 10:17; 11:15; 12:9; John 1:51; 10:34-35; Acts 19:27-28; 34-35; 1 Corinthians 6:3; 8:5; Hebrews 1:6-7; 12:22; 1 Peter 3:22; Jude 1:6; James 2:19; Revelation 5:11; 7:1; 8:2; 12:7; 16:4; 21:12.
2809. Seabrook, CBC, p. 106. Also see Blunt, s.v. "Christmas."
2810. See Weigall, passim.
2811. Evans-Wentz, p. 34.
2812. See Parsons, pp. 276-277.
2813. Comay, s.v. "Moses"; G. D. Young, s.v. "Moses."
2814. R. L. Fox, TUV, p. 253.
2815. Freud, MAM, pp. 3-4, 12.
2816. Fillmore, s.v. "Moses."
2817. Barbanell, p. 152.
2818. A. Pike, p. 422. Even more recent spiritual leaders, such as the 8th-Century "Second Buddha," Indian Buddhist teacher Padma-Sambhava, were known to possess the ability to strike a rock with their staff in order to procure water. Evans-Wentz, pp. 27, 184.
2819. Freud, MAM, p. 8.
2820. Inman, pp. 95-96.
2821. G. D. Young, s.v. "Moses."
2822. Romer, p. 55; Freud, MAM, p. 5.
2823. 2 Corinthians 3:12-18. Emphasis added.
2824. Littleton, GGAM, Vol. 4, s.v. "Faunus."
2825. Runes, see Plate 1, "The Prophet Moses."
2826. L. M. Graham, p. 150.
2827. Blavatsky, pp. 99-100.
2828. See L. M. Graham, pp. 18, 55, 57.
2829. Baumgartner, s.v. "Pan."
2830. See Genesis 1:26; 3:22.
2831. A. Pike, p. 727.
2832. Exodus 34:29.
2833. L. M. Graham, p. 149. Emphasis added.
2834. Today's orthodox Christians, of course, take the opposite view; namely, that Moses' horns as described in the Vulgate are a "grotesque embellishment" based on a mistranslation. What many mystics consider the astonishing naivete of the Church's exoteric writers continues. See Calvocoressi, s.v. "Moses."
2835. Cooper, s.v. "Horns."
2836. Biedermann, s.v. "Horns."
2837. Luke 1:69.
2838. Revelation 5:6.
2839. Revelation 12:3.
2840. Farrell and Presser, s.v. "Horn."
2841. B. G. Walker, TWEOMAS, s.v. "Goddess."
2842. See e.g., Acts 19:27.
2843. Baring and Cashford, pp. 547-608.
2844. B. G. Walker, TWDOSASO, pp. 76, 100, 108, 221, 303, 399, 446.
2845. John 19:25.
2846. See e.g., Attwater, passim; Farmer, passim; Delaney, passim; Kelly and Rogers, passim; R. M. Levy, passim; B. G. Walker, TWEOMAS, passim.
2847. See Gimbutas, TCOTG, passim; Gimbutas, TGAGOOE, passim; Streep, passim.
2848. B. G. Walker, TWEOMAS, s.v. "Goddess."
2849. Lasne and Gaultier, p. 251.
2850. Seabrook, CBC, p. 23.
2851. See Neumann, p. 313.

2852. See Monaghan, p. 388, passim.
2853. Revelation 12:1.
2854. B. G. Walker, TWEOMAS, s.v. "Aditi."
2855. Tenney, s.v. "Mount, Mountain."
2856. See e.g., Mark 3:13; 6:46; 9:2; Luke 6:12.
2857. See e.g., Isaiah 40:4; 54:10.
2858. Matthew 21:21.
2859. Zondervan, s.v. "Mouth."
2860. Yogananda, TSCOC, Vol. 1, p. 161.
2861. Yogananda, TSCOC, Vol. 1, pp. 265, 269.
2862. Revelation 1:4, 11.
2863. Revelation 1:20.
2864. See Yogananda, TSCOC, Vol. 1, p. 265.
2865. Farrell and Presser, s.v. "Pine"; "Thyrsus."
2866. M. P. Hall, p. 79.
2867. Cumont, TMOM, pp. 105, 136.
2868. A. Pike, pp. 204-205.
2869. Revelation 3:14. See also, John 1:1-3.
2870. John 8:58.
2871. John 1:1.
2872. Yogananda, AOAY, p. 422.
2873. Matthew 4:4.
2874. Schonfield, TPP, p. 61.
2875. Brewster, p. 39; Filson, pp. 153-154; Potter, pp. 77-78, 138-139, 155; Lamsa, IITBE, p. 86.
2876. H. S. Lewis, TSDOJ, p. 219.
2877. Neill, TIOTNT, pp. 162-163, 169-170.
2878. Zaehner, p. 43; M. Grant, J, pp. 136-138.
2879. Dentan, pp. 131, 140, 147.
2880. Sheehan, p. 74.
2881. Fysh, p. 118.
2882. Potter, pp. 81-84.
2883. Channing, p. 297.
2884. Randolph, p. 365. Emphasis added.
2885. Wiener, Vol. 1, pp. 13-14.
2886. Baigent and Leigh, p. 65.
2887. Goodspeed, HCTB, pp. 74-75, 79-80.
2888. Grusin, p. 44.
2889. Cabot, Vol. 1, p. 167.
2890. Wahr, p. 23.
2891. Mark 1:14.
2892. Schonfield, TPP, pp. 4-5.
2893. John 10:34.
2894. Matthew 1:18-25; 2:23; Luke 2:4-39.
2895. Burtt, p. 87.
2896. Encyc. Brit., s.v. "Buddha."
2897. The Ebionites, who were among the first Christians, believed that Matthew originally began with the Third Chapter. The Socinians held the same for Luke. For Matthew, see e.g., Priestly, Vol. 6, pp. 464-466. For Luke, see e.g., Trollope, Vol. 1, p. 486.
2898. Condon, pp. 7-15.
2899. Sharpe, pp. 17-19.
2900. Strauss, TLOJCE, Vol. 1, p. 114.
2901. Keck, pp. 51-52.
2902. O. C. Edwards, p. 19.
2903. Matthew 2:23.
2904. J. L. McKenzie, s.v. "Nazareth."

2905. Leishman, TCOTB, p. 27.
2906. Roddy and Sellier, pp. 36-37.
2907. Baigent, Leigh, and Lincoln, pp. 30-31; J. D. King, p. 137; Salm, passim.
2908. See Jeremiah 31:15.
2909. O. C. Edwards, p. 43.
2910. Strauss, TLOJCE, Vol. 1, pp. 163-165; Roddy and Sellier, p. 21.
2911. Some conservative Bible scholars assert that Mark and John left out the Nativity because it was already provided by Matthew and Luke; therefore, there was no need to cover it again. However, this is nonsensical since Mark was the first Gospel writer and John knew nothing of the Synoptic Gospels.
2912. J. M. Robertson, PC, pp. 234-237.
2913. Luke 2:8.
2914. Hoffman, pp. 53-59; M. P. Hall, p. 181.
2915. Hoffman, pp. 59-60.
2916. Hoffman, pp. 60-61.
2917. J. G. Jackson, POOTCM, pp. 6-8; Neill, WWKAJ, p. 8; Spivey and Smith, pp. 203-205.
2918. Keable, p. 3.
2919. Spivey and Smith, p. 249.
2920. M. Grant, J, p. 1.
2921. Sewall, pp. 72-73.
2922. See Helms, passim.
2923. Neill, TIOTNT, p. 194.
2924. Schweitzer, pp. 396-397. Emphasis added.
2925. Westbrook, p. 289.
2926. Spivey and Smith, p. 262.
2927. Neil, TIOTNT, pp. 144-145.
2928. Seabrook, CBC, p. 29. Note: the authentic letters of Paul are as follows: 1 Thessalonians (written about the year 52, this is perhaps the earliest known piece of orthodox Christian literature), Romans, 1 Corinthians, 2 Corinthians, and Galatians. Many religious scholars consider the rest of Paul's so-called "letters" to be late forgeries in his name, as they do not match his thoughts or the writing style of the time period (mid 1st Century). Some go even further, discounting *all* of the Pauline letters as *pseudographia* ("false writings").
2929. Spivey and Smith, pp. 322, 353.
2930. Sewall, p. 91.
2931. Neill, WWKAJ, p. 11.
2932. Schweitzer, TQOTHJ, p. 79. This is Schweitzer's paraphrase of Strauss.
2933. Mack, pp. 1-3, passim.
2934. See Kümmel, pp. 80-101.
2935. Neill, WWKAJ, pp. 53-54.
2936. Spivey and Smith, pp. 64, 74, 94-95.
2937. Schweitzer, TQOTHJ, p. 144.
2938. Helms, p. 17.
2939. The belief that Mark fabricated the Passion began many centuries ago. See e.g., Kümmel, p. 77.
2940. Attwater, s.v. "Peter."
2941. B. G. Walker, TWEOMAS, s.v. "Peter, Saint."
2942. See e.g., Luke 9:44-45.
2943. Mark 8:32-33.
2944. John 1:5.
2945. Spivey and Smith, p. 208.
2946. If this evidence ever existed it was no doubt long ago destroyed by the Catholic Church; or, it was permanently locked in a secret chamber in the Vatican's vast basement library.
2947. Herrmann, p. 53. See also Baigent, Leigh, and Lincoln, TML, p. 367, who attribute this quote to Pope Alexander VI.
2948. Titcomb, p. 105.
2949. Doane, p. 500.
2950. See Dupius, pp. 215-299.
2951. A. Pike, p. 591.

2952. M. P. Hall, p. 50.
2953. Spalding, Vol. 4, p. 33.
2954. Kingsford and Maitland, p. 142.
2955. Westbrook, p. 295.
2956. M. P. Hall, pp. 49-52.
2957. A. Pike, pp. 446-447.
2958. We will note here that since true astrology is based on the *mystical* signs of the Zodiac rather than on the actual *physical* Zodiacal constellations, astrology is not affected by the Precession of the Equinoxes (despite the claims of skeptics), and continues to accurately use the original ancient system of calculating horoscopes.
2959. Aquila derives its name from the mythological eagle sent to take Ganymedes to Olympus.
2960. M. P. Hall, pp. 49-52.
2961. During the formation of the mythological aspects of Jesus' life story, this name was applied to John the Baptist as the "Herald of the Son of God." See e.g., Matthew 3:1-3.
2962. Seabrook, CBC, pp. 104-107. See also Neumann, pp. 313-314; J. G. Jackson, POOTCM, pp. 10-11; J. G. Jackson, CBC, pp. 195, 199-200; J. M. Robertson, PC, pp. 168-169, 178, 331, 348; A. Pike, p. 455.
2963. Moses, pp. 256-257.
2964. Carpenter, pp. 27-33. Emphasis added.
2965. Luomanen, pp. 49-82.
2966. Baigent and Leigh, p. 174.
2967. See Potter, p. 154.
2968. Matthew 2:23. See also Terapeut, passim.
2969. Leishman, OAB, pp. 148-149; Neill, TIOTNT, p. 305.
2970. Acts 24:5.
2971. See Lemesurier, passim.
2972. Livingstone, s.v. "Nazarene."
2973. Baigent and Leigh, p. 174.
2974. Roddy and Sellier, pp. 36-37; G. D. Young, s.v. "Nazareth, Nazarene."
2975. Matthew 2:23.
2976. J. L. McKenzie, s.v. "Nazareth." Not even the word "Nazarene" appears in the Old Testament. Leishman, TCOTB, p. 27.
2977. For more on the questionable historicity of Nazareth, see Baigent, Leigh, and Lincoln, pp. 30-31; J. D. King, p. 137; Salm, passim.
2978. Schonfield, TANT, p. xvii.
2979. Schonfield, TPP, pp. 199-206.
2980. Dunlap, p. 488.
2981. Epiphanius, *Panarion*, 29, 1:3.
2982. Epiphanius, *Panarion*, 20, 3:2. See also Potter, p. 118.
2983. Livingstone, s.v. "Ebionites."
2984. Goring, s.v. "Ebionites."
2985. Dowley, p. 113.
2986. Livingstone, s.v. "Nazarene."
2987. Acts 24:5.
2988. Mark 12:31.
2989. For more on the topic of the Christian form of the Law of Attraction, see Seabrook, JATLOA, passim; Seabrook, TBATLOA, passim.
2990. See Seabrook, JATLOA, passim.
2991. Proverbs 23:7.
2992. Nelson's, s.v. "Noah." See Genesis 6:8-9:29.
2993. Colossians 3:11.
2994. Fillmore, s.v. "Noah."
2995. Jukes, pp. 104-105.
2996. See e.g., Larson, p. 29.
2997. See Revelation 13:11-16.
2998. Lamsa, IITBE, p. 70.
2999. Kee, p. 88.

3000. Revelation 12:1. See Massey, Vol. 1, p. 23.
3001. L. M. Graham, p. 375.
3002. See Curtiss and Curtiss, TKTTU, pp. 306-326.
3003. Gaskell, s.v. "Nine, number"; "Gates of the body, nine."
3004. Potter, pp. 24, 90.
3005. Revelation 14:1-3.
3006. Revelation 13:5.
3007. Revelation 11:2.
3008. Revelation 11:3.
3009. Revelation 12:6.
3010. Revelation 21:17.
3011. J. E. M. White, AE, p. 120.
3012. Farrell and Presser, s.v. "Three."
3013. A. Pike, pp. 13, 431.
3014. Finegan, Vol. 1, pp. 167-168, 173; Pritchard, passim.
3015. 1 Kings 10:14.
3016. B. G. Walker, TWEOMAS, s.v. "Solomon and Sheba."
3017. W. W. Westcott, pp. 30, 31.
3018. Farrell and Presser, s.v. "Six."
3019. Revelation 13:8.
3020. John 17:21; 1 Corinthians 6:17; 2 Corinthians 6:16; Ephesians 4:6.
3021. Spalding, Vol. 2, pp. 69-71.
3022. Yogananda, TSCOC, Vol. 2, p. 1587.
3023. Heindel, TRC, pp. 500-501.
3024. While the word numerology is of modern derivation (1911), as an art it has been practiced from time immemorial.
3025. Wall, pp. 102-106. Note: The word gematria is related to the Greek word *geometria*: "geometry."
3026. J. J. Davis, pp. 126-127.
3027. Wisdom 11:20.
3028. Revelation 21:14.
3029. Swedenborg, TAR, Vol. 1, p. 37.
3030. J. J. Davis, p. 130.
3031. Dods, Vol. 9, pp. 52-53. Emphasis added.
3032. Roberts and Donaldson, Vol. 6, p. 339.
3033. A. Pike, pp. 208-209.
3034. See e.g., Zondervan, s.v. "Oil."
3035. Ferguson, p. 43.
3036. Gaskell, s.v. "Oil, or Holy Oil."
3037. Colossians 3:11.
3038. Seabrook, JATLOA, p. 390.
3039. Farrell and Presser, s.v. "Chrism." See e.g., 1 Samuel 15:17; 2 Samuel 2:4, 7; 3:39; 5:3, 17; 12:7; 23:1; 1 Kings 1:45; 5:1; 2 Kings 9:3, 6, 12; 11:12; 23:30; 1 Chronicles 11:3; 14:8; 29:22; 2 Chronicles 23:11; Psalms 18:50.
3040. Psalms 45:7.
3041. Budge, EM, p. 186.
3042. Swedenborg, Vol. 1, p. 137.
3043. Seabrook, AT, p. 41.
3044. Examples of biblical prostitution: Hosea 4:10-19; 2 Kings 23:7; Judges 16:1; Numbers 25:1-5; 1 Samuel 2:22. In the New Testament *Horasis* is deceptively translated as the word "visions." See e.g., Acts 2:17.
3045. For more on the topic of religious prostitution, see Seabrook, AT, passim.
3046. See e.g., Deuteronomy 23:17.
3047. Genesis 14:6; 36:21, 29.
3048. B. G. Walker, TWEOMAS, s.v. "Prostitution."
3049. 2 Kings 23:7.
3050. See e.g., Genesis 3:5; 1 Kings 1:4; Matthew 1:25.

3051. See e.g., Exodus 30:30-31.
3052. See e.g., Psalms 89:20.
3053. Meissner, p. 116. "El Shaddai" is mistranslated in the Bible as "God Almighty." The Pagan mountain-god Shaddai was indeed "almighty." See e.g., Genesis 35:11.
3054. Genesis 28:18, 22.
3055. Genesis 35:14.
3056. Deuteronomy 32:18.
3057. See e.g., the original Hebrew word for "oil" in Exodus 30:25.
3058. Seabrook, AT, p. 55.
3059. For more on the topic of phallic worship, once important in early Christianity, see Wall, passim.
3060. Condon, pp. 12-13; Seabrook, AT, p. 55.
3061. Matthew 26:6-7.
3062. Luke 7:36-38.
3063. See Matthew 26:12.
3064. For more on the mystical sacrality of the Divine Whore, see Seabrook, AT, passim.
3065. B. G. Walker, TWEOMAS, s.v. "Trinity." See also R. Graves, TWG, passim.
3066. See e.g., Ezekiel 8:14.
3067. Jastrow and Clay, pp. 63-65.
3068. B. G. Walker, TWEOMAS, s.v. "Mary Magdalene."
3069. John 19:25. The "Three Marys" were the Virgin Mary (Jesus' mother), Mary Magdalene (according to many early traditions, Jesus' wife), and Mary the wife of Cleophas (Jesus' aunt).
3070. J. E. M. White, AE, p. 122; Lasne and Gaultier, p. 251.
3071. See Gimbutas, TGAGOOE, passim.
3072. B. G. Walker, C, pp. 101-102.
3073. Metford, s.v. "Ointment, jar of."
3074. Mark 16:1.
3075. Seabrook, AT, p. 57.
3076. Matthew 21:31. My paraphrasal.
3077. 1 Corinthians 2:7.
3078. G. D. Young, s.v. "Only Begotten."
3079. Hebrews 11:17.
3080. D. A. Carson, p. 92.
3081. Yogananda, TSCOC, Vol. 1, pp. 17, 178.
3082. 1 Corinthians 2:16; Philippians 2:5.
3083. Gaskell, s.v. "First-Born Son of God."
3084. Genesis 1:27.
3085. Colossians 3:11.
3086. Deussen, pp. 198-200.
3087. Colossians 1:12-16. Emphasis added.
3088. See John 1:14; 3:16; 1 John 4:9.
3089. Hoeller, p. 80.
3090. John 14:6.
3091. Colossians 3:11.
3092. See Evans-Wentz, pp. 4, 217-218.
3093. John 1:9. See Besant and Leadbetter, p. 295.
3094. Hardon, s.v. "Original Sin."
3095. See Romans 5:12.
3096. J. L. McKenzie, s.v. "Sin."
3097. Romans 6:23.
3098. Romans 3:23.
3099. Isaiah 40:6.
3100. Seabrook, JATLOA, pp. 504-505.
3101. Romans 5:10.
3102. See Seabrook, JATLOA, pp. 415-418.
3103. See H. S. Lewis, TSDOJ, pp. 220-222.

3104. Dupius, p. 218.
3105. For more on the topic of "sin," see Seabrook, JATLOA, pp. 240, 317, 399.
3106. Luke 3:6. See also Romans 10:13; Acts 2:17; 1 Timothy 2:4; 2 Peter 3:9.
3107. See Yogananda, TSCOC, Vol. 1, p. 148.
3108. Matthew 5:48.
3109. Seabrook, JATLOA, pp. 29, 75, 235-237, 324.
3110. M. P. Hall, p. 59.
3111. See Goguel, Vol. 2, p. 318.
3112. C. Wright, p. 17.
3113. Angus, p. 209.
3114. Montgomery, pp. 292-293. For more on how Orphism influenced Christianity, see Angus, pp. 150-156, passim.
3115. Kingsford and Maitland, p. 240.
3116. Exodus 3:14; Ezekiel 37:14; John 14:10-11; Romans 8:9, 11; 1 Corinthians 6:17; 2 Corinthians 6:16; Ephesians 2:22; 4:6.
3117. John 12:32; 14:20; 15:4; 17:21-23, 26; Colossians 1:27; 3:10-11; Romans 8:10; 1 Corinthians 6:15, 17; 2 Corinthians 5:16; 13:3, 5; Galatians 1:16; 2:20; 4:19; Ephesians 3:14-17; Philippians 1:20; 2:5; 1 Peter 1:11; 1 John 2:27; 3:24; 4:4.
3118. John 14:16-17; 1 Corinthians 6:19; 2 Timothy 1:14.
3119. Schweitzer, TQOTHJ, p. 97.
3120. See Kuhn, WITKOG, passim.
3121. Massey, Vol. 1, pp. 213-219.
3122. Massey, Vol. 1, p. 95.
3123. Massey, Vol. 1, p. 220.
3124. Lurker, TGASOAE, s.v. "Osiris"; Desroches-Noblecourt, p. 84; M. P. Hall, p. 35.
3125. See B. G. Walker, TWEOMAS, s.v. "Osiris"; Cotterrell, ADOWM, s.v. "Osiris."
3126. Desroches-Noblecourt, p. 269.
3127. J. M. Robertson, PC, p. 306.
3128. J. G. Jackson, CBC, p. 128.
3129. Freud, MAM, p. 20.
3130. Budge, OATER, Vol. 1, p. 1.
3131. B. G. Walker, TWEOMAS, s.v. "Osiris."
3132. Budge, TGOTE, Vol. 2, p. 126. Emphasis added.
3133. Angus, p. 139.
3134. Westbrook, p. 288.
3135. Massey, Vol. 1, pp. 213, 218.
3136. Massey, Vol. 1, pp. 500, 519.
3137. Massey, Vol. 1, p. 217.
3138. On this topic Massey writes: "The word krs denotes the embalmment of the mummy, and the krst, as the mummy, was made in the process of preparation by purifying, anointing, and embalming. To Karas the dead body was to embalm it, to bandage it, to make the mummy. The mummy was the Osirian *Corpus Christi*, prepared for burial as the laid-out dead, the karast by name. When raised to its feet, it was the risen mummy, or sahu. The place of embalmment was likewise the krs. Thus the process of making the mummy was to karas, the place in which it was laid is the karas, and the product was the krst, whose image is the upright mummy = the risen Christ. Hence the name of the Christ, Christos in Greek, Chrestus in Latin, for the anointed, was derived . . . from the Egyptian word krst. Karas also signifies the burial-place, and the word modifies into Kâs or Châs. Kasu the 'burial place' was a name of the 14th Nome in Upper Egypt. A god Kas is mentioned three or four times in the Book of the Dead, 'the god Kas who is in the Tuat.' This was a title of the mummy Osiris in the funerary dwelling. In one passage Kas is described as the deliverer or saviour from all mortal needs. In 'the chapter of raising the body' it is said of the deceased that he had been hungry and thirsty (on earth), but he will never hunger or thirst any more, for 'Kas delivers him' and does away with wants like these. That is, in the resurrection. Here the name of the god Osiris-Kas written at full is Osiris the Karast—the Egyptian Christ. Not only is the risen mummy or sahu called the karast, Osiris as lord of the bier is the Neb-karast, equivalent to the later Christ the Lord, and the lord of the bier is god of the resurrection from the house of death. The karast is literally the god or person who has been mummified, embalmed, and anointed or christified." Massey, Vol. 1, p. 218.

3139. J. E. M. White, AE, p. 28; B. G. Walker, TWEOMAS, s.v. "Osiris."
3140. Desroches-Noblecourt, p. 84.
3141. Goring, s.v. "Osiris."
3142. Littleton, M, p. 73; Cotterell, TMIEOMAL, s.v. "Osiris."
3143. Budge, OATER, Vol. 1, p. 9.
3144. Some say he was the son of the earth-god Geb rather than Ra. See Hart, s.v. "Osiris"; Sykes, s.v. "Osiris"; Desroches-Noblecourt, p. 103.
3145. Zimmerman, s.v. "Osiris."
3146. Littleton, M, p. 27; Hart, s.v. "Osiris"; Desroches-Noblecourt, pp. 239, 245, 253.
3147. B. G. Walker, TWEOMAS, s.v. "Osiris."
3148. B. G. Walker, TWEOMAS, s.v. "Osiris." Needless to say, Sirius was the real "Star of Bethlehem."
3149. B. G. Walker, TWEOMAS, s.v. "Osiris."
3150. B. G. Walker, TWEOMAS, s.v. "Osiris."
3151. Murnane, p. 62; Guirand, p. 17; J. G. Jackson, CBC, p. 109; Hart, s.v. "Osiris." Egyptian portrayals of Isis breast-feeding her infant Sun-god Horus, in particular, became the models for artistic depictions of the Virgin Mary and the infant Jesus. See e.g., M. P. Hall, p. 47; Westbrook, p. 291.
3152. Encyc. Brit., s.v. "Egypt."
3153. B. G. Walker, TWEOMAS, s.v. "Osiris." Jesus has about the same number of names and titles as Osiris. See Towns, passim; Derk, passim.
3154. J. M. Robertson, PC, p. 358.
3155. Massey, Vol. 1, pp. 95, 195, 213.
3156. B. G. Walker, TWEOMAS, s.v. "Osiris."
3157. Massey, Vol. 1, pp. 126, 406.
3158. J. E. M. White, ELIAE, p. 75.
3159. Lurker, TGASOAE, s.v. "Osiris."
3160. J. G. Jackson, CBC, p. 129.
3161. Littleton, M, p. 72.
3162. Cotterell, TMIEOMAL, s.v. "Osiris."
3163. B. G. Walker, TWEOMAS, s.v. "Osiris."
3164. Guirand, p. 16.
3165. Hart, s.v. "Osiris."
3166. Cotterell, ADOWM, s.v. "Osiris."
3167. Cotterell, ADOWM, s.v. "Osiris."
3168. A. Pike, p. 478.
3169. J. M. Robertson, PC, p. 306.
3170. R. Graves, TWG, p. 211.
3171. Massey, Vol. 1, pp. 17, 494.
3172. Littleton, M, p. 74; Massey, Vol. 1, p. 483. Jesus too had a throne. See e.g., Matthew 19:28; 25:31; Luke 1:32; 22:30; Acts 2:30.
3173. Guirand, p. 16; Budge, OATER, p. 2.
3174. J. E. M. White, ELIAE, p. 75.
3175. Bently, s.v. "Osiris."
3176. Massesy, Vol. 1, p. 205.
3177. Littleton, M, p. 73.
3178. Budge, TBOTD, pp. 29, 43, 138.
3179. Massey, Vol. 1, p. 296.
3180. Hart, s.v. "Osiris."
3181. Encyc. Brit., s.v. "Egypt"; Guirand, p. 16; Hart, s.v. "Osiris." Paul spoke of Jesus as a sort of vegetation god. See e.g., 1 Corinthians 15:35-38. See also A. Pike, p. 395.
3182. R. Graves, TWG, p. 177.
3183. Guirand, p. 17.
3184. Sykes, s.v. "Osiris." Jesus was born in the age of Aries the ram-god (which started about 2200 B.C.), and so became associated with sheep and the title the "Good Shepherd."
3185. M. Jordan, s.v. "Osiris."
3186. Baumgartner, s.v. "Osiris."

3187. Budge, TBOTD, p. 48.
3188. Hart, s.v. "Osiris."
3189. Sykes, s.v. "Osiris."
3190. M. Jordan, s.v. "Osiris."
3191. This Osirian teaching was used by the Church in John 12:24. See B. G. Walker, TWEOMAS, s.v. "Osiris."
3192. This Osirian teaching was used by the Church in John 14:2. See B. G. Walker, TWEOMAS, s.v. "Osiris."
3193. This Osirian teaching was used by the Church in John 4:43-54. See Budge, TGOTE, Vol. 2, pp. 40-41.
3194. Guirand, p. 17; Hart, s.v. "Osiris."
3195. Hart, s.v. "Osiris." Jesus was born at Bethlehem, which means "House of Bread."
3196. Murnane, p. 73; Cotterell, TMIEOMAL, s.v. "Osiris."
3197. Massey, Vol. 1, p. 195.
3198. Hart, s.v. "Osiris." Jesus was not only associated with truth (John 4:24; 8:32; 17), but (as the Indwelling Christ) He literally said "I AM the truth." John 14:6.
3199. Budge, OATER, Vol. 1, pp. 305-347; Cotterell, ADOWM, s.v. "Osiris." Jesus is also described as the "judge of the dead." See e.g., Acts 10:42; 17:31.
3200. Budge, OATER, Vol. 1, p. 30.
3201. Massey, Vol. 1, p. 487.
3202. Cotterell, ADOWM, s.v. "Osiris."
3203. Desroches-Noblecourt, p. 179.
3204. Hart, s.v. "Osiris." The worship of Jesus contained many "mysteries." See e.g. Matthew 13:11; Luke 8:10; 1 Corinthians 4:1; 13:2; 14:2.
3205. J. E. M. White, AE, p. 29.
3206. Hart, s.v. "Osiris."
3207. Cotterell, ADOWM, s.v. "Osiris." Osiris' paraclete was sometimes portrayed by his child the Sun/Son-god Horus. See Massey, Vol. 1, p. 206.
3208. Cotterell, ADOWM, s.v. "Osiris."
3209. Massey, Vol. 1, p. 363.
3210. Guirand, p. 17.
3211. Guirand, p. 16. Due to numerous similarities between the two, Jesus was also considered by many to be a Jewish Dionysus.
3212. Goguel, Vol. 2, p. 328.
3213. R. Graves, TWG, p. 134.
3214. J. M. Robertson, CAM, pp. 358-359.
3215. J. E. M. White, AE, p. 30.
3216. Budge, OATER, Vol. 1, p. 9.
3217. R. Graves, TWG, p. 278.
3218. Lemming, pp. 96-97.
3219. Murnane, p. 65; J. E. M. White, AE, p. 44.
3220. See Angus, pp. 45-46; J. E. M. White, ELIAE, p. 135; Hart, s.v. "Osiris." Jesus' life story, and in particular his death and resurrection, have long been celebrated in yearly passion plays, a custom which continues to this day.
3221. J. M. Robertson, CAM, p. 391; Massey, Vol. 1, p. 210; Guirand, p. 17; J. E. M. White, AE, p. 45. The universal Passion Play of the ancient dying and rising gods was transferred wholesale into the biography of Jesus, most popularly known today as "Christmas."
3222. J. E. M. White, ELIAE, p. 136; J. E. M. White, AE, pp. 44-45.
3223. Sykes, s.v. "Osiris."
3224. Bently, s.v. "Osiris"; Guirand, p. 17.
3225. Encyc. Brit., s.v. "Egypt."
3226. Budge, OATER, Vol. 1, p. 19.
3227. J. M. Robertson, PC, p. 407; Budge, OATER, Vol. 1, p. 15; Hart, s.v. "Osiris." Jesus was associated with various trees as well (see Jung, MAHS, p. 69), including the fig tree, the olive tree, and the dogwood tree. Jesus' crucifixion "crown" was a typical foliage crown found in the myths of hundreds of pre-Christian tree-gods.

3228. R. Graves, TWG, pp. 102, 264.
3229. Cotterell, ADOWM, s.v. "Osiris." According to Egyptian myth there were 72 "conspirators" and a Nubian queen who assisted Osiris' brother Set (Seth) in his murder. See Guirand, p. 17; Hart, s.v. "Osiris."
3230. Cotterell, ADOWM, s.v. "Osiris." Jesus later became associated with the astrological sign Pisces and one of the sacred animals of the Great Mother-Goddess, fish.
3231. See e.g., Leviticus 16:7-8.
3232. Leeming, p. 147.
3233. Cotterell, ADOWM, s.v. "Osiris."
3234. Massey, Vol. 1, p. 237.
3235. R. Graves, TWG, p. 264. Arks made of shittim (acacia) wood are also associated with Noah and Xisuthros.
3236. B. Evans, s.v. "Osiris."
3237. Guirand, p. 17.
3238. Guirand, p. 17. Jesus said "I AM the true vine." John 15:1. See also John 15:4-5.
3239. Budge, OATER, Vol. 1, p. 10; Massey, Vol. 1, p. 536.
3240. Guirand, p. 17; Hart, s.v. "Osiris." Jesus too is venerated in scores of annual festivals, such as Easter, Christmas, Lent, Palm Sunday, Maundy Thursday, Good Friday, Pentecost, and Advent.
3241. Cotterell, ADOWM, s.v. "Osiris."
3242. Sykes, s.v. "Osiris." Royal Egyptians assured their immortality through Osiris by performing the mystical ritual known as "the opening of the mouth and eyes," which was believed to restore to a mummy the use of its physical senses. Desroches-Noblecourt, pp. 170, 240.
3243. Hinnells, s.v. "Osirian Triad."
3244. Angus, p. 46.
3245. L. M. Graham, p. 148.
3246. Massey, Vol. 1, p. 213.
3247. 1 Corinthians 4:1.
3248. 1 Corinthians 2:7.
3249. Romans 16:25.
3250. M. P. Hall, p. 35.
3251. Jung, MAHS, pp. 68-69.
3252. W. R. Copper, passim. See also Murdock, CIE, passim.
3253. Massey, Vol. 1, p. 219.
3254. 2 Corinthians 4:16.
3255. Zondervan, s.v. "Parable."
3256. 1 Corinthians 2:7.
3257. Gaskell, s.v. Parable."
3258. Hardon, s.v. "Passion."
3259. Gaskell, s.v. "Passion of Jesus."
3260. Potter, pp. 81-83.
3261. See e.g., Ridderbos, passim.
3262. G. D. Young, s.v. "Paul."
3263. Elder, p. 46.
3264. Schweitzer, TQOTHJ, p. xxiii.
3265. Schweitzer, TQOTHJ, p. 318.
3266. John 10:34; 14:12.
3267. Dentan, p. 161.
3268. Galatians 2:20.
3269. See Ephesians 5:14.
3270. 1 Corinthians 1:18.
3271. See Pagels, TGP, passim.
3272. Richardson, p. 365.
3273. Ridderbos, p. 28.
3274. See Segal, passim.
3275. See e.g., 2 Peter 3:16.
3276. See e.g., Porter, pp. 503-508; J. H. Lee, p. 351.

3277. See De Bunsen, passim; Segal, p. 174.
3278. Acts 9:10-18; 22:14.
3279. Schonfield, TPP, p. 203.
3280. Angus, pp. 233-234.
3281. Schonfield, TPP, pp. 192-193.
3282. Schonfield, TANT, pp. 249-250; Ramm, p. 59.
3283. 2 Corinthians 5:16-17.
3284. Romans 10:6-8. Emphasis added.
3285. Romans 11:12, 25; 13:10; 15:29; 1 Corinthians 10:26, 28; Galatians 4:4; Ephesians 1:10, 23; 3:19; 4:13; Colossians 1:19; 2:9.
3286. Colossians 3:11. See my book of the same name.
3287. Schonfield, TANT, p. 250.
3288. G. N. Marshall, p. 62.
3289. 2 Corinthians 12:1-5. Emphasis added.
3290. Paul does mention "the twelve," see 1 Corinthians 15:5. But he is not referring to the 12 Apostles, but rather to the 12 leaders (symbolizing the 12 Tribes of Israel) of the "Council of the Community," an institution of the Essenic community at Qumran (see Vermes pp. 4, 72). This is borne out by the passages which follow, where Paul differentiates between "the twelve" and "all of the apostles." See 1 Corinthians 15:6-9.
3291. Potter, p. 134.
3292. Spong, p. 81.
3293. Spivey and Smith, p. 472; Sheehan, pp. 73-74.
3294. Brownrigg, s.v. "Mary, Mother of Jesus."
3295. Paul is not the only New Testament figure who is silent on important details. John, as another example, was an apostle who attended the Last Supper with Jesus. Yet strangely he makes no mention of the institution of the Eucharist, one of the most significant events in Christian history. These and other Johannine problems regarding Jesus' last night are addressed in Goguel, Vol. 2, pp. 460-462.
3296. See Schweitzer, TQOTHJ, pp. 343-344.
3297. Matthew 6:22-23.
3298. Westbrook, pp. 288-289. Emphasis added.
3299. See Neill, WWKAJ, p. 38.
3300. J. M. Robertson, PC, pp. 234-237. Emphasis added.
3301. Angus, pp. 295-296. Emphasis added.
3302. 1 Corinthians 3:16.
3303. Spivey and Smith, pp. 322, 353.
3304. Shillington, p. 15.
3305. Schonfield, TIC, p. 122.
3306. J. L. McKenzie, s.v. "Paul."
3307. Calvocoressi, s.v. "Paul."
3308. 1 Corinthians 1:10-13. Though Paul is here depicted as being against cults forming in his name, later he encourages it (see e.g., 1 Corinthians 4:16; 11:1), a sign of subsequent orthodox textual tampering.
3309. See e.g., Romans 2:16; 16:25; Philippians 3:17; 2 Timothy 2:8.
3310. See e.g, Matthew 13:11; Luke 8:10.
3311. See e.g., 1 Corinthians 4:1; 13:2; 14:2.
3312. Galatians 2:20.
3313. 1 Corinthians 13:1-13.
3314. See Burtt, pp. 46-47.
3315. Copan and Litwack, pp. 131-132; Covell, p. 17.
3316. Acts 17:28.
3317. Ephesians 3:9.
3318. Ridderbos, p. 47.
3319. Colossians 1:26.
3320. Colossians 1:27.
3321. Elder, p. 47.
3322. 2 Timothy 2:18.
3323. Galatians 1:16.

3324. 1 Corinthians 15:31.
3325. Galatians 2:20.
3326. Romans 6:6; Ephesians 4:22; Colossians 3:9.
3327. 1 Corinthians 6:14.
3328. 2 Corinthians 5:17. See also Galatians 6:15.
3329. Schonfield, TIC, p. 155.
3330. In nearby Bethlehem, only 5 miles from Jerusalem where Paul grew up, there was a shrine to Adonis or Tammuz which he would have been familiar with. Schonfield, TPP, p. 212.
3331. See Schonfield, TPP, p. 195.
3332. Guignebert, pp. 174, 182-188.
3333. Guignebert, p. 179.
3334. 1 Corinthians 15:31.
3335. Romans 6:3-10.
3336. See e.g., Romans 8:10; 2 Corinthians 11:10; 13:3, 5; Galatians 2:20; 4:19; Ephesians 3:17; Colossians 1:27; 3:11; 4:1
3337. See e.g., Ephesians 1:20-21.
3338. See e.g., Romans 6:3; 1 Corinthians 10:2; Galatians 3:27; Ephesians 5:26; 2 Timothy 3:5.
3339. See e.g., Romans 7:4; 1 Corinthians 12:14.
3340. See e.g., Romans 7:9.
3341. See e.g., Romans 4:17; Galatians 6:7.
3342. See e.g., Romans 8:14-19.
3343. See e.g., Romans 7:25; Philippians 2:5.
3344. See e.g., Romans 8:38-39; 1 Corinthians 13:4-8; 16:14.
3345. See e.g., Romans 10:8; Colossians 3:16.
3346. Spalding, Vol. 4, p. 33.
3347. See e.g., Romans 11:8; 15:21.
3348. See e.g., Romans 11:36; Ephesians 4:6; Philippians 2:10; Colossians 1:15-17; 3:11.
3349. See e.g., Romans 11:33; Colossians 1:9-10; 2:3. This as opposed to intellectually derived knowledge.
3350. See e.g., Romans 11:33; Ephesians 3:10; Colossians 1:9; 2:3. This as opposed to intellectually derived wisdom. See also Guignebert, p. 269.
3351. See e.g., Romans 12:2.
3352. See e.g., Romans 12:5; 1 Corinthians 10:16-17.
3353. Neil, TIOTNT, p. 159.
3354. Ridderbos, p. 388. See e.g., Romans 11:12, 25; 13:10; 15:29; 1 Corinthians 10:26, 28; Galatians 4:4; Ephesians 1:10, 23; 3:19; 4:13; Colossians 1:19; 2:9.
3355. See e.g., Romans 13:12.
3356. See e.g., Romans 14:17; 1 Corinthians 4:20.
3357. A. Pike, p. 769.
3358. See e.g., 1 Corinthians 2:6-7; Ephesians 4:13; Philippians 3:12, 15; Colossians 1:28. For more on this topic see the Introduction.
3359. See e.g., 1 Corinthians 2:10-16. See also Baba, pp. 37-38.
3360. See e.g., 1 Corinthians 2:16; Philemon 2:5. See also Guignebert, p. 271.
3361. See e.g., 1 Corinthians 3:16-17.
3362. See e.g., 1 Corinthians 4:1.
3363. See e.g., 1 Corinthians 6:3.
3364. See e.g., 1 Corinthians 6:12; 10:23; Ephesians 2:8-9.
3365. See e.g., 1 Corinthians 6:19.
3366. See e.g., 1 Corinthians 7:1-29.
3367. See e.g., 1 Corinthians 8:5; 14:18.
3368. See e.g., 1 Corinthians 9:25; 1 Thessalonians 5:8.
3369. See e.g., 1 Corinthians 10:4.
3370. See e.g., 1 Corinthians 11:12.
3371. Hoeller, p. xviii.
3372. Szekeley, TDOTEGOP, p. 9.

3373. See e.g., Romans 8:38; 1 Corinthians 6:3; 11:10; Galatians 3:19; Colossians 2:18; 1 Timothy 3:16; 5:21.
3374. M. P. Hall, pp. 83, 115-116.
3375. See e.g., 2 Corinthians 12:2; Ephesians 1:20; 2:6; 3:10; 4:9-10.
3376. See e.g., 1 Corinthians 15:10.
3377. Neil, TIOTNT, p. 157. See e.g., Romans 15:28; 2 Corinthians 1:22; Ephesians 1:13; 4:30.
3378. See e.g., 1 Corinthians 15:31.
3379. See e.g., 1 Corinthians 15:36-38; Galatians 3:16, 19. Mainline Protestants now admit that Paul borrowed this mythological vegetation motif from the Pagans he encountered in Greece. See e.g., Ramm, pp. 62-63. See also A. Pike, p. 395.
3380. See e.g., 1 Corinthians 15:42-43, 50; Galatians 5:17; Philippians 3:21.
3381. See e.g., 1 Corinthians 15:47, 50; Galatians 5:17.
3382. See e.g., 1 Corinthians 16:22.
3383. See e.g., 2 Corinthians 3:6; Philippians 4:7.
3384. Kelly, pp. 86-87; Pagels, TGG, pp. 147-148.
3385. Chernin, p. 165.
3386. See e.g., 2 Corinthians 4:4; Colossians 2:2. Gnostics believed that there was an evil god who ruled Earth (Yaldaboath or Jehovah) who was separate and distinct from the higher god, the Father, the "true God," known to them as Bythus. Jesus refers to the Gnostic Demiurge Yaldabaoth in John 12:31.
3387. Blunt, s.v. "Gnosticism."
3388. See e.g., 2 Corinthians 5:16; Galatians 1:11-12.
3389. See e.g., 2 Corinthians 6:14-15.
3390. See e.g., 2 Corinthians 6:16; Ephesians 4:6; Philippians 2:5-6.
3391. Versnel, p. 374.
3392. See e.g., 2 Corinthians 6:18.
3393. Meissner, p. 116.
3394. Philippians 2:12. See also Dowling, 100:17.
3395. Some 500 years before Paul, Buddha made this comment: "Work out your own salvation with diligence." Burtt, pp. 22, 49, 80. See also Bucke, p. 72.
3396. See e.g., 2 Corinthians 7:1.
3397. See e.g., 2 Corinthians 11:14.
3398. See e.g., 2 Corinthians 12:1-4.
3399. See e.g., Galatians 1:11.
3400. Galatians 1:11-16.
3401. See e.g., Galatians 2:21; 3:10-13, 23-26; Colossians 2:14.
3402. See e.g., Galatians 4:4; Philippians 2:5-8. See also Colossians 3:11.
3403. See e.g., Galatians 4:22-25, 28.
3404. See e.g., Galatians 4:26. See also G. D. Young, s.v. "Jerusalem."
3405. Neil, TIOTNT, p. 157. See e.g., Ephesians 1:18. Though non-Pauline, see also Hebrews 6:4; 10:32.
3406. See e.g., Galatians 5:14. The Pagan Golden Rule was also preached by Jesus. See e.g., Matthew 7:12.
3407. See e.g., Galatians 6:6.
3408. See e.g., Galatians 6:7.
3409. See e.g., Ephesians 1:4.
3410. Burtt, p. 69.
3411. See e.g., Galatians 3:24-25.
3412. See e.g., Ephesians 1:10.
3413. See e.g., Ephesians 1:17-18.
3414. See e.g., Ephesians 3:3-4; Philippians 3:8; Colossians 4:3.
3415. See e.g., Ephesians 3:9. See also Colossians 1:26.
3416. See e.g., Ephesians 4:6.
3417. See e.g., Ephesians 4:13.
3418. See e.g., Ephesians 4:13.
3419. See e.g., Ephesians 5:8.
3420. See e.g., Ephesians 5:14.
3421. Goring, s.v. "Sacred Marriage."

3422. See e.g., Ephesians 5:31-32.
3423. Shinn, p. 26.
3424. Davidson, p. 114.
3425. A. Pike, p. 404.
3426. See e.g., Colossians 1:15.
3427. See e.g., 1 Thessalonians 4:16. Here Paul displays a belief in archangels, which are considered minor or secondary gods and goddesses in Paganism.
3428. Spalding, Vol. 2, pp. 13-14; H. S. Lewis, TSDOJ, p. 90.
3429. See e.g., 1 Timothy 3:16. This doctrine has been firmly established by the Essenes' Dead Sea Scrolls, which reveal Jesus to have been a worldwide traveler who was knowledgeable in the religious doctrines of not only Rome, but Persia, Athens, and Alexandria as well. Potter, pp. 10, 52; Schweitzer, TQOTHJ, pp. 109-110; M. L. Prophet and E. C. Prophet, pp. xxx, 85, 126, 362.
3430. See e.g., 2 Timothy 1:14.
3431. Neil, TIOTNT, p. 161.
3432. Angus, p. 296.
3433. See e.g., Colossians 2:8.
3434. See e.g., 2 Timothy 2:18. In 2 Timothy 2:16-17 the "orthodox" Paul even names two Gnostic teachers, Hymenaeus and Philetus, whom he condemns.
3435. See e.g., Colossians 2:18.
3436. See e.g., Colossians 2:16-17.
3437. See e.g., Helms, passim; Strauss, TLOJCE, passim; L. M. Graham, passim; Frazier, FITOT, passim.
3438. For more on this topic see Seabrook, CBC, passim.
3439. Some have uncovered at least four separate portrayals of Paul in the New Testament. See e.g., Dewey, Hoover, McGaughy, and Schmidt, passim.
3440. Colossians 3:18. See also 1 Timothy 2:9-15.
3441. Galatians 3:28.
3442. See e.g., 1 Corinthians 7:1-40.
3443. See e.g., 1 Timothy 5:14. See also Ephesians 5:31-32; 1 Timothy 4:1-3.
3444. Romans 11:1; Galatians 1:13-14; Philippians 3:5-6.
3445. Titus 1:14.
3446. See e.g., 1 Thessalonians 2:14-16.
3447. 1 Corinthians 2:3.
3448. 2 Timothy 1:7.
3449. This biblical redaction process continues into the present day. See e.g., H. S. Lewis, TSDOJ, p. 153.
3450. The letters that were more or less written by Paul are: Romans, 1 Corinthians, 2 Corinthians, Galatians, and 1 Thessalonians. The disputed letters of Paul, but which are almost certainly forgeries, are: Ephesians, Philippians, Colossians, 2 Thessalonians, 1 Timothy, 2 Timothy, Titus, and Philemon. Definitely not by Paul: Hebrews.
3451. For more on John's Gnosticism, see Evans-Wentz, pp. 4, 217-218.
3452. Elder, p. 47.
3453. Matthew 19:34-36. These passages are contradicted by many others, e.g., Luke 2:14; Romans 5:1; Colossians 1:19-20.
3454. See e.g., Matthew 24:39-42.
3455. See Lindsay, passim; Walvoord, passim.
3456. Menzies, Vol. 9, p. 316.
3457. Brooke, pp. 13, 18.
3458. Tenney, s.v. "Pearl." See Matthew 13:45-46.
3459. Gaskell, s.v. "Pearl of Great Price."
3460. M. P. Hall, p. 52.
3461. Calvocoressi, s.v. "Peter."
3462. Gaskell, s.v. "Peter."
3463. 1 Corinthians 2:14.
3464. Matthew 16:22-23.
3465. See Job 37:21.
3466. Gregory, Vol. 3, pp. 251-252.

3467. See Matthew 16:18.
3468. Filson, p. 133.
3469. M. P. Hall, p. 25.
3470. B. G. Walker, TWEOMAS, s.v. "Peter, Saint."
3471. Filson, p. 133.
3472. J. L. McKenzie, s.v. "Romans, Epistle to the."
3473. Filson, p. 133.
3474. See Matthew 5:17. See also Goguel, Vol. 2, p. 585; Schweitzer, TQOTHJ, p. 17; Dunn, p. 105.
3475. See e.g., Parsons, pp. 276-277.
3476. B. G. Walker, TWEOMAS, s.v. "Peter, Saint."
3477. Calvocoressi, s.v. "Peter."
3478. Such noncanonical works include The Gospel of St. Peter, The Apocalypse of St. Peter, The Preaching of St. Peter, and The Acts of St. Peter. Farmer, s.v. "Peter (1)."
3479. Attwater, s.v. "Peter."
3480. Delaney, s.v. "Peter."
3481. Farmer, s.v. "Peter (1)."
3482. Farmer, s.v. "Peter (1)."
3483. Attwater, s.v. "Peter."
3484. See e.g., John 13:6-11, 36-38; 18:11.
3485. B. G. Walker, TWEOMAS, s.v. "Peter, Saint."
3486. Tripp, s.v. "Janus."
3487. M. P. Hall, p. 133.
3488. B. G. Walker, TWEOMAS, s.v. "Peter, Saint." St. Peter's Day was later moved to June 29, probably because of the obvious and discomforting fact that January 20 was the Feast of the god Janus, one of the Pagan key-holding deities on whom Peter's figure was based. See R. M. Levy, pp. 261-262.
3489. J. M. Robertson, PC, pp. 332-333.
3490. Cumont, TMOM, pp. 131-132.
3491. B. G. Walker, TWEOMAS, s.v. "Peter, Saint."
3492. Deuteronomy 32:18.
3493. Brownrigg, s.v. "Pharisees"; Tenney, s.v. "Pharisees." See John 10:30-33.
3494. Gaskell, s.v. "Pharisees."
3495. See e.g., Mark 4:11.
3496. Tenney, s.v. "Pilate."
3497. Gaskell, s.v. "Pilate, Pontius."
3498. John 5:2-9.
3499. Gaskell, s.v. "Pool of Bethesda."
3500. G. D. Young, s.v. "Prayer"; Tenney, s.v. "Prayer."
3501. Gaskell, s.v. "Prayer."
3502. Bushnell, pp. 186-187. Emphasis added.
3503. For more on the importance and power of prayer, see Seabrook, JATLOA, pp. 173-177.
3504. Ponder, p. 51.
3505. Jeremiah 33:3. Emphasis added.
3506. Job 22:27. Emphasis added.
3507. Luke 11:10. Emphasis added.
3508. See e.g., Luke 6:12. See also 1 Thessalonians 5:17.
3509. Doyle, TEOTU, p. 184.
3510. See e.g., G. D. Young, s.v. "Precious Stones."
3511. Galatians 5:22-23.
3512. Swedenborg, TAR, Vol. 1, pp. 166-167. Emphasis added.
3513. Revelation 21:19-20.
3514. See Fillmore, s.v. "Faculties."
3515. John 19:2-5.
3516. Gaskell, s.v. "Purple, Colour."
3517. J. P. Stuart, p. 16.
3518. Higgins, Vol. 1, pp. 150-151. Emphasis added.

3519. M. P. Hall, pp. 65-68; W. W. Westcott, pp. 11-15; Szekely, TEGOP, Vol. 1, pp. 48-49, passim.
3520. Genesis 9:8-17.
3521. Frazer, FITOT, pp. 46-152.
3522. Lasne and Gaultier, p. 142.
3523. Genesis 9:14.
3524. Jukes, p. 129. Emphasis added.
3525. Swedenborg, AC, Vol. 1, p. 420. Emphasis added.
3526. Böhme, p. 207. Emphasis added.
3527. Kingsford and Maitland, p. 147. Emphasis added.
3528. For example, Elijah raised the dead (1 Kings 17:17-24), as did Elisha (2 Kings 4:16-36), Peter (Acts 9:36-41), and Paul (Acts 20:7-12).
3529. John 3:1-21.
3530. Gaskell, s.v. "Rebirth."
3531. 2 Corinthians 5:17.
3532. Zondervan, s.v. "Redemption." See also Romans 6:4.
3533. Colossians 3:11.
3534. Gaskell, s.v. "Redeemer of the Soul."
3535. Shinn, p. 43.
3536. Job 19:25-27.
3537. Strauss, TOFATN, pp. 28-30. Emphasis added.
3538. Carus, TM, p. 615. Emphasis added.
3539. Tenney, s.v. "Redemption."
3540. Wahr, p. 23.
3541. Livingstone, s.v. "Emerson, Ralph Waldo."
3542. Greaves, p. 55.
3543. See Yogananda, TSCOC, Vol. 1, p. 244.
3544. Yogananda, TSCOC, Vol. 1, p. 10.
3545. Potter, p. 154.
3546. See A. Pike, p. 377.
3547. Baba, pp. 18-21.
3548. Bucke, p. 103.
3549. Mascaró, pp. 27-28.
3550. Matthew 23:27.
3551. Matthew 27:52-53.
3552. G. R. S. Mead, O, pp. 292-296. Emphasis added.
3553. See Fillmore, s.v. "Faculties."
3554. M. P. Hall, p. 35.
3555. Nath, Vol. 3, s.v. "Reincarnation." Emphasis added.
3556. Schopenhauer, Vol. 3, pp. 299, 300.
3557. E. D. Walker, p. 5.
3558. Seabrook, TGYC, pp. 27-48.
3559. See F. C. Grant, pp. 195-196.
3560. McClelland, s.v. "Metensomatosis."
3561. Matthew 16:13-14. Emphasis added.
3562. Matthew 26:52. This reincarnation passage deals with the ancient Law of Karma, which states that those who commit violence will have violence committed against them in a future lifetime.
3563. John 3:3-8. Emphasis added.
3564. John 8:56-58. Emphasis added.
3565. John 9:1-3. Again, this story concerns the Law of Karma and how if affects the Soul from incarnation to incarnation.
3566. John 10:9. Emphasis added. The "door" here is the portal between the spiritual world and the material world, and the phrase "go in and out" refers to reincarnation: involution (going *in* the gate of the earth plane) and evolution (going back *out* the gate to Heaven).
3567. John 14:1-3. Emphasis added.
3568. Malachi 4:5.

3569. Matthew 11:11-15. Emphasis added.
3570. Matthew 17:10-13. Emphasis added.
3571. Luke 1:13-17. Emphasis added.
3572. Romans 9:10-14. Emphasis added.
3573. Ephesians 1:4. Emphasis added.
3574. Hebrews 2:2-3. Emphasis added.
3575. See Potter, pp. 24, 99.
3576. Revelation 3:12.
3577. My interpretation.
3578. Genesis 9:6. Emphasis added.
3579. Deuteronomy 31:2. Emphasis added. "Go out and come in" refers to involution (incarnation) and evolution (resurrection), while the "Jordan" River here signifies the border between Heaven and earth.
3580. Jeremiah 1:5-6. Emphasis added.
3581. Job 33:27-30. Emphasis added.
3582. Proverbs 8:22-31. Emphasis added. This example, in particular, deals with the doctrine of the preexistence of the Soul.
3583. Obadiah 1:15. Emphasis added.
3584. See Proverbs 23:7.
3585. Greaves, p. 9.
3586. See Head and Cranston, passim.
3587. Yogananda, TSCOC, Vol. 1, p. 37.
3588. Greaves, p. 9.
3589. See H. S. Lewis, TSDOJ, p. 219.
3590. Leishman, OAB, pp. 46-47.
3591. Geddes MacGregor, p. 57.
3592. E. C. Prophet and E. L. Prophet, p. 222.
3593. McClelland, s.v. "Church Council of 553."
3594. Head and Cranston, pp. 51, 52.
3595. M. L. Prophet and E. C. Prophet, pp. 38, 138.
3596. Greaves, p. 10.
3597. Tingley, p. 515.
3598. Yogananda, TSCOC, Vol. 1, p. 148.
3599. John 1:9.
3600. Spalding, Vol. 4, p. 115.
3601. Watts, TWOZ, p. 58.
3602. 1 Corinthians 15:31. See also Philippians 1:21.
3603. Zondervan, s.v. "Resurrection."
3604. H. S. Lewis, TSDOJ, p. 185.
3605. Kingsford and Maitland, p. 26; A. Pike, pp. 406-407, 430, 594-595.
3606. Potter, p. 9.
3607. Spalding, Vol. 5, p. 104.
3608. Mackey, p. 354, s.v. "Resurrection."
3609. M. P. Hall, pp. 36, 48.
3610. Liddon, pp. 259, 263-264. Emphasis added.
3611. R. M. Jones, pp. 496-497. Emphasis added.
3612. Kingsford and Maitland, p. 227.
3613. Chatterjee, p. 598. Emphasis added.
3614. G. R. S. Mead, O, pp. 185-186. Emphasis added.
3615. Gulliver, p. 949.
3616. Sayce, pp. 164-165.
3617. Pagels, TGG, p. 12.
3618. A. Pike, pp. 594-595.
3619. Sheehan, p. 160.
3620. Mark 16:6. See Sheehan p. 133.
3621. Zondervan, s.v. "Revelation."

3622. Gaskell, s.v. "Revelation."
3623. Matthew 16:13-17. Emphasis added. We will note here that these same words as recorded in John 6:69, "thou art the Christ, the Son of the living God," are not original. They are "scribal assimilations," that is, intrusive additions by later orthodox editors. The original reading was: "Thou are the holy one of God." Neill, TIOTNT, pp. 112-113.
3624. Galatians 1:11-16. Emphasis added.
3625. Ladd, Vol. 2, pp. 419, 420, 421. Emphasis added.
3626. See 2 Corinthians 3:12-16.
3627. De Bunsen, p. 51.
3628. Jeremiah 31:33. Emphasis added. See also Job 38:36; Psalms 51:6; Proverbs 20:27.
3629. Filson, p. 44.
3630. G. D. Young, s.v. "Righteousness."
3631. See e.g., Spalding, Vol. 2, pp. 69-71.
3632. Barbanell, p. 152.
3633. See Proverbs 23:7.
3634. Proverbs 12:5.
3635. W. Smith, s.v. "River."
3636. Budge, TEHAH, Vol. 3, p. 124.
3637. Genesis 2:9-10.
3638. Psalms 65:9.
3639. Psalms 46:4.
3640. Maclaren, SPIM, pp. 47-48. Emphasis added.
3641. Zondervan, s.v. "Rock."
3642. See Matthew 16:18.
3643. B. G. Walker, TWEOMAS, s.v. "Peter, Saint."
3644. See e.g., Psalms 18:2, 31; Matthew 16:18; 21:42; 1 Corinthians 3:11.
3645. Luke 17:21.
3646. Hebrews 8:2. My paraphrasal. See also Hebrews 9:11.
3647. Galatians 5:22-23.
3648. Isaiah 33:13-19.
3649. Genesis 49:24.
3650. Deuteronomy 32.
3651. Zechariah 3:9.
3652. 1 Peter 2:4-5; 1 Corinthians 10:4. In the first case the Greek word is *lithos*; in the second *petra*. (Robertson's note).
3653. Matthew 16:18.
3654. J. M. Robertson, PC, pp. 316-318. Emphasis added.
3655. 1 Corinthians 10:1-4.
3656. John 1:9.
3657. Genesis 1:27.
3658. Deuteronomy 32:18.
3659. Tenney, s.v. "Sacrament."
3660. Colossians 3:11.
3661. B. G. Walker, TWEOMAS, s.v. "Hieros Gamos."
3662. John 10:34.
3663. A. Pike, p. 404.
3664. Goguel, Vol. 2, pp. 460-462.
3665. H. S. Lewis, TSDOJ, pp. 118-119.
3666. Evans-Wentz, p. 119.
3667. Murray, p. 86.
3668. Ide, YW, p. 31. My paraphrasal.
3669. Angus, p. 209. For more on how Orphism influenced Christianity, see Angus, pp. 150-156.
3670. Groton, p. x. Emphasis added.
3671. Carpenter, pp. 51-52.
3672. Goguel, Vol. 2, p. 328.

3673. Carpenter, pp. 52-53.
3674. Pfleiderer, TECCOC, pp. 129-133. Emphasis added.
3675. R. M. Jones, pp. 121-122. Emphasis added.
3676. Budge, TBOTD, Vol. 1, pp. 43-44. Emphasis added.
3677. Pfleiderer, TECCOC, p. 169. Emphasis added.
3678. Freud, MAM, p. 111.
3679. G. D. Young, s.v. "Salvation, Application of."
3680. See Seabrook, JATLOA, pp. 415-418.
3681. Luke 3:6. See also Romans 10:13; Acts 2:17; 1 Timothy 2:4; 2 Peter 3:9.
3682. See Seabrook, JATLOA, pp. 29, 75, 235-237, 324.
3683. See e.g., Genesis 8:21; Job 15:14; Psalms 14:2-3; 51:5; Proverbs 22:15; Ecclesiastes 9:3; Jeremiah 17:9; Romans 5:12; 6:23; 1 Corinthians 15:22; Ephesians 2:1-3. Some Christian groups attribute original sin to a pre-Adamic event in which angelic beings rebelled against God. See e.g., 2 Peter 2:4; Jude 6. Despite all the modern day scripture-twisting and unenlightened translating that has gone on, none of these passages actually say anything about the doctrine of "original sin." Indeed, the concept of hereditary sin being transmitted genetically to the entire human race is completely absent from both the Old and the New Testaments. Why? Because the idea was invented by the early Catholic Church out of "ecclesiastical necessity" hundreds of years after the writing of the New Testament. It was then later artificially linked to the above scriptures.
3684. Freud, MAM, p. 110.
3685. Romans 5:11.
3686. H. S. Lewis, TSDOJ, pp. 186-188.
3687. Note that this does not mean that our Lower Selves cannot sin. Only that our Higher Selves are not "born in sin"; that they are not "tainted" with the "sin of Adam." The Higher Self is, in other words, eternally pure and unsullied, even by life on earth.
3688. Bucke, p. 61.
3689. See Genesis 1:27.
3690. H. S. Lewis, TSDOJ, pp. 186-187.
3691. 1 Peter 3:4.
3692. Channing, p. 301.
3693. See Burtt, p. 124.
3694. Luke 3:6. See also Romans 10:13; Acts 2:17; 2 Peter 3:9.
3695. 1 Timothy 2:4.
3696. My paraphrasal of Acts 2:17.
3697. 2 Peter 3:9.
3698. See Romans 11:29.
3699. Mark 11:24. For more on the topic of the Laws of Karma and Reciprocity or Attraction, see Seabrook, JATLOA, passim; Seabrook, TBATLOA, passim.
3700. Genesis 1:26-27. See also 2 Corinthians 3:18.
3701. Barbanell, p. 152.
3702. Colossians 3:11.
3703. Isaiah 64:6.
3704. John 17:20-23.
3705. John 10:34.
3706. 1 John 4:8, 16.
3707. See e.g., Proverbs 1:20; Malachi 3:20; Luke 19:40; John 1:1-3, 9; 4:24; 1 Corinthians 10:4; Colossians 1:17; 6:33; Hebrews 12:29; 1 John 1:5; 4:8; Revelation 21:1.
3708. Genesis 1:27.
3709. Matthew 5:48.
3710. Luke 19:9. This is not to say that Jesus did not have a plan of salvation. He certainly did, and He preached almost nothing else but this plan—which He called "the mystery of Kingdom of God" (Mark 4:11)—during his final years.
3711. See J. G. Jackson, CBC, p. 122.
3712. The Aramaic version of Luke 19:9 reads: "Jesus said to him, 'Today *life* has come to this house, because he also is a son of Abraham.'"
3713. Maclaren, SPETTR, pp. 150-151. Emphasis added.

3714. See Hoeller, p. 114.
3715. Gaskell, s.v. "Salvation."
3716. Mascaró, p. 16.
3717. See Matthew 27:46.
3718. G. R. S. Mead, THOJ, pp. 20-30.
3719. See Apocalypse of Peter 83:1-3. See also Pagels, TGG, p. 87.
3720. Parker, p. 33. Emphasis added.
3721. Sheehan, pp. 69-71.
3722. Zondervan, s.v. "Satan."
3723. Matthew 4:1.
3724. Revelation 12:9-10.
3725. 1 Peter 5:8.
3726. Matthew 12:24.
3727. 2 Corinthians 6:15.
3728. Revelation 12:9.
3729. Revelation 12:9.
3730. Matthew 13:19, 38.
3731. John 8:44.
3732. 2 Corinthians 4:4.
3733. John 8:44.
3734. Revelation 12:9.
3735. Ephesians 2:2.
3736. John 12:31.
3737. Matthew 4:5.
3738. Shinn, p. 18.
3739. See Burtt, pp. 174, 195, 198.
3740. 2 Corinthians 4:4.
3741. Kelly, pp. 86-87.
3742. Pagels, TGG, pp. 147-148.
3743. Chernin, p. 165.
3744. Lamsa, IITBE, p. 57; Watts, G, p. 33.
3745. Curtiss and Curtiss, TKTTU, p. 291.
3746. B. G. Walker, TWEOMAS, s.v. "Satan."
3747. Hopfe, p. 266.
3748. Blavatsky, pp. 99-100.
3749. See L. M. Graham, pp. 18, 55, 57.
3750. See e.g., Ankerberg and Weldon, p. 27. The centuries old LDS doctrine of the brotherhood of Jesus and Satan has been preached since the Church's founding, as the official writings of numerous Mormon authorities reveal. Among them: Brigham Young, Spencer W. Kimball, George Q. Cannon, John A. Widtsoe, James E. Talmage, Neal A. Maxwell, and Bruce R. McConkie, to name but a few.
3751. Ide, YW, p. 17; L. M. Graham, p. 57.
3752. Isaiah 45:7.
3753. LaVey, TSR, p. 21.
3754. See 1 John 5:7.
3755. Romans 3:23.
3756. See Seabrook, JATLOA, passim; Seabrook, TBATLOA, passim.
3757. See Ponder, pp. 80-83.
3758. Matthew 5:39.
3759. A. Pike, p. 102.
3760. A. Pike, p. 102.
3761. Zondervan, s.v. "Saviour"; Tenney, s.v. "Saviour."
3762. See e.g., Titus 1:4; 2:13; 3:6; 2 Timothy 1:10; 2 Peter 1:1; 1 John 4:10.
3763. See e.g., Psalms 44:3,7; Isaiah 43:11; 45:21; 60:16; Jeremiah 14:8; Hosea 13:4.
3764. John 5:30-31; 8:28; 12:44-49; 14:10, 12; 28; 16:10, 16. See also Mark 3:11-12.
3765. See e.g., Judges 3:9-15; 2 Kings 13:5; Nehemiah 9:27, Obadiah 21.

3766. Mystically speaking, we are each a miniature Sun "lording" over our own miniature solar system. See e.g., Spalding, Vol. 5, p. 44.
3767. Malachi 4:2. See Dupuis, pp. 215-299.
3768. Ferguson, p. 150. See also Doane, pp. 507, 578, 588.
3769. Gaskell, s.v. "Saviours, The Twelve."
3770. M. P. Hall, p. 183.
3771. Luke 17:21.
3772. Bucke, p. 5.
3773. Doyle, TEOTU, p. 31; James, p. 47. In Christianity this concept first appeared in the writings of one Marcion (not Marcion of Sinope), an unknown eyewitness of the martyrdom of Polycarp around A.D. 155. See also Staniforth, p. 153.
3774. A. Pike, pp. 392-393.
3775. Another occult tradition, deriving from the ancient Mystery Schools, holds that the second "birth" of the twice-born experience refers to spiritual rebirth, the complete transformation that one goes through when attaining Cosmic Consciousness or Christ Consciousness, which Jesus called being "born again." See Eliade, Y, pp. 6, 145, 272-273.
3776. M. P. Hall, p. 92.
3777. Hicks, pp. 21,31.
3778. G. R. S. Mead, PS, pp. 10-11.
3779. To this day Buddhists consider Jesus a great yogi and Bodhisattva. See Evans-Wentz, p. 26.
3780. Burtt, pp. 125, 133-134.
3781. The Bhagavad Gita 4:8-9.
3782. Hoeller, p. 47.
3783. Colossian 3:11.
3784. Genesis 1:27.
3785. J. G. Jackson, CBC, pp. 192, 193, 199, 200.
3786. Seabrook, CBC, pp. 80-81; A. Pike, p. 277; Guignebert, pp. 182-185; Steiger, IMSIAF, pp. 145-146.
3787. See e.g., Deuteronomy 29:4; Ezekiel 12:2; Matthew 13:15-16; Ephesians 1:18.
3788. Spalding, Vol. 5, p. 129.
3789. Tenney, s.v. "Second Coming of Christ, The."
3790. G. D. Young, s.v. "Christ."
3791. 1 Thessalonians 3:13; 5:23.
3792. Philippians 3:20-21.
3793. 1 Corinthians 15:51-58.
3794. See Acts 1:11; Romans 8:19-23; 1 Corinthians 15:23-28; Ephesians 1:14.
3795. Luke 21:32.
3796. See Goodspeed, HCTB, pp. 69-71.
3797. John 18:36.
3798. Spalding, Vol. 1, p. 150.
3799. Colossians 3:11.
3800. M. L. Prophet and E. C. Prophet, pp. 227-228.
3801. See Yogananda, TSCOC, passim.
3802. G. D. Young, s.v. "Devil."
3803. Hoeller, p. 150.
3804. Blavatsky, pp. 99-100.
3805. A. Pike, p. 841.
3806. Hoeller, 74.
3807. L. M. Graham, pp. 18, 55.
3808. Isaiah 14:12.
3809. Revelation 22:16.
3810. Colossians 3:11.
3811. Job 38:7.
3812. Isaiah 45:7.
3813. 2 Corinthians 11:14.
3814. John 1:9. See Besant and Leadbetter, p. 295.

3815. B. G. Walker, TWEOMAS, s.v. "Serpent."
3816. Guirand, p. 72.
3817. Blavatsky, pp. 99-100.
3818. Daraul, p. 95.
3819. L. M. Graham, pp. 57-58.
3820. Hodson, Vol. 1, pp. 121-128.
3821. Cirlot, s.v. "Serpent." See also Yogananda, TSCOC, Vol. 1, p. 109.
3822. Revelation 1:4, 11, 20.
3823. 2 Kings 18:4; Numbers 21:8.
3824. B. G. Walker, TWEOMAS, s.v. "Serpent."
3825. See Potter, pp. 24, 90.
3826. This would make John some 1,000 years old. Steiger, IMSIAF, p. 190.
3827. Watts, MARIC, pp. 79, 196-198.
3828. John 3:14.
3829. Cirlot, s.v. "Serpent."
3830. Cirlot, s.v. "Serpent."
3831. Yogananda, TSCOC, Vol. 1, pp. 80-88; M. L. Prophet and E. C. Prophet, pp. xxx, 85, 126, 362; Potter, pp. 10, 19, 52, 147; Spalding, passim; Schweitzer, TQOTHJ, pp. 109-110; H. S. Lewis, TSDOJ, p. 90.
3832. Matthew 10:16. Emphasis added.
3833. Isaiah 45:7.
3834. See A. Pike, p. 377.
3835. John 12:31-32.
3836. John 20:11-12.
3837. Genesis 3.
3838. Revelation 12:9; 20:2.
3839. Revelation 22:16.
3840. John 12:31-32.
3841. Isaiah 14:12.
3842. Job 38:7.
3843. Isaiah 45:7.
3844. Evans-Wentz, pp. 4, 217-218.
3845. Renan, p. 20.
3846. Van Etten, p. 167.
3847. Farmer, s.v. "John the Apostle"; Metford, s.v. "Serpent."
3848. Cirlot, s.v. "Serpent."
3849. J. Campbell, TOMTT, p. 254.
3850. Revelation 1:16.
3851. See Trench, passim.
3852. Yogananda, TSCOC, Vol. 1, p. 109.
3853. M. P. Hall, p. 186.
3854. Spalding, Vol. 3, pp. 35-36.
3855. Yogananda, AOAY, p. 184.
3856. 1 Peter 5:4.
3857. 1 Corinthians 9:25. See M. P. Hall, pp. 93-94.
3858. See e.g., Exodus 7:9; Numbers 17:10.
3859. See e.g., Exodus 4:2.
3860. A. Pike, p. 422.
3861. See e.g., Genesis 2:9; Revelations 2:7; 22:2, 14.
3862. M. L. Prophet and E. C. Prophet, p. 174.
3863. Farrell and Presser, s.v. "Six."
3864. Walker, TWDOSASO, p. 68.
3865. Walker, TWDOSASO, p. 69.
3866. Biedermann, s.v. "Six."
3867. See Revelation 13:8.

3868. M. P. Hall, pp. 78, 121.
3869. See e.g., Genesis 2:1; 1 Chronicles 16:26; Psalms 68:33; Ephesians 3:10; 4:9-10; Hebrews 1:10; 2 Peter 3:13; Revelation 12:12. See also the Gnostic-Christian documents, On the Origin of the World and also The Apocalypse of Paul, in which the Seven Heavens are frequently and overtly referred to.
3870. See e.g., Philippians 2:10. Paul may be alluding to the seven levels of Hell here.
3871. 2 Corinthians 12:2.
3872. Ancient Hebrew women wore crescent Moon amulets in honor of the great Hebrew Mother-Goddess Ashtoreth (Asherah). See e.g., Isaiah 3:18. See also Finegan, Vol. 1, pp. 167-168, 173; Pritchard, passim.
3873. One of these, the great Temple of the Pagan goddess Diana (Artemis) at Ephesus, is alluded to in Acts 19:27, 35.
3874. The seven deadly sins are: pride, avarice, envy, wrath, lust, gluttony, and sloth.
3875. The seven virtues are: humility, generosity, love, kindness, chastity, temperance, and zeal.
3876. Genesis 2:2-3; Hebrews 4:4.
3877. Revelation 1:4, 11, 20. In mystical Christianity the "seven churches" of Revelation are considered an allegory of the seven chakras found along the human spine, referred to in Eastern literature as the "seven lotuses of light."
3878. In accordance with ancient Jewish and Christian numerology, the number seven, along with its numerological corollaries (e.g., 70, 77, 70,000, etc.), appears over 500 times in the Bible. Jesus, as just one example, appointed 70 additional Disciples (Luke 10:1, 17), and taught that we are to forgive someone not seven times, but "seventy times seven"; in other words, without end. (Matthew 18:22.)
3879. A. Pike, p. 10.
3880. Seabrook, JATLOA, pp. 354-355.
3881. B. G. Walker, TWEOMAS, s.v. "Hieros Gamos."
3882. See Shinn, p. 26.
3883. A. Pike, p. 404.
3884. Spalding, Vol. 4, p. 81.
3885. See e.g., Dowling, Sections 6 and 7.
3886. Mark 1:14.
3887. Yogananda, TSCOC, Vol. 1, pp. xxxiii, 56.
3888. Potter, pp. 77-78, 138-139.
3889. Spalding, Vol. 2, p. 106; H. S. Lewis, TSDOJ, p. 90; M. L. Prophet and E. C. Prophet, pp. xxx, 85, 126, 362.
3890. M. L. Prophet and E. C. Prophet, pp. xxx, 85, 126, 362.
3891. Potter, p. 147.
3892. Yogananda, TSCOC, Vol. 1, p. 56.
3893. M. P. Hall, p. 178.
3894. McCannon, p. 214.
3895. Notovitch, p. 91; Yogananda, TSCOC, Vol. 1, pp. 80-85.
3896. Notovitch, pp. 13-95.
3897. Yogananda, TSCOC, Vol. 1, pp. 80-81.
3898. Yogananda, TSCOC, Vol. 1, pp. 81-82. See also Faber-Kaiser, passim.
3899. Notovitch, p. 51.
3900. Notovitch, pp. 107-123.
3901. Yogananda, TSCOC, pp. 87-88.
3902. Potter, p. 21.
3903. McCannon, pp. 214-216; Schweitzer, TQOTHJ, pp. 291-293, 327.
3904. Matthew 24:14. Emphasis added.
3905. Mark 13:10. Emphasis added.
3906. Luke 24:47. Emphasis added.
3907. John 9:5. Emphasis added.
3908. 1 Timothy 3:16. Emphasis added.
3909. Bucke, p. 124.
3910. Matthew 16:17.
3911. Müller, TU, p. 92.
3912. Mark 4:12.

3913. The Bhagavad Gita 9:29.
3914. John 14:20.
3915. The Bhagavad Gita 9:31.
3916. John 6:47.
3917. The Bhagavad Gita 4:16.
3918. John 8:32.
3919. The Bhagavad Gita 6:19.
3920. Matthew 5:16.
3921. The Bhagavad Gita 7:6; 10:20.
3922. Revelation 22:13.
3923. The Bhagavad Gita 7:8.
3924. John 7:38.
3925. The Bhagavad Gita 7:13.
3926. Matthew 28:20.
3927. The Bhagavad Gita 8:9-10.
3928. Matthew 6:22-23.
3929. The Bhagavad Gita 9:2.
3930. Matthew 11:28-30.
3931. The Bhagavad Gita 9:18-19.
3932. John 14:6.
3933. The Bhagavad Gita 9:26.
3934. Mark 12: 41-44.
3935. The Bhagavad Gita 10:26.
3936. Revelation 2:7.
3937. The Bhagavad Gita 10:38.
3938. Mark 4:11.
3939. The Bhagavad Gita 13:9.
3940. Luke 14:26.
3941. The Bhagavad Gita 13:15.
3942. John 4:24.
3943. The Bhagavad Gita 13:28.
3944. John 10:34.
3945. See Yogananda, TSCOC, Vol. 1, p. xxv.
3946. Trollope, Vol. 1, p. 486.
3947. Schonfield, TPP, pp. 46-47.
3948. See e.g., Luke 1:1-2; John 21:24.
3949. Goguel, Vol. 2, p. 254.
3950. Roddy and Sellier, p. 47.
3951. John 21:25.
3952. Lamsa, IITBE, p. 57.
3953. Watts, G, p. 33.
3954. 1 John 4:6.
3955. Spalding, Vol. 4, p. 137.
3956. See e.g., Luke 18:9-14.
3957. See e.g., John 5:14; 8:11; Luke 18:42.
3958. One exception to this is Matthew 15:18-19.
3959. See Luke 15:11-32.
3960. John 4.
3961. H. S. Lewis, TSDOJ, pp. 220-222.
3962. See e.g., Romans 5:6-9. The doctrine of "original sin" was founded by the Catholic Church upon a "misreading" of Genesis 3:1-24, and also upon Paul's infamous comment: "Wherefore, as by one man [namely Adam] sin entered into the world, and death by sin; and so death passed upon all men, for that all have sinned" (Romans 5:12). Actually, the original meaning here has been greatly perverted over the centuries. What Paul is saying in this particular passage is merely that because "sin is death" (Romans 6:23), and because both sin (Romans 3:23) and death are universal (Isaiah 40:6), then all people must be sinners, nothing more. In fact,

in Romans 5:10, Paul wholly contradicts what would later become the idea of "original sin," which states that we must "pay" for the sins of Adam and Eve: "For if, when we were enemies, we were reconciled to God by the death of his Son, much more, being reconciled, we shall be saved by his life."
3963. Genesis 1:27.
3964. Colossians 3:11.
3965. Spalding, Vol. 1, p. 84.
3966. Luke 3:6. See also Romans 10:13; Acts 2:17; 2 Peter 3:9.
3967. Yogananda, TSCOC, Vol. 1, p. 276.
3968. John 5:48.
3969. Comay, s.v. "Solomon."
3970. Evans-Wentz, p. 46.
3971. B. G. Walker, TWEOMAS, s.v. "Solomon and Sheba."
3972. M. P. Hall, p. 91.
3973. M. P. Hall, p. 50.
3974. W. W. Westcott, pp. 30, 31.
3975. M. P. Hall, p. 175.
3976. G. D. Young, s.v. "God."
3977. See Mark 1:4-5, 9-11.
3978. John 3:16.
3979. Sheehan, p. 25.
3980. See e.g., Matthew 27:54 (this scripture is, of course, absent from the Gospel of Q). According to this theory, other "Son of God" passages, such as John 10:36 (also missing from Q), must be late interpolations as well, added after Jesus' death, but before the writing of the Codex Sinaiticus in the middle of the 4th Century.
3981. Baigent and Leight, p. 66.
3982. See Kertzer, pp. 38-39.
3983. John 1:12; Romans 8:14; Philippians 2:15; 1 John 3:1-2.
3984. Galatians 1:16.
3985. John 20:17.
3986. John 12:32; 14:20; 15:4; 17:21-23, 26; Colossians 1:27; 3:10-11; Romans 8:10; 1 Corinthians 6:15, 17; 2 Corinthians 5:16; 13:3, 5; Galatians 1:16; 2:20; 4:19; Ephesians 3:14-17; Philippians 1:20; 2:5; 1 Peter 1:11; 1 John 2:27; 3:24; 4:4.
3987. Yogananda, TSCOC, Vol. 1, pp. 201, 273.
3988. Malachi 4:2.
3989. H. S. Lewis, TSDOJ, p. 218; Dowley, p. 31.
3990. M. P. Hall, pp. 35-36.
3991. See Acts 20:7. Thus in Luke Jesus is shown "rising" from the dead on "the first day of the week," that is, Sunday. Luke 24:1.
3992. Seabrook, CBC, p. 68; Dowley, pp. 139-142.
3993. J. G. Jackson, CBC, p. 166; M. P. Hall, p. 178.
3994. Ferguson, p. 150.
3995. J. M. Robertson, p. 237.
3996. Metford, s.v. "Panthera."
3997. Bruce, p. 191.
3998. M. P. Hall, p. 178.
3999. J. G. Jackson, CBC, p. 166.
4000. Doane, p. 507.
4001. Jeremiah 31:33. See also Job 38:36; Psalms 51:6; Proverbs 20:27.
4002. Genesis 1:27.
4003. John 1:12; Romans 8:14; 1 John 3:1-2.
4004. Acts 11:26.
4005. Burtt, p. 154.
4006. Pfleiderer, TDOC, p. 152.
4007. Underhill, TLOTS, p. 98.
4008. Tenney, s.v. "Son of Man."
4009. Spivey and Smith, p. 239.

4010. Zondervan, s.v. "Son of Man."
4011. Burtt, p. 73.
4012. See e.g., Ezekiel 3:4-5.
4013. See e.g., Mark 8:38. Neill, WWKAJ, p. 70.
4014. Psalms 8:4-6.
4015. Schweitzer, TQOTHJ, pp. 91, 134.
4016. Schonfield, TPP, p. 75.
4017. Spivey and Smith, p. 238.
4018. Neill, WWKAJ, p. 70.
4019. See e.g., Ezekiel 2:1, passim.
4020. J. L. McKenzie, s.v. "Adam."
4021. See my book *Jesus and the Gospel of Q*, passim.
4022. See Eusebius' *History of the Church*, 3:39. See also Filson, p. 48; Neil, TIOTNT, p. 126; Kümmel, p. 55.
4023. See Acts 20:35.
4024. The one known reference Jesus makes to this phrase, John 10:36, is an obvious late priestly interpolation, for in all actuality, He never utters this statement anywhere else in the New Testament. Thus, we have yet another example of a self-reflexive passage artificially inserted by the Catholic Church to emphasize the divinity of Jesus.
4025. See Matthew 8:20 (from the first layer, known as Q1, of the Gospel of Q). Seabrook, JATGOQ, passim.
4026. Daniel 7:13-14.
4027. John 12:32; 14:20; 15:4; 17:21-23, 26; Colossians 1:27; 3:10-11; Romans 8:10; 1 Corinthians 6:15, 17; 2 Corinthians 5:16; 13:3, 5; Galatians 1:16; 2:20; 4:19; Ephesians 3:14-17; Philippians 1:20; 2:5; 1 Peter 1:11; 1 John 2:27; 3:24; 4:4.
4028. Schweitzer, TQOTHJ, p. 277.
4029. Schonfield, TPP, p. 213.
4030. Isaiah 51:12.
4031. Ezekiel 2:1-8.
4032. Daniel 8:17.
4033. Kloppenborg, TFOQ, pp. 207-208.
4034. Goguel, Vol. 2, p. 282.
4035. See Mark 3:28-29.
4036. Zondervan, s.v. "Son of Man."
4037. Potter, pp. 81-83.
4038. Whale, p. 115.
4039. Gordon, s.v. "Christianity."
4040. G. E. Kirk, p. 8.
4041. Hoeller, p. 43.
4042. See Townsend, passim; Kertzer, pp. 38-39.
4043. See e.g., Matthew 16:16; John 1:41; 1 John 5:1.
4044. Colossians 1:27; 3:11. See also Romans 8:10; 1 Corinthians 6:15, 17; 2 Corinthians 5:16; 13:3, 5.
4045. Philippians 2:7-8. Emphasis added.
4046. Romans 8:3. Emphasis added.
4047. 1 Corinthians 15:45.
4048. See the Hebrew "Adam" in Genesis 2:19.
4049. Mark 6:3; Matthew 13:55.
4050. Schweitzer, TQOTHJ, p. 212.
4051. See e.g., Mark 2:1; 9:33.
4052. Seabrook, JATLOA, pp. 262-263. Note: 17th-Century Quakers held that they lived and learned "in the School of Christ." See Van Etten, p. 168.
4053. Dowling, 87:11-12; 103:1. Emphasis added. See also Dowling, 90:16; 102:1; 119:1; 174:9.
4054. Mark 2:1 (ISV).
4055. Roddy and Sellier, p. 45.
4056. John 2-4.
4057. See e.g., Eyerly, pp. 120-126.
4058. John 6:9. See Schweitzer, TQOTHJ, pp. 323-324.

4059. Schaberg, pp. 154-155. See also, Leloup, p. 66, passim.
4060. Baigent, Leigh, and Lincoln, HBHG, pp. 313-314.
4061. Potter, p. 130.
4062. See Hebrews 3:3; 7:24; 10:12.
4063. Boer, p. 72.
4064. See Mark 1:4-5, 9-11.
4065. See Acts 13:33.
4066. See Matthew 3:13-17. An obvious interpolation occurs here in Matthew concerning John the Baptist and Jesus' baptism. After acknowledging Jesus early on in Chapter 3, much later, in Chapter 11, John does not recognize Jesus and asks Him to identify Himself. Matthew 11:1-4. The unknown author(s) of Matthew confused their various sources then failed to recheck their work.
4067. See Luke 3:16-17, 21-22.
4068. See John 1:19-34.
4069. See e.g., Ezekiel 2:1, passim. The phrase Son of Man should actually be written, "Son of Adam," or even more correctly, "son of adam," for here *adam* is used as a Hebrew noun for "man" (related to the Hebrew *damah*, "soil," "dust," "earth"). In the New Testament "man" is from the Greek word *anthropos*. Thus throughout the four Gospels we find the phrase *huios* ("son") *tou* ("of") *anthropos* ("man"), literally meaning, I am the "son of a mortal man." Jesus, of course, used this phrase in its metaphysical sense: "I represent the ideal man, God perfected in humanity."
4070. Luke 22:66-70.
4071. Mark 12:35-37. Some non-Marcan scriptures corroborate this view. While Mary did not descend from David, her husband Joseph did. According to Matthew and Luke, however, Joseph was not Jesus' biological father. See e.g., the contradiction in Matthew 1:1, 20. Some early Christians sought to correct this idea, stating that Mary too, like Joseph, descended from David. See e.g., The Gospel of the Birth of Mary, 1:1.
4072. See e.g., 2 Samuel 7:12-13; Isaiah 9:7. See also Luke 1:32-33; Romans 1:3.
4073. Compare, e.g., Matthew 1:1-17 with Luke 3:23-38.
4074. See J. G. Jackson, CBC, p. 122.
4075. Potter, p. 117.
4076. A. Pike, p. 564.
4077. Again, see Matthew 3:13-17, where many believe we have overt biblical proof of Adoptionism.
4078. Throughout the centuries, countless Christians besides Paul of Samosata, many of them of high authority, have embraced Adoptionism, among them: Lucian, Theodotus of Byzantium, Arius, Artemon, Elipandus of Toledo, Bishop Felix of Urgel, Abelard, Folmar, and Luitolph. One Christian sect in particular, the 1st-Century Ebionites (the *original* Christians), were strong supporters of Adoptionism.
4079. Livingstone, s.v. "Paul of Samosata."
4080. Tritheism holds that God, Jesus, and the Holy Spirit are gods, each one distinct from the other.
4081. Luke 3:22.
4082. As noted, this Adoptionist passage in the Codex Bezae is from Luke 3:22, but the original is from Psalms 2:7 (cited in Hebrews 1:5; 5:5). See also Isaiah 42:1. In the Gospel of the Ebionites, 4:3-4, we find the same sentiment: "You are my beloved Son, in you I am well pleased. . . . I have this day begotten you." Adding to its validity as an original canonical saying, this specific wording, or something close to it, was quoted by a number of early Church Fathers as well, including Augustine, Clement, Origen, Epiphanius, and Justin.
4083. See e.g., Matthew 8:27; 26:72, 74; Mark 14:71; John 4:29; 9:11. Jesus' critics and enemies also viewed Him as a mortal human being. See e.g., Luke 23:4, 6, 14, 47; John 7:46; 9:16; 10:33; 11:47; 18:17, 29; 19:5.
4084. See John 1:12; Romans 8:14; Philippians 2:15; 1 John 3:1-2.
4085. See e.g., Matthew 8:20, 9:6; 10:23; 12:8; 18:11; 25:13; Mark 2:10, 28; 10:45; 14:62; Luke 6:5; 9:22; 11:30; 17:30; 19:10; 24:7; John 1:51; 3:14; 6:27; 8:28; 12:23; 13:31.
4086. Hoeller, p. 139.
4087. See e.g., John 8:40.
4088. See Goguel, Vol. 2, pp. 259-260.
4089. See Mark 6:3.
4090. H. Brown, pp. 47-48. Emphasis added.
4091. Sheehan, pp. 5-7.
4092. Sheehan, p. 187.
4093. Neill, TIOTNT, p. 283.
4094. Moltmann, p. 85.

4095. John 1:12; Romans 8:14; Philippians 2:15; 1 John 3:1-2.
4096. See A. Pike, p. 377.
4097. See e.g., Matthew 13:55; Luke 2:41, 48; 3:23; 4:22; John 1:45; 6:42; Hebrews 3:3; 7:24; 10:12.
4098. The Gospel of Mary, 8:15-21. My paraphrasal. Emphasis added.
4099. Luke 17:21.
4100. Gaskell, s.v. "Bethlehem."
4101. Yogananda, TSCOC, Vol. 2, p. 1587.
4102. Yogananda, TSCOC, Vol. 1, pp. 17, 26, 207.
4103. A. Pike, p. 524.
4104. Tenney, s.v. "Soul."
4105. Spalding, Vol. 5, p. 111.
4106. Elliott Coues, "Modern Miracles," *Light: A Journal of Psychical, Occult, and Mystical Research*, Vol. 9, August 31, 1899, pp. 419-423 (London, UK: Eclectic Publishing).
4107. See e.g., Doyle, TEOTU, p. 190.
4108. Doyle, TEOTU, p. 170.
4109. Emerson, WORWE, p. 596. Emphasis added.
4110. Gaskell, s.v. "Soul, Spirit, and Body"; "Soul (Middle Aspect)."
4111. Colossians 3:11.
4112. G. R. S. Mead, TGH, Vol. 3, pp. 78-79.
4113. 1 Thessalonians 5:23.
4114. A. Pike, p. 239.
4115. Bucke, p. 169.
4116. Tenney, s.v. "Spirit."
4117. 1 Thessalonians 5:23.
4118. Christie-Murray, pp. 39, 57.
4119. John 1:9.
4120. Baba, p. 17; Yogananda, TSCOC, Vol. 1, p. 14; Steiger, IMSIAF, pp. 129-130; S. Smith, pp. 56-66.
4121. See Daraul, pp. 228-229.
4122. M. P. Hall, p. 92; Evans-Wentz, pp. 22, 84.
4123. A. Pike, p. 57.
4124. Biedermann, s.v. "Triads."
4125. John 14:20.
4126. Colossians 3:11.
4127. M. P. Hall, p. 51.
4128. Mark and John skipped Jesus' Nativity altogether, a problem which I address in my other works.
4129. See e.g., Tenney, s.v. "Astronomy"; Zondervan, s.v. "Astronomy."
4130. J. G. Jackson, CBC, p. 64.
4131. Riedel, Tracy, and Moskowitz, p. 268.
4132. Calvocoressi, s.v. "Jesus."
4133. Schonfield, TJP, p. 45.
4134. Roddy and Sellier, pp. 18, 31.
4135. J. L. McKenzie, s.v. "Star." See Numbers 24:17.
4136. Postulated by the 14th-Century Franciscan friar William of Ockham: "The simplest answer is usually the correct one."
4137. Farrell and Presser, s.v. "Stars."
4138. Biedermann, s.v. "angel."
4139. See Matthew 1:3-16; Revelation 5:5.
4140. Colossians 3:11.
4141. Yogananda, TSCOC, Vol. 1, p. 60. See also Luke 17:21.
4142. Ezekiel 43:1-2. Emphasis added.
4143. A. Pike, pp. 842, 843.
4144. See Gaskell, s.v. "Star in the East."
4145. Matthew 10:24.
4146. For more on the phenomenon of the Holy Spirit, fingerprints, and identical twins, see Yogananda, TSCOC, Vol. 1, p. 363.

4147. See Matthew 16:19; Revelation 1:18.
4148. Seabrook, JATLOA, p. 15.
4149. G. D. Young, s.v. "Sun."
4150. Hodson, Vol. 1, p. 129.
4151. Neander, Vol. 1, p. 480.
4152. Lessa and Vogt, pp. 116-119.
4153. John 12:32; 14:20; 15:4; 17:21-23, 26; Colossians 1:27; Romans 8:10; 1 Corinthians 6:15, 17; 2 Corinthians 5:16; 13:3, 5; Galatians 1:16; 2:20; 4:19; Ephesians 3:14-17; Philippians 1:20; 2:5; 1 Peter 1:11; 1 John 2:27; 3:24; 4:4.
4154. Colossians 3:11.
4155. 2 Corinthians 6:16.
4156. Note that the German word for son is *sohn*.
4157. Mackey, pp. 26-27.
4158. Malachi 4:2.
4159. Revelation 1:16.
4160. John 8:12.
4161. John 12:46.
4162. John 12:36.
4163. See Revelation 5:5.
4164. Cumont, TMOM, pp. 2, 10, 101-102, 116, 118, 133.
4165. Dowley, p. 140.
4166. M. Grant, CTG, pp. 135-136; Dowley, pp. 31, 141.
4167. See Acts 20:7.
4168. The Golden Manual, p. 98.
4169. Higgins, Vol. 1, p. 782; Andrews, pp. 59-60.
4170. Revelation 12:1.
4171. See M. Grant, CTG, pp. 121-186.
4172. Romer, p. 231.
4173. Higgins, Vol. 1, p. 584.
4174. Ferguson, p. 150.
4175. P. Robinson, p. 152.
4176. See Angus, p. 168.
4177. See Potter, passim.
4178. Dowley, pp. 140-141.
4179. Titcomb, p. 107.
4180. Dupius, pp. 215-217. Emphasis added.
4181. Volney, pp. 164-169. Emphasis added.
4182. Matthew 1:16.
4183. Luke 3:23.
4184. John 12:32; 14:20; 15:4; 17:21-23, 26; Colossians 1:27; 3:10-11; Romans 8:10; 1 Corinthians 6:15, 17; 2 Corinthians 5:16; 13:3, 5; Galatians 1:16; 2:20; 4:19; Ephesians 3:14-17; Philippians 1:20; 2:5; 1 Peter 1:11; 1 John 2:27; 3:24; 4:4.
4185. Matthew 27:46. Standard orthodox translation: "My God, my God, why hast thou forsaken me?"
4186. Malachi 4:2.
4187. Not a single one of the numerous Christian dictionaries and encyclopedias I own, for example, possess an entry on the "Sun of Righteousness." One lone reference to Jesus as the Sun of Righteousness appears, however, in the margins of my King James Bible (at Malachi 4:2), where our Lord is referred to in the great mystical Christian tradition as "Christ the Light," and in connection with Isaiah 9:2.
4188. See e.g., Revelation 11:15.
4189. Colossians 3:11.
4190. Burtt, p. 135.
4191. Genesis 17:1; Exodus 3:14-15; Psalms 46:10; Mark 8:29; 14:61-62; Luke 22:70; John 6:35; 8:12, 23, 58; 9:5; 10:7-11, 30-39; 11:25; 12:26, 46; 13:13; 14:3, 6, 10-11, 20; 15:1; 17:10, 16.
4192. See e.g., Philippians 4:3; Revelation 3:5; 20:12-15.
4193. 1 John 5:7.

4194. Seabrook, JATLOA, p. 15.
4195. Potter, p. 154.
4196. Malachi 4:2.
4197. Schonfield, TPP, p. 209.
4198. See Eisenman and Wise, p. 275; Neill, TIOTNT, p. 303; Wise, Abegg, and Cook, p. 19; Vermes, pp. 54, 56-57, 65-66; Schonfield, SOTDSS, pp. 21, 31, 39, 97, 126; Shanks, pp. 21, 135; Burrows, passim.
4199. H. S. Lewis, TSDOJ, pp. 29-31.
4200. Ramm, p. 65; Baigent and Leigh, p. 65.
4201. Bilde, pp. 183-188.
4202. Schweitzer, TQOTHJ, p. 329. See also G. R. S. Mead, *Did Jesus Live 100 B.C.?* Thirty years after Jesus' death, another Jew named Jesus roamed throughout Jerusalem warning of punishment and destruction. In the year A.D. 62 he preached at the Feast of Tabernacles, after which he was flogged and brought before the Roman governor, who questioned and released him. Such figures were no doubt later confused and combined with the figure of Jesus of Nazareth. See Goguel, Vol. 2, p. 511; R. L. Fox, TUV, p. 287.
4203. Szekely, TETOZ, pp. 9-10.
4204. J. L. McKenzie, s.v. "Jesus Christ"; "Joshua." Both names mean "Yahweh is salvation."
4205. Springett, pp. 94-95.
4206. Baigent and Leigh, pp. 44, 56.
4207. Brewster, p. 39; Filson, pp. 153-154; Potter, pp. 77-78, 138-139, 155; Lamsa, IITBE, p. 86.
4208. Mark 1:14.
4209. Mark 1:1. For more on this topic, see Seabrook, JATLOA, passim; Seabrook, JATGOQ, passim; Seabrook, CBC, passim.
4210. Matthew 19:17; Mark 10:18.
4211. Colossians 3:11.
4212. 1 Corinthians 6:19; 2 Timothy 1:14.
4213. Dods, Vol. 1, p. 300.
4214. 1 Corinthians 3:16-17. Emphasis added.
4215. Emerson, p. 401.
4216. Vaughn, p. 112.
4217. Dorner, Vol. 1, pp. 114-115. Emphasis added.
4218. Vaughn, p. 112.
4219. A. Pike, pp. 458-462.
4220. Cirlot, s.v. "Tetramorphs."
4221. Farrell and Presser, s.v. "Tetramorph."
4222. M. P. Hall, p. 44.
4223. Cirlot, s.v. "Tetramorphs."
4224. King James' scribes translated "Holy of Holies" as "most holy place." See e.g., Exodus 26:34; Numbers 18:10; 2 Chronicles 4:22.
4225. M. P. Hall, p. 77.
4226. See e.g., Ezekiel 41:4.
4227. A. Pike, pp. 5, 61. See also p. 209.
4228. Curtiss and Curtiss, TKTTU, p. 140.
4229. Seabrook, CIAAIA, p. 76.
4230. Curtiss and Curtiss, TKTTU, pp. 142-143.
4231. Cirlot, s.v. "Tetramorphs."
4232. Cumont, TMOM, pp. 116-118.
4233. Budge, TBOTD, Vol. 1, pp. 29, 99. See also pp. lxxiii, 93.
4234. Seabrook, JATLOA, p. 404; M. P. Hall, p. 60.
4235. Budge TBOTD, Vol. 1, p. 29.
4236. Hart, s.v. "Sons of Horus."
4237. Budge, EM, pp. 89, 91.
4238. M. P. Hall, p. 60.
4239. Ezekiel 1:4-10. Emphasis added.
4240. A. Pike, p. 58.
4241. Genesis 2:10-14.

4242. M. P. Hall, pp. 125-128.
4243. A. Pike, p. 291.
4244. Ferguson, p. 150.
4245. John 19:19.
4246. Seabrook, JATLOA, pp. 436-437; M. P. Hall, p. 184.
4247. Colossians 3:11. For more on this topic, see my book *Christ Is All and In All*.
4248. A. Pike, pp. 409-410.
4249. M. P. Hall, p. 185; Kümmel, p. 197.
4250. Potter, pp. 24, 90, 127.
4251. Revelation 4:1-7. Emphasis added.
4252. Legge, Vol. 1 and Vol. 2, passim; Potter, p. 154.
4253. J. G. Jackson, CBC, p. 196.
4254. Köstenberger, Kellum, and Quarles, p. 8.
4255. Bruce, p. 23.
4256. Oxford Society, pp. 117-118; Köstenberger, Kellum, and Quarles, pp. 8, 17-20.
4257. Yogananda, TSCOC, Vol. 1, p. 69. See also Finegan, Vol. 2, p. 525.
4258. Schonfield, TPP, pp. 239-240.
4259. Köstenberger, Kellum, and Quarles, p. 18.
4260. Romer, p. 201.
4261. J. G. Jackson, CBC, p. 200.
4262. We will note that Aquarius the Water-Bearer makes a number of mystical appearances in the Bible. See e.g., Mark 14:13. See also M. P. Hall, pp. 55, 156; A. Pike, p. 791.
4263. See M. P. Hall, p. 156; A. Pike, p. 791.
4264. Seabrook, JATLOA, p. 404. See also J. G. Jackson, CBC, pp. 145-150; M. P. Hall, pp. 55, 156; A. Pike, p. 791.
4265. See M. P. Hall, p. 156; A. Pike, p. 791.
4266. Seabrook, JATLOA, p. 404.
4267. Cirlot, s.v. "Tetramorphs."
4268. See e.g., Spivey and Smith, p. 170.
4269. See e.g., Metford, s.v. "Tetramorphs."
4270. See e.g., Seabrook, BR, passim; Seabrook, TBOK, passim; Seabrook, TGDOWAP, passim; Stone, WGWAW, passim; Stone, AMOW, passim; Reilly, AGWLLM, passim; Olson, passim; Ashe, TV, passim; Ashe, DBTD, passim; Lerner, passim.
4271. See e.g., Stone, WGWAW, passim; Reilly, AGWLLM, passim.
4272. Carey and Perry, p. 10.
4273. Carey and Perry, p. 10.
4274. Carey and Perry, p. 10.
4275. Carey and Perry, p. 10. See also Genesis 1:27; Psalms 82:6; Isaiah 41:23.
4276. Carey and Perry, p. 10.
4277. Carey and Perry, p. 10.
4278. Carey and Perry, p. 10.
4279. John 10:34.
4280. Carey and Perry, p. 10.
4281. 2 Corinthians 6:16. My view. See also 1 Corinthians 3:16.
4282. John 1:9. My view.
4283. 2 Peter 1:4. My view.
4284. G. Fox, p. 101. My view and my paraphrasal of Fox's central thought. See also Van Etten, p. 25, passim.
4285. Bucke, p. 162. My view. Named after William Blake.
4286. Whitman, p. 49. My view. Named after Walt Whitman.
4287. Wahr, p. 23. My view. Named after Ralph Waldo Emerson.
4288. Bucke, p. 70. My view. Named after Jakob Böhme.
4289. Trine, p. 13.
4290. Hoeller, p. 168.
4291. Genesis 1:27.

4292. For more on the Indwelling Christ of God, see Seabrook, JATLOA, passim.
4293. John 10:34.
4294. Colossians 3:11.
4295. John 1:9.
4296. 2 Peter 1:4.
4297. Hoeller, p. 172.
4298. James, p. 126.
4299. Psalms 82:6.
4300. John 10:34.
4301. Romans 8:14. See also John 1:12; 1 John 3:1-2.
4302. Galatians 3:28.
4303. Genesis 1:26-27; 3:5, 22.
4304. Baba, p. 53.
4305. John 14:9.
4306. My paraphrasal.
4307. Philippians 3:8.
4308. Hebrews 12:10.
4309. Leviticus 11:44-45.
4310. Psalms 86:2.
4311. The doctrine of the hypostatic union—as pertaining only to Jesus—is a late creation of the Catholic Church, which did not formally adopt the concept until the 6th Century, at the Fifth General Council of Constantinople held in A.D. 533. Before that Christians held a myriad of different beliefs on the subject. Among them were those forwarded by such doctrinal authorities as Eutyches, Arius, Apollinaris, and Nestorius.
4312. Colossians 2:9-10.
4313. Galatians 3:20.
4314. See Genesis 17:1; Exodus 3:14-15; Psalms 46:10; Mark 8:29; 14:61-62; Luke 22:70; John 6:35; 8:12, 23, 58; 9:5; 10:7-11, 30-39; 11:25; 12:26, 46; 13:13; 14:3, 6, 10-11, 20; 15:1; 17:10, 16.
4315. John 14:20.
4316. Matthew 5:48.
4317. See Goguel, Vol. 2, p. 557.
4318. Roberts and Donaldson, Vol. 5, p. 153. Emphasis added.
4319. Dods, Vol. 1, p. 468. Emphasis added.
4320. Dods, Vol. 1, p. 438. Emphasis added.
4321. From a letter to Adelphos. Emphasis added.
4322. Wace and Schaff, Vol. 7, p. 308. Emphasis added.
4323. John 10:34.
4324. From *The Stromata*, Chapter 10. Emphasis added.
4325. Emphasis added.
4326. *Summa Theologica*, Part 3, Question 16, Article 7. Emphasis added.
4327. Dorsey, p. 29.
4328. Philippians 2:5-6.
4329. Ragg and Ragg, p. 339. Emphasis added.
4330. Whitman, p. 299 ("Laws for Creations").
4331. Bucke, pp. 122, 123. Emphasis added.
4332. I have paraphrased John 17:10.
4333. Romans 8:16-17. Emphasis added.
4334. Wahr, p. 23.
4335. John 10:34. See my book, *Christ Is All and In All*.
4336. See Daraul, p. 220, for an example of this doctrine among the worshipers of the Hindu goddess Kali.
4337. 2 Corinthians 6:16.
4338. D. M. Jones, p. 137.
4339. Elder, pp. 10, 20
4340. Knight, p. 30.
4341. M. P. Hall, p. 92.
4342. See e.g., Numbers 23:22; 24:8; Job 39:9-10; Psalms 29:6; 92:10.

4343. Ephesians 1:18.
4344. Spalding, Vol. 4, p. 33.
4345. Matthew 6:22-23.
4346. Ephesians 5:8.
4347. M. P. Hall, pp. 79, 92.
4348. Mark 6:2-3.
4349. See e.g., Notovitch, passim; Dowling, Sections 6 and 7; Potter, pp. 10, 52.
4350. See e.g., Mark 8:31.
4351. Harrington, p. 92.
4352. Sheehan, p. 149.
4353. M. P. Hall, p. 183.
4354. A. Pike, p. 421.
4355. A. Pike, p. 423.
4356. Rogo, pp. 165-166.
4357. Brownrigg, s.v. "Mary, Mother of Jesus."
4358. Luke 2:46.
4359. J. G. Jackson, CBC, p. 192.
4360. Biedermann, s.v. "Phoneix."
4361. A. Pike, p. 81.
4362. See e.g., Kuhn, LL, pp. 17, 149-150, 258, 278, 303, 323, 352, 369, 492, 494, 495-496, 527, 639, 643.
4363. Gordon, s.v. "Christianity."
4364. See Cashford, pp. 9, 28-32, 53, 60, 289, 312, 341, passim.
4365. Exodus 10:22-23.
4366. Jonah 1:17.
4367. Hosea 6:2.
4368. Matthew 12:40.
4369. John 2:19.
4370. Mark 8:31. The three-day Pagan motif was added to the biography of Paul as well. See Acts 9:9.
4371. Curtiss and Curtiss, TKTTU, pp. 121-122.
4372. Potter, pp. 81-83.
4373. Gaskell, s.v. "Three Days."
4374. 2 Corinthians 3:6.
4375. Grusin, p. 20.
4376. See Channing, p. 302.
4377. Schweitzer, TQOTHJ, p. 153.
4378. Schweitzer, TQOTHJ, p. ix.
4379. Hardon, s.v. "Transfiguration of Our Lord"; Tenney, s.v. "Transfiguration."
4380. Matthew 17:1-8; Mark 9:2-8; Luke 9:28-36.
4381. Matthew 17:1-8. Emphasis added.
4382. Livingstone, s.v. "Transfiguration, The."
4383. Though three centuries later St. Cyril would claim that the incident took place on Mount Tabor, there is no evidence for this—for obvious reasons. See Metford, s.v. "Transfiguration of Christ."
4384. See e.g. J. L. McKenzie, s.v. "Transfiguration."
4385. John Reginald Campbell, "The Spiritual Meaning of Childhood" (sermon). Emphasis added.
4386. J. L. McKenzie, s.v. "Transfiguration."
4387. Carpenter, pp. 131, 242.
4388. Titcomb, p. 39.
4389. Chetwynd, p. 113.
4390. Titcomb, p. 54. Emphasis added.
4391. E. E. Evans, p. 57.
4392. See Matthew 17:10-13.
4393. Gaskell, s.v. "Transfiguration of Jesus."
4394. Kingsford and Maitland, pp. 247-248.
4395. Channing, p. 348.
4396. Tenney, s.v. "Tree of Life."

4397. Genesis 2:9.
4398. Gordon, s.v. "Trees"; G. D. Young, s.v. "Tree of Life."
4399. Revelation 22:2.
4400. Spence, s.v. "Tree of Life, The."
4401. Biedermann, s.v. "Tree."
4402. Lamsa, IITBE, p. 71.
4403. See Genesis 3:6.
4404. Leeming, p. 135; Graves, TWG, pp. 157, 255; M. Jordan, s.v. "Sophia."
4405. Daraul, p. 74.
4406. Loar, p. 377; Lash, p. 228.
4407. Monaghan, p. 378.
4408. See Patai, pp. 14, 17, 19, 96-111, 189-192, 202-206, 287-294, 323-324.
4409. Proverbs 3:13-20.
4410. Dods, Vol. 1, p. 545. See Proverbs 3:18.
4411. Hodson, Vol. 1, p. 134.
4412. Farrell and Presser, s.v. "Tree."
4413. Biedermann, s.v. "Tree."
4414. Runes, s.v. "Sefiroth."
4415. Hinnells, s.v. "Tarot."
4416. Holroyd, s.v. "Kabbalism" (p. 91).
4417. M. P. Hall, pp. 121-124.
4418. Daraul, p. 7.
4419. Chetwynd, pp. 214-215.
4420. Farrell and Presser, s.v. "Christmas Tree."
4421. See Jeremiah 10:3-4.
4422. Barlow, pp. 79-80. Emphasis added.
4423. M. P. Hall, p. 88.
4424. Watts, MARIC, pp. 79, 196.
4425. Mascaró, p. 16.
4426. Zondervan, s.v. "Tribe"; G. D. Young, s.v. "Tribes." See also Genesis 49:16, 28.
4427. Seiss, pp. 378-382. There are many alternate configurations of this list. See e.g., A. Pike, pp. 461-462.
4428. Jukes, p. 400.
4429. De Bunsen, p. 277.
4430. Swedenborg, AR, p. 349.
4431. Dunlap, p. 230.
4432. See 2 Esdras 12:11-15.
4433. Higgins, Vol. 1, p. 612.
4434. G. R. S. Mead, TGH, Vol. 1, p. 169.
4435. Metzger and Coogan, s.v. "Trinity."
4436. H. S. Lewis, TSDOJ, pp. 216-217.
4437. G. D. Young, s.v. "Apostles."
4438. Carlyle, p. 26.
4439. Lasne and Gaultier, p. 22.
4440. W. W. Westcott, p. 102.
4441. See Fillmore, s.v. "Faculties."
4442. See Davidson, pp. 171-172.
4443. R. Graves, TWG, p. 201.
4444. M. P. Hall, p. 145.
4445. Higgins, Vol. 1, p. 801.
4446. B. G. Walker, TWEOMAS, s.v. "Mithra."
4447. Gaskell, s.v. "Adityas, the Twelve."
4448. Gaskell, s.v. "Apostles, The Twelve."
4449. R. Graves, TWG, p. 201.
4450. Doane, p. 498.
4451. W. W. Westcott, pp. 102, 105, 107, 108.

4452. W. W. Westcott, p. 103.
4453. Scott-Moncrieff, pp. 158-163.
4454. Chernin, p. 165.
4455. Kelly, pp. 86-87; Pagels, TGG, pp. 147-148.
4456. G. R. S. Mead, PS, p. 42.
4457. Gaskell, s.v. "Aeon, the Thirteenth."
4458. Gaskell, s.v. "Aeons, the Twelve."
4459. Gaskell, s.v. "Apostles, The Twelve."
4460. Pearson, passim.
4461. Luke 2:46.
4462. G. D. Young, s.v. "Salvation, Application of."
4463. Watts, G, p. 19.
4464. Colossians 3:11.
4465. F. M. Müller, TOPR, p. 482.
4466. Fichte, pp. 514-515.
4467. Ueberweg, Vol. 1, pp. 480-481. Emphasis added.
4468. Barbanell, p. 152.
4469. See Proverbs 23:7.
4470. Steiger, IMSIAF, p. 125.
4471. Proverbs 15:26.
4472. G. D. Young, s.v. "Upper Room."
4473. Brownrigg, s.v. "Mary, Mother of Jesus."
4474. Mark 14:15; Luke 22:12; Acts 1:13.
4475. Acts 2:46; Luke 24:53. See H. S. Lewis, TSDOJ, pp. 163-164.
4476. Spalding, Vol. 4, p. 81.
4477. M. P. Hall, p. 121.
4478. M. P. Hall, p. 135.
4479. Matthew 27:33; Mark 15:22; John 19:17.
4480. Luke 23:33.
4481. Tenney, s.v. "Vale, Valley." See also Deuteronomy 34:6; Joshua 10:40; Luke 3:5.
4482. Yogananda, TSCOC, Vol. 1, p. 48.
4483. See Genesis 3:15.
4484. K. Graves, pp. 53-55.
4485. See e.g., Genesis 2:1; Psalms 48:3; Job 38:29; Isaiah 42:14; 46:3; 49:15; 66:13; Luke 15:8-10; Matthew 23:37.
4486. Yogananda, TSCOC, Vol. 1, p. 46.
4487. Kingsford and Maitland, pp. 140-142. Emphasis added.
4488. Kingsford and Maitland, pp. 239-240. Emphasis added.
4489. Pfleiderer, TDOC, pp. 152-153. Emphasis added.
4490. Jukes, pp. 66-67. Emphasis added.
4491. G. R. S. Mead, FOAFF, p. 203.
4492. Ueberweg, p. 482.
4493. See Neumann, p. 313.
4494. Seabrook, CBC, pp. 104-107. See also Neumann, pp. 313-314; J. G. Jackson, POOTCM, pp. 10-11; J. G. Jackson, CBC, p. 195; J. M. Robertson, PC, pp. 168-169, 178, 331, 348.
4495. Luke 1:26-27.
4496. Malachi 4:2.
4497. R. Graves, TWG, pp. 319, 469.
4498. Potter, pp. 24, 90.
4499. Potter, pp. 24, 90, 127.
4500. Revelation 12:1.
4501. John 4:24. The KJV says "God is *a* Spirit," a mistranslation. The original is: "God is Spirit." Spalding, Vol. 4, p. 24; Neill, WWKAJ, p. 78. See also Romans 1:20; 1 Timothy 1:17.
4502. Colossians 1:15-16.
4503. Gaskell, s.v. "Voice of God."

4504. Revelation 3:20-21.
4505. Matthew 14:22-36.
4506. J. M. Robertson, CAM, pp. 358-359.
4507. Zondervan, s.v. "Blood."
4508. See e.g., John 1:29; 1 John 1:7; Revelation 1:5.
4509. Pfleiderer, TECCOC, pp. 129-133.
4510. Budge, TEHAH, Vol. 3, pp. 105-106.
4511. Judges 8:33.
4512. See Acts 20:28.
4513. Hislop, pp. 102-106. Emphasis added.
4514. Colossians 3:11.
4515. Genesis 1:27.
4516. 1 Corinthians 2:16; Philippians 2:5.
4517. Luke 17:21.
4518. John 13:10.
4519. Dods, Vol. 11, p. 191.
4520. Shinn, p. 40.
4521. Goring, s.v. "Sacred Marriage."
4522. M. P. Hall, p. 135.
4523. 1 Corinthians 2:16; Philippians 2:5.
4524. Seabrook, JATLOA, p. 363, passim.
4525. Zondervan, s.v. "Water." See also Ezekiel 16:4, 9; 36:25; John 3:5.
4526. Fillmore, s.v. "Water."
4527. Gaskell, s.v. "Water (Higher Aspect)."
4528. Potter, p. 127.
4529. Revelation 22:17.
4530. Kingsley, TWOCK, pp. 3-4. Emphasis added.
4531. John 4:13-14.
4532. John 6:67-68.
4533. Barlow, pp. 59-62. Emphasis added.
4534. Mark 1:14.
4535. M. P. Hall, p. 35.
4536. John 4:14.
4537. Zondervan, s.v. "Way."
4538. The same holds true for liberal Bible scholars. See e.g., Schweitzer, TQOTHJ, pp. 226-229.
4539. See e.g., Goguel, Vol. 2, p. 585.
4540. Schweitzer, TQOTHJ, p. 17.
4541. See Matthew 5:17.
4542. See e.g., Parsons, pp. 276-277.
4543. Matthew 28:1-7. Some believe that Christianity began with Peter's protophany or "Easter experience," when he witnessed the risen Jesus for the first time. According to this view, Peter interpreted Jesus' resurrection as a revelation from God that Jesus had returned to usher in the Kingdom of God, there and then inaugurating the Christian religion. See Sheehan, pp. 91, 101-109.
4544. See Matthew 16:16. See also Sheehan, p. 8.
4545. Spivey and Smith, pp. 322, 353.
4546. Sheenhan, p. 183.
4547. See e.g., Matthew 7:13-14; 21:32; John 14:6.
4548. See e.g., Mark 1:3; 10:52; Luke 3:4; John 1:23; 14:4; Acts 9:2; 18:25-26; 19:9, 23; 22:4; 24:14, 22. Barnabas, an early disciple and a companion of Paul (Acts 13:43), more aptly called Jesus' "religion" the "Way of the Light." The Epistle of Barnabas 14:5.
4549. See e.g., Genesis 18:19; Exodus 32:8; Deuteronomy 9:16.
4550. See e.g., 2 Kings 21:22.
4551. See e.g., Job 31:7.
4552. See e.g., Psalms 25:8.

4553. Hermes Trismegistus, a mysterious ancient figure, is said to have founded the religion of Hermeticism and authored the wonderful mystic writings known as the *Corpus Hermeticum*.
4554. It was also known as "the Way." See Burtt, pp. 51-52, 148, 196-201.
4555. Seabrook, JATLOA, pp. 427-428. Note: Lao Tzu is the probable author of the ancient Chinese work entitled *Tao Te Ching*, "The Way of Virtue."
4556. See H. S. Lewis, TSDOJ, pp. 223-224.
4557. Matthew 18:3.
4558. W. Smith, s.v. "Wine."
4559. J. L. McKenzie, s.v. "Wine," s.v. "Eucharist"; Tenney, s.v. "Wine."
4560. Goguel, Vol. 2, p. 328.
4561. Farrell and Presser, s.v. "Wine."
4562. Hodson, Vol. 1, p. 144.
4563. John 14:6.
4564. Colossians 3:11.
4565. Nelson's, s.v. "Magi."
4566. See Matthew 2:11.
4567. Yogananda, TSCOC, Vol. 1, pp. 56-62.
4568. Ford, pp. 99, 122.
4569. Higgins, Vol. 2, pp. 96-97.
4570. K. Graves, p. 64.
4571. D. M. Bennett, Vol. 1, p. 108.
4572. Doane, p. 147.
4573. L. M. Graham, pp. 307-308.
4574. Matthew 2:7-8.
4575. Strauss, TLOJCE, Vol. 1, p. 158.
4576. See Spence, s.v. "Magi"; Yogananda, TSCOC, Vol. 1, pp. 58-59.
4577. Yogananda, TSCOC, Vol. 1, pp. 60-61.
4578. Martello, p. 146.
4579. Fillmore, s.v. "Herod."
4580. J. R. Allen, pp. 196-197.
4581. Yogananda, TSCOC, Vol. 1, p. 62.
4582. Godwin, p. 167.
4583. B. G. Walker, TWEOMAS, s.v. "Osiris."
4584. Fillmore, s.v. "Wise-men."
4585. Biedermann, s.v. "gold."
4586. Ramacharaka, p. 27.
4587. Ambauen, pp. 134-135.
4588. Sleater, Vol. 1, p. 523.
4589. Kingsford and Maitland, pp. 237-238. Emphasis added.
4590. Colossians 3:11.
4591. See Gaskell, s.v. "Word of God."
4592. Psalms 82:6.
4593. Genesis 1:27.
4594. Acts 17:26.
4595. J. L. McKenzie, s.v. "God."
4596. Exodus 3:13.
4597. Exodus 6:3.
4598. See e.g., Genesis 17:1.
4599. Versnel, p. 374.
4600. Murdock, DME, pp. 409-410.
4601. Meissner, p. 116.
4602. J. L. McKenzie, s.v. "God."
4603. Let us note here that the feminine singular of the plural Elohim is Eloah, "Goddess."
4604. Isaiah 63:14-15. Some of the first Christians, the Gnostics, also imaged God as a hermaphrodite. See Richardson, p. 364.

4605. Genesis 3:21.
4606. Hosea 11:1, 2, 4, 9.
4607. Jeremiah 31:20.
4608. Deuteronomy 32:18; Isaiah 42:13-14; 46:3-4.
4609. Ide, YW, p. 8.
4610. Genesis 1:26; 3:22.
4611. A. Pike, p. 727.
4612. Genesis 1:27.
4613. Hosea 2:16.
4614. Lurker, DOGAG, s.v. "Baal."
4615. M. Jordan, s.v. "Baal."
4616. My theory.
4617. Spence, s.v. "Adonai."
4618. See e.g., Genesis 2:4. Also Leishman, OAB, pp. 108-109.
4619. Exodus 6:3; Psalms 83:13; Isaiah 12:2; 26:4.
4620. Exodus 3:13-14.
4621. Young, s.v. "God, Names of."
4622. Spalding, Vol. 4, p. 33.
4623. Revelation 3:14. For John's corresponding Gospel text, see John 1:1-3.
4624. Colossians 3:11.
4625. Genesis 1:27.
4626. See Fillmore, s.v. "Jehovah."
4627. Doyle, TEOTU, p. 127.
4628. Richardson, p. 364.
4629. Hoeller, p. xviii.
4630. Chernin, p. 162.
4631. Szekeley, TDOTEGOP, p. 9.
4632. Freud, MAM, pp. 39, 47, 74-75.
4633. Exodus 19:20.
4634. Exodus 3:1.
4635. J. L. McKenzie, s.v. "Sinai."
4636. My theory.
4637. My theory.
4638. B. G. Walker, TWEOMAS, s.v. "Sin."
4639. M. P. Hall, p. 133.
4640. Mish, s.v. "demiurge."
4641. Kelly, pp. 86-87; Pagels, TGG, pp. 147-148.
4642. Chernin, p. 165. Jesus refers to the Gnostic Demiurge Yaldabaoth in John 12:31.
4643. See e.g., 2 Corinthians 4:4; Colossians 2:2.
4644. Blunt, s.v. "Gnosticism."
4645. Delaney, s.v. "Anne."
4646. Attwater, s.v. "Joachim and Ann." See 1 Samuel 1:1-28.
4647. B. G. Walker, TWEOMAS, s.v. "Anne, Saint"; "Anna-Nin."
4648. Graves and Patai, p. 28. See e.g., Isaiah 63:3.
4649. Monaghan, s.v. "Iahu Anat."
4650. Graves, TWG, pp. 286-287.
4651. Freud, MAM, pp. 55-56.
4652. See Streep, passim; Gimbutas, TGAGOOE, passim; Gimbutas, TCOTG, passim; Briffault, passim; Neumann, passim.
4653. Guignebert, p. 182.
4654. M. Jordan, s.v. "Baal."
4655. Graves, TWG, pp. 57, 118, 176, 264, 286-287, 335-337.
4656. See e.g., Tenney, s.v. "Yoke."
4657. Matthew 11:28-30.
4658. J. L. McKenzie, s.v. "Yoke."

4659. Zondervan, s.v. "Yoke."
4660. Spence, s.v. "Yoga."
4661. Cirlot, s.v. "Yoke."
4662. Biedermann, s.v. "Yoke."
4663. Eliade, Y, p. 4.
4664. Gordon, s.v. "Yoga."
4665. Farrell and Presser, s.v. "Yoke."
4666. van Buitenen, p. 17.
4667. The Bhagavad Gita, pp. 75-76; James, p. 400.
4668. Gordon, s.v. "Yoga."
4669. Colossians 3:11.
4670. Matthew 11:28-30.
4671. M. P. Hall, p. 88.
4672. Watts, MARIC, pp. 79, 196.
4673. Yogananda, AOAY, p. 266.
4674. Chetwynd, pp. 110-111.
4675. Oldenberg, p. 339.
4676. See M. L. Prophet and E. C. Prophet, pp. 141-142.
4677. Gaskell, s.v. "Yoke of Jesus."
4678. Yogananda, TSCOC, Vol. 1, pp. 26, 232.
4679. See e.g., Notovitch, passim; Dowling, Sections 6 and 7; Potter, pp. 10, 52.
4680. Nelson's, s.v. "Zion."
4681. Tenney, s.v. "Zion."
4682. Fillmore, s.v. "Zion."
4683. 2 Corinthians 6:16.
4684. See e.g., Zondervan, s.v. "Astrology"; s.v. "Astronomy."
4685. *Zedek* appears in such names as Melchizedek, literally the "King of Righteousness."
4686. M. P. Hall, p. 56.
4687. Mish, s.v. "zodiac."
4688. Proverbs 8:27.
4689. Ward, Vol. 2, pp. 358-359.
4690. A. Pike, pp. 445-446.
4691. A. Pike, pp. 437-438.
4692. Orthodox Christianity teaches that the six-month period between the birth of John the Baptist (in Cancer) and Jesus (in Capricorn) is because Luke states that the former was born six months before the latter. (See Luke 1:36.) This is Christian mysticism gone wrong, however, for John represents the astrological entrance gate of the Soul (Summer Solstice) and Jesus represents its exit gate (Winter Solstice). Additionally, no one knows when either John or Jesus was born, while Luke himself contradicts all of this by stating that Jesus was born in the Spring (the Spring Equinox or "Easter"), when shepherds were "keeping watch over their flock by night." (See Luke 2:8.) If this is true, then John was born in the Fall (the Autumnal Equinox or "Halloween").
4693. F. M. Müller, TOPR, pp. 144-145. Emphasis added.
4694. See Fillmore, s.v. "Faculties"; Gaskell, s.v. "Disciples, The Twelve, of Jesus."
4695. Chetwynd, p. 233.
4696. Houvet, p. 73.
4697. John 20:29-30.
4698. John 21:24.
4699. They could be true, but there is no need to literally claim this because mystically speaking Jesus was indeed "virgin-born," "the Christ," the "Son of God," "the Way, the truth, and the light," "crucified," and "resurrected."
4700. Mark 1:14.
4701. Mark 1:1.
4702. A. Pike, p. 308.
4703. Dowling, 127:6; John 14:12.
4704. Luke 3:6. See also Romans 10:13; Acts 2:17; 2 Peter 3:9; 1 Timothy 2:4.

4705. See e.g., John 6:44; 15:16; Acts 9:15; Romans 8:28-30; Ephesians 1:4-5; 2 Thessalonians 2:13; 2 Timothy 1:9.
4706. See e.g., John 1:12-13; 6:28-29; Philippians 1:29.
4707. John 10:34.
4708. Colossians 1:27; 3:11.
4709. John 14:12.
4710. Proverbs 23:7. We may logically conclude then that our lives are also governed by our beliefs, words, and deeds.
4711. Galatians 6:5-8; Ephesians 6:8.
4712. For a more in-depth discussion on these topics, see the entry in this book, "Gospel, The."
4713. Matthew 7:7-8; 21:22; Mark 11:24; John 14:13-14. See also Job 22:28.
4714. John 21:25.
4715. John 3:16.
4716. Luke 17:21.
4717. See e.g., Spalding, all five volumes, passim; Yogananda, TSCOC, Vol. 1, pp. xxvii-xxix, xxxi-xxxii.
4718. A Bodhisattva is a totally enlightened soul who incarnates in order to allay the suffering of humanity and offer redemption and salvation. See Burtt, pp. 125, 133-134; Evans-Wentz, p. 26.
4719. Luke 9:56.
4720. Ephesians 3:4.
4721. Romans 16:25.
4722. See e.g., Strauss, TLOJCE, passim; M. Grant, J, p. 1.
4723. Luke 8:50.
4724. John 5:30-31; 8:28; 12:44-45; 14:10.
4725. 2 Corinthians 3:6.
4726. John 15:17.
4727. Matthew 6:14-15; 18:21-22.
4728. Mark 9:40. See also John 8:7; Acts 10:28; Ephesians 4:2; Romans 14:1-4; 1 Peter 3:8-11.

Jesus in the Garden of Gethsemane.

Bibliography

Abbot, Walter M. (ed.). *The Documents of Vatican II*. New York, NY: Guild Press, 1966.
Akerley, Ben Edward. *The X-rated Bible: An Irreverent Survey of Sex in the Scriptures*. Austin, TX: American Atheist Press, 1989.
Albertson, Edward. *Understanding Zen for the Millions*. Los Angeles, CA: Sherbourne Press, 1970.
Alighieri, Dante. *The Banquet of Dante Alighieri* (Elizabeth Price Sayer, trans.,) London, UK: George Routledge and Sons, 1887.
Allen, John Romilly. *Early Christian Symbolism in Great Britain and Ireland Before the Thirteenth Century*. London, UK: Whiting and Co., 1887.
Allen, Paula Gunn. *The Sacred Hoop: Recovering the Feminine in American Indian Traditions*. Boston, MA: Beacon Press, 1986.
Alter, Robert. *The World of Biblical Literature*. New York, NY: Basic Books, 1992.
Altizer, Thomas J. J. *The Gospel of Christian Atheism*. Philadelphia, PA: Westminster Press, 1966.
Ambauen, Andrew Joseph. *The World's Symbolism, or Nature Voices and Other Voices*. Chicago, IL: J. S. Hyland and Co., 1916.
Ambrose, Saint. *The Letters of S. Ambrose, Bishop of Milan*. Oxford, UK: James Parker and Co., 1881.
Amery, Colin, and Brian Curran Jr. *The Lost World of Pompeii*. New York, NY: Getty Publications, 2002.
Anderson, Frederick (ed.). *A Pen Warmed-Up in Hell: Mark Twain in Protest*. New York, NY: Perennial Library, 1972.
Anderson, Hugh. *Jesus and Christian Origins*. Oxford, UK: Oxford University Press, 1964.
Anderson, J. N. D. *Christianity and Comparative Religion*. 1970. Downers Grove, IL: InterVarsity Press, 1974 ed.
Andrews, Ted. *The Occult Christ: Angelic Mysteries, Seasonal Rituals, and the Divine Feminine*. St. Paul, MN: Llewellyn, 1993.
Andrewes, Antony. *The Greeks*. 1967. New York, NY: W. W. Norton, 1978 ed.
Angus, Samuel. *The Mystery-Religions and Christianity*. New York, NY: Charles Scribner's Sons, 1925.
Ankerberg, John, and John Weldon. *Cult Watch: What You Need to Know About Spiritual Deception*. Eugene, OR: Harvest House, 1991.
Ardrey, Robert. *African Genesis*. 1961. New York, NY: Dell Publishing Co. (Laurel edition), 1972 ed.
———. *The Territorial Imperative*. 1966. New York, NY: Delta, 1968 ed.
Arieti, James A. *Philosophy in the Ancient World: An Introduction*. Lanham, MD: Rowman and Littlefield, 2005.
Armstrong, April Oursler. *What's Happening to the Catholic Church*. Garden City, NY: Echo Books, 1967.
Arnold, Edwin. *The Light of Asia; or, The Great Renunciation: Being the Life and Teaching of Gautama, Prince of India and Founder of Buddhism*. Boston, MA: Roberts Brothers, 1892.
Aron, Robert. *Jesus of Nazareth: The Hidden Years*. New York, NY: William Morrow and Co., 1962.
Arterburn, Stephen, and Jack Felton. *Toxic Faith: Understanding and Overcoming Religious Addiction*. Nashville, TN: Oliver-Nelson Books, 1991.
Ashe, Geoffrey. *The Virgin: Mary's Cult and the Re-emergence of the Goddess*. 1976. London, UK: Arkana, 1988 ed.
———. *Dawn Behind the Dawn: A Search for the Earthly Paradise*. New York, NY: Henry Holt, 1992.
Asimov, Isaac. *A Short History of Biology*. Garden City, NY: Natural History Press, 1964.
Astrov, Margot (ed.). *The Winged Serpent: An Anthology of American Indian Poetry*. 1946. Greenwich, CT: Fawcett, 1973 ed.
Atkins, Gaius Glenn, and Charles Samuel Braden. *Procession of the Gods*. 1930. New York, NY: Harper and Brothers Publishers, 1936 ed.

Attwater, Donald. *The Penguin Dictionary of Saints*. 1965. Harmondsworth, UK: Penguin, 1983 ed.
Augustine, Saint. *The Confessions of St. Augustine, Bishop of Hippo* (circa 400). (J. G. Pilkington, trans.). Edinburgh, Scotland: T. and T. Clark, 1886 ed.
Baba, Meher. *Life At Its Best*. 1957. New York, NY: E. P. Dutton, 1976 ed.
Baigent, Michael, and Richard Leigh. *The Dead Sea Scrolls Deception*. 1991. New York, NY: Touchstone, 1993 ed.
Baigent, Michael, Richard Leigh, and Henry Lincoln. *Holy Blood, Holy Grail*. 1982. New York, NY: Dell, 1983 ed.
———. *The Messianic Legacy*. New York, NY: Dell, 1986.
Bainton, Roland H. *Here I Stand: A Life of Martin Luther*. 1950. New York, NY: Mentor, 1962 ed.
———. *Behold the Christ*. 1970. New York, NY: Harper and Row, 1976 ed.
Balfour, Edward. *The Cyclopedia of India and of Eastern and Southern Asia, Commercial, Industrial, and Scientific*. 3 vols. London, UK: Bernard Quatrich, 1885.
Banton, Michael (ed.). *Anthropological Approaches to the Study of Religion*. 1966. London, UK: Tavistock Publications, 1973 ed.
Barbanell, Maurice. *This is Spiritualism*. 1959. New York, NY: Award Books, 1967 ed.
Barlow, Henry Clark. *Essays on Symbolism*. London, UK: Williams and Norgate, 1866.
Baring, Anne, and Jules Cashford. *The Myth of the Goddess: Evolution of an Image*. 1991. Harmondsworth, UK: Arkana, 1993 ed.
Baring-Gould, William S. (ed.). *The Annotated Sherlock Holmes*. Avenel, NJ: Wings Books, 1992 ed.
Barnouw, Victor. *An Introduction to Anthropology: Physical Anthropology and Archaeology*. Homewood, IL: Dorsey Press, 1971.
Barnstone, Willis (ed.). *The Other Bible*. New York, NY: Harper and Row, 1984.
———. *The Restored New Testament: A New Translation With Commentary, Including the Gnostic Gospels Thomas, Mary, and Judas*. 2002. New York, NY: W. W. Norton and Co., 2009 ed.
Barnstone, Willis, and Marvin Meyer (eds.). *The Gnostic Bible: Gnostic Texts of Mystical Wisdom From the Ancient and Medieval Worlds*. Boston, MA: New Seeds, 2006.
Barrett, C. K. *The New Testament Background: Selected Documents*. 1956. New York, NY: Harper and Row, 1961 ed.
Barrett, William (ed.). *Zen Buddhism: Selected Writings of D. T. Suzuki*. New York, NY: Doubleday, 1956.
Basalla, George. *The Evolution of Technology*. 1988. Cambridge, UK: Cambridge University Press, 1999 ed.
Basham, Don. *Can a Christian Have a Demon?* Monroeville, PA: Whitaker House, 1971.
Baumgartner, Anne S. *A Comprehensive Dictionary of the Gods: From Abaasy to Zvoruna*. Seacaucus, NJ: University Books, 1984.
Bauval, Robert, and Adrian Gilbert. *The Orion Mystery: Unlocking the Secrets of the Pyramids*. New York, NY: Crown, 1994.
Bede. *Historia Ecclesiastica Gentis Anglorum (A History of the English Church and People)*. C.E. 731. Harmondsworth, UK: Penguin, 1974 ed.
Begg, Ean. *The Cult of the Black Virgin*. Harmondsworth, UK: Arkana, 1985.
Bell, Robert E. *Women of Classical Mythology: A Biographical Dictionary*. 1991. Oxford, England: Oxford University Press, 1993 ed.
Ben-Abba, Dov. *Hebrew-English, English-Hebrew Dictionary*. Nazareth, Israel: Massada-Press, 1977.
Bennett, D. M. *The Gods and Religions and Ancient and Modern Times*. 2 vols. New York, NY: Liberal and Scientific Publishing House, 1880, 1881.
Bennett, Jonathan. *Rationality*. 1964. London, UK: Routledge and Kegan Paul Ltd., 1971 ed.
Bently, Peter (ed.). *The Dictionary of World Myth*. New York, NY: Facts on File, 1995.
Berens, Lewis Henry. *The Digger Movement in the Days of the Commonwealth as Revealed in the Writings of Gerrard Winstanley, the Digger*. London, UK: Simpkin, Marshall, Hamilton, Kent, and Co., 1906.
Bernstein, Morey. *The Search for Bridey Murphy*. 1956. New York, NY: Pocket Books, 1978 ed.

Berry, Thomas Sterling. *Christianity and Buddhism: A Comparison and Contrast.* London, UK: Society for Promoting Christian Knowledge, 1891.
Besant, Annie, and C. W. Leadbeater. *Man: Whence, How and Whither - A Record of Clairvoyant Investigation.* 1913. Madras, India: Theosophical Publishing House, 1971 ed.
Beston, Henry. *The Outermost House.* 1928. New York, NY: Holt, Rinehart and Winston, 1956 ed.
Bettelheim, Bruno. *The Uses of Enchantment: The Meaning and Importance of Fairy Tales.* New York, NY: Vintage, 1976.
Bhaktivedanta, A. C. (Swami Prabhupada). *The Science of Self Realization.* 1977. Los Angeles, CA: Bhaktivedanta Book Trust, 1983 ed.
Bidmead, Julye. *The Akitu Festival: Religious Continuity and Royal Legitimation in Mesopotamia.* 2002. Piscataway, NJ: Gorgias Press, 2004 ed.
Biedermann, Hans. *Dictionary of Symbolism: Cultural Icons and the Meanings Behind Them.* 1989. New York, NY: Facts on File, 1992 ed.
Bierce, Ambrose. *The Collected Works of Ambrose Bierce.* Vol. 7. New York, NY: Neal Publishing Co., 1911.
Bilde, Per. *The Originality of Jesus: A Critical Discussion and a Comparative Attempt.* Göttingen, Germany: Vandenhoeck and Ruprecht, 2013.
Blackman, Aylward M. *Gods, Priests and Men: Studies in the Religion of Pharaonic Egypt.* (Alan B. Lloyd, ed.) 1998. New York, NY: Routledge, 2011 ed.
Blackwelder, Boyce W. *Light From the Greek New Testament.* 1958. Anderson, IN: Warner Press, 1959 ed.
Blavatsky, Helena Petrovna. *Isis Unveiled: A Master-key to the Mysteries of Ancient and Modern Science and Theology.* 3 vols. 1877. New York, NY: J. W. Bouton, 1892 ed.
———. *The Secret Doctrine: The Synthesis of Science, Religion, and Philosophy.* 2 vols. London, UK: Theosophical Publishing Society, 1893.
Bloodworth, Venice. *Key To Yourself.* 1952. Marina del Rey, CA: DeVorss and Co., 1980 ed.
Bloom, Harold. *The American Religion: The Emergence of the Post-Christian Nation.* New York, NY: Touchstone, 1992.
Blunt, John Henry (ed.). *Dictionary of Doctrinal and Historical Theology.* London, UK: Rivingtons, 1872.
Bly, Robert. *Iron John: A Book About Men.* 1990. New York, NY: Vintage Books, 1992 ed.
Blyth, Reginald Horace. *Games Zen Masters Play.* New York, NY: Mentor, 1976.
Boardman, John, Jasper Griffin, and Oswyn Murray (eds.). *The Roman World.* 1986. Oxford, UK: Oxford University Press, 1988 ed.
Boates, Karen Scott (ed.). *The Goddess Within.* Philadelphia, PA: Running Press, 1990.
Boer, Harry R. *Above the Battle? The Bible and Its Critics.* 1975. Grand Rapids, MI: William B. Eerdmans, 1977 ed.
Böhme, Jakob. *Mysterium Magnum, or An Exposition of the First Book of Moses Called Genesis.* 1623. London, UK: Henry Blunden, 1656 English ed.
Bonhoeffer, Dietrich. *The Cost of Discipleship.* 1937. New York, NY: Macmillan, 1975 ed.
Bonwick, James. *Egyptian Belief and Modern Thought.* London, UK: C. Kegan Paul and Co., 1878.
Booty, John E. *The Church in History.* New York, NY: Seabury Press, 1979.
Borg, Victor Paul. *The Rough Guide to Malta and Gozo.* London, UK: Rough Guides, 2001.
Bowden, John. *Archaeology and the Bible.* Austin, TX: American Atheist Press, 1982.
Brantl, George. *Catholicism.* New York, NY: Washington Square Press, 1962.
Breasted, James Henry. *A History of Egypt: From the Earliest Times to the Persian Conquest.* New York, NY: Charles Scribner's Sons, 1905.
Brennan, J. H. *Five Keys to Past Lives.* 1971. New York, NY: Samuel Weiser, 1975 ed.
Breuilly, John (ed.). *The Oxford Handbook of the History of Nationalism.* Oxford, UK: Oxford University Press, 2013.
Briffault, Robert Stephen. *The Mothers: The Matriarchal Theory of Social Origins.* 1927. New York, NY: Macmillan, 1931 ed.

Briggs, Katherine. *The Vanishing People: Fairy Lore and Legends*. New York, NY: Pantheon Books, 1978.
Bright, Bill. *The Holy Spirit: The Key to Supernatural Living*. San Bernardino, CA: Campus Crusade for Christ International, 1980.
Brinkley, Dannion. *Saved by the Light: The True Story of a Man Who Died Twice and the Profound Revelations He Received*. New York, NY: Harper, 1995.
Bromiley, Geoffrey W. (ed.). *The International Standard Bible Encyclopedia*. 1915. Grand Rapids, MI: William B. Eerdmans Publishing, 1982 ed.
Bronowski, J. *Science and Human Values*. 1956. New York, NY: Harper Colophon Books, 1965 ed.
———. *The Ascent of Man*. Boston, MA: Little, Brown and Co., 1973.
Brooke, Stopford Augustus. *Faith and Freedom*. Boston, MA: George H. Ellis, 1881.
Brooks, Phillips. *Visions and Tasks and Other Sermons*. New York, NY: E. P. Dutton, 1886.
———. *The Mystery of Iniquity and Other Sermons*. London, UK: Macmillan and Co., 1893.
Brown, Dee. *Bury My Heart at Wounded Knee*. New York, NY: Bantam Books, 1970.
Brown, Henry (ed.). *Justin Martyr's Dialogue With Trypho the Jew*. 1745. Cambridge, UK: George Bell, 1846 ed.
Brown, Robert. *Semitic Influence in Hellenic Mythology*. New York, NY: Arno, 1977.
Bruce, F. F. *The New Testament Documents: Are They Reliable?* 1943. Downers Grove, IL: InterVarsity Press, 1980 ed.
Brunner, Hellmut. *An Outline of Middle Egyptian Grammar*. Graz, Austria: Akademische Druck, 1979.
Bucke, Richard Maurice. *Cosmic Consciousness: A Study in the Evolution of the Human Mind*. 1901. Philadelphia, PA: Innes and Sons, 1905 ed.
Budapest, Zsuzsanna Emese. *The Holy Book of Women's Mysteries*. 2 vols. 1979. Oakland, CA: Susan B. Anthony Coven, 1982 ed.
Budge, Ernest Alfred Wallis. *Egyptian Magic*. London, UK: Kegan Paul, Trench, Trübner and Co., 1901.
———. *The Book of the Dead*. 3 vols. Chicago, IL: Open Court, 1901.
———. *The Gods of the Egyptians, or Studies in Egyptian Mythology*. 2 vols. London, UK: Methuen and Co., 1904.
———. *The Egyptian Heaven and Hell* ("Books on Egypt and Chaldaea" series). London, UK: Kegan Paul, Trench, Trübner and Co., 1905.
———. *Egyptian Ideas of the Future Life*. ("Books on Egypt and Chaldaea" series, Vol. 3). London, UK: Kegan Paul, Trench, Trübner and Co., 1908.
———. *Osiris and the Egyptian Resurrection*. 2 vols. London, UK: Philip Lee Warner, 1911.
———. *Amulets and Talismans*. N.d. New York, NY: Citadel Press, 1992 ed.
Bulfinch, Thomas. *Bulfinch's Mythology*. 1855-1863. New York, NY: Modern Library, n.d.
Bullough, Sebastian. *The Church in the New Testament*. Westminster, MD: Newman Press, 1957.
Bullough, Vern L., and Bonnie Bullough. *The Subordinate Sex: A History of Attitudes Toward Women*. 1973. Baltimore, MD: Penguin, 1974 ed.
———. *Women and Prostitution: A Social History*. 1978. Buffalo, NY: Prometheus Books, 1987 ed.
Bultmann, Rudolf. *New Testament and Mythology and Other Basic Writings*. (Schubert M. Ogden, ed. and trans.) Philadelphia, PA: Fortress Press, 1984.
Bunsen, Christian Charles Josias. *Hippolytus and His Age; or, The Beginnings and Prospects of Christianity*. 3 vols. London, UK: Longman, Brown, Green, and Longmans, 1854.
Burke, James. *Connections*. Boston: Little, Brown and Co., 1978.
Burkitt, Francis Crawford. *Early Eastern Christianity: St. Margaret's Lectures, 1904, on the Syriac-Speaking Church*. New York, NY: E. P. Dutton, and Co., 1904.
Burnett, Frances Hodgson. *The Secret Garden*. 1911. New York, NY: Dell, 1974 ed.
Burr, William Henry. *Revelations of Antichrist, Concerning Christ and Christianity*. Boston, MA: J. P. Mendum, 1879.
Burrell, David James. *The Religions of the World: An Outline of the Great Religious Systems*. Philadelphia, PA: Presbyterian Board of Publication and Sabbath-School Work, 1888.
Burrell, Sidney A. *Handbook of Western Civilization: Beginnings to 1700* (Vol. 1). 1965. New York, NY:

John Wiley and Sons, 1972 ed.
Burrows, Millar. *The Dead Sea Scrolls.* 1955. New York, NY: Viking Press, 1961 ed.
Burtt, Edwin A (ed.). *The Teachings of the Compassionate Buddha.* New York, NY: Mentor, 1955.
Busenbark, Ernest. *Symbols, Sex, and the Stars, in Popular Beliefs: An Outline of the Origins of Moon and Sun Worship, Astrology, Sex Symbolism, Mystic Meaning of Numbers, the Cabals, and Many Popular Customs, Myths, Superstitions and Religious Beliefs.* New York, NY: Truth Seeker Co., 1949.
Bushnell, Horace. *Nature and the Supernatural, as Together Constituting the One System of God.* Edinburgh, Scotland: Alexander Strahan and Co., 1862.
Butler, Trent C. (ed.). *Holman Bible Dictionary.* Nashville, TN: Holman, 1991.
Cabot, James Elliot. *A Memoir of Ralph Waldo Emerson.* 2 vols. Boston, MA: Houghton, Mifflin and Co., 1887.
Caddy, Eileen. *The Spirit of Findhorn.* 1976. San Francisco, CA: Harper and Row, 1979 ed.
Caesar, Gaius Julius. *The Conquest of Gaul.* 52 B.C.E. Harmondsworth, UK: Penquin, 1951.
Calasso, Roberto. *The Marriage of Cadmus and Harmony* (Tim Parks, trans.). New York, NY: Knopf, 1993.
Calvocoressi, Peter. *Who's Who in the Bible.* 1987. Harmondsworth, UK: Penguin, 1990 ed.
Campanelli, Pauline. *Ancient Ways: Reclaiming Pagan Traditions.* 1991. St. Paul, MN: Llewellyn Publications, 1992 ed.
Campbell, Joseph. *The Hero With a Thousand Faces.* 1949. New York, NY: Bollingen Foundation, 1973 ed.
———. *The Masks of the Gods: Primitive Mythology.* Vol. 1. 1959. Harmondsworth, UK: Arkana, 1991 ed.
———. *The Masks of the Gods: Oriental Mythology.* Vol. 2. 1962. Harmondsworth, UK: Arkana, 1991 ed.
———. *The Masks of the Gods: Occidental Mythology.* Vol. 3. 1964. Harmondsworth, UK: Arkana, 1991 ed.
———. *The Masks of the Gods: Creative Mythology.* Vol. 4. 1968. Harmondsworth, UK: Arkana, 1991 ed.
———. *Myths to Live By.* New York, NY: Bantam, 1972.
———. *Transformations of Myth Through Time.* New York, NY: Harper and Row, 1990.
———. *The Power of Myth* (with Bill Moyers). New York, NY: Doubleday, 1988.
Campbell, Reginald John. *The New Theology.* New York, NY: Macmillan, 1908.
Camphausen, Rufus C. *The Encyclopedia of Erotic Wisdom.* Rochester, VT: Inner Traditions International, 1991.
Cantor, Norman F. *Inventing the Middle Ages.* New York, NY: William Morrow and Co., 1991.
Capra, Fritjof. *The Tao of Physics: An Exploration of the Parallels Bewteen Modern Physics and Eastern Mysticism.* 1975. Boston: Shambala Publications, 1991 ed.
Carey, George Washington, and Inez Eudora Perry. *God-Man: The Word Made Flesh.* Los Angeles, CA: Chemistry of Life, 1920.
Carlyle, Thomas. *Heroes, Hero-worship, and the Heroic in History.* New York, NY: Charles Scribner's Sons, 1841.
Carlyon, Richard. *A Guide to the Gods: An Essential Guide to World Mythology.* New York, NY: Quill, 1981.
Carpenter, Edward. *Pagan and Christian Creeds: Their Origin and Meaning.* New York, NY: Harcourt, Brace and Co., 1921.
Carson, Anne. *Goddesses and Wise Women: The Literature of Feminist Spirituality, An Annotated Bibliography.* Freedom, CA: The Crossing Press, 1992.
Carson, D. A. *The King James Version Debate: A Plea for Realism.* Grand Rapids, MI: Baker Book House, 1979.
Carter, Howard, and A. C. Mace. *The Discovery of the Tomb of Tutankhamen.* 1923. New York, NY: Dover, 1977 ed.
Carter, Mary Ellen. *Edgar Cayce on Prophecy.* New York, NY: Paperback Library, 1968.

Carus, Paul. *The Gospel of Buddha According to Old Records*. 1894. Chicago, IL: Open Court, 1895 ed.
——. *The History of the Devil and the Idea of Evil From the Earliest Times to the Present Day*. Chicago, IL: Open Court Publishing Co., 1900.
——. (ed.). *The Monist: A Quarterly Magazine Devoted to the Philosophy of Science*. Vol. 25. Chicago, IL: Open Court Publishing Co., 1915.
Case, Shirley Jackson. *The Historicity of Jesus*. Chicago, IL: University of Chicago Press, 1912.
Cashford, Jules. *The Moon: Myth and Image*. New York, NY: Four Walls Eight Windows, 2003.
Cassius, Dio. *The Roman History: The Reign of Augustus* (Ian Scott-Kilvert, trans.). C. 214-226. Harmondsworth, UK: Penguin, 1988.
Castaneda, Carlos. *A Separate Reality: Further Conversations with Don Juan*. 1971. New York, NY: Pocket Books, 1974 ed.
Cavalli-Sforza, Luigi Luca, and Francesco Cavalli-Sforza. *The Great Human Diasporas: The History of Diversity and Evolution*. 1993. Reading, MA: Helix Books, 1995 ed.
Cavendish, Richard. *A History of Magic*. 1987. Harmondsworth, UK: Arkana, 1990 ed.
Celeste. *The Messianic Legacy in the Age of Aquarius: Jesus, Redeemer of the World's Soul*. Bloomington, IN: AuthorHouse, 2007.
Cerminara, Gina. *Many Mansions*. 1950. New York, NY: Signet, 1967 ed.
——. *Many Lives, Many Loves*. 1963. New York, NY: Signet, 1974 ed.
Chadwick, Owen. *The Reformation*. 1964. Harmondsworth, UK: Penguin, 1976 ed.
Chaisson, Eric. *Cosmic Dawn*. New York, NY: Berkley Books, 1984.
Channing, William Ellery. *The Complete Works of W. E. Channing*. London, UK: Williams and Norgate, 1880.
Chapman, Graham, John Cleese, Terry Gilliam, Eric Idle, Terry Jones, and Michael Palin. *Monty Python's The Meaning of Life*. New York, NY: Grove Press, 1983.
Charig, Alan. *A New Look at the Dinosaurs*. London, UK: Heinemann Ltd. (published in association with the British Museum of Natural History), 1983 ed.
Chase, Mary Ellen. *The Bible and the Common Reader*. 1944. New York, NY: Macmillan, 1968 ed.
Chatterjee, Ramananda (ed.). *The Modern Review: A Monthly Review and Miscellany* (Vol. 9, January to June 1911). West Bengal, India: Prabasi Press, 1911.
Chernin, Kim. *Reinventing Eve: Modern Woman in Search of Herself*. 1987. New York, NY: Harper Collins, 1994 ed.
Chetwynd, Tom. *Dictionary of Sacred Myth*. London, UK: Aquarian Press, 1986.
Christian, C. W. *Friedrich Schleiermacher*. (From the book series: "Makers of the Modern Theological Mind.") Peabody, MA: Hendrickson, 1991.
Christie-Murray, David. *A History of Heresy*. Oxford, UK: Oxford University Press, 1976.
Chronicle of the World. Mount Kisco, NY: Ecam Publications, 1989.
Church History in the Fullness of Times. Church Educational System (eds.). Salt Lake City, UT: The Church of Jesus Christ of Latter-Day Saints, 1989.
Cirlot, J. E. *A Dictionary of Symbols*. 1962. New York, NY: Philosophical Library, 1983 ed.
Clark, Jerome. *Unexplained: 347 Strange Sightings, Incredible Occurrences, and Puzzling Physical Phenomena*. Detroit, MI: Visible Ink Press, 1993.
Clark, W. E. Le Gros. *History of the Primates*. 1949. Chicago, IL: University of Chicago Press, 1968 ed.
——. *The Antecedents of Man*. 1959. New York, NY: Quadrangle Books, 1978 ed.
Clarke, O. Fielding. *For Christ's Sake*. New York, NY: Morehouse-Barlow, 1963.
Clymer, Reuben Swinburne. *The Rosicrucians: Their Teachings and Mysteries According to the Manifestoes Issued at Various Times by the Fraternity Itself*. 1903. Allentown, PA: Philosophical Publishing Co., 1910 ed.
Coates, James. *In Mormon Circles: Gentiles, Jack Mormons, and Latter-Day Saints*. 1990. Reading, MA: Addison-Wesley, 1992 ed.
Cohen, Daniel. *The Encyclopedia of the Strange*. New York, NY: Avon Books, 1985.
Cohen, Edmund. *The Mind of the Bible-Believer*. 1986. Buffalo, NY: Prometheus Books, 1988 ed.

Coleman, Richard J. *Issues of Theological Conflict: Evangelicals and Liberals.* 1972. Grand Rapids, MI: William B. Eerdmans, 1980 ed.
Collignon, Maxime. *Manual of Mythology, in Relation to Greek Art* (Jane E. Harrison, trans.). London, UK: H. Grevel and Co., 1890.
Collins, Sheila D. *A Different Heaven and Earth.* Valley Forge, PA: Judson Press, 1974.
Comay, Joan. *Who's Who in the Old Testament.* 1971. New York, NY: Oxford University Press, 1993 ed.
Combes, Abbé (ed.). *Collected Poems of Saint Thérèse of Lisieux.* New York, NY: Sheed and Ward, 1949.
Compton's Encyclopedia and Fact-Index. 1922. Chicago, IL: F. E. Compton Co., 1969 ed.
Compton's Pictured Encyclopedia. 1922. Chicago, IL: F. E. Compton Co., 1957 ed.
Comte, Auguste. *Catéchisme Positiviste.* Paris, France: Ernest Leroux, 1874.
Conaty, Thomas James. *New Testament Studies: The Principal Events in the Life of Our Lord.* New York, NY: Benziger Brothers, 1898.
Condon, R. J. *Our Pagan Christmas.* Austin, TX: American Atheist Press, 1989.
Conway, J. D. *What the Church Teaches.* New York, NY: Harper and Brothers, 1962.
Coogan, Michael D. (ed.). *The Oxford History of the Biblical World.* Oxford, UK: Oxford University Press, 1998.
Cooper, J. C. *Symbolic and Mythological Animals.* London, UK: Aquarian Press, 1992.
Cooper, William Ricketts. *The Horus Myth in its Relation to Christianity.* London, UK: Hardwicke and Bogue, 1877.
Cooper-Oakley, Isabel. *Mystical Traditions.* Milan, Italy: Ars Regia, 1909.
Copan, Paul, and Kenneth D. Litwack. *The Gospel in the Marketplace of Ideas: Paul's Mars Hill Experience for Our Pluralistic World.* Downers Grove, IL: InterVarsity Press, 2014.
Corban, Jean. *Path to Freedom: Christian Experiences and the Bible.* New York, NY: Sheed and Ward, 1969.
Cotterell, Arthur. *A Dictionary of World Mythology.* 1979. New York, NY: Oxford University Press, 1990 ed.
———. *The Macmillan Illustrated Encyclopedia of Myths and Legends.* New York, NY: Macmillan, 1989.
Courtenay, William J. *The Judeo-Christian Heritage.* New York, NY: Holt, Rinehart and Winston, 1970.
Courtney, W. L. *The Literary Man's Bible.* London, UK: Chapman and Hall, 1908.
Cousteau, Jacques-Yves, and the staff of the Cousteau Society. *The Cousteau Almanac.* Garden City, NY: Doubleday, 1980.
Covell, Ralph. *Confucius, the Buddha, and Christ: A History of the Gospel in Chinese.* 1986. Eugene, OR: Wipf and Stock, 2004 ed.
Cover, Lois Brauer. *Anthropology For Our Times.* New York, NY: Oxford Book Co., 1971.
Cox, George W. *The Mythology of the Aryan Nations.* 2 vols. London, UK: Longmans, Green and Co., 1870.
Cramer, Raymond L. *The Psychology of Jesus and Mental Health.* 1959. Grand Rapids, MI: Zondervan, 1972 ed.
Cranston, Ruth. *The Miracle of Lourdes.* New York, NY: Popular Library, 1955.
Crisp, Oliver D. *God Incarnate: Explorations in Christology.* London, UK: T. and T. Clark, 2009.
Cross, Frank Leslie, and Elizabeth Anne Livingstone (eds.). *The Oxford Dictionary of the Christian Church.* 1957. London, UK: Oxford University Press, 1974 ed.
Crossley, Fred H. *English Church Design, 1040-1540 A.D.* 1945. London, UK: B. T. Batson, 1948 ed.
Cumont, Franz. *The Mysteries of Mithra.* London, UK: Kegan Paul, Trench, Trübner and Co., 1903.
———. *The Oriental Religions in Roman Paganism.* Chicago, IL: Open Court, 1911.
Curran, Charles E. *Transition and Tradition in Moral Theology.* Notre Dame, IN: University of Notre Dame Press, 1979.
Curtiss, Harriette Augusta, and F. Homer Curtiss. *The Key to the Universe, or a Spiritual Interpretation of Numbers and Symbols.* Washington, DC: The Curtiss Philosophic Book Co., 1917.
———. *The Key of Destiny: A Sequel to the Key of the Universe.* New York, NY: E. P. Dutton and Co.,

1919.
Daly, Mary. *Beyond God the Father*. Boston, MA: Beacon Press, 1973.
———. *Gyn/ecology: The Metaethics of Radical Feminism*. Boston, MA: Beacon Press, 1978.
Daniel, Alma, Timothy Wyllie, and Andrew Rammer. *Ask Your Angels*. New York, NY: Ballantine, 1992.
Dante, Alighieri. *Inferno* (Thomas G. Bergin, trans.). New York, NY: Appleton-Century, 1948.
Daraul, Arkon. *A History of Secret Societies*. 1962. New York, NY: Pocket Books, 1969 ed.
Dart, John. *The Jesus of Heresy and History: The Discovery and Meaning of the Nag Hammadi Gnostic Library*. New York, NY: Harper Collins, 1988.
Dasgupta, Amitava, with Lochlainn Seabrook. *Autobiography of a Non-Yogi: A Scientist's Journey From Hinduism to Christianity*. Franklin, TN: Sea Raven Press, 2015.
Das, Lama Surya. *Awakening the Buddha Within: Eight Steps to Enlightenment*. New York, NY: Broadway, 1998.
Dass, Baba Hari. *The Yellow Book: The Sayings of Bab Hari Dass*. San Cristobal, NM: Lama Foundation, 1973.
Dass, Ram. *The Only Dance There Is*. Garden City, NY: Anchor, 1974.
Daton, Lois. *Lilith*. Indianapolis, IN: Rod's Composing Service, 1977.
David, Bruno, Bryce Barker, and Ian J. McNiven (eds.). *The Social Archaeology of Australian Indigenous Societies*. Canberra, Australia: Aboriginal Studies Press, 2006.
David-Neel, Alexandra. *With Mystics and Magicians in Tibet*. Oxford, UK: Penguin, 1937.
David, Rosalie. *Handbook to Life in Ancient Egypt*. 1998. Oxford, UK: Oxford University Press, 1999 ed.
Davidson, Hilda Roderick Ellis. *Gods and Myths of Northern Europe*. 1964. Harmondsworth, UK: Penguin, 1990 ed.
Davies, A. Powell. *The Meaning of the Dead Sea Scrolls*. New York, NY: Mentor, 1956.
Davies, Owen. *The Omni Book of the Paranormal and the Mind*. New York, NY: Zebra, 1978.
Davis, F. Hadland. *Myths and Legends of Japan*. 1913. New York, NY: Dover, 1992 ed.
Davis, John J. *Biblical Numerology: A Basic Study of the Use of Numbers in the Bible*. 1968. Grand Rapids, MI: Baker Book House, 1988 ed.
Dawkins, Richard. *The Selfish Gene*. 1976. New York, NY: Oxford University Press, 1978 ed.
———. *The Blind Watchmaker*. New York, NY: W. W. Norton, 1987.
Dawson, Christopher. *Religion and the Rise of Western Culture*. 1950. Garden City, NY: Image Books, 1958 ed.
Day, Michael H. *Fossil Man*. New York, NY: Bantam, 1971.
De Bunsen, Ernest. *The Angel-Messiah of Buddhists, Essenes, and Christians*. London, UK: Longmans, Green, and Co., 1880.
De Chardin, Pierre Teilhard. *The Phenomenon of Man* (Bernard Wall, trans.). 1955. New York, NY: Harper and Row, 1965 ed.
Decker, Ed, and Dave Hunt. *The God Makers*. Eugene, OR: Harvest House Publishers, 1984.
———. *The God Makers II*. Eugene, OR: Harvest House Publishers, 1993.
DeHaan, M. R. *508 Answers to Bible Questions: With Answers to Seeming Bible Contradictions*. 1952. Grand Rapids, MI: Zondervan, 1961 ed.
Delaney, John J. *Pocket Dictionary of Saints*. 1980. New York, NY: Image, 1983 abridged ed.
Dellow, E. L. *Methods of Science*. New York, NY: Universe Books, 1970.
Dentan, Robert C. *The Holy Scriptures*. 1949. Greenwich, CT: Seabury Press, 1953 ed.
Derk, Francis H. *The Names of Christ*. 1969. Minneapolis, MN: Dimension, 1976 ed.
Derlon, Pierre. *The Secrets of the Gypsies*. New York, NY: Ballantine, 1977.
De Rosa, Peter. *Vicars of Christ*. New York, NY: Crown Publishers, 1988.
Desroches-Noblecourt, Christiane. *Tutankhamen*. Boston, MA: New York Graphic Society, 1963.
Deussen, Paul. *The Philosophy of the Upanishads*. Edinburgh, Scotland: T. and T. Clark, 1906.
Development Psychology Today. Del Mar, CA: CRM Books, 1971.
J. Dewey, Arthur, Roy W. Hoover, Lane C. McGaughy, and Daryl D. Schmidt. *The Authentic Letters*

of Paul: A New Reading of Paul's Rhetoric and Meaning (Scholars Version). Salem, OR: Polebridge Press, 2010.

Dickens, A. G. *Reformation and Society in Sixteenth-Century Europe.* New York, NY: Harcourt, Brace and World, 1966.

Dimont, Max I. *Jews, God and History.* New York, NY: Signet, 1962.

Dingle, R. D. (ed.). *The New Testament of Our Lord and Saviour Jesus Christ: According to the Authorized Version.* London, UK: London News, 1847.

Dixon, Dougal. *After Man: A Zoology of the Future.* New York, NY: St. Martin's Press, 1981.

Doane, Thomas William. *Bible Myths and Their Parallels in Other Religions.* New York, NY: Truth Seeker Co., 1882.

Dods, Marcus (ed.). *The Works of Aurelius Augustine, Bishop of Hippo.* 12 vols. Edinburgh, Scotland: T. and T. Clark, 1872-1874.

Donahue, Phil. *The Human Animal.* New York, NY: Fireside, 1985.

Donahue, Phil. *My Own Story.* 1979. New York, NY: Fawcett Crest, 1981 ed.

Donaldson, E. Talbot (trans.). *Beowulf.* New York, NY: W. W. Norton, 1966.

Doré, Gustave. *The Doré Bible Gallery.* Chicago, IL: Bedford, Clarke and Co., 1886.

Doresse, Jean. *The Secret Books of the Egyptian Gnostics: An Introduction to the Gnostic Coptic Manuscripts Discovered at Chenoboskion: Translated from the French by Philip Mairet, with an English Translation and Critical Evaluation of the Gospel According to Thomas.* London, UK: Hollis and Carter, 1960.

Dorner, J. August. *History of the Development of the Doctrine of the Person of Christ* (William L. Alexander, trans.). 2 Vols. Edinburgh, Scotland: T. and T. Clark, 1891.

Dorsey, John M. *Psychology of Emotion: Self Discipline by Conscious Emotional Continence.* Detroit, MI: Center for Health Education, 1971.

Douglas, Stephen. *The Redhead Dynasty.* Corona del Mar, CA: NewStyle Communications, 1987.

Douglas-Klotz, Neil. *Prayers of the Cosmos: Meditations on the Aramaic Words of Jesus.* San Francisco, CA: Harper and Row, 1990.

Dowley, Tim (ed.). *The History of Christianity.* 1977. Oxford, UK: Lion Publishing Co., 1990 ed.

Dowling, Levi. *The Aquarian Gospel of Jesus the Christ: The Philosophical and Practical Basis of the Religion of the Aquarian Age of the World and of the Church Universal.* Los Angeles, CA: Royal Publishing Co., 1909.

Downing, Christine. *The Goddess: Mythological Images of the Feminine.* New York, NY: Crossroad Publishing, 1984.

Doyle, Arthur Conan. *Adventures of Sherlock Holmes.* New York, NY: Harper and Brothers, 1892 ed.

———. *The New Revelation.* New York, NY: George H. Doran, 1918.

———. *The Coming of the Fairies.* New York, NY: George H. Doran Co., 1921.

———. *The Edge of the Unknown.* 1930. New York, NY: Berkley, 1968 ed.

Drake, Stillman. *Discoveries and Opinions of Galileo.* Garden City, NY: Anchor, 1957.

Drexel, Jeremias. *Zodiacus Christianus.* Munich, Germany: Anna Bergin, 1622.

Dudley, Dean. *History of the First Council of Nice: A World's Christian Convention, A.D. 325.* Boston, MA: C. W. Calkins and Co., 1880.

Dunlap, Samuel Fales. *The Ghebers of Hebron.* 1894. New York, NY: J. W. Bouton, 1898 ed.

Dunn, James D. G. *Unity and Diversity in the New Testament: An Inquiry Into the Character of Earliest Christianity.* Philadelphia, PA: Westminster Press, 1977.

Dunner, Joseph (ed.) *Handbook of World History: Concepts and Issues.* New York, NY: Philosophical Library, 1967.

Dunstan, J. Leslie (ed.). *Protestantism.* New York, NY: Washington Square Press, 1962.

Dupius, Charles F. *The Origin of All Religious Worship.* New Orleans, LA: self-published, 1872.

Dyer, Thomas H. *Pompeii: Its History, Buildings, and Antiquities.* London, UK: Bell and Daldy, 1871.

Easton, Matthew George. *Illustrated Bible Dictionary and Treasury of Biblical History, Biography, Geography, Doctrine, and Literature.* London, UK: T. Nelson and Sons, 1894.

Eban, Abba. *Heritage: Civilization and the Jews.* New York, NY: Summit Books, 1984.

Eddy, Mary Baker Glover. *Science and Health With Key to the Scriptures*. 1875. Boston, MA: self-published, 1889 ed.
Edwards, I. E. S. *The Pyramids of Egypt*. 1947. Harmondsworth, UK: Penguin, 1967 ed.
———. *Tutankhamun: His Tomb and Its Treasures*. 1977. New York, NY: Knopf, 1978 ed.
Edwards, Jonathan. *The Salvation of All Men Strictly Examined*. Boston, MA: C. Ewer and T. Bedlington, 1824.
Edwards, Otis Carl, Jr. *Luke's Story of Jesus*. Philadelphia, PA: Fortress Press, 1981.
Eimerl, Sarel, and Irven DeVore. *The Primates*. New York, NY: Time-Life Books, 1965.
Einstein, Albert. *The World as I See It*. New Jersey: Citadel Press, n.d.
Eisenman, Robert. *Maccabees, Zadokites, Christians, and Qumran: A New Hypothesis of Qumran Origins*. Leiden, The Netherlands: Brill, 1983.
Eisenman, Robert, and Michael Wise. *The Dead Sea Scrolls Uncovered*. Shaftesbury, Dorset, UK: Element Books, 1992.
Elder, Dorothy. *From Metaphysical to Mystical: A Study of the Way*. Denver, CO: Doriel Publishing Co., 1992.
Eliade, Mircea. *Images and Symbols: Studies in Religious Symbolism*. 1952. Princeton, NJ: Princeton University Press, 1991 ed.
———. *Yoga: Immortality and Freedom* (William R. Trask, trans.). 1954. Princeton, NJ: Princeton University Press, 1971 ed.
———. *From Primitives to Zen*. 1967. New York, NY: Harper and Row, 1977 ed.
———. *A History of Religious Ideas*. Vol. 1 (From the Stone Age to the Eleusinian Mysteries). Chicago, IL: University of Chicago Press, 1978.
———. *A History of Religious Ideas*. Vol. 2 (From Gautama Buddha to the Triumph of Christianity). Chicago, IL: University of Chicago Press, 1982.
———. *A History of Religious Ideas*. Vol. 3 (From Muhammad to the Age Reforms). Chicago: University of Chicago Press, 1985.
Eliot, Alexander. *The Universal Myths*. New York, NY: Meridian, 1976.
Ellis, Albert. *The Case Against Religion: A Psychotherapist's View*. Austin, TX: American Atheist Press, n.d.
Ellis, Edwin John, and William Butler Yeats (eds.). *The Works of William Blake: Poetic, Symbolic, and Critical*. Vol. 2. London, UK: Bernard Quaritch, 1893.
Ellis, Peter Berresford. *A Dictionary of Irish Mythology*. 1987. Oxford, UK: Oxford University Press, 1992 ed.
Emerson, Ralph Waldo. *Works of Ralph Waldo Emerson*. London, UK: George Routledge and Sons, 1883.
———. *The Essays of Emerson*. London, UK: Arthur L. Humphreys, 1908.
Encyclopedia Britannica: A New Study of Universal Knowledge. 1768. London, UK: Encyclopedia Britannica, 1955 ed.
Enslin, Morton Scott. *Christian Beginnings*. 1938. New York, NY: Harper and Brothers, 1956 ed.
Erasmus, Desiderius. *Praise of Folly* (1509). Betty Radice, trans. 1971. Harmondsworth, England: Penguin, 1987 ed.
Esslemont, J. E. *Bahá'u'lláh and the New Era: An Introduction to the Baha'i Faith*. 1923. Wilmette, IL: Baha'i Books, 1970 ed.
Eusebius (of Caesarea). *The History of the Church* (c. 315-325). G. A. Williamson, trans; Andrew Louth, ed. 1965. Harmondsworth, England: Penguin, 1989 ed.
———. *The Proof of the Gospel* (W. J. Ferrar, trans.). 2 vols. New York, NY: Macmillan, 1920.
Evans, Bergen. *Dictionary of Mythology*. 1970. New York, NY: Laurel, 1991 ed.
Evans, Elizabeth E. *The Christ Myth: A Study*. New York, NY: The Truth Seeker Co., 1900.
Evans-Wentz, Walter Yeeling. *The Tibetan Book of the Great Liberation, or the Method of Realizing Nirvana Through Knowing the Mind*. 1954. Oxford, UK: Oxford University Press, 1971 ed.
Eyerly, Dean R. *The Face of Jesus*. Mustang, OK: Tate Publishing, 2012.
Faber-Kaiser, Andreas. *Jesus Died in Kashmir: Jesus, Moses and the Ten Lost Tribes of Israel*. London, UK:

Gordon and Cremonesi, 1977.
Farmer, David Hugh. *The Oxford Dictionary of Saints.* 1978. Oxford, UK: Oxford University Press, 1992 ed.
Farnese, A. *A Wanderer in Spirit Lands.* Chicago, IL: Progressive Thinker, 1901.
Farren, David. *Sex and Magic.* New York, NY: Barnes and Noble Books, 1975.
Feder, Kenneth L. *Frauds, Myths, and Mysteries: Science and Pseudoscience in Archaeology.* Mountain View, CA: Mayfield Publishing Co., 1990.
Fell, Barry. *America B.C.* 1976. New York, NY: Pocket Books, 1989 ed.
Fenwick, Peter, and Elizabeth Fenwick. *The Truth in the Light: An Investigation of Over 300 Near-Death Experiences.* 1995. New York, NY: Berkley, 1997 ed.
Ferguson, George. *Signs and Symbols in Christian Art.* 1954. London, UK: Oxford University Press, 1975 ed.
Feuerbach, Ludwig. *The Essence of Christianity* (Maria Evans, trans.). London, UK: Trübner and Co., 1881.
Fichte, Johann Gottlieb. *John Gottlieb Fichte's Popular Works.* London, UK: Trübner and Co., 1873.
Fillmore, Charles. *Metaphysical Bible Dictionary.* Unity Village, MO: Unity School of Christianity, 1931.
Filson, Floyd V. *Opening the New Testament.* 1929. Philadelphia, PA: Westminster Press, 1952 ed.
Filthaut, Theodor. *Church Architecture and Liturgical Reform.* 1965. Baltimore, MD: Helicon Press, 1968 ed.
Finegan, Jack. *Light From the Ancient Past: The Archaeological Background of the Hebrew-Christian Religion.* 1946. 2 vols. Princeton, NJ: Princeton University Press, 1974 ed.
Finger, Ben, Jr. *Concise World History.* New York, NY: Philosophical Library, 1959.
Fischer, Carl. *The Myth and Legend of Greece.* Dayton, OH: George A. Pflaum, 1968.
Flew, Antony. *A Dictionary of Philosophy.* New York, NY: St. Martin's Press, 1979.
Forbes, R. J. *Studies in Ancient Technology* (Vol. 9). Leiden, The Netherlands: Brill, 1964.
Ford, Marvin. *On the Other Side.* Plainfield, NJ: Logos International, 1978.
Fox, George. *George Fox: An Autobiography* (Rufus M. Jones, ed.). Philadelphia, PA: Ferris and Leach, 1904 ed.
Fox, Matthew (ed.) *Western Spirituality: Historical Roots, Ecumenical Routes.* Santa Fe, NM: Bear and Co., 1981.
———. *The Coming of the Cosmic Christ.* New York, NY: Harper and Row, 1988.
———. *Christian Mystics: 365 Readings and Meditations.* Novato, CA: New World Library, 2011.
Fox, Robin Lane. *Pagans and Christians.* New York, NY: Knopf, 1986.
———. *The Unauthorized Version: Truth and Fiction in the Bible.* New York, NY: Knopf, 1991.
Frazer, James George. *Adonis, Attis, Osiris: Studies in the History of Oriental Religion.* London, UK: Macmillan, 1906.
———. *The Golden Bough.* 2 vols. London, UK: Macmillian, 1919.
———. *Folk-lore in the Old Testament: Studies in Comparative Religion, Legend, and Law.* 1918. Single abridged vol. New York, NY: Tudor, 1923 ed.
Freud, Sigmund. *Totem and Taboo: Resemblances Between the Psychic Lives of Savages and Neurotics.* New York, NY: Moffat, Yard and Co., 1918.
———. *The Future of an Illusion.* 1928. New York, NY: W. W. Norton, 1961.
———. *New Introductory Lectures Psychoanalysis.* Lecture no. 35: "A Philosophy of Life," 1932.
———. *Moses and Monotheism.* 1939. New York, NY: Vintage, 1958 ed.
Friend, David, and the editors of *Life. The Meaning of Life.* Boston, MA: Little, Brown and Co., 1991.
Frothingham, Octavius Brooks. *The Cradle of the Christ: A Study in Primitive Christianity.* New York, NY: G. P. Putnam's Sons, 1877.
Frye, Albert Myrton, and Albert William Levi. *Rational Belief: An Introduction to Logic.* New York, NY: Harcourt, Brace and Co., 1941.
Furnas, J. C. *The Americans: A Social History of United States (1587-1914).* New York, NY: G. P. Putnam's Sons, 1969.

Fysh, Frederic. *"The Beast and His Image," or the Pope and the Council of Trent.* London, UK: R. B. Seeley and W. Burnside, 1837.
Gadd, Laurence D. *The World Almanac Book of the Strange 2.* New York, NY: Signet, 1982.
Gaer, Joseph. *The Legend of the Wandering Jew.* New York, NY: Mentor, 1961.
Gantz, Jeffrey (trans.). *Early Irish Myths and Sagas.* 1981. Harmondsworth, UK: Penguin, 1988 ed.
Gardner, Alice. *Studies in John the Scot (Erigena): A Philosopher of the Dark Ages.* London, UK: Henry Frowde, 1900.
Gardner, Joseph L. (ed.). *Great Mysteries of the Past: Experts Unravel Fact and Fallacy Behind the Headlines of History.* Pleasantville, NY: Reader's Digest, 1991.
Gardner, Martin. *Science: Good, Bad, and Bogus.* New York, NY: Avon, 1981.
———. *The New Age: Notes of a Fringe Watcher.* Buffalo, NY: Prometheus, 1988.
Gaskell, G. A. *Dictionary of All Scriptures and Myths.* 1960. New York, NY: Julian Press, 1973 ed.
Gaskin, Stephen. *The Caravan.* New York, NY: Random House, 1972.
———. *Hey Beatnik! This is the Farm Book.* Summertown, TN: The Book Publishing Company, 1974.
———. *Mind at Play.* Summertown, TN: The Book Publishing Company, 1980.
Geller, L. D. *Sea Serpents of Coastal New England.* Plymouth, MA: Cape Cod Publications, 1979.
Gibbon, Edward. *Memoirs of My Life* (Betty Radice, ed.). 1788-1791. Harmondsworth, UK: Penguin, 1990.
———. *The History of the Decline and Fall of the Roman Empire.* 8 vols. Paris, France: Baudry's European Library, 1840.
Gibran, Kahlil. *The Prophet.* 1923. New York, NY: Knopf, 1980 ed.
———. *The Broken Wings* (Anthony R. Ferris, trans.). New York, NY: Citadel Press, 1957.
Gimbutas, Marija Alseikait. *The Goddesses and Gods of Old Europe: Myths and Cult Images.* 1974. Berkeley, CA: University of California Press, 1992 ed.
———. *The Civilization of the Goddess: The World of Old Europe.* San Francisco, CA: Harper, 1991.
Ginsburg, Christian David. *The Essenes: Their History and Doctrines.* London, UK: Longman, Green, Longman, Roberts, and Green, 1864.
Godfrey, Laurie R. (ed.). *Scientists Confront Creationism.* New York, NY: W. W. Norton, 1983.
Godwin, Joscelyn. *Arktos: The Polar Myth in Science, Symbolism, and Nazi Survival.* Kempton, IL: Adventures Unlimited Press, 1996.
Goguel, Maurice. *Jesus and the Origins of Christianity.* 2 vols. 1932. New York, NY: Harper and Brothers, 1960 ed.
Golas, Thaddeus. *The Lazy Man's Guide to Enlightenment.* 1971. New York, NY: Bantam, 1980 ed.
Goodrich-Freer, Ada. *Essays in Psychical Research.* London, UK: George Redway, 1899.
Goodspeed, Edgar J. *The Apocrypha: An American Translation.* 1938. New York, NY: Vintage Books, 1959 ed.
———. *How Came the Bible?* Nashville, TN: Abingdon Press, 1940.
Gordon, Stuart. *The Encyclopedia of Myths and Legends.* London, UK: Headline, 1994.
Goring, Rosemary (ed.). *Larousse Dictionary of Beliefs and Religions.* 1992. Edinburgh, Scotland: Larousse, 1995 ed.
Gottlieb, Lynn. *She Who Dwells Within: A Feminist Vision of a Renewed Judaism.* New York, NY: Harper Collins, 1995.
Gould, Stephen Jay. *Ever Since Darwin.* New York, NY: W. W. Norton, 1977.
———. *Hen's Teeth and Horse's Toes.* New York, NY: W. W. Norton, 1983.
———. *Bully for Brontosaurus.* New York, NY: W. W. Norton, 1991.
Graham, Billy. *Approaching Hoofbeats: The Four Horsemen of the Apocalypse.* Minneapolis, MN: Grason, 1983.
———. *Angels: Ringing Assurance That We Are Not Alone.* Nashville, TN: Thomas Nelson, 1996.
Graham, Lloyd M. *Deceptions and Myths of the Bible.* 1975. New York, NY: Citadel Press, 1991, ed.
Grant, Frederick C. (ed.). *Hellenistic Religions: The Age of Syncretism.* Indianapolis, IN: Bobbs-Merrill, 1953.
Grant, Michael. *Jesus: An Historian's Review of the Gospels.* New York, NY: Charles Scribner's Sons,

1977.

———. *Constantine the Great: The Man and His Times*. New York, NY: Charles Scribner's Sons, 1993.

Grant, Michael, and John Hazel. *Who's Who in Classical Mythology*. 1973. New York, NY: Oxford University Press, 1993 ed.

Graves, Frank Pierrepont. *What Did Jesus Teach? An Examination of the Educational Material and Method of the Master*. New York, NY: Macmillan, 1919.

Graves, Kersey. *The World's Sixteen Crucified Saviors, or Christianity Before Christ*. New York, NY: Peter Eckler, 1919.

Graves, Robert. *The White Goddess*. 1948. New York, NY: Noonday Press, 1991 ed.

———. (trans.) *The Golden Ass: The Transformation of Lucius*. 1950. New York, NY: Farrar, Straus and Giroux, 2009 ed.

———. *The Greek Myths*. Vol. 1. 1955. Harmondsworth, UK: Penguin, 1960 ed.

———. *The Greek Myths*. Vol. 2. 1955. Harmondsworth, UK: Penguin, 1990 ed.

Graves, Robert, and Joshua Podro. *The Nazarene Gospel Restored*. London, UK: Cassell and Co., 1953.

Graves, Robert, and Raphael Patai. *Hebrew Myths*. 1964. New York, NY: Anchor, 1989 ed.

Greaves, Helen. *Testimony of Light*. 1969. Saffron Walden, UK: Neville Spearman, 1988 ed.

Greenhouse, Herbert B. *The Book of Psychic Knowledge: All Your Questions Answered*. New York, NY: Mentor, 1973.

Greenstone, Julius H. *The Messiah Idea in Jewish History*. Philadelphia, PA: Jewish Publication Society, 1906.

Greenwood, Samuel. *Footsteps of Israel: From Eden to the City of God*. 1922. Freehold, NJ: Rare Book Co., 1958 ed.

Gregory, Saint, the Great. *Morals on the Book of Job*. 3 vols. Oxford, UK: John Henry Parker, 1847.

Grenfell, Bernard P., and Arthur S. Hunt (eds.). *New Sayings of Jesus and Fragment of a Lost Gospel From Oxyrhyncus*. London, UK: Henry Frowde, 1904.

Grimal, Pierre. *The Penguin Dictionary of Classical Mythology* (A. R. Maxwell-Hyslop, trans.). 1951. Harmondsworth, UK: Penguin, 1990 ed.

Grimes, Nikki. *Portrait of Mary*. New York, NY: Avon, 1994.

Grotjahn, Martin. *The Voice of the Symbol*. Los Angeles, CA: Mara Books, 1971.

Groton, William Mansfield. *The Christian Eucharist and the Pagan Cults*. New York, NY: Longmans, Green, and Co., 1914.

Grun, Bernard. *The Timetables of History*. New York, NY: Touchstone, 1975.

Grusin, Richard A. *Transcendentalist Hermeneutics: Institutional Authority and the Higher Criticism of the Bible*. Durham, NC: Duke University Press, 1991.

Guignebert, Charles. *The Christ*. New York, NY: Citadel, 1968.

Guinness Book of World Records. New York, NY: Bantam, 1990.

Guirand, Felix (ed.) *New Larousse Encyclopedia of Mythology*. 1959. London, UK: Hamlyn Publishing, 1976 ed.

Gulliver, John P. (ed.). *The Complete Works of John Bunyan*. Philadelphia, PA: Bradley, Garretson and Co., 1873.

Hadas, Moses (ed.). *A History of Rome*. Garden City, NY: Doubleday, 1956.

Haley, John Wesley. *An Examination of the Alleged Discrepancies of the Bible*. Andover, MA: Warren F. Draper, 1876.

Hall, J. A. *The Nature of God: A Series of Lectures*. Philadelphia, PA: The Lutheran Publication Society, 1910.

Hall, Manly Palmer. *The Secret Teachings of All Ages*. 1925. Los Angeles, CA: The Philosophical Research Society, 1989 ed.

Hall, Nor. *The Moon and the Virgin: Reflections on the Archetypal Feminine*. New York, NY: Harper and Row, 1980.

Hallo, William W., and William Kelly Simpson. *The Ancient Near East: A History*. New York, NY: Harcourt Brace, 1998.

Hamilton, Edith. *Mythology: Timeless Tales of Gods and Heroes*. 1940. New York, NY: Mentor Books,

1963 ed.
———. *The Roman Way*. 1932. New York, NY: Mentor Books, 1961 ed.
———. *The Greek Way*. 1930. New York, NY: Mentor Books, 1959 ed.
Hampson, Robert Thomas. *Medieval Kalendarium, or Dates, Charters, and Customs of the Middle Ages*. 2 vols. London, UK: Henry Kent Causton and Co., 1841.
Happold, F. C. *Mysticism: A Study and an Anthology*. Harmondsworth, UK: Penguin, 1991.
Hardon, John A. *Pocket Catholic Dictionary*. 1980. New York, NY: Image, 1985 ed.
Harnack, Adolf. *New Testament Studies 2: The Sayings of Jesus—The Second Source of St. Matthew and St. Luke* (J. R. Wilkinson, trans.). London, UK: Williams and Norgate, 1908.
Harpur, James. *The Atlas of Sacred Places: Meeting Points of Heaven and Earth*. New York, NY: Henry Holt, 1994.
Harrington, Daniel J. *Interpreting the New Testament: A Practical Guide*. 1979. Wilmington, DE: Michael Glazier, 1980 ed.
Harris, Marvin. *Our Kind*. New York, NY: Harper and Row, 1989.
Hart, George. *A Dictionary of Egyptian Gods and Goddesses*. 1986. London, UK: Routledge, 1992 ed.
Hartmann, Franz. *In the Pronaos of the Temple of Wisdom: Containing the History of the True and the False Rosicrucians*. London, UK: Theosophical Publishing Society, 1890.
———. *Magic White and Black: Or the Science of Finite and Infinite Life*. London, UK: Kegan Paul, Trench, Trübner, and Co., 1893.
Haskin, Frederic J. *5,000 Answers to Questions*. New York, NY: Grosset and Dunlap, 1933.
Haskins, Susan. *Mary Magdalen: Myth and Metaphor*. New York, NY: Harcourt Brace and Co., 1993.
Hawken, Paul. *The Magic of Findhorn*. New York, NY: Bantam, 1976.
Hawking, Stephen William. *A Brief History of Time: From the Big Bang to Black Holes*. New York, NY: Bantam, 1988.
Hay, Louise L. *You Can Heal Your Life*. 1984. Carlsbad, CA: Hay House, 1987 ed.
Head, Joseph, and S. L. Cranston (eds.). *Reincarnation: An East-West Anthology*. 1961. Wheaton, IL: Quest, 1975 ed.
Heaton, E. W. *Everyday Life in Old Testament Times*. New York, NY: Charles Scribner's Sons, 1956.
Heckethorn, Charles William. *The Secret Societies of All Ages and Countries*. 2 vols. London, UK: James Hogg, 1875.
Hefele, Charles Joseph. *A History of the Councils of the Church, From the Original Documents*. 5 vols. Edinburgh, Scotland: T. and T. Clark, 1871.
Heindel, Max. *The Rosicrucian Cosmo-Conception or Mystic Christianity*. Oceanside, CA: Rosicrucian Fellowship, 1911.
———. *Nature Spirits and Nature Forces*. Oceanside, CA: Rosicrucian Fellowship, 1937.
Helms, Randel. *Gospel Fictions*. Buffalo, NY: Prometheus Books, 1988.
Henry, Caleb Sprague. *A Compendium of Christian Antiquities: Being a Brief View of the Orders, Rites, Laws and Customs of the Ancient Church in the Early Ages*. Philadelphia, PA: Joseph Whetham, 1837.
Herbert W. Armstrong, Keith W. Stump, and John Halford. *The Plain Truth About Christmas*. Pasadena, CA: Worldwide Church of God, 1952, 1985, 1986.
Herm, Gerhard. *The Celts: The People Who Came Out of the Darkness*. New York, NY: St. Martin's Press, 1975.
Herrmann, Samuel O. (ed.). *The Black and Red*, Vol. 21, No. 2, May 1917. (A monthly magazine published by the students of Northwestern College.) Watertown, WI: Northwestern College, 1917.
Hertz, Joseph H. *Sayings of the Fathers: Pirke Aboth*. New York, NY: Behrman House, 1945.
Hesiod. *Theogonia; Erga kai Hemerai* (circa 8th Century B.C.) Martin Litchfield West, trans. In English: *Theogony and Work and Days*. 1988. Oxford, UK: Oxford University Press, 1991 ed.
Hesse, Hermann. *Siddhartha*. 1951. New York, NY: Bantam, 1974 ed.
Hewson, William. *The Hebrew and Greek Scriptures Compared With Oriental History, Dialling, Science, and Mythology*. London, UK: Simpkin and Co., 1870.
Hicks, Clive. *Green Man: The Archetype of Our Oneness With the Earth*. London, UK: Harper Collins,

1990.

Higgins, Godfrey. *Anacalypsis, An Attempt to Draw Aside the Veil of the Saitic Isis*. 2 vols. London, UK: Longman, Rees, Orme, Brown, Green and Longman, 1836.

Higginson, Edward. *Astro-Theology; or, The Religion of Astronomy: Four Lectures*. London, UK: E. T. Whitfield, 1855.

Hillman, James. *Insearch: Psychology and Religion*. New York, NY: Charles Scribner's Sons, 1967.

Hinckley, K. C. *A Compact Guide to the Christian Life*. Colorado Springs, CO: NavPress, 1989.

Hinnells, John R. (ed.). *The Penguin Dictionary of Religions*. Harmondsworth, UK: Penguin, 1984.

Hinsie, Leland E., and Robert Jean Campbell. *Psychiatric Dictionary*. New York, NY: Oxford University Press, 1970 ed.

Hislop, Alexander. *The Two Babylons, or The Papal Worship Proved to be the Worship of Nimrod and His Wife*. Edinburgh, Scotland: James Wood, 1862.

Hitching, Francis. *The Mysterious World: An Atlas of the Unexplained*. 1978. New York, NY: Holt, Rinehart and Winston, 1979 ed.

Hodson, Geoffrey. *The Hidden Wisdom in the Holy Bible*. Vol. 1. 1967. Wheaton, IL: Quest/Theosophical Publishing House, 1978 ed.

———. *The Hidden Wisdom in the Holy Bible*. Vol. 2. 1967. Wheaton, IL: Quest/Theosophical Publishing House, 1978 ed.

Hoeller, Stephan A. *Jung and the Lost Gospels: Insights into the Dead Sea Scrolls and the Nag Hammadi Library*. 1989. Wheaton, IL: Quest Books, 1990 ed.

Hoffer, Eric. *The True Believer*. New York, NY: Harper, 1951.

Hoffman, R. Joseph. *Jesus Outside the Gospels*. Buffalo, NY: Prometheus, 1984.

Holden, Joseph M., and Norman Geisler. *The Popular Handbook of Archaeology and the Bible*. Eugene, OR: Harvest House, 2013.

Holding, James Patrick. *Shattering the Christ Myth: Did Jesus Not Exist?* Maitland, FL: Xulon Press, 2008.

Holroyd, Stuart. *The Arkana Dictionary of New Perspectives*. Harmondsworth, UK: Arkana, 1989.

Hone, William (ed.). *The Apocryphal New Testament*. London, UK: self-published, 1820.

———. *Ancient Mysteries Described*. London, UK: self-published, 1823.

Hopfe, Lewis M. *Religions of the World*. New York, NY: Macmillan, 1987.

Hopkins, Emma Curtis. *High Mysticism*. New York, NY: Edwin S. Gorham, 1921.

Horne, Herman Harrell. *Jesus the Master Teacher*. New York, NY: Association Press, 1920.

Houvet, Etienne. *Chartres: Guide of the Cathedral*. Paris, France: Houvet-La Crypte, 1972.

Howell, F. Clark. *Early Man*. 1965. New York, NY: Time-Life Books, 1971 ed.

Howells, George. *The Bhagavad Gita and the New Testament: The Internal Relations of Their Fundamental Doctrines*. Cuttack, India: Orissa Mission Press, 1907.

Howitt, William. *The History of the Supernatural: In All Ages and Nations and in All Churches Christian and Pagan, Demonstrating a Universal Faith*. 2 vols. Philadelphia, PA: J. B. Lippincott and Co., 1863.

Hua-Ching, Ni. *The Taoist Inner View of the Universe and the Immortal Realm*. 1979. Malibu, CA: The Shrine of the Eternal Breath of Tao, 1986 ed.

Hughes, Philip. *A Popular History of the Catholic Church*. New York, NY: Macmillan, 1946.

Hume, David. *Dialogues Concerning Natural Religion*. London, UK: n.p., 1779.

Hutchinson, R. W. *Prehistoric Crete*. 1962. Harmondsworth, UK: Penguin, 1968 ed.

Hutchinson, Thomas (ed.). *The Poetical Works of Percy Bysshe Shelley*. London, UK: Henry Frowde, 1905.

Ide, Arthur Frederick. *Unzipped: The Popes Bare All - A Frank Study of Sex and Corruption in the Vatican*. Austin, TX: American Atheist Press, 1987.

———. *Yahweh's Wife: Sex in the Evolution of Monotheism - A Study of Yahweh, Asherah, Ritual Sodomy and Temple Prostitution*. Las Colinas, TX: Monument Press, 1991.

Inge, William Ralph. *Christian Mysticism: Considered in Eight Lectures Delivered Before the University of Oxford*. London, UK: Methuen and Co., 1899.

———. *Personal Idealism and Mysticism*. New York, NY: Longmans, Green, and Co., 1907.
Ingersoll, Robert Green. *Sixty-five Press Interviews with Robert G. Ingersoll*. Austin, TX: American Atheist Press, 1983.
Inman, Thomas. *Ancient Faiths Embodied in Ancient Names*. 2 vols. London, UK: Trübner and Co., 1872.
Ironside, H. A. *Illustrations of Bible Truth*. Chicago, IL: Moody Press, 1945.
Irudayaraj, Xavier (ed.). *Swamy Bede Dayananda: Testimonies and Tributes*. Thannirpalli, South India: Shantivanam Publications, 1994.
Irving, Edward. *The Collected Writings of Edward Irving*. 5 vols. London, UK: Alexander Strahan and Co., 1864.
Jackson, John G. *Christianity Before Christ*. Austin, TX: American Atheist Press, 1985.
———. *Pagan Origins of the Christ Myth*. Austin, TX: American Atheist Press, n.d.
———. *The Golden Ages of Africa*. Austin, TX: American Atheist Press, 1987.
Jacobi, Jolande. *The Psychology of C. G. Jung*. 1942. New Haven, CT: Yale University Press, 1973 ed.
Jacolliot, M. Louis. *The Bible in India: Hindoo Origin of Hebrew and Christian Revelation*. London, UK: John Camden Hotten, 1870.
James, William. *The Varieties of Religious Experience*. New York, NY: Mentor, 1902.
Jefferson, Thomas. *The Jefferson Bible: The Life and Morals of Jesus of Nazareth*. 1803. Chicago, IL: N. D. Thompson, 1902 ed.
John, DeWitt. *The Christian Science Way of Life*. Boston, MA: Christian Science Publishing Society, 1962.
Johns, Catherine. *Sex or Symbol? Erotic Images of Greece and Rome*. New York, NY: Routledge, 1982.
Johns, June. *Black Magic Today*. London, UK: New English Library, 1971.
Johnson, Robert A. *Inner Work: Using Dreams and Active Imagination for Personal Growth*. 1986. New York, NY: Harper Collins, 1989 ed.
———. *She: Understanding Feminine Psychology*. 1976. New York, NY: Perennial Library, 1977 ed.
Johnston, Charles. *Bhagavad Gita: The Songs of the Master*. New York, NY: J. J. Little and Ives, 1908.
Johnston, Sarah Iles (ed.). *Religions of the Ancient World: A Guide*. Cambridge, MA: Harvard University Press, 2004.
Jonas, Hans. *The Gnostic Religion: The Message of the Alien God and the Beginnings of Christianity*. 1958. London, UK: Routledge, 1992 ed.
Jones, A. H. M. *Constantine and the Conversion of Europe*. 1948. New York, NY: Collier, 1962 ed.
Jones, Dennis Merritt. *The Art of Being: 101 Ways to Practice Purpose in Your Life*. New York, NY: Penguin, 2008.
Jones, Gwyn. *A History of the Vikings*. 1968. Oxford, UK: Oxford University Press, 1984 ed.
Jones, Rufus Matthew. *Studies in Mystical Religion*. London, UK: Macmillan and Co., 1919.
Jones, William. *Manava Dharma Sastra, or the Institutes of Manu According to the Gloss of Kulluka*. Madras, India: J. Higginbotham, 1863.
Jordan, Louis Henry. *Comparative Religion: Its Adjuncts and Allies*. London, UK: Oxford University Press, 1915.
Jordan, Michael. *Encyclopedia of Gods: Over 2,500 Deities of the World*. New York, NY: Facts on File, 1993.
Josephus, Flavius. *The Genuine Works of Flavius Josephus* (William Whiston, trans.). 6 vols. New York, NY: William Borradaile, 1824.
Joyce, T. Athol, and N. W. Thomas. *Women of All Nations*. New York, NY: Metro Publications, 1942.
Jukes, Andrew. *The Types of Genesis Briefly Considered As Revealing the Development of Human Nature*. London, UK: Longmans, Green, and Co., 1885.
Julian of Norwich. *Revelations of Divine Love* (Clifton Wolters, trans.). 1373. Harmondsworth, UK: Penguin, 1966.
Jung, Carl Gustav. *Psychology and Religion*. 1938. New Haven, CT: Yale University Press, 1961 ed.
———. *Man and His Symbols*. 1964. New York, NY: Dell, 1968 ed.
Kaplan, Justin. *Walt Whitman: A Life*. New York, NY: Simon and Shuster, 1980.

Kavanagh, Morgan. *Origin of Language and Myths.* 2 vols. London, UK: Sampson Low, Son, and Marston, 1871.
Kavanaugh, James. *A Modern Priest Looks at His Outdated Church.* New York, NY: Trident Press, 1967.
———. *The Birth of God.* New York, NY: Trident Press, 1969.
Kawaguchi, Ekai. *Three Years in Tibet.* Madras, India: Theosophical Publishing Society, 1909.
Keable, Robert. *The Great Galilean.* Boston, MA: Little, Brown and Co., 1929.
Keck, Leander E. *Taking the Bible Seriously.* New York, NY: Association Press, 1962.
Kee, Howard Clark. *The Origins of Christianity: Sources and Documents.* Englewood Cliffs, NJ: Prentice-Hall, 1973.
Keller, Werner. *The Bible As History.* 1956. New York, NY: Bantam, 1980 ed.
Kelly, John Norman Davidson. *Early Christian Doctrines.* 1960. San Francisco, CA: Harper and Row, 1978 ed.
Kelly, Sean, and Rosemary Rogers. *Saints Preserve Us! Everything You Need to Know About Every Saint You'll Ever Need.* New York, NY: Random House, 1993.
Kennett, David. *Pharaoh: Life and Afterlife of a God.* New York, NY: Walker and Co., 2008.
Kerr, Adrian R. J. *Ancient Egypt and Us: The Impact of Ancient Egypt on the Modern World.* Ft. Myers, FL: Ferniehirst Trading, 2008.
Kertzer, Morris N. *What Is a Jew?* 1953. New York, NY: Macmillan, 1971 ed.
Khan, Pir Vilayat Inayat. *Toward the One.* London, UK: Harper Colophon, 1974.
King, Charles W. *The Gnostics and Their Remains, Ancient and Medieval.* London, UK: Bell and Daldy, 1864.
King, Jawara D. *The Awakening of Global Consciousness: A Guide to Self-Realization and Spirituality.* Bloomington, IN: AuthorHouse, 2010.
King, Karen L. *Images of the Feminine in Gnosticism.* 1988. Harrisburg, PA: Trinity Press, 2000 ed.
Kingsbury, Jack Dean. *Matthew: Structure, Christology, Kingdom.* 1975. Philadelphia, PA: Fortress Press, 1978 ed.
Kingsford, Anna, and Edward Maitland. *The Perfect Way; or, The Finding of Christ.* London, UK: Leadenhall Press, 1890.
Kingsley, Charles. *The Works of Charles Kingsley, Vol. 26: The Water of Life.* London, UK: Macmillan and Co., 1881.
Kirk, George E. *A Short History of the Middle East: From the Rise of Islam to Modern Times.* New York, NY: Praeger, 1959.
Kirk, G. S. *The Nature of the Greek Myths.* 1974. Harmondsworth, UK: Penguin, 1978 ed.
Kirk, Robert. *The Secret Commonwealth of Elves, Fauns, and Fairies: A Study in Folk-lore and Psychical Research.* 1691. London, UK: David Nutt, 1893 ed.
Kitto, John (ed.). *A Cyclopedia of Biblical Literature.* 2 vols. Edinburgh, Scotland: Adam and Charles Black, 1851.
———. *An Illustrated History of the Holy Bible.* Norwich, CT: Henry Bill, 1869.
Kloppenborg, John S. *The Formation of Q: Trajectories in Ancient Wisdom Collections.* 1987. Minneapolis, MN: Fortress Press, 2007 ed.
———. *Q Parallels: Synopsis, Critical Notes, and Concordance.* Sonoma, CA: Polebridge Press, 1988.
Knight, Richard Payne. *An Inquiry Into the Symbolic Language of Ancient Art and Mythology.* 1818. London, UK: Black and Armstrong, 1836 ed.
Knox, John. *The History of the Reformation of Religion in Scotland.* C. 1560. London, UK: Andrew Melrose, 1905.
Köstenberger, Andreas J. *John.* Grand Rapids, MI: Baker Publishing, 2004.
Köstenberger, Andreas J., L. Scott Kellum, and Charles L. Quarles. *The Cradle, the Cross, and the Crown: An Introduction to the New Testament.* Nashville, TN: B. and H., 2009.
Krippner, Stanley, and Daniel Rubin (eds.). *The Kirlian Aura: Photographing the Galaxies of Life.* New York, NY: Anchor Books, 1974.
Krishna, Gopi. *The Real Nature of Mystical Experience.* New York, NY: New Concepts, 1978.
———. *Kundalini in Time and Space.* New Delhi, India: Kundalini Research and Publication Trust, 1979.

Krishnamurti, Jiddu. *The First and Last Freedom*. 1954. Wheaton, IL: Quest, 1968 ed.
———. *Think on These Things* (D. Rajagopal, ed.). 1964. New York, NY: Perennial Library, 1970 ed.
———. *Talks and Dialogues*. 1968. New York, NY: Avon, 1970 ed.
———. *On Relationship*. New York, NY: Harper Collins, 1992.
Krutch, Joseph Wood. *Henry David Thoreau*. 1948. New York, NY: William Morrow and Co., 1974 ed.
Kuehl, Nancy L. *Becoming Christian: The Demise of the Jesus Movement*. Eugene, OR: Resource, 2014.
Kuhn, Alvin Boyd. *Who is This King of Glory?: A Critical Study of the Christos-Messiah Tradition*. Elizabeth, NJ: Academy Press, 1944.
———. *Lost Light: An Interpretation of Ancient Scriptures*. Minneapolis, MN: Filiquarian, 2007.
Kul, Djwal. *Intermediate Studies of the Human Aura*. 1974. Colorado Springs, CO: Summit University Press, 1976 ed.
Kümmel, W. G. *The New Testament: The History of the Investigation of Its Problems*. Nashville, TN: Abingdon, 1972.
Küng, Hans. *Christianity: Essence, History, and Future*. New York, NY: Continuum, 1995.
Küng, Hans, and Jürgen Moltmann (eds.). *Conflicts About the Holy Spirit*. New York, NY: Seabury Press, 1979.
Ladd, George Trumbull. *The Philosophy of Religion*. 2 vols. 1905. New York, NY: Charles Scribner's Sons, 1909 ed.
Lamsa, George M. *The Holy Bible From Ancient Eastern Manuscripts*. 1933. Philadelphia, PA: A. J. Holman Co., 1957 ed.
———. *Idioms in the Bible Explained and A Key to the Original Gospels*. 1931. New York, NY: Harper Collins, 1985 ed.
Landis, Benson Y. *An Outline of the Bible Book by Book*. 1963. New York, NY: Barnes and Noble, 1970 ed.
Lange, Johann Peter. *The Life of Jesus Christ: A Complete Critical Examination of the Origin, Contents, and Connection of the Gospels*. 4 vols. Edinburgh, Scotland: T. and T. Clark, 1872.
Langford, Norman F. *Fire Upon the Earth: The Story of the Christian Church*. Philadelphia, PA: Westminster Press, 1950.
Lao-Tsu. *Tao Te Ching*. New York, NY: Vintage Books, 1972.
Lapide, Pinchas E. *Three Popes and the Jews*. New York, NY: Hawthorne Books, 1967.
Larousse Encyclopedia of Archeology. 1969. New York, NY: Crescent Books, 1987 ed.
Larson, Bob. *Satanism: The Seduction of America's Youth*. Nashville, TN: Thomas Nelson, 1989.
Lash, John Lamb. *Not In His Image: Gnostic Vision, Sacred Ecology, and the Future of Belief*. White River Junction, VT: Chelsea Green, 2006.
Lasne, Sophie, and André Pascal Gaultier. *A Dictionary of Superstitions: From the Ridiculous to the Sublime*. Englewood Cliffs, NJ: Prentice-Hall, 1984.
Lass, Abraham H., David Kiremidjian, and Ruth M. Goldstein. *The Dictionary of Classical, Biblical, and Literary Allusions*. New York, NY: Fawcett Gold Medal, 1987.
LaVey, Anton Szandor. *The Satanic Bible*. New York, NY: Avon Books, 1969.
———. *The Satanic Rituals*. New York, NY: Avon Books, 1972.
Law, William. *The Works of the Reverend William Law, M.A., Sometime Fellow of the Emmanuel College, Cambridge*. 9 vols. 1762. Brockenhurst, Hampshire, UK: 1893 ed.
Layton, Bentley. *The Gnostic Scriptures: Ancient Wisdom for the New Age*. New York, NY: Doubleday, 1987.
Leakey, Richard E. *The Making of Mankind*. New York, NY: E. P. Dutton and Co., 1981.
Leakey, Richard E., and Roger Lewin. *Origins*. New York, NY: E. P. Dutton and Co., 1977.
———. *Origins Reconsidered: In Search of What Makes Us Human*. New York, NY: Doubleday, 1992.
Learsi, Rufus. *Israel: A History of the Jewish People*. 1949. Cleveland, OH: Meridian, 1966 ed.
Leboyer, Frederick. *Birth Without Violence*. 1975. New York, NY: Knopf, 1978 ed.
Lee, Arthur Patterson. *The Controversial Jesus and the Critics*. Toronto, Canada: Clements Publishing, 2002.

Lee, Dal. *Understanding the Occult: Secrets of Psychic Phenomena Revealed.* New York, NY: Paperback Library, 1969.
Lee, Jae Hyun. *Paul's Gospel in Romans: A Discourse Analysis of Rom. 1:16-8:39.* Leiden, The Netherlands, Brill, 2010.
Leek, Sybil. *The Complete Art of Witchcraft.* New York, NY: Signet, 1971.
Leeming, David Adams. *The World of Myth.* New York, NY: Oxford University Press, 1990.
Leggat, P. O., and D. V. Leggat. *The Healing Wells: Cornish Cults and Customs.* Kernow, Cornwall, UK: Truran, 1987.
Legge, Francis. *Forerunner and Rivals of Christianity: Being Studies in Religious History From 330 B.C. to 330 A.D.* 2 vols. Cambridge, UK: Cambridge University Press, 1915.
Leishman, Thomas Linton. *Our Ageless Bible: From Early Manuscripts to Modern Versions.* 1939. New York, NY: Thomas Nelson and Sons, 1962 ed.
———. *The Continuity of the Bible: The Gospels.* Boston, MA: Christian Science Publishing Society, 1976.
Leloup, Jean-Yves. *The Gospel of Philip: Jesus, Mary Magdalene, and the Gnosis of the Sacred Union.* Rochester, VT: Inner Traditions, 2004.
Lemesurier, Peter. *The Armageddon Script: Prophecy in Action.* Rockport, MA: Element, 1993.
Lenz, Frederick. *Lifetimes: True Accounts of Reincarnation.* New York, NY: Fawcett Crest, 1979.
Lerner, Gerda. *The Creation of Patriarchy.* 1986. Oxford, UK: Oxford University Press, 1987 ed.
Lessa, William A., and Evon Z. Vogt. *Reader in Comparative Religion: An Anthropological Approach.* New York, NY: Harper and Row, 1979.
Lewis, Abram Herbert. *Paganism Surviving In Christianity.* New York, NY: G. P. Putnam's Sons, 1892.
Lewis, C. S. *Mere Christianity.* 1943. New York, NY: Macmillan, 1973 ed.
———. *The Problem of Pain.* New York, NY: Collier, 1962.
Lewis, Harvey Spencer. *Mansions of the Soul: The Cosmic Conception.* 1930. San Jose, CA: Ancient Mystical Order Rosae Crucis (AMORC), 1969 ed.
———. *The Secret Doctrine of Jesus.* 1937. San Jose, CA: Rosicrucian Press, 1954 ed.
Lewis, I. M. *Ecstatic Religion: An Anthropological Study of Spirit Possession and Shamanism.* 1971. Harmondsworth, UK: Penguin, 1975 ed.
Levy, Rosalie Marie. *Heavenly Friends: A Saint For Each Day.* Boston, MA: Daughters of St. Paul, 1956.
Liddon, Henry Parry. *Sermons Preached Before the University of Oxford.* Oxford, UK: James Parker and Co., 1869.
Lieberman, E. James. *Acts of Will: The Life and Work of Otto Rank.* New York, NY: The Free Press, 1985.
Liebowitz, Michael R. *The Chemistry of Love.* 1983. New York, NY: Berkley Books, 1984 ed.
Life—How Did It Get Here? By Evolution or Creation? Brooklyn, NY: Watchtower Bible and Tract Society of New York, 1985.
Lillie, Arthur. *Buddhism in Christendom, or Jesus, the Essene.* London, UK: Kegan Paul, Trench and Co., 1887.
———. *The Influence of Buddhism on Primitive Christianity.* London, UK: Swan Sonnenschein and Co., 1893.
Lilly, John C. *The Human Biocomputer.* London: Abacus, 1967.
Lindsay, Hal. *The Rapture: Truth or Consequences.* New York, NY: Bantam, 1983.
Lindsay, Hal, and Carole C. Carlson. *The Late Great Planet Earth.* 1970. New York, NY: Bantam, 1990 ed.
———. *There's a New World Coming: A Prophetic Odyssey.* Santa Ana, CA: Vision House, 1973.
Link, John R. *Help In Understanding the Bible.* Valley Forge, PA: Judson Press, 1974.
Little, L. Gilbert. *Nervous Christians.* Chicago, IL: Moody Press, 1956.
Littleton, C. Scott (ed.). *Mythology: The Illustrated Anthology of World Myth and Storytelling.* London, UK: Duncan Baird, 2002.
———. (ed.) *Gods, Goddesses, and Mythology.* 11 vols. Tarrytown, NY: Marshall Cavendish, 2005.
Livingstone, Elizabeth Anne (ed.). *The Concise Oxford Dictionary of the Christian Church.* Oxford, UK: Oxford University Press, 1990 ed.

Llewelyn, Robert. *All Shall Be Well: The Spirituality of Julian of Norwich for Today*. Mahwah, NJ: Paulist Press, 1982.
Loar, Julie. *Goddesses For Every Day: Exploring the Wisdom and Power of the Divine Feminine Around the World*. Novato, CA: New World Library, 2011.
Lockyer, Herbert. *All the Women of the Bible*. 1967. Grand Rapids, MI: Zondervan, 1988 ed.
Locy, William A. *The Story of Biology*. Garden City, NY: Garden City Publishing Co., 1925.
Lohse, Eduard. *The New Testament Environment*. 1971. Nashville, TN: Abingdon, 1974 ed.
Loomis, Roger Sherman. *The Grail: From Celtic Myth to Christian Symbol*. 1963. Princeton, NJ: Princeton University Press, 1991 ed.
Lorberbaum, Yair. *Disempowered King: Monarchy in Classical Jewish Literature*. London, UK: Continuum International Publishing Group, 2011.
Lord, John. *The Old Pagan Civilizations*. New York, NY: Fords, Howard, and Hulbert, 1888.
Louis, David. *More Fascinating Facts*. New York, NY: The Ridge Press, 1979.
Lucas, Alfred, and John Richard Harris. *Ancient Egyptian Materials and Industries*. 1962. Mineola, NY: Dover, 1999 ed.
Ludlow, Daniel H. *Encyclopedia of Mormonism: The History, Scripture, Doctrine, and Procedure of the Church of Jesus Christ of Latter Day Saints*. New York, NY: Macmillan, 1992.
Lundy, John Patterson. *Monumental Christianity, or the Art and Symbolism of the Primitive Church As Witnesses and Teachers of the One Catholic Faith and Practice*. New York, NY: J. W. Bouton, 1876.
Luomanen, Petri. *Recovering Jewish-Christian Sects and Gospels*. Leiden, The Netherlands: Brill, 2012.
Lurker, Manfred. *Dictionary of Gods and Goddesses, Devils and Demons* (G. L. Campbell, trans.). 1984. London, UK: Routledge, 1988 ed.
———. *The Gods and Symbols of Ancient Egypt* (Barbara Cumming, trans.). 1974. London, UK: Thames and Hudson, 1984 ed.
Lyle, Anthony. *Ancient History: A Revised Chronology—An Updated Version of Ancient History Based on New Archaeology* (Vol. 1). Bloomington, IN: AuthorHouse, 2012.
Lynch, Frances. *Megalithic Tombs and Long Barrows in Britain*. 1997. Princes Risborough, UK: Shire Publications, 2004 ed.
MacCulloch, John Arnott. *Comparative Theology*. London, UK: Methuen and Co., 1902.
MacGregor, Geddes. *Reincarnation in Christianity: A New Vision of the Role of Rebirth in Christian Thought*. 1978. Wheaton, IL: Theosophical Publishing House, 1989 ed.
MacGregor, George Hogarth Carnaby. *The New Testament Basis of Pacifism*. 1936. New York, NY: Fellowship of Reconciliation, 1954 ed.
MacIntyre, Alisdair (ed.). *Hume's Ethical Writings*. London, UK: Collier, 1965.
Mack, Burton L. *The Lost Gospel: The Book of Q and Christian Origins*. New York, NY: Harper Collins, 1993.
Mackay, Robert William. *A Sketch of the Rise and Progress of Christianity*. London, UK: John Chapman, 1854.
Mackey, Albert Gallatin. *The Symbolism of Freemasonry: Illustrating and Explaining its Science and Philosophy, its Legends, Myths, and Symbols*. New York, NY: Clark and Maynard, 1869.
Maclaren, Alexander. *Sermons Preached in Manchester*. London, UK: Macmillan and Co., 1873.
———. *St. Paul's Epistle to the Romans*. New York, NY: A. C. Armstrong and Son, 1909.
Mader, Sylvia S. *Inquiry Into Life*. 1976. Dubuque, IA: William C. Brown Publishers, 1988 ed.
Magee, Bryan. *Philosophy and the Real World: An Inroduction to Karl Popper*. 1973. La Salle, IL: Open Court Publishing Co., 1990 ed.
Magli, Giulio. *Mysteries and Discoveries of Archaeoastronomy: From Giza to Easter Island*. 2005. New York, NY: Copernicus Books, 2009 ed.
Magoulias, Harry J. *Byzantine Christianity: Emperor, Church and the West*. Chicago, IL: Rand McNally and Co., 1970.
Maharshi, Ramana. *The Spiritual Teaching of Ramana Maharshi*. Berkeley, CA: Shambala, 1972.
Maitland, Edward. *Anna Kingsford: Her Life, Letters, Diary, and Work*. 2 vols. London, UK: George

Redway, 1896.
Manniche, Lise. *Sexual Life in Ancient Egypt.* 2002. London, UK: Kegan Paul, 2002.
Man's Place in Evolution. Cambridge, UK: British Museum of Natural History/Cambridge University Press, 1980.
Man's Search for God. Brooklyn, NY: Watchtower Bible and Tract Society of New York, 1990.
Marshall, George N. *Challenge of a Liberal Faith.* 1966. Boston, MA: Unitarian Universalist Association, 1975 ed.
Marshall, I. Howard. *Luke: Historian and Theologian.* 1970. Grand Rapids, MI: Zondervan, 1974 ed.
——. *I Believe in the Historical Jesus.* Vancouver, BC: Regent College Publishing, 2001.
Martello, Leo Louis. *Weird Ways of Witchcraft.* 1969. San Francisco, CA: Red Wheel, 2011 ed.
Martin, Joel, and Patricia Romanowski. *We Don't Die: George Anderson's Conversations With the Other Side.* New York, NY: G. P. Putnam's Sons, 1988.
Marty, Martin E. (ed.). *New Directions in Biblical Thought.* New York, NY: Association Press, 1960.
Massey, Gerald. *Ancient Egypt: The Light of the World - A Work of Reclamation and Restitution.* 12 vols. London, UK: T. Fisher Unwin, 1907.
Matthews, Caitlín. *Celtic Devotional: Daily Prayers and Blessings.* New York, NY: Harmony, 1996.
Maurice, Thomas. *The History of Hindostan.* 2 vols. London UK: self-published, 1820.
May, Rollo. *The Cry for Myth.* New York, NY: W. W. Norton, 1991.
McBee, Silas (ed.). *The Constructive Quarterly: A Journal of the Faith, Work and Thought of Christendom.* Vol. 1, March to December, 1913. New York, NY: George H., Doran Co., 1913.
McCannon, Tricia. *Jesus: The Explosive Story of the 30 Lost Years and the Ancient Mystery Religions.* Charlottesville, VA: Hampton Roads Publishing, 2010.
McClelland, Norman C. *Encyclopedia of Reincarnation and Karma.* Jefferson, NC: McFarland and Co., 2010.
McColman, Carl. *The Big Book of Christian Mysticism: The Essential Guide to Contemplative Spirituality.* Charlottesville, VA: Hampton Roads Publishing, 2010.
McConkie, Bruce R. *Mormon Doctrine.* 1966. Salt Lake City, UT: Bookcraft, 1992 ed.
McDonnell, Thomas P. *A Thomas Merton Reader.* Garden City, NY: Image Books, 1974.
McFague, Sally. *Metaphorical Theology.* Philadelphia, PA: Fortress Press, 1982.
McGovern, Patrick E. *Ancient Wine: The Search for the Origins of Viniculture.* 2003. Princeton, NJ: Princeton University Press, 2007 ed.
McGowan, Chris. *In the Beginning . . . .* Buffalo, NY: Prometheus Books, 1984.
McIntosh, Jane R. *Ancient Mesopotamia: New Perspectives.* Santa Barbara, CA: ABC-Clio, 2005.
McKenzie, J. Hewat. *Spirit Intercourse: Its Theory and Practice.* New York, NY: Mitchell Kennerley, 1917.
McKenzie, John L. *Dictionary of the Bible.* New York, NY: Collier, 1965.
Mead, Frank S. *Handbook of Denominations in the United States.* 1951. Nashville: Abingdon Press, 1989 ed.
Mead, George Robert Stow. *Orpheus.* London, UK: Theosophical Publishing Society, 1896.
——. (ed.). *Pistis Sophia: A Gnostic Gospel.* London, UK: Theosophical Publishing Society, 1896.
——. *Did Jesus Live 100 B.C.?* London, UK: Theosophical Publishing Society, 1903.
——. *Fragments of a Faith Forgotten: Some Short Sketches Among the Gnostics.* 1900. Theosophical Publishing Society, 1906 ed.
——. *Thrice-Greatest Hermes: Studies in Hellenistic Theosophy and Gnosis.* 3 vols. London, UK: Theosophical Publishing Society, 1906.
——. (trans.) *The Hymn of Jesus: Echos From the Gnosis.* 1907. Wheaton, IL: Theosophical Publishing House, 1973 ed.
Mead, Margaret. *Male and Female.* 1949. New York, NY: Mentor, 1959 ed.
Meeks, Wayne A. *The Origins of Christian Morality: The First Two Centuries.* New Haven, CT: Yale University Press, 1993.
Meissner, William W. *Psychoanalysis and Religious Experience.* New Haven, CT: Yale University Press, 1984.

Mendelssohn, Kurt. *The Riddle of the Pyramids*. 1974. London, UK: Thames and Hudson, 1986 ed.
Menzies, Allan (ed.). *The Ante-Nicene Fathers: Translations of the Fathers Down to A.D. 325* (original supplement to the American edition). 10 vols. New York, NY: The Christian Literature Co., 1896.
Mercatante, Anthony S. (ed.). *The Harper Book of Christian Poetry*. New York, NY: Harper and Row, 1972.
Merriam-Webster's Collegiate Encyclopedia. Springfield, MA: Merriam-Webster, 2000.
Metford, J. C. J. *Dictionary of Christian Lore and Legend*. London, UK: Thames and Hudson, 1983.
Metzger, Bruce M. *A Text of the New Testament: Its Transmission, Corruption, and Restoration*. Oxford, UK: Oxford University Press, 1968.
———. *The Text of the New Testament: Its Transmission, Corruption, and Restoration*. New York, NY: Oxford University Press, 1968.
Metzger, Bruce M., and Michael D. Coogan (eds.). *The Oxford Companion to the Bible*. Oxford, UK: Oxford University Press, 1993.
Meyer, Marvin W. *The Secret Teachings of Jesus: Four Gnostic Gospels*. New York, NY: Random House, 1984.
———. *The Ancient Mysteries: A Sourcebook*. New York, NY: Harper and Row, 1987.
Miller, Robert J. (ed.). *The Complete Gospels* (annotated scholars version). San Francisco, CA: Polebridge Press, 1994.
Milman, Henry Hart (ed.). *The Life of Edward Gibbon, Esq*. London, UK: John Murray, 1839.
Milton, John. *Selected Prose* (Malcom W. Wallace, ed.). 1641-1659. London, UK: Oxford University Press, 1959.
Mish, Frederick (ed.). *Webster's Ninth New Collegiate Dictionary*. 1828. Springfield, MA: Merriam-Webster, 1984.
Modi, Jivanji Jamshedji. *The Religious System of the Parsis: A Paper*. Bombay, India: Bombay Education Society's Press, 1903.
Mollenkott, Virginia Ramey. *The Divine Feminine: The Biblical Imagery of God as Female*. 1983. New York, NY: Crossroad, 1993 ed.
Moltmann, Jürgen. *The Crucified God: The Cross of Christ as the Foundation and Criticism of Christian Theology*. New York, NY: Harper and Row, 1973.
Monaghan, Patricia. *The Book of Goddesses and Heroines*. 1981. St. Paul, MN: Llewellyn Publications, 1990 ed.
Monk, Robert C., Walter C. Hofheinz, Kenneth T. Lawrence, Joseph D. Stamey, Bert Affleck, and Tetsunao Yamamori. *Exploring Religious Meaning*. Englewood Cliffs, NJ: Prentice-Hall, 1973.
Montagu, Ashley. *The Natural Superiority of Women*. 1952. New York, NY: Collier, 1992 ed.
———. *Man: His First Million Years*. New York, NY: Signet, 1962.
Montefiore, Hugh. *Paul the Apostle*. London, UK: Fount, 1981.
Montgomery, James A. (ed.). *Religions of the Past and Present*. Philadelphia, PA: J. B. Lippincott, 1918.
Moor, Edward. *The Hindu Pantheon*. Madras, India: J. Higginbotham, 1864.
Morgan, Elaine. *The Descent of Woman*. 1972. New York, NY: Bantam, 1973 ed.
———. *The Aquatic Ape*. New York, NY: Stein and Day, 1982.
Morris, Desmond. *The Naked Ape*. New York, NY: Dell, 1967.
———. *Bodywatching: A Field Guide to the Human Species*. New York, NY: Crown, 1985.
Morris, Henry M. *The Bible and Modern Science*. 1951. Chicago, IL: Moody Press, 1956 ed.
Morrison, Sarah Lyddon. *The Modern Witch's Spellbook*. Secaucus, NJ: Lyle Stuart, 1971.
Morrow, Louis Laravoire. *My Catholic Faith: A Manual of Religion*. 1949. Kenosha, WI: My Mission House, 1961 ed.
Moscati, Sabatino. *The Face of the Ancient Orient: Near Eastern Civilization in Pre-Classical Times*. 1960. Mineola, NY: Dover, 2001 ed.
Moses, William Stainton. *Spirit Teachings*. London, UK: London Spiritualist Alliance, 1907.
Mueller, David L. *Karl Barth*. Waco, TX: Word Books, 1972.

Muilenburg, James. *The Way of Israel: Biblical Faith and Ethics*. 1961. New York, NY: Harper and Row, 1965 ed.
Müller, Carl Otfried. *Introduction to a Scientific System of Mythology* (John Leitch, trans.) London, UK: Longman, Brown, Green, and Longmans, 1844.
Müller, Friedrich Max (trans.). *The Upanishads*. Oxford, UK: Clarendon Press, 1879.
——. *Theosophy or Psychological Religion*. London, UK: Longmans, Green, and Co., 1893.
——. *Ramakrishna: His Life and Sayings*. London, UK: Longmans, Green, and Co., 1898.
—— (ed.). *The Sacred Books of the East, Translated by Various Oriental Scholars*. 50 vols. Oxford, UK: Clarendon Press, 1900.
Mullins, E. Y., and H. W. Tribble. *The Baptist Faith*. Nashville, TN: Southern Baptist Convention, 1935.
Murdock, D. M. *Christ in Egypt: The Horus-Jesus Connection*. Seattle, WA: Stellar House, 2009.
——. *Did Moses Exist? The Myth of the Israelite Lawgiver*. Seattle, WA: Stellar House, 2014.
Murnane, William J. *The Penguin Guide to Ancient Egypt*. 1983. Harmondsworth, UK: Penguin, 1984 ed.
Murray, Gilbert (ed. and trans.). *The Bacchae of Euripides*. New York, NY: Longmans, Green, and Co., 1915.
Myer, Isaac. *Qabbalah: The Philosophical Writings of Solomon Ben Yehudah Ibn Gebirol*. Philadelphia, PA: self-published, 1888.
Narasu, Pokala Lakshmi. *The Essence of Buddhism*. Madras, India: Srinivasa Varadachari and Co., 1907.
Nath, Samir. *Encyclopaedic Dictionary of Buddhism*. 3 vols. New Delhi, India: Sarup and Sons, 1998.
Neander, Augustus. *General History of the Christian Religion and Church*. 2 vols. 1847. Boston, MA: Crocker and Brewster, 1854 ed.
Neher, Andrew. *The Psychology of Transcendence*. 1980. New York, NY: Dover, 1990 ed.
Neihardt, John G. *Black Elk Speaks*. 1932. New York, NY: Pocket Books, 1973 ed.
Neill, Stephen. *The Interpretation of the New Testament, 1861-1961*. 1964. Oxford, UK: Oxford University Press, 1970 ed.
——. *What We Know About Jesus*. 1970. Grand Rapids, MI: William B. Eermans Publishing Co., 1972 ed.
Nelson's New Compact Illustrated Bible Dictionary. Nashville, TN: Thomas Nelson, 1978.
Neumann, Erich. *The Great Mother: An Analysis of the Archetype*. New York, NY: Pantheon, 1955.
Newall, Venetia. *The Encyclopedia of Witchcraft and Magic*. A and W Visual Library, 1974.
Nicholson, Edward Byron. *The Gospel According to the Hebrews*. London, UK: C. Kegan Paul and Co., 1879.
Nietzche, Friedrich. *Thus Spoke Zarathustra* (1883-1885). R. J. Hollingdale, trans. 1961. Harmondsworth, England: Penguin, 1972 ed.
Notovitch, Nicolas. *The Unknown Life of Jesus Christ* (Alexina Loranger, trans.). Chicago, IL: Rand, McNally and Co., 1894.
Novak, Peter. *Original Christianity: A New Key to Understanding the Gospel of Thomas and Other Lost Scriptures*. Charlottesville, VA: Hampton Roads Publishing, 2005.
O'Brien, Isidore. *The Life of Christ*. 1937. Paterson, NJ: St. Anthony Guild Press, 1950 ed.
O'Dea, Thomas F. *The Mormons*. Chicago: University of Chicago Press, 1957.
Odent, Michael. *Water and Sexuality*. Harmondsworth, England: Arkana, 1990.
Oldenberg, Hermann. *Buddha: His Life, His Doctrine, His Order* (William Hoey, trans.). London, UK: Williams and Norgate, 1882.
Olson, Carl (ed.). *The Book of Goddess Past and Present: An Introduction to Her Religion*. New York, NY: Crossroad, 1989.
Otto, Rudolf. *Mysticism East and West: A Comparative Analysis of the Nature of Mysticism*. Wheaton, IL: Quest, 1987.
Ottum, Bob (ed.). *A Day in the Life of the Amish*. Greendale, WI: Reiman, 1994.
Owen, John B. *The Eighteenth Century: 1714-1815*. 1974. New York, NY: W. W. Norton, 1976 ed.
Oxford English Dictionary (compact edition). 2 vols. 1928. Oxford, UK: Oxford University Press,

1979 ed.
Oxford Society of Historical Theology. *The New Testament in the Apostolic Fathers*. Oxford, UK: Clarendon Press, 1905.
Pagels, Elaine. *The Gnostic Gospels*. 1979. New York, NY: Vintage Books, 1981 ed.
———. *Adam, Eve, and the Serpent: Sex and Politics in Early Christianity*. 1988. New York, NY: Vintage Books, 1989 ed.
———. *The Gnostic Paul: Gnostic Exegesis of the Pauline Letters*. London, UK: Continuum, 1992.
Paine, Lauran. *Witches in Fact and Fantasy*. 1971. New York, NY: Taplinger Publishing Co., 1972 ed.
Paine, Thomas. *The Age of Reason: Being an Investigation of True and Fabulous Theology*. 1794. New York, NY: D. M. Bennett, 1877 ed.
Paley, William. *The Works of William Paley*. Edinburgh, Scotland: Peter Brown and T. and W. Nelson, 1827.
Parker, Theodore. *The Transient and Permanent in Christianity*. Boston, MA: American Unitarian Association, 1908.
Parkes, James. *Whose Land? A History of the Peoples of Palestine*. 1940. Harmondsworth, UK: Penguin, 1979 ed.
———. *The Conflict of the Church and the Synagogue: A Study in the Origins of Antisemitism*. New York, NY: Meridian, 1961.
Parrinder, Geoffrey. *Encountering World Religions: Questions of Religious Truth*. New York, NY: Crossroad, 1987.
———. *Avatar and Incarnation: The Divine in Human Form in the World's Religions*. Oxford, UK: Oneworld, 1997.
Parsons, Albert Ross. *New Light From the Great Pyramid*. New York, NY: Metaphysical Publishing Co., 1893.
Pasachoff, Jay M. *Astronomy: From the Earth to the Universe*. Philadelphia: W. B. Saunders Co., 1979.
Patai, Raphael. *The Hebrew Goddess*. 1967. Detroit, MI: Wayne State University Press, 1990 ed.
Patterson, Stephen J., and James M. Robinson. *The Fifth Gospel: The Gospel of Thomas Comes of Age*. Harrisburg, PA: Trinity Press International, 1998.
Paul, John, II. *Crossing the Threshold of Hope*. New York, NY: Knopf, 1994.
Paulsen, Kathryn. *The Complete Book of Magic and Witchcraft*. 1970. New York, NY: Signet, 1980 ed.
Pearson, Carol S. *Awakening the Heroes Within: Twelve Archetypes to Help Us Find Ourselves and Transform Our World*. New York, NY: Harper San Francisco, 1991.
Peel, Robert. *Spiritual Healing in a Scientific Age*. San Francisco, CA: Harper and Row, 1988.
Peers, E. Allison (ed. and trans.). *Dark Night of the Soul* (Saint John of the Cross). 16th Century. 1959. New York, NY: Image, 1990 ed.
Pegis, Anton C. (ed.) *Introduction to Saint Thomas Aquinas*. 1945. New York, NY: Modern Library, 1948 ed.
Pelikan, Jaroslav (ed.). *The World Treasury of Modern Religious Thought*. Boston, MA: Little, Brown and Co., 1990.
Pennick, Nigel. *The Pagan Book of Days: A Guide to the Festivals, Traditions, and Sacred Days of the Year*. Rochester, VT: Destiny Books, 1992.
Pennock, Michael. *The New Testament: The Good News of Jesus*. Notre Dame, IN: Ave Maria Press, 1982.
Perowne, Stewart. *Roman Mythology*. 1969. Twickenham, UK: Newnes Books, 1986 ed.
Peters, F. E. *Children of Abraham: Judaism, Christianity, Islam*. 1982. Princeton, NJ: Princeton University Press, 1984 ed.
Pfleiderer, Otto. *The Philosophy of Religion on the Basis of Its History*. 2 vols. London, UK: Williams and Norgate, 1886.
———. *The Early Christian Conception of Christ: Its Significance and Value in the History of Religion*. London, UK: Williams and Norgate, 1905.
———. *The Development of Christianity*. London, UK: T. Fisher Unwin, 1910.
Philo of Alexandria. *The Works of Philo Judaeus, the Contemporary of Josephus* (C. D. Yonge, trans.). 4 vols. London, UK: Henry G. Bohn, 1855.

Pike, Albert. *Morals and Dogma of the Ancient and Accepted Scottish Rite of Freemasonry, Prepared for the Supreme Council of the Thirty-Third Degree for the Southern Jurisdiction of the United States and Published by Its Authority.* Charleston, SC: L. H. Jenkins, 1871.

Pike, James A. *If This Be Heresy.* New York, NY: Harper and Row, 1967.

Platt, Rutherford Hayes (ed.). *The Lost Books of the Bible and the Forgotten Books of Eden.* World Bible Publishers, 1926.

Plumb, J. H. *The Italian Renaissance: A Concise Survey of Its History and Culture.* 1961. New York, NY: Harper and Row, 1965 ed.

Plutarch. *Fall of the Roman Empire* (Rex Warner, trans.). C. 100 C.E. Harmondsworth, UK: Penguin, 1972.

———. *Plutarch's Morals: Theosophical Essays* (Charles W. King, trans.). London, UK: George Bell and Sons, 1898.

Pollock, Frederick. *Spinoza: His Life and Philosophy.* London, UK: C. Kegan Paul and Co., 1880.

Ponder, Catherine. *The Dynamic Laws of Prayer.* Marina Del Rey, CA: DeVorss and Co., 1987.

Porter, Stanley E. (ed.). *Handbook to Exegesis of the New Testament.* Leiden, The Netherlands: Brill, 1997.

Potter, Charles Francis. *The Lost Years of Jesus Revealed.* 1958. New York, NY: Fawcett, 1962 ed.

Powell, John. *The Christian Vision: The Truth That Sets Us Free.* Allen, TX: Argus Communications, 1984.

Powers, Joseph M. *Spirit and Sacrament: The Humanizing Experience.* New York, NY: Seabury Press, 1973.

Prabhavananda, Swami. *The Sermon on the Mount According to Vedanta.* New York, NY: Mentor, 1972.

Prahbupada, A. C. Bhaktivedanta Swami. *Bhagavad Gita As It Is.* 1968. Los Angeles, CA: The Bhaktivedanta Book Trust, 1981 ed.

———. *The Science of Self Realization.* 1971. Los Angeles, CA: The Bhaktivedanta Book Trust, 1981 ed.

———. *Beyond Birth and Death.* Los Angeles, CA: The Bhaktivedanta Book Trust, 1979.

———. *Message of Godhead.* Los Angeles, CA: The Bhaktivedanta Book Trust, 1990.

———. *Renunciation Through Wisdom.* Los Angeles, CA: International Society for Krishna Consciousness, 1992.

Preller, Victor. *Divine Science and the Science of God: A Reformulation of Thomas Aquinas.* Princeton, NJ: Princeton University Press, 1967.

Price, Ira Maurice. *The Ancestry of Our English Bible: An Account of the Bible Versions, Texts, and Manuscripts.* Philadelphia, PA: The Sunday School Times Co., 1907.

Price, Theron Douglas. *Europe Before Rome: A Site-by-Site Tour of the Stone, Bronze, and Iron Ages.* New York, NY: Oxford University Press, 2013.

Prichard, Marianna Nugent, and Norman Young Prichard. *Back to the Sources.* Boston, MA: United Church Press, 1964.

Priestley, Joseph. *The Theological and Miscellaneous Works of Joseph Priestly* (John T. Rutt, ed.). 1786. 25 vols. London, UK: G. Smallfield, 1817-1831 ed.

Pritchard, James B. *Palestinian Figurines in Relation to Certain Goddesses Known Through Literature.* New Haven, CT: American Oriental Society, 1943.

Prophet, Elizabeth Clare, and the Staff of Summit University. *Walking With the Master: Answering the Call of Jesus.* Gardiner, MT: Summit Lighthouse Library, 2002.

Prophet, Elizabeth Clare, and Erin L. Prophet. *Reincarnation: The Missing Link in Christianity.* Livingston, MT: Summit University Press, 1997.

Prophet, Mark L., and Elizabeth Clare Prophet. *The Lost Teachings of Jesus.* Livingston, MT: Summit University Press, 1986.

Pryse, James Morgan. *The Restored New Testament.* London, UK: John M. Watkins, 1914.

Qualls-Corbett, Nancy. *The Sacred Prostitute: Eternal Aspect of the Feminine.* Toronto, Canada: Inner City Books, 1988.

Radner, Daisie, and Michael Radner. *Science and Unreason.* Belmont, CA: Wadsworth Publishing Co., 1982.

Raftery, Barry. *Pagan Celtic Ireland: The Enigma of the Irish Iron Age*. London, UK: Thames and Hudson, 1994.
Ragg, Lonsdale, and Laura Ragg (eds. and trans.). *The Gospel of Barnabas: Edited and Translated From the Italian Ms. in the Imperial Library at Vienna*. Oxford, UK: Clarendon Press, 1907.
Ramacharaka, Yogi. *A Series of Lessons in Mystic Christianity*. Chicago, IL: Yogi Publication Society, 1907.
Ramm, Bernard L. *Hermeneutics*. 1967. Grand Rapids, MI: Baker Book House, 1988 ed.
Rampa, T. Lobsang. *The Third Eye: The Autobiography of a Tibetan Lama*. 1956. New York, NY: Ballantine, 1993 ed.
Randolph, Thomas Jefferson (ed.). *Memoir, Correspondence, and Miscellanies, From the Papers of Thomas Jefferson*. Charlottesville, VA: F. Carr and Co., 1829.
Rawlinson, George. *The History of Herodotus*. 4 vols. New York, NY: D. Appleton and Co., 1889.
Read, Anne. *Edgar Cayce on Jesus and His Church*. 1970. New York, NY: Warner, 1972 ed.
Reed, Henry (ed.). *The Complete Poetical Works of William Wordsworth*. Philadelphia, PA: James Kay Jr. and Brother, 1837.
Reed, Graham. *The Psychology of Anomalous Experience*. Buffalo, NY: Prometheus Books, 1988.
Reilly, Patrician Lynn. *A God Who Looks Like Me: Discovering a Woman-Affirming Spirituality*. New York, NY: Ballantine, 1995.
Renan, Ernest. *The Life of Jesus*. London, UK: Trübner and Co., 1864.
Reyes, E. Christopher. *In His Name: Who Wrote the Gospels?* Bloomington, IN: Trafford, 2014.
Ricciotti, Giuseppe. *The Life of Christ*. Milwaukee, WI: Bruce Publishing, 1947.
Rich, Benjamin E. (ed.) *Latter Day Saints Southern Star*. Vol. 2. Chattanooga, TN: The Southern States Mission, 1900.
Richard, Suzanne (ed.). *Near-Eastern Archaeology: A Reader*. Winona Lake, IN: Eisenbrauns, 2003.
Richards, Le Grand. *A Marvelous Work and a Wonder*. Salt Lake City, UT: Deseret Book Company, 1950.
Richardson, Cyril C. (ed.). *Early Church Fathers*. New York, NY: Collier, 1970.
Ridderbos, Herman. *Paul: An Outline of His Theology* (John R. De Witt, trans.). 1966. Grand Rapids, MI: Eerdmans, 1975 ed.
Riedel, Eunice, Thomas Tracy, and Barbra D. Moskowitz. *The Book of the Bible*. New York, NY: William Morrow and Co., 1979.
Ritchie, Jean. *Death's Door: True Stories of Near-Death Experiences*. New York, NY: Dell, 1996.
Robaldo, John E. (cathechetical notes by). *The Holy Gospel of Our Lord and Savior Jesus Christ*. Boston, MA: St. Paul Editions, 1984.
Roberts, Alexander, and James Donaldson (eds.). *The Ante-Nicene Fathers: Translations of the Fathers Down to A.D. 325* (American reprint of the Edinburgh edition). 10 vols. New York, NY: Charles Scribner's Sons, 1899.
Roberts, Jane. *Seth Speaks: The Eternal Validity of the Soul*. New York, NY: Bantam, 1972.
Roberts, Mark D. *Can We Trust the Gospels? Investigating the Reliability of Matthew, Mark, Luke, and John*. Wheaton, IL: Crossway, 2007.
Robertson, John Mackinnon. *Christianity and Mythology*. London, UK: Watts and Co., 1900.
———. *Pagan Christs: Studies in Comparative Hierology* (2nd ed.) London, UK: Watts and Co., 1911.
Robertson, Pat. *The Secret Kingdom*. Nashville, TN: Thomas Nelson, 1982.
Robinson, James M. (ed.). *The Nag Hammadi Library in English*. 1978. New York, NY: Harper Collins, 1988 ed.
Robinson, Lytle. *Edgar Cayce's Story of the Origin and Destiny of Man*. 1972. New York, NY: Berkley, 1984 ed.
Robinson, Paschal. *The Writings of Saint Francis of Assisi*. Philadelphia, PA: The Dolphin Press, 1905.
Roddy, Lee, and Charles E. Sellier Jr. *In Search of Historic Jesus*. 1960. New York, NY: Bantam, 1979 ed.
Rogo, D. Scott. *Man Does Survive Death: The Welcoming Silence*. 1973. Secaucus, NJ: Citadel Press, 1977 ed.

Romer, John. *Testament*. New York, NY: Henry Holt and Co., 1988.
Ross, Floyd H., and Tynette Hills. *The Great Religions By Which Men Live*. 1956. New York, NY: Premier, 1961 ed.
Rosten, Leo. *A Guide to the Religions of America*. New York, NY: Simon and Schuster, 1955.
Rouse, W. H. D. *Gods, Heroes and Men of Ancient Greece*. New York, NY: Mentor, 1957.
Rudrananda, Swami. *Spiritual Cannibalism*. New York, NY: Links Books, 1973.
Rubin, Zick, and Elton B. McNeil. *The Psychology of Being Human*. New York, NY: Harper and Row, 1983.
Rudolph, Kurt. *Gnosis: The Nature and History of Gnosticism*. 1977. Edinburgh, Scotland: T. and T. Clark, 1983 ed.
Ruether, Rosemary Radford. *The Radical Kingdom: The Western Experience of Messianic Hope*. New York, NY: Harper and Row, 1970.
Rufus, Anneli S., and Kristan Lawson. *Goddess Sites: Europe*. New York, NY: Harper Collins, 1991.
Runciman, Steven. *A History of the Crusades, Vol. 1: The First Crusade*. 1951. New York, NY: Harper Torchbooks, 1964 ed.
Runes, Dagobert D. (ed.). *Dictionary of Judaism*. 1959. New York, NY: Citadel Press, 1991 ed.
Russell, Bertrand. *A History of Western Philosophy*. 1945. New York, NY: Touchstone, 1972 ed.
———. *Why I Am Not a Christian*. 1930. New York, NY: Touchstone, 1957 ed.
Rutherford, Ward. *Celtic Mythology: The Nature and Influence of Celtic Myth—From Druidism to Arthurian Legend*. 1987. New York, NY: Sterling Publishing Co., 1990 ed.
Sagan, Carl. *Cosmos*. New York, NY: Random House, 1980.
Sagan, Carl, and Ann Druyan. *Shadows of Forgotten Ancestors: A Search for Who We Are*. New York, NY: Random House, 1992.
Salm, René. *The Myth of Nazareth: The Invented Town of Jesus*. Parsipanny, NJ: American Atheist Press, 2008.
Salmonson, Jessica Amanda. *The Encyclopedia of Amazons: Women Warriors from Antiquity to the Modern Era*. New York, NY: Paragon House, 1991.
Sanders, E. P. *The Historical Figure of Jesus*. Harmondsworth, UK: Penguin, 1993.
Sanford, John A. *Dreams: God's Forgotten Language*. Philadelphia, PA: J. B. Lippincott, 1968.
———. *The Kingdom Within*. New York, NY: Paulist Press, 1970.
Sayce, Archibald Henry. *The Religions of Ancient Egypt and Babylonia*. Edinburgh, Scotland: T. and T. Clark, 1903.
Schaberg, Jane. *The Resurrection of Mary Magdalene: Legends, Apocrypha, and the Christian Testament*. New York, NY: Continuum, 2004.
Schonfield, Hugh J. *Secrets of the Dead Sea Scrolls*. 1957. New York, NY: Perpetua, 1960 ed.
———. *The Authentic New Testament*. New York, NY: Mentor, 1958.
———. *The Passover Plot*. New York, NY: Bernard Geis Associates, 1965.
———. *Those Incredible Christians*. New York, NY: Bernard Geis Associates, 1968.
———. *The Jesus Party*. New York, NY: Macmillan, 1974.
Schopenhauer, Arthur. *The World as Will and Idea*. 4 vols. 1876. London, UK: Kegan Paul, Trench, Trübner, and Co., 1906 ed.
Schwartz, Howard. *Gabriel's Palace: Jewish Mystical Tales*. New York, NY: Oxford University Press, 1993.
Schweitzer, Albert. *The Quest of the Historical Jesus*. 1906. London, UK: Adam and Charles Black, 1910 ed.
———. *The Mystery of the Kingdom of God: The Secret of Jesus' Messiahship and Passion*. New York, NY: Dodd, Mead and Co., 1914.
———. *Out of My Life and Thought: An Autobiography*. 1933. New York, NY: Henry Holt and Co., 1949 ed.
Scott-Moncrieff, Philip David. *Paganism and Christianity in Ancient Egypt*. Cambridge, UK: University Press, 1913.
Scrivener, Frederick H. (Intro.). *A Full Collation of the Codex Sinaiticus With the Received Text of the New*

Testament. Cambridge, UK: Deighton, Bell, and Co., 1864.

Seabrook, Lochlainn. *Aphrodite's Trade: The Hidden History of Prostitution Unveiled*. 1994. Franklin, TN: Sea Raven Press, 2011 ed.

———. *The Goddess Dictionary of Words and Phrases: Introducing a New Core Vocabulary for the Women's Spirituality Movement*. 1997. Franklin, TN: Sea Raven Press, 2010 ed.

———. *Britannia Rules: Goddess-Worship in Ancient Anglo-Celtic Society - An Academic Look at the United Kingdom's Matricentric Spiritual Past*. 1999. Franklin, TN: Sea Raven Press, 2010 ed.

———. *The Book of Kelle: An Introduction to Goddess-Worship and the Great Celtic Mother-Goddess Kelle, Original Blessed Lady of Ireland*. 1999. Franklin, TN: Sea Raven Press, 2010 ed.

———. *Christmas Before Christianity: How the Birthday of the "Sun" Became the Birthday of the "Son."* Franklin, TN: Sea Raven Press, 2010.

———. *Everything You Were Taught About the Civil War is Wrong, Ask a Southerner!* 2010. Franklin, TN: Sea Raven Press, revised 2014 ed.

———. *Jesus and the Law of Attraction: The Bible-Based Guide to Creating Perfect Health, Wealth, and Happiness Following Christ's Simple Formula*. Franklin, TN: Sea Raven Press, 2013.

———. *The Bible and the Law of Attraction: 99 Teachings of Jesus, the Apostles, and the Prophets*. Franklin, TN: Sea Raven Press, 2013.

———. *Christ Is All and In All: Rediscovering Your Divine Nature and the Kingdom Within*. Franklin, TN: Sea Raven Press, 2014.

———. *Jesus and the Gospel of Q: Christ's Pre-Christian Teachings as Recorded in the New Testament*. Franklin, TN: Sea Raven Press, 2014.

———. *Confederacy 101: Amazing Facts You Never Knew About America's Oldest Political Tradition*. Franklin, TN: Sea Raven Press, 2015.

———. *Everything You Were Taught About American Slavery War is Wrong, Ask a Southerner!* Franklin, TN: Sea Raven Press, 2015.

———. *The Great Yankee Coverup: What the North Doesn't Want You to Know About Lincoln's War!* Franklin, TN: Sea Raven Press, 2015.

———. *The Way of Holiness: The Story of Religion and Myth From the Cave Bear Cult to Christianity*. Unpublished manuscript. Franklin, TN: Sea Raven Press.

Secret Teachings of Jesus, The: Four Gnostic Gospels (Marvin W. Meyer, trans.). New York, NY: Random House, 1984.

Segal, Alan F. *Paul the Convert: the Apostolate and Apostasy of Saul the Pharisee*. New Haven, CT: Yale University Press, 1990.

Seiss, Joseph Augustus. *The Gospel in the Stars; or, Primeval Astronomy*. Philadelphia, PA: E. Claxton and Co., 1882.

Sell, Henry T. *Bible Study By Books*. Chicago, IL: Fleming H. Revell Co., 1896.

Seton-Williams, Veronica, and Peter Stock. *Blue Guide: Egypt*. London, UK: Ernest Benn Ltd., and New York, NY: W. W. Norton, 1983.

Sewall, Charles G. *The Bible and Its Books*. Nashville, TN: Abingdon Press, 1941.

Shah, Idries. *The Sufis*. 1964. Garden City, NY: Anchor, 1971 ed.

Shanks, Hershel. *Understanding the Dead Sea Scrolls*. New York, NY: Random House, 1992.

Shapley, Harlow (ed.). *Science Ponders Religion*. New York, NY: Appleton-Century-Crofts, 1960.

Sharpe, Samuel. *Egyptian Mythology and Egyptian Christianity: With Their Influence on the Opinions of Modern Christendom*. London, UK: Carter and Co., 1896.

Sheehan, Thomas. *The First Coming: How the Kingdom of God Became Christianity*. 1986. New York, NY: Vintage, 1988 ed.

Shenkman, Richard. *Legends, Lies, and Cherished Myths of American History*. New York, NY: Harper and Row, 1988.

Shillington, V. George. *Jesus and Paul Before Christianity: Their World and Work in Retrospect*. Eugene, OR: Cascade, 2011.

Shinn, Florence Scovel. *The Game of Life and How to Play It*. Camarillo, CA: DeVorss, 1925.

Silk, Mark. *Spiritual Politics: Religion and American Since World War II*. New York, NY: Touchstone,

1988.

Sinetar, Marsha. *Ordinary People as Monks and Mystics: Lifestyles for Spiritual Wholeness.* Mahwah, NJ: Paulist Press, 2007.

Singh, Kirpal. *Man! Know Thyself.* 1954. Anaheim, CA: Divine Science of the Soul, 1988 ed.

———. *The Crown of Life: A Study in Yoga.* Delhi, India: Ruhani Satsang, 1974.

Sire, James W. *Scripture Twisting: 20 Ways the Cults Misread the Bible.* Downers Grove, IL: InterVarsity Press, 1980.

Sjöö, Monica, and Barbara Mor. *The Great Cosmic Mother: Rediscovering the Religion of the Earth.* San Francisco, CA: Harper and Row, 1987.

Skarin, Annalee. *Ye Are Gods.* New York, NY: Philosophical Library, 1952.

Skelton, Robin, and Margaret Blackwood. *Earth, Air, Fire, Water: Pre-Christian and Pagan Elements in British Songs, Rhymes and Ballads.* Harmondsworth, England: Arkana, 1990.

Skinner, Tom. *If Christ is the Answer, What Are the Questions?* 1974. Grand Rapids, MI: Zondervan, 1980 ed.

Slater, Philip E. *The Glory of Hera: Greek Mythology and the Greek Family.* Boston, MA: Beacon Press, 1968.

Sleater, Matthew. *A Complete History of the Holy Bible.* 2 vols. Dublin, Ireland: J. Charles, 1810.

Smith, Andrew Phillip. *The Gospel of Philip: Annontated and Explained.* Woodstock, VT: Skylight Paths, 2005.

Smith, Edward Reaugh. *The Disciple Whom Jesus Loved: Unveiling the Author of John's Gospel.* Great Barrington, MA: Anthroposophic Press, 2000.

Smith, Huston. *The Religions of Man.* 1958. New York, NY: Perennial Library, 1965 ed.

Smith, Morton. *Clement of Alexandria and a Secret Gospel of Mark.* Cambridge, MA: Harvard University Press, 1973.

Smith, Morton, and R. Joseph Hoffmann (eds.). *What the Bible Really Says.* Buffalo, NY: Prometheus, 1989.

Smith, Susy. *Out-of-Body Experiences for the Millions.* Los Angeles, CA: Dell, 1969.

Smith, William. *Nelson's Quick Reference Bible Dictionary.* Nashville, TN: Thomas Nelson, 1993.

Spalding, Baird Thomas. *Life and Teachings of the Masters of the Far East.* 5 vols. 1924. Marina Del Rey, CA: DeVorss, 1964-1976 ed.

Spence, Lewis. *An Encyclopedia of Occultism.* New York, NY: Dodd, Mead and Co., 1920.

Spivey, Robert A., and D. Moody Smith. *Anatomy of the New Testament: A Guide to Its Structure and Meaning.* 1969. New York, NY: Macmillan, 1982 ed.

Spivey, Thomas Sawyer. *The Last of the Gnostic Masters.* Beverly Hills, CA: self-published, 1926.

Spong, John Shelby. *Rescuing the Bible from Fundamentalism: A Bishop Rethinks the Meaning of Scripture.* 1991. San Francisco, CA: Harper San Francisco, 1992 ed.

Springett, Bernard H. *Secret Sects of Syria and the Lebanon: A Consideration of the Their Origin, Creeds and Religious Ceremonies, and Their Connection With and Influence Upon Modern Freemasonry.* London, UK: George Allen and Unwin, 1922.

Staniforth, Maxwell (trans.). *Early Christian Writings: The Apostolic Fathers.* 1968. Harmondsworth, UK: Penguin, 1984 ed.

Starbuck, Edwin Diller. *The Psychology of Religion: An Empirical Study of the Growth of Religious Consciousness.* London, UK: Walter Scott, 1900.

Stearn, Jess. *Edgar Cayce: The Sleeping Prophet.* 1967. New York, NY: Bantam, 1971 ed.

Steiger, Brad. *In My Soul I Am Free: The Incredible Paul Twitchell Story.* Menlo Park, CA: IWP, 1968.

———. *Encounters of the Angelic Kind.* Cottonwood, AZ: Esoteric Publications, 1979.

Stein, Diane. *The Goddess Book of Days.* 1988. Freedom, CA: The Crossing Press, 1992 ed.

Stein, Gordon. *The Encyclopedia of Unbelief.* Vol. 1, A-K. Buffalo, NY: Prometheus Books, 1985.

———. *The Encyclopedia of Unbelief.* Vol. 2, L-Z. Buffalo, NY: Prometheus Books, 1985.

Steinberg, Milton. *Basic Judaism.* 1947. San Diego, CA: Harvest, 1975 ed.

Steiner, Rudolf. *From Buddha to Christ.* Spring Valley, NY: Anthroposophic Press, 1978.

Stendahl, Krister. *Paul Among Jews and Gentiles.* Philadelphia, PA: Fortress Press, 1976.

Stern, Karl. *The Third Revolution: A Study of Psychiatry and Religion*. 1954. Garden City, NY: Image Books, 1961 ed.
Stevenson, Leslie. *Seven Theories of Human Nature*. 1974. Oxford, UK: Oxford University Press, 1987 ed.
Stewart, Thomas Milton. *Symbolic Teaching: Or, Masonry and Its Message*. 1914. Cincinnati, OH: Stewart and Kidd Co., 1917 ed.
Stirling, William. *The Canon: An Exposition of the Pagan Mystery Perpetuated in the Cabala as the Rule of All Arts*. London, UK: Elkin Mathews, 1897.
Stokes, Mack B. *The Bible in the Wesleyan Heritage*. 1979. Nashville, TN: Abingdon, 1981 ed.
Stone, Merlin. *When God was a Woman*. San Diego, CA: Harvest, 1976.
———. *Ancient Mirrors of Womanhood: A Treasury of Goddess and Heroine Lore From Around the World*. 1979. Boston, MA: Beacon Press, 1990 ed.
Stott, John R. W. *The Cross of Christ*. Downers Grove, IL: InterVarsity Press, 1986.
Strauss, David Friedrich. *The Life of Jesus Critically Examined* (Marian Evans, trans.). New York, NY: Calvin Blanchard, 1860.
———. *The Old Faith and the New: A Confession* (Mathilde Blind, trans.). London, UK: Asher and Co., 1874.
Streep, Peg. *Sanctuaries of the Goddess: The Sacred Landscapes and Objects*. Boston, MA: Bullfinch Press, 1994.
Strobel, Lee. *The Case for Christ: A Journalist's Personal Investigation of the Evidence for Jesus*. Grand Rapids, MI: Zondervan, 1998.
Strong, James. *Strong's Exhaustive Concordance of the Bible*. 1890. Nashville, TN: Abingdon Press, 1975 ed.
Suarès, Carlo. *The Cipher of Genesis: The Original Code of the Qabala as Applied to the Scriptures*. Berkeley, CA: Shambala, 1970.
Stuart, J. P. (ed.). *Popery Adjudged; or, The Roman Catholic Church Weighed in the Balance of God's Word and Found Wanting*. Boston, MA: Redding and Co., 1854.
Stuart, Micheline. *The Tarot: Path to Self Development*. Boulder, CO: Shambhala, 1977.
Stuart, Moses. *A Commentary on the Apocalypse*. 2 vols. Andover, MA: Allen, Morrill and Wardwell, 1845.
Sutphen, Dick. *You Were Born Again to Be Together*. New York, NY: Pocket Books, 1976.
Sutphen Dick, and Trenna Sutphen. *The Master of Life Manual*. Scottsdale, AZ: Valley of the Sun, 1980.
Suzuki, Shunryu. *Zen Mind, Beginner's Mind: Informal Talks on Zen Meditation and Practice*. Boulder, CO: Shambhala, 1993.
Swedenborg, Emanuel. *The Apocalypse Revealed, Wherein Are Disclosed the Arcana There Foretold, Which Have Heretofore Remained Concealed*. 2 vols. New York, NY: American Swedenborg Printing and Publishing Society, 1855 ed.
———. *Arcana Celestia: The Heavenly Mysteries Contained in the Holy Scripture*. 12 vols. London, UK: The Swedenborg Society, 1861 ed.
———. *The Heavenly Arcana Disclosed Which Are in the Sacred Scripture or the Word of the Lord*. 2 vols. 1749. New York, NY: American Swedenborg Printing and Publishing Society, 1896 ed.
———. *The True Christian Religion Containing The Universal Theology of the New Church*. 1771. New York, NY: American Swedenborg Printing and Publishing Society, 1906 ed.
Sykes, Egerton. *Who's Who in Non-Classical Mythology*. 1952. New York, NY: Oxford University Press, 1993 ed.
Szekely, Edmond Bordeaux. *The Essene Gospel of Peace*. Vol. 1. 1924. Cartago, Costa Rica: International Biogenic Society, l978 ed.
———. *The Essene Gospel of Peace: The Unknown Books of the Essenes*. Vol. 2. 1924. San Diego, CA: Academy Books, l974 ed.
———. *The Essene Gospel of Peace: Lost Scrolls of the Essene Brotherhood*. Vol. 3. 1924. Cartago, Costa Rica: International Biogenic Society, l978 ed.
———. *The Essene Teachings of Zarathustra*. San Diego, CA: Academy of Creative Living, 1970.

———. *The Essenes: By Josephus and his Contemporaries.* 1970. San Diego, CA: Academy of Creative Living, 1972 ed.
———. *The Evolution of Human Thought.* Cartago, Costa Rica: International Biogenic Society, 1971.
———. *The Zend Avesta of Zarathustra.* Cartago, Costa Rica: International Biogenic Society, 1973.
———. *Archeosophy, A New Science: Understanding Ancient Cultures.* Cartago, Costa Rica: International Biogenic Society, 1973.
———. *Pilgrim of the Himalayas: Life and Works of the Discoverer of Tibetan Buddhism.* Cartago, Costa Rica: International Biogenic Society, 1974.
———. *The Discovery of the Essene Gospel of Peace.* San Diego, CA: Academy Books, 1977.
Szlakmann, Charles. *Judaism for Beginners.* New York, NY: Writers and Readers Publishing, 1990.
Talbot, H. Fox. *The Antiquity of the Book of Genesis: Illustrated by Some New Arguments.* London, UK: Longman, Orme, Green, Brown, and Longman, 1839.
Talbot, Michael. *Mysticism and the New Physics.* New York, NY: Bantam, 1981.
Tannahill, Reay. *Sex in History.* 1980. Briarcliff Manor, NY: Scarborough, 1992 ed.
Tate, Karen. *Sacred Places of Goddess: 108 Destinations.* San Francisco, CA: Consortium of Collective Consciousness, 2006.
Tchakirides, Valjean. *The Shekhinah is Coming: Secrets of the Divine.* Bloomington, IN: Trafford, 2011.
Telushkin, Rabbi Joseph. *Jewish Literacy.* New York, NY: William Morrow and Co., 1991.
Temple, Theodore. *The Secret Discipline, Mentioned in Ancient Ecclesiastical History, Explained.* New York, NY: self-published (Samuel L. Knapp), 1833.
Tenney, Merrill C. (ed.). *Handy Dictionary of the Bible.* Grand Rapids, MI: Zondervan Publishing House, 1965.
Terapeut. *The Crucifixion, By an Eye-Witness: A Letter Written Seven Years After the Crucifixion, By a Personal Friend of Jesus in Jerusalem, to an Esseer [Essene] Brother in Alexandria.* 1907. Chicago, IL: Indo-American Book Co., 1911 ed.
Teresa, Saint (of Avila). *The Interior Castle, or the Mansions.* 1588. New York, NY: Benziger Brothers, 1912.
Testimonies of the Life, Character, Revelations and Doctrines of Mother Ann Lee, and the Elders With Her. Albany, NY: Shaker Heritage Society, 1888.
The Apocrypha: Translated Out of the Original Tongue. Cambridge, UK: Press Syndicate, n.d.
The Bhagavad Gita. Compiled from various writers. London, UK: The Christian Literature Society for India, 1899.
The Dhammapada: The Sayings of Buddha (6th Century B.C.). "Rendering" by Thomas Byrom. New York, NY: Vintage Books, 1976.
The Diamond Sutra and the Sutra of Hui Neng. Berkeley, CA: Shambala, 1973 ed.
The Epic of Gilgamesh (circa 3000 B.C.). N. K. Sandars, ed. 1960. Harmondsworth, England: Penguin, 1972 ed.
The Fortune Tellers. Baltimore: Black Watch, 1974.
The Fossil Record and Evolution: Collected articles from Scientific American. San Francisco, CA: W. H. Freeman and Co., 1982.
The Golden Manual: Or, Guide to Catholic Devotion, Public and Private. London, UK: Burns and Lambert, 1854.
The Illustrated World Encyclopedia. Woodbury, NY: Bobley Publishing Corp., 1977.
The Impersonal Life. 1941. San Gabriel, CA: C. A. Willing, 1973 ed.
The Koran (George Sale, trans.). 1734. London, UK: Frederick Warne and Co., n.d.
The Larousse Guide to Astronomy. David Baker. London, UK: Hamlyn Publishing, 1978.
The Layman's Parallel New Testament. 1970. Grand Rapids, MI.: Zondervan Publishing, 1977 ed.
The New American Desk Encyclopedia. New York, NY: Signet, 1982.
The Story of the Bible. (Vol. 1: Genesis to Daniel.) New York, NY: Wm. H. Wise and Co., 1958.
The Thompson Chain-Reference Bible. King James Version. Indianapolis, IN: B. B. Kirkbride Bible Co., 1964.
The Times Atlas of World History. Maplewood, NJ: Hammond, 1989.

The Urantia Book: Revealing the Mysteries of God, the Universe, World History, Jesus, and Ourselves. 1955. Chicago, IL: Urantia Foundation, 2010 ed.
The World Almanac and Book of Facts. New York, NY: Pharos Books, 1990 ed.
The World Almanac and Book of Facts. New York, NY: Pharos Books, 1991 ed.
The World Book Encyclopedia. Chicago, IL: Field Enterprises Educational Corp., 1966 ed.
Thoreau, Henry David. *A Week on the Concord and Merrimack Rivers*. 1849. Boston, MA: James R. Osgood and Co., 1873 ed.
———. *Walden, or Life in the Woods*. 1854. Philadelphia, PA: Henry Artemus Co., 1899 ed.
Tichenor, Henry Mulford. *Tales of Theology: Jehovah, Satan and the Christian Creed*. St. Louis, MO: Melting Pot Publishing, 1918.
Tillich, Paul. *Dynamics of Faith*. New York, NY: Harper and Row, 1957.
Titcomb, Sarah Elizabeth. *Aryan Sun-Myths: The Origin of Religions*. Troy, NY: Nims and Knight, 1889.
Tomlinson, Gerald. *Treasury of Religious Quotations*. Englewood Cliffs, NJ: Prentice Hall, 1991.
Tompkins, Peter. *Secrets of the Great Pyramid*. 1971. New York, NY: Harper Colophon Books, 1978 ed.
Torrey, Bradford (ed.). *The Writings of Henry David Thoreau: Journal, Vol. 1* (written 1837-1846). Boston, MA: Houghton, Mifflin and Co., 1906.
———. *The Writings of Henry David Thoreau: Journal, Vol. 3* (written 1851-1852). Boston, MA: Houghton, Mifflin and Co., 1906.
———. *The Writings of Henry David Thoreau: Journal, Vol. 9* (written 1856-1857). Boston, MA: Houghton, Mifflin and Co., 1906.
Towns, Elmer L. *The Names of Jesus*. Denver, CO: Accent Publications, 1987.
Townsend, George Fyler. *"He Descended Into Hell": Observations on the Descent of Christ Into Hell*. London, UK: J. G. F. and J. Rivington, 1842.
Toynbee, Arnold J. (trans.). *Greek Civilization and Character: The Self-Revelation of Ancient Greek Society*. New York, NY: Mentor, 1953.
Traupman, John C. *The New College Latin and English Dictionary*. 1966. New York, NY: Bantam, 1988 ed.
———. *The Bantam New College German and English Dictionary*. 1981. New York, NY: Bantam, 1986 ed.
Travis, Jerome. *Interspersed Harmony of the Life and Journeys of Christ*. Lansing, MI: Beacon Publishing Co., 1893.
Trine, Ralph Waldo. *In Tune With the Infinite; Or, Fullness of Peace, Power and Plenty*. 1897. New York, NY: Dodd, Mead and Co., 1921 ed.
Trollope, William. *Analecta Theologica: A Critical, Philological, and Exegetical Commentary on the New Testament*. 2 vols. London, UK: T. Cadell, 1830.
True Peace and Security: How Can You Find It? Brooklyn, NY: Watchtower Bible and Tract Society of New York, 1986.
Twain, Mark. *The Autobiography of Mark Twain*. 1917. New York, NY: Perennial Library, 1975 ed.
Tingley, Katherine (ed.). *The Theosophical Path* (illustrated monthly). Vol. 16, January-July 1919. Point Loma, CA: New Century, 1919.
Townsend, Mark. *Jesus Through Pagan Eyes: Bridging Neopagan Perspectives With a Progressive Vision of Christ*. Woodbury, MN: Llewellyn, 2012.
Trench, Richard Chenevix. *Commentary on the Epistles to the Seven Churches in Asia*. New York, NY: Charles Scribner and Co., 1872.
Trunga, Chögyam. *Shambhala: The Sacred Path of the Warrior*. Boston, MA: Shambhala, 1988.
Ueberweg, Friedrich. *A History of Philosophy, From Thales to the Present Time*. 2 Vols. London: UK, 1872.
Underhill, Evelyn. *Mysticism: A Study of the Nature and Development of Man's Spiritual Consciousness*. 1911. New York, NY: E. P. Dutton and Co., 1961 ed.
———. *The Mystic Way: A Psychological Study in Christian Origins*. London, UK: J. M. Dent and Sons, 1914.
———. *Practical Mysticism: A Little Book for Normal People*. London, UK: J. M. Dent and Sons, 1914.

———. *The Essentials of Mysticism and Other Essays*. London, UK: J. M. Dent and Sons, 1920.
———. *The Life of the Spirit and the Life of Today*. New York, NY: E. P. Dutton and Co., 1922.
van Buitenen, J. A. B. (ed.). *The Bhagavadgita in the Mahabharata*. Chicago, IL: University of Chicago Press, 1981.
van der Toorn, Karel. *Scribal Culture and the Making of the Hebrew Bible*. Cambridge, MA: Harvard University Press, 2007.
Van Etten, Henry. *George Fox and the Quakers: Men of Wisdom* (E. Kelvin Osborn, trans.). London, UK: Longmans, 1959.
van Gelder, Dora. *The Real World of the Fairies*. Wheaton, IL: Quest, 1978.
Van Kolken, Diana. *Introducing the Shakers: An Explanation and Directory*. Bowling Green, OH: Gabriel's Horn Publishing, 1985.
van Loon, Hendrik Willem. *The Story of Mankind*. New York, NY: Boni and Liveright, 1921.
Van Voorst, Robert E. *Jesus Outside the New Testament: An Introduction to the Ancient Evidence*. Grand Rapids, MI: William B. Eerdmans, 2000.
Vaughan, James. *The Trident, the Crescent, and the Cross: A View of the Religious History of India During the Hindu, Buddhist, Mohammedan, and Christian Periods*. London, UK: Longmans, Green, and Co., 1876.
Vermes, Geza (ed.). *The Dead Sea Scrolls in English*. 1962. Harmondsworth, UK: Penguin, 1987 ed.
Versnel, H. S. *Coping With the Gods: Wayward Readings in Greek Theology*. Leiden, The Netherlands: Brill, 2011.
Vick, Robert L. *Contemporary Medical Physiology*. Menlo Park, CA: Addison-Wesley, 1984.
Volney, Constantin-François. *Volney's Ruins: Or Meditation on the Revolution of Empires* (Count Daru, trans.). New York, NY: G. Vale, 1853.
Von Däniken, Erich. *Chariots of the Gods? Unsolved Mysteries of the Past*. New York, NY: Bantam, 1968.
Wace, Henry, and Philip Schaff (eds.). *A Select Library of Nicene and Post-Nicene Fathers of the Christian Church*. Oxford, UK: James Parker and Co., 1894.
Wach, Joachim. *Sociology of Religion*. 1944. Chicago, IL: University of Chicago Press, 1971 ed.
Waggoner, Hyatt H. *American Poets: From the Puritans to the Present*. Boston, MA: Houghton Mifflin Co., 1968.
Wahr, Frederick B. *Emerson and Goethe: Emerson and the Germans*. Ann Arbor, MI: George Wahr, 1915.
Waite, Arthur Edward. *A Book of Mystery and Vision*. London, UK: Philip Wellby, 1902.
Walker, Barbara G. *The Women's Encyclopedia of Myths and Secrets*. San Francisco, CA: Harper and Row, 1983.
———. *The Crone: Woman of Age, Wisdom, and Power*. New York, NY: Harper and Row, 1985.
———. *The Women's Dictionary of Symbols and Sacred Objects*. San Francisco, CA: Harper and Row, 1988.
Walker, Edward Dwight. *Reincarnation: A Study of Forgotten Truth*. New York, NY: John W. Lovell, 1888.
Wall, Otto Augustus. *Sex and Sex Worship*. St. Louis, MO: C. V. Mosby Co., 1919.
Wallace, Anthony F. C. *Religion: An Anthropological View*. New York, NY: Random House, 1966.
Walton, Robert C. *Chronological and Background Charts of Church History*. Grand Rapids, MI: Academie Books, 1986.
Walvoord, John F. *The Rapture Question: A Comprehensive Biblical Study of the Translation of the Church*. 1957. Grand Rapids, MI: Zondervan, 1970 ed.
Ward, John. *Zion's Works: New Light on the Bible*. 16 vols. London, UK: John MacQueen, 1899-1904.
Warnock, Robert, and George K. Anderson. *The Ancient Foundations*. 1950. Glenview, IL: Scott, Foresman and Co., 1967 ed.
Watts, Alan W. *The Supreme Identity*. 1950. New York, NY: Vintage, 1972 ed.
———. *Behold the Spirit (A Study in the Necessity of Mystical Religion)*. 1947. New York, NY: Vintage, 1972 ed.
———. *The Wisdom of Insecurity*. New York, NY: Vintage, 1951.
———. *The Way of Zen*. 1957. New York, NY: Mentor, 1960 ed.
———. *The Joyous Cosmology: Adventures in the Chemistry of Consciousness*. New York, NY: Vintage, 1962.

———. *The Book On the Taboo Against Knowing Who You Are*. 1966. New York, NY: Collier, 1971 ed.
———. *Does it Matter? Essays on Man's Relation to Materiality*. 1968. New York, NY: Vintage, 1971 ed.
———. *Myth and Ritual in Christianity*. Boston, MA: Beacon Press, 1968.
———. *Cloud-Hidden, Whereabouts Unknown*. 1968. New York, NY: Vintage, 1974 ed.
———. *This Is It and Other Essays On Zen and Spiritual Experience*. 1958. New York, NY: Collier, 1970 ed.
———. *In My Own Way: An Autobiography*. 1972. New York, NY: Vintage, 1973 ed.
———. *God* (Book 1 of the series, "The Essence of Alan Watts"). Millbrae, CA: Celestial Arts, 1974.
Webster's Biographical Dictionary. Springfield, MA: G. and C. Merriam Co., 1943.
Weems, Mason Locke. *The Life of Benjamin Franklin; With Many Choice Anecdotes and Admirable Sayings of This Great Man, Never Before Published By Any of His Biographers*. Philadelphia, PA: Uriah Hunt's Sons, 1873.
Weigall, Arthur Edward Pearse Brome. *The Paganism In Our Christianity*. London, UK: Hutchinson and Co., 1928.
Weigel, James, Jr. *Mythology*. Lincoln, NE: Cliff Notes, 1973.
Wells, G. A. *The Historical Evidence for Jesus*. Buffalo, NY: Prometheus Books, 1988.
Wells, H. G. *The Outline of History*. 2 Vols. 1920. Garden City, NY: Garden City Books, 1961 ed.
Westbrook, Richard Brodhead. *The Eliminator; or, Skeleton Keys to Sacerdotal Secrets*. Philadelphia, PA: J. B. Lippincott, 1894.
Westcott, Frank N. *Catholic Principles*. Milwaukee, WI: The Young Churchman Co., 1902.
Westcott, W. Wynn. *The Occult Power of Numbers*. North Hollywood, CA: Newcastle Publishing, 1984.
Whale, J. S. *Christian Doctrine*. 1941. London, UK: Collins, 1960 ed.
Wheeler, Joseph Mazzini. *Frauds and Follies of the Early Church Fathers: With a Review of The Worth of Their Testimony to the Four Gospels*. London, UK: Freethought Publishing Co., 1882.
White, Anne Terry. *The Golden Treasury of Myths and Legends*. New York, NY: Golden Press, 1959.
White, Ellen G. *The Desire of Ages: The Conflict of the Ages Illustrated in the Life of Christ*. 1898. Mountain View, CA: Pacific Press, 1940 ed.
White, Jon E. Manchip. *Everyday Life in Ancient Egypt*. New York, NY: Perigee, 1963.
———. *Ancient Egypt: Its Culture and History*. New York, NY: Dover, 1970.
Whitehead, Alfred North. *Religion in the Making*. 1926. New York, NY: Mentor, 1974 ed.
Whitehouse, Ruth, and John Wilkins. *The Making of Civilization*. London, UK: Roxby Archaeology, 1986.
Whitman, Walt. *Leaves of Grass*. 1855-1892. Philadelphia, PA: Rees Welsh and Co., 1882 ed.
Whitney, Loren Harper. *A Question of Miracles: Parallels in the Lives of Buddha and Jesus*. Chicago, IL: The Library Shelf, 1908.
Wickens, Rev. Paul A. *Christ Denied: Origin of the Present Day Problems in the Catholic Church*. Rockford, IL: Tan Books, 1982.
Wight, Fred H. *Manners and Customs of Bible Lands*. Chicago, IL: Moody Press, 1953.
Wiener, Leo (ed. and trans.). *The Complete Works of Count Tolstoy, Vol. 14: The Four Gospels Harmonized and Translated, by Tolstoy*. Boston, MA: Dana Estes and Co., 1904.
Wilbur, Sibyl. *The Life of Mary Baker Eddy*. 1907. Boston, MA: Christian Science Publishing, 1976 ed.
Wilhelm, Anthony J. *Christ Among Us: A Modern Presentation of the Catholic Faith*. New York, NY: Newman Press, 1967.
Williams, Watkin. *St. Bernard: The Man and His Message*. Manchester, UK: Manchester University Press, 1944.
William Shakespeare: The Complete Works. New York, NY: Dorset Press, 1988.
Wilson, Bryan R. *Religion in a Secular Society*. 1966. Harmondsworth, UK: Penguin, 1969 ed.
Wilson, Colin. *The Occult: A History*. New York, NY: Random House, 1972.
Wilson, Edward O. *Sociobiology: The New Synthesis*. Cambridge, MA: Belknap Press, 1975.
———. *On Human Nature*. New York, NY: Bantam New Age, 1979.
Wilson, John Rowan. *The Mind*. 1964. New York, NY: Time-Life Books, 1968 ed.

Winder, Delores, and Bill Keith. *Jesus Set Me Free.* Safety Harbor, FL: Fellowship Foundation, 1983.
Windle, Charles Augustus. *Christian vs. Pagan Civilization: Truth About the Catholic Church.* Chicago, IL: Iconoclast Publishing Co., 1914.
Wingeier, Douglas E. *Paul: His Life.* Nashville, TN: Graded Press, 1987.
Winick, Charles. *Dictionary of Anthropology.* Totowa, NJ: Littlefield, Adams and Co., 1970.
Wise, Micahel, Martin Abegg Jr., and Edward Cook. *The Dead Sea Scrolls: A New Translation.* San Francisco, CA: Harper Collins, 1996.
Wong, Kiew Kit. *Sukhavati, Western Paradise: Going to Heaven as Taught by the Buddha.* Sungai Petani, Kedah, Malaysia: Cosmos Internet Sdn Bhd, 2002.
Wood, James. *A Dictionary of the Holy Bible.* 2 vols. New York, NY: Griffin and Rudd, 1813.
Woolger, Jennifer Barker, and Roger J. Woolger. *The Goddess Within: A Guide to the Eternal Myths That Shape Women's Lives.* New York, NY: Fawcett Columbine, 1989.
Wordsworth, Christopher. *The New Testament of Our Lord and Saviour Jesus Christ, In the Original Greek.* London, UK: Rivingtons, 1861.
———. *The Holy Bible, In the Authorized Version.* 12 vols. London, UK: Rivingtons, 1873.
Wouk, Herman. *This Is My God.* 1959. New York, NY: Touchstone, 1986 ed.
Wright, Conrad (ed.). *Three Prophets of Religious Liberalism: Channing, Emerson, Parker.* 1961. Boston, MA: Unitarian Universalist Association, 1980 ed.
Wright, G. Frederick, William G. Ballantine, and Frank H. Foster (eds.). *The Bibliotheca Sacra.* Vol. 48. Oberlin, OH: E. J. Goodrich, 1891.
Yamada, Keichyu. *Scenes From the Life of Buddha.* Chicago, IL: Open Court, 1898.
Yoder, John H. *The Original Revolution: Essays on Christian Pacifism.* 1971. Scottsdale, PA: Herald Press, 1977 ed.
———. *The Politics of Jesus.* 1972. Grand Rapids, MI: William B. Eerdmans Publishing Co., 1983 ed.
Yogananda, Paramahansa. *Autobiography of a Yogi.* 1946. Los Angeles, CA: Self-Realization Fellowship, 1972 ed.
———. *Whispers From Eternity.* Los Angeles, CA: Self-Realization Fellowship, 1973.
———. *The Second Coming of Christ: The Resurrection of the Christ Within You.* 2 vols. Los Angeles, CA: Self-Realization Fellowship, 2004.
You Can Live Forever In Paradise on Earth. Brooklyn, NY: Watchtower Bible and Tract Society of New York, 1982, 1989.
Young, Dudley. *Origins of the Sacred: The Ecstacies of Love and War.* 1991. New York, NY: Harper Perennial, 1992 ed.
Young, G. Douglas (ed.). *Young's Compact Bible Dictionary.* 1984. Wheaton, IL: Tyndale House, 1989 ed.
Zaehner, R. C. (ed.). *Encyclopedia of the World's Religions.* 1959. New York, NY: Barnes and Noble, 1997 ed.
Zimmerman, J. E. *Dictionary of Classical Mythology.* New York, NY: Bantam, 1964.
Zinner, Samuel. *The Gospel of Thomas: In the Light of Early Jewish, Christian and Islamic Esoteric Trajectories.* London, UK: Matheson Trust, 2011.
Zolar. *Zolar's Encyclopedia of Ancient and Forbidden Knowledge.* 1970. New York, NY: Fireside, 1984 ed.
Zöllner, Johann Carl Friedrich. *Transcendental Physics: An Account of Experimental Investigations From the Scientific Treatises.* London, UK: W. H. Harrison, 1880.
Zondervan Compact Bible Dictionary. 1967. Grand Rapids, MI: Zondervan Publishing House, 1993 ed.

"I confess that it is all a mystery in which I am lost." — SAINT TERESA OF AVILA, 16th Century.

ON THE TEACHINGS OF JESUS
"A more beautiful or precious morsel of ethics I have never seen. [My little book on this subject] is a document in proof that I am a *real Christian*, that is to say, a disciple of the doctrines of Jesus, very different from the Platonists, who call *me* infidel and *themselves* Christians and preachers of the Gospel, while they draw all their characteristic dogmas from what its author never said nor saw. They have compounded from the heathen mysteries a system beyond the comprehension of man, of which the great reformer of the vicious ethics and deism of the Jews, were he to return on earth, would not recognize one feature." — THOMAS JEFFERSON, 1803

Meet the Author

LOCHLAINN SEABROOK, a Kentucky Colonel and the winner of the prestigious Jefferson Davis Historical Gold Medal for his "masterpiece," *A Rebel Born: A Defense of Nathan Bedford Forrest*, is an unreconstructed Southern historian, award-winning author, Civil War scholar, Bible authority, and traditional Southern Agrarian of Scottish, English, Irish, Welsh, German, and Italian extraction.

A child prodigy, Seabrook is today a true Renaissance Man whose occupational titles also include encyclopedist, lexicographer, musician, artist, graphic designer, genealogist, photographer, and award-winning poet. Also a songwriter and a screenwriter, he has a 40 year background in historical nonfiction writing and is a member of the Sons of Confederate Veterans, the Civil War Trust, and the National Grange. Due to similarities in their writing styles, ideas, and literary works, Seabrook is often referred to as the "new Shelby Foote," the "Southern Joseph Campbell," and the "American Robert Graves" (his English cousin).

A cousin of King James (whose Medieval English translation of the Bible is still the world's most popular version) and a descendant of both the Grail King Merovech (Frankish founder of the Merovingian dynasty) and Tiberius Caesar (emperor of Rome during the time of Jesus, Luke 3:1), Seabrook is the grandson of an Appalachian coal-mining family, a seventh-generation Kentuckian, co-chair of the Jent/Gent Family Committee (Kentucky), founder and director of the Blakeney Family Tree Project, and a board member of the Friends of Colonel Benjamin E. Caudill. Seabrook's literary works have been endorsed by leading authorities, museum curators, award-winning historians, bestselling authors, celebrities, noted scientists, well respected educators, TV show hosts and producers, renowned military artists, esteemed Southern organizations, and distinguished academicians from around the world.

Colonel Lochlainn Seabrook, award-winning historian, author, and Bible authority, is America's most popular and prolific pro-South author. His spiritual works have introduced hundreds of thousands to the truth about Jesus and the Bible.

Seabrook has authored over 45 popular adult books on the American Civil War, American and international slavery, the U.S. Confederacy (1781), the Southern Confederacy (1861), religion, theology and thealogy, Jesus, the Bible, the Apocrypha, the Law of Attraction, alternative health, spirituality, ghost stories, the paranormal, ufology, social issues, and cross-cultural studies of the family and marriage. His Confederate biographies, pro-South studies, genealogical monographs, family histories, military encyclopedias, self-help guides, and etymological dictionaries have received wide acclaim.

Seabrook's eight children's books include a Southern guide to the Civil War, a biography of Nathan Bedford Forrest, a dictionary of religion and myth, a rewriting of the King Arthur legend (which reinstates the original pre-Christian motifs), two bedtime stories for preschoolers, a naturalist's guidebook to owls, a worldwide look at the family, and an examination of the Near-Death Experience.

Of blue-blooded Southern stock through his Kentucky, Tennessee, Virginia, West Virginia, and North Carolina ancestors, he is a direct descendant of European royalty via his 6th great-grandfather, the Earl of Oxford, after which London's famous Harley Street is named. Among his celebrated male Celtic ancestors is Robert the Bruce, King of Scotland, Seabrook's 22nd great-grandfather. The 21st great-grandson of Edward I "Longshanks" Plantagenet, King of England, Seabrook is a thirteenth-generation Southerner through his descent from the colonists of Jamestown, Virginia (1607).

The 2nd, 3rd, and 4th great-grandson of dozens of Confederate soldiers, one of his closest connections to the War for Southern Independence is through his 3rd great-grandfather, Elias Jent, Sr., who fought for the Confederacy in the Thirteenth Cavalry Kentucky under Seabrook's 2nd cousin, Colonel Benjamin E. Caudill. The Thirteenth, also known as "Caudill's Army," fought in numerous conflicts, including the Battles of Saltville, Gladsville, Mill Cliff, Poor Fork, Whitesburg, and Leatherwood.

Seabrook is a descendant of the families of Alexander H. Stephens, John Singleton Mosby, and Edmund Winchester Rucker, and is related to the following Confederates and other 19th-Century luminaries: Robert E. Lee, Stephen Dill Lee, Stonewall Jackson, Nathan Bedford Forrest, James Longstreet, John Hunt Morgan, Jeb Stuart, P. G. T. Beauregard (approved the Confederate Battle Flag design), George W. Gordon, John Bell Hood, Alexander Peter Stewart, Arthur M. Manigault, Joseph Manigault, Charles Scott Venable, Thornton A. Washington, John A. Washington, Abraham Buford, Edmund W. Pettus, Theodrick "Tod" Carter, John B. Womack, John H. Winder, Gideon J. Pillow, States Rights Gist, Henry R. Jackson, John Lawton Seabrook, John C. Breckinridge, Leonidas Polk, Zachary Taylor, Sarah Knox Taylor (first wife of Jefferson Davis), Richard Taylor, Davy Crockett, Daniel Boone, Meriwether Lewis (of the Lewis and Clark Expedition) Andrew Jackson, James K. Polk, Abram Poindexter Maury (founder of Franklin, TN), William Giles Harding, Zebulon Vance, Thomas Jefferson, George Wythe Randolph (grandson of Jefferson), Felix K. Zollicoffer, Fitzhugh Lee, Nathaniel F. Cheairs, Jesse James, Frank James, Robert Brank Vance, Charles Sidney Winder, John W. McGavock, Caroline E. (Winder) McGavock, David Harding  McGavock, Lysander McGavock, James Randal McGavock, Randal William McGavock, Francis McGavock, Emily McGavock, William Henry F. Lee, Lucius E. Polk, Minor Meriwether (husband of noted pro-South author Elizabeth Avery Meriwether), Ellen Bourne Tynes (wife of Forrest's chief of artillery, Captain John W. Morton), South Carolina Senators Preston Smith Brooks and Andrew Pickens Butler, and famed South Carolina diarist Mary Chesnut.

Seabrook's modern day cousins include: Patrick J. Buchanan (conservative author), Cindy Crawford (model), Shelby Lee Adams (Letcher County, Kentucky, portrait photographer), Bertram Thomas Combs (Kentucky's fiftieth governor), Edith Bolling (wife of President Woodrow Wilson), and actors Robert Duvall, Reese Witherspoon, Lee Marvin, Rebecca Gayheart, Andy Griffith, and Tom Cruise.

Seabrook's screenplay, *A Rebel Born*, based on his book of the same name, has been signed with acclaimed filmmaker Christopher Forbes (of Forbes Film). It is now in pre-production, and is set for release in 2017 as a full-length feature film. This will be the first movie ever made of Nathan Bedford Forrest's life story, and as a historically accurate project written from the Southern perspective, is destined to be one of the most talked about Civil War films of all time.

Born with music in his blood, Seabrook is an award-winning, multi-genre, BMI-Nashville songwriter and lyricist who has composed some 3,000 songs (250 albums), and whose original music has been heard in film (*A Rebel Born, Cowgirls 'n Angels, Confederate Cavalry, Billy the Kid: Showdown in Lincoln County, Vengeance Without Mercy, Last Step, County Line, The Mark*) and on TV and radio worldwide. A musician, producer, multi-instrumentalist, and renown performer—whose keyboard work has been variously compared to pianists from Hargus Robbins and Vince Guaraldi to Elton John and Leonard Bernstein—Seabrook has opened for groups such as the Earl Scruggs Review, Ted Nugent, and Bob Seger, and has performed privately for such public figures as President Ronald Reagan, Burt Reynolds, Loni Anderson, and Senator Edward W. Brooke. Seabrook's cousins in the music business include: Johnny Cash, Elvis Presley, Billy Ray and Miley Cyrus, Patty Loveless, Tim McGraw, Lee Ann Womack, Dolly Parton, Pat Boone, Naomi, Wynonna, and Ashley Judd, Ricky Skaggs, the Sunshine Sisters, Martha Carson, and Chet Atkins.

Seabrook, a libertarian, lives with his wife and family in historic Middle Tennessee, the heart of Forrest country and the Confederacy, where his conservative Southern ancestors fought valiantly against Liberal Lincoln and the progressive North in defense of Jeffersonianism, constitutional government, and personal liberty.

LochlainnSeabrook.com

722 ~ SEABROOK'S BIBLE DICTIONARY

If you enjoyed this book you will be interested in Mr. Seabrook's other popular Jesus-related titles:

☛ CHRISTMAS BEFORE CHRISTIANITY: HOW THE BIRTHDAY OF THE "SUN" BECAME THE BIRTHDAY OF THE "SON"
☛ JESUS & THE GOSPEL OF Q: CHRIST'S PRE-CHRISTIAN TEACHINGS AS RECORDED IN THE NEW TESTAMENT
☛ CHRIST IS ALL & IN ALL: REDISCOVERING YOUR DIVINE NATURE & THE KINGDOM WITHIN
☛ JESUS & THE LAW OF ATTRACTION: THE BIBLE-BASED GUIDE TO CREATING PERFECT HEALTH, WEALTH, & HAPPINESS

Available from Sea Raven Press and wherever fine books are sold

ALL OF OUR BOOK COVERS ARE AVAILABLE AS 11" X 17" POSTERS, SUITABLE FOR FRAMING.

SeaRavenPress.com

LOCHLAINN SEABROOK ◦∞ 723

"Fear not, believe only."

Jesus

www.ingramcontent.com/pod-product-compliance
Lightning Source LLC
Chambersburg PA
CBHW020738020526
44115CB00030B/142